**Officially Licensed**

# NASCAR RECORD & FACT BOOK

**SportingNews BOOKS**

## PHOTO CREDITS

T = Top   B = Bottom   L = Left   R = Right

CONTRIBUTING PHOTOGRAPHERS

Bob Leverone/Sporting News: Cover (all photos), 17, 18, 20, 25, 33-96, 141R, 142, 143, 146, 147, 148, 149, 150, 151, 152L, 152R, 153, 155, 157R, 158, 159L, 159R, 161, 162T, 163, 165, 297-305, 328, 342-347, 353, 363, 368, 372

Dilip Vishwanat/Sporting News: 33-96, 141L, 157L, 369, 396L, 396B

Albert Dickson/Sporting News: 33-96

Harold Hinson for Sporting News: 145, 166

Bill Gutweiler for Sporting News: 154, 156, 162B, 164

NASCAR/ISC Publications: 8, 9, 10, 11, 12, 13, 14, 15, 26, 27, 30, 31, 99-133, 276-280, 297-305, 325-329, 342-347

Sherryl Creekmore/NASCAR: 33-96, 297-305

New Hampshire International Speedway: 383

Pocono Raceway: 388, 389

Richmond International Raceway: 392

Michigan International Speedway Archives: 7

AP/Wide World Photos: 144

## NASCAR RECORD & FACT BOOK

**Editors:** SPORTING NEWS—Jim Gilstrap, Kathy Sheldon, Carlyn Foster, Matt Crossman, Paul Grant, Dan Graf, David Bukovich, Chris Bergeron, Roger Kuznia, Jessica Daues, Dale Bye; NASCAR—Jennifer White, Ashley Costello, Tracey Judd, Tracey Eberts, Scott Bowman, Buz McKim
**Designers:** Christen Sager, Angie Pillman, Michael Behrens, Bob Parajon
**Photo editor:** August Miller
**Prepress specialists:** Steve Romer, Pamela Speh, Vern Kasal, Russ Carr

Copyright ©2004 by The Sporting News, a division of Vulcan Sports Media, Inc., 10176 Corporate Square Drive, Suite 200, St. Louis, MO 63132. All rights reserved. Printed in the U.S.A.

No part of the *NASCAR Record & Fact Book* may be reproduced or transmitted in any form or by any means, electronic or mechanical, including photocopy, recording or any information storage and retrieval system now known or to be invented, without permission in writing from the publisher, except by a reviewer who wishes to quote brief passages in connection with a review written for inclusion in a magazine, newspaper or broadcast.

THE SPORTING NEWS is a registered trademark of Vulcan Sports Media, Inc.

ISBN: 0-89204-728-3

# NASCAR NEXTEL Cup Series schedule

| Date | Race | Track | TV/Radio | 2003 winner |
|---|---|---|---|---|
| February 7 | Budweiser Shootout* | Daytona International Speedway | TNT/MRN | Dale Earnhardt Jr. |
| February 12 | Gatorade 125s* | Daytona International Speedway | TNT/MRN | Robby Gordon |
| | | | | Dale Earnhardt Jr. |
| February 15 | Daytona 500 | Daytona International Speedway | NBC/MRN | Michael Waltrip |
| February 22 | Subway 400 | North Carolina Speedway | FOX/MRN | Dale Jarrett |
| March 7 | UAW-DaimlerChrysler 400 | Las Vegas Motor Speedway | FOX/PRN | Matt Kenseth |
| March 14 | Golden Corral 500 | Atlanta Motor Speedway | FOX/PRN | Bobby Labonte |
| March 21 | Carolina Dodge Dealers 400 | Darlington Raceway | FOX/MRN | Ricky Craven |
| March 28 | Food City 500 | Bristol Motor Speedway | FOX/PRN | Kurt Busch |
| April 4 | Samsung/RadioShack 500 | Texas Motor Speedway | FOX/PRN | Ryan Newman |
| April 18 | Advance Auto Parts 500 | Martinsville Speedway | FOX/MRN | Jeff Gordon |
| April 25 | Aaron's 499 | Talladega Superspeedway | FOX/MRN | Dale Earnhardt Jr. |
| May 2 | Auto Club 500 | California Speedway | FOX/MRN | Kurt Busch |
| May 15 | Richmond 400 | Richmond International Raceway | FX/MRN | Joe Nemechek |
| May 22 | NASCAR NEXTEL All-Star Challenge* | Lowe's Motor Speedway | FX/MRN | Jimmie Johnson |
| May 30 | Coca-Cola 600 | Lowe's Motor Speedway | FOX/PRN | Jimmie Johnson |
| June 6 | MBNA America 400 | Dover International Speedway | FX/MRN | Ryan Newman |
| June 13 | Pocono 500 | Pocono Raceway | FOX/MRN | Tony Stewart |
| June 20 | Michigan 400 | Michigan International Speedway | FOX/MRN | Kurt Busch |
| June 27 | Dodge/Save Mart 350 | Infineon Raceway | FOX/PRN | Robby Gordon |
| July 3 | Pepsi 400 | Daytona International Speedway | FOX/MRN | Greg Biffle |
| July 11 | Tropicana 400 | Chicagoland Speedway | NBC/MRN | Ryan Newman |
| July 25 | New England 300 | New Hampshire International Speedway | TNT/MRN | Jimmie Johnson |
| August 1 | Pennsylvania 500 | Pocono Raceway | TNT/MRN | Ryan Newman |
| August 8 | Brickyard 400 | Indianapolis Motor Speedway | NBC/IMS | Kevin Harvick |
| August 15 | Sirius at The Glen | Watkins Glen International | TNT/MRN | Robby Gordon |
| August 22 | Michigan 400 | Michigan International Speedway | TNT/MRN | Ryan Newman |
| August 28 | Sharpie 500 | Bristol Motor Speedway | TNT/PRN | Kurt Busch |
| September 5 | Pop Secret 500 | California Speedway | NBC/MRN | inaugural event |
| September 11 | Chevy Monte Carlo 400 | Richmond International Raceway | TNT/MRN | Ryan Newman |
| September 19 | Sylvania 300 | New Hampshire International Speedway | TNT/MRN | Jimmie Johnson |
| September 26 | MBNA America 400 | Dover International Speedway | TNT/MRN | Ryan Newman |
| October 3 | EA SPORTS 500 | Talladega Superspeedway | NBC/MRN | Michael Waltrip |
| October 10 | Banquet 400 | Kansas Speedway | NBC/MRN | Ryan Newman |
| October 16 | UAW-GM Quality 500 | Lowe's Motor Speedway | NBC/PRN | Tony Stewart |
| October 24 | Subway 500 | Martinsville Speedway | NBC/MRN | Jeff Gordon |
| October 31 | Bass Pro Shops MBNA 500 | Atlanta Motor Speedway | NBC/PRN | Jeff Gordon |
| November 7 | Checker Auto Parts 500 | Phoenix International Raceway | NBC/MRN | Dale Earnhardt Jr. |
| November 14 | Mountain Dew Southern 500 | Darlington Raceway | NBC/MRN | Terry Labonte |
| November 21 | Ford 400 | Homestead-Miami Speedway | NBC/MRN | Bobby Labonte |

NOTE: Race names subject to change. *Non-points events.

# NASCAR Busch Series schedule

| Date | Race | Track | TV/Radio | 2003 winner |
|---|---|---|---|---|
| February 14 | Hershey's Kisses 300 | Daytona International Speedway | NBC/MRN | Dale Earnhardt Jr. |
| February 21 | Rockingham 200 | North Carolina Speedway | FX/MRN | Jamie McMurray |
| March 6 | Sam's Town 300 | Las Vegas Motor Speedway | FX/PRN | Joe Nemechek |
| March 20 | darlingtonraceway.com 200 | Darlington Raceway | FX/MRN | Todd Bodine |
| March 27 | TBA | Bristol Motor Speedway | FX/PRN | Kevin Harvick |
| April 3 | O'Reilly 300 | Texas Motor Speedway | FOX/MRN | Joe Nemechek |
| April 10 | Pepsi 300 pres. by Mapco | Nashville Superspeedway | FX/MRN | David Green |
| April 24 | Aaron's 312 | Talladega Superspeedway | FOX/MRN | Dale Earnhardt Jr. |
| May 1 | 1-800-PIT-SHOP.COM 300 | California Speedway | FOX/MRN | Matt Kenseth |
| May 8 | TBA | Gateway International Raceway | FX/MRN | Scott Riggs |
| May 14 | NASCAR Busch Series 250 | Richmond International Raceway | FX/MRN | Kevin Harvick |
| May 23 | TBA | Nazareth Speedway | FX/MRN | Ron Hornaday |
| May 29 | Carquest Auto Parts 300 | Lowe's Motor Speedway | FX/PRN | Matt Kenseth |
| June 5 | MBNA America 200 | Dover International Speedway | FX/MRN | Joe Nemechek |
| June 12 | Nashville 300 | Nashville Superspeedway | FX/MRN | Scott Riggs |
| June 19 | Meijer 300 | Kentucky Speedway | FX/MRN | Bobby Hamilton Jr. |
| June 26 | TBA | The Milwaukee Mile | FX/MRN | Jason Keller |
| July 2 | Winn-Dixie 250 pres. by PepsiCo | Daytona International Speedway | FX/MRN | Dale Earnhardt Jr. |
| July 10 | Twister 300 | Chicagoland Speedway | NBC/MRN | Bobby Hamilton Jr. |
| July 24 | New England 200 | New Hampshire International Speedway | TNT/MRN | David Green |
| July 31 | TBA | Pikes Peak International Raceway | TNT/MRN | Scott Wimmer |
| August 7 | Kroger 200 pres. by Tom Raper RVs | Indianapolis Raceway Park | TNT/MRN | Brian Vickers |
| August 21 | Cabela's 250 | Michigan International Speedway | TNT/MRN | Kevin Harvick |
| August 27 | Food City 250 | Bristol Motor Speedway | TNT/PRN | Michael Waltrip |
| September 4 | CaliforniaSpeedway.com 300 | California Speedway | NBC/MRN | inaugural event |
| September 10 | Funai 250 | Richmond International Raceway | TNT/MRN | Johnny Sauter |
| September 25 | Stacker 200 pres. by YJ Stinger | Dover International Speedway | TNT/MRN | Brian Vickers |
| October 9 | Mr. Goodcents 300 | Kansas Speedway | TNT/MRN | David Green |
| October 15 | Little Trees 300 | Lowe's Motor Speedway | TBD/PRN | Greg Biffle |
| October 23 | Sam's Town 250 | Memphis Motorsports Park | TNT/MRN | Bobby Hamilton Jr. |
| October 30 | Aaron's 312 | Atlanta Motor Speedway | TNT/PRN | Greg Biffle |
| November 6 | Bashas' Supermarkets 200 | Phoenix International Raceway | NBC/MRN | Bobby Hamilton Jr. |
| November 13 | South Carolina 200 | Darlington Raceway | TNT/MRN | Brian Vickers |
| November 20 | Ford 300 | Homestead-Miami Speedway | NBC/MRN | Kasey Kahne |

NOTE: Race names subject to change

# NASCAR Craftsman Truck Series schedule

| Date | Race | Track | TV/Radio | 2003 winner |
|---|---|---|---|---|
| February 13 | Florida Dodge Dealers 250 | Daytona International Speedway | SPD/MRN | Rick Crawford |
| March 13 | Atlanta 200 | Atlanta Motor Speedway | SPD/MRN | inaugural event |
| April 17 | Martinsville 250 | Martinsville Speedway | SPD/MRN | Dennis Setzer |
| May 16 | Ohio 250 | Mansfield Motorsports Speedway | SPD/MRN | inaugural event |
| May 21 | Hardee's 200 | Lowe's Motor Speedway | SPD/MRN | Ted Musgrave |
| June 4 | MBNA America 200 | Dover International Speedway | SPD/MRN | Jason Leffler |
| June 11 | O'Reilly 400K | Texas Motor Speedway | SPD/MRN | Brendan Gaughan |
| June 19 | O'Reilly 200 | Memphis Motorsports Park | SPD/MRN | Ted Musgrave |
| June 26 | GNC 200 | The Milwaukee Mile | SPD/MRN | Brendan Gaughan |
| July 3 | O'Reilly Auto Parts 250 | Kansas Speedway | SPD/MRN | Jon Wood |
| July 10 | Built Ford Tough 225 | Kentucky Speedway | SPD/MRN | Carl Edwards |
| July 17 | Dodge Ram Tough 200 | Gateway International Raceway | SPD/MRN | Brendan Gaughan |
| July 31 | Michigan 200 | Michigan International Speedway | SPD/MRN | Brendan Gaughan |
| August 6 | Power Stroke Diesel 200 | Indianapolis Raceway Park | SPD/MRN | Carl Edwards |
| August 14 | Toyota Tundra 200 | Nashville Superspeedway | SPD/MRN | Carl Edwards |
| August 25 | O'Reilly 200 | Bristol Motor Speedway | SPD/MRN | Travis Kvapil |
| September 9 | NASCAR Craftsman Truck Series 200 | Richmond International Raceway | SPD/MRN | Tony Stewart |
| September 18 | New Hampshire 200 | New Hampshire International Speedway | SPD/MRN | Jimmy Spencer |
| September 25 | Las Vegas 350 | Las Vegas Motor Speedway | SPD/MRN | Brendan Gaughan |
| October 2 | American Racing Wheels 200 | California Speedway | SPD/MRN | Ted Musgrave |
| October 16 | Silverado 350K | Texas Motor Speedway | SPD/MRN | Brendan Gaughan |
| October 23 | Martinsville 200 | Martinsville Speedway | SPD/MRN | Jon Wood |
| November 5 | Chevy Silverado 150 | Phoenix International Raceway | SPD/MRN | Kevin Harvick |
| November 12 | Darlington 200 | Darlington Raceway | SPD/MRN | Bobby Hamilton |
| November 19 | Ford 200 | Homestead-Miami Speedway | SPD/MRN | Bobby Hamilton |

NOTE: Race names subject to change

# Contents

2004 NASCAR NEXTEL Cup Series schedule .................................................. 3
2004 NASCAR Busch Series schedule ...................................................... 4
2004 NASCAR Craftsman Truck Series schedule ............................................. 5

## NASCAR at a glance — 7

| | |
|---|---|
| NASCAR milestones | 8-11 |
| NASCAR officials | 12-15 |
| Sponsors list | 16 |
| Race procedures | 17-19 |
| Glossary | 20-24 |
| Anatomy of a pit stop | 25 |
| Inside the cockpit | 26 |
| Car cutaway | 27 |
| Tech elements | 28 |
| NASCAR ladder system | 29 |

## NASCAR NEXTEL Cup Series — 30

| | |
|---|---|
| Nextel joins NASCAR | 31 |
| 2004 drivers roster | 32 |
| Top 43 drivers | 33-90 |
| Additional drivers | 91-96 |
| Champions section | 97-104 |
| Other notable drivers | 105-108 |
| Car owners | 109-121 |
| Crew chiefs | 122-132 |

## 2003 season — 133

| | |
|---|---|
| Points standings, lap leaders | 134-135 |
| Race results | 136 |
| Raybestos Rookie of the Year | 137 |
| NASCAR NEXTEL All-Star Challenge | 138-140 |
| Budweiser Shootout | 140 |
| Race by race recap | 141-166 |
| Race boxscores | 167-202 |

## Series history — 203

| | |
|---|---|
| Season by season recap | 204-257 |
| Records | 258-265 |
| Inactive drivers with 50-plus victories | 266-271 |
| Owners wins | 272 |

## NASCAR Busch Series — 273

| | |
|---|---|
| Milestones | 274-275 |
| Busch Series drivers | 276-280 |
| Busch/NEXTEL Cup Series drivers | 280-283 |
| Additional Busch Series drivers | 284-292 |
| 2003 race by race results | 293 |
| 2003 points standings | 294-295 |
| 2003 lap leaders | 296 |
| 2003 champion's race by race results | 297 |
| Previous champions | 298-305 |
| 2003 Raybestos Rookie of the Year | 306 |
| Series records | 307-209 |
| Season by season recaps | 310-320 |

## NASCAR Craftsman Truck Series — 321

| | |
|---|---|
| Milestones | 322-324 |
| Truck Series drivers | 325-329 |
| Additional drivers | 329-339 |
| 2003 race results | 340 |
| 2003 points standings | 341 |
| 2003 champion race by race results | 342 |
| Past champions | 343-344 |
| 2003 Raybestos Rookie of the Year | 345 |
| Series records | 346-348 |
| Season by season recap | 349-352 |

## NASCAR tracks — 353

| | |
|---|---|
| NEXTEL Cup Series tracks | 354-397 |
| Inactive Cup tracks | 398-400 |
| Busch Series and Craftsman Truck tracks | 401-406 |

**NASCAR on television** .................. **407-408**

# Milestones

Since its inception as the Strictly Stock division, the NASCAR NEXTEL Cup Series has seen many changes. In the beginning, the racecars were driven off the street and onto the track. But as safety technology advanced, changes were made, making the cars of today more complicated. NASCAR has grown from the small organization formed on the beaches of Daytona to a thriving sport that can be reached by anyone around the world through television and the Internet. This, along with an expanded schedule and more racetracks throughout the nation, has made the NASCAR NEXTEL Cup Series more accessible to fans. NASCAR is America's fastest growing sport. Important milestones for the NASCAR Cup series:

**December 14, 1947:** Bill France Sr. organizes a meeting at the Streamline Hotel in Daytona Beach, Fla., to discuss the future of stock car racing. NASCAR (the National Association for Stock Car Auto Racing) is conceived.

"Big" Bill France Sr. (seated at the head of the table) presides over the meeting in 1947 at the Streamline Hotel, where NASCAR was conceived.

**February 15, 1948:** NASCAR runs its first race in Daytona Beach at the beach-road course. The race is won by Red Byron.

**February 21, 1948:** NASCAR is incorporated.

**June 19, 1949:** The first NASCAR Strictly Stock (currently known as the NASCAR NEXTEL Cup Series) race is held at Charlotte Fairgrounds Speedway. Bob Flock wins the first pole, Jim Roper wins the race and Sara Christian, who finished 14th, is the first woman to start a NASCAR race.

**October 16, 1949:** Red Byron is the NASCAR Strictly Stock champion. Byron earned $5,800 in six starts and collected two wins.

**1950:** Bill France Sr. changes the name of NASCAR's top series from Strictly Stock to Grand National.

**September 4, 1950:** Darlington Raceway, NASCAR's first paved superspeedway, hosts the Southern 500. The first 500-mile event in NASCAR history is won by Johnny Mantz in a 1950 Plymouth. Seventy-five drivers started the event, which featured two caution periods and lasted more than 6 hours.

**April 8, 1951:** The first NASCAR Grand National race west of the Mississippi River is held at Carrell Speedway, a half-mile dirt track in Gardena, Calif.

**1952:** Sponsors step up in the NASCAR Grand National division. Pure Oil provides contingency monies and free gasoline during Daytona's SpeedWeeks and Champion Spark Plugs contributes $5,000 to the year-end point fund.

**June 13, 1954:** The International 100 is held at Linden Airport in New Jersey, becoming the first road race in what is now the NASCAR NEXTEL Cup Series.

**1955:** Car owner Carl Kiekhaefer enters cars in 40 Grand National events and wins 22 of them. Kiekhaefer becomes the first owner to use major sponsorships when he provides drivers with financial and technical backing.

**1958:** The Florida Sports Writers association votes Fireball Roberts as Professional Athlete of the Year. This is the first time the honor was given to a racecar driver.

**February 23, 1958:** Paul Goldsmith captures the final race on Daytona's famed Beach and Road Course.

**February 22, 1959:** The high-banked, 2.5-mile Daytona International Speedway hosts the first Daytona 500, attracting 41,000 fans. Sixty-one hours after the checkered flag

Stock cars raced on a 4.1-mile beach-road course during NASCAR sanctioned races in Daytona Beach, Fla., between 1948 and 1958. The race pictured above is from 1954 and was won by Lee Petty.

The first Daytona 500, in 1959, came down to this photo finish between Lee Petty (No. 42) and Johnny Beauchamp (No. 73). Petty was declared the winner, 61 hours after the checkered flag flew. Joe Weatherly (No. 48, on the outside) finished fifth, one lap down.

flew over an extremely close finish, Lee Petty is declared the winner by 2 feet after Bill France Sr. reviews footage from a news reel.

**January 31, 1960:** CBS Sports broadcasts its first live NASCAR Grand National events. *CBS Sports Spectacular* televises the Grand National Pole Position races from Daytona. The 2-hour program is the first devoted entirely to stock car racing.

**June 19, 1960:** Charlotte Motor Speedway plays host to its first NASCAR event. The World 600 is won by Joe Lee Johnson in a time of slightly more than 5½ hours.

**July 4, 1960:** Bud Moore and Jack Smith communicate by two-way radio in the Firecracker 250, marking the first time two-way radio communication is used in the sport.

**July 16, 1960:** ABC Sports televises the Firecracker 250 from Daytona International Speedway as part of *Wide World of Sports*.

**September 13, 1962:** Mamie Reynolds becomes the first woman to win as an owner when Fred Lorenzen takes the checkered flag at Augusta (Ga.) Speedway.

**February 24, 1963:** Tiny Lund subs for injured Marvin Panch and wins the Daytona 500.

**December 1, 1963:** Wendell Scott becomes the first black driver to win a race at NASCAR's highest level, beating Buck Baker at Jacksonville (Fla.) Speedway.

**1964:** The Goodyear Tire & Rubber Company tests and begins use of an inner liner for all NASCAR Grand National tires.

**1964:** Richard Petty, NASCAR's all-time wins leader, captures his first championship.

**1965:** The Firestone Racesafe Fuel Cell bladder is implemented.

**1967:** Richard Petty sets three records by collecting the most wins in one season (27), most consecutive wins (10) and most victories from the pole in one season (15).

**September 14, 1969:** Alabama International Speedway opens in Talladega, Ala., as the largest oval on the NASCAR circuit.

**March 24, 1970:** Buddy Baker becomes the first driver to break the 200 mph barrier in a stock car, doing so at a test run at Talladega.

**September 30, 1970:** The final NASCAR Grand National division race is run on dirt at State Fairgrounds Speedway in Raleigh, N.C.

**1971:** R.J. Reynolds Winston brand becomes the title sponsor of NASCAR's top division, which is renamed the NASCAR Winston Cup Grand National Division.

**February 14, 1971:** Motor Racing Network (MRN) broadcasts its first Daytona 500. Ken Squier anchors the broadcast for the racing-only network.

**January 10, 1972:** The founder of NASCAR, Bill France Sr., hands over the reins of leadership to his son Bill France, Jr., who becomes the second president in NASCAR's history.

Bill France Sr. (left) hands over the keys to his son, Bill France Jr., making Bill Jr. the second president in NASCAR history.

**1972:** The NASCAR Winston Cup Grand National Division schedule is trimmed from 48 races to 31, marking the beginning of the Modern Era.

**February 15, 1976:** David Pearson and Richard Petty battle at Daytona for a win on national television, as the two cars are involved in an accident near the finish line, with Pearson hobbling to the checkered flag first.

**February 20, 1977:** Janet Guthrie becomes the first woman to qualify for the Daytona 500. She qualifies 39th and finishes 12th.

**1978:** President Jimmy Carter and First Lady Rosalyn Carter invite NASCAR drivers to the White House, in the same year Cale Yarborough wins his third straight NASCAR Winston Cup title.

**February 18, 1979:** CBS Sports presents the first live flag-to-flag coverage of a NASCAR event with the Daytona 500. Richard Petty avoids a wreck between Cale Yarborough and Donnie Allison on the last lap to win the race.

**April 8, 1979:** The teaming of David Pearson and the Wood Brothers ends in Darlington.

Bill Elliott celebrates being awarded a $1 million bonus from series sponsor R.J. Reynolds for winning three of the four crown jewel races in 1985: the Daytona 500, the Winston 500 at Talladega and the Southern 500 at Darlington.

**September 3, 1979:** David Pearson sits in for rookie Dale Earnhardt and leads the final 70 laps of the Southern 500 at Darlington to win the race.

**1979:** Richard Petty wins his record seventh series points championship.

**April 29, 1982:** Benny Parsons becomes the first driver in NASCAR history to post an official qualifying lap over 200 mph, accomplishing the feat at Talladega.

**May 6, 1984:** At the most competitive race in NASCAR history, the lead changes 75 times among 13 drivers at Talladega.

**July 4, 1984:** In the Firecracker 400 at Daytona International Speedway, Richard Petty earns his 200th win, setting a mark that has yet to be challenged.

**May 5, 1985:** Bill Elliott falls to 26th and two laps down at Talladega in the Winston 500 but fights back to lead the last 20 laps and win the race.

**July 4, 1985:** Greg Sacks, with a limited number of team members, takes the lead with nine laps to go in the Firecracker 400 to win his only NASCAR Winston Cup Series race.

**September 1, 1985:** Bill Elliott claims a $1 million dollar bonus from R.J. Reynolds for winning three of the four crown jewel races on the schedule. Elliott won the Daytona 500, the Winston 500 at Talladega and the Southern 500 at Darlington.

**1985:** After trailing Bill Elliott by 206 points with eight races to go, Darrell Waltrip's late-season streak leads him to win the NASCAR Winston Cup Series championship.

**1986:** NASCAR drops "Grand National" from its top division, renaming it the NASCAR Winston Cup Series.

**April 30, 1987:** Bill Elliott sets the fastest lap time in NASCAR history, turning a blazing lap of 212.809 mph at Talladega Superspeedway.

**1987:** Dale Earnhardt makes his famous "pass in the grass" in The Winston, the all-star race at Charlotte Motor Speedway, shooting through the infield and back onto the track to maintain the lead and eventually win the race.

**February 14, 1988:** Bobby Allison and Davey Allison finish first and second, respectively, in the Daytona 500.

**1989:** For the first time, every NASCAR Winston Cup Series race is televised.

**February 18, 1990:** Dale Earnhardt leads 155 of 200 laps of the Daytona 500 but loses the race with a mile to go after blowing a tire on a piece of debris.

**September 1991:** Harry Gant, at 51, is tabbed "Mr. September" after winning four consecutive races in the month.

**May 16, 1992:** For the first time, Charlotte Motor Speedway holds The Winston under the lights, ending as Davey Allison takes the checkered flag before losing control of his car.

**November 15, 1992:** Richard Petty retires after 35 years of racing in NASCAR. He ends his career with 200 wins and 549 top five finishes in almost 1,200 races. The points championship is won by Alan Kulwicki, who leads one more lap than Bill Elliott in the final race at Atlanta Motor Speedway, to clinch the title by 10 points.

**Aug. 6, 1994:** The NASCAR championship schedule expands to include the famed 2.5-mile Indianapolis Motor Speedway. Jeff Gordon wins the first Cup race at the Brickyard.

**1994:** Dale Earnhardt joins Richard Petty as the only driver to win seven NASCAR championships.

**August 9, 1996:** Dale Earnhardt, with a broken collarbone, wheels around Watkins Glen to win the pole and sets a track record.

**November 24, 1996:** NASCAR runs a demonstration race in Suzuka, Japan.

**November 16, 1997:** Jeff Gordon clinches his second NASCAR championship, making him the youngest two-time winner.

In 1994, Dale Earnhardt captured his seventh NASCAR Winston Cup Series championship—tying Richard Petty—in convincing fashion after winning the AC Delco 500 at North Carolina Speedway.

**1997:** Two new tracks appear on the NASCAR schedule: Texas Motor Speedway and California Speedway. In front of sold-out crowds, Jeff Burton and Jeff Gordon, respectively, win the races.

**March 1, 1998:** NASCAR celebrates its 50th anniversary while adding Las Vegas Motor Speedway to the schedule. Mark Martin wins the inaugural event.

**February 1999:** NASCAR president Bill France Jr. hands over the day-to-day operations to senior vice president and chief operating officer Mike Helton, marking the first time someone from outside the France family has controlled the operations of the sport.

**November 11, 1999:** NASCAR announces multiyear partnerships with FOX, NBC and Turner Sports; the consolidated television package is set to begin in 2001.

**January 2000:** The NASCAR Winston Cup Point Fund increases from $5 million to $10 million; the champion's share increases to $3 million.

**November 28, 2000:** Mike Helton becomes the third president in NASCAR history as Bill France Jr., passes the torch of leadership to a non-France family member for the first time.

**February 18, 2001:** FOX Sports telecasts the Daytona 500, its first telecast as part of an eight-year network TV agreement along with its cable network partner FX. Michael Waltrip's victory in the Daytona 500 is his first win, coming in his 463rd start.

**July 7, 2001:** NBC Sports kicks off its six-year network TV agreement by telecasting the Pepsi 400. NBC's cable partner, TNT, will go on to televise seven of the season's races.

**September 25, 2001:** NASCAR Radio, the first 24-hour radio station dedicated to a single sport, debuts on XM Satellite Radio, the first commercial satellite radio service in the United States.

**2001:** NASCAR comes to two new tracks: Chicagoland Speedway and Kansas Speedway; Kevin Harvick and Jeff Gordon are the respective winners.

**September 2002:** NASCAR announces its NASCAR Craftsman Truck Series races will be televised live on the SPEED Channel in 2003.

**February 12, 2003:** NASCAR announces that Toyota will join the Craftsman Truck Series in 2004, marking the first time a NASCAR series will include a foreign automaker.

**June 19, 2003:** NASCAR announces that the sponsorship of its top series will shift from Winston to Nextel in 2004. In 2004, drivers will contend for the NASCAR NEXTEL Cup Series championship.

**November 16, 2003:** Matt Kenseth celebrates winning the final Winston Cup Series championship, marking the end of Winston's 33-year sponsorship of NASCAR's top series.

# NASCAR executives

## The France family

You need look no further than the France family tree to understand NASCAR's history and position at the pinnacle of American motorsports today.

William H.G. France founded the National Association for Stock Car Auto Racing (NASCAR) in 1948 to organize and promote racing on tracks such as the one carved out of the hard sand of Daytona Beach. With tracks scattered throughout the Southeast, each with different rules and facilities, the sport needed leadership. And that's exactly what Bill France Sr. delivered. Through dogged determination, he legitimized a sport that was, at the time, an unorganized hobby.

He also founded the International Speedway Corporation (ISC), which gave NASCAR two of its crown jewels in the form of Daytona International Speedway in 1959 and Talladega (Ala.) Superspeedway in 1969.

Bill and Anne's two sons, William (Bill) Jr. and Jim, were handed the reins upon Bill Sr.'s retirement. Bill Jr. became president while Jim took over the role of executive vice president and secretary, as well as president of ISC.

Other than the creation of the organization, Bill Jr.'s ascension to the leadership role of NASCAR is likely the most important event in the sanctioning body's history.

As rule maker, promoter, ambassador and salesman, Bill Jr. has set the standard by which all other forms of motorsports are measured. He has further involved his family as the sport continued its high-speed growth.

NASCAR's popularity during the 1970s and '80s grew primarily on a regional level, as Bill Jr. continued to work toward a vision of national recognition.

Today, millions of fans pack NASCAR venues across the country each year for what is arguably the most exciting form of motorsports entertainment.

In November 2000, Bill Jr. announced he would serve as chairman of a newly formed board of directors for NASCAR that would also consist of Jim France, Brian Z. France, Lesa France Kennedy and Mike Helton and would be responsible for developing policy and vision for the sport.

A third generation of Frances is following the path laid before them by their father and grandfather. Brian Z. France and Lesa France Kennedy are the son and daughter of Bill Jr. and his wife, Betty Jane.

Lesa France Kennedy joined the NASCAR board and has worked her way to president of ISC, and she serves on the ISC board, helping oversee the company's 11 racetracks and the successful Daytona USA motorsports attraction.

In September 2003, Brian Z. France was named NASCAR's chairman of the board and chief executive offi-

## Mike Helton
## President

Mike Helton assumed the role of NASCAR president in November 2000, succeeding Bill France Jr., who had served in the role since 1972. Helton became the first person outside the France family to take over the day-to-day operations of NASCAR when he was promoted from his position as vice president for competition and was named senior vice president and chief operating officer in February 1999.

Born and raised in Bristol, Va., Helton's motorsports experience allows him to look at all sides of the picture: from a sanctioning body's standpoint, from a track's standpoint (from his years running one), and even from a competitor's standpoint—he did a little racing at one time.

His motorsports management experience began in 1980 at what was then known as Atlanta International Raceway. Helton was promoted to general manager in 1985 before joining the management team at Daytona International Speedway in 1986. Eighteen months later, Helton became general manager at Talladega Superspeedway.

Within two years, he advanced to vice president of the International Speedway Corporation, and in 1989 was promoted to president of Talladega. He held that position until January 1994, when he relocated to Daytona Beach, Fla., as NASCAR's new vice president for competition—all before the age of 40.

Helton and his wife, Lynda, reside in Ormond Beach, Fla.

Clockwise from top left: Brian Z. France, Lesa France Kennedy, Mike Helton, Bill France Jr., Jim France.

minated with NASCAR Winston Cup Series and NASCAR Busch Series events being broadcast on FOX Sports, FX, NBC Sports and TNT.

Brian has been very successful in directing all aspects of marketing, including sponsorship sales and services, special projects, new business development and communications. In a short time, Brian has used his creativity and salesmanship to make the 1990s one of the most exciting decades the sport has seen.

Bill France Sr. died in 1992. His induction into the National Motorsports Press Hall of Fame in Darlington, S.C., is a testament not only to his accomplishments but also the efforts of his entire family. Now, after five decades, NASCAR is not just a successful sport; it is also one of the most successful family businesses in the country.

cer, replacing his father Bill Jr., who took over the position of vice chairman for NASCAR.

Brian has been at the forefront of NASCAR's dramatic sponsorship growth, including the recent ground-breaking announcement of Nextel Communications as the new sponsor of the NASCAR NEXTEL Cup Series, beginning in 2004. He has also led a host of marketing initiatives, including internalizing the sanctioning body's licensing efforts and developing NASCAR's consolidated television plans that cul-

# George Pyne
# Chief Operating Officer

George Pyne was named NASCAR's chief operating officer and was appointed to the board of directors in December 2002. Pyne has day-to-day operational responsibilities for each of NASCAR's departments and reports to NASCAR president Mike Helton.

Previously, Pyne was located in NASCAR's Charlotte office, where he oversaw NASCAR's marketing and licensing programs based out of its New York, Charlotte and Daytona Beach, Fla., offices. Leading a marketing staff of more than 100, Pyne boosted NASCAR's licensing business to $1.2 billion in 2000. Pyne was named head of NASCAR's licensing division in 1996 and took responsibility for the marketing division a year later. Pyne was instrumental in the successful rollout of various marketing and licensing initiatives, including NASCAR's 50th anniversary celebration in 1998 and NASCAR's Automotive Aftermarket program.

Under Pyne, NASCAR has entered into marketing partnerships with leading national and global brands and has seen significant expansion of cross-licensing and marketing agreements between NASCAR and drivers, teams and tracks. In 1998 and again in 2002, NASCAR received the "Sports and Special Event Licensor of the Year" award from LIMA, the international licensing trade association, and *License* magazine named NASCAR as its "Best Co-Branding Program of 2002."

Pyne has twice been named to *Sports Business Journal*'s "Forty Under Forty" list, and has received similar

13

# NASCAR executives

recognition from *License*. He has also been one of *Advertising Age*'s "Top 100 Marketers," *Sporting News*' "100 Most Powerful People in Sports" and the *Sports Marketing Letter*'s "Executive of the Year."

Before joining NASCAR, Pyne worked at the Portman Companies, where he helped develop a strategic plan for the company's $2 billion debt restructuring. He later was appointed executive director of AMC Events, a division of the Portman Companies that creates and manages marketing events for major sports properties. His clients included the NFL Players Association and NASCAR.

A native of Milford, Mass., Pyne attended Brown University. At Brown, he starred on the football team, serving as captain and earning All-Ivy League and All-New England honors. Pyne lives in Lake Mary, Fla., with his wife, Helene, and their children, Brendan, Shannon and Andrew.

## Gary Nelson
## Managing Director of Research and Development

Possessing a quarter-century of experience in NASCAR's top division, Gary Nelson was the ideal choice to be named as the managing director of research and development as well as the director for the NASCAR Research and Development Center in Concord, N.C., which officially opened in January 2003.

Nelson is the point person for the managing and prioritizing of the various safety, competition and cost-containment initiatives fostered in the R&D center. He moved into this position following a successful 10-year term as the series director for the NASCAR Winston Cup. He handed the series' reins over at the outset of the 2002 season to John Darby, who was promoted from director of the NASCAR Busch Series.

Before becoming the Winston Cup Series director in 1992, Nelson enjoyed a successful 15-year career as a crew chief that included capturing two of the most prestigious prizes in the sport. Nelson was the crew chief on the DiGard Racing team that won the 1983 championship with legendary driver Bobby Allison. Three years later, Nelson added a Daytona 500 crown when Geoffrey Bodine won the race in 1986.

In addition to Allison and Bodine, Nelson also crewed wins for Kyle Petty and Greg Sacks. Overall, Nelson's teams won 21 races and more than $5 million.

Nelson, a native of Redlands, Calif., resides in Concord, N.C., with his wife, Christine, and their three sons, William, Zachary and John.

## John Darby
## NASCAR NEXTEL Cup Series Director

John Darby reached the pinnacle of a racing career that spanned more than three decades when he was named the series director for NASCAR's premier division entering the 2002 season.

Darby, a native of Rockville, Ill., succeeded Gary Nelson as the Cup series director and culminated his climb through the racing ranks that began when he started his own race team in 1971 in the Street Stock division at Rockford (Ill.) Speedway. He moved on to the Late Model Stock Car Division as an owner and crew chief in 1976 and, a year later, he claimed his first championship at Rockford.

Darby retired as a team owner in 1982 to focus on a career as a race official. He began as a technical official at Rockford Speedway and moved through the ranks, which included the NASCAR Busch All-Star Tour, NASCAR Modified Tour, ARTGOP, All Pro and NASCAR Goody's Dash Series.

In 1989, he became the technical director for the NASCAR Sportsman Division and by 1993 was a technical inspector with the NASCAR Busch Series. A year later, he became a full-time NASCAR Busch Series official and was in

charge of overseeing the engine department.

In 1999, he moved into the role of the NASCAR Busch Series director after spending the previous season being groomed for the position by his predecessor, Ray Hill. Darby spent three seasons as the NASCAR Busch Series director (1999-2001).

Darby and his fiancée, Chrissy Massee, reside in Troutman, N.C. He has two daughters, Heather and Kelly.

# Brian DeHart
# NASCAR Busch Series Director

Brian DeHart began his first year as the NASCAR Busch Series director in 2002. His two seasons governing all aspects of competition in the NASCAR Busch Series—including technical inspections, rule enforcements and rule changes—have been successful.

DeHart was promoted to the position after a 10-year term as a senior inspector in NASCAR's top division, a position that gave him the insight, experience and knowledge to earn the move to series director. For DeHart, he achieved a dream when he moved from Christiansburg, Va., 12 years ago to Charlotte with the hope of one day becoming a NASCAR official. His desire and work ethic were apparent to former series director Gary Nelson, who gave DeHart the career opportunity.

While working for NASCAR, he has worked as a roll cage and chassis specialist and has maintained garage control. His ability to explain the technical side of the sport landed him a job as an analyst on TNN's *NASCAR Garage* and FOX Sports Net's *NASCAR Tech*.

Darby is single and resides in Concord, N.C.

# Wayne Auton
# NASCAR Craftsman Truck Series Director

Wayne Auton has directed the NASCAR Craftsman Truck Series since July 1995—virtually through its entire existence.

Auton is a second-generation official whose father, Robert "Hoot" Auton, served as a registrar for NASCAR's premier division, retiring in 1998 after more than three decades with the organization. His brother, Buster, is a longtime NASCAR inspector and pace car driver.

Auton's introduction to NASCAR racing came at age 10, doing odd jobs at Hickory (N.C.) Motor Speedway, where he became head of the track's safety crew seven years later. He was named chief steward at Tri-County (N.C.) Speedway in 1985.

In 1983, Auton began work as an inspector in NASCAR's premier division on a part-time basis. He joined the Goody's Dash Series, NASCAR Touring in the same position in 1986 and was named that division's director in 1990. Auton began the 1995 season as director of the what is known today as the NASCAR Autozone Elite Division, Southeast Series, and moved to the NASCAR Craftsman Truck Series the same year.

Auton, a United States Air Force veteran, lives with his wife, Libby, in Hickory, N.C. The couple has two daughters.

# 2004 NASCAR official sponsors

**America Online**
Official partner

**\*AutoZone**
Official series sponsor, Elite Division

**\*Best Western**
Official partner

**Budweiser**
Official beer

**Chevrolet (Monte Carlo)**
Official pace car

**Coca-Cola**
Official soft drink

**Craftsman Tools**
Official tools

**Dasani**
Official water

**Daytona USA**
Official attraction

**Dodge Intrepid**
Official passenger car

**Domino's Pizza**
Official pizza delivery

**DuPont Automotive**
Official finish

**Eastman Kodak**
Official film and single-use camera

**EXIDE**
Official battery

**Featherlite-Vantare**
Official trailers and luxury coaches

**Ford Trucks**
Official truck

**POWERADE**
Official sports beverage

**\*Gillette**
Official alkaline battery, official shaving product and official oral care products

**Goody's**
Official pain reliever

**Goodyear**
Official tire supplier

**The Home Depot**
Official home improvement warehouse

**International Truck & Engine Co.**
Official industrial tractor(semis)

**Kellogg's**
Official cereals

**McDonald's**
Official drive-thru

**Minute Maid**
Official juice

**Mobil 1**
Official lubricant

**\*Nextel**
Official series sponsor

**Pontiac Grand Prix**
Official pace car

**Raybestos**
Official brakes

**\*Sunoco**
Official fuel

**Toyota**
Official partner/manufacturer

**TrueValue**
Official hardware store

**UPS**
Official delivery service

**U.S. Army**
Official partner

**USG**
Official building products supplier

**Visa**
Official credit card

**XM Satellite Radio**
Exclusive satellite radio service

\*New sponsor

## Promotional partners

Cintas; DuPont Tyvek; Glidden; Husqvarna; Jack Links Beef Jerky; Just Born; Masterfoods USA (M&Ms/Combos); MeadWestvaco; Kraft/Nabisco; Old Spice; Outback Steakhouse; Tide; Unilever; Waste Management.

# Race procedures

NASCAR officials follow guidelines and rules, as any other sport or competition does. Race procedures include everything from the start of a race to flags, pit stops, restarts and, of course, the checkered flag. A pace or caution car leads the field before the start of a race.

## Pace laps

Normally, the pace car completes three laps before turning onto pit road, allowing the field to begin the race. The pace laps serve several purposes, the first of which is to allow each car to warm up its engine and its tires. Like most street vehicles, NASCAR racecars need to warm up their engines to perform to their potential. Drivers create better grip in their tires by warming them up through swerving back and forth during the pace laps.

The pace laps also serve another purpose. Because pit road has a speed limit and drivers do not have speedometers in the cars (they have tachometers that gauge the engine's revolutions per minute, or rpms), the pace car drives the pit road speed limit the first time by the frontstretch so drivers can locate that same speed on their tachometer.

A green flag marks the start of a race or the restart of a race after a caution flag has been waved.

## Flags

NASCAR officials signal messages to drivers during races by waving an assortment of colored flags. The flagman, who is always located on a stand high above the start/finish line, plays an important role.

**Green flag:** The green flag is displayed at the start of each race and for restarts during the race. Cars must maintain position as designated by NASCAR officials until they have crossed the start/finish line, and the No. 2 qualifier must not beat the No. 1 qualifier to the start/finish line. On restarts, the race will resume immediately when the green flag is waved.

**Yellow flag:** The yellow flag signifies caution and is given to the first car passing the starter immediately following the occurrence of the cause for caution. All cars receiving the yellow flag at the start/finish line shall slow down to a cautious pace, hold their position and form a single line behind the lead car.

**Red flag:** The red flag means the race must be stopped immediately, regardless of the position of the cars on the track. The red flag shall be used if, in the opinion of NASCAR officials, the race should be stopped. Cars should be brought to a stop in an area designated by NASCAR officials. Repairs, service of any nature, or refueling, whether on pit road or in the garage, will not be permitted when the race is halted due to a red flag unless the car has withdrawn from the event.

**Black flag:** The black flag means a car must go to the pits immediately and report to the NASCAR official at the car's pit area. It does not mean automatic disqualification. At the discretion of NASCAR officials, if the driver does not obey the black-flag directive, the driver might be given the black flag with a white cross at the start/finish line to inform the driver that any additional scoring of his or her car will be discontinued until further notice.

**Blue flag with diagonal yellow stripe:** Although the blue flag with its diagonal yellow stripe is typically displayed the most during races, it is probably the least recognized. This flag is displayed when drivers, who are a lap down or significantly slower, are about to be passed by lead-lap cars. Drivers who are shown the blue and diagonally yellow-striped flag must yield to the faster lead-lap cars.

**White flag:** The white flag waves when the driver in the lead begins his final lap.

**Checkered flag:** The most famous of all flags, the black and white checkered flag is displayed when the winner has crossed the finish line. All cars remaining on the track will take the checkered flag once.

Spotters are key behind-the-scenes members of any crew. They help drivers pass each other safely and avoid any debris on the track.

## Pit stops

Pit road, a road usually adjacent to the frontstretch, is where drivers come in for a pit stop. Teams choose which pit stall location they will use according to how they qualify. The pole winner has the first choice, followed by the outside pole winner and so on. The pit stall is where teams store their equipment used during the pits stops: tools, tires and fuel are just a few. When a driver enters pit road, he must enter into his designated pit box area.

Drivers who come onto pit road for service are usually in need of fuel, new tires and perhaps a mechanical adjustment to improve the handling. Crews might also make minor repairs to the vehicle on pit road. However, any major repairs must be made behind pit wall or in the garage area.

**Green-flag pit stops:** During green-flag competition, drivers are allowed to make pit stops as needed. However, drivers generally will try to stretch their fuel mileage as long as possible, hoping for a caution or yellow flag to make their pit stop. Generally, if a driver makes a green-flag pit stop for fuel, the leader might lap him one or more times. However, if the race stays "green" for the entire "fuel window," the driver might earn his lap back when the rest of the field pits for fuel.

However, if a caution flag comes out after a driver has made a green-flag pit stop, it might allow those drivers who have not yet pitted to do so under the caution and could keep those drivers who did pit under the green flag a lap down.

**Yellow-flag pit stops:** During a caution period, NASCAR will make the determination to open and close pit road. A NASCAR official, in front of the entrance to pit road, will use an open/closed flag to communicate to drivers when the pits are open or closed. Once the pits are open, only the lead-lap cars are allowed to pit the first time around. Cars that are down a lap or more must wait until the second time around to make their pit stop. Once all cars exit pit road, they must rejoin the field behind the pace car.

## Restarts

In 2003, NASCAR moved to prevent the practice of racing back to the start/finish line after a yellow flag was displayed. The rule provides for the first driver running one lap behind the leader when a caution is displayed to start in the last position on the lead lap when the race is restarted. All other cars one lap behind the leader will stay one lap behind the lead lap and in their respective positions from when the caution flag was displayed.

Following caution periods, NASCAR officials communicate to the drivers of a restart when there is one lap to go before the green flag is waved. The flag man signals one lap to go at the start/finish line by holding up one finger. Generally, team spotters and crew chiefs help communicate to their drivers over the radio when there is one lap remaining before the restart.

For restarts during the race, except those during the final 25 laps, cars on the lead lap line up on the outside toward the wall while the lapped cars line up to the inside for a double-file restart.

NASCAR uses a 25-lap rule and a 10-lap rule for restarts late in the race. The 25-lap rule states that if a restart occurs with less than 25 laps remaining and more than 10 laps remaining, only lead-lap cars are permitted to restart in the outside line.

The 10-lap rule states that if there are 10 or fewer laps remaining in an event, cars restart in single file with the leader of the race first in line and remaining lead-lap cars behind. All other cars must hold their respective track positions, regardless of running order.

When the green flag waves on restarts, all passing must be done on the righthand side until drivers cross the start/finish line.

# Qualifying and provisionals

For any given NASCAR NEXTEL Cup Series event, it is unknown how many cars will enter. But one thing is certain: a maximum of 43 cars will start. NASCAR uses time trials, known as qualifying, to choose which teams make "The Show."

## Qualifying draw

NASCAR officials use a draw to determine the qualifying order. Each team sends its crew chief or a representative to draw a number at the qualifying lottery, which is usually on the morning of qualifying. If 50 cars are entered, the NASCAR official will put Nos. 1-51 (always one more than there are entries) into a spinning ball. Each team representative draws one number, starting with the crew chief whose owner is highest in the owner point standings. After each team draws, officials record the number. When every team has drawn, the qualifying order is set.

## Qualifying

To qualify for a race, drivers take one or two timed laps, depending on the track. Drivers receive one warmup lap before taking the green flag. The driver with the quickest qualifying time starts on the pole, which is the inside (left side) of the front row. The one exception to these procedures is the Daytona 500, which follows a different qualifying method (see Daytona 500 qualifying).

## Provisionals

If a driver fails to make the race through qualifying, he or she can take a provisional spot. Provisional starting positions are 37-42. The process for determining provisional entries:

Through the first four races of the NASCAR NEXTEL Cup Series season, provisional starting positions 37-42 are assigned based on the previous year's final NASCAR series owner point standings. After the fourth race and until the conclusion of the NASCAR NEXTEL Cup Series season, provisional starting positions 37-42 are based on the current owner point standings.

Provisional starting positions are assigned beginning with the highest-ranked owner in the NASCAR NEXTEL Cup Series championship owner point standings who did not qualify for positions 1-36 and are assigned in descending order until all provisional spots are filled.

Each owner is allotted four provisionals at the start of the season. Owners are also given one provisional after his/her driver has attempted to qualify for eight races up to a maximum allotment of eight provisionals for the season.

Each provisional used during the first four races of the season does not count for owners who finished in the top 25 of the previous year's NASCAR championship owner standings. However, owners who finished outside the top 25 of the previous season's NASCAR championship owner standings are charged for each provisional used during the first four races.

Likewise, each provisional used after the fourth event does not count for owners who are in the top 25 of the NASCAR NEXTEL Cup Series championship owner standings. However, owners who are outside the top 25 of the NASCAR NEXTEL Cup championship owner standings are charged for each provisional used after the fourth event.

If the number of entrants eligible for a provisional starting position for an event is equal to or lesser than the number of starting positions available, provisionals assigned to starting positions 37-43 will not count toward the maximum season allotment.

## Champion provisional

The champion provisional is the 43rd and final position in a NASCAR NEXTEL Cup Series event. If, after provisional positions 37-42 have been assigned, an owner remains whose driver is a past NASCAR Cup champion who participated as a driver in the previous NASCAR Cup season and who was entered in the event for that owner, and in that car, before the entry deadline, the champion provisional will be assigned to that owner. A former champion may use up to eight champion provisionals during the season. If more than one former champion remains, the provisional is awarded to the most recent champion.

If there is not a former NASCAR Cup Series champion among drivers who have yet to be designated a starting position, the 43rd position is awarded to the next owner as described in the provisional section above.

## Daytona 500 qualifying

The Great American Race uses a unique qualifying procedure. In the first round of qualifying, the fastest car earns the pole position for both the Daytona 500 and the first of two 125-mile qualifying races known as the Gatorade 125s. The second-fastest car earns the outside pole for the Daytona 500 and starts on the pole for the second Gatorade 125 race.

Drivers qualifying in odd-numbered positions (first, third, fifth, etc.) compete in the first Gatorade 125 race and drivers qualifying in even-numbered positions (second, fourth, sixth, etc.) compete in the second.

The top 14 finishers, not including the pole sitter, in the first 125-mile qualifying race line up behind the pole sitter for the Daytona 500, while the top 14 finishers, not including the outside pole sitter, in the second 125-mile qualifying race line up behind the outside pole sitter. Thus, the first 30 of 43 positions are filled. The next six positions (31-36) are awarded to drivers who were the fastest in qualifying. The final seven positions (37-43) are given to teams entitled to provisionals as explained above.

# Glossary

## A

**Aerodynamics:** As applied to racing, the study of airflow and the forces of resistance and pressure that result from the flow of air over, under and around a moving car.

**A-frame:** Either the upper or lower connecting suspension piece (in the shape of an A) locking the frame to the spindle.

**Adhesion:** The "stick" between two touching objects. Adhesion implies a static condition, while traction implies a dynamic (moving) condition.

**Air box:** Housing for the air cleaner that connects the air intake at the base of the windshield to the carburetor.

**Air dam:** A metal strip that hangs beneath the front grill, often inches from the ground. The air dam helps provide aerodynamic downforce at the front of the car.

**Air filter:** Paper, gauze or a synthetic fiber element used to prevent dirt particles from entering the engine. Located in the air box.

**Air pressure:** Force exerted by air within a tire, expressed in pounds per square inch (psi).

**Alternator:** A belt-driven device mounted on the front of the engine that recharges the battery while the engine is running.

**A-post:** The post extending from the roofline to the base of the windshield on either side of the car.

**Apron:** The paved portion of a racetrack that separates the racing surface from the (usually unpaved) infield.

**Axle:** Rotating shafts that connect the rear differential gears to the rear wheels.

## B

**Ball joint:** A ball inside a socket that can turn and pivot in any direction. Used to allow suspension to travel while the driver steers the car.

**Banking:** The sloping of a racetrack, particularly at a curve or corner, from the apron to the outside wall. Degree of banking refers to the height of a track's slope at its outside edge.

**Bear grease:** Slang term used to describe patching material used to fill cracks and holes or smooth bumps on a track's surface. Can also be used as a sealer on the track.

**Bell housing:** A cover, shaped like a bell, that surrounds the flywheel, which is the clutch that connects the engine to the transmission.

**Bias-ply:** Layers of fabric within a tire woven in angles. Also used as a term to describe tires made in this manner.

**Binders:** Slang term for a racecar's brakes.

**Bite:** (1) "Round of bite" describes the turning or adjusting of a car's jacking screws found at each wheel. "Weight jacking" distributes the car's weight at each wheel. (2) Adhesion of a tire to the track surface.

**Bleeder valve:** A valve in the wheel used to reduce air pressure in tires.

**Blend line:** Line painted on the track near the apron and extending from the pit road exit into the first turn. When leaving the pits, a driver must stay below it to safely "blend" back into traffic.

**Blister:** An overheating of the tread compound resulting in bubbles on the tire surface.

**Bias-ply tires are composed of fabric woven in angles.**

**Blown motor:** Major engine failure. For instance, when a connecting rod goes through the engine block. Usually produces a lot of smoke and steam.

**Bodywork:** The fabricated sheet metal that encloses the chassis.

**Bore:** Pistons travel up and down within each cylinder, or bore, in the engine block.

**B-post:** Post extending from the roofline to the base of window behind the driver's head.

**Brake caliper:** The part of the braking system that, when applied by the driver through pressure on the pedal, clamps the brake disk/rotor to slow or stop the car.

## C

**Camber:** The amount a tire is tilted in or out from vertical. Described in degrees, either positive or negative.

**Camshaft:** A rotating shaft within the engine that opens and closes the intake and exhaust valves in the engine.

**Carburetor:** A device connected directly to the gas pedal and mounted on top of the intake manifold that controls the air-fuel mixture going to the engine.

20

**Chassis:** The steel structure or frame of the car.

**Chute:** A racetrack straightaway.

**Compound:** A formula or "recipe" of rubber composing a particular tire. Different tracks require different tire compounds. Left-side tires are considerably softer than right-side tires. It's against the rules to run left sides on the right. The rubber has four basic components: rubber polymers, carbon blacks, oils and curatives.

**Compression ratio:** Amount the air-fuel mixture is compressed as the piston reaches the top of the bore. The higher the compression, the more horsepower produced.

**Contact patch:** The portion of the tire that makes contact with the racing surface. The size of each tire's contact patch changes as the car travels.

**Cowl:** A removable metal scoop at the base of the windshield and rear of the hood that directs air into the air box.

**C-post:** The post extending from the roofline of a racecar to the base of the rear window to the top of the deck lid.

**Crankcase:** The area of the engine block that houses the crankshaft.

**Crankshaft:** The rotating shaft within the engine that delivers the power from the pistons to the flywheel, and from there to the transmission.

**Cubic-inch displacement:** The size of the engine measured in cubic inches.

**Cut tire:** A slice or puncture of the tread or sidewall due to high-speed contact with debris on the track or by contact with part of another racecar.

**Cylinder head:** Made of aluminum, it is bolted to the top of each side of the engine block. Cylinder heads hold the valves and spark plugs. Passages through the heads make up the intake and exhaust ports.

**Deck lid:** Slang term for the trunk lid of a racecar.

**Dirty air:** Aerodynamic term for the turbulent air currents caused by fast-moving cars that can cause a particular car to lose control.

**Donuts:** Slang term for black, circular, dent-line marks on the side panels of cars, usually caused after rubbing against other cars at high speed.

**Downforce:** A combination of aerodynamic and centrifugal forces. The more downforce, the more grip your car has. But more downforce also means more drag, which can rob a racecar of speed.

**Draft:** Slang term for the aerodynamic effect that allows two or more cars traveling nose-to-tail to run faster than a single car. When one car follows another closely, the front car cuts through the air, providing a cleaner path of air (less resistance) for the car in back.

**Drafting:** The practice of two or more cars, while racing, to run nose-to-tail, almost touching. The lead car, by displacing the air in front of it, creates a vacuum between its rear end and the nose of the following car, pulling the second car along with it.

**Drag:** The resistance a car experiences when passing through air at high speeds. A resisting force exerted on a car parallel to its airstream and opposite in direction to its motion.

**Driveshaft:** A steel tube that connects the transmission of a racecar to the rear-end housing.

**Dyno:** Shortened term for "dynamometer," a machine used to measure an engine's horsepower.

**Engine block:** An iron casting from the manufacturer that envelops the crankshaft, connecting rods and pistons.

**Equalized:** When the inner liner of a tire loses air pressure and that pressure becomes the same as that within the outer tire, creating a vibration. The inner shield should have a higher psi than the outer tire.

**Esses:** Slang term used for a series of acute lefthand and righthand turns on a road course, one turn immediately following another.

**Fabricator:** A person who specializes in creating the sheet metal body of a stock car. Most teams employ two or more.

**Factory:** A term designating the Big Three auto manufacturers: General Motors (GM), Ford, and DaimlerChrysler. The "factory days" refer to the periods in the 1950s and '60s when manufacturers actively and openly provided sponsorship money and technical support to race teams.

**Fan:** An electrically or mechanically driven device used to pull air through the radiator or oil cooler. Heat is transferred from the hot oil or water in the radiator to the moving air.

**Firewall:** A solid metal plate that separates the engine compartment from the driver's compartment of the racecar.

**Flat-out:** Slang term for racing a car as fast as possible under the given weather and track conditions.

**Flywheel:** A heavy metal rotating wheel that is part of the racecar's clutch system, used to keep elements such as the crank shaft turning steadily.

**Four-barrel:** A type of carburetor.

**Frame:** The metal skeleton or structure of a racecar, on which the sheet metal of the car's body is formed. Also referred to as a "chassis."

**Front clip:** Concluding at the firewall, the frontmost section of a racecar. Holds the engine and its associated electrical, lubricating and cooling apparatus, and the braking, steering and suspension mechanisms.

**Front steer:** A racecar in which the steering components are located ahead of the front axle.

**Fuel:** Also known as "gasoline."

**Fuel cell:** A holding tank for a racecar's supply of gasoline. Consists of a metal box that contains a flexible, tear-resistant bladder and foam baffling. A product of aerospace technology, it's designed to eliminate or minimize fuel spillage.

**Fuel pump:** A device that pumps fuel from the fuel cell through the fuel line into the carburetor.

**Gasket:** Made of thin paper, metal, silicone or other synthetic materials, it is used as a seal between two similarly machined metal surfaces such as cylinder heads and the engine block.

**Gauge:** An instrument, usually mounted on the dashboard, used to monitor engine conditions such as fuel pressure, oil pressure and temperature, water pressure and temperature, and revolutions per minute (rpms).

**Gears:** Circular, wheel-shaped parts with teeth along the edges. The interlocking of these two mechanisms enables one to turn the other.

**Give-up:** A reduction in lap times caused by aging tires.

**Greenhouse:** The upper area of the racecar that extends from the base of the windshield in the front, the tops of the doors on the sides and the base of the rear window in the back. Includes all of the A-, B- and C-posts, the entire glass area and the roof.

**Groove:** Slang term for the best route around the racetrack; the most efficient or quickest way around the track for a particular driver. The "high groove" takes a car closer to the outside wall for most of a lap, while the "low groove" takes a car closer to the apron than the outside wall. Road racers use the term "line." Drivers search for a fast groove, and that has been known to change depending on track and weather conditions.

**Happy Hour:** Slang term for the last official practice session held before an event. Usually takes place the day before the race and after all qualifying sessions and support races have been staged.

**Harmonic balancer:** An element used to reduce vibrations in the crankshaft.

**Handling:** Generally, a racecar's performance while racing, qualifying and practicing. How a car "handles" is determined by its tires, suspension geometry, aerodynamics and other factors.

**Hauler:** The 18-wheel tractor-trailer rig teams use to transport two racecars, engines, tools and support equipment to the racetracks. Cars are stowed in the top section, while the bottom floor is used for work space.

**Head wrench:** Slang term used for a race team's crew chief.

**Heat cycle:** Used to describe when a tire is raised to operating temperature.

**High heat:** Above-normal (260 degrees Fahrenheit) tire temperature.

**Horsepower:** A measurement of mechanical or engine power. Measured in the amount of power it takes to move 33,000 pounds one foot in one minute.

**Ignition:** An electrical system used to ignite the air-fuel mixture in an internal combustion engine.

**Intake manifold:** A housing that directs the air-fuel mixture through the port openings in the cylinder heads.

**Intermediate track:** Term describing a racetrack one mile to less than two miles in length.

**Interval:** The time-distance between two cars. Referred to roughly in car lengths or precisely in seconds.

**Jet:** When air is sent at a high velocity through the carburetor, jets direct the fuel into the airstream. Jets are made slightly larger to make a richer mixture or slightly smaller to make a more lean mixture, depending on track and weather conditions.

**Lapped traffic:** Cars that have completed at least one full lap less than the race leader.

**Lead lap:** The lap the race leader is currently on.

**Line:** See "groove."

**Loading:** Weight at a given tire position on a car due to aerodynamics, vehicle weight and lateral G-forces in a turn.

**Loose:** When the rear tires of the car have trouble sticking in the corners. Also known as "oversteer." This causes the car to "fishtail" as the rear end swings outward during turns. A minor amount of this effect can be desirable on certain tracks.

**Loose stuff:** Debris such as sand, pebbles or small pieces of rubber that collect on a track's apron or near the outside wall during a race.

**Lug nuts:** Large nuts applied with a high-pressure air wrench to a wheel during a pit stop to secure the tires in place. All NASCAR cars use five lug nuts on each wheel, and penalties are assessed if a team fails to put all five on during a pit stop.

# M

**Magnaflux:** Short for "magnetic particle inspection." A procedure for checking all ferrous (steel) parts (suspension pieces, connecting rods, cylinder heads, etc.) for cracks and other defects using a solution of metal particles and fluorescent dye and a black light. Surface cracks appear as red lines.

**Marbles:** Excess rubber build-up above the upper groove on the racetrack. Also known as "loose stuff."

# N

**Neutral:** A term drivers use when referring to how their car is handling. When a car is neither loose nor pushing ("tight").

# O

**Oil pump:** This device pumps oil to lubricate all moving engine parts.

# P

**P&G:** The procedure for checking the cubic-inch displacement of an engine. The term comes from the manufacturer of the particular gauge used.

**Panhard bar:** A lateral bar that keeps the rear tires centered within the body of the car. It connects the frame on one side and the rear axle on the other. Also called the "track bar."

**Piston:** A circular element that moves up and down in the cylinder, compressing the air-fuel mixture in the top of the chamber, helping produce horsepower.

**Pit road:** The area where pit crews service the cars. Generally located along the front straightaway, but because of space limitations, some racetracks sport pit roads on both the front and back straightaways.

**Pit stall:** The area along pit road designated for a particular team's use during pit stops. Each car stops in the team's pit stall before being serviced.

**Pole position:** Slang term for the foremost position on the starting grid, awarded to the fastest qualifier.

**Post-entry (PE):** A team or driver who submits an entry blank for a race after the deadline for submission has passed. A post-entry receives no driver or owner points.

**Push:** See "tight."

# Q

**Quarter-panel:** The sheet metal on both sides of the car from the C-post to the rear bumper below the deck lid and above the wheel well.

# R

**Rear clip:** The section of a racecar that begins at the base of the rear windshield and extends to the rear bumper. Contains the car's fuel cell and rear suspension components.

**Rear-steer:** A car in which the steering components are located behind the front axle.

**Restart:** The waving of the green flag following a caution period.

**Restrictor plate:** A thin metal plate with four holes that restrict airflow from the carburetor into the engine. Used to reduce horsepower and keep speeds down. The restrictor plates are used at Daytona International Speedway and Talladega Superspeedway, the two biggest and fastest tracks in NASCAR.

**Ride height:** The distance between the car's frame rails and the ground.

**RPM:** Short for revolutions per minute, a measurement of the speed of the engine's crankshaft.

**Roll cage:** The steel tubing inside the racecar's interior. Designed to protect the driver from impacts or rollovers, the roll cage must meet strict NASCAR safety guidelines and is inspected regularly.

**Round:** Slang term for a way of making chassis adjustments using the racecar's springs. A wrench is inserted in a jack bolt attached to the springs and is used to tighten or loosen the amount of play in the spring. This in turn can loosen or tighten the handling of a racecar.

# S

**Safety shield:** Also called a safety liner. A safety feature often referred to as a "tire within a tire." This inner tire is used in the NASCAR NEXTEL Cup Series and will support a car if the outer tire is cut down.

**Scuffs:** Slang term for tires used at least once and saved for further racing. A lap or two is enough to "scuff" them in. Most often used in qualifying.

**Setup:** Slang term for the tuning and adjustments made to a racecar's suspension before and during a race.

**Short track:** Racetracks that are less than a mile in length.

**Silly Season:** Slang for the period that begins during the latter part of the season, wherein teams announce driver, crew and/or sponsor changes for the following year.

**Slick:** A track condition where, for a number of reasons, it is hard for a car's tires to adhere to the surface or get a good "bite." A slick racetrack is not necessarily wet or slippery because of oil, water, etc.

**Slingshot:** A maneuver in which a car following the leader in a draft suddenly steers around it, breaking the vacuum; this provides an extra burst of speed that allows the second car to take the lead. See "drafting."

**Splash 'n' go:** A quick pit stop that involves nothing more than refueling the racecar with the amount of fuel necessary to finish the race.

**Spoiler:** A metal blade attached to the rear deck lid of the car. It helps restrict airflow over the rear of the car, providing downforce and traction.

**Sponsor:** An individual or business establishment that financially supports a driver, team, race or series of races in return for advertising and marketing benefits. Usually, the sponsor's name, colors and corporate or product logo are adorned on the car for the highest visibility and product identification.

**Stagger:** The difference in size between the tires on the left and right sides of a car. Because of a tire's makeup, slight variations in circumference result. Stagger between right-side and left-side tires might range from less than a half inch to more than an inch. Stagger applies to only bias-ply tires and not radials.

**Stick:** Slang term used for tire traction, as in "the car's sticking to the track."

**Stickers:** Slang term for new tires. The name is derived from the manufacturer's stickers that are affixed to each new tire's contact surface.

**Stop 'n' go:** A penalty, usually assessed for speeding on pit road or for unsafe driving. The car must be brought onto pit road at the appropriate speed and stopped for one full second in the team's pit stall before returning to the track.

**Superspeedway:** A racetrack of a mile or more in distance, road courses included. Drivers refer to three types of oval tracks. Short tracks are under one mile, intermediate tracks are at least a mile but under two miles, and speedways are two miles and longer.

**Sway bar:** Sometimes called an "antiroll bar." Bar used to resist or counteract the rolling force of the car body through the turns.

# T

**Template:** A device used to check the body shape and size, to ensure compliance with the rules. The template closely resembles the shape of the factory version of the car.

**Tight:** Also known as "understeer." A car is said to be tight if the front wheels lose traction before the rear wheels do. A tight racecar doesn't seem able to steer sharply enough through the turns. Instead, the front end continues toward the wall.

**Toe:** Looking at the car from the front, the amount the tires are turned in or out. If you imagine your feet to be the two front tires of a racecar, standing with your toes together would represent toe-in. Standing with your heels together would represent toe-out.

**Track bar:** See "panhard bar."

**Trading paint:** Slang term used to describe aggressive driving involving a lot of bumping and rubbing.

**Trailing arm:** A rear suspension piece holding the rear axle firmly fore and aft yet allowing it to travel up and down.

**Tri-oval:** A racetrack that has a "hump" or "fifth turn" in addition to the standard four corners. Not to be confused with a triangle-shaped speedway, which has only three distinct corners.

**200-mph tape:** Also known as "racer's tape." Duct tape so strong it will hold a banged-up racecar together long enough to finish a race.

# U

**Uniformity:** Tire-to-tire variation in size/properties. It's harder to control the size of a flexible tire made from rubber and fabric than it is something more solid such as wood, plastic or metal.

# V

**Victory lane:** Sometimes called the "winner's circle." The spot on each racetrack's infield where the race winner parks for the celebration.

# W

**Wedge, round of:** Adjusting the handling of the car by altering pressure on the rear springs.

**Wedge:** Term that refers to the cross-weight adjustment on a racecar.

**Window net:** A woven mesh that hangs across the driver's side window to prevent the driver's head and limbs from being exposed during an accident.

**Wrench:** Slang term for a racing mechanic.

# Anatomy of a pit stop

Tire carriers each carry a 50- to 55-pound tire to the car's right side and place each on the wheel after the tire changer removes the old tire. He repeats the process on the left side with new tires rolled to them by crew members behind pit wall. The rear tire carrier also might adjust the rear jack bolt to alter the car's handling.

The catch can man holds the can to collect overflow from the fuel cell. He signals the jackman with hand in the air when refueling is complete.

The gas man pours two 11-gallon (80-pound) dump cans of fuel into the 22-gallon fuel cell.

Tire changers each run to the car's right side and use an air-impact gun to remove five lug nuts off the old tire and bolt on a new tire. The process is repeated on the left side.

The jackman carries a 15-20 pound hydraulic jack from the pit wall to raise the car's right side. After the new tires are bolted on, he drops the car to the ground and repeats the process on the left side.

Only seven members of the pit crew are allowed over the wall. On occasion, and at the discretion of NASCAR officials, an eighth or extra man is allowed over the wall to clean the windshield or service the driver.

# Inside the cockpit

The cockpit of a NASCAR stock car serve as the "weekend office" for NASCAR NEXTEL Cup Series drivers. Configured uniquely by each team, it features an extensive array of safety features, as well as instrument gauges that allow the driver to monitor the car's performance.

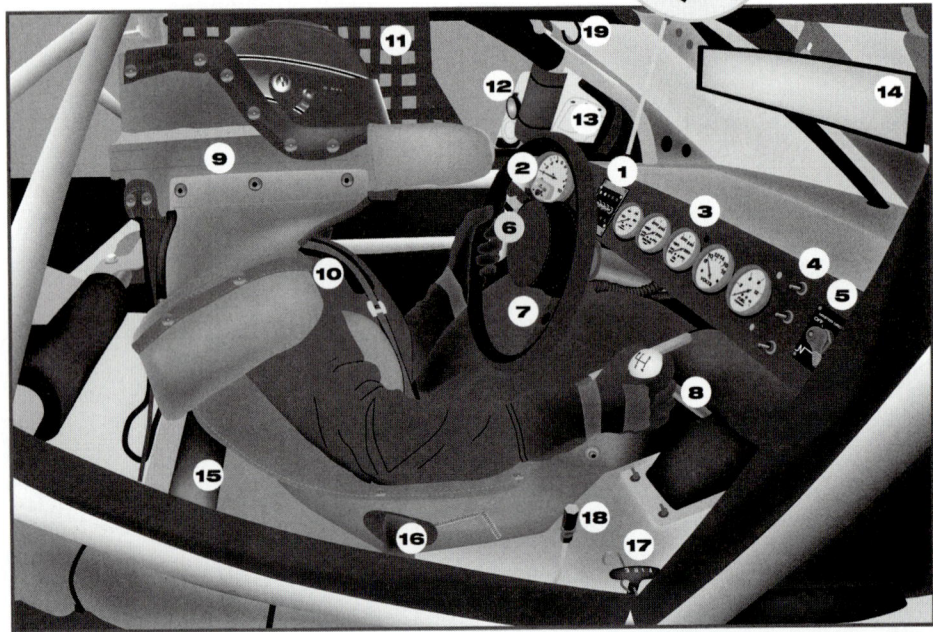

**1 Main Switch Panel**
Contains switches for starter, ignition and cooling fans

**2 Tachometer**
Monitors revolutions per minute (RPMs) of engine, assisting driver in selecting gears and monitoring engine power

**3 Engine Gauge Cluster**
Monitors engine oil pressure, water temperature, oil temperature, voltage and fuel pressure

**4 Auxillary Switches**
Can serve a number of purposes, including turning on the backup ignition system, ventilating fans or helmet cooling system.

**5 Master Switch**
Shuts down electrical system in emergency situations

**6 Ignition Kill Switch**
Shuts off engine in emergency situations

**7 Radio Button**
Controls communication to pits and race spotter

**8 Gearshift**
Controls four-speed manual transmission

**9 Safety Seat**
Provides extra support and protection for head, shoulders ribs and lower extremities

**10 Head and Neck Restraint**
NASCAR mandates the use of a head-and-neck restraint system, either the approved HANS Device or Hutchens Device, for all drivers competing in any of NASCAR's three national series (NASCAR NEXTEL Cup Series, NASCAR Busch Series, NASCAR Craftsman Truck Series), as well as its touring series

**11. Window Net**
Keeps driver's left arm inside the car during accidents

**12 Rear View Mirror**

**13 Fresh Air Vent**
Directs outside air into the driving compartment.

**14 Main Rear View Mirror**

**15 Fire Extinguisher**

**16 Seat Belt Harness**

**17 Fire Extinguisher Switch**
Discharges fire-suppressing chemicals into the driving compartment

**18 Fire Extinguisher Discharge Nozzle**

**19 Helmet Hook**

Source: NASCAR

# Cutaway car

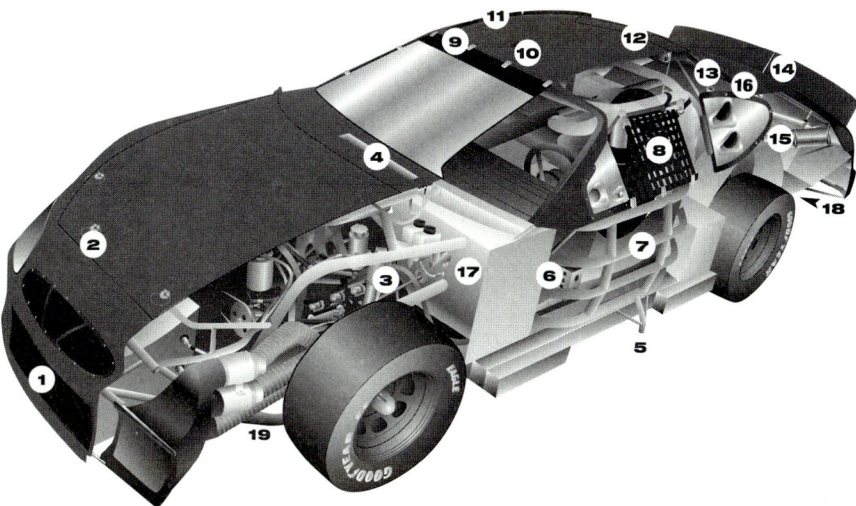

**1 Front Grill Openings** – These inlets allow air to pass through the radiator and ensure that the engine performs at the optimum temperature. Additional air ducts to the side help cool the brake systems.

**2 Hood Pins** – There are four metal-and-wire hood pins with wire tethers that serve as a safety feature by keeping the hood closed.

**3 Shock Absorbers** – Help control the compression and rebound of the suspension springs and provide a smooth and controlled ride to the driver.

**4 Cowl Induction** – Housing for the air cleaner that connects the air intake at the base of the windshield to the carburetor.

**5 Jack Post** – This is the area where the jackman must place the jack on each side of the car during a pit stop. Some teams place a piece of fluorescent or bright-colored tape on the body of the car to indicate the specific area of the jack brace.

**6 Impact Data Recorder** – The impact data recorder, which records numerous measurements such as G Forces and Delta V (change in speed) from an accident, is located on the left side of the driver's seat.

**7 Roll Cage** – A cage made of stell tubing inside the stock car's interior that is designed to protect the driver from impacts and rollovers. The roll cages must adhere to strict NASCAR safety guidelines and are inspected regularly.

**8 Window Net** – Safety device located on the driver's side window to keep his head and arms inside the car during an accident.

**9 Windshield Clips** – The clips attach the windshield to the chassis and allow for easy removal should a driver need to be extricated from the vehicle.

**10 Television Camera** – Miniature camera mounted on the roof of the car that allows NASCAR fans a great view of their favorite drivers in race traffic.

**11 Roof Strips** – The two half-inch tall aluminum strips that run lengthwise on the roof and help prevent the stock car from flipping when it is turned sideways during a spin or accident.

**12 Roof Flaps** – The flaps, which were first used in NASCAR competition in 1994, are a safety feature that was developed to help prevent the stock car from becoming airborne when it is turned sideways or backward during a spin or accident.

**13 Jacking Bolt** – Area where the crew uses a tool to adjust the handling of the car by altering pressure on the rear springs. A wrench is inserted into a jack bolt attached to the springs and is used to adjust the preload on the springs and, in turn, the handling of the race car. Sometimes will hear the slang reference that the team is putting in a round (one turn) of wedge.

**14 Rear Spoiler** – A metal blade that is attached to the deck lid of the car. The spoiler deflects the air coming off the roof and onto the rear deck lid, which, in turn, creates rear downforce and more rear traction for the car.

**15 Dry Break Fuel Cell** – Holding tank for race car's gasoline supply that consists of a metal box containing a flexible, tear-resistant bladder and foam baffling, both of which are safety enhancements. On most racetracks, the cell holds 22 gallons of fuel; at restrictor-plate tracks, it holds 13.5 gallons. The Dry Break Inlet is a spring-loaded tube, allowing fast refueling without fuel spillage.

**16 Deck Lid** – Slang term for the trunk lid of a stock car.

**17 Firewall** – Sheet steel plate that separates the engine compartment from the driver's compartment of the race car. Also used at the rear to separate the fuel cell compartment from the driver's compartment.

**18 Track Bar** – Lateral bar that keeps the rear tires centered within the body of the car. The bar connects the frame on one side to the rear axle on the opposite side and can be adjusted in height to alter the handling of the car.

**19 Sway or Anti-Roll Bar** – Used to resist or counteract the rolling force of the car body through the turns.

Source: NASCAR

# Tech elements

|  | NASCAR NEXTEL Cup Series | NASCAR Busch Series | NASCAR Craftsman Truck Series |
|---|---|---|---|
| ELIGIBLE MODELS | Chevrolet Monte Carlo<br>Dodge Intrepid<br>Ford Taurus<br>Pontiac Grand Prix** | Chevrolet Monte Carlo<br>Dodge Intrepid<br>Ford Taurus<br>Pontiac Grand Prix** | Chevrolet C1500 (Silverado)<br>Dodge Ram 1500<br>Ford F150<br>Toyota Tundra |
| YEARS | 2002-2004 | 2002-2004 | 2002-2004*** |
| ENGINE | Cast Iron 5.7L V8<br>Aluminum cylinder heads | Cast Iron 5.7L V8<br>Aluminum cylinder heads | Cast Iron 5.7L V8<br>Aluminum cylinder heads |
| HORSEPOWER* | 790 @ 9400 rpm | 660 @ 7900 rpm | 650 @ 8000 rpm |
| COMPRESSION RATIO | 12:1 | 12:1 | 12:1 |
| TORQUE | 550 ft/lb @ 7500 rpm | 540 ft/lb @ 6400 rpm | 535 ft/lb @ 6000 rpm |
| DISPLACEMENT | 358 c.i. max | 358 c.i. max | 358 c.i. max |
| INDUCTION | One 4V Holley carburetor | One 4V Holley carburetor | One 4V Holley carburetor |
| TOP SPEED | 200 mph (est.) | 195 mph (est.) | 185 mph (est.) |
| TRANSMISSION | 4-Speed | 4-Speed | 4-Speed |
| FUEL* | 110 octane<br>22-gallon capacity | 112 octane<br>22-gallon capacity | 112 octane<br>22-gallon capacity |
| FRONT SUSPENSION | Independent coil springs,<br>Twin control arms | Independent coil springs,<br>Twin control arms | Independent coil springs,<br>Twin control arms |
| REAR SUSPENSION | Trailing arms, coil springs,<br>panhard bar | Trailing arms, coil springs,<br>panhard bar | Trailing arms, coil springs,<br>panhard bar |
| CHASSIS | Rectangular steel tubing<br>w/integral roll-cage | Rectangular steel tubing<br>w/integral roll-cage | Rectangular steel tubing<br>w/integral roll-cage |
| BODY LENGTH | 200.7 inches | 203.5 inches | 206 inches |
| BODY WIDTH | 72.5 inches | 74.5 inches | 75 inches |
| HEIGHT | 51 inches (min) | 50.5 inches (min) | 59 inches (min) |
| WEIGHT | 3400 lbs (w/o driver) | 3,400 lbs (w/o driver) | 3,400 lbs (w/o driver) |
| FRONT AIR DAM* | 3.5 inches | 4 inches | 4 inches |
| GEAR RATIO | 2.90 to 6.33:1 | 2.91 to 5.29:1 | 3.60 to 6.83:1 |
| SPOILER* | 55" wide x 5.5" high<br>for 2003-2004 makes;<br>2002 makes vary | 57" wide x 5.75" high<br>for all makes | 66.75" wide x 8" high for all makes<br>68.75" wide x 8" high at designated speedways |
| WHEEL BASE | 110 inches | 105 inches | 112 inches |
| WHEELS | Steel 15" x 9.5" | Steel 15" x 9.5" | Steel 15" x 9.5" |
| TREAD WIDTH | 60.5 inches (max) | 60.5 inches (max) | 60.5 inches (max) |
| FRONT BRAKES | Disc | Disc | Disc |
| REAR BRAKES | Disc | Disc | Disc |

*Specifications may vary from restrictor-plate races; **Eligible model years for the Pontiac Grand Prix are 2002-2003. *** Only 2004 models are eligible for superspeedways (tracks one mile or more in length), and 2004 model for all tracks for Toyota Tundra.

# NASCAR ladder system

Reaching more than 110 racetracks in 36 states, NASCAR racing offers something for everyone, from the stars of the NEXTEL Cup Series to the weekend warriors in the NASCAR Weekly Racing Series presented by Dodge.

The Weekly Racing Series is the sport's foundation. Entry-level divisions at nearly 80 tracks provide drivers with their first racing opportunity. Drivers race at their home track for prizes and regional championships. Dale Earnhardt Jr., Dale Jarrett and Bobby Labonte are among those drivers who began their careers at this level.

The next step is the regional touring program, which is a training ground for NASCAR's national series in two divisions: Elite and Grand National. Within these divisions, different series compete in different parts of the country. These scaled-down versions of NASCAR's national series travel to short tracks, super-speedways and road courses. Kurt Busch, Kevin Harvick and Michael Waltrip are among those who took part in this program.

## NASCAR Weekly Racing Series presented by Dodge

Thousands of competitors race in the Weekly Racing Series at local dirt and asphalt short tracks from coast to coast, offering the best in local racing and a chance for drivers to become a NASCAR champion. A variety of cars compete in this series: Late Model Stock Cars, Sportsman, Limited Late Models, Dirt Late Models, Modifieds and Super Stocks. Dodge and other sponsors post $1.7 million in awards for the drivers.

Tracks are divided into eight regions. Track champions are compared using NASCAR's Competition Performance Index (CPI) to determine eight regional winners. The winners are then compared to determine the national champion. Each of the regional champions wins a point fund award of more than $40,000, while the national champion earns more than $160,000.

## NASCAR Grand National

**Busch North Series—West Series**

Modeled after the NASCAR Busch Series cars, the NASCAR Grand National Division is open to eligible models of American-made, steel-bodied passenger sedans. The cars are powered by 350 to 358 cubic-inch V-8 engines with a maximum compression ratio of 12:1. The cars have a 105-inch wheelbase, weigh 3,100 pounds and run on Goodyear bias-ply tires.

The Busch North Series competes on short tracks, speedways and road courses in Maine, New Hampshire, Vermont, Massachusetts, Connecticut, New York, Pennsylvania and Delaware. The 2003 champion was Andy Santerre of Cherryfield, Maine.

Entering its 51st season—making it the West Coast's oldest stock car racing circuit—the West Series competes in Arizona, California, Nevada, Oregon, Utah and Washington. This series is open to cars with the same specifications as the Busch North Series. The series traditionally used 110-inch wheelbase cars, similar to NASCAR NEXTEL Cup Series cars. The 2003 series winner was Scott Lynch of Burley, Idaho.

## NASCAR Elite Division

**AutoZone Elite Division, Southwest Series**
**AutoZone Elite Division, Southeast Series**
**AutoZone Elite Division, Midwest Series**
**AutoZone Elite Division, Northwest Series**

Each of the Elite Divisions operates with the same specifications: 2,900-pound cars use metal or fiberglass bodies, are powered by 350 to 358 cubic-inch engines and have a wheelbase between 101 inches and 105 inches. The cars drive on Hoosier bias-ply tires.

The AutoZone Elite Division, Midwest Series races in Illinois and Wisconsin. The 2003 winner was Steve Carlson of West Salem, Wis. The AutoZone Elite Division, Southeast Series has tracks in Virginia, South Carolina, Kentucky, Tennessee and other states in the South. The 2003 winner was Charlie Bradberry of Chelsea, Ala. The AutoZone Elite Division, Southwest Series competes in Arizona, California and Colorado. The 2003 winner was Auggie Vidovich Jr. of Lakeside, Calif. The AutoZone Elite Division, Northwest Series competes primarily in Washington state. The 2003 winner was Jeff Jefferson of Naches, Wash.

## Featherlite Modified

The Featherlite Modified Series is NASCAR's oldest and only open-wheeled division. Racing in Maine, New Hampshire, Massachusetts, Connecticut, New York and Pennsylvania, this series features low-slung and fenderless cars, a throwback design to NASCAR's earliest days when teams would modify their cars. Featherlite Modified Series cars weigh 2,610 pounds and have a wheelbase of 107 inches. Wider Hoosier bias-ply tires are used under small-block 350 to 360 cubic-inch engines. Todd Szegedy of Ridgefield, Conn., was the 2003 series champion.

## Goody's Dash Series

The Goody's Dash Series is the only NASCAR series to feature compact cars powered by six-cylinder engines. Approved models: Chevrolet Cavalier, Ford Escort, Mercury Cougar, Pontiac Sunfire and Toyota Celica. Goody's Dash Series cars have a wheelbase of 100 inches and weigh 2,750 pounds. (On superspeedways, 200 pounds are added to the cars.) The 2003 champion was Robert Huffman of Claremont, N.C.

The series was created in 1975 when a contingent of four-cylinder drivers from the Carolinas met in North Wilkesboro, N.C., to discuss the formation of a touring series for their cars. Originally dubbed "Baby Grands" for their resemblance to NASCAR's former Grand National Division cars, the series has also been known as the International Sedans, the Darlington Dash, the Charlotte-Daytona Dash, the Daytona Dash and the NASCAR Dash Series.

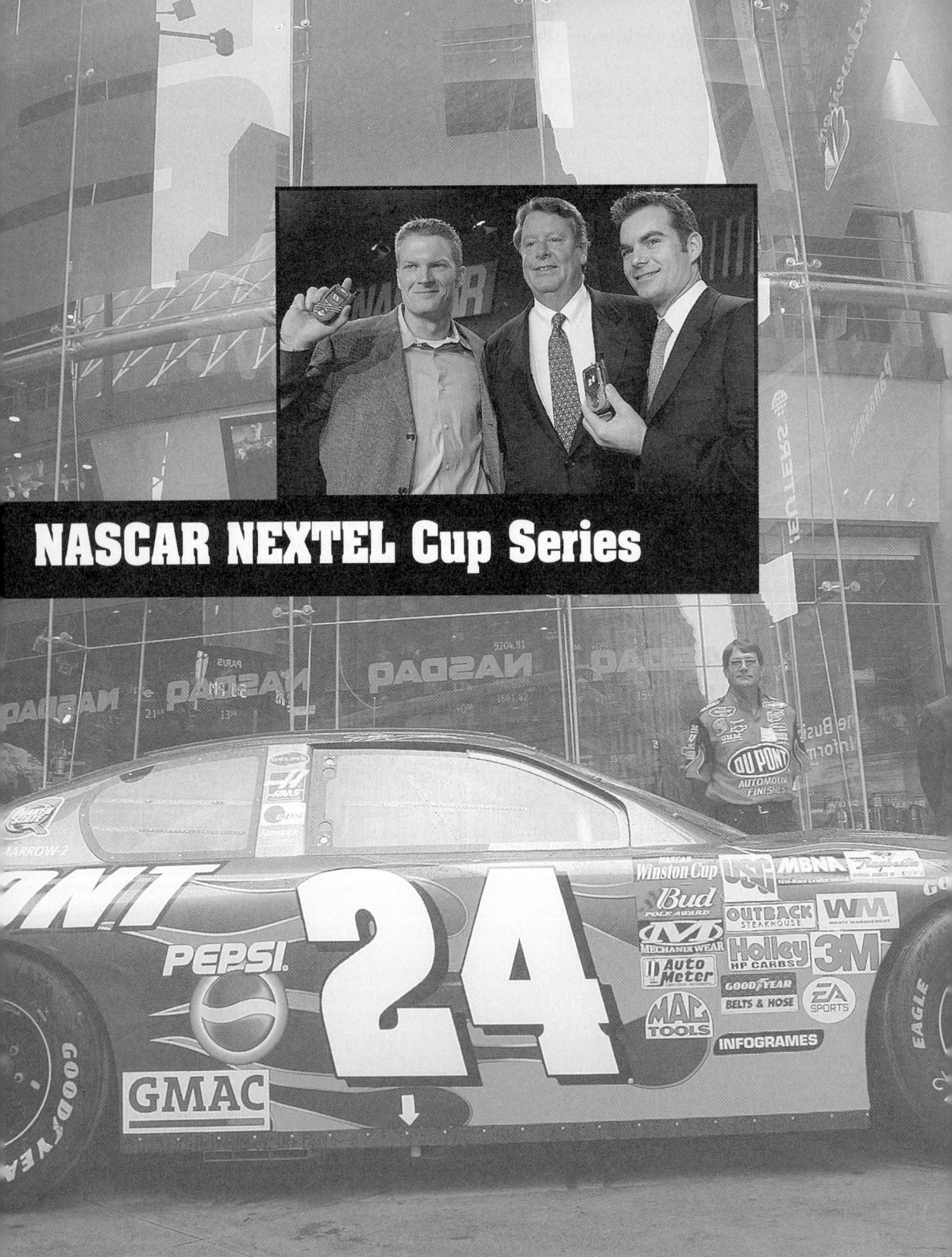

# NASCAR NEXTEL Cup Series

# NASCAR NEXTEL Cup Series debut

Electric guitars screamed and colored lights gleamed. Dale Earnhardt Jr. and Jeff Gordon flashed new cell phones that matched the paint schemes of their cars. From the loudspeakers, a voice sounded: "A new era has begun."

The reason for the splashy show in New York was big. For the first time since 1971, NASCAR's top series was getting a new sponsor: Nextel. NASCAR announced the new partnership with the wireless company on June 19, 2003, at the NASDAQ building in Times Square amid a laser light show and music by The Who.

The agreement has NASCAR and Nextel envisioning a new youth market for NASCAR. Having Nextel as the title sponsor will allow NASCAR access to markets it was previously unable to tap.

Nextel executive vice president and COO Tom Kelly said he hopes to reach out to NASCAR's existing fans through wireless communications by such features as being able to check qualifying times from their cell phones.

A more visible change for fans is that, starting next season, the NASCAR Winston Cup Series will be known as the NASCAR NEXTEL Cup Series. And the all-star race at Lowe's Motor Speedway, previously called The Winston, will also be sponsored by Nextel, becoming the NASCAR NEXTEL All-Star Challenge.

Although the NASCAR and Nextel deal is for 10 years, beginning for the 2004 season, Nextel president and CEO Tim Donahue said he hoped the sponsorship would become a lifetime arrangement.

Pairing up with NASCAR has proved to be a smart move for advertisers, and Nextel took note. According to NASCAR's research, NASCAR fans are three times as likely to purchase products from companies that sponsor NASCAR compared with other products. That kind of brand loyalty is unique in sports.

"For Nextel, I would add opportunities like this only come along once every 32 years," said Mark Schweitzer, Nextel's senior vice president of marketing. "We're a very competitive company in a competitive industry. We determined early on that this is something to go after, and enjoyed the process with NASCAR."

NASCAR talked to five companies about a possible sponsorship before striking a deal with Nextel.

Nextel Communications is a Fortune 500 company based in Reston, Va., and it is one of the leading providers of wireless communications services on the largest all-digital wireless network in the country. It serves 198 of the top 200 markets in the U.S.

R.J. Reynolds sponsored the NASCAR Winston Cup Series since the 1971 season. In February 2003, R.J. Reynolds asked NASCAR if it could get out of the five-year extension signed in 2002 because of the increasing number of laws regulating how the company could advertise, in addition to the company's new financial obligations.

"R.J. Reynolds has been an invaluable partner for more than 30 years," NASCAR vice chairman Bill France Jr. said. "The company and its people have invested heart and soul into our sport, helping to grow NASCAR into what it is today."

Looking to the future, NASCAR and Nextel see the sponsorship as an ideal match.

"I think our companies, Nextel and NASCAR, share cer-

**NASCAR vice chairman Bill France Jr. (left) and Nextel president and CEO Tim Donahue.**

tain similarities," Donahue said. "Both of our organizations began as up-starts. And, to be candid, not a lot of people took us seriously. But look at us now: America's No. 1 spectator sport and America's most successful wireless company joining forces."

France Jr., son of NASCAR founder Bill France Sr., said the deal paves the way for increased growth and popularity of the sport.

"My father would definitely be proud," France said. "We've come a long way toward fulfilling his vision, and we've come a long way toward making NASCAR racing a national sport with fans spread across America.

"We still have miles to go to achieve our goals, but we are confident we are well on our way with Nextel as our new partner."

# NASCAR NEXTEL Cup Series lineup

| Car | Driver | Make | Sponsor | Team | Crew chief |
|---|---|---|---|---|---|
| 0 | Ward Burton | Chevrolet | NetZero HiSpeed | Haas CNC Racing | Tony Furr |
| 01 | Joe Nemechek | Chevrolet | U.S. Army | MB2 Motorsports | Ryan Pemberton |
| 2 | Rusty Wallace | Dodge | Miller Lite | Penske Racing | TBA |
| 4 | Kevin Lepage | Chevrolet | TBA | Morgan-McClure | Tim Brewer |
| 5 | Terry Labonte | Chevrolet | Kellogg's/got milk? | Hendrick Motorsports | Jim Long |
| 6 | Mark Martin | Ford | Viagra | Roush Racing | Pat Tryson |
| 7 | Jimmy Spencer | Dodge | TBA | Ultra Motorsports | Gene Nead |
| 8 | Dale Earnhardt Jr. | Chevrolet | Budweiser | Dale Earnhardt Inc. | Tony Eury Sr. |
| 9 | Kasey Kahne* | Dodge | Dodge Dealers | Evernham Motorsports | Tommy Baldwin |
| 10 | Scott Riggs* | Chevrolet | Valvoline | MBV Motorsports | Doug Randolph |
| 12 | Ryan Newman | Dodge | ALLTEL | Penske Racing | Matt Borland |
| 14 | TBA | Dodge | TBA | A.J. Foyt Racing | TBA |
| 15 | Michael Waltrip | Chevrolet | NAPA Auto Parts | Dale Earnhardt Inc. | Richard Labbe |
| 16 | Greg Biffle | Ford | National Guard/Subway | Roush Racing | Doug Richert |
| 17 | Matt Kenseth | Ford | DeWalt Power Tools | Roush Racing | Robbie Reiser |
| 18 | Bobby Labonte | Chevrolet | Interstate Batteries | Joe Gibbs Racing | Michael McSwain |
| 19 | Jeremy Mayfield | Dodge | Dodge Dealers | Evernham Motorsports | Ken Francis |
| 20 | Tony Stewart | Chevrolet | Home Depot | Joe Gibbs Racing | Greg Zipadelli |
| 21 | Ricky Rudd | Ford | Motorcraft Quality Parts | Wood Brothers Racing | Ben Leslie |
| 22 | Scott Wimmer* | Dodge | Caterpillar | Bill Davis Racing | Frank Stoddard |
| 24 | Jeff Gordon | Chevrolet | DuPont | Hendrick Motorsports | Robbie Loomis |
| 25 | Brian Vickers* | Chevrolet | GMAC | Hendrick Motorsports | Peter Sospenzo |
| 26 | Todd Bodine | Ford | TBA | Travis Carter | TBA |
| 29 | Kevin Harvick | Chevrolet | GM Goodwrench Service | Richard Childress Racing | Todd Berrier |
| 30 | Johnny Sauter* | Chevrolet | America Online | Richard Childress Racing | Kevin Hamlin |
| 31 | Robby Gordon | Chevrolet | Cingular Wireless | Richard Childress Racing | Chris Andrews |
| 32 | Ricky Craven | Chevrolet | Tide | PPI Motorsports | Dave Charpentier |
| 37 | Derrike Cope | Chevrolet | Paramount Hospitality | Quest Motor Racing | Ernie Cope |
| 38 | Elliott Sadler | Ford | M&M's | Robert Yates Racing | Todd Parrott |
| 40 | Sterling Marlin | Dodge | Coors Light | Chip Ganassi Racing | Lee McCall |
| 41 | Casey Mears | Dodge | Target | Chip Ganassi Racing | Jimmy Elledge |
| 42 | Jamie McMurray | Dodge | Havoline | Chip Ganassi Racing | Donnie Wingo |
| 43 | Jeff Green | Dodge | Cheerios/Betty Crocker | Petty Enterprises | Gary Putnam |
| 45 | Kyle Petty | Dodge | Georgia Pacific/Brawny | Petty Enterprises | Greg Steadman |
| 48 | Jimmie Johnson | Chevrolet | Lowe's | Hendrick Motorsports | Chad Knaus |
| 49 | Ken Schrader | Dodge | BAM Racing | BAM Racing | Scott Eggleston |
| 74 | Tony Raines | Chevrolet | Staff America | BACE Motorsports | Larry Carter |
| 77 | TBA | Dodge | TBA | TBA | TBA |
| 88 | Dale Jarrett | Ford | UPS | Robert Yates Racing | Mike Ford |
| 91 | Bill Elliott** | Dodge | Dodge Dealers/UAW | Evernham Motorsports | TBA |
| 97 | Kurt Busch | Ford | Rubbermaid | Roush Racing | Jimmy Fennig |
| 99 | Jeff Burton | Ford | TBA | Roush Racing | Paul Andrews |

*Rookie. **Will run part-time schedule.
NOTE: Some information subject to change.

# John Andretti

**Date of birth**: March 12, 1963 **Hometown:** Indianapolis
**Resides:** Mooresville, N.C. **Spouse:** Nancy **Children:** Jarrett, Olivia, Amelia **Height:** 5-5 **Weight:** 140 **Hobbies:** Playing the stock market

## NASCAR ACHIEVEMENTS

**First NASCAR Cup start:** October 3, 1993 (North Wilkesboro)
**Best points finish:** 11 (1998)
**Career victories:** 2—Daytona (97b), Martinsville (99a)
**First victory:** July 5, 1997 (Daytona)
**Career poles:** 4—Atlanta (98a), Darlington (95b), Phoenix (99), Talladega (97a)
**First pole:** September 14, 1995 (Darlington)
**Best career finish:** 1  **Best career start:** 1

## FAST FACTS

- Began racing go-karts at age 11.
- Began open-wheel auto racing at the age 16, attending Andre Pilette's driving school in Belgium with cousin Michael Andretti.
- USAC Midget Rookie of the Year in 1983.
- Made CART debut in 1987, finishing sixth at Elkhart Lake.
- Raced in the 24 Hours of LeMans in 1988 with uncle Mario Andretti and cousin Michael.
- Raced in the Indianapolis 500 for the first time in 1988, finishing 21st.
- Co-drove to a Rolex 24 victory at Daytona International Speedway in 1989.
- Got first CART victory in 1991, at Gold Coast Grand Prix in Australia.
- Finished fifth in 1991 Indy 500.
- Reached the semifinals in his first NHRA Top Fuel event, in 1993.
- Andretti's father, Aldo, is Mario Andretti's twin brother.
- A.J. Foyt is his godfather.
- Graduated from Moravian College with a degree in business management.
- Thinks he would've been an investment banker or stock broker if he hadn't started racing.
- Younger brother Adam made his NASCAR debut in 2002, running three events in the Featherlite Southwest Series.

## CAREER BY YEAR

**2003** Andretti bounced from team to team and ran just 29 races. After being fired by Petty Enterprises in June, he ran races for Dale Earnhardt Inc., CNC Racing and Richard Childress Racing. For RCR, he piloted an experimental 2004 car to an impressive 15th-place finish in the September race at Talladega. His lone top 10 was in the Auto Club 500 at California in April.

**2002** Finished 28th in series points. … Had only three top 10 finishes, and two of those were in non-points events (eighth-place finishes in a Daytona 500 125-mile qualifying race and The Winston Open). … Season was highlighted by road-race efforts, a 10th at Infineon Raceway and an 11th at Watkins Glen International. … Best qualifying effort, second, was in season's next-to-last event at Rockingham.

**2001** Finished 31st in series points. … Season was marked by good qualifying performances and poor race finishes. … Had only one top five finish and one other top 10. … Struggles were part of an overall tough season for Petty Enterprises, which was one of the organizations that switched to the new Dodge Intrepids in 2001. … Season highlight was finishing second at Bristol's spring race, 0.426 seconds behind Elliott Sadler. … Other top 10 run came in the previous week, a sixth at Rockingham.

**2000** Finished 23rd in series points. … Had only two top 10 runs, the lowest total since 1994, his first full Winston Cup season. … Led only 11 laps. … Best finish was seventh at New Hampshire in September. … Team was in transition, preparing for the switch from Pontiacs to Dodges. … After the season, crew chief Robbie Loomis departed to join Jeff Gordon's team.

**1999** Finished 17th in series points. … Got the second Winston Cup victory of his career, in the spring Martinsville race, coming back after falling a lap down. … Had total of 10 top 10 runs, but also had 10 DNFs.

**1998** Finished a career-best 11th in series points. … First full season with Petty Enterprises. Had third-place finishes at Sonoma and Hew Hampshire and totals of three top fives and 10 top 10s. … Won the pole at the Atlanta spring race.

**1997** Finished 23rd in series points. … Won the Pepsi 400 at Daytona, for his first Winston Cup victory. … Drove a full season for Cale Yarborough. … Was strong in restrictor-plate races at Talladega, finishing third and fourth, and taking one pole. …Left Yarborough after the season, when the team lost its sponsorship.

**1996** Finished 31st in series points. … Drove for two teams, spending 22 races with Kranefuss-Haas—with 10 DNFs—before switching to Cale Yarborough Motorsports for eight races down the stretch. … Season highlight was two fifth-place finishes, one with each team.

**1995** Finished 18th in series points. … Raced the full season with Kranefuss-Haas Racing. … Won his first pole at the Southern 500 in Darlington.

**1994** Finished 32nd in points. … Started the season with Billy Hagan Racing and drove 18 races before the team has sponsorship problems. … Switched to Petty Enterprises in August, running 11 races. … Became the first driver to run the Indianapolis 500 and Coca-Cola 600 on the same day; finished 10th at Indy and 36th at Charlotte.

**1993** Finished 50th in series points. … Ran only four races for Billy Hagan Racing. … Made his Winston Cup debut at North Wilkesboro in October, finishing 24th despite four spins for his best finish of the four events.

### CAREER STATISTICS

| Year | Car Owner | Races | Champ. Finish | Won | Top 5 | Top 10 | DNF | Poles | Money Won |
|---|---|---|---|---|---|---|---|---|---|
| 1993 | Billy Hagan | 4 | 50 | 0 | 0 | 0 | 2 | 0 | $24,915 |
| 1994 | Billy Hagan | 18 | | 0 | 0 | 0 | 10 | 0 | 275,520 |
| | Petty Ent. | 11 | 32 | 0 | 0 | 0 | 2 | 0 | 116,400 |
| 1995 | M. Kranefuss | 31 | 18 | 0 | 1 | 5 | 7 | 1 | 593,542 |
| 1996 | M. Kranefuss | 22 | | 0 | 1 | 1 | 10 | 0 | 571,481 |
| | C. Yarborough | 8 | 31 | 0 | 1 | 1 | 1 | 0 | 117,030 |
| 1997 | C. Yarborough | 32 | 23 | 1 | 3 | 4 | 3 | 1 | 1,143,725 |
| 1998 | Petty Ent. | 33 | 11 | 0 | 3 | 10 | 5 | 1 | 1,838,379 |
| 1999 | Petty Ent. | 34 | 17 | 1 | 3 | 10 | 10 | 1 | 2,001,832 |
| 2000 | Petty Ent. | 34 | 23 | 0 | 0 | 2 | 7 | 0 | 2,035,902 |
| 2001 | Petty Ent. | 35 | 31 | 0 | 1 | 2 | 4 | 0 | 2,873,184 |
| 2002 | Petty Ent. | 36 | 28 | 0 | 0 | 1 | 7 | 0 | 2,954,229 |
| 2003 | Petty Ent. | 14 | | 0 | 0 | 1 | 2 | 0 | 1,490,636 |
| | Gene Haas | 3 | | 0 | 0 | 0 | 0 | 0 | 142,770 |
| | R. Childress | 1 | | 0 | 0 | 0 | 1 | 0 | 57,485 |
| | DEI | 11 | 38 | 0 | 0 | 0 | 1 | 0 | 886,729 |
| **TOTALS** | | 327 | | 2 | 13 | 37 | 72 | 4 | $17,123,759 |

### 2003 RESULTS

| Race | Start | Finish | Standing Pos. | Winnings |
|---|---|---|---|---|
| Daytona 500 (Daytona) | 12 | 34 | 34 | $183,283 |
| Subway 400 (Rockingham) | 32 | 39 | 42 | $81,568 |
| UAW-DaimlerChrysler 400 (Las Vegas) | 6 | 18 | 136 | $109,928 |
| Bass Pro Shops MBNA 500 (Atlanta) | 19 | 29 | 38 | $84,988 |
| Carolina Dodge Dealers 400 (Darlington) | 26 | 38 | 40 | $77,743 |
| Food City 500 (Bristol) | 43 | 31 | 39 | $96,168 |
| Samsung/RadioShack 500 (Texas) | 43 | 19 | 36 | $121,753 |
| Aaron's 499 (Talladega) | 40 | 14 | 34 | $109,388 |
| Virginia 500 (Martinsville) | 40 | 30 | 34 | $84,178 |
| Auto Club 500 (California) | 13 | 8 | 32 | $117,003 |
| Pontiac Excitement 400 (Richmond) | 24 | 30 | 31 | $86,253 |
| Coca-Cola 600 (Charlotte) | 42 | 39 | 32 | $104,538 |
| MBNA Armed Forces Family 400 (Dover) | 40 | 34 | 34 | $93,688 |
| Pocono 500 (Pocono) | 21 | 23 | 33 | $84,143 |
| New England 300 (New Hampshire) | 39 | 41 | 39 | $48,450 |
| Pennsylvania 500 (Pocono) | 5 | 33 | 39 | $44,265 |
| Brickyard 400 (Indianapolis) | 11 | 43 | 39 | $102,400 |
| Sirius at the Glen (Watkins Glen) | 15 | 19 | 38 | $50,055 |
| Chevy Rock & Roll 400 (Richmond) | 24 | 14 | 38 | $76,917 |
| Sylvania 300 (New Hampshire) | 16 | 12 | 38 | $85,637 |
| MBNA America 400 (Dover) | 30 | 34 | 38 | $77,532 |
| EA SPORTS 500 (Talladega) | 24 | 15 | 38 | $57,485 |
| Banquet 400 (Kansas) | 40 | 19 | 38 | $89,237 |
| UAW-GM Quality 500 (Charlotte) | 41 | 30 | 38 | $74,262 |
| Subway 500 (Martinsville) | 40 | 31 | 38 | $68,762 |
| Bass Pro Shops MBNA 500 (Atlanta) | 11 | 22 | 38 | $94,062 |
| Checker Auto Parts 500 (Phoenix) | 33 | 16 | 38 | $75,162 |
| Pop Secret 400 (Rockingham) | 36 | 30 | 38 | $75,142 |
| Ford 400 (Homestead) | 22 | 42 | 38 | $67,612 |

# Johnny Benson

**Date of birth:** June 27, 1963 **Hometown:** Grand Rapids, Mich. **Resides:** Cornelius, N.C. **Spouse:** Debbie **Children:** Katelyn **Height:** 6-0 **Weight:** 180 **Hobbies:** Golf, motorcycling

## NASCAR ACHIEVEMENTS

**First NASCAR Cup start:** February 18, 1996 (Daytona)
**Best points finish:** 11 (1997, 2001)
**Career victories:** 1—New Hampshire (02b)
**First victory:** November 3, 2002 (Rockingham)
**Career poles:** 2—Atlanta (96a), Michigan (97b)
**First pole:** March 10, 1996 (Atlanta)
**Best career finish:** 1   **Best career start:** 1

## FAST FACTS

- Won the Busch Series championship in 1995.
- Was the Busch Series Rookie of the Year in 1994, winning three races.
- Won the 1993 American Speed Association title and was the ASA Rookie of the Year in 1990.
- Began racing on dirt in 1982 and was the Rookie of the Year at Thunderbird (Mich.) Speedway in his first full year of competition.
- Followed his father, Johnny Benson Sr., into racing. Benson Sr., a local favorite in Michigan, competed in one Winston Cup race, the Motor State 400 at Michigan International Speedway in 1973. He finished 21st.
- Had vision correction surgery in 1999 after wearing glasses earlier in his career.
- Is an equity partner at Berlin Raceway in Michigan, the track where he began his asphalt career and where he father won seven track championships.

## CAREER BY YEAR

**2003** Benson was sixth in points after four races, but he plunged after that and never recovered. The bad stretch cost him the full-time ride in the No. 10. He was told in October he'd be replaced in 2004 by Scott Riggs. Benson's best finish was a fourth in the season finale at Homestead. He didn't fare any better qualifying—he had just three top 10 starts.

**2002** Finished 29th in series points. … Season was highlighted by his first Winston Cup win, at Rockingham, after starting 26th. … Missed five races, three due to a rib fracture suffered in a Busch Series race May 3 at Richmond, then two more after aggravating the injury in a July 5 crash at Daytona; also had eight DNFs, the most in his Winston

Cup career. ... Posted three top five finishes including a runner-up at Martinsville. ... Had seven top 10s with finishes of sixth (from 30th) and eighth (from 35th) at his home-state Michigan races. ... Finished 10th at the Daytona 500 ... Led a career-high 53 laps at New Hampshire.

**2001** Finished 11th in series points, tying his career best (1997). ... Had seven top 10 finishes in the season's first 11 races. ... Posted six top five finishes and 14 top 10s. ... Had third-place finishes at Texas, Indianapolis and North Carolina.

**2000** Finished 12th in series points. ... Scored three top five and seven top-10 finishes despite a season rife with sponsorship struggles. ... Held the Daytona 500 lead for 39 laps before being overcome by winner Dale Jarrett with four laps to go; finished 12th. ... Had two second-place finishes, at the time his career-bests in Winston Cup; moved up from 33rd on the starting grid at Bristol and from third at Dover. ... Landed his current deal with Nelson Bowers and Valvoline at season's end.

**1999** Finished 28th in series points. ... Scored two top 10 finishes, both seventh-place efforts, at Dover and at New Hampshire. ... Granted his release from Roush Racing in August to pursue other opportunities.

**1998** Finished 20th in series points. ... Collected three top five and 10 top 10 finishes; recovered to score seven of those top 10s after failing to qualify for the Daytona 500. ... Finished ninth after starting 39th at Charlotte. ... His three top fives were in his first six starts for his new team, Roush Racing.

**1997** Finished 11th in series points. ... Scored eight top 10 finishes, including two seventh-place results, at Indianapolis and Phoenix. ... Won his second career pole at Michigan. ... Finished 10th at Darlington after starting 36th.

**1996** Finished 21st in series points. ... Named Winston Cup Rookie of the Year. ... Drove for Chuck Rider. ... Scored one top five and six top 10 finishes, his best a fifth-place effort at Pocono. ... Won his first pole at the Atlanta spring race, in only his fourth Winston Cup start.

### CAREER STATISTICS

| Year | Car Owner | Races | Champ. Finish | Won | Top 5 | Top 10 | DNF | Poles | Money Won |
|---|---|---|---|---|---|---|---|---|---|
| 1996 | Chuck Rider | 30 | 21 | 0 | 1 | 6 | 5 | 1 | $947,080 |
| 1997 | Chuck Rider | 32 | 11 | 0 | 0 | 8 | 2 | 1 | 1,256,457 |
| 1998 | Jack Roush | 32 | 20 | 0 | 3 | 10 | 5 | 0 | 1,360,335 |
| 1999 | Jack Roush | 34 | 28 | 0 | 0 | 2 | 5 | 0 | 1,567,668 |
| 2000 | Tim Beverley | 18 | | 0 | 1 | 2 | 2 | 0 | 921,504 |
| | Nelson Bowers | 15 | 13 | 0 | 2 | 5 | 1 | 0 | 919,820 |
| 2001 | Nelson Bowers | 36 | 11 | 0 | 6 | 14 | 7 | 0 | 2,894,903 |
| 2002 | Nelson Bowers | 31 | 29 | 1 | 3 | 7 | 8 | 0 | 2,791,879 |
| 2003 | Nelson Bowers | 36 | 24 | 0 | 2 | 4 | 7 | 0 | 3,411,790 |
| TOTALS | | 264 | | 1 | 18 | 58 | 43 | 2 | $16,204,439 |

### 2003 RESULTS

| Race | Start | Finish | Standing Pos. | Winnings |
|---|---|---|---|---|
| Daytona 500 (Daytona) | 40 | 19 | 20 | $208,620 |
| Subway 400 (Rockingham) | 2 | 13 | 16 | $82,960 |
| UAW-DaimlerChrysler 400 (Las Vegas) | 16 | 12 | 9 | $107,725 |
| Bass Pro Shops MBNA 500 (Atlanta) | 23 | 11 | 6 | $84,400 |
| Carolina Dodge Dealers 400 (Darlington) | 22 | 25 | 11 | $73,670 |
| Food City 500 (Bristol) | 20 | 19 | 13 | $90,630 |
| Samsung/RadioShack 500 (Texas) | 13 | 32 | 16 | $92,450 |
| Aaron's 499 (Talladega) | 17 | 41 | 23 | $89,640 |
| Virginia 500 (Martinsville) | 28 | 32 | 26 | $74,200 |
| Auto Club 500 (California) | 32 | 36 | 29 | $92,425 |
| Pontiac Excitement 400 (Richmond) | 13 | 15 | 28 | $82,435 |
| Coca-Cola 600 (Charlotte) | 10 | 24 | 27 | $101,575 |
| MBNA Armed Forces Family 400 (Dover) | 30 | 5 | 27 | $110,975 |
| Pocono 500 (Pocono) | 24 | 24 | 25 | $75,765 |
| Sirius 400 (Michigan) | 26 | 26 | 25 | $79,790 |
| Dodge/Save Mart 350 (Sonoma) | 25 | 30 | 24 | $84,745 |
| Pepsi 400 (Daytona) | 22 | 27 | 25 | $95,000 |
| Tropicana 400 (Chicago) | 36 | 18 | 26 | $94,700 |
| New England 300 (New Hampshire) | 26 | 26 | 24 | $80,900 |
| Pennsylvania 500 (Pocono) | 29 | 20 | 26 | $78,265 |
| Brickyard 400 (Indianapolis) | 40 | 13 | 23 | $157,500 |
| Sirius at the Glen (Watkins Glen) | 27 | 27 | 23 | $74,565 |
| GFS Marketplace 400 (Michigan) | 35 | 10 | 22 | $94,690 |
| Sharpie 500 (Bristol) | 32 | 14 | 23 | $98,415 |
| Southern 500 (Darlington) | 11 | 40 | 24 | $76,800 |
| Chevy Rock & Roll 400 (Richmond) | 9 | 9 | 23 | $83,455 |
| Sylvania 300 (New Hampshire) | 22 | 25 | 26 | $81,600 |
| MBNA America 400 (Dover) | 26 | 21 | 25 | $84,490 |
| EA SPORTS 500 (Talladega) | 41 | 41 | 26 | $78,430 |
| Banquet 400 (Kansas) | 20 | 35 | 26 | $87,525 |
| UAW-GM Quality 500 (Charlotte) | 23 | 16 | 25 | $80,400 |
| Subway 500 (Martinsville) | 29 | 34 | 27 | $70,070 |
| Bass Pro Shops MBNA 500 (Atlanta) | 30 | 24 | 27 | $94,475 |
| Checker Auto Parts 500 (Phoenix) | 35 | 21 | 27 | $79,900 |
| Pop Secret 400 (Rockingham) | 25 | 29 | 25 | $76,825 |
| Ford 400 (Homestead) | 21 | 4 | 24 | $146,575 |

## Greg Biffle
### 16

**Date of birth:** December 23, 1969 **Hometown:** Vancouver, Wash. **Resides:** Mooresville, N.C. **Spouse:** Single **Children:** None **Height:** 5-9 **Weight:** 170 **Hobbies:** Flying, boating

### NASCAR ACHIEVEMENTS

**First NASCAR Cup start:** April 28, 2002
**Best points finish:** 20 (2003)
**Career victories:** 1—Daytona (03b)
**Career poles:** 0
**Best career finish:** 1   **Best career start:** 2

### FAST FACTS

● A superb example of NASCAR's developmental system, he progressed through every level in NASCAR racing before

making his Winston Cup Series debut in 2002.
- Was the 2002 Busch Series champion.
- Named 2001 Busch Series Rookie of the Year.
- Won 2000 NASCAR Craftsman Truck Series championship.
- Won nine trucks races in 1999 and finished second in points.
- Was the 1998 Craftsman Truck Series Rookie of the Year.
- Participated in the Raybestos Brakes Northwest Series in 1997, capturing one victory.
- Competed in the NASCAR Weekly Racing Series presented by Dodge from 1994-97, winning Late Model track championships at Tri City Raceway in West Richland, Wash., and at Portland (Ore.) Speedway.
- Is the only driver to win both the Craftsman Truck Series and the Busch Series championships; also is the only driver to win Raybestos Rookie of the Year awards in both series.
- Gave Roush Racing its first NASCAR championship when he won the 2000 trucks title.

### CAR FACTS

**Car:** No. 16 Ford
**Primary sponsor:** National Guard/Subway
**Owner:** Jack Roush
**Team:** Roush Racing
**Crew chief:** Doug Richert
**Engine builder:** Karl Bausman

## CAREER BY YEAR

**2003** At the beginning of the season, Biffle's goals were to win a race, finish in the top 15 and win the Rookie of the Year award. He went 1-for-3 by winning the night race at Daytona in July. His 20th-place points finish was more impressive when you consider he missed a race, failing to qualify at Las Vegas. He completed an impressive 96.9 percent of the season's laps. He finished one lap off the pace 12 times and on the lead lap 14 times.

**2002** Finished 48th in series points. ... Made his Winston Cup debut at California in the No. 16 Ford for Roush Racing. ... Also made four starts in the No. 55 Chevrolet—subbing for Bobby Hamilton—and two starts for Petty Enterprises. ... Qualified in the top five at three events. ... Finished a season-best 13th at California. ... Drove the No. 44 Dodge for Petty at Rockingham and in the season finale at Homestead-Miami Speedway, finishing 25th in both events. ... Won the 2002 Busch Series championship

### CAREER STATISTICS

| Year | Car Owner | Champ. Races | Finish | Won | Top 5 | Top 10 | DNF | Poles | Money Won |
|---|---|---|---|---|---|---|---|---|---|
| 2002 | Jack Roush | 1 | | 0 | 0 | 0 | 0 | 0 | $80,059 |
| | Andy Petree | 4 | | 0 | 0 | 0 | 1 | 0 | 218,700 |
| | Petty Ent. | 2 | 48 | 0 | 0 | 0 | 0 | 0 | 96,014 |
| 2003 | Jack Roush | 35 | 20 | 1 | 2 | 6 | 6 | 0 | 2,805,673 |
| | TOTALS | 42 | | 1 | 2 | 6 | 7 | 0 | $3,200,546 |

### 2003 RESULTS

| Race | Start | Finish | Standing Pos. | Winnings |
|---|---|---|---|---|
| Daytona 500 (Daytona) | 27 | 21 | 21 | $177,495 |
| Subway 400 (Rockingham) | 13 | 22 | 19 | $48,210 |
| Bass Pro Shops MBNA 500 (Atlanta) | 20 | 13 | 33 | $51,775 |
| Carolina Dodge Dealers 400 (Darlington) | 17 | 12 | 27 | $48,120 |
| Food City 500 (Bristol) | 15 | 5 | 24 | $71,120 |
| Samsung/RadioShack 500 (Texas) | 20 | 28 | 25 | $68,975 |
| Aaron's 499 (Talladega) | 33 | 22 | 25 | $66,375 |
| Virginia 500 (Martinsville) | 20 | 18 | 22 | $47,975 |
| Auto Club 500 (California) | 29 | 18 | 23 | $69,225 |
| Pontiac Excitement 400 (Richmond) | 15 | 17 | 21 | $49,150 |
| Coca-Cola 600 (Charlotte) | 26 | 16 | 22 | $76,520 |
| MBNA Armed Forces Family 400 (Dover) | 15 | 30 | 22 | $59,090 |
| Pocono 500 (Pocono) | 26 | 20 | 23 | $52,615 |
| Sirius 400 (Michigan) | 29 | 31 | 23 | $49,190 |
| Dodge/Save Mart 350 (Sonoma) | 32 | 37 | 25 | $54,765 |
| Pepsi 400 (Daytona) | 30 | 1 | 20 | $187,975 |
| Tropicana 400 (Chicago) | 7 | 20 | 20 | $69,650 |
| New England 300 (New Hampshire) | 20 | 10 | 20 | $66,350 |
| Pennsylvania 500 (Pocono) | 24 | 27 | 20 | $47,340 |
| Brickyard 400 (Indianapolis) | 18 | 21 | 20 | $121,825 |
| Sirius at the Glen (Watkins Glen) | 2 | 30 | 21 | $47,825 |
| GFS Marketplace 400 (Michigan) | 12 | 4 | 19 | $85,670 |
| Sharpie 500 (Bristol) | 34 | 22 | 19 | $69,610 |
| Southern 500 (Darlington) | 9 | 10 | 18 | $65,980 |
| Chevy Rock & Roll 400 (Richmond) | 2 | 20 | 18 | $54,680 |
| Sylvania 300 (New Hampshire) | 4 | 43 | 20 | $49,060 |
| MBNA America 400 (Dover) | 19 | 7 | 19 | $66,440 |
| EA SPORTS 500 (Talladega) | 36 | 24 | 19 | $56,975 |
| Banquet 400 (Kansas) | 22 | 12 | 18 | $70,825 |
| UAW-GM Quality 500 (Charlotte) | 22 | 17 | 18 | $53,000 |
| Subway 500 (Martinsville) | 19 | 19 | 18 | $48,925 |
| Bass Pro Shops MBNA 500 (Atlanta) | 27 | 34 | 18 | $62,425 |
| Checker Auto Parts 500 (Phoenix) | 25 | 15 | 18 | $56,130 |
| Pop Secret 400 (Rockingham) | 10 | 11 | 18 | $56,675 |
| Ford 400 (Homestead) | 25 | 35 | 20 | $43,975 |

# Dave Blaney

**Date of birth:** October 24, 1962 **Hometown:** Hartford, Ohio
**Resides:** Trinity, N.C. **Spouse:** Lisa **Children:** Emma, Ryan, Erin **Height:** 5-8 **Weight:** 170 **Hobbies:** Basketball, working with his World of Outlaws sprint car team

## NASCAR ACHIEVEMENTS

**First NASCAR Cup start:** October 25, 1992 (Rockingham)
**Best points finish:** 19 (2002)
**Career victories:** 0
**Career poles:** 1—Rockingham (03a)
**Best career finish:** 3  **Best career start:** 1

## FAST FACTS

- Finished seventh in the Busch Series in 1999, posting five top fives, 12 top 10s and four poles in 31 starts.
- Made his first Busch Series start in 1998 and won one pole while competing in 20 races.
- Won the 1995 World of Outlaws championship and was named that year's Sprint Car Driver of the Year.
- Was the runner-up in the World of Outlaws sprint car circuit

in 1993, 1994, 1996 and 1997.
- Won the Syracuse Nationals at the New York State Fairgrounds in 1987 and 1993).
- Won the Pacific Coast Nationals at Ascot Speedway (Calif.) in 1990.
- Posted 76 top five finishes in 85 races in sprints and modifieds in 1989.
- Won the Easter World Sprint Car championship in 1988 in Hagerstown, Md.
- Won first career World of Outlaws series race at Tri-City in 1985.
- Won USAC Silver Crown championship in 1984, becoming the youngest driver to win that division.
- Won Rookie of the Year honors on the All-Star Circuit of Champions sprint series in 1983.
- Began professional racing career in 1981, racing sprint cars.
- Has competed in all three major sprint car associations—World of Outlaws National Challenge Series, United Sprint Association and All-Star Circuit of Champions.
- Owns a World of Outlaws team for which his brother, Dale, is the driver.
- Owns "Outlaw Driving Experience" racing school for sprint cars, which is based in Hartford, Ohio.
- Brother, Dale, played college basketball at West Virginia, was drafted by the L.A. Lakers and played in the NBA and CBA.
- Owns Sharon Speedway in Hartford, Ohio, with his family.
- Father, Lou, also raced sprint cars.

## CAREER BY YEAR

**2003** Blaney completed a respectable 92.6 percent of laps, but he never finished on the lead lap in three consecutive races. Blaney had three top 10 finishes in the first five races but only one more after that. That hot start vaulted him to seventh place in the points standings, but he quickly dropped into the mid-20s and never made much progress from there. His best finish was third in the March race at Darlington.

**2002** Finished 19th in series points. ... Ran his first season with Jasper Motorsports in the No. 77 Ford. ... Had five top 10 finishes. ... Best finish was seventh at Phoenix. ... Was the top driver in series points without a top five finish. ... Matched his career-best start with a third at Richmond in September. ... Crew chief Ryan Pemberton left at season's end to work with Jerry Nadeau and MB2 Motorsports.

**2001** Finished 22nd in series points. ... Had six top 10 finishes, including career-best sixths at Texas, Michigan and Homestead. ... Qualified a career-best third at Atlanta in November and led 70 laps before mechanical problems ruined a strong run.

**2000** Finished 31st in series points. ... Finished the season on a high note with a fourth-place qualifying run at Atlanta, a season-best. ... Finished third in Raybestos Rookie of the Year standings. ... Scored two top 10s in the last three races. ... Had first top five locked up in Atlanta until a late-race incident knocked him down to 18th. ... Missed only one race all season (Rockingham's spring event), then came back to qualify in the top 25 in a fall race at that track.

**1999** Finished 51st in series points. ... Drove in five races. ... Best start (fourth) and finish (23rd) came at Homestead.

### CAREER STATISTICS

| Year | Car Owner | Champ. Races | Finish | Won | Top 5 | Top 10 | DNF | Poles | Money Won |
|---|---|---|---|---|---|---|---|---|---|
| 1992 | D. Blaney | 1 | | 0 | 0 | 0 | 1 | 0 | $4,500 |
| 1999 | B. Davis | 5 | 51 | 0 | 0 | 0 | 2 | 0 | 212,170 |
| 2000 | B. Davis | 33 | 31 | 0 | 0 | 2 | 7 | 0 | 1,272,689 |
| 2001 | B. Davis | 36 | 22 | 0 | 0 | 6 | 6 | 0 | 1,827,896 |
| 2002 | D. Bawel | 36 | 19 | 0 | 0 | 5 | 3 | 0 | 2,978,593 |
| 2003 | D. Bawel | 36 | 28 | 0 | 1 | 4 | 4 | 1 | 2,828,690 |
| TOTALS | | 147 | | 0 | 1 | 17 | 23 | 0 | $9,124,538 |

### 2003 RESULTS

| Race | Start | Finish | Standing Pos. | Winnings |
|---|---|---|---|---|
| Daytona 500 (Daytona) | 39 | 24 | 24 | $198,176 |
| Subway 400 (Rockingham) | 1 | 10 | 15 | $86,460 |
| UAW-DaimlerChrysler 400 (Las Vegas) | 35 | 34 | 23 | $67,300 |
| Bass Pro Shops MBNA 500 (Atlanta) | 27 | 8 | 15 | $80,125 |
| Carolina Dodge Dealers 400 (Darlington) | 18 | 3 | 7 | $91,945 |
| Food City 500 (Bristol) | 31 | 38 | 16 | $65,065 |
| Samsung/RadioShack 500 (Texas) | 39 | 36 | 22 | $67,075 |
| Aaron's 499 (Talladega) | 39 | 23 | 20 | $91,565 |
| Virginia 500 (Martinsville) | 15 | 31 | 24 | $64,064 |
| Auto Club 500 (California) | 18 | 13 | 22 | $101,350 |
| Pontiac Excitement 400 (Richmond) | 31 | 18 | 20 | $76,000 |
| Coca-Cola 600 (Charlotte) | 8 | 14 | 19 | $104,600 |
| MBNA Armed Forces Family 400 (Dover) | 26 | 20 | 19 | $73,335 |
| Pocono 500 (Pocono) | 22 | 26 | 21 | $66,090 |
| Sirius 400 (Michigan) | 38 | 38 | 24 | $56,585 |
| Dodge/Save Mart 350 (Sonoma) | 15 | 32 | 23 | $62,865 |
| Pepsi 400 (Daytona) | 39 | 35 | 26 | $71,750 |
| Tropicana 400 (Chicago) | 9 | 31 | 27 | $69,575 |
| New England 300 (New Hampshire) | 27 | 13 | 26 | $81,750 |
| Pennsylvania 500 (Pocono) | 22 | 9 | 24 | $79,390 |
| Brickyard 400 (Indianapolis) | 20 | 28 | 24 | $116,875 |
| Sirius at the Glen (Watkins Glen) | 16 | 25 | 26 | $65,189 |
| GFS Marketplace 400 (Michigan) | 9 | 25 | 25 | $72,065 |
| Sharpie 500 (Bristol) | 15 | 30 | 26 | $72,335 |
| Southern 500 (Darlington) | 10 | 30 | 28 | $60,000 |
| Chevy Rock & Roll 400 (Richmond) | 38 | 33 | 28 | $56,100 |
| Sylvania 300 (New Hampshire) | 26 | 14 | 28 | $81,950 |
| MBNA America 400 (Dover) | 28 | 24 | 28 | $75,490 |
| EA SPORTS 500 (Talladega) | 42 | 17 | 28 | $81,035 |
| Banquet 400 (Kansas) | 28 | 43 | 28 | $67,457 |
| UAW-GM Quality 500 (Charlotte) | 34 | 24 | 28 | $69,530 |
| Subway 500 (Martinsville) | 25 | 37 | 28 | $51,175 |
| Bass Pro Shops MBNA 500 (Atlanta) | 35 | 37 | 28 | $70,100 |
| Checker Auto Parts 500 (Phoenix) | 8 | 24 | 28 | $68,589 |
| Pop Secret 400 (Rockingham) | 22 | 27 | 28 | $66,849 |
| Ford 400 (Homestead) | 18 | 28 | 28 | $56,500 |

# Brett Bodine

**Date of birth**: January 11, 1959 **Hometown**: Chemung, N.Y.
**Resides**: Davidson, N.C. **Spouse**: Diane **Children**: Heidi
**Height**: 5-7 **Weight**: 160 **Hobbies**: Golf

## NASCAR ACHIEVEMENTS

**First NASCAR Cup start:** May 25, 1986 (Charlotte)
**Best points finish:** 12 (1990)
**Career victories:** 1—North Wilkesboro (90a)
**First victory:** April 22, 1990 (North Wilkesboro)
**Career poles:** 5—Charlotte (90b), Dover (92a), Michigan (93a), North Wilkesboro (91a, 93a)
**First pole:** October 4, 1990 (Charlotte)
**Best career finish:** 1   **Best career start:** 1

## FAST FACTS

- Began racing hobby cars at Chemung (N.Y.) Speedway in 1977.
- Won the 1984 track championship at Stafford (Conn.) Motor Speedway.
- Won the 1985 Modified Race of Champions at Pocono Raceway.
- Was the Busch Series championship runner-up in 1986.
- Named the Busch Series Most Popular Driver in 1987.
- Named one of top 50 modified drivers of all time.
- Graduated with honors from University of New York at Alfred with a degree in mechanical engineering.
- Was inducted into the Waverly (N.Y.) High School Sports Hall of Fame in 2000.

## CAREER BY YEAR

**2003** Bodine ran just six races in 2003. He had two DNFs due to accidents and never finished better than five laps off the pace. He completed just 82.4 percent of the laps in the races he entered. His average starting position was 33.8 and his average finish was 33.3. His best finish was 24th at the March race in Bristol.

**2002** Finished 36th in series points. … Competed in his seventh season as an owner/driver. … Best finishes were at restrictor-plate tracks, finishing 16th at the Daytona 500 and 13th at Talladega. … Struggled to qualify in the second half of the season, missing four races and taking provisionals in nine of his last 14 starts. … Best start was 14th at Las Vegas. … Nearly shut down the team before securing sponsorship from Hooters Restaurants in March.

**2001** Finished 30th in series points. … Recorded two top 10 finishes, including a season-best eighth-place finish at New Hampshire to end the season on a high note. … Finished ninth at Daytona in July. … Best start was 10th at Chicago.

**2000** Finished 35th in series points. … Set the fastest time for a Winston Cup driver in the history of Indianapolis Motor Speedway, a record that stood for two years. … Best finish was 14th at Miami in November.

**1999** Finished 35th in series points. … Had his best finishes on short tracks, 14th at Martinsville and 12th at Bristol.

**1998** Finished 25th in series points. … Started all 32 races and won over $1 million for the first time in his career. … Edged out Joe Nemechek by 10 points for the 25th and final paying position of Winston points fund. … Best runs were a pair of 11th-place finishes at Bristol and Talladega in the spring. … Started all 33 races and had just two DNFs.

**1997** Finished 29th in series points. … Posted two top 10 finishes despite losing his sponsor early in the season. … Best finish (sixth) was at the Sonoma road course, where he started fifth. … Best season start was third at New Hampshire.

**1996** Finished 24th in series points. … Purchased the once-heralded No. 11 team from legendary car owner Junior Johnson and began his first season as an owner/driver. … Led late in the race at Watkins Glen before settling for 14th place. …Scored one top 10, a ninth at the Pepsi 400 in Daytona.

**1995** Finished 20th in series points. … Scored two top 10 finishes. … Best performance of the season was qualifying second at North Wilkesboro and finishing ninth.

**1994** Finished 19th in series points. … Competed in his sixth and final season for car owner and famed drag racer Kenny Bernstein. … Recorded six top 10 finishes. … Finished second in the first Brickyard 400 at Indianapolis Motor Speedway. … Best start was second at North Wilkesboro.

**1993** Finished 20th in series points. … Scored nine top 10 finishes, including three top fives. … Won Bud Poles at Michigan and North Wilkesboro. … Scored three straight top 10s including a second-place finish at Darlington in the Southern 500. … Drove five races with a fractured left wrist following a practice accident at Dover in the fall. … Recorded eight top five starts.

**1992** Finished 15th in series points. … Collected two top fives and 13 top 10 finishes. … Strung together 10 straight qualifying efforts in the top 10 and started inside the top 10 21 times. … Best finish was third at Martinsville.

**1991** Finished 19th in series points. … Scored two top fives and six top 10 finishes. … Best finish was a second at Martinsville. … Took the pole at North Wilkesboro.

**1990** Finished 12th in series points. … Enjoyed career-best season in his first year under owner Kenny Bernstein and paired with crew chief Larry McReynolds. … Posted one win, five top fives and nine top 10 finishes. … Charged from the 20th starting position to win his first career race at North Wilkesboro. … Won his first pole late in the season, at Charlotte.

**1989** Finished 19th in series points. … Had one top five and six top 10 finishes in the second of two seasons driving for car owner Bud Moore. … Best finish was fifth at Michigan. … Started from the outside pole at Darlington and had a total of six starts inside the top 10.

**1988** Finished 20th in series points. … Competed on a full-time basis for the first time, for legendary car owner Bud Moore. … Scored two top five finishes—both at Charlotte—including a fourth in the Coca-Cola 600 and a season-best third in the fall. … Started in the top 10 10 times.

**1987** Finished 32nd in series points. … Made 14 starts for car owner Hoss Ellington. … Best finish was 11th at Daytona in July. … Also competed in the Busch Series, finishing third in points with five poles, eight top fives and 17 top 10s.

**1986** Finished 92nd in series points. ... Made his first Winston Cup start for Rick Hendrick at Charlotte. ... Finished runner-up to Larry Pearson in the Busch Series, scoring eight poles, two wins, 16 top fives and 24 top 10s.

## CAREER STATISTICS

| Year | Car Owner | Races | Champ. Finish | Won | Top 5 | Top 10 | DNF | Poles | Money Won |
|---|---|---|---|---|---|---|---|---|---|
| 1986 | Rick Hendrick | 1 | 92 | 0 | 0 | 0 | 0 | 0 | $10,100 |
| 1987 | Hoss Ellington | 14 | 32 | 0 | 0 | 0 | 7 | 0 | 51,145 |
| 1988 | Bud Moore | 29 | 20 | 0 | 5 | 3 | 11 | 0 | 433,658 |
| 1989 | Bud Moore | 29 | 19 | 0 | 1 | 5 | 9 | 0 | 281,274 |
| 1990 | K. Bernstein | 29 | 12 | 1 | 0 | 4 | 5 | 1 | 442,681 |
| 1991 | K. Bernstein | 29 | 19 | 0 | 0 | 4 | 13 | 1 | 376,220 |
| 1992 | K. Bernstein | 29 | 15 | 0 | 0 | 11 | 4 | 1 | 495,224 |
| 1993 | K. Bernstein | 29 | 20 | 0 | 2 | 6 | 6 | 2 | 582,014 |
| 1994 | K. Bernstein | 31 | 19 | 0 | 0 | 5 | 7 | 0 | 791,444 |
| 1995 | J. Johnson | 31 | 20 | 0 | 0 | 2 | 3 | 0 | 893,029 |
| 1996 | Brett Bodine | 30 | 24 | 0 | 0 | 1 | 3 | 0 | 767,716 |
| 1997 | Brett Bodine | 31 | 29 | 0 | 0 | 2 | 5 | 0 | 936,694 |
| 1998 | Brett Bodine | 33 | 25 | 0 | 0 | 0 | 2 | 0 | 1,281,673 |
| 1999 | Brett Bodine | 32 | 35 | 0 | 0 | 0 | 3 | 0 | 1,321,396 |
| 2000 | Brett Bodine | 29 | 35 | 0 | 0 | 0 | 7 | 0 | 1,020,659 |
| 2001 | Brett Bodine | 36 | 30 | 0 | 0 | 2 | 2 | 0 | 1,740,526 |
| 2002 | Brett Bodine | 32 | 36 | 0 | 0 | 0 | 5 | 0 | 1,766,820 |
| 2003 | Brett Bodine | 6 | 52 | 0 | 0 | 0 | 2 | 0 | 383,718 |
| TOTALS | | 480 | | 1 | 16 | 61 | 94 | 5 | $13,575,991 |

## 2003 RESULTS

| Race | Start | Finish | Standing Pos. | Winnings |
|---|---|---|---|---|
| Bass Pro Shops MBNA 500 (Atlanta) | 25 | 41 | 47 | $46,050 |
| Carolina Dodge Dealers 400 (Darlington) | 43 | 31 | 47 | $42,380 |
| Food City 500 (Bristol) | 33 | 24 | 45 | $62,515 |
| Samsung/RadioShack 500 (Texas) | 25 | 31 | 43 | $67,775 |
| Pontiac Excitement 400 (Richmond) | 43 | 31 | 43 | $49,825 |
| MBNA Armed Forces Family 400 (Dover) | 34 | 42 | 37 | $56,890 |

# Todd Bodine

**Date of birth**: February 27, 1964 **Hometown:** Chemung, N.Y. **Resides:** Concord, N.C. **Spouse:** Lynn **Children:** Ashlyn **Height:** 5-7 **Weight:** 190 **Hobbies:** Art

## NASCAR ACHIEVEMENTS

**First NASCAR Cup start:** August 9, 1992 (Watkins Glen)
**Best points finish:** 20 (1994)
**Career victories:** 0
**Career poles:** 5—Chicago (01), Las Vegas (02), Martinsville (01b), Pocono (01b), Watkins Glen (97)
**First pole:** August 19, 1997 (Watkins Glen)
**Best career finish:** 3  **Best career start:** 1

## FAST FACTS

- Finished 23rd in the 2002 Busch Series, competing in 28 races with one win, six top fives and eight top 10s.
- Finished fourth in 2000 Busch Series for the second straight year.
- Finished second in 1997 and third in the 1996 Busch Series.
- Won his first Busch Series race (Dover, 1991) in his 22nd start.
- Made his Busch Series debut in 1986, in a car owned by "Tiger" Tom Pistone.
- Began his racing career driving modifieds from 1983-85 at tracks such as Stafford Springs (Conn.) and Seekonk, (Mass.).
- Worked as a fabricator for Bobby Hillin's team and drove in the sportsman series before moving into Busch Series rides.
- Considers Friday the 13th his lucky day. He married his wife, Lynn, on Friday, November 13, 1987.
- Growing up, spent Saturday nights working at family-owned Chemung Speedrome in his hometown of Chemung, N.Y.

Drove late models, worked at Buck Baker Driving School and hung bodies on cars for Billy Standridge to pay the bills.

## CAREER BY YEAR

**2003** Bodine showed signs he could break through with strong runs, but he lacked consistency. He finished 31st in points while running 35 races. A better points finish was there for the taking, but he didn't finish eight races because of accidents and left another with a transmission problem.

**2002** Finished 38th in series points. ... Started 24 races. ... Best finish of season was fifth at Richmond. ... Started on the pole at Las Vegas. ... Was placed on probation on October 16 for several on-track incidents. ... Missed final race of season due to a back injury. ... Had off-season back surgery.

**2001** Finished 29th in series points in his first full Winston Cup season since 1995. ... Finished in the top five at Las Vegas and Watkins Glen. ... Qualified well all season; won poles at Chicagoland, Pocono and Martinsville.

**2000** Finished 49th in series points, driving in four Winston Cup races while running a full schedule in the Busch Series. ... Raced for Joe Falk at Richmond and Atlanta, where he finished seventh. ... Finished 15th at the Brickyard 400, substituting for injured Terry Labonte in the Hendrick Motorsports-owned Chevrolet.

**1999** Finished 46th in series points, competing in seven races for Jack Birmingham. ... Best start was fifth and best finish was 15th.

**1998** Finished 41st in series points. ... In Joe Falk-owned cars, had one top five and two top 10 finishes. ... For ISM Racing, had one top 10 finish.

**1997** Finished 52nd in series points, driving for five different owners in five races. ... Won the pole at Watkins Glen in a car owned by Frank Cicci.

**1996** Finished 40th in series points, competing in 10 races for three different owners. ... In four starts in a Bill Elliott-owned car, best finish was 10th at Pocono. ... Drove three races for David Blair and three for Andy Petree.

**1995** Finished 33rd in series points. ... Drove 28 races for Butch Mock-owned team. ... Finished fourth at Darlington, his best finish of the year.

**1994** Finished 20th in series points. ... Started 30 races for a Butch Mock-owned team and had two top five and seven top 10 finishes. ... At the season-ending race in Atlanta, scored a career-best finish of third.

**1993** Finished 40th in series points, driving in 10 races for car owner Butch Mock. ... Best start of season was sixth at Michigan.

**1992** Made first Winston Cup start at Watkins Glen. ... Won Goody's Headache award after an accident took him out of the race after 16 laps. ... That was only start of the season.

## CAREER STATISTICS

| Year | Car Owner | Races | Champ. Finish | Won | Top 5 | Top 10 | DNF | Poles | Money Won |
|---|---|---|---|---|---|---|---|---|---|
| 1992 | J. Donlavey | 1 | 87 | 0 | 0 | 0 | 1 | 0 | $3,485 |
| 1993 | Butch Mock | 10 | 40 | 0 | 0 | 0 | 5 | 0 | 63,245 |
| 1994 | Butch Mock | 30 | 20 | 0 | 2 | 7 | 6 | 0 | 494,316 |
| 1995 | Butch Mock | 28 | 33 | 0 | 1 | 3 | 10 | 0 | 664,620 |
| 1996 | B. Elliott | 4 | 40 | 0 | 0 | 1 | 1 | 0 | 92,945 |
|  | D. Blair | 3 |  | 0 | 0 | 0 | 0 | 0 | 32,800 |
|  | A. Petree | 3 |  | 0 | 0 | 0 | 1 | 0 | 72,780 |
| 1997 | R. Hendrick | 1 | 52 | 0 | 0 | 0 | 0 | 0 | 58,550 |
|  | G. Bodine | 1 |  | 0 | 0 | 0 | 1 | 0 | 25,400 |
|  | Cicci-Welliver | 1 |  | 0 | 0 | 0 | 1 | 1 | 16,465 |
|  | B. McCall | 1 |  | 0 | 0 | 0 | 1 | 0 | 12,270 |
|  | B. Hancher | 1 |  | 0 | 0 | 0 | 0 | 0 | 13,160 |
| 1998 | B. Hancher | 7 | 41 | 0 | 0 | 1 | 1 | 0 | 183,901 |
|  | J. Falk | 7 |  | 0 | 1 | 1 | 1 | 0 | 194,865 |
| 1999 | J. Birmingham | 7 | 46 | 0 | 0 | 0 | 2 | 0 | 208,382 |
| 2000 | J. Falk | 2 |  | 0 | 0 | 1 | 1 | 0 | 52,745 |
|  | R. Hendrick | 1 |  | 0 | 0 | 0 | 0 | 0 | 117,260 |
|  | F. Cicci | 1 |  | 0 | 0 | 0 | 1 | 0 | 24,760 |
|  | T. Carter | 1 | 49 | 0 | 0 | 0 | 0 | 0 | 39,300 |
| 2001 | T. Carter | 35 | 29 | 0 | 2 | 2 | 12 | 3 | 1,740,315 |
| 2002 | T. Carter | 24 | 38 | 0 | 1 | 4 | 9 | 1 | 1,879,767 |
| 2003 | Carter-Belnavis | 35 | 31 | 0 | 0 | 1 | 9 | 0 | 2,521,720 |
| **TOTALS** |  | **204** |  | **0** | **7** | **21** | **62** | **5** | **$8,513,051** |

## 2003 RESULTS

| Race | Start | Finish | Standing Pos. | Winnings |
|---|---|---|---|---|
| Daytona 500 (Daytona) | 6 | 18 | 17 | $208,051 |
| Subway 400 (Rockingham) | 40 | 42 | 34 | $45,615 |
| UAW-DaimlerChrysler 400 (Las Vegas) | 24 | 20 | 32 | $84,750 |
| Bass Pro Shops MBNA 500 (Atlanta) | 35 | 28 | 30 | $49,920 |
| Carolina Dodge Dealers 400 (Darlington) | 10 | 43 | 38 | $41,009 |
| Food City 500 (Bristol) | 41 | 40 | 40 | $56,965 |
| Samsung/RadioShack 500 (Texas) | 19 | 11 | 35 | $111,750 |
| Aaron's 499 (Talladega) | 35 | 28 | 36 | $79,045 |
| Virginia 500 (Martinsville) | 41 | 37 | 37 | $43,850 |
| Auto Club 500 (California) | 34 | 25 | 36 | $71,700 |
| Pontiac Excitement 400 (Richmond) | 34 | 23 | 35 | $65,375 |
| Coca-Cola 600 (Charlotte) | 16 | 23 | 35 | $84,314 |
| MBNA Armed Forces Family 400 (Dover) | 21 | 12 | 32 | $83,110 |
| Pocono 500 (Pocono) | 14 | 11 | 30 | $68,740 |
| Sirius 400 (Michigan) | 41 | 37 | 32 | $48,695 |
| Dodge/Save Mart 350 (Sonoma) | 22 | 23 | 31 | $70,125 |
| Pepsi 400 (Daytona) | 41 | 13 | 31 | $87,450 |
| Tropicana 400 (Chicago) | 39 | 33 | 31 | $62,075 |
| New England 300 (New Hampshire) | 32 | 19 | 31 | $57,200 |
| Pennsylvania 500 (Pocono) | 23 | 8 | 30 | $76,390 |
| Brickyard 400 (Indianapolis) | 31 | 23 | 29 | $125,605 |
| Sirius at the Glen (Watkins Glen) | 17 | 35 | 30 | $43,950 |
| GFS Marketplace 400 (Michigan) | 41 | 43 | 30 | $47,484 |
| Sharpie 500 (Bristol) | 40 | 37 | 32 | $60,420 |
| Southern 500 (Darlington) | 27 | 17 | 32 | $66,754 |
| Chevy Rock & Roll 400 (Richmond) | 12 | 42 | 32 | $46,790 |
| Sylvania 300 (New Hampshire) | 29 | 35 | 32 | $49,200 |
| MBNA America 400 (Dover) | 33 | 17 | 32 | $71,740 |
| Banquet 400 (Kansas) | 23 | 11 | 31 | $89,425 |
| UAW-GM Quality 500 (Charlotte) | 8 | 29 | 31 | $49,200 |
| Subway 500 (Martinsville) | 36 | 40 | 32 | $42,990 |
| Bass Pro Shops MBNA 500 (Atlanta) | 7 | 42 | 32 | $61,850 |
| Checker Auto Parts 500 (Phoenix) | 21 | 22 | 32 | $65,575 |
| Pop Secret 400 (Rockingham) | 27 | 16 | 31 | $69,475 |
| Ford 400 (Homestead) | 34 | 11 | 31 | $70,525 |

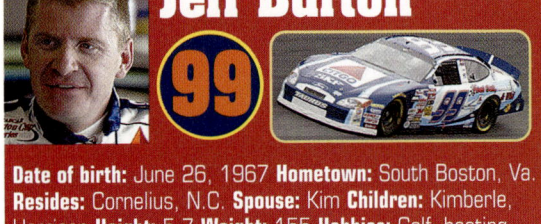

# Jeff Burton
## 99

**Date of birth:** June 26, 1967 **Hometown:** South Boston, Va. **Resides:** Cornelius, N.C. **Spouse:** Kim **Children:** Kimberle, Harrison **Height:** 5-7 **Weight:** 155 **Hobbies:** Golf, boating

## NASCAR ACHIEVEMENTS

**First NASCAR Cup start:** July 11, 1993 (New Hampshire)
**Best points finish:** 3 (2000)
**Career victories:** 17—Charlotte (99a, 01a), Darlington (99a, 99b), Daytona (00b), Las Vegas (99, 00), Martinsville (97b), New Hampshire (97a, 98a, 99a, 00b), Phoenix (00, 01), Richmond (98b), Rockingham (99b), Texas (97)
**First victory:** April 6, 1997 (Texas)
**Career poles:** 2—Michigan (96b), Richmond (00b)
**First pole:** August 16, 1996 (Michigan)
**Best career finish:** 1  **Best career start:** 1

## FAST FACTS

- Continues to compete part-time in the Busch Series.
- Won five Busch races in 2002, in only 13 starts.

- Won seven of 21 late model stock races at South Boston Speedway in 1988 and was voted the track's most popular driver.
- Began racing in the pure stock class at South Boston in 1984.
- Was a two-time Virginia state go-kart champion and finished second four times; began racing go-karts at age 8.
- Was an outstanding high school athlete in several sports.

## CAREER BY YEAR

**2003** An up-and-down season followed a promising start. He was ninth after four races but never reached that mark again. Engine failures at Atlanta, Darlington, New Hampshire and Talladega, combined with inconsistent performance to leave Burton with his second straight 12th place finish in the points race. He had zero wins, three top fives and 11 top 10s. His best finish of the season was a second at the second Daytona race.

**2002** Finished 12th in series points, his lowest finish since 1996, his first year with Roush Racing. … Posted five top fives and 14 top 10s. … For the first time since 1996, he didn't win a race. … Finished third at both Richmond and Dover.

**2001** Finished 10th in series points. … Finished 30th or worse in four of the first six races and had only two top 10 finishes in the first 11 races. … Was outside the top 30 in points until a third-place finish at Talladega in April. … Won the Coca-Cola 600 at Charlotte in May, his second victory in three seasons in NASCAR Winston Cup's longest event. … Won for the second straight year at Phoenix, capping a stretch of four straight top five finishes. … Had eight top fives and 16 top 10s.

**2000** Finished third in series points, behind Bobby Labonte and seven-time champion Dale Earnhardt. … Tied for second in races won (four), including leading all 300 laps at New Hampshire and winning the $1 million No Bull 5 bonus at Las Vegas. Other victories came at the Pepsi 400 in Daytona and Phoenix. … Compiled 15 top five finishes. … Two DNFs (at Atlanta and Dover) ranked him fourth behind Labonte (0), Earnhardt (0) and Ricky Rudd (1) for fewest of year. … Won his second career pole, at Richmond in September. … Two of his wins (at Las Vegas and Darlington) came ahead of his brother Ward, who finished second.

**1999** Finished fifth in series points. … Had 18 top fives and 23 top 10s. … Had his most wins in a single season (six) with triumphs at Charlotte, Las Vegas, New Hampshire, Rockingham and both Darlington races, both of which were rain-shortened.

**1998** Finished fifth in series points. … Had 18 top fives and 23 top 10s. … Won at New Hampshire and Richmond.

**1997** Finished fourth in series points, his first-ever top 10 finish. … Won first career Winston Cup race in the first race at Texas in April, then went on to victories at New Hampshire and Martinsville. … Had 13 top fives and 18 top 10s.

**1996** Finished 13th in series points. … Was his first year with Roush Racing. … Had six top fives and 12 top 10s. … Best start and finish was third at Richmond.

**1995** Finished 32nd in series points. … Was his final year driving with Stavola Brothers. … Had one top five and two top 10s. … Best finish was fifth at North Carolina.

**1994** Finished 24th in series points. … Drove for the Stavola Brothers. …Won Winston Cup Rookie of the Year honors with two top fives and three top 10s.

**1993** Made his Winston Cup debut at New Hampshire, qualifying sixth and finishing 37th in his only race.

### CAR FACTS

**Car:** No. 99 Ford
**Primary sponsor:** TBA
**Owner:** Jack Roush
**Team:** Roush Racing
**Crew chief:** Paul Andrews
**Engine builder:** Roush Racing

### CAREER STATISTICS

| Year | Car Owner | Races | Champ. Finish | Won | Top 5 | Top 10 | DNF | Poles | Money Won |
|---|---|---|---|---|---|---|---|---|---|
| 1993 | F. Martocci | 1 | 83 | 0 | 0 | 0 | 1 | 0 | $9,550 |
| 1994 | Stavola Bros. | 30 | 24 | 0 | 2 | 3 | 7 | 0 | 594,700 |
| 1995 | Stavola Bros. | 29 | 32 | 0 | 1 | 2 | 6 | 0 | 630,770 |
| 1996 | Jack Roush | 30 | 13 | 0 | 6 | 12 | 1 | 1 | 884,303 |
| 1997 | Jack Roush | 32 | 4 | 3 | 13 | 18 | 1 | 0 | 2,296,614 |
| 1998 | Jack Roush | 33 | 5 | 2 | 18 | 23 | 4 | 0 | 2,626,987 |
| 1999 | Jack Roush | 34 | 5 | 6 | 18 | 23 | 3 | 0 | 5,725,399 |
| 2000 | Jack Roush | 34 | 3 | 4 | 15 | 22 | 2 | 1 | 5,959,439 |
| 2001 | Jack Roush | 36 | 10 | 2 | 8 | 16 | 1 | 0 | 4,230,737 |
| 2002 | Jack Roush | 36 | 12 | 0 | 5 | 14 | 5 | 0 | 4,244,856 |
| 2003 | Jack Roush | 36 | 12 | 0 | 3 | 11 | 4 | 0 | 4,384,752 |
| TOTALS | | 331 | | 17 | 89 | 144 | 35 | 2 | $31,588,107 |

### 2003 RESULTS

| Race | Start | Finish | Standing Pos. | Winnings |
|---|---|---|---|---|
| Daytona 500 (Daytona) | 9 | 11 | 11 | $233,937 |
| Subway 400 (Rockingham) | 38 | 12 | 7 | $86,227 |
| UAW-DaimlerChrysler 400 (Las Vegas) | 7 | 6 | 4 | $127,067 |
| Bass Pro Shops MBNA 500 (Atlanta) | 26 | 33 | 9 | $80,687 |
| Carolina Dodge Dealers 400 (Darlington) | 37 | 42 | 22 | $75,107 |
| Food City 500 (Bristol) | 29 | 13 | 18 | $99,807 |
| Samsung/RadioShack 500 (Texas) | 29 | 20 | 18 | $120,492 |
| Aaron's 499 (Talladega) | 38 | 35 | 21 | $97,597 |
| Virginia 500 (Martinsville) | 10 | 4 | 18 | $101,592 |
| Auto Club 500 (California) | 10 | 19 | 15 | $102,442 |
| Pontiac Excitement 400 (Richmond) | 16 | 9 | 15 | $90,342 |
| Coca-Cola 600 (Charlotte) | 35 | 18 | 14 | $111,522 |
| MBNA Armed Forces Family 400 (Dover) | 28 | 14 | 14 | $98,652 |
| Pocono 500 (Pocono) | 16 | 14 | 14 | $84,507 |
| Sirius 400 (Michigan) | 23 | 11 | 14 | $93,447 |
| Dodge/Save Mart 350 (Sonoma) | 16 | 38 | 16 | $88,162 |
| Pepsi 400 (Daytona) | 36 | 2 | 14 | $168,142 |
| Tropicana 400 (Chicago) | 27 | 6 | 13 | $114,092 |
| New England 300 (New Hampshire) | 13 | 9 | 10 | $96,167 |
| Pennsylvania 500 (Pocono) | 19 | 6 | 10 | 200/200 |
| Brickyard 400 (Indianapolis) | 37 | 27 | 12 | $143,392 |
| Sirius at the Glen (Watkins Glen) | 23 | 31 | 13 | $80,157 |

| Race | Start | Standing Finish | Pos. | Winnings |
|---|---|---|---|---|
| GFS Marketplace 400 (Michigan) | 8 | 11 | 12 | $92,422 |
| Sharpie 500 (Bristol) | 37 | 32 | 13 | $96,547 |
| Southern 500 (Darlington) | 28 | 11 | 13 | $95,037 |
| Chevy Rock & Roll 400 (Richmond) | 7 | 4 | 12 | $116,897 |
| Sylvania 300 (New Hampshire) | 15 | 42 | 13 | $81,817 |
| MBNA America 400 (Dover) | 13 | 12 | 13 | $96,007 |
| EA SPORTS 500 (Talladega) | 40 | 32 | 13 | $88,727 |
| Banquet 400 (Kansas) | 33 | 13 | 15 | $108,692 |
| UAW-GM Quality 500 Charlotte | 37 | 20 | 14 | $87,167 |
| Subway 500 (Martinsville) | 21 | 10 | 13 | $90,142 |
| Bass Pro Shops MBNA 500 (Atlanta) | 38 | 23 | 12 | $102,442 |
| Checker Auto Parts 500 (Phoenix) | 27 | 8 | 13 | $98,917 |
| Pop Secret 400 (Rockingham) | 9 | 7 | 12 | $91,442 |
| Ford 400 (Homestead) | 36 | 14 | 12 | $85,742 |

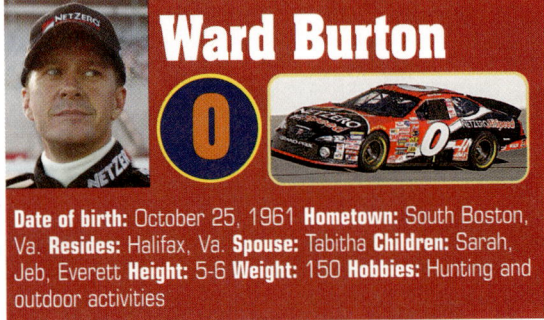

# Ward Burton

**Date of birth:** October 25, 1961 **Hometown:** South Boston, Va. **Resides:** Halifax, Va. **Spouse:** Tabitha **Children:** Sarah, Jeb, Everett **Height:** 5-6 **Weight:** 150 **Hobbies:** Hunting and outdoor activities

## NASCAR ACHIEVEMENTS

**First NASCAR Cup start:** March 6, 1994 (Richmond)
**Best points finish:** 9 (1999)
**Career victories:** 5—Darlington (00a, 01b), Daytona (02a), New Hampshire (02a), Rockingham (95b)
**First victory:** October 25, 1995 (Rockingham)
**Career poles:** 7—Charlotte (94b), Darlington (96a), Martinsville (97b), Michigan (96a, 99b), Pocono (98b), Richmond (02a)
**First pole:** October 5, 1994 (Charlotte)
**Best career finish:** 1  **Best career start:** 1

## FAST FACTS

- Competed in the Busch Series from 1990-93.
- Finished sixth in the Busch Series points in 1993, with three wins and four poles.
- Was second to Joe Nemechek in Busch Series Rookie of the Year points in 1990.
- Won three races and was voted Most Popular Driver at South Boston Speedway in 1989.

### CAR FACTS
**Car:** No. 0 Chevrolet
**Primary sponsor:** NetZero
**Owner:** Gene Haas
**Team:** Haas CNC Racing
**Crew chief:** Tony Furr
**Engine builder:** Hendrick Motorsports

- Began racing go-karts at age 8.
- Raced on Virginia Karting Association circuit until he was 16.
- Raced mini-stocks and street stocks in South Boston, Va., before moving into late model stock cars in 1986.
- Attended Hargrave Military Academy beginning in 10th grade and ranked first on the school's rifle team.
- After college, spent two years living in a cabin surviving off the land.
- Operates the Ward Burton Wildlife Foundation, which purchases land in an effort to conserve and protect wildlife habitats.

## CAREER BY YEAR

**2003** A mediocre season got worse when Burton was caught up in Silly Season and lost his ride with Bill Davis Racing. He quickly landed another full-time gig with Haas-CNC Racing, but his finishes didn't get much better. He had zero top fives on the year. His best finish was a sixth at Watkins Glen. He never posted back-to-back top 10s.

**2002** Finished 25th in series points. ... Led the final five laps of the Daytona 500, scoring the biggest win of his career. ... Won at New Hampshire, leading a total of 29 laps for his fifth career victory. ... Had nine DNFs. ... Richmond race began a six-race string of finishes 30th or worse that dropped him from 14th to 25th in points. ... Long-time crew chief Tommy Baldwin, Jr. was replaced by Frank Stoddard in the second half of the season. ... Capped the season with a 12th-place finish at Homestead to secure the final Winston points-paying position. ... Led 371 laps in 11 different events.

**2001** Finished 14th in series points. ... Charged from a 37th-place starting position to notch his third career win in September at Darlington. ... Had back-to-back third-place finishes at Charlotte and Martinsville in October. ... Struggled early in the season as he and his team adjusted to the Dodge Intrepid, scoring only one top 10 in the first 11 races. ... Beginning at Bristol in August, rallied to post top 15 finishes in eight of 12 races. ... Finished 14th in points despite nine DNFs. ... Had six top fives and 10 top 10s.

**2000** Finished 10th in series points. ... Scored his second career victory in a Pontiac at Darlington in March. ... Had eight top 10 finishes in the season's first 13 races and was second in points at that time. ... Stumbled in the second half of the season with four DNFs. ... Had four top fives and 17 top 10s. ... Started a season-best third in both Darlington races.

**1999** Finished ninth in series points. ... Didn't win a race but finished second three times, all three times behind his brother Jeff—at Rockingham, Las Vegas and Darlington. ... Had six top fives and 16 top 10s. ... Won the pole at Michigan in August.

**1998** Finished 16th in series points. ... Won two poles, at Michigan and Pocono. ... Finished second to Mark Martin at Charlotte in October for his lone top five of the season. ... Scored five top 10s.

**1997** Finished 24th in series points. ... Topped $1 million in season winnings for the first time in his career. ... Had seven top 10s and won the pole at Martinsville.

**1996** Finished 33rd in series points. ... Won one pole, at Darlington, in first full season with Bill Davis Racing. ... Scored four top 10s.

**1995** Finished 22nd in series points. ... Began the season driving for A.G. Dillard, finishing in the top 10 twice in 20 races. ... Joined Bill Davis Racing for the final nine races and proved it was a good move when he got his first career win at Rockingham. ... Also scored two other top fives for Davis.

**1994** Finished 35th in series points. ... Stepped up from the Busch Series for his first full season in Winston Cup. ... Struggled early, missing the first two races and recording two DNFs in the third and fourth races of the season. ... After seven straight finishes of 29th or worse, was second at Pocono. ... Scored first career pole at Charlotte in October.

### CAREER STATISTICS

| Year | Car Owner | Races | Champ. Finish | Won | Top 5 | Top 10 | DNF | Poles | Money Won |
|---|---|---|---|---|---|---|---|---|---|
| 1994 | A. Dillard | 26 | 35 | 0 | 1 | 2 | 12 | 1 | $304,700 |
| 1995 | A. Dillard | 20 |  | 0 | 0 | 2 | 4 | 0 | 334,330 |
|  | Bill Davis | 9 | 22 | 1 | 3 | 4 | 2 | 0 | 300,325 |
| 1996 | Bill Davis | 27 | 33 | 0 | 0 | 4 | 10 | 1 | 873,619 |
| 1997 | Bill Davis | 31 | 24 | 0 | 0 | 7 | 7 | 1 | 1,004,944 |
| 1998 | Bill Davis | 33 | 16 | 0 | 1 | 5 | 4 | 2 | 1,516,183 |
| 1999 | Bill Davis | 34 | 9 | 0 | 6 | 16 | 3 | 1 | 2,405,913 |
| 2000 | Bill Davis | 34 | 10 | 1 | 4 | 17 | 4 | 0 | 2,699,604 |
| 2001 | Bill Davis | 36 | 14 | 1 | 6 | 10 | 9 | 0 | 3,633,692 |
| 2002 | Bill Davis | 36 | 25 | 2 | 3 | 8 | 9 | 1 | 4,899,884 |
| 2003 | Bill Davis | 32 |  | 0 | 0 | 4 | 4 | 0 | 3,280,950 |
|  | Gene Haas | 4 | 21 | 0 | 0 | 0 | 2 | 0 | 347,650 |
| TOTALS |  | 322 |  | 5 | 24 | 79 | 70 | 7 | $21,551,794 |

### 2003 RESULTS

| Race | Start | Finish | Standing Pos. | Winnings |
|---|---|---|---|---|
| Daytona 500 (Daytona) | 17 | 38 | 38 | $203,751 |
| Subway 400 (Rockingham) | 15 | 18 | 31 | $85,316 |
| UAW-DaimlerChrysler 400 (Las Vegas) | 20 | 25 | 33 | $100,006 |
| Bass Pro Shops MBNA 500 (Atlanta) | 12 | 18 | 28 | $84,871 |
| Carolina Dodge Dealers 400 (Darlington) | 7 | 29 | 31 | $78,611 |
| Food City 500 (Bristol) | 11 | 33 | 32 | $94,256 |
| Samsung/RadioShack 500 (Texas) | 33 | 12 | 32 | $127,906 |
| Aaron's 499 (Talladega) | 24 | 7 | 26 | $114,386 |
| Virginia 500 (Martinsville) | 12 | 25 | 25 | $82,931 |
| Auto Club 500 (California) | 39 | 21 | 27 | $104,681 |
| Pontiac Excitement 400 (Richmond) | 20 | 11 | 25 | $90,781 |
| Coca-Cola 600 (Charlotte) | 41 | 10 | 21 | $120,331 |
| MBNA Armed Forces Family 400 (Dover) | 39 | 37 | 25 | $93,526 |
| Pocono 500 (Pocono) | 17 | 8 | 20 | $91,146 |
| Sirius 400 (Michigan) | 31 | 30 | 21 | $85,896 |
| Dodge/Save Mart 350 (Sonoma) | 19 | 16 | 21 | $93,406 |
| Pepsi 400 (Daytona) | 28 | 30 | 21 | $100,991 |
| Tropicana 400 (Chicago) | 30 | 19 | 21 | $100,106 |
| New England 300 (New Hampshire) | 21 | 25 | 22 | $87,806 |
| Pennsylvania 500 (Pocono) | 38 | 19 | 21 | $81,896 |
| Brickyard 400 (Indianapolis) | 4 | 26 | 22 | $145,081 |
| Sirius at the Glen (Watkins Glen) | 22 | 6 | 20 | $94,046 |
| GFS Marketplace 400 (Michigan) | 22 | 14 | 20 | $90,521 |
| Sharpie 500 (Bristol) | 24 | 13 | 18 | $105,996 |
| Southern 500 (Darlington) | 29 | 19 | 22 | $90,166 |
| Chevy Rock & Roll 400 (Richmond) | 8 | 15 | 19 | $88,811 |
| Sylvania 300 (New Hampshire) | 23 | 39 | 21 | $84,691 |
| MBNA America 400 (Dover) | 21 | 29 | 23 | $89,246 |
| EA SPORTS 500 (Talladega) | 20 | 14 | 21 | $92,801 |
| Banquet 400 (Kansas) | 39 | 21 | 20 | $99,706 |
| UAW-GM Quality 500 (Charlotte) | 38 | 28 | 21 | $81,941 |
| Subway 500 (Martinsville) | 2 | 18 | 21 | $84,036 |
| Bass Pro Shops MBNA 500 (Atlanta) | 29 | 13 | 21 | $74,125 |
| Checker Auto Parts 500 (Phoenix) | 20 | 41 | 22 | $47,185 |
| Pop Secret 400 (Rockingham) | 13 | 18 | 21 | $53,325 |
| Ford 400 (Homestead) | 24 | 32 | 21 | $44,575 |

## Kurt Busch — 97

**Date of birth:** August 4, 1978 **Hometown:** Las Vegas
**Resides:** Concord, N.C. **Spouse:** Single **Children:** None
**Height:** 5-11 **Weight:** 150 **Hobbies:** jet skiing, water skiing, snow skiing

### NASCAR ACHIEVEMENTS

**First NASCAR Cup start:** September 24, 2000 (Dover)
**Best points finish:** 3 (2002)
**Career victories:** 8—Atlanta (02b), Bristol (02a, 03a, 03b), California (03) Homestead (02), Martinsville (02b), Michigan (03)
**First victory:** March 24, 2002 (Bristol)
**Career poles:** 2—Darlington (01b), Homestead (02)
**First pole:** September 2, 2001 (Darlington)
**Best career finish:** 1  **Best career start:** 1

### FAST FACTS

- Was runner-up in the 2000 NASCAR Craftsman Truck Series and had four victories.
- In 1999, won the Featherlite Southwest Series, NASCAR Touring championship driving for Craig Keough. Was the youngest driver to win that series' championship at age 21.
- Named Featherlite Southwest Series Rookie of the Year in 1998.
- Competed in the Featherlite Southwest Series from 1997-1999, recording seven wins.
- Won the 1996 Hobby Stock track championship at the Las

### CAR FACTS

**Car:** No.97 Ford
**Primary sponsor:** Rubbermaid
**Owner:** Georgetta Roush
**Team:** Roush Racing
**Crew chief:** Jimmy Fenning
**Engine builder:** Guy Williams

Vegas Speedway Park.
- Was the 1996 Legend Cars National Rookie of the Year and Legend Cars Western States champion.
- Won the Nevada Dwarf Car championship in 1995.
- Was the 1994 Nevada State Dwarf Car Rookie of the Year.
- Began racing at age 14, in Dwarf Cars at Parhump Valley Speedway near Las Vegas.
- Won the 2002 Outback Steakhouse "Bloomin' Favorite Driver" award.

## CAREER BY YEAR

**2003** A hard-charging racer, Busch found more trouble than he avoided. His four wins were second-best on the circuit, but they were offset by controversy and 10 finishes outside the top 35. Three of those came in succession in October and cost him a top 10 finish in points. He showed his short-track prowess by sweeping the races at Bristol. He also won at Michigan and California.

**2002** Finished third in series points. ... Had a breakthrough season with four wins (Bristol, Martinsville, Atlanta and Homestead), three in the final five weeks of the season. ... Won from the pole at Homestead.

**2001** Finished 27th in series points. ... Finished third in the Talladega 500, fourth in the Harrah's 400 at Texas and fifth at Brickyard 400 at Indianapolis. ... Won his first career pole, at Darlington. ... Had seven DNFs.

**2000** Finished 48th in series points. ... Made his Winston Cup debut with seven starts for Roush Racing..

### CAREER STATISTICS

| Year | Car Owner | Races | Champ. Finish | Won | Top 5 | Top 10 | DNF | Poles | Money Won |
|---|---|---|---|---|---|---|---|---|---|
| 2000 | Jack Roush | 7 | 48 | 0 | 0 | 0 | 0 | 0 | $311,915 |
| 2001 | Jack Roush | 35 | 27 | 0 | 3 | 6 | 7 | 1 | 2,170,629 |
| 2002 | Jack Roush | 36 | 3 | 4 | 12 | 20 | 4 | 1 | 5,105,394 |
| 2003 | Jack Roush | 36 | 11 | 4 | 9 | 14 | 8 | 0 | 5,587,384 |
| TOTALS | | 114 | | 8 | 24 | 40 | 19 | 2 | $13,183,351 |

### 2003 RESULTS

| Race | Start | Finish | Standing Pos. | Winnings |
|---|---|---|---|---|
| Daytona 500 (Daytona) | 36 | 2 | 2 | $1,027,101 |
| Subway 400 (Rockingham) | 27 | 2 | 1 | $108,200 |
| UAW-DaimlerChrysler 400 (Las Vegas) | 5 | 38 | 6 | $78,475 |
| Bass Pro Shops MBNA 500 (Atlanta) | 9 | 40 | 14 | $66,090 |
| Carolina Dodge Dealers 400 (Darlington) | 6 | 2 | 6 | $103,725 |
| Food City 500 (Bristol) | 9 | 1 | 2 | $162,790 |
| Samsung/RadioShack 500 (Texas) | 30 | 9 | 2 | $133,150 |
| Aaron's 499 (Talladega) | 26 | 19 | 3 | $87,195 |
| Virginia 500 (Martinsville) | 36 | 28 | 5 | $64,910 |
| Auto Club 500 (California) | 16 | 1 | 4 | $213,150 |
| Pontiac Excitement 400 (Richmond) | 7 | 8 | 3 | $89,925 |
| Coca-Cola 600 (Charlotte) | 12 | 15 | 4 | $110,950 |
| MBNA Armed Forces Family 400 (Dover) | 7 | 15 | 5 | $95,685 |
| Pocono 500 (Pocono) | 10 | 36 | 5 | $62,790 |
| Sirius 400 (Michigan) | 4 | 1 | 5 | $172,650 |
| Dodge/Save Mart 350 (Sonoma) | 5 | 28 | 6 | $75,255 |
| Pepsi 400 (Daytona) | 31 | 36 | 7 | $83,600 |
| Tropicana 400 (Chicago) | 32 | 39 | 9 | $79,985 |
| New England 300 (New Hampshire) | 9 | 11 | 8 | $94,250 |
| Pennsylvania 500 (Pocono) | 13 | 2 | 8 | $152,695 |
| Brickyard 400 (Indianapolis) | 6 | 7 | 8 | $189,675 |
| Sirius at the Glen (Watkins Glen) | 8 | 12 | 8 | $85,100 |
| GFS Marketplace 400 (Michigan) | 20 | 18 | 9 | $96,690 |
| Sharpie 500 (Bristol) | 5 | 1 | 6 | $237,565 |
| Southern 500 (Darlington) | 31 | 13 | 6 | $92,135 |
| Chevy Rock & Roll 400 (Richmond) | 25 | 24 | 8 | $78,605 |
| Sylvania 300 (New Hampshire) | 28 | 15 | 7 | $89,375 |
| MBNA America 400 (Dover) | 7 | 38 | 8 | $71,750 |
| EA SPORTS 500 (Talladega) | 39 | 6 | 8 | $106,750 |
| Banquet 400 (Kansas) | 21 | 40 | 9 | $79,785 |
| UAW-GM Quality 500 (Charlotte) | 17 | 41 | 10 | $64,870 |
| Subway 500 (Martinsville) | 13 | 39 | 11 | $63,065 |
| Bass Pro Shops MBNA 500 (Atlanta) | 17 | 8 | 11 | $110,475 |
| Checker Auto Parts 500 (Phoenix) | 7 | 4 | 9 | $142,585 |
| Pop Secret 400 (Rockingham) | 19 | 17 | 10 | $82,925 |
| Ford 400 (Homestead) | 7 | 36 | 11 | $63,760 |

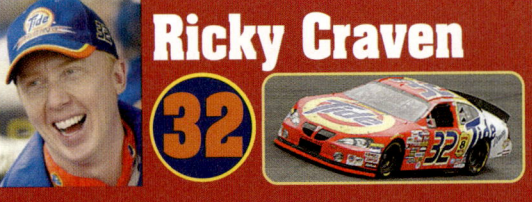

# Ricky Craven 32

**Date of birth:** May 24, 1966 **Hometown:** Newburgh, Maine **Resides:** Concord, N.C. **Spouse:** Cathleen **Children:** Riley Diane, Richard Everett **Height:** 5-9 **Weight:** 165 **Hobbies:** Riding snowmobiles.

## NASCAR ACHIEVEMENTS

**First NASCAR Cup start:** October 20, 1991 (Rockingham)
**Best points finish:** 15 (2002)
**Career victories:** 2—Darlington (03a), Martinsville (01b)
**First victory:** October 15, 2001 (Martinsville)
**Career poles:** 6—Darlington (02a), Martinsville (96a), Michigan (01b), New Hampshire (96b, 98a), North Carolina (02a)
**First pole:** April 21, 1996 (Martinsville)
**Best career finish:** 1  **Best career start:** 1

## FAST FACTS

- Won the 1997 Winston Open.
- Finished second in Busch Series standings in 1993 and 1994.
- Was the Busch Series Rookie of the Year in 1992.
- Won Busch North Series, NASCAR Touring title and was voted series' Most Popular

### CAR FACTS

**Car:** No.32 Chevrolet
**Primary sponsor:** Tide
**Owner:** Cal Wells
**Team:** PPI Motorsports
**Crew chief:** Dave Charpentier
**Engine builder:** PPI Motorsports

Driver in 1991.
- Was the Busch North Series Rookie of the Year and Most Popular Driver in 1990, winning two races in first full season on circuit.
- Finished fourth on the ACT Tour in 1988 with two wins.
- Was the Rookie of the Year in 1984 at Wiscasset (Maine) Speedway.
- Raced in the charger division at Unity (Maine) Raceway.
- Holds an annual snowmobile ride in Maine to raise money for various charities.

## CAREER BY YEAR

**2003** His bumping and banging, last-lap pass of Kurt Busch to win by .002 seconds at the Darlington spring race would be a season highlight for any driver in any season. Indeed, it was the most exciting finish to a Winston Cup race in years. But Craven struggled to string together good results. He showed flashes of strength, but they were surrounded by too many poor performances. The end of the season was particularly difficult: In an eight-race stretch, he had three accidents and two engine failures.

**2002** Finished 15th in series points. ... Won pole at Rockingham, the second race of the season. ... Finished third in the Coca-Cola 600. ... Season's other top fives were at Rockingham (fifth) and Atlanta (fifth), both in the spring.

**2001** Finished 21st in series points. ... Completed a long road back from injuries with an emotional win at Martinsville, battling Dale Jarrett door-to-door in a last-lap finish to score his first career win. ... Finished second at Michigan in August after starting on the pole and was fourth at Dover in June. ... Finished with four top fives and seven top 10s.

**2000** Finished 44th in series points. ... Ran only 16 races in the No. 50 Chevrolet for owner Hal Hicks. ... Best finish was 15th at Rockingham. ... Best start was fifth at New Hampshire.

**1999** Finished 41st in series points. ... Started 12 races for car owner Scott Barbour before switching to drive 12 races for Hal Hicks. ... Best finish was 13th at New Hampshire. ... Started sixth at Las Vegas, his best start of the season.

**1998** Finished 46th in series points. ... Began season with car owner Rick Hendrick. ... Finished 14th in the Daytona 500, his best finish of the season. ... Sidelined with post-concussion syndrome after the fourth race of season and sat out 12 weeks. ... Won the pole at New Hampshire in his return. ... After New Hampshire, made three more starts before resigning from Hendrick Motorsports. ... Subbed for injured Ernie Irvan in the last three events of the season.

**1997** Finished 19th in series points. ... Joined forces with Hendrick Motorsports, driving the formidable No. 25 Chevrolet. ... Posted four top fives and seven top 10s. ... Missed two races because of a practice accident at Texas. ... Finished a season-best third in the Daytona 500 and at Rockingham. ... Started second twice (Darlington and Charlotte). ... Won the Winston Open at Charlotte.

**1996** Finished 20th in series points. ... Started strong with two top fives and four top 10s in the season's first seven races, then won his first career pole at Martinsville. ... Ranked fourth in series points after a 12th-place finish at Martinsville. ... Streak included season-best third-place finishes at Rockingham and Darlington. ... Recorded just one more top 10—a fifth at Charlotte in October—the remainder of the year. ... Won his second career pole at New Hampshire.

**1995** Finished 24th in series points. ... Competed in his first full season driving for Larry Hedrick. ... Won Rookie of the Year honors in a heated battle with Robert Pressley. ... Qualified in the top 10 eight times. ... Best finish was seventh at Michigan.

### CAREER STATISTICS

| Year | Car Owner | Races | Champ. Finish | Won | Top 5 | Top 10 | DNF | Poles | Money Won |
|---|---|---|---|---|---|---|---|---|---|
| 1991 | D. Moroso | 1 | 82 | 0 | 0 | 0 | 1 | 0 | $3,750 |
| 1995 | L. Hedrick | 31 | 24 | 0 | 0 | 4 | 4 | 0 | 597,054 |
| 1996 | L. Hedrick | 31 | 20 | 0 | 3 | 5 | 7 | 2 | 941,959 |
| 1997 | R. Hendrick | 30 | 19 | 0 | 4 | 7 | 7 | 0 | 1,259,550 |
| 1998 | R. Hendrick | 8 |  | 0 | 0 | 1 | 0 | 1 | 422,200 |
|  | N. Bowers | 3 | 46 | 0 | 0 | 0 | 0 | 0 | 84,030 |
| 1999 | S. Barbour | 12 |  | 0 | 0 | 0 | 4 | 0 | 457,496 |
| 1999 | H. Hicks | 12 |  | 0 | 0 | 0 | 6 | 0 | 396,339 |
| 2000 | H. Hicks | 16 | 44 | 0 | 0 | 0 | 6 | 0 | 363,562 |
| 2001 | Cal Wells III | 36 | 21 | 1 | 4 | 7 | 9 | 1 | 1,996,981 |
| 2002 | Cal Wells III | 36 | 15 | 0 | 3 | 9 | 4 | 2 | 2,838,087 |
| 2003 | Cal Wells III | 36 | 27 | 1 | 3 | 8 | 10 | 0 | 3,216,211 |
| TOTALS |  | 252 |  | 2 | 17 | 41 | 58 | 6 | $12,871,864 |

### 2003 RESULTS

| Race | Start | Finish | Standing Pos. | Winnings |
|---|---|---|---|---|
| Daytona 500 (Daytona) | 25 | 26 | 25 | $194,259 |
| Subway 400 (Rockingham) | 6 | 4 | 8 | $103,725 |
| UAW-DaimlerChrysler 400 (Las Vegas) | 37 | 36 | 15 | $66,900 |
| Bass Pro Shops MBNA 500 (Atlanta) | 22 | 12 | 16 | $76,375 |
| Carolina Dodge Dealers 400 (Darlington) | 31 | 1 | 5 | $172,150 |
| Food City 500 (Bristol) | 14 | 15 | 7 | $84,815 |
| Samsung/RadioShack 500 (Texas) | 38 | 21 | 9 | $102,075 |
| Aaron's 499 (Talladega) | 15 | 4 | 6 | $139,575 |
| Virginia 500 (Martinsville) | 17 | 27 | 9 | $67,010 |
| Auto Club 500 (California) | 15 | 15 | 7 | $96,575 |
| Pontiac Excitement 400 (Richmond) | 38 | 38 | 11 | $54,375 |
| Coca-Cola 600 (Charlotte) | 33 | 38 | 15 | $76,860 |
| MBNA Armed Forces Family 400 (Dover) | 20 | 8 | 12 | $95,565 |
| Pocono 500 (Pocono) | 32 | 10 | 12 | $83,490 |
| Sirius 400 (Michigan) | 37 | 15 | 13 | $83,590 |
| Dodge/Save Mart 350 (Sonoma) | 38 | 21 | 14 | $80,050 |
| Pepsi 400 (Daytona) | 17 | 43 | 17 | $70,945 |
| Tropicana 400 (Chicago) | 26 | 25 | 17 | $84,925 |
| New England 300 (New Hampshire) | 17 | 21 | 17 | $63,375 |
| Pennsylvania 500 (Pocono) | 32 | 40 | 19 | $50,230 |
| Brickyard 400 (Indianapolis) | 35 | 17 | 18 | $141,525 |
| Sirius at the Glen (Watkins Glen) | 38 | 19 | 19 | $55,555 |
| GFS Marketplace 400 (Michigan) | 39 | 40 | 21 | $56,235 |
| Sharpie 500 (Bristol) | 14 | 8 | 21 | $102,740 |
| Southern 500 (Darlington) | 8 | 8 | 20 | $90,125 |
| Chevy Rock & Roll 400 (Richmond) | 35 | 30 | 21 | $67,189 |

| Race | Start | Standing Finish | Pos. | Winnings |
|---|---|---|---|---|
| Sylvania 300 (New Hampshire) | 21 | 38 | 22 | $56,700 |
| MBNA America 400 (Dover) | 22 | 40 | 24 | $59,465 |
| EA SPORTS 500 (Talladega) | 17 | 8 | 22 | $87,200 |
| Banquet 400 (Kansas) | 32 | 41 | 24 | $67,590 |
| UAW-GM Quality 500 (Charlotte) | 13 | 19 | 23 | $76,850 |
| Subway 500 (Martinsville) | 27 | 32 | 24 | $59,889 |
| Bass Pro Shops MBNA 500 (Atlanta) | 26 | 35 | 24 | $70,300 |
| Checker Auto Parts 500 (Phoenix) | 38 | 38 | 26 | $54,900 |
| Pop Secret 400 (Rockingham) | 30 | 39 | 27 | $54,090 |
| Ford 400 (Homestead) | 42 | 29 | 27 | $56,190 |

## Dale Earnhardt Jr.

**Date of birth:** October 10, 1974 **Hometown:** Kannapolis, N.C.
**Resides:** Mooresville, N.C. **Spouse:** Single **Children:** None.
**Height:** 6-0 **Weight:** 165. **Hobbies:** Car restoration, music, computers, video games

### NASCAR ACHIEVEMENTS

**First NASCAR Cup start:** May 30, 2000 (Charlotte)
**Best points finish:** 3 (2003)
**Career victories:** 9—Daytona (01b), Dover (01b), Phoenix (03), Richmond (00a), Talladega (01b, 02a, 02b, 03a), Texas (00)
**First victory:** April 2, 2000 (Texas)
**Career poles:** 6—Atlanta (02b), Charlotte (00a), Kansas (02), Michigan (00b, 02b), Texas (01)
**First pole:** May 28, 2000 (Charlotte)
**Best career finish:** 1 **Best career start:** 1

### FAST FACTS

- Won back-to-back Busch Series Championships in 1998 and 1999, his only two full seasons of Busch competition.
- Began his professional career at age 17, competing in the street stock division at Concord Motorsport Park and later moving up to late model stock division.
- Raced against brother Kerry and sister Kelley at the beginning of his career.
- Won three feature victories in his NASCAR late model stock career from 1994-96.
- When he raced in the Pepsi 400 at Michigan in 2000 along with his late father, Dale, and Kerry, it was the second time a father and two sons ran in the same Cup event. Lee Petty also raced against his sons, Richard and Maurice.

### CAR FACTS

**Car:** No.8 Chevrolet
**Primary sponsor:** Budweiser
**Owner:** Teresa Earnhardt
**Team:** Dale Earnhardt Inc.
**Crew chief:** Tony Eury Sr.
**Engine builder:** Richie Gilmore

- Says his hero is his father, seven-time NASCAR Winston Cup Series champion, Dale Earnhardt.
- Began his racing career when he and Kerry sold a go-kart for $500 to purchase a 1978 Chevy Monte Carlo street stock car for $200. Later sold the car to current Busch Series competitor Hank Parker Jr.

### CAREER BY YEAR

**2003** Earnhardt posted the best season of his career, finishing third in points with two wins, 13 top 5s and 21 top 10s. His most important race was at Phoenix, where he ended a long winless drought on non-superspeedway tracks. Resiliency was a key to his success—he followed four of his five finishes outside the top 30 with a top 10.

**2002** Finished 11th in series points. ... Won two races, both at Talladega. ... Won the Winston No Bull 5 Million-dollar bonus for the second consecutive season at Talladega with his October win. ... Won two poles, at Michigan (August) and Kansas. ... Led 1,068 laps, more laps than any other driver. ... Finished second in all three non-points races—the Budweiser Shootout (Daytona), Twin 125 qualifying race (Daytona) and The Winston. ... Had 11 top fives, 16 top 10s, 13 top five starts, led in 22 races and had only three DNFs. ... Had five short-track (Martinsville, Bristol and Richmond) finishes in the top five. ... Won in his first Busch Series race as a driver/owner at Richmond in September.

**2001** Finished eighth in series points. ... First win came in July at Daytona, the first race there since his father's death in the Daytona 500 on February 18. He held off DEI teammate Michael Waltrip, to whom he finished second in February, for that win. ... Next victory was at Dover in Winston Cup's first race back after the September 11 terrorist attacks; punctuated that win with a victory lap carrying an American flag. ... Third win was in October at Talladega, the site of his father's final career victory a year earlier. ... ... Was 26th in points after six races before rallying. ... Finished with nine top fives and 15 top 10s.

**2000** Finished 16th in series points. ... Made a big splash on the Winston Cup scene with two wins and two poles in his rookie season. ... Was 42 points shy of winning the Raybestos Rookie of the Year title behind former Busch Series foe Matt Kenseth. ... Joined Jeff Burton as the second first-time winner at Texas Motor Speedway with a win in DirecTV 500. ... Along with Tony Stewart, became the second rookie in two years to win at Richmond when he won the Pontiac Excitement 400. ... Matched a modern-era record (two wins in his first 16 races) set by the late Davey Allison in 1987. ... Became the first rookie to win The Winston all-star race.

**1999** Competed in five Winston Cup races. ... Best start was eighth in the Coca-Cola 600 at Charlotte. ... Best finish was 10th at Richmond.

### CAREER STATISTICS

| Year | Car Owner | Races | Champ. Finish | Won | Top 5 | Top 10 | DNF | Poles | Money Won |
|---|---|---|---|---|---|---|---|---|---|
| 1999 | D. Earnhardt | 5 | | 0 | 0 | 1 | 1 | 0 | $162,095 |

| Year | Car Owner | Champ. Races | Finish | Won | Top 5 | Top 10 | DNF | Poles | Money Won |
|---|---|---|---|---|---|---|---|---|---|
| 2000 | D. Earnhardt | 34 | 16 | 2 | 3 | 5 | 7 | 2 | 2,801,881 |
| 2001 | D. Earnhardt | 36 | 8 | 3 | 9 | 15 | 4 | 2 | 5,827,542 |
| 2002 | T. Earnhardt | 36 | 11 | 2 | 11 | 16 | 3 | 2 | 4,970,034 |
| 2003 | T. Earnhardt | 36 | 3 | 2 | 13 | 21 | 4 | 0 | 6,880,807 |
| TOTALS | | 147 | | 9 | 36 | 58 | 19 | 6 | $20,742,359 |

## 2003 RESULTS

| Race | Start | Finish | Standing Pos. | Winnings |
|---|---|---|---|---|
| Daytona 500 (Daytona) | 2 | 36 | 35 | $243,543 |
| Subway 400 (Rockingham) | 12 | 33 | 38 | $87,142 |
| UAW-DaimlerChrysler 400 (Las Vegas) | 4 | 2 | 18 | $267,167 |
| Bass Pro Shops MBNA 500 (Atlanta) | 37 | 3 | 10 | $113,917 |
| Carolina Dodge Dealers 400 (Darlington) | 16 | 6 | 4 | $98,392 |
| Food City 500 (Bristol) | 8 | 16 | 5 | $101,407 |
| Samsung/RadioShack 500 (Texas) | 11 | 2 | 3 | $299,667 |
| Aaron's 499 (Talladega) | 13 | 1 | 2 | $204,367 |
| Virginia 500 (Martinsville) | 2 | 3 | 2 | $112,542 |
| Auto Club 500 (California) | 8 | 6 | 2 | $120,217 |
| Pontiac Excitement 400 (Richmond) | 3 | 3 | 2 | $121,867 |
| Coca-Cola 600 (Charlotte) | 24 | 41 | 2 | $109,457 |
| MBNA Armed Forces Family 400 (Dover) | 12 | 11 | 2 | $106,692 |
| Pocono 500 (Pocono) | 5 | 4 | 2 | $116,272 |
| Sirius 400 (Michigan) | 3 | 7 | 2 | $100,607 |
| Dodge/Save Mart 350 (Sonoma) | 11 | 11 | 3 | $100,292 |
| Pepsi 400 (Daytona) | 5 | 7 | 2 | $133,067 |
| Tropicana 400 (Chicago) | 16 | 38 | 3 | $101,092 |
| New England 300 (New Hampshire) | 3 | 6 | 3 | $104,492 |
| Pennsylvania 500 (Pocono) | 18 | 3 | 2 | $131,037 |
| Brickyard 400 (Indianapolis) | 36 | 14 | 2 | $161,967 |
| Sirius at the Glen (Watkins Glen) | 6 | 3 | 2 | $127,202 |
| GFS Marketplace 400 (Michigan) | 19 | 32 | 2 | $89,782 |
| Sharpie 500 (Bristol) | 9 | 9 | 2 | $116,107 |
| Southern 500 (Darlington) | 12 | 25 | 2 | $93,932 |
| Chevy Rock & Roll 400 (Richmond) | 13 | 17 | 2 | $105,522 |
| Sylvania 300 (New Hampshire) | 6 | 5 | 2 | $111,992 |
| MBNA America 400 (Dover) | 2 | 37 | 4 | $97,792 |
| EA SPORTS 500 (Talladega) | 38 | 2 | 3 | $146,772 |
| Banquet 400 (Kansas) | 3 | 18 | 3 | $110,267 |
| UAW-GM Quality 500 (Charlotte) | 11 | 9 | 3 | $98,217 |
| Subway 500 (Martinsville) | 3 | 4 | 3 | $115,937 |
| Bass Pro Shops MBNA 500 (Atlanta) | 3 | 6 | 2 | $121,692 |
| Checker Auto Parts 500 (Phoenix) | 11 | 1 | 2 | $203,017 |
| Pop Secret 400 (Rockingham) | 26 | 13 | 3 | $92,042 |
| Ford 400 (Homestead) | 38 | 24 | 3 | $87,117 |

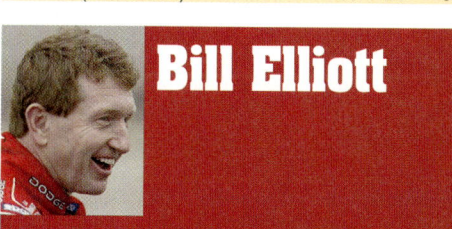

## Bill Elliott

**Date of birth:** October 8, 1955 **Hometown:** Dawsonville, Ga. **Resides:** Blairsville, Ga. **Spouse:** Cindy **Children:** Starr, Brittany, Chase **Height:** 6-1 **Weight:** 185 **Hobbies:** Skiing, snowboarding, flying

## NASCAR ACHIEVEMENTS

**First NASCAR Cup start:** February 29, 1976 (Rockingham)
**Best points finish:** 1 (1988)
**Career victories:** 44—Atlanta (85a, 85b, 87b, 92a, 92b), Bristol (88a), Charlotte (84b, 85a, 87b), Darlington (85a, 85b, 88b, 92a, 94b), Daytona (85a, 87a, 88b, 91b), Dover (85a, 88b, 88b, 91b), Homestead (01), Indianapolis (02), Michigan (84a, 85a, 85b, 86a, 86b, 87b, 89a), Phoenix (89), Pocono (85a, 85b, 88b, 89b, 02b), Richmond (92a), Riverside (83b), Rockingham (84b, 87b, 92a, 03b), Talladega (87b)

**First victory:** November 20, 1983 (Riverside)
**Career poles:** 55—Atlanta (84b, 86b, 87b, 91b, 02a), Bristol (91b), Charlotte (85a, 87a, 89b, 92a), Darlington (81a, 85a, 85b, 88a, 94a), Daytona (85a, 85b, 87a, 01a), Dover ( 87a, 90b), Homestead (01), Michigan (82a, 84a, 84b, 85a, 85b, 88a, 88b), New Hampshire (02a), North Wilkesboro (87a, 87b, 88b), Phoenix (93, 95), Pocono (84b, 85a, 85b, 95b, 02b), Richmond (89b, 92a, 97b), Rockingham (88a, 88b), Talladega (85a, 85b, 86a, 86b, 87a, 87b, 90a, 93b), Texas (02)

**First pole:** April 10, 1981 (Darlington)
**Best career finish:** 1    **Best career start:** 1

## FAST FACTS

- Began his racing career on short tracks in Georgia, working with his brothers Dan and Ernie, under the guidance of his father, George.
- Got his biggest break when Harry Melling bought the family's team in 1982.
- Shares the modern-era record with a streak of four straight victories in 1992.
- Named driver of the decade for the 1980s in an ESPN fans poll.
- Has won the National Motorsports Press Association's Most Popular Driver Award 16 times in his career. Upon his retirement from Winston Cup racing, the NMPA has voted to name the trophy for that award the Bill Elliott Trophy.

### CAR FACTS

**Car:** No. 91 Dodge
**Primary sponsor:** Dodge Dealers/UAW
**Owner:** Ray Evernham
**Team:** Evernham Motorsports
**Crew chief:** TBA
**Engine builder:** Doug Triplett

## CAREER BY CAREER BY YEAR

**2003** Considering all the speculation that he was going to retire, Elliott put together a remarkable ninth-place finish in the points race. He had one win, but he easily could have had three. He dominated at Kansas but finished second because of fuel mileage, and he was way out in front on the final lap at Homestead but cut a tire and finished eighth. His lone win had come the week before at Rockingham.

**2002** Finished 13th in series points. … Midseason surge included back-to-back poles at New Hampshire and Pocono.

... Won at Pocono from the pole and won the Brickyard 400 at Indianapolis in the next race. ... Dropped out of top 10 in points after five finishes of 30th or worse in the final six events. ... His four poles—Atlanta, Texas New Hampshire and Pocono—trailed only Ryan Newman's six for the season. ... Scored six top fives, the most since 1994, and 13 top 10s. ... Topped $4 million in season earnings for the first time.

**2001** Finished 15th in series points. ... First season teaming with owner Ray Evernham and driving Dodges. ... Won his 50th career pole for the Daytona 500 and finished fifth in the race. ... Won at Homestead for his first victory in 227 starts since 1994. ... Qualified in the top 10 17 times.

**2000** Finished 21st in series points. ... Celebrated his 25th season in NASCAR and drove his final season in self-owned No. 94 Ford. ... Won his Twin 125-mile qualifying race and finished third in the Daytona 500. ... Won the pole for The Winston at Charlotte. ... Made 600th career start at Talladega. ... Had 17 top 10 starting spots. ... Missed two races, Bristol and Darlington, after injuring himself doing yard work at his home.

**1999** Finished 21st in series points. ... Mechanical trouble and bad luck resulted in his fewest top 10 finishes (2) since 1977. ... Best finish was fifth at New Hampshire. ... Only other top 10 was at Talladega.

**1998** Finished 18th in series points. ... Began the season with seven straight top 15s, but accidents at Talladega and California stifled strong run. ... Posted five top 10s but also had seven DNFs. ... Missed season's second race at Dover to attend father's funeral. ... Scored season-best finishes of sixth at both Rockingham and Michigan. ... Inducted into the Georgia Sports Hall of Fame.

**1997** Finished eighth in series points. ... Rebounded from a disappointing season in 1996 with five top fives and 14 top 10s. ... Made 500th career start in April at Bristol. ... After having gone the previous season without a top five, posted a fourth-place finish in the season opener at Daytona. ... Best finish was second at Michigan. ... Won one pole at Richmond in September. ... Qualified in the top 10 12 times.

**1996** Finished 30th in series points. ... Missed five races after breaking his left thigh bone in an accident at Talladega. ... Best finish was eighth in the Daytona 500. ... Became sole owner of his race team after purchasing the other half of Elliott-Hardy Racing.

**1995** Finished eighth in series points. ... Partnered with Charles Hardy to begin tenure as owner/driver of the No. 94 Ford. ... Struggled early but fortunes turned with the arrival of crew chief Mike Beam. ... Won poles at Pocono and Phoenix and scored 11 top 10s in his last 19 races. ... Posted four top fives including season-best fourth-place finishes at Indianapolis and in the season finale at Atlanta.

**1994** Finished 10th in series points. ... Competed in his final season in the famed No. 11 Ford for Junior Johnson. ... Enjoyed success at both Darlington races, winning the pole and finishing third in the spring race, and posting his fifth win at the track in the fall. ... Ended the season with finishes of 33rd or worse in three of the final four events, dropping from eighth to 10th in the standings.

**1993** Finished eighth in series points. ... Battled uphill all year beginning with a blown engine in the Daytona 500. ... Had just two top 10s in the first 10 races. ... A sixth-place finish at the Coca-Cola 600 in Charlotte marked the beginning of a 20-race stretch of top 20s. ... Notched all six top fives in the second half of the season. ... Capped the year with three straight top fives. ... Best finish was a second at Richmond. ... Also notched two poles at Talladega, in July, and Phoenix.

**1992** Finished second in series standings. ... First season driving No. 11 Ford for Junior Johnson. ... Lost championship by 10 points to Alan Kulwicki, the smallest margin of victory in history. ... Won the season's final race, but led one lap fewer than Kulwicki; the bonus for leading the most laps in the race proved decisive. ... Won four straight races—Rockingham, Richmond, Atlanta and Darlington. ... Won poles at Richmond and Charlotte, both in the spring.

**1991** Finished 11th in series points. ... Broke an eight-year streak of top 10 points finishes in the previous 10 seasons driving for Melling Racing. ... His lone victory of the season, at Daytona in July, began a five-race string of top 10s. ... Won poles at Bristol and Atlanta.

**1990** Finished fourth in series points. ... After a pair of top fives to start the season, inconsistent finishes plagued the team for the next 13 races, ending with a 29th at Daytona in July. ... Completed the season with finishes of 15th or better including an impressive nine top fives. ... Won from the pole at Dover in his lone win of the season. ... Had four second-place finishes among a season total of 12 top fives. ... Won the pole at Talladega in the spring.

**1989** Finished sixth in series points, breaking a six-year streak of finishes inside the top five. ... Won poles at Richmond and Charlotte. ... Put together a midseason run that included six top 10s in seven starts and wins at Michigan and Pocono. ... Posted his third win of the year at Phoenix.

**1988** Was the Winston Cup Series champion. ... Was the first Ford driver to win the title since David Pearson in 1969. ... Won at Bristol, Daytona, Pocono, Darlington and both Dover races. ... Was a model of consistency, finishing all 29 races 19th or better. ... Scored 15 top 10s in his final 16 races, 11 of which were in the top five. ... Had six poles. ... Named American Driver of the Year. ... Named Professional Athlete of the Year in home state of Georgia.

**1987** Finished second in series points. ... Started the season by winning the pole for the Daytona 500, the Busch Clash and the Daytona 500. ... Also won at Talladega, Michigan, Charlotte, Rockingham and Atlanta—all in the second half of the season. ... Won eight poles.

**1986** Finished fourth in series points. ... Swept both races at Michigan. ... Won The Winston at Charlotte. ... Won four poles.

**1985** Finished second in series points. ... Won an astounding

11 races and 11 poles. ... Won the Winston Million in the first year it was offered, earned by winning three of the four "crown jewel" races—Daytona 500 (first), Coca-Cola 600 (18th at Charlotte), Winston 500 (first at Talladega) and Southern 500 (first at Darlington). ... Darlington victory earned him the cover of *Sports Illustrated* and the nickname "Million Dollar Bill." ... Won the Daytona 500 from the pole. ... Won twice at Michigan, Pocono, Darlington and Atlanta, in addition to his victories at Daytona, Talladega and Dover. ... Named American Driver of the Year. ... Named National Motorsports Press Association Driver of the Year. ... Named Auto Racing Digest Driver of the Year. ... Named Georgia Professional Athlete of the Year.

**1984** Finished third in series points. ... Victories came at Michigan, Charlotte and Rockingham. ... Won four poles. ... Named NASCAR's Most Popular Driver for the first time.

**1983** Finished third in series points. ... Began first year of a full Winston Cup schedule. ... Got his first victory in his 117th start at Riverside, a road course.

**1982** Finished 25th in series points. ... Began his first season driving No. 9 Ford for Harry Melling. ... Won one pole and finished second three times.

**1981** Finished 30th in series points. ... Won his first career pole at Darlington in April. ... Drove a Ford owned by the Elliott family in 13 races with seven top 10s.

**1980** Finished 34th in series points. ... In 11 starts, scored four top 10s. ... Best finish was sixth at Charlotte.

**1979** Finished 28th in series points. ... Made 14 total starts, 10 for his family-owned team and four for Roger Hamby. ... Had one second-place finish—in the Southern 500 at Darlington—and three other top 10s.

**1978** Finished 33rd in series points. ... Scored five top 10 finishes in 10 starts with his family-owned team. ... Recorded a pair of sixth-place finishes, season bests, at Talladega in May and Darlington in September.

**1977** Finished 35th in series points. ... Made 10 starts with his family-owned team. ... Posted two top 10s, at Darlington and Charlotte.

**1976** Finished 41st in series points. ... Made first career start at Rockingham, winning $640 after finishing 33rd. ... Best finish was 14th at Nashville in seven starts.

## CAREER STATISTICS

| Year | Car Owner | Champ. Races | Finish | Won | Top 5 | Top 10 | DNF | Poles | Money Won |
|---|---|---|---|---|---|---|---|---|---|
| 1976 | Elliott Rac. | 7 | 41 | 0 | 0 | 0 | 5 | 0 | $11,635 |
| 1977 | Elliott Rac. | 10 | 35 | 0 | 0 | 2 | 5 | 0 | 20,575 |
| 1978 | Elliott Rac. | 10 | 33 | 0 | 0 | 5 | 3 | 0 | 42,065 |
| 1979 | Elliott Rac. | 10 | 28 | 0 | 1 | 4 | 2 | 0 | 50,475 |
|  | Roger Hamby | 4 |  | 0 | 0 | 1 | 1 | 0 | 6,975 |
| 1980 | Elliott Rac. | 11 | 34 | 0 | 0 | 4 | 4 | 0 | 42,545 |
| 1981 | Elliott Rac. | 13 | 30 | 0 | 1 | 7 | 5 | 1 | 70,320 |
| 1982 | Harry Melling | 21 | 25 | 0 | 8 | 8 | 6 | 1 | 226,780 |
| 1983 | Harry Melling | 30 | 3 | 1 | 12 | 22 | 3 | 0 | 479,965 |
| 1984 | Harry Melling | 30 | 3 | 3 | 13 | 24 | 2 | 4 | 660,226 |
| 1985 | Harry Melling | 28 | 2 | 11 | 16 | 18 | 3 | 11 | 2,433,187 |
| 1986 | Harry Melling | 29 | 9 | 2 | 8 | 16 | 6 | 4 | 1,069,142 |
| 1987 | Harry Melling | 29 | 2 | 6 | 16 | 20 | 5 | 8 | 1,619,210 |
| 1988 | Harry Melling | 29 | 1 | 6 | 15 | 22 | 1 | 6 | 1,574,639 |
| 1989 | Harry Melling | 29 | 6 | 3 | 8 | 14 | 4 | 2 | 854,570 |
| 1990 | Harry Melling | 29 | 4 | 1 | 12 | 16 | 2 | 2 | 1,090,730 |
| 1991 | Harry Melling | 29 | 11 | 1 | 6 | 12 | 2 | 2 | 705,605 |
| 1992 | Junior Johnson | 29 | 2 | 5 | 14 | 17 | 2 | 2 | 1,692,381 |
| 1993 | Junior Johnson | 30 | 8 | 0 | 6 | 15 | 3 | 2 | 955,859 |
| 1994 | Junior Johnson | 31 | 10 | 1 | 6 | 12 | 5 | 1 | 936,779 |
| 1995 | B. Elliott | 31 | 8 | 0 | 4 | 11 | 4 | 2 | 996,816 |
| 1996 | B. Elliott | 24 | 30 | 0 | 0 | 6 | 3 | 0 | 716,506 |
| 1997 | B. Elliott | 32 | 8 | 0 | 5 | 14 | 3 | 1 | 1,607,827 |
| 1998 | B. Elliott | 32 | 18 | 0 | 0 | 5 | 7 | 0 | 1,618,421 |
| 1999 | B. Elliott | 34 | 21 | 0 | 1 | 2 | 4 | 0 | 1,624,101 |
| 2000 | B. Elliott | 32 | 21 | 0 | 3 | 7 | 8 | 0 | 2,580,823 |
| 2001 | R. Evernham | 36 | 15 | 1 | 5 | 9 | 2 | 2 | 3,618,017 |
| 2002 | R. Evernham | 36 | 13 | 2 | 6 | 13 | 4 | 4 | 4,122,699 |
| 2003 | R. Evernham | 36 | 9 | 1 | 9 | 12 | 2 | 0 | 5,008,530 |
| **TOTALS** |  | **731** |  | **44** | **175** | **309** | **106** | **55** | **$36,427,403** |

## 2003 RESULTS

| Race | Start | Finish | Standing Pos. | Winnings |
|---|---|---|---|---|
| Daytona 500 (Daytona) | 14 | 32 | 32 | $211,484 |
| Subway 400 (Rockingham) | 5 | 32 | 36 | $85,283 |
| UAW-DaimlerChrysler 400 (Las Vegas) | 30 | 14 | 31 | $113,383 |
| Bass Pro Shops MBNA 500 (Atlanta) | 2 | 39 | 36 | $85,723 |
| Carolina Dodge Dealers 400 (Darlington) | 25 | 9 | 29 | $86,743 |
| Food City 500 (Bristol) | 5 | 18 | 28 | $99,023 |
| Samsung/RadioShack 500 (Texas) | 6 | 43 | 33 | $100,781 |
| Aaron's 499 (Talladega) | 5 | 13 | 32 | $109,823 |
| Virginia 500 (Martinsville) | 31 | 13 | 29 | $88,358 |
| Auto Club 500 (California) | 2 | 4 | 21 | $148,683 |
| Pontiac Excitement 400 (Richmond) | 28 | 20 | 19 | $89,058 |
| Coca-Cola 600 (Charlotte) | 32 | 26 | 23 | $109,258 |
| MBNA Armed Forces Family 400 (Dover) | 14 | 22 | 23 | $98,668 |
| Pocono 500 (Pocono) | 8 | 19 | 22 | $84,673 |
| Sirius 400 (Michigan) | 16 | 24 | 20 | $89,223 |
| Dodge/Save Mart 350 (Sonoma) | 12 | 4 | 19 | $119,748 |
| Pepsi 400 (Daytona) | 14 | 16 | 19 | $107,183 |
| Tropicana 400 (Chicago) | 3 | 11 | 19 | $106,908 |
| New England 300 (New Hampshire) | 19 | 31 | 19 | $88,858 |
| Pennsylvania 500 (Pocono) | 11 | 17 | 18 | $85,123 |
| Brickyard 400 (Indianapolis) | 3 | 5 | 17 | $235,542 |
| Sirius at the Glen (Watkins Glen) | 25 | 20 | 17 | $86,693 |
| GFS Marketplace 400 (Michigan) | 32 | 15 | 17 | $92,598 |
| Sharpie 500 (Bristol) | 25 | 16 | 17 | $106,018 |
| Southern 500 (Darlington) | 22 | 5 | 14 | $113,028 |
| Chevy Rock & Roll 400 (Richmond) | 15 | 37 | 16 | $85,863 |
| Sylvania 300 (New Hampshire) | 12 | 4 | 15 | $144,108 |
| MBNA America 400 (Dover) | 15 | 14 | 15 | $94,673 |
| EA SPORTS 500 (Talladega) | 9 | 13 | 15 | $98,138 |
| Banquet 400 (Kansas) | 8 | 2 | 13 | $203,623 |
| UAW-GM Quality 500 (Charlotte) | 4 | 4 | 12 | $125,233 |
| Subway 500 (Martinsville) | 28 | 9 | 10 | $89,758 |
| Bass Pro Shops MBNA 500 (Atlanta) | 5 | 4 | 9 | $133,833 |
| Checker Auto Parts 500 (Phoenix) | 18 | 14 | 10 | $90,633 |
| Pop Secret 400 (Rockingham) | 5 | 1 | 9 | $207,648 |
| Ford 400 (Homestead) | 20 | 8 | 9 | $116,358 |

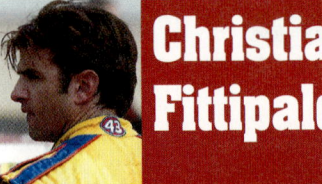

# Christian Fittipaldi

**Date of birth**: January 18, 1971 **Hometown**: Sao Paulo, Brazil
**Resides**: Key Biscayne, Fla. **Spouse**: Andrea **Children**: None.
**Height**: 5-10 **Weight**: 160 **Hobbies**: Waveboarding, jet skiing, cycling

## NASCAR ACHIEVEMENTS

**First NASCAR Cup start:** November 10, 2002 (Phoenix)
**Best points finish:** 44 (2003)
**Career victories:** 0
**Career poles:** 0
**Best career finish:** 41 **Best career start:** 17

## FAST FACTS

- Spent eight seasons in the CART series, including the last seven with Newman/Haas Racing.
- Posted two wins in his CART career (1999 Road America, 2000 California Speedway).
- Competed in Formula One from 1992-94.
- Made his stock-car debut at the 2001 Busch Series season finale at Homestead, finishing 39th.
- Started racing go-karts at age 11.
- Is the nephew of open-wheel legend Emerson Fittipaldi, who is a two-time Indianapolis 500 winner and a former champion on the CART and Formula One circuits.
- Chosen as one of the honorary Olympic torch bearers in 1996, carrying the flame—which was bound for Atlanta—in the Orlando area.
- Raises cattle with his father in his native Brazil.
- Speaks three languages—English, Portuguese and Italian.

## CAREER BY YEAR

**2003** Fittipaldi ran 15 races, 14 for Petty Enterprises. He had only three finishes in the top 30, the best being a 24th at the July race at Pocono. He did not finish a single race on the lead lap. In one four-race stretch, he had an engine problem and three crashes, completing just 33.4 percent of the laps in those four races.

**2002** Made his Winston Cup debut with Petty Enterprises at Phoenix, qualifying 17th and finishing 41st because of an accident. ... His first start was the first by a Brazilian and third by a South American in Winston Cup history.

### CAREER STATISTICS

| Year | Car Owner | Champ. Races | Finish | Won | Top 5 | Top 10 | DNF | Poles | Money Won |
|------|-----------|-------|--------|-----|-------|--------|-----|-------|-----------|
| 2002 | Petty Ent. | 1 | 81 | 0 | 0 | 0 | 1 | 0 | $39,600 |
| 2003 | Andy Petree | 1 | | 0 | 0 | 0 | 0 | 0 | 177,856 |
|      | Petty Ent. | 14 | 44 | 0 | 0 | 0 | 6 | 0 | 1,087,974 |
|      | TOTALS | 16 | | 0 | 0 | 0 | 7 | 0 | $1,295,430 |

### 2003 RESULTS

| Race | Start | Finish | Standing Pos. | Winnings |
|------|-------|--------|------|----------|
| Daytona 500 (Daytona) | 34 | 35 | 36 | $177,856 |
| Samsung/Radio Shack 500 (Texas) | 28 | 38 | 46 | $64,950 |
| Sirius 500 (Michigan) | 36 | 35 | 46 | $84,573 |
| Dodge/Save Mart 350 (Sonoma) | 41 | 40 | 46 | $90,463 |
| Tropicana 400 (Chicago) | 42 | 29 | 46 | $100,303 |
| New England 300 (New Hampshire) | 37 | 37 | 45 | $84,628 |
| Pennsylvania 500 (Pocono) | 36 | 24 | 44 | $83,893 |
| Sirus at the Glen (Watkins Glen) | 36 | 40 | 44 | $43,615 |
| GFS Marketplace 400 (Michigan) | 7 | 33 | 44 | $87,068 |
| Sharpie 500 (Bristol) | 43 | 41 | 44 | $95,953 |
| Southern 500 (Darlington) | 23 | 43 | 44 | $85,927 |
| Chevy Rock & Roll 400 (Richmond) | 41 | 43 | 44 | $82,778 |
| Sylvania 300 (New Hampshire) | 43 | 31 | 44 | $85,803 |
| EA Sports 500 (Talladega) | 26 | 28 | 44 | $52,800 |
| UAW-GM Quality 500 (Charlotte) | 31 | 34 | 43 | $45,225 |

# Larry Foyt

**Date of birth:** February 22, 1977 **Hometown:** Houston
**Resides:** Cornelius, N.C. **Spouse:** Single **Children:** None
**Height:** 5-9 **Weight:** 170 **Hobbies:** Volleyball, golf, tennis, books, movies, video games

## NASCAR ACHIEVEMENTS

**First NASCAR Cup start:** February 23, 2003 (Rockingham)
**Best points finish:** 41 (2003)
**Career victories:** 0
**Career poles:** 0
**Best career finish:** 16 **Best career start:** 12

## FAST FACTS

- Competed in the Busch Series in 2001 and 2002.
- Finished fourth in the Busch Series Raybestos Rookie of the Year standings in 2001.
- In 2000, competed in the American Speed Association; had four top 10s and one pole.
- In 1999, competed on a limited basis in the Sports Car Club of America, winning the regional event at Cabaniss in Corpus Christi, Texas, and the national event at Texas World Speedway.
- Started five U.S. Auto Club Formula 2000 Series events in 1998, finishing fourth at Phoenix International Raceway.
- Competed in seven USAC F-2000 Series events in 1997

### CAR FACTS

**Car:** No. 14 Dodge
**Primary sponsor:** TBA
**Owner:** A.J. Foyt
**Team:** A.J. Foyt Racing
**Crew chief:** Mike Hillman
**Engine builder:** Evernham Motorsports

- Won the Texas go-kart championship in 1996 in the 125 cc-shifter kart division.
- Began competing in go-karts in 1993.
- His father, A.J. Foyt, won the 1972 Daytona 500 and is four-time Indy 500 winner.
- Has attended every Indianapolis 500 since he was born.

## CAREER BY YEAR

**2003** A 16th-place run in the season's last race (Homestead) gave the team a boost going into the offseason. There wasn't much else to get excited about. The son of legendary driver A.J. Foyt, Larry never competed with any consistency on stock car's elite circuit. Other than the 16th-place finish, he never placed better than 28th. In the 20 races he ran, he completed just 79.3 percent of the laps.

### CAREER STATISTICS

| Year | Car Owner | Races | Champ. Finish | Won | Top 5 | Top 10 | DNF | Poles | Money Won |
|---|---|---|---|---|---|---|---|---|---|
| 2003 | A.J. Foyt | 20 | 41 | 0 | 0 | 0 | 8 | 0 | $1,180,990 |

### 2003 RESULTS

| Race | Start | Finish | Standing Pos. | Winnings |
|---|---|---|---|---|
| Subway 400 (Rockingham) | 41 | 36 | 44 | $45,950 |
| UAW-DaimlerChrysler 400 (Las Vegas) | 31 | 35 | 43 | $59,100 |
| Bass Pro Shops MBNA 500 (Atlanta) | 41 | 43 | 42 | $45,069 |
| Carolina Dodge Dealers 400 (Darlington) | 42 | 32 | 42 | $44,825 |
| Samsung/RadioShack 500 (Texas) | 35 | 30 | 42 | $69,185 |
| Auto Club 500 (California) | 42 | 38 | 42 | $65,300 |
| Pontiac Excitement 400 (Richmond) | 42 | 33 | 42 | $49,625 |
| Coca-Cola 600 (Charlotte) | 29 | 34 | 42 | $73,290 |
| MBNA Armed Forces Family 400 (Dover) | 43 | 28 | 42 | $58,880 |
| Pocono 500 (Pocono) | 43 | 41 | 42 | $42,090 |
| Pepsi 400 (Daytona) | 26 | 34 | 42 | $63,875 |
| Tropicana 400 (Chicago) | 31 | 41 | 42 | $59,590 |
| Pennsylvania 500 (Pocono) | 43 | 29 | 43 | $44,015 |
| Brickyard 400 (Indianapolis) | 42 | 32 | 42 | $103,780 |
| GFS Marketplace 400 (Michigan) | 14 | 39 | 41 | $48,295 |
| Sharpie 500 (Bristol) | 33 | 39 | 41 | $60,300 |
| EA SPORTS 500 (Talladega) | 35 | 43 | 42 | $51,832 |
| Checker Auto Parts 500 (Phoenix) | 32 | 28 | 42 | $49,200 |
| Pop Secret 400 (Rockingham) | 42 | 28 | 42 | $47,260 |
| Ford 400 (Homestead) | 12 | 16 | 41 | $47,800 |

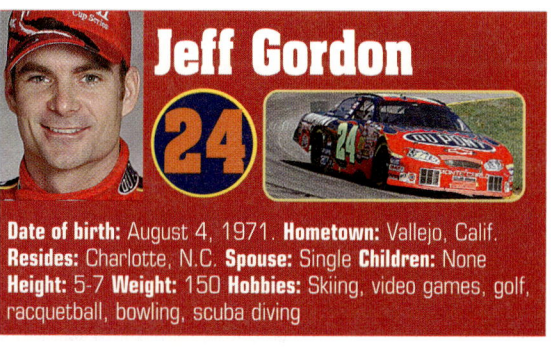

**Jeff Gordon**
**24**
**Date of birth:** August 4, 1971. **Hometown:** Vallejo, Calif. **Resides:** Charlotte, N.C. **Spouse:** Single **Children:** None **Height:** 5-7 **Weight:** 150 **Hobbies:** Skiing, video games, golf, racquetball, bowling, scuba diving

## NASCAR ACHIEVEMENTS

**First NASCAR Cup start:** November 15, 1992 (Atlanta)
**Best points finish:** 1 (1995, 1997, 1998, 2001)
**Career victories:** 64—Atlanta (95a, 98b, 99a, 03b), Bristol (95a, 96a, 97, 98a, 02b), California (97, 99), Charlotte (94a, 97a, 98a, 99b), Darlington (95b, 96a, 96b, 97b, 98b, 02b), Daytona (95b, 97a, 98b, 99a), Dover (95b, 96a, 96b, 01a), Indianapolis (94, 98, 01), Kansas (01, 02), Las Vegas (01), Martinsville (96b, 97a, 99b, 03a, 03b), Michigan (98b, 01a), North Wilkesboro (96b), New Hampshire (95, 97b, 98b), Pocono (96a, 97a, 98b), Richmond (96a, 00b), Rockingham (95a, 97a, 98a, 98b), Sonoma (98, 99, 00), Talladega (96b, 00a), Watkins Glen (97, 98, 99, 01, 03)
**First victory:** May 29, 1994 (Charlotte)
**Career poles:** 46—Atlanta (00b), Bristol (02a, 02b, 03b), California (98), Charlotte (93b, 94a, 95a, 96a, 97a, 98a, 00b), Darlington (95a, 99a, 00a), Daytona (96b, 99a), Dover (95a, 96a), Indianapolis (95, 96, 99), Martinsville (01a, 02a, 03a, 03b), Michigan (95a, 99a, 01a), New Hampshire (98b, 99a, 01a), North Wilkesboro (95a), Pocono (96a, 98a), Richmond (95a, 98a, 99a, 01b), Rockingham (95a, 01a), Sonoma (98, 99, 01), Watkins Glen (98)
**First pole:** October 6, 1993 (Charlotte)
**Best career finish:** 1   **Best career start:** 1

## FAST FACTS

- Set the Busch Series record with 11 poles in 1992; also won three races that season—all from the pole.
- Named Busch Series Rookie of the Year in 1991 following an 11th place finish in the points standings.
- Won the USAC Silver Crown Series championship in 1991.
- Was the 1990 USAC Midget champion at age 19, making him the youngest driver ever to win the title; was also the youngest driver ever awarded a USAC license at 16.
- Won three quarter-midget national championships and four karting titles.
- Won more than 600 short-track races as a youngster after beginning in the sport in his native California at age 5; the family later relocated to Pittsboro, Ind., where he honed his skills.
- Gordon is one of NASCAR's most active drivers on behalf of charitable causes. The Jeff Gordon Foundation, founded in 1999, primarily supports charities working on behalf of children in need. The Foundation supports the Leukemia & Lymphoma Society, the Make-A-Wish Foundation, the Hendrick Bone Marrow Foundation and Riley Hospital for Children in Indianapolis.

### CAR FACTS

**Car:** No. 24 Chevrolet
**Primary sponsor:** DuPont
**Owners:** Rick Hendrick, Jeff Gordon
**Team:** Hendrick Motorsports
**Crew chief:** Robbie Loomis
**Engine builder:** Rick Wetzel

- Along with Darrell Waltrip, was named 1997 NASCAR Person of the Year by *Winston Cup Illustrated*.
- Won the True Value Man of the Year Award in 1996 for his work on behalf of leukemia research.

## CAREER BY YEAR

**2003** The season would be considered a success for anybody else, but for Gordon it was a bit of an off year. He won three races—including back-to-back victories at Martinsville and Atlanta—and posted 15 top fives and 20 top 10s. A rough midseason stretch with five of six finishes outside the top 20 left him out of the championship race. He led more laps than any driver on the circuit.

**2002** Finished fourth in series points. … Was Gordon's first year as part-owner with Rick Hendrick of Jimmie Johnson's No. 48 Lowe's team. … A win at Bristol's night race broke a career-long streak of 30 races without a win. … Won at Darlington the next week, marking the 13th time in his career he's registered back-to-back victories. … The Darlington win pushed him to second in the points with 11 races to go, but four finishes of 36th or lower in the following seven races ended his shot at a fifth title. … Had his first DNF in 57 races in September at Richmond. … Final win of the year was at Kansas, the track where he last won prior to snapping his winless string. … Registered 13 top fives and 20 top 10s, the 10th straight season in which he finished in the top 10 in both categories. … Built on his lead in active driver wins (61) as well as on his lead on the all-time money list, topping the $50 million mark. … Used a provisional for the first time in 329 Winston Cup events to start the season's final race at Homestead; was 37th on the grid but finished fifth.

**2001** Won his fourth Winston Cup championship, placing him third on the all-time list behind only seven-time winners Richard Petty and Dale Earnhardt. … Won a Winston Cup single-season record $10,879,757, breaking his own mark set in 1998 and passed Earnhardt to take over the all-time money-winning lead. … Led the circuit in victories and poles with six, the sixth time in seven years he posted more wins than any other driver. … Finished second six times and totaled 18 top fives and 24 top 10s, best in the series in all three categories. … Won The Winston for the third time in his career, tying Earnhardt for the most wins in the event. … Became the first three-time winner of the Brickyard 400 and scored his seventh career road course win at Watkins Glen the next week, extending his Winston Cup record for road-course wins. … Won the inaugural event at Kansas in September.

**2000** Finished ninth in series points, his lowest finish in points since 1994. … His three wins—at Talladega, Sonoma and Richmond—were the fewest in his Winston Cup career since 1994. … Did not win back-to-back races at least once for the first time since 1995. … Despite a slow start, scored 10 top 10s in the final 11 races of the season. … Had 11 top fives and 22 top 10s.

**1999** Finished sixth in series points. … Won seven times, breaking a streak of three seasons in which he won at least 10 races. … Set the all-time Winston Cup record for road course wins, taking the checkered flag at Sonoma and Watkins Glen for the second straight year. … Won the Winston No Bull 5 $1 million bonus with his victory at the Daytona 500. … Had 18 top fives and 21 top 10s.

**1998** Won his third Winston Cup championship in four years and became the youngest three-time Cup champion at age 27. … Tied Richard Petty for the modern era season win record with 13 and tied the modern era mark with four straight wins (Pocono, Indianapolis, Watkins Glen, Michigan). … Won a then-record $9,306,584. … Became the first repeat winner at the Brickyard 400. … Scored career bests with 26 top fives, 28 top 10s and seven poles. … Won the Winston No Bull 5 $1 million bonus at Indy and Darlington.

**1997** Won his second Winston Cup championship as well as 10 races for the second straight season. … Became the first driver to win more than $6 million in a season; $1 million came from a Winston Million victory. … Became the youngest driver to win the Daytona 500, at 26. … Had one pole, 22 top fives and 23 top 10s.

**1996** Finished second in series points, 37 points behind champion and Hendrick Motorsports teammate Terry Labonte. … Mechanical problems in the season finale at Atlanta put him two laps down in the 10th lap and ended his chance to catch Labonte. … Won a series-high 10 races. … Had five poles, 21 top fives and 24 top 10s.

**1995** Won his first Winston Cup championship, becoming the youngest champion in the modern era at age 24. … Had seven wins, a career-high eight poles, 17 top fives and 23 top 10s. … Won back-to-back races for the first time in his career, July 1 at Daytona and July 9 at New Hampshire. … Had only three DNFs after having 21 in his first two seasons.

**1994** Finished eighth in series points despite 10 DNFs. … Won his first Winston Cup race after starting on the pole at the Coca-Cola 600 at Charlotte. … Won the inaugural Brickyard 400 in his adopted home state of Indiana.

**1993** Finished 14th in series points. … Named Rookie of the Year, becoming the first driver to win rookie honors in both the Winston Cup and Busch Series. … Took first career pole at the Charlotte fall race, and at 23 was the youngest driver in 30 years to win a Gatorade 125 qualifying race at Daytona. … His first career top five was at the Daytona 500, where he finished fifth

**1992** Made first Winston Cup start came at Atlanta in the final race of the season; he started 21st and finished 31st. … Gordon's first race was the last in the illustrious career of "The King," Richard Petty.

## CAREER STATISTICS

| Year | Car Owner | Races | Champ. Finish | Won | Top 5 | Top 10 | DNF | Poles | Money Won |
|---|---|---|---|---|---|---|---|---|---|
| 1992 | Rick Hendrick | 1 | 79 | 0 | 0 | 0 | 1 | 0 | $6,285 |
| 1993 | Rick Hendrick | 30 | 14 | 0 | 7 | 11 | 11 | 1 | 765,168 |
| 1994 | Rick Hendrick | 31 | 8 | 2 | 7 | 14 | 10 | 1 | 1,779,523 |
| 1995 | Rick Hendrick | 31 | 1 | 7 | 17 | 23 | 3 | 8 | 4,347,343 |
| 1996 | Rick Hendrick | 31 | 2 | 10 | 21 | 24 | 5 | 5 | 3,428,485 |
| 1997 | Rick Hendrick | 32 | 1 | 10 | 22 | 23 | 2 | 1 | 6,375,658 |
| 1998 | Rick Hendrick | 33 | 1 | 13 | 26 | 28 | 2 | 7 | 9,306,584 |
| 1999 | Rick Hendrick | 34 | 6 | 7 | 18 | 21 | 7 | 7 | 5,858,633 |
| 2000 | Rick Hendrick | 34 | 9 | 3 | 11 | 22 | 2 | 3 | 3,001,144 |
| 2001 | Rick Hendrick | 36 | 1 | 6 | 18 | 24 | 2 | 6 | 10,879,757 |
| 2002 | Rick Hendrick | 36 | 4 | 3 | 13 | 20 | 3 | 3 | 6,154,475 |
| 2003 | Rick Hendrick | 36 | 4 | 3 | 15 | 20 | 5 | 4 | 6,622,002 |
| TOTALS | | 365 | | 64 | 175 | 230 | 53 | 46 | $58,525,057 |

## 2003 RESULTS

| Race | Start | Finish | Standing Pos. | Winnings |
|---|---|---|---|---|
| Daytona 500 (Daytona) | 13 | 12 | 12 | $238,648 |
| Subway 400 (Rockingham) | 23 | 15 | 13 | $98,988 |
| UAW-DaimlerChrysler 400 (Las Vegas) | 2 | 37 | 20 | $106,053 |
| Bass Pro Shops MBNA 500 (Atlanta) | 30 | 2 | 8 | $142,778 |
| Carolina Dodge Dealers 400 (Darlington) | 5 | 33 | 15 | $90,503 |
| Food City 500 (Bristol) | 2 | 9 | 10 | $115,643 |
| Samsung/RadioShack 500 (Texas) | 7 | 3 | 6 | $249,753 |
| Aaron's 499 (Talladega) | 4 | 8 | 5 | $128,458 |
| Virginia 500 (Martinsville) | 1 | 1 | 3 | $219,143 |
| Auto Club 500 (California) | 14 | 11 | 3 | $120,628 |
| Pontiac Excitement 400 (Richmond) | 6 | 16 | 4 | $97,228 |
| Coca-Cola 600 (Charlotte) | 4 | 8 | 3 | $135,103 |
| MBNA Armed Forces Family 400 (Dover) | 9 | 2 | 3 | $176,228 |
| Pocono 500 (Pocono) | 12 | 13 | 3 | $95,568 |
| Sirius 400 (Michigan) | 6 | 3 | 3 | $126,228 |
| Dodge/Save Mart 350 (Sonoma) | 8 | 2 | 2 | $143,203 |
| Pepsi 400 (Daytona) | 3 | 14 | 3 | $117,303 |
| Tropicana 400 (Chicago) | 2 | 4 | 2 | $158,178 |
| New England 300 (New Hampshire) | 2 | 24 | 2 | $103,928 |
| Pennsylvania 500 (Pocono) | 25 | 36 | 3 | $90,168 |
| Brickyard 400 (Indianapolis) | 19 | 4 | 3 | $260,853 |
| Sirius at the Glen (Watkins Glen) | 1 | 33 | 3 | $97,353 |
| GFS Marketplace 400 (Michigan) | 21 | 30 | 3 | $96,943 |
| Sharpie 500 (Bristol) | 1 | 28 | 5 | $118,973 |
| Southern 500 (Darlington) | 14 | 32 | 5 | $98,443 |
| Chevy Rock & Roll 400 (Richmond) | 5 | 10 | 5 | $102,333 |
| Sylvania 300 (New Hampshire) | 7 | 19 | 6 | $99,978 |
| MBNA America 400 (Dover) | 6 | 5 | 6 | $123,923 |
| EA SPORTS 500 (Talladega) | 5 | 5 | 6 | $138,193 |
| Banquet 400 (Kansas) | 7 | 5 | 6 | $127,753 |
| UAW-GM Quality 500 (Charlotte) | 2 | 5 | 6 | $123,578 |
| Subway 500 (Martinsville) | 1 | 1 | 6 | $183,018 |
| Bass Pro Shops MBNA 500 (Atlanta) | 19 | 1 | 5 | $249,978 |
| Checker Auto Parts 500 (Phoenix) | 4 | 7 | 4 | $111,778 |
| Pop Secret 400 (Rockingham) | 16 | 22 | 5 | $96,203 |
| Ford 400 (Homestead) | 5 | 5 | 4 | $147,628 |

# Robby Gordon
## 31

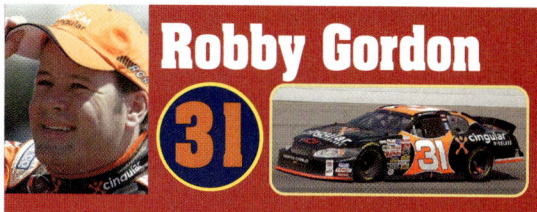

**Date of birth:** January 2, 1969 **Hometown:** Cerritos, Calif.
**Resides:** Orange, Calif. and Parker, Ariz. **Spouse:** Single
**Children:** None **Height:** 5-10 **Weight:** 180 **Hobbies:** Boating, mountain biking, water skiing

## NASCAR ACHIEVEMENTS

**First NASCAR Cup start:** February 17, 1991 (Daytona)
**Best points finish:** 16 (2003)
**Career victories:** 3—New Hampshire (01b), Sonoma (03), Watkins Glen (03)
**First victory:** November 23, 2001 (New Hampshire)
**Career poles:** 1—Atlanta (97)
**First pole:** March 7, 1997 (Atlanta)
**Best career finish:** 1   **Best career start:** 1

## FAST FACTS

- Runs in the Indy 500 each year; finished a career-best fourth there in 1999.
- Drove for his own CART series team in 1999 and for Arcieo-Wells Racing in 1998.
- Finished second in the 1996 and 1997 IROC series.
- Won the 1996 SCORE Off-Road Trophy Truck Championship with four wins.
- Won CART races at Detroit and Phoenix in 1995 and finished fifth in the point standings.
- Voted most improved driver by his peers in the 1994 PPG IndyCar World Series.
- First full IndyCar season was in 1993, driving for the legendary A.J. Foyt.
- Won GTS class in IMSA 24 Hours of Daytona in 1993, his fourth straight victory in that event, all for car owner Jack Roush.
- Won Sports Car Club of America Trans-Am race at Long Beach, Calif., in 1992, also for Roush Racing.
- In 1991, won five IMSA GTO races in a Roush Racing Ford Mustang.
- Finished second in 1990 GTO season standings.
- Overall winner of the Baja 1000 in 1987 and 1989.
- Won the Mickey Thompson Stadium Series championships in 1988 and 1989.
- Was the SCORE Off-Road champion for five straight years, beginning in 1985.

## CAR FACTS

**Car:** No. 31 Chevrolet
**Primary sponsor:** Cingular Wireless
**Owner:** Richard Childress
**Team:** Richard Childress Racing
**Crew chief:** Chris Andrews
**Engine builder:** Todd Overby

- Elected to the American Auto Racing Writers and Broadcasters Association All-American Team in 1989.
- Sometimes goes by the nickname of "Flash."
- His only pre-race ritual is eating a turkey sandwich for lunch.
- First job was working in his dad's feed yard raking chaff (strands left over from bales of hay).

## CAREER BY YEAR

**2003** A sweep of the season's road course races highlighted an up-and-down year. The two wins were a personal best for Gordon, as was his 16th-place finish in the points race. The best stretch of the season—a win sandwiched between two sixth-place finishes—was followed by his worst stretch: in the last 13 races, his best finish was 12th; the rest of his finishes were 20th or worse.

**2002** Finished 20th in series points. ... First complete NASCAR Winston Cup Series season. ... After leading 21 laps on the road course at Watkins Glen, earned his best finish of the season (third). ... Competing in both the Indianapolis 500 and Coca-Cola 600 on May 26, finishing eighth and 16th. ... Posted one top five and five top 10s.

**2001** Finished 44th in series points. ... Drove for three different teams. ... Won his first career Winston Cup race in his 10th start for Richard Childress Racing at the New Hampshire 300 on November 23. ... Began the season with Morgan-McClure Racing for five races. ... What began as a substitute situation at Sonoma with the Jimmy Smith-owned Ford, turned into a semi-permanent deal in July. ... Offered to drive the Richard Childress-owned Chevrolet in September, filling in for injured Mike Skinner. ... Qualified third and led 22 laps in the Indianapolis 500 in a car co-owned by Childress and A.J. Foyt.

**2000** Finished 43rd in series points. ... Returned to Winston Cup racing in 17 events as a driver for team he co-owned with Mike Held and John Menard. ... Had two top 10s, both at road course events, Sears Point (ninth) and Watkins Glen (fourth).

**1998** Drove one race for car owner Buz McCall, finishing 37th at Sonoma.

**1997** Finished 40th in series points. ... Competed in 20 races for car owner Felix Sabates. ... Won his only career pole at Atlanta. ... Finished fourth at Watkins Glen.

**1996** Finished 57th in series points, starting only three races. ... Drove at Charlotte for DEI. ... Drove in two races, Rockingham and Phoenix, for Felix Sabates.

**1994** Made only one start, for Kranefuss-Haas Racing at Michigan, starting 38th and finishing 38th.

**1993** Made only one start, but a highly significant one. Drove the No. 28 Texaco Havoline Ford at Talladega in that team's first race since the death of Davey Allison. ... Finished 42nd.

**1991** Finished 55th in series points. ... Started only two races. ... Made Winston Cup debut in the Daytona 500, finishing 18th. ... Also competed at Richmond, finishing 26th.

... Drove both races for car owner Junie Donlavey.

## CAREER STATISTICS

| Year | Car Owner | Champ. Races | Finish | Won | Top 5 | Top 10 | DNF | Poles | Money Won |
|---|---|---|---|---|---|---|---|---|---|
| 1991 | J. Donlavey | 2 | 55 | 0 | 0 | 0 | 0 | 0 | $27,265 |
| 1993 | R. Yates | 1 | 94 | 0 | 0 | 0 | 1 | 0 | 17,665 |
| 1994 | Kranefuss-Haas | 1 | 76 | 0 | 0 | 0 | 1 | 0 | 7,965 |
| 1996 | D. Earnhardt | 1 | 57 | 0 | 0 | 0 | 1 | 0 | 4,800 |
|  | F. Sabates | 2 |  | 0 | 0 | 0 | 2 | 0 | 29,115 |
| 1997 | F. Sabates | 20 | 40 | 0 | 1 | 1 | 7 | 1 | 622,439 |
| 1998 | Buz McCall | 1 | 67 | 0 | 0 | 0 | 1 | 0 | 24,765 |
| 2000 | R. Gordon | 17 | 43 | 0 | 1 | 2 | 7 | 0 | 620,781 |
| 2001 | Morgan-McClure | 5 | 44 | 0 | 0 | 0 | 1 | 0 | 287,545 |
|  | Jim Smith | 2 | 0 | 1 | 0 | 0 | 0 | 0 | 167,335 |
|  | R. Childress | 10 |  | 1 | 1 | 2 | 0 | 0 | 917,020 |
| 2002 | R. Childress | 36 | 20 | 0 | 1 | 5 | 4 | 0 | 3,342,703 |
| 2003 | R. Childress | 36 | 16 | 2 | 4 | 10 | 2 | 0 | 4,157,064 |
| TOTALS |  | 134 |  | 3 | 9 | 21 | 28 | 1 | $10,226,462 |

## 2003 RESULTS

| Race | Start | Finish | Standing Pos. | Winnings |
|---|---|---|---|---|
| Daytona 500 (Daytona) | 3 | 6 | 7 | $362,807 |
| Subway 400 (Rockingham) | 19 | 29 | 17 | $74,921 |
| UAW-DaimlerChrysler 400 (Las Vegas) | 21 | 23 | 14 | $94,737 |
| Bass Pro Shops MBNA 500 (Atlanta) | 18 | 17 | 17 | $77,912 |
| Carolina Dodge Dealers 400 (Darlington) | 30 | 28 | 21 | $70,942 |
| Food City 500 (Bristol) | 36 | 17 | 19 | $89,527 |
| Samsung/RadioShack 500 (Texas) | 21 | 18 | 19 | $112,387 |
| Aaron's 499 (Talladega) | 6 | 10 | 13 | $105,367 |
| Virginia 500 (Martinsville) | 38 | 21 | 14 | $75,262 |
| Auto Club 500 (California) | 26 | 27 | 16 | $95,837 |
| Pontiac Excitement 400 (Richmond) | 32 | 4 | 13 | $101,212 |
| Coca-Cola 600 (Charlotte) | 38 | 17 | 12 | $104,087 |
| MBNA Armed Forces Family 400 (Dover) | 38 | 9 | 12 | $99,747 |
| Pocono 500 (Pocono) | 37 | 28 | 15 | $72,377 |
| Sirius 400 (Michigan) | 19 | 22 | 16 | $79,427 |
| Dodge/Save Mart 350 (Sonoma) | 2 | 1 | 13 | $204,512 |
| Pepsi 400 (Daytona) | 18 | 40 | 15 | $88,247 |
| Tropicana 400 (Chicago) | 35 | 7 | 15 | $106,812 |
| New England 300 (New Hampshire) | 15 | 5 | 14 | $101,912 |
| Pennsylvania 500 (Pocono) | 37 | 18 | 12 | $74,977 |
| Brickyard 400 (Indianapolis) | 13 | 6 | 11 | $189,112 |
| Sirius at the Glen (Watkins Glen) | 14 | 1 | 10 | $156,272 |
| GFS Marketplace 400 (Michigan) | 3 | 6 | 10 | $89,402 |
| Sharpie 500 (Bristol) | 22 | 35 | 10 | $86,602 |
| Southern 500 (Darlington) | 25 | 28 | 12 | $80,072 |
| Chevy Rock & Roll 400 (Richmond) | 21 | 29 | 13 | $75,647 |
| Sylvania 300 (New Hampshire) | 17 | 21 | 12 | $80,762 |
| MBNA America 400 (Dover) | 12 | 23 | 12 | $83,327 |
| EA SPORTS 500 (Talladega) | 34 | 12 | 12 | $87,002 |
| Banquet 400 (Kansas) | 25 | 25 | 12 | $91,512 |
| UAW-GM Quality 500 (Charlotte) | 15 | 38 | 15 | $70,162 |
| Subway 500 (Martinsville) | 37 | 36 | 16 | $68,412 |
| Bass Pro Shops MBNA 500 (Atlanta) | 16 | 21 | 16 | $94,712 |
| Checker Auto Parts 500 (Phoenix) | 31 | 32 | 16 | $75,862 |
| Pop Secret 400 (Rockingham) | 17 | 20 | 16 | $79,612 |
| Ford 400 (Homestead) | 39 | 30 | 16 | $73,662 |

# Jeff Green

**Date of birth:** September 6, 1962 **Hometown:** Owensboro, Ky. **Resides:** Davidson, N.C. **Spouse:** Michelle **Children:** None **Height:** 5-8 **Weight:** 190 **Hobbies:** Hunting, radio-controlled cars

## NASCAR ACHIEVEMENTS

**First NASCAR Cup start:** September 10, 1994 (Richmond)
**Best points finish:** 17 (2002)
**Career victories:** 0
**Career poles:** 2—Bristol (01b), Daytona (03a)
**First pole:** August 24, 2001 (Bristol)
**Best career finish:** 2  **Best career start:** 1

## FAST FACTS

- Won the 2000 Busch Series championship by a record 616 points over second-place Jason Keller.
- First racing experience was in go-karts.
- Green and brother David, the 1994 Busch Series champion, were the first siblings to both win a major auto racing championship.

## CAREER BY YEAR

**2003** In one season, he drove for legendary teams Richard Childress Racing, Dale Earnhardt Inc. and Petty Enterprises. Those big names didn't help on the track, though, as he posted just two top 10s, one at Texas and one at Michigan. He won the pole at Daytona but was involved in a wreck that left him in 39th position.

**2002** Finished 17th in series points. ... First full season in Winston Cup. ... Season-best finish was a runner-up at the New Hampshire July race. ... Finished third at the Richmond fall race. ... Qualified in the top 10 only twice.

**2001** Finished 48th in series points. ... Made only eight starts, driving for Richard Childress Racing. ... Started on the pole for Bristol night race ... Finished second in the Busch Series. ... During the summer, announced three-year full-time Winston Cup deal with Childress.

**1998** Finished 40th in series points. ... Ran total of 22 races, 18 for owner Felix Sabates. ... Started the season driving for Gary Bechtel. ... Season highlight was a fifth-place qualifying run at the Brickyard 400. ... Best finish was 12th at the New Hampshire race in July.

**1997** Finished 39th in series points. ... Started 20 races. ... Left Busch Series in midseason to drive for Gary Bechtel. In his first race, the Coca-Cola 600, qualified fourth. ... Season-best finish was fourth at Atlanta, in the season finale. ... Finished third in Raybestos Rookie of Year points behind Mike Skinner and brother David Green.

### CAR FACTS

**Car:** No. 43 Dodge
**Primary sponsor:** Cheerios/Betty Crocker
**Owners:** Richard and Kyle Petty
**Team:** Petty Enterprises
**Crew chief:** Gary Putnam
**Engine builder:** Mike Ege

## CAREER STATISTICS

| Year | Car Owner | Races | Champ. Finish | Won | Top 5 | Top 10 | DNF | Poles | Money Won |
|---|---|---|---|---|---|---|---|---|---|
| 1994 | E. Sadler | 2 | 51 | 0 | 0 | 0 | 1 | 0 | $11,455 |
|  | J. Johnson | 1 |  | 0 | 0 | 0 | 0 | 0 | 8,815 |
| 1996 | D. Earnhardt | 2 | 49 | 0 | 0 | 0 | 2 | 0 | 16,835 |
|  | G. Bechtel | 2 |  | 0 | 0 | 0 | 0 | 0 | 30,040 |
| 1997 | G. Bechtel | 20 | 39 | 0 | 1 | 2 | 4 | 0 | 434,685 |
| 1998 | G. Bechtel | 3 | 40 | 0 | 0 | 0 | 0 | 0 | 107,880 |
|  | C. Rider | 1 |  | 0 | 0 | 0 | 0 | 0 | 32,350 |
|  | F. Sabates | 18 |  | 0 | 0 | 0 | 7 | 0 | 449,611 |
| 1999 | B. Moore | 0 | 60 | 0 | 0 | 0 | 0 | 0 | 31,506 |
|  | F. Sebates | 1 |  | 0 | 0 | 0 | 0 | 0 | 31,415 |
| 2001 | R. Childress | 8 | 48 | 0 | 0 | 1 | 3 | 1 | 441,449 |
| 2002 | R. Childress | 36 | 17 | 0 | 4 | 6 | 2 | 0 | 2,531,339 |
| 2003 | R. Childress | 11 | 32 | 0 | 0 | 1 | 2 | 1 | 906,135 |
|  | D. Earnhardt | 12 | 33 | 0 | 0 | 0 | 2 | 0 | 1,072,355 |
|  | Petty Ent. | 8 | 34 | 0 | 0 | 0 | 2 | 0 | 629,094 |
| **TOTALS** |  | **125** |  | **0** | **5** | **10** | **25** | **2** | **$6,112,074** |

## 2003 RESULTS

| Race | Start | Finish | Standing Pos. | Winnings |
|---|---|---|---|---|
| Daytona 500 (Daytona) | 1 | 39 | 39 | $202,720 |
| Subway 400 (Rockingham) | 39 | 31 | 40 | $56,975 |
| UAW-DaimlerChrysler 400 (Las Vegas) | 14 | 27 | 40 | $72,550 |
| Bass Pro Shops MBNA 500 (Atlanta) | 28 | 25 | 39 | $59,035 |
| Carolina Dodge Dealers 400 (Darlington) | 32 | 19 | 35 | $56,365 |
| Food City 500 (Bristol) | 21 | 20 | 33 | $73,575 |
| Samsung/RadioShack 500 (Texas) | 14 | 7 | 27 | $118,575 |
| Aaron's 499 (Talladega) | 30 | 29 | 31 | $76,285 |
| Virginia 500 (Martinsville) | 35 | 26 | 31 | $56,825 |
| Auto Club 500 (California) | 40 | 26 | 31 | $79,000 |
| Pontiac Excitement 400 (Richmond) | 41 | 40 | 32 | $54,230 |
| Coca-Cola 600 (Charlotte) | 15 | 19 | 30 | $92,900 |
| MBNA Armed Forces 400 (Dover) | 33 | 25 | 30 | $84,942 |
| Pocono 500 (Pocono) | 35 | 33 | 31 | $68,552 |
| Sirius 400 (Michigan) | 13 | 28 | 31 | $77,812 |
| Pepsi 400 (Daytona) | 34 | 29 | 32 | $92,969 |
| Tropicana 400 (Chicago) | 15 | 16 | 32 | $89,937 |
| New England 300 (New Hampshire) | 30 | 30 | 32 | $75,912 |
| Pennsylvania 500 (Pocono) | 39 | 31 | 33 | $71,402 |
| Brickyard 400 (Indianapolis) | 30 | 20 | 33 | $141,212 |
| GFS Marketplace 400 (Michigan) | 34 | 21 | 33 | $76,027 |
| Sharpie 500 (Bristol) | 39 | 40 | 33 | $85,412 |
| Southern 500 (Darlington) | )35 | 18 | 33 | $79,577 |
| EA Sports 500 (Talladega) | 13 | 18 | 33 | $95,498 |
| Banquet 400 (Kansas) | 9 | 27 | 33 | $101,203 |
| UAW-GM Quality 500 (Charlotte) | 36 | 27 | 33 | $84,963 |

| Race | Start | Finish | Standing Pos. | Winnings |
|---|---|---|---|---|
| Subway 500 (Martinsville) | 10 | 24 | 33 | $85,353 |
| Checker Auto Parts 500 (Phoenix) | 42 | 37 | 33 | $82,803 |
| Pop Secret 400 (Rockingham) | 41 | 19 | 34 | $88,703 |
| Ford 400 (Homestead) | 26 | 40 | 34 | $78,703 |

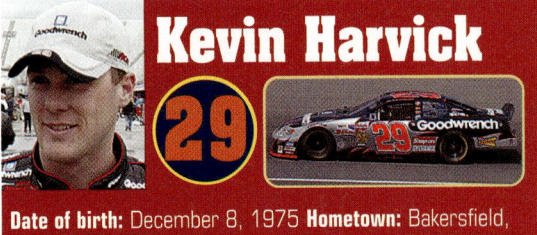

**Kevin Harvick — 29**

**Date of birth:** December 8, 1975 **Hometown:** Bakersfield, Calif. **Resides:** Winston-Salem, N.C. **Spouse:** DeLana **Children:** None **Height:** 5-10 **Weight:** 175 **Hobbies:** Radio-controlled race cars

## NASCAR ACHIEVEMENTS

**First NASCAR Cup start:** February 25, 2001 (Rockingham)
**Best points finish:** 5 (2003)
**Career victories:** 4—Atlanta (01a), Chicagoland (01, 02), Indianapolis (03)
**First victory:** March 11, 2001 (Atlanta)
**Career poles:** 2—Daytona (02b), Indianapolis (03)
**First pole:** July 6, 2002 (Daytona)
**Best career finish:** 1  **Best career start:** 1

## FAST FACTS

- Won the 2002 IROC championship.
- Won Busch Series Raybestos Rookie of the Year honors in 2000, winning three races and two poles on his way to a third-place finish in points.
- Had 11 top 10 finishes in Craftsman Truck Series in 1999.
- Won the 1998 NASCAR Winston West Series championship.
- Was Rookie of the Year in the Featherlite Southwest Series in 1995, winning at Tucson and finishing 11th in points.
- Won the 1993 late model championship at Mesa Marin Raceway in his hometown of Bakersfield, Calif.
- Began racing go-karts at age 5, winning seven national titles and two Grand National championships.
- Has a dog named Backup, which he got just before the start of the 2001 season after another pet died.
- Kevin and his wife, DeLana, were married in Las Vegas in February 2001, two days after he made his NASCAR Winston Cup debut at Rockingham.
- Won the 2002 IROC championship.

### CAR FACTS

**Car:** No. 29 Chevrolet
**Primary sponsor:** GM Goodwrench Service
**Owner:** Richard Childress
**Team:** Richard Childress Racing
**Crew chief:** Todd Berrier
**Engine builder:** Gary Wagoner

## CAREER BY YEAR

**2003** Harvick finished a career high fifth in points. Inconsistency and a sluggish start were his biggest foes. He finished 25th or worse in five of the first 14 races, but he got hot early in the second half of the season. Starting with a win from the pole August 3 at the Brickyard 400, Harvick had five straight top fives.

**2002** Finished 21st in series points. … Won at Chicagoland Speedway, his second consecutive win at the track. …. Finished the season with five top fives and eight top 10s. … Started on the pole at Daytona in the Pepsi 400. … Placed on probation in April for an incident in the Craftsman Truck Series. … In the 75th start in the Craftsman Truck Series, won his first race at Phoenix. … Is one of only five drivers who have won in all three of NASCAR's national series.

**2001** Finished ninth in series points. … Was the Winston Cup Raybestos Rookie of the Year and Busch Series champion. … Competed in 35 races, taking over as driver of the Chevrolets owned by Richard Childress after the death of seven-time champion Dale Earnhardt in the Daytona 500. … Won in his third career Winston Cup start, edging Jeff Gordon at Atlanta Motor Speedway. … Won the inaugural race at Chicagoland Speedway as well. …Counting one start in the Craftsman Truck Series, he ran 70 races in NASCAR's top three series at 30 different tracks, logging over 20,000 racing miles.

### CAREER STATISTICS

| Year | Car Owner | Champ. Races | Finish | Won | Top 5 | Top 10 | DNF | Poles | Money Won |
|---|---|---|---|---|---|---|---|---|---|
| 2001 | R. Childress | 35 | 9 | 2 | 6 | 16 | 1 | 0 | $4,302,202 |
| 2002 | R. Childress | 35 | 21 | 1 | 5 | 8 | 6 | 1 | 3,849,216 |
| 2003 | R. Childress | 36 | 5 | 1 | 11 | 18 | 0 | 1 | 6,237,119 |
| TOTALS | | 106 | | 4 | 22 | 42 | 7 | 2 | $14,388,537 |

### 2003 RESULTS

| Race | Start | Finish | Standing Pos. | Winnings |
|---|---|---|---|---|
| Daytona 500 (Daytona) | 31 | 4 | 4 | $569,630 |
| Subway 400 (Rockingham) | 26 | 25 | 10 | $87,138 |
| UAW-DaimlerChrysler 400 (Las Vegas) | 22 | 13 | 7 | $116,553 |
| Bass Pro Shops MBNA 500 (Atlanta) | 17 | 19 | 7 | $87,968 |
| Carolina Dodge Dealers 400 (Darlington) | 33 | 36 | 18 | $77,843 |
| Food City 500 (Bristol) | 27 | 7 | 11 | $104,448 |
| Samsung/RadioShack 500 (Texas) | 8 | 15 | 10 | $128,128 |
| Aaron's 499 (Talladega) | 2 | 2 | 8 | $179,233 |
| Virginia 500 (Martinsville) | 29 | 16 | 6 | $87,678 |
| Auto Club 500 (California) | 37 | 29 | 9 | $105,828 |
| Pontiac Excitement 400 (Richmond) | 36 | 6 | 8 | $100,928 |
| Coca-Cola 600 (Charlotte) | 20 | 13 | 8 | $119,003 |
| MBNA Armed Forces Family 400 (Dover) | 23 | 27 | 9 | $97,833 |
| Pocono 500 (Pocono) | 20 | 25 | 9 | $84,018 |
| Sirius 400 (Michigan) | 10 | 18 | 11 | $91,468 |
| Dodge/Save Mart 350 (Sonoma) | 6 | 3 | 9 | $119,128 |
| Pepsi 400 (Daytona) | 2 | 9 | 8 | $113,553 |
| Tropicana 400 (Chicago) | 11 | 17 | 7 | $104,028 |
| New England 300 (New Hampshire) | 7 | 2 | 7 | $165,033 |
| Pennsylvania 500 (Pocono) | 31 | 12 | 7 | $88,428 |

| Race | Start | Standing Finish | Pos. | Winnings |
|---|---|---|---|---|
| Brickyard 400 (Indianapolis) | 1 | 1 | 7 | $418,253 |
| Sirius at the Glen (Watkins Glen) | 11 | 5 | 5 | $96,408 |
| GFS Marketplace 400 (Michigan) | 11 | 2 | 4 | $147,758 |
| Sharpie 500 (Bristol) | 23 | 2 | 3 | $174,223 |
| Southern 500 (Darlington) | 18 | 2 | 3 | $149,063 |
| Chevy Rock & Roll 400 (Richmond) | 28 | 16 | 3 | $89,383 |
| Sylvania 300 (New Hampshire) | 13 | 13 | 3 | $96,528 |
| MBNA America 400 (Dover) | 3 | 4 | 2 | $119,533 |
| EA SPORTS 500 (Talladega) | 30 | 7 | 2 | $101,953 |
| Banquet 400 (Kansas) | 24 | 6 | 2 | $115,053 |
| UAW-GM Quality 500 (Charlotte) | 9 | 10 | 2 | $97,853 |
| Subway 500 (Martinsville) | 5 | 7 | 2 | $92,228 |
| Bass Pro Shops MBNA 500 (Atlanta) | 10 | 20 | 3 | $110,753 |
| Checker Auto Parts 500 (Phoenix) | 13 | 34 | 6 | $86,603 |
| Pop Secret 400 (Rockingham) | 34 | 15 | 6 | $91,403 |
| Ford 400 (Homestead) | 6 | 2 | 5 | $240,583 |

# Dale Jarrett

**Date of birth:** November 26, 1956 **Hometown:** Hickory, N.C. **Resides:** Hickory, N.C. **Spouse:** Kelley **Children:** Jason, Natalee, Karsyn, Zachary **Height:** 6-2 **Weight:** 215 **Hobbies:** Golf, outdoor sports

## NASCAR ACHIEVEMENTS

**First NASCAR Cup start:** April 29, 1984 (Martinsville)
**Best points finish:** 1 (1999)
**Career victories:** 31—Atlanta (97a), Bristol (97b), Charlotte (94b, 96a, 97b), Darlington (97a, 98a, 01a), Daytona (93a, 96a, 99b, 00a), Dover (98a), Indianapolis (96, 99), Martinsville (01a), Michigan (91b, 96b, 99a, 02b), New Hampshire (01a), Phoenix (97), Pocono (95b, 97b, 02a) Richmond (97b, 99a), Rockingham (00b, 03a), Talladega (98b), Texas (01)
**First victory:** August 18, 1991 (Michigan)
**Career poles:** 15—Atlanta (00a, 01a), Darlington (96b, 97a, 98b), Daytona (95a, 00a, 00b), Dover (01b), Las Vegas (98, 01), Michigan (02a), Rockingham (96b) Texas (97), Watkins Glen (01)
**First pole:** February 11, 1995 (Daytona)
**Best career finish:** 1 **Best career start:** 1

## FAST FACTS

- Began racing in 1977 in the Limited Sportsman division at Hickory Motor Speedway, where his father, two-time NASCAR champion Ned Jarrett, once was a track promoter.
- Is considered one of the charter drivers in the Busch Series, competing as a regular in 1982, the first year of competition for the division.
- Won 11 races and 14 poles in the Busch Series.
- Competed in IROC seven times (1994, '97, '98, '99, '00, '01 and '02).
- Has two IROC wins, Daytona ('01) and Indianapolis ('02).
- Was all-conference in football, basketball and golf at Newton-Conover (N.C.) High School. Also played baseball and was offered a full golf scholarship to the University of South Carolina.
- Winston Cup team owner Andy Petree helped build and was part-owner of Jarrett's first race car.
- An excellent golfer, Jarrett has played some of America's most famous courses. If not for racing, he would have attempted a professional golf career.
- Won the True Value Man of the Year Award in NASCAR in 2000 for his charity work on behalf of the Susan G. Komen Breast Cancer Foundation. Also was nominated for the award in 1996 for his fundraising efforts for Brenner Children's Hospital and for Carly Brayton, son of driver Scott Brayton, who was fatally injured in an accident during Indianapolis 500 practice that year.

## CAR FACTS

**Car:** No. 88 Ford
**Primary sponsor:** UPS
**Owner:** Robert Yates
**Team:** Robert Yates Racing
**Crew chief:** Mike Ford
**Engine builder:** Nick Ramey

## CAREER BY YEAR

**2003** A win in the second race of the season, at Rockingham, was the lone highlight for Jarrett. After that, the year was a disaster of ill-handling cars, bad luck and constant personnel moves. The 25th-place finish in the points race was Jarrett's worst as a full-time driver. He struggled even at tracks where he has had success—he finished 32nd and 23rd at Michigan, where he has four career wins.
**2002** Finished ninth in series points. ... Won at Pocono in June and Michigan in August. ... Ended a six-year streak of finishes inside the top five in the points standings. ... Had nine top 15s in the final 10 races. ... Had 10 top fives and 18 top 10s and won the pole at Michigan in June. ... Led 15 races and led the most laps at Texas and Michigan in June. ... Todd Parrott was renamed crew chief following Jimmy Elledge's departure in early April.
**2001** Finished fifth in series points. ... Won three times in a four-race stretch early in the season, with a victory at Darlington and then back-to-back wins at Martinsville and Talladega. ... July victory at New Hampshire drew him even with Jeff Gordon in the standings, but Jarrett's bid for a second championship unraveled with four finishes of 30th or worse in the next six races. ... Won poles at Las Vegas, Atlanta, Watkins Glen and Dover. ... Had 12 top fives and 19 top 10s. ... Topped the $5 million mark in earnings for the third straight year. ... Won the first race in the IROC series.
**2000** Finished fourth in series points. ... Won the Daytona 500 for the third time, from the pole, winning a Winston No Bull 5 race for the second time. ... Won the Bud Shootout

Qualifier and Bud Shootout. … Became the fourth driver to win three or more Daytona 500s. … Had two wins and three poles and finished in a three-way tie for the most top 10 finishes with 24.

**1999** Won the Winston Cup Series championship. … With father Ned, became only the second father-son combination to win championship, after Lee and Richard Petty. … Won four races, including his second Brickyard 400. … Was named Driver of the Year by TNN, National Motorsports Press Association, American Auto Racing Writers and Broadcasters Association. … Led the circuit with 24 top fives and 29 top 10s.

**1998** Finished third in series points. … Scored three wins, 19 top fives and 22 top 10s. … Collected a $1 million No Bull 5 bonus for winning the Winston 500 at Talladega.

**1997** Finished second in series points. … Won a career-high seven races. … Had 17 top fives and 20 top 10s on his way to being named Driver of the Year by the National Motorsports Press Association.

**1996** Finished third in series points. … Was in his second season with Robert Yates Racing but his first full season with the No. 88 team and crew chief Todd Parrott. … Captured his second Daytona 500 victory and first Brickyard 400 win. … Won four races and had 21 top 10s.

**1995** Finished 13th in series points. … Joined Yates' No. 28 Ford team at the start of 1995, taking over a vacant seat after Ernie Irvan's career-threatening injury at Michigan the previous season. … Jump-started the season by winning the pole for the Daytona 500; it was his first career pole. … Won at Pocono in his 130th career start. … Capped the season with nine top fives and 14 top 10s.

**1994** Finished 16th in series points. … Was in his third and final season competing for Joe Gibbs Racing. … After failing to qualify at North Wilkesboro, won at Charlotte the following week. … Had four top fives and nine top 10s.

**1993** Finished fourth in series points. … Won the Daytona 500 while driving Gibbs' No. 18 Pontiac. … Scored 10 of his 13 top fives in the first 18 races. … Won over $1 million for the first time.

**1992** Finished 19th in series points. … Became the first driver for Gibbs' new team. … Best finish was a second at Bristol. … Finished third at Daytona in July. … Had two top fives and eight top 10s.

**1991** Finished 17th in series points. … Got first career victory at Michigan, snapping a 134-race winless streak by the Wood Brothers. … Had eight top 10s.

**1990** Finished 25th in series points. … Replaced Neil Bonnett in the Wood Brothers' famed No. 21 six races into the season. … Scored six of his seven top 10s in the second half of the season. … Best finish was fourth at the season finale at Atlanta.

**1989** Finished 24th in series points. … Notched a career-first top five finish at Martinsville in September. … Was his first full-time season for a single team.

**1988** Finished 23rd in series points. … Made 29 starts driving with four different car owners. … Best finish was eighth at Riverside, a road course.

**1987** Finished 26th in series points. … Finished second to Davey Allison for Rookie of the Year honors. … Posted a best finish of 10th twice. … Competed full-time in the Busch Series, finishing sixth in the standings with one win.

**1986** Finished 107th in series points. … Competed in just one race for car owner Mike Curb. … Finished fourth in Busch Series standings with five poles and one win.

**1985** Finished 72nd in series points. … Made three starts for two different owners. … Finished 14th in his first career start at Martinsville. … Competed full-time in the Busch Series, finishing fourth in points.

## CAREER STATISTICS

| Year | Car Owner | Races | Champ. Finish | Won | Top 5 | Top 10 | DNF | Poles | Money Won |
|---|---|---|---|---|---|---|---|---|---|
| 1984 | E. Zervakis | 2 | | 0 | 0 | 0 | 1 | 0 | $2,350 |
| | Means | 1 | 72 | 0 | 0 | 0 | 0 | 0 | 4,995 |
| 1986 | Mike Curb | 1 | 108 | 0 | 0 | 0 | 1 | 0 | 990 |
| 1987 | Freedlander | 24 | | 0 | 0 | 2 | 11 | 0 | 143,405 |
| 1988 | C. Yarborough | 19 | | 0 | 0 | 1 | 8 | 0 | 60,610 |
| | H. Ellington | 8 | | 0 | 0 | 0 | 4 | 0 | 51,655 |
| | Ralph Ball | 1 | | 0 | 0 | 0 | 1 | 0 | 2,175 |
| | B. Arrington | 1 | 23 | 0 | 0 | 0 | 1 | 0 | 4,200 |
| 1989 | C. Yarborough | 29 | 24 | 0 | 2 | 5 | 11 | 0 | 232,317 |
| 1990 | Wood Brothers | 24 | 25 | 0 | 1 | 7 | 9 | 0 | 214,495 |
| 1991 | Wood Brothers | 29 | 17 | 1 | 3 | 8 | 9 | 0 | 444,256 |
| 1992 | Joe Gibbs | 29 | 19 | 0 | 2 | 8 | 5 | 0 | 418,648 |
| 1993 | Joe Gibbs | 30 | 4 | 1 | 13 | 18 | 5 | 0 | 1,242,394 |
| 1994 | Joe Gibbs | 30 | 16 | 1 | 4 | 9 | 7 | 0 | 881,754 |
| 1995 | Robert Yates | 31 | 13 | 1 | 9 | 14 | 6 | 1 | 1,363,158 |
| 1996 | Robert Yates | 31 | 3 | 4 | 17 | 21 | 3 | 2 | 2,985,418 |
| 1997 | Robert Yates | 32 | 2 | 7 | 20 | 23 | 1 | 2 | 3,240,542 |
| 1998 | Robert Yates | 33 | 3 | 3 | 19 | 22 | 3 | 2 | 4,019,657 |
| 1999 | Robert Yates | 34 | 1 | 4 | 24 | 29 | 1 | 0 | 6,649,596 |
| 2000 | Robert Yates | 34 | 4 | 2 | 15 | 24 | 2 | 3 | 5,934,475 |
| 2001 | Robert Yates | 36 | 5 | 4 | 12 | 19 | 4 | 4 | 5,377,742 |
| 2002 | Robert Yates | 36 | 9 | 2 | 10 | 18 | 5 | 1 | 4,421,951 |
| 2003 | Robert Yates | 36 | 26 | 1 | 1 | 7 | 9 | 0 | 4,121,487 |
| **TOTALS** | | 531 | | 31 | 152 | 235 | 107 | 15 | $41,818,270 |

## 2003 RESULTS

| Race | Start | Finish | Standing Pos. | Winnings |
|---|---|---|---|---|
| Daytona 500 (Daytona) | 11 | 10 | 10 | $256,098 |
| Subway 400 (Rockingham) | 9 | 1 | 2 | $177,828 |
| UAW-DaimlerChrysler 400 (Las Vegas) | 27 | 41 | 10 | $103,633 |
| Bass Pro Shops MBNA 500 (Atlanta) | 16 | 21 | 12 | $93,968 |
| Carolina Dodge Dealers 400 (Darlington) | 36 | 18 | 13 | $90,673 |
| Food City 500 (Bristol) | 38 | 36 | 20 | $102,923 |
| Samsung/RadioShack 500 (Texas) | 23 | 13 | 15 | $136,528 |
| Aaron's 499 (Talladega) | 18 | 12 | 12 | $116,473 |
| Virginia 500 (Martinsville) | 37 | 20 | 13 | $94,303 |
| Auto Club 500 (California) | 38 | 37 | 17 | $111,253 |
| Pontiac Excitement 400 (Richmond) | 40 | 36 | 23 | $92,253 |
| Coca-Cola 600 (Charlotte) | 23 | 9 | 18 | $129,152 |
| MBNA Armed Forces Family 400 (Dover) | 29 | 39 | 24 | $103,028 |
| Pocono 500 (Pocono) | 7 | 42 | 27 | $87,778 |
| Sirius 400 (Michigan) | 25 | 32 | 26 | $94,893 |
| Dodge/Save Mart 350 (Sonoma) | 29 | 42 | 29 | $100,403 |
| Pepsi 400 (Daytona) | 16 | 10 | 28 | $120,203 |

| Race | Start | Finish | Standing Pos. | Winnings |
|---|---|---|---|---|
| Tropicana 400 (Chicago) | 33 | 30 | 29 | $108,063 |
| New England 300 (New Hampshire) | 29 | 7 | 28 | $107,228 |
| Pennsylvania 500 (Pocono) | 8 | 21 | 27 | $91,168 |
| Brickyard 400 (Indianapolis) | 34 | 39 | 28 | $148,333 |
| Sirius at the Glen (Watkins Glen) | 30 | 7 | 27 | $98,688 |
| GFS Marketplace 400 (Michigan) | 29 | 23 | 27 | $97,093 |
| Sharpie 500 (Bristol) | 27 | 7 | 25 | $122,418 |
| Southern 500 (Darlington) | 19 | 34 | 25 | $96,543 |
| Chevy Rock & Roll 400 (Richmond) | 37 | 21 | 27 | $94,333 |
| Sylvania 300 (New Hampshire) | 27 | 41 | 27 | $94,228 |
| MBNA America 400 (Dover) | 27 | 18 | 27 | $100,703 |
| EA SPORTS 500 (Talladega) | 6 | 19 | 27 | $101,228 |
| Banquet 400 (Kansas) | 13 | 33 | 27 | $107,853 |
| UAW-GM Quality 500 (Charlotte) | 16 | 22 | 27 | $93,053 |
| Subway 500 (Martinsville) | 39 | 11 | 26 | $94,003 |
| Bass Pro Shops MBNA 500 (Atlanta) | 31 | 12 | 26 | $115,403 |
| Checker Auto Parts 500 (Phoenix) | 39 | 29 | 25 | $93,853 |
| Pop Secret 400 (Rockingham) | 32 | 38 | 26 | $91,923 |
| Ford 400 (Homestead) | 32 | 26 | 26 | $91,578 |

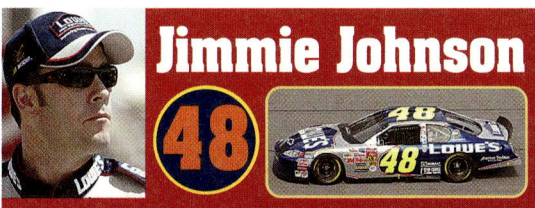

# Jimmie Johnson

**Date of birth:** September 17, 1975 **Hometown:** El Cajon, Calif. **Resides:** Mooresville, N.C. **Spouse:** Single **Children:** None **Height:** 5-11 **Weight:** 175 **Hobbies:** Water sports

## NASCAR ACHIEVEMENTS

**First NASCAR Cup start:** October 7, 2001 (Charlotte)
**Best points finish:** 2 (2003)
**Career victories:** 5—California (02), Charlotte (03a), Dover (02a, 02b), New Hampshire (03a, 03b)
**First victory:** April 28, 2002 (California)
**Career poles:** 7—Charlotte (02a), Daytona (02a), Kansas (03), Pocono (03a), Richmond (02b), Talladega (02a, 02b)
**First pole:** February 17, 2002 (Daytona)
**Best career finish:** 1 **Best career start:** 1

## FAST FACTS

- Finished eighth in Busch Series points in 2001, driving for Herzog Motorsports.
- Got his first career Busch Series victory in the series' inaugural race at Chicagoland Speedway.
- Won $1,556,668 in 72 Busch Series events from 1998-2001.
- Won Rookie of the Year honors in the ASA ACDelco Challenge Series in 1998.
- Prior to racing stock cars, he won six off-road racing titles—the 1992, '93, and '94 Mickey Thompson Stadium Truck Series championships, the '94 SCORE Desert championship and the '96 and '97 SODA Winter Series championship.
- Competed in the 1995 SCORE Trophy Truck Series and the 1991 MTEG Series.
- Began racing in motocross events at age 4.
- Johnson and Jeff Gordon joined World Superbike champion Colin Edwards in Europe and won the 2002 Race of Champions Nations Cup, an annual event pitting the world's best rally, motorcycle and circuit racers against one another.
- During the 2000 season, Johnson was selected as one of *People*'s "Sexiest Men in the Fast Lane," along with other Winston Cup and Busch Series drivers.
- Johnson was the youngest driver ever in the Mickey Thompson Stadium Truck Series.

## CAR FACTS

**Car:** No. 48 Chevrolet
**Primary sponsor:** Lowe's
**Owners:** Jeff Gordon, Rick Hendrick
**Team:** Hendrick Motorsports
**Crew chief:** Chad Knaus
**Engine builder:** Tom Karas

## CAREER BY YEAR

**2003** Johnson has been in the top 10 in points for all but the first three weeks of his two-year career in NASCAR's elite stock car series. A late-season charge—he finished in the top three in the final six races—helped him end up second in points. His finishes revealed no weaknesses—he had at least one top 10 at a superspeedway, intermediate track, short track and road course.

**2002** Finished fifth in series points, in one of the best rookie performances since Tony Stewart's three-win season in 1999. … Won the Daytona 500 pole in just his fourth career start. … His first career victory (at California) came in his 13th Winston Cup start. … Overall, had three wins (California and both Dover races). … Became the first rookie in Winston Cup history to sweep both races at a single venue. … Led the championship point standings for one week after the Kansas Kansas race in September.

**2001** Finished 52nd in series points in Winston Cup debut. … Best finish was 25th at Homestead.

### CAREER STATISTICS

| Year | Car Owner | Races | Champ. Finish | Won | Top 5 | Top 10 | DNF | Poles | Money Won |
|---|---|---|---|---|---|---|---|---|---|
| 2001 | Rick Hendrick | 3 | 52 | 0 | 0 | 0 | 1 | 0 | $122,320 |
| 2002 | Jeff Gordon | 36 | 5 | 3 | 6 | 21 | 3 | 5 | 3,788,268 |
| 2003 | Jeff Gordon | 36 | 2 | 3 | 14 | 20 | 3 | 2 | 7,745,530 |
| TOTALS | | 75 | | 6 | 20 | 41 | 7 | 7 | $11,656,118 |

### 2003 RESULTS

| Race | Start | Finish | Standing Pos. | Winnings |
|---|---|---|---|---|
| Daytona 500 (Daytona) | 10 | 3 | 3 | $707,526 |
| Subway 400 (Rockingham) | 37 | 8 | 3 | $77,110 |
| UAW-DaimlerChrysler 400 (Las Vegas) | 10 | 11 | 3 | $97,675 |
| Bass Pro Shops MBNA 500 (Atlanta) | 11 | 32 | 4 | $65,835 |
| Carolina Dodge Dealers 400 (Darlington) | 14 | 27 | 8 | $62,310 |

| Race | Standing Start | Finish | Pos. | Winnings |
|---|---|---|---|---|
| Food City 500 (Bristol) | 23 | 8 | 6 | $82,570 |
| Samsung/RadioShack 500 (Texas) | 4 | 8 | 5 | $119,575 |
| Aaron's 499 (Talladega) | 7 | 15 | 4 | $89,930 |
| Virginia 500 (Martinsville) | 7 | 9 | 4 | $70,250 |
| Auto Club 500 (California) | 20 | 16 | 5 | $89,025 |
| Pontiac Excitement 400 (Richmond) | 10 | 19 | 6 | $68,275 |
| Coca-Cola 600 (Charlotte) | 37 | 1 | 5 | $271,900 |
| MBNA Armed Forces Family 400 (Dover) | 5 | 38 | 7 | $76,760 |
| Pocono 500 (Pocono) | 1 | 12 | 7 | $80,375 |
| Sirius 400 (Michigan) | 11 | 16 | 7 | $71,890 |
| Dodge/Save Mart 350 (Sonoma) | 37 | 17 | 7 | $75,630 |
| Pepsi 400 (Daytona) | 11 | 18 | 6 | $87,075 |
| Tropicana 400 (Chicago) | 6 | 3 | 6 | $134,575 |
| New England 300 (New Hampshire) | 6 | 1 | 5 | $200,225 |
| Pennsylvania 500 (Pocono) | 2 | 15 | 4 | $67,840 |
| Brickyard 400 (Indianapolis) | 9 | 18 | 4 | $135,225 |
| Sirius at the Glen (Watkins Glen) | 20 | 4 | 4 | $86,850 |
| GFS Marketplace 400 (Michigan) | 15 | 27 | 6 | $73,875 |
| Sharpie 500 (Bristol) | 16 | 5 | 4 | $100,775 |
| Southern 500 (Darlington) | 2 | 3 | 4 | $112,575 |
| Chevy Rock & Roll 400 (Richmond) | 26 | 11 | 4 | $70,605 |
| Sylvania 300 (New Hampshire) | 8 | 1 | 4 | $200,225 |
| MBNA America 400 (Dover) | 4 | 8 | 3 | $79,940 |
| EA SPORTS 500 (Talladega) | 3 | 34 | 4 | $71,930 |
| Banquet 400 (Kansas) | 1 | 7 | 5 | $96,525 |
| UAW-GM Quality 500 (Charlotte) | 3 | 3 | 5 | $144,550 |
| Subway 500 (Martinsville) | 26 | 2 | 5 | $100,250 |
| Bass Pro Shops MBNA 500 (Atlanta) | 9 | 3 | 4 | $122,800 |
| Checker Auto Parts 500 (Phoenix) | 3 | 2 | 3 | $173,625 |
| Pop Secret 400 (Rockingham) | 18 | 2 | 2 | $105,590 |
| Ford 400 (Homestead) | 10 | 3 | 2 | $183,855 |

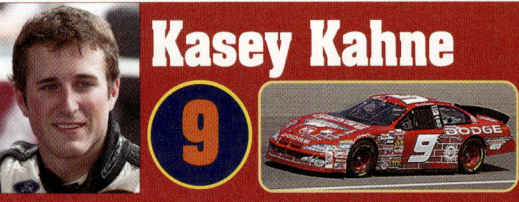

## Kasey Kahne

**Date of birth**: April 10, 1980 **Hometown:** Enumclaw, Wash.
**Resides:** Huntersville, N.C. **Spouse:** Single **Children:** None

### NASCAR ACHIEVEMENTS

**First NASCAR Cup start:** n/a
**Best points finish:** n/a
**Career victories:** 0
**Career poles:** 0
**Best career finish:** n/a
**Best career start:** n/a

### FAST FACTS

- Began racing Micro Midgets at age 14 in 1994.
- Won the Mini-Sprint Class Hannigan (Wash.)

### CAR FACTS

**Car:** No. 9 Dodge
**Primary sponsor:** Dodge Dealers/UAW
**Owner:** Ray Evernham
**Team:** Evernham Motorsports
**Crew chief:** Tommy Baldwin
**Engine builder:** Danny Triplett

Speedway championship and Northwest Mini-Sprint Car championship in 1996.
- Second in the Northern Sprint Tour championship in 1997.
- Won 2000 USAC Midget championship and was named the 2000 USAC Rookie of the Year and Midget Driver of the Year.
- Ran on the USAC Midget, USAC Silver Crown, Northern Sprint Tour and Toyota Atlantic Series circuits in 2001.
- Finished seventh in the Busch Series in 2003 and 33rd as a rookie in 2002.

## Matt Kenseth

**Date of birth:** March 10, 1972 **Hometown:** Cambridge, Wis.
**Resides:** Terrell, N.C. **Spouse:** Katie **Children:** Ross
**Height:** 5-9 **Weight:** 150 **Hobbies:** Motorcycling, boating, golf, computer games

### NASCAR ACHIEVEMENTS

**First NASCAR Cup start:** September 20, 1998 (Dover)
**Best points finish:** 1 (2003)
**Career victories:** 7—Charlotte (00a), Las Vegas (03), Michigan (02), North Carolina (02a), Phoenix (02), Richmond (02), Texas (02)
**First victory:** May 28, 2000 (Charlotte)
**Career poles:** 1—Dover (02a)
**First pole:** June 2, 2002 (Dover)
**Best career finish:** 1 **Best career start:** 1

### FAST FACTS

- Finished third in 1999 Busch Series standings with four wins and two poles.
- Was second in 1998 Busch Series points race with three victories.
- Finished second in the 1997 Busch Series Rookie of the Year race despite starting only 21 races.
- Was running second in the ASA standings when he left for the Busch Series in 1997.
- Began his short-track career at age 16, winning his first feature in his third race while he was a high school junior.
- Won 10 features in his first two seasons at tracks in Wisconsin and had 46 super late-model victories over the next three seasons.
- Won the Alan Kulwicki Memorial race in 1993 and track titles at Madison International and Wisconsin International tracks the following year.
- Won another track title at Wisconsin International in 1995, with 15 wins in 60 races.
- Made his NASCAR All-Pro Series debut in 1995, finishing in the top three in three of four starts.
- Won one race and finished third in the Hooters ProCup

Series in 1996.
- Worked on his father's racecar for three years before starting to drive it.
- Won ARTGO Challenge Series race at La Crosse, Wis., at age 19, becoming the youngest winner ever in that series. He broke the record held by Mark Martin, his eventual Winston Cup mentor.

### CAR FACTS
**Car:** No. 17 Ford
**Primary sponsor:** DeWalt Power Tools
**Owners:** Mark Martin, Jack Roush
**Team:** Roush Racing
**Crew chief:** Robbie Reiser
**Engine builder:** Jerry Carcone

## CAREER BY YEAR

**2003** Kenseth's only win came at Las Vegas in February. He took the points lead after the next race and never relinquished it. Kenseth built an insurmountable early-season lead in the points race by finishing in the top 10 in 12 of the first 14 races. His season was remarkably consistent—he never went more than three races without a top 10 finish. He ended the season with a series-best 25 top 10s.

**2002** Finished eighth in series points. ... Won five races—Texas, Phoenix, Michigan, North Carolina and Richmond—the most of any driver on the circuit. ... Finished with 11 top fives and 19 top 10s. ... Won the pole at Dover spring race.

**2001** Finished 13th in series points. ... Finished fourth at Michigan, Talladega, New Hampshire and Phoenix for his only top fives. ... Had nine top 10s ... Had only six qualifying attempts of 20th or better and none better than 13th. ... His team won the Pit Crew Competition in Rockingham in October.

**2000** Finished 14th in series points. ... Won Winston Cup Raybestos Rookie of the Year title over Dale Earnhardt Jr. and a group of other talented first-year drivers. ... Won the circuit's longest race, the Coca-Cola 600, at Lowe's Motor Speedway for his first career win. ... Followed that performance with a second-place finish the following weekend at Dover. ... Posted 11 top 10s, including in the Daytona 500. ... Managed only two top 10 starting positions, a fourth at Atlanta and a sixth at Rockingham's early-season race.

**1999** Finished 49th in series points. ... Drove five races for Roush Racing in preparation for his rookie season. ... Scored his first career top five finish at Dover, where he was fourth. ... Also ran at Michigan, Darlington, Charlotte and Rockingham in the second half of the season.

**1999** Finished 57th in series points, driving in only one race. ... Drove the No. 94 Ford in place of Bill Elliott at Dover so Elliott could attend his father's funeral; finished sixth in the race.

### CAREER STATISTICS

| Year | Car Owner | Champ. Races | Finish | Won | Top 5 | Top 10 | DNF | Poles | Money Won |
|---|---|---|---|---|---|---|---|---|---|
| 1998 | Bill Elliott | 1 | 57 | 0 | 0 | 1 | 0 | 0 | $42,340 |
| 1999 | Jack Roush | 5 | 49 | 0 | 1 | 1 | 3 | 0 | 143,561 |
| 2000 | Jack Roush | 34 | 14 | 1 | 4 | 11 | 5 | 0 | 2,408,138 |
| 2001 | Jack Roush | 36 | 13 | 0 | 4 | 9 | 5 | 0 | 2,565,579 |
| 2002 | Jack Roush | 36 | 8 | 5 | 11 | 19 | 3 | 1 | 4,514,203 |
| 2003 | Jack Roush | 36 | 1 | 1 | 11 | 25 | 2 | 0 | 9,422,764 |
| TOTALS | | 148 | | 7 | 20 | 41 | 16 | 1 | $19,096,585 |

### 2003 RESULTS

| Race | Start | Finish | Standing Pos. | Winnings |
|---|---|---|---|---|
| Daytona 500 (Daytona) | 35 | 20 | 19 | $200,345 |
| Subway 400 (Rockingham) | 18 | 3 | 6 | $94,350 |
| UAW-DaimlerChrysler 400 (Las Vegas) | 17 | 1 | 2 | $365,875 |
| Bass Pro Shops MBNA 500 (Atlanta) | 24 | 4 | 1 | $91,850 |
| Carolina Dodge Dealers 400 (Darlington) | 12 | 8 | 1 | $69,440 |
| Food City 500 (Bristol) | 37 | 2 | 1 | $118,870 |
| Samsung/RadioShack 500 (Texas) | 17 | 6 | 1 | $142,950 |
| Aaron's 499 (Talladega) | 27 | 9 | 1 | $104,730 |
| Virginia 500 (Martinsville) | 34 | 22 | 1 | $66,725 |
| Auto Club 500 (California) | 23 | 9 | 1 | $95,425 |
| Pontiac Excitement 400 (Richmond) | 18 | 7 | 1 | $73,675 |
| Coca-Cola 600 (Charlotte) | 18 | 2 | 1 | $206,500 |
| MBNA Armed Forces Family 400 (Dover) | 4 | 7 | 1 | $87,985 |
| Pocono 500 (Pocono) | 25 | 3 | 1 | $109,870 |
| Sirius 400 (Michigan) | 21 | 4 | 1 | $93,275 |
| Dodge/Save Mart 350 (Sonoma) | 4 | 14 | 1 | $78,975 |
| Pepsi 400 (Daytona) | 37 | 6 | 1 | $98,475 |
| Tropicana 400 (Chicago) | 24 | 12 | 1 | $87,725 |
| New England 300 (New Hampshire) | 1 | 3 | 1 | $124,030 |
| Pennsylvania 500 (Pocono) | 9 | 13 | 1 | $68,590 |
| Brickyard 400 (Indianapolis) | 17 | 2 | 1 | $314,425 |
| Sirius at the Glen (Watkins Glen) | 7 | 8 | 1 | $70,535 |
| GFS Marketplace 400 (Michigan) | 33 | 9 | 1 | $76,540 |
| Sharpie 500 (Bristol) | 10 | 4 | 1 | $122,905 |
| Southern 500 (Darlington) | 6 | 14 | 1 | $75,720 |
| Chevy Rock & Roll 400 (Richmond) | 18 | 7 | 1 | $75,230g |
| Sylvania 300 (New Hampshire) | 19 | 7 | 1 | $80,750 |
| MBNA America 400 (Dover) | 1 | 9 | 1 | $79,840 |
| EA SPORTS 500 (Talladega) | 37 | 33 | 1 | $61,125 |
| Banquet 400 (Kansas) | 37 | 36 | 1 | $68,575 |
| UAW-GM Quality 500 (Charlotte) | 29 | 8 | 1 | $82,425 |
| Subway 500 (Martinsville) | 14 | 13 | 1 | $68,400 |
| Bass Pro Shops MBNA 500 (Atlanta) | 37 | 11 | 1 | $95,825 |
| Checker Auto Parts 500 (Phoenix) | 37 | 6 | 1 | $86,000 |
| Pop Secret 400 (Rockingham) | 23 | 4 | 1 | $92,650 |
| Ford 400 (Homestead) | 37 | 43 | 1 | $62,665 |

## Bobby Labonte
**Date of birth:** May 8, 1964  **Hometown:** Corpus Christi, Texas
**Resides:** Trinity, N.C.  **Spouse:** Donna  **Children:** Robert, Madison  **Height:** 5-9  **Weight:** 175  **Hobbies:** Fishing

## NASCAR ACHIEVEMENTS

**First NASCAR Cup start:** June 2, 1991 (Dover)
**Best points finish:** 1 (2000)
**Career victories:** 21—Atlanta (96b, 97b, 98a, 99b, 01b, 03a), Charlotte (95a, 00b), Darlington (00b), Dover (99a), Homestead (03), Indianapolis (00), Martinsville (02a), Michigan (95a, 95b, 99b), Pocono (99a, 99b, 01b), Rockingham (00a), Talladega (98a)
**First victory:** May 28, 1995 (Charlotte)
**Career poles:** 25—Atlanta (96b, 99a), California (01), Charlotte (96b, 99a, 99b), Darlington (97b), Daytona (98a, 98b), Dover (96b, 97a, 99a), Las Vegas (99, 03), Martinsville (95a), Michigan (94a, 00a, 03a, 03b), New Hampshire (00b), Phoenix (96), Richmond (93b), Rockingham (97b), Talladega (98a), Texas (03)
**First pole:** September 9, 1993 (Richmond)
**Best career finish:** 1    **Best career start:** 1

## FAST FACTS

- Began his career in 1984 as a Hagan Racing crew member; his brother Terry was the team's driver.
- Raced late model stock cars at Caraway Speedway in Asheboro, N.C., winning the 1987 track championship with 12 victories in 23 races.
- Won the Busch Series championship in 1991 and finished second in 1992 behind Joe Nemechek; Nemechek's winning margin of three points was closest in the history of NASCAR's three national series.
- Ran quarter-midgets in Texas as a boy.
- In 2001, Bobby and Terry had a park named in their honor, in their hometown of Corpus Christi, Texas.
- With Terry, was inducted into the Texas Sports Hall of Fame in 2001, nearly doubling the class of four inductees from the racing community. The Labontes' class included Texas football greats Troy Aikman, Dick "Night Train" Lane, Bruce Matthews and Mike Munchak, along with baseball great Norm Cash.

### CAR FACTS

**Car:** No. 18 Chevrolet
**Primary sponsor:** Interstate Batteries
**Owner:** Joe Gibbs
**Team:** Joe Gibbs Racing
**Crew chief:** Michael McSwain
**Engine builder:** Mark Cronquist

## CAREER BY YEAR

**2003** His season ended on a high note with a win at Homestead on a last-lap pass as Bill Elliott cut a tire. That victory further solidified Labonte's reputation as stout on mile-and-a-half tracks; his other win in 2003 came at Atlanta, a track similar to Homestead. Labonte looked great with a streak of eight top 10s in nine races early in the season, but he faltered after that, with seven consecutive finishes of 14th or worse.

**2002** Finished 16th in series points. ... Snapped a run of five consecutive seasons of finishing among the top seven in points. ... Won at Martinsville in the spring, extending streak of seasons with at least one win to eight. ... Posted seven top 10s and five top fives.

**2001** Finished sixth in series points. ... Posted wins at Pocono and Atlanta, extending his streak of consecutive multiple-win seasons to four and streak of at least one victory to seven consecutive seasons. ... Recorded 20 top 10 finishes, including nine top fives.

**2000** Was the Winston Cup Series champion. ... Posted four wins and 19 top fives for Joe Gibbs Racing, winning the title by 265 points over runner-up Dale Earnhardt. ... Joined his brother Terry as a Winston Cup champion, making them the only brothers to have won the title. ... Grabbed the points lead following the third race of the season (Las Vegas) and fell out of the top spot just once the rest of the way. ... Had just two finishes outside the top 20 and failed to finish only nine laps out of 10,167 on the season. ... First win of the season was at Rockingham and was followed with triumphs at Indianapolis, Darlington and Charlotte. ... Won two poles (Michigan, New Hampshire), marking his sixth consecutive multiple-pole season.

**1999** Finished second in series points, 201 points behind champion Dale Jarrett. ... Established career bests for wins (five), top 10s (26), top 5s (23) and poles (five). ... Swept the Pocono races and also won at Dover, Michigan and at the season-ending race at Atlanta. ... Broke his shoulder blade during a Busch Series practice at Darlington in March but amazingly did not miss a Winston Cup start.

**1998** Finished sixth in series points. ... Had 18 top 10s and 11 top fives, including wins at Talladega and Atlanta. ... Won three poles (Daytona sweep, Talladega), giving him 12 in his first four seasons with Joe Gibbs Racing.

**1997** Finished seventh in series points. ... Won the season finale at Atlanta for the second consecutive year, both times marking his only win of the season. ... Had 18 top 10s, including five top fives. ... Won three poles (Darlington, Dover, Rockingham).

**1996** Finished 11th in series points. ... Another solid season with Joe Gibbs Racing, with one win and 14 top 10s. ... Got his win in the season finale at Atlanta, which was where his brother Terry celebrated clinching the Winston Cup title. ... Surpassed his previous career total for poles (three) with four—at Atlanta, Charlotte, Dover and Phoenix.

**1995** Finished 10th in series points. ... Moved from Bill Davis Racing to Joe Gibbs Racing, where he enjoyed a breakthrough season, replacing Dale Jarrett as driver of the No. 18 car. ... Got the first three victories of his career, and had 14 top 10s and two poles. ... First career win came on May 28 in the Coca-Cola 600 at Charlotte, his 74th career start. Swept the Michigan events for his other two wins.

**1994** Finished 21st in series points. ... Posted two top 10s in his second and final season with Bill Davis Racing. ... Got the first top five of his career, taking fifth at Watkins Glen.

**1993** Finished 19th in series points. ... A strong career in the Busch Series helped land a full-time ride with Bill Davis

Racing. ... Had a solid rookie season with six top 10s and a pole .... Lost out to Jeff Gordon for the Rookie of the Year honors.

**1991** Made his Winston Cup debut as a driver/owner, competing in two events. ... First start was on June 2 at Dover, where he started 33rd and finished 34th. ... Ran full-time in the Busch Series and won that series' title.

## CAREER STATISTICS

| Year | Car Owner | Races | Champ. Finish | Won | Top 5 | Top 10 | DNF | Poles | Money Won |
|---|---|---|---|---|---|---|---|---|---|
| 1991 | Bobby Labonte | 2 | 66 | 0 | 0 | 0 | 2 | 0 | $8,350 |
| 1993 | Bill Davis | 30 | 19 | 0 | 0 | 6 | 6 | 1 | 395,660 |
| 1994 | Bill Davis | 31 | 21 | 0 | 1 | 2 | 7 | 0 | 550,305 |
| 1995 | Joe Gibbs | 31 | 10 | 3 | 7 | 14 | 6 | 2 | 1,413,682 |
| 1996 | Joe Gibbs | 31 | 11 | 1 | 5 | 14 | 5 | 4 | 1,475,196 |
| 1997 | Joe Gibbs | 32 | 7 | 1 | 9 | 18 | 1 | 3 | 2,217,999 |
| 1998 | Joe Gibbs | 33 | 6 | 2 | 11 | 18 | 6 | 3 | 2,980,052 |
| 1999 | Joe Gibbs | 34 | 2 | 5 | 23 | 26 | 1 | 5 | 4,763,615 |
| 2000 | Joe Gibbs | 34 | 1 | 4 | 19 | 24 | 0 | 2 | 7,361,386 |
| 2001 | Joe Gibbs | 36 | 6 | 2 | 9 | 20 | 6 | 1 | 4,786,779 |
| 2002 | Joe Gibbs | 36 | 16 | 1 | 5 | 7 | 4 | 0 | 4,183,715 |
| 2003 | Joe Gibbs | 36 | 8 | 2 | 12 | 17 | 5 | 4 | 5,505,018 |
| TOTALS | | 366 | | 21 | 101 | 166 | 49 | 25 | $35,641,757 |

## 2003 RESULTS

| Race | Start | Finish | Standing Pos. | Winnings |
|---|---|---|---|---|
| Daytona 500 (Daytona) | 22 | 41 | 41 | $202,134 |
| Subway 400 (Rockingham) | 10 | 16 | 28 | $88,743 |
| UAW-DaimlerChrysler 400 (Las Vegas) | 1 | 4 | 13 | $178,908 |
| Bass Pro Shops MBNA 500 (Atlanta) | 4 | 1 | 5 | $209,233 |
| Carolina Dodge Dealers 400 (Darlington) | 20 | 37 | 14 | $87,108 |
| Food City 500 (Bristol) | 12 | 3 | 8 | $126,558 |
| Samsung/RadioShack 500 (Texas) | 1 | 37 | 11 | $117,108 |
| Aaron's 499 (Talladega) | 22 | 32 | 15 | $109,658 |
| Virginia 500 (Martinsville) | 39 | 2 | 11 | $138,348 |
| Auto Club 500 (California) | 19 | 2 | 8 | $172,708 |
| Pontiac Excitement 400 (Richmond) | 4 | 2 | 5 | $157,758 |
| Coca-Cola 600 (Charlotte) | 11 | 3 | 6 | $184,633 |
| MBNA Armed Forces Family 400 (Dover) | 13 | 3 | 4 | $139,333 |
| Pocono 500 (Pocono) | 3 | 17 | 4 | $91,973 |
| Sirius 400 (Michigan) | 1 | 2 | 4 | $142,858 |
| Dodge/Save Mart 350 (Sonoma) | 14 | 9 | 4 | $105,223 |
| Pepsi 400 (Daytona) | 15 | 5 | 4 | $129,283 |
| Tropicana 400 (Chicago) | 18 | 36 | 4 | $105,658 |
| New England 300 (New Hampshire) | 4 | 14 | 4 | $100,533 |
| Pennsylvania 500 (Pocono) | 4 | 30 | 5 | $89,448 |
| Brickyard 400 (Indianapolis) | 8 | 22 | 6 | $156,913 |
| Sirius at the Glen (Watkins Glen) | 9 | 14 | 7 | $93,443 |
| GFS Marketplace 400 (Michigan) | 1 | 37 | 7 | $99,023 |
| Sharpie 500 (Bristol) | 19 | 27 | 9 | $107,688 |
| Southern 500 (Darlington) | 5 | 7 | 8 | $112,568 |
| Chevy Rock & Roll 400 (Richmond) | 16 | 6 | 7 | $104,513 |
| Sylvania 300 (New Hampshire) | 37 | 16 | 8 | $99,308 |
| MBNA America 400 (Dover) | 8 | 31 | 7 | $97,948 |
| EA SPORTS 500 (Talladega) | 10 | 11 | 7 | $102,598 |
| Banquet 400 (Kansas) | 4 | 17 | 7 | $109,633 |
| UAW-GM Quality 500 (Charlotte) | 12 | 6 | 8 | $110,258 |
| Subway 500 (Martinsville) | 20 | 41 | 8 | $88,023 |
| Bass Pro Shops MBNA 500 (Atlanta) | 2 | 5 | 8 | $133,383 |
| Checker Auto Parts 500 (Phoenix) | 24 | 36 | 8 | $92,233 |
| Pop Secret 400 (Rockingham) | 14 | 8 | 8 | $98,208 |
| Ford 400 (Homestead) | 2 | 1 | 8 | $331,058 |

# Terry Labonte
## 5

**Date of birth:** November 16, 1956 **Hometown:** Corpus Christi, Texas **Resides:** Thomasville, N.C. **Spouse:** Kim **Children:** Justin, Kristen **Height:** 5-10 **Weight:** 165 **Hobbies:** Hunting, fishing

## NASCAR ACHIEVEMENTS

**First NASCAR Cup start:** September 4, 1978 (Darlington)
**Best points finish:** 1 (1984, 1996)
**Career victories:** 22—Bristol (84b, 95b), Charlotte (96b), Darlington (80b, 03b), North Wilkesboro (87b, 88a, 94a, 96a), Phoenix (94), Pocono (89a, 95s), Richmond (94b, 95a, 98a), Rockingham (83b, 86a), Talladega (89b, 97b), Texas (99)
**First victory:** September 1, 1980 (Darlington)
**Career poles:** 27—Atlanta (81a), Bristol (87b), Dover (83b, 85a), Martinsville (82a), North Wilkesboro (88a, 96a), Pocono (87a), Richmond (96a, 03a), Riverside (82a, 84a, 84b, 85a, 87a), Rockingham (85a, 85b, 86a, 96a), Sonoma (96), Talladega (95a), Texas (00), Texas World (81), Watkins Glen (87, 91)
**First pole:** March 13, 1981 (Atlanta)
**Best career finish:** 1  **Best career start:** 1

## FAST FACTS

- Started racing in quarter-midgets when he was 7.
- At age 16, moved into stock cars that were first owned by his father, Bob, then by former Winston Cup owner Billy Hagan.
- His family moved to North Carolina in the late 1970s to get Labonte closer to the Winston Cup scene, where he debuted with Hagan in 1978.
- Won his first Busch Series race in 1985 and won 11 total in that series.
- Has competed in the Craftsman Truck Series, winning at Richmond in 1995, which made him one of only five drivers

## CAR FACTS

**Car:** No. 5 Chevrolet
**Primary sponsor:** Kellogg's/got milk?
**Owner:** Rick Hendrick
**Team:** Hendrick Motorsports
**Crew chief:** Jim Long
**Engine builder:** Keith Chrisco

to win a race in each of NASCAR's national series.
- Was inducted into the Texas Sports Hall of Fame in 2001. Labonte and his brother, Bobby, are among the four auto racing inductees in the Hall, which also includes Carroll Shelby and Johnny Rutherford.
- Labonte's son, Justin, has competed on the Busch and ARCA circuits.

## CAREER BY YEAR

**2003** The Iceman finished 10th, his best standing since 1998. His season already was impressive before his win at the final Southern 500, his first trip to victory lane in three years. The key to his resurgence was consistency. He had only nine top 10s, but he didn't have a DNF and completed a ton of laps. He finished 39th in the spring race at Bristol but didn't miss the top 25 again until the October race at Atlanta.

**2002** Finished 24th in series points. … Had only one top five finish and four top 10s. … Posted six DNFs, including at the Daytona 500. … Did not have a victory for the third season in a row. … His Winston Cup record streak of 655 straight starts was broken by Ricky Rudd. … Went over $30 million in career earnings and made his 745th career Winston Cup start in the season's final race.

**2001** Finished 23rd in series points. … Had one top five and two top 10s, both at Bristol. … His eight DNFs were the most since 1991.

**2000** Finished 17th in series points. … Second half of his season was impacted by injuries suffered in an accident at Daytona on July 1; was forced to miss races at Indianapolis and Watkins Glen, ending his Winston Cup record of 655 consecutive starts. … Finished second at Richmond in May. … Started his 700th career race on September 23 at Dover. … Won his first pole since 1996.

**1999** Finished 12th in series points, ending a five-year streak of top 10 finishes. … Won at Texas in March. … Had seven top 10s.

**1998** Finished ninth in series points. … Won at Richmond in June and had four other top fives, including two at Talladega. … Had 15 top 10s. … Started second at the Daytona 500 next to brother Bobby, the only time brothers have shared the front row for the prestigious event.

**1997** Finished sixth in series points and helped cap another great season for Hendrick Motorsports as teammate Jeff Gordon won the Winston Cup championship, bumping Labonte's 1984 mark as the youngest champion. … Won at Talladega in October and posted three runner-up finishes. … Had 20 top 10s.

**1996** Won his second Winston Cup championship. … Became the fifth driver in the modern era and one of 13 in 54 overall years of NASCAR competition to win multiple titles. … Won two races, at North Wilkesboro in April from the pole (his career-best fourth victory at one track) and at Sonoma in May. … Finished second a career-high seven times and tied his career best with six thirds; had 21 top fives and 24 top 10s, both career bests. … Teammate Jeff Gordon's finish put Hendrick at 1-2 in the final points standings. … Broke Richard Petty's record with his 514th consecutive start on April 21 at Martinsville.

**1995** Finished sixth in series points while Hendrick teammate Jeff Gordon won the first of four Winston Cup championships. … Won three races for the second straight year. … Won a pole for the first time in three years, in April at Talladega. … Had 14 top fives and 17 top 10s.

**1994** Finished seventh in series points. … First year with Hendrick Motorsports resulted in his best points finish in six seasons. … Had three wins—April 17 at North Wilkesboro, September 10 at Richmond and October 30 at Phoenix.

**1993** Finished 18th in series points. … Didn't win a race for the fourth straight year and had no poles or top fives. … Had 14 finishes of 11th or lower, including six DNFs. … Ran his final season in his second of two stints with Billy Hagan (1978-86, 1991-93).

**1992** Finished eighth in series points. … Did not win a race or a pole, but his resurgence was built on 16 top 10s, including four top fives.

**1991** Finished 18th in series points. … Reunited with car owner Billy Hagan after a four-year separation. … Had one top five and seven top 10s. … Raced against brother Bobby for the first time in Winston Cup at the Dover spring race; Terry finished 24th, Bobby 34th.

**1990** Finished 15th in series points. … First and only season driving for Richard Jackson. … Did not win a race for the first time since 1982. … Four top fives were his lowest since 1979.

**1989** Finished 10th in series points. … Had two wins, June 18 at Pocono and July 30 at Talladega. … Had nine top fives and 11 top 10s in his final year driving for Junior Johnson. … Did not win a pole for the first season since 1980. … Won the IROC title.

**1988** Finished fourth in series points. … Won for the second straight season at North Wilkesboro on April 17. … Won one pole and has 18 top 10s and 11 top fives.

**1987** Finished third in series points in his first year driving for Junior Johnson. … Had one win, October 4 at North Wilkesboro. … Won four poles and had 13 top fives and 22 top 10s. … Qualified in excess of 210 mph in May at Talladega; his 13 qualifying laps at 200-plus mph put him behind only Cale Yarborough (15) and Bill Elliott (14).

**1986** Finished 12th in series points, his first year out of the top 10 since 1979 … Had 12 DNFs, tying the most in his career. … Won from the pole at Rockingham on March 2, his only win and pole of the year. … Had five top fives and 10 top 10s. … Final season with Billy Hagan following nine years, eight full-time, before moving to Junior Johnson's camp.

**1985** Finished seventh in series points. … Won the season-opening non-points race at Daytona, the Busch Clash. … Set a career mark with four poles and qualified second four times. … Won for a second straight season at Riverside on June 2. … Had eight top fives and 13 top 10s.

**1984** Won the Winston Cup championship. … Won two races in a season for the first time in his career, from the pole on June 3 at Riverside and on August 25 at Bristol. … Had six seconds and six thirds among 17 top fives and 24 top 10s, his career best in that category.

**1983** Finished fifth in series points. ... Won for the first time in more than two years on October 30 at Rockingham and grabbed three poles to go along with 20 top 10s and 11 top fives.

**1982** Finished third in series points, marking the fourth straight year with a jump in the final standings despite a second straight season without a win. ... Won two poles and had 21 top 10s and 17 top fives. ... His fourth-place finish at Martinsville on October 17 made him the youngest driver in motorsports history to win $1 million and the 12th NASCAR driver to reach that mark.

**1981** Finished fourth in series points. ... Won his first Winston Cup pole at the Atlanta spring race and grabbed a second pole at his home track at Texas. ... His surge in the final points standings was buoyed by eight top fives and 17 top 10s.

**1980** Finished eighth in series points. ... Got his first Winston Cup win September 1 at Darlington in his 59th start. ... Claimed five other top fives and 16 top 10s overall despite 12 DNFs.

**1979** Finished 10th in series points, beginning a run of seven straight years in the top 10. ... First full season in Winston Cup resulted in a runner-up finish in the Rookie of the Year battle to Dale Earnhardt. ... Had two top fives and 13 top 10s.

**1978** Finished 39th in series points. ... Ran only five races for car owner Billy Hagan and placed in the top 10 in his first three Winston Cup events; his first event was the Southern 500, where he finished fourth; he was seventh at Richmond and ninth at Martinsville.

### CAREER STATISTICS

| Year | Car Owner | Races | Champ. Finish | Won | Top 5 | Top 10 | DNF | Poles | Money Won |
|---|---|---|---|---|---|---|---|---|---|
| 1978 | Billy Hagan | 5 | 39 | 0 | 1 | 3 | 2 | 0 | $20,545 |
| 1979 | Billy Hagan | 31 | 10 | 0 | 2 | 13 | 10 | 0 | 130,057 |
| 1980 | Billy Hagan | 31 | 8 | 1 | 6 | 16 | 12 | 0 | 215,889 |
| 1981 | Billy Hagan | 31 | 4 | 0 | 8 | 17 | 8 | 2 | 334,987 |
| 1982 | Billy Hagan | 30 | 3 | 0 | 17 | 21 | 8 | 2 | 363,970 |
| 1983 | Billy Hagan | 30 | 5 | 1 | 11 | 20 | 7 | 3 | 362,790 |
| 1984 | Billy Hagan | 30 | 1 | 2 | 17 | 24 | 3 | 2 | 713,010 |
| 1985 | Billy Hagan | 28 | 7 | 1 | 8 | 17 | 8 | 4 | 694,510 |
| 1986 | Billy Hagan | 29 | 12 | 1 | 5 | 10 | 12 | 1 | 522,235 |
| 1987 | Junior Johnson | 29 | 3 | 1 | 13 | 22 | 5 | 4 | 825,369 |
| 1988 | Junior Johnson | 29 | 4 | 1 | 11 | 18 | 3 | 1 | 950,781 |
| 1989 | Junior Johnson | 29 | 10 | 2 | 9 | 11 | 6 | 0 | 704,806 |
| 1990 | Richard Jackson | 29 | 15 | 0 | 4 | 9 | 5 | 0 | 450,230 |
| 1991 | Billy Hagan | 29 | 18 | 0 | 1 | 7 | 8 | 1 | 348,898 |
| 1992 | Billy Hagan | 29 | 8 | 0 | 4 | 16 | 3 | 0 | 600,381 |
| 1993 | Billy Hagan | 30 | 18 | 0 | 0 | 10 | 6 | 0 | 531,717 |
| 1994 | Rick Hendrick | 31 | 7 | 3 | 6 | 14 | 4 | 0 | 1,125,921 |
| 1995 | Rick Hendrick | 31 | 6 | 3 | 14 | 17 | 3 | 1 | 1,558,659 |
| 1996 | Rick Hendrick | 31 | 1 | 2 | 21 | 24 | 3 | 4 | 4,030,648 |
| 1997 | Rick Hendrick | 32 | 6 | 1 | 8 | 20 | 3 | 0 | 2,270,144 |
| 1998 | Rick Hendrick | 33 | 9 | 1 | 5 | 15 | 4 | 0 | 2,054,163 |
| 1999 | Rick Hendrick | 34 | 12 | 1 | 1 | 7 | 6 | 0 | 2,475,365 |
| 2000 | Rick Hendrick | 32 | 17 | 0 | 3 | 6 | 3 | 1 | 2,239,716 |
| 2001 | Rick Hendrick | 36 | 23 | 0 | 1 | 3 | 8 | 0 | 3,011,901 |
| 2002 | Rick Hendrick | 36 | 24 | 0 | 1 | 4 | 6 | 0 | 3,244,240 |
| 2003 | Rick Hendrick | 36 | 10 | 1 | 4 | 9 | 0 | 1 | 4,283,625 |
| TOTALS | | 781 | | 22 | 181 | 353 | 146 | 27 | $34,064,557 |

### 2003 RESULTS

| Race | Start | Finish | Standing Pos. | Winnings |
|---|---|---|---|---|
| Daytona 500 (Daytona) | 41 | 30 | 30 | $200,576 |
| Subway 400 (Rockingham) | 31 | 27 | 33 | $76,312 |
| UAW-DaimlerChrysler 400 (Las Vegas) | 36 | 16 | 26 | $102,406 |
| Bass Pro Shops MBNA 500 (Atlanta) | 39 | 20 | 26 | $80,196 |
| Carolina Dodge Dealers 400 (Darlington) | 29 | 24 | 25 | $72,891 |
| Food City 500 (Bristol) | 17 | 39 | 30 | $83,086 |
| Samsung/RadioShack 500 (Texas) | 12 | 16 | 31 | $115,656 |
| Aaron's 499 (Talladega) | 28 | 5 | 24 | $122,221 |
| Virginia 500 (Martinsville) | 16 | 14 | 21 | $78,581 |
| Auto Club 500 (California) | 21 | 12 | 19 | $102,806 |
| Pontiac Excitement 400 (Richmond) | 1 | 21 | 18 | $83,456 |
| Coca-Cola 600 (Charlotte) | 39 | 21 | 17 | $102,031 |
| MBNA Armed Forces Family 400 (Dover) | 8 | 10 | 17 | $97,641 |
| Pocono 500 (Pocono) | 11 | 7 | 17 | $87,946 |
| Sirius 400 (Michigan) | 5 | 10 | 15 | $89,571 |
| Dodge/Save Mart 350 (Sonoma) | 23 | 25 | 15 | $84,886 |
| Pepsi 400 (Daytona) | 25 | 4 | 13 | $128,806 |
| Tropicana 400 (Chicago) | 28 | 15 | 14 | $96,356 |
| New England 300 (New Hampshire) | 14 | 20 | 16 | $84,056 |
| Pennsylvania 500 (Pocono) | 6 | 5 | 13 | $100,581 |
| Brickyard 400 (Indianapolis) | 38 | 19 | 14 | $144,481 |
| Sirius at the Glen (Watkins Glen) | 19 | 18 | 14 | $76,566 |
| GFS Marketplace 400 (Michigan) | 5 | 13 | 13 | $84,421 |
| Sharpie 500 (Bristol) | 13 | 11 | 12 | $102,346 |
| Southern 500 (Darlington) | 3 | 1 | 11 | $204,736 |
| Chevy Rock & Roll 400 (Richmond) | 32 | 8 | 9 | $83,161 |
| Sylvania 300 (New Hampshire) | 2 | 18 | 9 | $84,856 |
| MBNA America 400 (Dover) | 9 | 20 | 9 | $86,346 |
| EA SPORTS 500 (Talladega) | 14 | 22 | 10 | $83,796 |
| Banquet 400 (Kansas) | 34 | 16 | 10 | $94,406 |
| UAW-GM Quality 500 (Charlotte) | 21 | 18 | 9 | $78,406 |
| Subway 500 (Martinsville) | 31 | 6 | 9 | $85,456 |
| Bass Pro Shops MBNA 500 (Atlanta) | 32 | 33 | 10 | $89,531 |
| Checker Auto Parts 500 (Phoenix) | 19 | 30 | 11 | $77,706 |
| Pop Secret 400 (Rockingham) | 20 | 12 | 11 | $81,681 |
| Ford 400 (Homestead) | 14 | 15 | 10 | $79,606 |

## Sterling Marlin

**Date of birth:** June 30, 1957 **Hometown:** Columbia, Tenn.
**Resides:** Columbia, Tenn. **Spouse:** Paula **Children:** Steadman, Sutherlin **Height:** 6-0 **Weight:** 180 **Hobbies:** Civil War history, collecting artifacts, following University of Tennessee football

### NASCAR ACHIEVEMENTS

**First NASCAR Cup start:** May 8, 1976 (Nashville)
**Best points finish:** 3 (2001)
**Career victories:** 10—Charlotte (01b), Darlington (95a, 02a), Daytona (94a, 95a, 96b), Las Vegas (02), Michigan (01b), Talladega (95b, 96a)

**First victory:** February 20, 1994 (Daytona)
**Career poles:** 11—Darlington (92a, 92b), Daytona (91b, 92a, 92b, 01b), Phoenix (94), Pocono (99a), Talladega (95b, 96a)
**First pole:** July 4, 1991 (Daytona)
**Best career finish:** 1   **Best career start:** 1

## FAST FACTS

- Won three consecutive track championships at Nashville Raceway from 1980-82.
- Has two career victories in the Busch Series.
- Marlin was named Professional Athlete of the Year in Tennessee in 1995 and '96.
- Was the team captain and an All Mid-State selection, playing quarterback and linebacker at Spring Hill (Tenn.) High School.
- Played basketball in high school.

### CAR FACTS
**Car:** No. 40 Dodge
**Primary sponsor:** Coors Light
**Owner:** Chip Ganassi
**Team:** Chip Ganassi Racing
**Crew chief:** Lee McCall
**Engine builder:** Ernie Elliott

## CAREER BY YEAR

**2003** Marlin posted zero top fives and only 11 top 10s. He finished 18th for the second straight year, but in 2002 he did so despite missing seven races. He appeared on the verge of a strong season with eight top 10s—four sixths, two sevenths, an eighth and a 10th—in the first 15 races. But he never finished better than 10th the rest of the season.

**2002** Finished 18th in series points. … Was having the most productive year of career when a neck injury that was a result of an accident at Kansas City on September 29 ended his season. Was in pursuit of his first Winston Cup title, having led in points for 25 consecutive races. The run spanned from the second race of the season, Rockingham, through Richmond in September.… Was fifth in the points when his injury sidelined him and was replaced by Jamie McMurray. … Made 29 starts for Chip Ganassi Racing and posted two wins, at Las Vegas and Darlington (spring). … Was red-flagged while he was leading the Daytona 500. While the cars were stopped, he got out of his car and began working on some body damage. He was penalized for the infraction and finished eighth.

**2001** Finished third in series points, matching a career best established in 1995 with Morgan-McClure. … First full season with Chip Ganassi running the operation and driving a Dodge resulted in a pair of wins (Michigan, Charlotte) and a career-best 12 top fives. … Victory at Michigan in August was his first since winning the Pepsi 400 at Daytona in July 1996. … Led Dodge in its return to NASCAR Winston Cup with a win at Michigan, giving the manufacturer its first victory since Neil Bonnett won November 20, 1977 at Ontario, Calif. … Won a pole at the Pepsi 400, his first since 1999.

**2000** Finished 19th in series points. … Had seven top 10s, highlighted by a season-best second at Sonoma. … Was his final season with Chevrolet and owner Felix Sabates, who sold majority interest of the team to Chip Ganassi.

**1999** Finished 16th in series points. … Notched two season-best fourth-place finishes, marking his first top fives as a driver for Team Sabco. … Had five top 10s and his first pole since 1995.

**1998** Finished 13th in series points. … Parted ways with Morgan-McClure after four seasons and joined Felix Sabates' operation, Team Sabco. … Did not record a top five, but had six top 10s.

**1997** Finished 25th in series points. … Final season with Morgan-McClure was the least productive of his four there; was winless after registering six wins in the previous three seasons. … Had six top 10s. … Points finish was his lowest since running a limited schedule in 1986.

**1996** Finished eighth in series points. … Enjoyed another strong campaign with Morgan-McClure with a second consecutive multiple-win season. … Had two wins, the Pepsi 400 at Daytona and Talladega, and 10 top 10s.

**1995** Finished third in series points, breaking into the top five for the first time. … Won three races, including his second consecutive Daytona 500. Other wins came at Darlington and Talladega, which he won from his lone pole of the season. … Posted 22 top 10s, including nine top fives.

**1994** Finished 14th in series points. … Left Stavola Brothers for Morgan-McClure, and the move paid off when he finally got his first Winston Cup victory at the Daytona 500 in his first start for the team and his 279th overall. … Had 11 top 10s and took the pole at Phoenix.

**1993** Finished 15th in series points. … Moved from Junior Johnson to the Stavola Brothers, his only season with the team. … Posted eight top 10s, including a season-best second at the Pepsi 400 at Daytona.

**1992** Finished 10th in series points. … Second and final season with Junior Johnson was solid, but Marlin was unable to land his elusive first win. Had 13 top 10s, including three runner-ups. … Won five poles, which ranked second in the series to Alan Kulwicki's six.

**1991** Finished seventh in series points. … Left Billy Hagen's team for an opportunity with legendary Junior Johnson, and it paid off immediately. … Had best finish in points up to this point of his career, topping 10th in 1988, and had career-high totals for top fives (seven) and top 10s (16). … Had second-place finishes at the Daytona 500 and Bristol. … Won his first Winston Cup pole, for the Pepsi 400 at Daytona, in his 205th career start. Also won the pole two races later at Talladega.

**1990** Finished 14th in series points. … Ran his fourth and final season with Billy Hagen. … Had 10 top 10s, including five top fives.

**1989** Finished 12th in series points. … Enjoyed another productive season with Billy Hagen with 13 top 10s. … Season-best finish was second at Charlotte.

**1988** Finished 10th in series points. … Had 13 top 10s in 29 starts and finished second at Martinsville.

**1987** Finished 11th in series points. ... Signed with Billy Hagen for his first full season since winning Winston Cup Rookie of the Year honors in 1983. ... Had eight top 10s in 29 starts.

**1986** Finished 36th in series points. ... Moved to Hoss Ellington's operation and competed in 10 races. ... Posted four top 10s, including a runner-up to Tim Richmond in the Pepsi 400 at Daytona.

**1985** Finished 37th in series points. ... Competed in only eight races, running seven for Earl Sadler and one for Helen Rae.

**1984** Finished 37th in series points. ... Made 11 starts for Earl Sadler, which included a pair of top 10s; also ran for Dick Bahre (two starts) and Jimmy Means (one).

**1983** Finished 19th in series points. ... After winning track championships at Nashville Raceway the previous three years, landed his first full-time Winston Cup ride with owner Roger Hamby. ... Won the Rookie of the Year award. ... Competed in 30 events and posted one top 10.

**1982** Made one start for Matthews Racing, finishing 23rd at the Charlotte fall race.

**1981** Made two starts, one for Coo Coo Marlin and the other for D.K. Ulrich. ... Did not finish either race.

**1980** Made five starts, driving for three different owners—Coo Coo Marlin, Jim Stacy and D.K. Ulrich. ... Had two top 10s.

**1979** Made one start for Coo Coo Marlin, at Nashville, finishing 15th.

**1978** Made two starts for his father Coo Coo's Winston Cup operation. ... Finished ninth at the World 600.

**1976** Made first Winston Cup appearance on May 8 at Nashville, where he started 30th and finished 29th. The start was the result of his father, Coo Coo, sustaining a broken shoulder and putting his 18-year-old son in the family entry.

## CAREER STATISTICS

| Year | Car Owner | Races | Champ. Finish | Won | Top 5 | Top 10 | DNF | Poles | Money Won |
|---|---|---|---|---|---|---|---|---|---|
| 1976 | Coo Coo Marlin | 1 | 101 | 0 | 0 | 0 | 1 | 0 | $ 565 |
| 1978 | Coo Coo Marlin | 2 | 67 | 0 | 0 | 1 | 1 | 0 | 10,170 |
| 1979 | Coo Coo Marlin | 1 | 85 | 0 | 0 | 0 | 1 | 0 | 505 |
| 1980 | Coo Coo Marlin | 2 | | 0 | 0 | 1 | 1 | 0 | 18,750 |
| | Jim Stacy | 2 | | 0 | 0 | 0 | 0 | 0 | 6,725 |
| | D.K. Ulrich | 1 | 49 | 0 | 0 | 1 | 0 | 0 | 4,335 |
| 1981 | Coo Coo Marlin | 1 | | 0 | 0 | 0 | 1 | 0 | 1,225 |
| | D.K. Ulrich | 1 | 93 | 0 | 0 | 0 | 1 | 0 | 730 |
| 1982 | Matthews Racing | 1 | | 0 | 0 | 0 | 1 | 0 | 4,015 |
| 1983 | Roger Hamby | 30 | 19 | 0 | 0 | 1 | 11 | 0 | 143,564 |
| 1984 | Earl Sadler | 11 | | 0 | 0 | 2 | 7 | 0 | 35,320 |
| | Dick Bahre | 2 | | 0 | 0 | 0 | 1 | 0 | 16,235 |
| | Jimmy Means | 1 | 37 | 0 | 0 | 0 | 1 | 0 | 2,800 |
| 1985 | Earl Sadler | 7 | | 0 | 0 | 0 | 5 | 0 | 29,805 |
| | Helen Rae | 1 | 37 | 0 | 0 | 0 | 1 | 0 | 1,350 |
| 1986 | Hoss Ellington | 10 | 36 | 0 | 2 | 4 | 7 | 0 | 113,070 |
| 1987 | Billy Hagan | 29 | 11 | 0 | 4 | 8 | 6 | 0 | 306,412 |
| 1988 | Billy Hagan | 29 | 10 | 0 | 6 | 13 | 6 | 0 | 521,464 |
| 1989 | Billy Hagan | 29 | 12 | 0 | 4 | 13 | 5 | 0 | 473,267 |
| 1990 | Billy Hagan | 29 | 14 | 0 | 5 | 10 | 8 | 0 | 369,167 |
| 1991 | Junior Johnson | 29 | 7 | 0 | 7 | 16 | 2 | 2 | 633,690 |
| 1992 | Junior Johnson | 29 | 10 | 0 | 6 | 13 | 4 | 5 | 649,048 |
| 1993 | Stavola Bros. | 30 | 15 | 0 | 1 | 8 | 3 | 0 | 628,835 |
| 1994 | Morgan-McClure | 31 | 14 | 1 | 5 | 11 | 7 | 1 | 1,127,683 |
| 1995 | Morgan-McClure | 31 | 3 | 3 | 9 | 22 | 2 | 1 | 2,253,502 |
| 1996 | Morgan-McClure | 31 | 8 | 2 | 5 | 10 | 6 | 0 | 1,588,425 |
| 1997 | Morgan-McClure | 32 | 25 | 0 | 2 | 6 | 8 | 0 | 1,301,370 |
| 1998 | Felix Sabates | 32 | 13 | 0 | 0 | 6 | 1 | 0 | 1,350,161 |
| 1999 | Felix Sabates | 34 | 16 | 0 | 2 | 5 | 3 | 1 | 1,797,416 |
| 2000 | Felix Sabates | 19 | | 0 | 1 | 4 | 2 | 0 | 1,091,964 |
| | | 15 | 19 | 0 | 0 | 3 | 2 | 0 | 900,337 |
| 2001 | Chip Ganassi | 36 | 3 | 2 | 12 | 20 | 2 | 1 | 4,517,634 |
| 2002 | Chip Ganassi | 29 | 18 | 2 | 8 | 14 | 3 | 0 | 4,228,889 |
| 2003 | Chip Ganassi | 36 | 18 | 0 | 0 | 11 | 8 | 0 | 4,384,491 |
| **TOTALS** | | **604** | | **10** | **79** | **203** | **118** | **11** | **$28,512,919** |

## 2003 RESULTS

| Race | Start | Finish | Standing Pos. | Winnings |
|---|---|---|---|---|
| Daytona 500 (Daytona) | 7 | 17 | 18 | $229,745 |
| Subway 400 (Rockingham) | 4 | 40 | 29 | $89,790 |
| UAW-DaimlerChrysler 400 (Las Vegas) | 34 | 8 | 19 | $136,000 |
| Bass Pro Shops MBNA 500 (Atlanta) | 34 | 14 | 20 | $93,675 |
| Carolina Dodge Dealers 400 (Darlington) | 8 | 39 | 24 | $85,915 |
| Food City 500 (Bristol) | 16 | 6 | 22 | $110,795 |
| Samsung/RadioShack 500 (Texas) | 36 | 29 | 23 | $111,475 |
| Aaron's 499 (Talladega) | 11 | 6 | 16 | $126,380 |
| Virginia 500 (Martinsville) | 25 | 7 | 12 | $97,275 |
| Auto Club 500 (California) | 30 | 10 | 13 | $121,125 |
| Pontiac Excitement 400 (Richmond) | 21 | 13 | 10 | $95,425 |
| Coca-Cola 600 (Charlotte) | 36 | 7 | 9 | $132,225 |
| MBNA Armed Forces Family 400 (Dover) | 6 | 35 | 11 | $101,695 |
| Pocono 500 (Pocono) | 23 | 6 | 10 | $104,490 |
| Sirius 400 (Michigan) | 30 | 6 | 9 | $114,540 |
| Dodge/Save Mart 350 (Sonoma) | 27 | 18 | 10 | $99,775 |
| Pepsi 400 (Daytona) | 4 | 19 | 10 | $111,225 |
| Tropicana 400 (Chicago) | 19 | 21 | 10 | $107,650 |
| New England 300 (New Hampshire) | 10 | 39 | 15 | $92,635 |
| Pennsylvania 500 (Pocono) | 20 | 10 | 15 | $97,790 |
| Brickyard 400 (Indianapolis) | 12 | 34 | 16 | $147,230 |
| Sirius at the Glen (Watkins Glen) | 37 | 43 | 16 | $86,809 |
| GFS Marketplace 400 (Michigan) | 38 | 19 | 16 | $95,390 |
| Sharpie 500 (Bristol) | 36 | 17 | 16 | $121,035 |
| Southern 500 (Darlington) | 13 | 31 | 16 | $95,255 |
| Chevy Rock & Roll 400 (Richmond) | 6 | 22 | 17 | $92,430 |
| Sylvania 300 (New Hampshire) | 9 | 29 | 17 | $94,465 |
| MBNA America 400 (Dover) | 17 | 13 | 17 | $102,540 |
| EA SPORTS 500 (Talladega) | 4 | 39 | 18 | $95,810 |
| Banquet 400 (Kansas) | 29 | 34 | 19 | $104,975 |
| UAW-GM Quality 500 (Charlotte) | 33 | 15 | 19 | $96,600 |
| Subway 500 (Martinsville) | 9 | 43 | 19 | $86,191 |
| Bass Pro Shops MBNA 500 (Atlanta) | 40 | 16 | 21 | $111,150 |
| Checker Auto Parts 500 (Phoenix) | 15 | 11 | 19 | $100,000 |
| Pop Secret 400 (Rockingham) | 31 | 10 | 19 | $99,425 |
| Ford 400 (Homestead) | 41 | 10 | 18 | $103,025 |

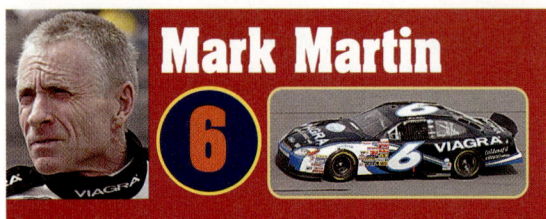

# Mark Martin

**Date of birth:** January 9, 1959 **Hometown:** Batesville, Ark. **Resides:** Daytona Beach, Fla. **Spouse:** Arlene **Children:** Amy, Rachel, Heather, Stacy, Matthew **Height:** 5-6 **Weight:** 135 **Hobbies:** Weight training, quarter-midget racing with son.

## NASCAR ACHIEVEMENTS

**First NASCAR Cup start:** April 5, 1981 (North Wilkesboro)
**Best points finish:** 2 (1990, 1994, 1998, 2002)
**Career victories:** 33—Atlanta (91b, 94b), Bristol (93b, 98b), California (98), Charlotte (92b, 95b, 98b, 02a), Darlington (93b), Dover (97b, 98b, 99b), Las Vegas (98), Martinsville (92a, 00a), Michigan (90b, 93b, 97b, 98a), North Wilkesboro (90b, 95b), Phoenix (93), Richmond (90a), Rockingham (89b, 99a), Sonoma (97), Talladega (95a, 97a), Texas (98), Watkins Glen (93, 94, 95)
**First victory:** October 22, 1989 (Rockingham)
**Career poles:** 41—Atlanta (92a), Bristol (89a, 93b, 95b, 96a, 96b, 01a), Charlotte (91a, 91b), Darlington (89a, 98a), Daytona (89b), Dover (88b, 89a, 97b, 98b), Martinsville (90b, 91a, 91b), Nashville (81b), New Hampshire (93, 95), North Wilkesboro (90a), Pocono (90b, 91a, 96b), Richmond (81b, 96b, 01a), Rockingham (93a, 93b, 97a, 98b, 99b), Sonoma (97), Talladega (89a, 89b), Watkins Glen (93, 94, 95)
**First pole:** July 9, 1981 (Nashville)
**Best career finish:** 1 **Best career start:** 1

### CAR FACTS

**Car:** No. 6 Ford
**Primary sponsor:** Viagra
**Owner:** Jack Roush
**Team:** Roush Racing
**Crew chief:** Pat Tryson
**Engine builder:** Mike Kasch

## FAST FACTS

- Has a series-leading 45 victories in the Busch Series.
- Grew up racing up short tracks throughout the Midwest.
- Won three consecutive ASA championships from 1978-80 before moving to NASCAR; returned to ASA and won the 1986 title before making a permanent move to NASCAR.
- Owns Mark Martin Performance, a company that sells quarter-midget racing chassis.
- Helped build the quarter-midget track at the New Smyrna (Fla.) Speedway.

## CAREER BY YEAR

**2003** One of several 40-something drivers to have an off year, Martin never visited victory lane and had just 10 top 10s. Four engine failures and three accidents led to Martin completing only 89.4 percent of the laps on the way to a 17th place finish in the points race. He couldn't maintain positive momentum; he never had consecutive top fives and never had more than two straight top 10s.

**2002** Finished runner-up in series points, 38 behind champion Tony Stewart. It was the fourth time in his career that he has finished second in the championship (1992, '94, '99) and 13th time he was among the top eight in points. … Had one win, which came at the Coca-Cola 600 in May at Charlotte, breaking a 73-race winless streak. … Scored 22 top 10s for Roush Racing, tying him for the series lead with rookie Ryan Newman. … Held the championship lead for two weeks late in the season.

**2001** Finished 12th in series points, his first time out of the top 10 since finishing 15th in his first season with Roush Racing in 1988. … Went winless for only the second time in the past 13 seasons and did not finish in the top three for the first time since joining Roush. … Had 15 top 10s, including pair of season-best fourths. … Won two poles, at Richmond and Bristol.

**2000** Finished eighth in series points. … Was his 12th consecutive season finishing among the top 10 in points but snapped a run of seven consecutive years among the top five. … Won at Martinsville, giving him at least one win for four straight seasons and 11 of the last 12. … Had 20 top 10s, including seven thirds. … Did not win a pole, marking the first time since joining Jack Roush in 1988 he was shut out.

**1999** Finished third in series points. … Was his third consecutive season among the top three and seventh among the top five. … Posted two wins—Rockingham and Dover—in his eighth multiple-win season. … Had 26 top 10s and 19 top fives. … Won his lone pole at Rockingham, extending his streak to 12 consecutive seasons with at least one pole.

**1998** Finished second in series points, 364 behind champion Jeff Gordon. … Had career-high victory total, with seven; previous best was five in 1993. … Was second in series in wins, trailing Gordon's 13. Victories came at Bristol, Las Vegas, California, Charlotte, Dover, Michigan and Texas. Wins at Las Vegas (inaugural event), California and Texas were the first of his career at those tracks. … Posted 17 top threes and 26 top 10s. … Tied for third in the series with three poles. … Won from the pole at Dover and added other poles at Rockingham and Darlington.

**1997** Finished third in series points. … Fifth straight season among the top five and fifth time in his career among the top three. … After going winless the previous season for the first time since 1988, bounced back with four wins. … Victory total was third in the series. Won at Sonoma, Dover, Michigan and Talladega. … The win at Sonoma came from the pole. … Had 24 top 10s, including 16 among the top five. … Co-shared the series lead for poles with Bobby Labonte, with three. Won at Dover, Rockingham and Sonoma.

**1996** Finished fifth in series points—the fourth consecutive season among the top five. … Had 23 top 10s, including 14 top fives, but did not win. … Snapped a run of seven straight seasons with at least one win. … Had four season-best runner-ups. … Ranked second in the series in poles with four, trailing only Jeff Gordon (five). … Poles came at Bristol, where he swept the top spot for both events for the second consecutive year, Pocono and Richmond.

**1995** Finished fourth in series points. … Finished third in wins (four) and second in poles (four). … Had 22 top 10s and 13 top fives. … Won at Charlotte, North Wilkesboro, Talladega and Watkins Glen. Captured Watkins Glen from the pole for the third consecutive season. … Other poles came at Bristol (twice) and New Hampshire.

**1994** Finished second in series points for second time in five seasons. Finished behind Dale Earnhardt again, but this time it was a distant 444 points. … Had two wins—at Watkins Glen from the pole for the second consecutive year and at Atlanta—and 20 top 10s. … His only pole of the season was at Watkins Glen, but it extended his streak of consecutive seasons with at least one pole to seven.

**1993** Finished third in series points for the second time in his career. … Was third in the series with a career-best five wins and second with five poles. … Wins were at Watkins Glen, Bristol, Darlington, Michigan and Phoenix. … Poles were at New Hampshire, Bristol, Watkins Glen and Rockingham (twice). … Extended string of seasons with at least one pole to six.

**1992** Finished sixth in series points for the second consecutive year. … Had two wins—Martinsville and Charlotte—and 17 top 10s. … Had one pole (Atlanta), giving him at least one pole for five consecutive years.

**1991** Finished sixth in series points. … Had one win, at Atlanta, and 14 top fives. … Led the series in poles for the first time, with five. …Won poles in both races at Charlotte and Martinsville; his other pole was at Pocono.

**1990** Finished second in series points, just 26 behind champion Dale Earnhardt. … Tied for second in series wins (three) and poles (three). … Wins came at Richmond, North Wilkesboro and Michigan; poles came at North Wilkesboro, Pocono and Martinsville. … Made 10 front-row starts. … Posted 23 top 10s and 16 top fives.

**1989** Finished third in series points. … Made a dramatic jump to a championship contender in just his second season with Jack Roush and his third full season overall. … Got his first Winston Cup win in his 113th career start, October 22 at Rockingham. … Had five runner-up finishes and 14 top fives. … Won six poles, tying Alan Kulwicki for the series' season high.

**1988** Finished 15th in series points. … Joined owner Jack Roush in what would become a long and successful relationship. … Notched 10 top 10s, including a career-best second at Bristol. … Won the pole at Dover.

**1987** Finished 101st in points, starting only one race. … Ran for Roger Hamby.

**1986** Finished 48th in series points after not running Winston Cup in 1984 and '85. … Ran five events for Gunderman Racing. … Did not record a top 10.

**1983** Finished 30th in series points. … Ran a partial schedule for four different teams, J.D. Stacy (seven races), Morgan-McClure (six), D.K. Ulrich (two) and his own (one). … Best finish came while running with Stacy; he matched his career best with a third-place finish at Darlington.

**1982** Finished 14th in series points. … Competed in his first full season as a driver/owner and finished runner-up to Geoff Bodine for Winston Cup Rookie of the Year. … Competed in 30 races, including one for Bob Rogers, and had eight top 10s.

**1981** Finished 42nd in series points. … Made his initial venture into the Winston Cup Series as a driver/owner. … Competed in five races, which included an impressive third-place finish at Martinsville and poles at Nashville and Richmond Fairgrounds. … His first career pole, at Nashville, came in just his third career start. … First career start was April 5 at North Wilkesboro, where he started fifth and finished 27th.

## CAREER STATISTICS

| Year | Car Owner | Races | Champ. Finish | Won | Top 5 | Top 10 | DNF | Poles | Money Won |
|---|---|---|---|---|---|---|---|---|---|
| 1981 | Mark Martin | 5 | 42 | 0 | 1 | 2 | 2 | 2 | $13,950 |
| 1982 | Mark Martin | 29 | | 0 | 2 | 8 | 11 | 0 | 124,215 |
| | Bob Rogers | 1 | 14 | 0 | 0 | 0 | 1 | 0 | 2,440 |
| 1983 | J.D. Stacy | 7 | | 0 | 1 | 2 | 3 | 0 | 75,240 |
| | D.K. Ulrich | 2 | | 0 | 0 | 0 | 2 | 0 | 5,745 |
| | Mark Martin | 1 | | 0 | 0 | 0 | 1 | 0 | 1,640 |
| | Morgan-McClure | 6 | 30 | 0 | 0 | 1 | 2 | 0 | 17,030 |
| 1986 | J. Gunderman | 5 | 48 | 0 | 0 | 0 | 2 | 0 | 20,515 |
| 1987 | Roger Hamby | 1 | 101 | 0 | 0 | 0 | 1 | 0 | 3,550 |
| 1988 | Jack Roush | 29 | 15 | 0 | 3 | 10 | 10 | 1 | 223,630 |
| 1989 | Jack Roush | 29 | 3 | 1 | 14 | 18 | 4 | 6 | 1,019,250 |
| 1990 | Jack Roush | 29 | 2 | 3 | 16 | 23 | 1 | 3 | 1,302,958 |
| 1991 | Jack Roush | 29 | 6 | 1 | 14 | 17 | 5 | 5 | 1,039,991 |
| 1992 | Jack Roush | 29 | 6 | 2 | 10 | 17 | 5 | 1 | 1,000,571 |
| 1993 | Jack Roush | 30 | 3 | 5 | 12 | 19 | 5 | 5 | 1,657,662 |
| 1994 | Jack Roush | 31 | 2 | 2 | 15 | 20 | 8 | 1 | 1,628,906 |
| 1995 | Jack Roush | 31 | 4 | 4 | 13 | 22 | 1 | 4 | 1,893,519 |
| 1996 | Jack Roush | 31 | 5 | 0 | 14 | 23 | 4 | 4 | 1,887,396 |
| 1997 | Jack Roush | 32 | 3 | 4 | 16 | 24 | 3 | 3 | 2,532,484 |
| 1998 | Jack Roush | 33 | 2 | 7 | 22 | 26 | 1 | 3 | 4,309,006 |
| 1999 | Jack Roush | 34 | 3 | 2 | 19 | 26 | 3 | 1 | 3,509,744 |
| 2000 | Jack Roush | 34 | 8 | 1 | 13 | 20 | 6 | 0 | 3,098,874 |
| 2001 | Jack Roush | 36 | 12 | 0 | 3 | 15 | 4 | 2 | 3,797,006 |
| 2002 | Jack Roush | 36 | 2 | 1 | 12 | 22 | 3 | 0 | 7,004,893 |
| 2003 | Jack Roush | 36 | 17 | 0 | 5 | 10 | 7 | 0 | 4,048,850 |
| **TOTALS** | | 566 | | 33 | 205 | 325 | 95 | 41 | $40,656,775 |

## 2003 RESULTS

| Race | Start | Finish | Standing Pos. | Winnings |
|---|---|---|---|---|
| Daytona 500 (Daytona) | 26 | 5 | 5 | $444,609 |
| Subway 400 (Rockingham) | 3 | 7 | 4 | $93,443 |
| UAW-DaimlerChrysler 400 (Las Vegas) | 29 | 43 | 11 | $91,542 |
| Bass Pro Shops MBNA 500 (Atlanta) | 29 | 42 | 25 | $79,843 |
| Carolina Dodge Dealers 400 (Darlington) | 27 | 4 | 16 | $114,813 |
| Food City 500 (Bristol) | 19 | 29 | 23 | $95,368 |
| Samsung/RadioShack 500 (Texas) | 32 | 5 | 13 | $173,058 |
| Aaron's 499 (Talladega) | 9 | 26 | 14 | $102,783 |

| Race | Start | Standing Finish | Pos. | Winnings |
|---|---|---|---|---|
| Virginia 500 (Martinsville) | 24 | 17 | 15 | $85,433 |
| Auto Club 500 (California) | 22 | 17 | 14 | $107,358 |
| Pontiac Excitement 400 (Richmond) | 30 | 5 | 12 | $102,533 |
| Coca-Cola 600 (Charlotte) | 21 | 29 | 13 | $107,183 |
| MBNA Armed Forces Family 400 (Dover) | 32 | 18 | 15 | $97,968 |
| Pocono 500 (Pocono) | 6 | 2 | 11 | $152,278 |
| Sirius 400 (Michigan) | 15 | 9 | 10 | $96,248 |
| Dodge/Save Mart 350 (Sonoma) | 17 | 19 | 12 | $93,208 |
| Pepsi 400 (Daytona) | 33 | 20 | 12 | $106,708 |
| Tropicana 400 (Chicago) | 13 | 14 | 12 | $103,883 |
| New England 300 (New Hampshire) | 12 | 18 | 12 | $90,133 |
| Pennsylvania 500 (Pocono) | 14 | 41 | 16 | $75,923 |
| Brickyard 400 (Indianapolis) | 25 | 9 | 15 | $180,433 |
| Sirius at the Glen (Watkins Glen) | 3 | 10 | 15 | $90,598 |
| GFS Marketplace 400 (Michigan) | 37 | 17 | 14 | $89,323 |
| Sharpie 500 (Bristol) | 2 | 36 | 14 | $94,813 |
| Southern 500 (Darlington) | 7 | 33 | 15 | $85,638 |
| Chevy Rock & Roll 400 (Richmond) | 3 | 13 | 14 | $89,463 |
| Sylvania 300 (New Hampshire) | 33 | 28 | 16 | $87,583 |
| MBNA America 400 (Dover) | 16 | 22 | 16 | $91,323 |
| EA SPORTS 500 (Talladega) | 15 | 23 | 16 | $92,103 |
| Banquet 400 (Kansas) | 38 | 20 | 16 | $103,483 |
| UAW-GM Quality 500 (Charlotte) | 27 | 11 | 17 | $93,108 |
| Subway 500 (Martinsville) | 23 | 14 | 17 | $85,008 |
| Bass Pro Shops MBNA 500 (Atlanta) | 39 | 39 | 17 | $95,833 |
| Checker Auto Parts 500 (Phoenix) | 12 | 10 | 17 | $99,133 |
| Pop Secret 400 (Rockingham) | 12 | 41 | 17 | $79,773 |
| Ford 400 (Homestead) | 40 | 33 | 17 | $79,113 |

## Jeremy Mayfield

**Date of birth**: May 27, 1969 **Hometown**: Owensboro, Ky.
**Resides**: Mooresville, N.C. **Spouse**: Shana **Children**: None
**Height**: 6-0 **Weight**: 190 **Hobbies**: Four-wheel vehicles

## NASCAR ACHIEVEMENTS

**First NASCAR Cup start:** October 10, 1993 (Charlotte)
**Best points finish:** 7 (1998)
**Career victories:** 3—California (00), Pocono (98a, 00a)
**First victory:** June 1, 1998 (Pocono)
**Career poles:** 7—Darlington (00b), Dover (00b), Rockingham (00b), Talladega (96b, 00a, 03a), Texas (98)
**First pole:** July 6, 1998 (Talladega)
**Best career finish:** 1  **Best career start:** 1

## FAST FACTS

- Began racing go-karts in 1982 and then moved up through the weekly programs at tracks in central Tennessee.
- Raced street stocks, sportsman and late-model stocks in Tennessee.
- Was the 1987 Kentucky Motor Speedway Rookie of the Year.
- Was the ARCA Rookie of the Year in 1993, with eight top fives and 10 top 10s.
- Favorite driver is childhood hero Darrell Waltrip.

## CAR FACTS

**Car:** No. 19 Dodge
**Primary sponsor:** Dodge Dealers/UAW
**Owner:** Ray Evernham
**Team:** Evernham Motorsports
**Crew chief:** Ken Francis
**Engine builder:** Evernham Engine Technologies

## CAREER BY YEAR

**2003** Mayfield had a rough first half but a strong second half. After 21 races, he was 30th in points, but a strong surge helped him finish 19th. After finishing eighth in the season opener at Daytona, he didn't crack the top 10 again until the season's 16th race, when he started a stretch of three straight top 10s. All told, he had four top fives, all in the last 11 races, and 12 top 10s.
**2002** Finished 26th in series points, his third consecutive finish out of the top 20. … Completed first season for Evernham Motorsports. … Scored a pair of top fives, a second at Las Vegas and fifth in the Richmond spring race.
**2001** Finished 35th in series points. … Finished second twice but parted ways with the No. 12 Penske South team after the inaugural Protection One 400 at Kansas Speedway.
**2000** Finished 24th in series points. … His roller-coaster season included two wins, four poles and 11 DNFs. … Won the NAPA Auto Parts 500 at California in April, then passed Dale Earnhardt on the final lap to win Pocono 500 in June. … Missed two races after sustaining a head injury in a practice accident at the Brickyard 400 in Indianapolis.
**1999** Finished 11th in series points. … Highlight of his year was a second-place finish at Darlington in the spring.
**1998** Finished seventh in series points, leading the points race four times in the first 16 races. … First career victory was at Pocono, passing Darrell Waltrip for the lead 20 laps from the end. … Won the No Bull Sprint qualifier and the Winston Open. … Won his second career pole at Texas.
**1997** Finished 13th in series points in his first full year with Michael Kranefuss. … Best finish was fourth at Daytona in July, after starting 25th.
**1996** Finished 26th in series points. … Went through a mid-season driver swap, starting the season with Cale Yarborough, then switching to the Michael Kranefuss team when John Andretti did the reverse. … Scored a fourth- and fifth-place finish with Yarborough, winning his first career pole in July at Talladega.
**1995** Finished 31st in series points in his first full Winston Cup season. … Registered one top 10, at Pocono.
**1994** Finished 37th in series points. … Ran four races each with Earl Sadler and T.W. Taylor before moving to Cale Yarborough's team for final 12 races of the season.
**1993** Made his Winston Cup debut at Charlotte in October, finishing 29th in his only start of the season.

## CAREER STATISTICS

| Year | Car Owner | Champ. Races | Finish | Won | Top 5 | Top 10 | DNF | Poles | Money Won |
|---|---|---|---|---|---|---|---|---|---|
| 1993 | E. Sadler | 1 | 74 | 0 | 0 | 0 | 0 | 0 | $4,830 |
| 1994 | E. Sadler | 4 | | 0 | 0 | 0 | 2 | 0 | 48,255 |
| | T.W. Taylor | 4 | | 0 | 0 | 0 | 0 | 0 | 40,145 |
| | C. Yarborough | 12 | 37 | 0 | 0 | 0 | 3 | 0 | 137,865 |
| 1995 | C. Yarborough | 27 | 31 | 0 | 0 | 1 | 2 | 0 | 436,805 |
| 1996 | C. Yarborough | 23 | | 0 | 2 | 2 | 4 | 1 | 463,863 |
| | M. Kranefuss | 7 | 26 | 0 | 0 | 0 | 4 | 0 | 128,990 |
| 1997 | M. Kranefuss | 32 | 13 | 0 | 3 | 8 | 3 | 0 | 1,067,203 |
| 1998 | Penske-Kranefuss | 33 | 7 | 1 | 12 | 16 | 2 | 1 | 2,332,034 |
| 1999 | Penske-Kranefuss | 34 | 11 | 0 | 5 | 12 | 4 | 0 | 2,125,227 |
| 2000 | Penske-Kranefuss | 27 | | 2 | 4 | 10 | 9 | 3 | 1,617,951 |
| | Roger Penske | 5 | 24 | 0 | 2 | 2 | 2 | 1 | 551,300 |
| 2001 | Roger Penske | 28 | 35 | 0 | 5 | 7 | 4 | 0 | 2,682,603 |
| 2002 | Ray Evernham | 36 | 26 | 0 | 2 | 4 | 7 | 0 | 2,494,583 |
| 2003 | Ray Evernham | 36 | 19 | 0 | 4 | 12 | 6 | 1 | 3,371,879 |
| TOTALS | | 309 | | 3 | 39 | 74 | 52 | 7 | $17,595,675 |

## 2003 RESULTS

| Race | Start | Finish | Standing Pos. | Winnings |
|---|---|---|---|---|
| Daytona 500 (Daytona) | 20 | 8 | 8 | $245,026 |
| Subway 400 (Rockingham) | 29 | 41 | 22 | $53,670 |
| UAW-DaimlerChrysler 400 (Las Vegas) | 13 | 21 | 24 | $78,850 |
| Bass Pro Shops MBNA 500 (Atlanta) | 10 | 22 | 24 | $59,435 |
| Carolina Dodge Dealers 400 (Darlington) | 11 | 30 | 26 | $53,985 |
| Food City 500 (Bristol) | 18 | 23 | 29 | $72,045 |
| Samsung/RadioShack 500 (Texas) | 27 | 25 | 29 | $85,525 |
| Aaron's 499 (Talladega) | 1 | 18 | 29 | $84,285 |
| Virginia 500 (Martinsville) | 23 | 40 | 32 | $51,665 |
| Auto Club 500 (California) | 11 | 35 | 33 | $73,750 |
| Pontiac Excitement 400 (Richmond) | 19 | 25 | 30 | $59,050 |
| Coca-Cola 600 (Charlotte) | 22 | 43 | 33 | $76,590 |
| MBNA Armed Forces Family 400 (Dover) | 3 | 21 | 33 | $71,885 |
| Pocono 500 (Pocono) | 33 | 15 | 32 | $59,640 |
| Sirius 400 (Michigan) | 20 | 13 | 29 | $67,290 |
| Dodge/Save Mart 350 (Sonoma) | 31 | 10 | 27 | $80,335 |
| Pepsi 400 (Daytona) | 10 | 8 | 27 | $87,175 |
| Tropicana 400 (Chicago) | 5 | 10 | 25 | $85,075 |
| New England 300 (New Hampshire) | 25 | 34 | 27 | $57,400 |
| Pennsylvania 500 (Pocono) | 15 | 38 | 28 | $50,500 |
| Brickyard 400 (Indianapolis) | 10 | 41 | 30 | $113,703 |
| Sirius at the Glen (Watkins Glen) | 40 | 16 | 29 | $59,600 |
| GFS Marketplace 400 (Michigan) | 40 | 28 | 29 | $60,325 |
| Sharpie 500 (Bristol) | 29 | 10 | 28 | $88,740 |
| Southern 500 (Darlington) | )15 | 6 | 27 | $78,355 |
| Chevy Rock & Roll 400 (Richmond) | 23 | 2 | 24 | $136,365 |
| Sylvania 300 (New Hampshire) | 10 | 11 | 25 | $69,750 |
| MBNA America 400 (Dover) | 25 | 2 | 22 | $140,635 |
| EA SPORTS 500 (Talladega) | 22 | 38 | 24 | $59,875 |
| Banquet 400 (Kansas) | 16 | 3 | 21 | $127,175 |
| UAW-GM Quality 500 (Charlotte) | 32 | 12 | 20 | $65,125 |
| Subway 500 (Martinsville) | 30 | 33 | 20 | $52,270 |
| Bass Pro Shops MBNA 500 (Atlanta) | 15 | 7 | 19 | $89,200 |
| Checker Auto Parts 500 (Phoenix) | 16 | 43 | 20 | $54,471 |
| Pop Secret 400 (Rockingham) | 3 | 3 | 20 | $88,700 |
| Ford 400 (Homestead) | 9 | 6 | 19 | $90,975 |

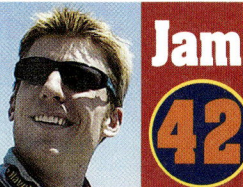

# Jamie McMurray
## 42

**Date of birth:** June 3, 1976 **Hometown:** Joplin, Mo. **Spouse:** Single **Children:** None **Height:** 5-8 **Weight:** 150 **Hobbies:** Radio-controlled cars

## NASCAR ACHIEVEMENTS

**First NASCAR Cup start:** October 6, 2002 (Talladega)
**Best points finish:** 46 (2002)
**Career victories:** 1—Charlotte (02b)
**First victory:** October 13, 2002 (Charlotte)
**Career poles:** 1
**First pole:** November 14, 2003 (Homestead)
**Best career finish:** 1  **Best career start:** 1

## FAST FACTS

- NASCAR's version of Mr. October won his first two Busch Series races and his first Winston Cup event within a four-week period in 2002.
- Ran in 69 Busch Series races from 2000-02, winning twice and earning six top fives and 17 top 10s.
- Finished third in the Busch Series Raybestos Rookie of the Year standings in 2001.
- Finishing 22nd in the 2000 Craftsman Truck Series standings.
- Ran five Craftsman Truck Series races in 1999 while also racing in the NASCAR RE/MAX Challenge Series.
- Ran in the NASCAR Winston Racing Series at several tracks in his home state of Missouri, most notably the I-44 Speedway, where he was track champion in 1997.
- Competed in the Grand American Late Model class from 1996-98 and in the Grand American Modified division from 1994-95.
- Began racing Late Models at age 16 and go-karts at age 8.
- Won four U.S. Go-Kart titles between 1986-92 and was the World Go-Kart champion in 1991.
- Selected as one of only 10 Americans to represent the U.S. in an international karting event in the former Soviet Union in 1989.
- His Busch Series victory on October 26, 2002, gave him

## CAR FACTS

**Car:** No. 42 Dodge
**Primary sponsor:** Havoline
**Owners:** Chip Ganassi/Felix Sabates
**Team:** Chip Ganassi Racing with Felix Sabates
**Crew chief:** Donnie Wingo
**Engine builder:** Robert Fisher

the distinction of becoming the 100th driver to win a Busch race.
- Became associated with 2002 Winston Cup champion Tony Stewart during their days on the go-kart circuit while Stewart was in the junior class and McMurray was in the rookie-junior class.

## CAREER BY YEAR

**2003** The Raybestos Rookie of the Year, McMurray didn't visit victory lane but was consistent in the second half of the season. He finished outside the top 20 just once in the last 13 races. His best finishes were a pair of thirds, one at Indianapolis and the other in the second Bristol race. He struggled at the two superspeeedways (Daytona and Talladega), with an average finish of 28th. McMurray won his first career Cup pole at the season finale at Homestead.

**2002** Finished 46th in series points. ... Won his first Winston Cup race in only his second start—at Charlotte in October, by holding off Bobby Labonte on the last lap; became just the 11th time a driver won within two Winston Cup starts. ... Was announced in early September as the surprising selection for Chip Ganassi with Felix Sabates' Havoline Dodge ride in 2003 but got the nod to finish the season's six remaining Winston Cup races following a neck injury to Sterling Marlin that ended the veteran's chase for the championship after the Kansas race in September.

### CAREER STATISTICS

| Year | Car Owner | Champ. Races | Finish | Won | Top 5 | Top 10 | DNF | Poles | Money Won |
|---|---|---|---|---|---|---|---|---|---|
| 2002 | Chip Ganassi | 6 | 46 | 1 | 1 | 2 | 1 | 0 | $717,942 |
| 2003 | Chip Ganassi | 36 | 13 | 0 | 5 | 13 | 4 | 1 | 3,258,806 |
| TOTALS | | 42 | | 1 | 6 | 15 | 5 | 1 | $3,976,748 |

### 2003 RESULTS

| Race | Start | Finish | Standing Pos. | Winnings |
|---|---|---|---|---|
| Daytona 500 (Daytona) | 19 | 31 | 31 | $171,195 |
| Subway 400 (Rockingham) | 7 | 5 | 18 | $59,375 |
| UAW-DaimlerChrysler 400 (Las Vegas) | 12 | 32 | 21 | $59,700 |
| Bass Pro Shops MBNA 500 (Atlanta) | 31 | 36 | 29 | $46,255 |
| Carolina Dodge Dealers 400 (Darlington) | 19 | 22 | 28 | $43,965 |
| Food City 500 (Bristol) | 26 | 11 | 26 | $63,245 |
| Samsung/RadioShack 500 (Texas) | 24 | 10 | 21 | $101,150 |
| Aaron's 499 (Talladega) | 14 | 27 | 22 | $65,395 |
| Virginia 500 (Martinsville) | 11 | 39 | 30 | $43,740 |
| Auto Club 500 (California) | 25 | 5 | 24 | $101,575 |
| Pontiac Excitement 400 (Richmond) | 22 | 22 | 24 | $47,975 |
| Coca-Cola 600 (Charlotte) | 17 | 25 | 25 | $71,125 |
| MBNA Armed Forces Family 400 (Dover) | 19 | 13 | 21 | $68,970 |
| Pocono 500 (Pocono) | 28 | 32 | 24 | $43,565 |
| Sirius 400 (Michigan) | 39 | 14 | 22 | $63,590 |
| Dodge/Save Mart 350 (Sonoma) | 26 | 20 | 22 | $62,525 |
| Pepsi 400 (Daytona) | 8 | 37 | 23 | $63,475 |
| Tropicana 400 (Chicago) | 10 | 8 | 22 | $77,375 |
| New England 300 (New Hampshire) | 22 | 40 | 23 | $48,550 |
| Pennsylvania 500 (Pocono) | 12 | 28 | 25 | $47,190 |
| Brickyard 400 (Indianapolis) | 22 | 3 | 21 | $258,275 |
| Sirius at the Glen (Watkins Glen) | 29 | 22 | 22 | $50,715 |
| GFS Marketplace 400 (Michigan) | 26 | 36 | 23 | $48,490 |
| Sharpie 500 (Bristol) | 31 | 3 | 22 | $127,390 |
| Southern 500 (Darlington) | 17 | 4 | 21 | $90,765 |
| Chevy Rock & Roll 400 (Richmond) | 29 | 19 | 20 | $53,930 |
| Sylvania 300 (New Hampshire) | 3 | 10 | 18 | $68,650 |
| MBNA America 400 (Dover) | 18 | 6 | 18 | $71,890 |
| EA SPORTS 500 (Talladega) | 2 | 16 | 17 | $67,425 |
| Banquet 400 (Kansas) | 15 | 8 | 17 | $77,175 |
| UAW-GM Quality 500 (Charlotte) | 19 | 7 | 16 | $67,225 |
| Subway 500 (Martinsville) | 17 | 8 | 15 | $57,125 |
| Bass Pro Shops MBNA 500 (Atlanta) | 18 | 15 | 15 | $74,400 |
| Checker Auto Parts 500 (Phoenix) | 22 | 12 | 14 | $59,900 |
| Pop Secret 400 (Rockingham) | 21 | 35 | 15 | $46,300 |
| Ford 400 (Homestead) | 1 | 9 | 13 | $65,725 |

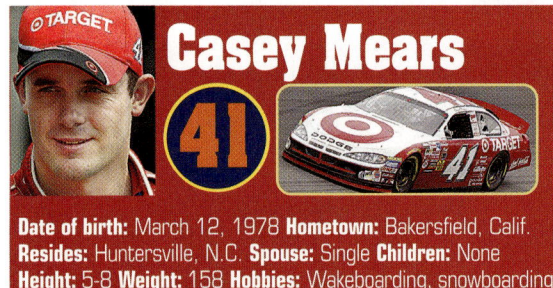

**Casey Mears** · 41

**Date of birth:** March 12, 1978 **Hometown:** Bakersfield, Calif. **Resides:** Huntersville, N.C. **Spouse:** Single **Children:** None **Height:** 5-8 **Weight:** 158 **Hobbies:** Wakeboarding, snowboarding

## NASCAR ACHIEVEMENTS

**First NASCAR Cup start:** February 16, 2003 (Daytona)
**Best points finish:** 35 (2003)
**Career victories:** 0
**Career poles:** 0
**Best career finish:** 15  **Best career start:** 4

## FAST FACTS

- Finished 21st in his rookie season in the Busch Series in 2002, scoring one top five.
- In 2001, had two top 10s in four starts in CART after replacing Alex Zanardi, who was involved in a career-ending crash.
- Finished ninth at Talladega in his lone ARCA start in 2001.
- In 2000, finished third in the Indy Lights Series, scoring his first win at the Grand Prix of Houston.
- Made his first CART start at California Speedway in 2000, finishing a career-best fourth.
- Finished second in the

### CAR FACTS

**Car:** No. 41 Dodge
**Primary sponsor:** Target
**Owners:** Chip Ganassi/Felix Sabates
**Team:** Chip Ganassi Racing with Felix Sabates
**Crew chief:** Jimmy Elledge
**Engine builder:** Robert Fisher

Indy Lights Series in 1999, becoming only the fourth driver in series history to complete every lap.
- Won three races in off-road stadium SuperLites in 1996.
- Won the 1995 Jim Russell USAC Triple Crown Championship at age 17.
- Is the nephew of four-time Indy 500 winner Rick Mears.
- Is the son of two-time Indy 500 starter and off-road legend Roger Mears.
- Was the second-youngest driver in USAC history to win a feature race (Mesa Marin, 1994) at age 16.
- Began racing BMX bicycles at age 4.

## CAREER BY YEAR

**2003** Coming from open-wheel racing, Mears still is figuring out stock cars. Driving in good equipment for Chip Ganassi, his average finish was 30th.

### CAREER STATISTICS

| Year | Car Owner | Races | Champ. Finish | Won | Top 5 | Top 10 | DNF | Poles | Money Won |
|---|---|---|---|---|---|---|---|---|---|
| 2003 | Chip Ganassi | 36 | 35 | 0 | 0 | 0 | 10 | 0 | $2,639,180 |

### 2003 RESULTS

| Race | Start | Finish | Standing Pos. | Winnings |
|---|---|---|---|---|
| Daytona 500 (Daytona) | 29 | 27 | 27 | $184,420 |
| Subway 400 (Rockingham) | 16 | 30 | 30 | $58,100 |
| UAW-DaimlerChrysler 400 (Las Vegas) | 18 | 15 | 25 | $105,100 |
| Bass Pro Shops MBNA 500 (Atlanta) | 33 | 23 | 27 | $70,535 |
| Carolina Dodge Dealers 400 (Darlington) | 24 | 34 | 30 | $50,165 |
| Food City 500 (Bristol) | 39 | 32 | 31 | $67,845 |
| Samsung/RadioShack 500 (Texas) | 26 | 27 | 34 | $82,475 |
| Aaron's 499 (Talladega) | 10 | 40 | 35 | $71,090 |
| Virginia 500 (Martinsville) | 22 | 36 | 36 | $54,400 |
| Auto Club 500 (California) | 17 | 34 | 37 | $76,425 |
| Pontiac Excitement 400 (Richmond) | 11 | 28 | 37 | $66,864 |
| Coca-Cola 600 (Charlotte) | 19 | 35 | 39 | $79,700 |
| MBNA Armed Forces Family 400 (Dover) | 22 | 40 | 39 | $65,120 |
| Pocono 500 (Pocono) | 19 | 21 | 36 | $69,990 |
| Sirius 400 (Michigan) | 22 | 20 | 36 | $80,190 |
| Dodge/Save Mart 350 (Sonoma) | 33 | 26 | 34 | $66,300 |
| Pepsi 400 (Daytona) | 12 | 25 | 34 | $85,639 |
| Tropicana 400 (Chicago) | 4 | 34 | 34 | $68,975 |
| New England 300 (New Hampshire) | 35 | 16 | 34 | $75,514 |
| Pennsylvania 500 (Pocono) | 10 | 35 | 34 | $50,990 |
| Brickyard 400 (Indianapolis) | 28 | 29 | 34 | $116,275 |
| Sirius at the Glen (Watkins Glen) | 12 | 32 | 34 | $52,150 |
| GFS Marketplace 400 (Michigan) | 16 | 41 | 34 | $56,200 |
| Sharpie 500 (Bristol) | 41 | 21 | 34 | $86,249 |
| Southern 500 (Darlington) | 21 | 35 | 34 | $58,580 |
| Chevy Rock & Roll 400 (Richmond) | 31 | 41 | 34 | $54,830 |
| Sylvania 300 (New Hampshire) | 18 | 17 | 33 | $75,500 |
| MBNA America 400 (Dover) | 35 | 36 | 34 | $60,000 |
| EA SPORTS 500 (Talladega) | 8 | 37 | 34 | $59,925 |
| Banquet 400 (Kansas) | 12 | 24 | 34 | $85,625 |
| UAW-GM Quality 500 (Charlotte) | 28 | 42 | 34 | $52,830 |
| Subway 500 (Martinsville) | 35 | 17 | 34 | $71,175 |
| Bass Pro Shops MBNA 500 (Atlanta) | 14 | 28 | 34 | $82,864 |
| Checker Auto Parts 500 (Phoenix) | 9 | 42 | 35 | $54,350 |
| Pop Secret 400 (Rockingham) | 39 | 33 | 35 | $55,450 |
| Ford 400 (Homestead) | 15 | 27 | 35 | $56,800 |

# Joe Nemechek

**Date of birth:** September 26, 1963 **Hometown:** Lakeland, Fla.
**Resides:** Mooresville, N.C. **Spouse:** Andrea **Children:** John, Blair
**Height:** 5-9 **Weight:** 185 **Hobbies:** Fishing, skiing

## NASCAR ACHIEVEMENTS

**First NASCAR Cup start:** July 11, 1993 (New Hampshire)
**Best points finish:** 15 (2000)
**Career victories:** 3—New Hampshire (99b), Richmond (03a), Rockingham (01b)
**First victory:** September 19, 1999 (New Hampshire)
**Career poles:** 6—California (97), Daytona (99b), Martinsville (99b), Pocono (97b), Talladega (99b, 00b)
**First pole:** June 22, 1997 (California)
**Best career finish:** 1  **Best career start:** 1

## FAST FACTS

- Finished second in a Craftsman Truck event at Watkins Glen in 1996.
- Won 1992 Busch Series championship, edging Bobby Labonte by three points, the closest champion's margin in the history of NASCAR's three national series.
- Named the Busch Series Rookie of the Year in 1990.
- Won the championship and Rookie of the Year honors in NASCAR's All-Pro Series in 1989.
- Won the championship and Rookie of the Year honors in the United Stock Car Alliance series in 1988.
- Named Lakeland Interstate Speedway's Rookie of the Year in 1987.
- Began racing in 1983, in motocross; won more than 300 trophies in six years of competition.

### CAR FACTS

**Car:** No. 01 Chevrolet
**Primary sponsor:** U.S. Army
**Owner:** Nelson Bowers
**Team:** MB2 Motorsports
**Crew chief:** Ryan Pemberton
**Engine builder:** Hendrick Motorsports

## CAREER BY YEAR

**2003** Front Row Joe looked primed for a strong season after winning at Richmond in May. But Nemechek had only three top 10s the rest of the season and eventually lost his job with Hendrick Motorsports. He ran the last four races of the season for MB2. Overall, he had two top fives, six top 10s and six DNFs.

**2002** Finished 34th in series points … Had three top fives, which tied his career high for a season that was established in 2000 with Andy Petree. … Finished a season-best second at Atlanta in the fall and at Homestead in the season finale. … Began the season with Haas-Carter Motorsports but was limited to only seven starts before the team ceased operations; his last start for the team was at California. … Started the next race at Richmond as a replacement for injured Johnny Benson and finished 12th. … Got a major break the following event as well, replacing Jerry Nadeau in the No. 25 Henrick Motorsports entry for the remainder of the season.

**2001** Finished 28th in series points. … Second season with Andy Petree was not as strong as the first, but he got the second victory of his career when he won the November race at Rockingham. … Added three other top 10s.

**2000** Finished a career-best 15th in series points. … Departed from Felix Sabates' operation after three seasons and joined Andy Petree. … Posted a career-best nine top 10s, including three top fives. … Finished a season-best second at New Hampshire and won a pole at Talladega.

**1999** Finished 30th in series points. … Season was highlighted by his first career victory, on September 19 at New Hampshire, also the site of his first start in 1993. … Won a career-best three poles—at Daytona's Pepsi 400, Martinsville and Talladega.

**1998** Finished 26th in series points. … Posted four top 10s in his second season with Felix Sabates. … Posted his first top five since 1995, finishing fourth at Texas.

**1997** Finished 28th in series points. … After two seasons as an owner/driver, opted to focus solely on driving and run for owner Felix Sabates. … Had only three top 10s but started on the front row five times and from the pole twice.

**1996** Finished 34th in series points. … Ran his second full season as an owner/driver. … Competed in 29 races and scored two top 10s.

**1995** Finished 28th in series points. … Returned to being an owner/driver, competing in his own entry in 29 events. … Had four top 10, including a season-best of fourth at Dover.

**1994** Finished 27th in series points. … Completed his first full season in the series, running for owner Larry Hedrick. … Competed in 29 races and recorded three top 10s. … Notched his first career top five, a third at Pocono.

**1993** Finished 44th in series points. … Following a Busch Series championship in 1992, ventured into the Winston Cup ranks for a limited five-race schedule. Ran three races for his own organization and another two for Morgan-McClure. … First start was July 11 at New Hampshire, where he began 15th and finished 36th.

## CAREER STATISTICS

| Year | Car Owner | Champ. Races | Champ. Finish | Won | Top 5 | Top 10 | DNF | Poles | Money Won |
|---|---|---|---|---|---|---|---|---|---|
| 1993 | J. Nemechek | 3 | | 0 | 0 | 0 | 2 | 0 | $24,300 |
| | Morgan-McClure | 2 | 44 | 0 | 0 | 0 | 0 | 0 | 32,280 |
| 1994 | L. Hedrick | 29 | 27 | 0 | 1 | 3 | 9 | 0 | 389,565 |
| 1995 | J. Nemechek | 29 | 28 | 0 | 1 | 4 | 5 | 0 | 428,925 |
| 1996 | J. Nemechek | 29 | 34 | 0 | 0 | 2 | 8 | 0 | 666,247 |
| 1997 | F. Sabates | 30 | 28 | 0 | 0 | 3 | 5 | 2 | 732,194 |
| 1998 | F. Sabates | 32 | 26 | 0 | 1 | 4 | 5 | 0 | 1,343,991 |
| 1999 | F. Sabates | 34 | 30 | 1 | 1 | 3 | 5 | 3 | 1,634,946 |
| 2000 | A. Petree | 34 | 15 | 0 | 3 | 9 | 6 | 1 | 2,105,041 |
| 2001 | A. Petree | 31 | 28 | 1 | 1 | 4 | 6 | 0 | 2,543,660 |
| 2002 | T. Carter | 7 | | 0 | 0 | 0 | | 0 | 612,062 |
| | N. Bowers | 1 | | 0 | 0 | 0 | | 0 | 74,710 |
| | R. Hendrick | 25 | 34 | 0 | 3 | 3 | | 0 | 1,766,252 |
| | Rick Hendrick | 25 | 34 | 0 | 3 | 3 | | 0 | $1,766,252 |
| 2003 | Rick Hendrick | 32 | | 1 | 2 | 5 | 7 | 0 | $2,289,060 |
| | Nelson Bowers | 4 | 25 | 0 | 0 | 1 | 0 | 0 | $337,424 |
| **TOTALS** | | 322 | | 3 | 13 | 41 | 58 | 6 | $14,982,115 |

## 2003 RESULTS

| Race | Start | Finish | Standing Pos. | Winnings |
|---|---|---|---|---|
| Daytona 500 (Daytona) | 15 | 22 | 22 | $180,595 |
| Subway 400 (Rockingham) | 14 | 23 | 20 | $52,360 |
| UAW-DaimlerChrysler 400 (Las Vegas) | 26 | 9 | 12 | $87,200 |
| Bass Pro Shops MBNA 500 (Atlanta) | 13 | 9 | 11 | $58,225 |
| Carolina Dodge Dealers 400 (Darlington) | 38 | 13 | 9 | $51,465 |
| Food City 500 (Bristol) | 25 | 27 | 12 | $62,005 |
| Samsung/RadioShack 500 (Texas) | 9 | 35 | 17 | $60,125 |
| Aaron's 499 (Talladega) | 29 | 21 | 17 | $70,695 |
| Virginia 500 (Martinsville) | 6 | 15 | 17 | $53,750 |
| Auto Club 500 (California) | 9 | 32 | 20 | $69,325 |
| Pontiac Excitement 400 (Richmond) | 2 | 1 | 14 | $159,375 |
| Coca-Cola 600 (Charlotte) | 7 | 11 | 11 | $84,740 |
| MBNA Armed Forces Family 400 (Dover) | 37 | 24 | 13 | $62,630 |
| Pocono 500 (Pocono) | 15 | 38 | 18 | $42,500 |
| Sirius 400 (Michigan) | 12 | 21 | 18 | $54,540 |
| Dodge/Save Mart 350 (Sonoma) | 21 | 35 | 20 | $54,805 |
| Pepsi 400 (Daytona) | 20 | 38 | 22 | $63,325 |
| Tropicana 400 (Chicago) | 17 | 42 | 24 | $59,395 |
| New England 300 (New Hampshire) | 24 | 29 | 25 | $52,965 |
| Pennsylvania 500 (Pocono) | 26 | 7 | 22 | $65,190 |
| Brickyard 400 (Indianapolis) | 7 | 37 | 25 | $102,790 |
| Sirius at the Glen (Watkins Glen) | 21 | 17 | 24 | $50,830 |
| GFS Marketplace 400 (Michigan) | 25 | 20 | 24 | $56,790 |
| Sharpie 500 (Bristol) | 38 | 19 | 24 | $70,325 |
| Southern 500 (Darlington) | 26 | 21 | 23 | $57,415 |
| Chevy Rock & Roll 400 (Richmond) | 11 | 26 | 26 | $51,030 |
| Sylvania 300 (New Hampshire) | 25 | 3 | 24 | $101,980 |
| MBNA America 400 (Dover) | 24 | 43 | 26 | $51,330 |
| EA SPORTS 500 (Talladega) | 27 | 25 | 25 | $57,005 |
| Banquet 400 (Kansas) | 30 | 37 | 25 | $60,375 |
| UAW-GM Quality 500 (Charlotte) | 40 | 31 | 26 | $47,950 |
| Subway 500 (Martinsville) | 22 | 20 | 25 | $50,925 |
| Bass Pro Shops MBNA 500 (Atlanta) | 8 | 10 | 25 | $92,225 |
| Checker Auto Parts 500 (Phoenix) | 10 | 31 | 24 | $50,925 |
| Pop Secret 400 (Rockingham) | 6 | 25 | 24 | $61,875 |
| Ford 400 (Homestead) | 8 | 17 | 25 | $66,400 |

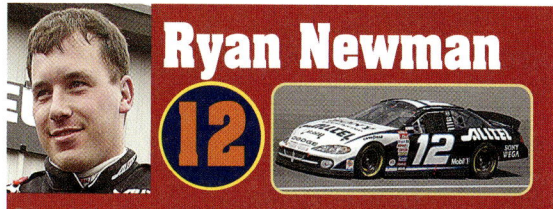

# Ryan Newman

**Date of birth:** December 8, 1977 **Hometown:** South Bend, Ind. **Resides:** Sherrills Ford, N.C. **Spouse:** Single **Children:** None **Height:** 5-11 **Weight:** 207 **Hobbies:** Fishing, radio-controlled cars

## NASCAR ACHIEVEMENTS

**First NASCAR Cup start:** November 5, 2000 (Phoenix)
**Best points finish:** 6 (2002, 2003)
**Career victories:** 9—Chicago (03), Dover (03a, 03b), Kansas (03), Michigan (03b), New Hampshire (02b), Pocono (03b), Richmond (03b), Texas (03)
**First victory:** September 15, 2002 (New Hampshire)
**Career poles:** 18—Atlanta (03a, 03b), Bristol (03a), California (02), Charlotte (01a, 03a, 03b), Chicago (02), Darlington (03b), Dover (03a), Martinsville (02b), New Hampshire (02b, 03b), Phoenix (02, 03), Pocono (03b), Rockingham (02b, 03b)
**First pole:** May 25, 2001 (Charlotte)
**Best career finish:** 1 **Best career start:** 1

## FAST FACTS

- Ran 15 Busch Series races in 2001, winning one.
- Made his stock-car debut in an ARCA race at Michigan in 2000, then won the next race he entered at Pocono; also won ARCA races that year at Kentucky and Charlotte.
- Won the 1999 USAC Coors Light Silver Bullet Series national championship with two wins and 12 top 10s.
- Won seven times in midgets and once in sprint cars.
- Named Rookie of the Year in Sprint Cars (1999), USAC Silver Crown (1996) and USAC National Midgets (1995).
- Was the 1993 All-American Midget Series champion and Rookie of the Year.
- Is a member of the Quarter-Midget Hall of Fame.
- Started racing quarter-midgets at age 4.
- Graduated from Purdue University in August 2001 with a degree in Vehicle Structural Engineering.
- Enjoys working on vintage cars.

### CAR FACTS

**Car:** No. 12 Dodge
**Primary sponsor:** ALLTEL
**Owner:** Roger Penske
**Team:** Penske South
**Crew chief:** Matt Borland
**Engine builder:** Scott Carriher

## CAREER BY YEAR

**2003** The circuit's biggest boom or bust driver, Newman had more wins (eight) than any two drivers combined. He also led the circuit in top fives (17) and was second in top 10s (22). But Newman was unlucky and inconsistent early in the season and never could dig himself out of the early-season points hole. In one stretch, he finished outside the top 35 in five of seven races.

**2002** Finished sixth in series points. … Topped Jimmie Johnson for Raybestos Rookie of the Year honors in one of the most heated rookie battles in years. … Tied Mark Martin for the most top 10s (22) in a season, which set a new rookie record. … Scored his career-first win at New Hampshire in September in his 34th career start. … Became just the second Raybestos Rookie to win The Winston, following Dale Earnhardt Jr. in 2000. … Led the series with six poles, setting a new rookie record for most poles in a season and topping Davey Allison's five poles in 1987. … Had 14 top fives, second only to series champion Tony Stewart's 15. … Tied Stewart in races led (22).

**2001** Finished 49th in series points. … Drove the ALLTEL-sponsored Ford for car owner Roger Penske. … Scored his first pole in his third career Winston Cup start, at the Coca-Cola 600 in Charlotte. That tied Mark Martin's record for earliest career pole. … Competed in seven races, finishing a season-best second at Kansas.

### CAREER STATISTICS

| Year | Car Owner | Races | Champ. Finish | Won | Top 5 | Top 10 | DNF | Poles | Money Won |
|---|---|---|---|---|---|---|---|---|---|
| 2000 | Roger Penske | 1 | | 0 | 0 | 0 | 1 | 0 | $37,825 |
| 2001 | Roger Penske | 7 | 49 | 0 | 2 | 2 | 2 | 1 | 465,276 |
| 2002 | Roger Penske | 36 | 6 | 1 | 14 | 22 | 5 | 6 | 5,346,651 |
| 2003 | Roger Penske | 36 | 6 | 8 | 17 | 22 | 7 | 11 | 6,100,877 |
| **TOTALS** | | 80 | | 9 | 33 | 46 | 15 | 18 | $11,950,629 |

### 2003 RESULTS

| Race | Start | Finish | Standing Pos. | Winnings |
|---|---|---|---|---|
| Daytona 500 (Daytona) | 37 | 43 | 43 | $195,663 |
| Subway 400 (Rockingham) | 21 | 14 | 32 | $84,335 |
| UAW-DaimlerChrysler 400 (Las Vegas) | 3 | 7 | 17 | $128,025 |
| Bass Pro Shops MBNA 500 (Atlanta) | 1 | 10 | 13 | $94,450 |
| Carolina Dodge Dealers 400 (Darlington) | 2 | 14 | 12 | $80,060 |
| Food City 500 (Bristol) | 1 | 22 | 15 | $97,940 |
| Samsung/RadioShack 500 (Texas) | 3 | 1 | 8 | $406,500 |
| Aaron's 499 (Talladega) | 8 | 39 | 11 | $93,215 |
| Virginia 500 (Martinsville) | 3 | 38 | 20 | $74,665 |
| Auto Club 500 (California) | 4 | 42 | 25 | $94,960 |
| Pontiac Excitement 400 (Richmond) | 5 | 39 | 27 | $76,185 |
| Coca-Cola 600 (Charlotte) | 1 | 5 | 24 | $186,850 |
| MBNA Armed Forces Family 400 (Dover) | 1 | 1 | 18 | $199,325 |
| Pocono 500 (Pocono) | 2 | 5 | 16 | $98,700 |
| Sirius 400 (Michigan) | 8 | 41 | 17 | $78,355 |
| Dodge/Save Mart 350 (Sonoma) | 13 | 5 | 17 | $101,140 |
| Pepsi 400 (Daytona) | 24 | 22 | 16 | $99,800 |
| Tropicana 400 (Chicago) | 14 | 1 | 16 | $191,000 |
| New England 300 (New Hampshire) | 16 | 4 | 13 | $114,425 |
| Pennsylvania 500 (Pocono) | 1 | 1 | 9 | $180,575 |
| Brickyard 400 (Indianapolis) | 2 | 11 | 9 | $172,750 |
| Sirius at the Glen (Watkins Glen) | 13 | 9 | 9 | $83,930 |
| GFS Marketplace 400 (Michigan) | 2 | 1 | 8 | $155,505 |
| Sharpie 500 (Bristol) | 6 | 6 | 7 | $111,940 |
| Southern 500 (Darlington) | 1 | 23 | 7 | $101,775 |

| Race | Start | Finish | Standing Pos. | Winnings |
|---|---|---|---|---|
| Chevy Rock & Roll 400 (Richmond) | 4 | 1 | 6 | $160,970 |
| Sylvania 300 (New Hampshire) | 1 | 9 | 5 | $98,925 |
| MBNA America 400 (Dover) | 5 | 1 | 5 | $160,460 |
| EA SPORTS 500 (Talladega) | 12 | 4 | 5 | |
| $113,165 Banquet 400 (Kansas) | 11 | 1 | 4 | $191,000 |
| UAW-GM Quality 500 (Charlotte) | 1 | 2 | 4 | $164,425 |
| Subway 500 (Martinsville) | 8 | 5 | 4 | $90,225 |
| Bass Pro Shops MBNA 500 (Atlanta) | 1 | 29 | 6 | $107,900 |
| Checker Auto Parts 500 (Phoenix) | 1 | 3 | 5 | $152,625 |
| Pop Secret 400 (Rockingham) | 1 | 5 | 4 | $98,785 |
| Ford 400 (Homestead) | 4 | 37 | 6 | $73,525 |

## Kyle Petty

**Date of birth:** June 20, 1960 **Hometown:** Trinity, N.C. **Resides:** Trinity, N.C. **Spouse:** Pattie **Children:** Adam, Austin, Montgomery **Height:** 6-2 **Weight:** 195 **Hobbies:** Reading, riding motorcycles, collecting books, collecting Elvis memorabilia

### NASCAR ACHIEVEMENTS

**First NASCAR Cup start:** August 5, 1979 (Talladega)
**Best points finish:** 5 (1992, 1993)
**Career victories:** 8—Charlotte (87a), Dover (95a), Pocono (93a), Richmond (86a), Rockingham (90a, 91a, 92b), Watkins Glen (92)
**First victory:** February 23, 1986 (Richmond)
**Career poles:** 8—Daytona (93a), Martinsville (92b), North Wilkesboro (90b), Rockingham (90a, 91a, 91b, 92a, 92b)
**First pole:** March 2, 1990 (Rockingham)
**Best career finish:** 1 **Best career start:** 1

### FAST FACTS

- Won the ARCA 200 at Daytona International Speedway in February 1979. It was his first race on a closed course, and the victory led to the beginning of his Winston Cup Series career that same season.
- With five poles at North Carolina Speedway, Petty is tied for first on that track's all-time pole winner's list with Mark Martin, David Pearson and Cale Yarborough.
- Petty, his father Richard and the entire Petty family were named Persons of the Year for 2000 by *NASCAR Winston Cup Illustrated*, for their charitable work.
- Kyle Petty's Charity Ride Across America was founded in 1995. Petty also works with the Make-A-Wish Foundation, the Boy Scouts of America, and the Winston Cup Racing Wives Auxiliary.
- Named NASCAR True Value Man of the Year in 1998, 2002.
- Petty was recruited by several colleges as a quarterback; others talked to him about a baseball scholarship.

### CAR FACTS

**Car:** No. 45 Dodge
**Primary sponsor:** Georgia Pacific/Brawney
**Owner:** Pattie Petty
**Team:** Petty Enterprises
**Crew chief:** Greg Steadman
**Engine builder:** Mike Ege Racing Engines

## CAREER BY YEAR

**2003** It was another down season for Petty, who hasn't finished a season in the top 10 in points since 1993. His hallmark consistency still was evident—he completed more than 93 percent of the laps in races he entered—despite six DNFs. But he wasn't running those laps near the front. He had only three top 20s in 33 starts. He qualified in the top 10 just twice, and his average starting spot was 33.2.

**2002** Finished 22nd in series points. ... Best finish was 10th at Talladega. ... Seventh consecutive season without a victory. ... Completed 97.4 percent of the season's laps.

**2001** Finished 43rd in series points. ... Best finish was 16th, at the Daytona 500 and at Homestead-Miami. ... Made his 600th career start in June, placing him 13th on the all-time list of Winston Cup starts.

**2000** Finished 41st in series points. ... Competed in 19 Winston Cup races before moving from his No. 44 Winston Cup team to drive his late son Adam's No. 45 car in the Busch Series. ... Best finish was ninth at Talladega. ... Awarded the Myers Brothers Award by the National Motorsports Press Association for his contributions to racing.

**1999** Finished 26th in series points. ... Finished a season best seventh five times.

**1998** Finished 30th in series points. ... Finished a season-best sixth at Watkins Glen.

**1997** Finished 15th in series points. ... Finished a season-best third at Dover.

**1996** Finished 27th in series points in his final season with Felix Sabates' Team Sabco. ... Finished a season-best eighth at Dover and Martinsville. ... Sustained an injury in the Brickyard 400 that caused him to miss races at Watkins Glen, Michigan and Bristol.

**1995** Finished 30th in series points. ... Got his eighth career victory, at Dover. ... Had five top fives.

**1994** Finished 15th in series points. ... Finished a season-best fourth at North Wilkesboro.

**1993** Finished fifth in series points, matching his career-best finish in 1992. ... Won the Daytona 500 pole. ... Had one victory, at Pocono.

**1992** Finished fifth in series points. ... Won two races, Watkins Glen and Rockingham. ... The Rockingham win was his third there in three consecutive seasons. ... Made a late bid for the Winston Cup championship with seven top fives in the last 10 races.

**1991** Finished 31st in series points. ... Had one victory, at Rockingham, and three poles. ... Sat out 11 races after being involved in an accident at Talladega that left him with a broken thigh bone.

**1990** Finished 11th in series points. ... His only win, at Rockingham, was achieved in dominating style, leading 433 of 492 laps. ... Car owner Felix Sabates was so elated by the Rockingham victory he presented Petty with a Rolls Royce. ... Won two poles.

**1989** Finished 30th in series points. ... First year driving for team owner Felix Sabates. ... Best finish was fourth, at

Atlanta. … Finished in the top 10 twice in the final three races.

**1988** Finished 13th in series points in the final season driving for Wood Brothers Racing. … Best finish was fifth, at Atlanta and North Wilkesboro.

**1987** Finished seventh in series points. … Won two races, including the prestigious Coca-Cola 600 at Charlotte.

**1986** Finished 10th in series points. … Got his first career victory, at Richmond; became the first third-generation driver to win a Winston Cup Series race, following grandfather Lee and father Richard.

**1985** Finished ninth in series points. … Joined the Wood Brothers Racing team … Won the Comeback Driver of the Year award.

**1984** Finished 16th in series points. … Had only one top five. … Ran his last season for Petty Enterprises until rejoining the operation in 1999.

**1983** Finished 13th in series points. … Made 30 starts, posting two top fives.

**1982** Finished 15th in series points. … Best finish was second, at Dover. … Drove the Petty Enterprises STP Pontiac but also made a few starts in the Hoss Ellington/UNO Buick.

**1981** Finished 12th in series points. … Finished a season-best fifth at Charlotte and attempted to compete in every race for the first time.

**1980** Finished 28th in series points after competing in 15 events. … Finished third in the Rookie of the Year standings behind Jody Ridley and Lake Speed. … Had six top 10s.

**1979** Finished 37th in series points. … Made his Winston Cup Series debut, running five races for Petty Enterprises. … His first Winston Cup race was at Talladega Superspeedway, where he finished ninth.

## CAREER STATISTICS

| Year | Car Owner | Races | Champ. Finish | Won | Top 5 | Top 10 | DNF | Poles | Money Won |
|---|---|---|---|---|---|---|---|---|---|
| 1979 | Petty Enter. | 5 | 37 | 0 | 0 | 1 | 1 | 0 | $10,810 |
| 1980 | Petty Enter. | 14 | | 0 | 0 | 6 | 5 | 0 | 35,575 |
| | Rahmoc | 1 | 28 | 0 | 0 | 0 | 0 | 0 | 775 |
| 1981 | Petty Enter. | 31 | 12 | 0 | 1 | 10 | 18 | 0 | 112,289 |
| 1982 | Petty Enter. | 23 | | 0 | 2 | 4 | 13 | 0 | 108,715 |
| | Hoss Ellington | 6 | 15 | 0 | 0 | 0 | 3 | 0 | 12,015 |
| 1983 | Petty Enter. | 30 | 13 | 0 | 0 | 2 | 10 | 0 | 157,820 |
| 1984 | Petty Enter. | 30 | 16 | 0 | 1 | 6 | 7 | 0 | 324,555 |
| 1985 | Wood Brothers | 28 | 9 | 0 | 7 | 12 | 4 | 0 | 296,367 |
| 1986 | Wood Brothers | 29 | 10 | 1 | 4 | 14 | 6 | 0 | 403,242 |
| 1987 | Wood Brothers | 29 | 7 | 1 | 6 | 14 | 4 | 0 | 544,437 |
| 1988 | Wood Brothers | 29 | 13 | 0 | 2 | 8 | 6 | 0 | 377,092 |
| 1989 | SABCO Racing | 19 | 30 | 0 | 1 | 5 | 7 | 0 | 117,022 |
| 1990 | Felix Sabates | 29 | 11 | 1 | 2 | 14 | 5 | 2 | 746,326 |
| 1991 | Felix Sabates | 18 | 31 | 1 | 2 | 4 | 5 | 2 | 413,727 |
| 1992 | Felix Sabates | 29 | 5 | 2 | 9 | 17 | 5 | 3 | 1,107,063 |
| 1993 | Felix Sabates | 30 | 5 | 1 | 9 | 15 | 5 | 1 | 914,662 |
| 1994 | Felix Sabates | 31 | 15 | 0 | 2 | 7 | 3 | 0 | 806,332 |
| 1995 | Felix Sabates | 31 | 30 | 1 | 1 | 5 | 10 | 0 | 698,875 |
| 1996 | Felix Sabates | 28 | 27 | 0 | 0 | 2 | 4 | 0 | 689,041 |
| 1997 | Kyle Petty | 32 | 15 | 0 | 2 | 9 | 2 | 0 | 984,314 |
| 1998 | Kyle Petty | 33 | 30 | 0 | 0 | 2 | 8 | 0 | 1,287,731 |
| 1999 | Petty Ent. | 32 | 26 | 0 | 0 | 9 | 4 | 0 | 1,278,953 |
| 2000 | Petty Ent. | 19 | 41 | 0 | 0 | 1 | 6 | 0 | 894,911 |
| 2001 | Petty Ent. | 24 | 43 | 0 | 0 | 0 | 0 | 0 | 1,008,919 |
| 2002 | Petty Ent. | 36 | 22 | 0 | 0 | 1 | 1 | 0 | 2,198,073 |
| 2003 | Petty Ent. | 33 | 37 | 0 | 0 | 0 | 6 | 0 | 2,293,220 |
| **TOTALS** | | 678 | | 8 | 51 | 168 | 156 | 8 | $17,822,861 |

## 2003 RESULTS

| Race | Start | Finish | Standing Pos. | Winnings |
|---|---|---|---|---|
| Daytona 500 (Daytona) | 30 | 13 | 13 | $198,176 |
| Subway 400 (Rockingham) | 30 | 35 | 21 | $54,000 |
| UAW-DaimlerChrysler 400 (Las Vegas) | 19 | 31 | 30 | $70,400 |
| Bass Pro Shops MBNA 500 (Atlanta) | 38 | 34 | 35 | $54,325 |
| Carolina Dodge Dealers 400 (Darlington) | 40 | 26 | 34 | $54,210 |
| Food City 500 (Bristol) | 32 | 34 | 35 | $65,235 |
| Aaron's 499 (Talladega) | 21 | 11 | 37 | $84,375 |
| Virginia 500 (Martinsville) | 33 | 34 | 38 | $55,000 |
| Auto Club 500 (California) | 36 | 28 | 38 | $78,350 |
| Pontiac Excitement 400 (Richmond) | 8 | 27 | 38 | $58,700 |
| Coca-Cola 600 (Charlotte) | 31 | 30 | 36 | $81,635 |
| MBNA Armed Forces Family 400 (Dover) | 27 | 43 | 37 | $65,028 |
| Pocono 500 (Pocono) | 40 | 27 | 38 | $55,340 |
| Sirius 400 (Michigan) | 42 | 34 | 38 | $56,935 |
| Dodge/Save Mart 350 (Sonoma) | 35 | 27 | 37 | $66,160 |
| Pepsi 400 (Daytona) | 42 | 23 | 36 | $77,550 |
| Tropicana 400 (Chicago) | 41 | 27 | 35 | $73,425 |
| New England 300 (New Hampshire) | 36 | 32 | 35 | $57,825 |
| Pennsylvania 500 (Pocono) | 35 | 34 | 35 | $51,165 |
| Brickyard 400 (Indianapolis) | 41 | 40 | 35 | $110,475 |
| Sirius at the Glen (Watkins Glen) | 31 | 42 | 36 | $51,485 |
| GFS Marketplace 400 (Michigan) | 36 | 16 | 35 | $64,540 |
| Sharpie 500 (Bristol) | 42 | 34 | 37 | $68,560 |
| Southern 500 (Darlington) | )40 | 27 | 35 | $63,095 |
| Chevy Rock & Roll 400 (Richmond) | 10 | 34 | 36 | $55,135 |
| Sylvania 300 (New Hampshire) | 40 | 30 | 35 | $61,225 |
| MBNA America 400 (Dover) | 36 | 32 | 35 | $60,705 |
| Banquet 400 (Kansas) | 36 | 23 | 37 | $74,550 |
| UAW-GM Quality 500 (Charlotte) | 42 | 40 | 37 | $52,905 |
| Subway 500 (Martinsville) | 32 | 25 | 37 | $55,725 |
| Bass Pro Shops MBNA 500 (Atlanta) | 25 | 25 | 37 | $75,725 |
| Checker Auto Parts 500 (Phoenix) | 36 | 35 | 37 | $55,300 |
| Pop Secret 400 (Rockingham) | 33 | 32 | 37 | $54,675 |

**Scott Riggs** 10

**Date of birth:** January 1, 1971 **Hometown:** Bahama, N.C. **Resides:** Bahama, N.C. **Spouse:** Jai **Children:** Lane **Height:** 5-6 **Weight:** 175 **Hobbies:** Horseback riding, riding dirt and road bikes and water sports

## NASCAR ACHIEVEMENTS

**First NASCAR Cup start:** n/a
**Best points finish:** n/a

Career victories: 0
Career poles: 0
Best career finish: n/a  Best career start: n/a

## FAST FACTS

- Finished 10th in the 2002 Busch Series, winning the Raybestos Rookie of the Year award.
- Finished fifth in the Craftsman Truck Series in 2001, with five wins and 14 top fives; also ran on that circuit in 1999 and 2000.
- Was a two-time champion at the Southern National Speedway in Kenley, N.C., where he has 60 victories.
- Has competed on the Hills Bros All-Pro Series of NASCAR Touring, posting eight top 10s in 13 races in 1998.

### CAR FACTS

**Car:** No. 10 Chevrolet
**Primary sponsor:** Valvoline
**Owner:** Nelson Bowers, James Rocco, Tom Beard
**Team:** MBV Motorsports
**Crew chief:** Doug Randolph
**Engine builder:** Hendrick Motorsports

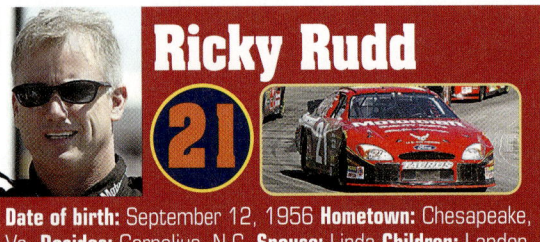

# Ricky Rudd
## 21

**Date of birth:** September 12, 1956  **Hometown:** Chesapeake, Va.  **Resides:** Cornelius, N.C.  **Spouse:** Linda  **Children:** Landon  **Height:** 5-8  **Weight:** 160  **Hobbies:** Flying, outdoors, boating, water sports

## NASCAR ACHIEVEMENTS

**First NASCAR Cup start:** March 2, 1975 (Rockingham)
**Best points finish:** 2 (1991)
**Career victories:** 23—Atlanta (87), Darlington (91a), Dover (86b, 87b, 92b, 97a), Indianapolis (97), Martinsville (83b, 86a, 98b), Michigan (93a), New Hampshire (94), Phoenix (95), Pocono (01a), Richmond (84b, 01b), Rockingham (96b), Sonoma (89, 02), Watkins Glen (88,90)
**First victory:** June 5, 1983
**Career poles:** 28—Bristol (84b), Charlotte (96b), Daytona (83a), Dover (81b, 82b, 84, 88a), Indianapolis (00), Las Vegas (00), Martinsville (81a, 82a, 83a, 88a), Nashville (81a, 84b), North Wilkesboro (84a), Pocono (01a), Richmond (83a, 90a), Riverside (88), Rockingham (83a, 94b, 99a), Sonoma (90, 91, 91, 95), Watkins Glen (02)
**First pole:** April 24, 1981 (Martinsville)
**Best career finish:** 1  **Best career start:** 1

## FAST FACTS

- Started racing at age 9 and raced in motorcross and go-karts as a teenager.
- Won the IROC championship in 1992.
- Father, Al Rudd Jr., owned an auto salvage business that led to Ricky's interest in cars.
- NASCAR's iron man, with 716 consecutive starts dating back to 1981.

## CAREER BY YEAR

**2003** Rudd had nine DNFs and completed only 92.5 percent of the season's laps in his first year with Wood Brothers Racing. He had just five top 10 finishes. The season highlight was a second-place finish in the fall at New Hampshire. Rudd's problems began with qualifying—his average starting position was 27.1. His average finish was 22.3.

**2002** Finished 10th in series points. ... Started his 656th consecutive race on May 26 at Charlotte, breaking Terry Labonte's record of 655 consecutive starts. ... Won the road-course race at Sonoma, his 23rd career victory. ... Had four third-place finishes. ... Won the pole at Watkins Glen. ... Broke into the top 10 in points after season's seventh race and stayed in the top 10 for the rest of the season.

**2001** Finished fourth in series points. ... Ended an 88-race winless streak with victory from the pole at Pocono in June, his first win since 1988 at Martinsville. ... Won the Richmond fall race, taking the lead with six laps remaining. ... Was in championship contention until August.

**2000** Finished fifth in series points. ... First season with Robert Yates Racing after six years of owning his own team. ... Failed to win a race for second consecutive season. ... Won a Daytona 500 125-mile qualifying race. ... Season-best finish was second at Michigan in August. ... Had five top fives in six-race span in September and October. ... Won poles at Las Vegas and Indianapolis. ... Finished in the top 10 in points for the 17th time.

### CAR FACTS

**Car:** No. 21 Ford
**Primary sponsor:** Motorcraft Quality Parts
**Owners:** Glen Wood, Eddie Wood, Len Wood, Kim Wood Hall
**Team:** Wood Brothers Racing
**Crew chief:** Ben Leslie
**Engine builder:** Roush Racing

**1999** Finished 31st in series points. ... Had the worst season of his Winston Cup career in his final season as an owner-driver. ... Sold race shop to Robert Yates Racing; shop became home of the No. 28. ... Ended his streak of winning at least one race in 16 consecutive years.

**1998** Finished 22nd in series points. ... Won at Martinsville in September. ... Made his 600th career start.

**1997** Finished 17th in series points. ... Got two victories in a season for the first time since 1987, winning at Dover and Indianapolis.

**1996** Finished sixth in series points. ... Won at Rockingham in October and had two second-place finishes.

**1995** Finished ninth in series points. ... Won at Phoenix in October. ... Six DNFs hurt his chances for a higher finish in the series standings.

**1994** Finished fifth in series points. ... First season as owner-driver. ... Had 15 top 10s, including a victory at New Hampshire.

**1993** Finished 10th in series points. ... Last season with Hendrick Motorsports. ... Had one victory, at Michigan.

**1992** Finished seventh in series points. ... Won at the Dover fall race and had 18 top 10s.

**1991** Finished career-high second in series points, ending up 195 points behind Dale Earnhardt. ... Was ninth in points with eight races left in the season. ... Won at Darlington in the spring.

**1990** Finished seventh in series points. ... First season with Hendrick Motorsports. ... Won road-course race at Watkins Glen. ... Had poles at the Richmond spring race and the road race at Sonoma.

**1989** Finished eighth in series points. ... Ran his second and last season with Kenny Bernstein's team. Won the road race at Sonoma.

**1988** Finished 11th in series points. ... First season with King Racing Team, owned by drag-racing legend Kenny Bernstein. ... Won the road race at Watkins Glen. ... Had three second-place finishes ... Had two poles, at the Martinsville spring race and Riverside.

**1987** Finished sixth in series points. ... Had two victories, at the Atlanta spring race and the Dover fall race. ... Last season with Bud Moore Engineering.

**1986** Finished fifth in series points. ... Won in the Martinsville spring race and the Dover fall event. ... Had four runner-up finishes.

**1985** Finished sixth in series points. ... Had 19 top 10s, including a victory at Riverside.

**1984** Finished seventh in series points. ... First season with Bud Moore Engineering. ... Won the Richmond fall race and had four poles.

**1983** Finished ninth in series points. ...Got his first Winston Cup win, in his 161st start, on June 5 at Riverside. ... Won in September at Martinsville. ... Won the Daytona 500 pole, one of four poles overall.

**1982** Finished ninth in series points. ... First of two seasons with Richard Childress Racing. ... Had two second-place runs. ... Won poles at the Martinsville and Dover fall races.

**1981** Finished sixth in series points on the strength of 17 top 10s. ... Joined DiGard Racing. ... Won his first career Winston Cup pole on April 24 at Martinsville. ... Also won poles at Nashville and Dover.

**1980** Finished 35th in series points. ... Ran 13 races with father Al Rudd Jr.'s team. ... Gained attention by qualifying second and finishing fourth at the Charlotte fall race.

**1979** Finished ninth in series points. ... Ran 28 races for Junie Donlavey. ... Had two third-place finishes.

**1978** Finished 31st in series points. ... Ran 13 races with his father's team and had four top 10s.

**1977** Finished 17th in series points. ... Was the Winston Cup Rookie of the Year. ... Ran 25 races with his father's team.

**1976** Finished 53rd in series points. ... Ran four races with hi father's team and had one top 10.

**1975** Finished 47th in series points. ... Ran four races for Bill Champion. ... Made his Winston Cup debut on March 2 at Rockingham, finishing 11th.

## CAREER STATISTICS

| Year | Car Owner | Champ. Races | Finish | Won | Top 5 | Top 10 | DNF | Poles | Money Won |
|---|---|---|---|---|---|---|---|---|---|
| 1975 | Bill Champion | 4 | 47 | 0 | 0 | 1 | 2 | 0 | 4,345 |
| 1976 | Al Rudd Sr. | 4 | 53 | 0 | 0 | 1 | 2 | 0 | 7,525 |
| 1977 | Al Rudd Sr. | 25 | 17 | 0 | 1 | 10 | 11 | 0 | 68,448 |
| 1978 | Al Rudd Sr. | 13 | 31 | 0 | 0 | 4 | 7 | 0 | 49,610 |
| 1979 | J. Donlavey | 28 | 17 | 0 | 4 | 17 | 6 | 0 | 146,302 |
| 1980 | Al Rudd Sr. | 13 | 35 | 0 | 1 | 3 | 6 | 0 | 50,500 |
| 1981 | Bill Gardner | 31 | 6 | 0 | 14 | 17 | 9 | 3 | 381,968 |
| 1982 | R. Childress | 30 | 9 | 0 | 6 | 13 | 13 | 2 | 201,130 |
| 1983 | R. Childress | 30 | 9 | 2 | 7 | 14 | 8 | 4 | 257,585 |
| 1984 | Bud Moore | 30 | 7 | 1 | 7 | 16 | 6 | 4 | 476,602 |
| 1985 | Bud Moore | 28 | 6 | 1 | 13 | 19 | 5 | 0 | 512,441 |
| 1986 | Bud Moore | 29 | 5 | 2 | 11 | 17 | 7 | 1 | 671,548 |
| 1987 | Bud Moore | 29 | 6 | 2 | 10 | 13 | 9 | 0 | 653,508 |
| 1988 | K. Bernstein | 29 | 11 | 1 | 6 | 11 | 12 | 2 | 410,954 |
| 1989 | K. Bernstein | 29 | 8 | 1 | 7 | 15 | 5 | 0 | 534,824 |
| 1990 | R. Hendrick | 29 | 7 | 1 | 8 | 15 | 5 | 2 | 573,650 |
| 1991 | R. Hendrick | 29 | 2 | 1 | 9 | 17 | 1 | 1 | 1,093,765 |
| 1992 | R. Hendrick | 29 | 7 | 1 | 9 | 18 | 4 | 1 | 793,903 |
| 1993 | R. Hendrick | 30 | 10 | 1 | 9 | 14 | 6 | 0 | 752,562 |
| 1994 | Ricky Rudd | 31 | 5 | 1 | 6 | 15 | 2 | 1 | 1,044,441 |
| 1995 | Ricky Rudd | 31 | 9 | 1 | 10 | 16 | 6 | 2 | 1,337,703 |
| 1996 | Ricky Rudd | 31 | 6 | 1 | 5 | 16 | 1 | 0 | 1,503,025 |
| 1997 | Ricky Rudd | 32 | 17 | 2 | 6 | 11 | 7 | 0 | 1,975,981 |
| 1998 | Ricky Rudd | 33 | 22 | 1 | 1 | 5 | 7 | 0 | 1,602,895 |
| 1999 | Ricky Rudd | 34 | 31 | 0 | 3 | 5 | 7 | 1 | 1,632,011 |
| 2000 | Robert Yates | 34 | 5 | 0 | 12 | 19 | 1 | 2 | 2,914,970 |
| 2001 | Robert Yates | 36 | 4 | 2 | 14 | 22 | 4 | 1 | 4,878,027 |
| 2002 | Robert Yates | 36 | 10 | 1 | 8 | 12 | 4 | 1 | 4,444,614 |
| 2003 | Wood Bros. | 36 | 23 | 0 | 4 | 5 | 9 | 0 | 3,240,614 |
| **TOTALS** | | **803** | | **23** | **191** | **361** | **172** | **28** | **$32,215,451** |

## 2003 RESULTS

| Race | Start | Finish | Standing Pos. | Winnings |
|---|---|---|---|---|
| Daytona 500 (Daytona) | 5 | 15 | 15 | $222,595 |
| Subway 400 (Rockingham) | 28 | 11 | 12 | $76,685 |
| UAW-DaimlerChrysler 400 (Las Vegas) | 38 | 19 | 8 | $94,050 |
| Bass Pro Shops MBNA 500 (Atlanta) | 21 | 35 | 21 | $54,290 |
| Carolina Dodge Dealers 400 (Darlington) | 39 | 15 | 17 | $69,055 |
| Food City 500 (Bristol) | 34 | 4 | 9 | $103,475 |
| Samsung/RadioShack 500 (Texas) | 16 | 26 | 12 | $84,175 |
| Aaron's 499 (Talladega) | 37 | 42 | 19 | $70,690 |
| Virginia 500 (Martinsville) | 19 | 11 | 19 | $78,650 |
| Auto Club 500 (California) | 35 | 24 | 18 | $79,600 |
| Pontiac Excitement 400 (Richmond) | 27 | 34 | 22 | $57,075 |
| Coca-Cola 600 (Charlotte) | 40 | 33 | 26 | $80,550 |
| MBNA Armed Forces Family 400 (Dover) | 24 | 17 | 26 | $82,950 |
| Pocono 500 (Pocono) | 29 | 37 | 26 | $50,625 |
| Sirius 400 (Michigan) | 32 | 43 | 27 | $55,765 |
| Dodge/Save Mart 350 (Sonoma) | 9 | 15 | 26 | $84,825 |
| Pepsi 400 (Daytona) | 27 | 3 | 24 | $127,600 |
| Tropicana 400 (Chicago) | 37 | 13 | 23 | $94,475 |
| New England 300 (New Hampshire) | 23 | 12 | 21 | $83,550 |
| Pennsylvania 500 (Pocono) | 27 | 39 | 23 | $50,385 |
| Brickyard 400 (Indianapolis) | 39 | 38 | 26 | $110,660 |
| Sirius at the Glen (Watkins Glen) | 26 | 21 | 25 | $72,535 |
| GFS Marketplace 400 (Michigan) | 27 | 29 | 26 | $60,140 |

| Race | Start | Finish | Standing Pos. | Winnings |
|---|---|---|---|---|
| Sharpie 500 (Bristol) | 8 | 33 | 27 | $68,595 |
| Southern 500 (Darlington) | 30 | 16 | 26 | $77,235 |
| Chevy Rock & Roll 400 (Richmond) | 19 | 3 | 25 | $104,130 |
| Sylvania 300 (New Hampshire) | 31 | 2 | 23 | $145,055 |
| MBNA America 400 (Dover) | 23 | 11 | 21 | $87,155 |
| EA SPORTS 500 (Talladega) | 32 | 36 | 23 | $62,475 |
| Banquet 400 (Kansas) | 19 | 10 | 22 | $99,125 |
| UAW-GM Quality 500 (Charlotte) | 39 | 23 | 22 | $71,475 |
| Subway 500 (Martinsville) | 12 | 15 | 22 | $76,825 |
| Bass Pro Shops MBNA 500 (Atlanta) | 42 | 31 | 22 | $73,425 |
| Checker Auto Parts 500 (Phoenix) | 30 | 17 | 21 | $76,875 |
| Pop Secret 400 (Rockingham) | 24 | 40 | 22 | $54,015 |
| Ford 400 (Homestead) | 30 | 31 | 23 | $55,275 |

**Elliott Sadler**

**Date of birth:** April 30, 1975  **Hometown:** Emporia, Va.
**Resides:** Emporia, Va.  **Spouse:** Single  **Children:** None  **Height:** 6-2
**Weight:** 195  **Hobbies:** Golf, hunting, basketball, water sports

## NASCAR ACHIEVEMENTS

**First NASCAR Cup start:** May 24, 1998 (Charlotte)
**Best points finish:** 20 (2001)
**Career victories:** 1—Bristol (01a)
**First victory:** March 25, 2001 (Bristol)
**Career poles:** 2—Darlington (03a), Talladega (03b)
**Best career finish:** 1   **Best career start:** 1

## FAST FACTS

- Had five races, five pole positions and 12 top fives in 76 career Busch Series starts before moving into Winston Cup full-time.
- Crowned track champion at South Boston Speedway in 1995, winning 13 races.
- Moved into the Winston Racing Series at age 18.
- Began racing at age in go-karts at age 7 and won more than 200 races; also won the 1983-84 Virginia State Karting Championship.
- Is a hunting guide and raises Walker hunting dogs in the winter months.
- His father, Herman, raced late model stocks in Virginia.
- Received a basketball scholarship to James Madison University to play for coach Lefty Driessell but suffered a knee injury that "allowed him to pursue a sit-down job."

## CAR FACTS

**Car:** No. 38 Ford
**Primary sponsor:** M&Ms
**Owner:** Robert Yates
**Team:** Robert Yates Racing
**Crew chief:** Todd Parrott
**Engine builder:** Robert Yates Racing

## CAREER BY YEAR

**2003** Horrific crashes and bad luck doomed his first season with Robert Yates Racing. The season started out well—he was 10th in points race after 10 races. But consecutive finishes of 37th, 36th and 33rd pushed him out of the top 10 for good. He had two top fives and nine top 10s, with his best finish a third at the April race at Talladega.

**2002** Finished 23rd in series points in his last season with the Wood Brothers operation. ... Started by grabbing the runner-up spots in the Daytona 500 and the spring race at Darlington. ... Had two top fives and seven top 10s.

**2001** Finished 20th in series points, a career best. ... Took the Wood Brothers back to victory lane for the first time since 1993 with a victory at Bristol in March. It was Sadler's 75th Winston Cup start. ... Was third behind Dale Earnhardt Jr. and Michael Waltrip in the Pepsi 400 at Daytona for his only other top 10.

**2000** Finished 29th in series points. ... Had only one top 10. ... Low point of his season was at Talladega in April, when he failed to qualify. ... Qualified 25th and finished 17th in the second Talladega race, using a car built by Roush Racing. Also used Roush chassis in two other races to prepare for the 2001 season. ... Finished a season-best seventh in the Bristol night race. ... Best start was sixth at Darlington in March. ... Used six provisionals and had four DNFs. ... Lost crew chief Mike Beam, who left the team with four races remaining. ... Was joined by crew chief Pat Tryson for final race of the season.

**1999** Finished 24th in series points. ... Finished second to Tony Stewart in the Raybestos Rookie of the Year race. ... Scored just one top 10 but finished all but two races.

**1998** Made his Winston Cup debut in the Coca-Cola 600 at Charlotte. ... Drove two races for car owner Gary Bechtel and Diamond Ridge Motorsports. ... Also started fourth and finished 20th in the Motegi Coca-Cola 500 exhibition race in Japan for the Wood Brothers.

## CAREER STATISTICS

| Year | Car Owner | Champ. Races | Finish | Won | Top 5 | Top 10 | DNF | Poles | Money Won |
|---|---|---|---|---|---|---|---|---|---|
| 1998 | G. Bechtel | 2 | 59 | 0 | 0 | 0 | 1 | 0 | $45,325 |
| 1999 | Wood Brothers | 34 | 24 | 0 | 0 | 1 | 2 | 0 | 1,589,221 |
| 2000 | Wood Brothers | 33 | 29 | 0 | 0 | 1 | 5 | 0 | 1,579,656 |
| 2001 | Wood Brothers | 36 | 20 | 1 | 2 | 2 | 2 | 0 | 2,683,225 |
| 2002 | Wood Brothers | 36 | 23 | 0 | 2 | 7 | 6 | 0 | 3,491,694 |
| 2003 | Robert Yates | 36 | 22 | 0 | 1 | 9 | 9 | 2 | 3,795,174 |
| **TOTALS** | | 177 | | 1 | 5 | 20 | 25 | 2 | $13,184,295 |

## 2003 RESULTS

| Race | Start | Finish | Standing Pos. | Winnings |
|---|---|---|---|---|
| Daytona 500 (Daytona) | 16 | 23 | 23 | $215,901 |
| Subway 400 (Rockingham) | 11 | 9 | 14 | $91,060 |
| UAW-DaimlerChrysler 400 (Las Vegas) | 23 | 42 | 27 | $91,915 |
| Bass Pro Shops MBNA 500 (Atlanta) | 3 | 6 | 19 | $94,450 |
| Carolina Dodge Dealers 400 (Darlington) | 1 | 7 | 10 | $94,470 |
| Food City 500 (Bristol) | 30 | 21 | 14 | $97,565 |

| Race | Start | Finish | Standing Pos. | Winnings |
|---|---|---|---|---|
| Samsung/RadioShack 500 (Texas) | 2 | 41 | 20 | $92,060 |
| Aaron's 499 (Talladega) | 3 | 3 | 10 | $162,955 |
| Virginia 500 (Martinsville) | 18 | 5 | 10 | $98,950 |
| Auto Club 500 (California) | 5 | 23 | 10 | $107,075 |
| Pontiac Excitement 400 (Richmond) | 39 | 37 | 16 | $80,675 |
| Coca-Cola 600 (Charlotte) | 2 | 36 | 16 | $108,525 |
| MBNA Armed Forces Family 400 (Dover) | 17 | 33 | 20 | $93,270 |
| Pocono 500 (Pocono) | 9 | 9 | 19 | $101,040 |
| Sirius 400 (Michigan) | 7 | 17 | 19 | $90,440 |
| Dodge/Save Mart 350 (Sonoma) | 24 | 22 | 18 | $93,125 |
| Pepsi 400 (Daytona) | 9 | 24 | 18 | $104,350 |
| Tropicana 400 (Chicago) | 8 | 9 | 18 | $108,375 |
| New England 300 (New Hampshire) | 18 | 27 | 18 | $88,175 |
| Pennsylvania 500 (Pocono) | 3 | 14 | 17 | $85,240 |
| Brickyard 400 (Indianapolis) | 16 | 42 | 19 | $136,515 |
| Sirius at the Glen (Watkins Glen) | 24 | 15 | 8 | $86,820 |
| GFS Marketplace 400 (Michigan) | 17 | 12 | 18 | $92,515 |
| Sharpie 500 (Bristol) | 17 | 38 | 20 | $94,600 |
| Southern 500 (Darlington) | 4 | 9 | 19 | $98,335 |
| Chevy Rock & Roll 400 (Richmond) | 30 | 39 | 22 | $81,195 |
| Sylvania 300 (New Hampshire) | 24 | 8 | 19 | $97,700 |
| MBNA America 400 (Dover) | 20 | 19 | 20 | $92,490 |
| EA SPORTS 500 (Talladega) | 1 | 30 | 20 | $96,330 |
| Banquet 400 (Kansas) | 10 | 42 | 23 | $93,645 |
| UAW-GM Quality 500 (Charlotte) | 7 | 43 | 24 | $78,999 |
| Subway 500 (Martinsville) | 38 | 28 | 23 | $80,610 |
| Bass Pro Shops MBNA 500 (Atlanta) | 6 | 17 | 23 | $105,300 |
| Checker Auto Parts 500 (Phoenix) | 14 | 20 | 23 | $89,225 |
| Pop Secret 400 (Rockingham) | 15 | 21 | 23 | $86,325 |
| Ford 400 (Homestead) | 29 | 21 | 22 | $84,650 |

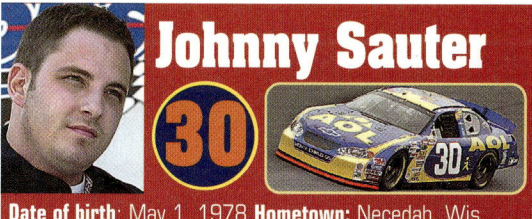

# Johnny Sauter

**Date of birth:** May 1, 1978 **Hometown:** Necedah, Wis. **Resides:** Salisbury, N.C. **Spouse:** Single **Children:** None

## NASCAR ACHIEVEMENTS

**First NASCAR Cup start:** July 13, 2003
**Best points finish:** 51 (2003)
**Career victories:** 0
**Career poles:** 0
**Best career finish:** 23  **Best career start:** 20

## FAST FACTS

- Finished eighth in the 2003 Busch Series and 15th on that circuit in 2002.
- Was the 2001 ASA national champion and Rookie of the Year, winning 10 events.

### CAR FACTS
**Car:** No. 30 Chevrolet
**Primary sponsor:** AOL
**Owner:** Richard Childress
**Team:** Richard Childress Racing
**Crew chief:** Kevin Hamlin
**Engine builder:** Ron Liddell

# CAREER BY YEAR

**2003** Sauter ran five Cup races for Morgan-McClure but never cracked the top 10.

## CAREER STATISTICS

| Year | Car Owner | Champ. Races | Finish | Won | Top 5 | Top 10 | DNF | Poles | Money Won |
|---|---|---|---|---|---|---|---|---|---|
| 2003 | Morgan-McClure | 5 | 51 | 0 | 0 | 0 | 0 | 0 | $281,335 |
| **TOTALS** | | **5** | | **0** | **0** | **0** | **0** | **0** | **$281,335** |

## 2003 RESULTS

| Race | Start | Finish | Standing Pos. | Winnings |
|---|---|---|---|---|
| Tropicana 400 (Chicago) | 20 | 35 | 57 | $60,775 |
| New England 300 (New Hampshire) | 41 | 23 | 48 | $55,750 |
| Sharpie 500 (Bristol) | 21 | 25 | 47 | $67,990 |
| Chevy Rock & Roll 400 (Richmond) | 36 | 38 | 48 | $46,995 |
| Sylvania 300 (New Hampshire) | 30 | 32 | 47 | $49,825 |

# Ken Schrader

**Date of birth:** May 29, 1955 **Hometown:** Fenton, Mo. **Resides:** Concord, N.C. **Spouse:** Ann **Children:** Dorothy Lynn, Sheldon Bradley **Height:** 5-9 **Weight:** 200 **Hobbies:** Driving in a number of racing series, riding dirt bikes and motorcycles

## NASCAR ACHIEVEMENTS

**First NASCAR Cup start:** July 14, 1984 (Nashville)
**Best points finish:** 4 (1994)
**Career victories:** 4—Atlanta (91a), Charlotte (89a), Dover (91a), Talladega (88b)
**First victory:** July 31, 1988 (Talladega)
**Career poles:** 23—Charlotte (90a, 93a), Darlington (87a, 88a, 90a), Daytona (88a, 89a, 90a), Michigan (89a, 93b), New Hampshire (97a, 97b), Phoenix (89, 98), Pocono (89b, 92a, 93a, 93b, 95a), Richmond (93a), Rockingham (90b) Talladega (98b, 99a)
**First pole:** March 27, 1987 (Darlington)
**Best career finish:** 1  **Best career start:** 1

## FAST FACTS

- Won a Sprint Car national championship in 1983.
- Named USAC's stock car Rookie of the Year in 1990.
- Won the 1982 USAC Silver Crown title and the 1983 USAC Sprint Car championship.

### CAR FACTS
**Car:** No. 49 Dodge
**Primary sponsor:** BAM Racing
**Owner:** Troy and Beth Ann Morgenthau
**Team:** BAM Racing
**Crew chief:** Scott Eggleston
**Engine builder:** Joey Arrington

- Won four USAC sprint races, six in the USAC Silver Crown division and 21 in USAC Midgets; won 24 midget races in other divisions.
- Has won races on in the Busch Series, the Craftsman Truck Series and in three NASCAR Touring divisions—Busch North, Featherlite Southwest and Winston West; is one of five drivers to win in all three of NASCAR's national series.
- Began racing on local tracks around his home in Missouri in 1971, primarily in open-wheel competition.
- Owns I-55 Raceway in Pevely, Mo.

## CAREER BY YEAR

**2003** Schrader ran in 32 races and finished in the top 10 just twice. He put together consecutive top 15 finishes just once all season, with an eighth at Michigan and a 12th at Bristol. He was an inconsistent qualifier, starting in the top 10 four times but 40th or worse eight times—but it didn't matter. His average finish when starting 40th or worse: 29.9; when starting in the top 10: 27.3.

**2002** Finished 30th in series points. … First season out of top 20 in series points since racing full-time in 1985. … Struggled with nine DNFs, seven of them mechanical. … Led 46 laps in the Daytona 500. … Best finish was 13th at New Hampshire in September. … Departed MB2 Motorsports at season's end.

**2001** Finished 19th in series points. … Best finish was eighth in the season finale at Atlanta. … Made his 500th start eight races into the season at Martinsville. … Was running at the end of each of the season's final 30 races.

**2000** Finished 18th in series points. … Tabbed as the new MB2 Motorsports driver following Ernie Irvan's retirement. … Flirted with the top 10 in points early in the season but scored only one top 10 in the second half of the year. … Had only two DNFs. … Finished a season-high ninth at the Daytona 500.

**1999** Finished 15th in series points. … Posted four of his six top 10s in the first half of the season. …Proved tough on superspeedways, posting two season-best sixth-place finishes at the Daytona 500 and Talladega in April, where he won the pole. … Had six top 10s. … Joined by new teammate Kenny Wallace to start the season as car owner Andy Petree expanded to two teams.

**1998** Finished 12th in series points. … Won poles at Talladega and two races later at Phoenix, where he led the first 53 laps. … Had 10 starts inside the top 10. … Had three top fives and 11 top 10s. … Posted season-best finishes (fourth) at the Daytona 500 and both Richmond races.

**1997** Finished 10th in series points. … Joined the new team for upstart Andy Petree Racing. … Started slow with three finishes of 25th or worse in the first four races, including 33rd in the season opener at Daytona. …Rebounded with a strong second half, posting just three finishes outside the top 15. … Scored a pair of season-best fourth-place finishes at Talladega and Rockingham in the final four races. … Won two poles, both at New Hampshire. … Had two top fives and eight top 10s.

**1996** Finished 12th in series points. … Posted three top fives and 10 top 10s in his final season driving for Rick Hendrick. …Best finish was third at the Daytona 500. … Led 45 laps during the season. … Qualified in the top 10 11 times. … Fell out of the top 10 in series points after finishing 35th and 30th in the final two races.

**1995** Finished 17th in series points. … Hopes of chasing the series championship were doused by nine DNFs. … Teammate Jeff Gordon won the championship, but Schrader's No. 25 team suffered 15 finishes of 25th or worse. … Won the pole at Pocono and finished a season-best third. … Qualified in the top 10 13 times. … Led nine races and a total of 238 laps. … Had two top fives and eight top 10s.

**1994** Finished fourth in series points, a career best. … Did not reach victory lane despite nine top fives. … Ran second to Dale Earnhardt at Bristol. … Scored back-to-back third-place finishes at Dover and Pocono, followed by a sixth at Michigan and a fifth at Daytona in July. … Started in the top 10 14 times.

**1993** Finished ninth in series points. … Four finishes of 20th or worse left the No. 25 team 19th in points after just six races. … Battled back to fifth in points by midseason after scoring five top fives in six races capped by a third at Daytona. … Led the series with six poles. … Had nine top fives and 15 top 10s. … Finished second twice, at Pocono and Dover.

**1992** Finished 17th in series points, breaking a five-year streak of top 10 finishes. … Struggled to find consistency, scattering four top fives and 11 top 10s among nine finishes of 23rd or worse. … Won the pole at Pocono. …Best finish was third Bristol in the spring.

**1991** Finished ninth in series points. … Won at Atlanta and Dover and had 18 top 10s and 10 top fives. … Five finishes of 30th or worse in the last 14 races kept him out of title hunt. … Led 16 races for a career-high 440 laps led.

**1990** Finished 10th in series points. … Won his third straight pole at the Daytona 500 but finished 40th. … Won the Busch Clash for second consecutive season. … Had a string of 10 top 10 starts. … Had two runner-up finishes, seven top fives and 14 top 10s.

**1989** Finished fifth in series points. … Won his second straight Daytona 500 pole; also won the Busch Clash and a 125-mile qualifying race before finishing second in the Daytona 500. … Finished with four poles and qualified 10th or better in 24 of 29 races. … Won at Charlotte. … Had 10 top fives and 14 top 10s.

**1988** Finished fifth in series points. … Enjoyed a breakthrough season with four top fives and 17 top 10s. … First of nine seasons driving for Rick Hendrick. … Held off Geoff Bodine to win his first career race, at Talladega in August. … Won the pole for the Daytona 500.

**1987** Finished 10th in series points. … Won his first career pole, at Darlington. … Won one of two 125-mile qualifying races for the Daytona 500. … Had 10 top 10s.

**1986** Finished 16th in series points. … Had four top 10s, driving the second of three seasons for Junie Donlavey. … Finished a season-best seventh at both Martinsville races.

**1985** Finished 16th in series points. … Known for helping young drivers, car owner Junie Donlavey gave Schrader his first full-time ride. … Won Rookie of the Year honors, topping Eddie Bierschwale by 14 points. … Had three top 10s.

**1984** Finished 53rd in series points. … Broke into the series by renting Fords from car owner Elmo Langley for his first three starts. … Langley rewarded him with two more starts after taking care of his equipment. … Best finish was 17th at North Wilkesboro.

### CAREER STATISTICS

| Year | Car Owner | Races | Champ. Finish | Won | Top 5 | Top 10 | DNF | Poles | Money Won |
|---|---|---|---|---|---|---|---|---|---|
| 1984 | Elmo Langley | 5 | 53 | 0 | 0 | 0 | 0 | 0 | $16,425 |
| 1985 | Junie Donlavey | 28 | 16 | 0 | 0 | 3 | 7 | 0 | 211,523 |
| 1986 | Junie Donlavey | 29 | 16 | 0 | 0 | 4 | 9 | 0 | 235,904 |
| 1987 | Junie Donlavey | 29 | 10 | 0 | 1 | 10 | 8 | 1 | 375,918 |
| 1988 | R. Hendrick | 28 | | 1 | 4 | 17 | 1 | 2 | 626,934 |
| | B. Arrington | 1 | 5 | 0 | 0 | 0 | 0 | 0 | 4,610 |
| 1989 | R. Hendrick | 29 | 5 | 1 | 10 | 14 | 6 | 4 | 1,039,441 |
| 1990 | R. Hendrick | 29 | 10 | 0 | 7 | 14 | 8 | 3 | 769,934 |
| 1991 | R. Hendrick | 29 | 9 | 2 | 10 | 18 | 6 | 0 | 772,439 |
| 1992 | R. Hendrick | 29 | 17 | 0 | 4 | 11 | 6 | 1 | 639,679 |
| 1993 | R. Hendrick | 30 | 9 | 0 | 9 | 15 | 4 | 6 | 952,748 |
| 1994 | R. Hendrick | 31 | 4 | 0 | 9 | 18 | 2 | 0 | 1,171,062 |
| 1995 | R. Hendrick | 31 | 17 | 0 | 2 | 10 | 9 | 1 | 886,566 |
| 1996 | R. Hendrick | 31 | 12 | 0 | 3 | 10 | 2 | 0 | 1,089,603 |
| 1997 | A. Petree | 32 | 10 | 0 | 2 | 8 | 1 | 2 | 1,355,292 |
| 1998 | A. Petree | 33 | 12 | 0 | 3 | 11 | 5 | 2 | 1,887,399 |
| 1999 | A. Petree | 34 | 15 | 0 | 0 | 6 | 1 | 1 | 1,939,147 |
| 2000 | N. Bowers | 34 | 18 | 0 | 0 | 2 | 2 | 0 | 1,711,476 |
| 2001 | N. Bowers | 36 | 19 | 0 | 0 | 5 | 2 | 0 | 2,418,181 |
| 2002 | T. Beard | 36 | 30 | 0 | 0 | 0 | 9 | 0 | 2,460,140 |
| 2003 | B. Morgenthau | 32 | 36 | 0 | 0 | 2 | 8 | 0 | 2,007,420 |
| **TOTALS** | | 596 | | 4 | 64 | 178 | 96 | 23 | $22,571,841 |

### 2003 RESULTS

| Race | Start | Finish | Standing Pos. | Winnings |
|---|---|---|---|---|
| Daytona 500 (Daytona) | 28 | 42 | 42 | $166,476 |
| Subway 400 (Rockingham) | 35 | 24 | 37 | $47,760 |
| UAW-DaimlerChrysler 400 (Las Vegas) | 28 | 28 | 38 | $60,550 |
| Bass Pro Shops MBNA 500 (Atlanta) | 42 | 38 | 41 | $46,175 |
| Carolina Dodge Dealers 400 (Darlington) | 15 | 17 | 37 | $45,715 |
| Food City 500 (Bristol) | 3 | 37 | 38 | $57,410 |
| Samsung/RadioShack 500 (Texas) | 42 | 24 | 38 | $75,975 |
| Aaron's 499 (Talladega) | 41 | 33 | 39 | $65,350 |
| Virginia 500 (Martinsville) | 4 | 10 | 35 | $54,050 |
| Auto Club 500 (California) | 41 | 30 | 35 | $67,210 |
| Pontiac Excitement 400 (Richmond) | 33 | 24 | 34 | $58,100 |
| Coca-Cola 600 (Charlotte) | 30 | 28 | 34 | $70,175 |
| MBNA Armed Forces Family 400 (Dover) | 25 | 26 | 35 | $62,205 |
| Pocono 500 (Pocono) | 39 | 43 | 35 | $42,186 |
| Sirius 400 (Michigan) | 28 | 42 | 37 | $48,440 |
| Dodge/Save Mart 350 (Sonoma) | 42 | 33 | 35 | $55,745 |
| Pepsi 400 (Daytona) | 7 | 41 | 37 | $62,935 |
| Tropicana 400 (Chicago) | 43 | 28 | 36 | $73,614 |
| New England 300 (New Hampshire) | 38 | 36 | 36 | $49,010 |
| Pennsylvania 500 (Pocono) | 34 | 26 | 36 | $47,590 |
| GFS Marketplace 400 (Michigan) | 30 | 8 | 37 | $79,790 |
| Sharpie 500 (Bristol) | 26 | 12 | 36 | $74,090 |
| Southern 500 (Darlington) | 39 | 38 | 36 | $50,160 |
| Chevy Rock & Roll 400 (Richmond) | 27 | 25 | 35 | $51,655 |
| Sylvania 300 (New Hampshire) | 20 | 37 | 36 | $48,850 |
| MBNA America 400 (Dover) | 38 | 33 | 36 | $53,455 |
| EA SPORTS 500 (Talladega) | 7 | 21 | 35 | $58,060 |
| Banquet 400 (Kansas) | 43 | 28 | 35 | $64,725 |
| Subway 500 (Martinsville) | 18 | 22 | 36 | $48,075 |
| Bass Pro Shops MBNA 500 (Atlanta) | 43 | 26 | 36 | $67,025 |
| Checker Auto Parts 500 (Phoenix) | 34 | 27 | 36 | $51,625 |
| Pop Secret 400 (Rockingham) | 28 | 36 | 36 | $46,255 |

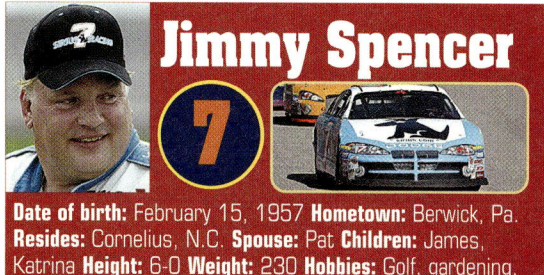

# Jimmy Spencer

**Date of birth:** February 15, 1957 **Hometown:** Berwick, Pa. **Resides:** Cornelius, N.C. **Spouse:** Pat **Children:** James, Katrina **Height:** 6-0 **Weight:** 230 **Hobbies:** Golf, gardening, helping son pursue racing

### NASCAR ACHIEVEMENTS

**First NASCAR Cup start:** June 4, 1999 (Dover)
**Best points finish:** 12 (1993)
**Career victories:** 2—Daytona (94b), Talladega (94b)
**First victory:** July 2, 1994 (Daytona)
**Career poles:** 3—Charlotte (01b), Indianapolis (01), North Wilkesboro (94b)
**First pole:** September 30, 1994 (North Wilkesboro)
**Best career finish:** 1 **Best career start:** 1

### FAST FACTS

- Was the NASCAR Winston Modified champion in 1986, '87.
- Ran full time in the Busch Series in 1988 and '92 and remains a frequent competitor in the series.
- Began racing at Port Royal (Pa.) Speedway.
- Named 1979 Rookie of the Year at Shangri-La Speedway in Owego, N.Y., in the modified division.
- Spencer's father, Ed, and brother, Paul, both were racers.
- When he was 15, Spencer snuck into the garage area at Pocono Raceway during an IndyCar weekend and met A.J. Foyt.

### CAR FACTS

**Car:** No. 7 Dodge
**Primary sponsor:** TBA
**Owner:** Jim Smith
**Team:** Ultra Motorsports
**Crew chief:** Gene Nead
**Engine builder:** Mike Ege

### CAREER BY YEAR

**2003** Spencer's 29th-place finish in points his worst since 1994. Four accidents in the first 11 races set the tone for a disappointing season. His best finish, and only top five, was a fourth at Charlotte in May. Spencer never finished consecutive races in the top 15. Qualifying was a problem—he had to use five provisionals, and his average starting spot was 23.9.

**2002** Finished 27th in series points. ... Concluded a long relationship with owner Travis Carter, moving from Haas-Carter Motorsports to Chip Ganassi Racing. ... Had six top 10s and two top fives. ... Season-best finish was second at the spring event at Bristol. ... Made 34 of 36 starts; did not qualify for the Daytona 500 or Watkins Glen. ... Released by Ganassi at end of the season.

**2001** Finished 16th in series points, his best championship finish with owner Travis Carter since 1998 in what would be their final season together. ... Had eight top 10s, his highest total since 1998, including season-best fourth-place efforts at Darlington, New Hampshire. ... Won two poles—at Indy and Charlotte—his first since his first career pole in 1994.

**2000** Finished 22nd in series points. ... Posted five top 10s, including a pair of fifth-place finishes, in his sixth consecutive season with Travis Carter.

**1999** Finished 20th in series points. ... Matched his career-best finish of second. ... Had four top 10s overall.

**1998** Finished 14th in series points. ... Had eight top 10s, including a runner-up finish at Talladega.

**1997** Finished 20th in series points. ... Had four top 10s.

**1996** Finished 15th in series points. ... Had nine top 10s and two top fives.

**1995** Finished 26th in series points. ... Reunited with team owner Travis Carter, whom he ran for in 1991 and '92, after one season with Junior Johnson. ... Posted four top 10s.

**1994** Finished 29th in series points. ... Moved from one legend to another, leaving Bobby Allison's operation for Junior Johnson. ... Despite his relatively low finish in the points, it was a breakthrough season as he posted the first two wins of his Winston Cup career as well as his first pole. ... His first win came at the Pepsi 400 at Daytona, in his 129th career start, and he added another triumph at Talladega. ... First pole came at North Wilkesboro in September, in his 139th career start.

**1993** Finished 12th in series points. ... An impressive four-race stint with Bobby Allison the previous season earned him a full-time ride, and he turned in a strong performance. In addition to his championship standing, he posted 10 top 10s and five top fives.

**1992** Finished 33rd in series points. ... Ran a limited schedule for three owners—Travis Carter (seven races), Bobby Allison (four) and Dick Moroso (one). ... Had three top fives in four starts for Allison.

**1991** Finished 25th in series points. ... Moved to his third team in three seasons, joining Travis Carter. ... Registered six top 10s, including his first career top five, a third at North Wilkesboro.

**1990** Finished 24th in series points. ... Moved from the Baker-Schiff operation to owner Rod Osterlund's team. ... Competed in 26 races and had a pair of top 10s.

**1989** Finished 34th in series points, running a limited schedule for Baker-Schiff. ... Competed in 17 races and posted three top 10s. ... First career start was June 4 at Dover, where he started 20th and finished 34th.

## CAREER STATISTICS

| Year | Car Owner | Champ. Races | Finish | Won | Top 5 | Top 10 | DNF | Poles | Money Won |
|---|---|---|---|---|---|---|---|---|---|
| 1989 | Baker-Schiff | 17 | 34 | 0 | 0 | 3 | 9 | 0 | $121,065 |
| 1990 | Rod Osterlund | 26 | 24 | 0 | 0 | 2 | 5 | 0 | 219,775 |
| 1991 | Travis Carter | 29 | 25 | 0 | 1 | 6 | 14 | 0 | 283,620 |
| 1992 | Travis Carter | 7 | | 0 | 0 | 0 | 4 | 0 | 76,055 |
| | Dick Moroso | 1 | | 0 | 0 | 0 | 0 | 0 | 6,125 |
| | Bobby Allison | 4 | | 0 | 3 | 3 | 0 | 0 | 103,905 |
| 1993 | Bobby Allison | 30 | 12 | 0 | 5 | 10 | 4 | 0 | 686,026 |
| 1994 | Junior Johnson | 29 | 29 | 2 | 3 | 4 | 11 | 1 | 479,235 |
| 1995 | T. Carter | 29 | 26 | 0 | 0 | 4 | 2 | 0 | 507,210 |
| 1996 | T. Carter | 31 | 15 | 0 | 2 | 9 | 2 | 0 | 1,090,876 |
| 1997 | T. Carter | 32 | 20 | 0 | 1 | 4 | 6 | 0 | 1,073,779 |
| 1998 | T. Carter | 31 | 14 | 0 | 3 | 8 | 2 | 0 | 1,741,012 |
| 1999 | T. Carter | 34 | 20 | 0 | 2 | 4 | 6 | 0 | 1,752,299 |
| 2000 | T. Carter | 34 | 22 | 0 | 2 | 5 | 8 | 0 | 1,936,762 |
| 2001 | T. Carter | 36 | 16 | 0 | 3 | 8 | 7 | 2 | 2,669,638 |
| 2002 | Chip Ganassi | 34 | 27 | 0 | 2 | 6 | 7 | 0 | 2,136,792 |
| 2003 | Jim Smith | 35 | 29 | 0 | 1 | 4 | 8 | 0 | 2,565,800 |
| TOTALS | | 439 | | 2 | 28 | 80 | 95 | 3 | $17,449,974 |

## 2003 RESULTS

| Race | Start | Finish | Standing Pos. | Winnings |
|---|---|---|---|---|
| Daytona 500 (Daytona) | 23 | 40 | 40 | $166,620 |
| Subway 400 (Rockingham) | 36 | 28 | 39 | $50,085 |
| UAW-DaimlerChrysler 400 (Las Vegas) | 15 | 17 | 35 | $90,250 |
| Bass Pro Shops MBNA 500 (Atlanta) | 5 | 7 | 23 | $79,550 |
| Carolina Dodge Dealers 400 (Darlington) | 4 | 21 | 23 | $56,569 |
| Food City 500 (Bristol) | 7 | 12 | 21 | $88,865 |
| Samsung/RadioShack 500 (Texas) | 18 | 33 | 24 | $63,075 |
| Aaron's 499 (Talladega) | 34 | 38 | 30 | $66,025 |
| Virginia 500 (Martinsville) | 13 | 19 | 28 | $63,575 |
| Auto Club 500 (California) | 24 | 33 | 28 | $70,025 |
| Pontiac Excitement 400 (Richmond) | 25 | 42 | 29 | $46,110 |
| Coca-Cola 600 (Charlotte) | 14 | 4 | 28 | $137,350 |
| MBNA Armed Forces Family 400 (Dover) | 31 | 29 | 29 | $61,230 |
| Pocono 500 (Pocono) | 30 | 39 | 29 | $42,385 |
| Sirius 400 (Michigan) | 40 | 29 | 30 | $60,304 |
| Dodge/Save Mart 350 (Sonoma) | 39 | 36 | 30 | $54,785 |
| Pepsi 400 (Daytona) | 40 | 12 | 30 | $89,175 |
| Tropicana 400 (Chicago) | 21 | 23 | 30 | $82,550 |
| New England 300 (New Hampshire) | 31 | 15 | 29 | $70,475 |
| Pennsylvania 500 (Pocono) | 21 | 22 | 29 | $61,690 |
| Brickyard 400 (Indianapolis) | 32 | 8 | 27 | $165,500 |
| Sirius at the Glen (Watkins Glen) | 39 | 23 | 29 | $62,795 |
| GFS Marketplace 400 (Michigan) | 10 | 26 | 28 | $61,154 |
| Southern 500 (Darlington) | 38 | 22 | 29 | $56,745 |
| Chevy Rock & Roll 400 (Richmond) | 22 | 36 | 29 | $47,065 |
| Sylvania 300 (New Hampshire) | 34 | 23 | 29 | $55,850 |
| MBNA America 400 (Dover) | 29 | 15 | 29 | $75,890 |
| EA SPORTS 500 (Talladega) | 31 | 42 | 29 | $51,630 |
| Banquet 400 (Kansas) | 27 | 15 | 29 | $83,200 |
| UAW-GM Quality 500 (Charlotte) | 25 | 26 | 29 | $57,889 |
| Subway 500 (Martinsville) | 6 | 38 | 29 | $43,115 |
| Bass Pro Shops MBNA 500 (Atlanta) | 22 | 9 | 29 | $92,450 |
| Checker Auto Parts 500 (Phoenix) | 29 | 40 | 29 | $46,625 |
| Pop Secret 400 (Rockingham) | 8 | 14 | 29 | $72,825 |
| Ford 400 (Homestead) | 16 | 25 | 29 | $58,989 |

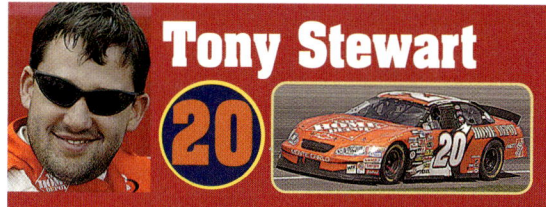

# Tony Stewart

**Date of birth:** May 20, 1971 **Hometown:** Rushville, Ind.
**Resides:** Columbus, Ind. and Cornelius, N.C. **Spouse:** Single
**Children:** None **Height:** 5-9 **Weight:** 170 **Hobbies:** Pool, bowling, boating, fishing

## NASCAR ACHIEVEMENTS

**First NASCAR Cup start:** February 14, 1999 (Daytona)
**Best points finish:** 1 (2002)
**Career victories:** 17—Atlanta (02a), Bristol (01b), Dover (00a, 00b), Homestead (99, 00), Martinsville (00b), Michigan (00a), New Hampshire (00a), Phoenix (99), Pocono (03a), Richmond (99b, 01a, 02a, 02b), Sonoma (01), Watkins Glen (02)
**First victory:** September 11, 1999 (Richmond)
**Career poles:** 7—Atlanta (02b), Bristol (99b), Charlotte (02b, 03b), Chicago (03), Indianapolis (02), Martinsville (99a, 00b), Pocono (00b), Sonoma (02)
**First pole:** October 1, 1999 (Martinsville)
**Best career finish:** 1  **Best career start:** 1

## FAST FACTS

- Ran 22 Busch Series races for Joe Gibbs Racing in 1998, winning two poles and posting five top fives.
- Ran a full Indy Racing League schedule in 1998.
- Ran five Busch races for Gibbs in 1997 and nine for Ranier/Walsh in 1996.
- Won the Indy Racing League championship in 1997 and was the IRL Rookie of the Year in 1996.
- Was the Indianapolis 500 Rookie of the Year in 1996.
- Swept championships in the USAC Midget, Sprint Car and Silver Crown competition in 1995, becoming first driver to do so.
- Was the 1994 USAC Midget national champ.
- Was the 1991 USAC Sprint Car Rookie of the Year.
- Won the 1987 World Karting Association national title.
- Won the 1983 International Karting Foundation Grand National title.
- Has a World of Outlaws sprint car team.
- Stewart's favorite driver is A.J. Foyt.

## CAR FACTS

**Car:** No. 20 Chevrolet
**Primary sponsor:** Home Depot
**Owner:** Joe Gibbs
**Team:** Joe Gibbs Racing
**Crew chief:** Greg Zipadelli
**Engine builder:** Mark Cronquist

## CAREER BY YEAR

**2003** A switch from Pontiac to Chevrolets and a horsepower problem had the defending champion struggling early in the season. He finished 40th or worse in three straight races in late April and early May. He salvaged his season with six straight top fives, starting at Dover on September 21 and ending at Atlanta on October 27. He won at Charlotte and Watkins Glen.

**2002** Won the Winston Cup Series championship, giving team owner Joe Gibbs his second championship in the last three seasons. … Won three races—Atlanta in March, Richmond in May and Watkins Glen in August. … Bounced back after a last-place finish in the Daytona 500. … Took the series lead in points after the Talladega race in October. … March to the top began at New Hampshire in July with the first of nine consecutive top 15s. … Clinched the championship in the season finale at Homestead with an 18th-place finish.

**2001** Finished second in series points, behind four-time champion Jeff Gordon. … Started the season by winning the Budweiser Shootout at Daytona, a non-points event; that was his first victory in restrictor-plate racing. … Won three races—at Sonoma and Richmond and at the Bristol night race. … Completed 1,100 miles of racing on May 27, finishing sixth in the Indianapolis 500 and third in the Coca-Cola 600 at Charlotte.

**2000** Finished sixth in series points. … A slow start had him outside the top 10 after nine races. … Won six races, including a sweep of Dover's two events. Also won at Michigan, New Hampshire, Martinsville and in season finale at Homestead. … Homestead win came on day Joe Gibbs Racing teammate Bobby Labonte clinched the Winston Cup championship. … Won two poles.

**1999** Finished fourth in series points. … Was the Raybestos Rookie of the Year in his first season with Joe Gibbs Racing. … Won three races during great second half of season. … First career win came at Richmond, on September 11, in his 25th start. … Also won back-to-back events at Phoenix and Homestead. … Became the first Winston Cup rookie to win three races. … Won two poles and qualified second for the Daytona 500. … Won the Winston Open, then finished second in The Winston. … Raced in the Indianapolis 500 and Coca-Cola 600 on May 30, finishing ninth at Indy and fourth at Charlotte.

## CAREER STATISTICS

| Year | Car Owner | Races | Champ. Finish | Won | Top 5 | Top 10 | DNF | Poles | Money Won |
|---|---|---|---|---|---|---|---|---|---|
| 1999 | Joe Gibbs | 34 | 4 | 3 | 12 | 21 | 1 | 2 | $3,190,149 |
| 2000 | Joe Gibbs | 34 | 6 | 6 | 12 | 23 | 5 | 2 | 3,642,348 |
| 2001 | Joe Gibbs | 36 | 2 | 3 | 15 | 22 | 4 | 0 | 4,941,463 |
| 2002 | Joe Gibbs | 36 | 1 | 3 | 15 | 21 | 6 | 2 | 9,163,761 |
| 2003 | Joe Gibbs | 36 | 7 | 2 | 12 | 18 | 5 | 1 | 6,131,633 |
| TOTALS | | 176 | | 17 | 66 | 105 | 21 | 7 | $27,069,354 |

## 2003 RESULTS

| Race | Start | Finish | Standing Pos. | Winnings |
|---|---|---|---|---|
| Daytona 500 (Daytona) | 8 | 7 | 6 | $315,454 |
| Subway 400 (Rockingham) | 33 | 20 | 9 | $103,538 |
| UAW-DaimlerChrysler 400 (Las Vegas) | 8 | 5 | 5 | $163,503 |
| Bass Pro Shops MBNA 500 (Atlanta) | 8 | 5 | 2 | $113,328 |
| Carolina Dodge Dealers 400 (Darlington) | 28 | 10 | 2 | $103,158 |
| Food City 500 (Bristol) | 10 | 26 | 3 | $111,518 |
| Samsung/RadioShack 500 (Texas) | 22 | 34 | 7 | $113,728 |
| Aaron's 499 (Talladega) | 19 | 25 | 9 | $118,708 |
| Virginia 500 (Martinsville) | 8 | 6 | 7 | $105,953 |
| Auto Club 500 (California | 3 | 41 | 11 | $117,708 |

| Race | Start | Finish | Standing Pos. | Winnings |
|---|---|---|---|---|
| Pontiac Excitement 400 (Richmond) | 9 | 41 | 17 | $98,748 |
| Coca-Cola 600 (Charlotte) | 6 | 40 | 20 | $140,528 |
| MBNA Armed Forces Family 400 (Dover) | 11 | 4 | 16 | $145,253 |
| Pocono 500 (Pocono) | 4 | 1 | 13 | $214,253 |
| Sirius 400 (Michigan) | 2 | 8 | 12 | $110,843 |
| Dodge/Save Mart 350 (Sonoma) | 10 | 12 | 11 | $110,988 |
| Pepsi 400 (Daytona) | 13 | 21 | 11 | $114,128 |
| Tropicana 400 (Chicago) | 1 | 2 | 8 | $213,468 |
| New England 300 (New Hampshire) | 8 | 22 | 9 | $104,528 |
| Pennsylvania 500 (Pocono) | 33 | 37 | 14 | $105,203 |
| Brickyard 400 (Indianapolis) | 15 | 12 | 13 | $224,728 |
| Sirius at the Glen (Watkins Glen) | 4 | 11 | 11 | $101,233 |
| GFS Marketplace 400 (Michigan) | 23 | 3 | 11 | $140,063 |
| Sharpie 500 (Bristol) | 18 | 23 | 11 | $119,138 |
| Southern 500 (Darlington) | 20 | 12 | 10 | $109,503 |
| Chevy Rock & Roll 400 (Richmond) | 14 | 27 | 11 | $100,283 |
| Sylvania 300 (New Hampshire) | 32 | 20 | 11 | $107,278 |
| MBNA America 400 (Dover) | 11 | 3 | 10 | $153,408 |
| EA SPORTS 500 (Talladega) | 11 | 3 | 9 | $163,333 |
| Banquet 400 (Kansas) | 14 | 4 | 8 | $155,578 |
| UAW-GM Quality 500 (Charlotte) | 6 | 1 | 7 | $312,478 |
| Subway 500 (Martinsville) | 16 | 3 | 7 | $129,478 |
| Bass Pro Shops MBNA 500 (Atlanta) | 24 | 2 | 7 | $207,678 |
| Checker Auto Parts 500 (Phoenix) | 6 | 18 | 7 | $102,128 |
| Pop Secret 400 (Rockingham) | 29 | 9 | 7 | $100,403 |
| Ford 400 (Homestead) | 13 | 7 | 7 | $120,703 |

## Brian Vickers

**Date of birth:** October 24, 1983 **Hometown:** Thomasville, N.C.
**Resides:** Thomasville, N.C. **Spouse:** Single **Children:** None
**Height:** 5-11 **Weight:** 160 **Hobbies:** Golf and video games

### NASCAR ACHIEVEMENTS

**First NASCAR Cup start:** October 11, 2003 (Charlotte)
**Best points finish:** 49 (2003)
**Career victories:** 0
**Career poles:** 0
**Best career finish:** 13 **Best career start:** 2

### FAST FACTS

- Ran partial Busch Series schedules in 2001 and 2002 before winning the series championship in his first full season in 2003.
- Was a three-time World Karting Association national champion in the mid-1990s.
- Began racing late model stocks in the NASCAR

### CAR FACTS

**Car:** No. 25 Chevrolet
**Primary sponsor:** GMAC
**Owner:** Papa Joe Hendrick
**Team:** Hendrick Motorsports
**Crew chief:** Peter Sospenzo
**Engine builder:** Hendrick Motorsports

Weekly Racing Series in 1999. Was named the series Rookie of the Year and Most Popular Driver.
- Was the 2000 USAR ProCup Series Rookie of the Year and finished second in that series in 2001.

## CAREER BY YEAR

**2003** Vickers got his feet wet by running the last four races for Hendrick Motorsports. He had stellar qualifying efforts and decent races. The 20-year-old faced huge pressure and didn't flinch—he didn't clinch the Busch championship until he crossed the finish line in the final race.

### CAREER STATISTICS

| Year | Car Owner | Races | Champ. Finish | Won | Top 5 | Top 10 | DNF | Poles | Money Won |
|---|---|---|---|---|---|---|---|---|---|
| 2003 | Rick Hendrick | 5 | 49 | 0 | 0 | 0 | 1 | 0 | $263,484 |

### 2003 RESULTS

| Race | Start | Finish | Standing Pos. | Winnings |
|---|---|---|---|---|
| UAW-GM Quality 500 (Charlotte) | 20 | 33 | 68 | $46,175 |
| Bass Pro Sops MBNA 500 (Atlanta) | 4 | 43 | 62 | $62,059 |
| Checker Auto Parts 500 (Phoenix) | 2 | 13 | 53 | $58,900 |
| Pop Secret 400 (Rockingham) | 2 | 24 | 51 | $52,175 |
| Ford 400 (Homestead) | 3 | 34 | 50 | $44,175 |

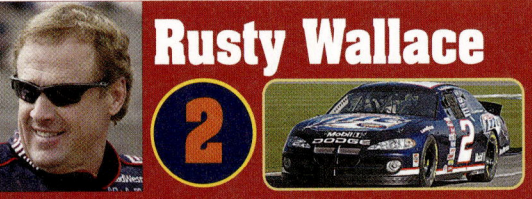

## Rusty Wallace

**Date of birth:** August 14, 1956 **Hometown:** Fenton, Mo.
**Resides:** Lake Norman, N.C. **Spouse:** Patti **Children:** Greg, Katie, Stephen **Height:** 6-0 **Weight:** 185 **Hobbies:** Flying, boating, golf

### NASCAR ACHIEVEMENTS

**First NASCAR Cup start:** March 16, 1980 (Atlanta)
**Best points finish:** 1 (1989)
**Career victories:** 54—Atlanta (88b, 93b), Bristol (86a, 89a, 91a, 93a, 94b, 96a, 99a, 00a, 00b), California (01), Charlotte (88b, 90a), Dover (93b, 94a, 94b), Martinsville (86b, 93a, 94a, 94b, 95a, 96a), Michigan (88a, 89b, 94a, 96a, 00b), New Hampshire (90), North Wilkesboro (88b, 93b, 93b), Phoenix (98), Pocono (91b, 94a, 96b, 00b), Richmond (89a, 89b, 92b, 93b, 95b, 97a), Riverside (87b, 88a), Rockingham (88b, 89a, 93a, 93b, 94a), Sonoma (90, 96), Watkins Glen (87, 89)
**First victory:** April 6, 1986 (Bristol)
**Career poles:** 36—Atlanta (88b, 90b, 93a), Bristol (91a, 93a, 97a, 98a, 99a, 00b), Dover (93b, 98a, 99b, 00a, 02b), Martinsville (88b, 94a, 00a), New Hampshire (99b, 00a), North Wilkesboro (89a), Phoenix (90, 92, 000, Pocono (89a, 94a, 00a), Richmond (91b, 98b, 00a), Rockingham

(89a, 00a), Sonoma (89, 00), Watkins Glen (99)
**First pole:** June 6, 1987 (Michigan)
**Best career finish:** 1   **Best career start:** 1

## FAST FACTS

- Made his driving debut at Lakehill Speedway in Valley Park, Mo., in 1973.
- Named 1973 Central Racing Association Rookie of the Year.
- Won more than 200 stock car features from 1974-78 before joining the USAC stock car circuit in 1979.
- Named USAC's Rookie of the Year in 1979, winning five races and finishing second in points.
- Won the 1983 ASA championship.
- Is a nine-time IROC participant, with four victories in the series.
- Is an avid aviator who owns his own airplanes and helicopter; is a jet-rated pilot and says he likely would be a commercial pilot if he were not a racer.
- Father was a three-time track champion in the St. Louis area.
- Once crashed while waving to the crowd after winning a race in Springfield, Mo.

### CAR FACTS
**Car:** No. 2 Dodge
**Primary sponsor:** Miller Lite
**Owner:** Roger Penske
**Team:** Penske South
**Crew chief:** TBA
**Engine builder:** Scott Carriher

## CAREER BY YEAR

**2003** For the second straight season, Wallace was winless. He qualified well but wasn't able to back that up with good finishes. He led only four races and picked up just two top fives and 12 top 10s. His 14th-place finish in the points standings was his worst in 18 seasons. He finished off the lead lap in the last five races of the season.

**2002** Finished seventh in series points for the third consecutive season. … Did not record a victory, ending the second-longest streak in NASCAR history for most consecutive seasons with at least one win at 16. … Came close to extending the streak, finishing runner-up three times. … Had seven top fives and 17 top 10s and led 202 laps. … Had just one DNF. …Started the season with a crew chief change, from Robin Pemberton to Bill Wilburn.

**2001** Finished seventh in series points for the second consecutive season. … Scored his only victory of the season at California Speedway, a track built by his car owner, Roger Penske. … Season was hampered by three 43rd-place finishes in which he completed a total of 33 of a possible 657 laps. … Won the pole for The Winston. … Had eight top fives and 14 top 10s.

**2000** Finished seventh in series points. … Cracked the 50-victory barrier at Bristol, winning the Food City 500 on March 26. … Posted four wins, sweeping at Bristol and also winning at Pocono and Michigan. … Won a career-best nine poles.

**1999** Finished eighth in series points. … Recorded one win (Bristol), seven top fives, 16 top 10s and four poles. … Had only three DNFs, all because of accidents.

**1998** Finished fourth in series points. … Posted a win (Phoenix), 15 top fives and 21 top 10s. … Had four pole positions, his first multiple-pole season 1994.

**1997** Finished ninth in series points. … Had a win (Martinsville) and six top threes. … Had 11 DNFs in 32 starts. …Captured the pole at Bristol, his first since 1994.

**1996** Finished seventh in series points. … Registered five victories for his fourth consecutive multiple-win season and 10th in the last 11 seasons. … Season win total ranked second in the series. … Had eight top fives and 18 top 10s. … Ranked third in the series in laps led. … Five wins gave him 46 for his career, tying him with Buddy Baker for 11th on the all-time list.

**1995** Finished fifth in series points, his third consecutive finish among the top five in the championship. … Had two wins, 15 top fives and 19 top 10s. … Ended the new Chevy Monte Carlos' early-season dominance, winning the first race for Ford, at Martinsville in the eighth race of the year.

**1994** Finished third in series points. … Led the series in wins (eight) and laps led. … Won the second race of the season at Rockingham, proving the switch from Pontiac to Ford was a success. … Posted 17 top fives and 20 top 10s.

**1993** Finished runner-up in series points behind Dale Earnhardt. … Won a career-high 10 races and had 19 top fives and 21 top 10s, along with three pole positions. … His team won the annual Unocal Pit Crew Championship at Rockingham. … Led the most laps during the season—2,860 of 10,004.

**1992** Finished 13th in series points, his first season outside the top 10 since 1985. … In his second year as driver/co-owner, scored a win at Richmond and a pole at Phoenix. … Posted five top fives, 12 top 10s and one pole.

**1991** Finished 10th in series points in his first season as driver/co-owner of the Miller Genuine Draft Pontiac. … Recorded two wins, nine top fives and 14 top 10s.

**1990** Finished sixth in series points, his final season with drag racer-team owner Raymond Beadle. … Three engine failures in the final four races dropped him from a top five spot in the point standings. … Posted two wins, nine top fives and 16 top 10s. … Won two poles.

**1989** Won the Winston Cup championship, edging Dale Earnhardt by 12 points for his first title. … Posted six wins in 29 races, along with 13 top fives and 20 top 10s. … Became the eighth driver to win $5 million in a career.

**1988** Finished second in series points, 24 points shy of Bill Elliott for the Winston Cup championship. … Posted six wins, 19 top fives, 23 top 10s and two poles. … Won the last NASCAR event on the road course at Riverside.

**1987** Finished fifth in series points. … Won two races, both on road courses. … Won his first career pole on August 9 at Michigan. … Had nine top fives and 16 top 10s.

**1986** Finished sixth in series points. … Won two races In his first season as driver of the No. 27 Raymond Beadle-owned Pontiacs. …Had four top fives and 16 top 10s. … First career win came on April 6 at Bristol, in his 72nd career start. … Showed his early mastery of road courses, finishing fourth, sixth and eighth in three starts.

**1985** Finished 19th in series points. … Had two top fives and eight top 10s in his second year driving for Cliff Stewart. … Parted ways with Stewart at the end of the season to join Raymond Beadle's Blue Max Racing.

**1984** Finished 14th in series points in his first full season. ... Won NASCAR Rookie of the Year honors. ... Posted two top fives and four top 10s. ... Led the first lap of his career on lap 49 at Darlington in the spring. ... Drew "wild card" entry for the 1985 Busch Clash, a non-points race.

**1982** Finished 65th in series points. ... Drove his own car in three races. .... Finished a season-best 29th at Charlotte.

**1981** Finished 64th in series points. ... Ran in four races with a season-best finish of sixth at Charlotte. ... Ran two races as a driver-owner and another two races for Ron Benfield.

**1980** Finished 57th in series points. ... Drove two races for Roger Penske. ... In his first Winston Cup race, the Atlanta 500 on March 16, Wallace started seventh and finished second to Dale Earnhardt. ... Drove the No. 16 Chevrolet at Charlotte on October 5, starting 15th and finishing 14th.

## CAREER STATISTICS

| Year | Car Owner | Races | Champ. Finish | Won | Top 5 | Top 10 | DNF | Poles | Money Won |
|---|---|---|---|---|---|---|---|---|---|
| 1980 | Roger Penske | 2 | 57 | 0 | 1 | 1 | 0 | 0 | $22,760 |
| 1981 | Ron Benfield | 2 | | 0 | 0 | 0 | 2 | 0 | 4,245 |
| | Rusty Wallace | 2 | 64 | 0 | 0 | 1 | 1 | 0 | 8,650 |
| 1982 | Rusty Wallace | 3 | 65 | 0 | 0 | 0 | 3 | 0 | 7,655 |
| 1983 | John Childs | 0 | | 0 | 0 | 0 | 0 | 0 | 1,100 |
| 1984 | Cliff Stewart | 30 | 14 | 0 | 2 | 4 | 9 | 0 | 195,927 |
| 1985 | Cliff Stewart | 28 | 19 | 0 | 2 | 8 | 12 | 0 | 233,670 |
| 1986 | Ray Beadle | 29 | 6 | 2 | 4 | 16 | 4 | 0 | 557,354 |
| 1987 | Ray Beadle | 29 | 5 | 2 | 9 | 16 | 7 | 1 | 690,652 |
| 1988 | Ray Beadle | 29 | 2 | 6 | 19 | 23 | 2 | 2 | 1,411,567 |
| 1989 | Ray Beadle | 29 | 1 | 6 | 13 | 20 | 4 | 4 | 2,247,950 |
| 1990 | Ray Beadle | 29 | 6 | 2 | 9 | 16 | 8 | 2 | 954,129 |
| 1991 | Roger Penske | 29 | 10 | 2 | 9 | 14 | 10 | 2 | 502,073 |
| 1992 | Roger Penske | 29 | 13 | 1 | 5 | 12 | 5 | 1 | 657,925 |
| 1993 | Roger Penske | 30 | 2 | 10 | 19 | 21 | 5 | 3 | 1,702,154 |
| 1994 | Roger Penske | 31 | 3 | 8 | 17 | 20 | 5 | 2 | 1,914,072 |
| 1995 | Roger Penske | 31 | 5 | 2 | 15 | 19 | 4 | 0 | 1,642,837 |
| 1996 | Roger Penske | 31 | 7 | 5 | 8 | 18 | 6 | 0 | 1,665,315 |
| 1997 | Roger Penske | 32 | 9 | 1 | 8 | 12 | 11 | 1 | 1,705,625 |
| 1998 | Roger Penske | 33 | 4 | 1 | 15 | 21 | 2 | 4 | 2,667,889 |
| 1999 | Roger Penske | 34 | 8 | 1 | 7 | 16 | 3 | 4 | 2,454,050 |
| 2000 | Roger Penske | 34 | 7 | 4 | 12 | 20 | 3 | 9 | 3,621,468 |
| 2001 | Roger Penske | 36 | 7 | 1 | 8 | 14 | 3 | 0 | 4,788,652 |
| 2002 | Roger Penske | 36 | 7 | 0 | 7 | 17 | 1 | 1 | 4,785,134 |
| 2003 | Roger Penske | 36 | 14 | 0 | 2 | 12 | 4 | 0 | 4,246,547 |
| **TOTALS** | | **634** | | **54** | **191** | **321** | **114** | **36** | **$38,689,400** |

## 2003 RESULTS

| Race | Start | Finish | Standing Pos. | Winnings |
|---|---|---|---|---|
| Daytona 500 (Daytona) | 38 | 25 | 26 | $190,692 |
| Subway 400 (Rockingham) | 8 | 6 | 11 | $104,127 |
| UAW-DaimlerChrysler 400 (Las Vegas) | 25 | 40 | 22 | $92,717 |
| Bass Pro Shops MBNA 500 (Atlanta) | 7 | 15 | 22 | $88,392 |
| Carolina Dodge Dealers 400 (Darlington) | 13 | 16 | 20 | $83,827 |
| Food City 500 (Bristol) | 4 | 14 | 17 | $99,882 |
| Samsung/RadioShack 500 (Texas) | 10 | 14 | 14 | $126,692 |
| Aaron's 499 (Talladega) | 31 | 37 | 18 | $101,567 |
| Virginia 500 (Martinsville) | 5 | 8 | 16 | $91,217 |
| Auto Club 500 (California) | 7 | 3 | 12 | $146,917 |
| Pontiac Excitement 400 (Richmond) | 17 | 10 | 9 | $91,942 |
| Coca-Cola 600 (Charlotte) | 34 | 12 | 10 | $117,542 |
| MBNA Armed Forces Family 400 (Dover) | 2 | 6 | 8 | $110,097 |
| Pocono 500 (Pocono) | 27 | 16 | 8 | $84,957 |
| Sirius 400 (Michigan) | 17 | 12 | 8 | $93,457 |
| Dodge/Save Mart 350 (Sonoma) | 7 | 8 | 8 | $99,482 |
| Pepsi 400 (Daytona) | 38 | 28 | 9 | $102,592 |
| Tropicana 400 (Chicago) | 22 | 32 | 11 | $96,042 |
| New England 300 (New Hampshire) | 11 | 17 | 11 | $91,667 |
| Pennsylvania 500 (Pocono) | 7 | 11 | 11 | $88,107 |
| Brickyard 400 (Indianapolis) | 14 | 10 | 10 | $175,967 |
| Sirius at the Glen (Watkins Glen) | 5 | 37 | 12 | $78,492 |
| GFS Marketplace 400 (Michigan) | 31 | 38 | 15 | $82,997 |
| Sharpie 500 (Bristol) | 20 | 43 | 15 | $94,737 |
| Southern 500 (Darlington) | 34 | 36 | 17 | $85,172 |
| Chevy Rock & Roll 400 (Richmond) | 17 | 5 | 15 | $99,047 |
| Sylvania 300 (New Hampshire) | 11 | 6 | 14 | $106,317 |
| MBNA America 400 (Dover) | 14 | 10 | 14 | $98,707 |
| EA SPORTS 500 (Talladega) | 33 | 9 | 14 | $97,742 |
| Banquet 400 (Kansas) | 5 | 9 | 14 | $108,592 |
| UAW-GM Quality 500 (Charlotte) | 14 | 13 | 13 | $90,842 |
| Subway 500 (Martinsville) | 7 | 29 | 14 | $78,392 |
| Bass Pro Shops MBNA 500 (Atlanta) | 21 | 19 | 13 | $104,692 |
| Checker Auto Parts 500 (Phoenix) | 5 | 33 | 15 | $85,217 |
| Pop Secret 400 (Rockingham) | 7 | 23 | 14 | $86,242 |
| Ford 400 (Homestead) | 11 | 23 | 14 | $84,467 |

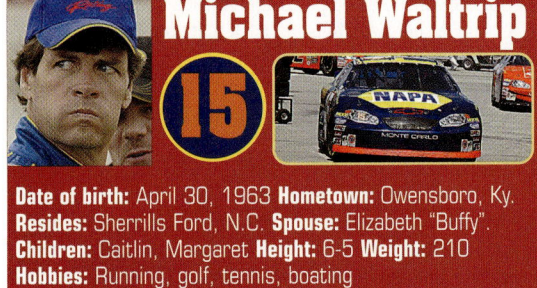

# Michael Waltrip #15

**Date of birth:** April 30, 1963   **Hometown:** Owensboro, Ky.
**Resides:** Sherrills Ford, N.C.   **Spouse:** Elizabeth "Buffy"
**Children:** Caitlin, Margaret   **Height:** 6-5   **Weight:** 210
**Hobbies:** Running, golf, tennis, boating

## NASCAR ACHIEVEMENTS

**First NASCAR Cup start:** May 26, 1985 (Charlotte)
**Best points finish:** 12 (1994, 1995)
**Career victories:** 4—Daytona (01a, 02b, 03a), Talladega (03b)
**First victory:** February 18, 2001 (Daytona)
**Career poles:** 2—Dover (91a), Michigan (91a)
**First pole:** May 30, 1991 (Dover)
**Best career finish:** 1   **Best career start:** 1

## FAST FACTS

● Began racing in go-karts in the mid-1970s and won numerous races.
● Started in stock cars in 1981, when he was the Kentucky Motor Speedway champion in the Mini-Modified Division.
● Won the Goody's Dash Series championship in 1983 and

was that series' Most Popular Driver in 1983 and '84.
- Still is a regular on the NASCAR Busch Series.
- Cites winning The Winston in 1996 and a Busch race at Bristol in 1993 as top memories.
- After taking the first-ever backward victory lap in memory of Alan Kulwicki at Bristol, he proposed in victory lane to his wife, Buffy.
- An avid distance runner, Waltrip has competed in several marathons including the prestigious Boston Marathon. He also had the honor of being a torch bearer in the 2002 Olympic Torch Relay to Salt Lake City.
- Waltrip lived with Richard and Lynda Petty when he first moved to North Carolina from his native Kentucky in order to establish himself in Winston Cup racing.

## CAR FACTS

**Car:** No. 15 Chevrolet
**Primary sponsor:** NAPA Auto Parts
**Owner:** Teresa Earnhardt
**Team:** Dale Earnhardt Inc.
**Crew chief:** Richard Labbe
**Engine builder:** Richie Gilmore

## CAREER BY YEAR

**2003** Waltrip ended the season a disappointing 15th in points, but there were several bright spots. The first was a victory in the Daytona 500. The second was a victory at Talladega. His strong season fell apart starting with the 24th race (Bristol). From there on, he finished outside the top 25 in 10 of 13 races. Still, with eight top fives, he showed signs that he's not just a restrictor-plate racer.

**2002** Finished 14th in series points. … Continued to show dominance in restrictor-plate races as he won the Pepsi 400 and finished fifth at the Daytona 500; he was second and eighth at Talladega. … Surged from 24th to 12th in points with three of his four total top fives and six of his 10 top 10s within a nine-race span beginning with a second-place effort at Talladega in April. … Had seven top 15s in the final 14 events. … Had only four DNFs. … Ended speculation about his immediate future by signing a four-year deal with Dale Earnhardt, Inc. in July to remain in the No. 15 NAPA Chevrolet.

**2001** Finished 24th in series points. … Won his first Winston Cup race in 463 career starts at the Daytona 500. … Finished second behind teammate Dale Earnhardt Jr., in the Pepsi 400 at Daytona five months later. … Also finished second at Homestead in November for a total of three top fives.

**2000** Finished 27th in series points. … Had one top five, a season-best third at Martinsville in April. … Ran season's first 19 races for Jim Mattei and finished driving for Jim Smith.

**1999** Finished 29th in series points. … First season with Mattei Mortorsports produced his first top five in three seasons, a fifth-place finish at the Daytona 500. Had two top 10s and a career-high 10 DNFs.

**1998** Finished 17th in series points. … In his final season with the Wood Brothers, had five top 10s, including a season-best sixth in the Daytona 500. … Had string of 387 consecutive starts snapped when he failed to qualify at Phoenix.

**1997** Finished 18th in series points. … Had six top 10s, included four seventh-place finishes … Best start of the season (sixth) was on the Sonoma road course.

**1996** Finished 14th in series points in his first year with the Wood Brothers. … Won The Winston, becoming the first driver to win the all-star event after transferring from the Winston Open. … Had one top five and 10 top 10s.

**1995** Finished 12th in series points. … Final season with Chuck Rider, ending a eight-year association. … Had two top fives and six top 10s.

**1994** Finished 12th in series points. … Finished a season-best third at Talladega and had eight top 10s.

**1993** Finished 17th in series points. … Had five top 10s, including a season-best seventh at Talladega in July.

**1992** Finished 23rd in series points, his first finish outside the top 20 in his career. … Had one top five and two top 10s in a season of struggles that included eight DNFs.

**1991** Finished 15th in series points. … Won the first two pole positions of his Winston Cup career within a four-race span—June 2 at Dover and June 23 at Michigan. … Had four top fives and 12 top 10s.

**1990** Finished 16th in series points. …Had five top fives and 10 top 10s.

**1989** Finished 18th in series points. … Had five top 10s despite nine DNFs in 29 starts.

**1998** Finished 18th in points in his first season driving for Chuck Rider. … Finished a season-best second at Pocono.

**1987** Finished 20th in series points. … Scored his first career top 10 with a 10th-place finish in April at Martinsville.

**1986** Finished 19th in series points in his first full season in Winston Cup driving for Dick Bahre. … Was runner-up to Alan Kulwicki for Rookie of the Year honors. … Best finishes were 11th-place efforts in April at Martinsville and July at Pocono.

**1985** Finished 57th in series points after running in only five races. … First Winston Cup start was on May 27 at Charlotte and was a great day for the Waltrip clan as brother Darrell won the event; Michael finished 28th.

## CAREER STATISTICS

| Year | Car Owner | Races | Champ. Finish | Won | Top 5 | Top 10 | DNF | Poles | Money Won |
|---|---|---|---|---|---|---|---|---|---|
| 1985 | Dick Bahre | 5 | 57 | 0 | 0 | 0 | 4 | 0 | $9,540 |
| 1986 | Dick Bahre | 28 | 19 | 0 | 0 | 0 | 8 | 0 | 108,767 |
| 1987 | Dick Bahre | 29 | 20 | 0 | 0 | 1 | 8 | 0 | 205,370 |
| 1988 | Chuck Rider | 29 | 18 | 0 | 1 | 3 | 8 | 0 | 240,400 |
| 1989 | Chuck Rider | 29 | 18 | 0 | 0 | 5 | 9 | 0 | 249,233 |
| 1990 | Chuck Rider | 29 | 16 | 0 | 5 | 10 | 7 | 0 | 395,507 |
| 1991 | Chuck Rider | 29 | 15 | 0 | 4 | 12 | 6 | 2 | 440,812 |
| 1992 | Chuck Rider | 29 | 23 | 0 | 1 | 2 | 8 | 0 | 410,545 |
| 1993 | Chuck Rider | 30 | 17 | 0 | 0 | 5 | 4 | 0 | 529,923 |
| 1994 | Chuck Rider | 31 | 12 | 0 | 2 | 10 | 3 | 0 | 706,426 |
| 1995 | Chuck Rider | 31 | 12 | 0 | 2 | 8 | 2 | 0 | 898,338 |
| 1996 | Wood Brothers | 31 | 14 | 0 | 1 | 11 | 3 | 0 | 1,182,811 |
| 1997 | Wood Brothers | 32 | 18 | 0 | 0 | 6 | 4 | 0 | 1,138,599 |
| 1998 | Wood Brothers | 32 | 17 | 0 | 0 | 5 | 3 | 0 | 1,508,680 |

## Career Statistics

| Year | Car Owner | Races | Champ. Finish | Won | Top 5 | Top 10 | DNF | Poles | Money Won |
|---|---|---|---|---|---|---|---|---|---|
| 1999 | Jim Mattei | 34 | 29 | 0 | 1 | 3 | 10 | 0 | 1,702,460 |
| 2000 | Jim Mattei | 19 |  | 0 | 1 | 1 | 6 | 0 | 993,886 |
|  | Jim Smith | 15 | 27 | 0 | 0 | 0 | 4 | 0 | 696,935 |
| 2001 | Dale Earnhardt | 36 | 24 | 1 | 3 | 3 | 6 | 0 | 3,411,644 |
| 2002 | T. Earnhardt | 36 | 14 | 1 | 4 | 10 | 4 | 0 | 3,185,969 |
| 2003 | T. Earnhardt | 36 | 15 | 2 | 8 | 11 | 6 | 0 | 4,929,620 |
| TOTALS |  | 570 |  | 4 | 33 | 106 | 113 | 2 | $22,945,465 |

### 2003 RESULTS

| Race | Start | Finish | Standing Pos. | Winnings |
|---|---|---|---|---|
| Daytona 500 (Daytona) | 4 | 1 | 1 | $1,419,406 |
| Subway 400 (Rockingham) | 22 | 19 | 5 | $66,910 |
| UAW-DaimlerChrysler 400 (Las Vegas) | 9 | 3 | 1 | $190,550 |
| Bass Pro Shops MBNA 500 (Atlanta) | 6 | 27 | 3 | $68,070 |
| Carolina Dodge Dealers 400 (Darlington) | 9 | 5 | 3 | $74,450 |
| Food City 500 (Bristol) | 28 | 25 | 4 | $77,470 |
| Samsung/RadioShack 500 (Texas) | 37 | 17 | 4 | $102,500 |
| Aaron's 499 (Talladega) | 16 | 24 | 7 | $83,935 |
| Virginia 500 (Martinsville) | 30 | 23 | 8 | $63,975 |
| Auto Club 500 (California) | 27 | 7 | 6 | $95,025 |
| Pontiac Excitement 400 (Richmond) | 37 | 12 | 7 | $69,910 |
| Coca-Cola 600 (Charlotte) | 9 | 6 | 7 | $112,875 |
| MBNA Armed Forces Family 400 (Dover) | 16 | 16 | 6 | $78,935 |
| Pocono 500 (Pocono) | 13 | 18 | 6 | $64,090 |
| Sirius 400 (Michigan) | 9 | 5 | 6 | $81,475 |
| Dodge/Save Mart 350 (Sonoma) | 20 | 13 | 5 | $75,950 |
| Pepsi 400 (Daytona) | 6 | 11 | 5 | $90,275 |
| Tropicana 400 (Chicago) | 12 | 5 | 5 | $100,975 |
| New England 300 (New Hampshire) | 5 | 28 | 6 | $68,750 |
| Pennsylvania 500 (Pocono) | 17 | 4 | 6 | $94,355 |
| Brickyard 400 (Indianapolis) | 5 | 16 | 5 | $137,450 |
| Sirius at the Glen (Watkins Glen) | 34 | 13 | 6 | $65,800 |
| GFS Marketplace 400 (Michigan) | 13 | 7 | 5 | $77,915 |
| Sharpie 500 (Bristol) | 3 | 42 | 8 | $78,430 |
| Southern 500 (Darlington) | 37 | 37 | 9 | $68,325 |
| Chevy Rock & Roll 400 (Richmond) | 33 | 32 | 10 | $65,230 |
| Sylvania 300 (New Hampshire) | 5 | 26 | 10 | $69,150 |
| MBNA America 400 (Dover) | 10 | 42 | 11 | $69,200 |
| EA SPORTS 500 (Talladega) | 18 | 1 | 11 | $157,090 |
| Banquet 400 (Kansas) | 31 | 39 | 11 | $77,985 |
| UAW-GM Quality 500 (Charlotte) | 30 | 14 | 11 | $68,950 |
| Subway 500 (Martinsville) | 15 | 26 | 12 | $62,175 |
| Bass Pro Shops MBNA 500 (Atlanta) | 13 | 38 | 14 | $80,050 |
| Checker Auto Parts 500 (Phoenix) | 17 | 5 | 12 | $100,925 |
| Pop Secret 400 (Rockingham) | 11 | 37 | 13 | $64,200 |
| Ford 400 (Homestead) | 23 | 41 | 15 | $60,735 |

# Scott Wimmer
## 22

**Date of birth:** January 26, 1976 **Hometown:** Wausau, Wis.
**Resides:** High Point, N.C. **Spouse:** Single **Children:** None
**Hobbies:** Hunting and fishing

## NASCAR ACHIEVEMENTS

**First NASCAR Cup start:** November 19, 2000 (Atlanta)
**Best points finish:** 48 (2003)
**Career victories:** 0
**Career poles:** 0
**Best career finish:** 9 **Best career start:** 27

### FAST FACTS

- Finished third in the Busch Series in 2002 and ninth in 2003.
- Was 11th in the Busch Series in 2001, finishing second to Greg Biffle for Raybestos Rookie of the Year honors.
- Was the 1997 Hooters Pro Cup Series Rookie of the Year.
- Finished second in the 2000 ASA rookie standings.

### CAR FACTS

**Car:** No. 22 Dodge
**Primary sponsor:** Caterpillar
**Owner:** Bill Davis
**Team:** Bill Davis Racing
**Crew chief:** Frank Stoddard
**Engine builder:** Terry Elledge

## CAREER BY YEAR

**2003** He drove six races for Bill Davis Racing and had impressive finishes at Phoenix (ninth) and Homestead (12th).

### CAREER STATISTICS

| Year | Car Owner | Races | Champ. Finish | Won | Top 5 | Top 10 | DNF | Poles | Money Won |
|---|---|---|---|---|---|---|---|---|---|
| 2000 | Bill Davis | 1 | 74 | 0 | 0 | 0 | 0 | 0 | $37,780 |
| 2002 | Bill Davis | 3 | 56 | 0 | 0 | 0 | 2 | 0 | 143,110 |
| 2003 | Bill Davis | 6 | 48 | 0 | 0 | 1 | 0 | 0 | 479,504 |
| TOTALS |  | 10 |  | 0 | 0 | 1 | 2 | 0 | $660,394 |

### 2003 RESULTS

| Race | Start | Finish | Standing Pos. | Winnings |
|---|---|---|---|---|
| Sharpie 500 (Bristol) | 28 | 24 | 58 | $65,085 |
| Sylvania 300 (New Hampshire) | 35 | 24 | 54 | $51,550 |
| Bass Pro Shops MBNA 500 (Atlanta) | 41 | 32 | 51 | $98,801 |
| Checker Auto Parts 500 (Phoenix) | 28 | 9 | 48 | $95,656 |
| Pop Secret 400 (Rockingham) | 37 | 26 | 48 | $83,731 |
| Ford 400 (Homestead) | 27 | 12 | 48 | $84,681 |

# Other NASCAR NEXTEL Cup Series drivers

## Casey Atwood

**Date of birth:** 8/25/80. **Hometown:** Antioch, Tenn.

### CAREER STATISTICS

| Year | Car Owner | Races | Won | Top 5 | Top 10 | DNF | Poles | Money Won |
|---|---|---|---|---|---|---|---|---|
| 2000 | R. Evernham | 3 | 0 | 0 | 1 | 0 | 0 | $97,030 |
| 2001 | R. Evernham | 35 | 0 | 1 | 3 | 6 | 1 | 1,797,111 |
| 2002 | James Smith | 34 | 0 | 0 | 0 | 5 | 0 | 1,951,079 |
|  | R. Evernham | 1 | 0 | 0 | 0 | 0 | 0 | 37,175 |
| 2003 | R. Evernham | 2 | 0 | 0 | 0 | 1 | 0 | 149,838 |
| **TOTALS** |  | **75** | **0** | **1** | **4** | **12** | **1** | **$4,032,233** |

## Stacy Compton

**Date of birth:** 5/26/67. **Hometown:** Hurt, Va.

### CAREER STATISTICS

| Year | Car Owner | Races | Won | Top 5 | Top 10 | DNF | Poles | Money Won |
|---|---|---|---|---|---|---|---|---|
| 1996 | Dean Monroe | 2 | 0 | 0 | 0 | 1 | 0 | $18,115 |
| 1999 | H. Melling | 3 | 0 | 0 | 0 | 0 | 0 | 92,600 |
| 2000 | M. Melling | 27 | 0 | 0 | 0 | 6 | 0 | 1,069,649 |
| 2001 | M. Melling | 34 | 0 | 0 | 1 | 7 | 2 | 1,704,962 |
| 2002 | A.J. Foyt | 18 | 0 | 0 | 0 | 4 | 0 | 1,053,464 |
|  | M. Melling | 1 | 0 | 0 | 0 | 0 | 0 | 41,615 |
|  | B.A. Morganthau | 20 | 0 | 0 | 0 | 1 | 0 | 90,630 |
| 2003 | Morgan-McClure | 1 | 0 | 0 | 0 | 0 | 0 | 67,400 |
| **TOTALS** |  | **88** | **0** | **0** | **1** | **19** | **2** | **$4,138,435** |

## Geoffrey Bodine

**Date of birth:** 4/18/49. **Hometown:** Chemung, N.Y.

### CAREER STATISTICS

| Year | Car Owner | Races | Won | Top 5 | Top 10 | DNF | Poles | Money Won |
|---|---|---|---|---|---|---|---|---|
| 1979 | Jack Beebe | 3 | 0 | 0 | 0 | 3 | 0 | $1,224,820 |
| 1981 | Dick Bahre | 2 | 0 | 0 | 0 | 1 | 0 | 6,390 |
|  | E. Zervakis | 3 | 0 | 0 | 1 | 2 | 0 | 8,610 |
| 1982 | Dick Bahre | 1 | 0 | 0 | 0 | 1 | 0 | 3,450 |
|  | Cliff Stewart | 24 | 0 | 4 | 10 | 8 | 2 | 255,050 |
| 1983 | Cliff Stewart | 28 | 0 | 5 | 8 | 15 | 1 | 194,476 |
| 1984 | Rick Hendrick | 30 | 3 | 7 | 14 | 8 | 3 | 393,924 |
| 1985 | Rick Hendrick | 28 | 0 | 10 | 14 | 5 | 3 | 565,865 |
| 1986 | Rick Hendrick | 29 | 2 | 10 | 14 | 12 | 8 | 795,111 |
| 1987 | Rick Hendrick | 29 | 0 | 3 | 10 | 11 | 0 | 449,816 |
| 1988 | Rick Hendrick | 29 | 1 | 10 | 16 | 4 | 3 | 570,643 |
| 1989 | Rick Hendrick | 29 | 1 | 9 | 11 | 6 | 3 | 620,594 |
| 1990 | Junior Johnson | 29 | 3 | 11 | 19 | 3 | 2 | 1,131,222 |
| 1991 | Junior Johnson | 27 | 1 | 6 | 12 | 7 | 2 | 625,256 |
| 1992 | Bud Moore | 29 | 2 | 7 | 11 | 7 | 0 | 716,583 |
| 1993 | Bud Moore | 23 | 1 | 2 | 8 | 5 | 1 | 613,750 |
|  | Geoff Bodine | 7 | 0 | 0 | 1 | 4 | 0 | 170,012 |
| 1994 | Geoff Bodine | 31 | 3 | 7 | 10 | 15 | 5 | 1,276,126 |
| 1995 | Geoff Bodine | 31 | 0 | 1 | 4 | 5 | 0 | 1,011,090 |
| 1996 | Geoff Bodine | 31 | 1 | 2 | 6 | 5 | 0 | 1,031,762 |
| 1997 | Geoff Bodine | 29 | 0 | 3 | 10 | 8 | 2 | 1,092,734 |
| 1998 | Jim Mattei | 32 | 0 | 1 | 5 | 10 | 0 | 1,247,255 |
| 1999 | Joe Bessey | 34 | 0 | 1 | 2 | 6 | 0 | 1,258,894 |
| 2000 | Joe Bessey | 12 | 0 | 0 | 0 | 4 | 0 | 636,124 |
|  | C. MacPherson | 1 | 0 | 0 | 0 | 1 | 0 | 33,875 |
|  | Andy Petree | 1 | 0 | 0 | 0 | 1 | 0 | 34,982 |
| 2001 | B. Bodine | 2 | 0 | 0 | 0 | 0 | 0 | 80,855 |
| 2002 | James Finch | 7 | 0 | 1 | 2 | 2 | 0 | 946,906 |
|  | Bill Davis | 1 | 0 | 0 | 0 | 0 | 0 | 35,615 |
|  | Travis Carter | 4 | 0 | 0 | 0 | 2 | 0 | 241,980 |
| 2003 | B. Bodine | 1 | 0 | 0 | 0 | 1 | 0 | 78,150 |
| **TOTALS** |  | **566** | **18** | **100** | **188** | **161** | **37** | **$16,131,920** |

## Derrike Cope

**Date of birth:** 11/3/58. **Hometown:** Spanaway, Wash.

### CAREER STATISTICS

| Year | Car Owner | Races | Won | Top 5 | Top 10 | DNF | Poles | Money Won |
|---|---|---|---|---|---|---|---|---|
| 1982 | George Jefferson | 1 | 0 | 0 | 0 | 1 | 0 | $625 |
| 1984 | George Jefferson | 3 | 0 | 0 | 0 | 1 | 0 | 6,500 |
| 1985 | George Jefferson | 2 | 0 | 0 | 0 | 1 | 0 | 7,100 |
| 1986 | Rabanco Racing | 5 | 0 | 0 | 1 | 2 | 0 | 8,025 |
| 1987 | Fred Stoke | 11 | 0 | 0 | 0 | 8 | 0 | 33,750 |
| 1988 | Jim Testa | 26 | 0 | 0 | 0 | 16 | 0 | 132,835 |
| 1989 | Jim Testa | 3 | 0 | 0 | 0 | 3 | 0 | 5,440 |
|  | Bob Whitcomb | 20 | 0 | 0 | 4 | 9 | 0 | 120,190 |
| 1990 | Bob Whitcomb | 29 | 2 | 2 | 6 | 10 | 0 | 569,451 |
| 1991 | Bob Whitcomb | 28 | 0 | 1 | 2 | 14 | 0 | 419,380 |
| 1992 | Bob Whitcomb | 29 | 0 | 0 | 3 | 6 | 0 | 277,215 |
| 1993 | C. Yarborough | 30 | 0 | 0 | 1 | 8 | 0 | 402,515 |
| 1994 | C. Yarborough | 16 | 0 | 0 | 0 | 7 | 0 | 185,186 |
|  | T.W. Taylor | 2 | 0 | 0 | 0 | 0 | 0 | 35,110 |
|  | B. Allison | 12 | 0 | 0 | 2 | 3 | 0 | 178,140 |
| 1995 | B. Allison | 31 | 0 | 2 | 8 | 5 | 0 | 683,075 |
| 1996 | B. Allison | 29 | 0 | 0 | 3 | 11 | 0 | 675,781 |
| 1997 | N. Bowers | 31 | 0 | 1 | 2 | 6 | 0 | 707,404 |
| 1998 | C. Rider | 28 | 0 | 0 | 0 | 9 | 1 | 985,730 |
| 1999 | C. Rider | 10 | 0 | 0 | 0 | 3 | 0 | 424,626 |
|  | J. Birmingham | 1 | 0 | 0 | 0 | 0 | 0 | 82,385 |
|  | R. Fenley | 1 | 0 | 0 | 0 | 0 | 0 | 19,740 |
|  | L. Hedrick | 3 | 0 | 0 | 0 | 1 | 0 | 91,225 |
| 2000 | R. Fenley | 3 | 0 | 0 | 0 | 1 | 0 | 179,151 |
| 2001 | E. Campbell | 1 | 0 | 0 | 0 | 0 | 0 | 47,500 |
|  | W. Johnson | 0 | 0 | 0 | 0 | 0 | 0 | 34,371 |
| 2002 | D. Cope | 2 | 0 | 0 | 0 | 1 | 0 | 108,826 |
|  | B. A. Morganthau | 5 | 0 | 0 | 0 | 2 | 0 | 224,390 |
| 2003 | D. Cope | 18 | 0 | 0 | 0 | 12 | 0 | 1,030,690 |
| **TOTALS** |  | **380** | **2** | **6** | **32** | **139** | **1** | **$7,676,356** |

## Ron Fellows

**Date of birth:** 9/28/59. **Hometown:** Mississaugua, Ontario

### CAREER STATISTICS

| Year | Car Owner | Races | Won | Top 5 | Top 10 | DNF | Poles | Money Won |
|---|---|---|---|---|---|---|---|---|
| 1995 | Canaska Racing | 1 | 0 | 0 | 0 | 1 | 0 | $49,035 |
| 1998 | B. McCall | 2 | 0 | 0 | 0 | 0 | 0 | 46,310 |
| 1999 | J. Nemechek | 1 | 0 | 1 | 1 | 0 | 0 | 67,270 |
| 2000 | J. Nemechek | 1 | 0 | 0 | 0 | 1 | 0 | 24,725 |
| 2001 | J. Nemechek | 2 | 0 | 0 | 0 | 2 | 0 | 72,055 |
| 2002 | J. Nemechek | 1 | 0 | 0 | 0 | 0 | 0 | 47,930 |
| 2003 | Dale Earnhardt Inc. | 2 | 0 | 0 | 1 | 1 | 0 | 161,854 |
| **TOTALS** | | 10 | 0 | 1 | 2 | 5 | 0 | $429,179 |

## Steve Grissom

**Date of birth:** 6/26/63. **Hometown:** Gadsden, Ala.

### CAREER STATISTICS

| Year | Car Owner | Races | Won | Top 5 | Top 10 | DNF | Poles | Money Won |
|---|---|---|---|---|---|---|---|---|
| 1990 | D. Moroso | 1 | 0 | 0 | 0 | 0 | 0 | $1,074,275 |
| 1993 | G. Bechtel | 1 | 0 | 0 | 0 | 0 | 0 | 6,485 |
| 1994 | G. Bechtel | 28 | 0 | 0 | 3 | 4 | 0 | 303,215 |
| 1995 | G. Bechtel | 29 | 0 | 1 | 4 | 3 | 0 | 511,647 |
| 1996 | G. Bechtel | 13 | 0 | 1 | 2 | 3 | 0 | 314,983 |
| 1997 | L. Hedrick | 31 | 0 | 3 | 6 | 5 | 0 | 1,074,374 |
| 1998 | L. Hedrick | 24 | 0 | 0 | 2 | 2 | 0 | 962,446 |
| | Buz McCall | 3 | 0 | 0 | 0 | 1 | 0 | 67,595 |
| 1999 | J. Falk | 2 | 0 | 0 | 0 | 1 | 0 | 82,059 |
| | H. Melling | 3 | 0 | 0 | 0 | 2 | 0 | 78,625 |
| | F. Sabates | 1 | 0 | 0 | 0 | 0 | 0 | 32,845 |
| 2000 | Petty Ent. | 5 | 0 | 0 | 0 | 0 | 0 | 231,850 |
| 2002 | Petty Ent. | 11 | 0 | 0 | 1 | 1 | 0 | 529,781 |
| **TOTALS** | | 152 | 0 | 5 | 18 | 22 | 0 | $4,200,180 |

## Bobby Hamilton

**Date of birth:** 5/29/57. **Hometown:** Nashville

### CAREER STATISTICS

| Year | Car Owner | Races | Won | Top 5 | Top 10 | DNF | Poles | Money Won |
|---|---|---|---|---|---|---|---|---|
| 1989 | Paramount | 1 | 0 | 0 | 0 | 1 | 0 | $3,075 |
| 1990 | G. Bradshaw | 3 | 0 | 0 | 0 | 2 | 0 | 13,065 |
| 1991 | G. Bradshaw | 28 | 0 | 0 | 4 | 4 | 0 | 259,105 |
| 1992 | G. Bradshaw | 29 | 0 | 0 | 2 | 5 | 0 | 367,065 |
| 1993 | G. Bradshaw | 8 | 0 | 0 | 0 | 3 | 0 | 84,710 |
| | Akins-Sutton | 2 | 0 | 0 | 1 | 0 | 0 | 21,715 |
| | D. Moroso | 5 | 0 | 0 | 0 | 1 | 0 | 36,315 |
| 1994 | Felix Sabates | 30 | 0 | 0 | 1 | 11 | 0 | 514,520 |
| 1995 | Petty Ent. | 31 | 0 | 4 | 10 | 2 | 0 | 804,505 |
| 1996 | Petty Ent. | 31 | 1 | 3 | 11 | 4 | 2 | 1,151,235 |
| 1997 | Petty Ent. | 32 | 1 | 6 | 8 | 4 | 2 | 1,478,843 |

| Year | Car Owner | Races | Won | Top 5 | Top 10 | DNF | Poles | Money Won |
|---|---|---|---|---|---|---|---|---|
| 1998 | Morgan-McClure | 33 | 1 | 3 | 8 | 1 | 1 | 2,089,566 |
| 1999 | Morgan-McClure | 34 | 0 | 1 | 10 | 3 | 0 | 2,019,255 |
| 2000 | Morgan-McClure | 34 | 0 | 0 | 2 | 11 | 0 | 1,619,775 |
| 2001 | Andy Petree | 36 | 1 | 3 | 7 | 0 | 0 | 2,527,310 |
| 2002 | Andy Petree | 31 | 0 | 0 | 3 | 1 | 0 | 3,196,956 |
| **TOTALS** | | 368 | 4 | 20 | 67 | 53 | 5 | $15,187,015 |

## Bobby Hamilton Jr.

**Date of birth:** 1/8/78. **Hometown:** Nashville

### CAREER STATISTICS

| Year | Car Owner | Races | Won | Top 5 | Top 10 | DNF | Poles | Money Won |
|---|---|---|---|---|---|---|---|---|
| 2000 | B. Hamilton | 1 | 0 | 0 | 0 | 0 | 0 | $35,500 |
| | C. Ganassi | 1 | 0 | 0 | 0 | 0 | 0 | 46,890 |
| 2001 | Andy Petree | 3 | 0 | 0 | 0 | 2 | 0 | 241,142 |
| | Morgan-McClure | 7 | 0 | 0 | 0 | 2 | 0 | 305,705 |
| 2003 | E. Rensi | 2 | 0 | 0 | 0 | 0 | 0 | 128,725 |
| **TOTALS** | | 14 | 0 | 0 | 0 | 4 | 0 | $757,962 |

## Ron Hornaday

**Date of birth:** 6/20/58. **Hometown:** Palmdale, Calif.

### CAREER STATISTICS

| Year | Car Owner | Races | Won | Top 5 | Top 10 | DNF | Poles | Money Won |
|---|---|---|---|---|---|---|---|---|
| 1992 | B. Fisher | 2 | 0 | 0 | 0 | 0 | 0 | $11,290 |
| 1993 | W. Spears | 1 | 0 | 0 | 0 | 0 | 0 | 6,660 |
| 1994 | W. Spears | 2 | 0 | 0 | 0 | 0 | 0 | 13,710 |
| 1995 | J. Strauser | 1 | 0 | 0 | 0 | 0 | 0 | 9,660 |
| 1998 | T. Beverley | 1 | 0 | 0 | 0 | 0 | 0 | 27,850 |
| 1999 | F. Sabates | 1 | 0 | 0 | 0 | 0 | 0 | 22,810 |
| 2000 | R. Hendrick | 1 | 0 | 0 | 0 | 0 | 0 | 47,020 |
| 2001 | A.J. Foyt | 32 | 0 | 0 | 1 | 8 | 0 | 1,435,857 |
| 2002 | B. A. Morgenthau | 1 | 0 | 0 | 0 | 1 | 0 | 88,476 |
| | A. Petree | 1 | 0 | 0 | 0 | 0 | 0 | 52,860 |
| | A. Fritz | 1 | 0 | 0 | 0 | 0 | 0 | 40,275 |
| 2003 | R. Childress | 1 | 0 | 0 | 0 | 0 | 0 | 48,950 |
| **TOTALS** | | 45 | 0 | 0 | 1 | 9 | 0 | $1,805,418 |

## P.J. Jones

**Date of birth:** 4/23/69. **Hometown:** Rolling Hills, Calif.

### CAREER STATISTICS

| Year | Car Owner | Races | Won | Top 5 | Top 10 | DNF | Poles | Money Won |
|---|---|---|---|---|---|---|---|---|
| 1993 | H. Melling | 6 | 0 | 0 | 0 | 2 | 0 | $50,070 |
| 1994 | D. K. Ulric | 1 | 0 | 0 | 1 | 0 | 0 | 6,085 |
| | G. Chilson | 1 | 0 | 0 | 0 | 0 | 0 | 6,960 |
| 2000 | M. Held | 1 | 0 | 0 | 0 | 0 | 0 | 33,345 |
| | F. Sabatas | 1 | 0 | 0 | 0 | 0 | 0 | 37,555 |
| 2002 | A. J. Foyt | 1 | 0 | 1 | 1 | 0 | 0 | 65,950 |
| 2003 | Morgan-McClure | 1 | 0 | 0 | 0 | 1 | 0 | 59,135 |
| **TOTALS** | | 12 | 0 | 1 | 1 | 3 | 0 | $295,100 |

## Jason Leffler

**Date of birth:** 9/18/75. **Hometown:** Long Beach, Calif.

### CAREER STATISTICS

| Year | Car Owner | Races | Won | Top 5 | Top 10 | DNF | Poles | Money Won |
|---|---|---|---|---|---|---|---|---|
| 2001 | Chip Ganassi | 30 | 0 | 0 | 1 | 8 | 1 | $1,724,692 |
| 2002 | Jim Smith | 2 | 0 | 0 | 0 | 0 | 0 | 78,500 |
| 2003 | G. Haas | 10 | 0 | 0 | 0 | 0 | 0 | 594,500 |
| **TOTALS** | | 42 | 0 | 0 | 1 | 8 | 1 | $2,397,692 |

## Kevin Lepage

**Date of birth:** 6/26/62. **Hometown:** Shelbourne, Vt.

### CAREER STATISTICS

| Year | Car Owner | Races | Won | Top 5 | Top 10 | DNF | Poles | Money Won |
|---|---|---|---|---|---|---|---|---|
| 1997 | Joe Falk | 3 | 0 | 0 | 0 | 1 | 0 | $1,557,720 |
| 1998 | Joe Falk | 13 | 0 | 0 | 0 | 3 | 0 | 384,591 |
| | Buz McCall | 1 | 0 | 0 | 0 | 1 | 0 | 20,385 |
| | Jack Roush | 13 | 0 | 0 | 2 | 5 | 0 | 447,745 |
| 1999 | Jack Roush | 34 | 0 | 1 | 2 | 3 | 1 | 1,587,841 |
| 2000 | Jack Roush | 32 | 0 | 1 | 3 | 5 | 0 | 1,679,186 |
| 2001 | Morgan-McClure | 21 | 0 | 0 | 1 | 3 | 0 | 987,976 |
| | Jim Smith | 8 | 0 | 0 | 0 | 0 | 0 | 436,876 |
| 2002 | Derrike Cope | 2 | 0 | 0 | 0 | 2 | 0 | 97,809 |
| | B. A. Morgenthau | 1 | 0 | 0 | 0 | 1 | 0 | 44,650 |
| 2003 | Morgan-McClure | 11 | 0 | 0 | 0 | 1 | 0 | 742,077 |
| **TOTALS** | | 139 | 0 | 2 | 8 | 25 | 1 | $6,486,856 |

## Chad Little

**Date of birth:** 4/23/63. **Hometown:** Spokane, Wash.

### CAREER STATISTICS

| Year | Car Owner | Races | Won | Top 5 | Top 10 | DNF | Poles | Money Won |
|---|---|---|---|---|---|---|---|---|
| 1986 | G. Jefferson | 2 | 0 | 0 | 0 | 1 | 0 | $1,446,065 |
| 1987 | G. Jefferson | 2 | 0 | 0 | 0 | 0 | 0 | 8,810 |
| 1988 | Fred Stoke | 4 | 0 | 0 | 0 | 0 | 0 | 14,225 |
| 1989 | J. Donlavey | 8 | 0 | 0 | 0 | 4 | 0 | 44,690 |
| 1990 | C. Little | 17 | 0 | 0 | 0 | 3 | 0 | 77,390 |
| | D. Moroso | 1 | 0 | 0 | 0 | 0 | 0 | 4,450 |
| 1991 | C. Little | 27 | 0 | 0 | 1 | 6 | 0 | 179,265 |
| | D. Close | 1 | 0 | 0 | 0 | 0 | 0 | 4,925 |
| 1992 | C. Yarborough | 6 | 0 | 0 | 0 | 2 | 0 | 65,810 |
| | H. Melling | 13 | 0 | 0 | 1 | 5 | 0 | 79,995 |
| 1993 | H. Melling | 2 | 0 | 0 | 0 | 1 | 0 | 34,865 |
| | M. Rypien | 1 | 0 | 0 | 0 | 0 | 0 | 6,275 |
| 1994 | M. Rypien | 1 | 0 | 0 | 0 | 0 | 0 | 30,805 |
| 1995 | M. Rypien | 2 | 0 | 0 | 0 | 1 | 0 | 22,775 |
| 1996 | M. Rypien | 6 | 0 | 0 | 0 | 3 | 0 | 100,432 |
| | G. Bechtel | 3 | 0 | 0 | 0 | 1 | 0 | 64,320 |
| 1997 | M. Rypien | 16 | 0 | 0 | 1 | 4 | 0 | 343,324 |

| Year | Car Owner | Races | Won | Top 5 | Top 10 | DNF | Poles | Money Won |
|---|---|---|---|---|---|---|---|---|
| 1998 | J. Roush | 32 | 0 | 1 | 7 | 7 | 0 | 1,449,659 |
| 1999 | J. Roush | 34 | 0 | 0 | 5 | 4 | 0 | 1,623,976 |
| 2000 | J. Roush | 27 | 0 | 0 | 1 | 3 | 0 | 1,449,854 |
| 2002 | B. Baumgardner | 1 | 0 | 0 | 0 | 0 | 0 | 49,745 |
| **TOTALS** | | 217 | 0 | 1 | 16 | 46 | 0 | $5,843,269 |

## Carl Long

**Date of birth:** 9/20/67. **Hometown:** Roxboro, N.C.

### CAREER STATISTICS

| Year | Car Owner | Races | Won | Top 5 | Top 10 | DNF | Poles | Money Won |
|---|---|---|---|---|---|---|---|---|
| 2000 | Thee Dixon | 2 | 0 | 0 | 0 | 1 | 0 | $82,571 |
| 2001 | Thee Dixon | 3 | 0 | 0 | 0 | 2 | 0 | 152,376 |
| 2002 | Thee Dixon | 1 | 0 | 0 | 0 | 1 | 0 | 86,413 |
| | Foster Price | 1 | 0 | 0 | 0 | 0 | 0 | 54,100 |
| **TOTALS** | | 7 | 0 | 0 | 0 | 4 | 0 | $375,460 |

## Ted Musgrave

**Date of birth:** 12/18/55. **Hometown:** Evanston, Ill.

### CAREER STATISTICS

| Year | Car Owner | Races | Won | Top 5 | Top 10 | DNF | Poles | Money Won |
|---|---|---|---|---|---|---|---|---|
| 1990 | Ray DeWitt | 4 | 0 | 0 | 0 | 2 | 0 | $1,117,190 |
| 1991 | DeWitts-Ulrich | 29 | 0 | 0 | 0 | 4 | 0 | 200,910 |
| 1992 | DeWitts-Ulrich | 29 | 0 | 1 | 7 | 3 | 0 | 449,121 |
| 1993 | DeWitts-Ulrich | 29 | 0 | 2 | 5 | 6 | 0 | 458,615 |
| 1994 | Jack Roush | 31 | 0 | 1 | 8 | 5 | 3 | 656,187 |
| 1995 | Jack Roush | 31 | 0 | 7 | 13 | 1 | 1 | 1,147,445 |
| 1996 | Jack Roush | 31 | 0 | 2 | 7 | 2 | 1 | 961,512 |
| 1997 | Jack Roush | 32 | 0 | 5 | 8 | 4 | 0 | 1,256,680 |
| 1998 | Jack Roush | 20 | 0 | 1 | 4 | 3 | 0 | 965,076 |
| | Bud Moore | 2 | 0 | 0 | 0 | 2 | 0 | 39,725 |
| | Travis Carter | 1 | 0 | 0 | 0 | 0 | 0 | 35,310 |
| | Buz McCall | 1 | 0 | 0 | 0 | 0 | 0 | 20,405 |
| | Elliott-Marino | 7 | 0 | 1 | 1 | 2 | 0 | 166,110 |
| | Doug Bawel | 1 | 0 | 0 | 0 | 0 | 0 | 27,000 |
| 1999 | Butch Mock | 32 | 0 | 0 | 2 | 2 | 0 | 1,162,403 |
| 2000 | Joe Bessey | 5 | 0 | 0 | 0 | 2 | 0 | 205,491 |
| | Robert Fenley | 1 | 0 | 0 | 0 | 1 | 0 | 34,305 |
| | Felix Sabates | 1 | 0 | 0 | 0 | 0 | 0 | 46,590 |
| | Chip Ganassi | 11 | 0 | 0 | 0 | 1 | 0 | 540,830 |
| 2001 | Junie Donlavey | 0 | 0 | 0 | 0 | 0 | 0 | 29,722 |
| | Jim Smith | 1 | 0 | 0 | 0 | 0 | 0 | 43,565 |
| 2002 | Jim Smith | 4 | 0 | 0 | 0 | 0 | 0 | 225,320 |
| | Petty Ent. | 1 | 0 | 0 | 0 | 0 | 0 | 58,450 |
| 2003 | Jim Smith | 1 | 0 | 0 | 0 | 0 | 0 | 63,715 |
| **TOTALS** | | 305 | 0 | 20 | 55 | 40 | 5 | $8,811,677 |

## Jerry Nadeau

**Date of birth**: 9/9/70. **Hometown**: Danbury, Conn.

### CAREER STATISTICS

| Year | Car Owner | Races | Won | Top 5 | Top 10 | DNF | Poles | Money Won |
|---|---|---|---|---|---|---|---|---|
| 1997 | R. Jackson | 5 | 0 | 0 | 0 | 2 | 0 | $118,545 |
| 1998 | Elliott-Marino | 14 | 0 | 0 | 0 | 3 | 0 | 377,062 |
| | Harry Melling | 16 | 0 | 0 | 0 | 4 | 0 | 427,805 |
| 1999 | Harry Melling | 22 | 0 | 1 | 2 | 4 | 0 | 919,454 |
| | N. Bowers | 12 | 0 | 0 | 0 | 2 | 0 | 450,775 |
| 2000 | R. Hendrick | 34 | 1 | 3 | 5 | 9 | 0 | 2,164,778 |
| 2001 | R. Hendrick | 36 | 0 | 4 | 10 | 8 | 0 | 2,507,827 |
| 2002 | R. Hendrick | 11 | 0 | 0 | 1 | 3 | 0 | 754,275 |
| | N. Bowers | 3 | 0 | 0 | 0 | 0 | | 280,056 |
| | Kyle Petty | 13 | 0 | 0 | 0 | 5 | 0 | 718,202 |
| | B. Waltrip | 1 | 0 | 0 | 0 | 1 | | 53,600 |
| 2003 | N. Bowers | 10 | 0 | 1 | 1 | 3 | 0 | 861,628 |
| TOTALS | | 177 | 1 | 9 | 189 | 44 | 0 | $9,634,007 |

## Steve Park

**Date of birth:** August 23, 1967 **Hometown:** East Northport, N.Y.

### CAREER STATISTICS

| Year | Car Owner | Races | Won | Top 5 | Top 10 | DNF | Poles | Money Won |
|---|---|---|---|---|---|---|---|---|
| 1997 | D. Earnhardt | 4 | 0 | 0 | 0 | 1 | 0 | $60,405 |
| | F. Sabates | 1 | 0 | 0 | 0 | 1 | 0 | 14,075 |
| 1998 | D. Earnhardt | 17 | 0 | 0 | 0 | 5 | 0 | 487,265 |
| 1999 | D. Earnhardt | 34 | 0 | 0 | 5 | 4 | 0 | 1,767,690 |
| 2000 | D. Earnhardt | 34 | 1 | 6 | 13 | 4 | 2 | 2,283,629 |
| 2001 | D. Earnhardt | 24 | 1 | 5 | 12 | 2 | 0 | 2,495,490 |
| 2002 | T. Earnhardt | 32 | 0 | 0 | 2 | 5 | 0 | 2,681,594 |
| 2003 | T. Earnhardt | 11 | 0 | 0 | 1 | 3 | 1 | 1,033,202 |
| | R. Childress | 24 | 0 | 1 | 3 | 3 | 1 | 1,653,708 |
| TOTALS | | 181 | 2 | 12 | 36 | 28 | 4 | $12,477,058 |

## Robert Pressley

**Date of birth:** 4/8/59. **Hometown:** Asheville, N.C.

### CAREER STATISTICS

| Year | Car Owner | Races | Won | Top 5 | Top 10 | DNF | Poles | Money Won |
|---|---|---|---|---|---|---|---|---|
| 1994 | Leo Jackson | 3 | 0 | 0 | 0 | 1 | 0 | $39,485 |
| 1995 | Leo Jackson | 31 | 0 | 0 | 1 | 7 | 0 | 698,425 |
| 1996 | Leo Jackson | 26 | 0 | 2 | 3 | 8 | 0 | 619,820 |
| | A. Petree | 1 | 0 | 0 | 0 | 0 | 0 | 14,995 |
| | G. Bechtel | 3 | 0 | 0 | 0 | 2 | 0 | 55,650 |
| 1997 | G. Bechtel | 7 | 0 | 0 | 0 | 3 | 0 | 148,668 |
| | D. Bawel | 7 | 0 | 0 | 0 | 3 | 0 | 103,810 |
| 1998 | Doug Bawel | 30 | 0 | 1 | 1 | 7 | 0 | 996,721 |
| 1999 | Doug Bawel | 28 | 0 | 0 | 0 | 5 | 0 | 1,033,223 |
| 2000 | Doug Bawel | 34 | 0 | 1 | 1 | 10 | 0 | 1,460,317 |
| 2001 | Doug Bawel | 34 | 0 | 1 | 5 | 9 | 0 | 2,171,520 |
| 2002 | M. Melling | 1 | 0 | 0 | 0 | 1 | 0 | 150,859 |
| TOTALS | | 205 | 0 | 5 | 11 | 56 | 0 | $7,493,493 |

## Scott Pruett

**Date of birth**: 3/24/60. **Hometown**: Sacramento

### CAREER STATISTICS

| Year | Car Owner | Races | Won | Top 5 | Top 10 | DNF | Poles | Money Won |
|---|---|---|---|---|---|---|---|---|
| 2000 | C. Wells III | 28 | 0 | 0 | 1 | 11 | 0 | $1,135,854 |
| 2001 | Andy Petree | 1 | 0 | 0 | 0 | 0 | 0 | 77,020 |
| | Chip Ganassi | 1 | 0 | 0 | 0 | 0 | 0 | 57,025 |
| 2002 | Chip Ganassi | 1 | 0 | 0 | 1 | 0 | 0 | 66,690 |
| 2003 | Chip Ganassi | 2 | 0 | 1 | 1 | 0 | 0 | 143,035 |
| TOTALS | | 33 | 0 | 1 | 3 | 11 | 0 | $1,479,624 |

## Shawna Robinson

**Date of birth**: 11/30/64. **Hometown**: Des Moines, Iowa

### CAREER STATISTICS

| Year | Car Owner | Races | Won | Top 5 | Top 10 | DNF | Poles | Money Won |
|---|---|---|---|---|---|---|---|---|
| 2001 | M. Kranefuss | 1 | 0 | 0 | 0 | 0 | 0 | $35,190 |
| 2002 | B. Morgenthau | 7 | 0 | 0 | 0 | 4 | 0 | 428,519 |
| TOTALS | | 8 | 0 | 0 | 0 | 4 | 0 | $463,709 |

## Hermie Sadler

**Date of birth**: 4/24/69. **Hometown**: Emporia, Va.

### CAREER STATISTICS

| Year | Car Owner | Races | Won | Top 5 | Top 10 | DNF | Poles | Money Won |
|---|---|---|---|---|---|---|---|---|
| 1996 | Hermie Sadler | 1 | 0 | 0 | 0 | 1 | 0 | $13,055 |
| 2001 | Hermie Sadler | 3 | 0 | 0 | 0 | 0 | 0 | 121,865 |
| 2002 | Angela Sadler | 8 | 0 | 0 | 0 | 3 | 0 | 379,775 |
| | J. Donlavey | 2 | 0 | 0 | 0 | 0 | 0 | 93,915 |
| 2003 | Hermie Sadler | 10 | 0 | 0 | 0 | 8 | 0 | 552,741 |
| TOTALS | | 24 | 0 | 0 | 0 | 12 | 0 | $1,161,351 |

## Boris Said

**Date of birth**: 9/18/62. **Hometown**: Carlsbad, Calif.

### CAREER STATISTICS

| Year | Car Owner | Races | Won | Top 5 | Top 10 | DNF | Poles | Money Won |
|---|---|---|---|---|---|---|---|---|
| 1999 | E. Irvan | 2 | 0 | 0 | 0 | 1 | 0 | $68,657 |
| 2000 | J. Spencer | 1 | 0 | 0 | 0 | 1 | 0 | 36,940 |
| 2001 | Doug Bawel | 2 | 0 | 0 | 1 | 0 | 0 | 124,340 |
| 2002 | Doug Bawel | 2 | 0 | 0 | 1 | 1 | 0 | 87,400 |
| 2003 | Nelson Bowers | 2 | 0 | 0 | 1 | 0 | 1 | 134,680 |
| TOTALS | | 9 | 0 | 0 | 3 | 3 | 1 | $452,017 |

## Morgan Shepherd

**Date of birth:** 10/21/41. **Hometown:** Conover, N.C.

### CAREER STATISTICS

| Year | Car Owner | Races | Won | Top 5 | Top 10 | DNF | Poles | Money Won |
|---|---|---|---|---|---|---|---|---|
| 1970 | M. Shepherd | 3 | 0 | 0 | 0 | 3 | 0 | $269,965 |
| 1977 | Jim Makar | 3 | 0 | 0 | 1 | 0 | 0 | 7,465 |
| 1978 | Jim Makar | 2 | 0 | 0 | 0 | 1 | 0 | 8,115 |
| 1979 | Jim Makar | 0 | 0 | 0 | 0 | 0 | 0 | 256 |
| 1981 | Cliff Stewart | 18 | 1 | 3 | 8 | 7 | 1 | 132,879 |
| | Cecil Gordon | 7 | 0 | 0 | 2 | 2 | 0 | 28,925 |
| | Ron Benfield | 3 | 0 | 0 | 0 | 3 | 0 | 2,405 |
| | Mark Martin | 1 | 0 | 0 | 0 | 1 | 0 | 1,120 |
| 1982 | Ron Benfield | 29 | 0 | 6 | 13 | 14 | 2 | 150,475 |
| 1983 | Jim Stacy | 23 | 0 | 3 | 13 | 8 | 0 | 269,001 |
| | E. Zervakis | 1 | 0 | 0 | 0 | 1 | 0 | 1,000 |
| | Beare Racing | 1 | 0 | 0 | 0 | 1 | 0 | 850 |
| 1984 | R. Harrington | 1 | 0 | 0 | 0 | 0 | 0 | 1,735 |
| | Dick Bahre | 4 | 0 | 0 | 0 | 3 | 0 | 7,450 |
| | M. Shepherd | 3 | 0 | 0 | 0 | 1 | 0 | 3,950 |
| | D.K. Ulrich | 2 | 0 | 0 | 0 | 1 | 0 | 5,545 |
| | Jimmy Means | 1 | 0 | 0 | 0 | 1 | 0 | 4,655 |
| | Roger Hamby | 6 | 0 | 0 | 0 | 3 | 0 | 19,035 |
| | Ron Benfield | 3 | 0 | 0 | 1 | 0 | 0 | 17,300 |
| 1985 | B. Arrington | 1 | 0 | 0 | 0 | 0 | 0 | 15,300 |
| | Dick Bahre | 1 | 0 | 0 | 0 | 1 | 0 | 1,150 |
| | Petty Enter. | 1 | 0 | 0 | 0 | 0 | 0 | 3,415 |
| | Bobby Hawkins | 4 | 0 | 1 | 2 | 2 | 0 | 18,575 |
| | Helen Smith | 7 | 0 | 0 | 0 | 7 | 0 | 11,130 |
| | M. Shepherd | 2 | 0 | 0 | 0 | 1 | 0 | 6,415 |
| 1986 | Jack Beebe | 13 | 1 | 3 | 6 | 6 | 0 | 145,380 |
| | Elmo Langley | 1 | 0 | 0 | 0 | 1 | 0 | 2,940 |
| | James Hylton | 1 | 0 | 0 | 0 | 0 | 0 | 3,880 |
| | Buster Mathis | 1 | 0 | 0 | 0 | 0 | 0 | 1,525 |
| | Rahmoc | 11 | 0 | 1 | 2 | 8 | 0 | 90,421 |
| 1987 | K. Bernstein | 29 | 0 | 7 | 11 | 13 | 1 | 317,034 |
| 1988 | Tom Winkle | 3 | 0 | 0 | 1 | 1 | 1 | 37,645 |
| | M. Shepherd | 9 | 0 | 0 | 0 | 6 | 0 | 37,755 |
| | Mach I | 5 | 0 | 1 | 2 | 2 | 0 | 57,570 |
| | Rahmoc | 3 | 0 | 0 | 1 | 2 | 1 | 27,685 |
| | Baker-Schiff | 3 | 0 | 1 | 2 | 1 | 0 | 36,770 |
| 1989 | Rahmoc | 29 | 0 | 5 | 13 | 9 | 1 | 544,255 |
| 1990 | Bud Moore | 29 | 1 | 7 | 16 | 6 | 0 | 666,915 |
| 1991 | Bud Moore | 29 | 0 | 4 | 14 | 6 | 0 | 521,147 |
| 1992 | Wood Brothers | 29 | 0 | 3 | 11 | 3 | 0 | 634,222 |
| 1993 | Wood Brothers | 30 | 1 | 3 | 15 | 2 | 0 | 782,523 |
| 1994 | Wood Brothers | 31 | 0 | 9 | 16 | 2 | 0 | 1,089,038 |
| 1995 | Wood Brothers | 31 | 0 | 4 | 10 | 2 | 0 | 966,374 |
| 1996 | Butch Mock | 31 | 0 | 1 | 5 | 3 | 0 | 719,059 |
| 1997 | R. Jackson | 18 | 0 | 1 | 3 | 3 | 0 | 578,524 |
| | Doug Bawel | 5 | 0 | 0 | 0 | 0 | 0 | 84,475 |
| 1998 | F. Sabates | 2 | 0 | 0 | 0 | 0 | 0 | 61,611 |
| | R. Childress | 2 | 0 | 0 | 0 | 1 | 0 | 50,140 |
| | Stavola Bros. | 2 | 0 | 0 | 0 | 2 | 0 | 45,955 |
| | Joe Falk | 6 | 0 | 0 | 0 | 3 | 0 | 206,835 |
| 1999 | M. Collins | 0 | 0 | 0 | 0 | 0 | 0 | 30,756 |
| | J. Donlavey | 1 | 0 | 0 | 0 | 0 | 0 | 29,400 |
| | M. Shepherd | 0 | 0 | 0 | 0 | 0 | 0 | 9,147 |
| 2001 | S. Hover Jr. | 0 | 0 | 0 | 0 | 0 | 0 | 21,059 |
| 2002 | C. Shepherd | 5 | 0 | 0 | 0 | 5 | 0 | 214,397 |
| 2003 | M. Shepherd | 2 | 0 | 0 | 0 | 2 | 0 | 120,034 |
| TOTALS | | 488 | 4 | 63 | 168 | 150 | 7 | $8,853,582 |

## Mike Skinner

**Date of birth:** 6/28/57. **Hometown:** Susanville, Calif.

### CAREER STATISTICS

| Year | Car Owner | Races | Won | Top 5 | Top 10 | DNF | Poles | Money Won |
|---|---|---|---|---|---|---|---|---|
| 1986 | Zanworth Rac. | 3 | 0 | 0 | 0 | 1 | 0 | $4,255 |
| 1990 | Thee Dixon | 1 | 0 | 0 | 0 | 1 | 0 | 2,825 |
| 1991 | Thee Dixon | 2 | 0 | 0 | 0 | 1 | 0 | 8,505 |
| 1992 | Thee Dixon | 1 | 0 | 0 | 0 | 0 | 0 | 8,550 |
| | A. Aroneck | 1 | 0 | 0 | 0 | 0 | 0 | 4,900 |
| 1993 | J. Means | 1 | 0 | 0 | 0 | 1 | 0 | 5,180 |
| 1994 | J. Means | 1 | 0 | 0 | 0 | 0 | 0 | 9,550 |
| 1996 | R. Childress | 5 | 0 | 0 | 0 | 1 | 0 | 65,850 |
| 1997 | R. Childress | 31 | 0 | 0 | 3 | 7 | 2 | 900,569 |
| 1998 | R. Childress | 30 | 0 | 4 | 9 | 3 | 0 | 1,518,901 |
| 1999 | R. Childress | 34 | 0 | 5 | 14 | 1 | 2 | 2,499,877 |
| 2000 | R. Childress | 34 | 0 | 1 | 11 | 2 | 1 | 2,205,320 |
| 2001 | R. Childress | 23 | 0 | 0 | 1 | 4 | 0 | 1,921,186 |
| 2002 | L. McClure | 36 | 0 | 0 | 1 | 6 | 0 | 2,094,232 |
| 2003 | Morgan-McClure | 14 | 0 | 0 | 0 | 4 | 0 | 945,373 |
| | N. Bowers | 11 | 0 | 0 | 0 | 2 | 1 | 794,327 |
| | M. Waltrip | 1 | 0 | 0 | 0 | 1 | 0 | 43,150 |
| TOTALS | | 229 | 0 | 10 | 39 | 35 | 6 | $13,032,500 |

## Jack Sprague

**Date of birth:** 8/8/64. **Hometown:** Spring Lake, Mich.

### CAREER STATISTICS

| Year | Car Owner | Races | Won | Top 5 | Top 10 | DNF | Poles | Money Won |
|---|---|---|---|---|---|---|---|---|
| 1996 | J. Hendrick | 2 | 0 | 0 | 0 | 1 | 0 | $22,720 |
| 1997 | J. Hendrick | 1 | 0 | 0 | 0 | 1 | 0 | 18,650 |
| 2002 | Gene Haas | 3 | 0 | 0 | 0 | 2 | 0 | 132,000 |
| 2003 | Gene Haas | 18 | 0 | 0 | 0 | 5 | 0 | 1,187,830 |
| TOTAL | | 24 | 0 | 0 | 0 | 9 | 0 | $1,361,200 |

## Hut Stricklin

**Date of birth**: 6/24/61. **Hometown**: Calera, Ala.

### CAREER STATISTICS

| Year | Car Owner | Races | Won | Top 5 | Top 10 | DNF | Poles | Money Won |
|---|---|---|---|---|---|---|---|---|
| 1987 | Skip Jaehne | 3 | 0 | 0 | 0 | 2 | 0 | $6,085 |
| 1989 | Rod Osterlund | 27 | 0 | 1 | 4 | 6 | 0 | 152,504 |
| 1990 | G. Bradshaw | 2 | 0 | 0 | 0 | 1 | 0 | 21,525 |
|  | Rick Hendrick | 1 | 0 | 0 | 0 | 1 | 0 | 2,765 |
|  | Bobby Allison | 21 | 0 | 0 | 2 | 7 | 0 | 143,909 |
| 1991 | Bobby Allison | 29 | 0 | 2 | 6 | 7 | 0 | 426,524 |
| 1992 | Bobby Allison | 21 | 0 | 0 | 4 | 7 | 0 | 299,935 |
|  | Junie Donlavey | 4 | 0 | 0 | 0 | 0 | 0 | 18,810 |
|  | Junior Johnson | 1 | 0 | 0 | 0 | 1 | 0 | 3,800 |
|  | Larry Hendrick | 2 | 0 | 0 | 0 | 1 | 0 | 14,420 |
| 1993 | Junior Johnson | 30 | 0 | 1 | 2 | 8 | 0 | 494,600 |
| 1994 | Travis Carter | 29 | 0 | 0 | 1 | 3 | 0 | 333,495 |
| 1995 | K. Bernstein | 24 | 0 | 2 | 5 | 9 | 1 | 486,065 |
| 1996 | Stavola Bros. | 31 | 0 | 2 | 2 | 3 | 0 | 631,055 |
| 1997 | Stavola Bros. | 29 | 0 | 0 | 1 | 6 | 0 | 802,904 |
| 1998 | Stavola Bros. | 6 | 0 | 0 | 0 | 3 | 0 | 178,266 |
|  | Buz McCall | 5 | 0 | 0 | 0 | 4 | 0 | 114,275 |
|  | Doug Bawel | 1 | 0 | 0 | 0 | 0 | 0 | 20,265 |
|  | Andy Petree | 1 | 0 | 0 | 0 | 1 | 0 | 24,250 |
| 1999 | J. Donlavey | 1 | 0 | 0 | 0 | 0 | 0 | 47,112 |
|  | S. Barbour | 9 | 0 | 0 | 1 | 1 | 0 | 331,830 |
| 2000 | J. Donlavey | 7 | 0 | 0 | 0 | 5 | 0 | 255,200 |
| 2001 | J. Donlavey | 21 | 0 | 0 | 1 | 3 | 0 | 951,071 |
|  | Michael Brown | 1 | 0 | 0 | 0 | 0 | 0 | 54,950 |
| 2002 | Bill Davis | 22 | 0 | 0 | 0 | 5 | 0 | 1,313,548 |
| **TOTALS** |  | **328** | **0** | **8** | **29** | **83** | **1** | **$7,129,213** |

## Kenny Wallace

**Date of birth**: 8/23/63. **Hometown**: St. Louis

### CAREER STATISTICS

| Year | Car Owner | Races | Won | Top 5 | Top 10 | DNF | Poles | Money Won |
|---|---|---|---|---|---|---|---|---|
| 1990 | Randy Hope | 1 | 0 | 0 | 0 | 1 | 0 | $6,050 |
| 1991 | Felix Sabates | 2 | 0 | 0 | 0 | 0 | 0 | 46,900 |
|  | S. McMahon III | 3 | 0 | 0 | 0 | 2 | 0 | 11,425 |
| 1993 | Felix Sabates | 30 | 0 | 0 | 3 | 6 | 0 | 330,325 |

| Year | Car Owner | Races | Won | Top 5 | Top 10 | DNF | Poles | Money Won |
|---|---|---|---|---|---|---|---|---|
| 1994 | F. Martocci | 1 | 0 | 0 | 0 | 0 | 0 | 9,825 |
|  | C. Hardy | 1 | 0 | 0 | 1 | 0 | 0 | 13,370 |
|  | R. Yates | 10 | 0 | 1 | 2 | 1 | 0 | 211,810 |
| 1995 | F. Martocci | 11 | 0 | 0 | 0 | 3 | 0 | 151,700 |
| 1996 | F. Martocci | 30 | 0 | 0 | 2 | 9 | 0 | 457,665 |
| 1997 | F. Martocci | 31 | 0 | 0 | 2 | 11 | 2 | 939,001 |
| 1998 | F. Martocci | 31 | 0 | 0 | 7 | 13 | 0 | 1,019,861 |
| 1999 | A. Petree | 34 | 0 | 3 | 5 | 7 | 0 | 1,416,208 |
| 2000 | A. Petree | 34 | 0 | 1 | 1 | 6 | 0 | 1,723,966 |
| 2001 | J. Birmingham | 12 | 0 | 0 | 0 | 5 | 0 | 597,651 |
|  | Dale Earnhardt | 12 | 0 | 1 | 2 | 1 | 1 | 965,030 |
| 2002 | Teresa Earnhardt | 4 | 0 | 0 | 1 | 0 | 0 | 454,060 |
|  | R. Childress | 1 | 0 | 0 | 0 | 0 | 0 | 85,567 |
|  | Michael Waltrip | 1 | 0 | 0 | 0 | 0 | 0 | 54,570 |
|  | George Debidart | 4 | 0 | 0 | 0 | 2 | 0 | 240,635 |
|  | B. Davis | 10 | 0 | 0 | 0 | 0 | 0 | 503,085 |
|  | A. Petree | 1 | 0 | 0 | 0 | 0 | 0 | 44,775 |
| 2003 | Bill Davis | 36 | 0 | 0 | 1 | 5 | 0 | 2,480,490 |
| **TOTALS** |  | **300** | **0** | **6** | **27** | **67** | **3** | **$11,763,969** |

## Mike Wallace

**Date of birth**: 3/10/59. **Hometown**: St. Louis

### CAREER STATISTICS

| Year | Car Owner | Races | Won | Top 5 | Top 10 | DNF | Poles | Money Won |
|---|---|---|---|---|---|---|---|---|
| 1991 | J. Means | 2 | 0 | 0 | 0 | 1 | 0 | $7,000 |
| 1992 | D. Moroso | 1 | 0 | 0 | 0 | 0 | 0 | 7,980 |
|  | P. Rissi | 2 | 0 | 0 | 0 | 0 | 0 | 12,235 |
| 1993 | M. Pritchard | 3 | 0 | 0 | 0 | 1 | 0 | 25,400 |
|  | J. Means | 1 | 0 | 0 | 0 | 0 | 0 | 4,725 |
| 1994 | J. Donlavey | 22 | 0 | 1 | 1 | 3 | 0 | 265,115 |
| 1995 | J. Donlavey | 26 | 0 | 0 | 1 | 9 | 0 | 428,006 |
| 1996 | J. Donlavey | 10 | 0 | 0 | 0 | 6 | 0 | 152,417 |
|  | M. Smith | 1 | 0 | 0 | 0 | 0 | 0 | 16,665 |
| 1997 | J. Falk | 7 | 0 | 0 | 0 | 1 | 0 | 159,303 |
| 1998 | P. Barkdoll | 1 | 0 | 0 | 0 | 0 | 0 | 86,105 |
| 1999 | J. Donlavey | 1 | 0 | 0 | 0 | 0 | 0 | 11,806 |
|  | J. Smith | 1 | 0 | 0 | 0 | 0 | 0 | 23,455 |
| 2001 | J. Smith | 21 | 0 | 0 | 4 | 3 | 0 | 1,394,697 |
|  | Roger Penske | 8 | 0 | 1 | 2 | 1 | 0 | 706,673 |
| 2002 | Andy Petree | 4 | 0 | 0 | 0 | 2 | 0 | 390,812 |
|  | A. J. Foyt | 17 | 0 | 0 | 1 | 5 | 0 | 883,891 |
| 2003 |  | 14 | 0 | 0 | 2 | 3 | 0 | 1,031,100 |
| **TOTALS** |  | **142** | **0** | **2** | **11** | **35** | **0** | **$5,707,385** |

## Series champions

| Year | Car No. | Driver | Car owner | Car make | Wins | Poles | Money won |
|---|---|---|---|---|---|---|---|
| 1949 | 22 | Red Byron | Raymond Parks | Oldsmobile | 2 | 1 | $5,800 |
| 1950 | 60 | Bill Rexford | Julian Buesink | Oldsmobile | 1 | 0 | 6,175 |
| 1951 | 92 | Herb Thomas | Herb Thomas | Hudson | 7 | 4 | 18,200 |
| 1952 | 91 | Tim Flock | Ted Chester | Hudson | 8 | 4 | 20,210 |
| 1953 | 92 | Herb Thomas | Herb Thomas | Hudson | 12 | 10 | 27,300 |
| 1954 | 92 | — | Herb Thomas | Hudson | 12 | 8 | 27,540 |
| 1954 | 42 | Lee Petty | — | Chrysler | 7 | 3 | 26,706 |
| 1955 | 300 | Tim Flock | Carl Kiekhaefer | Chrysler | 18 | 19 | 33,750 |
| 1956 | 300B | Buck Baker | Carl Kiekhaefer | Chrysler | 14 | 12 | 29,790 |
| 1957 | 87 | Buck Baker | Buck Baker | Chevrolet | 10 | 5 | 24,712 |
| 1958 | 42 | Lee Petty | Petty Ent. | Oldsmobile | 7 | 4 | 20,600 |
| 1959 | 42 | Lee Petty | Petty Ent. | Plymouth | 11 | 2 | 45,570 |
| 1960 | 4 | Rex White | White-Clements | Chevrolet | 6 | 3 | 45,260 |
| 1961 | 11 | Ned Jarrett | W.G. Holloway Jr. | Chevrolet | 1 | 4 | 27,285 |
| 1962 | 8 | Joe Weatherly | Bud Moore | Pontiac | 9 | 6 | 56,110 |
| 1963 | 21 | — | Wood Brothers | Ford | 3 | 5 | 77,636 |
| 1963 | 8 | Joe Weatherly | — | Mercury | 3 | 6 | 58,110 |
| 1964 | 43 | Richard Petty | Petty Ent. | Plymouth | 9 | 8 | 98,810 |
| 1965 | 11 | Ned Jarrett | Bondy Long | Ford | 13 | 9 | 77,966 |
| 1966 | 6 | David Pearson | Cotton Owens | Dodge | 14 | 7 | 59,205 |
| 1967 | 43 | Richard Petty | Petty Ent. | Plymouth | 27 | 18 | 130,275 |
| 1968 | 17 | David Pearson | Holman-Moody | Ford | 16 | 12 | 118,842 |
| 1969 | 17 | David Pearson | Holman-Moody | Ford | 11 | 14 | 183,700 |
| 1970 | 71 | Bobby Isaac | Nord Krauskopf | Dodge | 11 | 13 | 121,470 |
| 1971 | 43 | Richard Petty | Petty Ent. | Plymouth | 21 | 9 | 309,225 |
| 1972 | 43 | Richard Petty | Petty Ent. | Plymouth | 8 | 3 | 227,015 |
| 1973 | 72 | Benny Parsons | L.G. DeWitt | Chevrolet | 1 | 0 | 114,345 |
| 1974 | 43 | Richard Petty | Petty Ent. | Dodge | 10 | 7 | 299,175 |
| 1975 | 43 | Richard Petty | Petty Ent. | Dodge | 13 | 3 | 378,865 |
| 1976 | 11 | Cale Yarborough | Junior Johnson | Chevrolet | 9 | 2 | 387,173 |
| 1977 | 11 | Cale Yarborough | Junior Johnson | Chevrolet | 9 | 3 | 477,499 |
| 1978 | 11 | Cale Yarborough | Junior Johnson | Oldsmobile | 10 | 8 | 530,751 |
| 1979 | 43 | Richard Petty | Petty Ent. | Chevrolet | 5 | 1 | 531,292 |
| 1980 | 2 | Dale Earnhardt | Rod Osterlund | Chevrolet | 5 | 0 | 588,926 |
| 1981 | 11 | Darrell Waltrip | Junior Johnson | Buick | 12 | 11 | 693,342 |
| 1982 | 11 | Darrell Waltrip | Junior Johnson | Buick | 12 | 7 | 873,118 |
| 1983 | 22 | Bobby Allison | Bill Gardner | Buick | 6 | 0 | 828,355 |
| 1984 | 44 | Terry Labonte | Billy Hagan | Chevrolet | 2 | 2 | 713,010 |
| 1985 | 11 | Darrell Waltrip | Junior Johnson | Chevrolet | 3 | 4 | 1,318,735 |
| 1986 | 3 | Dale Earnhardt | Richard Childress | Chevrolet | 5 | 1 | 1,783,880 |
| 1987 | 3 | Dale Earnhardt | Richard Childress | Chevrolet | 11 | 1 | 2,099,243 |
| 1988 | 9 | Bill Elliott | Harry Melling | Ford | 6 | 6 | 1,574,639 |
| 1989 | 27 | Rusty Wallace | Raymond Beadle | Pontiac | 6 | 4 | 2,247,950 |
| 1990 | 3 | Dale Earnhardt | Richard Childress | Chevrolet | 9 | 4 | 3,083,056 |
| 1991 | 3 | Dale Earnhardt | Richard Childress | Chevrolet | 4 | 0 | 2,396,685 |
| 1992 | 7 | Alan Kulwicki | Alan Kulwicki | Ford | 2 | 6 | 2,322,561 |
| 1993 | 3 | Dale Earnhardt | Richard Childress | Chevrolet | 6 | 2 | 3,353,789 |
| 1994 | 3 | Dale Earnhardt | Richard Childress | Chevrolet | 4 | 2 | 3,400,733 |
| 1995 | 24 | Jeff Gordon | Rick Hendrick | Chevrolet | 7 | 8 | 4,347,343 |
| 1996 | 5 | Terry Labonte | Rick Hendrick | Chevrolet | 2 | 4 | 4,030,648 |
| 1997 | 24 | Jeff Gordon | Rick Hendrick | Chevrolet | 10 | 1 | 6,375,658 |
| 1998 | 24 | Jeff Gordon | Rick Hendrick | Chevrolet | 13 | 7 | 9,306,584 |
| 1999 | 88 | Dale Jarrett | Robert Yates | Ford | 4 | 0 | 6,649,596 |
| 2000 | 18 | Bobby Labonte | Joe Gibbs | Pontiac | 4 | 2 | 7,361,387 |
| 2001 | 24 | Jeff Gordon | Rick Hendrick | Chevrolet | 6 | 6 | 10,879,757 |
| 2002 | 20 | Tony Stewart | Joe Gibbs | Pontiac | 3 | 2 | 9,163,761 |
| 2003 | 17 | Matt Kenseth | Jack Roush | Ford | 1 | 2 | 9,422,764 |

Note: In 1954 and 1963 the driver champion and car owner champion were on separate teams.

LEGENDS

# Champion crew chiefs

1949: Red Vogt; 1950: Julian Bueskink; 1951: Smokey Yunick; 1952: B.B. Blackburn; 1953: Smokey Yunick; 1954: Lee Petty; 1955: Carl Kiekhafer; 1956: Carl Kiekhafer; 1957: Bud Moore; 1958: Lee Petty; 1959: Lee Petty; 1960: Louis Clements; 1961: Bud Allman; 1962: Bud Moore; 1963: Bud Moore; 1964: Dale Inman; 1965: John Ervin; 1966: Cotton Owens; 1967: Dale Inman; 1968: Jake Elder; 1969: Jake Elder; 1970: Harry Hyde; 1971: Dale Inman; 1972: Dale Inman; 1973: Travis Carter; 1974: Dale Inman; 1975: Dale Inman; 1976: Herb Nab; 1977: Herb Nab; 1978: Tim Brewer/Travis Carter; 1979: Dale Inman; 1980: Doug Richert; 1981: Tim Brewer; 1982: Jeff Hammond; 1983: Gary Nelson; 1984: Dale Inman; 1985: Jeff Hammond; 1986: Kirk Shelmerdine; 1987: Kirk Shelmerdine; 1988: Ernie Elliott; 1989: Barry Dodson; 1990: Kirk Shelmerdine; 1991: Kirk Shelmerdine; 1992: Paul Andrews; 1993: Andy Petree; 1994: Andy Petree; 1995: Ray Evernham; 1996: Gary DeHart; 1997: Ray Evernham; 1998: Ray Evernham; 1999: Todd Parrott; 2000: Jimmy Makar; 2001: Robbie Loomis; 2002: Greg Zipadelli; 2003 Robbie Reiser.

# Champions and runners-up

## Modern Era – Since 1972

| Year | Champion | Runner-Up | Point Margin | Year | Champion | Runner-Up | Point Margin |
|---|---|---|---|---|---|---|---|
| 1972 | Richard Petty | Bobby Allison | 127.90 | 1988 | Bill Elliott | Rusty Wallace | 24 |
| 1973 | Benny Parsons | Cale Yarborough | 67.15 | 1989 | Rusty Wallace | Dale Earnhardt | 12 |
| 1974 | Richard Petty | Cale Yarborough | 567.45 | 1990 | Dale Earnhardt | Mark Martin | 26 |
| *1975 | Richard Petty | Dave Marcis | 722 | 1991 | Dale Earnhardt | Ricky Rudd | 195 |
| 1976 | Cale Yarborough | Richard Petty | 195 | 1992 | Alan Kulwicki | Bill Elliott | 10 |
| 1977 | Cale Yarborough | Richard Petty | 386 | 1993 | Dale Earnhardt | Rusty Wallace | 80 |
| 1978 | Cale Yarborough | Bobby Allison | 474 | 1994 | Dale Earnhardt | Mark Martin | 444 |
| 1979 | Richard Petty | Darrell Waltrip | 11 | 1995 | Jeff Gordon | Dale Earnhardt | 34 |
| 1980 | Dale Earnhardt | Cale Yarborough | 19 | 1996 | Terry Labonte | Jeff Gordon | 37 |
| 1981 | Darrell Waltrip | Bobby Allison | 53 | 1997 | Jeff Gordon | Dale Jarrett | 14 |
| 1982 | Darrell Waltrip | Bobby Allison | 72 | 1998 | Jeff Gordon | Mark Martin | 364 |
| 1983 | Bobby Allison | Darrell Waltrip | 47 | 1999 | Dale Jarrett | Bobby Labonte | 201 |
| 1984 | Terry Labonte | Harry Gant | 65 | 2000 | Bobby Labonte | Dale Earnhardt | 265 |
| 1985 | Darrell Waltrip | Bill Elliott | 101 | 2001 | Jeff Gordon | Tony Stewart | 349 |
| 1986 | Dale Earnhardt | Darrell Waltrip | 288 | 2002 | Tony Stewart | Mark Martin | 38 |
| 1987 | Dale Earnhardt | Bill Elliott | 489 | 2003 | Matt Kenseth | Jimmie Johnson | 90 |

* Current point system instituted.

# Top 10 closest champion points margins

| | Year | Champion | Runner-Up | Point Margin | | Year | Champion | Runner-Up | Point Margin |
|---|---|---|---|---|---|---|---|---|---|
| 1. | 1992 | Alan Kulwicki | Bill Elliott | 10 | 6. | 1988 | Bill Elliott | Rusty Wallace | 24 |
| 2. | 1979 | Richard Petty | Darrell Waltrip | 11 | 7. | 1990 | Dale Earnhardt | Mark Martin | 26 |
| 3. | 1989 | Rusty Wallace | Dale Earnhardt | 12 | 8. | 1995 | Jeff Gordon | Dale Earnhardt | 34 |
| 4. | 1997 | Jeff Gordon | Dale Jarrett | 14 | 9. | 1996 | Terry Labonte | Jeff Gordon | 37 |
| 5. | 1980 | Dale Earnhardt | Cale Yarborough | 19 | 10. | 2002 | Tony Stewart | Mark Martin | 38 |

# Closest points battles

## (Modern Era – Since 1972)

Six Races to go — 1981 – Darrell Waltrip leads Bobby Allison by two points.
Five Races to Go — 1985 – Bill Elliott leads Darrell Waltrip by 23 points.
Four Races to Go — 1985 – Darrell Waltrip leads Bill Elliott by 20 points.
Three Races to go — 1996 – Jeff Gordon leads Terry Labonte by one point.
Two races To Go — 1979 – Richard Petty leads Darrell Waltrip by eight points.
One Race To Go — 1979 – Darrell Waltrip leads Richard Petty by two points.

# Inactive champions

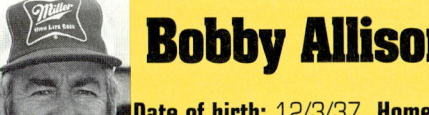

## Bobby Allison

**Date of birth:** 12/3/37. **Hometown:** Hueytown, Ala. **Years of competition:** 1961-88 (717 races). **NASCAR Winston Cup: Titles:** 1. **Years:** '83. **Victories:** 84. **Poles:** 57. **Career earnings:** $7,102,233.

**Personal:** Resides in Hueytown, Ala. ... Married (Judy). ... Career ended 13 races into the 1988 season because of injuries suffered in accident at Pocono Raceway. ... Son Davey Allison raced in NASCAR Winston Cup prior to his 1993 death in a helicopter crash. Son Clifford Allison raced in ARCA and the NASCAR Busch Series prior to his 1992 death in a crash at Michigan International Speedway, during Busch Series practice.

### CAREER HIGHLIGHTS

84 race victories third on all-time list (tied with Darrell Waltrip). ... Won Daytona 500 three times – 1978, '82, '88; in '88, son Davey Allison finished second. ... Brother Donnie Allison raced in NASCAR Winston Cup. ... Had best statistical season in 1972, driving for car owner Junior Johnson, winning 10 races, finishing second 12 times and taking 11 poles; finished second in series standings to Richard Petty. ... Member of NASCAR's famed "Alabama Gang." ... Inducted into International Motorsports Hall of Fame in 1993. ... Named one of NASCAR's 50 Greatest Drivers.

## Buck Baker

**Date of birth:** 3/4/19. **Hometown:** Charlotte, N.C. **Years of competition:** 1949-76 (631 races). **NASCAR Winston Cup: Titles:** 2. **Years:** '56, '57. **Victories:** 46. **Poles:** 44. **Career earnings:** $325,570.

**Personal:** Deceased 4-14-02. ... Full name Elzie Wylie Baker. ... Son Buddy also was Winston Cup standout. ... Drove a bus before deciding to try auto racing, in 1939. ... Founded high-performance driving schools at Atlanta Motor Speedway, Bristol Motor Speedway, Darlington Raceway and North Carolina Speedway.

### CAREER HIGHLIGHTS

First driver to win consecutive Winston Cup titles. ... Finished second in Winston Cup point standings twice (1955, '58). ... Known for versatility. Won races in NASCAR's Modified, Speedway, Grand American and Winston Cup circuits. ... Career victory total of 46 is 13th-best all-time. ... Inducted into International Motorsports Hall of Fame in 1990. ... Named one of NASCAR's 50 Greatest Drivers.

## Red Byron

**Date of birth:** 3/12/15. **Hometown:** Anniston, Ala. **Years of competition:** 1949-51 (15 races). **NASCAR Winston Cup: Titles:** 1. **Years:** '49. **Victories:** 2. **Poles:** 2. **Career earnings:** $10,100.

**Personal:** Deceased 11-7-60. ... Real name was Robert. ... Bomber tail-gunner during World War II. ... Health problems led to early exit from racing.

### CAREER HIGHLIGHTS

First two-time Winston Cup champion. ... Won first NASCAR-sanctioned race, in 1948, on the Daytona Beach road-beach course. ... Was one of key early supporters of Bill France Sr.'s formation of NASCAR. ... After retiring from stock car racing, became interested in sports cars; at the time of his death, was striving to develop an American car capable of winning the 24 Hours of LeMans. ... Named one of NASCAR's 50 Greatest Drivers.

## Dale Earnhardt

**Date of birth:** 4/29/51. **Hometown:** Kannapolis, N.C. **Years of competition:** 1975-2001 (676 races). **NASCAR Winston Cup: Titles:** 7. **Years:** '80, '86, '87, '90, '91, '93, '94. **Victories:** 76. **Poles:** 22. **Career earnings:** $41,742,384.

**Personal:** Deceased 2-18-01, in accident on last lap of Daytona 500. ... Son Dale Jr. races in NASCAR Winston Cup circuit. Son Kerry races in NASCAR Busch Series. ... Father Ralph Earnhardt raced in Winston Cup. ... Full name Ralph Dale Earnhardt. ... Had two nicknames during career, "Ironhead" and "The Intimidator."

## CAREER HIGHLIGHTS

Co-holder of record for most NASCAR Winston Cup championships with Richard Petty. ... Victory total sixth-best all-time. ... Second-leading all-time money winner in Winston Cup. ... Won Daytona 500 in 1998; all-time leader in race victories at Daytona International Speedway, with 34. ... Finished second in Winston Cup points three times, including 2000 season. ... Named NASCAR's 2001 Most Popular Driver posthumously. ... First Winston Cup start was in 1975 World 600 at Charlotte. Finished 22nd, one spot ahead of future car owner Richard Childress. ... Named one of NASCAR's 50 Greatest Drivers.

# Tim Flock

**Date of birth:** 5/11/24. **Hometown:** Fort Payne, Ala. **Years of competition:** 1949-61 (189 races). **NASCAR Winston Cup: Titles:** 2. **Years:** '52, '55. **Victories:** 40. **Poles:** 39. **Career earnings:** $103,515

**Personal:** Deceased 3-31-98. ... Father Carl Flock was a tightrope walker. ... Tim, brothers Bob and Fonty and sister Ethel all were in a race in the 1950s, the only time four siblings have been in the same Winston Cup race. Ethel finished ahead of her brothers.

## CAREER HIGHLIGHTS

Won 18 races in 1955, a single-season victory record that stood until Richard Petty won 27 in 1967. ... Winning percentage of 21.2 (40 wins in 189 starts) is highest in Winston Cup history. ... Won NASCAR's only sports car race, in 1955, driving a Mercedes-Benz 300 SL. ... Occasionally drove with a monkey named Jocko Flocko as a "co-pilot." ... Father was a daredevil. ... Said "I always thought you could do both – win and have fun." ... Inducted into International Motorsports Hall of Fame in 1991. ... Named one of NASCAR's 50 Greatest Drivers.

# Bobby Isaac

**Date of birth:** 8/1/32. **Hometown:** Catawba, N.C. **Years of competition:** 1964-79 (308 races). **NASCAR Winston Cup: Titles:** 1. **Years:** '70. **Victories:** 37. **Poles:** 50. **Career earnings:** $585,297

**Personal:** Deceased 8-14-77. ... After parents died, quit school as teenager to work in a sawmill. ... Died after suffering a heart attack during a Late Model Sportsman race at Hickory (N.C.) Speedway.

## CAREER HIGHLIGHTS

Holds record for most poles in a season (20-1969). ... In 1964, his first full season, led every race entered. ... Won 11 races in championship season, driving futuristic-looking Dodge Daytonas. ... 50-pole total sixth-best all-time. ... Holds record for most poles in a season, with 20 in 1969. ... Set a then-record speed of 201.104 mph in a closed-course test at Talladega in 1970. ... Inducted into International Motorsports Hall of Fame in 1996. ... Named one of NASCAR's 50 Greatest Drivers.

# Ned Jarrett

**Date of birth:** 3/27/40. **Hometown:** Newton, N.C. **Years of competition:** 1953-66 (351 races). **NASCAR Winston Cup: Titles:** 2. **Years:** '61, '65. **Victories:** 50. **Poles:** 35. **Career earnings:** $289,146

**Personal:** Resides in Hickory, N.C. ... Married (Martha). ... Nicknamed "Gentleman Ned" during career. ... Since retiring, has become recognized as one of NASCAR's greatest ambassadors, and considered instrumental to NASCAR's growth via his television work. ... Son Dale competes in Winston Cup, and won the series championship in 1999.

## CAREER HIGHLIGHTS

50 race victories 10th on all-time list (tied with Junior Johnson). ... 48 victories on short tracks; short-track victory total third-best all-time. ... Won total of 28 races during 1964 and '65 seasons. ... Became television commentator. Remembered for emotional call of

son Dale Jarrett winning Daytona 500 in 1993. ... Inducted into International Motorsports Association Hall of Fame in 1991. ... Named one of NASCAR's 50 Greatest Drivers.

## Alan Kulwicki

**Date of birth:** 12/14/54. **Hometown:** Greenfield, Wis. **Years of competition:** 1985-93 (207 races). **NASCAR Winston Cup: Titles:** 1. **Years:** '92. **Victories:** 5. **Poles:** 24. **Career earnings:** $5,059,052

**Personal:** Deceased 4-1-93 in plane crash, en route to NASCAR Winston Cup race at Bristol Motor Speedway. ... Held degree in mechanical engineering from the University of Wisconsin.

### CAREER HIGHLIGHTS

First Northern driver to win the NASCAR Winston Cup title since New York's Bill Rexford in 1950. ... Won title by closest margin in series history, 10 points ahead of Bill Elliott. Was 278 points out of first place with six races remaining in season. ... Inducted into International Motorsports Hall of Fame in 2002. ... Named one of NASCAR's 50 Greatest Drivers.

## Benny Parsons

**Date of birth:** 4/12/41. **Hometown:** Detroit. **Years of competition:** 1970-88 (526 races). **NASCAR Winston Cup: Titles:** 1. **Years:** '73. **Victories:** 21. **Poles:** 20. **Career earnings:** $3,926,539

**Personal:** Married (Terri). ... Resides in Concord, N.C. ... Avid golfer. ... Does television commentary for NASCAR events on NBC and TNT. ... Nicknamed the "Taxi Cab Driver from Detroit," for listing it as his occupation on race entry forms.

### CAREER HIGHLIGHTS

First driver to qualify a stock car at more than 200 mph (200.176), at 1982 Winston 500 at Talladega Superspeedway. ... Won 1975 Daytona 500. ... Finished second in Winston Cup standings twice (1955, '58). ... Finished in the top 10 in 283 of 526 events (54%.) ... Inducted into International Motorsports Hall of Fame in 1994. ... Named one of NASCAR's 50 Greatest Drivers.

## David Pearson

**Date of birth:** 12/22/34. **Hometown:** Spartanburg, S.C. **Years of competition:** 1960-86 (574 races). **NASCAR Winston Cup: Titles:** 3. **Years:** '66, '68, '69. **Victories:** 105. **Poles:** 113. **Career earnings:** $2,482,596

**Personal:** Resides in Spartanburg, S.C. ... Nicknamed "The Silver Fox" during racing career. ... Son, Larry, is a former NASCAR Busch Series champion.

### CAREER HIGHLIGHTS

105 victories second-best total all-time. ... During 1968-69, had combined totals of 27 victories and 30 runner-up finishes. ... Won career-high 16 races in 1968. ... Won Daytona 500 only once, in 1976, but had six victories overall at Daytona International Speedway (tied for third all-time with Bobby Allison) via five Firecracker 400 victories. ... Drove for legendary Wood Brothers from 1972-79. ... Inducted into International Motorsports Hall of Fame in 1993. ... Named one of NASCAR's 50 Greatest Drivers.

## Lee Petty

**Date of birth:** 3/14/14. **Hometown:** Level Cross, N.C. **Years of competition:** 1949-64 (429 races). **NASCAR Winston Cup: Titles:** 3. **Years:** '54, '58, '59. **Victories:** 54. **Poles:** 18. **Career earnings:** $209,780

**Personal:** Deceased 4-5-00. ... Father of seven-time Winston Cup champion Richard Petty, grandfather of Winston Cup driver Kyle Petty. ... Helped develop race car safety innovations such as roll bars and window webs.

### CAREER HIGHLIGHTS

First driver to win three Winston Cup titles. ... Won the first Daytona 500, edging Johnny Beauchamp in a photo finish; the result took three days to be determined. ... Upon retirement, 54 victories was best all-time total. Son Richard broke that record in 1964. Now tied for eighth all-time with Rusty Wallace. ... Inducted into International Motorsports Hall of Fame in 1990. ... Named one of NASCAR's 50 Greatest Drivers.

## Richard Petty

**Date of birth:** 7/2/37. **Hometown:** Randleman, N.C. **Years of competition:** 1958-92 (1,177 races). **NASCAR Winston Cup: Titles:** 7. **Years:** '64, '67, '71, '72, '74, '75, '79. **Victories:** 200. **Poles:** 127. **Career earnings:** $7,755,409.

**Personal:** Married (Lynda). ... Resides in Level Cross, N.C. ... Father Lee Petty won three NASCAR Winston Cup championships. ... Nicknamed "The King."

### CAREER HIGHLIGHTS

Co-holds record for most NASCAR Winston Cup championships (7) with the late Dale Earnhardt. ... Holds records for most NASCAR Winston Cup victories (200), poles (127), victories in a season (27, 1967), consecutive victories (10, 1967) and starts (1,177). ... Last victory came in Firecracker 400 at Daytona International Speedway on July 4, 1984, with President Ronald Reagan in attendance. ... Won Daytona 500 a record seven times. ... Now heads multi-car Petty Enterprises team in NASCAR Winston Cup Series, with son Kyle Petty as lead driver. ... Inducted into International Motorsports Hall of Fame in 1997. ... Named one of NASCAR's 50 Greatest Drivers.

## Bill Rexford

**Date of birth:** 3/14/27. **Hometown:** Conowango Valley, N.Y. **Years of competition:** 1949-53 (36 races). **NASCAR Winston Cup: Titles:** 1. **Years:** '50. **Victories:** 1. **Poles:** 1. **Career earnings:** $7,535.

**Personal:** Deceased 4-18-94. ... Stopped racing at the age of 26. ... Lived in California after retirement.

### CAREER HIGHLIGHTS

Youngest driver – 23 – to win the NASCAR Winston Cup championship. ... Championship came in controversial manner; benefited from NASCAR penalizing Red Byron and Lee Petty (deducting points) for running in non-NASCAR events.

## Herb Thomas

**Date of birth:** 4/6/23. **Hometown:** Sanford, N.C. **Years of competition:** 1949-62 (230 races). **NASCAR Winston Cup: Titles:** 2. **Years:** '51, '53. **Victories:** 48. **Poles:** 39. **Career earnings:** $126,570.

**Personal:** Deceased 8-9-00. ... Survived near-fatal racing accident in October, 1956 that curtailed career. ... After several comeback attempts, retired from racing, founded a trucking company and ran a sawmill.

### CAREER HIGHLIGHTS

First two-time NASCAR Winston Cup Series champion. ... First three-time (1951, '54, '55) winner of the Southern 500. ... 48 career victories 12th-best total all-time. ... Series runner-up twice (1952, '54). ... Inducted into International Motorsports Hall of Fame in 1994. ... Named one of NASCAR's 50 Greatest Drivers.

## Darrell Waltrip

**Date of birth:** 2/5/47. **Hometown:** Owensboro, Ky. **Years of competition:** 1972-2000 (809 races). **NASCAR Winston Cup: Titles:** 3. **Years:** '81, '82, '85. **Victories:** 84. **Poles:** 59. **Career earnings:** $19,416,618.

**Personal:** Married (Stevie). ... Resides in Franklin, Tenn. ... Nicknamed "Jaws" during his career, because of outspoken demeanor. ... Younger brother Michael competes in NASCAR Winston Cup.

### CAREER HIGHLIGHTS

84 career victories third all-time (tied with Bobby Allison). ... ... Won his three series titles driving for

the legendary driver/owner Junior Johnson. ... Was first driver in a Tide-sponsored car. "Tide Machine" Chevrolet started one of NASCAR's longest-running and most well-known sponsorships ... Ended career-long frustration by finally winning Daytona 500 in 1989, driving Rick Hendrick-owned Chevrolet. ... Now works as television commentator on FOX Network's NASCAR Winston Cup broadcasts. ... Named one of NASCAR's 50 Greatest Drivers.

## Joe Weatherly

**Date of birth:** 5/29/22. **Hometown:** Norfolk, Va. **Years of competition:** 1960-64 (230 races). **NASCAR Winston Cup: Titles:** 2. **Years:** '62, '63. **Victories:** 25. **Poles:** 19. **Career earnings:** $193,620

**Personal:** Deceased 1-19-64, in racing accident at Riverside, Calif. ... One of first NASCAR "personalities" that attracted fans to the sport. ... Raced motorcycles before moving to stock cars. ... Nicknamed "Little Joe" and the "Clown Prince of Stock Car Racing" during his career.

### CAREER HIGHLIGHTS

One of six two-time Winston Cup champions. ... Accumulated 25 victories in only four seasons. ... Won 101 races in the 1952 and '53 seasons in NASCAR Modified division, winning division title in '53. ... From 1956-59 drove in NASCAR Convertible division. ... 1962 Winston Cup title was first for legendary car owner/crew chief Bud Moore. ... Inducted into International Motorsports Hall of Fame in 1994. ... Named one of NASCAR's 50 Greatest Drivers,

## Rex White

**Date of birth:** 8/17/29. **Hometown:** Spartanburg, S.C. **Years of competition:** 1956-64 (233 races). **NASCAR Winston Cup: Titles:** 1. **Years:** '60. **Victories:** 28. **Poles:** 35. **Career earnings:** $190,283

**Personal:** Resides in Forest Park, Ga. ... Drove for a trucking company after leaving racing; retired in summer of 2001 – at the age of 72. ... Often mistaken during his racing days for popular comedian George Gobel.

### CAREER HIGHLIGHTS

In championship season, finished 3,936 points ahead of runner-up Richard Petty. ... Career victory total of 28 is 20th-best all-time. ... Series runner-up in 1961. ... Finished in series standings top 10 in six of nine years. ... Consistency was hallmark of career. Finished in top five in 110 of 233 races; finished outside of the top 10 only 30% of the time. ... A short-track expert; only one victory came on a superspeedway, the 1962 Dixie 400 at Atlanta Motor Speedway. ... Named one of NASCAR's 50 Greatest Drivers.

## Cale Yarborough

**Date of birth:** 3/27/40. **Hometown:** Sardis, S.C. **Years of competition:** 1957-88 (559 races). **NASCAR Winston Cup: Titles:** 3. **Years:** '76, '77, '78. **Victories:** 83. **Poles:** 70. **Career earnings:** $5,003,616

**Personal:** Resides in Sardis, S.C. ... Married (Betty Jo). ... Full name William Caleb Yarborough. ... Runs car dealership in Florence, S.C.

### CAREER HIGHLIGHTS

83 race victories fifth-best total all-time. ... Only driver to win three consecutive NASCAR Winston Cup championships. ... Finished second in series standings three times. ... Won Daytona 500 four times (1968, '77, '83, '84), second behind Richard Petty's seven victories. ... Tied with Buddy Baker and Bill Elliott for most Daytona 500 poles (four). ... Holds record for most poles overall at Daytona International Speedway (12). ... Inducted into International Motorsports Hall of Fame in 1993. ... Named one of NASCAR's 50 Greatest Drivers.

# Other notable NASCAR drivers

## Davey Allison

**Date of birth:** 2/25/61. **Hometown:** Hueytown, Ala. **Years of competition:** 1985-93 (191 races). **Victories:** 19. **Poles:** 14. **Career winnings:** $6,726,974

**Personal:** Deceased 7/13/93 after a helicopter crash the day before in the Talladega Superspeedway infield. ... First job was sweeping floors at his father's auto shop, Bobby Allison Racing in Hueytown, Ala. ... Brother Clifford Allison raced in NASCAR until his death in a 1992 Busch Series practice crash at Michigan International Speedway. ... Father Bobby won the 1983 Winston Cup championship.

### CAREER HIGHLIGHTS

Helped popularize the No. 28 Texaco/Havoline-sponsored Ford among NASCAR fans. ... Finished second in 1988 Daytona 500 behind father Bobby. ... Won 1992 Daytona 500. ... 1987 Rookie of the Year, becoming first rookie to win two races. ... In 1987, became first rookie to qualify on front row (outside pole) for Daytona 500. ... Had 66 top-five finishes and 92 top-10 finishes. ... Inducted into International Motorsports Hall of Fame in 1998. ... Named one of NASCAR's 50 Greatest Drivers.

## Donnie Allison

**Date of birth:** 9/7/39. **Hometown:** Hueytown, Ala. **Years of competition:** 1966-88 (241 races). **Victories:** 10. **Poles:** 17. **Career winnings:** $1,034,923

**Personal:** Resides Salisbury, N.C. ... Married (Pat). ... Original member of stock car racing's "Alabama Gang." ... Perhaps best remembered for his involvement in his and brother Bobby's nationally-televised fight with Cale Yarborough after the 1979 Daytona 500.

### CAREER HIGHLIGHTS

In 1970, won the World 600 on May 24 and six days later finished fourth in the Indianapolis 500, taking Indy Rookie of the Year honor. ... Career curtailed after accident in 1981 World 600. Competed in only 13 races from that point, with his final race at Michigan International Speedway in August, 1988. ... Had 115 top-10 finishes.

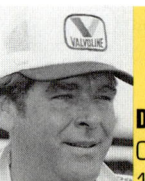

## Buddy Baker

**Date of birth:** 1/25/41. **Hometown:** Charlotte, N.C. **Years of competition:** 1959-92 (698 races). **Victories:** 19. **Poles:** 40. **Career winnings:** $3,640,371

**Personal:** Resides in Sherrills Ford, N.C. ... At 6-foot-6, one of tallest drivers in history. ... Nicknamed "Leadfoot" and the "Gentle Giant" during career. ... Did television race commentary after retiring from competition. ... Son of racing legend Buck Baker, who won NASCAR Winston Cup titles in 1956 and '57. ... Full name Elzie Wylie Baker Jr.

### CAREER HIGHLIGHTS

Won 1980 Daytona 500. ... Won consecutive (1972-73) World 600s. ... Average speed of 177.602 mph in winning Daytona 500 is still the race record, going into 2003 season. ... Finished career-high fifth in 1977 Winston Cup points. ... Inducted into International Motorsports Association Hall of Fame in 1997. ... Named one of NASCAR's 50 Greatest Drivers.

## Neil Bonnett

**Date of birth:** 7/30/46. **Hometown:** Bessemer, Ala. **Years of competition:** 1974-93 (363 races). **Victories:** 18. **Poles:** 20. **Career winnings:** $3,861,661

**Personal:** Deceased 2/11/94 in accident at Daytona International Speedway, in practice for the Daytona 500. ... Original "Alabama Gang" member. ... Became television commentator in latter stages of racing career, and hosted his own race show on The Nashville Network. ... Was out of action for three years after April 1990 crash at Darlington Raceway. ... Full name Lawrence Neil Bonnett.

## CAREER HIGHLIGHTS

Won consecutive World 600s in 1982 and '83. ... Finished a career-high fourth in series points in 1985. .... Had 156 top-10 finishes. ... Won consecutive Busch Clash titles at Daytona International Speedway in 1983 and '84. ... Named one of NASCAR's 50 Greatest Drivers.

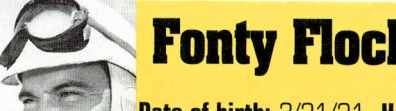

# Fonty Flock

**Date of birth:** 3/21/21. **Hometown:** Decatur, Ga. **Years of competition:** 1949-57 (154 races). **Victories:** 19. **Poles:** 33. **Career winnings:** $73,758

**Personal:** Deceased 7/15/72. Full name Truman Fontello Flock. ... Younger brother Tim Flock won Winston Cup championship in 1952 and '55. ... Older brother Bob Flock made four Winston Cup starts between 1949-52. ... Sister Ethel also raced.

## CAREER HIGHLIGHTS

Biggest victory came in 1952 Southern 500. ... Finished a career-high second in series points in 1951. ... Had 20 runner-up finishes in career. ... Won Raleigh 300 in May 1953 after starting 43rd. ... In nine of his 19 victories, started on the pole.

# A.J. Foyt

**Date of birth:** 1/16/35. **Hometown:** Houston. **Years of competition:** 1963-94 (128 races). **Victories:** 7. **Poles:** 10. **Career winnings:** $706,684

**Personal:** Resides in Hockley, Texas. ... Married (Lucy). ... Son Larry Foyt, a NASCAR Busch Series rookie in 2002, is slated to drive in NASCAR Winston Cup Series in 2003. ... Inducted into International Motorsports Hall of Fame in 2000.

## CAREER HIGHLIGHTS

Never raced more than seven times in a NASCAR Winston Cup season; concentrated on legendary Indy-car career that included a record four Indianapolis 500 victories. ... Won 1971 Daytona 500; also won the Firecracker 400 at Daytona International Speedway in 1964 and '65. ... Had six second-place finishes and four third-place finishes. ... Has fielded a NASCAR Winston Cup team since retiring from driving.

# Harry Gant

**Date of birth:** 1/10/40. **Hometown:** Taylorsville, N.C. **Years of competition:** 1973-94 (474 races). **Victories:** 18. **Poles:** 17. **Career winnings:** $8,456,104

**Personal:** Resides in Taylorsville, N.C. ... Married (Peggy). ... Nicknamed "Handsome Harry" for years, then "Mr. September" after September 1991 run of four consecutive victories.

## CAREER HIGHLIGHTS

Runner-up in 1984 series championship standings. ... Won four consecutive races in September 1991 (Darlington, Richmond, Dover and Martinsville) en route to a career-best fourth-place finish in series standings. ... Three-time runner-up in NASCAR Busch Series standings (1969, '76, '77). ... Named one of NASCAR's 50 Greatest Drivers.

# Janet Guthrie

**Date of birth:** 3/7/38. **Hometown:** Iowa City, Iowa. **Years of competition:** 1976-78, 1980 (33 races). **Victories:** None. **Poles:** 0. **Career winnings:** $75,309

**Personal:** Resides in Miami, Fl. ... Married (Warren Levene). ... Earned her pilot's license by age 17 and was able to fly more than 20 types of aircraft. ... Graduated from University of Michigan in 1960 with a degree in physics. ... Worked as aviation engineer and qualified for NASA astronaut program but was disqualified when a Ph.D. was subsequently made a requirement. ... Also served as a flight instructor.

## CAREER HIGHLIGHTS

In 1977, became first woman to qualify for the Daytona 500 and finished 12th; placed 11th in her only other appearance, in 1980. ... Only woman to lead a Winston Cup race (Ontario, 1977). ...Career-best finish was sixth at Bristol. ... Finished in the top 15 in 17 of her 33 career races with four top 10s. ... First woman to qualify for a Winston Cup race since Louise Smith in 1949 when she finished 15th at Charlotte in 1976. ... Did not succeed in her first attempt to become the first woman to qualify for the Indianapolis 500 in 1976 but did qualify in 1977 and had a career-best finish of ninth in 1978. ... Inducted into Women's Sports Hall of Fame in 1980.

# Ernie Irvan

**Date of birth:** 1/13/59. **Hometown:** Salinas Calif. **Years of competition:** 1987-99 (313 races). **Victories:** 15. **Poles:** 22. **Career winnings:** $11,625,817

**Personal:** Resides in Mooresville, N.C. ... Married (Kim). ... Retired from racing in September 1999, following an Aug. 20 accident at Michigan – five years to the day after his previous bad accident at the track. ... Fielding race team that competes in ARCA Series, with Kevin Conway driving.

## CAREER HIGHLIGHTS

Won 1991 Daytona 500 ... Finished career-best fifth in points, in 1991. ... Was polesitter in consecutive years (1997 and '98) for the Brickyard 400 at Indianapolis Motor Speedway. ... Made remarkable comeback from serious August 20, 1994 accident at Michigan International Speedway, returning to racing in October 1995 and finishing sixth at North Wilkesboro Speedway. ... Followed late Davey Allison as driver of popular No. 28 Texaco/Havoline Ford. ... Four of 15 career victories came in restrictor-plate events (two at Daytona International Speedway, two at Talladega Superspeedway). ... Named one of NASCAR's 50 Greatest Drivers.

# Junior Johnson

**Date of birth:** 6/28/31. **Hometown:** Ronda N.C. **Years of competition:** 1953-66 (313 races). **Victories:** 50. **Poles:** 47. **Career winnings:** $275,910

**Personal:** Resides in Wilkesboro, N.C. ... Full name Robert Glenn Johnson. ... Married (Lisa).

## CAREER HIGHLIGHTS

Won second annual Daytona 500 in 1960. ... Victory total ties for eighth (with Ned Jarrett) on all-time list. ... Pole total also eighth all-time. ... After retiring from driving, added to legend as car owner. His drivers won 132 races and six Winston Cup championships. ... Car owner victory total of 139, second all-time. ... Inducted into International Motorsports Hall of Fame in 1990. ... Named one of NASCAR's 50 Greatest Drivers.

# Fred Lorenzen

**Date of birth:** 12/30/34. **Hometown:** Elmhurst, Ill. **Years of competition:** 1956-72 (158 races). **Victories:** 26. **Poles:** 33. **Career winnings:** $496,574

**Personal:** Resides in Oakwood, Ill. ... Immensely popular with fans. Had several nicknames, including "Golden Boy," "Fearless Freddie" and the "Elmhurst Express." ... Retired in 1967 at age of 33, became successful in real estate in his native Illinois.

## CAREER HIGHLIGHTS

First Winston Cup driver to win more than $100,000 in a season, winning $113,570 in 1963. ... Won 1965 Daytona 500 in 1963. ... Won World 600 in 1965 after starting on the pole. ... Excelled especially at Martinsville Speedway, winning five of seven races there between 1963-66. ... Inducted into International Motorsports Hall of Fame in 1990. ... Named one of NASCAR's 50 Greatest Drivers.

# Tiny Lund

**Date of birth:** 3/3/36. **Hometown:** Harlan, Iowa. **Years of competition:** 1955-75 (303 races). **Victories:** 5. **Poles:** 6. **Career winnings:** $185,703

**Personal:** Deceased 8/17/75 in racing accident at Talladega Superspeedway. ... Full name DeWayne Louis Lund. ... Stature – 6-5, 250 pounds – belied his nickname.

## CAREER HIGHLIGHTS

Recorded one of the most dramatic victories in auto racing history at 1963 Daytona 500. During practice for race, rescued fellow driver Marvin Panch from a burning car. Panch asked Lund to replace him in his Wood Brothers-owned Ford. Lund agreed and went on to win the race. Lund was awarded Carnegie Medal For Heroism, for saving Panch. ... Inducted into International Motorsports Hall of Fame in 1994. ... Named one of NASCAR's 50 Greatest Drivers.

# Dave Marcis

**Date of birth:** 3/1/41. **Hometown:** Wausau, Wis. **Years of competition:** 1968-2002, (882 races). **Victories:** 5. **Poles:** 14. **Career winnings:** $7,349,818

**Personal:** Resides in Avery's Creek, N.C. ... Married (Helen). ... Retired from driving after the 2002 Daytona 500 but still is a car owner.

## CAREER HIGHLIGHTS

An independent for most of his career, Marcis always chose to do things his way—from the shoestring budget he operated on as an owner/driver to the wing tips he preferred over state-of-the-art driving shoes. ... Had his best season driving Nord Krauskopf's No. 71 K&K Insurance Dodge in 1976, when he notched three of his five career victories and won seven poles. A victory in the Talladega 500, in which he finished 29.5 seconds ahead of Buddy Baker, was Marcis' first on a superspeedway. ... His best points finish was second, to Richard Petty, in 1975. Marcis had 16 top-five finishes that season.

# Hershel McGriff

**Date of birth:** 12/14/27. **Hometown:** Bridal Veil, Ore. **Years of competition:** 1950-93 (86 races). **Victories:** 4. **Poles:** 5. **Career winnings:** $130,190

**Personal:** Married (Sheri). ... Resides in Green Valley, Ariz.

## CAREER HIGHLIGHTS

Had three stints in Winston Cup – 1950-54, 1971-78, 1980-93. ... Finished sixth in series standings in 1954, when he won four of the season's last nine races. ... Retired at end of 2001 season, in which he competed in NASCAR Winston West Series, at the age of 74. ... Finished 12th in his last race, at Irwindale Speedway. ... Named one of NASCAR's 50 Greatest Drivers.

# Tim Richmond

**Date of birth:** 6/7/55. **Hometown:** Ashland, Ohio. **Years of competition:** 1980-87 (185 races). **Victories:** 13. **Poles:** 14. **Career winnings:** $2,310,018

**Personal:** Deceased 8/13/89, from complications caused by Acquired Immune Deficiency Syndrome.

## CAREER HIGHLIGHTS

It's arguable that no other driver has made such an impression on NASCAR in such a short period. ... In 1986 season won a series-high seven races, finishing a career-high third in the series standings. ... Won 1986 Southern 500 after starting on the pole. ... Four victories came at Riverside International Raceway, including first career victory in 1982 and last career victory in 1987. ... Inducted into International Motorsports Hall of Fame in 2002. ... Named one of NASCAR's 50 Greatest Drivers.

# Fireball Roberts

**Date of birth:** 1/20/29. **Hometown:** Daytona Beach, Fla. **Years of competition:** 1950-64 (207 races). **Victories:** 33. **Poles:** 36. **Career winnings:** $290,309

**Personal:** Deceased 7/2/64, 39 days after a fiery crash at Charlotte seven laps into the World 600 and is buried near Turn 3 at Daytona International Speedway in Daytona Memorial Park. ... Full name Edward Glenn Roberts; nicknamed "Fireball" from his days as a hard-throwing pitcher in high school. ... Thought of as one of NASCAR's smartest drivers, Roberts was one of the first to utilize a fitness regimen.

## CAREER HIGHLIGHTS

Perhaps the greatest driver never to win a NASCAR title and arguably stock car racing's first superstar,

Roberts won some of NASCAR's most-famous events – the Daytona 500 (1962), the Southern 500 (1958, '63) and the Firecracker 400 (1963). ... Accumulated 93 top-five and 122 top-10 finishes along with 36 career poles. ... Was second in the points standings in his rookie season, and placed in the top 10 five other times. ... Despite running only 10 NASCAR races in 1958, Roberts still had six wins, one second and a third and finished 11th in points. ... Inducted into International Motorsports Hall of Fame in 1990. ... Named one of NASCAR's "50 Greatest Drivers" in 1998.

## Wendell Scott

**Date of birth:** 8/29/21. **Hometown:** Danville, Va. **Years of competition:** 1961-1973 (495 races). **Victories:** 1. **Poles:** 1. **Career winnings:** $180,629

**Personal:** Deceased 12/22/90 ... Forced to end career due to a broken pelvis suffered in 1973 crash at Talladega Superspeedway. ... Former cab driver was an Army mechanic in World War II and ran his own garage upon his return from the war, fixing cars while perfecting his driving skills on Virginia tracks.

### CAREER HIGHLIGHTS

First African-American driver to compete in NASCAR Winston Cup. ... Had 20 top-five and 147 top-10 finishes. ... Finished in the top 10 in championship points four consecutive seasons with his best effort a sixth-place showing in 1966 ... Only victory came at Turkey Day 200 in 1964 at Jacksonville Speedway ... Inducted into the International Motorsports Hall of Fame in 1999.

## Curtis Turner

**Date of birth:** 4/12/24. **Hometown:** Roanoke, Va. **Years of competition:** 1949-68 (184 races). **Victories:** 17. **Poles:** 17. **Career winnings:** $122,155

**Personal:** Deceased 10/4/70, in airplane crash. ... Sports Illustrated called him the "Babe Ruth of Stock Car Racing."

### CAREER HIGHLIGHTS

Won fourth race of NASCAR's first season – 1949. ... Had 73 top-10 finishes in 184 starts. ...Started on the pole in five of his victories. ... Inducted into International Motorsports Hall of Fame in 1992. ... Named one of NASCAR's 50 Greatest Drivers.

## LeeRoy Yarbrough

**Date of birth:** 9/17/38. **Hometown:** Jacksonville, Fla. **Years of competition:** 1960-72 (198 races). **Victories:** 14. **Poles:** 11. **Career winnings:** $450,329

**Personal:** Deceased 12/7/84. ... His life away from racing was marked by personal problems; he died in a mental hospital.

### CAREER HIGHLIGHTS

Most successful season in 1969, with seven wins, all on superspeedways, also becoming first driver to win NASCAR's "Triple Crown" – the Daytona 500, the World 600 and the Southern 500 all in the same year. ... His seven superspeedway victories set the record for big track wins at the time. ... Also posted career highs with 16 top-five and 21 top-10 finishes that year. ... Accumulated 56 top-five finishes in addition to 92 top-10 efforts while averaging only 16.5 races per year. ... Also drove in three Indianapolis 500s. ... Named one of NASCAR's "50 Greatest Drivers" in 1998.

# Car owners

## Bill Baumgardner

**Hometown:** Charlotte. **Resides:** Charlotte. **Years as NNCS Owner:** 1. **Best points finish:** 33. **Career victories:** 0. **Career poles:** 0.

### CAREER NASCAR WINSTON CUP SERIES STATS

| Year | Driver | Races | Won | Top 5 | Top 10 | DNF | Poles | Money Won |
|---|---|---|---|---|---|---|---|---|
| 2003 | T. Raines | 35 | 0 | 0 | 1 | 5 | 0 | $2,122,740 |

## Doug Bawel

**Date of birth:** 7/10/55. **Hometown:** Jasper, Ind. **Resides:** Jasper, Ind. **Years as NNCS Owner:** 10. **Best points finish:** 25. **Career victories:** 0. **First victory:** None. **Career poles:** 1. **First pole:** 1994 Atlanta.

### CAREER NASCAR WINSTON CUP SERIES STATS

| Year | Driver | Races | Won | Top 5 | Top 10 | DNF | Poles | Money Won |
|---|---|---|---|---|---|---|---|---|
| 1994 | G. Sacks | 31 | 0 | 0 | 3 | 10 | 1 | $411,728 |
|  | P.J. Jones | 1 | 0 | 0 | 0 | 1 | 0 | 6,085 |
| 1995 | B. Hillin Jr. | 18 | 0 | 0 | 1 | 4 | 0 | 241,520 |
|  | D. Jones | 7 | 0 | 0 | 0 | 2 | 0 | 109,925 |
| 1996 | B. Hillin Jr. | 25 | 0 | 0 | 0 | 6 | 0 | 369,489 |
| 1997 | B. Hillin Jr. | 10 | 0 | 0 | 0 | 5 | 0 | 211,978 |
|  | M. Shepherd | 5 | 0 | 0 | 0 | 0 | 0 | 84,475 |
|  | R. Pressley | 7 | 0 | 0 | 0 | 3 | 0 | 103,810 |
| 1998 | R. Pressley | 30 | 0 | 1 | 1 | 7 | 0 | 996,721 |
|  | H. Stricklin | 1 | 0 | 0 | 0 | 0 | 0 | 20,265 |
|  | T. Musgrave | 1 | 0 | 0 | 0 | 0 | 0 | 27,000 |
| 1999 | R. Pressley | 28 | 0 | 0 | 0 | 5 | 0 | 1,033,223 |
| 2000 | R. Pressley | 34 | 0 | 1 | 1 | 10 | 0 | 1,460,317 |
| 2001 | R. Pressley | 34 | 0 | 0 | 4 | 9 | 0 | 2,171,520 |
|  | B. Said | 2 | 0 | 0 | 1 | 0 | 0 | 124,340 |
| 2002 | D. Blaney | 36 | 0 | 0 | 5 | 3 | 0 | 2,978,593 |
|  | B. Said | 2 | 0 | 0 | 0 | 1 | 0 | 87,400 |
| 2003 | D. Blaney | 36 | 0 | 1 | 4 | 4 | 1 | $2,828,690 |
| **TOTALS** |  | **308** | **0** | **3** | **20** | **70** | **2** | **$13,267,079** |

\* Co-owner with D.K. Ulrich 1994 through Oct. 2, 1995
\*\* Co-owner with Mark Harrah and Mark Wallace since 1996

## Tom Beard

**Date of birth:** 1/5/46. **Hometown:** Moultrie, Ga. **Resides:** Atlanta. **Years as NNCS Owner:** 7\*. **Best points finish:** 15. **Career victories:** 1. **First victory:** 2002 Rockingham. **Career poles:** 14. **First pole:** 1998 Indianapolis

• All three MB2 team owners (Tom Beard, Nelson Bowers and James Rocco) are graduates of the University of Georgia. They met after graduation and are now business partners.

### CAREER NASCAR WINSTON CUP SERIES STATS

| Year | Driver | Races | Won | Top 5 | Top 10 | DNF | Poles | Money Won |
|---|---|---|---|---|---|---|---|---|
| 1997 | D. Cope | 31 | 0 | 1 | 1 | 6 | 0 | $707,404 |
| 1998 | E. Irvan | 30 | 0 | 0 | 11 | 3 | 3 | 1,600,452 |
|  | R. Craven | 3 | 0 | 0 | 0 | 0 | 0 | 84,030 |
| 1999 | E. Irvan | 21 | 0 | 0 | 5 | 5 | 0 | 1,073,775 |
|  | J. Nadeau | 12 | 0 | 0 | 0 | 2 | 0 | 450,775 |
|  | D. Trickle | 1 | 0 | 0 | 0 | 0 | 0 | 27,620 |
| 2000 | K. Schrader | 34 | 0 | 0 | 2 | 2 | 0 | 1,711,476 |
|  | J. Benson | 33 | 0 | 0 | 3 | 7 | 3 | 1,841,325 |
| 2001 | K. Schrader | 36 | 0 | 0 | 5 | 2 | 0 | 2,418,181 |
|  | J. Benson | 36 | 0 | 0 | 6 | 14 | 8 | 2,894,903 |
| 2002 | K. Schrader | 36 | 0 | 0 | 0 | 9 | 0 | 2,460,140 |
|  | J. Benson | 31 | 1 | 3 | 7 | 8 | 0 | 2,791,879 |
|  | J. Nadeau | 3 | 0 | 0 | 0 | 0 | 0 | 275,681 |
|  | J. Nemechek | 1 | 0 | 0 | 0 | 0 | 0 | 74,710 |
|  | M. Wallace | 1 | 0 | 0 | 0 | 1 | 0 | 80,150 |
| 2003 | Mike Skinner | 11 | 0 | 0 | 0 | 2 | 1 | 945,373 |
|  | J. Nadeau | 10 | 0 | 1 | 1 | 3 | 0 | 861,628 |
|  | Boris Said | 2 | 0 | 0 | 1 | 0 | 1 | 134,680 |
|  | J. Benson | 36 | 0 | 2 | 4 | 7 | 0 | 3,411,790 |
| **TOTALS** |  | **383** | **1** | **7** | **46** | **71** | **16** | **$24,683,399** |

\* Co-owners are Tom Beard, Nelson Bowers and James Rocco.

## Brett Bodine

**Date of birth:** 1/11/59. **Hometown:** Chemung, N.Y. **Resides:** Davidson, N.C. **Years as NNCS Owner:** 8. **Best points finish:** 24. **Career victories:** 0. **First victory:** None. **Career poles:** 0. **First pole:** None

### CAREER NASCAR WINSTON CUP SERIES STATS

| Year | Driver | Races | Won | Top 5 | Top 10 | DNF | Poles | Money Won |
|---|---|---|---|---|---|---|---|---|
| 1996 | B. Bodine | 30 | 0 | 0 | 1 | 3 | 0 | $767,716 |
| 1997 | B. Bodine | 31 | 0 | 0 | 2 | 5 | 0 | 936,694 |
| 1998 | B. Bodine | 33 | 0 | 0 | 0 | 2 | 0 | 1,281,673 |
| 1999 | B. Bodine | 32 | 0 | 0 | 0 | 3 | 0 | 1,321,396 |
| 2000 | B. Bodine | 29 | 0 | 0 | 0 | 7 | 0 | 1,020,659 |
| 2001 | B. Bodine | 36 | 0 | 0 | 2 | 2 | 0 | 1,740,526 |
| 2002 | B. Bodine | 32 | 0 | 0 | 0 | 5 | 0 | 1,766,820 |
| 2003 | B. Bodine | 6 | 0 | 0 | 0 | 2 | 0 | $383,718 |
|  | G. Bodine | 1 | 0 | 0 | 0 | 1 | 0 | $78,150 |
| **TOTALS** |  | **230** | **0** | **0** | **5** | **30** | **0** | **$9,297,352** |

## OWNERS

# Travis Carter

**Date of birth:** 11/21/49. **Hometown:** Ellerbe, N.C. **Resides:** Denver, N.C. **Years as NNCS Owner:** 13. **Best points finish:** 14. **Career victories:** 0. **First victory:** None. **Career poles:** 6. **First pole:** 2001 Chicagoland

- Won Winston Cup Championship in rookie year as crew chief.
- Crew Chief for Bobby Allison, Harry Gant, Rick Mast, Cale Yarborough and Benny Parsons.
- Began motorsports career in 1971 with L. G. DeWitt.

### CAREER NASCAR WINSTON CUP SERIES STATS

| Year | Driver | Races | Won | Top 5 | Top 10 | DNF | Poles | Money Won |
|---|---|---|---|---|---|---|---|---|
| 1989 | R. Mast | 13 | 0 | 0 | 1 | 5 | 0 | $128,102 |
| 1990 | B. Miller | 23 | 0 | 0 | 1 | 4 | 0 | 151,941 |
| | R. Mast | 6 | 0 | 0 | 1 | 3 | 0 | 27,305 |
| 1991 | J. Spencer | 29 | 0 | 1 | 6 | 14 | 0 | 283,620 |
| 1992 | J. Spencer | 7 | 0 | 0 | 0 | 4 | 0 | 76,055 |
| 1994 | H. Stricklin | 29 | 0 | 0 | 1 | 3 | 0 | 333,495 |
| 1995 | J. Spencer | 29 | 0 | 0 | 4 | 2 | 0 | 507,210 |
| 1996 | J. Spencer | 31 | 0 | 2 | 9 | 2 | 0 | 1,090,876 |
| 1997 | J. Spencer | 32 | 0 | 1 | 4 | 6 | 0 | 1,073,779 |
| 1998 | J. Spencer | 31 | 0 | 3 | 8 | 2 | 0 | 1,741,012 |
| | F. Kimmel | 1 | 0 | 0 | 0 | 0 | 0 | 28,065 |
| | T. Musgrave | 1 | 0 | 0 | 0 | 0 | 0 | 35,310 |
| 1999 | J. Spencer | 34 | 0 | 2 | 4 | 6 | 0 | 1,752,299 |
| | D. Waltrip | 27 | 0 | 0 | 0 | 4 | 0 | 973,133 |
| 2000 | J. Spencer | 34 | 0 | 2 | 3 | 8 | 0 | 1,936,762 |
| | D. Waltrip | 28 | 0 | 0 | 0 | 7 | 0 | 1,212,940 |
| | T. Bodine | 1 | 0 | 0 | 0 | 0 | 0 | 39,300 |
| 2001 | J. Spencer | 36 | 0 | 3 | 8 | 7 | 2 | 2,669,638 |
| | T. Bodine | 35 | 0 | 2 | 0 | 12 | 3 | 1,740,315 |
| 2002 | T. Bodine | 24 | 0 | 1 | 4 | 9 | 1 | 1,879,767 |
| | J. Nemechek | 7 | 0 | 0 | 0 | 0 | 0 | 612,062 |
| | F. Kimmel | 5 | 0 | 0 | 0 | 0 | 0 | 372,510 |
| | G. Bodine | 4 | 0 | 0 | 0 | 0 | 0 | 241,980 |
| | H. Fukuyama | 2 | 0 | 0 | 0 | 2 | 0 | 79,005 |
| 2003 | T. Bodine | 35 | 0 | 0 | 1 | 9 | 0 | 2,521,720 |
| | H. Fukuyama | 2 | 0 | 0 | 0 | 1 | 0 | 115,229 |
| **TOTALS** | | 506 | 0 | 17 | 55 | 110 | 6 | $21,623,430 |

# Richard Childress

**Date of birth:** 9/21/45. **Hometown:** Winston-Salem, N.C. **Resides:** Lexington, N.C. **Years as NNCS Owner:** 29. **Best points finish:** 1. **Career victories:** 76. **First victory:** 1983 Riverside. **Career poles:** 33. **First pole:** 1982 Martinsville

- Drove at the first Talladega race in 1969.
- Only car owner to win a championship in NASCAR's three top divisions.
- Car owner for six of the late Dale Earnhardt's seven championship seasons.

### CAREER NASCAR WINSTON CUP SERIES STATS

| Year | Driver | Races | Won | Top 5 | Top 10 | DNF | Poles | Money Won |
|---|---|---|---|---|---|---|---|---|
| 1972 | R Childress | 15 | 0 | 0 | 0 | 12 | 0 | $7,245 |
| 1976 | R. Childress | 30 | 0 | 0 | 11 | 9 | 0 | 85,780 |
| 1977 | R. Childress | 30 | 0 | 0 | 11 | 9 | 0 | 97,012 |
| 1978 | R. Childress | 30 | 0 | 1 | 12 | 4 | 0 | 108,106 |
| 1979 | R. Childress | 31 | 0 | 1 | 10 | 5 | 0 | 132,922 |
| 1980 | R. Childress | 31 | 0 | 0 | 10 | 4 | 0 | 157,420 |
| 1981 | R. Childress | 20 | 0 | 1 | 1 | 7 | 0 | 70,665 |
| | D. Earnhardt | 11 | 0 | 2 | 6 | 4 | 0 | 92,728 |
| 1982 | R. Rudd | 30 | 0 | 6 | 13 | 13 | 2 | 211,130 |
| 1983 | R. Rudd | 30 | 2 | 7 | 14 | 9 | 4 | 267,585 |
| 1984 | D. Earnhardt | 30 | 2 | 12 | 22 | 2 | 0 | 616,788 |
| 1985 | D. Earnhardt | 28 | 4 | 10 | 16 | 9 | 1 | 546,596 |
| 1986 | D. Earnhardt | 29 | 5 | 16 | 23 | 4 | 1 | 1,783,880 |
| 1987 | D. Earnhardt | 29 | 11 | 21 | 24 | 2 | 1 | 2,099,243 |
| 1988 | D. Earnhardt | 29 | 3 | 13 | 19 | 1 | 0 | 1,214,089 |
| | R. Combs | 1 | 0 | 0 | 0 | 1 | 0 | 1,500 |
| 1989 | D. Earnhardt | 29 | 5 | 14 | 19 | 2 | 0 | 1,435,730 |
| | J. Hensley | 0 | 0 | 0 | 0 | 0 | 1 | 0 |
| 1990 | D. Earnhardt | 29 | 9 | 18 | 23 | 1 | 4 | 3,083,056 |
| 1991 | D. Earnhardt | 29 | 4 | 14 | 21 | 2 | 0 | 2,396,685 |
| 1992 | D. Earnhardt | 29 | 1 | 6 | 15 | 4 | 1 | 915,463 |
| 1993 | D. Earnhardt | 30 | 6 | 17 | 21 | 2 | 2 | 3,353,789 |
| | N. Bonnett | 2 | 0 | 0 | 0 | 2 | 0 | 14,515 |
| 1994 | D. Earnhardt | 31 | 4 | 20 | 25 | 3 | 2 | 3,300,733 |
| 1995 | D. Earnhardt | 31 | 5 | 19 | 23 | 2 | 3 | 3,154,241 |
| 1996 | D. Earnhardt | 31 | 2 | 13 | 17 | 2 | 2 | 2,285,926 |
| | M. Skinner | 5 | 0 | 0 | 0 | 1 | 0 | 65,850 |
| 1997 | D. Earnhardt | 32 | 0 | 7 | 16 | 0 | 0 | 2,151,909 |
| | M. Skinner | 31 | 0 | 0 | 3 | 7 | 2 | 900,569 |
| 1998 | D. Earnhardt | 33 | 1 | 5 | 13 | 3 | 0 | 2,990,749 |
| | M. Skinner | 30 | 0 | 4 | 9 | 3 | 0 | 1,518,901 |
| | M. Shepherd | 2 | 0 | 0 | 0 | 1 | 0 | 50,146 |
| | M. Dillon | 1 | 0 | 0 | 0 | 0 | 0 | 28,050 |
| 1999 | D. Earnhardt | 34 | 3 | 7 | 21 | 3 | 0 | 3,149,536 |
| | M. Skinner | 34 | 0 | 0 | 9 | 1 | 2 | 2,499,877 |
| 2000 | D. Earnhardt | 34 | 2 | 13 | 24 | 0 | 0 | 4,918,886 |
| | M. Skinner | 34 | 0 | 1 | 11 | 2 | 0 | 2,205,320 |
| 2001 | D. Earnhardt | 1 | 0 | 0 | 0 | 1 | 0 | 293,833 |
| | M. Skinner | 23 | 0 | 0 | 1 | 4 | 0 | 1,921,186 |
| | K. Harvick | 35 | 2 | 6 | 16 | 1 | 0 | 4,302,202 |
| | J. Green | 8 | 0 | 0 | 1 | 3 | 1 | 441,449 |
| | R. Gordon | 10 | 1 | 1 | 2 | 1 | 0 | 917,020 |
| 2002 | J. Green | 36 | 0 | 4 | 6 | 2 | 0 | 2,531,339 |
| | R. Gordon | 36 | 0 | 1 | 5 | 4 | 0 | 3,342,703 |
| | K. Harvick | 35 | 1 | 5 | 8 | 6 | 1 | 3,849,216 |
| | K. Wallace | 1 | 0 | 0 | 0 | 0 | 0 | 85,567 |
| 2003 | K. Harvick | 36 | 1 | 11 | 18 | 0 | 1 | 4,994,250 |
| | Robby Gordon | 36 | 2 | 4 | 10 | 2 | 0 | 3,705,320 |
| | Steve Park | 24 | 0 | 1 | 3 | 3 | 0 | 1,653,708 |
| | R. Hornaday | 1 | 0 | 0 | 0 | 0 | 0 | 48,950 |
| **TOTALS** | | 1197 | 76 | 281 | 532 | 163 | 33 | $75,999,357 |

# Derrike Cope

**Date of birth:** 11/3/58. **Hometown:** Spanaway, Wash. **Resides:** Huntersville, N.C. **Years as NNCS Owner:** 1. **Best points finish:** 46. **Career victories:** 0. **First victory:** None. **Career poles:** 0. **First pole:** None

## CAREER NASCAR WINSTON CUP SERIES STATS

| Year | Driver | Races | Won | Top 5 | Top 10 | DNF | Poles | Money Won |
|---|---|---|---|---|---|---|---|---|
| 2003 | D. Cope | 18 | 0 | 0 | 0 | 12 | 0 | $1,030,690 |

# Bill Davis

**Date of birth:** 1/18/51. **Hometown:** Little Rock, Ark. **Resides:** High Point, N.C. **Years as NNCS Owner:** 10. **Best points finish:** 9. **Career victories:** 5. **First victory:** 1995 Rockingham. **Career poles:** 7. **First pole:** 1993 Richmond

- Owned NASCAR Busch Series car once driven by Jeff Gordon.

## CAREER NASCAR WINSTON CUP SERIES STATS

| Year | Driver | Races | Won | Top 5 | Top 10 | DNF | Poles | Money Won |
|---|---|---|---|---|---|---|---|---|
| 1993 | B. Labonte | 30 | 0 | 0 | 6 | 6 | $1 | $395,660 |
| 1994 | B. Labonte | 31 | 0 | 1 | 1 | 7 | 0 | 550,305 |
| 1995 | R. LaJoie | 13 | 0 | 0 | 0 | 3 | 0 | 265,770 |
|  | J. Hensley | 5 | 0 | 0 | 0 | 2 | 0 | 129,595 |
|  | W. Dallenbach | 1 | 0 | 1 | 1 | 0 | 0 | 54,140 |
|  | W. Burton | 9 | 1 | 3 | 4 | 2 | 0 | 300,325 |
| 1996 | W. Burton | 27 | 0 | 0 | 4 | 10 | 1 | 873,619 |
| 1997 | W. Burton | 31 | 0 | 0 | 7 | 7 | 1 | 1,004,944 |
| 1998 | W. Burton | 33 | 0 | 1 | 5 | 4 | 2 | 1,516,183 |
| 1999 | W. Burton | 34 | 0 | 6 | 16 | 3 | 1 | 2,405,913 |
|  | D. Blaney | 5 | 0 | 0 | 0 | 2 | 0 | 212,170 |
| 2000 | W. Burton | 34 | 1 | 4 | 17 | 4 | 0 | 2,699,604 |
|  | D. Blaney | 33 | 0 | 0 | 2 | 7 | 0 | 1,272,689 |
| 2001 | W. Burton | 36 | 1 | 7 | 11 | 9 | 0 | 3,583,692 |
|  | D. Blaney | 36 | 0 | 0 | 6 | 6 | 0 | 1,827,896 |
| 2002 | W. Burton | 36 | 2 | 3 | 8 | 9 | 1 | 4,899,884 |
|  | K. Wallace | 10 | 0 | 0 | 0 | 0 | 0 | 503,085 |
|  | H. Stricklin | 22 | 0 | 0 | 0 | 5 | 0 | 1,313,548 |
|  | S. Wimmer | 3 | 0 | 0 | 0 | 2 | 0 | 143,110 |
|  | T. Hubert | 1 | 0 | 0 | 0 | 0 | 0 | 41,925 |
|  | G. Bodine | 1 | 0 | 0 | 0 | 0 | 0 | 35,615 |
| 2003 | Kenny Wallace | 36 | 0 | 0 | 1 | 5 | 0 | 2,480,490 |
|  | Ward Burton | 32 | 0 | 0 | 4 | 4 | 0 | 3,280,950 |
|  | Scott Wimmer | 6 | 0 | 0 | 1 | 0 | 0 | 479,504 |
| **TOTALS** |  | **505** | **5** | **26** | **94** | **97** | **7** | **$30,270,616** |

# Junie Donlavey

**Date of birth:** 4/8/24. **Hometown:** Richmond, Va. **Resides:** Richmond, Va. **Years as NNCS Owner:** 53. **Best points finish:** 4. **Career victories:** 1. **First victory:** 1981 Dover. **Career poles:** 3. **First pole:** 1974 Richmond

- Navy Veteran.
- 2001 recipient of the H. Clay Earles Award.
- 1999 recipient of the NMPA/Myers Bros. Award.
- 1999 recipient of the Ford Motor Company Spirit of Ford Award.
- 1998 recipient of the STP Richard Petty Achievement Award.

## CAREER NASCAR WINSTON CUP SERIES STATS

| Year | Driver | Races | Won | Top 5 | Top 10 | DNF | Poles | Money Won |
|---|---|---|---|---|---|---|---|---|
| 1950 | B. Apperson | 1 | 0 | 0 | 0 | 1 | 0 | 0 |
|  | R. Harris | 1 | 0 | 0 | 0 | 1 | 0 | 0 |
| 1952 | J. Weatherly | 1 | 0 | 0 | 0 | 0 | 0 | $150 |
| 1957 | R. Harris | 1 | 0 | 0 | 0 | 1 | 0 | 100 |
| 1958 | E. Zervakis | 4 | 0 | 0 | 0 | 4 | 0 | 365 |
| 1959 | N. Castles | 1 | 0 | 0 | 0 | 0 | 0 | 150 |
|  | R. Harris | 1 | 0 | 1 | 1 | 0 | 0 | 250 |
| 1960 | R. Harris | 3 | 0 | 0 | 0 | 3 | 0 | 350 |
|  | S. Thompson | 3 | 0 | 0 | 0 | 3 | 0 | 1,450 |
|  | L. Frank | 1 | 0 | 0 | 0 | 1 | 0 | 400 |
|  | T. Lund | 1 | 0 | 0 | 0 | 1 | 0 | 250 |
| 1961 | J. Roberts | 1 | 0 | 0 | 0 | 1 | 0 | 75 |
|  | B. Woodward | 1 | 0 | 0 | 1 | 0 | 0 | 400 |
| 1965 | S. Hutchins | 10 | 0 | 1 | 1 | 7 | 0 | 3,585 |
| 1966 | S. Hutchins | 4 | 0 | 0 | 0 | 3 | 0 | 2,190 |
| 1967 | S. Hutchins | 7 | 0 | 0 | 2 | 4 | 0 | 6,385 |
| 1968 | S. Hutchins | 4 | 0 | 0 | 0 | 4 | 0 | 2,810 |
| 1969 | S. Hutchins | 8 | 0 | 2 | 2 | 5 | 0 | 9,552 |
| 1970 | B. Dennis | 3 | 0 | 0 | 0 | 2 | 0 | 2,460 |
|  | S. Hutchins | 2 | 0 | 1 | 1 | 1 | 0 | 2,575 |
|  | L. Yarbrough | 1 | 0 | 0 | 0 | 1 | 0 | 320 |
| 1971 | B. Dennis | 26 | 0 | 4 | 10 | 12 | 1 | 26,408 |
|  | J. Oliver | 1 | 0 | 0 | 0 | 1 | 0 | 605 |
|  | L. Yarbrough | 1 | 0 | 0 | 0 | 1 | 0 | 1,054 |
| 1972 | J. Oliver | 7 | 0 | 1 | 1 | 6 | 0 | 8,075 |
|  | D. Brooks | 5 | 0 | 0 | 1 | 3 | 0 | 5,815 |
|  | B. Dennis | 2 | 0 | 1 | 0 | 1 | 0 | 2,425 |
|  | J. Hensley | 2 | 0 | 1 | 0 | 1 | 0 | 1,400 |
|  | L. Yarbrough | 2 | 0 | 1 | 1 | 1 | 0 | 4,495 |
|  | R. Stott | 2 | 0 | 2 | 2 | 0 | 0 | 13,390 |
|  | F. Lorenzen | 1 | 0 | 1 | 1 | 0 | 0 | 1,225 |
|  | D. Pearson | 1 | 0 | 0 | 0 | 1 | 0 | 430 |
|  | M. Berrier | 1 | 0 | 0 | 0 | 0 | 1 | 490 |
|  | B. Hartman | 1 | 0 | 1 | 1 | 0 | 0 | 3,070 |
|  | R. Hutcherson | 1 | 0 | 0 | 0 | 1 | 0 | 550 |
|  | J. Rutherford | 1 | 0 | 0 | 0 | 1 | 0 | 780 |
|  | R. Brown | 1 | 0 | 0 | 0 | 1 | 0 | 663 |
|  | B. Isaac | 1 | 0 | 0 | 0 | 1 | 0 | 250 |
| 1973 | D. Brooks | 8 | 0 | 1 | 3 | 4 | 0 | 14,175 |
|  | R. Panch | 4 | 0 | 0 | 3 | 0 | 0 | 4,010 |
|  | R. Stott | 2 | 0 | 0 | 1 | 0 | 0 | 4,650 |
|  | Ray Hendrick | 2 | 0 | 0 | 0 | 1 | 0 | 1,450 |
|  | Y. DuHamel | 1 | 0 | 0 | 1 | 0 | 0 | 550 |
|  | J. Hensley | 1 | 0 | 0 | 1 | 0 | 0 | 1,300 |
|  | E. Pettyjohn | 2 | 0 | 0 | 1 | 1 | 0 | 2,145 |
|  | J. Ridley | 2 | 0 | 1 | 0 | 1 | 0 | 5,175 |
|  | B. Moore | 1 | 0 | 0 | 0 | 1 | 0 | 1,225 |
|  | H. Gant | 1 | 0 | 0 | 0 | 0 | 0 | 1,760 |
|  | C. Glotzbach | 1 | 0 | 0 | 1 | 0 | 0 | 2,125 |
|  | W. Andrews | 1 | 0 | 0 | 0 | 1 | 0 | 1,005 |
| 1974 | C. Glotzbach | 11 | 0 | 3 | 4 | 7 | 0 | 18,447 |
|  | B. Dennis | 3 | 0 | 0 | 2 | 1 | 0 | 6,785 |
|  | J. Ridley | 2 | 0 | 0 | 0 | 2 | 0 | 1,935 |
|  | E. Pettyjohn | 2 | 0 | 0 | 0 | 2 | 0 | 1,885 |
|  | B. Isaac | 1 | 0 | 0 | 0 | 1 | 0 | 615 |
|  | H. Gant | 1 | 0 | 0 | 1 | 0 | 0 | 805 |
|  | J. Hensley | 1 | 0 | 0 | 1 | 0 | 0 | 1,400 |
|  | P. Radford | 1 | 0 | 0 | 0 | 1 | 0 | 500 |
|  | G. Follmer | 1 | 0 | 0 | 0 | 1 | 0 | 1,000 |
|  | R. Panch | 1 | 0 | 0 | 0 | 1 | 0 | 54 |

# OWNERS

| Year | Driver | Races | Won | Top 5 | Top 10 | DNF | Poles | Money Won |
|---|---|---|---|---|---|---|---|---|
| 1975 | D. Brooks | 25 | 0 | 6 | 15 | 8 | 0 | 76,818 |
|  | J. Ridley | 2 | 0 | 0 | 0 | 1 | 0 | 3,000 |
|  | K. Brightbill | 1 | 0 | 0 | 1 | 0 | 0 | 2,000 |
|  | D. May | 1 | 0 | 0 | 0 | 1 | 0 | 505 |
|  | E. Ross | 1 | 0 | 0 | 0 | 0 | 0 | 2,965 |
| 1976 | D. Brooks | 26 | 0 | 3 | 17 | 8 | 0 | 104,717 |
|  | Buck Baker | 1 | 0 | 0 | 1 | 0 | 0 | 3,670 |
|  | G. Felton | 1 | 0 | 0 | 0 | 0 | 0 | 1,635 |
|  | D. Trickle | 1 | 0 | 0 | 0 | 1 | 0 | 1,225 |
| 1977 | D. Brooks | 27 | 0 | 6 | 18 | 9 | 0 | 137,677 |
|  | C. Beckers | 1 | 0 | 0 | 0 | 1 | 0 | 695 |
| 1978 | D. Brooks | 27 | 0 | 5 | 16 | 7 | 0 | 126,235 |
| 1979 | R. Rudd | 28 | 0 | 4 | 17 | 6 | 0 | 146,302 |
|  | J. Ridley | 3 | 0 | 1 | 1 | 1 | 0 | 11,245 |
| 1980 | J. Ridley | 31 | 0 | 2 | 16 | 4 | 0 | 196,617 |
| 1981 | J. Ridley | 30 | 1 | 3 | 18 | 7 | 0 | 253,028 |
| 1982 | J. Ridley | 30 | 0 | 0 | 10 | 12 | 0 | 304,960 |
| 1983 | D. Brooks | 30 | 0 | 2 | 6 | 12 | 0 | 175,471 |
| 1984 | D. Brooks | 30 | 0 | 1 | 5 | 11 | 0 | 186,819 |
| 1985 | K. Schrader | 28 | 0 | 0 | 3 | 7 | 0 | 211,523 |
| 1986 | K. Schrader | 29 | 0 | 0 | 4 | 9 | 0 | 235,904 |
| 1987 | K. Schrader | 29 | 0 | 1 | 9 | 8 | 1 | 375,918 |
| 1988 | B. Parsons | 27 | 0 | 0 | 1 | 9 | 0 | 210,755 |
|  | J. Means | 1 | 0 | 0 | 0 | 0 | 0 | 3,650 |
| 1989 | C. Little | 8 | 0 | 0 | 0 | 4 | 0 | 44,690 |
|  | S. Barrett | 4 | 0 | 0 | 0 | 3 | 0 | 11,500 |
|  | L. Pond | 1 | 0 | 0 | 0 | 0 | 0 | 3,475 |
| 1990 | Buddy Baker | 8 | 0 | 0 | 0 | 5 | 0 | 40,085 |
|  | E. Irvan | 3 | 0 | 0 | 0 | 2 | 0 | 37,605 |
|  | C. Glotzbach | 1 | 0 | 0 | 0 | 0 | 0 | 3,100 |
| 1991 | W. Dallenbach Jr. | 11 | 0 | 0 | 0 | 6 | 0 | 54,020 |
|  | R. Gordon | 2 | 0 | 0 | 0 | 0 | 0 | 27,265 |
|  | S. Perry | 1 | 0 | 0 | 0 | 1 | 0 | 4,150 |
| 1992 | C. Glotzbach | 7 | 0 | 0 | 0 | 2 | 0 | 48,060 |
|  | D. Schroeder | 1 | 0 | 0 | 0 | 0 | 0 | 25,720 |
|  | K. Teague | 1 | 0 | 0 | 0 | 1 | 0 | 3,790 |
|  | T. Bodine | 1 | 0 | 0 | 0 | 1 | 0 | 3,485 |
|  | H. Stricklin | 4 | 0 | 0 | 0 | 0 | 0 | 18,810 |
|  | P. Carter | 1 | 0 | 0 | 0 | 0 | 0 | 3,735 |
|  | B. Hillin Jr. | 1 | 0 | 0 | 0 | 1 | 0 | 4,350 |
| 1993 | B. Hillin Jr. | 30 | 0 | 0 | 0 | 9 | 0 | 263,540 |
| 1994 | M. Wallace | 22 | 0 | 1 | 0 | 3 | 0 | 265,115 |
|  | B. Hillin Jr. | 3 | 0 | 0 | 0 | 0 | 0 | 48,455 |
| 1995 | M. Wallace | 26 | 0 | 0 | 1 | 9 | 0 | 428,006 |
| 1996 | D. Trickle | 17 | 0 | 0 | 0 | 7 | 0 | 268,905 |
|  | M. Wallace | 10 | 0 | 0 | 0 | 6 | 0 | 152,417 |
| 1997 | D. Trickle | 28 | 0 | 2 | 2 | 6 | 0 | 656,189 |
|  | D. Schroeder | 1 | 0 | 0 | 0 | 0 | 0 | 11,630 |
| 1998 | D. Trickle | 32 | 0 | 0 | 1 | 10 | 0 | 1,208,771 |
| 1999 | E. Barrier | 4 | 0 | 0 | 0 | 0 | 0 | 120,325 |
|  | S. Barrett Jr. | 2 | 0 | 0 | 0 | 1 | 0 | 84,665 |
|  | M. Wallace | 1 | 0 | 0 | 0 | 0 | 0 | 111,806 |
|  | M. Shepherd | 1 | 0 | 0 | 0 | 0 | 0 | 29,400 |
|  | H. Stricklin | 1 | 0 | 0 | 0 | 0 | 0 | 47,112 |
| 2000 | E. Berrier | 10 | 0 | 0 | 0 | 4 | 0 | 417,144 |
|  | B. Simo | 1 | 0 | 0 | 0 | 0 | 0 | 37,110 |
|  | H. Stricklin | 7 | 0 | 0 | 0 | 5 | 0 | 255,200 |
| 2001 | H. Stricklin | 21 | 0 | 0 | 1 | 3 | 0 | 951,071 |
|  | B. Simo | 2 | 0 | 0 | 0 | 2 | 0 | 72,175 |
|  | R. Mast | 3 | 0 | 0 | 0 | 0 | 0 | 113,725 |
|  | T. Musgrave | 0 | 0 | 0 | 0 | 0 | 0 | 29,722 |
| 2002 | R. Mast | 9 | 0 | 0 | 0 | 0 | 0 | 417,580 |
|  | H. Sadler | 2 | 0 | 0 | 0 | 0 | 0 | 93,915 |
|  | L. Hooper | 1 | 0 | 0 | 0 | 0 | 0 | 51,840 |
|  | G. Bradberry | 1 | 0 | 0 | 0 | 0 | 0 | 40,399 |
|  | J. Hedlesky | 1 | 0 | 0 | 0 | 0 | 0 | 39,160 |
| **TOTALS** |  | 866 | 1 | 59 | 204 | 317 | 3 | $9,500,489 |

## Dale Earnhardt, Inc.

**Owner:** Teresa Earnhardt. **Hometown:** Conover, N.C. **Resides:** Mooresville, N.C. **Years as NNCS Owner:** 8. **Best points finish:** 3. **Career victories:** 15. **First victory:** 2000 Texas. **Career poles:** 9. **First pole:** 2000 Bristol

### CAREER NASCAR WINSTON CUP SERIES STATS

| Year | Driver | Races | Won | Top 5 | Top 10 | DNF | Poles | Money Won |
|---|---|---|---|---|---|---|---|---|
| 1996 | J. Green | 2 | 0 | 0 | 0 | 2 | 0 | $16,835 |
|  | R. Gordon | 1 | 0 | 0 | 0 | 1 | 0 | 4,800 |
| 1997 | S. Park | 4 | 0 | 0 | 0 | 1 | 0 | 60,405 |
| 1998 | S. Park | 17 | 0 | 0 | 0 | 5 | 0 | 487,265 |
|  | D. Waltrip | 13 | 0 | 1 | 2 | 2 | 0 | 398,615 |
| 1999 | S. Park | 34 | 0 | 0 | 5 | 4 | 0 | 1,767,690 |
|  | D. Earnhardt Jr. | 5 | 0 | 0 | 1 | 1 | 0 | 162,095 |
| 2000 | S. Park | 34 | 1 | 6 | 13 | 4 | 2 | 2,283,629 |
|  | D. Earnhardt Jr. | 34 | 2 | 3 | 5 | 7 | 2 | 2,801,880 |
| 2001 | S. Park | 24 | 1 | 5 | 12 | 2 | 0 | 2,495,490 |
|  | D. Earnhardt Jr. | 36 | 3 | 9 | 15 | 4 | 2 | 5,827,542 |
|  | M. Waltrip | 36 | 1 | 3 | 3 | 6 | 0 | 3,411,644 |
|  | K. Wallace | 12 | 0 | 1 | 2 | 1 | 1 | 965,030 |
| 2002 | D. Earnhardt Jr. | 36 | 2 | 11 | 16 | 3 | 2 | 4,970,034 |
|  | M. Waltrip | 36 | 1 | 4 | 10 | 4 | 0 | 3,185,969 |
|  | S. Park | 32 | 0 | 0 | 2 | 5 | 0 | 2,681,594 |
|  | K. Wallace | 4 | 0 | 0 | 1 | 0 | 0 | 454,060 |
| 2003 | D. Earnhardt Jr. | 36 | 2 | 13 | 21 | 4 | 0 | 4,923,500 |
|  | M. Waltrip | 36 | 2 | 8 | 11 | 6 | 0 | 4,463,840 |
|  | J. Andretti | 11 | 0 | 0 | 0 | 1 | 0 | 886,729 |
|  | R. Fellows | 2 | 0 | 0 | 1 | 1 | 0 | 161,854 |
|  | J. Keller | 2 | 0 | 0 | 0 | 0 | 0 | 128,007 |
| **TOTALS** |  | 447 | 15 | 64 | 120 | 64 | 9 | $38,538,507 |

## Ray Evernham

**Date of birth:** 8/26/57. **Hometown:** Hazlet, N.J. **Resides:** Cornelius, N.C. **Years as NNCS Owner:** 6. **Best points finish:** 9. **Career victories:** 4. **First victory:** 2001 Homestead-Miami. **Career poles:** 8. **First pole:** 2001 Daytona

- Rides a Harley.
- Has spoken at NASA.
- Won three Winston Cup titles as crew chief for Jeff Gordon.

### CAREER NASCAR WINSTON CUP SERIES STATS

| Year | Driver | Races | Won | Top 5 | Top 10 | DNF | Poles | Money Won |
|---|---|---|---|---|---|---|---|---|
| 1989 | D. Johnson | 4 | 0 | 0 | 0 | 1 | 0 | $11,515 |
| 1990 | D. Johnson | 3 | 0 | 0 | 0 | 3 | 0 | 10,550 |
| | Jim Sauter | 1 | 0 | 0 | 0 | 0 | 0 | 3,925 |
| 2000 | C. Atwood | 3 | 0 | 0 | 1 | 0 | 0 | 97,030 |
| 2001 | C. Atwood | 35 | 0 | 1 | 3 | 6 | 1 | 1,797,111 |
| | B. Elliott | 36 | 1 | 5 | 9 | 2 | 2 | 3,618,017 |
| 2002 | B. Elliott | 36 | 2 | 6 | 13 | 4 | 4 | 4,122,699 |
| | J. Mayfield | 36 | 0 | 2 | 4 | 7 | 0 | 2,494,583 |
| | C. Atwood | 1 | 0 | 0 | 0 | 0 | 0 | 37,175 |
| | H. Parker Jr. | 1 | 0 | 0 | 0 | 0 | 0 | 39,325 |
| 2003 | Bill Elliott | 36 | 1 | 9 | 12 | 2 | 0 | 4,321,190 |
| | J. Mayfield | 36 | 0 | 4 | 12 | 6 | 1 | 2,962,230 |
| | C. Atwood | 2 | 0 | 0 | 0 | 1 | 0 | 149,838 |
| TOTALS | | 230 | 4 | 27 | 54 | 32 | 8 | $19,665,188 |

## James Finch

**Date of birth:** 6/16/50. **Hometown:** Lynn Haven, Fla. **Resides:** Lynn Haven, Fla. **Years as NNCS Owner:** 1. **Best points finish:** 42. **Career victories:** 0. **Career poles:** 0.

### CAREER NASCAR WINSTON CUP SERIES STATS

| Year | Driver | Races | Won | Top 5 | Top 10 | DNF | Poles | Money Won |
|---|---|---|---|---|---|---|---|---|
| 2003 | M. Wallace | 14 | 0 | 0 | 2 | 3 | 0 | $1,031,100 |

## A.J. Foyt

**Date of birth:** 1/16/35. **Hometown:** Houston. **Resides:** Houston. **Years as NNCS Owner:** 23. **Best points finish:** 35. **Career victories:** 0. **First victory:** None. **Career poles:** 1. **First pole:** 1977 Talladega

- A.J.'s NASCAR career as a driver spanned more than 30 years. In that time, he made 128 starts and made it to victory lane seven times. He started on the front row 16 times including nine poles. His record includes 32 top five finishes and 38 top 10s.

### CAREER NASCAR WINSTON CUP SERIES STATS

| Year | Driver | Races | Won | Top 5 | Top 10 | DNF | Poles | Money Won |
|---|---|---|---|---|---|---|---|---|
| 1973 | A.J. Foyt | 3 | 0 | 1 | 1 | 2 | 0 | $8,555 |
| 1974 | A.J. Foyt | 2 | 0 | 1 | 0 | 1 | 0 | 7,655 |
| 1977 | A.J. Foyt | 6 | 0 | 1 | 2 | 2 | 1 | 28,850 |
| | J. Rutherford | 1 | 0 | 0 | 0 | 1 | 0 | 1,865 |
| 1978 | A.J. Foyt | 2 | 0 | 1 | 1 | 1 | 0 | 22,575 |
| | R. Hutcherson | 3 | 0 | 1 | 1 | 2 | 0 | 22,420 |
| 1979 | A.J. Foyt | 2 | 0 | 1 | 2 | 0 | 0 | 41,690 |
| 1980 | A.J. Foyt | 1 | 0 | 0 | 0 | 1 | 0 | 3,575 |
| 1981 | A.J. Foyt | 3 | 0 | 0 | 1 | 2 | 0 | 9,210 |
| 1982 | A.J. Foyt | 2 | 0 | 0 | 0 | 2 | 0 | 9,405 |
| 1983 | A.J. Foyt | 3 | 0 | 0 | 0 | 2 | 0 | 22,935 |
| | C. Yarborough | 0 | 0 | 0 | 0 | 0 | 0 | 10,500 |
| 1984 | A.J. Foyt | 3 | 0 | 0 | 0 | 3 | 0 | 8,830 |
| 1985 | A.J. Foyt | 7 | 0 | 1 | 0 | 6 | 0 | 29,750 |
| 1986 | A.J. Foyt | 5 | 0 | 0 | 0 | 4 | 0 | 24,135 |
| 1987 | A.J. Foyt | 6 | 0 | 0 | 0 | 5 | 0 | 21,075 |
| 1988 | A.J. Foyt | 7 | 0 | 0 | 0 | 6 | 0 | 29,660 |
| 1989 | A.J. Foyt | 7 | 0 | 0 | 0 | 5 | 0 | 31,995 |
| | T. Leslie | 2 | 0 | 0 | 0 | 1 | 0 | 8,800 |
| 1990 | A.J. Foyt | 3 | 0 | 0 | 0 | 2 | 0 | 26,725 |
| 1991 | M. Chase | 4 | 0 | 0 | 0 | 2 | 0 | 19,225 |
| 1992 | A.J. Foyt | 1 | 0 | 0 | 0 | 0 | 0 | 23,055 |
| 1994 | A.J. Foyt | 1 | 0 | 0 | 0 | 0 | 0 | 29,000 |
| 2000 | M. Bliss | 1 | 0 | 0 | 0 | 0 | 0 | 103,996 |
| | D. Trickle | 2 | 0 | 0 | 0 | 0 | 0 | 52,150 |
| | R. Mast | 24 | 0 | 0 | 2 | 4 | 0 | 912,773 |
| 2001 | R. Hornaday | 32 | 0 | 0 | 1 | 8 | 0 | 1,435,857 |
| 2002 | S. Compton | 18 | 0 | 0 | 0 | 4 | 0 | 992,684 |
| | M. Wallace | 16 | 0 | 0 | 0 | 4 | 0 | 802,283 |
| | P.J. Jones | 1 | 0 | 1 | 1 | 0 | 0 | 65,950 |
| 2003 | Larry Foyt | 20 | 0 | 0 | 0 | 8 | 0 | 1,180,990 |
| TOTALS | | 188 | 0 | 8 | 12 | 78 | 1 | $5,988,168 |

## Chip Ganassi Racing with Felix Sabates

**Owner:** Chip Ganassi. **Date of birth:** 5/24/58. **Hometown:** Pittsburgh. **Resides:** Pittsburgh. **Years as NNCS Owner:** 3. **Best points finish:** 3. **Career victories:** 5. **First victory:** 2001 Michigan. **Career poles:** 3. **First pole:** 2001 Daytona

- Ganassi became the primary owner of team following Race 18 in 2000; Felix Sabates was the owner prior to that date.
- Ganassi's CART teams won four consecutive championships from 1996-99.
- Became second owner in CART history to win CART and NASCAR events on the same day – Bruno Junqueira won CART's Motorola 220 at Road America; Sterling Marlin won Pepsi 400 at Michigan International Speedway.

### CAREER NASCAR WINSTON CUP SERIES STATS

| Year | Driver | Races | Won | Top 5 | Top 10 | DNF | Poles | Money Won |
|---|---|---|---|---|---|---|---|---|
| 1988 | R. Moroso | 1 | 0 | 0 | 0 | 0 | 0 | $4,500 |
| 1989 | K. Petty | 19 | 0 | 0 | 0 | 7 | 0 | 117,022 |
| 1990 | K. Petty | 29 | 1 | 2 | 14 | 5 | 2 | 746,326 |
| 1991 | K. Petty | 18 | 1 | 2 | 4 | 5 | 2 | 413,727 |
| | K. Wallace | 2 | 0 | 0 | 0 | 0 | 0 | 46,900 |
| | T. Kendall | 1 | 0 | 0 | 0 | 0 | 0 | 12,450 |
| | B. Hillin Jr. | 8 | 0 | 0 | 0 | 1 | 0 | 103,005 |
| 1992 | K. Petty | 29 | 2 | 9 | 17 | 5 | 3 | 1,107,063 |
| | T. Kendall | 1 | 0 | 0 | 0 | 0 | 0 | 6,755 |
| | S. Sharp | 1 | 0 | 0 | 0 | 0 | 0 | 7,155 |
| 1993 | K. Petty | 30 | 1 | 9 | 15 | 5 | 1 | 914,662 |
| | K. Wallace | 30 | 0 | 0 | 3 | 6 | 0 | 330,325 |

## OWNERS

| Year | Driver | Races | Won | Top 5 | Top 10 | DNF | Poles | Money Won |
|---|---|---|---|---|---|---|---|---|
| 1994 | K. Petty | 31 | 0 | 2 | 7 | 3 | 0 | 806,332 |
| | B. Hamilton | 30 | 0 | 0 | 1 | 10 | 0 | 514,520 |
| 1995 | K. Petty | 30 | 1 | 1 | 5 | 10 | 0 | 698,875 |
| 1996 | K. Petty | 28 | 0 | 0 | 0 | 4 | 0 | 689,041 |
| | Jim Sauter | 2 | 0 | 0 | 0 | 1 | 0 | 47,700 |
| | G. Sacks | 2 | 0 | 0 | 0 | 0 | 0 | 21,190 |
| | R. Gordon | 2 | 0 | 0 | 0 | 2 | 0 | 18,565 |
| | Jay Sauter | 0 | 0 | 0 | 0 | 0 | 0 | 2,400 |
| 1997 | R. Gordon | 20 | 0 | 0 | 0 | 7 | 1 | 622,439 |
| | J. Nemechek | 29 | 0 | 0 | 3 | 4 | 2 | 679,954 |
| | W. Dallenbach Jr. | 22 | 0 | 0 | 0 | 10 | 0 | 471,479 |
| | G. Sacks | 5 | 0 | 0 | 0 | 3 | 0 | 114,035 |
| | P. Parsons | 1 | 0 | 0 | 0 | 0 | 0 | 12,854 |
| | S. Park | 1 | 0 | 0 | 0 | 1 | 0 | 14,075 |
| 1998 | J. Nemechek | 32 | 0 | 1 | 4 | 5 | 0 | 1,343,991 |
| | S. Marlin | 32 | 0 | 2 | 5 | 1 | 0 | 1,350,161 |
| | J. Green | 18 | 0 | 0 | 0 | 7 | 0 | 449,611 |
| | W. Dallenbach Jr. | 4 | 0 | 0 | 0 | 1 | 0 | 162,100 |
| | M. Shepherd | 2 | 0 | 0 | 0 | 0 | 0 | 61,611 |
| | T. Kendall | 1 | 0 | 0 | 0 | 0 | 0 | 19,405 |
| 1999 | J. Nemechek | 34 | 1 | 0 | 0 | 5 | 3 | 1,634,946 |
| | S. Marlin | 34 | 0 | 0 | 0 | 3 | 1 | 1,797,416 |
| | J. Green | 1 | 0 | 0 | 0 | 0 | 0 | 31,415 |
| | S. Grissom | 1 | 0 | 0 | 0 | 0 | 0 | 32,845 |
| | R. Hornaday Jr. | 1 | 0 | 0 | 0 | 0 | 0 | 22,810 |
| *2000 | S. Marlin | 34 | 0 | 1 | 7 | 4 | 0 | 1,992,301 |
| | K. Irwin Jr. | 17 | 0 | 1 | 1 | 2 | 0 | 949,436 |
| | T. Musgrave | 12 | 0 | 0 | 0 | 1 | 0 | 587,420 |
| | P.J. Jones | 1 | 0 | 0 | 0 | 0 | 0 | 37,555 |
| | B. Hamilton Jr. | 1 | 0 | 0 | 0 | 0 | 0 | 46,890 |
| 2001 | S. Marlin | 36 | 2 | 12 | 20 | 2 | 1 | 4,517,634 |
| | J. Leffler | 30 | 0 | 0 | 1 | 8 | 1 | 1,724,692 |
| | D. Schroeder | 1 | 0 | 0 | 0 | 0 | 0 | 52,805 |
| | S. Pruett | 1 | 0 | 0 | 0 | 0 | 0 | 57,025 |
| 2002 | S. Marlin | 29 | 2 | 8 | 14 | 3 | 0 | 4,228,889 |
| | J. Spencer | 34 | 0 | 2 | 6 | 7 | 0 | 2,136,792 |
| | J. McMurray | 6 | 1 | 1 | 2 | 1 | 0 | 717,942 |
| | M. Bliss | 1 | 0 | 0 | 0 | 0 | 0 | 90,083 |
| | S. Pruett | 1 | 0 | 0 | 1 | 0 | 0 | 66,690 |
| 2003 | S. Marlin | 36 | 0 | 0 | 11 | 8 | 0 | 3,960,810 |
| | J. McMurray | 36 | 0 | 5 | 13 | 4 | 1 | 2,699,970 |
| | C. Mears | 36 | 0 | 0 | 0 | 10 | 0 | 2,639,180 |
| | S. Pruett | 2 | 0 | 1 | 1 | 0 | 0 | 143,035 |
| *TOTALS | | 846 | 12 | 59 | 155 | 161 | 18 | $42,078,809 |

\* Ganassi became primary owner following Race No. 18 (New Hampshire) in 2000; Felix Sabates was owner before that date

## Joe Gibbs

**Date of birth:** 11/25/40. **Hometown:** Mocksville, N.C. **Resides:** Cornelius, N.C. **Years as NNCS Owner:** 12. **Best points finish:** 1. **Career victories:** 40. **First victory:** 1993 Daytona. **Career poles:** 31. **First pole:** 1995 Martinsville

- Son, J.D., is president of Joe Gibbs Racing, while youngest son, Coy, runs in the NASCAR Busch Series.
- NFL coach for 12 years – four Super Bowl appearances, three Super Bowl wins, with Washington Redskins.
- Associated Press Coach of the Year (1982 and 1983).
- Graduated from San Diego State University in 1964.

### CAREER NASCAR WINSTON CUP SERIES STATS

| Year | Driver | Races | Won | Top 5 | Top 10 | DNF | Poles | Money Won |
|---|---|---|---|---|---|---|---|---|
| 1992 | D. Jarrett | 29 | 0 | 2 | 8 | 5 | 0 | $418,648 |
| 1993 | D. Jarrett | 30 | 1 | 13 | 18 | 5 | 0 | 1,242,394 |
| 1994 | D. Jarrett | 30 | 1 | 4 | 9 | 7 | 0 | 881,754 |
| 1995 | B. Labonte | 31 | 3 | 7 | 14 | 6 | 2 | 1,413,682 |
| 1996 | B. Labonte | 31 | 1 | 5 | 14 | 5 | 4 | 1,475,196 |
| 1997 | B. Labonte | 32 | 1 | 9 | 18 | 1 | 3 | 2,217,999 |
| 1998 | B. Labonte | 33 | 2 | 11 | 18 | 6 | 3 | 2,980,052 |
| 1999 | B. Labonte | 34 | 5 | 23 | 26 | 1 | 5 | 4,763,615 |
| | T. Stewart | 34 | 3 | 12 | 21 | 1 | 2 | 3,190,149 |
| 2000 | B. Labonte | 34 | 4 | 19 | 24 | 0 | 2 | 7,361,386 |
| | T. Stewart | 34 | 6 | 12 | 23 | 5 | 2 | 3,642,348 |
| 2001 | T. Stewart | 36 | 3 | 15 | 22 | 4 | 0 | 4,941,463 |
| | B. Labonte | 36 | 2 | 9 | 20 | 6 | 1 | 4,786,779 |
| 2002 | T. Stewart | 36 | 3 | 15 | 21 | 6 | 2 | 9,163,761 |
| | B. Labonte | 36 | 1 | 5 | 7 | 4 | 0 | 4,183,715 |
| 2003 | T. Stewart | 36 | 2 | 12 | 18 | 5 | 1 | 5,227,500 |
| | B. Labonte | 36 | 2 | 12 | 17 | 5 | 4 | 4,745,260 |
| | M. Bliss | 1 | 0 | 0 | 0 | 0 | 0 | 65,300 |
| TOTALS | | 569 | 40 | 185 | 298 | 72 | 31 | $62,701,001 |

## Gene Haas

**Hometown:** Oxnard, Calif. **Resides:** Harrisburg, N.C. **Years as NNCS Owner:** 1. **Best points finish:** 21. **Career victories:** 0. **First victory:** None **Career poles:** 0. **First pole:** None

### CAREER NASCAR WINSTON CUP SERIES STATS

| Year | Driver | Races | Won | Top 5 | Top 10 | DNF | Poles | Money Won |
|---|---|---|---|---|---|---|---|---|
| 2003 | J. Sprague | 18 | 0 | 0 | 0 | 5 | 0 | 1,187,830 |
| | J. Leffler | 10 | 0 | 0 | 0 | 0 | 0 | 594,500 |
| | J. Andretti | 3 | 0 | 0 | 0 | 0 | 0 | 142,770 |
| | W. Burton | 4 | 0 | 0 | 0 | 2 | 0 | 219,206 |
| TOTALS | | 35 | 0 | 0 | 0 | 7 | 0 | $2,144,306 |

## Rick Hendrick

**Date of birth:** 7/12/49. **Hometown:** Warrenton, N.C. **Resides:** Charlotte, N.C. **Years as NNCS Owner:** 20. **Best points finish:** 1. **Career victories:** 109. **First victory:** 1984 Martinsville. **Career poles:** 107. **First pole:** 1984 Bristol

- Founder of Hendrick Automotive Group.
- Attended North Carolina State University.
- Drafted by Pittsburgh Pirates.

- Owned drag boat team (Nitro Fever), won national championships in 1981-83.
- One of the original owners of the NBA's Charlotte Hornets.
- Technical advisor on Tom Cruise movie Days of Thunder.
- For car owner points purposes, Jeff Gordon is the listed owner for Jimmie Johnson (No. 48).
- For car owner points purposes, Joe Hendrick, Jr. is the listed car owner for Joe Nemechek (No. 25).

### CAREER NASCAR WINSTON CUP SERIES STATS

| Year | Driver | Races | Won | Top 5 | Top 10 | DNF | Poles | Money Won |
|---|---|---|---|---|---|---|---|---|
| 1984 | G. Bodine | 30 | 3 | 7 | 14 | 8 | 3 | $393,924 |
| 1985 | G. Bodine | 28 | 0 | 10 | 14 | 5 | 3 | 565,865 |
|  | D. Brooks | 1 | 0 | 0 | 1 | 0 | 0 | 9,000 |
| 1986 | G. Bodine | 29 | 2 | 10 | 14 | 12 | 8 | 795,111 |
|  | T. Richmond | 29 | 7 | 13 | 17 | 2 | 8 | 988,221 |
|  | B. Bodine | 1 | 0 | 0 | 0 | 0 | 0 | 10,100 |
| 1987 | G. Bodine | 29 | 0 | 3 | 10 | 11 | 2 | 449,816 |
|  | D. Waltrip | 29 | 1 | 6 | 16 | 2 | 0 | 511,768 |
|  | B. Parsons | 29 | 0 | 6 | 9 | 12 | 0 | 555,584 |
|  | T. Richmond | 8 | 2 | 3 | 4 | 2 | 1 | 151,850 |
|  | J. Fitzgerald | 1 | 0 | 0 | 0 | 0 | 0 | 1,675 |
|  | J. Means | 1 | 0 | 0 | 0 | 1 | 0 | 5,960 |
|  | Rick Hendrick | 1 | 0 | 0 | 0 | 1 | 0 | 1,150 |
| 1988 | G. Bodine | 29 | 1 | 10 | 16 | 4 | 3 | 570,643 |
|  | D. Waltrip | 29 | 2 | 10 | 14 | 4 | 2 | 731,659 |
|  | K. Schrader | 28 | 1 | 4 | 17 | 1 | 2 | 626,934 |
|  | Rick Hendrick | 1 | 0 | 0 | 0 | 0 | 0 | 2,550 |
| 1989 | G. Bodine | 29 | 1 | 9 | 11 | 6 | 3 | 620,594 |
|  | D. Waltrip | 29 | 6 | 14 | 18 | 3 | 0 | 1,323,079 |
|  | K. Schrader | 29 | 1 | 10 | 14 | 6 | 4 | 1,039,441 |
|  | T. Kendall | 1 | 0 | 0 | 0 | 1 | 0 | 3,015 |
| 1990 | D. Waltrip | 23 | 0 | 5 | 12 | 0 | 0 | 530,420 |
|  | K. Schrader | 29 | 0 | 7 | 14 | 8 | 3 | 769,934 |
|  | R. Rudd | 29 | 1 | 8 | 15 | 5 | 2 | 573,650 |
|  | G. Sacks | 4 | 0 | 1 | 1 | 2 | 0 | 93,315 |
|  | J. Horton | 2 | 0 | 0 | 0 | 0 | 0 | 30,475 |
|  | H. Stricklin | 1 | 0 | 0 | 0 | 1 | 0 | 2,765 |
|  | S. Van der Merwe | 1 | 0 | 0 | 0 | 1 | 0 | 12,070 |
| 1991 | K. Schrader | 29 | 2 | 10 | 18 | 6 | 0 | 772,439 |
|  | R. Rudd | 29 | 1 | 9 | 17 | 1 | 1 | 1,093,765 |
| 1992 | K. Schrader | 29 | 0 | 4 | 11 | 5 | 1 | 639,679 |
|  | R. Rudd | 29 | 1 | 9 | 18 | 4 | 1 | 793,903 |
|  | J. Gordon | 1 | 0 | 0 | 0 | 1 | 0 | 6,285 |
| 1993 | K. Schrader | 30 | 0 | 9 | 15 | 4 | 6 | 952,748 |
|  | Rudd | 30 | 1 | 9 | 14 | 6 | 0 | 752,562 |
|  | J. Gordon | 30 | 0 | 7 | 11 | 11 | 1 | 765,168 |
|  | A. Unser Jr. | 1 | 0 | 0 | 0 | 1 | 0 | 23,005 |
| 1994 | K. Schrader | 31 | 0 | 9 | 18 | 2 | 0 | 1,171,062 |
|  | J. Gordon | 31 | 2 | 7 | 14 | 10 | 1 | 1,779,523 |
|  | T. Labonte | 31 | 3 | 6 | 14 | 4 | 0 | 1,125,921 |
| 1995 | K. Schrader | 31 | 0 | 2 | 10 | 9 | 1 | 886,566 |
|  | J. Gordon | 31 | 7 | 17 | 23 | 3 | 8 | 4,347,343 |
|  | T. Labonte | 31 | 3 | 14 | 17 | 3 | 1 | 1,558,659 |
|  | J. Purvis | 1 | 0 | 0 | 0 | 0 | 0 | 7,370 |
| 1996 | K. Schrader | 31 | 0 | 3 | 10 | 2 | 0 | 1,089,603 |
|  | J. Gordon | 31 | 10 | 21 | 24 | 5 | 5 | 3,428,485 |
|  | T. Labonte | 31 | 2 | 21 | 24 | 3 | 4 | 4,030,648 |
| 1997 | J. Gordon | 32 | 10 | 22 | 23 | 2 | 1 | 6,375,658 |
|  | T. Labonte | 32 | 1 | 8 | 20 | 3 | 0 | 2,270,144 |
|  | R. Craven | 30 | 0 | 4 | 7 | 7 | 0 | 1,259,550 |
|  | T. Bodine | 1 | 0 | 0 | 0 | 0 | 0 | 58,550 |
|  | J. Sprague | 1 | 0 | 0 | 1 | 0 | 0 | 18,650 |
| 1998 | J. Gordon | 33 | 13 | 26 | 28 | 2 | 7 | 9,306,584 |
|  | T. Labonte | 33 | 1 | 5 | 15 | 4 | 0 | 2,054,163 |
|  | W. Dallenbach Jr. | 16 | 0 | 0 | 3 | 3 | 0 | 522,996 |
|  | R. LaJoie | 9 | 0 | 1 | 3 | 3 | 0 | 336,905 |
|  | R. Craven | 8 | 0 | 0 | 1 | 0 | 1 | 442,200 |
| 1999 | J. Gordon | 34 | 7 | 18 | 21 | 7 | 7 | 5,858,633 |
|  | T. Labonte | 34 | 1 | 1 | 6 | 6 | 0 | 2,475,365 |
|  | W. Dallenbach Jr. | 34 | 0 | 1 | 6 | 5 | 0 | 1,741,176 |
| 2000 | J. Gordon | 34 | 3 | 11 | 22 | 2 | 3 | 3,001,144 |
|  | T. Labonte | 32 | 0 | 3 | 6 | 3 | 1 | 2,239,716 |
|  | J. Nadeau | 34 | 1 | 3 | 5 | 9 | 0 | 2,164,778 |
|  | T. Bodine | 1 | 0 | 0 | 0 | 0 | 0 | 117,260 |
|  | R. Hornaday Jr. | 1 | 0 | 0 | 0 | 0 | 0 | 47,020 |
| 2001 | J. Gordon | 36 | 6 | 18 | 24 | 2 | 6 | 10,879,757 |
|  | T. Labonte | 36 | 0 | 1 | 3 | 8 | 0 | 3,011,901 |
|  | J. Nadeau | 36 | 0 | 4 | 10 | 8 | 0 | 2,507,827 |
|  | J. Johnson | 3 | 0 | 0 | 0 | 1 | 0 | 122,320 |
| 2002 | J. Gordon | 36 | 3 | 13 | 20 | 3 | 3 | 6,154,475 |
|  | J. Johnson | 36 | 3 | 6 | 21 | 3 | 4 | 3,788,268 |
|  | T. Labonte | 36 | 0 | 1 | 4 | 6 | 0 | 3,244,240 |
|  | J. Nadeau | 11 | 0 | 0 | 1 | 3 | 0 | 754,275 |
|  | J. Nemechek | 25 | 0 | 3 | 8 | 0 | 0 | 1,766,252 |
| 2003 | J. Gordon | 36 | 3 | 15 | 20 | 5 | 4 | 5,107,760 |
|  | J. Johnson | 36 | 3 | 14 | 20 | 3 | 2 | 5,517,850 |
|  | T. Labonte | 36 | 1 | 4 | 9 | 0 | 1 | 3,643,690 |
|  | J. Nemechek | 32 | 1 | 2 | 5 | 7 | 0 | 2,289,060 |
|  | D. Green | 11 | 0 | 0 | 1 | 2 | 1 | 906,135 |
|  | B. Vickers | 5 | 0 | 0 | 0 | 1 | 0 | 263,484 |
| TOTALS |  | 1622 | 109 | 442 | 741 | 277 | 107 | $126,843,088 |

## Larry McClure

**Date of birth:** 3/21/44. **Hometown:** Harmon, Va. **Resides:** Abingdon, Va. **Years as NNCS Owner:** 21. **Best points finish:** 3. **Career victories:** 14. **First victory:** 1990 Bristol. **Career poles:** 13. **First pole:** 1998 Bristol

- Morgan-McClure Motorsports is one of only three active Winston Cup teams to win at both road courses (Hendrick Motorsports and Roush Racing are the other two).
- Ernie Irvan and Sterling Marlin posted first career NASCAR Winston Cup Series wins with Morgan-McClure.
- Kodak has been with Morgan-McClure since 1986, making it the longest running, continuous primary sponsor in Winston Cup.

### CAREER NASCAR WINSTON CUP SERIES STATS

| Year | Driver | Races | Won | Top 5 | Top 10 | DNF | Poles | Money Won |
|---|---|---|---|---|---|---|---|---|
| 1983 | L. Pond | 5 | 0 | 0 | 2 | 2 | 0 | $23,475 |
|  | M. Martin | 6 | 0 | 0 | 1 | 2 | 0 | 17,030 |
| 1984 | L. Pond | 4 | 0 | 0 | 0 | 2 | 0 | 21,590 |
|  | T. Ellis | 20 | 0 | 0 | 1 | 11 | 0 | 44,315 |
|  | J. Ruttman | 3 | 0 | 0 | 1 | 2 | 0 | 5,525 |
| 1985 | J. Ruttman | 16 | 0 | 1 | 4 | 10 | 0 | 71,425 |
| 1986 | R. Wilson | 17 | 0 | 0 | 4 | 8 | 0 | 88,820 |

## OWNERS

| Year | Driver | Races | Won | Top 5 | Top 10 | DNF | Poles | Money Won |
|---|---|---|---|---|---|---|---|---|
| 1987 | R. Wilson | 19 | 0 | 0 | 1 | 11 | 0 | 65,935 |
| 1988 | R. Wilson | 28 | 0 | 2 | 5 | 11 | 1 | 209,925 |
| 1989 | R. Wilson | 29 | 0 | 2 | 7 | 8 | 0 | 312,402 |
| 1990 | P. Parsons | 3 | 0 | 0 | 0 | 1 | 0 | 39,350 |
|  | E. Irvan | 26 | 1 | 6 | 13 | 3 | 3 | 497,675 |
| 1991 | E. Irvan | 29 | 2 | 11 | 19 | 6 | 1 | 1,079,017 |
| 1992 | E. Irvan | 29 | 3 | 9 | 11 | 7 | 3 | 996,885 |
| 1993 | E. Irvan | 21 | 1 | 7 | 8 | 9 | 2 | 815,985 |
|  | J. Purvis | 5 | 0 | 0 | 0 | 0 | 0 | 81,370 |
|  | J. Nemechek | 2 | 0 | 0 | 0 | 0 | 0 | 32,280 |
|  | J. Hensley | 2 | 0 | 0 | 0 | 1 | 0 | 31,895 |
| 1994 | S. Marlin | 31 | 1 | 5 | 11 | 7 | 1 | 1,127,683 |
| 1995 | S. Marlin | 31 | 3 | 9 | 22 | 2 | 1 | 2,253,502 |
| 1996 | S. Marlin | 31 | 2 | 5 | 10 | 6 | 0 | 1,588,425 |
| 1997 | S. Marlin | 32 | 0 | 2 | 6 | 8 | 0 | 1,301,370 |
| 1998 | B. Hamilton | 33 | 1 | 3 | 8 | 1 | 1 | 2,089,566 |
| 1999 | B. Hamilton | 34 | 0 | 1 | 10 | 3 | 0 | 2,019,255 |
| 2000 | B. Hamilton | 34 | 0 | 0 | 2 | 11 | 0 | 1,619,775 |
| 2001 | K. Lepage | 21 | 0 | 0 | 0 | 3 | 0 | 987,976 |
|  | B. Hamilton Jr. | 7 | 0 | 0 | 0 | 0 | 0 | 305,705 |
|  | R. Gordon | 5 | 0 | 0 | 0 | 1 | 0 | 287,545 |
|  | R. Bickle Jr. | 1 | 0 | 0 | 0 | 0 | 0 | 30,300 |
| 2002 | M. Skinner | 36 | 0 | 0 | 1 | 6 | 0 | 2,094,232 |
| 2003 | K. Lepage | 11 | 0 | 0 | 0 | 1 | 0 | 742,077 |
|  | J. Sauter | 5 | 0 | 0 | 0 | 0 | 0 | 281,335 |
|  | J. Miller | 2 | 0 | 0 | 0 | 0 | 0 | 110,814 |
|  | P.J. Jones | 1 | 0 | 0 | 0 | 0 | 0 | 59,135 |
|  | S. Compton | 1 | 0 | 0 | 0 | 0 | 0 | 67,400 |
| TOTALS |  | 580 | 14 | 63 | 147 | 143 | 13 | $21,400,994 |

## Beth Ann Morgenthau

**Hometown:** Baltimore, Md. **Resides:** Coral Gables, Fla. **Years as NNCS Owner:** 2. **Best points finish:** 36. **Career victories:** 0. **First victory:** 0. **Career poles:** 0. **First pole:** 0

- Active in Miami Association of Charities.

### CAREER NASCAR WINSTON CUP SERIES STATS

| Year | Driver | Races | Won | Top 5 | Top 10 | DNF | Poles | Money Won |
|---|---|---|---|---|---|---|---|---|
| 2002 | S. Robinson | 7 | 0 | 0 | 0 | 4 | 0 | $428,519 |
|  | D. Cope | 5 | 0 | 0 | 0 | 0 | 0 | 224,390 |
|  | S. Compton | 2 | 0 | 0 | 0 | 1 | 0 | 90,630 |
|  | R. Hornaday | 1 | 0 | 0 | 0 | 1 | 0 | 88,476 |
|  | K. Lepage | 1 | 0 | 0 | 0 | 1 | 0 | 44,650 |
|  | S. Kirby | 1 | 0 | 0 | 0 | 0 | 0 | 53,100 |
| 2003 | K. Schrader | 32 | 0 | 0 | 2 | 8 | 0 | 2,007,420 |
| TOTALS |  | 49 | 0 | 0 | 2 | 15 | 0 | $2,937,185 |

## Roger Penske

**Hometown:** Shaker Heights, Ohio. **Resides:** Bloomfield Hills, Mich. **Years as NNCS Owner:** 32. **Best points finish:** 2. **Career victories:** 50. **First victory:** 1973 Riverside. **Career poles:** 53. **First pole:** 1974 Riverside

- 1962 New York Times Driver of the Year (USAC Champion).
- Won Indy 500 11 times as owner.
- 11-time CART Series Champion owner.

### CAREER NASCAR WINSTON CUP SERIES STATS

| Year | Driver | Races | Won | Top 5 | Top 10 | DNF | Poles | Money Won |
|---|---|---|---|---|---|---|---|---|
| 1972 | D. Marcis | 7 | 0 | 0 | 3 | 4 | 0 | $9,406 |
|  | M. Donohue | 4 | 0 | 0 | 0 | 3 | 0 | 5,130 |
|  | D. Allison | 1 | 0 | 1 | 1 | 0 | 0 | 4,025 |
| 1973 | D. Marcis | 8 | 0 | 1 | 2 | 6 | 0 | 10,625 |
|  | M. Donohue | 2 | 1 | 1 | 1 | 1 | 0 | 16,120 |
| 1974 | B. Allison | 10 | 1 | 6 | 6 | 4 | 0 | 53,885 |
|  | G. Bettenhausen | 5 | 0 | 1 | 3 | 1 | 0 | 12,730 |
|  | D. Marcis | 1 | 0 | 0 | 1 | 0 | 0 | 2,025 |
|  | G. Follmer | 1 | 0 | 0 | 0 | 1 | 1 | 1,000 |
| 1975 | B. Allison | 19 | 3 | 10 | 10 | 9 | 3 | 122,435 |
| 1976 | B. Allison | 30 | 0 | 15 | 19 | 9 | 2 | 210,377 |
|  | N. Bonnett* | 0 | 0 | 0 | 0 | 0 | 1 | 0 |
| 1977 | D. Marcis | 14 | 0 | 5 | 7 | 3 | 0 | 66,545 |
| 1980 | R. Wallace | 2 | 0 | 1 | 1 | 0 | 0 | 22,760 |
| 1991 | R. Wallace | 29 | 2 | 9 | 14 | 10 | 2 | 502,073 |
| 1992 | R. Wallace | 29 | 1 | 5 | 12 | 5 | 1 | 657,925 |
| 1993 | R. Wallace | 30 | 10 | 19 | 21 | 5 | 3 | 1,702,154 |
| 1994 | R. Wallace | 31 | 8 | 17 | 20 | 5 | 2 | 1,914,072 |
| 1995 | R. Wallace | 31 | 2 | 15 | 19 | 4 | 0 | 1,642,837 |
| 1996 | R. Wallace | 31 | 5 | 8 | 18 | 6 | 0 | 1,665,315 |
| 1997 | R. Wallace | 32 | 1 | 8 | 12 | 11 | 1 | 1,705,625 |
| 1998 | R. Wallace | 33 | 1 | 15 | 21 | 2 | 4 | 2,667,889 |
| 1999 | R. Wallace | 34 | 1 | 7 | 16 | 3 | 4 | 2,454,050 |
| 2000 | R. Wallace | 34 | 4 | 12 | 20 | 3 | 9 | 3,621,468 |
|  | J. Mayfield | 5 | 0 | 2 | 2 | 2 | 1 | 551,300 |
|  | R. Newman | 1 | 0 | 0 | 0 | 1 | 0 | 37,825 |
| 2001 | R. Wallace | 36 | 1 | 8 | 12 | 3 | 0 | 4,788,652 |
|  | J. Mayfield | 28 | 0 | 5 | 7 | 4 | 0 | 2,682,603 |
|  | R. Newman | 7 | 0 | 2 | 2 | 2 | 1 | 465,276 |
|  | M. Wallace | 8 | 0 | 1 | 2 | 1 | 0 | 706,673 |
| 2002 | R. Newman | 36 | 1 | 14 | 22 | 5 | 6 | 5,346,651 |
|  | R. Wallace | 36 | 0 | 7 | 17 | 1 | 1 | 4,785,134 |
| 2003 | R. Newman | 36 | 8 | 17 | 22 | 7 | 11 | 4,827,380 |
|  | R. Wallace | 36 | 0 | 2 | 12 | 4 | 0 | 3,766,740 |
| TOTALS |  | 640 | 50 | 214 | 322 | 121 | 53 | $47,019,299 |

* Bonnett substituted in qualifying for Allison at Nashville and won pole; Allison started the race with Bonnett relieving him after one lap

## Andy Petree

**Date of birth:** 8/15/58. **Hometown:** Newton, N.C. **Resides:** Hendersonville, N.C. **Years as NNCS Owner:** 8. **Best points finish:** 10. **Career victories:** 2. **First victory:** 2001 Talladega. **Career poles:** 6. **First pole:** 1997 Loudon

- 1993 & '94 Winston Cup champion crew chief with driver Dale Earnhardt.

### CAREER NASCAR WINSTON CUP SERIES STATS

| Year | Driver | Races | Won | Top 5 | Top 10 | DNF | Poles | Money Won |
|---|---|---|---|---|---|---|---|---|
| 1996 | T. Bodine | 3 | 0 | 0 | 0 | 0 | 0 | $72,780 |
| | R. Pressley | 1 | 0 | 0 | 0 | 0 | 0 | 4,995 |
| 1997 | K. Schrader | 32 | 0 | 2 | 8 | 1 | 2 | 1,355,292 |
| 1998 | K. Schrader | 33 | 0 | 3 | 11 | 5 | 2 | 1,907,399 |
| | H. Stricklin | 1 | 0 | 0 | 0 | 1 | 0 | 24,250 |
| 1999 | K. Schrader | 34 | 0 | 0 | 6 | 1 | 1 | 1,939,147 |
| | K. Wallace | 34 | 0 | 3 | 5 | 7 | 0 | 1,416,208 |
| 2000 | K. Wallace | 34 | 0 | 1 | 1 | 6 | 0 | 1,723,966 |
| | J. Nemechek | 34 | 0 | 3 | 9 | 6 | 1 | 2,105,041 |
| | G. Bodine | 1 | 0 | 0 | 0 | 1 | 0 | 34,982 |
| 2001 | B. Hamilton | 36 | 1 | 3 | 7 | 0 | 0 | 2,527,310 |
| | J. Nemechek | 31 | 1 | 1 | 4 | 6 | 0 | 2,543,660 |
| | B. Hamilton Jr. | 3 | 0 | 0 | 0 | 2 | 0 | 241,142 |
| | W. Dallenbach | 1 | 0 | 0 | 0 | 0 | 0 | 64,410 |
| | S. Pruett | 1 | 0 | 0 | 0 | 0 | 0 | 77,020 |
| | L. Hooper | 1 | 0 | 0 | 0 | 1 | 0 | 47,700 |
| 2002 | B. Hamilton | 31 | 0 | 0 | 3 | 1 | 0 | 2,196,956 |
| | M. Wallace | 4 | 0 | 0 | 0 | 2 | 0 | 316,357 |
| | G. Biffle | 4 | 0 | 0 | 0 | 1 | 0 | 218,700 |
| | K. Wallace | 1 | 0 | 0 | 0 | 0 | 0 | 44,775 |
| | R. Hornaday | 1 | 0 | 0 | 0 | 0 | 0 | 52,860 |
| 2003 | Paul Menard | 1 | 0 | 0 | 0 | 0 | 0 | 52,410 |
| **TOTALS** | | **319** | **2** | **16** | **54** | **41** | **6** | **$18,894,580** |

## Petty Enterprises

**Owner:** Richard Petty. **Date of birth:** 7/2/37. **Hometown:** Newton, N.C. **Resides:** Level Cross, N.C. **Years as NNCS Owner:** 55*. **Best points finish:** 1. **Career victories:** 271. **First victory:** 1949 Heidelberg, Pa. **Career poles:** 152. **First pole:** 1954 Daytona Beach Course

- Petty Enterprises founded in 1949 by Lee Petty.
- Petty Enterprises has 10 Winston Cup titles (3-Lee Petty; 7-Richard Petty).
- For car owner points purposes, Pattie Petty is the listed owner for Kyle Petty (No. 45).
- For car owner points purposes, Kyle Petty is the listed owner for Christian Fittipaldi (No. 44).

### CAREER NASCAR WINSTON CUP SERIES STATS

| Year | Driver | Races | Won | Top 5 | Top 10 | DNF | Poles | Money Won |
|---|---|---|---|---|---|---|---|---|
| 1949 | L. Petty | 10 | 1 | 5 | 8 | 2 | 0 | $3,875 |
| 1950 | L. Petty | 17 | 2 | 10 | 14 | 1 | 0 | 6,225 |
| 1951 | L. Petty | 33 | 1 | 11 | 19 | 10 | 0 | 7,790 |
| 1952 | L. Petty | 32 | 3 | 21 | 27 | 5 | 0 | 15,520 |
| 1953 | L. Petty | 37 | 5 | 26 | 32 | 2 | 0 | 15,550 |
| 1954 | L. Petty | 34 | 7 | 24 | 32 | 2 | 3 | 18,325 |
| 1955 | L. Petty | 42 | 6 | 20 | 30 | 9 | 1 | 16,400 |
| 1956 | L. Petty | 47 | 2 | 17 | 28 | 13 | 1 | 13,555 |
| 1957 | L. Petty | 41 | 4 | 20 | 33 | 5 | 3 | 15,620 |
| | T. Lund | 6 | 0 | 1 | 2 | 2 | 0 | 810 |
| | Bobby Myers | 1 | 0 | 0 | 0 | 1 | 0 | 260 |
| 1958 | L. Petty | 49 | 7 | 27 | 42 | 3 | 5 | 20,385 |
| | R. Petty | 9 | 0 | 0 | 1 | 5 | 0 | 760 |
| | J. Reed | 1 | 0 | 0 | 0 | 1 | 0 | 315 |
| 1959 | L. Petty | 43 | 11 | 27 | 35 | 6 | 2 | 43,765 |
| | R. Petty | 22 | 0 | 5 | 8 | 12 | 0 | 7,630 |
| | J. Beauchamp | 1 | 0 | 0 | 0 | 0 | 0 | 300 |
| 1960 | L. Petty | 39 | 5 | 21 | 30 | 7 | 3 | 26,650 |
| | R. Petty | 40 | 3 | 17 | 30 | 8 | 2 | 35,180 |
| | M. Petty | 2 | 0 | 0 | 2 | 0 | 0 | 290 |
| | J. Paschal | 8 | 0 | 3 | 7 | 1 | 0 | 13,595 |
| | B. Johns | 1 | 0 | 1 | 1 | 0 | 0 | 6,975 |
| 1961 | R. Petty | 42 | 2 | 16 | 20 | 18 | 2 | 22,696 |
| | L. Petty | 3 | 1 | 2 | 2 | 1 | 1 | 1,260 |
| | M. Petty | 9 | 0 | 2 | 4 | 3 | 0 | 1,460 |
| | M. Porter | 2 | 0 | 1 | 1 | 1 | 0 | 450 |
| | M. Panch | 1 | 0 | 0 | 0 | 1 | 0 | 200 |
| | D. Dieringer | 1 | 0 | 0 | 1 | 0 | 0 | 1,375 |
| | J. Paschal | 1 | 0 | 0 | 0 | 1 | 0 | 100 |
| 1962 | R. Petty | 52 | 8 | 32 | 38 | 11 | 4 | 52,885 |
| | J. Paschal | 9 | 3 | 5 | 8 | 0 | 0 | 15,580 |
| | M. Petty | 5 | 0 | 2 | 3 | 2 | 0 | 965 |
| | B. Blackburn | 6 | 0 | 0 | 2 | 2 | 0 | 2,740 |
| | L. Petty | 1 | 0 | 1 | 1 | 0 | 0 | 750 |
| | S. Thompson | 1 | 0 | 0 | 1 | 0 | 0 | 900 |
| 1963 | R. Petty | 54 | 14 | 31 | 39 | 12 | 8 | 47,765 |
| | J. Paschal | 29 | 5 | 15 | 18 | 10 | 1 | 18,515 |
| | B. James | 4 | 0 | 0 | 0 | 3 | 0 | 1,700 |
| | B. Welborn | 4 | 0 | 3 | 3 | 1 | 0 | 2,330 |
| | M. Petty | 4 | 0 | 1 | 2 | 2 | 0 | 575 |
| | L. Petty | 3 | 0 | 1 | 2 | 1 | 0 | 600 |
| | J. Hurtubise | 3 | 0 | 0 | 0 | 3 | 0 | 975 |
| | J. Weatherly | 1 | 0 | 1 | 1 | 0 | 0 | 500 |
| | J. Massey | 1 | 0 | 0 | 0 | 1 | 0 | 125 |
| 1964 | R. Petty | 61 | 9 | 36 | 41 | 19 | 8 | 98,810 |
| | J. Paschal | 13 | 1 | 7 | 8 | 5 | 0 | 47,845 |
| | Buck Baker | 6 | 0 | 3 | 4 | 1 | 0 | 5,825 |
| | M. Petty | 6 | 0 | 2 | 5 | 1 | 0 | 1,540 |
| | L. Petty | 2 | 0 | 0 | 0 | 2 | 0 | 250 |
| 1965 | R. Petty | 14 | 4 | 10 | 10 | 4 | 7 | 16,450 |
| | J. Paschal | 3 | 0 | 3 | 3 | 0 | 0 | 2,450 |
| | L. Yarbrough | 1 | 0 | 0 | 0 | 1 | 0 | 150 |
| 1966 | R. Petty | 39 | 8 | 20 | 21 | 17 | 15 | 78,930 |
| | M. Panch | 5 | 1 | 2 | 4 | 1 | 0 | 32,900 |
| | J. Paschal | 1 | 0 | 0 | 0 | 1 | 0 | 325 |
| | D. Dieringer | 1 | 0 | 0 | 0 | 1 | 0 | 570 |
| | P. Lewis | 1 | 0 | 0 | 0 | 1 | 0 | 670 |
| 1967 | R. Petty | 48 | 27 | 38 | 39 | 8 | 18 | 130,275 |
| | T. Lund | 4 | 0 | 3 | 3 | 1 | 0 | 11,525 |
| | G.C. Spencer | 3 | 0 | 2 | 2 | 1 | 0 | 10,105 |
| 1968 | R. Petty | 49 | 16 | 31 | 33 | 16 | 12 | 89,103 |
| 1969 | R. Petty | 50 | 10 | 31 | 35 | 15 | 6 | 109,180 |
| 1970 | R. Petty | 40 | 18 | 25 | 29 | 10 | 9 | 138,969 |
| | P. Hamilton | 15 | 3 | 9 | 11 | 4 | 1 | 130,806 |
| | D. Gurney | 1 | 0 | 0 | 1 | 0 | 1 | 2,400 |
| | J. Paschal | 1 | 0 | 0 | 0 | 0 | 0 | 1,800 |
| 1971 | R. Petty | 46 | 21 | 38 | 41 | 5 | 9 | 309,225 |
| | Buddy Baker | 18 | 1 | 12 | 15 | 3 | 1 | 112,170 |

## OWNERS

| Year | Driver | Races | Won | Top 5 | Top 10 | DNF | Poles | Money Won |
|---|---|---|---|---|---|---|---|---|
| 1972 | R. Petty | 31 | 8 | 25 | 27 | 4 | 3 | 227,015 |
|  | Buddy Baker | 10 | 1 | 3 | 4 | 6 | 0 | 51,875 |
| 1973 | R. Petty | 28 | 6 | 15 | 16 | 10 | 3 | 159,655 |
| 1974 | R. Petty | 30 | 10 | 22 | 23 | 7 | 7 | 299,175 |
|  | H. McGriff | 4 | 0 | 0 | 1 | 2 | 0 | 7,430 |
| 1975 | R. Petty | 30 | 13 | 21 | 24 | 6 | 3 | 378,865 |
| 1976 | R. Petty | 30 | 3 | 19 | 22 | 8 | 1 | 338,265 |
| 1977 | R. Petty | 30 | 5 | 20 | 23 | 6 | 5 | 345,886 |
| 1978 | R. Petty | 30 | 0 | 11 | 17 | 12 | 0 | 215,491 |
| 1979 | R. Petty | 31 | 5 | 23 | 27 | 3 | 1 | 531,292 |
|  | K. Petty | 5 | 0 | 0 | 1 | 1 | 0 | 10,810 |
| 1980 | R. Petty | 31 | 2 | 15 | 18 | 10 | 0 | 374,092 |
|  | K. Petty | 14 | 0 | 0 | 6 | 5 | 0 | 35,575 |
| 1981 | R. Petty | 31 | 3 | 11 | 15 | 14 | 0 | 389,214 |
|  | K. Petty | 31 | 0 | 1 | 10 | 18 | 0 | 112,289 |
| 1982 | R. Petty | 30 | 0 | 9 | 16 | 13 | 0 | 453,832 |
|  | K. Petty | 23 | 0 | 2 | 4 | 13 | 0 | 108,715 |
| 1983 | R. Petty | 30 | 3 | 9 | 21 | 5 | 0 | 491,022 |
|  | K. Petty | 30 | 0 | 0 | 2 | 10 | 0 | 157,820 |
| 1984 | K. Petty | 30 | 0 | 1 | 6 | 7 | 0 | 324,555 |
| 1985 | D. Brooks | 3 | 0 | 0 | 0 | 3 | 0 | 20,340 |
|  | M. Shepherd | 1 | 0 | 0 | 0 | 0 | 0 | 3,415 |
| 1986 | R. Petty | 29 | 0 | 4 | 11 | 10 | 0 | 280,657 |
| 1987 | R. Petty | 29 | 0 | 9 | 14 | 5 | 0 | 468,602 |
| 1988 | R. Petty | 29 | 0 | 1 | 5 | 15 | 0 | 190,155 |
| 1989 | R. Petty | 25 | 0 | 0 | 0 | 12 | 0 | 133,050 |
| 1990 | R. Petty | 29 | 0 | 0 | 1 | 12 | 0 | 169,465 |
| 1991 | R. Petty | 29 | 0 | 0 | 1 | 10 | 0 | 268,035 |
| 1992 | R. Petty | 29 | 0 | 0 | 0 | 5 | 0 | 348,870 |
| 1993 | R. Wilson | 29 | 0 | 0 | 1 | 6 | 0 | 299,725 |
|  | J. Hensley | 1 | 0 | 0 | 0 | 1 | 0 | 5,875 |
| 1994 | W. Dallenbach Jr. | 14 | 0 | 1 | 3 | 3 | 0 | 241,492 |
|  | J. Andretti | 11 | 0 | 0 | 0 | 2 | 0 | 116,400 |
| 1995 | B. Hamilton | 31 | 0 | 4 | 10 | 2 | 0 | 804,505 |
| 1996 | B. Hamilton | 31 | 1 | 3 | 11 | 4 | 2 | 1,151,235 |
| 1997 | B. Hamilton | 32 | 1 | 6 | 8 | 4 | 2 | 1,478,843 |
| 1998 | J. Andretti | 33 | 0 | 3 | 10 | 4 | 1 | 1,838,379 |
| 1999 | J. Andretti | 34 | 1 | 3 | 10 | 10 | 1 | 2,001,832 |
|  | K. Petty | 32 | 0 | 0 | 9 | 4 | 0 | 1,278,953 |
| 2000 | J. Andretti | 34 | 0 | 0 | 2 | 7 | 0 | 2,035,902 |
|  | K. Petty | 18 | 0 | 0 | 1 | 6 | 0 | 797,176 |
|  | S. Grissom | 5 | 0 | 0 | 0 | 0 | 0 | 231,850 |
|  | A. Petty | 1 | 0 | 0 | 0 | 1 | 0 | 38,675 |
| 2001 | J. Andretti | 35 | 0 | 1 | 2 | 4 | 0 | 2,873,184 |
|  | K. Petty | 24 | 0 | 0 | 0 | 8 | 0 | 1,008,919 |
|  | B. Jones | 30 | 0 | 0 | 0 | 10 | 0 | 1,631,488 |
| 2002 | J. Andretti | 36 | 0 | 0 | 1 | 7 | 0 | 2,954,229 |
|  | K. Petty | 36 | 0 | 0 | 1 | 1 | 0 | 2,198,073 |
|  | J. Nadeau | 13 | 0 | 0 | 0 | 5 | 0 | 718,202 |
|  | S. Grissom | 10 | 0 | 0 | 0 | 1 | 0 | 529,781 |
|  | B. Jones | 7 | 0 | 0 | 0 | 2 | 0 | 394,223 |
|  | G. Biffle | 2 | 0 | 0 | 0 | 0 | 0 | 96,014 |
|  | T. Musgrave | 1 | 0 | 0 | 0 | 0 | 0 | 58,450 |
|  | C. Fittipaldi | 1 | 0 | 0 | 0 | 1 | 0 | 39,600 |
| 2003 | J. Green | 8 | 0 | 0 | 0 | 2 | 0 | 629,094 |
|  | K. Petty | 33 | 0 | 0 | 0 | 6 | 0 | 2,293,220 |
|  | C. Fittipaldi | 14 | 0 | 0 | 0 | 6 | 0 | 1,087,974 |
| **TOTALS** |  | 2447 | 271 | 883 | 1216 | 624 | 152 | $37,505,249 |

* Petty Enterprises was founded in 1949 by Lee Petty

## Edward Rensi

**Hometown:** Hopedale, Ohio **Resides:** Hopedale, Ohio **Years as NNCS Owner:** 1. **Best points finish:** 54. **Career victories:** 0. **Career poles:** 0.

### CAREER NASCAR WINSTON CUP SERIES STATS

| Year | Driver | Races | Won | Top 5 | Top 10 | DNF | Poles | Money Won |
|---|---|---|---|---|---|---|---|---|
| 2003 | B. Hamilton Jr. | 2 | 0 | 0 | 0 | 0 | 0 | 128,725 |

## Jack Roush

**Date of birth:** 4/19/42. **Hometown:** Manchester, Ohio. **Resides:** Northville, Mich. **Years as NNCS Owner:** 16. **Best points finish:** 2. **Career victories:** 66. **First victory:** 1989 Rockingham. **Career poles:** 50. **First pole:** 1988 Nashville

- First Winston Cup owner to field a five-car team in 1998.
- CEO of Roush Industries, an engineering and prototype development company servicing the automotive transportation industry, employing about 2,000 people.
- For car owner points purposes, Georgetta Roush is the listed owner for Kurt Busch (No. 97).
- For car owner points purposes, Mark Martin is the listed owner for Matt Kenseth (No. 17).

### CAREER NASCAR WINSTON CUP SERIES STATS

| Year | Driver | Races | Won | Top 5 | Top 10 | DNF | Poles | Money Won |
|---|---|---|---|---|---|---|---|---|
| 1988 | Martin | 29 | 0 | 3 | 10 | 10 | 1 | $223,630 |
| 1989 | Martin | 29 | 1 | 14 | 18 | 4 | 6 | 1,019,250 |
| 1990 | Martin | 29 | 3 | 17 | 24 | 1 | 3 | 1,302,958 |
| 1991 | Martin | 29 | 1 | 14 | 17 | 5 | 5 | 1,039,991 |
| 1992 | Martin | 29 | 2 | 10 | 17 | 5 | 1 | 1,000,571 |
|  | W. Dallenbach Jr. | 29 | 0 | 1 | 1 | 7 | 0 | 220,245 |
| 1993 | Martin | 30 | 5 | 12 | 19 | 5 | 5 | 1,657,662 |
|  | W. Dallenbach Jr. | 30 | 0 | 1 | 4 | 7 | 0 | 474,340 |
| 1994 | Martin | 31 | 2 | 15 | 20 | 8 | 1 | 1,628,906 |
|  | Musgrave | 31 | 0 | 1 | 8 | 5 | 3 | 656,187 |

| Year | Driver | Races | Won | Top 5 | Top 10 | DNF | Poles | Money Won |
|---|---|---|---|---|---|---|---|---|
| 1995 | Martin | 31 | 4 | 13 | 22 | 1 | 4 | 1,893,519 |
|  | Musgrave | 31 | 0 | 7 | 13 | 1 | 1 | 1,147,445 |
| 1996 | Martin | 31 | 0 | 14 | 23 | 4 | 4 | 1,887,396 |
|  | Musgrave | 31 | 0 | 2 | 7 | 2 | 1 | 961,512 |
|  | J. Burton | 30 | 0 | 6 | 12 | 1 | 1 | 884,303 |
| 1997 | Martin | 32 | 4 | 16 | 23 | 3 | 3 | 2,532,484 |
|  | Musgrave | 32 | 0 | 5 | 8 | 4 | 0 | 1,256,680 |
|  | J. Burton | 32 | 3 | 13 | 18 | 1 | 0 | 2,296,614 |
|  | C. Little | 11 | 0 | 0 | 0 | 1 | 0 | 212,590 |
| 1998 | Martin | 33 | 7 | 22 | 26 | 1 | 3 | 4,309,006 |
|  | T. Musgrave | 20 | 0 | 1 | 4 | 3 | 0 | 965,076 |
|  | J. Burton | 33 | 2 | 18 | 23 | 4 | 0 | 2,626,987 |
|  | C. Little | 32 | 0 | 1 | 7 | 7 | 0 | 1,449,659 |
|  | J. Benson | 32 | 0 | 3 | 10 | 5 | 0 | 1,360,335 |
|  | K. Lepage | 13 | 0 | 0 | 2 | 5 | 0 | 447,745 |
| 1999 | Martin | 34 | 2 | 19 | 26 | 3 | 1 | 3,509,744 |
|  | J. Burton | 34 | 6 | 18 | 23 | 3 | 0 | 5,725,399 |
|  | C. Little | 34 | 0 | 0 | 5 | 4 | 0 | 1,623,976 |
|  | J. Benson | 34 | 0 | 0 | 2 | 4 | 0 | 1,567,668 |
|  | K. Lepage | 34 | 0 | 1 | 2 | 3 | 1 | 1,587,841 |
|  | M. Kenseth | 5 | 0 | 1 | 1 | 3 | 0 | 143,561 |
| 2000 | Martin | 34 | 1 | 13 | 20 | 6 | 0 | 3,098,874 |
|  | J. Burton | 34 | 4 | 15 | 22 | 2 | 1 | 5,959,439 |
|  | C. Little | 27 | 0 | 0 | 1 | 3 | 0 | 1,418,884 |
|  | K. Lepage | 32 | 0 | 1 | 3 | 5 | 0 | 1,679,186 |
|  | M. Kenseth | 34 | 1 | 4 | 11 | 5 | 0 | 2,408,138 |
| 2001 | M. Martin | 36 | 0 | 3 | 15 | 4 | 2 | 3,797,006 |
|  | K. Busch | 7 | 0 | 0 | 0 | 0 | 0 | 311,915 |
|  | J. Burton | 36 | 2 | 8 | 16 | 1 | 0 | 4,230,737 |
|  | M. Kenseth | 36 | 0 | 4 | 9 | 5 | 0 | 2,565,579 |
|  | K. Busch | 35 | 0 | 3 | 6 | 7 | 1 | 2,170,629 |
| 2002 | M. Martin | 36 | 1 | 12 | 22 | 3 | 0 | 7,004,893 |
|  | J. Burton | 36 | 0 | 5 | 14 | 5 | 0 | 4,244,856 |
|  | K. Busch | 36 | 4 | 12 | 20 | 4 | 1 | 5,105,394 |
|  | M. Kenseth | 36 | 5 | 11 | 19 | 3 | 1 | 4,514,203 |
|  | G Biffle | 1 | 0 | 0 | 0 | 0 | 0 | 80,059 |
| 2003 | M. Kenseth | 36 | 1 | 11 | 25 | 2 | 0 | 4,038,120 |
|  | M. Martin | 36 | 0 | 5 | 10 | 7 | 0 | 4,048,850 |
|  | K. Busch | 36 | 4 | 9 | 14 | 8 | 0 | 5,020,480 |
|  | G. Biffle | 35 | 1 | 2 | 6 | 6 | 0 | 2,410,050 |
|  | J. Burton | 36 | 0 | 3 | 11 | 4 | 0 | 3,846,880 |
| TOTALS |  | 1530 | 66 | 369 | 639 | 200 | 50 | $115,567,452 |

## Morgan Shepherd

**Date of birth:** 10/12/41. **Hometown:** Conover, N.C. **Resides:** Conover, N.C. **Years as NNCS Owner:** 1. **Best points finish:** 69. **Career victories:** 0. **Career poles:** 0.

### CAREER NASCAR WINSTON CUP SERIES STATS

| Year | Driver | Races | Won | Top 5 | Top 10 | DNF | Poles | Money Won |
|---|---|---|---|---|---|---|---|---|
| 2003 | M. Shepard | 2 | 0 | 0 | 0 | 2 | 0 | $120,034 |

## Jim Smith

**Date of birth:** 3/28/4. **Hometown:** Altadena, Calif. **Resides:** Orange, Calif. **Years as NNCS Owner:** 6. **Best points finish:** 27. **Career victories:** 0. **First victory:** 0. **Career poles:** 0. **First pole:** 0

- Owner in NASCAR Craftsman Truck Series since its inception.

### CAREER NASCAR WINSTON CUP SERIES STATS

| Year | Driver | Races | Won | Top 5 | Top 10 | DNF | Poles | Money Won |
|---|---|---|---|---|---|---|---|---|
| 1998 | G. Bodine | 32 | 0 | 1 | 5 | 10 | 0 | $1,247,255 |
| 1999 | M. Waltrip | 34 | 0 | 1 | 3 | 10 | 0 | 1,702,460 |
| 2000 | M. Waltrip | 34 | 0 | 1 | 1 | 10 | 0 | 1,690,821 |
| 2001 | M. Wallace | 21 | 0 | 0 | 4 | 3 | 0 | 1,394,697 |
|  | K. Lepage | 8 | 0 | 0 | 0 | 0 | 0 | 458,860 |
|  | R. Gordon | 2 | 0 | 1 | 1 | 0 | 0 | 167,335 |
|  | T. Musgrave | 1 | 0 | 0 | 0 | 0 | 0 | 43,565 |
| 2002 | C. Atwood | 34 | 0 | 0 | 0 | 5 | 0 | 1,951,079 |
|  | T. Musgrave | 4 | 0 | 0 | 0 | 0 | 0 | 225,320 |
|  | J. Leffler | 2 | 0 | 0 | 0 | 0 | 0 | 78,500 |
| 2003 | J. Spencer | 35 | 0 | 1 | 4 | 8 | 0 | 2,565,800 |
|  | T. Musgrave | 1 | 0 | 0 | 0 | 0 | 0 | 63,715 |
| TOTALS |  | 208 | 0 | 5 | 18 | 46 | 0 | $11,589,407 |

* Co-owner with Jim Mattei 1998 through Oct. 22, 2000

## Cal Wells

**Date of birth:** 10/12/55. **Hometown:** Pomona, Calif. **Resides:** San Juan Capistrano, Calif. and Hickory, N.C. **Years as NNCS Owner:** 4. **Best points finish:** 15. **Career victories:** 2. **First victory:** 2001 Martinsville. **Career poles:** 3. **First pole:** 2001 Michigan

- Built and raced his own off-road truck at age 15.
- Has fielded competitive teams in off-road, CART, Formula Atlantic and NASCAR.
- Earned 25 off-road championships and one Formula Atlantic title as a car owner.
- Founded Precision Preparation, Inc., in 1979 as his sole business interest; remains so today.

## OWNERS

### CAREER NASCAR WINSTON CUP SERIES STATS

| Year | Driver | Races | Won | Top 5 | Top 10 | DNF | Poles | Money Won |
|------|--------|-------|-----|-------|--------|-----|-------|-----------|
| 2000 | S. Pruett | 28 | 0 | 0 | 1 | 11 | 0 | $1,135,854 |
|      | A. Houston | 5 | 0 | 0 | 0 | 2 | 0 | 141,850 |
| 2001 | R. Craven | 36 | 1 | 4 | 7 | 9 | 1 | 1,996,981 |
|      | A. Houston | 17 | 0 | 0 | 0 | 9 | 0 | 865,263 |
| 2002 | R. Craven | 36 | 0 | 3 | 9 | 4 | 2 | 2,838,087 |
| 2003 | R. Craven | 36 | 1 | 3 | 8 | 10 | 0 | 3,116,210 |
| TOTALS | | 158 | 2 | 10 | 25 | 45 | 3 | $10,094,245 |

## Wood Brothers

**Owner:** Glen Wood. **Date of birth:** 7/18/25. **Hometown:** Stuart, Va. **Resides:** Stuart, Va. **Years as NNCS Owner:** 51. **Best points finish:** 1. **Career victories:** 97. **First victory:** 1960 Winston-Salem. **Career poles:** 115. **First pole:** 1958 N.Wilkesboro

- At least one win in each of past 5 decades – 60s, 70s, 80s, 90s and 2000s.
- Ran Sportsman Class on the beach at Daytona in 1953 and '54.
- 13 of NASCAR's 50 greatest drivers list drove for Wood Brothers Racing.
- Wood Brothers Racing has been in existence for 52 years.
- Drivers have included David Pearson, Cale Yarborough, Neil Bonnett, Marvin Panch, A.J. Foyt, Dan Gurney, Kyle Petty, Buddy Baker and Dale Jarrett.

### CAREER NASCAR WINSTON CUP SERIES STATS

| Year | Driver | Races | Won | Top 5 | Top 10 | DNF | Poles | Money Won |
|------|--------|-------|-----|-------|--------|-----|-------|-----------|
| 1953 | G. Wood | 2 | 0 | 0 | 0 | 1 | 0 | $125 |
| 1954 | G. Wood | 1 | 0 | 0 | 0 | 1 | 0 | 0 |
| 1955 | G. Wood | 1 | 0 | 0 | 0 | 1 | 0 | 0 |
| 1956 | G. Wood | 1 | 0 | 0 | 0 | 1 | 0 | 50 |
| 1957 | G. Wood | 2 | 0 | 0 | 0 | 1 | 0 | 300 |
| 1958 | G. Wood | 5 | 0 | 1 | 5 | 0 | 1 | 1,500 |
| 1959 | G. Wood | 16 | 0 | 7 | 10 | 4 | 2 | 4,010 |
| 1960 | G. Wood | 9 | 3 | 6 | 7 | 2 | 4 | 4,910 |
|      | J. Massey | 3 | 0 | 2 | 2 | 1 | 0 | 2,085 |
|      | S. Thompson | 3 | 2 | 3 | 3 | 0 | 0 | 15,985 |
|      | F. Harb | 2 | 0 | 0 | 1 | 1 | 0 | 475 |
|      | J. Johnson | 2 | 0 | 1 | 1 | 1 | 1 | 345 |
|      | C. Turner | 1 | 0 | 0 | 0 | 1 | 0 | 50 |
|      | B. Welborn | 1 | 0 | 0 | 0 | 1 | 0 | 125 |

| Year | Driver | Races | Won | Top 5 | Top 10 | DNF | Poles | Money Won |
|------|--------|-------|-----|-------|--------|-----|-------|-----------|
| 1961 | G. Wood | 6 | 0 | 3 | 3 | 3 | 1 | 2,000 |
|      | C. Turner | 7 | 0 | 1 | 1 | 6 | 0 | 5,960 |
|      | B. Matthews | 1 | 0 | 0 | 0 | 1 | 0 | 100 |
|      | S. Thompson | 1 | 0 | 0 | 0 | 1 | 0 | 825 |
| 1962 | M. Panch | 14 | 0 | 5 | 8 | 5 | 0 | 23,470 |
| 1963 | M. Panch | 12 | 1 | 9 | 12 | 0 | 3 | 37,461 |
|      | T. Lund | 7 | 1 | 5 | 6 | 1 | 0 | 33,645 |
|      | G. Wood | 3 | 1 | 2 | 2 | 1 | 2 | 1,070 |
|      | D. MacDonald | 1 | 0 | 1 | 1 | 0 | 0 | 4,655 |
|      | F. Lorenzen | 1 | 0 | 0 | 0 | 1 | 0 | 530 |
| 1964 | M. Panch | 29 | 3 | 17 | 18 | 10 | 5 | 31,785 |
|      | D. Gurney | 1 | 1 | 1 | 1 | 0 | 0 | 12,870 |
|      | G. Wood | 2 | 0 | 1 | 1 | 1 | 1 | 530 |
| 1965 | M. Panch | 20 | 4 | 12 | 14 | 6 | 5 | 54,045 |
|      | C. Turner | 4 | 1 | 3 | 3 | 1 | 0 | 16,643 |
|      | D. Gurney | 1 | 1 | 1 | 1 | 0 | 0 | 13,625 |
|      | A.J. Foyt | 1 | 0 | 0 | 1 | 0 | 0 | 1,775 |
| 1966 | M. Panch | 6 | 0 | 1 | 1 | 5 | 0 | 3,700 |
|      | C. Turner | 6 | 0 | 2 | 2 | 3 | 0 | 6,760 |
|      | D. Gurney | 1 | 1 | 1 | 1 | 0 | 0 | 18,445 |
|      | C. Yarborough | 5 | 0 | 1 | 1 | 3 | 0 | 4,350 |
| 1967 | C. Yarborough | 15 | 2 | 7 | 7 | 8 | 4 | 56,310 |
|      | P. Jones | 1 | 1 | 1 | 1 | 0 | 0 | 18,720 |
|      | Balmer | 1 | 0 | 0 | 0 | 1 | 0 | 625 |
| 1968 | C. Yarborough | 20 | 6 | 12 | 12 | 8 | 4 | 136,536 |
|      | D. Gurney | 1 | 1 | 1 | 1 | 0 | 1 | 21,250 |
| 1969 | C. Yarborough | 19 | 2 | 7 | 8 | 11 | 6 | 74,240 |
| 1970 | C. Yarborough | 18 | 3 | 11 | 12 | 6 | 5 | 114,675 |
| 1971 | D. Allison | 11 | 1 | 7 | 8 | 3 | 5 | 68,245 |
|      | A.J. Foyt | 4 | 2 | 4 | 4 | 0 | 4 | 86,775 |
| 1972 | D. Pearson | 14 | 6 | 11 | 11 | 3 | 4 | 131,415 |
|      | A.J. Foyt | 6 | 2 | 5 | 5 | 1 | 3 | 94,440 |
| 1973 | D. Pearson | 18 | 11 | 14 | 14 | 4 | 8 | 213,966 |
| 1974 | D. Pearson | 19 | 7 | 15 | 15 | 4 | 11 | 221,615 |
| 1975 | D. Pearson | 21 | 3 | 13 | 13 | 8 | 7 | 179,208 |
| 1976 | D. Pearson | 22 | 10 | 16 | 18 | 4 | 8 | 283,686 |
| 1977 | D. Pearson | 22 | 2 | 16 | 16 | 6 | 5 | 180,999 |
| 1978 | D. Pearson | 22 | 4 | 11 | 11 | 11 | 7 | 151,837 |
| 1979 | D. Pearson | 5 | 0 | 1 | 1 | 4 | 1 | 22,815 |
|      | N. Bonnett | 17 | 3 | 4 | 6 | 11 | 4 | 131,875 |
| 1980 | N. Bonnett | 22 | 2 | 10 | 13 | 9 | 0 | 210,547 |
| 1981 | N. Bonnett | 22 | 3 | 7 | 8 | 14 | 1 | 181,670 |
| 1982 | N. Bonnett | 22 | 1 | 6 | 8 | 13 | 0 | 130,964 |
| 1983 | Buddy Baker | 21 | 1 | 5 | 12 | 8 | 1 | 206,355 |
| 1984 | Buddy Baker | 21 | 0 | 4 | 12 | 7 | 1 | 133,635 |
|      | B. Rahal | 1 | 0 | 0 | 0 | 1 | 0 | 875 |
| 1985 | K. Petty | 28 | 0 | 7 | 12 | 4 | 0 | 296,367 |
| 1986 | K. Petty | 29 | 0 | 4 | 14 | 6 | 0 | 403,242 |
| 1987 | K. Petty | 29 | 1 | 6 | 14 | 4 | 0 | 544,437 |
| 1988 | K. Petty | 29 | 0 | 2 | 8 | 6 | 0 | 377,092 |
| 1989 | N. Bonnett | 26 | 0 | 0 | 11 | 5 | 0 | 271,628 |
|      | T. Ellis | 3 | 0 | 0 | 0 | 1 | 0 | 15,385 |

| Year | Driver | Races | Won | Top 5 | Top 10 | DNF | Poles | Money Won |
|---|---|---|---|---|---|---|---|---|
| 1990 | D. Jarrett | 24 | 0 | 1 | 7 | 9 | 0 | 214,495 |
|  | N. Bonnett | 5 | 0 | 0 | 0 | 3 | 0 | 62,600 |
| 1991 | D. Jarrett | 29 | 1 | 3 | 8 | 9 | 0 | 444,256 |
| 1992 | M. Shepherd | 29 | 0 | 3 | 11 | 3 | 0 | 634,222 |
| 1993 | M. Shepherd | 30 | 1 | 3 | 15 | 2 | 0 | 782,523 |
| 1994 | M. Shepherd | 31 | 0 | 9 | 16 | 2 | 0 | 1,089,038 |
| 1995 | M. Shepherd | 31 | 0 | 4 | 10 | 2 | 0 | 966,374 |
| 1996 | M. Waltrip | 31 | 0 | 1 | 11 | 3 | 0 | 1,182,811 |
| 1997 | M. Waltrip | 32 | 0 | 0 | 6 | 4 | 0 | 1,138,599 |
| 1998 | M. Waltrip | 32 | 0 | 0 | 5 | 3 | 0 | 1,508,680 |
| 1999 | E. Sadler | 34 | 0 | 0 | 1 | 2 | 0 | 1,589,221 |
| 2000 | E. Sadler | 33 | 0 | 0 | 1 | 5 | 0 | 1,578,356 |
| 2001 | E. Sadler | 36 | 1 | 2 | 2 | 2 | 0 | 2,683,225 |
| 2002 | E. Sadler | 36 | 0 | 2 | 7 | 6 | 0 | 3,491,694 |
| 2003 | R. Rudd | 36 | 0 | 4 | 5 | 9 | 0 | 3,106,610 |
| TOTALS |  | 1136 | 97 | 325 | 486 | 299 | 115 | $25,738,337 |

## Robert Yates

**Date of birth:** 4/19/43. **Hometown:** Charlotte, N.C. **Resides:** Cornelius, N.C. **Years as NNCS Owner:** 15. **Best points finish:** 1. **Career victories:** 54. **First victory:** 1989 Talladega. **Career poles:** 40. **First pole:** 1989 Dover.

- Enjoys motorcycles.
- Father was a pastor.

## CAREER NASCAR WINSTON CUP SERIES STATS

| Year | Driver | Races | Won | Top 5 | Top 10 | DNF | Poles | Money Won |
|---|---|---|---|---|---|---|---|---|
| 1989 | Da. Allison | 29 | 2 | 7 | 13 | 6 | 1 | $640,956 |
| 1990 | Da. Allison | 29 | 2 | 5 | 10 | 2 | 0 | 640,684 |
| 1991 | Da. Allison | 29 | 5 | 12 | 16 | 4 | 3 | 1,732,924 |
| 1992 | Da. Allison | 29 | 5 | 15 | 17 | 3 | 2 | 1,955,628 |
| 1993 | Da. Allison | 16 | 1 | 6 | 8 | 1 | 0 | 513,585 |
|  | E. Irvan | 9 | 2 | 5 | 6 | 1 | 2 | 584,483 |
|  | L. Speed | 3 | 0 | 0 | 1 | 0 | 0 | 60,620 |
|  | R. Gordon | 1 | 0 | 0 | 0 | 1 | 0 | 17,665 |
| 1994 | E. Irvan | 20 | 3 | 13 | 15 | 3 | 5 | 1,311,522 |
|  | K. Wallace | 10 | 0 | 1 | 2 | 1 | 0 | 211,810 |
| 1995 | E. Irvan | 3 | 0 | 0 | 2 | 1 | 0 | 54,875 |
|  | D. Jarrett | 31 | 1 | 9 | 14 | 6 | 1 | 1,363,158 |
| 1996 | E. Irvan | 31 | 2 | 12 | 16 | 5 | 1 | 1,683,313 |
|  | D. Jarrett | 31 | 4 | 17 | 21 | 3 | 2 | 2,985,418 |
| 1997 | E. Irvan | 32 | 1 | 5 | 13 | 8 | 2 | 1,614,281 |
|  | D. Jarrett | 32 | 7 | 20 | 23 | 1 | 2 | 3,240,542 |
| 1998 | D. Jarrett | 33 | 3 | 19 | 22 | 3 | 2 | 4,019,657 |
|  | K. Irwin | 32 | 0 | 1 | 4 | 8 | 1 | 1,459,867 |
| 1999 | D. Jarrett | 34 | 4 | 24 | 29 | 1 | 0 | 6,649,596 |
|  | K. Irwin | 34 | 0 | 2 | 6 | 5 | 2 | 2,125,810 |
| 2000 | D. Jarrett | 34 | 2 | 15 | 24 | 2 | 3 | 5,934,475 |
|  | R. Rudd | 34 | 0 | 12 | 19 | 1 | 2 | 2,914,970 |
| 2001 | D. Jarrett | 36 | 4 | 12 | 19 | 4 | 4 | 5,377,742 |
|  | R. Rudd | 36 | 2 | 14 | 22 | 4 | 1 | 4,878,027 |
| 2002 | D. Jarrett | 36 | 2 | 10 | 18 | 5 | 1 | 4,421,951 |
|  | R. Rudd | 36 | 1 | 8 | 12 | 4 | 1 | 4,444,614 |
| 2003 | D. Jarrett | 36 | 1 | 1 | 7 | 9 | 0 | 4,055,490 |
|  | E. Sadler | 36 | 0 | 1 | 9 | 9 | 2 | 3,660,170 |
|  | J. Jarrett | 1 | 0 | 0 | 0 | 0 | 0 | 52,640 |
| TOTALS |  | 753 | 54 | 246 | 368 | 101 | 40 | $68,606,473 |

# Crew chiefs

## Paul Andrews

**Date of birth:** 5/25/57. **Hometown:** Bangor, Maine. **Resides:** Harrisburg, N.C. **Team:** No. 99 Ford. **Years with current team:** 2. **Years as crew chief:** 2. **Overall years as crew chief:** 16. **Best points finish:** 1. **Career victories:** 12. **First victory:** 1988 Phoenix. **Career poles:** 30. **First pole:** 1988 Dover.

### CAREER NASCAR WINSTON CUP SERIES STATS

| Year | Driver | Races | Won | Top 5 | Top 10 | DNF | Poles | Money Won |
|---|---|---|---|---|---|---|---|---|
| 1988 | A. Kulwicki | 29 | 1 | 7 | 9 | 12 | 4 | $448,547 |
| 1989 | A. Kulwicki | 29 | 0 | 5 | 9 | 11 | 6 | 501,295 |
| 1990 | A. Kulwicki | 29 | 1 | 5 | 13 | 6 | 1 | 550,936 |
| 1991 | A. Kulwicki | 29 | 1 | 4 | 11 | 7 | 4 | 595,614 |
| 1992 | A. Kulwicki | 29 | 2 | 11 | 17 | 2 | 6 | 2,322,561 |
| 1993 | A. Kulwicki | 5 | 0 | 2 | 3 | 1 | 0 | 165,470 |
|  | J. Hensley | 15 | 0 | 0 | 2 | 3 | 0 | 294,970 |
|  | T. Kendall | 2 | 0 | 0 | 0 | 0 | 0 | 32,190 |
|  | G. Bodine | 7 | 0 | 0 | 1 | 4 | 0 | 170,012 |
| 1994 | G. Bodine | 31 | 3 | 7 | 10 | 15 | 5 | 1,276,126 |
| 1995 | G. Bodine | 31 | 0 | 1 | 4 | 5 | 0 | 1,011,090 |
| 1996 | G. Bodine | 31 | 1 | 2 | 6 | 5 | 0 | 1,031,762 |
| 1997 | J. Mayfield | 32 | 0 | 3 | 8 | 3 | 0 | 1,067,203 |
| 1998 | J. Mayfield | 33 | 1 | 12 | 16 | 2 | 1 | 2,332,034 |
| 1999 | J. Mayfield | 11 | 0 | 3 | 4 | 1 | 0 | 733,894 |
|  | S. Park | 23 | 0 | 0 | 5 | 3 | 0 | 1,243,389 |
| 2000 | S. Park | 34 | 1 | 6 | 13 | 4 | 2 | 2,283,629 |
| 2001 | S. Park | 24 | 1 | 5 | 12 | 2 | 0 | 2,495,490 |
|  | K. Wallace | 12 | 0 | 1 | 2 | 1 | 1 | 965,030 |
| 2002 | S. Park | 21 | 0 | 0 | 2 | 5 | 0 | 1,750,949 |
|  | K. Wallace | 4 | 0 | 0 | 0 | 0 | 0 | 418,105 |
|  | J. Burton | 11 | 0 | 2 | 4 | 1 | 0 | 1,163,762 |
| 2003 | J. Burton | 36 | 0 | 3 | 11 | 4 | 0 | 4,384,752 |
| TOTALS |  | 508 | 12 | 79 | 162 | 97 | 30 | $27,238,806 |

## Tommy Baldwin

**Date of birth:** 10/27/66. **Hometown:** Bellport, N.Y. **Resides:** Mooresville, N.C. **Team:** No. 9 Dodge. **Years with current team:** First. **Years as crew chief:** First. **Overall years as crew chief:** 7. **Best points finish:** 9. **Career victories:** 4. **First victory:** 2000 Darlington. **Career poles:** 2. **First pole:** 1999 Michigan.

### CAREER NASCAR WINSTON CUP SERIES STATS

| Year | Driver | Races | Won | Top 5 | Top 10 | DNF | Poles | Money Won |
|---|---|---|---|---|---|---|---|---|
| 1997 | Greg Sacks | 6 | 0 | 0 | 3 | 0 | 0 | $149,269 |
|  | Lance Hooper | 1 | 0 | 0 | 0 | 0 | 0 | 21,820 |
|  | Dick Trickle | 19 | 0 | 2 | 2 | 4 | 0 | 422,759 |
|  | D. Schroeder | 1 | 0 | 0 | 0 | 0 | 0 | 11,630 |
| 1998 | D. Trickle | 24 | 0 | 0 | 1 | 6 | 0 | 978,646 |
|  | W. Burton | 8 | 0 | 5 | 6 | 1 | 0 | 954,592 |
| 1999 | W. Burton | 34 | 0 | 6 | 16 | 3 | 1 | 2,405,913 |
| 2000 | W. Burton | 34 | 1 | 4 | 17 | 4 | 0 | 2,669,604 |
| 2001 | W. Burton | 36 | 1 | 6 | 10 | 9 | 0 | 3,583,692 |
| 2002 | W. Burton | 29 | 2 | 2 | 6 | 7 | 1 | 4,205,319 |
| 2003 | J. Spencer | 35 | 0 | 1 | 4 | 8 | 0 | 2,565,800 |
| TOTALS |  | 227 | 4 | 26 | 62 | 46 | 2 | $17,969,044 |

## Robert Barker

**Date of birth:** 3/2/71. **Hometown:** Brookneal, Va. **Resides:** Mooresville, N.C. **Years as crew chief:** 1. **Overall years as crew chief:** 1. **Best points finish:** N/A. **Career victories:** 0. **Career poles:** 1.

### CAREER NASCAR WINSTON CUP SERIES STATS

| Year | Driver | Races | Won | Top 5 | Top 10 | DNF | Poles | Money Won |
|---|---|---|---|---|---|---|---|---|
| 2003 | D. Blaney | 31 | 0 | 1 | 4 | 3 | 1 | $2,515,477 |

## Mike Beam

**Date of birth:** 12/17/55. **Hometown:** Hickory, N.C. **Resides:** Hickory, N.C. **Overall years as crew chief:** 21. **Best points finish:** 4. **Career victories:** 3. **First victory:** 1990 Dover. **Career poles:** 17. **First pole:** 1990 Talladega.

### CAREER NASCAR WINSTON CUP SERIES STATS

| Year | Driver | Races | Won | Top 5 | Top 10 | DNF | Poles | Money Won |
|---|---|---|---|---|---|---|---|---|
| 1981 | K. Petty | 31 | 0 | 1 | 10 | 18 | 0 | $112,289 |
| 1982 | K. Petty | 23 | 0 | 2 | 4 | 13 | 0 | 108,715 |
| 1983 | K. Petty | 30 | 0 | 0 | 2 | 10 | 0 | 157,820 |
| 1984 | K. Petty | 19 | 0 | 1 | 4 | 6 | 0 | 203,195 |
| 1985 | R. Petty | 28 | 0 | 1 | 13 | 12 | 0 | 306,142 |
| 1986 | R. Bouchard | 3 | 0 | 0 | 1 | 0 | 0 | 59,870 |
| 1988 | M. Waltrip | 29 | 0 | 1 | 3 | 8 | 0 | 240,400 |
| 1989 | M. Waltrip | 26 | 0 | 0 | 4 | 9 | 0 | 195,240 |
| 1990 | B. Elliott | 29 | 1 | 12 | 16 | 2 | 2 | 1,090,730 |
| 1991 | S. Marlin | 29 | 0 | 7 | 16 | 2 | 2 | 633,690 |
| 1992 | S. Marlin | 29 | 0 | 6 | 13 | 3 | 5 | 649,048 |
| 1993 | B. Elliott | 30 | 0 | 6 | 15 | 3 | 2 | 955,859 |
| 1994 | B. Elliott | 31 | 1 | 6 | 12 | 5 | 1 | 936,779 |
| 1995 | B. Bodine | 10 | 0 | 0 | 1 | 0 | 0 | 259,481 |
| 1996 | B. Elliott | 24 | 0 | 0 | 6 | 2 | 0 | 716,506 |
|  | T. Kendall | 1 | 0 | 0 | 0 | 0 | 0 | 20,730 |
|  | H. Gant | 0 | 0 | 0 | 0 | 0 | 0 | 18,000 |
|  | T. Bodine | 4 | 0 | 0 | 1 | 1 | 0 | 92,945 |
|  | D. Schroeder | 1 | 0 | 0 | 0 | 0 | 0 | 22,745 |
|  | B. Hillin Jr. | 1 | 0 | 0 | 0 | 0 | 0 | 25,735 |
| 1997 | B. Elliott | 32 | 0 | 5 | 14 | 3 | 1 | 1,607,827 |

| Year | Driver | Races | Won | Top 5 | Top 10 | DNF | Poles | Money Won |
|---|---|---|---|---|---|---|---|---|
| 1999 | E. Sadler | 34 | 0 | 0 | 1 | 2 | 0 | 1,589,221 |
| 2000 | E. Sadler | 29 | 0 | 0 | 1 | 4 | 0 | 1,393,356 |
| 2001 | R. Craven | 36 | 1 | 4 | 7 | 9 | 1 | 1,996,981 |
| 2002 | R. Craven | 36 | 0 | 3 | 9 | 4 | 2 | 2,838,087 |
| 2003 | J. Green | 11 | 0 | 0 | 0 | 2 | 1 | 788,253 |
|  | S. Park | 24 | 0 | 1 | 2 | 3 | 0 | 1,621,925 |
| TOTALS | | 580 | 3 | 56 | 155 | 121 | 17 | $18,641,569 |

## Todd Berrier

**Date of birth:** 5/29/70. **Hometown:** Kernersville, N.C. **Resides:** Winston-Salem, N.C. **Team:** No. 29 Chevrolet. **Years with current team:** 1. **Years as crew chief:** 1. **Overall years as crew chief:** 1. **Best points finish:** 5. **Career victories:** 1. **First victory:** 2003 Indianapolis. **Career poles:** 1. **First pole:** 2003 Rockingham.

### CAREER NASCAR WINSTON CUP SERIES STATS

| Year | Driver | Races | Won | Top 5 | Top 10 | DNF | Poles | Money Won |
|---|---|---|---|---|---|---|---|---|
| 2003 | K. Harvick | 31 | 1 | 10 | 17 | 0 | 1 | $6,237,119 |

## Matt Borland

**Date of birth:** 9/2/71. **Hometown:** Haslett, Mich. **Resides:** Cornelius, N.C. **Team:** No. 12 Dodge. **Years with current team:** 4. **Years as crew chief:** 4. **Overall years as crew chief:** 4. **Best points finish:** 6. **Career victories:** 9. **First victory:** 2002 New Hampshire. **Career poles:** 18. **First pole:** 2001 Charlotte.

### CAREER NASCAR WINSTON CUP SERIES STATS

| Year | Driver | Races | Won | Top 5 | Top 10 | DNF | Poles | Money Won |
|---|---|---|---|---|---|---|---|---|
| 2000 | R. Newman | 1 | 0 | 0 | 0 | 1 | 0 | $37,825 |
| 2001 | R. Newman | 7 | 0 | 2 | 2 | 2 | 1 | 465,276 |
| 2002 | R. Newman | 36 | 1 | 14 | 22 | 5 | 6 | 5,346,651 |
| 2003 | R. Newman | 36 | 8 | 17 | 22 | 7 | 11 | 6,100,877 |
| TOTALS | | 80 | 9 | 33 | 46 | 15 | 18 | $11,950,629 |

## Tim Brewer

**Date of birth:** 2/4/55. **Hometown:** Winston-Salem, N.C. **Resides:** Denver, N.C. **Team:** No. 4 Chevrolet. **Years with current team:** 1. **Years as crew chief:** 1. **Overall years as crew chief:** 28. **Best points finish:** 1. **Career victories:** 53. **First victory:** None. **Career poles:** 54. **First pole:** None.

### CAREER NASCAR WINSTON CUP SERIES STATS

| Year | Driver | Races | Won | Top 5 | Top 10 | DNF | Poles | Money Won |
|---|---|---|---|---|---|---|---|---|
| 1973 | R. Childress | 25 | 0 | 1 | 2 | 11 | 0 | $28,359 |
| 1974 | R. Childress | 29 | 0 | 0 | 3 | 19 | 0 | 32,914 |
| 1975 | R. Childress | 30 | 0 | 2 | 15 | 4 | 0 | 84,280 |
| 1976 | R. Childress | 30 | 0 | 0 | 11 | 9 | 0 | 85,780 |
| 1977 | R. Childress | 30 | 0 | 0 | 11 | 9 | 0 | 97,012 |
| 1978 | C. Yarborough | 30 | 10 | 22 | 23 | 2 | 8 | 530,751 |
| 1979 | C. Yarborough | 31 | 4 | 18 | 21 | 6 | 1 | 413,872 |
| 1980 | C. Yarborough | 31 | 6 | 19 | 22 | 5 | 14 | 537,358 |
| 1981 | D. Waltrip | 31 | 12 | 21 | 25 | 4 | 11 | 693,342 |
| 1982 | C. Yarborough | 16 | 3 | 8 | 8 | 8 | 2 | 219,090 |
| 1983 | T. Richmond | 30 | 1 | 10 | 15 | 13 | 4 | 245,664 |
| 1984 | T. Richmond | 30 | 1 | 6 | 11 | 12 | 0 | 329,589 |
| 1985 | N. Bonnett | 28 | 2 | 11 | 17 | 5 | 1 | 530,145 |
| 1986 | N. Bonnett | 28 | 1 | 6 | 12 | 10 | 0 | 485,930 |
|  | Da. Allison | 1 | 0 | 1 | 1 | 0 | 0 | 17,820 |
| 1987 | T. Labonte | 29 | 1 | 13 | 22 | 5 | 4 | 825,369 |
| 1988 | T. Labonte | 29 | 1 | 11 | 18 | 3 | 1 | 950,781 |
| 1989 | T. Labonte | 29 | 2 | 9 | 11 | 6 | 0 | 704,806 |
| 1990 | G. Bodine | 29 | 3 | 11 | 19 | 3 | 2 | 1,131,222 |
| 1991 | G. Bodine | 25 | 1 | 5 | 10 | 7 | 2 | 602,481 |
|  | T. Ellis | 0 | 0 | 0 | 0 | 0 | 0 | 18,000 |
| 1992 | B. Elliott | 29 | 5 | 13 | 16 | 2 | 2 | 1,692,381 |
| 1993 | B. Labonte | 30 | 0 | 0 | 6 | 6 | 1 | 395,660 |
| 1994 | R. Gordon | 1 | 0 | 0 | 0 | 1 | 0 | 7,965 |
|  | G. Brabham | 1 | 0 | 0 | 0 | 1 | 0 | 27,400 |
| 1995 | J. Andretti | 31 | 0 | 1 | 5 | 7 | 1 | 593,542 |
| 1996 | J. Andretti | 17 | 0 | 0 | 1 | 8 | 0 | 404,391 |
| 1997 | S. Marlin | 14 | 0 | 1 | 3 | 2 | 0 | 636,415 |
| 1998 | G. Bodine | 8 | 0 | 1 | 1 | 4 | 0 | 372,085 |
|  | S. Grissom | 8 | 0 | 0 | 0 | 1 | 0 | 283,172 |
|  | D. Green | 4 | 0 | 0 | 0 | 2 | 0 | 100,595 |
| 1999 | D. Green | 0 | 0 | 0 | 0 | 0 | 0 | 14,359 |
| 2003 | K. Lepage | 11 | 0 | 0 | 0 | 1 | 0 | 742,077 |
| TOTALS | | 695 | 53 | 191 | 311 | 176 | 54 | $13,834,577 |

## Jeff Buckner

**Team:** No. 02 Chevrolet. **Years with current team:** 2. **Years as crew chief:** 2. **Overall years as crew chief:** 2. **Best points finish:** 45. **Career victories:** 0. **Career poles:** 0

### CAREER NASCAR WINSTON CUP SERIES STATS

| Year | Driver | Races | Won | Top 5 | Top 10 | DNF | Poles | Money Won |
|---|---|---|---|---|---|---|---|---|
| 2002 | H. Sadler | 10 | 0 | 0 | 0 | 3 | 0 | $473,690 |
| 2003 | H. Sadler | 10 | 0 | 0 | 0 | 8 | 0 | 552,741 |
| TOTALS | | 20 | 0 | 0 | 0 | 11 | 0 | $1,026,431 |

## Chris Carrier

**Date of birth:** 4/6/60. **Hometown:** Bristol, Tenn. **Resides:** Fariview, N.C. **Overall years as crew chief:** 3. **Best points finish:** 28. **Career victories:** 1. **First victory:** 2001 Rockingham. **Career poles:** 0

# CREW CHIEFS

## CAREER NASCAR WINSTON CUP SERIES STATS

| Year | Driver | Races | Won | Top 5 | Top 10 | DNF | Poles | Money Won |
|---|---|---|---|---|---|---|---|---|
| 2001 | J. Nemechek | 31 | 1 | 1 | 4 | 6 | 0 | $2,543,660 |
| 2002 | M. Wallace | 3 | 0 | 0 | 0 | 1 | 0 | 316,357 |
| | M. Skinner | 25 | 0 | 0 | 1 | 5 | 0 | 1,364,330 |
| 2003 | M. Skinner | 14 | 0 | 0 | 0 | 4 | 0 | 945,373 |
| | J. Sauter | 2 | 0 | 0 | 0 | 0 | 0 | 116,525 |
| TOTALS | | 75 | 1 | 0 | 5 | 16 | 0 | $5,306,636 |

## Larry Carter

**Date of birth:** 9/21/62. **Hometown:** Raleigh, N.C. **Resides:** Mooresville, N.C. **Team:** No. 74 Chevrolet. **Years with current team:** 1 **Years as crew chief:** 3. **Overall years as crew chief:** 3. **Best points finish:** 29. **Career victories:** 0. **Career poles:** 3 **First pole:** 1997 Watkins Glen

### CAREER NASCAR WINSTON CUP SERIES STATS

| Year | Driver | Races | Won | Top 5 | Top 10 | DNF | Poles | Money Won |
|---|---|---|---|---|---|---|---|---|
| 2000 | D. Waltrip | 28 | 0 | 0 | 0 | 7 | 0 | $1,212,940 |
| 2001 | T. Bodine | 35 | 0 | 2 | 2 | 12 | 3 | 1,740,315 |
| 2003 | T. Raines | 35 | 0 | 0 | 0 | 3 | 0 | 2,448,782 |
| TOTALS | | 98 | 0 | 2 | 2 | 22 | 3 | $5,402,037 |

## Dennis Conner

**Date of birth:** 1/5/51. **Hometown:** Sylva, N.C. **Resides:** Concord, N.C. **Overall years as crew chief:** 26. **Best points finish:** 5. **Career victories:** 2. **First victory:** 1987 Pocono. **Career poles:** 9. **First pole:** 1987 Pocono.

### CAREER NASCAR WINSTON CUP SERIES STATS

| Year | Driver | Races | Won | Top 5 | Top 10 | DNF | Poles | Money Won |
|---|---|---|---|---|---|---|---|---|
| 1987 | T. Richmond | 7 | 1 | 2 | 3 | 2 | 1 | $71,525 |
| | J. Means | 1 | 0 | 0 | 0 | 1 | 0 | 5,960 |
| | R. Hendrick | 1 | 0 | 0 | 0 | 1 | 0 | 1,150 |
| 1988 | K. Schrader | 28 | 1 | 4 | 17 | 6 | 2 | 626,934 |
| 1989 | K. Schrader | 22 | 0 | 6 | 9 | 6 | 3 | 686,140 |
| | J. Spencer | 5 | 0 | 0 | 1 | 2 | 0 | 34,995 |
| 1990 | H. Stricklin | 1 | 0 | 0 | 0 | 1 | 0 | 2,765 |
| 1991 | Venturini | 1 | 0 | 0 | 0 | 1 | 0 | 3,375 |
| | L. Pearson | 2 | 0 | 0 | 0 | 1 | 0 | 8,700 |
| 1992 | G. Sacks | 20 | 0 | 0 | 0 | 6 | 0 | 178,120 |
| | D. Marcis | 7 | 0 | 0 | 0 | 3 | 0 | 43,060 |
| | H. Stricklin | 2 | 0 | 0 | 0 | 1 | 0 | 13,670 |
| 1993 | J. O'Neil | 1 | 0 | 0 | 0 | 1 | 0 | 10,950 |
| | G. Sacks | 3 | 0 | 0 | 0 | 0 | 0 | 18,750 |
| | Loy Allen Jr. | 1 | 0 | 0 | 0 | 0 | 0 | 6,560 |
| 1994 | Loy Allen Jr. | 12 | 0 | 0 | 0 | 4 | 3 | 169,656 |
| | J. Hensley | 1 | 0 | 0 | 0 | 1 | 0 | 4,455 |
| | B. Hillin Jr. | 1 | 0 | 0 | 0 | 1 | 0 | 6,100 |
| 2003 | L. Foyt | 3 | 0 | 0 | 0 | 0 | 0 | 144,260 |
| TOTALS | | 119 | 2 | 12 | 29 | 33 | 9 | $2,048,075 |

## Ernie Cope

**Date of birth:** 7/17/69. **Hometown:** Tacoma, Wash. **Resides:** Huntersville, N.C. **Team:** No. 37 Chevrolet. **Years as crew chief:** 1. **Overall years as crew chief:** 1. **Best points finish:** 46. **Career victories:** 0. **Career poles:** 0

### CAREER NASCAR WINSTON CUP SERIES STATS

| Year | Driver | Races | Won | Top 5 | Top 10 | DNF | Poles | Money Won |
|---|---|---|---|---|---|---|---|---|
| 2003 | D. Cope | 18 | 0 | 0 | 0 | 12 | 0 | $1,030,690 |

## Scott Eggleston

**Date of birth:** 5/13/62. **Hometown:** Springfield, Va. **Resides:** Mooresville, N.C. **Team:** No. 49 Dodge. **Years with current team:** 1. **Years as crew chief:** 1. **Overall years as crew chief:** 6. **Best points finish:** 14. **Career victories:** 1. **First victory:** 2001 Daytona. **Career poles:** 1. **First pole:** 1999 Pocono.

### CAREER NASCAR WINSTON CUP SERIES STATS

| Year | Driver | Races | Won | Top 5 | Top 10 | DNF | Poles | Money Won |
|---|---|---|---|---|---|---|---|---|
| 1998 | J. Nemechek | 32 | 0 | 1 | 4 | 5 | 0 | $1,343,991 |
| 1999 | J. Nemechek | 12 | 0 | 0 | 1 | 3 | 0 | 567,511 |
| | S. Marlin | 22 | 0 | 2 | 4 | 1 | 1 | 1,148,795 |
| 2000 | S. Marlin | 34 | 0 | 1 | 7 | 4 | 0 | 1,992,301 |
| 2001 | M. Waltrip | 13 | 1 | 1 | 1 | 2 | 0 | 1,983,799 |
| | K. Lepage | 13 | 0 | 0 | 0 | 2 | 0 | 579,161 |
| | B. Hamilton Jr. | 7 | 0 | 0 | 0 | 2 | 0 | 305,705 |
| | R. Bickle Jr. | 1 | 0 | 0 | 0 | 0 | 0 | 30,300 |
| 2002 | M. Skinner | 11 | 0 | 0 | 0 | 1 | 0 | 762,478 |
| 2003 | K. Schrader | 32 | 0 | 0 | 2 | 8 | 0 | 2,007,420 |
| TOTALS | | 177 | 1 | 5 | 19 | 28 | 1 | $10,721,461 |

## Jimmy Elledge

**Date of birth:** 7/14/70. **Hometown:** Redding, Calif. **Resides:** Arden, N.C. **Team:** No. 41 Dodge. **Years with current team:** 1. **Years as crew chief:** 1. **Overall years as crew chief:** 6. **Best points finish:** 18. **Career victories:** 1. **First victory:** 2001 Talladega. **Career poles:** 0

### CAREER NASCAR WINSTON CUP SERIES STATS

| Year | Driver | Races | Won | Top 5 | Top 10 | DNF | Poles | Money Won |
|---|---|---|---|---|---|---|---|---|
| 1998 | H. Stricklin | 1 | 0 | 0 | 0 | 1 | 0 | $24,250 |
| 1999 | K. Wallace | 34 | 0 | 3 | 5 | 7 | 0 | 1,416,208 |
| 2000 | K. Wallace | 34 | 0 | 1 | 1 | 6 | 0 | 1,723,966 |
| 2001 | B. Hamilton | 36 | 1 | 3 | 7 | 0 | 0 | 2,527,310 |
| 2002 | D. Jarrett | 6 | 0 | 0 | 1 | 2 | 0 | 663,433 |
| | B. Hamilton | 20 | 0 | 0 | 2 | 0 | 0 | 1,385,577 |
| 2003 | C. Mears | 36 | 0 | 0 | 0 | 10 | 0 | 2,639,180 |
| TOTALS | | 131 | 1 | 7 | 16 | 26 | 0 | $10,379,924 |

## Tony Eury Sr.

**Date of birth:** 12/11/53. **Hometown:** Kannapolis, N.C. **Resides:** Kannapolis, N.C. **Team:** No. 8 Budweiser Chevrolet. **Years with current team:** 5. **Years as crew chief:** 5. **Overall years as crew chief:** 5. **Best points finish:** 3. **Career victories:** 9. **First victory:** 2000 Texas. **Career poles:** 6. **First pole:** 2000 Charlotte

### CAREER NASCAR WINSTON CUP SERIES STATS

| Year | Driver | Races | Won | Top 5 | Top 10 | DNF | Poles | Money Won |
|---|---|---|---|---|---|---|---|---|
| 1999 | Earnhardt Jr. | 5 | 0 | 0 | 1 | 1 | 0 | $162,095 |
| 2000 | Earnhardt Jr. | 34 | 2 | 3 | 5 | 7 | 2 | 2,801,881 |
| 2001 | Earnhardt Jr. | 36 | 3 | 9 | 15 | 4 | 2 | 5,827,542 |
| 2002 | Earnhardt Jr. | 36 | 2 | 11 | 16 | 3 | 2 | 4,970,034 |
| 2003 | Earnhardt Jr. | 36 | 2 | 13 | 21 | 4 | 0 | 6,880,807 |
| TOTALS | | 147 | 9 | 36 | 58 | 19 | 6 | $20,742,359 |

## Jimmy Fennig

**Date of birth:** 9/15/53. **Hometown:** Milwaukee, Wis. **Resides:** Charlotte, N.C. **Team:** No. 97 Ford. **Years with current team:** 2. **Years as crew chief:** 2. **Overall years as crew chief:** 18. **Best points finish:** 2. **Career victories:** 24. **First victory:** 1987 Daytona. **Career poles:** 12. **First pole:** 1987 Charlotte

### CAREER NASCAR WINSTON CUP SERIES STATS

| Year | Driver | Races | Won | Top 5 | Top 10 | DNF | Poles | Money Won |
|---|---|---|---|---|---|---|---|---|
| 1986 | M. Martin | 5 | 0 | 0 | 0 | 2 | 0 | $20,515 |
| 1987 | B. Allison | 29 | 1 | 4 | 13 | 9 | 1 | 515,894 |
| 1988 | B. Allison | 13 | 1 | 3 | 6 | 1 | 0 | 409,295 |
| | M. Alexander | 16 | 0 | 2 | 6 | 2 | 0 | 200,709 |
| 1989 | M. Alexander | 1 | 0 | 0 | 0 | 0 | 0 | 16,275 |
| | D. Trickle | 28 | 0 | 6 | 9 | 8 | 0 | 343,728 |
| 1990 | M. Alexander | 7 | 0 | 0 | 0 | 2 | 0 | 41,080 |
| | J. Purvis | 1 | 0 | 0 | 0 | 1 | 0 | 3,300 |
| | H. Stricklin | 21 | 0 | 0 | 2 | 7 | 0 | 143,909 |
| 1991 | H. Stricklin | 29 | 0 | 3 | 7 | 6 | 0 | 426,524 |
| 1992 | H. Stricklin | 21 | 0 | 0 | 4 | 7 | 0 | 299,935 |
| | J. Purvis | 4 | 0 | 0 | 0 | 2 | 0 | 34,920 |
| | J. Spencer | 4 | 0 | 3 | 3 | 0 | 0 | 103,905 |
| 1993 | J. Spencer | 30 | 0 | 5 | 10 | 4 | 0 | 686,026 |
| 1994 | C. Bown | 13 | 0 | 0 | 1 | 3 | 1 | 225,260 |
| | T. Steele | 5 | 0 | 0 | 0 | 4 | 0 | 65,000 |
| | D. Cope | 12 | 0 | 0 | 2 | 3 | 0 | 178,140 |
| 1995 | D. Cope | 31 | 0 | 2 | 8 | 5 | 0 | 683,075 |
| 1996 | D. Cope | 27 | 0 | 0 | 3 | 9 | 0 | 640,641 |
| 1997 | M. Martin | 32 | 4 | 16 | 23 | 3 | 3 | 2,532,484 |
| 1998 | M. Martin | 33 | 7 | 22 | 26 | 1 | 3 | 4,309,006 |
| 1999 | M. Martin | 34 | 2 | 19 | 26 | 3 | 1 | 3,509,744 |
| 2000 | M. Martin | 34 | 1 | 13 | 20 | 6 | 0 | 3,098,874 |
| 2001 | M. Martin | 36 | 0 | 3 | 15 | 4 | 2 | 3,797,006 |
| 2002 | K. Busch | 36 | 4 | 12 | 20 | 4 | 1 | 5,105,394 |
| 2003 | K. Busch | 36 | 4 | 9 | 14 | 8 | 0 | 5,587,384 |
| TOTALS | | 538 | 24 | 122 | 228 | 104 | 12 | $32,978,018 |

## Mike Ford

**Date of birth:** 4/13/70. **Hometown:** Morristown, Tenn. **Resides:** Stanley, N.C. **Team:** No. 88 Ford. **Years with current team:** First. **Years as crew chief:** First. **Overall years as crew chief:** 4. **Best points finish:** 9. **Career victories:** 4. **First victory:** 2001 Homestead-Miami. **Career poles:** 6. **First pole:** 2001 Daytona

### CAREER NASCAR WINSTON CUP SERIES STATS

| Year | Driver | Races | Won | Top 5 | Top 10 | DNF | Poles | Money Won |
|---|---|---|---|---|---|---|---|---|
| 2000 | C. Atwood | 3 | 0 | 0 | 1 | 0 | 0 | $97,030 |
| 2001 | B. Elliott | 36 | 1 | 5 | 9 | 2 | 2 | 3,618,017 |
| 2002 | B. Elliott | 36 | 2 | 6 | 13 | 4 | 4 | 4,122,699 |
| 2003 | B. Elliott | 36 | 1 | 9 | 12 | 2 | 0 | 5,008,530 |
| TOTALS | | 111 | 4 | 20 | 35 | 8 | 6 | $12,846,281 |

## Raymond Fox III

**Date of birth:** 7/26/71. **Hometown:** Concord, N.C. **Resides:** Concord, N.C. **Overall years as crew chief:** 3. **Career victories:** 0. **Career poles:** 1. **First pole:** 2003 Darlington

### CAREER NASCAR WINSTON CUP SERIES STATS

| Year | Driver | Races | Won | Top 5 | Top 10 | DNF | Poles | Money Won |
|---|---|---|---|---|---|---|---|---|
| 1999 | K. Irwin | 3 | 0 | 0 | 0 | 0 | 0 | $263,394 |
| 2002 | R. Rudd | 3 | 0 | 0 | 0 | 0 | 0 | 271,476 |
| 2003 | E. Sadler | 24 | 0 | 1 | 7 | 4 | 1 | 2,480,766 |
| TOTALS | | 30 | 0 | 1 | 7 | 4 | 1 | $3,015,636 |

## Kenny Francis

**Date of birth:** 12/1/69. **Hometown:** Jacksonville, Fla. **Overall years as crew chief:** 1. **Best points finish:** 19. **Career victories:** 0. **Career poles:** 1. **First pole:** 2003 Talladega

### CAREER NASCAR WINSTON CUP SERIES STATS

| Year | Driver | Races | Won | Top 5 | Top 10 | DNF | Poles | Money Won |
|---|---|---|---|---|---|---|---|---|
| 2003 | J. Mayfield | 36 | 0 | 4 | 12 | 6 | 1 | $3,371,879 |

## Tony Furr

**Date of birth:** 9/14/56. **Hometown:** Concord, N.C. **Resides:** Concord, N.C. **Team:** No. 0 Chevrolet. **Years with current team:** 1. **Years as crew chief:** 1. **Overall years as crew chief:** 9. **Best points finish:** 17. **Career victories:** 2. **First victory:** 1997 Talladega. **Career poles:** 4. **First pole:** 1994 Atlanta

# CREW CHIEFS

### CAREER NASCAR WINSTON CUP SERIES STATS

| Year | Driver | Races | Won | Top 5 | Top 10 | DNF | Poles | Money Won |
|---|---|---|---|---|---|---|---|---|
| 1994 | G. Sacks | 31 | 0 | 0 | 3 | 10 | 1 | $411,728 |
| 1995 | J. Nemechek | 7 | 0 | 0 | 0 | 2 | 0 | 89,595 |
| | J. Mayfield | 21 | 0 | 0 | 1 | 0 | 0 | 348,230 |
| 1996 | J. Mayfield | 23 | 0 | 2 | 2 | 4 | 1 | 463,863 |
| 1997 | J. Andretti | 32 | 1 | 3 | 3 | 3 | 1 | 1,143,725 |
| 1998 | R. Craven | 8 | 0 | 0 | 1 | 0 | 1 | 422,200 |
| | R. LaJoie | 9 | 0 | 1 | 3 | 3 | 0 | 336,905 |
| | W. Dallenbach | 16 | 0 | 0 | 3 | 3 | 0 | 522,996 |
| 1999 | W. Dallenbach | 34 | 0 | 1 | 5 | 5 | 0 | 1,741,176 |
| 2000 | R. Nadeau | 34 | 1 | 3 | 5 | 9 | 0 | 2,164,778 |
| 2001 | R. Nadeau | 36 | 0 | 4 | 10 | 8 | 0 | 2,507,827 |
| 2003 | J. Sprague | 18 | 0 | 0 | 0 | 4 | 0 | 1,187,830 |
| | J. Leffler | 10 | 0 | 0 | 0 | 0 | 0 | 594,500 |
| | J. Andretti | 3 | 0 | 0 | 0 | 0 | 0 | 142,770 |
| | W. Burton | 4 | 0 | 0 | 0 | 2 | 0 | 347,650 |
| | **TOTALS** | **294** | **2** | **15** | **37** | **54** | **4** | **$12,542,803** |

## Tony Gibson

**Date of birth:** 11/3/64. **Hometown:** Daytona Beach, Fla. **Resides:** Concord, N.C. **Team:** No. 1 Chevrolet. **Years with current team:** 1. **Years as crew chief:** 1. **Overall years as crew chief:** 1. **Best points finish:** 56. **Career victories:** 0. **First victory:** None. **Career poles:** 1. **First pole:** 2003 California

### CAREER NASCAR WINSTON CUP SERIES STATS

| Year | Driver | Races | Won | Top 5 | Top 10 | DNF | Poles | Money Won |
|---|---|---|---|---|---|---|---|---|
| 2003 | S. Park | 11 | 0 | 0 | 1 | 3 | 1 | $1,033,202 |
| | J. Green | 12 | 0 | 0 | 0 | 2 | 0 | 1,072,355 |
| | J. Andretti | 11 | 0 | 0 | 0 | 1 | 0 | 886,729 |
| | R. Fellows | 2 | 0 | 0 | 0 | 1 | 0 | 161,854 |
| | **TOTALS** | **36** | **0** | **0** | **1** | **7** | **1** | **$3,154,140** |

## Randy Goss

**Date of birth:** 1/12/56. **Hometown:** Flint, Mich. **Resides:** Mooresville, N.C. **Overall years as crew chief:** 1. **Career victories:** 1. **First victory:** 2003 Daytona. **Career poles:** 0.

### CAREER NASCAR WINSTON CUP SERIES STATS

| Year | Driver | Races | Won | Top 5 | Top 10 | DNF | Poles | Money Won |
|---|---|---|---|---|---|---|---|---|
| 2003 | G. Biffle | 24 | 1 | 3 | 5 | 3 | 0 | $1,724,960 |

## Jay Guy

**Overall years as crew chief:** 1. **Best points finish:** 24. **Career victories:** 0. **Career poles:** 0

### CAREER NASCAR WINSTON CUP SERIES STATS

| Year | Driver | Races | Won | Top 5 | Top 10 | DNF | Poles | Money Won |
|---|---|---|---|---|---|---|---|---|
| 2003 | J. Benson | 7 | 0 | 1 | 1 | 1 | 0 | $635,770 |

## Kevin Hamlin

**Date of birth:** 6/17/59. **Hometown:** Kalamazoo, Mich. **Resides:** Winston-Salem, N.C. **Team:** No. 30 Chevrolet. **Years with current team:** First. **Years as crew chief:** First. **Overall years as crew chief:** 10. **Best points finish:** 2. **Career victories:** 9. **First victory:** 1999 Talladega. **Career poles:** 4. **First pole:** 1994 Indianapolis

### CAREER NASCAR WINSTON CUP SERIES STATS

| Year | Driver | Races | Won | Top 5 | Top 10 | DNF | Poles | Money Won |
|---|---|---|---|---|---|---|---|---|
| 1994 | R. Mast | 31 | 0 | 4 | 10 | 10 | 1 | $722,361 |
| 1995 | R. Mast | 31 | 0 | 0 | 3 | 9 | 1 | 749,550 |
| 1996 | R. Mast | 31 | 0 | 1 | 5 | 6 | 0 | 924,559 |
| 1997 | M. Skinner | 31 | 0 | 0 | 3 | 7 | 2 | 900,569 |
| 1998 | M. Skinner | 10 | 0 | 0 | 1 | 3 | 0 | 399,046 |
| | M. Shepherd | 2 | 0 | 0 | 0 | 1 | 0 | 50,140 |
| | M. Dillon | 1 | 0 | 0 | 0 | 0 | 0 | 28,050 |
| | D. Earnhardt | 20 | 0 | 3 | 9 | 1 | 0 | 1,397,219 |
| 1999 | D. Earnhardt | 34 | 3 | 7 | 21 | 3 | 0 | 3,149,536 |
| 2000 | D. Earnhardt | 34 | 2 | 13 | 24 | 0 | 0 | 4,918,886 |
| 2001 | D. Earnhardt | 1 | 0 | 0 | 0 | 1 | 0 | 296,833 |
| | K. Harvick | 35 | 2 | 6 | 16 | 1 | 0 | 4,302,202 |
| 2002 | K. Harvick | 11 | 0 | 2 | 3 | 3 | 0 | 1,221,143 |
| | K. Wallace | 1 | 0 | 0 | 0 | 0 | 0 | 82,678 |
| | R. Gordon | 24 | 0 | 1 | 5 | 1 | 0 | 2,269,421 |
| 2003 | Robby Gordon | 36 | 2 | 4 | 10 | 2 | 0 | 4,157,064 |
| | **TOTALS** | **33** | **9** | **41** | **120** | **48** | **4** | **$25,569,257** |

## Mark Harrah

**Overall years as crew chief:** 1. **Best points finish:** 28. **Career victories:** 0. **Career poles:** 0

### CAREER NASCAR WINSTON CUP SERIES STATS

| Year | Driver | Races | Won | Top 5 | Top 10 | DNF | Poles | Money Won |
|---|---|---|---|---|---|---|---|---|
| 2003 | D. Blaney | 5 | 0 | 0 | 0 | 1 | 0 | $313,213 |

## Mike Hillman

**Date of birth:** 8/27/57. **Hometown:** Lockport, N.Y. **Resides:** Mooresville, N.C. **Team:** No. 11 Ford. **Years with current team:** 2. **Years as crew chief:** 2. **Overall years as crew chief:** 11. **Best points finish:** 25. **Career victories:** 0. **Career poles:** 0

### CAREER NASCAR WINSTON CUP SERIES STATS

| Year | Driver | Races | Won | Top 5 | Top 10 | DNF | Poles | Money Won |
|---|---|---|---|---|---|---|---|---|
| 1993 | J. Horton | 13 | 0 | 0 | 0 | 10 | 0 | $115,105 |
| 1994 | D. Trickle | 25 | 0 | 0 | 1 | 10 | 0 | 224,806 |
| 1995 | M. Chase | 0 | 0 | 0 | 0 | 0 | 0 | 2,100 |
| | J. Hensley | 2 | 0 | 0 | 0 | 2 | 0 | 17,650 |
| | C. Bown | 4 | 0 | 0 | 0 | 1 | 0 | 44,164 |
| 1996 | B. Hillin Jr. | 12 | 0 | 0 | 0 | 1 | 0 | 191,800 |

| Year | Driver | Races | Won | Top 5 | Top 10 | DNF | Poles | Money Won |
|---|---|---|---|---|---|---|---|---|
| 1997 | J. Nemechek | 8 | 0 | 0 | 0 | 3 | 0 | 201,164 |
| | P. Parsons | 1 | 0 | 0 | 0 | 0 | 0 | 12,845 |
| | R. Gordon | 12 | 0 | 1 | 1 | 4 | 0 | 377,694 |
| | W. Dallenbach | 1 | 0 | 0 | 0 | 1 | 0 | 22,515 |
| | G. Sacks | 5 | 0 | 0 | 0 | 3 | 0 | 114,035 |
| | S. Park | 1 | 0 | 0 | 0 | 1 | 0 | 14,075 |
| 1998 | G. Sacks | 7 | 0 | 0 | 0 | 2 | 0 | 296,880 |
| | R. Bickle | 13 | 0 | 0 | 0 | 3 | 0 | 429,675 |
| | D. Trickle | 7 | 0 | 0 | 0 | 2 | 0 | 239,466 |
| 1999 | R. Craven | 12 | 0 | 0 | 0 | 4 | 0 | 424,799 |
| | L. Allen Jr. | 2 | 0 | 0 | 0 | 0 | 0 | 53,135 |
| | H. Stricklin | 6 | 0 | 0 | 1 | 1 | 0 | 236,905 |
| 2000 | A. Hillenberg | 0 | 0 | 0 | 0 | 0 | 0 | 15,171 |
| | R. Gordon | 4 | 0 | 0 | 0 | 0 | 0 | 140,265 |
| | B. Bodine | 17 | 0 | 0 | 0 | 5 | 0 | 613,660 |
| 2001 | B. Bodine | 21 | 0 | 0 | 2 | 2 | 0 | 994,229 |
| 2003 | B. Bodine | 6 | 0 | 0 | 0 | 2 | 0 | $383,718 |
| TOTALS | | 152 | 0 | 1 | 5 | 51 | 0 | $4,033,042 |

## Ben Holm

**Career victories:** 0. **Career poles:** 0

### CAREER NASCAR WINSTON CUP SERIES STATS

| Year | Driver | Races | Won | Top 5 | Top 10 | DNF | Poles | Money Won |
|---|---|---|---|---|---|---|---|---|
| 2003 | L. Foyt | 17 | 0 | 0 | 0 | 8 | 0 | $1,036,730 |

## James Ince

**Date of birth:** 11/24/70. **Hometown:** Springfield, Mo. **Resides:** Charlotte, N.C. **Overall years as crew chief:** 8. **Best points finish:** 11. **Career victories:** 1. **First victory:** 2002 Rockingham. **Career poles:** 1. **First pole:** 1999 Homestead-Miami.

### CAREER NASCAR WINSTON CUP SERIES STATS

| Year | Driver | Races | Won | Top 5 | Top 10 | DNF | Poles | Money Won |
|---|---|---|---|---|---|---|---|---|
| 1996 | T. Musgrave | 4 | 0 | 1 | 1 | 0 | 0 | $192,400 |
| 1997 | T. Musgrave | 32 | 0 | 5 | 8 | 4 | 0 | 1,256,680 |
| 1998 | T. Musgrave | 20 | 0 | 1 | 4 | 3 | 0 | 965,076 |
| | K. Lepage | 13 | 0 | 0 | 2 | 5 | 0 | 447,745 |
| 1999 | K. Lepage | 7 | 0 | 0 | 0 | 2 | 0 | 369,219 |
| | R. Bickle | 12 | 0 | 0 | 2 | 0 | 0 | 405,962 |
| | D. Green | 9 | 0 | 0 | 0 | 3 | 1 | 293,790 |
| 2000 | J. Benson | 33 | 0 | 3 | 7 | 3 | 0 | 1,841,324 |
| 2001 | J. Benson | 36 | 0 | 6 | 14 | 7 | 0 | 2,894,903 |
| 2002 | J. Benson Jr. | 31 | 1 | 3 | 7 | 8 | 0 | 2,791,879 |
| | J. Nadeau | 3 | 0 | 0 | 0 | 0 | 0 | 275,681 |
| | J. Nemechek III | 1 | 0 | 0 | 0 | 0 | 0 | 74,710 |
| | Mike Wallace | 1 | 0 | 0 | 0 | 1 | 0 | 80,150 |
| 2003 | J. Benson | 29 | 0 | 1 | 3 | 6 | 0 | 2,909,020 |
| TOTALS | | 231 | 1 | 20 | 48 | 42 | 1 | $12,022,519 |

# CREW CHIEFS

## Chad Knaus

**Date of birth:** 8/5/71. **Hometown:** Rockford, Ill. **Resides:** Charlotte, N.C. **Team:** No. 48 Chevrolet. **Years with current team:** 2. **Years as crew chief:** 2. **Overall years as crew chief:** 4. **Best points finish:** 2. **Career victories:** 6. **First victory:** 2002 California. **Career poles:** 8. **First pole:** 2001 Talladega.

### CAREER NASCAR WINSTON CUP SERIES STATS

| Year | Driver | Races | Won | Top 5 | Top 10 | DNF | Poles | Money Won |
|---|---|---|---|---|---|---|---|---|
| 2000 | S. Compton | 1 | 0 | 0 | 0 | 1 | 0 | $34,500 |
| 2001 | S. Compton | 34 | 0 | 0 | 1 | 7 | 2 | 1,704,500 |
| 2002 | J. Johnson | 36 | 3 | 6 | 21 | 3 | 4 | 3,788,268 |
| 2003 | J. Johnson | 36 | 3 | 14 | 20 | 3 | 2 | 7,745,530 |
| TOTALS | | 107 | 6 | 20 | 42 | 14 | 8 | $13,272,798 |

## Richard Labbe

**Date of birth:** 6/14/68. **Hometown:** Biddeford, Maine. **Resides:** Kannapolis, N.C. **Team:** No. 15 Chevrolet. **Years with current team:** 3. **Years as crew chief:** 3. **Overall years as crew chief:** 4. **Best points finish:** 14. **Career victories:** 3. **First victory:** Pepsi 400. **Career poles:** 1. **First pole:** 1998 Atlanta.

### CAREER NASCAR WINSTON CUP SERIES STATS

| Year | Driver | Races | Won | Top 5 | Top 10 | DNF | Poles | Money Won |
|---|---|---|---|---|---|---|---|---|
| 1998 | K. Irwin | 29 | 0 | 1 | 4 | 8 | 1 | $1,264,847 |
| 2001 | M. Waltrip | 11 | 0 | 1 | 1 | 3 | 0 | 734,785 |
| 2002 | M. Waltrip | 36 | 1 | 4 | 10 | 4 | 0 | 3,185,969 |
| 2003 | M. Waltrip | 36 | 2 | 8 | 11 | 6 | 0 | 4,929,620 |
| TOTALS | | 112 | 3 | 14 | 26 | 21 | 1 | $10,115,216 |

## Steven Lane

**Date of birth:** 11/15/71. **Hometown:** Winston-Salem, N.C. **Resides:** Mooresville, N.C. **Overall years as crew chief:** 3. **Best points finish:** 22. **Career victories:** 0. **Career poles:** 0

### CAREER NASCAR WINSTON CUP SERIES STATS

| Year | Driver | Races | Won | Top 5 | Top 10 | DNF | Poles | Money Won |
|---|---|---|---|---|---|---|---|---|
| 2001 | K. Petty | 5 | 0 | 0 | 0 | 2 | 0 | $214,319 |
| 2002 | K. Petty | 36 | 0 | 0 | 1 | 1 | 0 | 2,198,073 |
| 2003 | K. Petty | 31 | 0 | 0 | 0 | 5 | 0 | 2,183,245 |
| TOTALS | | 72 | 0 | 0 | 1 | 8 | 0 | $4,595,637 |

## Ben Leslie

**Date of birth:** 9/23/72. **Hometown:** Puroin, Mo. **Resides:** Concord, N.C. **Team:** No. 21 Ford. **Years with current team:** 1. **Years as crew chief:** 1. **Overall years as crew chief:** 5. **Best points finish:** 2. **Career victories:** 1. **First victory:** 2002 Charlotte. **Career poles:** 1. **First pole:** 2001 Darlington.

## CAREER NASCAR WINSTON CUP SERIES STATS

| Year | Driver | Races | Won | Top 5 | Top 10 | DNF | Poles | Money Won |
|---|---|---|---|---|---|---|---|---|
| 1999 | J. Benson | 10 | 0 | 0 | 0 | 1 | 0 | $521,061 |
| 2000 | K. Petty | 6 | 0 | 0 | 0 | 0 | 0 | 313,915 |
| 2001 | K. Busch | 29 | 0 | 3 | 5 | 6 | 1 | 1,781,030 |
| 2002 | M. Martin | 36 | 1 | 12 | 22 | 3 | 0 | 7,004,803 |
| 2003 | M. Martin | 34 | 0 | 5 | 10 | 5 | 0 | 3,889,964 |
|  | R. Rudd | 2 | 0 | 0 | 0 | 2 | 0 | 243,290 |
| TOTALS |  | 111 | 1 | 20 | 39 | 18 | 1 | $13,235,577 |

## CREW CHIEFS

# Jim Long

**Date of birth:** 2/17/57. **Hometown:** Toledo, Ohio. **Resides:** Denver, N.C. **Team:** No. 5 Chevrolet. **Years with current team:** 2. **Years as crew chief:** 2. **Overall years as crew chief:** 9. **Best points finish:** 10. **Career victories:** 3. **First victory:** 1997 Dover. **Career poles:** 1. **First pole:** 2003 Richmond

### CAREER NASCAR WINSTON CUP SERIES STATS

| Year | Driver | Races | Won | Top 5 | Top 10 | DNF | Poles | Money Won |
|---|---|---|---|---|---|---|---|---|
| 1994 | K. Petty | 31 | 0 | 2 | 7 | 3 | 0 | $806,332 |
| 1996 | L. Speed | 31 | 0 | 0 | 2 | 9 | 0 | 817,175 |
| 1997 | Ricky Rudd | 32 | 2 | 6 | 11 | 7 | 0 | 1,975,981 |
| 1998 | Ricky Rudd | 5 | 0 | 0 | 0 | 2 | 0 | 266,345 |
|  | H. Stricklin | 2 | 0 | 0 | 0 | 1 | 0 | 82,576 |
|  | B. Jones | 1 | 0 | 0 | 1 | 0 | 0 | 26,580 |
|  | M. Shepherd | 2 | 0 | 0 | 0 | 2 | 0 | 45,955 |
| 1999 | G. Bodine | 34 | 0 | 1 | 2 | 6 | 0 | 1,258,894 |
| 2000 | T. Musgrave | 5 | 0 | 0 | 0 | 2 | 0 | 205,491 |
|  | D. Trickle | 4 | 0 | 0 | 0 | 2 | 0 | 181,715 |
|  | R. Bickle Jr. | 3 | 0 | 0 | 0 | 0 | 0 | 135,960 |
|  | G. Bodine | 12 | 0 | 0 | 0 | 4 | 0 | 636,124 |
|  | J. Bessey | 1 | 0 | 0 | 0 | 0 | 0 | 48,975 |
| 2001 | M. Wallace | 12 | 0 | 0 | 3 | 1 | 0 | 678,936 |
|  | R. Gordon | 2 | 0 | 1 | 1 | 0 | 0 | 167,335 |
|  | H. Sadler | 3 | 0 | 0 | 0 | 0 | 0 | 121,862 |
| 2002 | T. Labonte | 36 | 0 | 1 | 4 | 6 | 0 | 3,244,240 |
| 2003 | T. Labonte | 36 | 1 | 4 | 9 | 0 | 1 | 4,283,625 |
| TOTALS |  | 252 | 3 | 15 | 40 | 45 | 1 | $14,984,099 |

# Robbie Loomis

**Date of birth:** 6/7/64. **Hometown:** Forest City, Fla. **Resides:** Charlotte, N.C. **Team:** No. 24 Chevrolet. **Years with current team:** 4. **Years as crew chief:** 4. **Overall years as crew chief:** 13. **Best points finish:** 1. **Career victories:** 18. **First victory:** 1996 Phoenix. **Career poles:** 22. **First pole:** 1996 Martinsville

### CAREER NASCAR WINSTON CUP SERIES STATS

| Year | Driver | Races | Won | Top 5 | Top 10 | DNF | Poles | Money Won |
|---|---|---|---|---|---|---|---|---|
| 1991 | R. Petty | 29 | 0 | 0 | 1 | 10 | 0 | $268,035 |
| 1992 | R. Petty | 29 | 0 | 0 | 0 | 5 | 0 | 348,870 |
| 1993 | R. Wilson | 29 | 0 | 0 | 1 | 6 | 0 | 299,725 |
|  | J. Hensley | 1 | 0 | 0 | 0 | 1 | 0 | 5,875 |

| Year | Driver | Races | Won | Top 5 | Top 10 | DNF | Poles | Money Won |
|---|---|---|---|---|---|---|---|---|
| 1994 | Dallenbach Jr. | 14 | 0 | 1 | 3 | 3 | 0 | 241,492 |
|  | J. Andretti | 11 | 0 | 0 | 0 | 2 | 0 | 116,400 |
| 1995 | B. Hamilton | 31 | 0 | 4 | 10 | 2 | 0 | 804,505 |
| 1996 | B. Hamilton | 31 | 1 | 3 | 11 | 4 | 2 | 1,151,235 |
| 1997 | B. Hamilton | 32 | 1 | 6 | 8 | 4 | 2 | 1,478,843 |
| 1998 | J. Andretti | 33 | 0 | 3 | 10 | 4 | 1 | 1,838,379 |
| 1999 | J. Andretti | 34 | 1 | 3 | 10 | 10 | 1 | 2,001,832 |
| 2000 | J. Gordon | 34 | 3 | 11 | 22 | 2 | 3 | 3,001,144 |
| 2001 | J. Gordon | 36 | 6 | 18 | 24 | 2 | 6 | 10,879,757 |
| 2002 | J. Gordon | 36 | 3 | 13 | 20 | 3 | 3 | 6,154,475 |
| 2003 | J. Gordon | 36 | 3 | 15 | 20 | 5 | 4 | 6,622,002 |
| TOTALS |  | 416 | 18 | 77 | 140 | 63 | 22 | $35,212,567 |

# Phillipe Lopez

**Date of birth:** 1/28/63. **Hometown:** Verdun, France. **Resides:** Mooresville, N.C. **Overall years as crew chief:** 10. **Best points finish:** 22. **Career victories:** 0. **Career poles:** 1. **First pole:** 1994 Charlotte

### CAREER NASCAR WINSTON CUP SERIES STATS

| Year | Driver | Races | Won | Top 5 | Top 10 | DNF | Poles | Money Won |
|---|---|---|---|---|---|---|---|---|
| 1994 | W. Burton | 15 | 0 | 1 | 2 | 6 | 1 | $187,785 |
| 1995 | W. Burton | 20 | 0 | 0 | 2 | 4 | 0 | 334,330 |
|  | G. Sacks | 3 | 0 | 0 | 0 | 2 | 0 | 34,240 |
|  | J. Hensley | 2 | 0 | 0 | 0 | 1 | 0 | 13,780 |
|  | G. Bradberry | 2 | 0 | 0 | 0 | 1 | 0 | 19,280 |
| 1996 | H. Stricklin | 31 | 0 | 1 | 1 | 3 | 0 | 631,055 |
| 1997 | H. Stricklin | 2 | 0 | 0 | 0 | 0 | 0 | 93,314 |
|  | S. Park | 4 | 0 | 0 | 0 | 1 | 0 | 60,405 |
| 1998 | S. Park | 17 | 0 | 0 | 0 | 5 | 0 | 487,265 |
|  | D. Waltrip | 13 | 0 | 1 | 2 | 2 | 0 | 398,615 |
| 1999 | S. Park | 10 | 0 | 0 | 0 | 1 | 0 | 495,376 |
|  | D. Waltrip | 14 | 0 | 0 | 0 | 3 | 0 | 483,127 |
| 2000 | R. Mast | 28 | 0 | 0 | 2 | 5 | 0 | 1,090,227 |
|  | G. Bradberry | 2 | 0 | 0 | 0 | 2 | 0 | 63,700 |
| 2001 | R. Hornaday | 7 | 0 | 0 | 1 | 2 | 0 | 395,964 |
|  | D. Blaney | 4 | 0 | 0 | 1 | 1 | 0 | 257,550 |
| 2002 | H. Stricklin | 22 | 0 | 0 | 0 | 5 | 0 | 1,313,548 |
|  | K. Wallace | 10 | 0 | 0 | 0 | 0 | 0 | 503,085 |
|  | G. Bodine | 1 | 0 | 0 | 0 | 0 | 0 | 35,615 |
|  | T. Hubert | 1 | 0 | 0 | 0 | 0 | 0 | 41,925 |
|  | S. Wimmer | 1 | 0 | 0 | 0 | 0 | 0 | 52,285 |
| 2003 | K. Wallace | 36 | 0 | 0 | 1 | 5 | 0 | 2,480,490 |
| TOTALS |  | 245 | 0 | 3 | 12 | 49 | 1 | $9,472,961 |

# Bob Marcis

**Date of birth:** 7/15/64. **Hometown:** Wausau, Wis. **Resides:** Horse Shoe, N.C. **Overall years as crew chief:** 6. **Best points finish:** 42. **Career victories:** 0. **Career poles:** 0

### CAREER NASCAR WINSTON CUP SERIES STATS

| Year | Driver | Races | Won | Top 5 | Top 10 | DNF | Poles | Money Won |
|---|---|---|---|---|---|---|---|---|
| 1997 | D. Marcis | 8 | 0 | 0 | 0 | 2 | 0 | $156,074 |
| 1998 | D. Marcis | 13 | 0 | 0 | 0 | 3 | 0 | 444,946 |

| Year | Driver | Races | Won | Top 5 | Top 10 | DNF | Poles | Money Won |
|---|---|---|---|---|---|---|---|---|
| 1999 | D. Marcis | 20 | 0 | 0 | 0 | 3 | 0 | 731,221 |
| 2000 | D. Marcis | 11 | 0 | 0 | 0 | 4 | 0 | 405,572 |
|  | K. Earnhardt | 1 | 0 | 0 | 0 | 1 | 0 | 21,830 |
| 2001 | D. Marcis | 3 | 0 | 0 | 0 | 0 | 0 | 153,196 |
|  | D. Trickle | 1 | 0 | 0 | 0 | 0 | 0 | 33,850 |
| 2002 | D. Marcis | 3 | 0 | 0 | 0 | 1 | 0 | 137,110 |
|  | A. Hillenburg | 2 | 0 | 0 | 0 | 2 | 0 | 101,629 |
|  | Jay Sauter | 2 | 0 | 0 | 0 | 1 | 0 | 94,682 |
|  | Tim Sauter | 2 | 0 | 0 | 0 | 1 | 0 | 85,060 |
|  | D. Trickle | 3 | 0 | 0 | 0 | 3 | 0 | 136,830 |
| **TOTALS** |  | **67** | **0** | **0** | **0** | **21** | **0** | **$2,502,000** |

## Gil Martin

**Date of birth:** 1/31/66. **Hometown:** Nashville. **Resides:** Harrisburg, N.C. **Team:** Overall years as crew chief: 9. **Best points finish:** 20. **Career victories:** 2. **First victory:** 2001 Loudon. **Career poles:** 2. **First pole:** 1997 Martinsville.

### CAREER NASCAR WINSTON CUP SERIES STATS

| Year | Driver | Races | Won | Top 5 | Top 10 | DNF | Poles | Money Won |
|---|---|---|---|---|---|---|---|---|
| 1993 | J. Burton | 1 | 0 | 0 | 0 | 1 | 0 | $9,550 |
| 1994 | K. Wallace | 1 | 0 | 0 | 0 | 0 | 0 | 9,825 |
| 1995 | K. Wallace | 11 | 0 | 0 | 0 | 3 | 0 | 151,700 |
| 1996 | K. Wallace | 30 | 0 | 0 | 2 | 9 | 0 | 457,665 |
| 1997 | K. Wallace | 11 | 0 | 0 | 1 | 6 | 1 | 378,329 |
| 2000 | D. Blaney | 17 | 0 | 0 | 0 | 4 | 0 | 685,144 |
| 2001 | R. Gordon | 3 | 1 | 1 | 2 | 0 | 0 | 353,647 |
|  | J. Green | 1 | 0 | 0 | 1 | 0 | 0 | 83,899 |
| 2002 | R. Gordon | 12 | 0 | 0 | 0 | 3 | 0 | 1,073,282 |
|  | K. Harvick | 24 | 1 | 4 | 6 | 3 | 1 | 2,628,073 |
| 2003 | K. Harvick | 5 | 0 | 1 | 1 | 0 | 0 | 939,132 |
| **TOTALS** |  | **116** | **2** | **5** | **7** | **29** | **2** | **$6,770,246** |

## Lee McCall

**Date of birth:** 8/24/68. **Hometown:** Travelers Rest, S.C. **Resides:** Mooresville, N.C. **Team:** No. 40 Dodge. **Years with current team:** 3. **Years as crew chief:** 3. **Overall years as crew chief:** 3. **Best points finish:** 3. **Career victories:** 5. **First victory:** 2001 Michigan. **Career poles:** 2. **First pole:** 2001 Daytona.

### CAREER NASCAR WINSTON CUP SERIES STATS

| Year | Driver | Races | Won | Top 5 | Top 10 | DNF | Poles | Money Won |
|---|---|---|---|---|---|---|---|---|
| 2001 | S. Marlin | 36 | 2 | 12 | 20 | 2 | 1 | $4,517,634 |
| 2002 | S. Marlin | 29 | 2 | 8 | 14 | 3 | 1 | 4,228,889 |
|  | J. McMurray | 6 | 1 | 1 | 2 | 1 | 0 | 717,942 |
|  | Mike Bliss | 1 | 0 | 0 | 0 | 0 | 0 | 90,083 |
| 2003 | S. Marlin | 36 | 0 | 0 | 11 | 8 | 0 | 4,384,491 |
| **TOTALS** |  | **108** | **5** | **21** | **47** | **14** | **2** | **$13,939,040** |

## Michael McSwain

**Date of birth:** 1/17/67. **Hometown:** Mount Holly, N.C. **Resides:** Huntersville, N.C. **Team:** No. 18 Interstate Batteries Chevrolet. **Years with current team:** 1. **Years as crew chief:** 1. **Overall years as crew chief:** 8. **Best points finish:** 4. **Career victories:** 5. **First victory:** 2001 Pocono. **Career poles:** 8. **First pole:** 2000 Las Vegas.

### CAREER NASCAR WINSTON CUP SERIES STATS

| Year | Driver | Races | Won | Top 5 | Top 10 | DNF | Poles | Money Won |
|---|---|---|---|---|---|---|---|---|
| 1997 | M. Shepherd | 13 | 0 | 1 | 3 | 3 | 0 | $447,529 |
|  | J. Nadeau | 5 | 0 | 0 | 0 | 2 | 0 | 118,545 |
|  | R. Pressley | 7 | 0 | 0 | 0 | 3 | 0 | 103,810 |
| 1998 | R. Pressley | 24 | 0 | 1 | 1 | 5 | 0 | 854,795 |
|  | R. Bickle | 3 | 0 | 0 | 0 | 1 | 0 | 93,855 |
| 1999 | R. Mast | 10 | 0 | 0 | 1 | 0 | 0 | 483,096 |
|  | R. Rudd | 24 | 0 | 3 | 5 | 4 | 0 | 1,148,330 |
| 2000 | R. Rudd | 34 | 0 | 12 | 19 | 3 | 2 | 2,914,970 |
| 2001 | R. Rudd | 36 | 2 | 14 | 22 | 4 | 1 | 4,878,027 |
| 2002 | R. Rudd | 33 | 1 | 8 | 12 | 4 | 1 | 4,173,138 |
| 2003 | B. Labonte | 36 | 2 | 12 | 17 | 5 | 4 | 5,505,018 |
| **TOTALS** |  | **225** | **5** | **51** | **80** | **32** | **8** | **$20,721,115** |

## Scott Miller

**Date of birth:** 8/23/57. **Hometown:** Bardstown, Ky. **Resides:** Mooresville, N.C. **Overall years as crew chief:** 1. **Best points finish:** 27. **Career victories:** 1. **First victory:** 2003 Darlington. **Career poles:** 0

### CAREER NASCAR WINSTON CUP SERIES STATS

| Year | Driver | Races | Won | Top 5 | Top 10 | DNF | Poles | Money Won |
|---|---|---|---|---|---|---|---|---|
| 2003 | R. Craven | 36 | 1 | 3 | 8 | 103 | 0 | $3,216,211 |

## Newt Moore

**Date of birth:** 9/15/62. **Hometown:** Nashville. **Resides:** Concord, N.C. **Overall years as crew chief:** 7. **Best points finish:** 19. **Career victories:** 0. **Career poles:** 1. **First pole:** 1997 Bristol.

### CAREER NASCAR WINSTON CUP SERIES STATS

| Year | Driver | Races | Won | Top 5 | Top 10 | DNF | Poles | Money Won |
|---|---|---|---|---|---|---|---|---|
| 1997 | K. Wallace | 20 | 0 | 0 | 1 | 5 | 1 | $571,211 |
| 1998 | K. Wallace | 22 | 0 | 0 | 6 | 9 | 0 | 773,701 |
|  | R. Pressley | 6 | 0 | 0 | 0 | 2 | 0 | 141,926 |
|  | H. Stricklin | 1 | 0 | 0 | 0 | 0 | 0 | 20,265 |
|  | T. Musgrave | 1 | 0 | 0 | 0 | 0 | 0 | 27,000 |
| 1999 | R. Pressley | 9 | 0 | 0 | 0 | 1 | 0 | 413,876 |
|  | J. Nadeau | 9 | 0 | 1 | 1 | 1 | 0 | 343,441 |
|  | S. Grissom | 3 | 0 | 0 | 0 | 2 | 0 | 78,625 |
|  | R. Bickle Jr. | 5 | 0 | 0 | 0 | 2 | 0 | 142,485 |
|  | S. Compton | 3 | 0 | 0 | 0 | 0 | 0 | 92,600 |

**CREW CHIEFS**

| Year | Driver | Races | Won | Top 5 | Top 10 | DNF | Poles | Money Won |
|---|---|---|---|---|---|---|---|---|
| 2000 | W. Dallenbach | 24 | 0 | 0 | 1 | 6 | 0 | 892,493 |
| 2001 | K. Schrader | 34 | 0 | 0 | 5 | 1 | 0 | 2,181,085 |
| 2002 | K. Schrader | 36 | 0 | 0 | 0 | 9 | 0 | 2,460,140 |
| 2003 | P. Menard | 1 | 0 | 0 | 0 | 0 | 0 | 52,410 |
| TOTALS | | 174 | 0 | 1 | 14 | 38 | 1 | $8,191,258 |

## Shawn Parker

**Date of birth:** 1/24/74. **Hometown:** Canandaigua, N.Y. **Resides:** Cornelius, N.C. **Overall years as crew chief:** 1. **Career victories:** 0. **Career poles:** 0

### CAREER NASCAR WINSTON CUP SERIES STATS

| Year | Driver | Races | Won | Top 5 | Top 10 | DNF | Poles | Money Won |
|---|---|---|---|---|---|---|---|---|
| 2003 | D. Jarrett | 28 | 0 | 0 | 6 | 8 | 0 | $2,977,366 |

## Brad Parrott

**Date of birth:** 7/13/67. **Hometown:** Charlotte, N.C. **Resides:** Huntersville, N.C. **Overall years as crew chief:** 1. **Career victories:** 1. **First victory:** 2003 Rockingham **Career poles:** 0

### CAREER NASCAR WINSTON CUP SERIES STATS

| Year | Driver | Races | Won | Top 5 | Top 10 | DNF | Poles | Money Won |
|---|---|---|---|---|---|---|---|---|
| 2000 | S. Pruett | 9 | 0 | 0 | 1 | 4 | 0 | $381,770 |
| 2003 | D. Jarrett | 8 | 1 | 1 | 1 | 1 | 0 | 1,144,124 |
| TOTALS | | 17 | 1 | 1 | 2 | 5 | 0 | $1,525,894 |

## Todd Parrott

**Date of birth:** 2/9/64. **Hometown:** Charlotte, N.C. **Resides:** Mooresville, N.C. **Team:** No. 38 Ford. **Years with current team:** 1. **Years as crew chief:** 8. **Overall years as crew chief:** 8. **Best points finish:** 1. **Career victories:** 24. **First victory:** 1996 Daytona. **Career poles:** 13 **First pole:** 1996 Darlington

### CAREER NASCAR WINSTON CUP SERIES STATS

| Year | Driver | Races | Won | Top 5 | Top 10 | DNF | Poles | Money Won |
|---|---|---|---|---|---|---|---|---|
| 1995 | E. Irvan | 2 | 0 | 0 | 1 | 1 | 0 | $40,160 |
| 1996 | D. Jarrett | 31 | 4 | 17 | 21 | 3 | 2 | 2,985,418 |
| 1997 | D. Jarrett | 32 | 7 | 18 | 26 | 1 | 2 | 3,240,542 |
| 1998 | D. Jarrett | 33 | 3 | 19 | 27 | 3 | 2 | 4,019,657 |
| 1999 | D. Jarrett | 34 | 4 | 24 | 29 | 1 | 0 | 6,649,596 |
| 2000 | D. Jarrett | 34 | 2 | 15 | 24 | 2 | 3 | 5,934,475 |
| 2001 | D. Jarrett | 36 | 4 | 12 | 19 | 4 | 4 | 5,934,475 |
| 2003 | E. Sadler | 12 | 0 | 0 | 2 | 5 | 0 | $1,314,410 |
| TOTALS | | 214 | 24 | 107 | 141 | 20 | 13 | $30,118,733 |

## Ryan Pemberton

**Date of birth:** 6/1/69. **Hometown:** Saratoga Springs, N.Y. **Resides:** Mooresville, N.C. **Team:** No. 01 U.S. Army Pontiac. **Years with current team:** 1. **Years as crew chief:** 1. **Overall years as crew chief:** 7. **Best points finish:** 19. **Career victories:** 0. **Career poles:** 5. **First pole:** 1998 Indianapolis

### CAREER NASCAR WINSTON CUP SERIES STATS

| Year | Driver | Races | Won | Top 5 | Top 10 | DNF | Poles | Money Won |
|---|---|---|---|---|---|---|---|---|
| 1997 | D. Cope | 31 | 0 | 1 | 2 | 6 | 0 | $707,404 |
| 1998 | E. Irvan | 30 | 0 | 0 | 11 | 3 | 3 | 1,600,452 |
| | R. Craven | 3 | 0 | 0 | 0 | 0 | 0 | 84,030 |
| 1999 | E. Irvan | 21 | 0 | 0 | 5 | 5 | 0 | 1,073,775 |
| | D. Trickle | 1 | 0 | 0 | 0 | 0 | 0 | 27,620 |
| | J. Nadeau | 12 | 0 | 0 | 0 | 2 | 0 | 450,775 |
| 2000 | R. Pressley | 34 | 0 | 1 | 1 | 10 | 0 | 1,460,317 |
| 2001 | R. Pressley | 34 | 0 | 1 | 4 | 9 | 0 | 2,171,520 |
| | B. Said | 2 | 0 | 0 | 1 | 0 | 0 | 124,340 |
| 2002 | D. Blaney | 36 | 0 | 0 | 5 | 3 | 0 | 2,978,593 |
| 2003 | J. Nadeau | 10 | 0 | 1 | 1 | 3 | 0 | 861,628 |
| | J. Keller | 1 | 0 | 0 | 0 | 0 | 0 | 49,675 |
| | M. Wallace | 8 | 0 | 0 | 0 | 2 | 0 | 487,959 |
| | B. Said | 2 | 0 | 0 | 1 | 0 | 1 | 134,680 |
| | M. Skinner | 11 | 0 | 0 | 0 | 1 | 1 | 735,502 |
| | J. Nemecheck | 4 | 0 | 0 | 1 | 0 | 0 | 271,424 |
| TOTALS | | 240 | 0 | 4 | 32 | 44 | 5 | $13,216,694 |

## Gary Putnam

**Date of birth:** 2/10/70. **Hometown:** Vernon, Conn. **Resides:** Concord, N.C. **Team:** No. 43 Dodge. **Years with current team:** 2. **Years as crew chief:** 2. **Overall years as crew chief:** 2. **Best points finish:** 0. **Career victories:** 0. **Career poles:** 0

### CAREER NASCAR WINSTON CUP SERIES STATS

| Year | Driver | Races | Won | Top 5 | Top 10 | DNF | Poles | Money Won |
|---|---|---|---|---|---|---|---|---|
| 2002 | J. Nadeau | 5 | 0 | 0 | 0 | 2 | 0 | $285,164 |
| | G. Biffle | 2 | 0 | 0 | 0 | 0 | 0 | 96,014 |
| | S. Grissom | 1 | 0 | 0 | 0 | 0 | 0 | 35,540 |
| | T. Musgrave | 1 | 0 | 0 | 0 | 0 | 0 | 58,450 |
| | C. Fittipaldi | 1 | 0 | 0 | 0 | 1 | 0 | 39,600 |
| 2003 | J. Andretti | 14 | 0 | 0 | 1 | 2 | 0 | 1,490,636 |
| | C. Fittipaldi | 14 | 0 | 0 | 0 | 6 | 0 | 177,856 |
| | J. Green | 8 | 0 | 0 | 0 | 2 | 0 | 629,094 |
| TOTALS | | 46 | 0 | 0 | 1 | 13 | 0 | $2,297,586 |

## Robbie Reiser

**Date of birth:** 6/27/63. **Hometown:** Allenton, Wis. **Resides:** Denver, N.C. **Team:** No. 17 Ford. **Years with current team:** 4. **Years as crew chief:** 4. **Overall years as crew chief:** 4. **Best points finish:** 5. **Career victories:** 7. **First victory:** 2000 Charlotte. **Career poles:** 2. **First pole:** 2002 Dover

## CAREER NASCAR WINSTON CUP SERIES STATS

| Year | Driver | Races | Won | Top 5 | Top 10 | DNF | Poles | Money Won |
|---|---|---|---|---|---|---|---|---|
| 2000 | M. Kenseth | 34 | 1 | 4 | 11 | 5 | 0 | $2,408,138 |
| 2001 | M. Kenseth | 36 | 0 | 4 | 9 | 5 | 0 | 2,565,579 |
| 2002 | M. Kenseth | 36 | 5 | 11 | 19 | 3 | 1 | 4,514,203 |
| 2003 | M. Kenseth | 36 | 1 | 11 | 18 | 0 | 1 | 9,422,764 |
| TOTALS | | 142 | 7 | 30 | 57 | 13 | 2 | $18,910,684 |

## Doug Richert

**Date of birth:** 6/14/60. **Hometown:** San Jose, Calif. **Team:** No. 16 Ford. **Years as crew chief:** 1. **Overall years as crew chief:** 15. **Best points finish:** 1. **Career victories:** 5. **First victory:** 1980 Nashville. **Career poles:** 4. **First pole:** 1984 Pocono.

### CAREER NASCAR WINSTON CUP SERIES STATS

| Year | Driver | Races | Won | Top 5 | Top 10 | DNF | Poles | Money Won |
|---|---|---|---|---|---|---|---|---|
| 1980 | D. Earnhardt | 18 | 3 | 12 | 14 | 2 | 0 | $379,166 |
| 1981 | D. Earnhardt | 20 | 0 | 7 | 11 | 6 | 0 | 254,385 |
| 1984 | N. Bonnett | 30 | 0 | 7 | 14 | 6 | 1 | 223,592 |
| 1985 | N. Bonnett | 28 | 2 | 11 | 17 | 5 | 1 | 530,145 |
| 1986 | N. Bonnett | 18 | 0 | 2 | 5 | 9 | 0 | 265,110 |
| | Da. Allison | 1 | 0 | 0 | 1 | 0 | 0 | 17,820 |
| | Baker | 6 | 0 | 4 | 4 | 2 | 0 | 45,065 |
| 1987 | Baker | 19 | 0 | 3 | 9 | 7 | 0 | 239,240 |
| | Hoerr | 1 | 0 | 0 | 0 | 0 | 0 | 1,705 |
| 1988 | B. Parsons | 26 | 0 | 0 | 1 | 8 | 0 | 204,695 |
| | Means | 1 | 0 | 0 | 0 | 0 | 0 | 3,650 |
| 1989 | Hess | 9 | 0 | 0 | 0 | 0 | 0 | 48,490 |
| | Stricklin | 16 | 0 | 1 | 3 | 2 | 0 | 93,012 |
| 1990 | J. Spencer | 15 | 0 | 0 | 2 | 3 | 0 | 149,465 |
| | P. Parsons | 3 | 0 | 0 | 0 | 1 | 0 | 14,755 |
| 1993 | P. Parsons | 25 | 0 | 0 | 1 | 9 | 0 | 281,000 |
| | D. Trickle | 5 | 0 | 1 | 2 | 1 | 0 | 61,700 |
| 1994 | J. Nemechek | 29 | 0 | 0 | 3 | 9 | 0 | 389,565 |
| 1997 | K. Lepage | 3 | 0 | 0 | 0 | 1 | 0 | 57,720 |
| 1998 | K. Lepage | 13 | 0 | 0 | 0 | 3 | 0 | 384,591 |
| | T. Kendall | 1 | 0 | 0 | 0 | 0 | 0 | 33,800 |
| | A. Hillenburg | 3 | 0 | 0 | 0 | 0 | 0 | 96,000 |
| | M. Shepard | 6 | 0 | 0 | 0 | 3 | 0 | 206,835 |
| | T. Bodine | 7 | 0 | 1 | 1 | 1 | 0 | 194,865 |
| 1999 | K. Irwin | 30 | 0 | 1 | 5 | 5 | 2 | 1,823,366 |
| 2003 | G. Biffle | 11 | 0 | 0 | 1 | 3 | 0 | 1,020,710 |
| TOTALS | | 344 | 5 | 52 | 93 | 86 | 4 | $6,395,447 |

## Peter Sospenzo

**Date of birth:** 12/23/56. **Hometown:** New York. **Resides:** Cornelius, N.C. **Team:** No. 25 Chevrolet. **Years with current team:** 1. **Years as crew chief:** 1. **Overall years as crew chief:** 8. **Best points finish:** 11. **Career victories:** 3. **First victory:** 2000 California. **Career poles:** 4. **First pole:** 2000 Talladega.

## CAREER NASCAR WINSTON CUP SERIES STATS

| Year | Driver | Races | Won | Top 5 | Top 10 | DNF | Poles | Money Won |
|---|---|---|---|---|---|---|---|---|
| 1994 | P. J. Jones | 0 | 0 | 0 | 0 | 0 | 0 | $10,000 |
| | J. Ruttman | 1 | 0 | 0 | 0 | 0 | 0 | 34,005 |
| | R. Bickle Jr. | 10 | 0 | 0 | 0 | 5 | 0 | 100,845 |
| | P. Parsons | 3 | 0 | 0 | 0 | 1 | 0 | 21,415 |
| 1995 | L. Speed | 31 | 0 | 0 | 2 | 3 | 0 | 529,435 |
| 1996 | L. Allen Jr. | 9 | 0 | 0 | 0 | 5 | 0 | 130,667 |
| | D. Trickle | 8 | 0 | 0 | 1 | 1 | 0 | 99,470 |
| | M. Wallace | 1 | 0 | 0 | 0 | 0 | 0 | 16,665 |
| 1997 | L. Allen Jr. | 2 | 0 | 0 | 0 | 1 | 0 | 75,239 |
| | G. Bradberry | 8 | 0 | 0 | 0 | 3 | 0 | 117,184 |
| 1999 | J. Mayfield | 23 | 0 | 2 | 7 | 3 | 0 | 1,391,333 |
| 2000 | J. Mayfield | 32 | 2 | 6 | 12 | 11 | 4 | 2,169,251 |
| | K. Petty | 1 | 0 | 0 | 0 | 0 | 0 | 97,735 |
| | T. Hubert | 1 | 0 | 0 | 0 | 0 | 0 | 33,175 |
| 2001 | J. Mayfield | 28 | 0 | 5 | 7 | 4 | 0 | 2,682,603 |
| | M. Wallace | 8 | 0 | 1 | 2 | 1 | 0 | 706,673 |
| 2003 | J. Nemechek | 32 | 1 | 2 | 5 | 7 | 0 | 2,289,060 |
| | B. Vickers | 4 | 0 | 0 | 0 | 1 | 0 | 217,309 |
| TOTALS | | 202 | 3 | 16 | 36 | 46 | 4 | $10,722,064 |

## Greg Steadman

**Date of birth:** 7/25/69. **Hometown:** Tampa. **Resides:** Randleman, N.C. **Team:** No. 45 Dodge. **Years as crew chief:** 5. **Overall years as crew chief:** 5. **Best points finish:** 23. **Career victories:** 0. **Career poles:** 0.

### CAREER NASCAR WINSTON CUP SERIES STATS

| Year | Driver | Races | Won | Top 5 | Top 10 | DNF | Poles | Money Won |
|---|---|---|---|---|---|---|---|---|
| 2000 | J. Andretti | 34 | 0 | 0 | 2 | 7 | 0 | $2,035,902 |
| 2001 | J. Andretti | 35 | 0 | 1 | 2 | 4 | 0 | 2,873,184 |
| 2002 | J. Andretti | 13 | 0 | 0 | 1 | 4 | 0 | 2,954,230 |
| | J. Nadeau | 10 | 0 | 0 | 0 | 4 | 0 | 563,463 |
| 2003 | K. Petty | 2 | 0 | 0 | 0 | 1 | 0 | 107,795 |
| TOTALS | | 94 | 0 | 2 | 5 | 20 | 0 | $9,534,574 |

## Frank Stoddard

**Date of birth:** 4/20/68. **Hometown:** North Haverhill, N.H. **Resides:** Cornelius, N.C. **Team:** No. 22 Dodge. **Years with current team:** 2. **Years as crew chief:** 2. **Overall years as crew chief:** 6. **Best points finish:** 3. **Career victories:** 14. **First victory:** 1998 Loudon. **Career poles:** 1. **First pole:** 2000 Richmond.

### CAREER NASCAR WINSTON CUP SERIES STATS

| Year | Driver | Races | Won | Top 5 | Top 10 | DNF | Poles | Money Won |
|---|---|---|---|---|---|---|---|---|
| 1998 | J. Burton | 33 | 2 | 18 | 23 | 4 | 0 | $2,626,987 |
| 1999 | J. Burton | 34 | 6 | 18 | 23 | 3 | 0 | 5,725,399 |
| 2000 | J. Burton | 34 | 4 | 15 | 22 | 2 | 1 | 5,959,439 |
| 2001 | J. Burton | 36 | 2 | 8 | 16 | 1 | 0 | 4,230,737 |
| 2002 | J. Burton | 25 | 0 | 3 | 10 | 4 | 0 | 2,699,459 |
| | W. Burton | 7 | 0 | 1 | 2 | 1 | 0 | 694,565 |
| 2003 | W. Burton | 32 | 0 | 0 | 4 | 4 | 0 | 3,280,950 |
| | S. Wimmer | 4 | 0 | 0 | 1 | 0 | 0 | 487,060 |
| TOTALS | | 205 | 14 | 63 | 101 | 19 | 1 | $25,587,961 |

# CREW CHIEFS

## Pat Tryson

**Date of birth:** 3/4/64. **Hometown:** Bryn Mawr, Pa. **Resides:** Troutman, N.C. **Team:** No. 6 Ford. **Years with current team:** 1. **Years as crew chief:** 1. **Overall years as crew chief:** 7. **Best points finish:** 18. **Career victories:** 1. **First victory:** 2001 Bristol. **Career poles:** 1. **First pole:** 1999 Atlanta.

### CAREER NASCAR WINSTON CUP SERIES STATS

| Year | Driver | Races | Won | Top 5 | Top 10 | DNF | Poles | Money Won |
|---|---|---|---|---|---|---|---|---|
| 1997 | G. Bodine | 19 | 0 | 2 | 7 | 7 | 0 | $689,914 |
| 1998 | T. Bodine | 7 | 0 | 0 | 1 | 1 | 0 | 183,901 |
|  | W. Dallenbach | 1 | 0 | 0 | 0 | 0 | 0 | 29,225 |
|  | G. Bradberry | 1 | 0 | 0 | 0 | 1 | 0 | 29,200 |
| 1999 | J. Benson Jr. | 13 | 0 | 0 | 1 | 1 | 0 | 589,325 |
|  | K. Lepage | 11 | 0 | 1 | 2 | 0 | 1 | 528,990 |
| 2000 | K. Lepage | 32 | 0 | 0 | 3 | 5 | 0 | 1,679,186 |
| 2001 | E. Sadler | 36 | 1 | 2 | 2 | 2 | 0 | 2,683,225 |
| 2002 | E. Sadler | 36 | 0 | 2 | 7 | 6 | 0 | 3,491,694 |
| 2003 | R. Rudd | 34 | 0 | 4 | 4 | 7 | 0 | 2,997,320 |
|  | M. Martin | 2 | 0 | 0 | 0 | 2 | 0 | 596,599 |
| **TOTALS** |  | **192** | **1** | **12** | **23** | **32** | **1** | **$13,498,579** |

## Bill Wilburn

**Date of birth:** 7/11/66. **Hometown:** Kernersville, N.C. **Resides:** Kernersville, N.C. **Overall years as crew chief:** 2. **Best points finish:** 7. **Career victories:** 0. **Career poles:** 0

### CAREER NASCAR WINSTON CUP SERIES STATS

| Year | Driver | Races | Won | Top 5 | Top 10 | DNF | Poles | Money Won |
|---|---|---|---|---|---|---|---|---|
| 2002 | R. Wallace | 36 | 0 | 7 | 17 | 1 | 0 | $4,785,134 |
| 2003 | R. Wallace | 36 | 0 | 2 | 12 | 4 | 0 | 4,246,547 |
| **TOTALS** |  | **72** | **0** | **9** | **29** | **5** | **0** | **$9,031,680** |

## Donnie Wingo

**Date of birth:** 2/13/60. **Hometown:** Spartanburg, S.C. **Resides:** Mooresville, N.C. **Team:** No. 42 Dodge. **Years with current team:** 1. **Years as crew chief:** 1. **Overall years as crew chief:** 12. **Best points finish:** 5. **Career victories:** 4. **First victory:** 1990 Atlanta. **Career poles:** 4. **First polejon:** 1993 Martinsville

### CAREER NASCAR WINSTON CUP SERIES STATS

| Year | Driver | Races | Won | Top 5 | Top 10 | DNF | Poles | Money Won |
|---|---|---|---|---|---|---|---|---|
| 1989 | B. Bodine | 22 | 0 | 1 | 6 | 3 | 0 | $237,684 |
| 1990 | Shepherd | 29 | 1 | 7 | 16 | 6 | 0 | 666,915 |
| 1991 | Shepherd | 29 | 0 | 4 | 14 | 6 | 0 | 521,147 |
| 1992 | G. Bodine | 29 | 2 | 7 | 11 | 7 | 0 | 716,583 |
| 1993 | G. Bodine | 23 | 1 | 2 | 8 | 5 | 1 | 613,750 |
|  | L. Speed | 7 | 0 | 0 | 0 | 1 | 0 | 134,825 |
| 1994 | L. Speed | 31 | 0 | 4 | 9 | 4 | 0 | 832,463 |
| 1995 | D. Trickle | 31 | 0 | 0 | 1 | 5 | 0 | 694,920 |
| 1996 | J. Spencer | 31 | 0 | 2 | 9 | 2 | 0 | 1,090,876 |
| 1997 | J. Spencer | 32 | 0 | 1 | 4 | 6 | 0 | 1,073,779 |
| 1998 | J. Spencer | 31 | 0 | 3 | 8 | 2 | 0 | 1,741,012 |
|  | F. Kimmel | 1 | 0 | 0 | 0 | 0 | 0 | 28,065 |
|  | T. Musgrave | 1 | 0 | 0 | 0 | 0 | 0 | 35,310 |
| 1999 | J. Spencer | 34 | 0 | 2 | 4 | 6 | 0 | 1,752,299 |
| 2000 | J. Spencer | 34 | 0 | 2 | 5 | 8 | 0 | 1,936,762 |
| 2001 | J. Spencer | 36 | 0 | 3 | 8 | 7 | 2 | 2,669,638 |
| 2002 | J. Nemechek | 7 | 0 | 0 | 0 | 2 | 0 | 612,062 |
|  | G. Bodine | 4 | 0 | 0 | 0 | 0 | 0 | 241,980 |
|  | F. Kimmel | 5 | 0 | 0 | 0 | 3 | 0 | 328,042 |
|  | T. Bodine | 20 | 0 | 1 | 4 | 7 | 0 | 1,530,950 |
| 2003 | J. McMurray | 36 | 0 | 5 | 13 | 4 | 1 | 3,258,806 |
| **TOTALS** |  | **473** | **4** | **44** | **120** | **86** | **4** | **$20,717,869** |

## Jon Wolfe

**Date of birth:** 2/2/63. **Hometown:** Strasburg, Ohio. **Resides:** Mooresville, N.C. **Overall years as crew chief:** 2. **Best points finish:** 33. **Career victories:** 0. **Career poles:** 0

### CAREER NASCAR WINSTON CUP SERIES STATS

| Year | Driver | Races | Won | Top 5 | Top 10 | DNF | Poles | Money Won |
|---|---|---|---|---|---|---|---|---|
| 1999 | T. Musgrave | 19 | 0 | 0 | 1 | 0 | 0 | $759,356 |
| 2002 | B. Bodine | 4 | 0 | 0 | 0 | 0 | 0 | 188,205 |
| **TOTALS** |  | **23** | **0** | **0** | **1** | **0** | **0** | **$947,561** |

## Greg Zipadelli

**Date of birth:** 4/21/67. **Hometown:** New Britain, Conn. **Resides:** Huntersville, N.C. **Team:** No. 20 Chevrolet. **Years with current team:** 5. **Years as crew chief:** 5. **Overall years as crew chief:** 5. **Best points finish:** 1. **Career victories:** 17. **First victory:** 1999 Richmond. **Career poles:** 7. **First pole:** 1999 Martinsville.

### CAREER NASCAR WINSTON CUP SERIES STATS

| Year | Driver | Races | Won | Top 5 | Top 10 | DNF | Poles | Money Won |
|---|---|---|---|---|---|---|---|---|
| 1999 | T. Stewart | 34 | 3 | 12 | 21 | 1 | 2 | $3,190,149 |
| 2000 | T. Stewart | 34 | 6 | 12 | 23 | 5 | 2 | 3,642,348 |
| 2001 | T. Stewart | 36 | 3 | 15 | 22 | 4 | 0 | 4,941,463 |
| 2002 | T. Stewart | 36 | 3 | 15 | 21 | 6 | 2 | 9,163,761 |
| 2003 | T. Stewart | 36 | 2 | 12 | 18 | 5 | 1 | 6,131,633 |
| **TOTALS** |  | **176** | **17** | **66** | **105** | **21** | **7** | **$27,069,354** |

## 2003 season

# 2003 points standings

| Rk. | Driver | Points | Behind | Starts | Wins | Top 5 | Top 10 | Winnings |
|---|---|---|---|---|---|---|---|---|
| 1. | Matt Kenseth | 5,022 | — | 36 | 1 | 11 | 25 | $9,422,764 |
| 2. | Jimmie Johnson | 4,932 | -90 | 36 | 3 | 14 | 20 | $7,745,530 |
| 3. | Dale Earnhardt Jr. | 4,815 | -207 | 36 | 2 | 13 | 21 | $6,880,807 |
| 4. | Jeff Gordon | 4,785 | -237 | 36 | 3 | 15 | 20 | $6,622,002 |
| 5. | Kevin Harvick | 4,770 | -252 | 36 | 1 | 11 | 18 | $6,237,119 |
| 6. | Ryan Newman | 4,711 | -311 | 36 | 8 | 17 | 22 | $6,100,877 |
| 7. | Tony Stewart | 4,549 | -473 | 36 | 2 | 12 | 18 | $6,131,633 |
| 8. | Bobby Labonte | 4,377 | -645 | 36 | 2 | 12 | 17 | $5,505,018 |
| 9. | Bill Elliott | 4,303 | -719 | 36 | 1 | 9 | 12 | $5,008,530 |
| 10. | Terry Labonte | 4,162 | -860 | 36 | 1 | 4 | 9 | $4,283,625 |
| 11. | Kurt Busch | 4,150 | -872 | 36 | 4 | 9 | 14 | $5,587,384 |
| 12. | Jeff Burton | 4,109 | -913 | 36 | 0 | 3 | 11 | $4,384,752 |
| 13. | Jamie McMurray* | 3,965 | -1,057 | 36 | 0 | 5 | 13 | $3,258,806 |
| 14. | Rusty Wallace | 3,950 | -1,072 | 36 | 0 | 2 | 12 | $4,246,547 |
| 15. | Michael Waltrip | 3,934 | -1,088 | 36 | 2 | 8 | 11 | $4,929,620 |
| 16. | Robby Gordon | 3,856 | -1,166 | 36 | 2 | 4 | 10 | $4,157,064 |
| 17. | Mark Martin | 3,769 | -1,253 | 36 | 0 | 5 | 10 | $4,486,560 |
| 18. | Sterling Marlin | 3,745 | -1,277 | 36 | 0 | 0 | 11 | $4,384,491 |
| 19. | Jeremy Mayfield | 3,736 | -1,286 | 36 | 0 | 4 | 12 | $3,371,879 |
| 20. | Greg Biffle* | 3,696 | -1,326 | 35 | 1 | 3 | 6 | $2,805,673 |
| 21. | Ward Burton | 3,550 | -1,472 | 36 | 0 | 0 | 4 | $3,628,600 |
| 22. | Elliott Sadler | 3,525 | -1,497 | 36 | 0 | 2 | 9 | $3,795,174 |
| 23. | Ricky Rudd | 3,521 | -1,501 | 36 | 0 | 4 | 5 | $3,240,614 |
| 24. | Johnny Benson | 3,448 | -1,574 | 36 | 0 | 2 | 4 | $3,544,793 |
| 25. | Joe Nemechek | 3,426 | -1,596 | 36 | 1 | 2 | 6 | $2,626,484 |
| 26. | Dale Jarrett | 3,358 | -1,664 | 36 | 1 | 1 | 7 | $4,121,847 |
| 27. | Ricky Craven | 3,334 | -1,688 | 36 | 1 | 3 | 8 | $3,216,211 |
| 28. | Dave Blaney | 3,194 | -1,828 | 36 | 0 | 1 | 4 | $2,828,690 |
| 29. | Jimmy Spencer | 3,147 | -1,875 | 35 | 0 | 1 | 4 | $2,565,800 |
| 30. | Kenny Wallace | 3,061 | -1,961 | 36 | 0 | 0 | 1 | $2,480,490 |
| 31. | Todd Bodine | 2,976 | -2,046 | 35 | 0 | 0 | 1 | $2,521,727 |
| 32. | Steve Park | 2,923 | -2,099 | 35 | 0 | 1 | 3 | $2,686,910 |
| 33. | Tony Raines* | 2,772 | -2,250 | 35 | 0 | 0 | 1 | $2,122,740 |
| 34. | Jeff Green | 2,656 | -2,366 | 31 | 0 | 0 | 1 | $2,693,530 |
| 35. | Casey Mears* | 2,638 | -2,384 | 36 | 0 | 0 | 0 | $2,639,180 |
| 36. | Ken Schrader | 2,451 | -2,571 | 32 | 0 | 0 | 2 | $2,007,420 |
| 37. | Kyle Petty | 2,414 | -2,608 | 33 | 0 | 0 | 0 | $2,293,220 |
| 38. | John Andretti | 2,379 | -2,643 | 29 | 0 | 0 | 1 | $2,577,620 |
| 39. | Mike Skinner | 1,960 | -3,062 | 26 | 0 | 0 | 0 | $1,782,800 |
| 40. | Jack Sprague* | 1,284 | -3,738 | 18 | 0 | 0 | 0 | $1,187,830 |
| 41. | Larry Foyt* | 1,228 | -3,794 | 20 | 0 | 0 | 0 | $1,180,990 |
| 42. | Mike Wallace | 1,189 | -3,833 | 14 | 0 | 0 | 2 | $1,031,100 |
| 43. | Kevin Lepage | 877 | -4,145 | 11 | 0 | 0 | 0 | $742,077 |
| 44. | Christian Fittipaldi | 857 | -4,165 | 15 | 0 | 0 | 0 | $1,265,830 |
| 45. | Jerry Nadeau | 844 | -4,178 | 10 | 0 | 1 | 1 | $861,628 |
| 46. | Derrike Cope | 822 | -4,200 | 18 | 0 | 0 | 0 | $1,030,690 |
| 47. | Jason Leffler | 764 | -4,258 | 10 | 0 | 0 | 0 | $594,500 |
| 48. | Scott Wimmer | 599 | -4,423 | 6 | 0 | 0 | 1 | $487,060 |
| 49. | Brian Vickers | 379 | -4,643 | 5 | 0 | 0 | 0 | $263,484 |
| 50. | Hermie Sadler | 373 | -4,649 | 10 | 0 | 0 | 0 | $552,741 |
| 51. | Johnny Sauter | 356 | -4,666 | 5 | 0 | 0 | 0 | $281,335 |
| 52. | Brett Bodine | 308 | -4,714 | 6 | 0 | 0 | 0 | $383,718 |
| 53. | Scott Pruett | 236 | -4,786 | 2 | 0 | 1 | 1 | $143,035 |
| 54. | Bobby Hamilton Jr. | 203 | -4,819 | 2 | 0 | 0 | 0 | $128,725 |
| 55. | Boris Said | 201 | -4,821 | 2 | 0 | 0 | 1 | $134,680 |
| 56. | Ron Fellows | 200 | -4,822 | 2 | 0 | 0 | 1 | $161,854 |
| 57. | Buckshot Jones | 160 | -4,862 | 2 | 0 | 0 | 0 | $119,730 |
| 58. | Jason Keller | 152 | -4,870 | 2 | 0 | 0 | 0 | $128,007 |
| 59. | Johnny Miller | 146 | -4,876 | 2 | 0 | 0 | 0 | $110,814 |
| 60. | David Green | 125 | -4,897 | 2 | 0 | 0 | 0 | $138,070 |
| 61. | Casey Atwood | 113 | -4,909 | 2 | 0 | 0 | 0 | $149,838 |
| 62. | Ron Hornaday | 103 | -4,919 | 1 | 0 | 0 | 0 | $48,950 |

2003 SEASON

| Rk. | Driver | Points | Behind | Starts | Wins | Top 5 | Top 10 | Winnings |
|---|---|---|---|---|---|---|---|---|
| 63. | Hideo Fukuyama* | 98 | -4,924 | 2 | 0 | 0 | 0 | $115,229 |
| 64. | P.J. Jones | 91 | -4,931 | 1 | 0 | 0 | 0 | $59,135 |
| 65. | Mike Bliss | 85 | -4,937 | 1 | 0 | 0 | 0 | $65,300 |
| 66. | Paul Menard | 76 | -4,946 | 1 | 0 | 0 | 0 | $52,410 |
| 67. | Jason Jarrett | 76 | -4,946 | 1 | 0 | 0 | 0 | $52,640 |
| 68. | Ted Musgrave | 70 | -4,952 | 1 | 0 | 0 | 0 | $63,715 |
| 69. | Morgan Shepherd | 68 | -4,954 | 2 | 0 | 0 | 0 | $120,034 |
| 70. | Geoffrey Bodine | 46 | -4,976 | 1 | 0 | 0 | 0 | $78,150 |
| 71. | Stacy Compton | 39 | -4,983 | 1 | 0 | 0 | 0 | $67,400 |

*Rookie

## 2003 miles leaders standings

| | Driver | Miles Led | Times Led | Races Led | Miles Run | Possible Miles | Unfinished Miles | Laps Led | Wins | Starts |
|---|---|---|---|---|---|---|---|---|---|---|
| 1. | Ryan Newman | 1,509.13 | 52 | 24 | 12,186.19 | 13,933.63 | 1,747.45 | 1,173 | 8 | 36 |
| 2. | Jeff Gordon | 1,497.69 | 57 | 22 | 13,579.39 | 13,933.63 | 354.25 | 1,639 | 3 | 36 |
| 3. | Tony Stewart | 1,425.88 | 48 | 16 | 13,237.06 | 13,933.63 | 696.57 | 882 | 2 | 36 |
| 4. | Dale Earnhardt Jr. | 1,292.36 | 57 | 24 | 13,710.44 | 13,933.63 | 223.20 | 1,046 | 2 | 36 |
| 5. | Jimmie Johnson | 987.03 | 51 | 20 | 13,694.73 | 13,933.63 | 238.91 | 644 | 3 | 36 |
| 6. | Bill Elliott | 823.05 | 25 | 12 | 13,165.46 | 13,933.63 | 768.17 | 600 | 1 | 36 |
| 7. | Kevin Harvick | 787.05 | 38 | 19 | 13,875.73 | 13,933.63 | 57.91 | 569 | 1 | 36 |
| 8. | Kurt Busch | 681.04 | 29 | 19 | 12,684.97 | 13,933.63 | 1,248.66 | 680 | 4 | 36 |
| 9. | Bobby Labonte | 638.04 | 36 | 18 | 13,038.79 | 13,933.63 | 894.84 | 497 | 2 | 36 |
| 10. | Matt Kenseth | 543.47 | 31 | 17 | 13,422.81 | 13,933.63 | 510.83 | 354 | 1 | 36 |
| 11. | Rusty Wallace | 487.83 | 23 | 10 | 12,698.24 | 13,933.63 | 1,235.39 | 379 | 0 | 36 |
| 12. | Sterling Marlin | 368.73 | 14 | 8 | 12,696.85 | 13,933.63 | 1,236.78 | 237 | 0 | 36 |
| 13. | Michael Waltrip | 356.20 | 22 | 10 | 12,580.97 | 13,933.63 | 1,352.66 | 159 | 2 | 36 |
| 14. | Elliott Sadler | 321.44 | 17 | 10 | 12,541.50 | 13,933.63 | 1,392.13 | 174 | 0 | 36 |
| 15. | Robby Gordon | 291.49 | 12 | 8 | 13,525.68 | 13,933.63 | 407.95 | 158 | 2 | 36 |
| 16. | Greg Biffle | 245.97 | 8 | 6 | 13,125.58 | 13,533.13 | 407.55 | 136 | 1 | 35 |
| 17. | Jamie McMurray | 238.09 | 16 | 8 | 13,369.26 | 13,933.63 | 584.38 | 120 | 0 | 36 |
| 18. | Jeremy Mayfield | 209.67 | 9 | 4 | 12,619.44 | 13,933.63 | 1,314.19 | 156 | 0 | 36 |
| 19. | Mark Martin | 174.66 | 13 | 7 | 12,349.45 | 13,933.63 | 1,584.18 | 159 | 0 | 36 |
| 20. | Jeff Burton | 163.83 | 10 | 8 | 13,009.74 | 13,933.63 | 923.90 | 98 | 0 | 36 |
| 21. | Joe Nemechek | 160.35 | 9 | 4 | 12,801.23 | 13,933.63 | 1,132.40 | 197 | 1 | 36 |
| 22. | Jimmy Spencer | 113.10 | 12 | 10 | 12,051.96 | 13,667.13 | 1,615.17 | 163 | 0 | 35 |
| 23. | Terry Labonte | 105.96 | 11 | 9 | 13,816.84 | 13,933.63 | 116.79 | 118 | 1 | 36 |
| 24. | Ward Burton | 77.59 | 9 | 5 | 13,505.89 | 13,933.63 | 427.74 | 48 | 0 | 36 |
| 25. | Dale Jarrett | 73.04 | 8 | 6 | 12,676.26 | 13,933.63 | 1,257.37 | 49 | 1 | 36 |
| 26. | Buckshot Jones | 50.54 | 1 | 1 | 634.08 | 900.08 | 266.00 | 19 | 0 | 2 |
| 27. | Ron Fellows | 42.00 | 2 | 1 | 420.90 | 440.50 | 19.60 | 21 | 0 | 2 |
| 28. | Ricky Rudd | 32.82 | 4 | 4 | 12,370.02 | 13,933.63 | 1,563.62 | 29 | 0 | 36 |
| 29. | Johnny Benson | 27.00 | 3 | 3 | 12,609.58 | 13,933.63 | 1,324.06 | 15 | 0 | 36 |
| 30. | Casey Mears | 22.50 | 2 | 2 | 11,942.60 | 13,919.97 | 1,977.37 | 9 | 0 | 36 |
| 31. | Scott Pruett | 22.05 | 1 | 1 | 438.50 | 440.50 | 2.00 | 9 | 0 | 2 |
| 32. | Jason Leffler | 21.75 | 3 | 2 | 3,605.39 | 3,749.72 | 144.33 | 24 | 0 | 10 |
| 33. | Ricky Craven | 20.04 | 6 | 6 | 12,429.05 | 13,933.63 | 1,504.59 | 16 | 1 | 36 |
| 34. | Jeff Green | 16.53 | 4 | 4 | 11,481.91 | 12,375.23 | 893.32 | 20 | 0 | 31 |
| 35. | Brian Vickers | 16.50 | 1 | 1 | 1,559.85 | 2,113.68 | 553.83 | 11 | 0 | 5 |
| 36. | Kevin Lepage | 14.83 | 3 | 3 | 4,186.88 | 4,492.00 | 305.12 | 11 | 0 | 11 |
| 37. | Dave Blaney | 13.68 | 3 | 3 | 12,960.83 | 13,933.63 | 972.80 | 11 | 0 | 36 |
| 38. | Larry Foyt | 12.50 | 1 | 1 | 6,297.48 | 8,289.93 | 1,992.45 | 5 | 0 | 20 |
| 39. | Todd Bodine | 10.00 | 2 | 2 | 11,477.87 | 13,433.55 | 1,955.68 | 4 | 0 | 35 |
| 40. | Mike Skinner | 8.17 | 4 | 4 | 8,873.30 | 10,263.05 | 1,289.76 | 8 | 0 | 26 |
| 41. | John Andretti | 7.16 | 2 | 2 | 10,176.95 | 11,345.31 | 1,168.36 | 4 | 0 | 29 |
| 42. | Mike Wallace | 5.25 | 1 | 1 | 4947.62 | 5,617.06 | 669.44 | 7 | 0 | 14 |
| 43. | Steve Park | 5.22 | 3 | 3 | 12,166.53 | 13,433.55 | 1,267.02 | 3 | 0 | 35 |
| 44. | Kyle Petty | 4.88 | 3 | 3 | 11,806.70 | 12,532.05 | 725.36 | 3 | 0 | 33 |
| 45. | Boris Said | 2.00 | 1 | 1 | 416.00 | 440.50 | 24.50 | 1 | 0 | 2 |
| 46. | Christian Fittipaldi | 2.00 | 1 | 1 | 4,426.06 | 5618.20 | 1,192.14 | 1 | 0 | 15 |
| 47. | Hermie Sadler | 2.00 | 1 | 1 | 1,763.60 | 3,845.80 | 2,082.21 | 1 | 0 | 10 |
| 48. | Tony Raines | 1.54 | 1 | 1 | 12,037.96 | 13,533.62 | 1,495.67 | 1 | 0 | 35 |

# 2003 NASCAR Winston Cup Series race results

| Race | Location | Pole | Winner | Winning Owner | Time of race | Avg. Speed | Victory margin | Race leaders | Lead changes | Caution flags | Caution laps | Cars on lead lap | DNFs |
|---|---|---|---|---|---|---|---|---|---|---|---|---|---|
| Daytona 500 | Daytona Beach, Fla. | Jeff Green | Michael Waltrip | Teresa Earnhardt | 2:02:08 | 133.87 | Under Caution | 8 | 11 | 5 | 23 | 33 | 5 |
| Subway 400 | Rockingham, N.C. | Dave Blaney * | Dale Jarrett | Robert Yates | 3:23:29 | 117.852 | .966 sec. | 11 | 20 | 7 | 46 | 11 | 4 |
| UAW-Daimler Chrysler 400 | Las Vegas | Bobby Labonte | Matt Kenseth | Jack Roush | 3:00:46 | 132.934 | 1.274 sec. | 10 | 17 | 6 | 30 | 11 | 9 |
| Bass Pro Shops MBNA 500 | Hampton, Ga. | Ryan Newman | Bobby Labonte | Joe Gibbs | 3:25:37 | 146.048 | 1.274 sec. | 10 | 23 | 7 | 34 | 9 | 12 |
| Carolina Dodge Dealers 400 | Darlington, S.C. | Elliott Sadler * | Ricky Craven | Cal Wells III | 3:10:16 | 126.214 | .002 sec. | 11 | 15 | 7 | 33 | 10 | 5 |
| Food City 500 | Bristol, Tenn. | Ryan Newman | Kurt Busch | Jack Roush | 3:29:53 | 76.185 | .390 sec. | 7 | 11 | 17 | 121 | 6 | 8 |
| Samsung/RadioShack 500 | Fort Worth, Tex. | Bobby Labonte | Ryan Newman | Roger Penske | 3:43:28 | 134.517 | 3.405 sec. | 11 | 19 | 10 | 52 | 13 | 12 |
| Aaron's 499 | Talladega, Ala. | Jeremy Mayfield | Dale Earnhardt Jr. | Teresa Earnhardt | 3:27:28 | 144.625 | .125 sec. | 16 | 43 | 6 | 32 | 17 | 10 |
| Virginia 500 | Martinsville, Va. | Jeff Gordon | Jeff Gordon | Rick Hendrick | 3:28:51 | 75.557 | Under Caution | 9 | 14 | 11 | 64 | 12 | 9 |
| Auto Club 500 | Fontana, Calif. | Steve Park | Kurt Busch | Jack Roush | 3:34:07 | 140.111 | 2.294 sec. | 9 | 19 | 8 | 34 | 16 | 9 |
| Pontiac Excitement 400 | Richmond, Va. | Terry Labonte | Joe Nemechek | Rick Hendrick | 3:23:47 | 86.783 | Under Caution | 11 | 20 | 15 | 91 | 23 | 10 |
| Coca-Cola 600 | Harrisburg, N.C. | Ryan Newman | Jimmie Johnson | Rick Hendrick | 3:16:50 | 126.198 | Under Caution | 8 | 16 | 8 | 46 | 18 | 7 |
| MBNA Armed ForcesFamily 400 | Dover, Del. | Ryan Newman | Ryan Newman | Roger Penske | 3:44:31 | 106.896 | .834 sec. | 10 | 16 | 9 | 68 | 13 | 9 |
| Pocono 500 | Long Pond, Pa. | Jimmie Johnson | Tony Stewart | Joe Gibbs | 3:42:24 | 134.892 | Under Caution | 16 | 28 | 5 | 25 | 19 | 10 |
| Sirius 400 | Brooklyn, Mich. | Bobby Labonte | Kurt Busch | Jack Roush | 3:02:54 | 131.219 | .774 sec. | 9 | 22 | 9 | 41 | 15 | 7 |
| Dodge/Save Mart 350 | Sonoma, Calif. | Boris Said ^ | Robby Gordon | Richard Childress | 2:57:55 | 73.821 | .553 sec. | 4 | 6 | 5 | 16 | 29 | 5 |
| Pepsi 400 | Daytona Beach, Fla. | Steve Park | Greg Biffle ^ | Jack Roush | 2:24:29 | 166.109 | 4.102 sec. | 11 | 17 | 2 | 10 | 23 | 4 |
| Tropicana 400 | Joliet, Ill. | Tony Stewart | Ryan Newman | Roger Penske | 2:59:15 | 134.059 | 2.633 sec. | 7 | 13 | 7 | 36 | 11 | 10 |
| New England 300 | Loudon, N.H. | Matt Kenseth # | Jimmie Johnson | Rick Hendrick | 3:16:29 | 96.924 | 1.582 sec. | 9 | 14 | 12 | 63 | 24 | 4 |
| Pennsylvania 500 | Long Pond, Pa. | Ryan Newman | Ryan Newman | Roger Penske | 3:54:55 | 127.705 | .307 sec. | 11 | 18 | 8 | 36 | 22 | 10 |
| Brickyard 400 | Indianapolis | Kevin Harvick | Kevin Harvick | Richard Childress | 2:58:22 | 134.554 | 2.758 sec. | 12 | 17 | 5 | 25 | 21 | 4 |
| Sirius at The Glen | Watkins Glen, N.Y. | Jeff Gordon | Robby Gordon | Richard Childress | 2:26:17 | 90.441 | 2.335 sec. | 8 | 8 | 6 | 14 | 32 | 2 |
| GFS Marketplace 400 | Brooklyn, Mich. | Bobby Labonte | Ryan Newman | Roger Penske | 3:08:31 | 127.31 | 1.652 | 8 | 14 | 8 | 46 | 26 | 10 |
| Sharpie 500 | Bristol, Tenn. | Jeff Gordon | Kurt Busch | Jack Roush | 3:26:32 | 77.421 | .818 sec. | 8 | 11 | 20 | 119 | 22 | 8 |
| Mountain Dew Southern 500 | Darlington, S.C. | Ryan Newman | Terry Labonte | Rick Hendrick | 4:09:07 | 120.744 | 1.651 sec. | 12 | 24 | 9 | 55 | 16 | 9 |
| Chevy Rock & Roll 400 | Richmond, Va. | Mike Skinner | Ryan Newman | Roger Penske | 3:09:35 | 94.945 | .159 sec. | 12 | 20 | 14 | 76 | 16 | 6 |
| Sylvania 300 | Loudon, N.H. | Ryan Newman | Jimmie Johnson | Rick Hendrick | 2:58:41 | 106.58 | 6.240 sec. | 11 | 20 | 6 | 38 | 13 | 5 |
| MBNA America 400 | Dover, Del. | Matt Kenseth # | Ryan Newman | Roger Penske | 3:40:35 | 108.802 | 1.152 sec. | 7 | 13 | 7 | 63 | 19 | 7 |
| EA Sports 500 | Talladega, Ala. | Elliott Sadler | Michael Waltrip | Teresa Earnhardt | 3:12:17 | 156.045 | .095 sec. | 17 | 41 | 5 | 23 | 23 | 13 |
| Banquet 400 | Kansas City, Kan. | Jimmie Johnson | Ryan Newman | Roger Penske | 3:17:34 | 121.63 | .863 sec. | 11 | 23 | 9 | 47 | 24 | 9 |
| UAW-GM Quality 500 | Harrisburg, N.C. | Ryan Newman | Tony Stewart | Joe Gibbs | 3:30:24 | 142.871 | .608 sec. | 8 | 15 | 6 | 31 | 15 | 4 |
| Subway 500 | Martinsville, Va. | Jeff Gordon | Jeff Gordon | Rick Hendrick | 3:53:14 | 67.658 | 1.036 sec. | 8 | 9 | 19 | 119 | 15 | 5 |
| Georgia 500 | Hampton, Ga. | Jeff Gordon | Jeff Gordon | Rick Hendrick | 3:55:02 | 127.769 | Under Caution | 12 | 28 | 10 | 63 | 14 | 11 |
| Checker Auto Parts 500 | Phoenix | Ryan Newman | Dale Earnhardt Jr. | Teresa Earnhardt | 3:19:11 | 93.984 | .735 sec. | 6 | 10 | 10 | 66 | 29 | 8 |
| Pop Secret Microwave Popcorn 400 | Rockingham, N.C. | Bill Elliott | Ray Evernham | | 3:34:44 | 111.677 | 1.230 sec. | 5 | 14 | 10 | 65 | 10 | 7 |
| Ford 400 | Homestead, Fla. | Jamie McMurray * | Bobby Labonte | Joe Gibbs | 3:25:37 | 116.868 | 1.749 sec. | 12 | 21 | 10 | 60 | 21 | 11 |

\* First-time Bud Pole winner  ^ First-time race winner  # Pole position awarded by points

2003 SEASON

# 2003 Raybestos Rookie of the Year

## Jamie McMurray

**Car:** No. 42 Dodge. **Team Owner:** Chip Ganassi/Felix Sabates. **Birthdate:** June 3, 1976. **Hometown:** Huntersville, N.C.

### NASCAR BUSCH SERIES STATISTICS

Seasons Competed: 2 (2002, 2003)   Career Starts: 42
Career Wins: 1                      Career Poles: 1

**Rookie Season Recap:** McMurray won the Raybestos Rookie of the Year award because he was consistently solid in the second half of the season. In the last 13 races, he had eight top 10s and finished outside the top 20 just once. His best finishes for the season were a pair of thirds, one at Indianapolis and the other at the Brickyard. McMurray's measured driving style and willingness to learn won him the respect of veteran drivers and helped keep his equipment together. He completed an impressive 95.6 percent of possible laps on the season. His consistency was noteworthy, as well—his longest stretch outside of the top 10 was seven races, and even then he had three top 15s. He won his first career Cup pole in the season finale at Homestead.

## 2003 rookie points standings

| Rk. | Driver | Rookie Points | Points behind | Starts | Wins | Top 5 | Top 10 | Winnings |
|---|---|---|---|---|---|---|---|---|
| 1 | Jamie McMurray | 320 | — | 36 | 0 | 5 | 13 | $2,699,970 |
| 2 | Greg Biffle | 283 | -37 | 35 | 1 | 3 | 6 | $2,410,050 |
| 3 | Tony Raines | 239 | -81 | 35 | 0 | 0 | 1 | $2,122,740 |
| 4 | Casey Mears | 238 | -82 | 36 | 0 | 0 | 0 | $2,639,180 |
| 5 | Jack Sprague | 183 | -137 | 18 | 0 | 0 | 0 | $1,187,830 |
| 6 | Larry Foyt | 176 | -144 | 20 | 0 | 0 | 0 | $1,180,990 |

## Raybestos Rookies of the Year: 1957-2003

| Year | Driver | Pt Pos | Races | Poles | Wins | Top 5 | Top 10 | Winnings |
|---|---|---|---|---|---|---|---|---|
| 2003 | Jamie McMurray | 13 | 36 | 1 | 0 | 5 | 13 | $3,258,806 |
| 2002 | Ryan Newman | 6th | 36 | 6 | 1 | 14 | 22 | $5,346,651 |
| 2001 | Kevin Harvick | 9th | 35 | 0 | 2 | 6 | 16 | $4,302,202 |
| 2000 | Matt Kenseth | 14th | 34 | 0 | 1 | 4 | 11 | $2,408,138 |
| 1999 | Tony Stewart | 4th | 34 | 2 | 3 | 12 | 21 | $3,190,149 |
| 1998 | Kenny Irwin | 28th | 32 | 1 | 0 | 1 | 4 | $1,459,967 |
| 1997 | Mike Skinner | 30th | 31 | 2 | 0 | 0 | 3 | $900,569 |
| 1996 | Johnny Benson | 21st | 30 | 1 | 0 | 1 | 6 | $932,580 |
| 1995 | Ricky Craven | 24th | 31 | 0 | 0 | 0 | 4 | $597,054 |
| 1994 | Jeff Burton | 24th | 30 | 0 | 0 | 2 | 3 | $594,700 |
| 1993 | Jeff Gordon | 14th | 30 | 1 | 0 | 7 | 11 | $765,168 |
| 1992 | Jimmy Hensley | 28th | 22 | 0 | 0 | 0 | 4 | $247,660 |
| 1991 | Bobby Hamilton | 22nd | 28 | 0 | 0 | 0 | 4 | $259,105 |
| 1990 | Rob Moroso | 30th | 25 | 0 | 0 | 0 | 1 | $162,002 |
| 1989 | Dick Trickle | 15th | 28 | 0 | 0 | 6 | 9 | $343,728 |
| 1988 | Ken Bouchard | 25th | 24 | 0 | 0 | 0 | 1 | $109,410 |
| 1987 | Davey Allison | 21st | 22 | 5 | 2 | 9 | 10 | $361,060 |
| 1986 | Alan Kulwicki | 21st | 23 | 0 | 0 | 1 | 4 | $94,450 |
| 1985 | Ken Schrader | 16th | 28 | 0 | 0 | 0 | 3 | $211,523 |
| 1984 | Rusty Wallace | 14th | 30 | 0 | 0 | 2 | 4 | $196,617 |
| 1983 | Sterling Marlin | 19th | 30 | 0 | 0 | 0 | 1 | $143,564 |
| 1982 | Geoffrey Bodine | 22nd | 25 | 2 | 0 | 4 | 10 | $258,500 |
| 1981 | Ron Bouchard | 22nd | 22 | 1 | 1 | 5 | 12 | $152,855 |
| 1980 | Jody Ridley | 7th | 31 | 0 | 0 | 2 | 18 | $196,617 |
| 1979 | Dale Earnhardt | 7th | 27 | 4 | 1 | 11 | 17 | $264,086 |
| 1978 | Ronnie Thomas | 18th | 27 | 0 | 0 | 0 | 2 | $73,037 |
| 1977 | Ricky Rudd | 17th | 25 | 0 | 0 | 1 | 10 | $68,448 |
| 1976 | Skip Manning | 18th | 27 | 0 | 0 | 0 | 4 | $55,820 |
| 1975 | Bruce Hill | 16th | 26 | 0 | 0 | 3 | 11 | $58,138 |
| 1974 | Earl Ross | 8th | 21 | 0 | 1 | 5 | 10 | $64,830 |
| 1973 | Lennie Pond | 23rd | 23 | 0 | 0 | 1 | 9 | $25,155 |
| 1972 | Larry Smith | 23rd | 23 | 0 | 0 | 0 | 7 | $24,215 |
| 1971 | Walter Ballard | 10th | 41 | 0 | 0 | 3 | 11 | $25,598 |
| 1970 | Bill Dennis | 25th | 25 | 0 | 0 | 0 | 5 | $15,670 |
| 1969 | Dick Brooks | 21st | 28 | 0 | 0 | 3 | 12 | $27,532 |
| 1968 | Pete Hamilton | 32nd | 16 | 0 | 0 | 3 | 6 | $8,239 |
| 1967 | Donnie Allison | 16th | 20 | 0 | 0 | 4 | 7 | $16,440 |
| 1966 | James Hylton | 2nd | 41 | 1 | 0 | 20 | 32 | $29,575 |
| 1965 | Sam McQuagg | 24th | 15 | 0 | 0 | 2 | 5 | $10,555 |
| 1964 | Doug Cooper | 21st | 39 | 0 | 0 | 4 | 11 | $10,445 |
| 1963 | Billy Wade | 16th | 22 | 0 | 0 | 4 | 11 | $8,710 |
| 1962 | Tom Cox | 18th | 40 | 0 | 0 | 12 | 20 | $8,980 |
| 1961 | Woody Wilson | 41st | 5 | 0 | 0 | 0 | 1 | $2,625 |
| 1960 | David Pearson | 23rd | 22 | 0 | 3 | 3 | 7 | $5,030 |
| 1959 | Richard Petty | 15th | 22 | 0 | 0 | 6 | 9 | $7,630 |
| 1958 | Shorty Rollins | 4th | 21 | 0 | 1 | 10 | 17 | $8,515 |
| 1957 | Ken Rush | 38th | 16 | 1 | 0 | 1 | 6 | $2,045 |

# NASCAR NEXTEL All-Star Challenge

## Survival of the Fastest

The NASCAR NEXTEL All-Star Challenge, the "all-star" spectacle of the NASCAR NEXTEL Cup Series and one of the season's biggest events, will be contested for the 20th time this year. The prize for the survivor of "Survival of the Fastest" is $1 million.

From Dale Earnhardt's famous 1987 "Pass in the Grass" to Jeff Gordon's 2001 victory in a backup car to Ryan Newman's win as a rookie in 2002 after transferring from the Winston Open, the star-studded event has played host to some of NASCAR's most dramatic moments since its inception in 1985.

The winners-only event returns to Lowe's Motor Speedway, which has hosted it since 1987. The 2004 NASCAR NEXTEL All-Star challenge will be run under the lights on May 22.

The race will be 90 laps around the 1.5-mile tri-oval. There will be three segments, one each of 40, 30 and 20 laps.

Drivers will be eliminated after each segment. After the first segment, which mandates a four-tire, green-flag pit stop, the field will be reduced to 20 competitors. After the second segment, only the fastest 14 will advance to the final 20-lap shootout and take aim at $1 million. Naturally, inverting part of the field for the final segment could figure into the equation.

The NEXTEL Open will consist of 30 laps and will be run in segments of 20 and 10 laps. After the first segment, the field will be reduced to 14 cars to challenge for the one transfer spot to the NASCAR NEXTEL All-Star Challenge. The NEXTEL Open is for all NASCAR NEXTEL Cup teams that competed in a NASCAR Cup Series event in 2003 or 2004 that are not already eligible for the NASCAR NEXTEL All-Star Challenge. Following are the rules, subject to change, for the 2004 running of NASCAR NEXTEL All-Star Challenge and the NEXTEL Open.

### THE NASCAR NEXTEL All-Star Challenge

- The NASCAR NEXTEL All-Star Challenge will consist of a minimum of 20 cars and drivers comprised of:
  – Drivers and car owners who have won races in the preceding and current years.
  – Any active driver who has won the NASCAR Cup points championship.
  – Any active driver who has won the event within the five preceding years.
  – The winner of the NEXTEL Open.
- The NASCAR NEXTEL All-Star Challenge will be 90 laps total and consists of three segments of 40, 30 and 20 laps. The field will be inverted for the final segment as determined at the track in a random fashion.
- First Segment—40 laps
  – Teams must make a green-flag, four-tire pit stop during this segment.
  – All restarts will be double-file.
  – All laps count, including caution laps. If a late-segment caution occurs, efforts will be made to ensure a green-flag finish.
  – The top 20 finishers from the first segment will advance to the second segment.
  – The winner of the first segment will earn $50,000.
- There will be a 10-minute break following the first segment, at which time teams may change tires and make chassis adjustments without losing track position.
- Second Segment—30 laps
  – The finish of the first segment will determine the double-file starting order of the 20-car field for the second segment.
  – There are no pit-stop requirements, but teams may pit if they wish. All laps count, including caution laps. If a late-segment caution occurs, efforts will be made to ensure a green-flag finish.
  – Only the top 14 finishers in the second segment will advance to the final segment.
  – The winner of the second segment will earn $50,000.
- There will be a 10-minute break following the second segment, during which time teams may change tires and make chassis adjustments without losing track position.
  During the break, the determination will be made as to how many cars will be inverted from their finishing position in the second segment. A maximum of 10 and a minimum of three cars will be inverted prior to the start of the final segment. The number to invert will be randomly determined on site.
- Third Segment—20 laps.
  – The top 14 finishers in the second segment will compete in the third and final segment with the field inverted as determined during the 10-minute break. The start of the final segment will be double-file. Only green-flag laps count.
  – The winner of the final segment will earn $1 million.

### NASCAR NEXTEL All-Star Challenge Qualifying

- Qualifying will consist of three laps with a mandatory four-tire pit stop. The total elapsed time will make up each team's qualifying effort. The NASCAR NEXTEL All-Star Challenge qualifying will be Friday night.
- The winning team will earn $50,000.

### NEXTEL Open

- This NEXTEL Open is for all NASCAR NEXTEL Cup

teams that competed in a NASCAR Cup Series event in 2003 or 2004 that are not already eligible for The NASCAR NEXTEL All-Star Challenge.

• The NEXTEL Open will consist of 30 laps and be run in two segments of 20 laps and 10 laps.

• First Segment—20 Laps

− All laps count, including caution laps. If a late-segment caution occurs, efforts will be made to ensure a green-flag finish.

− All restarts will be double-file.

− The top 14 finishers will advance to the second and final segment.

• There will be a five-minute break following the first segment, at which time teams may change tires and make chassis adjustments without losing track position.

• Second Segment—10 laps

− The top 14 finishers will compete in the final 10-lap segment.

− All restarts will be double-file.

− Only green-flag laps count.

• The winner of The NEXTEL Open will advance to The NASCAR NEXTEL All-Star Challenge.

# 2004 fact sheet

**Where:** Lowe's Motor Speedway
**When:** May 22, 2004
**Time:** 9 p.m. ET (approximately)
**Length:** Three segments (40, 30 and 20 laps)
**Purse:** $3,500,000 (includes Nextel Open)
**Winner:** $1,000,000

## THE NASCAR NEXTEL ALL-STAR CHALLENGE 2004 ELIGIBILITY LIST (as of 1/1/2004)

| Driver | Race Won | Car Owner |
|---|---|---|
| 1. Michael Waltrip | 2003 Daytona 500, Daytona Beach, Fla. | Teresa Earnhardt |
| 2. Dale Jarrett | 2003 Subway 400, Rockingham, N.C. | Robert Yates |
| 3. Matt Kenseth | 2003 UAW-Daimler Chrysler 400, Las Vegas | Jack Roush |
| 4. Bobby Labonte | 2003 Bass Pro Shops MBNA 500, Hampton, Ga. | Joe Gibbs |
| 5. Ricky Craven | 2003 Carolina Dodge Dealers 400, Darlington, S.C. | Cal Wells |
|  | 2002 Food City 500, Bristol, Tenn. | Jack Roush |
| 6. Kurt Busch | 2003 Food City 500, Bristol, Tenn. | Jack Roush |
| 7. Ryan Newman | 2003 Samsung/Radio Shack 500, Fort Worth, Texas | Roger Penske |
| 8. Dale Earnhardt Jr. | 2003 Aaron's 499, Talladega, Ala. | Teresa Earnhardt |
| 9. Jeff Gordon | 2003 Virginia 500, Martinsville, Va. | Rick Hendrick |
| 10. Joe Nemechek | 2003 Pontiac Excitement 400, Richmond, Va. | Rick Hendrick |
| 11. Jimmie Johnson | 2003 Coca-Cola 600, Charlotte, N.C. | Rick Hendrick |
| 12. Tony Stewart | 2003 Pocono 500, Long Pond, Pa. | Joe Gibbs |
| 13. Robby Gordon | 2003 Dodge/Save Mart 350, Sonoma, Calif. | Richard Childress |
| 14. Greg Biffle | 2003 Pepsi 400, Daytona Beach, Fla. | Jack Roush |
| 15. Kevin Harvick | 2003 Brickyard 400, Indianapolis, Ind. | Richard Childress |
| 16. Terry Labonte | 2003 Southern 500, Darlington, S.C. | Rick Hendrick |
| 17. Bill Elliott | 2003 Pop Secret 400; Rockingham, N.C. | Ray Evernham |

## Previous NASCAR Winston Cup champions

(Not otherwise exempt)

| Drivers | Year(s) Won |
|---|---|
| Rusty Wallace | 1989 |

## Owner exemption

(Not otherwise exempt, one-year owner exemption)

| Drivers | Year(s) Won | Car Owner |
|---|---|---|
| Brian Vickers | 2003 Pontiac Excitement 400 | Rick Hendrick |

## Other qualified drivers

(Not otherwise eligible)
NEXTEL Open Winner

**2003 SEASON**

## YEAR BY YEAR All-Star event winners

| Year | Winner | Runner-Up | Open Winner | Year | Winner | Runner-Up | Open Winner |
|---|---|---|---|---|---|---|---|
| 1985 | Darrell Waltrip | Harry Gant | None | 1995 | Jeff Gordon | Sterling Marlin | Todd Bodine |
| 1986 | Bill Elliott | Dale Earnhardt | Benny Parsons* | 1996 | Michael Waltrip | Rusty Wallace | Jimmy Spencer |
| 1987 | Dale Earnhardt | Terry Labonte | Buddy Baker | 1997 | Jeff Gordon | Bobby Labonte | Ricky Craven |
| 1988 | Terry Labonte | Sterling Marlin | Sterling Marlin | 1998 | Mark Martin | Bobby Labonte | Jeremy Mayfield |
| 1989 | Rusty Wallace | Ken Schrader | Sterling Marlin | 1999 | Terry Labonte | Tony Stewart | Tony Stewart |
| 1990 | Dale Earnhardt | Ken Schrader | Dick Trickle | 2000 | Dale Earnhardt Jr. | Dale Jarrett | Steve Park |
| 1991 | Davey Allison | Ken Schrader | Michael Waltrip | 2001 | Jeff Gordon | Dale Jarrett | Johnny Benson |
| 1992 | Davey Allison | Kyle Petty | Michael Waltrip | 2002 | Ryan Newman | Dale Earnhardt Jr. | Ryan Newman |
| 1993 | Dale Earnhardt | Mark Martin | Sterling Marlin | 2003 | Jimmie Johnson | Kurt Busch | Jeff Burton |
| 1994 | Geoffrey Bodine | Sterling Marlin | Jeff Gordon | | *Winner of the Atlanta Invitational | | |

# Budweiser Shootout at Daytona

## HISTORY

The 26th Budweiser Shootout At Daytona will be held Saturday, February 7, at Daytona International Speedway. The Budweiser Shootout traditionally had been scheduled during Speedweeks on a Sunday afternoon, a week before the Daytona 500. However, the 2004 Budweiser Shootout will be televised by FOX Sports in prime time. The non-points event has jump-started the NASCAR Cup Series season since 1979.

Dale Earnhardt Jr. won his first Budweiser Shootout in 2003, beating Jeff Gordon and Matt Kenseth to the finish line.

## PAST WINNERS

The late Dale Earnhardt leads all drivers with six victories in Budweiser Shootout events. The late Neil Bonnett, Jeff Gordon, Dale Jarrett, Ken Schrader and Tony Stewart have two wins each.

**2003 SEASON**

| Year | Winner | Year | Winner | Year | Winner | Year | Winner |
|---|---|---|---|---|---|---|---|
| 2003 | Dale Earnhardt Jr. | 1996 | Dale Jarrett | 1989 | Ken Schrader | 1982 | Bobby Allison |
| 2002 | Tony Stewart | 1995 | Dale Earnhardt | 1988 | Dale Earnhardt | 1981 | Darrell Waltrip |
| 2001 | Tony Stewart | 1994 | Jeff Gordon | 1987 | Bill Elliott | 1980 | Dale Earnhardt |
| 2000 | Dale Jarrett | 1993 | Dale Earnhardt | 1986 | Dale Earnhardt | 1979 | Buddy Baker |
| 1999 | Mark Martin | 1992 | Geoffrey Bodine | 1985 | Terry Labonte | | |
| 1998 | Rusty Wallace | 1991 | Dale Earnhardt | 1984 | Neil Bonnett | | |
| 1997 | Jeff Gordon | 1990 | Ken Schrader | 1983 | Neil Bonnett | | |

Note: From 1979-97 the race was named the "Busch Clash." In 1998, the event name was changed to the "Bud Shootout," and was renamed the "Budweiser Shootout" in 2001.

## FORMAT

The Budweiser Shootout features drivers who earned a Bud Pole Award in the previous season and past champions of the Budweiser Shootout who did not earn a Bud Pole during the previous year but finished in the top 50 in the season's final point standings.

### 2003 Bud Pole winners

| Driver | Bud Poles | Driver | Bud Poles | Driver | Bud Poles |
|---|---|---|---|---|---|
| Ryan Newman | 11 | Steve Park | 2 | Jeremy Mayfield | 1 |
| Bobby Labonte | 4 | Jeff Green | 1 | Terry Labonte | 1 |
| Jeff Gordon | 4 | Dave Blaney | 1 | Boris Said | 1 |
| Jimmie Johnson | 2 | Kevin Harvick | 1 | Tony Stewart | 1 |
| Elliott Sadler | 2 | Jamie McMurray | 1 | Mike Skinner | 1 |

# 2003 race by race review

## DAYTONA 500

Give NASCAR drivers the opportunity to pick the race they most would like to win, and the majority would respond with the Daytona 500, the sport's Super Bowl that kicks off each season.

Is it the biggest race for Michael Waltrip? You don't even have to ask. Waltrip's first NASCAR Winston Cup victory was the Daytona 500 in 2001, but that celebration quickly turned somber after he learned that Dale Earnhardt, his car owner, was killed on the last lap of the race.

Two years later Waltrip found himself in victory lane again. And nothing spoiled the party after his second Daytona 500 win—not even a little rain. Actually, it was the Daytona 272.5 because the race was called after 109 laps and two red flags for rain.

With the help of Dale Earnhardt Inc. teammate and race favorite Dale Earnhardt Jr., who won three races during a spectacular showing in Speedweeks, Waltrip passed leader Jimmie Johnson on the last green-flag lap before the rain that eventually ended the race began falling. Junior had a strong car and led 22 laps early in the race, but a bad alternator and dying battery ended any chances of him scoring the victory. He finished 36th.

Waltrip's second career victory also came at Daytona in the 2002 Pepsi 400. He had no qualms about his third victory at Daytona not going its 500-mile distance. "Oh, yeah, it's just ruining me," Waltrip said. "You know what I heard? They're still going to pay me the whole amount. That's kind of crazy, isn't it?"

Though the Chevrolets appeared to be the dominant cars throughout Speedweeks, including the 500—five of the top seven finishers drove Monte Carlos—Kurt Busch managed to take second place in a Ford, carrying over his strong finish in 2002 to the '03 opener. He was disappointed that the race ended prematurely. "It's difficult to accept and to swallow," Busch said. "It's the greatest race that we go to every year. It's the beginning of the season for us. Whether or not we continued forward, it was the weather's decision."

Pole-sitter Jeff Green never was a factor, finishing 39th after a blown right rear tire put him into the wall.

Rain shortened the Daytona 500 to 272.5 miles, forcing drivers such as Terry Labonte (left) to take cover during two red-flag delays. Michael Waltrip (right) passed Jimmie Johnson on the last green-flag lap and got the victory when the race failed to resume. It was the second Daytona 500 victory for Waltrip, who also won the race in 2001.

Dale Jarrett (88) took the Subway 400 lead from Kurt Busch on Lap 390 of 393. They changed places three times in the last 10 laps before Jarrett won the race. The victory, in the year's second race, was Jarrett's only win of the season. Busch finished second for the second straight event but went on to win four races.

## SUBWAY 400

Much is made of the young guns who are taking NASCAR by storm and putting a fresh, and sometimes rowdy, face on the sport. But on this afternoon at North Carolina Speedway, a graybeard took a youngster to school.

Dale Jarrett, 46, beat Kurt Busch, 25, because he conserved his tires when Busch was dominating the latter stages of the race. That strategy allowed Jarrett to get past Busch on Lap 390 of 393—they swapped the lead three times in the final 10 laps—on his way to victory.

Lapped traffic helped Jarrett pass Busch with 10 laps to go. Busch, also aided by slower cars, returned the favor with five laps left. But Busch burned up too much of the grip in his tires in retaking the lead and didn't have enough left to hold off Jarrett at the end.

"I'm 46 years old, but I don't think my age has a thing to do with my performance on the racetrack," Jarrett said. "I can hang with them (young guns) at any track that we go to, but they're tough competitors. So this strikes one for the older guys."

Busch led a race-high 150 laps and took a 31-point lead in the points standings with his second consecutive second-place finish of the season. Roush Racing teammate Matt Kenseth finished third, and Ricky Craven and Jamie McMurray rounded out the top five. First-time pole-sitter Dave Blaney acquitted himself well, finishing 10th.

"I'm real proud of the way Dale Jarrett and I raced," Busch said. "That was a lot of fun. We were just a little bit too aggressive on the rear tires."

The victory was Jarrett's first working with new crew chief Brad Parrott, the younger brother of Todd Parrott, the team manager and Jarrett's long-time crew chief.

## UAW-DAIMLERCHRYSLER 400

Las Vegas native Kurt Busch might have been the favorite entering the race, but it was no surprise to see Matt Kenseth end up in victory lane.

Helped by a lightning-fast 13-second pit stop on the last stop of the day, Kenseth cruised to a nine-second victory over Dale Earnhardt Jr., giving car owner Jack Roush his fourth win in the six NASCAR Winston Cup races at Las Vegas. Jeff Burton (two) and Mark Martin have Roush's other victories.

Kenseth's victory was set up when he decided not to pit

with most of the leaders midway through the race. Kenseth, in fourth at the time, decided to remain on the track with then-leader Earnhardt, but the rest of the top contenders pitted with the knowledge that the race could be finished with one additional pit stop if green-flag conditions remained.

Staying out earned Kenseth valuable track position that he ended up keeping when a caution flag flew about 40 laps later, getting everyone back on the same pit sequence. Kenseth's crew then got him out of the pits first on the final stop of the day, and he was untouchable once he got into the clean air.

"We just have an awesome pit crew," Kenseth said. "We had some turnover this winter, but these guys are still the world champions. The guys worked really hard to get me out of the pits, and it was key to be out front."

Busch, meanwhile, had a day to forget. He damaged the rear end of his car early in the race after brushing the wall, then was caught in an incident that began when Mike Skinner's car got loose and ran into Rusty Wallace's, starting a chain reaction that also ended the day for Jeff Gordon.

## BASS PRO SHOPS MBNA 500

It's no wonder Bobby Labonte loves Atlanta. For the sixth time in his career, Labonte took the checkered flag at the track, but he had to work for it at the end.

On the day's final restart following a caution, Jeff Gordon took advantage of Labonte's slow restart on Lap 313 to take the lead on the back stretch. However, Labonte stayed close with Gordon, nudging Gordon's bumper in Turn 4, causing both cars to wiggle. Gordon had to slow down just enough to regain traction, allowing Labonte the chance to get by the No. 24 on the outside as the two cars came to the start/finish line. Labonte then sped away in the final laps, winning by 1.274 seconds—half a straightaway—and leading a race-high 172 laps.

"I just had a fast car, and I tried to pass him when I could get to him," Labonte said. "When I got close, I thought, 'Man, I've got to take this opportunity right now.' If you wait, you never know what's going to happen."

The victory was the 20th of Labonte's career, and it also was his first under new crew chief Michael "Fatback" McSwain, who left Robert Yates Racing in October 2002 to lead the No. 18 team. It also went a long way toward giving Labonte needed confidence; his team, which won the NASCAR Winston Cup championship in 2000, finished a disappointing 16th in points last season.

"I have no idea why we're so good here," Labonte said. "All I know is it's a combination of a lot of things—team, car, motor, pit stops—and I really like this place."

The race was a typical one at NASCAR's fastest track; there were 23 lead changes, but only nine cars finished on the lead lap. The race further advanced the notion that Chevrolets had the most competitive car make; four Chevys finished among the top five, and the best Dodge (Jimmy Spencer) finished seventh. Three Fords finished in the top 10, and Johnny Benson had the highest finishing Pontiac at 11th.

## CAROLINA DODGE DEALERS 400

NASCAR drivers often refer to the second-place finisher as the first loser. Their reasoning: No one remembers who comes in second. But on this afternoon at Darlington—a race no one will forget anytime soon—the driver who finished second was just as big a part of the story as the winner.

**Dave Blaney gets into the No. 77 Ford as crew chief Robert Barker watches before the Carolina Dodge Dealers 400 at Darlington. Blaney finished third, giving him three finishes in the top 10 in the first five races of the season.**

Ricky Craven's sheet metal-swapping victory over Kurt Busch in the Dodge Dealers 400 at Darlington easily was the most dramatic moment of the 2003 season and also the closest finish—Craven won by .002 seconds—in NASCAR history since the sport introduced electronic scoring in 1993.

In fact, the winner wasn't even sure he was the winner—even a couple of hours after the race.

In one of the most compelling finishes in stock car racing history, Craven won a remarkable physical duel in the final lap to beat Kurt Busch by .002 seconds, the closest finish in NASCAR history since the sport introduced electronic scoring in 1993.

The only other finish that looked this close was during the inaugural Daytona 500 in 1959, when it took three days to determine that Lee Petty had edged Johnny Beauchamp in a photo finish.

But the story at Darlington wasn't so much the margin of victory as the body-slamming style in which it was attained. During the final two laps, Busch and Craven banged and bounced off one another several times, producing smoke from the friction of sheet metal. Remarkably, neither lost control, and there were no cheap shots.

Busch overtook Jeff Gordon and Elliott Sadler with a daring three-wide pass to take the lead on lap 270, and he appeared to have the race won.

But Craven, whose car was better on long runs all day, eventually caught Busch, who had lost his power steering, with two laps left. The two took turns swapping the lead and nearly putting each other into the wall during that lap, setting up the most dramatic action on the final lap.

Craven got a remarkable run coming off Turn 4 to get side by side with Busch, and the two rubbed and banged doors the entire way to the checkered flag. Craven didn't know that he had won until he saw the scoreboard coming off Turn 2 on the cool-down lap. That's when the moment struck him.

"The last five laps were just—I'm not really sure," Craven said. "I'm going to have to watch it because ... looking back, it's the most fun I've ever had in my life. This is exactly what you dream of. It will probably never happen again, but it's the perfect way to win a race at the perfect track."

Busch, who earlier in the season lost a stirring back-and-forth duel in the closing laps at Rockingham to Dale Jarrett, scored his third second-place finish of the year, and Dave Blaney finished a career-best third.

Though NASCAR drivers of yesteryear might have come out of their cars swinging after an ending such as this, there was no animosity between Craven and Busch. Busch even went to victory lane to congratulate Craven.

"This was the coolest finish I've ever seen, and I'm glad I got to be a part of it," Busch said. "It's a bit stale that I was on the wrong end of it, but it was just an awesome duel between two guys who don't win all that often and ones who excel at conserving tires."

# FOOD CITY 500

After three second-place finishes in the first five races of the season, Kurt Busch put the icing on his hot start by defending his win in the Food City 500 at Bristol. Busch led the final 96 laps and had no problem keeping teammate and points leader Matt Kenseth behind him.

"We've been so close so many times this year, it's somewhat bittersweet," Busch said. "But I knew we'd eventually piece things together and make sure our car was competitive at the end of a run."

Long green-flag runs were rare in a race that featured 17 cautions—three shy of the record. But when the race ran under green for 129 laps in the latter stages, many drivers were forced to pit to avoid running out of fuel. However, five cars managed to stay out long enough to get the long-awaited caution, and one of those was Busch.

Busch said he was going to pit two laps earlier, but a gut instinct told him to stay out on the track after he saw some debris. A lap later, a caution was issued, keeping Busch on the lead lap. He then passed Bobby Labonte on the restart and went on to victory.

Kenseth's points lead after six races stood at 138 with his fifth consecutive top 10 finish. He finished 20th in the season-opening Daytona 500.

Ryan Newman, who ran the first sub-15 second lap at Bristol to win the pole, finished 22nd. An ill-handling car forced Newman to pit early in the race, and that was too much for him to overcome.

# SAMSUNG/ RADIOSHACK 500

Even though Ryan Newman took just two fresh tires on the final round of pit stops while the rest of the leaders took four, he simply was too good for the field at Texas Motor Speedway.

Newman became the seventh driver to win in seven NASCAR Winston Cup races at the track, but his tire strategy appeared shaky initially when Dale Earnhardt Jr. raced around Newman with four new tires on the restart at Lap 289. But as Newman's tire pressure rose on the right-side replacements, his car's handling improved. He eventually caught Junior, who was battling a tight car, and passed him with 11 laps to go. Newman then pulled away

**Michael Waltrip (15) and Dave Blaney had a rough time at the Food City 500. Waltrip finished 25th and Blaney 38th in a race that was marred by 17 cautions—three short of the record for the spring race at Bristol.**

After several laps of side-by-side racing in the Virginia 500, Jeff Gordon (24) passed Bobby Labonte for the lead with 14 laps to go and went on to win. The victory was Gordon's first since September 2002 at Kansas.

and won by half the final straightaway for his second career series victory.

"Even if we would have finished second, I feel that (taking two tires) was the right decision," Newman said. "If we had taken four tires and three cars had taken two tires and beat us out, then we were pretty much guaranteed not to have a shot at winning the race."

The bigger battle was for second, as Jeff Gordon caught Earnhardt in the closing laps and fought him hard for the position. Earnhardt barely edged Gordon, and the two banged doors for an instant coming to the finish line. "He made it hard on us," Gordon said. "If we'd have been going for the win, we probably would've wrecked."

Texas is one of only four active NASCAR Winston Cup tracks where Gordon has yet to win.

## AARON'S 499

Dale Earnhardt Jr. drove into victory lane and the record book at Talladega, where he became the only driver in NASCAR history to win four consecutive races at the high-speed track. Junior broke the mark he shared with Buddy Baker with a controversial pass of Matt Kenseth below the yellow out-of-bounds line with four laps to go to win a race that had 43 lead changes among 16 drivers.

Passing below that line, which separates the apron from the banked surface, was outlawed in July 2001 to keep a driver from taking the risk of losing control of his car because of the difference in banking. The enforcement of the rule has been subject to interpretation by NASCAR since.

NASCAR ruled Earnhardt's maneuver was legal because he already was in the act of passing Kenseth when his left tires dipped below the yellow line.

The victory capped a remarkable comeback for Earnhardt, one of 27 drivers whose cars were damaged when Ryan Newman cut a left rear tire to start off the feared "Big One" on Lap 5. However, with the help of 15 pit stops under the lengthy caution periods early in the race, Junior stayed on the lead lap and picked his way through the field. He even lost the lead draft twice, but well-timed cautions allowed him to get back each time.

Kevin Harvick, who pushed Junior past Kenseth in the closing laps, finished second, and Elliott Sadler was third, his fourth top 10 of the season. Sadler had only seven top 10 finishes in 2002 racing for Wood Brothers.

Despite Junior's record-setting performance, he still has some ground to cover before he catches his late father. Dale Earnhardt won a career-best 10 races at Talladega.

## VIRGINIA 500

When it comes to short track racing, Jeff Gordon might be NASCAR's best driver. Let's just say that you don't want to be the leader with a rearview mirror full of Gordon late in the race.

After beating out Ryan Newman for the pole, Gordon won the Virginia 500 by nudging Bobby Labonte out of the way with 14 laps to go for his first win since September 2002 at Kansas.

Gordon has become the master of the bump-and-run, having won his last two short-track races with the technique. Gordon won the fall race at Bristol in 2002 the same way, punting Rusty Wallace out of the way.

For several laps, Gordon and Labonte were engaged in a side-by-side duel for the lead, with Labonte keeping Gordon pinned down on the inside of the track and unable to accelerate out of the corners and get enough speed to pass the No. 18.

"I race guys the way they race me," Gordon said. "Bobby raced me clean, but he was definitely crowding me. He was cutting the entry of the corners pretty short."

Despite the bump, Labonte had no ill will toward Gordon after the race, and even congratulated Gordon in victory lane.

"He passed us fair and square," Labonte said. "His car was fast, and we tried to hold him off. But he is obviously really good here, so we were fortunate to finish second after we got two tires."

Dale Earnhardt Jr. finished third, his third consecutive

**Matt Kenseth continued his steady season at the Pontiac Excitement 400. He finished seventh after qualifying 18th and maintained a 20-point lead over second-place Dale Earnhardt Jr. in the championship standings.**

top five finish at Martinsville. He returned to the track in second behind Labonte after the leaders made their final pit stop, but he bumped into Ricky Craven's car on the restart after Craven struggled to get up to speed.

It sent both cars up the racetrack and pushed Earnhardt back to fifth. However, Junior regained two spots in the final 55 laps.

## AUTO CLUB 500

Often one to charge full-speed ahead at any cost, Kurt Busch put two disappointing finishes in his rearview mirror and became the season's first two-time winner because he played it more conservatively. In a race full of cautions, Rusty Wallace and Bobby Labonte pushed high and grasped the lead from Jamie McMurray on Lap 239. While those three were watching each other, Busch laid back and slid underneath Wallace. Once in front, the ride to victory lane was smooth for Busch, who had hit bumps with 19th- and 28th-place finishes at Talledega and Martinsville.

"I'm just real proud that we can sit down and look at our poor efforts and produce such a great result," Busch said. "It's just a total team effort—to have that kind of car, to have that kind of motor and just produce results like that on pit road to maintain track position."

Wallace, who desperately was trying to win his first race in two years, nearly passed both McMurray and Busch on the high side, but he just couldn't make it work and ultimately finished third behind Labonte.

"I flew up the racetrack a little bit," Wallace said. "I just couldn't hold that bottom line. I let the 97 (Busch) get underneath me. I tried to get him back in (Turn) 3. I drove it in real deep and slid up again, and that was it."

Bill Elliott finished fourth for his first top five of the season, and McMurray finished fifth for his first top five since Rockingham, the second race of the season.

Tony Stewart had the day's strongest car early in the event, leading 100 of the first 128 laps, but a broken rod in his engine forced him to the garage.

## PONTIAC EXCITEMENT 400

It's not often a team can make a major mistake during a race and still end up winning. But Joe Nemechek's car was so good at Richmond that a severe pit road blunder couldn't keep him out of victory lane for the first time since November 2001.

"When you get a car that'll go that well—high, low, wherever you want it to go—it is fun," Nemechek said. "We've been so close to winning, and here we are."

Nemechek was stunningly fast in the first half of the race but missed the entrance to pit road during a caution while talking strategy with crew chief Peter Sospenzo. Nemechek was forced to pit the next lap, which caused him to go from first to 25th, his blood rising as quickly as his name fell among the leaders.

"I wanted to get out and wrestle (Sospenzo) right there," Nemechek said.

But Nemechek passed cars in droves and then opted to regain more track position by staying out during a caution with 100 laps to go. He restarted in fifth, then drove to the lead by passing Jeff Gordon on Lap 330.

Late-race cautions helped Nemechek hold his advantage over Dale Earnhardt Jr., Bobby Labonte and a host of other

The smoke barely had cleared from Jimmie Johnson's victory celebration following The Winston at Lowe's Motor Speedway when Johnson won the Coca-Cola 600 eight days later at the same track.

cars with fresher tires. The race eventually was called on Lap 393 of 400 because of rain.

Labonte finished second, his third consecutive second-place finish, and Earnhardt finished third, putting him 20 points behind Winston Cup leader Matt Kenseth.

The day before the race, Jerry Nadeau was seriously injured when he crashed driver's side-first into the wall during final practice. Nadeau suffered head, lung and rib injuries.

## THE WINSTON

Jimmie Johnson's victory in The Winston, NASCAR's all-star race, was no surprise to those who followed his rise to fifth place in points during his rookie season in 2002. One quality that stands out above all others: He's a quick learner. This time, quick thinking got Johnson $1 million.

After being disappointed in 2002 in The Winston, Johnson determined that the third and final segment of the race was the only one that mattered.

Knowing that the fans like to mix things up and were sure to vote to invert the maximum 10 cars for the final 20-lap segment, Johnson positioned himself to finish the second segment of the race near the back of the top 10.

Finishing the second segment seventh put Johnson in fourth for the restart after the inversion. Driving an extremely fast Hendrick Motorsports car, Johnson quickly picked his way to the front and passed car owner and teammate Jeff Gordon three laps into the final segment, then cruised to an easy victory.

The victory was sweet redemption for Johnson, who won the first two segments the previous year but ended up finishing fifth.

"Last year we thought we had it after the first two segments, but it didn't work out," Johnson said. "So this year we played our cards right and focused on the big prize and went out and got it."

Kurt Busch, who won the second segment, finished second, and Bobby Labonte finished third. Tony Stewart, who won the first segment, fell from contention late in the second segment after he got together with Terry Labonte, creating a multicar accident.

Dale Earnhardt Jr., Dale Jarrett, Mark Martin and Bill Elliott were collected in the melee, knocking them out of the race, too.

# COCA-COLA 600

Eight days after winning The Winston at Lowe's Motor Speedway, Jimmie Johnson struck again by winning the rain-shortened Coca-Cola 600 at the track.

The race was called after 276 of the scheduled 400 laps. NASCAR officials determined that efforts to dry the asphalt likely would have taken three hours, pushing the finish past midnight, so the plug was pulled on the race.

"I am dumbfounded," Johnson said. "I expected to be doing doughnuts on the front stretch to celebrate. But we'll take it this way."

Johnson's team made a remarkable comeback.

Engine problems kept him from making his qualifying run at the start of the weekend, threatening his prospects. He was supposed to start 37th after taking a provisional, but he was shuffled back to 43rd after changing engines.

Johnson also had a great opportunity to win this race a year before, but he overshot his pit stall on his final stop, which cost him track position and ultimately the race.

"The success we had last year, we did so well, but we just couldn't close the deal," Johnson said. "This makes it all worth it."

Points leader Matt Kenseth finished second after starting 18th, but he was a little upset that the race was called.

"I sure wish we would have waited it out a little bit," Kenseth said. "I'm real thankful and real grateful to finish second and to be with such a great race team, but the racer in me still wanted to race."

Bobby Labonte, Jimmy Spencer and pole-sitter Ryan

**Drivers come off a restart in the Coca-Cola 600 at Lowe's Motor Speedway. The race was called after 276 of the scheduled 400 laps because of rain. Jimmie Johnson won after starting 37th on a provisional.**

Dale Earnhardt Jr. makes a pit stop during the Coca-Cola 600. It was a frustrating day for Earnhardt, who completed only 240 of 276 laps because a problem with his brakes cut his day short. He finished 41st.

Newman rounded out the top five.

Robby Gordon, who finished 22nd earlier in the day in the Indianapolis 500, finished 17th at Charlotte. It was Gordon's fourth attempt at racing's daily double. He also was disappointed that the race was cut short.

"As far as going the distance, 17th place is pretty weak, and we had a better car than that," Gordon said. "We could have had a top 10 car, and I could have continued racing."

## MBNA ARMED FORCES FAMILY 400

Try driving your car without power steering for a week, and that might resemble what it felt like to be Ryan Newman for nearly two hours at Dover.

Newman lost the power steering in his No. 12 just past the midpoint of the 400-lap race but had enough muscle and grit to hold off Jeff Gordon on a restart with six laps to go and won his second race of the season.

"This is one of the hardest places to have that problem and overcome it, but we had a fast racecar, and I wasn't about to pull it in the garage and say, 'That's it,'" Newman said.

Newman, who led a race-high 162 laps, won the race from the pole, his fourth of the season. Newman's victory also was Dodge's first at Dover since Richard Petty won there in 1975.

Gordon tried to make it a race when the green flag flew for the final time on Lap 395, but Newman blocked him going into Turn 1. Newman then cruised on to the victory, beating Gordon by almost 1 second.

"Ryan is very smooth and runs a great line," Gordon said. "He has a great team behind him, and he deserves to be in victory lane today."

Jamie McMurray had the best finish, 13th, among the six rookies in the race.

"Overall, I'm happy with our finish," McMurray said. "I think we had a top 10 car, but we were just better on longer runs. On the initial restarts, it would take the Havoline Dodge a few laps to come to life, and there at the end, we had a short run to the finish and just didn't have the chance to work our way into the top 10."

## POCONO 500

For Tony Stewart, there was nothing quite like winning on the mountaintop at Pocono, especially given the misfortune and frustration that had plagued the defending NASCAR Winston Cup champion.

Stewart easily had cars capable of winning the previous two races, but a blown engine in the Coca-Cola 600 and a pit road violation at Dover cost him chances at victory.

Thoughts of bad luck crept back into his mind in the

final stages of this race, but everything fell into place for Stewart. He led Mark Martin to the finish line and broke his winless streak at 27 races. The race ended under caution because of a wreck in the final laps.

"You look at all those places, and we were doing our job, but we didn't have the luck on our side," Stewart said. "We knew in our hearts and minds that it was just a matter of time before it finally turned back around in our favor."

Fuel mileage dictated that every competitor was about 10 laps short of having enough gas to finish the race, which gave teams the opportunity to use some interesting pit strategies.

Knowing they could pit under green flag conditions and not lose a lap to the leaders on the 2½-mile circuit, some drivers started pitting with about 30 laps left in the race in order to position themselves to get to the front if a caution came out. If that had happened, everyone who hadn't stopped would have been forced to pit and lose track position to those who pitted under green. Fortunately for Stewart, all of the cars had to make their stops under green, which cycled him back to the lead.

Martin posted his best finish of the season and moved up to 11th in the points standings. Matt Kenseth, Dale Earnhardt Jr. and Ryan Newman rounded out the top five.

"We couldn't beat Tony unless something happened, but I was sure going to try to make something happen there at the end," Martin said. "I wanted to run it out. We had a great car on the long run, and it's just a tribute to (crew chief) Ben Leslie and the whole Viagra team."

## SIRIUS 400

Considering that Ford Motor Co. celebrated its 100th anniversary during the weekend, it was fitting that Kurt Busch drove a Ford Taurus to victory lane at Michigan.

Busch overtook Jeff Gordon with 24 laps to go— the first time he took the lead in the 200-lap race— and went on and won his third race of the year, the most in the series at the time.

The win wasn't surprising because Busch drove the same car to victory in April at California Speedway. That track is the same length and has nearly the same amount of banking in the turns as Michigan, so a team's setup notes translate well.

It was fortuitous for Busch that a short run decided the outcome. Busch said he didn't think his car could have won if the race had been decided during a long green flag run.

"It just seemed like the car came right at the end, just like it did at California Speedway," Busch said. "There are adjustments that (crew chief) Jimmy Fennig has found that are keys for shorter runs, so with 40 laps to go he made those adjustments, and I think that paid dividends."

For the fourth time in seven races, Bobby Labonte finished second. Labonte overtook Gordon for second position late in the race and tried to pass Busch off the final restart, driving to the top of the track.

"I knew it was going to be tough to get away from

**Jeff Gordon had eight top four finishes in the first 21 races but only one win. He moved as high as second in the points standings midway through the season but hit a rough patch in August and ended up finishing fourth in the championship race.**

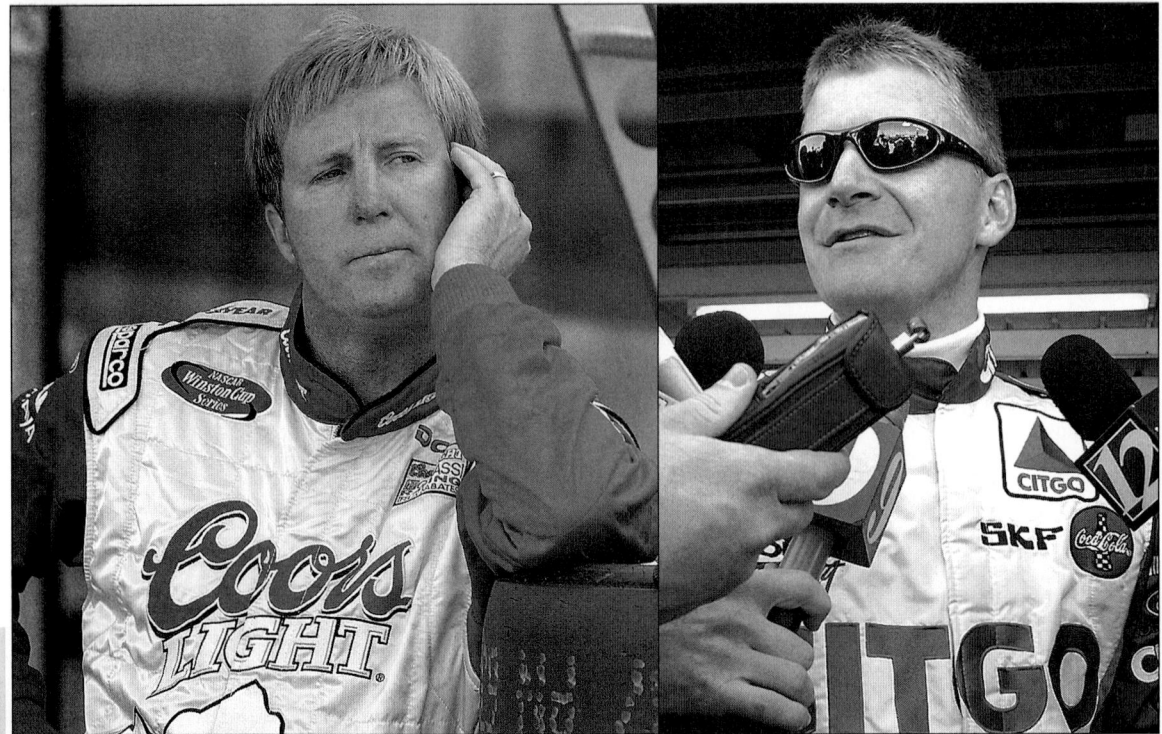

Sterling Marlin (left) finished a season-high sixth for the fourth time in the Sirius 400 but never fared that well again and ended up 18th in the championship standings. Jeff Burton finished a season-high second in the Pepsi 400, beginning a season-best streak of four straight top 10s, but ended up 12th in points.

Bobby," Busch said.

"All I needed to do was hit Turns 3 and 4. If I could stretch it out from there, he wouldn't be able to draft up on us, and I knew we could pull away."

There were several accidents in the race. The most harrowing came on Lap 36, when Ryan Newman's car turned into a huge fireball after his engine blew up. Fire engulfed Newman in the cockpit, and he tried to put it out with the fire extinguisher before he could escape.

"(The fire) was getting the right side of my body pretty good," Newman said. "On top of that, trying to stop the car and get out and all those things; it was pretty tough. It got my face pretty good."

Newman likened his facial burns to bad sunburn.

## DODGE/SAVE MART 350

Robby Gordon held off Jeff Gordon for the final 25 laps and got his second career series victory, his first on a road course. The victory ended the heartache of several near-misses for Robby Gordon in road races.

Gordon had chances to win both road races in 2001. His preoccupation with keeping Kevin Harvick one lap down allowed Tony Stewart to slip by for the win at Sonoma. At Watkins Glen, his television telemetry box caught on fire, forcing him out of contention in a race he had well in hand.

This victory didn't come without controversy. Gordon's pass of Harvick with the caution out on Lap 71 was questioned by Harvick and Jeff Gordon, even though NASCAR reiterated in the prerace drivers meeting that such a maneuver was legal.

"It was good, hard racing except for that chicken move under yellow," Harvick said.

"Robby became an animal when that caution came out," Jeff Gordon said. "It doesn't surprise me, but that just doesn't happen in our sport."

Robby Gordon remained unperturbed.

"Do you think I really care what Jeff Gordon says?" Robby said. "He's won enough races. I guess he just doesn't like it when someone comes in and rains on his parade a little bit. Kevin Harvick may be mad at me, but it is what it is."

Two of the four road racing specialists brought in for the race, Boris Said and Ron Fellows, finished in the top 10. Said, subbing for injured Jerry Nadeau, won the pole and finished sixth. Fellows, driving in place of Jeff Green, finished seventh. The other specialists, Johnny Miller and Scott Pruett, finished 24th and 34th.

# PEPSI 400

Much of the first half of Greg Biffle's rookie season was about as pleasant as running coarse sandpaper over your skin. But no matter how much disappointment there has been, there's nothing like a victory at NASCAR's most renowned track to smooth over frustrations.

Aided by a spur-of-the-moment fuel decision that Biffle and crew chief Randy Goss made, Biffle drove his No. 16 Ford to victory lane, proving the racing adage that it's not always the fastest car that wins.

Biffle was one of a handful of drivers who pitted on Lap 79 under caution to top off his gas tank, knowing that doing so would allow him to finish with just one more stop. Biffle's car wasn't nearly as stout as those driven by Michael Waltrip and Dale Earnhardt Jr., who race for restrictor-plate power Dale Earnhardt Inc. But those drivers weren't within the same fuel window as Biffle.

After Waltrip, Junior and the rest of the leaders made their final pit stops for fuel, Biffle ended up cycling through to the lead, with Matt Kenseth and Bobby Labonte his closest pursuers. When Kenseth ducked into the pits on Lap 156 of 160, it gave Labonte the chance to close on Biffle's bumper, but he couldn't complete the pass.

Biffle caught a big break when Labonte's No. 18 ran out of gas on the back stretch of the final lap. Biffle's spotter relayed the good news.

"He said, 'Just bring it home. You've got the race won,'" Biffle said. "What a relief because I thought when Bobby got to my bumper he'd beat me, and I'd learn a lesson tonight, and I'd finish second."

Labonte was able to coast to a fifth-place finish. Brother Terry finished one spot better in fourth. Waltrip, trying for his third consecutive Daytona victory, finished 11th.

# TROPICANA 400

Kevin Harvick owned Chicagoland Speedway in its first two years of existence, but he couldn't hold off Ryan Newman for the three-peat.

Newman cruised to his third victory of the season after Harvick ran out of gas with three laps to go, winning the race by 2.6 seconds over Tony Stewart. The victory was especially vindicating for Newman, who led the most laps in the race last year but lost to Harvick because of fuel strategy.

"He had a fast racecar, and I was really worried about him until he ran out of gas," Newman said. "I got out there in the clean air, and that was pretty much the biggest thing."

Newman and Harvick both pitted with 70 laps remaining to top off their gas tanks in an effort to make it to the end without another stop. Newman beat Harvick out of the pits, which was critical because track position has proved important at Chicagoland.

Newman took the lead for good on Lap 210 of the

**After 15 straight finishes of 10th or worse, Jeremy Mayfield ended up eighth in the Pepsi 400 at Daytona. Mayfield also finished eighth in the season-opening race at Daytona.**

267-lap event after the rest of the field pitted under caution. Newman had worked his way to a one-second lead over Harvick when Harvick's No. 29 slowed and ultimately finished 17th.

"We all thought we had the pit strategy worked to perfection," Harvick said. "Before we came in that last time, we took a gas-and-go that we thought would make up for about six laps that we thought we'd be short. Unfortunately, it didn't work out that way for some reason."

Later in the week, NASCAR officials announced that Todd Berrier, Harvick's crew chief, had been fined $25,000 because of a rule infraction. NASCAR also penalized Harvick 25 driver points and Richard Childress 25 owner points. During prerace inspection, the rear suspension of the No. 29 Chevrolet was found to have an unapproved travel limiting device.

Tony Stewart (20) was among the cars taking qualifying practice at the Tropicana 400. He won the pole, but Ryan Newman, who started 14th, won the race. Stewart finished second, 2.6 seconds behind Newman.

## NEW ENGLAND 300

For the third time in as many weeks, fuel mileage made the difference in the outcome of a race. The driver benefiting at Loudon was Jimmie Johnson, who parlayed that into his second victory of the season and Chevrolet's 400th win in series history.

Johnson went 93 laps on his final fuel run, beating out Kevin Harvick on the newly paved surface at New Hampshire International Speedway. Johnson took the lead from Ryan Newman, who was stretching his fuel load, with 37 laps left in the 300-lap event. Johnson then guided the car to the finish, striking a perfect balance between fuel conservation and maintaining his lead.

Johnson's victory wasn't the only notable outcome of the race. Matt Kenseth finished third, and his points lead grew to 234 over Jeff Gordon. It was Kenseth's largest lead since taking over the top spot in March.

"I don't know where everyone else finished, but I know we finished in front of them, so that was good," he said.

Another of Kenseth's closest pursuers in the points battle, Dale Earnhardt Jr., finished a career-best sixth at New Hampshire. Despite that, the gap between Kenseth and Earnhardt grew to 273.

"We're not chipping away at Matt's lead in the points, but you have to hand it to him and his team," Junior said. "We're having our best year ever, and we can only keep working hard and focusing on our own effort. We can't let it bother us if we keep knocking off top five and top 10 finishes while Matt is doing the same."

## PENNSYLVANIA 500

Because it can be difficult to pass at Pocono Raceway—the straightaways are huge but the turns are tight—the best place to be is in front. With the help of excellent pit strategy and timely cautions, Ryan Newman ended up there when it mattered most.

Newman took the lead on Lap 157 of 200, holding off Kurt Busch to win the Pennsylvania 500. Two cautions that slowed a field that had dwindled to 12 lead-lap cars for the final 44 laps allowed Newman to stretch his fuel and finish without pitting.

"The cautions played out to our favor for sure," he said. "I think in hindsight we wouldn't have been able to make it if we hadn't had those cautions."

When the green flag waved for the final time on Lap 189, Busch tracked down Newman and engaged him in a high-speed game of cat and mouse. Busch was making incredible runs on Newman in Turn 1, but Busch lost just as much coming out of Turn 3 on the triangular track. With all the seesawing in the closing laps, Busch couldn't make the pass, and Newman held on to win his fourth race of the season and second in three weeks.

"It was a great day," Busch said. "But (Newman) was in position to win."

Newman's victory vaulted him to ninth in the points standings. He also won the pole, his fifth of the season.

Dale Earnhardt Jr., who elected to gamble on fuel, finished third and reclaimed second place in the standings after Jeff Gordon finished 36th. Gordon accidentally was tapped from behind by Dave Blaney on Lap 124, causing Gordon's No. 24 to spin and hit the wall. It was Gordon's worst run since he finished 37th at Las Vegas, the third race of the season.

## BRICKYARD 400

Dreams really do come true. Just ask Kevin Harvick. As a youngster, Harvick met Rick Mears and received an autographed picture from the open-wheel star who won four Indianapolis 500s. On the picture, Mears wrote, "Good luck, hope to see you here someday."

Little did he or anyone know that Harvick would win a pole and a race at the Brickyard. The only difference is that Harvick accomplished his feat in a stock car.

"Man, I didn't know I'd be sitting here in victory lane and be getting to do all this," Harvick said. "It means a lot to me, and I've looked at that picture for a long time. It's hard to explain how good I feel."

Harvick easily beat Robby Gordon, his teammate, and Jamie McMurray and Matt Kenseth in a 10-lap battle to the finish. Six laps earlier, Harvick passed McMurray on a frantic restart that caused a multicar pileup behind the leaders.

"I always look forward to restarts because I usually make up some ground," Harvick said. "Jamie went high, we went low, Robby followed us, and it was like the seas parted. That was pretty much the race."

Harvick's victory had open-wheel flavor, as he climbed the fence on the front stretch to celebrate, imitating what Helio Castroneves did when he won consecutive Indianapolis 500s in 2001 and 2002.

Harvick, whose relationship with Gordon is contentious at best credited Gordon for holding back his competitors in the final laps. Gordon, who was second with 10 laps to go, finished sixth. Harvick won by almost three seconds. Kenseth finished second, and Dale Earnhardt Jr. finished 14th. Kenseth held a 286-point lead over Earnhardt after Harvick's victory.

## SIRIUS AT THE GLEN

Considering a fluke fire robbed Robby Gordon of a chance at victory two years ago at Watkins Glen, maybe the

**Joe Gibbs Racing teammates Tony Stewart (left) and Bobby Labonte talk strategy at the Pennsylvania 500. Both drivers had engine problems and finished 37th and 30th, respectively.**

Kevin Harvick's team kisses the bricks at Indianapolis after Harvick won the Brickyard 400. Harvick, who started on the pole, reclaimed the lead on a restart late in the race and scored his only victory of the season.

road course owed him a make-up call.

He was running ninth when Rusty Wallace spun just before the entrance of pit road on Lap 51. Gordon dove into the pits for fuel and tires just before the caution flag was displayed.

That move paid off because many cars pitted under caution two laps later, which put Gordon ahead of them. The drivers who remained ahead of Gordon then pitted on Lap 61, giving him a lead he did not relinquish for the remainder of the 90-lap event.

"Track position is so important," Gordon said. "I don't know if we had the best car today, but we won. That's what teamwork is all about."

The victory was indeed sweet justice for Gordon, who looked to be on his way to a win in 2001 at The Glen when the television telemetry box located inside his cockpit caught fire, forcing him out of the race. The win also gave him a season sweep of the road course races; he became the first driver to complete the feat since Jeff Gordon won both in 1999.

Scott Pruett, a road racing ace hired by Chip Ganassi to run both road course races in 2003, finished second. He made the pass for second on the day's final restart, driving hard into Turn 1 to get past Robby Gordon's teammate Kevin Harvick, who finished fifth. Pruett credited unique pit strategy for his solid finish.

"We did something different than everybody else, and it was all predicated on how many yellows we got at the start of the race," Pruett said. "We got enough yellows where we thought we were going to take a gamble. We got a little behind the eight ball because at the end we really had to conserve fuel."

## GFS MARKETPLACE 400

After Ryan Newman pitted on Lap 149 of 200 at Michigan, crew chief Matt Borland calculated whether his driver could make it the rest of the way without refueling. The numbers indicated Newman would be four laps short. The numbers were wrong. Newman finished with enough gas to win the race, complete a slow victory lap, turn a few burnouts and cruise to victory lane.

Clearly, he was good to the last drop.

Newman bided his time for much of the race in an effort to conserve as much fuel as possible. But he wanted more than just second place, so he asked for his team's permission to go for the win in the final laps. After getting the go-ahead, Newman quickly chased down leader Kurt Busch,

Robby Gordon (left) celebrated his second win of the year after the Sirius at the Glen. Kurt Busch (above) got his chance to smile after winning the Sharpie 500, his fourth victory of the season.

who was thought to be in greater danger of running out of fuel. Newman took the lead on Lap 197 and never looked back, winning his fifth race of the year.

"I didn't want to jeopardize the team because of my greed," Newman said. "Seeing that there was, I think, five laps to go and we had a shot at catching Kurt just from a speed standpoint, I didn't want him to be able to make it on fuel, us to be able to make it on fuel and have plenty of fuel left over and say, 'Man, we could have chased him down, but we were too conservative.' I would rather be on the aggressive side than the conservative side. It always looks better in the win column."

After giving way to Newman, Busch ran out of fuel with one lap left and finished 18th.

"The thing Kurt didn't have going for him," Newman said, "was that I don't think his car would work on the bottom as ours would. If you can take a 2-mile racetrack and make it a mile and three-quarters vs. 2 miles and a quarter, then you're going to have better fuel mileage. I think that was a contributing factor also."

## SHARPIE 500

With a swollen nose and chipped tooth courtesy of Jimmy Spencer, Kurt Busch rode into Bristol as racing's newest villain. The 160,000 fans reminded Busch of his newfound infamy with a chorus of boos during pre-race introductions. It would have been understandable for the 25-year-old driver to have trouble staying focused for the tension-packed night race on the circuit's most demanding short track.

But once Busch strapped on his helmet, he was back in the groove and passed former Public Enemy No. 1 Kevin

Harvick for the lead 120 laps from the finish and held on for his third Bristol win in the last four races run at the track.

However, Busch's victory didn't come without additional controversy. In working his way to the lead, he spun out Sterling Marlin, a favorite of fans at Bristol because he is from Tennessee, on Lap 373 to take over second place. Busch quickly apologized over the team's radio, calling it unintentional. But in a race in which Busch wanted to get back into the good graces of his fellow competitors, he alienated another.

Busch tempered his postrace celebration by skipping the celebratory burnouts that have become commonplace for race winners. Instead, he drove to victory lane and enjoyed the moment with his crew, exchanging high fives as the boos rained down.

"This has to be the sweetest of all—to be able to conquer what we've been able to overcome this week, put everything behind us and march forward," Busch said. "This group of guys behind me, I can't do it without them, and they're the ones who are the most important."

Harvick, who scored his second straight second-place finish, didn't hide his disdain for Busch after the race. Yet he also commended Busch's ability.

"He's a cocky, arrogant punk," Harvick said. "He just has a really, really bad attitude. Sometimes he just spins people out, runs into them and drives like an idiot. But he can wheel a racecar, there's no doubt about it."

Rusty Wallace, a contender almost every time he races at Bristol, was running 15th on Lap 87 when Michael Waltrip spun into the wall in Turn 4. As Waltrip slid back down the 36-degree banking, Wallace couldn't avoid slamming into the No. 15 Chevrolet.

## SOUTHERN 500

Terry Labonte had serious doubts he ever would win another NASCAR race. Despite the team's obvious improvement during 2003, it had been more than four years since Labonte's last victory, and the 47-year-old won't keep racing forever.

He carried a winless streak of 156 races into Darlington for the 54th consecutive Southern 500 to be run on Labor Day weekend. Both streaks ended on this day.

Labonte, whose first career start (1978) and victory (1980) came in the Southern 500, won the race, an appropriate epilogue to the Lady in Black's Labor Day tradition. Next season, the race will be run in November.

"It's really special for me," Labonte said. "I was running with Bill Elliott (late in the race) and thinking to myself, 'I hope one of us wins it because we appreciate this place more than some of the young guys do.' "

The record crowd of 75,000 roared its approval for Labonte, who has two NASCAR Winston Cup championships but hadn't won a race since March 1999 at Texas. Instead of doing victory burnouts, the celebration of choice for many of the sport's young guns, Labonte took the checkered flag from the flag man and held it out the window while completing a lap around the speedway.

Dale Earnhardt Jr. (left) and Matt Kenseth share a laugh at the Sharpie 500. Earnhardt finished ninth and Kenseth fourth in a race won by Kurt Busch. Kenseth emerged from the race still in charge in the points standings; Earnhardt was second.

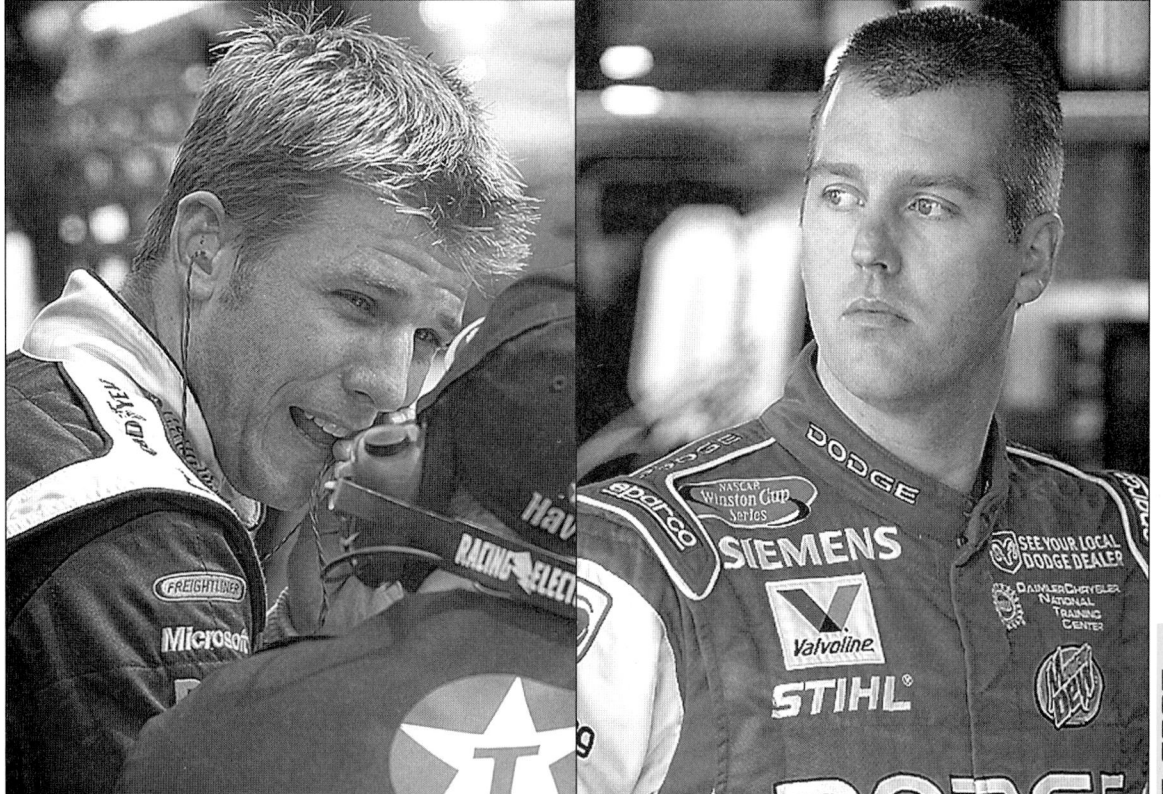

Jamie McMurray (left) finished a season-best third in the Sharpie 500. Jeremy Mayfield finished a season-best second in the Chevy Rock & Roll 400. McMurray, the Raybestos Rookie of the Year, ended the season 13th in points; Mayfield was 19th.

"I was really tired of a losing streak from hell," Labonte said. "With 15 (laps) to go, it was about the longest 14 laps I've ever run. Even though you feel you still can (win), all the pieces have to come together. I'm just glad it's over."

Labonte took control late in the race with a 13.11-second pit stop, beating everyone out and assuming the lead on Lap 335. He never was seriously challenged by Kevin Harvick, who was running second but got caught up in lapped traffic. That allowed Labonte to build a comfortable cushion and beat Harvick to the checkered flag by about 15 car lengths.

"I think everybody is happy to see him win," Harvick said. "If there's anybody who should win the last Southern 500 on Labor Day (weekend), it's somebody like Terry Labonte, who is a legend in our sport."

Labonte's victory gave all four Hendrick Motorsports drivers at least one victory this season. Elliott, a five-time winner at the track, finished fifth.

## CHEVY ROCK & ROLL 400

Ryan Newman's series-high sixth victory of the season wasn't even the biggest story of the race. The tempers characteristic of short-track racing were on display at Richmond, as Kevin Harvick pulled alongside the car of Ricky Rudd on pit road at the end of the race and exchanged heated words with Rudd for spinning him out with nine laps to go.

Harvick, running second at the time, had no chance to save his car from hitting the outside wall because Rudd bumped him going into the corner. Harvick finished 16th, ending his string of three straight second-place finishes.

Harvick's crew restrained its driver from getting close to Rudd, though Harvick threw his head-and-neck restraint at Rudd. "If he's going to take a cheap shot at us, he's going to get one back," Harvick said.

Rudd explained that the contact was unavoidable, as Harvick applied the brakes at a part of the straightaway where he shouldn't have.

This wasn't the first time these two tangled at Richmond. Harvick bumped Rudd out of the way two years ago to take the lead with 18 laps left in the fall race. Rudd saved the car and caught Harvick six laps later, gladly returning the favor on the way to his win.

Rudd understood why Harvick was upset, but he wasn't in a forgiving mood because Harvick dented the right side of the No. 21 with his own car. And in an attempt to restrain their driver, Harvick's crew members dented Rudd's hood by walking on it.

"This is kind of a one-of-a-kind piece that (my team) just put together, and we didn't have a scratch on it until the end of the race," Rudd said. "It's unfortunate that crew members tore our car up and it didn't happen on the racetrack."

During the race, Newman kept his front bumper clean, and that was all that mattered to him. He took the lead with 124 laps to go and never relinquished it. With the benefit of a handful of cautions the rest of the way, Newman easily finished the race with enough fuel and held off Jeremy Mayfield in the closing laps.

"(Crew chief) Matt (Borland) and (engineer) Mike (Nelson) did an awesome job on strategy," Newman said. "We were just fortunate to be in the position that we were at the end of the night. They've been right a couple of times, but it just happens the way it happens."

## SYLVANIA 300

Not even injuries to three of Jimmie Johnson's crewmen during the day's first pit stop could keep the No. 48 from sweeping both races of the season at New Hampshire International Speedway.

As the lead-lap cars came to pit road on Lap 124, Jeff Gordon tried to squeeze between the cars of Johnson, who was pitting behind Gordon, and Michael Waltrip, who was pitting in front of Gordon's No. 24.

Gordon, unaware of Waltrip's pit position, dived to the inside of the No. 15 to get to his pit more quickly. But as Waltrip moved down to make the entrance into his pit box, the two cars collided, with the No. 24 hitting three members of Johnson's pit crew. Two of them slid onto Gordon's hood, and the third was sideswiped by the right side of the car.

Though stunned, the injured crewmen rushed back to Johnson's pit stall and remarkably finished the stop. Johnson came back under caution to examine his car for damage, and went back on the track in 22nd.

"After that, I thought, 'We're just going to salvage what we can,'" Johnson said. "I thought it was virtually impossible to get to the front, but once everybody began to string out, I was able to pass."

Johnson's decision to pit for fuel with 25 laps left proved to be the right one, as the race remained under green. That forced every other driver who was trying to stay out in hopes of getting caution laps to pit and eventually put Johnson in front after Robby Gordon pitted with seven laps to go.

Though the team's strategy played out to perfection, crew chief Chad Knaus was quick to thank his injured crewmen.

"It's just a testament to the training and athleticism that these guys have ... they came back from the infield care center, and we did a four-tire stop directly afterwards, and that was a 13.7-second stop," Knaus said. "That's just awesome after the trauma they went through."

Ricky Rudd finished second in a Ford, his fourth top five of the season. Joe Nemechek, who scored the first victory of his NASCAR Winston Cup career at New Hampshire in 1999, finished third.

## MBNA AMERICA 400

Considering the high level of competition, Jeff Gordon's 13 victories in 1998 once seemed ready to stand as the last double-digit victory season for quite a while. However, Ryan Newman is proving that 10 wins might be a possibility because of his driving talent and the work of his pit crew.

Newman won his seventh race of the season, completing a sweep at Dover despite being almost two laps down because of a cut tire. The race was the first run under a new rule that gives a lap back to the first car one lap down to the leader when a caution comes out. The rule was in response to the danger Dale Jarrett faced when his car sat motionless in the middle of the front straightaway last week at New Hampshire while the field raced to the caution. Drivers no longer will race back to the yellow flag.

Newman got a lap back under the new rule and used his strong fuel-mileage strategy to outlast Jeremy Mayfield.

"We finished with a little bit more fuel than I thought we would've had, but I was able to save quite a bit," Newman said. (Crew chief Matt Borland was) definitely on the radio because his job is to make sure that we finish first, and we need to finish in order to finish first."

Mayfield pushed Newman hard in the closing laps, getting on the inside of Newman twice in an effort to make the pass, but Mayfield couldn't pull it off. The two even touched fenders. Newman pulled away from Mayfield in the final 15 laps, winning easily.

"Jeremy raced me really clean, and I thank him for that," Newman said. "He never cut me a fender when he could've, and that goes a long way."

Two other drivers swept events at other venues this season—Jimmie Johnson at New Hampshire and Kurt Busch at Bristol.

## EA SPORTS 500

Leave it to Michael Waltrip to make his presence known after winning another restrictor-plate race. Waltrip, never shy around television cameras, whipped off a few doughnuts in the infield grass, then emerged waving to the crowd from the newly installed escape hatch in the roof of his car.

The move was met with resounding approval from the Talladega fans, who witnessed another harrowing, yet exciting race at NASCAR's biggest track. The race featured 41 lead changes among 17 drivers.

Coming off Turn 4 on the final lap, Waltrip noticed

Dale Earnhardt Jr. finished the season strong, beginning with a fifth-place finish in the Sylvania 300. He had six top 10s in the last 10 races and picked up his second win of the year in November at Phoenix.

the car landed on its tires and he got out under his own power. A visibly shaken Sadler was taken to an area hospital and was released later that day.

That incident set up a four-lap dash to the finish that Waltrip managed to win. And though his four career victories all have come at either Daytona or Talladega, Waltrip doesn't mind being labeled a restrictor plate specialist.

"I got told for a long time I didn't know how to do anything right," Waltrip said. "So now at least I can do restrictor plates right. I've got that going for me."

## BANQUET 400

Ryan Newman and his team were magicians with fuel mileage during the second half of the season, and that continued at Kansas Speedway.

Newman topped off on Lap 189 and stretched his fuel load for 79 laps to win

Jeff Gordon getting a good run on him on the high side of the track. Waltrip shot up the track to block Gordon's momentum, then quickly darted back down in front of Dale Earnhardt Jr., his Dale Earnhardt Inc. teammate, to win his fourth career race—but first at Talladega.

"I firmly believe that if I just stayed on the bottom of the track and tried to ride to the checkered flag, Gordon would pass me," Waltrip said. "He got a run on the outside, and he was coming up strong."

Waltrip was fortunate to come out with the victory; pole-sitter Elliott Sadler wasn't so lucky. Sadler was driving side-by-side with Earnhardt seven laps from the finish, when Junior's No. 8 dove down toward Sadler, who took evasive action by pulling down farther on the track.

But Sadler got into the path of Kurt Busch, which sent Sadler's No. 38 flipping into the air, landing on its roof and skidding across the infield grass before going back onto the track and flipping four more times.

Miraculously, Sadler was alert throughout the crash,

the Banquet 400 despite the advances of Bill Elliott, who had tested at the track, had the day's strongest car and led the most laps (119).

Newman pitted on Lap 186 for fuel and four tires, then topped off his gas tank two more times before the green flag flew on Lap 190. Six other cars also topped off with fuel, and everyone else opted to pit later.

How Newman won while others had to pit was a point of contention.

Elliott didn't want to discuss the matter and left the track without attending his news conference. Third-place finisher Jeremy Mayfield wondered aloud about Newman's mileage after the race, even though he made it under the same strategy. The day before the race, Jeff Gordon questioned whether Newman was cheating. Kevin Harvick, who finished seventh and closed the gap on points leader Matt Kenseth, had the clearest stance.

"I'm just ticked off that a 15th-place car wins the race and can go 15 laps farther on fuel than the rest of us," Harvick said. "If he can do that with his foot, then he's a

Jeff Burton (top left) had to settle for a 13th-place finish at the Banquet 400, but Ryan Newman was No. 1. Newman's victory was his eighth and final win of 2003. Once again, he stretched his fuel load further than his competitors and ended up winning without having the fastest car.

magician, and I'll kiss his butt if he's doing it with his foot."

Kenseth's wreck on the back stretch on Lap 69 was the day's other big story. After Michael Waltrip spun and hit the wall, Kenseth slowed down to avoid contact with Waltrip, but he lost the car all by himself and careened into the inside wall, causing heavy damage to the front of his car. After much work on the car in the garage, Kenseth managed to get back into the race but finished 36th.

"I wasn't even going fast, so I'm kind of puzzled with what happened," Kenseth said.

With six races left, Harvick trailed Kenseth by 259 points.

## UAW-GM QUALITY 500

Once Tony Stewart caught a glimpse of Ryan Newman, nothing could stop him from tracking Newman down.

Stewart passed Newman with eight laps to go and went on to win the UAW-GM Quality 500, his second victory in what had been an otherwise disappointing defense of his championship.

Stewart, who was dominant throughout the race, gave up the lead with 38 laps left, when he made his final pit stop. After Jamie McMurray led the next lap and pitted himself, Stewart found himself eight seconds down to Newman, who had taken the lead after short-pitting because of a vibration earlier.

Stewart slowly gained ground on Newman, confidently saying at one point over his radio, "I can see him. I'm getting him." Newman's lead then shrank quickly while he apparently attempted to save fuel. When Newman had Stewart on his bumper, he did everything he could to hold him back. But even with aero push working in Newman's favor, Stewart was not to be denied.

"It's about time in the Winston Cup Series that the fastest car won the race," Stewart said. "That fuel stuff is getting old, and all these fans deserve to see the fastest car win the race."

Despite his second-place finish and his 12th top 10 in the last 14 races, Newman wasn't in a celebratory mood.

"I'm just disappointed in having a shot to win the race and not being able to follow through," Newman said. "When you're that close to the No. 1 spot, you tend to think about it for 15 minutes after the race."

Stewart continued his pattern of finishing the year strong; this was his fourth top five finish in a row. Perhaps settling his contract issue in late August by re-signing with Joe Gibbs Racing through 2009 helped him focus. Stewart's sponsor, Home Depot, also signed through 2009.

## SUBWAY 500

This season's theme could be "one good win deserves another." Jeff Gordon became the fourth driver to sweep both races at a NASCAR Winston Cup track, winning the Subway 500 at Martinsville. A superb short-track racer, Gordon won each race from the pole position.

He dominated long stretches, leading 313 of the 500 laps in joining Kurt Busch (Bristol), Ryan Newman (Dover) and teammate Jimmie Johnson (New Hampshire) as the drivers who swept two races at one venue.

Gordon and Johnson finished 1-2 in the race, but the outcome never was in question. Gordon did all he could to keep distance between himself and his teammate because he knew the No. 48 would be driving hard for another victory. Gordon negotiated traffic well and never had to worry about Johnson getting to his bumper.

"This team is on top of its short-track game so well, and really altogether is on top of its game the last five races," Gordon said. "I really hate that we had that August and part of September like we did. I'd love to be up there battling for that championship, but that kind of took us back a little bit."

With the championship out of reach, Gordon made it a goal to finish second in the point standings. With four races left, he was 106 points behind second-place Kevin Harvick.

Meanwhile, Johnson would have loved to win his fourth race of the year. But he was pleased with a second-place finish, especially considering how badly he struggled with his car on Friday and Saturday.

**Dale Earnhardt Jr. qualified third in three of the four October races—the Banquet 400, Subway 500 and Bass Pro Shops MBNA 500. His best finish in those races was fourth, in the Subway 500.**

"To be able to get things figured out and sorted out on how to drive the track and finish second is such a cool accomplishment," Johnson said. "This is one of the places that is hardest mentally to drive, and even after being spun out, we still ended up with a good finish."

## BASS PRO SHOPS MBNA 500

Jeff Gordon continued his outstanding late-season run by doing something no one else had in 2003—win consecutive races. Gordon followed his victory at Martinsville with one at Atlanta, holding off Tony Stewart in the late stages for his third victory of the year.

Gordon's victory was made somewhat easier because the caution flag flew on Lap 322, just three laps from the finish. The race was beyond the point at which NASCAR could red flag the event to ensure a green-flag finish, so it ended under caution.

"The 20 (Stewart) made a heck of an effort and certainly kept it exciting," Gordon said. "I didn't know whether we were going to win it or not. He came up there and got to me, and I saw where once he got to me, he stopped gaining. I thought, 'Ooh, we might have something for him now.' I started adjusting my line and then we were just battling it out. Then the caution came out. Great victory."

Gordon has finished no worse than fifth in his last six races. That's a reversal from the six before that, when he had just one top 10 finish and four of 28th or worse.

Gordon said the surge reminded him of the end of the 2000 season, when he finished strong and carried that momentum into a 2001 championship.

"This is all about not only trying to get as far up in the points as we can this year but to build momentum for that offseason," Gordon said. "How you do that is by having good runs and winning races."

Series points leader Matt Kenseth gained additional breathing room with an 11th-place finish. Kenseth's closest competitor, Kevin Harvick, finished 20th. Harvick never got his car handling right after getting caught up in Dave Blaney's wreck midway through the race. Harvick tried going high to avoid contact, but Blaney's car slid up the track and into Harvick's path.

The race was completed on Monday because of rain. Only 39 of the 325 laps were run Sunday.

## CHECKER AUTO PARTS 500

Victory lane celebrations are exhilarating by nature, but it was easy to see that being there at Phoenix was extra special for Dale Earnhardt Jr. Junior took the lead from Jimmie Johnson 51 laps from the finish and went on to win his second race of the season. More important, it was Junior's first victory at a non-restrictor plate racetrack since September 2001, when he won at Dover. Junior's three wins since then had come at Talladega, including one in April of this year.

"We wanted to be in victory lane so bad this year," Earnhardt said. "We wanted to show that we're not just a restrictor plate team. These guys just gave me such a good car."

Junior had no difficulty keeping Johnson behind him despite several caution flags late in the race. What Junior enjoyed most was the fact he had no trouble reeling in Johnson at a time of his choosing.

"I was just sitting there and waiting behind Jimmie," Earnhardt said. "I patiently waited and waited, and he got easier and easier to catch. I didn't want to burn myself up trying to keep up with him. And it finally came to me. We saved all we had for the end."

Though Earnhardt's prospects for winning the champi-

**Kurt Busch was in the top 10 in points for all but one week of the season until he dropped to 11th after the Subway 500. He ended up finishing 11th in the standings.**

**Bill Elliott scored his first victory since August 2002 when he took the checkered flag in the Pop Secret 400 despite starting from the back of the field.**

onship appeared slim—Matt Kenseth finished sixth and was 230 points ahead of Junior—he made it clear what his plans are for next year.

"We've been pretty good all year, and we've improved in a lot of places," Earnhardt said. "We've got a lot of guys who have been with us and some new guys and, if we keep everybody next year, we're going to win a championship."

Looking at Kenseth's day, it was fairly typical of his season. He qualified poorly (37th) but still had the savvy, skills and car to work his way into another top 10 finish. He tried hard to pass Michael Waltrip for fifth place in the final laps, but he understood that driving any harder would have caused him to wreck. He settled for sixth.

## POP SECRET 400

Finally, Matt Kenseth exhaled. Bill Elliott won his first race of the year, and the 44th of his career, but his story was secondary on this day at North Carolina Speedway. Kenseth, a native of Wisconsin, finished fourth and locked up a first NASCAR Winston Cup championship for himself and for car owner Jack Roush.

Kenseth said that despite holding such a big points lead for much of the second half of the season, he felt pressure not to blow it. "I feel like the world has been lifted off my shoulders today," he said.

Kenseth took a slow celebratory victory lap around Rockingham in his No. 17 Ford, while his crew members did the same, riding around the track in the back of two pickup trucks. Kenseth maintained his usual cool demeanor even after getting out of the car, but there was a reason for that.

"I got all this stuff bottled up inside because I didn't want to get too excited the last few months," Kenseth said. "I don't know what I'm going to do now. It's an awesome feeling."

The championship was Ford's first since Dale Jarrett won it in 1999.

Meanwhile, Elliott reveled in his good fortune. With retirement rumors swirling around him, the driver of the No. 9 Dodge collected his first win since August 2002 despite starting from the back of the field because of an engine change.

He led a race-high 140 of 393 laps and had no trouble holding off Jimmie Johnson on the final restart with 11 laps to go.

"It seems like everything has just come together for this team the last few months," Elliott said. "We had a great car here today. That thing just came on when the race started and stayed good all day."

Elliott remained noncommittal when asked about his plans for 2004. "Right now, I want to concentrate on that last race and what we're going to do there," he said, "and we'll think about next year after that."

## FORD 400

Bobby Labonte didn't have the best car of the day, but he had the one that led the final lap.

When Bill Elliott's right rear tire blew on the white flag lap, Labonte took the lead on the back stretch—the only time he led all day—and notched a victory in the season finale at reconfigured Homestead-Miami Speedway.

Labonte's victory, his second of the season, came as a major surprise because Elliott's car had led 189 of the 267 laps and held off every challenge Labonte and others could muster. With encouragement from crew chief Michael "Fatback" McSwain not to give up, Labonte was in position to take advantage of Elliott's misfortune.

"Oh man, I couldn't believe it, I just couldn't believe it," Labonte said. "Fatback kept saying, 'Keep going, he'll make a mistake.' But I told him Bill was just playing with me."

Elliott, who won the week before at Rockingham, finished eighth.

"Our Dodge ran so well today and it's just an unfortunate thing," Elliott said. "I don't know if I've ever won one

Bobby Labonte fortified his eighth-place points finish by winning the season-ending Ford 400. It was Labonte's first victory since Atlanta in March. He finished the season with 12 top fives but had only two in the second half of the year.

like that, but I've sure lost them like that. Obviously, it wasn't our day."

Despite Elliott's dominance throughout the race, the reconfigured track, which features 18 to 20 degrees of banking in each corner, provided entertaining side-by-side racing. The track previously had just 6 degrees of banking in the corners, leaving only one preferred groove in the turns and making passing extremely difficult. International Speedway Corporation, which owns the track, spent $10 million on the renovation.

Series champion Matt Kenseth no doubt was glad he clinched the title a week ago at Rockingham; his engine blew on Lap 28. He finished 43rd, and only 90 points ahead of Jimmie Johnson, who finished third. Kenseth also blew an engine in this race in 2002.

# Daytona 500 — race 1 of 36

| Fin. | St. | Car | Driver | Make | Sponsor | Pts./Bonus | Laps | Status | Winnings |
|---|---|---|---|---|---|---|---|---|---|
| 1. | 4 | 15 | Michael Waltrip | Chevrolet | NAPA Auto Parts | 185/10 | 109 | Running | $1,419,406 |
| 2. | 36 | 97 | Kurt Busch | Ford | Rubbermaid | 170/0 | 109 | Running | $1,027,101 |
| 3. | 10 | 48 | Jimmie Johnson | Chevrolet | Lowe's | 170/5 | 109 | Running | $707,526 |
| 4. | 31 | 29 | Kevin Harvick | Chevrolet | GM Goodwrench Service | 160/0 | 109 | Running | $569,630 |
| 5. | 26 | 6 | Mark Martin | Ford | Viagra | 155/0 | 109 | Running | $444,609 |
| 6. | 3 | 31 | Robby Gordon | Chevrolet | Cingular Wireless | 150/0 | 109 | Running | $362,807 |
| 7. | 8 | 20 | Tony Stewart | Chevrolet | Home Depot | 151/5 | 109 | Running | $315,454 |
| 8. | 20 | 19 | Jeremy Mayfield | Dodge | Dodge Dealers/UAW | 142/0 | 109 | Running | $245,026 |
| 9. | 18 | 09 | Mike Wallace | Dodge | Miccosukee Resort | 138/0 | 109 | Running | $220,051 |
| 10. | 11 | 88 | Dale Jarrett | Ford | UPS | 134/0 | 109 | Running | $256,098 |
| 11. | 9 | 99 | Jeff Burton | Ford | CITGO | 130/0 | 109 | Running | $233,937 |
| 12. | 13 | 24 | Jeff Gordon | Chevrolet | DuPont | 127/0 | 109 | Running | $238,648 |
| 13. | 30 | 45 | Kyle Petty | Dodge | Georgia Pacific | 124/0 | 109 | Running | $198,176 |
| 14. | 24 | 0 | Jack Sprague* | Pontiac | NetZero | 121/0 | 109 | Running | $184,901 |
| 15. | 5 | 21 | Ricky Rudd | Ford | Motorcraft Quality Parts | 118/0 | 109 | Running | $222,595 |
| 16. | 21 | 23 | Kenny Wallace | Dodge | Stacker 2 | 115/0 | 109 | Running | $199,420 |
| 17. | 7 | 40 | Sterling Marlin | Dodge | Coors Light | 112/0 | 109 | Running | $229,745 |
| 18. | 6 | 54 | Todd Bodine | Ford | National Guard | 114/5 | 109 | Running | $208,051 |
| 19. | 40 | 10 | Johnny Benson | Pontiac | Valvoline | 106/0 | 109 | Running | $208,620 |
| 20. | 35 | 17 | Matt Kenseth | Ford | DeWalt Power Tools | 108/5 | 109 | Running | $200,345 |
| 21. | 27 | 16 | Greg Biffle* | Ford | Grainger | 100/0 | 109 | Running | $177,495 |
| 22. | 15 | 25 | Joe Nemechek | Chevrolet | UAW/Delphi | 97/0 | 109 | Running | $180,595 |
| 23. | 16 | 38 | Elliott Sadler | Ford | M&M's | 94/0 | 109 | Running | $215,901 |
| 24. | 39 | 77 | Dave Blaney | Ford | Jasper Engines & Trans. | 91/0 | 109 | Running | $198,176 |
| 25. | 38 | 2 | Rusty Wallace | Dodge | Miller Lite | 88/0 | 109 | Running | $190,692 |
| 26. | 25 | 32 | Ricky Craven | Pontiac | Tide | 90/5 | 109 | Running | $194,259 |
| 27. | 29 | 41 | Casey Mears* | Dodge | Target | 87/5 | 109 | Running | $184,420 |
| 28. | 42 | 01 | Jerry Nadeau | Pontiac | U.S. Army | 79/0 | 109 | Running | $176,526 |
| 29. | 32 | 1 | Steve Park | Chevrolet | Pennzoil | 76/0 | 109 | Running | $191,957 |
| 30. | 41 | 5 | Terry Labonte | Chevrolet | Kellogg's/got milk? | 73/0 | 109 | Running | $200,576 |
| 31. | 19 | 42 | Jamie McMurray* | Dodge | Havoline | 70/0 | 109 | Running | $171,195 |
| 32. | 14 | 9 | Bill Elliott | Dodge | Dodge Dealers/UAW | 67/0 | 109 | Running | $211,484 |
| 33. | 33 | 74 | Tony Raines* | Chevrolet | Staff America | 64/0 | 109 | Running | $171,851 |
| 34. | 12 | 43 | John Andretti | Dodge | Cheerios | 61/0 | 108 | Running | $208,509 |
| 35. | 34 | 33 | Christian Fittipaldi | Chevrolet | Monaco Coaches | 58/0 | 108 | Running | $177,856 |
| 36. | 2 | 8 | Dale Earnhardt Jr. | Chevrolet | Budweiser | 60/5 | 108 | Running | $243,543 |
| 37. | 43 | 4 | Mike Skinner | Pontiac | Kodak | 52/0 | 108 | Running | $167,870 |
| 38. | 17 | 22 | Ward Burton | Dodge | Caterpillar | 49/0 | 105 | Accident | $203,751 |
| 39. | 1 | 30 | Jeff Green | Chevrolet | America Online | 46/0 | 94 | Accident | $202,720 |
| 40. | 23 | 7 | Jimmy Spencer | Dodge | Sirius Satellite Radio | 43/0 | 94 | Accident | $166,620 |
| 41. | 22 | 18 | Bobby Labonte | Chevrolet | Interstate Batteries | 40/0 | 81 | Running | $202,134 |
| 42. | 28 | 49 | Ken Schrader | Dodge | 1-800-CALLATT | 37/0 | 57 | Accident | $166,476 |
| 43. | 37 | 12 | Ryan Newman | Dodge | ALLTEL | 34/0 | 56 | Accident | $195,663 |

*Rookie. Time of race: 2 hours, 2 minutes, 8 seconds. Average speed: 133.870 mph. Margin of victory: Under caution. Caution flags: Five for 23 laps. 43-45 (Car 18—spin, back stretch); 58-67 (Cars 12, 18, 22 and 49—accident, trioval), 96-99 (Cars 7 and 30—accident, Turn 4), 103-105 (debris), 107-109 (Car 22—accident, Turn 4). Lap leaders: 11 lead changes among eight drivers. Michael Waltrip 1-34, Matt Kenseth 35-36, Tony Stewart 37-42, Dale Earnhardt Jr. 43-64, Casey Mears 65, Waltrip 66-95, Jimmie Johnson 96, Todd Bodine 97, Ricky Craven 98, Johnson 99-105, Waltrip 106-109. Pole winner: Jeff Green, 186.606 mph. Notes: The race was halted by rain after 109 laps of the scheduled 200. It was red-flagged twice for rain. The first red-flag period, on Lap 63, lasted 1 hour, 8 minutes. The second was called on Lap 109, and the race was not resumed after 65 minutes. Dropped to rear: Mark Martin (backup car), Casey Mears (backup car), Johnny Benson (backup car), Kevin Harvick (engine change). Failed to qualify: David Green, Hermie Sadler, Brett Bodine, Larry Foyt, Derrike Cope, Kirk Shelmerdine, Mike Harmon. Estimated attendance: 200,000.

**Daytona International Speedway**
Daytona Beach, Fla.—2.5-mile banked paved trioval
February 16, 2003—272.5 miles—109 laps (shortened by rain)

**2003 SEASON**

## Points standings

| Rank | Driver | Behind |
|---|---|---|
| 1. | Michael Waltrip | Leader |
| 2. | Kurt Busch | -15 |
| 3. | Jimmie Johnson | -15 |
| 4. | Kevin Harvick | -25 |
| 5. | Mark Martin | -30 |
| 6. | Tony Stewart | -34 |
| 7. | Robby Gordon | -35 |
| 8. | Jeremy Mayfield | -43 |
| 9. | Mike Wallace | -47 |
| 10. | Dale Jarrett | -51 |

# Subway 400 — race 2 of 36

| Fin. | St. | Car | Driver | Make | Sponsor | Pts./Bonus | Laps | Status | Winnings |
|---|---|---|---|---|---|---|---|---|---|
| 1. | 9 | 88 | Dale Jarrett | Ford | UPS | 180/5 | 393 | Running | $177,828 |
| 2. | 27 | 97 | Kurt Busch | Ford | Rubbermaid | 175/5 | 393 | Running | $108,200 |
| 3. | 18 | 17 | Matt Kenseth | Ford | DeWalt Power Tools | 170/5 | 393 | Running | $94,350 |
| 4. | 6 | 32 | Ricky Craven | Pontiac | Tide | 165/5 | 393 | Running | $103,725 |
| 5. | 7 | 42 | Jamie McMurray* | Dodge | Havoline | 155/0 | 393 | Running | $59,375 |
| 6. | 8 | 2 | Rusty Wallace | Dodge | Miller Lite | 160/10 | 393 | Running | $104,127 |
| 7. | 3 | 6 | Mark Martin | Ford | Viagra | 151/5 | 393 | Running | $93,443 |
| 8. | 37 | 48 | Jimmie Johnson | Chevrolet | Lowe's | 142/0 | 393 | Running | $77,110 |
| 9. | 11 | 38 | Elliott Sadler | Ford | M&M's | 138/0 | 393 | Running | $91,060 |
| 10. | 1 | 77 | Dave Blaney | Ford | Jasper Engines & Trans. | 139/5 | 393 | Running | $86,460 |
| 11. | 28 | 21 | Ricky Rudd | Ford | Motorcraft Quality Parts | 130/0 | 393 | Running | $76,685 |
| 12. | 38 | 99 | Jeff Burton | Ford | CITGO | 132/5 | 392 | Running | $86,227 |
| 13. | 2 | 10 | Johnny Benson | Pontiac | Valvoline | 124/0 | 392 | Running | $82,960 |
| 14. | 21 | 12 | Ryan Newman | Dodge | ALLTEL | 121/0 | 392 | Running | $84,335 |
| 15. | 23 | 24 | Jeff Gordon | Chevrolet | DuPont | 118/0 | 392 | Running | $98,988 |
| 16. | 10 | 18 | Bobby Labonte | Chevrolet | Interstate Batteries | 120/5 | 392 | Running | $88,743 |
| 17. | 20 | 4 | Mike Skinner | Pontiac | Kodak | 112/0 | 392 | Running | $63,760 |
| 18. | 15 | 22 | Ward Burton | Dodge | Caterpillar | 109/0 | 392 | Running | $85,316 |
| 19. | 22 | 15 | Michael Waltrip | Chevrolet | NAPA Auto Parts | 106/0 | 392 | Running | $66,910 |
| 20. | 33 | 20 | Tony Stewart | Chevrolet | Home Depot | 103/0 | 392 | Running | $103,538 |
| 21. | 25 | 1 | Steve Park | Chevrolet | Pennzoil | 100/0 | 392 | Running | $69,197 |
| 22. | 13 | 16 | Greg Biffle* | Ford | Grainger | 97/0 | 392 | Running | $48,210 |
| 23. | 14 | 25 | Joe Nemechek | Chevrolet | UAW/Delphi | 94/0 | 392 | Running | $52,360 |
| 24. | 35 | 49 | Ken Schrader | Dodge | 1-800-CALLATT | 91/0 | 392 | Running | $47,760 |
| 25. | 26 | 29 | Kevin Harvick | Chevrolet | GM Goodwrench Service | 88/0 | 391 | Running | $87,138 |
| 26. | 24 | 01 | Jerry Nadeau | Pontiac | U.S. Army | 85/0 | 391 | Running | $59,039 |
| 27. | 31 | 5 | Terry Labonte | Chevrolet | Kellogg's/got milk? | 82/0 | 391 | Running | $76,312 |
| 28. | 36 | 7 | Jimmy Spencer | Dodge | Sirius Satellite Radio | 79/0 | 391 | Running | $50,085 |
| 29. | 19 | 31 | Robby Gordon | Chevrolet | Cingular Wireless | 76/0 | 391 | Running | $74,921 |
| 30. | 16 | 41 | Casey Mears* | Dodge | Target | 73/0 | 390 | Running | $58,100 |
| 31. | 39 | 30 | Jeff Green | Chevrolet | America Online | 70/0 | 390 | Running | $56,975 |
| 32. | 5 | 9 | Bill Elliott | Dodge | Dodge Dealers/UAW | 67/0 | 390 | Running | $85,283 |
| 33. | 12 | 8 | Dale Earnhardt Jr. | Chevrolet | Budweiser | 64/0 | 390 | Running | $87,142 |
| 34. | 34 | 0 | Jack Sprague* | Pontiac | NetZero | 61/0 | 390 | Running | $47,050 |
| 35. | 30 | 45 | Kyle Petty | Dodge | Georgia Pacific | 63/5 | 389 | Running | $54,000 |
| 36. | 41 | 14 | Larry Foyt* | Dodge | Harrah's | 55/0 | 388 | Running | $45,950 |
| 37. | 42 | 74 | Tony Raines* | Chevrolet | Staff America | 52/0 | 387 | Running | $45,900 |
| 38. | 17 | 23 | Kenny Wallace | Dodge | Stacker 2 | 49/0 | 386 | Running | $45,840 |
| 39. | 32 | 43 | John Andretti | Dodge | Cheerios | 46/0 | 347 | Running | $81,568 |
| 40. | 4 | 40 | Sterling Marlin | Dodge | Coors Light | 48/5 | 319 | Water pump | $89,790 |
| 41. | 29 | 19 | Jeremy Mayfield | Dodge | Dodge Dealers/UAW | 40/0 | 271 | Accident | $53,670 |
| 42. | 40 | 54 | Todd Bodine | Ford | National Guard | 37/0 | 85 | Accident | $45,615 |
| 43. | 43 | 37 | Derrike Cope | Chevrolet | Friendly's | 34/0 | 34 | Clutch | $44,922 |

*Rookie. Time of race: 3 hours, 23 minutes, 29 seconds. Average speed: 117.852 mph. Margin of victory: .966 seconds. Caution flags: 7 for 46 laps. 47-54 (Competition caution—debris); 88-92 (Car 54—accident, Turn 2), 108-112 (Car 23—accident, back stretch), 123-126 (Cars 19 and 01—accident, Turn 4), 174-177 (Car 8—spin, back stretch), 276-291 (Cars 19 and 8—accident, Turn 2), 299-302 (Car 24—spin, Turn 4; Car 01—spin, front stretch). Lap leaders: 20 lead changes among 11 drivers. Dave Blaney 1-8, Mark Martin 9-16, Ricky Craven 17-26, Rusty Wallace 27-88, Kyle Petty 89, Martin 90-92, R. Wallace 93-123, Martin 124-126, R. Wallace, 127-174, Martin 175-178, R. Wallace 179-219, Kurt Busch 220-255, Matt Kenseth 256-257, Sterling Marlin 258-260, Busch 261-299, Bobby Labonte 300-303, Jeff Burton 304-309, Busch 310-383, Dale Jarrett 384-388, Busch 389, Jarrett 390-393. Pole winner: Dave Blaney, 154.683 mph. Failed to qualify: None. Estimated attendance: 40,000.

**North Carolina Speedway**
Rockingham, N.C.—1.017-mile banked paved oval
February 23, 2003—400 miles—393 laps

## Points standings

| Rk. | Driver | Behind |
|---|---|---|
| 1. | Kurt Busch | Leader |
| 2. | Dale Jarrett | -31 |
| 3. | Jimmie Johnson | -33 |
| 4. | Mark Martin | -39 |
| 5. | Michael Waltrip | -54 |
| 6. | Matt Kenseth | -67 |
| 7. | Jeff Burton | -83 |
| 8. | Ricky Craven | -90 |
| 9. | Tony Stewart | -91 |
| 10. | Kevin Harvick | -97 |

# UAW-DaimlerChrysler 400 — race 3 of 36

| Fin. | St. | Car | Driver | Make | Sponsor | Pts./Bonus | Laps | Status | Winnings |
|---|---|---|---|---|---|---|---|---|---|
| 1. | 17 | 17 | Matt Kenseth | Ford | DeWalt Power Tools | 180/5 | 267 | Running | $365,875 |
| 2. | 4 | 8 | Dale Earnhardt Jr. | Chevrolet | Budweiser | 180/10 | 267 | Running | $267,167 |
| 3. | 9 | 15 | Michael Waltrip | Chevrolet | NAPA Auto Parts | 170/5 | 267 | Running | $190,550 |
| 4. | 1 | 18 | Bobby Labonte | Chevrolet | Interstate Batteries | 165/5 | 267 | Running | $179,658 |
| 5. | 8 | 20 | Tony Stewart | Chevrolet | Home Depot | 155/0 | 267 | Running | $162,753 |
| 6. | 7 | 99 | Jeff Burton | Ford | CITGO | 150/0 | 267 | Running | $127,067 |
| 7. | 3 | 12 | Ryan Newman | Dodge | ALLTEL | 151/5 | 267 | Running | $128,025 |
| 8. | 34 | 40 | Sterling Marlin | Dodge | Coors Light | 142/0 | 267 | Running | $136,000 |
| 9. | 26 | 25 | Joe Nemechek | Chevrolet | UAW/Delphi | 138/0 | 267 | Running | $87,200 |
| 10. | 39 | 1 | Steve Park | Chevrolet | Pennzoil | 134/0 | 267 | Running | $111,862 |
| 11. | 10 | 48 | Jimmie Johnson | Chevrolet | Lowe's | 135/5 | 267 | Running | $97,675 |
| 12. | 16 | 10 | Johnny Benson | Pontiac | Valvoline | 127/0 | 266 | Running | $107,725 |
| 13. | 22 | 29 | Kevin Harvick | Chevrolet | GM Goodwrench Service | 124/0 | 266 | Running | $116,553 |
| 14. | 30 | 9 | Bill Elliott | Dodge | Dodge Dealers/UAW | 121/0 | 266 | Running | $113,383 |
| 15. | 18 | 41 | Casey Mears* | Dodge | Target | 118/0 | 266 | Running | $105,100 |
| 16. | 36 | 5 | Terry Labonte | Chevrolet | Kellogg's/got milk? | 115/0 | 266 | Running | $102,406 |
| 17. | 15 | 7 | Jimmy Spencer | Dodge | Sirius Satellite Radio | 112/0 | 266 | Running | $90,250 |
| 18. | 6 | 43 | John Andretti | Dodge | Cheerios | 114/5 | 266 | Running | $109,928 |
| 19. | 38 | 21 | Ricky Rudd | Ford | Motorcraft Quality Parts | 111/5 | 266 | Running | $94,050 |
| 20. | 24 | 54 | Todd Bodine | Ford | National Guard | 103/0 | 266 | Running | $84,750 |
| 21. | 13 | 19 | Jeremy Mayfield | Dodge | Dodge Dealers/UAW | 100/0 | 266 | Running | $78,850 |
| 22. | 11 | 01 | Jerry Nadeau | Pontiac | U.S. Army | 97/0 | 266 | Running | $78,139 |
| 23. | 21 | 31 | Robby Gordon | Chevrolet | Cingular Wireless | 94/0 | 266 | Running | $94,737 |
| 24. | 32 | 74 | Tony Raines* | Chevrolet | Staff America | 91/0 | 265 | Running | $64,550 |
| 25. | 20 | 22 | Ward Burton | Dodge | Caterpillar | 88/0 | 265 | Running | $100,006 |
| 26. | 42 | 0 | Jack Sprague* | Pontiac | NetZero | 85/0 | 265 | Running | $62,550 |
| 27. | 14 | 30 | Jeff Green | Chevrolet | America Online | 82/0 | 265 | Running | $72,550 |
| 28. | 28 | 49 | Ken Schrader | Dodge | BAM Racing | 79/0 | 263 | Running | $60,550 |
| 29. | 43 | 37 | Derrike Cope | Chevrolet | Friendly's | 76/0 | 263 | Running | $60,350 |
| 30. | 33 | 23 | Kenny Wallace | Dodge | Stacker 2 | 73/0 | 261 | Running | $63,600 |
| 31. | 19 | 45 | Kyle Petty | Dodge | Georgia Pacific | 70/0 | 261 | Running | $70,400 |
| 32. | 12 | 42 | Jamie McMurray* | Dodge | Havoline | 67/0 | 258 | Running | $59,700 |
| 33. | 41 | 66 | Hideo Fukuyama* | Ford | Kikkoman | 64/0 | 258 | Running | $60,400 |
| 34. | 35 | 77 | Dave Blaney | Ford | Jasper Engines & Trans. | 61/0 | 231 | Clutch | $67,300 |
| 35. | 31 | 14 | Larry Foyt* | Dodge | Harrah's | 58/0 | 216 | Vibration | $59,100 |
| 36. | 37 | 32 | Ricky Craven | Pontiac | Tide | 55/0 | 211 | Running | $66,900 |
| 37. | 2 | 24 | Jeff Gordon | Chevrolet | DuPont | 57/5 | 193 | Accident | $106,053 |
| 38. | 5 | 97 | Kurt Busch | Ford | Rubbermaid | 54/5 | 179 | Accident | $78,475 |
| 39. | 40 | 4 | Mike Skinner | Pontiac | Kodak | 46/0 | 174 | Accident | $58,275 |
| 40. | 25 | 2 | Rusty Wallace | Dodge | Miller Lite | 43/0 | 174 | Accident | $92,717 |
| 41. | 27 | 88 | Dale Jarrett | Ford | UPS | 40/0 | 131 | Accident | $103,633 |
| 42. | 23 | 38 | Elliott Sadler | Ford | M&M's | 37/0 | 125 | Engine | $91,915 |
| 43. | 29 | 6 | Mark Martin | Ford | Viagra | 34/0 | 114 | Engine | $91,542 |

*Rookie. Time of race: 3 hours, 0 minutes, 46 seconds. Average speed: 132.934 mph. Margin of victory: 9.104 seconds. Caution flags: 6 for 30 laps. 101-106 (Cars 14 and 32—accident, front stretch); 117-120 (oil on track); 127-130 (oil on track); 133-137 (Car 88—accident, Turn 2); 167-170 (Car 42—spin, Turn 4); 177-183 (Cars 2, 4, 7, 14, 24, 54 and 97—accident, Turn 2). Lap leaders: 17 lead changes among 10 drivers. Bobby Labonte—pole, Jeff Gordon 1-50, Dale Earnhardt Jr. 51-56, Michael Waltrip 57, B. Labonte 58, Kurt Busch 59-60, Earnhardt Jr. 61-90, Waltrip 91-101, Earnhardt Jr. 102-116, Waltrip 117-121, Earnhardt Jr. 122-167, Ricky Rudd 168, J. Gordon 169-171, Matt Kenseth 172-227, Jimmie Johnson 228-229, Ryan Newman 230-232, John Andretti 233-235, Kenseth 236-267. Pole winner: Bobby Labonte, 173.016 mph, track record. Failed to qualify: Greg Biffle, Brandon Ash. Estimated attendance: 140,000.

**Las Vegas Motor Speedway**
Las Vegas —1.5-mile banked paved trioval
March 2, 2003—400 miles—267 laps

## Points standings

| Rk. | Driver | Behind |
|---|---|---|
| 1. | Michael Waltrip | Leader |
| 2. | Matt Kenseth | -3 |
| 3. | Jimmie Johnson | -14 |
| 4. | Jeff Burton | -49 |
| 5. | Tony Stewart | -52 |
| 6. | Kurt Busch | -62 |
| 7. | Kevin Harvick | -89 |
| 8. | Ricky Rudd | -102 |
| 9. | Johnny Benson | -104 |
| 10. | Dale Jarrett | -107 |

2003 SEASON

# Bass Pro Shops MBNA 500 — race 4 of 36

| Fin. | St. | Car | Driver | Make | Sponsor | Pts./Bonus | Laps | Status | Winnings |
|---|---|---|---|---|---|---|---|---|---|
| 1. | 4 | 18 | Bobby Labonte | Chevrolet | Interstate Batteries | 185/10 | 325 | Running | $209,233 |
| 2. | 30 | 24 | Jeff Gordon | Chevrolet | DuPont | 175/5 | 325 | Running | $142,778 |
| 3. | 37 | 8 | Dale Earnhardt Jr. | Chevrolet | Budweiser | 170/5 | 325 | Running | $113,917 |
| 4. | 24 | 17 | Matt Kenseth | Ford | DeWalt Power Tools | 160/0 | 325 | Running | $92,600 |
| 5. | 8 | 20 | Tony Stewart | Chevrolet | Home Depot | 160/5 | 325 | Running | $112,578 |
| 6. | 3 | 38 | Elliott Sadler | Ford | M&M's | 155/5 | 325 | Running | $94,450 |
| 7. | 5 | 7 | Jimmy Spencer | Dodge | Sirius Satellite Radio | 151/5 | 325 | Running | $79,550 |
| 8. | 27 | 77 | Dave Blaney | Ford | Jasper Engines & Trans. | 147/5 | 325 | Running | $80,125 |
| 9. | 13 | 25 | Joe Nemechek | Chevrolet | UAW/Delphi | 143/5 | 325 | Running | $58,225 |
| 10. | 1 | 12 | Ryan Newman | Dodge | ALLTEL | 139/5 | 324 | Running | $94,450 |
| 11. | 23 | 10 | Johnny Benson | Pontiac | Valvoline | 130/0 | 324 | Running | $84,400 |
| 12. | 22 | 32 | Ricky Craven | Pontiac | Tide | 127/0 | 324 | Running | $76,375 |
| 13. | 20 | 16 | Greg Biffle* | Ford | Grainger | 124/0 | 324 | Running | $51,775 |
| 14. | 34 | 40 | Sterling Marlin | Dodge | Coors Light | 121/0 | 324 | Running | $93,675 |
| 15. | 7 | 2 | Rusty Wallace | Dodge | Miller Lite | 118/0 | 324 | Running | $88,392 |
| 16. | 15 | 1 | Steve Park | Chevrolet | Pennzoil | 115/0 | 324 | Running | $75,512 |
| 17. | 18 | 31 | Robby Gordon | Chevrolet | Cingular Wireless | 112/0 | 323 | Running | $77,912 |
| 18. | 12 | 22 | Ward Burton | Dodge | Caterpillar | 109/0 | 323 | Running | $84,871 |
| 19. | 17 | 29 | Kevin Harvick | Chevrolet | GM Goodwrench Service | 106/0 | 323 | Running | $87,968 |
| 20. | 39 | 5 | Terry Labonte | Chevrolet | Kellogg's/got milk? | 103/0 | 323 | Running | $80,196 |
| 21. | 16 | 88 | Dale Jarrett | Ford | UPS | 100/0 | 323 | Running | $93,968 |
| 22. | 10 | 19 | Jeremy Mayfield | Dodge | Dodge Dealers/UAW | 97/0 | 322 | Running | $59,435 |
| 23. | 33 | 41 | Casey Mears* | Dodge | Target | 94/0 | 322 | Running | $70,535 |
| 24. | 36 | 74 | Tony Raines* | Chevrolet | Staff America | 91/0 | 322 | Running | $47,635 |
| 25. | 28 | 30 | Jeff Green | Chevrolet | America Online | 88/0 | 322 | Running | $59,035 |
| 26. | 40 | 23 | Kenny Wallace | Dodge | Stacker 2 | 85/0 | 322 | Running | $58,774 |
| 27. | 6 | 15 | Michael Waltrip | Chevrolet | NAPA Auto Parts | 82/0 | 321 | Running | $68,070 |
| 28. | 35 | 54 | Todd Bodine | Ford | National Guard | 79/0 | 321 | Running | $49,920 |
| 29. | 19 | 43 | John Andretti | Dodge | Cheerios | 76/0 | 320 | Running | $84,988 |
| 30. | 32 | 4 | Mike Skinner | Pontiac | Kodak | 73/0 | 318 | Running | $47,085 |
| 31. | 14 | 01 | Jerry Nadeau | Pontiac | U.S. Army | 70/0 | 316 | Accident | $46,510 |
| 32. | 11 | 48 | Jimmie Johnson | Chevrolet | Lowe's | 72/5 | 308 | Engine | $65,835 |
| 33. | 26 | 99 | Jeff Burton | Ford | CITGO | 64/0 | 305 | Engine | $80,687 |
| 34. | 38 | 45 | Kyle Petty | Dodge | Georgia Pacific | 61/0 | 296 | Running | $54,325 |
| 35. | 21 | 21 | Ricky Rudd | Ford | Motorcraft Quality Parts | 58/0 | 295 | Engine | $54,290 |
| 36. | 31 | 42 | Jamie McMurray* | Dodge | Havoline | 55/0 | 293 | Engine | $46,255 |
| 37. | 43 | 0 | Jack Sprague* | Pontiac | NetZero | 52/0 | 267 | Overheating | $46,220 |
| 38. | 42 | 49 | Ken Schrader | Dodge | 1-800-CALLATT | 49/0 | 182 | Engine | $46,175 |
| 39. | 2 | 9 | Bill Elliott | Dodge | Dodge Dealers/UAW | 46/0 | 164 | Engine | $85,723 |
| 40. | 9 | 97 | Kurt Busch | Ford | Rubbermaid | 43/0 | 143 | Engine | $66,090 |
| 41. | 25 | 11 | Brett Bodine | Ford | Hooters Restaurants | 40/0 | 141 | Accident | $46,050 |
| 42. | 29 | 6 | Mark Martin | Ford | Viagra | 37/0 | 133 | Engine | $79,843 |
| 43. | 41 | 14 | Larry Foyt* | Dodge | Harrah's | 34/0 | 104 | Engine | $45,069 |

*Rookie. Time of race: 3 hours, 25 minutes. Average speed: 146.048 mph. Margin of victory: 1.274 seconds. Caution flags: 7 for 34 laps. 136-140 (oil on track); 146-154 (oil on track and Car 11 and 23—accident, back stretch); 175-178 (Car 2—accident, Turn 2); 186-189 (oil on track); 209-212 (debris in Turn 2); 303-306 (Car 21—accident, Turn 3), 309-312 (Cars 43 and 99—accident, Turn 2). Lap leaders: 23 lead changes among 10 drivers. Ryan Newman 1-20, Bobby Labonte 21-36, Joe Nemechek 37-55, B. Labonte 56-57, Tony Stewart 58-59, Jeff Gordon 60-68, B. Labonte 69-118, Stewart 119-120, B. Labonte 121-136, Elliott Sadler 137, B. Labonte 138-175, Dave Blaney 176, B. Labonte 177-185, Dale Earnhardt Jr. 186-208, Newman 209, Stewart 210-222, J. Gordon 223-268, Jimmie Johnson 269-270, J. Gordon 271-281, B. Labonte 282-303, Jimmy Spencer 304, B. Labonte 305-312, J. Gordon 313-314, B. Labonte 315-325. Pole winner: Ryan Newman, 191.417 mph. Failed to qualify: Bobby Hamilton Jr., Jeff Fultz. Estimated attendance: 106,000.

**Atlanta Motor Speedway**
Hampton, Ga.—1.54-mile banked paved speedway
March 9, 2003—500 miles—325 laps

## Points standings

| Rk. | Driver | Behind |
|---|---|---|
| 1. | Matt Kenseth | Leader |
| 2. | Tony Stewart | -49 |
| 3. | Michael Waltrip | -75 |
| 4. | Jimmie Johnson | -99 |
| 5. | Bobby Labonte | -108 |
| 6. | Johnny Benson | -131 |
| 7. | Kevin Harvick | -140 |
| 8. | Jeff Gordon | -141 |
| 9. | Jeff Burton | -142 |
| 10. | Dale Earnhardt Jr. | -144 |

2003 SEASON

# Carolina Dodge Dealers 400 — race 5 of 36

| Fin. | St. | Car | Driver | Make | Sponsor | Pts./Bonus | Laps | Status | Winnings |
|---|---|---|---|---|---|---|---|---|---|
| 1. | 31 | 32 | Ricky Craven | Pontiac | Tide | 180/5 | 293 | Running | $172,150 |
| 2. | 6 | 97 | Kurt Busch | Ford | Rubbermaid | 175/5 | 293 | Running | $103,725 |
| 3. | 18 | 77 | Dave Blaney | Ford | Jasper Engines & Trans. | 165/0 | 293 | Running | $91,945 |
| 4. | 27 | 6 | Mark Martin | Ford | Viagra | 165/5 | 293 | Running | $115,563 |
| 5. | 9 | 15 | Michael Waltrip | Chevrolet | NAPA Auto Parts | 155/0 | 293 | Running | $73,700 |
| 6. | 16 | 8 | Dale Earnhardt Jr. | Chevrolet | Budweiser | 160/10 | 293 | Running | $98,392 |
| 7. | 1 | 38 | Elliott Sadler | Ford | M&M's | 151/5 | 293 | Running | $94,470 |
| 8. | 12 | 17 | Matt Kenseth | Ford | DeWalt Power Tools | 142/0 | 293 | Running | $69,440 |
| 9. | 25 | 9 | Bill Elliott | Dodge | Dodge Dealers/UAW | 138/0 | 293 | Running | $86,743 |
| 10. | 28 | 20 | Tony Stewart | Chevrolet | Home Depot | 134/0 | 293 | Running | $103,158 |
| 11. | 23 | 4 | Mike Skinner | Pontiac | Kodak | 130/0 | 292 | Running | $64,250 |
| 12. | 17 | 16 | Greg Biffle* | Ford | Grainger | 127/0 | 292 | Running | $48,120 |
| 13. | 38 | 25 | Joe Nemechek | Chevrolet | UAW/Delphi | 129/5 | 292 | Running | $51,465 |
| 14. | 2 | 12 | Ryan Newman | Dodge | ALLTEL | 126/5 | 292 | Running | $80,060 |
| 15. | 39 | 21 | Ricky Rudd | Ford | Motorcraft Quality Parts | 118/0 | 292 | Running | $69,055 |
| 16. | 13 | 2 | Rusty Wallace | Dodge | Miller Lite | 115/0 | 291 | Running | $83,827 |
| 17. | 15 | 49 | Ken Schrader | Dodge | 1-800-CALLATT | 112/0 | 291 | Running | $45,715 |
| 18. | 36 | 88 | Dale Jarrett | Ford | UPS | 114/5 | 291 | Running | $90,673 |
| 19. | 32 | 30 | Jeff Green | Chevrolet | America Online | 106/0 | 291 | Running | $56,365 |
| 20. | 35 | 1 | Steve Park | Chevrolet | Pennzoil | 103/0 | 291 | Running | $74,982 |
| 21. | 4 | 7 | Jimmy Spencer | Dodge | Sirius Satellite Radio | 105/5 | 291 | Running | $56,569 |
| 22. | 19 | 42 | Jamie McMurray* | Dodge | Havoline | 97/0 | 291 | Accident | $43,965 |
| 23. | 21 | 23 | Kenny Wallace | Dodge | Stacker 2 | 94/0 | 291 | Accident | $48,050 |
| 24. | 29 | 5 | Terry Labonte | Chevrolet | Kellogg's/got milk? | 91/0 | 291 | Accident | $72,891 |
| 25. | 22 | 10 | Johnny Benson | Pontiac | Valvoline | 88/0 | 291 | Accident | $73,670 |
| 26. | 40 | 45 | Kyle Petty | Dodge | Georgia Pacific | 85/0 | 291 | Accident | $54,210 |
| 27. | 14 | 48 | Jimmie Johnson | Chevrolet | Lowe's | 82/0 | 291 | Running | $62,310 |
| 28. | 30 | 31 | Robby Gordon | Chevrolet | Cingular Wireless | 84/5 | 291 | Running | $70,942 |
| 29. | 7 | 22 | Ward Burton | Dodge | Caterpillar | 76/0 | 290 | Running | $78,611 |
| 30. | 11 | 19 | Jeremy Mayfield | Dodge | Dodge Dealers/UAW | 73/0 | 289 | Running | $53,985 |
| 31. | 43 | 57 | Brett Bodine** | Ford | CLR | PE | 288 | Running | $42,380 |
| 32. | 42 | 14 | Larry Foyt* | Dodge | Harrah's | 67/0 | 288 | Running | $44,825 |
| 33. | 5 | 24 | Jeff Gordon | Chevrolet | DuPont | 69/5 | 286 | Running | $90,503 |
| 34. | 24 | 41 | Casey Mears* | Dodge | Target | 61/0 | 286 | Running | $50,165 |
| 35. | 3 | 01 | Jerry Nadeau | Pontiac | U.S. Army | 58/0 | 286 | Running | $42,210 |
| 36. | 33 | 29 | Kevin Harvick | Chevrolet | GM Goodwrench Service | 55/0 | 283 | Running | $77,843 |
| 37. | 20 | 18 | Bobby Labonte | Chevrolet | Interstate Batteries | 52/0 | 240 | Running | $87,108 |
| 38. | 26 | 43 | John Andretti | Dodge | Cheerios | 49/0 | 187 | Accident | $77,743 |
| 39. | 8 | 40 | Sterling Marlin | Dodge | Coors Light | 46/0 | 145 | Accident | $85,915 |
| 40. | 34 | 0 | Jack Sprague* | Pontiac | NetZero | 43/0 | 144 | Running | $41,815 |
| 41. | 41 | 74 | Tony Raines* | Chevrolet | Staff America | 40/0 | 60 | Accident | $41,750 |
| 42. | 37 | 99 | Jeff Burton | Ford | CITGO | 37/0 | 32 | Engine | $75,107 |
| 43. | 10 | 54 | Todd Bodine | Ford | National Guard | 34/0 | 22 | Accident | $41,009 |

*Rookie. **Brett Bodine was not awarded points because he entered the race after the entry deadline. Time of race: 3 hours, 10 minutes, 16 seconds. Average speed: 126.214 mph. Margin of victory: .002 seconds. Caution flags: Seven for 33 laps. 7-9 (Car 01—spin, Turn 1 and Cars 42 and 17—accident, Turn 2); 14-16 (Car 0—spin, front stretch); 24-28 (Cars 54, 29, 0, 18, 40, 74, 31 and 48—accident, Turn 1); 34-39 (oil on track); 69-74 (Car 22—spin, Turn 1); 191-196 (Car 43—accident, front stretch); 238-241 (debris in Turns 3-4). Lap leaders: 15 lead changes among 11 drivers. Ryan Newman 1, Elliott Sadler 2-13, Jimmy Spencer 14-17, Dale Earnhardt Jr. 18-24, Dale Jarrett, 25-31, Earnhardt Jr. 32-69, Robby Gordon 70, Earnhardt Jr. 71-116, Mark Martin 117-131, Jeff Gordon 132, Joe Nemechek 133-135, Martin 136-191, J. Gordon 192-269, Kurt Busch 270-292, Ricky Craven 293. Pole winner: Elliott Sadler, 170.147 mph. Dropped to rear: Kurt Busch (engine change), Michael Waltrip (backup car). Failed to qualify: None. Estimated attendance: 55,000.

**Darlington Raceway**
Darlington, S.C.—1.366-mile banked paved oval
March 16, 2003—400 miles—293 laps

## Points standings

| Rk. | Driver | Behind |
|---|---|---|
| 1. | Matt Kenseth | Leader |
| 2. | Tony Stewart | -57 |
| 3. | Michael Waltrip | -62 |
| 4. | Dale Earnhardt Jr. | -126 |
| T5. | Ricky Craven | -143 |
| T5. | Kurt Busch | -143 |
| 7. | Dave Blaney | -157 |
| T8. | Jimmie Johnson | -159 |
| T8. | Joe Nemechek | -159 |
| 10. | Elliott Sadler | -185 |

2003 SEASON

# Food City 500 — race 6 of 36

| Fin. | St. | Car | Driver | Make | Sponsor | Pts./Bonus | Laps | Status | Winnings |
|---|---|---|---|---|---|---|---|---|---|
| 1. | 9 | 97 | Kurt Busch | Ford | Rubbermaid | 180/5 | 500 | Running | $162,790 |
| 2. | 37 | 17 | Matt Kenseth | Ford | DeWalt Power Tools | 175/5 | 500 | Running | $118,870 |
| 3. | 12 | 18 | Bobby Labonte | Chevrolet | Interstate Batteries/Advair | 170/5 | 500 | Running | $126,558 |
| 4. | 34 | 21 | Ricky Rudd | Ford | Motorcraft Quality Parts | 160/0 | 500 | Running | $104,225 |
| 5. | 15 | 16 | Greg Biffle* | Ford | Grainger | 155/0 | 500 | Running | $70,370 |
| 6. | 16 | 40 | Sterling Marlin | Dodge | Coors Light | 150/0 | 500 | Running | $110,795 |
| 7. | 27 | 29 | Kevin Harvick | Chevrolet | GM Goodwrench Service | 151/5 | 499 | Running | $104,448 |
| 8. | 23 | 48 | Jimmie Johnson | Chevrolet | Lowe's | 142/0 | 499 | Running | $82,570 |
| 9. | 2 | 24 | Jeff Gordon | Chevrolet | DuPont | 148/10 | 499 | Running | $115,643 |
| 10. | 40 | 23 | Kenny Wallace | Dodge | Stacker 2 | 134/0 | 499 | Running | $86,615 |
| 11. | 26 | 42 | Jamie McMurray* | Dodge | Havoline | 130/0 | 499 | Running | $63,245 |
| 12. | 7 | 7 | Jimmy Spencer | Dodge | Sirius Satellite Radio | 132/5 | 498 | Running | $88,865 |
| 13. | 29 | 99 | Jeff Burton | Ford | CITGO | 124/0 | 498 | Running | $99,807 |
| 14. | 4 | 2 | Rusty Wallace | Dodge | Miller Lite | 126/5 | 498 | Running | $99,882 |
| 15. | 14 | 32 | Ricky Craven | Pontiac | Tide | 118/0 | 498 | Running | $84,815 |
| 16. | 8 | 8 | Dale Earnhardt Jr. | Chevrolet | Budweiser | 115/0 | 498 | Running | $101,407 |
| 17. | 36 | 31 | Robby Gordon | Chevrolet | Cingular Wireless | 112/0 | 498 | Running | $89,527 |
| 18. | 5 | 9 | Bill Elliott | Dodge | Dodge Dealers/UAW | 109/0 | 497 | Running | $99,023 |
| 19. | 20 | 10 | Johnny Benson | Pontiac | Valvoline | 106/0 | 497 | Running | $90,630 |
| 20. | 21 | 30 | Jeff Green | Chevrolet | America Online | 103/0 | 497 | Running | $73,575 |
| 21. | 30 | 38 | Elliott Sadler | Ford | M&M's | 100/0 | 497 | Running | $97,565 |
| 22. | 1 | 12 | Ryan Newman | Dodge | ALLTEL | 97/0 | 496 | Running | $97,940 |
| 23. | 18 | 19 | Jeremy Mayfield | Dodge | Dodge Dealers/UAW | 94/0 | 494 | Running | $72,045 |
| 24. | 33 | 11 | Brett Bodine | Ford | Hooters Restaurants | 91/0 | 494 | Running | $62,515 |
| 25. | 28 | 15 | Michael Waltrip | Chevrolet | NAPA Auto Parts | 88/0 | 488 | Running | $77,470 |
| 26. | 10 | 20 | Tony Stewart | Chevrolet | Home Depot | 85/0 | 487 | Accident | $111,518 |
| 27. | 25 | 25 | Joe Nemechek | Chevrolet | UAW/Delphi | 82/0 | 469 | Accident | $62,005 |
| 28. | 13 | 01 | Jerry Nadeau | Pontiac | U.S. Army | 79/0 | 456 | Running | $70,139 |
| 29. | 19 | 6 | Mark Martin | Ford | Viagra | 76/0 | 451 | Running | $95,368 |
| 30. | 35 | 1 | Steve Park | Chevrolet | Pennzoil | 73/0 | 446 | Running | $83,872 |
| 31. | 43 | 43 | John Andretti | Dodge | Cheerios | 70/0 | 440 | Running | $96,168 |
| 32. | 39 | 41 | Casey Mears* | Dodge | Target | 67/0 | 423 | Running | $67,845 |
| 33. | 11 | 22 | Ward Burton | Dodge | Caterpillar | 64/0 | 422 | Accident | $94,256 |
| 34. | 32 | 45 | Kyle Petty | Dodge | Georgia Pacific | 61/0 | 422 | Accident | $65,235 |
| 35. | 42 | 0 | Jack Sprague* | Pontiac | NetZero | 58/0 | 409 | Running | $57,190 |
| 36. | 38 | 88 | Dale Jarrett | Ford | UPS | 55/0 | 397 | Running | $102,923 |
| 37. | 3 | 49 | Ken Schrader | Dodge | 1-800-CALLATT | 52/0 | 385 | Accident | $57,410 |
| 38. | 31 | 77 | Dave Blaney | Ford | Jasper Engines & Trans. | 49/0 | 371 | Running | $65,065 |
| 39. | 17 | 5 | Terry Labonte | Chevrolet | Kellogg's/got milk? | 46/0 | 349 | Running | $83,086 |
| 40. | 41 | 54 | Todd Bodine | Ford | National Guard | 43/0 | 342 | Accident | $56,965 |
| 41. | 6 | 4 | Mike Skinner | Pontiac | Kodak | 40/0 | 310 | Running | $56,915 |
| 42. | 22 | 74 | Tony Raines* | Chevrolet | Staff America | 37/0 | 52 | Engine | $56,860 |
| 43. | 24 | 37 | Derrike Cope | Chevrolet | Friendly's | 34/0 | 31 | Engine | $56,178 |

*Rookie. Time of race: 3 hours, 29 minutes, 53 seconds. Average speed: 76.185 mph. Margin of victory: .39 seconds. Caution flags: 17 for 121 laps. 4-6 (Car 45—spin, Turn 1); 15-19 (Cars 15, 41, 77 and 88—accident, Turn 2); 21-28 (Cars 41, 43 and 54—accident, Turn 3); 56-63 (Car 74—accident, Turn 2); 69-73 (Car 12—spin, Turn 1); 136-141 (Car 4—accident, Turn 2); 150-153 (Cars 0 and 10—accident, Turn 2); 182-186 (Car 0—accident, Turn 2); 200-204 (Car 6—accident, front stretch); 219-222 (Car 01—accident, front stretch); 227-240 (Cars 18 and 97—spin, Turn 2); 244-249 (Cars 5, 11, 23, 31, 45 and 49—accident, Turn 2); 257-262 (Cars 20, 21 and 42—accident, back stretch); 390-403 (Car 88—accident, Turn 2); 407-411 (Car 45—spin, Turn 4); 425-438 (Cars 22 and 45—accident, Turn 1); 473-481 (Cars 20 and 25—accident, Turn 1). Lap leaders: 11 lead changes among seven drivers. Jeff Gordon 1-28, Rusty Wallace 29-33, J. Gordon 34-160; Jimmy Spencer 161-182, J. Gordon 183-201, Kevin Harvick 202-216, Spencer 217-333, Matt Kenseth 334-358, Kurt Busch 359-377, Bobby Labonte 378-403, Busch 404-500. Pole winner: Ryan Newman, 128.709 mph, track record. Dropped to rear: Jamie McMurray (engine change). Failed to qualify: Hermie Sadler, Larry Foyt. Estimated attendance: 160,000.

**Bristol Motor Speedway**
Bristol, Tenn.—.533-mile banked concrete oval
March 23, 2003—266.5 miles—500 laps

## Points standings

| Rk. | Driver | Behind |
|---|---|---|
| 1. | Matt Kenseth | Leader |
| 2. | Kurt Busch | -138 |
| 3. | Tony Stewart | -147 |
| 4. | Michael Waltrip | -149 |
| 5. | Dale Earnhardt Jr. | -186 |
| 6. | Jimmie Johnson | -192 |
| 7. | Ricky Craven | -200 |
| 8. | Bobby Labonte | -203 |
| 9. | Ricky Rudd | -240 |
| 10. | Jeff Gordon | -241 |

# Samsung/RadioShack 500 — race 7 of 36

| Fin. | St. | Car | Driver | Make | Sponsor | Pts./Bonus | Laps | Status | Winnings |
|---|---|---|---|---|---|---|---|---|---|
| 1. | 3 | 12 | Ryan Newman | Dodge | ALLTEL | 180/5 | 334 | Running | $406,500 |
| 2. | 11 | 8 | Dale Earnhardt Jr. | Chevrolet | Budweiser | 175/5 | 334 | Running | $299,667 |
| 3. | 7 | 24 | Jeff Gordon | Chevrolet | DuPont | 170/5 | 334 | Running | $249,753 |
| 4. | 5 | 01 | Jerry Nadeau | Pontiac | U.S. Army | 160/0 | 334 | Running | $188,475 |
| 5. | 32 | 6 | Mark Martin | Ford | Viagra | 155/0 | 334 | Running | $172,308 |
| 6. | 17 | 17 | Matt Kenseth | Ford | Smirnoff Ice/DeWalt | 155/5 | 334 | Running | $142,950 |
| 7. | 14 | 30 | Jeff Green | Chevrolet | America Online | 151/5 | 334 | Running | $118,575 |
| 8. | 4 | 48 | Jimmie Johnson | Chevrolet | Lowe's | 142/0 | 334 | Running | $119,575 |
| 9. | 30 | 97 | Kurt Busch | Ford | Rubbermaid | 138/0 | 334 | Running | $133,150 |
| 10. | 24 | 42 | Jamie McMurray* | Dodge | Havoline | 134/0 | 334 | Running | $101,150 |
| 11. | 19 | 54 | Todd Bodine | Ford | National Guard | 130/0 | 334 | Running | $111,750 |
| 12. | 33 | 22 | Ward Burton | Dodge | Caterpillar | 127/0 | 334 | Running | $127,906 |
| 13. | 23 | 88 | Dale Jarrett | Ford | UPS | 129/5 | 334 | Running | $136,528 |
| 14. | 10 | 2 | Rusty Wallace | Dodge | Miller Lite | 121/0 | 333 | Running | $126,692 |
| 15. | 8 | 29 | Kevin Harvick | Chevrolet | GM Goodwrench Service | 118/0 | 333 | Running | $128,128 |
| 16. | 12 | 5 | Terry Labonte | Chevrolet | Kellogg's/got milk? | 115/0 | 333 | Running | $115,656 |
| 17. | 37 | 15 | Michael Waltrip | Chevrolet | NAPA Auto Parts | 112/0 | 333 | Running | $102,500 |
| 18. | 21 | 31 | Robby Gordon | Chevrolet | Cingular Wireless | 109/0 | 333 | Running | $112,387 |
| 19. | 43 | 43 | John Andretti | Dodge | Cheerios | 106/0 | 333 | Running | $121,753 |
| 20. | 29 | 99 | Jeff Burton | Ford | CITGO | 103/0 | 333 | Running | $120,492 |
| 21. | 38 | 32 | Ricky Craven | Pontiac | Tide | 105/5 | 333 | Running | $102,075 |
| 22. | 31 | 0 | Jack Sprague* | Pontiac | NetZero | 97/0 | 333 | Running | $78,975 |
| 23. | 40 | 23 | Kenny Wallace | Dodge | Stacker 2 | 94/0 | 333 | Running | $90,164 |
| 24. | 42 | 49 | Ken Schrader | Dodge | BAM Racing | 91/0 | 333 | Running | $75,975 |
| 25. | 27 | 19 | Jeremy Mayfield | Dodge | Dodge Dealers/UAW | 88/0 | 332 | Running | $85,525 |
| 26. | 16 | 21 | Ricky Rudd | Ford | Motorcraft Quality Parts | 85/0 | 332 | Running | $84,175 |
| 27. | 26 | 41 | Casey Mears* | Dodge | Target | 82/0 | 331 | Running | $82,475 |
| 28. | 20 | 16 | Greg Biffle* | Ford | Grainger | 79/0 | 330 | Running | $68,975 |
| 29. | 36 | 40 | Sterling Marlin | Dodge | Coors Light | 76/0 | 328 | Running | $111,475 |
| 30. | 35 | 14 | Larry Foyt* | Dodge | Harrah's | 73/0 | 326 | Running | $69,185 |
| 31. | 25 | 11 | Brett Bodine | Ford | Hooters Restaurants | 70/0 | 325 | Running | $67,775 |
| 32. | 13 | 10 | Johnny Benson | Pontiac | Valvoline | 67/0 | 322 | Engine | $92,450 |
| 33. | 18 | 7 | Jimmy Spencer | Dodge | Sirius Satellite Radio | 69/5 | 294 | Accident | $63,075 |
| 34. | 22 | 20 | Tony Stewart | Chevrolet | Home Depot | 61/0 | 293 | Engine | $113,728 |
| 35. | 9 | 25 | Joe Nemechek | Chevrolet | UAW/Delphi | 58/0 | 279 | Accident | $60,125 |
| 36. | 39 | 77 | Dave Blaney | Ford | Jasper Engines & Trans. | 55/0 | 268 | Engine | $67,075 |
| 37. | 1 | 18 | Bobby Labonte | Chevrolet | Interstate Batteries | 52/0 | 260 | Accident | $117,108 |
| 38. | 28 | 45 | Christian Fittipaldi | Dodge | Georgia Pacific | 49/0 | 240 | Accident | $64,950 |
| 39. | 15 | 1 | Steve Park | Chevrolet | Pennzoil | 51/5 | 234 | Accident | $82,087 |
| 40. | 41 | 4 | Mike Skinner | Pontiac | Kodak | 43/0 | 233 | Accident | $56,850 |
| 41. | 2 | 38 | Elliott Sadler | Ford | M&M's | 50/10 | 167 | Accident | $92,060 |
| 42. | 34 | 74 | Tony Raines* | Chevrolet | Staff America | 37/0 | 152 | Engine | $56,765 |
| 43. | 6 | 9 | Bill Elliott | Dodge | Dodge Dealers/UAW | 39/5 | 46 | Engine | $100,781 |

*Rookie. Time of race: 3 hours, 43 minutes, 28 seconds. Average speed: 134.517 mph. Margin of victory: 3.405 seconds. Caution flags: 10 for 52 laps. 14-17 (oil on track); 43-46 (Car 1—spin, Turn 4); 48-50 (oil on track); 157-160 (debris on front stretch); 169-178 (Car 38—accident, back stretch); 227-232 (Cars 7 and 21—accident, front stretch); 236-240 (Cars 0, 1, 4 and 40—accident, back stretch); 243-249 (Cars 45 and 88—accident, Turn 4); 252-254 (Car 18—accident, back stretch); 283-288 (Car 25—accident, Turn 3). Lap leaders: 19 lead changes among 11 drivers. Elliott Sadler 1-3, Bill Elliott 4-46, Sadler 47-88, Jeff Gordon 89-102, Matt Kenseth 103, Ryan Newman 104-105, Jeff Green 106-107, Jimmy Spencer 108, Steve Park 109, Ricky Craven 110-111, Sadler 112-157, Kenseth 158-220, J. Gordon 221-222, Kenseth 223, Newman 224-285, Dale Jarrett 286, Newman 287-288, Dale Earnhardt Jr. 289-323, Newman 324-334. Pole winner: Bobby Labonte, 193.514 mph. Dropped to rear: Jimmie Johnson, Brett Bodine and Sterling Marlin (engine changes); Kyle Petty (driver change). Failed to qualify: Kerry Earnhardt, David Starr. Estimated attendance: 215,000.

**Texas Motor Speedway**
Justin, Texas—1.5-mile banked paved trioval
March 30, 2003—500 miles—334 laps

## Points standings

| Rk. | Driver | Behind |
|---|---|---|
| 1. | Matt Kenseth | Leader |
| 2. | Kurt Busch | -155 |
| 3. | Dale Earnhardt Jr. | -166 |
| 4. | Michael Waltrip | -192 |
| 5. | Jimmie Johnson | -205 |
| 6. | Jeff Gordon | -226 |
| 7. | Tony Stewart | -241 |
| 8. | Ryan Newman | -242 |
| 9. | Ricky Craven | -250 |
| 10. | Kevin Harvick | -288 |

# Aaron's 499 — race 8 of 36

| Fin. | St. | Car | Driver | Make | Sponsor | Pts./Bonus | Laps | Status | Winnings |
|---|---|---|---|---|---|---|---|---|---|
| 1. | 13 | 8 | Dale Earnhardt Jr. | Chevrolet | Budweiser | 180/5 | 188 | Running | $204,367 |
| 2. | 2 | 29 | Kevin Harvick | Chevrolet | GM Goodwrench Service | 175/5 | 188 | Running | $179,233 |
| 3. | 3 | 38 | Elliott Sadler | Ford | M&M's | 170/5 | 188 | Running | $162,955 |
| 4. | 15 | 32 | Ricky Craven | Pontiac | Tide | 160/0 | 188 | Running | $139,575 |
| 5. | 28 | 5 | Terry Labonte | Chevrolet | Kellogg's/got milk? | 160/0 | 188 | Running | $121,471 |
| 6. | 11 | 40 | Sterling Marlin | Dodge | Coors Light | 155/5 | 188 | Running | $127,130 |
| 7. | 24 | 22 | Ward Burton | Dodge | Caterpillar | 151/5 | 188 | Running | $114,386 |
| 8. | 4 | 24 | Jeff Gordon | Chevrolet | DuPont | 147/5 | 188 | Running | $128,458 |
| 9. | 27 | 17 | Matt Kenseth | Ford | DeWalt Power Tools | 143/5 | 188 | Running | $104,730 |
| 10. | 6 | 31 | Robby Gordon | Chevrolet | Cingular Wireless | 134/0 | 188 | Running | $105,367 |
| 11. | 21 | 45 | Kyle Petty | Dodge | Georgia Pacific | 130/0 | 188 | Running | $84,375 |
| 12. | 18 | 88 | Dale Jarrett | Ford | UPS | 132/5 | 188 | Running | $116,473 |
| 13. | 5 | 9 | Bill Elliott | Dodge | Dodge Dealers/UAW | 129/5 | 188 | Running | $109,823 |
| 14. | 40 | 43 | John Andretti | Dodge | Cheerios | 126/5 | 188 | Running | $109,388 |
| 15. | 7 | 48 | Jimmie Johnson | Chevrolet | Lowe's | 128/10 | 188 | Running | $89,930 |
| 16. | 43 | 74 | Tony Raines* | Chevrolet | Staff America | 115/0 | 188 | Running | $74,640 |
| 17. | 25 | 23 | Kenny Wallace | Dodge | Stacker 2 | 112/0 | 188 | Running | $86,825 |
| 18. | 1 | 19 | Jeremy Mayfield | Dodge | Dodge Dealers/UAW | 114/5 | 187 | Running | $84,285 |
| 19. | 26 | 97 | Kurt Busch | Ford | Rubbermaid | 111/5 | 186 | Running | $87,195 |
| 20. | 12 | 1 | Steve Park | Chevrolet | Pennzoil | 108/5 | 184 | Running | $97,302 |
| 21. | 29 | 25 | Joe Nemechek | Chevrolet | UAW/Delphi | 100/0 | 182 | Running | $70,695 |
| 22. | 33 | 16 | Greg Biffle* | Ford | Grainger | 97/0 | 178 | Running | $66,375 |
| 23. | 39 | 77 | Dave Blaney | Ford | Jasper Engines & Trans. | 94/0 | 178 | Running | $91,565 |
| 24. | 16 | 15 | Michael Waltrip | Chevrolet | NAPA Auto Parts | 96/5 | 177 | Running | $83,935 |
| 25. | 19 | 20 | Tony Stewart | Chevrolet | Home Depot | 88/0 | 156 | Running | $118,708 |
| 26. | 9 | 6 | Mark Martin | Ford | Viagra | 85/0 | 154 | Running | $102,783 |
| 27. | 14 | 42 | Jamie McMurray* | Dodge | Havoline | 82/0 | 154 | Running | $65,395 |
| 28. | 35 | 54 | Todd Bodine | Ford | National Guard | 79/0 | 152 | Running | $79,045 |
| 29. | 30 | 30 | Jeff Green | Chevrolet | America Online | 76/0 | 124 | Running | $76,285 |
| 30. | 36 | 09 | Mike Wallace | Dodge | Miccosukee Resort | 73/0 | 120 | Electrical | $65,390 |
| 31. | 42 | 4 | Mike Skinner | Pontiac | Kodak | 70/0 | 120 | Running | $76,214 |
| 32. | 22 | 18 | Bobby Labonte | Chevrolet | Interstate Batteries | 67/0 | 118 | Running | $109,658 |
| 33. | 41 | 49 | Ken Schrader | Dodge | 1-800-CALLATT | 64/0 | 110 | Running | $65,350 |
| 34. | 20 | 0 | Jack Sprague* | Pontiac | NetZero | 61/0 | 109 | Running | $64,310 |
| 35. | 38 | 99 | Jeff Burton | Ford | CITGO | 58/0 | 107 | Running | $97,597 |
| 36. | 23 | 01 | Jerry Nadeau | Pontiac | U.S. Army | 55/0 | 73 | Accident | $67,050 |
| 37. | 31 | 2 | Rusty Wallace | Dodge | Miller Lite | 52/0 | 12 | Accident | $101,567 |
| 38. | 34 | 7 | Jimmy Spencer | Dodge | Sirius Satellite Radio | 49/0 | 9 | Accident | $66,025 |
| 39. | 8 | 12 | Ryan Newman | Dodge | ALLTEL | 46/0 | 3 | Accident | $93,215 |
| 40. | 10 | 41 | Casey Mears* | Dodge | Target | 43/0 | 3 | Accident | $71,090 |
| 41. | 17 | 10 | Johnny Benson | Pontiac | Valvoline | 40/0 | 3 | Accident | $89,640 |
| 42. | 37 | 21 | Ricky Rudd | Ford | Motorcraft Quality Parts | 37/0 | 3 | Accident | $70,690 |
| 43. | 32 | 02 | Hermie Sadler | Chevrolet | Total Non-Stop Wrestling | 34/0 | 3 | Accident | $62,746 |

*Rookie. Time of race: 3 hours, 27 minutes, 28 seconds. Average speed: 144.625 mph. Margin of victory: .125 seconds. Caution flags: Six for 32 laps. 5-13 (Cars 0, 01, 02, 09, 1, 2, 4, 6, 8, 10, 12, 16, 17, 18, 20, 21, 25, 30, 31, 41, 42, 43, 45, 49, 54, 77 and 99—accident, Turn 2); 37-40 (debris on track); 64-67 (debris in trioval); 84-89 (Cars 15 and 38—accident, Turn 3); 91-94 (Cars 97, 20 and 16—accident, Turn 4); 133-137 (debris on track). Lap leaders: 43 lead changes among 16 drivers. Jeremy Mayfield 1-8; Kevin Harvick 9-19; Michael Waltrip 20-29; Steve Park 30; Sterling Marlin 31-32; Jimmie Johnson 33-36; Terry Labonte 37; Johnson 38-47; Mayfield 48-49; Johnson 50-53; Mayfield 54-57; Jeff Gordon 58; Mayfield 59-63; Bill Elliott 64; Johnson 65-79; Matt Kenseth 80-83; Kurt Busch 84; Johnson 85-99; Kenseth 100-103; Harvick 104; Ward Burton 105-106; Dale Earnhardt Jr. 107-112; J. Gordon 113-118; Earnhardt Jr. 119-121; J. Gordon 122-125; John Andretti 126; J. Gordon 127-128; J. Gordon 129-141; W. Burton 142-143; Earnhardt Jr. 144-154; Johnson 155-156; Earnhardt Jr. 157-160; Dale Jarrett 161-162; Elliott Sadler 163; Johnson 164-171; Earnhardt Jr. 172-175; Johnson 176; Earnhardt Jr. 177; Johnson 178; W. Burton 179; Johnson 180-184; Earnhardt Jr. 185; Kenseth 186; Earnhardt Jr. 187-188. Pole winner: Jeremy Mayfield, 186.489 mph. Dropped to rear: Mike Skinner, Dale Earnhardt Jr., Bobby Labonte and Jeff Green (engine changes). Failed to qualify: Brett Bodine, Larry Foyt, David Green. Estimated attendance: 190,000.

**Talladega Superspeedway**
Talladega, Ala.—2.66-mile banked paved trioval
April 6, 2003—500 miles—188 laps

## Points standings

| Rk. | Driver | Behind |
|---|---|---|
| 1. | Matt Kenseth | Leader |
| 2. | Dale Earnhardt Jr. | -129 |
| 3. | Kurt Busch | -187 |
| 4. | Jimmie Johnson | -220 |
| 5. | Jeff Gordon | -222 |
| 6. | Ricky Craven | -233 |
| 7. | Michael Waltrip | -239 |
| 8. | Kevin Harvick | -256 |
| 9. | Tony Stewart | -296 |
| 10. | Elliott Sadler | -338 |

# Virginia 500 — race 9 of 36

| Fin. | St. | Car | Driver | Make | Sponsor | Pts./Bonus | Laps | Status | Winnings |
|---|---|---|---|---|---|---|---|---|---|
| 1. | 1 | 24 | Jeff Gordon | Chevrolet | DuPont | 180/5 | 500 | Running | $219,143 |
| 2. | 39 | 18 | Bobby Labonte | Chevrolet | Interstate Batteries | 175/5 | 500 | Running | $138,348 |
| 3. | 2 | 8 | Dale Earnhardt Jr. | Chevrolet | Budweiser | 175/10 | 500 | Running | $112,542 |
| 4. | 10 | 99 | Jeff Burton | Ford | CITGO | 160/0 | 500 | Running | $102,342 |
| 5. | 18 | 38 | Elliott Sadler | Ford | M&M's | 160/5 | 500 | Running | $98,950 |
| 6. | 8 | 20 | Tony Stewart | Chevrolet | Home Depot | 155/5 | 500 | Running | $105,203 |
| 7. | 25 | 40 | Sterling Marlin | Dodge | Coors Light | 151/5 | 500 | Running | $97,275 |
| 8. | 5 | 2 | Rusty Wallace | Dodge | Miller Lite | 147/5 | 500 | Running | $91,217 |
| 9. | 7 | 48 | Jimmie Johnson | Chevrolet | Lowe's | 138/0 | 500 | Running | $70,250 |
| 10. | 4 | 49 | Ken Schrader | Dodge | BAM Racing | 134/0 | 500 | Running | $54,050 |
| 11. | 19 | 21 | Ricky Rudd | Ford | Motorcraft Quality Parts | 130/0 | 500 | Running | $78,650 |
| 12. | 9 | 23 | Kenny Wallace | Dodge | Stacker 2 | 127/0 | 500 | Running | $68,225 |
| 13. | 31 | 9 | Bill Elliott | Dodge | Dodge Dealers/UAW | 124/0 | 499 | Running | $88,358 |
| 14. | 16 | 5 | Terry Labonte | Chevrolet | Kellogg's/got milk? | 126/5 | 499 | Running | $78,581 |
| 15. | 6 | 25 | Joe Nemechek | Chevrolet | UAW/Delphi | 118/0 | 499 | Running | $53,750 |
| 16. | 29 | 29 | Kevin Harvick | Chevrolet | GM Goodwrench Service | 120/5 | 499 | Running | $87,678 |
| 17. | 24 | 6 | Mark Martin | Ford | Viagra | 112/0 | 499 | Running | $85,433 |
| 18. | 20 | 16 | Greg Biffle* | Ford | Grainger | 109/0 | 499 | Running | $47,975 |
| 19. | 13 | 7 | Jimmy Spencer | Dodge | Sirius Satellite Radio | 106/0 | 499 | Running | $63,575 |
| 20. | 37 | 88 | Dale Jarrett | Ford | UPS | 103/0 | 499 | Running | $94,303 |
| 21. | 38 | 31 | Robby Gordon | Chevrolet | Cingular Wireless | 100/0 | 499 | Running | $75,262 |
| 22. | 34 | 17 | Matt Kenseth | Ford | DeWalt Power Tools | 97/0 | 499 | Running | $66,725 |
| 23. | 30 | 15 | Michael Waltrip | Chevrolet | NAPA Auto Parts | 94/0 | 499 | Running | $63,975 |
| 24. | 32 | 1 | Steve Park | Chevrolet | Pennzoil | 91/0 | 499 | Running | $74,562 |
| 25. | 12 | 22 | Ward Burton | Dodge | Caterpillar | 88/0 | 499 | Running | $82,931 |
| 26. | 35 | 30 | Jeff Green | Chevrolet | America Online | 85/0 | 498 | Running | $56,825 |
| 27. | 17 | 32 | Ricky Craven | Pontiac | Tide | 82/0 | 498 | Running | $67,010 |
| 28. | 36 | 97 | Kurt Busch | Ford | Rubbermaid | 79/0 | 498 | Running | $64,910 |
| 29. | 14 | 0 | Jack Sprague* | Pontiac | NetZero | 76/0 | 497 | Running | $44,725 |
| 30. | 40 | 43 | John Andretti | Dodge | Cheerios | 73/0 | 497 | Running | $84,178 |
| 31. | 15 | 77 | Dave Blaney | Ford | Jasper Engines & Trans. | 70/0 | 497 | Running | $64,064 |
| 32. | 28 | 10 | Johnny Benson | Pontiac | Valvoline | 67/0 | 496 | Running | $74,200 |
| 33. | 27 | 74 | Tony Raines* | Chevrolet | Staff America | 64/0 | 496 | Running | $45,025 |
| 34. | 33 | 45 | Kyle Petty | Dodge | Georgia Pacific | 61/0 | 496 | Running | $55,000 |
| 35. | 21 | 4 | Mike Skinner | Pontiac | Kodak | 58/0 | 496 | Running | $46,950 |
| 36. | 22 | 41 | Casey Mears* | Dodge | Target | 55/0 | 496 | Running | $54,400 |
| 37. | 41 | 54 | Todd Bodine | Ford | National Guard | 52/0 | 492 | Running | $43,850 |
| 38. | 3 | 12 | Ryan Newman | Dodge | ALLTEL | 49/0 | 436 | Brakes | $74,665 |
| 39. | 11 | 42 | Jamie McMurray* | Dodge | Havoline | 46/0 | 319 | Engine | $43,740 |
| 40. | 23 | 19 | Jeremy Mayfield | Dodge | Dodge Dealers/UAW | 43/0 | 308 | Overheating | $51,665 |
| 41. | 26 | 01 | Jerry Nadeau | Pontiac | U.S. Army | 40/0 | 267 | Oil pump | $43,615 |
| 42. | 42 | 37 | Derrike Cope | Chevrolet | Friendly's | 37/0 | 230 | Throttle linkage | $43,575 |
| 43. | 43 | 02 | Hermie Sadler | Chevrolet | GoTeamVa.com | 34/0 | 133 | Engine | $42,866 |

*Rookie. Time of race: 3 hours, 28 minutes, 51 seconds. Average speed: 75.557 mph. Margin of victory: Under caution. Caution flags: 11 for 64 laps. 80-84 (Car 01—spin, Turn 2); 120-126 (Car 21—spin, Turn 4); 244-249 (Car 19—spin, Turn 2); 272-281 (Car 0—stalled, Turn 3); 295-299 (Car 0—spin, Turn 4); 319-324 (debris); 349-354 (Car 77—spin, front stretch); 436-443 (Car 12—spin, Turn 2); 447-451 (Car 32—stalled, Turn 2); 489-492 (Car 5—spin, Turn 4); 499-500 (Car 97—spin, Turn 2). Lap leaders: 14 lead changes among nine drivers. Jeff Gordon 1-120; Tony Stewart 121-131; Rusty Wallace 132-144; Dale Earnhardt Jr. 145-239; J. Gordon 240-295; Sterling Marlin 296-318; Terry Labonte 319; Earnhardt Jr. 320-349; Kevin Harvick 350-361; Elliott Sadler 362; Harvick 363; E. Sadler 364-367; Earnhardt Jr. 368-437; Bobby Labonte 438-486; J. Gordon 487-500. Pole winner: Jeff Gordon, 94.307 mph. Dropped to rear: Ward Burton (backup car), Hermie Sadler (driver change). Failed to qualify: None. Estimated attendance: 86,000.

**Martinsville Speedway**
Martinsville, Va.—.526-mile paved speedway
April 13, 2003—263 miles—500 laps

**2003 SEASON**

## Points standings

| Rk. | Driver | Behind |
|---|---|---|
| 1. | Matt Kenseth | Leader |
| 2. | Dale Earnhardt Jr. | -51 |
| 3. | Jeff Gordon | -139 |
| 4. | Jimmie Johnson | -179 |
| 5. | Kurt Busch | -205 |
| 6. | Kevin Harvick | -233 |
| 7. | Tony Stewart | -238 |
| 8. | Michael Waltrip | -242 |
| 9. | Ricky Craven | -248 |
| 10. | Elliott Sadler | -275 |

# Auto Club 500 — race 10 of 36

**2003 SEASON**

| Fin. | St. | Car | Driver | Make | Sponsor | Pts./Bonus | Laps | Status | Winnings |
|---|---|---|---|---|---|---|---|---|---|
| 1. | 16 | 97 | Kurt Busch | Ford | Rubbermaid | 180/5 | 250 | Running | $213,150 |
| 2. | 19 | 18 | Bobby Labonte | Chevrolet | Interstate Batteries | 175/5 | 250 | Running | $172,708 |
| 3. | 7 | 2 | Rusty Wallace | Dodge | Miller Lite | 170/5 | 250 | Running | $146,917 |
| 4. | 2 | 9 | Bill Elliott | Dodge | Dodge Dealers/UAW | 165/5 | 250 | Running | $149,433 |
| 5. | 25 | 42 | Jamie McMurray* | Dodge | Havoline | 160/5 | 250 | Running | $100,825 |
| 6. | 8 | 8 | Dale Earnhardt Jr. | Chevrolet | Budweiser | 150/0 | 250 | Running | $120,217 |
| 7. | 27 | 15 | Michael Waltrip | Chevrolet | NAPA Auto Parts | 146/0 | 250 | Running | $95,025 |
| 8. | 13 | 43 | John Andretti | Dodge | Cheerios | 142/0 | 250 | Running | $117,003 |
| 9. | 23 | 17 | Matt Kenseth | Ford | DeWalt Power Tools | 143/0 | 250 | Running | $95,425 |
| 10. | 30 | 40 | Sterling Marlin | Dodge | Coors Light | 134/0 | 250 | Running | $121,525 |
| 11. | 14 | 24 | Jeff Gordon | Chevrolet | DuPont | 130/0 | 250 | Running | $120,628 |
| 12. | 21 | 5 | Terry Labonte | Chevrolet | Kellogg's/got milk? | 127/0 | 250 | Running | $102,806 |
| 13. | 18 | 77 | Dave Blaney | Ford | Jasper Engines & Trans. | 129/5 | 250 | Running | $101,350 |
| 14. | 6 | 01 | Jerry Nadeau | Pontiac | U.S. Army | 121/0 | 250 | Running | $89,925 |
| 15. | 15 | 32 | Ricky Craven | Pontiac | Tide | 123/5 | 250 | Running | $96,575 |
| 16. | 20 | 48 | Jimmie Johnson | Chevrolet | Lowe's | 115/0 | 250 | Running | $89,025 |
| 17. | 22 | 6 | Mark Martin | Ford | Viagra | 112/0 | 249 | Running | $107,358 |
| 18. | 29 | 16 | Greg Biffle* | Ford | Grainger | 109/0 | 249 | Running | $69,225 |
| 19. | 10 | 99 | Jeff Burton | Ford | CITGO | 106/0 | 249 | Running | $102,442 |
| 20. | 28 | 4 | Mike Skinner | Pontiac | Kodak | 103/0 | 249 | Running | $85,625 |
| 21. | 39 | 22 | Ward Burton | Dodge | Caterpillar | 100/0 | 249 | Running | $104,681 |
| 22. | 31 | 23 | Kenny Wallace | Dodge | Stacker 2 | 97/0 | 249 | Running | $80,614 |
| 23. | 5 | 38 | Elliott Sadler | Ford | M&M's | 94/0 | 249 | Running | $107,075 |
| 24. | 35 | 21 | Ricky Rudd | Ford | Motorcraft Quality Parts | 91/0 | 249 | Running | $79,600 |
| 25. | 34 | 54 | Todd Bodine | Ford | National Guard | 88/0 | 249 | Running | $71,700 |
| 26. | 40 | 30 | Jeff Green | Chevrolet | America Online | 85/0 | 249 | Running | $79,000 |
| 27. | 26 | 31 | Robby Gordon | Chevrolet | Cingular Wireless | 82/0 | 249 | Running | $95,837 |
| 28. | 36 | 45 | Kyle Petty | Dodge | Georgia Pacific | 79/0 | 249 | Running | $78,350 |
| 29. | 37 | 29 | Kevin Harvick | Chevrolet | GM Goodwrench Service | 76/0 | 248 | Running | $105,828 |
| 30. | 41 | 49 | Ken Schrader | Dodge | BAM Racing | 73/0 | 248 | Running | $67,210 |
| 31. | 33 | 74 | Tony Raines* | Chevrolet | Staff America | 70/0 | 248 | Running | $66,525 |
| 32. | 9 | 25 | Joe Nemechek | Chevrolet | UAW/Delphi | 67/0 | 248 | Running | $69,325 |
| 33. | 24 | 7 | Jimmy Spencer | Dodge | Sirius Satellite Radio | 64/0 | 247 | Running | $70,025 |
| 34. | 17 | 41 | Casey Mears* | Dodge | Target | 61/0 | 247 | Running | $76,425 |
| 35. | 11 | 19 | Jeremy Mayfield | Dodge | Dodge Dealers/UAW | 58/0 | 233 | Accident | $73,750 |
| 36. | 32 | 10 | Johnny Benson | Pontiac | Valvoline | 55/0 | 229 | Accident | $92,425 |
| 37. | 38 | 88 | Dale Jarrett | Ford | UPS | 52/0 | 228 | Accident | $111,253 |
| 38. | 42 | 14 | Larry Foyt* | Dodge | Harrah's | 49/0 | 226 | Accident | $65,300 |
| 39. | 12 | 0 | Jack Sprague* | Pontiac | NetZero | 46/0 | 199 | Accident | $65,255 |
| 40. | 1 | 1 | Steve Park | Chevrolet | Pennzoil | 43/0 | 138 | Accident | $100,367 |
| 41. | 3 | 20 | Tony Stewart | Chevrolet | Home Depot | 50/10 | 128 | Engine | $117,708 |
| 42. | 4 | 12 | Ryan Newman | Dodge | ALLTEL | 37/0 | 34 | Accident | $94,960 |
| 43. | 43 | 37 | Derrike Cope | Chevrolet | GBROnline.com | 34/0 | 9 | Engine | $65,281 |

*Rookie. Time of race: 3 hours, 34 minutes, 7 seconds. Average speed: 140.111 mph. Margin of victory: 2.294 seconds. Caution flags: Eight for 34 laps. 2-4 (Car 1 and 12—accident, back stretch); 9-11 (Car 0—accident, back stretch); 41-44 (Car 16—accident, Turn 4); 130-134 (oil on track); 156-159 (debris); 210-213 (Car 01 and 32—spin, Turn 4); 220-223 (Car 01—spin, Turn 2); 231-237 (Car 88, 10, 19, 14, 31, 25 and 41—accident, Turn 3). Lap leaders: 19 lead changes among nine drivers. Steve Park-pole, Bill Elliott 1-12, Tony Stewart 13-92, Ricky Craven 93, Dave Blaney 94-95, Stewart 96-114, Jamie McMurray 115, Stewart 116, McMurray 117-130, Kurt Busch 131-145, McMurray 146-156, Rusty Wallace 157-201, McMurray 202-204, Matt Kenseth 205-206, R. Wallace 207-215, Bobby Labonte 216, McMurray 217, B. Labonte 218-227, McMurray 228-238, Busch 239-250. Pole winner: Steve Park, 186.838 mph. Dropped to rear: Sterling Marlin and Johnny Benson (backup cars); Jerry Nadeau, Dale Earnhardt Jr., Ward Burton, Jeff Green and Derrike Cope (engine changes). Failed to qualify: Kerry Earnhardt, Hideo Fukuyama. Estimated attendance: 120,000.

**California Speedway**
Fontana, Calif.—2-mile banked paved trioval
April 27, 2003—500 miles—250 laps

## Points standings

| Rk. | Driver | Behind |
|---|---|---|
| 1. | Matt Kenseth | Leader |
| 2. | Dale Earnhardt Jr. | -44 |
| 3. | Jeff Gordon | -152 |
| 4. | Kurt Busch | -168 |
| 5. | Jimmie Johnson | -207 |
| 6. | Michael Waltrip | -239 |
| 7. | Ricky Craven | -268 |
| 8. | Bobby Labonte | -272 |
| 9. | Kevin Harvick | -300 |
| 10. | Elliott Sadler | -324 |

# Pontiac Excitement 400 — race 11 of 36

| Fin. | St. | Car | Driver | Make | Sponsor | Pts./Bonus | Laps | Status | Winnings |
|---|---|---|---|---|---|---|---|---|---|
| 1. | 2 | 25 | Joe Nemechek | Chevrolet | UAW/Delphi | 185/10 | 393 | Running | $159,375 |
| 2. | 4 | 18 | Bobby Labonte | Chevrolet | Interstate Batteries | 175/5 | 393 | Running | $157,758 |
| 3. | 3 | 8 | Dale Earnhardt Jr. | Chevrolet | Budweiser | 170/5 | 393 | Running | $121,867 |
| 4. | 32 | 31 | Robby Gordon | Chevrolet | Cingular Wireless | 165/5 | 393 | Running | $101,212 |
| 5. | 30 | 6 | Mark Martin | Ford | Viagra | 160/5 | 393 | Running | $102,533 |
| 6. | 36 | 29 | Kevin Harvick | Chevrolet | GM Goodwrench Service | 155/5 | 393 | Running | $100,928 |
| 7. | 18 | 17 | Matt Kenseth | Ford | DeWalt Power Tools | 146/0 | 393 | Running | $73,675 |
| 8. | 7 | 97 | Kurt Busch | Ford | Rubbermaid | 147/5 | 393 | Running | $89,925 |
| 9. | 16 | 99 | Jeff Burton | Ford | CITGO | 138/0 | 393 | Running | $90,342 |
| 10. | 17 | 2 | Rusty Wallace | Dodge | Miller Lite | 134/0 | 393 | Running | $91,942 |
| 11. | 20 | 22 | Ward Burton | Dodge | Caterpillar | 130/0 | 393 | Running | $90,781 |
| 12. | 37 | 15 | Michael Waltrip | Chevrolet | NAPA Auto Parts | 127/0 | 393 | Running | $69,910 |
| 13. | 21 | 40 | Sterling Marlin | Dodge | Coors Light | 124/0 | 393 | Running | $95,425 |
| 14. | 35 | 74 | Tony Raines* | Chevrolet | Staff America | 121/0 | 393 | Running | $51,325 |
| 15. | 13 | 10 | Johnny Benson | Pontiac | Valvoline | 118/0 | 393 | Running | $82,435 |
| 16. | 6 | 24 | Jeff Gordon | Chevrolet | DuPont | 120/0 | 393 | Running | $97,228 |
| 17. | 15 | 16 | Greg Biffle* | Ford | Grainger | 112/0 | 393 | Running | $49,150 |
| 18. | 31 | 77 | Dave Blaney | Ford | Jasper Engines & Trans. | 109/0 | 393 | Running | $76,000 |
| 19. | 10 | 48 | Jimmie Johnson | Chevrolet | Lowe's | 106/0 | 393 | Running | $68,275 |
| 20. | 28 | 9 | Bill Elliott | Dodge | Dodge Dealers/UAW | 108/5 | 393 | Running | $89,058 |
| 21. | 1 | 5 | Terry Labonte | Chevrolet | Kellogg's/got milk? | 105/5 | 393 | Running | $83,456 |
| 22. | 22 | 42 | Jamie McMurray* | Dodge | Havoline | 97/0 | 393 | Running | $47,975 |
| 23. | 34 | 54 | Todd Bodine | Ford | National Guard | 94/0 | 393 | Running | $65,375 |
| 24. | 33 | 49 | Ken Schrader | Dodge | BAM Racing | 91/0 | 392 | Running | $58,100 |
| 25. | 19 | 19 | Jeremy Mayfield | Dodge | Dodge Dealers/UAW | 88/0 | 392 | Running | $59,050 |
| 26. | 29 | 0 | Jack Sprague* | Pontiac | NetZero | 85/0 | 392 | Running | $47,725 |
| 27. | 8 | 45 | Kyle Petty | Dodge | Georgia Pacific | 82/0 | 391 | Running | $58,700 |
| 28. | 11 | 41 | Casey Mears* | Dodge | Target | 79/0 | 391 | Running | $66,864 |
| 29. | 14 | 23 | Kenny Wallace | Dodge | Stacker 2 | 76/0 | 390 | Accident | $50,250 |
| 30. | 24 | 43 | John Andretti | Dodge | Cheerios | 73/0 | 390 | Running | $86,253 |
| 31. | 43 | 11 | Brett Bodine | Ford | Hooters Restaurants | 70/0 | 389 | Running | $49,825 |
| 32. | 12 | 01 | Jason Keller | Pontiac | U.S. Army | 67/0 | 388 | Running | $49,675 |
| 33. | 42 | 14 | Larry Foyt* | Dodge | Harrah's | 64/0 | 387 | Running | $49,625 |
| 34. | 27 | 21 | Ricky Rudd | Ford | Motorcraft Quality Parts | 61/0 | 378 | Accident | $57,075 |
| 35. | 26 | 4 | Mike Skinner | Pontiac | Kodak | 58/0 | 378 | Accident | $47,425 |
| 36. | 40 | 88 | Dale Jarrett | Ford | UPS | 55/0 | 363 | Accident | $92,253 |
| 37. | 39 | 38 | Elliott Sadler | Ford | M&M's | 52/0 | 338 | Running | $80,675 |
| 38. | 38 | 32 | Ricky Craven | Pontiac | Tide | 49/0 | 287 | Accident | $54,375 |
| 39. | 5 | 12 | Ryan Newman | Dodge | ALLTEL | 51/5 | 277 | Running | $76,185 |
| 40. | 41 | 30 | Jeff Green | Chevrolet | America Online | 43/0 | 267 | Accident | $54,230 |
| 41. | 9 | 20 | Tony Stewart | Chevrolet | Home Depot | 40/0 | 223 | Accident | $98,748 |
| 42. | 25 | 7 | Jimmy Spencer | Dodge | Sirius Satellite Radio | 37/0 | 139 | Accident | $46,110 |
| 43. | 23 | 1 | Steve Park | Chevrolet | Pennzoil | 34/0 | 42 | Accident | $71,502 |

*Rookie. Time of race: 3 hours, 23 minutes, 47 seconds. Average speed: 86.783 mph. Margin of victory: under caution for rain. Caution flags: 15 for 91 laps. 45-53 (Car 1—accident, Turn 2); 64-67 (Cars 0 and 11—accident, front stretch); 142-157 (Car 7—accident, Turn 3); 211-218 (rain); 225-230 (Cars 20 and 38—accident, Turn 2); 232-235 (Car 41—accident, Turn 3); 251-254 (Car 14—accident, front stretch); 262-265 (Car 32—accident, Turn 2); 269-277 (Cars 01, 2, 12 and 30—accident, Turn 2); 300-303 (Car 0—spin, Turn 4); 318-321 (Car 43—spin, Turn 2); 364-367 (Car 88—accident, back stretch); 371-374 (Cars 48 and 54—accident, back stretch); 381-388 (Cars 4 and 21—accident, Turn 4); 391-393 (Cars 0 and 23—accident, front stretch). Lap leaders: 20 lead changes among 11 drivers. Joe Nemechek 1-2, Terry Labonte 3, Nemechek 4-45, T. Labonte 46-74, Ryan Newman 75-98, Nemechek 99-120, Kurt Busch 121-127, Nemechek 128-129, Busch 130-139, Dale Earnhardt Jr. 140-144, Bobby Labonte 145-204, Nemechek 205-228, Jeff Gordon 229-260, Mark Martin 261-270, J. Gordon 271-280, Bill Elliott 281-286, Kevin Harvick 287-298, B. Labonte 299-300, Robby Gordon 301-329, Nemechek 330-393. Pole winner: Terry Labonte, 126.511 mph. Dropped to rear: Jason Keller (driver change); Bill Elliott (engine change). Failed to qualify: Hermie Sadler, Derrike Cope, Hideo Fukuyama. Estimated attendance: 110,000.

**Richmond International Raceway**
Richmond, Va.—.75-mile paved oval
May 3, 2003—295 miles—393 laps (shortened by rain)

## Points standings

| Rk. | Driver | Behind |
|---|---|---|
| 1. | Matt Kenseth | Leader |
| 2. | Dale Earnhardt Jr. | -20 |
| 3. | Kurt Busch | -167 |
| 4. | Jeff Gordon | -178 |
| 5. | Bobby Labonte | -243 |
| 6. | Jimmie Johnson | -247 |
| 7. | Michael Waltrip | -258 |
| 8. | Kevin Harvick | -291 |
| 9. | Rusty Wallace | -345 |
| 10. | Sterling Marlin | -360 |

**2003 SEASON**

# Coca-Cola 600 — race 12 of 36

| Fin. | St. | Car | Driver | Make | Sponsor | Pts./Bonus | Laps | Status | Winnings |
|---|---|---|---|---|---|---|---|---|---|
| 1. | 37 | 48 | Jimmie Johnson | Chevrolet | Lowe's | 180/5 | 276 | Running | $271,900 |
| 2. | 18 | 17 | Matt Kenseth | Ford | DeWalt Power Tools | 180/10 | 276 | Running | $206,500 |
| 3. | 11 | 18 | Bobby Labonte | Chevrolet | Interstate Batteries | 170/5 | 276 | Running | $184,633 |
| 4. | 14 | 7 | Jimmy Spencer | Dodge | Sirius Satellite Radio | 160/0 | 276 | Running | $137,350 |
| 5. | 1 | 12 | Ryan Newman | Dodge | ALLTEL | 160/5 | 276 | Running | $186,850 |
| 6. | 9 | 15 | Michael Waltrip | Chevrolet | NAPA Auto Parts | 150/0 | 276 | Running | $112,875 |
| 7. | 36 | 40 | Sterling Marlin | Dodge | Coors Light | 146/0 | 276 | Running | $132,225 |
| 8. | 4 | 24 | Jeff Gordon | Chevrolet | DuPont | 142/0 | 276 | Running | $135,103 |
| 9. | 23 | 88 | Dale Jarrett | Ford | UPS | 138/0 | 275 | Running | $129,153 |
| 10. | 41 | 22 | Ward Burton | Dodge | Caterpillar | 134/0 | 275 | Running | $120,331 |
| 11. | 7 | 25 | Joe Nemechek | Chevrolet | UAW/Delphi | 130/0 | 275 | Running | $84,740 |
| 12. | 34 | 2 | Rusty Wallace | Dodge | Miller Lite | 127/0 | 275 | Running | $117,542 |
| 13. | 20 | 29 | Kevin Harvick | Chevrolet | GM Goodwrench Service | 129/5 | 275 | Running | $119,003 |
| 14. | 8 | 77 | Dave Blaney | Ford | Jasper Engines & Trans. | 121/0 | 275 | Running | $104,600 |
| 15. | 12 | 97 | Kurt Busch | Ford | Rubbermaid | 123/5 | 275 | Running | $110,950 |
| 16. | 26 | 16 | Greg Biffle* | Ford | Grainger | 115/0 | 275 | Running | $76,500 |
| 17. | 38 | 31 | Robby Gordon | Chevrolet | Cingular Wireless | 112/0 | 275 | Running | $104,087 |
| 18. | 35 | 99 | Jeff Burton | Ford | CITGO | 109/0 | 275 | Running | $111,522 |
| 19. | 15 | 1 | Jeff Green | Chevrolet | Pennzoil | 106/0 | 274 | Running | $98,512 |
| 20. | 3 | 4 | Mike Skinner | Pontiac | Kodak | 103/0 | 274 | Running | $92,900 |
| 21. | 39 | 5 | Terry Labonte | Chevrolet | Kellogg's/got milk? | 100/0 | 274 | Running | $102,031 |
| 22. | 5 | 0 | Jack Sprague* | Pontiac | NetZero | 97/0 | 274 | Running | $73,350 |
| 23. | 16 | 54 | Todd Bodine | Ford | National Guard | 94/0 | 274 | Running | $84,314 |
| 24. | 10 | 10 | Johnny Benson | Pontiac | Valvoline | 91/0 | 274 | Running | $101,575 |
| 25. | 17 | 42 | Jamie McMurray* | Dodge | Havoline | 88/0 | 274 | Running | $71,125 |
| 26. | 32 | 9 | Bill Elliott | Dodge | Dodge Dealers/UAW | 85/0 | 274 | Running | $109,258 |
| 27. | 13 | 30 | Steve Park | Chevrolet | America Online | 82/0 | 274 | Running | $81,700 |
| 28. | 30 | 49 | Ken Schrader | Dodge | Freightliner Trucks | 79/0 | 273 | Running | $70,175 |
| 29. | 21 | 6 | Mark Martin | Ford | Viagra | 76/0 | 273 | Running | $107,183 |
| 30. | 31 | 45 | Kyle Petty | Dodge | Georgia Pacific | 73/0 | 273 | Running | $81,635 |
| 31. | 43 | 01 | Mike Wallace | Pontiac | U.S. Army | 70/0 | 272 | Running | $72,900 |
| 32. | 27 | 71 | Kevin Lepage** | Ford | Warranty Gold | PE | 271 | Running | $69,675 |
| 33. | 40 | 21 | Ricky Rudd | Ford | U.S. Air Force | 64/0 | 271 | Running | $80,550 |
| 34. | 29 | 14 | Larry Foyt* | Dodge | Harrah's | 61/0 | 269 | Running | $73,290 |
| 35. | 19 | 41 | Casey Mears* | Dodge | Target | 58/0 | 263 | Trans. | $79,700 |
| 36. | 2 | 38 | Elliott Sadler | Ford | Pedigree | 60/5 | 262 | Accident | $108,525 |
| 37. | 25 | 74 | Tony Raines* | Chevrolet | Staff America | 52/0 | 260 | Running | $68,970 |
| 38. | 33 | 32 | Ricky Craven | Pontiac | Tide | 49/0 | 259 | Engine | $76,860 |
| 39. | 42 | 43 | John Andretti | Dodge | Cheerios | 46/0 | 259 | Accident | $104,538 |
| 40. | 6 | 20 | Tony Stewart | Chevrolet | Home Depot | 48/5 | 245 | Running | $140,528 |
| 41. | 24 | 8 | Dale Earnhardt Jr. | Chevrolet | Budweiser | 40/0 | 240 | Brakes | $109,457 |
| 42. | 28 | 23 | Kenny Wallace | Dodge | Stacker 2 | 37/0 | 216 | Engine | $68,435 |
| 43. | 22 | 19 | Jeremy Mayfield | Dodge | Dodge Dealers/UAW | 34/0 | 123 | Accident | $76,590 |

*Rookie. **Kevin Lepage was not awarded points because he entered the race after the entry deadline. Time of race: 3 hours, 16 minutes, 50 seconds. Average speed: 126.198 mph. Margin of victory: Under caution. Caution flags: Eight for 46 laps. 1-3 (green/yellow displayed at race start); 104-110 (rain, red flag); 128-134 (Car 19—accident, Turn 2); 200-204 (Car 21—spin, front stretch); 223-227 (Car 8—spin, Turn 4); 230-232 (Car 30—spin, Turn 2); 241-244 (debris in Turn 1); 265-276 (Cars 14, 32, 38 and 43—accident, Turn 4; caution extended by rain). Lap leaders: 16 lead changes among eight drivers. Ryan Newman 1-49, Tony Stewart 50-54, Newman 55, Kurt Busch 56, Matt Kenseth 57-58, Stewart 59-104, Kevin Harvick 105, Stewart 106-122, Kenseth 123-128, Elliott Sadler 129, Kenseth 130-196, Bobby Labonte 197-233, Kenseth 234-240, B. Labonte 241, Jimmie Johnson 242-264, B. Labonte 265, Johnson 266-276. Pole winner: Ryan Newman, 185.312 mph. Note: During the second caution period, the race was red flagged for 17 minutes because of rain. Dropped to rear: Jimmie Johnson (engine change), Robby Gordon (missed drivers meeting). Failed to qualify: Hermie Sadler, Brett Bodine, Derrike Cope. Estimated attendance: 165,000.

**Lowe's Motor Speedway**
Harrisburg, N.C.—1.5-mile banked paved oval
May 25, 2003—414 miles—276 laps (shortened by rain)

## Points standings

| Rk. | Driver | Behind |
|---|---|---|
| 1. | Matt Kenseth | Leader |
| 2. | Dale Earnhardt Jr. | -160 |
| 3. | Jeff Gordon | -216 |
| 4. | Kurt Busch | -224 |
| 5. | Jimmie Johnson | -247 |
| 6. | Bobby Labonte | -253 |
| 7. | Michael Waltrip | -288 |
| 8. | Kevin Harvick | -342 |
| 9. | Sterling Marlin | -394 |
| 10. | Rusty Wallace | -398 |

2003 SEASON

# MBNA Armed Forces Family 400 — race 13 of 36

| Fin. | St. | Car | Driver | Make | Sponsor | Pts./Bonus | Laps | Status | Winnings |
|---|---|---|---|---|---|---|---|---|---|
| 1. | 1 | 12 | Ryan Newman | Dodge | ALLTEL | 185/10 | 400 | Running | $199,325 |
| 2. | 9 | 24 | Jeff Gordon | Chevrolet | DuPont | 175/5 | 400 | Running | $176,228 |
| 3. | 13 | 18 | Bobby Labonte | Chevrolet | Interstate Batteries | 170/5 | 400 | Running | $139,333 |
| 4. | 11 | 20 | Tony Stewart | Chevrolet | Home Depot | 165/5 | 400 | Running | $145,253 |
| 5. | 30 | 10 | Johnny Benson | Pontiac | Valvoline | 155/0 | 400 | Running | $110,975 |
| 6. | 2 | 2 | Rusty Wallace | Dodge | Miller Lite | 155/5 | 400 | Running | $110,097 |
| 7. | 4 | 17 | Matt Kenseth | Ford | DeWalt Power Tools | 146/0 | 400 | Running | $87,985 |
| 8. | 20 | 32 | Ricky Craven | Pontiac | Tide | 142/0 | 400 | Running | $95,565 |
| 9. | 38 | 31 | Robby Gordon | Chevrolet | Cingular Wireless | 143/5 | 400 | Running | $99,747 |
| 10. | 8 | 5 | Terry Labonte | Chevrolet | Kellogg's/got milk? | 134/0 | 400 | Running | $97,641 |
| 11. | 12 | 8 | Dale Earnhardt Jr. | Chevrolet | Budweiser | 135/5 | 400 | Running | $106,692 |
| 12. | 21 | 54 | Todd Bodine | Ford | National Guard | 127/0 | 400 | Running | $83,110 |
| 13. | 19 | 42 | Jamie McMurray* | Dodge | Havoline | 124/0 | 400 | Running | $68,970 |
| 14. | 28 | 99 | Jeff Burton | Ford | CITGO | 121/0 | 399 | Running | $98,652 |
| 15. | 7 | 97 | Kurt Busch | Ford | Rubbermaid | 123/5 | 399 | Running | $95,685 |
| 16. | 16 | 15 | Michael Waltrip | Chevrolet | NAPA Auto Parts | 120/5 | 399 | Running | $78,935 |
| 17. | 24 | 21 | Ricky Rudd | Ford | Motorcraft Quality Parts | 112/0 | 399 | Running | $82,950 |
| 18. | 32 | 6 | Mark Martin | Ford | Viagra | 109/0 | 399 | Running | $97,968 |
| 19. | 18 | 01 | Mike Wallace | Pontiac | U.S. Army | 106/0 | 398 | Running | $72,199 |
| 20. | 26 | 77 | Dave Blaney | Ford | Jasper Engines & Trans. | 103/0 | 398 | Running | $73,335 |
| 21. | 3 | 19 | Jeremy Mayfield | Dodge | Dodge Dealers/UAW | 100/0 | 398 | Running | $71,885 |
| 22. | 14 | 9 | Bill Elliott | Dodge | Dodge Dealers/UAW | 97/0 | 398 | Running | $98,668 |
| 23. | 36 | 23 | Kenny Wallace | Dodge | Stacker 2 | 94/0 | 398 | Running | $63,785 |
| 24. | 37 | 25 | Joe Nemechek | Chevrolet | UAW/Delphi | 91/0 | 397 | Running | $62,630 |
| 25. | 33 | 1 | Jeff Green | Chevrolet | Pennzoil | 88/0 | 396 | Running | $84,942 |
| 26. | 25 | 49 | Ken Schrader | Dodge | BAM Racing | 85/0 | 396 | Running | $62,205 |
| 27. | 23 | 29 | Kevin Harvick | Chevrolet | GM Goodwrench Service | 82/0 | 395 | Running | $97,833 |
| 28. | 43 | 14 | Larry Foyt* | Dodge | Harrah's | 79/0 | 394 | Running | $58,880 |
| 29. | 31 | 7 | Jimmy Spencer | Dodge | Sirius Satellite Radio | 76/0 | 393 | Running | $61,230 |
| 30. | 15 | 16 | Greg Biffle* | Ford | Grainger | 73/0 | 387 | Accident | $59,090 |
| 31. | 42 | 74 | Tony Raines* | Chevrolet | America's Second Harvest | 70/0 | 382 | Running | $58,430 |
| 32. | 10 | 30 | Steve Park | Chevrolet | America Online | 67/0 | 367 | Running | $66,270 |
| 33. | 17 | 38 | Elliott Sadler | Ford | M&M's | 64/0 | 331 | Running | $93,270 |
| 34. | 40 | 43 | John Andretti | Dodge | Cheerios | 61/0 | 309 | Running | $93,688 |
| 35. | 6 | 40 | Sterling Marlin | Dodge | Coors Light | 58/0 | 301 | Accident | $101,695 |
| 36. | 35 | 4 | Mike Skinner | Pontiac | Kodak | 55/0 | 298 | Running | $57,580 |
| 37. | 39 | 22 | Ward Burton | Dodge | Caterpillar | 52/0 | 279 | Accident | $93,526 |
| 38. | 5 | 48 | Jimmie Johnson | Chevrolet | Lowe's | 54/5 | 277 | Accident | $76,760 |
| 39. | 29 | 88 | Dale Jarrett | Ford | UPS | 46/0 | 255 | Engine | $103,028 |
| 40. | 22 | 41 | Casey Mears* | Dodge | Target | 43/0 | 244 | Accident | $65,120 |
| 41. | 41 | 0 | Jack Sprague* | Pontiac | NetZero HiSpeed | 40/0 | 215 | Accident | $56,995 |
| 42. | 34 | 11 | Brett Bodine | Ford | Hooters Restaurants | 37/0 | 213 | Accident | $56,890 |
| 43. | 27 | 45 | Kyle Petty | Dodge | Georgia Pacific | 34/0 | 207 | Accident | $65,028 |

*Rookie. Time of race: 3 hours, 44 minutes, 31 seconds. Average speed: 106.896 mph. Margin of victory: .834 seconds. Caution flags: Nine for 68 laps. 3-22 (Cars 0, 1, 4, 7, 8, 22, 41 and 74—accident, front stretch; rain); 40-44 (Car 7—accident, front stretch); 78-89 (rain); 115-119 (Car 40—accident, back stretch); 139-142 (Car 16—accident, front stretch); 203-208 (debris); 212-218 (Cars 0, 6, 11, 43, 45, 49 and 97—accident, front stretch); 278-281 (Car 48—accident, back stretch); 390-394 (Car 41—accident, Turn 1). Lap leaders: 16 lead changes among 10 drivers. Rusty Wallace 1-41, Ryan Newman 42-69, Tony Stewart 70-116, Robby Gordon 117-119, Stewart 120-139, Newman 140-203, Jimmie Johnson 204-239, Jeff Gordon 240-278, Michael Waltrip 279, J. Gordon 280-285, Bobby Labonte 286-319, J. Gordon 320-327, Newman 328-364, Dale Earnhardt Jr. 365-366, Kurt Busch 367, Newman 368-400. Pole winner: Ryan Newman, 158.716 mph. Dropped to rear: Dale Earnhardt Jr. and Joe Nemechek (backup cars), Tony Raines (engine change), Robby Gordon (pit stop). Failed to qualify: Derrike Cope, Hermie Sadler. Estimated attendance: 135,000.

**Dover International Speedway**
Dover, Del.— 1-mile banked concrete oval
June 1, 2003—400 miles—400 laps

## Points standings

| Rk. | Driver | Behind |
|---|---|---|
| 1. | Matt Kenseth | Leader |
| 2. | Dale Earnhardt Jr. | -171 |
| 3. | Jeff Gordon | -187 |
| 4. | Bobby Labonte | -229 |
| 5. | Kurt Busch | -247 |
| 6. | Michael Waltrip | -314 |
| 7. | Jimmie Johnson | -339 |
| 8. | Rusty Wallace | -389 |
| 9. | Kevin Harvick | -406 |
| 10. | Robby Gordon | -472 |

**2003 SEASON**

# Pocono 500 — race 14 of 36

| Fin. | St. | Car | Driver | Make | Sponsor | Pts./Bonus | Laps | Status | Winnings |
|---|---|---|---|---|---|---|---|---|---|
| 1. | 4 | 20 | Tony Stewart | Chevrolet | Home Depot | 180/5 | 200 | Running | $214,253 |
| 2. | 6 | 6 | Mark Martin | Ford | Viagra | 175/5 | 200 | Running | $152,278 |
| 3. | 25 | 17 | Matt Kenseth | Ford | DeWalt Power Tools | 170/5 | 200 | Running | $109,870 |
| 4. | 5 | 8 | Dale Earnhardt Jr. | Chevrolet | Budweiser | 165/5 | 200 | Running | $116,272 |
| 5. | 2 | 12 | Ryan Newman | Dodge | ALLTEL | 160/5 | 200 | Running | $98,700 |
| 6. | 23 | 40 | Sterling Marlin | Dodge | Coors Light | 160/10 | 200 | Running | $104,490 |
| 7. | 11 | 5 | Terry Labonte | Chevrolet | Kellogg's/got milk? | 151/5 | 200 | Running | $87,946 |
| 8. | 17 | 22 | Ward Burton | Dodge | Caterpillar | 147/5 | 200 | Running | $91,146 |
| 9. | 9 | 38 | Elliott Sadler | Ford | M&M's | 143/5 | 200 | Running | $101,040 |
| 10. | 32 | 32 | Ricky Craven | Pontiac | Tide | 134/0 | 200 | Running | $83,490 |
| 11. | 14 | 54 | Todd Bodine | Ford | National Guard | 135/5 | 200 | Running | $68,740 |
| 12. | 1 | 48 | Jimmie Johnson | Chevrolet | Lowe's | 132/5 | 200 | Running | $80,375 |
| 13. | 12 | 24 | Jeff Gordon | Chevrolet | DuPont | 124/0 | 200 | Running | $95,568 |
| 14. | 16 | 99 | Jeff Burton | Ford | CITGO | 126/0 | 200 | Running | $84,507 |
| 15. | 33 | 19 | Jeremy Mayfield | Dodge | Dodge Dealers/UAW | 118/0 | 200 | Running | $59,640 |
| 16. | 27 | 2 | Rusty Wallace | Dodge | Miller Lite | 115/0 | 200 | Running | $84,957 |
| 17. | 3 | 18 | Bobby Labonte | Chevrolet | Interstate Batteries | 112/0 | 200 | Running | $91,973 |
| 18. | 13 | 15 | Michael Waltrip | Chevrolet | NAPA Auto Parts | 114/5 | 200 | Running | $64,090 |
| 19. | 8 | 9 | Bill Elliott | Dodge | Dodge Dealers/UAW | 111/5 | 200 | Running | $84,673 |
| 20. | 26 | 16 | Greg Biffle* | Ford | Grainger | 103/0 | 199 | Accident | $52,615 |
| 21. | 19 | 41 | Casey Mears* | Dodge | Target | 100/0 | 199 | Running | $69,990 |
| 22. | 18 | 0 | Jack Sprague* | Pontiac | NetZero HiSpeed | 97/0 | 199 | Running | $48,690 |
| 23. | 21 | 43 | John Andretti | Dodge | Cheerios | 94/0 | 199 | Running | $84,143 |
| 24. | 24 | 10 | Johnny Benson | Pontiac | Valvoline | 91/0 | 199 | Running | $75,765 |
| 25. | 20 | 29 | Kevin Harvick | Chevrolet | GM Goodwrench Service | 88/0 | 199 | Running | $84,018 |
| 26. | 22 | 77 | Dave Blaney | Ford | Jasper Engines & Trans. | 85/0 | 199 | Running | $66,090 |
| 27. | 40 | 45 | Kyle Petty | Dodge | Georgia Pacific | 82/0 | 199 | Running | $55,340 |
| 28. | 37 | 31 | Robby Gordon | Chevrolet | Cingular Wireless | 79/0 | 199 | Running | $72,377 |
| 29. | 38 | 23 | Kenny Wallace | Dodge | Stacker 2 | 76/0 | 199 | Running | $54,904 |
| 30. | 42 | 74 | Tony Raines* | Chevrolet | Staff America | 73/0 | 199 | Running | $44,365 |
| 31. | 31 | 01 | Mike Wallace | Pontiac | U.S. Army | 70/0 | 198 | Running | $43,715 |
| 32. | 28 | 42 | Jamie McMurray* | Dodge | Havoline | 67/0 | 198 | Running | $43,565 |
| 33. | 35 | 1 | Jeff Green | Chevrolet | Pennzoil | 69/5 | 197 | Accident | $68,552 |
| 34. | 41 | 4 | Mike Skinner | Pontiac | Kodak | 61/0 | 197 | Accident | $44,065 |
| 35. | 36 | 30 | Steve Park | Chevrolet | America Online | 58/0 | 195 | Running | $50,990 |
| 36. | 10 | 97 | Kurt Busch | Ford | Rubbermaid | 55/0 | 193 | Accident | $62,790 |
| 37. | 29 | 21 | Ricky Rudd | Ford | Motorcraft Quality Parts | 52/0 | 171 | Running | $50,625 |
| 38. | 15 | 25 | Joe Nemechek | Chevrolet | UAW/Delphi | 49/0 | 166 | Trans. | $42,500 |
| 39. | 30 | 7 | Jimmy Spencer | Dodge | Sirius Satellite Radio | 46/0 | 156 | Handling | $42,385 |
| 40. | 34 | 91 | Casey Atwood | Dodge | Mountain Dew Live Wire | 43/0 | 77 | Engine | $42,230 |
| 41. | 43 | 14 | Larry Foyt* | Dodge | Harrah's | 45/5 | 71 | Brakes | $42,090 |
| 42. | 7 | 88 | Dale Jarrett | Ford | UPS | 37/0 | 53 | Accident | $87,778 |
| 43. | 39 | 49 | Ken Schrader | Dodge | Blair.com | 34/0 | 7 | Accident | $42,186 |

*Rookie. Time of race: 3 hours, 42 minutes, 24 seconds. Average speed: 134.892 mph. Margin of victory: under caution. Caution flags: Five for 25 laps. 9-16 (Car 49—accident, Turn 1); 55-61 (Car 88—accident, Turn 1); 154-157 (Car 21—stalled, Turn 2); 194-197 (Car 97—accident, Turn 2); 199-200 (Cars 1, 4 and 16—accident, Long Pond straightaway). Lap leaders: 28 lead changes among 16 drivers. Jimmie Johnson 1-9, Larry Foyt 10-14, Bill Elliott 15-16, Johnson 17-30, Dale Earnhardt Jr. 31-47, Ryan Newman 48, Matt Kenseth 49-50, Earnhardt Jr. 51-53, Tony Stewart 54-55, Elliott Sadler 56-85, Kenseth 86-89, Stewart 90-91, Mark Martin 92-93, Terry Labonte 94, Ward Burton 95-96, E. Sadler 97-101, Sterling Marlin 102-121, Kenseth 122-125, Stewart 126-127, Martin 128-130, Marlin 131-154, Michael Waltrip 155, Stewart 156-175, Martin 176-177, Earnhardt Jr. 178-179, Jeff Green 180, Jeff Burton 181-186, Todd Bodine 187-189, Stewart 190-200. Pole winner: Jimmie Johnson, 170.645 mph. Failed to qualify: Derrike Cope, Morgan Shepherd. Estimated attendance: 100,000.

**Pocono Raceway**
Pocono, Pa.— 2.5-mile banked paved oval
June 8, 2003—500 miles—200 laps

## Points standings

| Rk. | Driver | Behind |
|---|---|---|
| 1. | Matt Kenseth | Leader |
| 2. | Dale Earnhardt Jr. | -176 |
| 3. | Jeff Gordon | -233 |
| 4. | Bobby Labonte | -287 |
| 5. | Kurt Busch | -362 |
| 6. | Michael Waltrip | -370 |
| 7. | Jimmie Johnson | -377 |
| 8. | Rusty Wallace | -444 |
| 9. | Kevin Harvick | -488 |
| 10. | Sterling Marlin | -492 |

2003 SEASON

# Sirius 400 — race 15 of 36

| Fin. | St. | Car | Driver | Make | Sponsor | Pts./Bonus | Laps | Status | Winnings |
|---|---|---|---|---|---|---|---|---|---|
| 1. | 4 | 97 | Kurt Busch | Ford | Rubbermaid | 180/5 | 200 | Running | $172,650 |
| 2. | 1 | 18 | Bobby Labonte | Chevrolet | Interstate Batteries/The Hulk | 170/0 | 200 | Running | $142,858 |
| 3. | 6 | 24 | Jeff Gordon | Chevrolet | DuPont | 170/0 | 200 | Running | $126,228 |
| 4. | 21 | 17 | Matt Kenseth | Ford | DeWalt Power Tools | 160/0 | 200 | Running | $93,275 |
| 5. | 9 | 15 | Michael Waltrip | Chevrolet | NAPA Auto Parts | 155/0 | 200 | Running | $81,475 |
| 6. | 30 | 40 | Sterling Marlin | Dodge | Coors Light | 160/10 | 200 | Running | $114,540 |
| 7. | 3 | 8 | Dale Earnhardt Jr. | Chevrolet | Budweiser | 151/5 | 200 | Running | $100,607 |
| 8. | 2 | 20 | Tony Stewart | Chevrolet | Home Depot | 147/5 | 200 | Running | $110,843 |
| 9. | 15 | 6 | Mark Martin | Ford | Viagra | 138/0 | 200 | Running | $96,248 |
| 10. | 5 | 5 | Terry Labonte | Chevrolet | Kellogg's/got milk? | 134/0 | 200 | Running | $89,571 |
| 11. | 23 | 99 | Jeff Burton | Ford | CITGO | 130/0 | 200 | Running | $93,447 |
| 12. | 17 | 2 | Rusty Wallace | Dodge | Miller Lite | 127/0 | 200 | Running | $93,457 |
| 13. | 20 | 19 | Jeremy Mayfield | Dodge | Dodge Dealers/UAW | 124/0 | 200 | Running | $67,290 |
| 14. | 39 | 42 | Jamie McMurray* | Dodge | Havoline | 121/0 | 200 | Running | $63,590 |
| 15. | 37 | 32 | Ricky Craven | Pontiac | Tide | 118/0 | 200 | Running | $83,590 |
| 16. | 11 | 48 | Jimmie Johnson | Chevrolet | Lowe's | 115/0 | 199 | Running | $71,890 |
| 17. | 7 | 38 | Elliott Sadler | Ford | M&M's | 112/0 | 199 | Running | $90,440 |
| 18. | 10 | 29 | Kevin Harvick | Chevrolet | GM Goodwrench Service | 109/0 | 199 | Running | $91,468 |
| 19. | 14 | 0 | Jack Sprague* | Pontiac | NetZero HiSpeed | 106/0 | 199 | Running | $55,290 |
| 20. | 22 | 41 | Casey Mears* | Dodge | Target | 103/0 | 199 | Running | $80,190 |
| 21. | 12 | 25 | Joe Nemechek | Chevrolet | UAW/Delphi | 100/0 | 199 | Running | $54,540 |
| 22. | 19 | 31 | Robby Gordon | Chevrolet | Cingular Wireless | 97/0 | 199 | Running | $79,427 |
| 23. | 34 | 01 | Mike Wallace | Pontiac | U.S. Army | 94/0 | 199 | Running | $67,790 |
| 24. | 16 | 9 | Bill Elliott | Dodge | Dodge Dealers/UAW | 91/0 | 199 | Running | $89,223 |
| 25. | 24 | 23 | Kenny Wallace | Dodge | Stacker 2 | 88/0 | 199 | Running | $64,290 |
| 26. | 26 | 10 | Johnny Benson | Pontiac | Valvoline | 85/0 | 199 | Running | $79,790 |
| 27. | 33 | 30 | Steve Park | Chevrolet | America Online | 82/0 | 199 | Running | $60,775 |
| 28. | 13 | 1 | Jeff Green | Chevrolet | Pennzoil | 79/0 | 199 | Running | $77,812 |
| 29. | 40 | 7 | Jimmy Spencer | Dodge | Sirius Satellite Radio | 76/0 | 199 | Running | $60,304 |
| 30. | 31 | 22 | Ward Burton | Dodge | Caterpillar | 73/0 | 199 | Running | $85,896 |
| 31. | 29 | 16 | Greg Biffle* | Ford | Grainger | 75/5 | 199 | Running | $49,190 |
| 32. | 25 | 88 | Dale Jarrett | Ford | UPS | 67/0 | 199 | Running | $94,893 |
| 33. | 43 | 74 | Tony Raines* | Chevrolet | Staff America | 64/0 | 199 | Running | $49,940 |
| 34. | 42 | 45 | Kyle Petty | Dodge | Georgia Pacific | 61/0 | 199 | Running | $56,935 |
| 35. | 36 | 43 | Christian Fittipaldi | Dodge | Cheerios | 63/5 | 199 | Running | $84,573 |
| 36. | 18 | 02 | Hermie Sadler | Chevrolet | Total Non-Stop Action Wrestling | 60/5 | 198 | Running | $48,745 |
| 37. | 41 | 54 | Todd Bodine | Ford | National Guard | 52/0 | 191 | Accident | $48,695 |
| 38. | 38 | 77 | Dave Blaney | Ford | Jasper Engines & Trans. | 49/0 | 167 | Running | $56,585 |
| 39. | 27 | 11 | Geoffrey Bodine | Ford | Hooters Restaurants | 46/0 | 119 | Vibration | $48,550 |
| 40. | 35 | 37 | Derrike Cope | Chevrolet | GBR Online/Friendly's | 43/0 | 68 | Engine | $48,515 |
| 41. | 8 | 12 | Ryan Newman | Dodge | ALLTEL | 45/5 | 36 | Engine | $78,355 |
| 42. | 28 | 49 | Ken Schrader | Dodge | BAM Racing | 37/0 | 1 | Accident | $48,440 |
| 43. | 32 | 21 | Ricky Rudd | Ford | Motorcraft Quality Parts | 34/0 | 1 | Accident | $55,765 |

*Rookie. Time of race: 3 hours, 2 minutes, 54 seconds. Average speed: 131.219 mph. Margin of victory: .774 seconds. Caution flags: 9 for 41 laps. 3-6 (Cars 21 and 49—accident, Turns 1 and 2); 12-14 (Car 77—spin, Turn 4); 38-47 (oil on track); 49-51 (Car 30—spin, Turn 2); 72-77 (oil on track); 159-162 (debris on back stretch); 172-175 (Cars 16 and 32—accident, Turn 4); 180-182 (Car 74—accident, Turn 2); 192-195 (Car 54—accident, back stretch). Lap leaders: 22 lead changes among nine drivers. Tony Stewart 1-19, Dale Earnhardt Jr. 20, Stewart 21-28, Sterling Marlin 29, Stewart 30-31, Ryan Newman 32, Stewart 33, Newman 34, Stewart 35-38, Christian Fittipaldi 39, Marlin 40-47, Stewart 48-58, Marlin 59-69, Stewart 70-72, Hermie Sadler 73, Marlin 74-119, Stewart 120-121, Greg Biffle 122, Marlin 123-158, Stewart 159, Jeff Gordon 160-176, Kurt Busch 177-200. Pole winner: Bobby Labonte, 190.365 mph. Dropped to rear: Geoffrey Bodine (backup car); Terry Labonte, Jimmy Spencer, Dale Earnhardt Jr. and Christian Fittipaldi (engine changes). Failed to qualify: Mike Skinner, Larry Foyt. Estimated attendance: 160,000.

**Michigan International Speedway**
Brooklyn, Mich.— 2-mile banked paved oval
June 15, 2003—400 miles—200 laps

## Points standings

| Rk. | Driver | Behind |
|---|---|---|
| 1. | Matt Kenseth | Leader |
| 2. | Dale Earnhardt Jr. | -185 |
| 3. | Jeff Gordon | -223 |
| 4. | Bobby Labonte | -277 |
| 5. | Kurt Busch | -342 |
| 6. | Michael Waltrip | -375 |
| 7. | Jimmie Johnson | -422 |
| 8. | Rusty Wallace | -477 |
| 9. | Sterling Marlin | -492 |
| 10. | Mark Martin | -535 |

# Dodge/Save Mart 350 — race 16 of 36

| Fin. | St. | Car | Driver | Make | Sponsor | Pts./Bonus | Laps | Status | Winnings |
|---|---|---|---|---|---|---|---|---|---|
| 1. | 2 | 31 | Robby Gordon | Chevrolet | Cingular Wireless | 185/10 | 110 | Running | $204,512 |
| 2. | 8 | 24 | Jeff Gordon | Chevrolet | DuPont | 170/0 | 110 | Running | $143,203 |
| 3. | 6 | 29 | Kevin Harvick | Chevrolet | GM Goodwrench Service | 165/0 | 110 | Running | $119,128 |
| 4. | 12 | 9 | Bill Elliott | Dodge | Dodge Dealers/UAW | 160/0 | 110 | Running | $119,748 |
| 5. | 13 | 12 | Ryan Newman | Dodge | ALLTEL | 155/0 | 110 | Running | $101,140 |
| 6. | 1 | 01 | Boris Said | Pontiac | U.S. Army | 155/5 | 110 | Running | $90,990 |
| 7. | 3 | 1 | Ron Fellows | Chevrolet | Pennzoil | 151/5 | 110 | Running | $92,927 |
| 8. | 7 | 2 | Rusty Wallace | Dodge | Miller Lite | 142/0 | 110 | Running | $99,482 |
| 9. | 14 | 18 | Bobby Labonte | Chevrolet | Interstate Batteries | 138/0 | 110 | Running | $105,223 |
| 10. | 31 | 19 | Jeremy Mayfield | Dodge | Dodge Dealers/UAW | 134/0 | 110 | Running | $80,335 |
| 11. | 11 | 8 | Dale Earnhardt Jr. | Chevrolet | Budweiser | 130/0 | 110 | Running | $100,292 |
| 12. | 10 | 20 | Tony Stewart | Chevrolet | Home Depot | 127/0 | 110 | Running | $110,988 |
| 13. | 20 | 15 | Michael Waltrip | Chevrolet | NAPA Auto Parts | 124/0 | 110 | Running | $75,950 |
| 14. | 4 | 17 | Matt Kenseth | Ford | DeWalt Power Tools | 121/0 | 110 | Running | $78,975 |
| 15. | 9 | 21 | Ricky Rudd | Ford | Motorcraft Quality Parts | 118/0 | 110 | Running | $84,825 |
| 16. | 19 | 22 | Ward Burton | Dodge | Caterpillar | 115/0 | 110 | Running | $93,406 |
| 17. | 37 | 48 | Jimmie Johnson | Chevrolet | Lowe's | 112/0 | 110 | Running | $75,630 |
| 18. | 27 | 40 | Sterling Marlin | Dodge | Coors Light | 109/0 | 110 | Running | $99,775 |
| 19. | 17 | 6 | Mark Martin | Ford | Viagra | 106/0 | 110 | Running | $93,208 |
| 20. | 26 | 42 | Jamie McMurray* | Dodge | Havoline | 103/0 | 110 | Running | $62,525 |
| 21. | 38 | 32 | Ricky Craven | Pontiac | Tide | 100/0 | 110 | Running | $80,050 |
| 22. | 24 | 38 | Elliott Sadler | Ford | M&M's | 97/0 | 110 | Running | $93,125 |
| 23. | 22 | 54 | Todd Bodine | Ford | National Guard | 94/0 | 110 | Running | $70,125 |
| 24. | 36 | 4 | Johnny Miller | Pontiac | Kodak | 91/0 | 110 | Running | $66,939 |
| 25. | 23 | 5 | Terry Labonte | Chevrolet | Kellogg's/got milk? | 88/0 | 110 | Running | $84,886 |
| 26. | 33 | 41 | Casey Mears* | Dodge | Target | 85/0 | 110 | Running | $66,300 |
| 27. | 35 | 45 | Kyle Petty | Dodge | Georgia Pacific | 82/0 | 110 | Running | $66,160 |
| 28. | 5 | 97 | Kurt Busch | Ford | Rubbermaid | 79/0 | 110 | Running | $75,255 |
| 29. | 30 | 23 | Kenny Wallace | Dodge | Stacker 2 | 76/0 | 110 | Running | $58,035 |
| 30. | 25 | 10 | Johnny Benson | Pontiac | Valvoline | 78/5 | 109 | Running | $84,745 |
| 31. | 34 | 74 | Tony Raines* | Chevrolet | Staff America | 70/0 | 109 | Running | $54,925 |
| 32. | 15 | 77 | Dave Blaney | Ford | Jasper Engines & Trans. | 67/0 | 109 | Running | $62,865 |
| 33. | 42 | 49 | Ken Schrader | Dodge | BAM Racing | 64/0 | 109 | Running | $55,745 |
| 34. | 18 | 09 | Scott Pruett | Dodge | Target | 61/0 | 109 | Running | $54,825 |
| 35. | 21 | 25 | Joe Nemechek | Chevrolet | UAW/Delphi | 58/0 | 109 | Running | $54,805 |
| 36. | 39 | 7 | Jimmy Spencer | Dodge | Sirius Satellite Radio | 55/0 | 109 | Running | $54,785 |
| 37. | 32 | 16 | Greg Biffle* | Ford | Grainger | 52/0 | 106 | Fuel pump | $54,765 |
| 38. | 16 | 99 | Jeff Burton | Ford | CITGO | 49/0 | 102 | Running | $88,162 |
| 39. | 28 | 0 | Jack Sprague* | Pontiac | NetZero HiSpeed | 46/0 | 95 | Gas | $54,720 |
| 40. | 41 | 43 | Christian Fittipaldi | Dodge | Cheerios | 43/0 | 86 | Trans. | $90,463 |
| 41. | 40 | 30 | Steve Park | Chevrolet | America Online | 40/0 | 85 | Accident | $62,650 |
| 42. | 29 | 88 | Dale Jarrett | Ford | UPS | 37/0 | 83 | Trans. | $100,403 |
| 43. | 43 | 66 | Hideo Fukuyama* | Ford | Kikkoman | 34/0 | 68 | Rear end | $54,829 |

*Rookie. Time of race: 2 hours, 57 minutes, 55 seconds. Average speed: 73.821 mph. Margin of victory: .553 seconds. Caution flags: 6 for 16 laps. 37-40 (debris); 52-53 (Car 66—spin, Turn 7); 59-61 (Cars 0, 30 and 45—accident, Turn 7); 63-64 (Cars 2 and 8—spin, Turn 4); 72-74 (Car 43—spin, Turn 10); 90-91 (Car 74-Spin, Turn 2). Lap leaders: Six lead changes among four drivers. Boris Said 1, Robby Gordon 2-30, Ron Fellows 31-35, R. Gordon 36-56, Fellows 57-72, Johnny Benson 73-79, R. Gordon 80-110. Pole winner: Boris Said, 93.620 mph. Dropped to rear: Ricky Craven (engine change). Failed to qualify: P.J. Jones, Brandon Ash, Paul Menard, Jim Inglebright. Estimated attendance: 100,000.

**Infineon Raceway**
Sonoma, Calif.— 2-mile paved road course
June 22, 2003—218.9 miles, 350 K—110 laps

## Points standings

| Rk. | Driver | Behind |
|---|---|---|
| 1. | Matt Kenseth | Leader |
| 2. | Jeff Gordon | -174 |
| 3. | Dale Earnhardt Jr. | -176 |
| 4. | Bobby Labonte | -260 |
| 5. | Michael Waltrip | -372 |
| 6. | Kurt Busch | -384 |
| 7. | Jimmie Johnson | -431 |
| 8. | Rusty Wallace | -456 |
| 9. | Kevin Harvick | -495 |
| 10. | Sterling Marlin | -504 |

2003 SEASON

# Pepsi 400 — race 17 of 36

| Fin. | St. | Car | Driver | Make | Sponsor | Pts./Bonus | Laps | Status | Winnings |
|---|---|---|---|---|---|---|---|---|---|
| 1. | 30 | 16 | Greg Biffle* | Ford | Grainger | 180/5 | 160 | Running | $187,975 |
| 2. | 36 | 99 | Jeff Burton | Ford | CITGO | 170/0 | 160 | Running | $168,142 |
| 3. | 27 | 21 | Ricky Rudd | Ford | Motorcraft Quality Parts | 165/0 | 160 | Running | $127,600 |
| 4. | 25 | 5 | Terry Labonte | Chevrolet | Kellogg's/got milk? | 160/0 | 160 | Running | $128,806 |
| 5. | 15 | 18 | Bobby Labonte | Chevrolet | Interstate Batteries | 160/5 | 160 | Running | $129,283 |
| 6. | 37 | 17 | Matt Kenseth | Ford | Smirnoff Ice/DeWalt | 155/5 | 160 | Running | $98,475 |
| 7. | 5 | 8 | Dale Earnhardt Jr. | Chevrolet | Budweiser | 151/5 | 160 | Running | $133,067 |
| 8. | 10 | 19 | Jeremy Mayfield | Dodge | Dodge Dealers/UAW | 142/0 | 160 | Running | $87,175 |
| 9. | 2 | 29 | Kevin Harvick | Chevrolet | GM Goodwrench Service | 148/10 | 160 | Running | $113,553 |
| 10. | 16 | 88 | Dale Jarrett | Ford | UPS | 134/0 | 160 | Running | $120,203 |
| 11. | 6 | 15 | Michael Waltrip | Chevrolet | NAPA Auto Parts | 110/5 | 160 | Running | $90,275 |
| 12. | 40 | 7 | Jimmy Spencer | Dodge | Sirius Satellite Radio | 127/0 | 160 | Running | $89,175 |
| 13. | 41 | 54 | Todd Bodine | Ford | National Guard | 124/0 | 160 | Running | $87,450 |
| 14. | 3 | 24 | Jeff Gordon | Chevrolet | DuPont | 126/0 | 160 | Running | $117,303 |
| 15. | 29 | 23 | Kenny Wallace | Dodge | Stacker 2 | 118/0 | 160 | Running | $84,475 |
| 16. | 14 | 9 | Bill Elliott | Dodge | Dodge Dealers/UAW | 115/0 | 160 | Running | $107,183 |
| 17. | 19 | 09 | Buckshot Jones | Dodge | Miccosukee Resort | 112/0 | 160 | Running | $68,000 |
| 18. | 11 | 48 | Jimmie Johnson | Chevrolet | Lowe's | 114/5 | 160 | Running | $87,075 |
| 19. | 4 | 40 | Sterling Marlin | Dodge | Coors Light | 106/0 | 160 | Running | $111,225 |
| 20. | 33 | 6 | Mark Martin | Ford | Viagra | 103/0 | 160 | Running | $106,708 |
| 21. | 13 | 20 | Tony Stewart | Chevrolet | Home Depot | 100/0 | 160 | Running | $114,128 |
| 22. | 24 | 12 | Ryan Newman | Dodge | ALLTEL | 97/0 | 160 | Running | $99,800 |
| 23. | 42 | 45 | Kyle Petty | Dodge | Georgia Pacific | 74/0 | 160 | Running | $77,550 |
| 24. | 9 | 38 | Elliott Sadler | Ford | M&M's | 96/5 | 159 | Running | $104,350 |
| 25. | 12 | 41 | Casey Mears* | Dodge | Target | 88/0 | 159 | Running | $85,639 |
| 26. | 32 | 80 | Mike Bliss | Chevrolet | Advair | 85/0 | 159 | Running | $65,300 |
| 27. | 22 | 10 | Johnny Benson | Pontiac | Valvoline | 82/0 | 159 | Running | $95,000 |
| 28. | 38 | 2 | Rusty Wallace | Dodge | Miller Lite | 79/0 | 159 | Running | $102,592 |
| 29. | 34 | 1 | Jeff Green | Chevrolet | Pennzoil | 76/0 | 159 | Running | $92,969 |
| 30. | 28 | 22 | Ward Burton | Dodge | Caterpillar | 78/5 | 159 | Running | $100,991 |
| 31. | 35 | 0 | Jack Sprague* | Pontiac | NetZero HiSpeed | 70/0 | 159 | Running | $67,250 |
| 32. | 21 | 60 | David Green | Chevrolet | Haas Automation | 67/0 | 157 | Running | $64,125 |
| 33. | 43 | 4 | Stacy Compton | Pontiac | Kodak/Pirates of the Caribbean | 39/0 | 157 | Running | $67,400 |
| 34. | 26 | 14 | Larry Foyt* | Dodge | Harrah's | 61/0 | 155 | Running | $63,875 |
| 35. | 39 | 77 | Dave Blaney | Ford | Jasper Engines & Trans. | 58/0 | 154 | Running | $71,750 |
| 36. | 31 | 97 | Kurt Busch | Ford | Irwin/Lenox/Rubbermaid | 55/0 | 151 | Running | $83,600 |
| 37. | 8 | 42 | Jamie McMurray* | Dodge | Havoline/Terminator 3 | 52/0 | 143 | Running | $63,475 |
| 38. | 20 | 25 | Joe Nemechek | Chevrolet | UAW/Delphi | 49/0 | 113 | Running | $63,325 |
| 39. | 1 | 30 | Steve Park | Chevrolet | America Online | 46/0 | 112 | Running | $78,210 |
| 40. | 18 | 31 | Robby Gordon | Chevrolet | Cingular Wireless | 43/0 | 86 | Accident | $88,247 |
| 41. | 7 | 49 | Ken Schrader | Dodge | 1-800-CALLATT | 40/0 | 85 | Engine | $62,935 |
| 42. | 23 | 01 | Mike Wallace | Pontiac | U.S. Army | 37/0 | 84 | Running | $62,815 |
| 43. | 17 | 32 | Ricky Craven | Pontiac | Tide | 34/0 | 79 | Accident | $70,945 |

*Rookie. Time of race: 2 hours, 24 minutes, 29 seconds. Average speed: 166.109 mph. Margin of victory: 4.102 seconds. Caution flags: Two for 10 laps. 64-68 (Car 77—spin, back stretch); 75-79 (Cars 97, 31, 01, 32, 25, 42 and 30—accident, Turn 2). Lap leaders: 17 lead changes among 11 drivers. Kevin Harvick 1-37, Ward Burton 38, Harvick 39-54, Michael Waltrip 55-63, Jimmie Johnson 64, Kyle Petty 65, Elliott Sadler 66-69, Johnson 70, Dale Earnhardt Jr. 71-101, Harvick 102, Jeff Gordon 103, W. Burton 104-105, Matt Kenseth 106-115, Bobby Labonte 116-126, Earnhardt Jr. 127-138, Johnson 139, Greg Biffle 140-160. Pole winner: Steve Park, 184.752 mph. Dropped to rear: Rusty Walllace and Stacy Compton (engine changes). Failed to qualify: Kerry Earnhardt, Tony Raines, Shane Hmiel, Christian Fittipaldi. Estimated attendance: 155,000.

**Daytona International Speedway**
Daytona Beach, Fla.— 2.5-mile high-banked paved oval
July 5, 2003—400 miles—160 laps

## Points standings

| Rk. | Driver | Behind |
|---|---|---|
| 1. | Matt Kenseth | Leader |
| 2. | Dale Earnhardt Jr. | -180 |
| 3. | Jeff Gordon | -203 |
| 4. | Bobby Labonte | -255 |
| 5. | Michael Waltrip | -392 |
| 6. | Jimmie Johnson | -472 |
| 7. | Kurt Busch | -484 |
| 8. | Kevin Harvick | -502 |
| 9. | Rusty Wallace | -532 |
| 10. | Sterling Marlin | -553 |

# Tropicana 400 — race 18 of 36

| Fin. | St. | Car | Driver | Make | Sponsor | Pts./Bonus | Laps | Status | Winnings |
|---|---|---|---|---|---|---|---|---|---|
| 1. | 14 | 12 | Ryan Newman | Dodge | ALLTEL | 180/5 | 267 | Running | $191,000 |
| 2. | 1 | 20 | Tony Stewart | Chevrolet | Home Depot | 180/10 | 267 | Running | $213,468 |
| 3. | 6 | 48 | Jimmie Johnson | Chevrolet | Lowe's | 170/5 | 267 | Running | $134,575 |
| 4. | 2 | 24 | Jeff Gordon | Chevrolet | DuPont | 165/5 | 267 | Running | $158,178 |
| 5. | 12 | 15 | Michael Waltrip | Chevrolet | NAPA Auto Parts | 160/5 | 267 | Running | $100,975 |
| 6. | 27 | 99 | Jeff Burton | Ford | CITGO | 150/0 | 267 | Running | $114,092 |
| 7. | 35 | 31 | Robby Gordon | Chevrolet | Cingular Wireless | 146/0 | 267 | Running | $106,812 |
| 8. | 10 | 42 | Jamie McMurray* | Dodge | Havoline | 147/5 | 267 | Running | $77,375 |
| 9. | 8 | 38 | Elliott Sadler | Ford | M&M's | 138/0 | 267 | Running | $108,375 |
| 10. | 5 | 19 | Jeremy Mayfield | Dodge | Dodge Dealers/UAW | 134/0 | 267 | Running | $85,075 |
| 11. | 3 | 9 | Bill Elliott | Dodge | Dodge Dealers/UAW | 130/0 | 267 | Running | $106,908 |
| 12. | 24 | 17 | Matt Kenseth | Ford | DeWalt Power Tools | 127/0 | 266 | Running | $87,725 |
| 13. | 37 | 21 | Ricky Rudd | Ford | Motorcraft Quality Parts | 124/0 | 266 | Running | $94,475 |
| 14. | 13 | 6 | Mark Martin | Ford | Viagra | 121/0 | 266 | Running | $103,883 |
| 15. | 28 | 5 | Terry Labonte | Chevrolet | Kellogg's/got milk? | 118/0 | 266 | Running | $96,356 |
| 16. | 15 | 1 | Jeff Green | Chevrolet | Pennzoil Synthetic | 115/0 | 266 | Running | $89,937 |
| 17. | 11 | 29 | Kevin Harvick | Chevrolet | GM Goodwrench Service | 92/5 | 266 | Running | $104,028 |
| 18. | 36 | 10 | Johnny Benson | Pontiac | Valvoline | 109/0 | 265 | Running | $94,700 |
| 19. | 30 | 22 | Ward Burton | Dodge | Caterpillar | 106/0 | 265 | Running | $100,106 |
| 20. | 7 | 16 | Greg Biffle* | Ford | Grainger | 103/0 | 265 | Running | $69,650 |
| 21. | 19 | 40 | Sterling Marlin | Dodge | Coors Light | 100/0 | 265 | Running | $107,650 |
| 22. | 29 | 74 | Tony Raines* | Chevrolet | Staff America | 97/0 | 265 | Running | $63,450 |
| 23. | 21 | 7 | Jimmy Spencer | Dodge | Sirius Satellite Radio | 94/0 | 265 | Running | $82,550 |
| 24. | 38 | 23 | Kenny Wallace | Dodge | Stacker 2 | 91/0 | 265 | Running | $79,325 |
| 25. | 26 | 32 | Ricky Craven | Pontiac | Tide | 88/0 | 265 | Running | $84,925 |
| 26. | 23 | 30 | Steve Park | Chevrolet | America Online | 85/0 | 265 | Running | $73,725 |
| 27. | 41 | 45 | Kyle Petty | Dodge | Georgia Pacific | 82/0 | 264 | Running | $73,425 |
| 28. | 43 | 49 | Ken Schrader | Dodge | BAM Racing | 79/0 | 263 | Running | $73,614 |
| 29. | 42 | 43 | Christian Fittipaldi | Dodge | Cheerios | 76/0 | 263 | Running | $100,303 |
| 30. | 33 | 88 | Dale Jarrett | Ford | UPS | 73/0 | 263 | Running | $108,063 |
| 31. | 9 | 77 | Dave Blaney | Ford | Jasper Engines & Trans. | 70/0 | 262 | Running | $69,575 |
| 32. | 22 | 2 | Rusty Wallace | Dodge | Miller Lite | 67/0 | 249 | Running | $96,042 |
| 33. | 39 | 54 | Todd Bodine | Ford | National Guard | 64/0 | 237 | Trans. | $62,075 |
| 34. | 4 | 41 | Casey Mears* | Dodge | Fujifilm | 61/0 | 232 | Accident | $68,975 |
| 35. | 20 | 4 | Johnny Sauter | Pontiac | Kodak | 58/0 | 213 | Running | $60,775 |
| 36. | 18 | 18 | Bobby Labonte | Chevrolet | Interstate Batteries | 55/0 | 212 | Accident | $105,658 |
| 37. | 40 | 01 | Mike Wallace | Pontiac | USG | 52/0 | 211 | Accident | $60,375 |
| 38. | 16 | 8 | Dale Earnhardt Jr. | Chevrolet | Budweiser | 49/0 | 206 | Accident | $101,092 |
| 39. | 32 | 97 | Kurt Busch | Ford | Rubbermaid | 46/0 | 124 | Engine | $79,985 |
| 40. | 34 | 0 | Jack Sprague* | Pontiac | NetZero HiSpeed | 43/0 | 117 | Engine | $59,785 |
| 41. | 31 | 14 | Larry Foyt* | Dodge | Harrah's | 40/0 | 88 | Accident | $59,590 |
| 42. | 17 | 25 | Joe Nemechek | Chevrolet | UAW/Delphi | 37/0 | 45 | Engine | $59,395 |
| 43. | 25 | 37 | Derrike Cope | Chevrolet | Great Barrier Reef Online | 34/0 | 6 | Trans. | $59,457 |

*Rookie. Time of race: 2 hours, 59 minutes, 15 seconds. Average speed: 134.059 mph. Margin of victory: 2.633 seconds. Caution flags: Seven for 36 laps. 83-86 (debris on track); 92-95 (Car 14—accident, Turn 4); 107-113 (debris on track); 128-131 (oil on track); 209-212 (Car 8—accident, Turn 2); 215-222 (Cars 10, 18, 01, 30, 9, 31 and 41—accident, Turn 4); 235-239 (Car 41—accident, Turn 2). Lap leaders: 13 lead changes among seven drivers. Tony Stewart 1-60, Kevin Harvick 61-64, Michael Waltrip 65, Stewart 66-83, Harvick 84-104, Stewart 105-106, Harvick 107-127, Jeff Gordon 128-173, Jimmie Johnson 174-188, Jamie McMurray 189, Ryan Newman 190-198, Johnson 199-208, J. Gordon 209, Newman 210-267. Pole winner: Tony Stewart, 184.786 mph. Dropped to rear: Derrike Cope (backup car); Jimmie Johnson and Larry Foyt (engine changes). Failed to qualify: Jason Keller. Estimated attendance: 85,000.

## Points standings

| Rk. | Driver | Behind |
|---|---|---|
| 1. | Matt Kenseth | Leader |
| 2. | Jeff Gordon | -165 |
| 3. | Dale Earnhardt Jr. | -258 |
| 4. | Bobby Labonte | -327 |
| 5. | Michael Waltrip | -384 |
| 6. | Jimmie Johnson | -429 |
| 7. | Kevin Harvick | -512 |
| 8. | Tony Stewart | -549 |
| 9. | Kurt Busch | -565 |
| 10. | Sterling Marlin | -580 |

**Chicagoland Speedway**
Joliet, Ill.— 1.5-mile paved oval
July 13, 2003—400 miles—267 laps

# New England 300 — race 19 of 36

| Fin. | St. | Car | Driver | Make | Sponsor | Pts./Bonus | Laps | Status | Winnings |
|---|---|---|---|---|---|---|---|---|---|
| 1. | 6 | 48 | Jimmie Johnson | Chevrolet | Lowe's | 180/5 | 300 | Running | $200,225 |
| 2. | 7 | 29 | Kevin Harvick | Chevrolet | GM Goodwrench Service | 175/5 | 300 | Running | $165,033 |
| 3. | 1 | 17 | Matt Kenseth | Ford | DeWalt Power Tools | 170/5 | 300 | Running | $124,030 |
| 4. | 16 | 12 | Ryan Newman | Dodge | ALLTEL | 165/5 | 300 | Running | $114,425 |
| 5. | 15 | 31 | Robby Gordon | Chevrolet | Cingular Wireless | 155/0 | 300 | Running | $101,912 |
| 6. | 3 | 8 | Dale Earnhardt Jr. | Chevrolet | Budweiser | 155/0 | 300 | Running | $104,492 |
| 7. | 29 | 88 | Dale Jarrett | Ford | UPS | 146/0 | 300 | Running | $107,228 |
| 8. | 34 | 30 | Steve Park | Chevrolet | America Online | 142/0 | 300 | Running | $76,450 |
| 9. | 13 | 99 | Jeff Burton | Ford | CITGO/Bassmaster Classic | 143/5 | 300 | Running | $96,167 |
| 10. | 20 | 16 | Greg Biffle* | Ford | Grainger | 134/0 | 300 | Running | $66,350 |
| 11. | 9 | 97 | Kurt Busch | Ford | Rubbermaid | 130/0 | 300 | Running | $94,250 |
| 12. | 23 | 21 | Ricky Rudd | Ford | Motorcraft Quality Parts | 127/0 | 300 | Running | $83,550 |
| 13. | 27 | 77 | Dave Blaney | Ford | Jasper Engines & Trans. | 124/0 | 300 | Running | $81,750 |
| 14. | 4 | 18 | Bobby Labonte | Chevrolet | Interstate Batteries | 121/0 | 300 | Running | $100,533 |
| 15. | 31 | 7 | Jimmy Spencer | Dodge | Sirius Satellite Radio | 123/5 | 300 | Running | $70,475 |
| 16. | 35 | 41 | Casey Mears* | Dodge | Target | 115/0 | 300 | Running | $75,514 |
| 17. | 11 | 2 | Rusty Wallace | Dodge | Miller Lite | 112/0 | 300 | Running | $91,667 |
| 18. | 12 | 6 | Mark Martin | Ford | Viagra | 109/0 | 300 | Running | $90,133 |
| 19. | 32 | 54 | Todd Bodine | Ford | National Guard | 106/0 | 300 | Running | $57,200 |
| 20. | 14 | 5 | Terry Labonte | Chevrolet | Kellogg's/got milk? | 103/0 | 300 | Running | $84,056 |
| 21. | 17 | 32 | Ricky Craven | Pontiac | Tide | 100/0 | 300 | Running | $63,375 |
| 22. | 8 | 20 | Tony Stewart | Chevrolet | Home Depot | 97/0 | 300 | Running | $104,528 |
| 23. | 41 | 4 | Johnny Sauter | Pontiac | Kodak | 94/0 | 300 | Running | $55,750 |
| 24. | 2 | 24 | Jeff Gordon | Chevrolet | DuPont | 101/10 | 300 | Running | $103,928 |
| 25. | 21 | 22 | Ward Burton | Dodge | Caterpillar | 88/0 | 299 | Running | $87,806 |
| 26. | 26 | 10 | Johnny Benson | Pontiac | Valvoline | 85/0 | 299 | Running | $80,900 |
| 27. | 18 | 38 | Elliott Sadler | Ford | M&M's | 82/0 | 299 | Running | $88,175 |
| 28. | 5 | 15 | Michael Waltrip | Chevrolet | NAPA Auto Parts | 79/0 | 299 | Running | $68,750 |
| 29. | 24 | 25 | Joe Nemechek | Chevrolet | UAW/Delphi | 76/0 | 299 | Running | $52,965 |
| 30. | 30 | 1 | Jeff Green | Chevrolet | Pennzoil | 73/0 | 299 | Running | $75,912 |
| 31. | 19 | 9 | Bill Elliott | Dodge | Dodge Dealers/UAW | 70/0 | 299 | Running | $88,858 |
| 32. | 36 | 45 | Kyle Petty | Dodge | Georgia Pacific | 67/0 | 299 | Running | $57,825 |
| 33. | 40 | 74 | Tony Raines* | Chevrolet | Staff America | 64/0 | 297 | Running | $50,530 |
| 34. | 25 | 19 | Jeremy Mayfield | Dodge | Dodge Dealers/UAW | 61/0 | 296 | Running | $57,400 |
| 35. | 42 | 37 | Derrike Cope | Chevrolet | Friendly's | 58/0 | 295 | Running | $49,200 |
| 36. | 38 | 49 | Ken Schrader | Dodge | AT&T | 55/0 | 292 | Running | $49,010 |
| 37. | 37 | 43 | Christian Fittipaldi | Dodge | Cheerios | 52/0 | 268 | Running | $84,628 |
| 38. | 28 | 23 | Kenny Wallace | Dodge | Stacker 2 | 49/0 | 260 | Running | $48,700 |
| 39. | 10 | 40 | Sterling Marlin | Dodge | Coors Light | 46/0 | 196 | Accident | $92,635 |
| 40. | 22 | 42 | Jamie McMurray* | Dodge | Havoline | 48/5 | 195 | Accident | $48,550 |
| 41. | 39 | 0 | John Andretti | Pontiac | NetZero HiSpeed | 40/0 | 179 | Running | $48,450 |
| 42. | 33 | 01 | Mike Wallace | Pontiac | U.S. Army | 37/0 | 118 | Accident | $48,400 |
| 43. | 43 | 89 | Morgan Shepherd | Ford | Racing With Jesus/Red Line Oil | 34/0 | 43 | Brakes | $48,560 |

*Rookie. Time of race: 3 hours, 16 minutes, 29 seconds. Average speed: 96.924 mph. Margin of victory: 1.582 seconds. Caution flags: 12 for 63 laps. 10-15 (Cars 0, 4 and 49—accident, Turn 1); 22-27 (debris on back stretch); 62-65 (Car 40—accident, Turn 3); 101-107 (debris); 110-113 (Car 2—spin, back stretch); 118-121 (Car 01—spin, back stretch); 146-150 (Car 19—accident, Turn 1); 154-156 (Cars 23 and 99—accident, Turn 4); 166-169 (debris); 197-202 (Car 42—accident, front stretch); 204-211 (debris); 234-239 (Car 43—accident, front stretch). Lap leaders: 14 lead changes among nine drivers. Matt Kenseth 1, Jeff Gordon 2, Dale Earnhardt Jr. 3-4, J. Gordon 5-62, Jimmy Spencer 63, Kevin Harvick 64-79, Jimmie Johnson 80-100, J. Gordon 101-146, Jamie McMurray 147-159, Harvick 160-196, J. Gordon 197, Jeff Burton 198-207, J. Gordon 208-234, Ryan Newman 235-263, Johnson 264-300. Pole winner: Qualifying cancelled because of rain; starting grid based on car owner points. Dropped to rear: Johnny Sauter (engine change). Failed to qualify: Tim Sauter, David Reutimann, Carl Long, Larry Foyt. Estimated attendance: 101,000.

**New Hampshire International Speedway**
Loudon, N.H.— 1.058-mile flat paved oval
July 20, 2003—317.4 miles—300 laps

## Points standings

| Rk. | Driver | Behind |
|---|---|---|
| 1. | Matt Kenseth | Leader |
| 2. | Jeff Gordon | -234 |
| 3. | Dale Earnhardt Jr. | -273 |
| 4. | Bobby Labonte | -376 |
| 5. | Jimmie Johnson | -419 |
| 6. | Michael Waltrip | -475 |
| 7. | Kevin Harvick | -532 |
| 8. | Tony Stewart | -622 |
| 10. | Jeff Burton | -648 |

# Pennsylvania 500 — race 20 of 36

| Fin. | St. | Car | Driver | Make | Sponsor | Pts./Bonus | Laps | Status | Winnings |
|---|---|---|---|---|---|---|---|---|---|
| 1. | 1 | 12 | Ryan Newman | Dodge | ALLTEL | 185/10 | 200 | Running | $180,575 |
| 2. | 13 | 97 | Kurt Busch | Ford | Rubbermaid | 175/5 | 200 | Running | $152,695 |
| 3. | 18 | 8 | Dale Earnhardt Jr. | Chevrolet | Budweiser | 170/5 | 200 | Running | $131,037 |
| 4. | 17 | 15 | Michael Waltrip | Chevrolet | NAPA Auto Parts | 165/5 | 200 | Running | $94,355 |
| 5. | 6 | 5 | Terry Labonte | Chevrolet | Kellogg's/got milk? | 155/0 | 200 | Running | $100,581 |
| 6. | 19 | 99 | Jeff Burton | Ford | CITGO | 155/0 | 200 | Running | $97,107 |
| 7. | 26 | 25 | Joe Nemechek | Chevrolet | UAW/Delphi | 146/0 | 200 | Running | $65,190 |
| 8. | 23 | 54 | Todd Bodine | Ford | National Guard | 142/0 | 200 | Running | $76,390 |
| 9. | 22 | 77 | Dave Blaney | Ford | Jasper Engines & Trans. | 138/0 | 200 | Running | $79,390 |
| 10. | 20 | 40 | Sterling Marlin | Dodge | Coors Light | 134/0 | 200 | Running | $97,790 |
| 11. | 7 | 2 | Rusty Wallace | Dodge | Miller Lite | 135/5 | 200 | Running | $88,107 |
| 12. | 31 | 29 | Kevin Harvick | Chevrolet | GM Goodwrench Service | 127/0 | 200 | Running | $88,428 |
| 13. | 9 | 17 | Matt Kenseth | Ford | DeWalt Power Tools | 129/5 | 200 | Running | $68,590 |
| 14. | 3 | 38 | Elliott Sadler | Ford | M&M's | 121/0 | 200 | Running | $85,240 |
| 15. | 2 | 48 | Jimmie Johnson | Chevrolet | Lowe's | 118/0 | 200 | Running | $67,840 |
| 16. | 30 | 74 | Tony Raines* | Chevrolet | Staff America | 115/0 | 200 | Running | $47,490 |
| 17. | 11 | 9 | Bill Elliott | Dodge | Dodge Dealers/UAW | 112/0 | 200 | Running | $85,123 |
| 18. | 37 | 31 | Robby Gordon | Chevrolet | Cingular Wireless | 109/0 | 200 | Running | $74,977 |
| 19. | 38 | 22 | Ward Burton | Dodge | Caterpillar | 106/0 | 200 | Running | $81,896 |
| 20. | 29 | 10 | Johnny Benson | Pontiac | Valvoline | 108/5 | 200 | Running | $78,265 |
| 21. | 8 | 88 | Dale Jarrett | Ford | UPS | 100/0 | 200 | Running | $91,168 |
| 22. | 21 | 7 | Jimmy Spencer | Dodge | Sirius Satellite Radio | 102/5 | 200 | Running | $61,690 |
| 23. | 40 | 01 | Mike Wallace | Pontiac | U.S. Army | 94/0 | 199 | Running | $59,765 |
| 24. | 36 | 43 | Christian Fittipaldi | Dodge | Cheerios | 91/0 | 199 | Running | $83,893 |
| 25. | 16 | 30 | Steve Park | Chevrolet | America Online | 88/0 | 198 | Running | $56,240 |
| 26. | 34 | 49 | Ken Schrader | Dodge | AT&T | 85/0 | 198 | Running | $47,590 |
| 27. | 24 | 16 | Greg Biffle* | Ford | Grainger | 82/0 | 197 | Running | $47,340 |
| 28. | 12 | 42 | Jamie McMurray* | Dodge | Havoline | 79/0 | 195 | Running | $47,190 |
| 29. | 43 | 50 | Larry Foyt* | Dodge | Harrah's | 76/0 | 188 | Running | $44,015 |
| 30. | 4 | 18 | Bobby Labonte | Chevrolet | Interstate Batteries | 73/0 | 180 | Engine | $89,448 |
| 31. | 39 | 1 | Jeff Green | Chevrolet | Pennzoil | 70/0 | 180 | Running | $71,402 |
| 32. | 28 | 23 | Kenny Wallace | Dodge | Stacker 2 | 67/0 | 178 | Running | $51,954 |
| 33. | 5 | 0 | John Andretti | Pontiac | NetZero HiSpeed | 64/0 | 176 | Running | $44,265 |
| 34. | 35 | 45 | Kyle Petty | Dodge | Georgia Pacific | 61/0 | 170 | Running | $51,165 |
| 35. | 10 | 41 | Casey Mears* | Dodge | Target | 63/5 | 164 | Accident | $50,990 |
| 36. | 25 | 24 | Jeff Gordon | Chevrolet | DuPont | 55/0 | 155 | Accident | $90,168 |
| 37. | 33 | 20 | Tony Stewart | Chevrolet | Home Depot | 57/5 | 153 | Engine | $105,203 |
| 38. | 15 | 19 | Jeremy Mayfield | Dodge | Dodge Dealers/UAW | 49/0 | 123 | Accident | $50,500 |
| 39. | 27 | 21 | Ricky Rudd | Ford | Motorcraft Quality Parts | 46/0 | 121 | Engine | $50,385 |
| 40. | 32 | 32 | Ricky Craven | Pontiac | Tide | 43/0 | 115 | Engine | $50,230 |
| 41. | 14 | 6 | Mark Martin | Ford | Viagra | 40/0 | 74 | Accident | $75,923 |
| 42. | 41 | 37 | Derrike Cope | Chevrolet | Friendly's | 37/0 | 66 | Fuel pump | $42,000 |
| 43. | 42 | 89 | Morgan Shepherd | Ford | Racing With Jesus/Red Line Oil | 34/0 | 44 | Handling | $42,186 |

*Rookie. Time of race: 3 hours, 54 minutes, 55 seconds. Average speed: 127.705 mph. Margin of victory: .307 seconds. Caution flags: Eight for 36 laps. 50-53 (oil on Track); 69-72 (Car 19—accident, Long Pond straight); 75-77 (Car 6—accident, Tunnel Turn); 119-123 (Car 32—stalled, Turn 3); 125-129 (Car 24—accident, Turn 3); 154-158 (oil on track); 167-170 (Car 41—accident, Turn 1); 183-188 (Car 18—spin, Turn 2). Lap leaders: 18 lead changes among 11 drivers. Ryan Newman 1-31, Rusty Wallace 32-34, Matt Kenseth 35-36, Michael Waltrip 37, Newman 38-50, Johnny Benson 51, R. Wallace 52-69, Jimmy Spencer 70, Casey Mears 71-78, R. Wallace 79-80, Jeff Burton 81-97, Tony Stewart 98-108, Kurt Busch 109, Waltrip 110-116, Stewart 117-119, Waltrip 120-129, Dale Earnhardt Jr. 130-154, Spencer 155-156, Newman 157-200. Pole winner: Ryan Newman, 170.358 mph. Dropped to rear: Kyle Petty and Jeff Green (engine changes). Failed to qualify: None. Estimated attendance: 100,000.

**Pocono Raceway**
Pocono, Pa. — 2.5-mile banked paved oval
July 27, 2003—500 miles—200 laps

## Points standings

| Rk. | Driver | Behind |
|---|---|---|
| 1. | Matt Kenseth | Leader |
| 2. | Dale Earnhardt Jr. | -232 |
| 3. | Jeff Gordon | -308 |
| 4. | Jimmie Johnson | -430 |
| 5. | Bobby Labonte | -432 |
| 6. | Michael Waltrip | -439 |
| 7. | Kevin Harvick | -534 |
| 8. | Kurt Busch | -559 |
| 9. | Ryan Newman | -614 |
| 10. | Jeff Burton | -622 |

2003 SEASON

# Brickyard 400 — race 21 of 36

| Fin. | St. | Car | Driver | Make | Sponsor | Pts./Bonus | Laps | Status | Winnings |
|---|---|---|---|---|---|---|---|---|---|
| 1. | 1 | 29 | Kevin Harvick | Chevrolet | GM Goodwrench Service | 180/5 | 160 | Running | $418,253 |
| 2. | 17 | 17 | Matt Kenseth | Ford | Smirnoff Ice/DeWalt | 175/5 | 160 | Running | $314,425 |
| 3. | 22 | 42 | Jamie McMurray* | Dodge | Havoline | 170/5 | 160 | Running | $258,275 |
| 4. | 19 | 24 | Jeff Gordon | Chevrolet | DuPont | 165/5 | 160 | Running | $260,853 |
| 5. | 3 | 9 | Bill Elliott | Dodge | Dodge Dealers/UAW | 160/5 | 160 | Running | $235,542 |
| 6. | 13 | 31 | Robby Gordon | Chevrolet | Cingular Wireless | 155/5 | 160 | Running | $189,112 |
| 7. | 6 | 97 | Kurt Busch | Ford | Rubbermaid | 151/5 | 160 | Running | $189,675 |
| 8. | 32 | 7 | Jimmy Spencer | Dodge | Sirius Satellite Radio | 142/0 | 160 | Running | $165,500 |
| 9. | 25 | 6 | Mark Martin | Ford | Viagra | 143/5 | 160 | Running | $180,433 |
| 10. | 14 | 2 | Rusty Wallace | Dodge | Miller Lite | 134/0 | 160 | Running | $175,967 |
| 11. | 2 | 12 | Ryan Newman | Dodge | ALLTEL | 135/0 | 160 | Running | $172,750 |
| 12. | 15 | 20 | Tony Stewart | Chevrolet | Home Depot | 137/10 | 160 | Running | $224,728 |
| 13. | 40 | 10 | Johnny Benson | Pontiac | Valvoline | 124/0 | 160 | Running | $157,500 |
| 14. | 36 | 8 | Dale Earnhardt Jr. | Chevrolet | Budweiser | 121/0 | 160 | Running | $161,967 |
| 15. | 23 | 30 | Steve Park | Chevrolet | America Online | 118/0 | 160 | Running | $131,750 |
| 16. | 5 | 15 | Michael Waltrip | Chevrolet | NAPA Auto Parts | 115/0 | 160 | Running | $137,450 |
| 17. | 35 | 32 | Ricky Craven | Pontiac | Tide | 112/0 | 160 | Running | $141,525 |
| 18. | 9 | 48 | Jimmie Johnson | Chevrolet | Lowe's | 109/0 | 160 | Running | $135,225 |
| 19. | 38 | 5 | Terry Labonte | Chevrolet | Kellogg's/got milk? | 106/0 | 160 | Running | $144,481 |
| 20. | 30 | 1 | Jeff Green | Chevrolet | Pennzoil | 108/5 | 160 | Running | $141,212 |
| 21. | 18 | 16 | Greg Biffle* | Ford | Grainger | 100/0 | 160 | Running | $121,825 |
| 22. | 8 | 18 | Bobby Labonte | Chevrolet | Interstate Batteries | 97/0 | 159 | Running | $156,913 |
| 23. | 31 | 54 | Todd Bodine | Ford | National Guard | 94/0 | 159 | Running | $125,605 |
| 24. | 29 | 23 | Kenny Wallace | Dodge | Stacker 2 | 91/0 | 159 | Running | $121,494 |
| 25. | 33 | 74 | Tony Raines* | Chevrolet | Aaron's | 88/0 | 159 | Running | $109,205 |
| 26. | 4 | 22 | Ward Burton | Dodge | Caterpillar | 85/0 | 159 | Running | $145,081 |
| 27. | 37 | 99 | Jeff Burton | Ford | CITGO | 82/0 | 159 | Running | $143,392 |
| 28. | 20 | 77 | Dave Blaney | Ford | Jasper Engines & Trans. | 79/0 | 159 | Running | $116,875 |
| 29. | 28 | 41 | Casey Mears* | Dodge | Target | 76/0 | 159 | Running | $116,275 |
| 30. | 21 | 57 | Kevin Lepage | Ford | CLR | 73/0 | 158 | Running | $105,280 |
| 31. | 27 | 91 | Casey Atwood | Dodge | Evernham Motorsports | 70/0 | 158 | Running | $107,608 |
| 32. | 42 | 14 | Larry Foyt* | Dodge | Harrah's | 67/0 | 156 | Running | $103,780 |
| 33. | 26 | 0 | Jason Leffler | Pontiac | NetZero HiSpeed | 64/0 | 154 | Running | $107,425 |
| 34. | 12 | 40 | Sterling Marlin | Dodge | Coors Light | 61/0 | 154 | Running | $147,230 |
| 35. | 24 | 01 | Mike Skinner | Pontiac | U.S. Army | 63/5 | 146 | Accident | $105,875 |
| 36. | 43 | 37 | Derrike Cope | Chevrolet | Friendly's | 55/0 | 146 | Running | $102,875 |
| 37. | 7 | 25 | Joe Nemechek | Chevrolet | UAW/Delphi | 52/0 | 145 | Accident | $102,790 |
| 38. | 39 | 21 | Ricky Rudd | Ford | Motorcraft Quality Parts | 49/0 | 143 | Accident | $110,660 |
| 39. | 34 | 88 | Dale Jarrett | Ford | UPS | 46/0 | 143 | Running | $148,333 |
| 40. | 41 | 45 | Kyle Petty | Dodge | Georgia Pacific | 43/0 | 141 | Running | $110,475 |
| 41. | 10 | 19 | Jeremy Mayfield | Dodge | Dodge Dealers/UAW | 40/0 | 122 | Running | $113,703 |
| 42. | 16 | 38 | Elliott Sadler | Ford | Pedigree | 37/0 | 108 | Engine | $136,515 |
| 43. | 11 | 81 | John Andretti | Chevrolet | Kraft Foods 100th Anniversary | 34/0 | 46 | Accident | $102,400 |

*Rookie. Time of race: 2 hours, 58 minutes, 22 seconds. Average speed: 134.554 mph. Margin of victory: 2.758 seconds. Caution flags: Five for 25 laps. 38-44 (Car 88—accident, pit road); 47-50 (Car 81—accident, Turn 2); 106-109 (oil on track); 140-144 (debris on back stretch); 146-150 (Cars 5, 40, 01, 25, 21 and 48—accident, back stretch). Lap leaders: 17 lead changes among 12 drivers. Kevin Harvick 1-17, Bill Elliott 18-25, Tony Stewart 26-34, Ryan Newman 35, Jeff Gordon 36-38, Kurt Busch 39-40, Newman 41-50, Stewart 51-81, Matt Kenseth 82, Jeff Green 83, Mark Martin 84-86, Stewart 87-106, Mike Skinner 107, Robby Gordon 108-113, Jamie McMurray 114-132, Kenseth 133-141, McMurray 142-144, Harvick 145-160. Pole winner: Kevin Harvick, 184.343 mph. Dropped to rear: John Andretti and Jason Leffler (engine changes); Larry Foyt (backup car). Failed to qualify: Brett Bodine, Ken Schrader, Billy Bigley Jr., Ted Musgrave, Robert Pressley, Jim Sauter, Christian Fittapaldi, David Reutimann, Hermie Sadler. Estimated attendance: 300,000.

**Indianapolis Motor Speedway**
Indianapolis — 2.5-mile semi-banked paved oval
August 3, 2003—400 miles—160 laps

## Points standings

| Rk. | Driver | Behind |
|---|---|---|
| 1. | Matt Kenseth | Leader |
| 2. | Dale Earnhardt Jr. | -286 |
| 3. | Jeff Gordon | -318 |
| 4. | Jimmie Johnson | -496 |
| 5. | Michael Waltrip | -499 |
| 6. | Bobby Labonte | -510 |
| 7. | Kevin Harvick | -529 |
| 8. | Kurt Busch | -583 |
| 9. | Ryan Newman | -654 |
| 10. | Rusty Wallace | -685 |

## Sirius at the Glen — race 22 of 36

**2003 SEASON**

| Fin. | St. | Car | Driver | Make | Sponsor | Pts./Bonus | Laps | Status | Winnings |
|---|---|---|---|---|---|---|---|---|---|
| 1. | 14 | 31 | Robby Gordon | Chevrolet | Cingular Wireless | 185/10 | 90 | Running | $156,272 |
| 2. | 28 | 39 | Scott Pruett | Dodge | Target | 175/5 | 90 | Running | $88,210 |
| 3. | 6 | 8 | Dale Earnhardt Jr. | Chevrolet | Budweiser | 170/5 | 90 | Running | $127,202 |
| 4. | 20 | 48 | Jimmie Johnson | Chevrolet | Lowe's | 160/0 | 90 | Running | $86,850 |
| 5. | 11 | 29 | Kevin Harvick | Chevrolet | GM Goodwrench Service | 155/0 | 90 | Running | $96,408 |
| 6. | 22 | 22 | Ward Burton | Dodge | Caterpillar | 150/0 | 90 | Running | $94,046 |
| 7. | 30 | 88 | Dale Jarrett | Ford | UPS | 146/0 | 90 | Running | $98,688 |
| 8. | 7 | 17 | Matt Kenseth | Ford | DeWalt Power Tools | 142/0 | 90 | Running | $70,535 |
| 9. | 13 | 12 | Ryan Newman | Dodge | ALLTEL | 138/0 | 90 | Running | $83,930 |
| 10. | 3 | 6 | Mark Martin | Ford | Viagra | 134/0 | 90 | Running | $90,598 |
| 11. | 4 | 20 | Tony Stewart | Chevrolet | Home Depot | 130/0 | 90 | Running | $101,233 |
| 12. | 8 | 97 | Kurt Busch | Ford | Rubbermaid | 127/0 | 90 | Running | $85,100 |
| 13. | 34 | 15 | Michael Waltrip | Chevrolet | NAPA Auto Parts | 124/0 | 90 | Running | $65,800 |
| 14. | 9 | 18 | Bobby Labonte | Chevrolet | Interstate Batteries | 126/5 | 90 | Running | $93,443 |
| 15. | 24 | 38 | Elliott Sadler | Ford | M&M's | 118/0 | 90 | Running | $86,820 |
| 16. | 40 | 19 | Jeremy Mayfield | Dodge | Dodge Dealers/UAW | 115/0 | 90 | Running | $59,600 |
| 17. | 21 | 25 | Joe Nemechek | Chevrolet | UAW/Delphi | 112/0 | 90 | Running | $50,830 |
| 18. | 19 | 5 | Terry Labonte | Chevrolet | Kellogg's/got milk? | 109/0 | 90 | Running | $76,566 |
| 19. | 15 | 0 | John Andretti | Pontiac | NetZero HiSpeed | 106/0 | 90 | Running | $50,055 |
| 20. | 25 | 9 | Bill Elliott | Dodge | Dodge Dealers/UAW | 103/0 | 90 | Running | $86,693 |
| 21. | 26 | 21 | Ricky Rudd | Ford | Motorcraft Quality Parts | 105/5 | 90 | Running | $72,535 |
| 22. | 29 | 42 | Jamie McMurray* | Dodge | Havoline | 102/5 | 90 | Running | $50,715 |
| 23. | 39 | 7 | Jimmy Spencer | Dodge | Sirius Satellite Radio | 94/0 | 90 | Running | $62,795 |
| 24. | 33 | 4 | P.J. Jones | Pontiac | Kodak | 91/0 | 90 | Running | $59,135 |
| 25. | 16 | 77 | Dave Blaney | Ford | Jasper Engines & Trans. | 88/0 | 90 | Running | $65,189 |
| 26. | 41 | 30 | Steve Park | Chevrolet | America Online | 85/0 | 90 | Running | $56,140 |
| 27. | 27 | 10 | Johnny Benson | Pontiac | Valvoline | 82/0 | 90 | Running | $74,565 |
| 28. | 38 | 32 | Ricky Craven | Pontiac | Tide | 79/0 | 90 | Running | $55,555 |
| 29. | 43 | 33 | Paul Menard | Chevrolet | Turtle Wax | 76/0 | 90 | Running | $52,410 |
| 30. | 2 | 16 | Greg Biffle* | Ford | Grainger | 78/5 | 90 | Running | $47,825 |
| 31. | 23 | 99 | Jeff Burton | Ford | CITGO | 75/5 | 90 | Running | $80,157 |
| 32. | 12 | 41 | Casey Mears* | Dodge | Target | 67/0 | 90 | Running | $52,150 |
| 33. | 1 | 24 | Jeff Gordon | Chevrolet | DuPont | 64/0 | 89 | Accident | $97,353 |
| 34. | 35 | 23 | Kenny Wallace | Dodge | Stacker 2 | 61/0 | 89 | Accident | $44,015 |
| 35. | 17 | 54 | Todd Bodine | Ford | National Guard | 58/0 | 89 | Running | $43,950 |
| 36. | 32 | 04 | Johnny Miller | Pontiac | Kodak | 55/0 | 89 | Running | $43,875 |
| 37. | 5 | 2 | Rusty Wallace | Dodge | Miller Lite | 52/0 | 84 | Running | $78,492 |
| 38. | 18 | 1 | Ron Fellows | Chevrolet | Pennzoil | 49/0 | 82 | Handling | $68,927 |
| 39. | 10 | 01 | Boris Said | Pontiac | USG | 46/0 | 80 | Running | $43,690 |
| 40. | 36 | 44 | Christian Fittipaldi | Dodge | New York Yankees | 43/0 | 80 | Running | $43,615 |
| 41. | 42 | 74 | Tony Raines* | Chevrolet | Staff America | 40/0 | 78 | Running | $43,555 |
| 42. | 31 | 45 | Kyle Petty | Dodge | Georgia Pacific | 37/0 | 74 | Running | $51,485 |
| 43. | 37 | 40 | Sterling Marlin | Dodge | Coors Light | 34/0 | 1 | Engine | $86,809 |

*Rookie. Time of race: 2 hours, 26 minutes, 17 seconds. Average speed: 90.411 mph. Margin of victory: 2.335 seconds. Caution flags: 6 for 14 laps. 2-4 (Car 45—accident, Turn 8); 23-24 (fire on pit road); 35-36 (Car 44—accident, Turn 11; Car 30—spin); 44-45 (Car 74—accident, back stretch); 53-55 (Car 2—spin, Turn 6); 77-78 (Car 54—spin, Turn 1). Lap leaders: Eight lead changes among eight drivers. Greg Biffle 1-23, Scott Pruett 24-32, Jeff Burton 33-42, Dale Earnhardt Jr. 43-53, Bobby Labonte 54-58, Ricky Rudd 59, Jamie McMurray 60, Robby Gordon 61-90. Pole winner: Jeff Gordon, 124.580 mph, track record. Dropped to rear: Jimmy Spencer, Tony Stewart, Boris Said, Jimmie Johnson and Christian Fittapaldi (engine changes). Failed to qualify: Ken Schrader, Joe Varde, Scott Maxwell, Larry Foyt. Estimated attendance: 100,000.

### Points standings

| Rk. | Driver | Behind |
|---|---|---|
| 1. | Matt Kenseth | Leader |
| 2. | Dale Earnhardt Jr. | -258 |
| 3. | Jeff Gordon | -396 |
| 4. | Jimmie Johnson | -478 |
| 5. | Kevin Harvick | -516 |
| 6. | Michael Waltrip | -517 |
| 7. | Bobby Labonte | -526 |
| 8. | Kurt Busch | -598 |
| 9. | Ryan Newman | -658 |
| 10. | Robby Gordon | -667 |

**Watkins Glen International**
Watkins Glen, N.Y.— 2.45-mile paved road course
August 10, 2003—220.5 miles—90 laps

# GFS Marketplace 400 — race 23 of 36

| Fin. | St. | Car | Driver | Make | Sponsor | Pts./Bonus | Laps | Status | Winnings |
|---|---|---|---|---|---|---|---|---|---|
| 1. | 2 | 12 | Ryan Newman | Dodge | ALLTEL | 180/5 | 200 | Running | $155,505 |
| 2. | 11 | 29 | Kevin Harvick | Chevrolet | GM Goodwrench Service | 175/5 | 200 | Running | $147,758 |
| 3. | 23 | 20 | Tony Stewart | Chevrolet | Home Depot | 165/0 | 200 | Running | $140,063 |
| 4. | 12 | 16 | Greg Biffle* | Ford | Grainger | 165/5 | 200 | Running | $85,670 |
| 5. | 18 | 30 | Steve Park | Chevrolet | America Online | 155/0 | 200 | Running | $76,980 |
| 6. | 3 | 31 | Robby Gordon | Chevrolet | Cingular Wireless | 150/0 | 200 | Running | $89,402 |
| 7. | 13 | 15 | Michael Waltrip | Chevrolet | NAPA Auto Parts | 146/0 | 200 | Running | $77,915 |
| 8. | 30 | 49 | Ken Schrader | Dodge | SEM Products | 142/0 | 200 | Running | $79,790 |
| 9. | 33 | 17 | Matt Kenseth | Ford | DeWalt Power Tools | 138/0 | 200 | Running | $76,540 |
| 10. | 35 | 10 | Johnny Benson | Pontiac | Valvoline | 134/0 | 200 | Running | $94,690 |
| 11. | 8 | 99 | Jeff Burton | Ford | CITGO | 130/0 | 200 | Running | $92,422 |
| 12. | 17 | 38 | Elliott Sadler | Ford | M&M's | 127/0 | 200 | Running | $92,515 |
| 13. | 5 | 5 | Terry Labonte | Chevrolet | Kellogg's/got milk? | 124/0 | 200 | Running | $84,421 |
| 14. | 22 | 22 | Ward Burton | Dodge | Caterpillar | 121/0 | 200 | Running | $90,521 |
| 15. | 32 | 9 | Bill Elliott | Dodge | Dodge Dealers/UAW | 118/0 | 200 | Running | $92,598 |
| 16. | 36 | 45 | Kyle Petty | Dodge | Georgia Pacific | 115/0 | 200 | Running | $64,540 |
| 17. | 37 | 6 | Mark Martin | Ford | Viagra | 112/0 | 200 | Running | $89,323 |
| 18. | 20 | 97 | Kurt Busch | Ford | Rubbermaid | 114/5 | 200 | Running | $96,690 |
| 19. | 38 | 40 | Sterling Marlin | Dodge | Coors Light | 106/0 | 200 | Running | $95,390 |
| 20. | 25 | 25 | Joe Nemechek | Chevrolet | UAW/Delphi | 103/0 | 200 | Running | $56,790 |
| 21. | 34 | 1 | Jeff Green | Chevrolet | Pennzoil | 100/0 | 200 | Running | $76,027 |
| 22. | 42 | 01 | Mike Skinner | Pontiac | U.S. Army | 97/0 | 200 | Running | $66,940 |
| 23. | 29 | 88 | Dale Jarrett | Ford | UPS | 99/5 | 200 | Running | $97,093 |
| 24. | 24 | 74 | Tony Raines* | Chevrolet | GFS Marketplace | 91/0 | 200 | Running | $50,215 |
| 25. | 9 | 77 | Dave Blaney | Ford | Jasper Engines & Trans. | 88/0 | 200 | Running | $72,065 |
| 26. | 10 | 7 | Jimmy Spencer | Dodge | Sirius Satellite Radio | 90/5 | 200 | Running | $61,154 |
| 27. | 15 | 48 | Jimmie Johnson | Chevrolet | Lowe's | 92/10 | 199 | Running | $73,875 |
| 28. | 40 | 19 | Jeremy Mayfield | Dodge | Dodge Dealers/UAW | 79/0 | 199 | Running | $60,325 |
| 29. | 27 | 21 | Ricky Rudd | Ford | Motorcraft Quality Parts | 76/0 | 199 | Running | $60,140 |
| 30. | 21 | 24 | Jeff Gordon | Chevrolet | DuPont | 73/0 | 198 | Running | $96,943 |
| 31. | 4 | 57 | Kevin Lepage | Ford | CLR | 70/0 | 197 | Running | $49,065 |
| 32. | 19 | 8 | Dale Earnhardt Jr. | Chevrolet | Budweiser | 67/0 | 192 | Accident | $89,782 |
| 33. | 7 | 43 | Christian Fittipaldi | Dodge | Cheerios | 64/0 | 176 | Engine | $87,068 |
| 34. | 43 | 37 | Derrike Cope | Chevrolet | Friendly's | 61/0 | 173 | Engine | $49,585 |
| 35. | 6 | 0 | Jason Leffler | Pontiac | NetZero HiSpeed | 58/0 | 166 | Running | $48,540 |
| 36. | 26 | 42 | Jamie McMurray* | Dodge | Havoline | 55/0 | 141 | Accident | $48,490 |
| 37. | 1 | 18 | Bobby Labonte | Chevrolet | Interstate Batteries | 57/5 | 140 | Engine | $99,023 |
| 38. | 31 | 2 | Rusty Wallace | Dodge | Miller Lite | 49/0 | 105 | Engine | $82,997 |
| 39. | 14 | 50 | Larry Foyt* | Dodge | Harrah's | 46/0 | 81 | Trans. | $48,295 |
| 40. | 39 | 32 | Ricky Craven | Pontiac | Tide | 43/0 | 76 | Accident | $56,235 |
| 41. | 16 | 41 | Casey Mears* | Dodge | Target | 40/0 | 76 | Accident | $56,200 |
| 42. | 28 | 23 | Kenny Wallace | Dodge | Stacker 2 | 37/0 | 62 | Accident | $48,160 |
| 43. | 41 | 54 | Todd Bodine | Ford | National Guard | 34/0 | 62 | Accident | $47,484 |

*Rookie. Time of race: 3 hours, 8 minutes, 31 seconds. Average speed: 127.310 mph. Margin of victory: 1.652 seconds. Caution flags: Eight for 46 laps. 17-19 (Car 42—accident, Turn 3); 55-58 (debris on track); 64-71 (Cars 54 and 23—accident, back stretch); 78-82 (Cars 32 and 41—accident, Turn 2); 90-95 (debris on track); 106-113 (Car 2—stalled, front stretch); 135-138 (debris on track); 142-149 (oil on track). Lap leaders: 14 lead changes among eight drivers. Ryan Newman 1-17, B. Labonte 18-20, Jimmie Johnson 21-43, Kevin Harvick 44-77, Newman 78-89, Johnson 90-108, Greg Biffle 109-127, Johnson 128-135, Harvick 136-147, Jimmy Spencer 148-149, Kurt Busch 150-151, Dale Jarrett 152-156, Busch 157-197, Newman 198-200. Pole winner: Bobby Labonte, 190.240 mph. Dropped to rear: Sterling Marlin (engine change), Jeremy Mayfield (backup car). Failed to qualify: Stacy Compton. Estimated attendance: 150,000.

**Michigan International Speedway**
Brooklyn, Mich.— 2-mile banked paved oval
August 17, 2003—400 miles—200 laps

## Points standings

| Rk. | Driver | Behind |
|---|---|---|
| 1. | Matt Kenseth | Leader |
| 2. | Dale Earnhardt Jr. | -329 |
| 3. | Jeff Gordon | -461 |
| 4. | Kevin Harvick | -479 |
| 5. | Michael Waltrip | -509 |
| 6. | Jimmie Johnson | -524 |
| 7. | Bobby Labonte | -607 |
| 8. | Ryan Newman | -616 |
| 9. | Kurt Busch | -622 |
| 10. | Robby Gordon | -655 |

2003 SEASON

# Sharpie 500 — race 24 of 36

## 2003 SEASON

| Fin. | St. | Car | Driver | Make | Sponsor | Pts./Bonus | Laps | Status | Winnings |
|---|---|---|---|---|---|---|---|---|---|
| 1. | 5 | 97 | Kurt Busch | Ford | Rubbermaid | 180/5 | 500 | Running | $237,565 |
| 2. | 23 | 29 | Kevin Harvick | Chevrolet | GM Goodwrench Service | 175/5 | 500 | Running | $174,223 |
| 3. | 31 | 42 | Jamie McMurray* | Dodge | Havoline | 165/0 | 500 | Running | $127,390 |
| 4. | 10 | 17 | Matt Kenseth | Ford | DeWalt Power Tools | 160/0 | 500 | Running | $122,905 |
| 5. | 16 | 48 | Jimmie Johnson | Chevrolet | Lowe's | 155/0 | 500 | Running | $100,775 |
| 6. | 6 | 12 | Ryan Newman | Dodge | ALLTEL | 155/5 | 500 | Running | $111,940 |
| 7. | 27 | 88 | Dale Jarrett | Ford | UPS | 146/0 | 500 | Running | $122,418 |
| 8. | 14 | 32 | Ricky Craven | Pontiac | Tide | 142/0 | 500 | Running | $102,740 |
| 9. | 9 | 8 | Dale Earnhardt Jr. | Chevrolet | Budweiser | 138/0 | 500 | Running | $116,107 |
| 10. | 29 | 19 | Jeremy Mayfield | Dodge | Dodge Dealers/UAW | 134/0 | 500 | Running | $88,740 |
| 11. | 13 | 5 | Terry Labonte | Chevrolet | Kellogg's/got milk? | 130/0 | 500 | Running | $102,346 |
| 12. | 26 | 49 | Ken Schrader | Dodge | SEM Products | 127/0 | 500 | Running | $74,090 |
| 13. | 24 | 22 | Ward Burton | Dodge | Caterpillar | 124/0 | 500 | Running | $105,996 |
| 14. | 32 | 10 | Johnny Benson | Pontiac | Valvoline | 121/0 | 500 | Running | $98,415 |
| 15. | 11 | 23 | Kenny Wallace | Dodge | Stacker 2 | 118/0 | 500 | Running | $85,735 |
| 16. | 25 | 9 | Bill Elliott | Dodge | Dodge Dealers/UAW | 115/0 | 500 | Running | $106,018 |
| 17. | 36 | 40 | Sterling Marlin | Dodge | Coors Light | 117/5 | 500 | Running | $121,035 |
| 18. | 4 | 01 | Mike Skinner | Pontiac | U.S. Army | 114/5 | 500 | Running | $81,175 |
| 19. | 38 | 25 | Joe Nemechek | Chevrolet | UAW/Delphi | 106/0 | 500 | Running | $70,325 |
| 20. | 12 | 74 | Tony Raines* | Chevrolet | BACE Motorsports | 103/0 | 500 | Running | $68,885 |
| 21. | 41 | 41 | Casey Mears* | Dodge | Target | 100/0 | 500 | Running | $86,249 |
| 22. | 34 | 16 | Greg Biffle* | Ford | Grainger | 97/0 | 500 | Running | $69,610 |
| 23. | 18 | 20 | Tony Stewart | Chevrolet | Home Depot | 94/0 | 494 | Running | $119,138 |
| 24. | 28 | 27 | Scott Wimmer | Chevrolet | YJ Stinger | 91/0 | 494 | Running | $65,085 |
| 25. | 21 | 4 | Johnny Sauter | Pontiac | Kodak | 88/0 | 459 | Running | $67,990 |
| 26. | 30 | 0 | Jason Leffler | Pontiac | NetZero HiSpeed | 85/0 | 458 | Running | $66,815 |
| 27. | 19 | 18 | Bobby Labonte | Chevrolet | Interstate Batteries | 82/0 | 448 | Running | $107,688 |
| 28. | 1 | 24 | Jeff Gordon | Chevrolet | DuPont | 89/10 | 444 | Accident | $118,973 |
| 29. | 35 | 30 | Steve Park | Chevrolet | America Online | 76/0 | 440 | Running | $72,185 |
| 30. | 15 | 77 | Dave Blaney | Ford | First Tennessee Bank/Jasper | 73/0 | 436 | Running | $72,335 |
| 31. | 7 | 7 | Ted Musgrave | Dodge | Sirius Satellite Radio | 70/0 | 430 | Running | $63,715 |
| 32. | 37 | 99 | Jeff Burton | Ford | CITGO | 67/0 | 419 | Running | $96,547 |
| 33. | 8 | 21 | Ricky Rudd | Ford | Motorcraft Quality Parts | 64/0 | 415 | Running | $68,595 |
| 34. | 42 | 45 | Kyle Petty | Dodge | Georgia Pacific | 61/0 | 400 | Running | $68,560 |
| 35. | 22 | 31 | Robby Gordon | Chevrolet | Cingular Wireless | 58/0 | 392 | Running | $86,602 |
| 36. | 2 | 6 | Mark Martin | Ford | Viagra | 60/5 | 346 | Accident | $94,813 |
| 37. | 40 | 54 | Todd Bodine | Ford | National Guard | 52/0 | 315 | Running | $60,420 |
| 38. | 17 | 38 | Elliott Sadler | Ford | Combos | 49/0 | 305 | Accident | $94,600 |
| 39. | 33 | 50 | Larry Foyt* | Dodge | Harrah's | 46/0 | 273 | Accident | $60,300 |
| 40. | 39 | 1 | Jeff Green | Chevrolet | Pennzoil | 48/5 | 193 | Engine | $85,412 |
| 41. | 43 | 43 | Christian Fittipaldi | Dodge | Cheerios Heart Health | 40/0 | 175 | Accident | $95,953 |
| 42. | 3 | 15 | Michael Waltrip | Chevrolet | NAPA Auto Parts | 37/0 | 87 | Accident | $78,430 |
| 43. | 20 | 2 | Rusty Wallace | Dodge | Miller Lite | 34/0 | 87 | Accident | $94,737 |

*Rookie. Time of race: 3 hours, 26 minutes, 32 seconds. Average speed: 77.421 mph. Margin of victory: .818 seconds. Caution flags: 20 for 119 laps. 7-12 (Cars 1, 30, 45, 54, 41 and 43—accident, Turn 4); 65-70 (Cars 16, 0 and 27—accident, back stretch); 77-80 (Car 12—spin, front stretch); 90-100 (Cars 2 and 15—accident, Turn 4); 104-107 (Cars 1, 50, 25, 9, 42 and 10—accident, Turn 3); 161-166 (Cars 41, 25, 20, 18 and 97—accident, Turn 3); 178-186 (Cars 99, 7, 12 and 77—accident, front stretch); 194-197 (Car 1—accident, Turn 3); 223-228 (Cars 7 and 32—accident, Turn 3); 256-261 (Car 31—spin, front stretch); 276-282 (Car 43—accident, front stretch); 287-292 (Car 50—accident, back stretch); 300-304 (debris); 307-313 (Car 38—accident, back stretch); 339-344 (Car 18—accident, Turn 4); 348-353 (Cars 6 and 4—accident, front stretch); 373-378 (Cars 40 and 21—accident, Turn 2); 423-427 (debris); 445-449 (Cars 24 and 49—accident, front stretch); 461-464 (Car 74—accident, Turn 2). Lap leaders: 11 lead changes among eight drivers. Jeff Gordon 1-66, Jeff Green 67-82, J. Gordon 83-162, Kevin Harvick 163-187, Mike Skinner 188-192, J. Gordon 193-225, Sterling Marlin 226-261, Mark Martin 262-310, Ryan Newman 311-340, Marlin 341-365, Harvick 366-379, Kurt Busch 380-500. Pole winner: Jeff Gordon, 127.597 mph. Failed to qualify: Hermie Sadler, Billy Bigley Jr., Derrike Cope. Estimated attendance: 160,000.

**Bristol Motor Speedway**
Bristol, Tenn. — .533-mile banked concrete oval
August 23, 2003—266.5 miles—500 laps

## Points standings

| Rk. | Driver | Behind |
|---|---|---|
| 1. | Matt Kenseth | Leader |
| 2. | Dale Earnhardt Jr. | -351 |
| 3. | Kevin Harvick | -464 |
| 4. | Jimmie Johnson | -529 |
| 5. | Jeff Gordon | -532 |
| 6. | Kurt Busch | -602 |
| 7. | Ryan Newman | -621 |
| 8. | Michael Waltrip | -632 |
| 9. | Bobby Labonte | -685 |
| 10. | Robby Gordon | -757 |

# Mountain Dew Southern 500 — race 25 of 36

| Fin. | St. | Car | Driver | Make | Sponsor | Pts./Bonus | Laps | Status | Winnings |
|---|---|---|---|---|---|---|---|---|---|
| 1. | 3 | 5 | Terry Labonte | Chevrolet | Kellogg's/got milk? | 180/5 | 367 | Running | $204,736 |
| 2. | 18 | 29 | Kevin Harvick | Chevrolet | GM Goodwrench Service | 175/5 | 367 | Running | $149,063 |
| 3. | 2 | 48 | Jimmie Johnson | Chevrolet | Lowe's | 170/5 | 367 | Running | $112,575 |
| 4. | 17 | 42 | Jamie McMurray* | Dodge | Havoline | 165/5 | 367 | Running | $90,765 |
| 5. | 22 | 9 | Bill Elliott | Dodge | Dodge Dealers/UAW | 155/0 | 367 | Running | $113,028 |
| 6. | 15 | 19 | Jeremy Mayfield | Dodge | Dodge Dealers/UAW | 150/0 | 367 | Running | $78,355 |
| 7. | 5 | 18 | Bobby Labonte | Chevrolet | Interstate Batteries | 146/0 | 367 | Running | $112,568 |
| 8. | 8 | 32 | Ricky Craven | Pontiac | Give Kids The World/Tide | 142/0 | 367 | Running | $90,125 |
| 9. | 4 | 38 | Elliott Sadler | Ford | M&M's | 138/0 | 367 | Running | $98,335 |
| 10. | 9 | 16 | Greg Biffle* | Ford | Grainger | 139/5 | 367 | Running | $65,980 |
| 11. | 28 | 99 | Jeff Burton | Ford | CITGO | 135/5 | 367 | Running | $95,037 |
| 12. | 20 | 20 | Tony Stewart | Chevrolet | Home Depot | 127/0 | 367 | Running | $109,503 |
| 13. | 31 | 97 | Kurt Busch | Ford | Rubbermaid | 124/0 | 367 | Running | $92,135 |
| 14. | 6 | 17 | Matt Kenseth | Ford | Smirnoff Ice/DeWalt | 126/5 | 367 | Running | $75,720 |
| 15. | 41 | 4 | Kevin Lepage | Pontiac | Kodak | 123/5 | 367 | Running | $74,780 |
| 16. | 30 | 21 | Ricky Rudd | Ford | Motorcraft Quality Parts | 120/5 | 367 | Running | $77,235 |
| 17. | 27 | 54 | Todd Bodine | Ford | National Guard | 112/0 | 366 | Running | $66,754 |
| 18. | 35 | 1 | Jeff Green | Chevrolet | Pennzoil | 109/0 | 365 | Running | $79,577 |
| 19. | 29 | 22 | Ward Burton | Dodge | Caterpillar | 106/0 | 364 | Running | $90,166 |
| 20. | 32 | 30 | Steve Park | Chevrolet | America Online | 103/0 | 364 | Running | $67,390 |
| 21. | 26 | 25 | Joe Nemechek | Chevrolet | UAW/Delphi | 100/0 | 363 | Running | $57,415 |
| 22. | 38 | 7 | Jimmy Spencer | Dodge | Sirius Satellite Radio | 102/5 | 361 | Running | $56,745 |
| 23. | 1 | 12 | Ryan Newman | Dodge | ALLTEL | 104/10 | 359 | Running | $101,775 |
| 24. | 24 | 23 | Kenny Wallace | Dodge | Stacker 2 | 91/0 | 358 | Running | $56,925 |
| 25. | 12 | 8 | Dale Earnhardt Jr. | Chevrolet | Budweiser | 88/0 | 358 | Running | $93,932 |
| 26. | 36 | 0 | Jason Leffler | Pontiac | NetZero HiSpeed | 85/0 | 356 | Running | $55,455 |
| 27. | 40 | 45 | Kyle Petty | Dodge | Georgia Pacific | 87/5 | 345 | Engine | $63,095 |
| 28. | 25 | 31 | Robby Gordon | Chevrolet | Cingular Wireless | 79/0 | 336 | Accident | $80,072 |
| 29. | 16 | 01 | Mike Skinner | Pontiac | U.S. Army | 76/0 | 318 | Running | $54,165 |
| 30. | 10 | 77 | Dave Blaney | Ford | Jasper Engines & Trans. | 73/0 | 316 | Running | $60,000 |
| 31. | 13 | 40 | Sterling Marlin | Dodge | Coors Light | 70/0 | 315 | Running | $95,255 |
| 32. | 14 | 24 | Jeff Gordon | Chevrolet | DuPont | 67/0 | 309 | Accident | $98,443 |
| 33. | 7 | 6 | Mark Martin | Ford | Viagra | 64/0 | 307 | Running | $85,638 |
| 34. | 19 | 88 | Dale Jarrett | Ford | UPS | 61/0 | 302 | Running | $96,543 |
| 35. | 21 | 41 | Casey Mears* | Dodge | Target | 58/0 | 266 | Running | $58,580 |
| 36. | 34 | 2 | Rusty Wallace | Dodge | Miller Lite | 55/0 | 258 | Running | $85,172 |
| 37. | 37 | 15 | Michael Waltrip | Chevrolet | NAPA Auto Parts | 52/0 | 251 | Running | $68,325 |
| 38. | 39 | 49 | Ken Schrader | Dodge | 1-800-CALLATT | 49/0 | 184 | Accident | $50,160 |
| 39. | 42 | 37 | Derrike Cope | Chevrolet | Friendly's/SP Films | 46/0 | 168 | Accident | $50,125 |
| 40. | 11 | 10 | Johnny Benson | Pontiac | Valvoline | 43/0 | 165 | Accident | $76,800 |
| 41. | 43 | 02 | Hermie Sadler | Pontiac | goteamva.com | PE | 61 | Electrical | $50,000 |
| 42. | 33 | 74 | Tony Raines* | Chevrolet | BACE Motorsports | 37/0 | 9 | Accident | $49,950 |
| 43. | 23 | 43 | Christian Fittipaldi | Dodge | Cheerios Heart Health | 34/0 | 9 | Accident | $85,927 |

*Rookie. Time of race: 4 hours, 9 minutes, 7 seconds. Average speed: 120.744 mph. Margin of victory: 1.651 seconds. Caution flags: 10 for 55 laps. 7-13 (Cars 0, 43, 15, 88, 2 and 74—accident, Turn 3); 73-76 (debris in Turn 1); 100-103 (Car 01—accident, Turn 4); 148-153 (debris in Turn 1); 167-175 (Cars 41, 24, 23, 10, 77 and 49—accident, Turn 3); 229-232 (Car 25—accident, Turn 2); 240-247 (Car 49—accident, Turn 3); 275-278 (debris in Turn 4); 311-315 (debris in Turn 2); 334-337 (Car 31—accident, Turn 1). Lap leaders: 24 lead changes among 12 drivers. Ryan Newman 1-10, Jimmy Spencer 11, Newman 12-65, Matt Kenseth 66-72, Newman 73, Kenseth 74-99, Newman 100, Jeff Burton 101-103, Kenseth 104-107, J. Burton 108-147, Jimmie Johnson 148, Kevin Harvick 149-158, Johnson 159-170, Kyle Petty 171, Johnson 172-175, Newman 176-229, Greg Biffle 230-240, Kevin Lepage 241-249, Harvick 250, Biffle 251-275, Harvick 276-278, Biffle 279-312, Ricky Rudd 313, Jamie McMurray 314-334, Terry Labonte 335-367. Pole winner: Ryan Newman, 169.048 mph. Dropped to rear: Dale Jarrett and Derrike Cope (engine changes); Jimmy Spencer (backup car). Failed to qualify: Larry Foyt. Estimated attendance: 75,000.

**Darlington Raceway**
Darlington, S.C. — 1.366-mile banked paved oval
August 31, 2003—500 miles—367 laps

## 2003 SEASON

## Points standings

| Rk. | Driver | Behind |
|---|---|---|
| 1. | Matt Kenseth | Leader |
| 2. | Dale Earnhardt Jr. | -389 |
| 3. | Kevin Harvick | -415 |
| 4. | Jimmie Johnson | -485 |
| 5. | Jeff Gordon | -591 |
| 6. | Kurt Busch | -604 |
| 7. | Ryan Newman | -643 |
| 8. | Bobby Labonte | -665 |
| 9. | Michael Waltrip | -706 |
| 10. | Tony Stewart | -782 |

## Chevy Rock & Roll 400 — race 26 of 36

| Fin. | St. | Car | Driver | Make | Sponsor | Pts./Bonus | Laps | Status | Winnings |
|---|---|---|---|---|---|---|---|---|---|
| 1. | 4 | 12 | Ryan Newman | Dodge | ALLTEL | 180/5 | 400 | Running | $160,970 |
| 2. | 23 | 19 | Jeremy Mayfield | Dodge | Dodge Dealers/UAW | 170/0 | 400 | Running | $136,365 |
| 3. | 19 | 21 | Ricky Rudd | Ford | Motorcraft Quality Parts | 165/0 | 400 | Running | $104,130 |
| 4. | 7 | 99 | Jeff Burton | Ford | CITGO | 165/5 | 400 | Running | $116,897 |
| 5. | 17 | 2 | Rusty Wallace | Dodge | Miller Lite | 155/0 | 400 | Running | $99,047 |
| 6. | 16 | 18 | Bobby Labonte | Chevrolet | Interstate Batteries | 155/5 | 400 | Running | $104,513 |
| 7. | 18 | 17 | Matt Kenseth | Ford | Smirnoff Ice/DeWalt | 146/0 | 400 | Running | $75,230 |
| 8. | 32 | 5 | Terry Labonte | Chevrolet | Kellogg's/got milk? | 147/5 | 400 | Running | $83,161 |
| 9. | 9 | 10 | Johnny Benson | Pontiac | Valvoline | 138/0 | 400 | Running | $83,455 |
| 10. | 5 | 24 | Jeff Gordon | Chevrolet | DuPont | 144/10 | 400 | Running | $102,333 |
| 11. | 26 | 48 | Jimmie Johnson | Chevrolet | Lowe's | 130/0 | 400 | Running | $70,605 |
| 12. | 42 | 09 | Mike Wallace | Dodge | Miccosukee Resort | 132/5 | 400 | Running | $56,290 |
| 13. | 3 | 6 | Mark Martin | Ford | Viagra | 129/5 | 400 | Running | $89,463 |
| 14. | 24 | 1 | John Andretti | Chevrolet | Pennzoil | 121/0 | 400 | Running | $76,917 |
| 15. | 8 | 22 | Ward Burton | Dodge | Caterpillar | 118/0 | 400 | Running | $88,811 |
| 16. | 28 | 29 | Kevin Harvick | Chevrolet | GM Goodwrench Service | 120/5 | 400 | Running | $89,383 |
| 17. | 13 | 8 | Dale Earnhardt Jr. | Chevrolet | Budweiser | 117/5 | 399 | Running | $105,522 |
| 18. | 1 | 01 | Mike Skinner | Pontiac | U.S. Army | 109/0 | 399 | Running | $73,155 |
| 19. | 29 | 42 | Jamie McMurray* | Dodge | Havoline | 106/0 | 399 | Running | $53,930 |
| 20. | 2 | 16 | Greg Biffle* | Ford | Grainger | 108/0 | 399 | Running | $54,680 |
| 21. | 37 | 88 | Dale Jarrett | Ford | UPS | 100/0 | 399 | Running | $94,333 |
| 22. | 6 | 40 | Sterling Marlin | Dodge | Coors Light | 102/5 | 399 | Running | $92,430 |
| 23. | 34 | 23 | Kenny Wallace | Dodge | Stacker 2 | 94/0 | 399 | Running | $65,555 |
| 24. | 25 | 97 | Kurt Busch | Ford | Rubbermaid | 91/0 | 398 | Running | $78,605 |
| 25. | 27 | 49 | Ken Schrader | Dodge | BAM Racing | 88/0 | 398 | Running | $51,655 |
| 26. | 11 | 25 | Joe Nemechek | Chevrolet | UAW/Delphi | 85/0 | 397 | Running | $51,030 |
| 27. | 14 | 20 | Tony Stewart | Chevrolet | Home Depot | 82/0 | 397 | Running | $100,283 |
| 28. | 40 | 0 | Jason Leffler | Pontiac | NetZero HiSpeed | 84/5 | 397 | Running | $50,680 |
| 29. | 21 | 31 | Robby Gordon | Chevrolet | Cingular Wireless | 76/0 | 397 | Running | $75,647 |
| 30. | 35 | 32 | Ricky Craven | Pontiac | Tide | 73/0 | 396 | Running | $67,189 |
| 31. | 39 | 30 | Steve Park | Chevrolet | AOL/Third Eye Blind | 70/0 | 394 | Running | $57,765 |
| 32. | 33 | 15 | Michael Waltrip | Chevrolet | NAPA Auto Parts | 67/0 | 388 | Running | $65,230 |
| 33. | 38 | 77 | Dave Blaney | Ford | Jasper Engines & Trans. | 64/0 | 377 | Running | $56,100 |
| 34. | 10 | 45 | Kyle Petty | Dodge | Georgia Pacific | 61/0 | 373 | Running | $55,135 |
| 35. | 20 | 74 | Tony Raines* | Chevrolet | BACE Motorsports | 58/0 | 360 | Running | $47,100 |
| 36. | 22 | 7 | Jimmy Spencer | Dodge | Sirius Satellite Radio | 55/0 | 324 | Engine | $47,065 |
| 37. | 15 | 9 | Bill Elliott | Dodge | Dodge Dealers/UAW | 52/0 | 302 | Running | $85,863 |
| 38. | 36 | 4 | Johnny Sauter | Pontiac | Kodak | 49/0 | 291 | Running | $46,995 |
| 39. | 30 | 38 | Elliott Sadler | Ford | M&M's | 46/0 | 280 | Accident | $81,195 |
| 40. | 43 | 02 | Hermie Sadler | Chevrolet | Dollar Tree | 43/0 | 266 | Accident | $46,885 |
| 41. | 31 | 41 | Casey Mears* | Dodge | Target | 40/0 | 247 | Accident | $54,830 |
| 42. | 12 | 54 | Todd Bodine | Ford | National Guard | 37/0 | 230 | Accident | $46,790 |
| 43. | 41 | 43 | Christian Fittipaldi | Dodge | Cheerios | 34/0 | 130 | Accident | $82,778 |

*Rookie. Time of race: 3 hours, 9 minutes, 35 seconds. Average speed: 94.945 mph. Margin of victory: .159 seconds. Caution flags: 14 for 76 laps. 25-28 (Car 31—accident, back stretch); 65-68 (Car 16—spin, Turn 3); 85-88 (Cars 17 and 38—spin, front stretch); 95-112 (Cars 77, 23, 45, 30, 4 and 88—accident, back stretch); 121-126 (Cars 0, 97, 1, 88, 42, 43 and 16—accident, back stretch); 130-133 (Car 20—accident, Turn 3); 145-148 (Cars 17 and 38—accident, front stretch); 196-200 (Car 20—accident, front stretch); 269-274 (Car 42—spin, front stretch); 287-293 (Car 38—accident, Turn 1); 320-323 (debris in Turn 2); 383-386 (Car 31—accident, Turn 3); 389-391 (debris in Turn 1); 394-396 (Car 29—accident, Turn 1). Lap leaders: 20 lead changes among 12 drivers. Mark Martin 1, Greg Biffle 2-3, Jeff Gordon 4-64, Ryan Newman 65, Jason Leffler 66-84, Mike Wallace 85-91, J. Gordon 92-120, Jeff Burton 121, Kevin Harvick 122-144, Terry Labonte 145-151, Bobby Labonte 152-156, T. Labonte 157-159, J. Burton 160-163, Dale Earnhardt Jr. 164-196, Sterling Marlin 197, Earnhardt Jr. 198-213, J. Gordon 214-242, Earnhardt Jr. 243-269, J. Gordon 270-276, Newman 277-400. Pole winner: Mike Skinner, 125.792 mph. Dropped to rear: Mike Skinner (backup car). Failed to qualify: Larry Foyt, Billy Bigley Jr. Estimated attendance: 105,000.

**Richmond International Speedway**
Richmond, Va.— .75-mile paved oval
September 6, 2003—300 miles—400 laps

2003 SEASON

### Points standings

| Rk. | Driver | Behind |
|---|---|---|
| 1. | Matt Kenseth | Leader |
| 2. | Dale Earnhardt Jr. | -418 |
| 3. | Kevin Harvick | -441 |
| 4. | Jimmie Johnson | -501 |
| 5. | Jeff Gordon | -593 |
| 6. | Ryan Newman | -609 |
| 7. | Bobby Labonte | -656 |
| 8. | Kurt Busch | -659 |
| 9. | Terry Labonte | -782 |
| 10. | Michael Waltrip | -785 |

# Sylvania 300 — race 27 of 36

| Fin. | St. | Car | Driver | Make | Sponsor | Pts./Bonus | Laps | Status | Winnings |
|---|---|---|---|---|---|---|---|---|---|
| 1. | 8 | 48 | Jimmie Johnson | Chevrolet | Lowe's | 180/5 | 300 | Running | $200,225 |
| 2. | 31 | 21 | Ricky Rudd | Ford | Motorcraft Quality Parts | 175/5 | 300 | Running | $145,055 |
| 3. | 25 | 25 | Joe Nemechek | Chevrolet | UAW/Delphi | 165/0 | 300 | Running | $101,980 |
| 4. | 12 | 9 | Bill Elliott | Dodge | Dodge Dealers/UAW | 165/5 | 300 | Running | $144,108 |
| 5. | 6 | 8 | Dale Earnhardt Jr. | Chevrolet | Budweiser | 165/10 | 300 | Running | $111,992 |
| 6. | 11 | 2 | Rusty Wallace | Dodge | Miller Lite | 150/0 | 300 | Running | $106,317 |
| 7. | 19 | 17 | Matt Kenseth | Ford | DeWalt Power Tools | 151/5 | 300 | Running | $80,750 |
| 8. | 24 | 38 | Elliott Sadler | Ford | M&M's | 142/0 | 300 | Running | $97,700 |
| 9. | 1 | 12 | Ryan Newman | Dodge | ALLTEL | 143/5 | 300 | Running | $98,925 |
| 10. | 3 | 42 | Jamie McMurray* | Dodge | Havoline | 134/0 | 300 | Running | $68,650 |
| 11. | 10 | 19 | Jeremy Mayfield | Dodge | Dodge Dealers/UAW | 130/0 | 300 | Running | $69,750 |
| 12. | 16 | 1 | John Andretti | Chevrolet | Pennzoil | 127/0 | 300 | Running | $85,637 |
| 13. | 13 | 29 | Kevin Harvick | Chevrolet | GM Goodwrench Service | 129/5 | 300 | Running | $96,528 |
| 14. | 26 | 77 | Dave Blaney | Ford | Jasper Engines & Trans. | 121/0 | 299 | Running | $81,950 |
| 15. | 28 | 97 | Kurt Busch | Ford | Rubbermaid | 118/0 | 299 | Running | $89,375 |
| 16. | 37 | 18 | Bobby Labonte | Chevrolet | Interstate Batteries | 115/0 | 299 | Running | $99,308 |
| 17. | 18 | 41 | Casey Mears* | Dodge | Target | 112/0 | 299 | Running | $75,500 |
| 18. | 2 | 5 | Terry Labonte | Chevrolet | Kellogg's/got milk? | 109/0 | 299 | Running | $84,856 |
| 19. | 7 | 24 | Jeff Gordon | Chevrolet | DuPont | 111/5 | 299 | Running | $99,978 |
| 20. | 32 | 20 | Tony Stewart | Chevrolet | Home Depot | 103/0 | 299 | Running | $107,278 |
| 21. | 17 | 31 | Robby Gordon | Chevrolet | Cingular Wireless | 105/5 | 299 | Running | $80,762 |
| 22. | 14 | 01 | Mike Skinner | Pontiac | U.S. Army | 97/0 | 299 | Running | $63,639 |
| 23. | 34 | 7 | Jimmy Spencer | Dodge | Sirius Satellite Radio | 94/0 | 299 | Running | $55,850 |
| 24. | 35 | 27 | Scott Wimmer | Chevrolet | YJ Stinger | 91/0 | 299 | Running | $51,550 |
| 25. | 22 | 10 | Johnny Benson | Pontiac | Valvoline | 88/0 | 299 | Running | $81,600 |
| 26. | 5 | 15 | Michael Waltrip | Chevrolet | NAPA Auto Parts | 90/5 | 299 | Running | $69,150 |
| 27. | 41 | 0 | Jason Leffler | Pontiac | NetZero HiSpeed | 82/0 | 298 | Running | $53,925 |
| 28. | 33 | 6 | Mark Martin | Ford | Viagra | 79/0 | 298 | Running | $87,583 |
| 29. | 9 | 40 | Sterling Marlin | Dodge | Coors Light | 76/0 | 298 | Running | $94,465 |
| 30. | 40 | 45 | Kyle Petty | Dodge | Georgia Pacific | 73/0 | 298 | Running | $61,225 |
| 31. | 43 | 43 | Christian Fittipaldi | Dodge | Cheerios | 70/0 | 298 | Running | $85,803 |
| 32. | 30 | 4 | Johnny Sauter | Pontiac | Kodak | 67/0 | 297 | Running | $49,825 |
| 33. | 42 | 74 | Tony Raines* | Chevrolet | BACE Motorsports | 64/0 | 297 | Running | $50,530 |
| 34. | 39 | 30 | Steve Park | Chevrolet | America Online | 66/5 | 297 | Running | $57,400 |
| 35. | 29 | 54 | Todd Bodine | Ford | National Guard | 58/0 | 296 | Running | $49,200 |
| 36. | 38 | 23 | Kenny Wallace | Dodge | Stacker 2 | 55/0 | 295 | Running | $49,010 |
| 37. | 20 | 49 | Ken Schrader | Dodge | BAM Racing | 52/0 | 292 | Running | $48,850 |
| 38. | 21 | 32 | Ricky Craven | Pontiac | Tide | 49/0 | 291 | Running | $56,700 |
| 39. | 23 | 22 | Ward Burton | Dodge | Caterpillar | 46/0 | 270 | Accident | $84,691 |
| 40. | 36 | 02 | Hermie Sadler | Pontiac | GoTeamVa.com | 43/0 | 179 | Engine | $48,550 |
| 41. | 27 | 88 | Dale Jarrett | Ford | UPS | 40/0 | 159 | Accident | $94,228 |
| 42. | 15 | 99 | Jeff Burton | Ford | CITGO | 37/0 | 117 | Engine | $81,817 |
| 43. | 4 | 16 | Greg Biffle* | Ford | Grainger | 34/0 | 108 | Engine | $49,060 |

*Rookie. Time of race: 2 hours, 58 minutes, 41 seconds. Average speed: 106.580 mph. Margin of victory: 6.240 seconds. Caution flags: 6 for 38 laps. 127-138 (debris on track); 148-151 (Car 22—accident, Turn 1); 156-159 (Car 31—spin, back stretch); 162-171 (Car 88—accident, Turn 4); 184-187 (oil on track); 196-199 (Car 20—accident, Turn 2). Lap leaders: 20 lead changes among 11 drivers. Ryan Newman 1-45, Dale Earnhardt Jr. 46-83, Michael Waltrip 84-85, Jimmie Johnson 86, Matt Kenseth 87-88, Robby Gordon 89, Steve Park 90, Earnhardt Jr. 91-126, Newman 127, Bill Elliott 128-146, Newman 147, Elliott 148-183, Earnhardt Jr. 184-229, Ricky Rudd 230-255, Waltrip 256-271, Johnson 272-275, Jeff Gordon 276, Kevin Harvick 277-285, Kenseth 286-290, R. Gordon 291-293, Johnson 294-300. Pole winner: Ryan Newman, 133.357 mph. Dropped to rear: Rusty Wallace (engine change); Dave Blaney and Ricky Craven (backup cars). Failed to qualify: Larry Foyt, Derrike Cope, Morgan Shepherd, Carl Long. Estimated attendance: 101,000.

**New Hampshire International Speedway**
Loudon, N.H. — 1.058-mile flat paved oval
September 14, 2003—300 miles—300 laps

2003 SEASON

## Points standings

| Rk. | Driver | Behind |
|---|---|---|
| 1. | Matt Kenseth | Leader |
| 2. | Dale Earnhardt Jr. | -404 |
| 3. | Kevin Harvick | -463 |
| 4. | Jimmie Johnson | -472 |
| 5. | Ryan Newman | -617 |
| 6. | Jeff Gordon | -633 |
| T7. | Kurt Busch | -692 |
| T7. | Bobby Labonte | -692 |
| 9. | Terry Labonte | -824 |
| 10. | Michael Waltrip | -846 |

# MBNA America 400 — race 28 of 36

| Fin. | St. | Car | Driver | Make | Sponsor | Pts./Bonus | Laps | Status | Winnings |
|---|---|---|---|---|---|---|---|---|---|
| 1. | 5 | 12 | Ryan Newman | Dodge | ALLTEL | 180/5 | 400 | Running | $160,460 |
| 2. | 25 | 19 | Jeremy Mayfield | Dodge | Dodge Dealers/UAW | 170/0 | 400 | Running | $140,635 |
| 3 | 11 | 20 | Tony Stewart | Chevrolet | Home Depot | 170/5 | 400 | Running | $153,408 |
| 4. | 3 | 29 | Kevin Harvick | Chevrolet | GM Goodwrench Service | 170/10 | 400 | Running | $119,533 |
| 5 | 6 | 24 | Jeff Gordon | Chevrolet | DuPont | 160/5 | 400 | Running | $123,923 |
| 6. | 18 | 42 | Jamie McMurray* | Dodge | Havoline | 150/0 | 400 | Running | $71,890 |
| 7. | 19 | 16 | Greg Biffle* | Ford | Grainger | 146/0 | 400 | Running | $66,440 |
| 8. | 4 | 48 | Jimmie Johnson | Chevrolet | Lowe's | 142/0 | 400 | Running | $79,940 |
| 9. | 1 | 17 | Matt Kenseth | Ford | DeWalt Power Tools | 143/5 | 400 | Running | $79,840 |
| 10. | 14 | 2 | Rusty Wallace | Dodge | Miller Lite | 134/0 | 400 | Running | $98,707 |
| 11. | 23 | 21 | Ricky Rudd | Ford | Motorcraft Quality Parts | 130/0 | 400 | Running | $87,155 |
| 12. | 13 | 99 | Jeff Burton | Ford | CITGO | 127/0 | 400 | Running | $96,007 |
| 13. | 17 | 40 | Sterling Marlin | Dodge | Coors Light | 129/5 | 400 | Running | $102,540 |
| 14. | 15 | 9 | Bill Elliott | Dodge | Dodge Dealers/UAW | 121/0 | 400 | Running | $94,673 |
| 15. | 29 | 7 | Jimmy Spencer | Dodge | Sirius Satellite Radio | 118/0 | 400 | Running | $75,890 |
| 16. | 41 | 43 | Jeff Green | Dodge | Cheerios | 115/0 | 400 | Running | $99,818 |
| 17. | 33 | 54 | Todd Bodine | Ford | National Guard | 112/0 | 400 | Running | $71,740 |
| 18. | 27 | 88 | Dale Jarrett | Ford | UPS | 109/0 | 400 | Running | $100,703 |
| 19. | 20 | 38 | Elliott Sadler | Ford | M&M's | 106/0 | 400 | Running | $92,490 |
| 20. | 9 | 5 | Terry Labonte | Chevrolet | Kellogg's/got milk? | 103/0 | 399 | Running | $86,346 |
| 21. | 26 | 10 | Johnny Benson | Pontiac | Valvoline | 100/0 | 399 | Running | $84,490 |
| 22. | 16 | 6 | Mark Martin | Ford | Viagra | 97/0 | 398 | Running | $91,323 |
| 23. | 12 | 31 | Robby Gordon | Chevrolet | Cingular Wireless | 94/0 | 398 | Running | $83,327 |
| 24. | 28 | 77 | Dave Blaney | Ford | Jasper Engines & Trans. | 91/0 | 398 | Running | $75,490 |
| 25. | 37 | 0 | Jason Leffler | Pontiac | NetZero HiSpeed | 88/0 | 398 | Running | $57,215 |
| 26. | 32 | 30 | Steve Park | Chevrolet | America Online | 85/0 | 397 | Running | $64,165 |
| 27. | 40 | 4 | Kevin Lepage | Pontiac | Kodak | 82/0 | 397 | Running | $61,904 |
| 28. | 31 | 23 | Kenny Wallace | Dodge | Stacker 2 | 79/0 | 397 | Running | $53,340 |
| 29. | 21 | 22 | Ward Burton | Dodge | Caterpillar | 76/0 | 397 | Running | $89,246 |
| 30. | 39 | 74 | Tony Raines* | Chevrolet | Staff America | 73/0 | 395 | Running | $53,540 |
| 31. | 8 | 18 | Bobby Labonte | Chevrolet | Interstate Batteries | 70/0 | 395 | Running | $97,948 |
| 32. | 36 | 45 | Kyle Petty | Dodge | Georgia Pacific | 67/0 | 394 | Running | $60,705 |
| 33. | 38 | 49 | Ken Schrader | Dodge | BAM Racing | 64/0 | 393 | Running | $53,455 |
| 34. | 30 | 1 | John Andretti | Chevrolet | Pennzoil | 61/0 | 393 | Running | $77,532 |
| 35. | 42 | 37 | Derrike Cope | Chevrolet | Friendly's/GBR Online | 58/0 | 393 | Running | $52,130 |
| 36. | 35 | 41 | Casey Mears* | Dodge | Target | 55/0 | 392 | Running | $60,000 |
| 37. | 2 | 8 | Dale Earnhardt Jr. | Chevrolet | Budweiser | 57/5 | 362 | Accident | $97,792 |
| 38. | 7 | 97 | Kurt Busch | Ford | Rubbermaid | 49/0 | 347 | Engine | $71,750 |
| 39. | 43 | 02 | Hermie Sadler | Pontiac | VCU Rams/Dollar Tree Pontiac | 46/0 | 257 | Engine | $51,635 |
| 40. | 22 | 32 | Ricky Craven | Pontiac | Tide | 43/0 | 249 | Engine | $59,465 |
| 41. | 34 | 01 | Mike Skinner | Pontiac | U.S. Army | 40/0 | 195 | Engine | $51,325 |
| 42. | 10 | 15 | Michael Waltrip | Chevrolet | NAPA Auto Parts | 37/0 | 171 | Engine | $69,200 |
| 43. | 24 | 25 | Joe Nemechek | Chevrolet | UAW/Delphi | 34/0 | 78 | Accident | $51,330 |

*Rookie. Time of race: 3 hours, 40 minutes, 35 seconds. Average speed: 108.802 mph. Margin of victory: 1.152 seconds. Caution flags: Seven for 63 laps. 4-7 (Cars 01 and 49—accident, Turn 2); 81-105 (Car 25—accident, Turn 1); 165-170 (Car 18—accident, Turn 4); 236-241 (debris on track); 288-296 (debris on track); 326-330 (Car 23—accident, Turn 4); 365-372 (Car 8—accident, Turn 2). Lap leaders: 13 lead changes among seven drivers. Kevin Harvick 1-11, Ryan Newman 12-44, Harvick 45-166, Sterling Marlin 167, Jeff Gordon 168-180, Dale Earnhardt Jr. 181-198, Tony Stewart 199-212, Earnhardt Jr. 213-237, Kenseth 238, Earnhardt Jr. 239-243, J. Gordon 244, Stewart 245-327, Newman 328-400. Pole winner: Qualifying cancelled because of rain; starting grid based on car owner points. Dropped to rear: Ricky Craven (engine change). Failed to qualify: Larry Foyt, Morgan Shepherd, Billy Bigley Jr., Scott Wimmer, Christian Fittipaldi, Tim Sauter. Estimated attendance: 137,000.

**Dover International Speedway**
Dover, Del.— 1-mile banked concrete oval
September 21, 2003—400 miles—400 laps

## Points standings

| Rk. | Driver | Behind |
|---|---|---|
| 1. | Matt Kenseth | Leader |
| 2. | Kevin Harvick | -436 |
| 3. | Jimmie Johnson | -473 |
| 4. | Dale Earnhardt Jr. | -490 |
| 5. | Ryan Newman | -580 |
| 6. | Jeff Gordon | -616 |
| 7. | Bobby Labonte | -765 |
| 8. | Kurt Busch | -786 |
| 9. | Terry Labonte | -864 |
| 10. | Tony Stewart | -867 |

2003 SEASON

# EA Sports 500 — race 29 of 36

| Fin. | St. | Car | Driver | Make | Sponsor | Pts./Bonus | Laps | Status | Winnings |
|---|---|---|---|---|---|---|---|---|---|
| 1. | 18 | 15 | Michael Waltrip | Chevrolet | NAPA Auto Parts | 180/5 | 188 | Running | $157,090 |
| 2. | 38 | 8 | Dale Earnhardt Jr. | Chevrolet | Budweiser | 175/5 | 188 | Running | $146,772 |
| 3. | 11 | 20 | Tony Stewart | Chevrolet | Home Depot | 165/0 | 188 | Running | $163,333 |
| 4. | 12 | 12 | Ryan Newman | Dodge | ALLTEL | 160/0 | 188 | Running | $113,165 |
| 5. | 5 | 24 | Jeff Gordon | Chevrolet | DuPont | 165/10 | 188 | Running | $138,193 |
| 6. | 39 | 97 | Kurt Busch | Ford | Rubbermaid | 155/5 | 188 | Running | $106,750 |
| 7. | 30 | 29 | Kevin Harvick | Chevrolet | GM Goodwrench Service | 151/5 | 188 | Running | $101,953 |
| 8. | 17 | 32 | Ricky Craven | Pontiac | Tide | 142/0 | 188 | Running | $87,200 |
| 9. | 33 | 2 | Rusty Wallace | Dodge | Miller Lite | 143/5 | 188 | Running | $97,742 |
| 10. | 23 | 09 | Mike Wallace | Dodge | Miccosukee Resort | 134/0 | 188 | Running | $61,600 |
| 11. | 10 | 18 | Bobby Labonte | Chevrolet | Interstate Batteries | 135/5 | 188 | Running | $102,998 |
| 12. | 34 | 31 | Robby Gordon | Chevrolet | Cingular Wireless | 132/5 | 188 | Running | $87,002 |
| 13. | 9 | 9 | Bill Elliott | Dodge | Dodge Dealers/UAW | 129/5 | 188 | Running | $98,138 |
| 14. | 20 | 22 | Ward Burton | Dodge | Caterpillar | 126/5 | 188 | Running | $92,801 |
| 15. | 24 | 90 | John Andretti | Chevrolet | America Online | 118/0 | 188 | Running | $57,485 |
| 16. | 2 | 42 | Jamie McMurray* | Dodge | Havoline | 120/5 | 188 | Running | $67,425 |
| 17. | 42 | 77 | Dave Blaney | Ford | Jasper Engines & Trans. | 112/0 | 188 | Running | $81,035 |
| 18. | 13 | 43 | Jeff Green | Dodge | Cheerios | 109/0 | 188 | Running | $95,498 |
| 19. | 6 | 88 | Dale Jarrett | Ford | UPS | 106/0 | 188 | Running | $101,228 |
| 20. | 19 | 23 | Kenny Wallace | Dodge | Stacker 2 | 103/0 | 188 | Running | $71,405 |
| 21. | 7 | 49 | Ken Schrader | Dodge | BAM Racing | 100/0 | 188 | Running | $58,060 |
| 22. | 14 | 5 | Terry Labonte | Chevrolet | Kellogg's/got milk? | 102/5 | 188 | Running | $83,796 |
| 23. | 15 | 6 | Mark Martin | Ford | Viagra | 94/0 | 188 | Running | $92,103 |
| 24. | 36 | 16 | Greg Biffle* | Ford | Grainger | 91/0 | 187 | Running | $56,975 |
| 25. | 27 | 25 | Joe Nemechek | Chevrolet | UAW/Delphi | 88/0 | 187 | Running | $57,005 |
| 26. | 43 | 1 | Jason Keller | Chevrolet | Pennzoil | 85/0 | 187 | Running | $78,352 |
| 27. | 28 | 01 | Mike Skinner | Pontiac | U.S. Army | 82/0 | 186 | Running | $64,549 |
| 28. | 26 | 44 | Christian Fittipaldi | Dodge | Bugles | 79/0 | 186 | Running | $52,800 |
| 29. | 25 | 98 | Jason Jarrett | Ford | C.H.I. Overhead Doors | 76/0 | 184 | Running | $52,640 |
| 30. | 1 | 38 | Elliott Sadler | Ford | M&M's | 78/5 | 181 | Accident | $96,330 |
| 31. | 29 | 74 | Tony Raines* | Chevrolet | Staff America | 70/0 | 179 | Accident | $55,395 |
| 32. | 40 | 99 | Jeff Burton | Ford | CITGO | 72/5 | 168 | Engine | $88,727 |
| 33. | 37 | 17 | Matt Kenseth | Ford | DeWalt Power Tools | 69/5 | 158 | Engine | $61,125 |
| 34. | 3 | 48 | Jimmie Johnson | Chevrolet | Lowe's | 66/5 | 157 | Engine | $71,930 |
| 35. | 21 | 60 | David Green | Chevrolet | Haas Automation | 58/0 | 150 | Accident | $52,025 |
| 36. | 32 | 21 | Ricky Rudd | Ford | Motorcraft Quality Parts | 55/0 | 138 | Engine | $62,475 |
| 37. | 8 | 41 | Casey Mears* | Dodge | Target | 52/0 | 113 | Overheating | $59,925 |
| 38. | 22 | 19 | Jeremy Mayfield | Dodge | Dodge Dealers/UAW | 49/0 | 104 | Running | $59,875 |
| 39. | 4 | 40 | Sterling Marlin | Dodge | Coors Light | 46/0 | 103 | Overheating | $95,810 |
| 40. | 16 | 00 | Buckshot Jones | Chevrolet | TBA | 48/5 | 88 | Accident | $51,730 |
| 41. | 41 | 10 | Johnny Benson | Pontiac | Valvoline | 40/0 | 29 | Accident | $78,430 |
| 42. | 31 | 7 | Jimmy Spencer | Dodge | Sirius Satellite Radio | 37/0 | 11 | Accident | $51,630 |
| 43. | 35 | 14 | Larry Foyt* | Dodge | Harrah's | 34/0 | 9 | Accident | $51,832 |

*Rookie. Time of race: 3 hours, 12 minutes, 17 seconds. Average speed: 156.045 mph. Margin of victory: .095 seconds. Caution flags: Five for 23 laps. 11-17 (Cars 14, 19, 74, 60, 10, 7 and 25—accident, Turn 4); 91-94 (debris on track); 144-148 (Car 48—accident, Turn 2); 170-174 (oil on track); 183-184 (Car 38—accident, back stretch). Lap leaders: 41 lead changes among 17 drivers. Elliott Sadler 1, Jamie McMurray 2-13, Michael Waltrip 14, Terry Labonte 15, McMurray 16-22, Buckshot Jones 23-41, Waltrip 42-43, Ward Burton 44-48, Jeff Gordon 49-50, Jimmie Johnson 51, Matt Kenseth 52, Kevin Harvick 53, J. Gordon 54-85, Rusty Wallace 86-87, Harvick 88, Robby Gordon 89-90, J. Gordon 91-101, Harvick 102, Sadler 103-104, J. Gordon 105-106, Harvick 107, Johnson 108, Sadler 109-122, Waltrip 123, Kurt Busch 124-125, Jeff Burton 126, R. Gordon 127-128, Johnson 129-141, Waltrip 142-143, Bill Elliott 144-145, McMurray 146, Sadler 147-152, Ward Burton 153-155, Rusty Wallace 156-164, Dale Earnhardt Jr. 165-166, Bobby Labonte 167, Earnhardt 168, B. Labonte 169, Busch 170-176, Waltrip 177, Busch 178-179, Waltrip 180-188. Pole winner: Elliott Sadler, 189.943 mph. Dropped to rear: Ryan Newman and Jason Jarrett (engine changes). Failed to qualify: Kyle Petty, Kevin Lepage, Jason Leffler, Mike Bliss, Steve Park, Todd Bodine. Estimated attendance: 170,000.

**Talladega Superspeedway**
Talladega, Ala. — 2.66-mile banked trioval
September 28, 2003—500 miles—188 laps

## Points standings

| Rk. | Driver | Behind |
|---|---|---|
| 1. | Matt Kenseth | Leader |
| 2. | Kevin Harvick | -354 |
| 3. | Dale Earnhardt Jr. | -384 |
| 4. | Jimmie Johnson | -476 |
| 5. | Ryan Newman | -489 |
| 6. | Jeff Gordon | -520 |
| 7. | Bobby Labonte | -699 |
| 8. | Kurt Busch | -700 |
| 9. | Tony Stewart | -771 |
| 10. | Terry Labonte | -831 |

2003 SEASON

## Banquet 400 — race 30 of 36

| Fin. | St. | Car | Driver | Make | Sponsor | Pts./Bonus | Laps | Status | Winnings |
|---|---|---|---|---|---|---|---|---|---|
| 1. | 11 | 12 | Ryan Newman | Dodge | ALLTEL | 180/5 | 267 | Running | $191,000 |
| 2. | 8 | 9 | Bill Elliott | Dodge | Dodge Dealers/UAW | 180/10 | 267 | Running | $203,623 |
| 3. | 16 | 19 | Jeremy Mayfield | Dodge | Dodge Dealers/UAW | 170/5 | 267 | Running | $127,175 |
| 4. | 14 | 20 | Tony Stewart | Chevrolet | Home Depot | 160/0 | 267 | Running | $155,578 |
| 5. | 7 | 24 | Jeff Gordon | Chevrolet | DuPont | 155/0 | 267 | Running | $127,753 |
| 6. | 24 | 29 | Kevin Harvick | Chevrolet | GM Goodwrench Service | 150/0 | 267 | Running | $115,053 |
| 7. | 1 | 48 | Jimmie Johnson | Chevrolet | Lowe's | 151/5 | 267 | Running | $96,525 |
| 8. | 15 | 42 | Jamie McMurray* | Dodge | Havoline | 142/0 | 267 | Running | $77,175 |
| 9. | 5 | 2 | Rusty Wallace | Dodge | Miller Lite | 143/5 | 267 | Running | $108,592 |
| 10. | 19 | 21 | Ricky Rudd | Ford | Motorcraft Quality Parts | 134/0 | 267 | Running | $99,125 |
| 11. | 23 | 54 | Todd Bodine | Ford | National Guard | 130/0 | 267 | Running | $89,425 |
| 12. | 22 | 16 | Greg Biffle* | Ford | Grainger | 127/0 | 267 | Running | $70,825 |
| 13. | 33 | 99 | Jeff Burton | Ford | CITGO | 124/0 | 267 | Running | $108,692 |
| 14. | 18 | 35 | Bobby Hamilton Jr. | Ford | Wawa/Marines | 121/0 | 267 | Running | $65,150 |
| 15. | 27 | 7 | Jimmy Spencer | Dodge | Sirius Satellite Radio | 118/0 | 267 | Running | $83,200 |
| 16. | 34 | 5 | Terry Labonte | Chevrolet | Kellogg's/got milk? | 115/0 | 267 | Running | $94,406 |
| 17. | 4 | 18 | Bobby Labonte | Chevrolet | Interstate Batteries | 117/5 | 267 | Running | $109,633 |
| 18. | 3 | 8 | Dale Earnhardt Jr. | Chevrolet | Budweiser | 114/5 | 267 | Running | $110,267 |
| 19. | 40 | 1 | John Andretti | Chevrolet | Pennzoil | 106/0 | 267 | Running | $89,237 |
| 20. | 38 | 6 | Mark Martin | Ford | Viagra | 103/0 | 267 | Running | $103,483 |
| 21. | 39 | 22 | Ward Burton | Dodge | Caterpillar | 100/0 | 267 | Running | $99,706 |
| 22. | 17 | 30 | Steve Park | Chevrolet | America Online | 97/0 | 267 | Running | $74,850 |
| 23. | 36 | 45 | Kyle Petty | Dodge | Georgia Pacific | 94/0 | 267 | Running | $74,550 |
| 24. | 12 | 41 | Casey Mears* | Dodge | Target | 91/0 | 267 | Running | $85,625 |
| 25. | 25 | 31 | Robby Gordon | Chevrolet | Cingular Wireless | 88/0 | 266 | Running | $91,512 |
| 26. | 35 | 74 | Tony Raines* | Chevrolet | Staff America | 85/0 | 266 | Running | $65,625 |
| 27. | 9 | 43 | Jeff Green | Dodge | Cheerios | 82/0 | 266 | Running | $101,203 |
| 28. | 43 | 49 | Ken Schrader | Dodge | BAM Racing | 79/0 | 266 | Running | $64,725 |
| 29. | 2 | 01 | Mike Skinner | Pontiac | U.S. Army | 81/5 | 265 | Running | $70,414 |
| 30. | 6 | 0 | Jason Leffler | Pontiac | NetZero HiSpeed | 78/0 | 265 | Running | $62,285 |
| 31. | 26 | 23 | Kenny Wallace | Dodge | Stacker 2 | 70/0 | 264 | Running | $61,575 |
| 32. | 42 | 09 | Mike Wallace | Dodge | Miccosukee Resort | 67/0 | 264 | Running | $61,375 |
| 33. | 13 | 88 | Dale Jarrett | Ford | UPS | 69/5 | 263 | Engine | $107,853 |
| 34. | 29 | 40 | Sterling Marlin | Dodge | Coors Light | 61/0 | 263 | Gas | $104,975 |
| 35. | 20 | 10 | Johnny Benson | Pontiac | Valvoline | 58/0 | 248 | Accident | $87,525 |
| 36. | 37 | 17 | Matt Kenseth | Ford | DeWalt Power Tools | 55/0 | 220 | Running | $68,575 |
| 37. | 30 | 25 | Joe Nemechek | Chevrolet | UAW/Delphi | 52/0 | 211 | Running | $60,375 |
| 38. | 41 | 37 | Derrike Cope | Chevrolet | Friendly's/GBR Online | 49/0 | 199 | Engine | $60,175 |
| 39. | 31 | 15 | Michael Waltrip | Chevrolet | NAPA Auto Parts | 46/0 | 197 | Accident | $77,985 |
| 40. | 21 | 97 | Kurt Busch | Ford | Rubbermaid | 48/5 | 181 | Engine | $79,785 |
| 41. | 32 | 32 | Ricky Craven | Pontiac | Tide | 40/0 | 174 | Engine | $67,590 |
| 42. | 10 | 38 | Elliott Sadler | Ford | M&M's | 37/0 | 104 | Accident | $93,645 |
| 43. | 28 | 77 | Dave Blaney | Ford | Jasper Engines & Trans. | 34/0 | 80 | Accident | $67,457 |

*Rookie. Time of race: 3 hours, 17 minutes, 34 seconds. Average speed: 121.630 mph, race record. Margin of victory: .863 seconds. Caution flags: Nine for 47 laps. 70-76 (Cars 15 and 17—accident, back stretch); 83-87 (Car 77—accident, Turn 2); 106-110 (Car 38—accident, Turn 2); 160-165 (debris on front stretch); 171-174 (Car 25–accident, Turn 2); 183-190 (oil on track); 202-205 (Car 15—accident, Turn 4); 236-239 (Car 6—spin, front stretch); 250-253 (Car 10—accident, front stretch). Lap leaders: 23 lead changes among 11 drivers. Jimmie Johnson-pole, Mike Skinner 1, Dale Earnhardt Jr. 2-4, Rusty Wallace 5, Earnhardt Jr. 6-11, R. Wallace 12-17, Bill Elliott 18-56, R. Wallace 57-58, Dale Jarrett 59, Bobby Labonte 60-61, Kurt Busch 62-63, Elliott 64-69, R. Wallace 70-82, Jarrett 83-106, Jason Leffler 107-110, R. Wallace 111, Leffler 112, Johnson 113-130, Elliott 131-159, Johnson 160, Elliott 161-201, Johnson 202, Jeremy Mayfield 203-239, Ryan Newman 240-267. Pole winner: Jimmie Johnson, 180.373 mph, track record. Dropped to rear: Jimmie Johnson (backup car), Joe Nemechek (engine change). Failed to qualify: Larry Foyt, Johnny Sauter. Estimated attendance: 80,000.

**Kansas Speedway**
Kansas City, Kan.— 1.5-mile paved trioval
October 5, 2003—400.5 miles—267 laps

### Points standings

| Rk. | Driver | Behind |
|---|---|---|
| 1. | Matt Kenseth | Leader |
| 2. | Kevin Harvick | -259 |
| 3. | Dale Earnhardt Jr. | -325 |
| 4. | Ryan Newman | -364 |
| 5. | Jimmie Johnson | -380 |
| 6. | Jeff Gordon | -420 |
| 7. | Bobby Labonte | -637 |
| 8. | Tony Stewart | -666 |
| 9. | Kurt Busch | -707 |
| 10. | Terry Labonte | -771 |

# UAW-GM Quality 500 — race 31 of 36

| Fin. | St. | Car | Driver | Make | Sponsor | Pts./Bonus | Laps | Status | Winnings |
|---|---|---|---|---|---|---|---|---|---|
| 1. | 6 | 20 | Tony Stewart | Chevrolet | Home Depot | 185/10 | 334 | Running | $312,478 |
| 2. | 1 | 12 | Ryan Newman | Dodge | ALLTEL | 175/5 | 334 | Running | $164,425 |
| 3. | 3 | 48 | Jimmie Johnson | Chevrolet | Lowe's | 170/5 | 334 | Running | $144,550 |
| 4. | 4 | 9 | Bill Elliott | Dodge | Dodge Dealers/UAW | 165/5 | 334 | Running | $125,233 |
| 5. | 2 | 24 | Jeff Gordon | Chevrolet | DuPont | 155/0 | 334 | Running | $123,578 |
| 6. | 12 | 18 | Bobby Labonte | Chevrolet | Interstate Batteries | 155/5 | 334 | Running | $110,258 |
| 7. | 19 | 42 | Jamie McMurray* | Dodge | Havoline | 151/5 | 334 | Running | $67,225 |
| 8. | 29 | 17 | Matt Kenseth | Ford | DeWalt Power Tools | 142/0 | 334 | Running | $82,425 |
| 9. | 11 | 8 | Dale Earnhardt Jr. | Chevrolet | Budweiser | 143/5 | 334 | Running | $98,217 |
| 10. | 9 | 29 | Kevin Harvick | Chevrolet | GM Goodwrench Service | 134/0 | 334 | Running | $97,853 |
| 11. | 27 | 6 | Mark Martin | Ford | Viagra | 130/0 | 334 | Running | $93,108 |
| 12. | 32 | 19 | Jeremy Mayfield | Dodge | Dodge Dealers/UAW | 127/0 | 334 | Running | $65,125 |
| 13. | 14 | 2 | Rusty Wallace | Dodge | Miller Lite | 124/0 | 334 | Running | $90,842 |
| 14. | 30 | 15 | Michael Waltrip | Chevrolet | NAPA Auto Parts | 121/0 | 334 | Running | $68,950 |
| 15. | 33 | 40 | Sterling Marlin | Dodge | Coors Light | 118/0 | 334 | Running | $96,600 |
| 16. | 23 | 10 | Johnny Benson | Pontiac | Valvoline | 115/0 | 333 | Running | $80,400 |
| 17. | 22 | 16 | Greg Biffle* | Ford | Grainger | 112/0 | 333 | Running | $53,000 |
| 18. | 21 | 5 | Terry Labonte | Chevrolet | Kellogg's/got milk? | 109/0 | 333 | Running | $78,406 |
| 19. | 13 | 32 | Ricky Craven | Pontiac | Tide | 106/0 | 333 | Running | $76,850 |
| 20. | 37 | 99 | Jeff Burton | Ford | CITGO | 103/0 | 332 | Running | $87,167 |
| 21. | 5 | 4 | Kevin Lepage | Pontiac | Kodak | 100/0 | 332 | Running | $64,050 |
| 22. | 16 | 88 | Dale Jarrett | Ford | UPS | 97/0 | 331 | Running | $93,053 |
| 23. | 39 | 21 | Ricky Rudd | Ford | Motorcraft Quality Parts | 94/0 | 331 | Running | $71,475 |
| 24. | 34 | 77 | Dave Blaney | Ford | Jasper Engines & Trans. | 91/0 | 331 | Running | $69,530 |
| 25. | 35 | 74 | Tony Raines* | Chevrolet | Aaron's | 88/0 | 331 | Running | $50,200 |
| 26. | 25 | 7 | Jimmy Spencer | Dodge | Sirius Satellite Radio | 85/0 | 331 | Running | $57,889 |
| 27. | 36 | 43 | Jeff Green | Dodge | Cheerios | 82/0 | 331 | Running | $84,963 |
| 28. | 38 | 22 | Ward Burton | Dodge | Caterpillar | 79/0 | 331 | Running | $81,941 |
| 29. | 8 | 54 | Todd Bodine | Ford | National Guard | 76/0 | 331 | Running | $49,200 |
| 30. | 41 | 1 | John Andretti | Chevrolet | Pennzoil | 73/0 | 331 | Running | $74,262 |
| 31. | 40 | 25 | Joe Nemechek | Chevrolet | UAW/Delphi | 70/0 | 330 | Running | $47,950 |
| 32. | 18 | 23 | Kenny Wallace | Dodge | Stacker 2 | 67/0 | 330 | Running | $45,325 |
| 33. | 20 | 60 | Brian Vickers | Chevrolet | Haas Automation | 64/0 | 329 | Running | $46,175 |
| 34. | 31 | 44 | Christian Fittipaldi | Dodge | Bugles | 61/0 | 329 | Running | $45,225 |
| 35. | 24 | 0 | Jason Leffler | Pontiac | NetZero HiSpeed | 58/0 | 325 | Running | $45,150 |
| 36. | 26 | 30 | Steve Park | Chevrolet | America Online | 55/0 | 310 | Running | $53,065 |
| 37. | 43 | 37 | Derrike Cope | Chevrolet | GBROnline.com/Friendly's | 52/0 | 297 | Running | $45,020 |
| 38. | 15 | 31 | Robby Gordon | Chevrolet | Cingular Wireless | 49/0 | 293 | Running | $70,162 |
| 39. | 10 | 01 | Mike Skinner | Pontiac | U.S. Army | 51/5 | 275 | Running | $45,440 |
| 40. | 42 | 45 | Kyle Petty | Dodge | Georgia Pacific | 43/0 | 271 | Suspension | $52,905 |
| 41. | 17 | 97 | Kurt Busch | Ford | Rubbermaid | 40/0 | 229 | Accident | $64,870 |
| 42. | 28 | 41 | Casey Mears* | Dodge | Target | 37/0 | 217 | Engine | $52,830 |
| 43. | 7 | 38 | Elliott Sadler | Ford | M&M's | 34/0 | 204 | Accident | $78,999 |

*Rookie. Time of race: 3 hours, 30 minutes, 24 seconds. Average speed: 142.871 mph. Margin of victory: .608 seconds. Caution flags: Five for 31 laps. 87-94 (Car 97—spin, Turn 2); 161-164 (Cars 38 and 01—accident, Turn 4); 169-172 (Car 31—accident, Turn 4); 206-213 (Cars 38 and 54—accident, front stretch); 232-238 (Car 97—accident, Turn 1). Lap leaders: 15 lead changes among eight drivers. Ryan Newman 1-17, Jimmie Johnson 18-59, Tony Stewart 60, Bobby Labonte 61-64, Johnson 65-86, Stewart 87, Mike Skinner 88, Johnson 89-128, Stewart 129-155, Dale Earnhardt Jr. 156-157, Stewart 158-206, Bill Elliott 207-233, Stewart 234-296, Jamie McMurray 297, Newman 298-326, Stewart 327-334. Pole winner: Ryan Newman, 186.657 mph, track record. Dropped to rear: Jeff Green (engine change). Failed to qualify: Ken Schrader, Hermie Sadler, Mark Green, Jeff Fultz. Estimated attendance: 160,000.

**Lowe's Motor Speedway**
Harrisburg, N.C. — 1.5-mile high-banked paved oval
October 11, 2003—501 miles—334 laps

## 2003 SEASON

## Points standings

| Rk. | Driver | Behind |
|---|---|---|
| 1. | Matt Kenseth | Leader |
| 2. | Kevin Harvick | -267 |
| 3. | Dale Earnhardt Jr. | -324 |
| 4. | Ryan Newman | -331 |
| 5. | Jimmie Johnson | -352 |
| 6. | Jeff Gordon | -407 |
| 7. | Tony Stewart | -623 |
| 8. | Bobby Labonte | -624 |
| 9. | Terry Labonte | -804 |
| 10. | Kurt Busch | -809 |

# Subway 500 — race 32 of 36

| Fin. | St. | Car | Driver | Make | Sponsor | Pts./Bonus | Laps | Status | Winnings |
|---|---|---|---|---|---|---|---|---|---|
| 1. | 1 | 24 | Jeff Gordon | Chevrolet | DuPont | 185/10 | 500 | Running | $183,018 |
| 2. | 26 | 48 | Jimmie Johnson | Chevrolet | Lowe's | 170/0 | 500 | Running | $100,250 |
| 3. | 16 | 20 | Tony Stewart | Chevrolet | Home Depot | 170/5 | 500 | Running | $129,478 |
| 4. | 3 | 8 | Dale Earnhardt Jr. | Chevrolet | Budweiser | 165/5 | 500 | Running | $115,937 |
| 5. | 8 | 12 | Ryan Newman | Dodge | ALLTEL | 155/0 | 500 | Running | $90,225 |
| 6. | 31 | 5 | Terry Labonte | Chevrolet | Kellogg's/got milk? | 155/5 | 500 | Running | $85,456 |
| 7. | 5 | 29 | Kevin Harvick | Chevrolet | GM Goodwrench Service | 151/5 | 500 | Running | $92,228 |
| 8. | 17 | 42 | Jamie McMurray* | Dodge | Havoline | 142/0 | 500 | Running | $57,125 |
| 9. | 28 | 9 | Bill Elliott | Dodge | Dodge Dealers/UAW | 138/0 | 500 | Running | $89,758 |
| 10. | 21 | 99 | Jeff Burton | Ford | CITGO | 134/0 | 500 | Running | $90,142 |
| 11. | 39 | 88 | Dale Jarrett | Ford | UPS | 130/0 | 500 | Running | $94,003 |
| 12. | 41 | 30 | Steve Park | Chevrolet | America Online | 127/0 | 500 | Running | $64,900 |
| 13. | 14 | 17 | Matt Kenseth | Ford | DeWalt Power Tools | 124/0 | 500 | Running | $68,400 |
| 14. | 23 | 6 | Mark Martin | Ford | Viagra | 121/0 | 500 | Running | $85,008 |
| 15. | 12 | 21 | Ricky Rudd | Ford | Motorcraft Quality Parts | 118/0 | 500 | Running | $76,825 |
| 16. | 4 | 23 | Kenny Wallace | Dodge | Stacker 2 | 115/0 | 500 | Running | $66,575 |
| 17. | 35 | 41 | Casey Mears* | Dodge | Target | 112/0 | 500 | Running | $71,175 |
| 18. | 2 | 22 | Ward Burton | Dodge | Caterpillar | 109/0 | 500 | Running | $84,036 |
| 19. | 19 | 16 | Greg Biffle* | Ford | Grainger | 106/0 | 500 | Running | $48,925 |
| 20. | 22 | 25 | Joe Nemechek | Chevrolet | UAW/Delphi | 108/5 | 499 | Running | $50,925 |
| 21. | 11 | 01 | Mike Skinner | Pontiac | U.S. Army | 100/0 | 499 | Running | $58,825 |
| 22. | 18 | 49 | Ken Schrader | Dodge | SEM Products | 97/0 | 499 | Running | $48,075 |
| 23. | 33 | 74 | Tony Raines* | Chevrolet | Staff America | 94/0 | 499 | Running | $48,725 |
| 24. | 10 | 43 | Jeff Green | Dodge | Cheerios | 91/0 | 498 | Running | $83,353 |
| 25. | 32 | 45 | Kyle Petty | Dodge | Georgia Pacific | 88/0 | 498 | Running | $55,725 |
| 26. | 15 | 15 | Michael Waltrip | Chevrolet | NAPA Auto Parts | 85/0 | 498 | Running | $62,175 |
| 27. | 34 | 0 | Jason Leffler | Pontiac | NetZero HiSpeed | 82/0 | 498 | Running | $47,010 |
| 28. | 38 | 38 | Elliott Sadler | Ford | M&M's | 79/0 | 497 | Running | $80,610 |
| 29. | 7 | 2 | Rusty Wallace | Dodge | Miller Lite | 81/5 | 497 | Running | $78,392 |
| 30. | 43 | 02 | Hermie Sadler | Pontiac | James Madison University | 73/0 | 495 | Running | $44,150 |
| 31. | 40 | 1 | John Andretti | Chevrolet | Pennzoil | 70/0 | 495 | Running | $68,762 |
| 32. | 27 | 32 | Ricky Craven | Pontiac | Tide | 67/0 | 495 | Running | $59,889 |
| 33. | 30 | 19 | Jeremy Mayfield | Dodge | Dodge Dealers/UAW | 64/0 | 490 | Running | $52,270 |
| 34. | 29 | 10 | Johnny Benson | Pontiac | Valvoline | 61/0 | 488 | Running | $70,070 |
| 35. | 24 | 4 | Kevin Lepage | Pontiac | Kodak | 58/0 | 475 | Running | $43,275 |
| 36. | 37 | 31 | Robby Gordon | Chevrolet | Cingular Wireless | 55/0 | 473 | Running | $68,412 |
| 37. | 25 | 77 | Dave Blaney | Ford | Jasper Engines & Trans. | 52/0 | 471 | Running | $51,175 |
| 38. | 6 | 7 | Jimmy Spencer | Dodge | Sirius Satellite Radio | 49/0 | 459 | Running | $43,115 |
| 39. | 13 | 97 | Kurt Busch | Ford | Rubbermaid | 51/5 | 407 | Engine | $63,065 |
| 40. | 36 | 54 | Todd Bodine | Ford | Subway/National Guard | 43/0 | 385 | Accident | $42,990 |
| 41. | 20 | 18 | Bobby Labonte | Chevrolet | Interstate Batteries | 40/0 | 271 | Engine | $88,023 |
| 42. | 42 | 37 | Derrike Cope | Chevrolet | PHM/Friendly's | 37/0 | 260 | Overheating | $42,900 |
| 43. | 9 | 40 | Sterling Marlin | Dodge | Coors Light | 34/0 | 127 | Engine | $86,191 |

*Rookie. Time of race: 3 hours, 53 minutes, 14 seconds. Average speed: 67.658 mph. Margin of victory: 1.036 seconds. Caution flags: 15 for 119 laps. 55-62 (Cars 7 and 2—accident, Turn 4); 65-69 (Car 40—spin, Turn 4); 80-85 (Car 12—spin, Turn 2); 107-112 (Car 88—spin, Turn 2); 122-129 (Car 45—spin, Turn 2); 138-143 (Cars 2, 48, 02 and 42—accident, Turn 4); 177-188 (Cars 22 and 23—accident, back stretch); 231-237 (Car 23—spin, Turn 3); 275-281 (Car 77—accident, Turn 1); 288-293 (Car 38—spin, Turn 4); 355-362 (Cars 6 and 02—accident, Turn 4); 375-380 (Car 88—spin, Turn 4); 388-393 (Cars 54, 77 and 31—accident, front stretch); 405-427 (Cars 97 and 2—accident, front stretch); 436-440 (debris on track). Lap leaders: Nine lead changes among eight drivers. Jeff Gordon 1-107, Terry Labonte 108-147, Dale Earnhardt Jr. 148-180, Rusty Wallace 181-198, Kevin Harvick 199-208, Kurt Busch 209-245, Earnhardt Jr. 246-273, Tony Stewart 274-275, Joe Nemechek 276-294, J. Gordon 295-500. Pole winner: Jeff Gordon, 93.650 mph. Dropped to rear: Dale Jarrett and Todd Bodine (backup cars). Failed to qualify: Mark Green, Morgan Shepherd. Estimated attendance: 88,000.

**Martinsville Speedway**
Martinsville, Va.— .526-mile paved oval
October 19, 2003—263 miles—500 laps

## Points standings

| Rk. | Driver | Behind |
|---|---|---|
| 1. | Matt Kenseth | Leader |
| 2. | Kevin Harvick | -240 |
| 3. | Dale Earnhardt Jr. | -283 |
| 4. | Ryan Newman | -300 |
| 5. | Jimmie Johnson | -306 |
| 6. | Jeff Gordon | -346 |
| 7. | Tony Stewart | -577 |
| 8. | Bobby Labonte | -708 |
| 9. | Terry Labonte | -773 |
| 10. | Bill Elliott | -863 |

2003 SEASON

# Bass Pro Shops MBNA 500 — race 33 of 36

| Fin. | St. | Car | Driver | Make | Sponsor | Pts./Bonus | Laps | Status | Winnings |
|---|---|---|---|---|---|---|---|---|---|
| 1. | 19 | 24 | Jeff Gordon | Chevrolet | DuPont | 180/5 | 325 | Running | $249,978 |
| 2. | 24 | 20 | Tony Stewart | Chevrolet | Home Depot | 180/10 | 325 | Running | $207,678 |
| 3. | 9 | 48 | Jimmie Johnson | Chevrolet | Lowe's | 170/5 | 325 | Running | $122,800 |
| 4. | 5 | 9 | Bill Elliott | Dodge | Dodge Dealers/UAW | 160/5 | 325 | Running | $133,833 |
| 5. | 2 | 18 | Bobby Labonte | Chevrolet | Interstate Batteries | 160/5 | 325 | Running | $133,383 |
| 6. | 3 | 8 | Dale Earnhardt Jr. | Chevrolet | Budweiser | 155/5 | 325 | Running | $121,692 |
| 7. | 15 | 19 | Jeremy Mayfield | Dodge | Dodge Dealers/UAW | 146/0 | 325 | Running | $89,200 |
| 8. | 17 | 97 | Kurt Busch | Ford | Rubbermaid | 147/5 | 325 | Running | $110,475 |
| 9. | 22 | 7 | Jimmy Spencer | Dodge | Sirius Satellite Radio | 143/5 | 325 | Running | $92,450 |
| 10. | 8 | 01 | Joe Nemechek | Pontiac | U.S. Army | 134/0 | 325 | Running | $92,225 |
| 11. | 37 | 17 | Matt Kenseth | Ford | Smirnoff Ice/DeWalt | 130/0 | 325 | Running | $95,825 |
| 12. | 31 | 88 | Dale Jarrett | Ford | The UPS Store | 127/0 | 325 | Running | $115,403 |
| 13. | 29 | 0 | Ward Burton | Pontiac | NetZero HiSpeed | 99/0 | 325 | Running | $74,125 |
| 14. | 12 | 4 | Kevin Lepage | Pontiac | Kodak | 126/5 | 325 | Running | $78,550 |
| 15. | 18 | 42 | Jamie McMurray* | Dodge | Havoline | 118/0 | 324 | Running | $74,400 |
| 16. | 40 | 40 | Sterling Marlin | Dodge | Coors Light/St. Jude Hospital | 115/0 | 324 | Running | $111,150 |
| 17. | 6 | 38 | Elliott Sadler | Ford | M&M's | 117/5 | 324 | Running | $105,300 |
| 18. | 33 | 74 | Tony Raines* | Chevrolet | Staff America | 114/0 | 324 | Running | $70,550 |
| 19. | 21 | 2 | Rusty Wallace | Dodge | Miller Lite | 106/0 | 324 | Running | $104,692 |
| 20. | 10 | 29 | Kevin Harvick | Chevrolet | GM Goodwrench Service | 108/5 | 324 | Running | $110,753 |
| 21. | 16 | 31 | Robby Gordon | Chevrolet | Cingular Wireless | 100/0 | 324 | Running | $94,712 |
| 22. | 11 | 1 | John Andretti | Chevrolet | Pennzoil | 97/0 | 324 | Running | $94,062 |
| 23. | 38 | 99 | Jeff Burton | Ford | CITGO | 94/0 | 324 | Running | $102,442 |
| 24. | 30 | 10 | Johnny Benson | Pontiac | Valvoline | 91/0 | 323 | Running | $94,475 |
| 25. | 25 | 45 | Kyle Petty | Dodge | Georgia Pacific | 88/0 | 323 | Running | $75,725 |
| 26. | 43 | 49 | Ken Schrader | Dodge | 1-800-CALLATT | 85/0 | 323 | Running | $67,025 |
| 27. | 36 | 35 | Bobby Hamilton Jr. | Ford | U.S. Marines/WaWa | 82/0 | 323 | Running | $63,575 |
| 28. | 14 | 41 | Casey Mears* | Dodge | Target | 79/0 | 321 | Running | $82,864 |
| 29. | 1 | 12 | Ryan Newman | Dodge | Mobil 1/ALLTEL | 81/5 | 320 | Accident | $107,900 |
| 30. | 28 | 23 | Kenny Wallace | Dodge | Stacker 2 | 73/0 | 320 | Running | $66,585 |
| 31. | 42 | 21 | Ricky Rudd | Ford | Motorcraft Quality Parts | 70/0 | 319 | Running | $73,425 |
| 32. | 41 | 22 | Scott Wimmer | Dodge | Caterpillar | 67/0 | 316 | Running | $98,801 |
| 33. | 32 | 5 | Terry Labonte | Chevrolet | Kellogg's/got milk? | 64/0 | 316 | Running | $89,531 |
| 34. | 27 | 16 | Greg Biffle* | Ford | Grainger | 61/0 | 314 | Trans. | $62,425 |
| 35. | 26 | 32 | Ricky Craven | Pontiac | Tide | 58/0 | 222 | Accident | $70,300 |
| 36. | 20 | 30 | Steve Park | Chevrolet | America Online | 55/0 | 221 | Accident | $70,225 |
| 37. | 35 | 77 | Dave Blaney | Ford | Jasper Engines & Trans. | 52/0 | 201 | Accident | $70,100 |
| 38. | 13 | 15 | Michael Waltrip | Chevrolet | NAPA Auto Parts | 49/0 | 170 | Engine | $80,050 |
| 39. | 39 | 6 | Mark Martin | Ford | Viagra | 46/0 | 159 | Engine | $95,833 |
| 40. | 23 | 37 | Derrike Cope | Chevrolet | PHM/Friendly's | 43/0 | 132 | Engine | $61,950 |
| 41. | 34 | 02 | Hermie Sadler | Chevrolet | Zapf Creation | 40/0 | 77 | Accident | $61,900 |
| 42. | 7 | 54 | Todd Bodine | Ford | National Guard | 37/0 | 44 | Accident | $61,850 |
| 43. | 4 | 25 | Brian Vickers | Chevrolet | UAW/Delphi | 34/0 | 18 | Overheating | $62,059 |

*Rookie. Time of race: 3 hours, 55 minutes, 2 seconds. Average speed: 127.769 mph. Margin of victory: Under caution. Caution flags: 10 for 63 laps. 4-6 (debris on track); 34-44 (rain); 46-51 (Cars 54, 23, 4, 15, 17 and 40—accident, back stretch); 104-113 (Car 21—spin, front stretch); 153-157 (debris in Turn 1); 162-168 (oil on track); 172-178 (Car 32—accident, Turn 1); 201-205 (Car 77—accident, Turn 4); 224-229 (Car 30—accident, Turn 2); 323-325 (Car 12—accident, Turn 3). Lap leaders: 28 lead changes among 12 drivers: Ryan Newman 1-12, Kevin Harvick 13-33, Dale Earnhardt Jr. 34, Elliott Sadler 35, Harvick 36-55, Bobby Labonte 56-61, Tony Stewart 62-99, Earnhardt Jr. 100-101, Kurt Busch 102-104, Earnhardt Jr. 105-128, Stewart 129-152, Earnhardt Jr. 153, Stewart 154-200, B. Labonte 201, Jimmy Spencer 202-203, Jeff Gordon 204-205, B. Labonte 206-224, J. Gordon 225-231, B. Labonte 232-239, Earnhardt Jr. 240-243, B. Labonte 244-274, J. Gordon 275, B. Labonte 276, J. Gordon 277-285, Jimmie Johnson 286, Newman 287, Kevin Lepage 288, Tony Raines 289, J. Gordon 290-325. Note: The race was run over two days because of rain. Pole winner: Ryan Newman, 194.295 mph, track record. Dropped to rear: Ward Burton (backup car), Mark Martin (engine change). Failed to qualify: Jeff Green, Buckshot Jones, Larry Foyt, Mike Wallace, Billy Bigley Jr., Shelby Howard.

**Atlanta Motor Speedway**
Hampton, Ga.— 1.54-mile banked paved oval
October 26 and 27, 2003—500 miles—325 laps

## Points standings

| Rk. | Driver | Behind |
|---|---|---|
| 1. | Matt Kenseth | Leader |
| 2. | Dale Earnhardt Jr. | -258 |
| 3. | Kevin Harvick | -262 |
| 4. | Jimmie Johnson | -266 |
| 5. | Jeff Gordon | -296 |
| 6. | Ryan Newman | -349 |
| 7. | Tony Stewart | -527 |
| 8. | Bobby Labonte | -678 |
| 9. | Bill Elliott | -833 |
| 10. | Terry Labonte | -839 |

**2003 SEASON**

# Checker Auto Parts 500 — race 34 of 36

| Fin. | St. | Car | Driver | Make | Sponsor | Pts./Bonus | Laps | Status | Winnings |
|---|---|---|---|---|---|---|---|---|---|
| 1. | 11 | 8 | Dale Earnhardt Jr. | Chevrolet | Budweiser | 180/5 | 312 | Running | $203,017 |
| 2. | 3 | 48 | Jimmie Johnson | Chevrolet | Lowe's | 175/5 | 312 | Running | $173,625 |
| 3. | 1 | 12 | Ryan Newman | Dodge | ALLTEL | 170/5 | 312 | Running | $152,625 |
| 4. | 7 | 97 | Kurt Busch | Ford | Rubbermaid | 170/10 | 312 | Running | $142,585 |
| 5. | 17 | 15 | Michael Waltrip | Chevrolet | NAPA Auto Parts | 155/0 | 312 | Running | $100,925 |
| 6. | 37 | 17 | Matt Kenseth | Ford | DeWalt Power Tools | 150/0 | 312 | Running | $86,000 |
| 7. | 4 | 24 | Jeff Gordon | Chevrolet | DuPont | 146/0 | 312 | Running | $111,778 |
| 8. | 27 | 99 | Jeff Burton | Ford | CITGO | 142/0 | 312 | Running | $98,917 |
| 9. | 28 | 22 | Scott Wimmer | Dodge | Caterpillar | 138/0 | 312 | Running | $95,656 |
| 10. | 12 | 6 | Mark Martin | Ford | Viagra | 134/0 | 312 | Running | $99,133 |
| 11. | 15 | 40 | Sterling Marlin | Dodge | Coors Light | 130/0 | 312 | Running | $100,000 |
| 12. | 22 | 42 | Jamie McMurray* | Dodge | Havoline | 127/0 | 312 | Running | $59,900 |
| 13. | 2 | 25 | Brian Vickers | Chevrolet | UAW/Delphi | 124/0 | 312 | Running | $58,900 |
| 14. | 18 | 9 | Bill Elliott | Dodge | Dodge Dealers/UAW | 121/0 | 312 | Running | $90,633 |
| 15. | 25 | 16 | Greg Biffle* | Ford | Grainger | 118/0 | 312 | Running | $56,130 |
| 16. | 33 | 1 | John Andretti | Chevrolet | Pennzoil | 115/0 | 312 | Running | $75,162 |
| 17. | 30 | 21 | Ricky Rudd | Ford | Motorcraft Quality Parts | 112/0 | 312 | Running | $76,875 |
| 18. | 6 | 20 | Tony Stewart | Chevrolet | Home Depot | 109/0 | 312 | Running | $102,128 |
| 19. | 41 | 74 | Tony Raines* | Chevrolet | Staff America | 106/0 | 312 | Running | $53,350 |
| 20. | 14 | 38 | Elliott Sadler | Ford | Pedigree | 103/0 | 312 | Running | $89,225 |
| 21. | 35 | 10 | Johnny Benson | Pontiac | Valvoline | 100/0 | 312 | Running | $79,900 |
| 22. | 21 | 54 | Todd Bodine | Ford | National Guard | 97/0 | 312 | Running | $65,575 |
| 23. | 43 | 4 | Kevin Lepage | Pontiac | Kodak | 99/5 | 312 | Running | $60,250 |
| 24. | 8 | 77 | Dave Blaney | Ford | Jasper Engines & Trans. | 91/0 | 312 | Running | $68,589 |
| 25. | 26 | 23 | Kenny Wallace | Dodge | Stacker 2 | 88/0 | 312 | Running | $52,375 |
| 26. | 23 | 09 | Mike Wallace | Dodge | Miccosukee Resort | 85/0 | 312 | Running | $48,450 |
| 27. | 34 | 49 | Ken Schrader | Dodge | BAM Racing | 82/0 | 312 | Running | $51,625 |
| 28. | 32 | 14 | Larry Foyt* | Dodge | Harrah's | 79/0 | 312 | Running | $49,200 |
| 29. | 39 | 88 | Dale Jarrett | Ford | UPS | 76/0 | 312 | Running | $93,853 |
| 30. | 19 | 5 | Terry Labonte | Chevrolet | Kellogg's/got milk? | 73/0 | 310 | Running | $77,706 |
| 31. | 10 | 01 | Joe Nemechek | Pontiac | U.S. Army | 70/0 | 310 | Running | $50,925 |
| 32. | 31 | 31 | Robby Gordon | Chevrolet | Cingular Wireless | 67/0 | 310 | Running | $75,862 |
| 33. | 5 | 2 | Rusty Wallace | Dodge | Miller Lite | 64/0 | 305 | Running | $85,217 |
| 34. | 13 | 29 | Kevin Harvick | Chevrolet | GM Goodwrench Service | 61/0 | 297 | Running | $86,603 |
| 35. | 36 | 45 | Kyle Petty | Dodge | Georgia Pacific | 58/0 | 280 | Engine | $55,300 |
| 36. | 24 | 18 | Bobby Labonte | Chevrolet | Interstate Batteries | 55/0 | 267 | Running | $92,233 |
| 37. | 42 | 43 | Jeff Green | Dodge | Cheerios | 52/0 | 266 | Engine | $82,803 |
| 38. | 38 | 32 | Ricky Craven | Pontiac | Tide | 54/5 | 207 | Accident | $54,900 |
| 39. | 40 | 30 | Steve Park | Chevrolet | America Online | 46/0 | 206 | Accident | $54,775 |
| 40. | 29 | 7 | Jimmy Spencer | Dodge | Sirius Satellite Radio | PE | 167 | Accident | $46,625 |
| 41. | 20 | 0 | Ward Burton | Pontiac | NetZero HiSpeed | 40/0 | 167 | Accident | $47,185 |
| 42. | 9 | 41 | Casey Mears* | Dodge | Target | 37/0 | 117 | Engine | $54,350 |
| 43. | 16 | 19 | Jeremy Mayfield | Dodge | Dodge Dealers/UAW | 34/0 | 32 | Engine | $54,471 |

*Rookie. Time of race: 3 hours, 19 minutes, 11 seconds. Average speed: 93.984 mph. Margin of victory: .735 seconds. Caution flags: 10 for 66 laps. 35-43 (oil on track); 120-124 (oil on track); 140-144 (Car 32—accident, Turn 1); 170-178 (Cars 7 and 0—accident, Turn 3); 187-190 (Car 99—accident, Turn 3); 210-217 (Car 30—accident, Turn 3); 230-237 (Cars 2, 29, 20 and 18—accident, Turn 2); 269-275 (oil on track); 282-288 (oil on track); 300-303 (Car 09—spin, Turn 3). Lap leaders: 10 lead changes among six drivers. Ryan Newman 1, Jimmie Johnson 2-38, Dale Earnhardt Jr. 39, Ricky Craven 40, Kurt Busch 41-85, Earnhardt Jr. 86-120, Busch 121-173, Newman 174-213, Kevin Lepage 214, Johnson 215-261, Earnhardt Jr. 262-312. Pole winner: Ryan Newman, 133.675 mph. Failed to qualify: Derrike Cope, Brandon Ash. Estimated attendance: 100,000.

## Points standings

| Rk. | Driver | Behind |
|---|---|---|
| 1. | Matt Kenseth | Leader |
| 2. | Dale Earnhardt Jr. | -228 |
| 3. | Jimmie Johnson | -241 |
| 4. | Jeff Gordon | -300 |
| 5. | Ryan Newman | -329 |
| 6. | Kevin Harvick | -351 |
| 7. | Tony Stewart | -568 |
| 8. | Bobby Labonte | -773 |
| 9. | Kurt Busch | -845 |
| 10. | Bill Elliott | -862 |

**Phoenix International Raceway**
Avondale, Ariz. — 1-mile paved oval
November 2, 2003—312 miles—312 laps

# Pop Secret 400 — race 35 of 36

| Fin. | St. | Car | Driver | Make | Sponsor | Pts./Bonus | Laps | Status | Winnings |
|---|---|---|---|---|---|---|---|---|---|
| 1. | 5 | 9 | Bill Elliott | Dodge | Dodge Dealers/UAW | 185/10 | 393 | Running | $207,648 |
| 2. | 18 | 48 | Jimmie Johnson | Chevrolet | Lowe's | 175/5 | 393 | Running | $105,590 |
| 3. | 3 | 19 | Jeremy Mayfield | Dodge | Dodge Dealers/UAW | 170/5 | 393 | Running | $88,700 |
| 4. | 23 | 17 | Matt Kenseth | Ford | Smirnoff Ice/DeWalt | 160/0 | 393 | Running | $92,650 |
| 5. | 1 | 12 | Ryan Newman | Dodge | ALLTEL | 160/5 | 393 | Running | $98,785 |
| 6. | 4 | 74 | Tony Raines* | Chevrolet | Staff America | 150/0 | 393 | Running | $61,775 |
| 7. | 9 | 99 | Jeff Burton | Ford | CITGO | 146/0 | 393 | Running | $91,442 |
| 8. | 14 | 18 | Bobby Labonte | Chevrolet | Interstate Batteries | 142/0 | 393 | Running | $98,208 |
| 9. | 29 | 20 | Tony Stewart | Chevrolet | Home Depot | 138/0 | 393 | Running | $100,403 |
| 10. | 31 | 40 | Sterling Marlin | Dodge | Coors Light | 134/0 | 393 | Running | $99,425 |
| 11. | 10 | 16 | Greg Biffle* | Ford | Grainger | 130/0 | 392 | Running | $56,675 |
| 12. | 20 | 5 | Terry Labonte | Chevrolet | Kellogg's/got milk? | 127/0 | 392 | Running | $81,681 |
| 13. | 26 | 8 | Dale Earnhardt Jr. | Chevrolet | Budweiser | 124/0 | 391 | Running | $92,042 |
| 14. | 8 | 7 | Jimmy Spencer | Dodge | Sirius Satellite Radio | 121/0 | 391 | Running | $72,825 |
| 15. | 34 | 29 | Kevin Harvick | Chevrolet | GM Goodwrench Service | 118/0 | 391 | Running | $91,403 |
| 16. | 27 | 54 | Todd Bodine | Ford | National Guard | 115/0 | 391 | Running | $69,475 |
| 17. | 19 | 97 | Kurt Busch | Ford | Rubbermaid | 112/0 | 391 | Running | $82,925 |
| 18. | 13 | 0 | Ward Burton | Pontiac | NetZero HiSpeed | 114/5 | 390 | Running | $53,325 |
| 19. | 41 | 43 | Jeff Green | Dodge | Pop Secret | 106/0 | 390 | Running | $88,703 |
| 20. | 17 | 31 | Robby Gordon | Chevrolet | Cingular Wireless | 103/0 | 390 | Running | $79,612 |
| 21. | 15 | 38 | Elliott Sadler | Ford | M&M's | 100/0 | 390 | Running | $86,325 |
| 22. | 16 | 24 | Jeff Gordon | Chevrolet | DuPont | 97/0 | 390 | Running | $96,203 |
| 23. | 7 | 2 | Rusty Wallace | Dodge | Miller Lite | 94/0 | 390 | Running | $86,242 |
| 24. | 2 | 25 | Brian Vickers | Chevrolet | UAW/Delphi | 91/0 | 390 | Running | $52,175 |
| 25. | 6 | 01 | Joe Nemechek | Pontiac | U.S. Army | 88/0 | 390 | Running | $61,875 |
| 26. | 37 | 22 | Scott Wimmer | Dodge | Caterpillar | 85/0 | 389 | Running | $83,731 |
| 27. | 22 | 77 | Dave Blaney | Ford | Jasper Engines & Trans. | 82/0 | 389 | Running | $66,849 |
| 28. | 42 | 14 | Larry Foyt* | Dodge | Harrah's | 79/0 | 389 | Running | $47,260 |
| 29. | 25 | 10 | Johnny Benson | Pontiac | Valvoline | 76/0 | 388 | Running | $76,825 |
| 30. | 36 | 1 | John Andretti | Chevrolet | Pennzoil | 73/0 | 388 | Running | $75,142 |
| 31. | 35 | 23 | Kenny Wallace | Dodge | Stacker 2 | 70/0 | 387 | Running | $46,800 |
| 32. | 33 | 45 | Kyle Petty | Dodge | G. Pacific/Brawny/V. Junction | 67/0 | 387 | Running | $54,675 |
| 33. | 39 | 41 | Casey Mears* | Dodge | Target House | 64/0 | 386 | Running | $55,450 |
| 34. | 38 | 30 | Steve Park | Chevrolet | America Online | 61/0 | 386 | Running | $54,425 |
| 35. | 21 | 42 | Jamie McMurray* | Dodge | Havoline | 58/0 | 375 | Running | $46,300 |
| 36. | 28 | 49 | Ken Schrader | Dodge | BAM Racing | 55/0 | 374 | Accident | $46,255 |
| 37. | 11 | 15 | Michael Waltrip | Chevrolet | NAPA Auto Parts | 52/0 | 343 | Engine | $64,200 |
| 38. | 32 | 88 | Dale Jarrett | Ford | UPS | 49/0 | 339 | Engine | $91,923 |
| 39. | 30 | 32 | Ricky Craven | Pontiac | Tide | 46/0 | 325 | Accident | $54,090 |
| 40. | 24 | 21 | Ricky Rudd | Ford | Motorcraft Quality Parts | 43/0 | 325 | Accident | $54,015 |
| 41. | 12 | 6 | Mark Martin | Ford | Viagra | 40/0 | 239 | Engine | $79,773 |
| 42. | 40 | 4 | Kevin Lepage | Pontiac | Kodak | 37/0 | 130 | Engine | $45,860 |
| 43. | 43 | 37 | Derrike Cope | Chevrolet | PHM/Friendly's | 34/0 | 127 | Broken axle | $45,170 |

*Rookie. Time of race: 3 hours, 34 minutes, 44 seconds. Average speed: 111.677 mph. Margin of victory: 1.230 seconds. Caution flags: 10 for 65 laps. 77-81 (Car 37—accident, back stretch); 85-89 (Car 12—accident, Turn 2); 94-98 (debris on front stretch); 101-105 (Car 99—spin, front stretch); 108-117 (Cars 16 and 42—accident, back stretch); 156-160 (Car 45—accident, Turn 4); 243-253 (oil on track); 330-336 (Cars 21 and 32—accident, Turn 1); 369-373 (Car 20—spin, Turn 2); 376-382 (Car 49—accident, Turn 1). Lap leaders: 14 lead changes among five drivers. Ryan Newman 1-47, Ward Burton 48-77, Jeremy Mayfield 78-169, Jimmie Johnson 170, Mayfield 171-173, Johnson 174-185, Bill Elliott 186-243, Mayfield 244, Elliott 245-254, Johnson 255-319, Elliott 320-329, Newman 330, Elliott 331-368, Newman 369, Elliott 370-393. Pole winner: Ryan Newman, 155.577 mph. Dropped to rear: Bill Elliott (engine change). Failed to qualify: Hermie Sadler, Tim Sauter, Rich Bickle. Estimated attendance: 60,000.

**North Carolina Speedway**
Rockingham, N.C.— 1.017-mile banked paved oval
November 9, 2003—400 miles—393 laps

## 2003 SEASON

### Points standings

| Rk. | Driver | Behind |
|---|---|---|
| 1. | Matt Kenseth | Leader |
| 2. | Jimmie Johnson | -226 |
| 3. | Dale Earnhardt Jr. | -264 |
| 4. | Ryan Newman | -329 |
| 5. | Jeff Gordon | -363 |
| 6. | Kevin Harvick | -393 |
| 7. | Tony Stewart | -590 |
| 8. | Bobby Labonte | -791 |
| 9. | Bill Elliott | -837 |
| 10. | Kurt Busch | -893 |

# Ford 400 — race 36 of 36

| Fin. | St. | Car | Driver | Make | Sponsor | Pts./Bonus | Laps | Status | Winnings |
|---|---|---|---|---|---|---|---|---|---|
| 1. | 2 | 18 | Bobby Labonte | Chevrolet | Interstate Batteries | 180/5 | 267 | Running | $331,058 |
| 2. | 6 | 29 | Kevin Harvick | Chevrolet | GM Goodwrench Service | 175/5 | 267 | Running | $240,583 |
| 3. | 10 | 48 | Jimmie Johnson | Chevrolet | Lowe's | 170/5 | 267 | Running | $183,855 |
| 4. | 21 | 10 | Johnny Benson | Pontiac | Valvoline | 165/5 | 267 | Running | $146,575 |
| 5. | 5 | 24 | Jeff Gordon | Chevrolet | DuPont | 160/5 | 267 | Running | $147,628 |
| 6. | 9 | 19 | Jeremy Mayfield | Dodge | Dodge Dealers/UAW | 155/5 | 267 | Running | $90,975 |
| 7. | 13 | 20 | Tony Stewart | Chevrolet | Home Depot | 151/5 | 267 | Running | $120,703 |
| 8. | 20 | 9 | Bill Elliott | Dodge | Dodge Dealers/UAW | 152/10 | 267 | Running | $116,358 |
| 9. | 1 | 42 | Jamie McMurray* | Dodge | Havoline | 138/5 | 267 | Running | $65,725 |
| 10. | 41 | 40 | Sterling Marlin | Dodge | Coors Light | 134/5 | 267 | Running | $103,025 |
| 11. | 34 | 54 | Todd Bodine | Ford | National Guard | 130/5 | 267 | Running | $70,525 |
| 12. | 27 | 22 | Scott Wimmer | Dodge | Caterpillar | 127/0 | 267 | Running | $84,681 |
| 13. | 19 | 74 | Tony Raines* | Chevrolet | Speed Racer | 124/0 | 267 | Running | $53,525 |
| 14. | 36 | 99 | Jeff Burton | Ford | CITGO | 121/0 | 267 | Running | $85,742 |
| 15. | 14 | 5 | Terry Labonte | Chevrolet | Kellogg's/got milk? | 123/5 | 267 | Running | $79,606 |
| 16. | 12 | 14 | Larry Foyt* | Dodge | Harrah's | 115/0 | 267 | Running | $47,800 |
| 17. | 8 | 01 | Joe Nemechek | Pontiac | U.S. Army | 112/0 | 267 | Running | $66,400 |
| 18. | 31 | 4 | Kevin Lepage | Pontiac | Kodak | 109/0 | 267 | Running | $60,400 |
| 19. | 35 | 30 | Steve Park | Chevrolet | America Online | 106/0 | 267 | Running | $58,900 |
| 20. | 28 | 90 | Ron Hornaday | Chevrolet | Childress Vineyards | 103/0 | 267 | Running | $48,950 |
| 21. | 29 | 38 | Elliott Sadler | Ford | M&M's | 100/0 | 267 | Running | $84,650 |
| 22. | 43 | 23 | Kenny Wallace | Dodge | Stacker 2 | 97/0 | 266 | Running | $60,950 |
| 23. | 11 | 2 | Rusty Wallace | Dodge | Miller Lite | 99/5 | 265 | Running | $84,467 |
| 24. | 38 | 8 | Dale Earnhardt Jr. | Chevrolet | Budweiser | 91/0 | 265 | Running | $87,117 |
| 25. | 16 | 7 | Jimmy Spencer | Dodge | Sirius Satellite Radio | 93/5 | 265 | Running | $58,989 |
| 26. | 32 | 88 | Dale Jarrett | Ford | UPS | 85/0 | 265 | Running | $91,578 |
| 27. | 15 | 41 | Casey Mears* | Dodge | Target | 82/0 | 264 | Running | $56,800 |
| 28. | 18 | 77 | Dave Blaney | Ford | Jasper Engines & Trans. | 79/0 | 264 | Running | $56,500 |
| 29. | 42 | 32 | Ricky Craven | Pontiac | Tide | 76/0 | 264 | Running | $56,190 |
| 30. | 39 | 31 | Robby Gordon | Chevrolet | Cingular Wireless | 73/0 | 258 | Running | $73,662 |
| 31. | 30 | 21 | Ricky Rudd | Ford | Motorcraft Quality Parts | 70/0 | 252 | Engine | $55,275 |
| 32. | 24 | 0 | Ward Burton | Pontiac | NetZero HiSpeed | 67/0 | 242 | Accident | $44,575 |
| 33. | 40 | 6 | Mark Martin | Ford | Viagra | 64/0 | 242 | Accident | $79,113 |
| 34. | 3 | 25 | Brian Vickers | Chevrolet | UAW/Delphi | 66/5 | 220 | Running | $44,175 |
| 35. | 25 | 16 | Greg Biffle* | Ford | Grainger | 58/0 | 197 | Accident | $43,975 |
| 36. | 7 | 97 | Kurt Busch | Ford | Rubbermaid | 55/0 | 147 | Running | $63,760 |
| 37. | 4 | 12 | Ryan Newman | Dodge | ALLTEL | 52/0 | 122 | Accident | $73,425 |
| 38. | 33 | 02 | Hermie Sadler** | Chevrolet | Sadler GM | PE | 121 | Overheating | $43,350 |
| 39. | 17 | 00 | Mike Skinner | Chevrolet | Bacardi Silver Raz | 46/0 | 89 | Accident | $43,150 |
| 40. | 26 | 43 | Jeff Green | Dodge | Chex | 43/0 | 81 | Engine | $78,703 |
| 41. | 23 | 15 | Michael Waltrip | Chevrolet | NAPA Auto Parts | 40/0 | 72 | Accident | $60,735 |
| 42. | 22 | 1 | John Andretti | Chevrolet | Pennzoil | 37/0 | 57 | Engine | $67,612 |
| 43. | 37 | 17 | Matt Kenseth | Ford | DeWalt Power Tools | 34/0 | 28 | Engine | $62,665 |

*Rookie. **Hermie Sadler was not awarded points because he entered the race after the entry deadline. Time of race: 3 hours, 25 minutes, 37 seconds. Average speed: 116.868 mph. Margin of victory: 1.749 seconds. Caution flags: 10 for 60 laps. 5-9 (Cars 12, 29 and 97—accident, back stretch); 30-34 (oil on track); 74-78 (Car 15—accident, Turn 2); 82-86 (oil on track); 122-128 (Car 25—accident, Turn 1); 143-151 (debris on track); 200-207 (Car 16—accident, Turn 3); 210-214 (Car 01—accident, front stretch); 244-249 (Cars 0 and 6—accident, Turn 1); 254-258 (oil on track). Lap leaders: 21 lead changes among 12 drivers. Jamie McMurray-pole, Brian Vickers 1-11, Jeff Gordon 12-15, Rusty Wallace 16-22, Jimmie Johnson 23-29, R. Wallace 30, Jimmy Spencer 31-39, Johnny Benson 40-46, Bill Elliott 47-73, R. Wallace 74, Bill Elliott 75-87, Jeremy Mayfield 88-91, Elliott 92-121, Kevin Harvick 122, Terry Labonte 123, Harvick 124-132, Elliott 133-142, Harvick 143, Elliott 144-201, Tony Stewart 202-215, Elliott 216-266, Bobby Labonte 267. Pole winner: Jamie McMurray, 181.111 mph, track record. Failed to qualify: Kyle Petty, Ken Schrader, Mike Wallace, Derrike Cope, Rich Bickle. Estimated attendance: 75,000.

**Homestead-Miami Speedway**
Homestead, Fla.— 1.5-mile banked paved oval
November 16, 2003—400 miles—267 laps

# Series history

# 2002 NASCAR WINSTON CUP SEASON

| Race No. | Location | Date | Winner | Car owner |
|---|---|---|---|---|
| 1. | Daytona Beach, Fla. | Feb. 17 | Ward Burton | Bill Davis |
| 2. | Rockingham, N.C. | Feb. 24 | Matt Kenseth | Jack Roush |
| 3. | Las Vegas | March 3 | Sterling Marlin | Chip Ganassi |
| 4. | Hampton, Ga. | March 10 | Tony Stewart | Joe Gibbs |
| 5. | Darlington, S.C. | March 17 | Sterling Marlin | Chip Ganassi |
| 6. | Bristol, Tenn. | March 24 | Kurt Busch | Jack Roush |
| 7. | Justin, Texas | April 7 | Matt Kenseth | Jack Roush |
| 8. | Martinsville, Va. | April 14 | Bobby Labonte | Joe Gibbs |
| 9. | Talladega, Ala. | April 21 | Dale Earnhardt Jr. | Teresa Earnhardt |
| 10. | Fontana, Calif. | April 28 | Jimmie Johnson | Rick Hendrick |
| 11. | Richmond, Va. | May 4 | Tony Stewart | Joe Gibbs |
| 12. | Harrisburg, N.C. | May 26 | Mark Martin | Jack Roush |
| 13. | Dover, Del. | June 2 | Jimmie Johnson | Rick Hendrick |
| 14. | Long Pond, Pa. | June 9 | Dale Jarrett | Robert Yates |
| 15. | Brooklyn, Mich. | June 16 | Matt Kenseth | Jack Roush |
| 16. | Sonoma, Calif. | June 23 | Ricky Rudd | Robert Yates |
| 17. | Daytona Beach, Fla. | July 6 | Michael Waltrip | Teresa Earnhardt |
| 18. | Joliet, Ill. | July 14 | Kevin Harvick | Richard Childress |
| 19. | Loudon, N.H. | July 21 | Ward Burton | Bill Davis |
| 20. | Long Pond, Pa. | July 28 | Bill Elliott | Ray Evernham |
| 21. | Indianapolis | Aug. 4 | Bill Elliott | Ray Evernham |
| 22. | Watkins Glen, N.Y. | Aug. 11 | Tony Stewart | Joe Gibbs |
| 23. | Brooklyn, Mich. | Aug. 18 | Dale Jarrett | Robert Yates |
| 24. | Bristol, Tenn. | Aug. 24 | Jeff Gordon | Rick Hendrick |
| 25. | Darlington, S.C. | Sept. 1 | Jeff Gordon | Rick Hendrick |
| 26. | Richmond, Va. | Sept. 7 | Matt Kenseth | Jack Roush |
| 27. | Loudon, N.H. | Sept. 15 | Ryan Newman | Roger Penske |
| 28. | Dover, Del. | Sept. 22 | Jimmie Johnson | Rick Hendrick |
| 29. | Kansas City, Kan. | Sept. 29 | Jeff Gordon | Rick Hendrick |
| 30. | Talladega, Ala. | Oct. 6 | Dale Earnhardt Jr. | Teresa Earnhardt |
| 31. | Harrisburg, N.C. | Oct. 13 | Jamie McMurray | Chip Ganassi |
| 32. | Martinsville, Va. | Oct. 20 | Kurt Busch | Jack Roush |
| 33. | Hampton, Ga. | Oct. 27 | Kurt Busch | Jack Roush |
| 34. | Rockingham, N.C. | Nov. 3 | Johnny Benson | Nelson Bowers |
| 35. | Phoenix | Nov. 10 | Matt Kenseth | Jack Roush |
| 36. | Homestead, Fla. | Nov. 17 | Kurt Busch | Jack Roush |

\# Qualifying was rained out at Pocono 1, Darlington 2, Talladega 2, Charlotte 2 and Atlanta 2. Starting order at those races determined by car owner points.

## Points standings
1. Tony Stewart .............4,800
2. Mark Martin ..............4,762
3. Kurt Busch ................4,641
4. Jeff Gordon ...............4,607
5. Jimmie Johnson .......4,600
6. Ryan Newman ..........4,593
7. Rusty Wallace ...........4,574
8. Matt Kenseth ............4,432
9. Dale Jarrett ...............4,415
10. Ricky Rudd ................4,323

## Race winners (18)
1. Matt Kenseth ...................5
2. Kurt Busch........................4
3. Tony Stewart ....................3
   Jeff Gordon .......................3
   Jimmie Johnson ................3
6. Dale Jarrett .......................2
   Dale Earnhardt Jr. .............2
   Bill Elliott ..........................2
   Sterling Marlin ..................2
   Ward Burton .....................2
11. Mark Martin......................1
    Ryan Newman ..................1
    Ricky Rudd .......................1
    Michael Waltrip ................1
    Bobby Labonte .................1
    Kevin Harvick....................1
    Johnny Benson .................1
    Jamie McMurray ...............1

## Money won leaders
1. Tony Stewart ......$9,163,761
2. Mark Martin ........$7,004,893
3. Jeff Gordon ........$6,154,475
4. Ryan Newman ....$5,346,651
5. Kurt Busch .........$5,105,394
6. Dale Earnhardt Jr.$4,970,034
7. Ward Burton........$4,899,884
8. Rusty Wallace ....$4,785,134
9. Matt Kenseth ......$4,514,203
10. Ricky Rudd..........$4,444,614

## Pole winners (15)
1. Ryan Newman ....................6
2. Bill Elliott ............................4
   Jimmie Johnson .................4
4. Jeff Gordon .........................3
5. Ricky Craven ......................2
   Dale Earnhardt Jr. ..............2
   Tony Stewart ......................2
8. Todd Bodine .......................1
   Ward Burton .......................1
   Kurt Busch ..........................1
   Kevin Harvick .....................1
   Dale Jarrett ........................1
   Matt Kenseth .....................1
   Ricky Rudd .........................1
   Rusty Wallace ....................1

In 2002, there were 36 NASCAR Winston Cup events.

# 2001 NASCAR WINSTON CUP SEASON

| Race No. | Location | Date | Winner | Car owner |
|---|---|---|---|---|
| 1. | Daytona Beach, Fla. | Feb. 18 | Michael Waltrip | Dale Earnhardt |
| 2. | Rockingham, N.C. | Feb. 25 | Steve Park | Dale Earnhardt |
| 3. | Las Vegas | March 4 | Jeff Gordon | Rick Hendrick. |
| 4. | Atlanta | March 11 | Kevin Harvick | Richard Childress |
| 5. | Darlington, S.C. | March 18 | Dale Jarrett | Robert Yates |
| 6. | Bristol, Tenn. | March 25 | Elliott Sadler | Glen Wood |
| 7. | Ft. Worth, Texas | April 1 | Dale Jarrett | Robert Yates |
| 8. | Martinsville, Va. | April 8 | Dale Jarrett | Robert Yates |
| 9. | Talladega, Ala. | April 22 | Bobby Hamilton | Andy Petree |
| 10. | Los Angeles | April 29 | Rusty Wallace | Roger Penske |
| 11. | Richmond, Va. | May 5 | Tony Stewart | Joe Gibbs |
| 12. | Charlotte, N.C. | May 27 | Jeff Burton | Jack Roush |
| 13. | Dover, Del. | June 3 | Jeff Gordon | Rick Hendrick |
| 14. | Brooklyn, Mich. | June 10 | Jeff Gordon | Rick Hendrick |
| 15. | Long Pond, Pa. | June 17 | Ricky Rudd | Robert Yates |
| 16. | Sonoma, Calif. | June 24 | Tony Stewart | Joe Gibbs |
| 17. | Daytona Beach, Fla. | July 7 | Dale Earnhardt, Jr. | Dale Earnhardt |
| 18. | Chicago | July 15 | Kevin Harvick | Richard Childress |
| 19. | Loudon, N.H. | July 22 | Dale Jarrett | Robert Yates |
| 20. | Long Pond, Pa. | July 29 | Bobby Labonte | Joe Gibbs |
| 21. | Indianapolis | Aug. 5 | Jeff Gordon | Rick Hendrick |
| 22. | Watkins Glen, N.Y. | Aug. 12 | Jeff Gordon | Rick Hendrick |
| 23. | Brooklyn, Mich. | Aug. 19 | Sterling Marlin | Chip Ganassi |
| 24. | Bristol, Tenn. | Aug. 25 | Tony Stewart | Joe Gibbs |
| 25. | Darlington, S.C. | Sept. 2 | Ward Burton | Bill Davis |
| 26. | Richmond, Va. | Sept. 8 | Ricky Rudd | Robert Yates |
| 27. | Dover, Del. | Sept. 23 | Dale Earnhardt, Jr. | Dale Earnhardt |
| 28. | Kansas City, Kan. | Sept. 30 | Jeff Gordon | Rick Hendrick |
| 29. | Charlotte, N.C. | Oct. 7 | Sterling Marlin | Chip Ganassi |
| 30. | Martinsville, Va. | Oct. 14 | Ricky Craven | Cal Wells III |
| 31. | Talladega, Ala. | Oct. 21 | Dale Earnhardt, Jr. | Dale Earnhardt |
| 32. | Phoenix | Oct. 28 | Jeff Burton | Jack Roush |
| 33. | Rockingham, N.C. | Nov. 4 | Joe Nemechek | Andy Petree |
| 34. | Miami | Nov. 11 | Bill Elliott | Ray Evernham |
| 35. | Atlanta | Nov. 18 | Bobby Labonte | Joe Gibbs |
| 36. | Loudon, N.H. | Nov. 23 | Robby Gordon | Richard Childress |

Starting order was set car owner points for Darlington (March 18), Dover (June 3) and New Hampshire (Nov. 23).

## Points standings
1. JEFF GORDON .............5,112
2. Tony Stewart ...............4,763
3. Sterling Marlin .............4,741
4. Ricky Rudd .................4,706
5. Dale Jarrett .................4,612
6. Bobby Labonte.............4,561
7. Rusty Wallace .............4,481
8. Dale Earnhardt Jr. ........4,460
9. Kevin Harvick...............4,406
10. Jeff Burton .................4,394

## Race winners (19)
1. Jeff Gordon ........................6
2. Dale Jarrett ........................4
3. Tony Stewart .....................3
   Dale Earnhardt, Jr. .............3
5. Jeff Burton.........................2
   Kevin Harvick.....................2
   Bobby Labonte ..................2
   Sterling Marlin ...................2
   Ricky Rudd ........................2
10. Ward Burton .....................1
    Ricky Craven .....................1
    Bill Elliott ..........................1
    Robby Gordon ...................1
    Bobby Hamilton .................1
    Joe Nemechek ..................1
    Steve Park ........................1
    Elliott Sadler ......................1
    Rusty Wallace ...................1
    Michael Waltrip .................1

## Money won leaders
1. Jeff Gordon ......$10,879,757
2. Dale Earnhardt, Jr. 5,827,542
3. Dale Jarrett............5,377,742
4. Tony Stewart .......4,941,463
5. Ricky Rudd ..........4,828,027
6. Rusty Wallace ......4,788,652
7. Bobby Labonte ......4,786,779
8. Sterling Marlin ......4,517,634
9. Kevin Harvick .......4,302,202
10. Jeff Burton ..........4,230,737

## Pole winners (18)
1. Jeff Gordon ........................6
2. Dale Jarrett ........................4
3. Todd Bodine ......................3
4. Stacy Compton ..................2
   Dale Earnhardt, Jr. .............2
   Bill Elliott ..........................2
   Mark Martin .......................2
   Jimmy Spencer ..................2
9. Casey Atwood ....................1
   Kurt Busch .........................1
   Ricky Craven .....................1
   Jeff Green ..........................1
   Bobby Labonte ..................1
   Jason Leffler ......................1
   Sterling Marlin...................1
   Ryan Newman ...................1
   Ricky Rudd ........................1
   Kenny Wallace ...................1

In 2001, there were 36 NASCAR Winston Cup events. Race No. 36 at New Hampshire originally was scheduled for Sept. 16, but was postponed because of terrorist attacks.

# 2000 NASCAR WINSTON CUP SEASON

| Race No. | Location | Date | Winner | Car owner |
|---|---|---|---|---|
| 1. | Daytona Beach, Fla. | Feb. 20 | Dale Jarrett | Robert Yates |
| 2. | Rockingham, N.C. | Feb. 27 | Bobby Labonte | Joe Gibbs |
| 3. | Las Vegas | Mar. 5 | Jeff Burton | Robert Corn |
| 4. | Hampton, Ga. | Mar. 12 | Dale Earnhardt | Richard Childress |
| 5. | Darlington, S.C. | Mar. 19 | Ward Burton | Bill Davis |
| 6. | Bristol, Tenn. | Mar. 26 | Rusty Wallace | Roger Penske |
| 7. | Fort Worth, Texas | April 2 | Dale Earnhardt, Jr. | Dale Earnhardt |
| 8. | Martinsville, Va. | April 9 | Mark Martin | Jack Roush |
| 9. | Talladega, Ala. | April 16 | Jeff Gordon | Rick Hendrick |
| 10. | Fontana, Calif. | April 30 | Jeremy Mayfield | Michael Kranefuss |
| 11. | Richmond, Va. | May 6 | Dale Earnhardt, Jr. | Dale Earnhardt |
| 12. | Charlotte, N.C. | May 28 | Matt Kenseth | Mark Martin |
| 13. | Dover, Del. | June 4 | Tony Stewart | Joe Gibbs |
| 14. | Brooklyn, Mich. | June 11 | Tony Stewart | Joe Gibbs |
| 15. | Long Pond, Pa. | June 19 | Jeremy Mayfield | Michael Kranefuss |
| 16. | Sonoma, Calif. | June 25 | Jeff Gordon | Rick Hendrick |
| 17. | Daytona Beach, Fla. | July 1 | Jeff Burton | Robert Corn |
| 18. | Loudon, N.H. | July 9 | Tony Stewart | Joe Gibbs |
| 19. | Long Pond, Pa. | July 23 | Rusty Wallace | Roger Penske |
| 20. | Indianapolis | Aug. 5 | Bobby Labonte | Joe Gibbs |
| 21. | Watkins Glen, N.Y. | Aug. 13 | Steve Park | Dale Earnhardt |
| 22. | Brooklyn, Mich. | Aug. 20 | Rusty Wallace | Roger Penske |
| 23. | Bristol, Tenn. | Aug. 26 | Rusty Wallace | Roger Penske |
| 24. | Darlington, S.C. | Sept. 3 | Bobby Labonte | Joe Gibbs |
| 25. | Richmond, Va. | Sept. 9 | Jeff Gordon | Rick Hendrick |
| 26. | Loudon, N.H. | Sept. 17 | Jeff Burton | Robert Corn |
| 27. | Dover, Del. | Sept. 24 | Tony Stewart | Joe Gibbs |
| 28. | Martinsville, Va. | Oct. 1 | Tony Stewart | Joe Gibbs |
| 29. | Charlotte, N.C. | Oct. 8 | Bobby Labonte | Joe Gibbs |
| 30. | Talladega, Ala. | Oct. 15 | Dale Earnhardt | Richard Childress |
| 31. | Rockingham, N.C. | Oct. 22 | Dale Jarrett | Robert Yates |
| 32. | Phoenix, Ariz. | Nov. 5 | Jeff Burton | Robert Corn |
| 33. | Homestead, Fla. | Nov. 12 | Tony Stewart | Joe Gibbs |
| 34. | Hampton, Ga. | Nov. 20 | Jerry Nadeau | Joe Hendrick, Jr. |

## Points standings
1. Bobby Labonte..............5,130
2. Dale Earnhardt..............4,865
3. Jeff Burton....................4,836
4. Dale Jarrett...................4,684
5. Ricky Rudd...................4,575
6. Tony Stewart.................4,570
7. Rusty Wallace...............4,544
8. Mark Martin..................4,410
9. Jeff Gordon...................4,361
10. Ward Burton................4,152

## Race winners (14)
1. Tony Stewart .......................6
2. Bobby Labonte ..................4
   Jeff Burton............................4
   Rusty Wallace .....................4
5. Jeff Gordon..........................3
6. Dale Earnhardt ...................2
   Dale Earnhardt, Jr. ..............2
   Dale Jarrett ..........................2
   Jeremy Mayfield .................2
10. Mark Martin........................1
    Ward Burton .......................1
    Steve Park ..........................1
    Matt Kenseth ......................1
    Jerry Nadeau ......................1

## Money won leaders
1. Bobby Labonte ....$7,361,386
2. Jeff Burton ............5,959,439
3. Dale Jarrett .......... 5,934,475
4. Dale Earnhardt ..... 4,918,886
5. Tony Stewart ........ 3,642,348
6. Rusty Wallace.......3,621,468
7. Mark Martin ......... 3,098,874
8. Jeff Gordon .......... 3,001,144
9. Rick Rudd.............2,914,970
10. Dale Earnhardt Jr 2,801,880

## Pole winners (13)
1. Rusty Wallace ......................9
2. Jeremy Mayfield ..................4
3. Jeff Gordon ..........................3
   Dale Jarrett...........................3
5. Bobby Labonte R..................2
   Dale Earnhardt.....................2
   Steve Park ...........................2
   Dale Earnhardt, Jr. ...............2
   Ricky Rudd ..........................2
10. Jeff Burton...........................1
    Terry Labonte ......................1
    Joe Nemechek.....................1
    Mike Skinner .......................1

In 2000, there were 34 NASCAR Winston Cup Series events.

Qualifying was rained out at Watkins Glen.

# 1999 NASCAR WINSTON CUP SEASON

| Race No. | Location | Date | Winner | Car owner |
|---|---|---|---|---|
| 1. | Daytona Beach, Fla. | Feb. 14 | Jeff Gordon | Rick Hendrick |
| 2. | Rockingham, N.C. | Feb. 21 | Mark Martin | Jack Roush |
| 3. | Las Vegas | Mar. 7 | Jeff Burton | Jack Roush |
| 4. | Hampton, Ga. | Mar. 14 | Jeff Gordon | Rick Hendrick |
| 5. | Darlington, S.C. | Mar. 21 | Jeff Burton | Jack Roush |
| 6. | Justin, Texas | Mar. 28 | Terry Labonte | Rick Hendrick |
| 7. | Bristol, Tenn. | April 11 | Rusty Wallace | Roger Penske |
| 8. | Martinsville, Va. | April 18 | John Andretti | Richard Petty |
| 9. | Talladega, Ala. | April 25 | Dale Earnhardt | Richard Childress |
| 10. | Fontana, Calif. | May 2 | Jeff Gordon | Rick Hendrick |
| 11. | Richmond, Va. | May 15 | Dale Jarrett | Robert Yates |
| 12. | Harrisburg, N.C. | May 30 | Jeff Burton | Rick Hendrick |
| 13. | Dover, Del. | June 6 | Bobby Labonte | Joe Gibbs |
| 14. | Brooklyn, Mich. | June 13 | Dale Jarrett | Robert Yates |
| 15. | Long Pond, Pa. | June 20 | Bobby Labonte | Joe Gibbs |
| 16. | Sonoma, Calif. | June 27 | Jeff Gordon | Rick Hendrick |
| 17. | Daytona Beach, Fla. | July 3 | Dale Jarrett | Robert Yates |
| 18. | Loudon, N.H. | July 11 | Jeff Burton | Jack Roush |
| 19. | Long Pond, Pa. | July 25 | Bobby Labonte | Joe Gibbs |
| 20. | Indianapolis | Aug. 8 | Dale Jarrett | Robert Yates |
| 21. | Watkins Glen, N.Y. | Aug. 15 | Jeff Gordon | Rick Hendrick |
| 22. | Brooklyn, Mich. | Aug. 22 | Bobby Labonte | Joe Gibbs |
| 23. | Bristol, Tenn. | Aug. 28 | Dale Earnhardt | Richard Childress |
| 24. | Darlington, S.C. | Sept. 5 | Jeff Burton | Jack Roush |
| 25. | Richmond, Va. | Sept. 11 | Tony Stewart | Joe Gibbs |
| 26. | Loudon, N.H. | Sept. 19 | Joe Nemechek | Felix Sabates |
| 27. | Dover, Del. | Sept. 26 | Mark Martin | Jack Roush |
| 28. | Martinsville, Va. | Oct. 3 | Jeff Gordon | Rick Hendrick |
| 29. | Harrisburg, N.C. | Oct. 11 | Jeff Gordon | Rick Hendrick |
| 30. | Talladega, Ala. | Oct. 17 | Dale Earnhardt | Richard Childress |
| 31. | Rockingham, N.C. | Oct. 24 | Jeff Burton | Jack Roush |
| 32. | Phoenix | Nov. 7 | Tony Stewart | Joe Gibbs |
| 33. | Homestead, Fla. | Nov. 14 | Tony Stewart | Joe Gibbs |
| 34. | Hampton, Ga. | Nov. 21 | Bobby Labonte | Joe Gibbs |

## Points standings
1. Dale Jarrett ................5,262
2. Bobby Labonte............5,061
3. Mark Martin ...............4,943
4. Tony Stewart ..............4,774
5. Jeff Burton..................4,733
6. Jeff Gordon .................4,620
7. Dale Earnhardt ............4,492
8. Rusty Wallace .............4,155
9. Ward Burton ................4,062
10. Mike Skinner ..............4,003

## Race winners (11)
1. Jeff Gordon ........................7
2. Jeff Burton..........................6
3. Bobby Labonte ..................5
4. Dale Jarrett .......................4
5. Dale Earnhardt ..................3
   Tony Stewart ....................3
7. Mark Martin .......................2
8. Rusty Wallace ...................1
   Terry Labonte ...................1
   John Andretti.....................1
   Joe Nemechek ..................1

## Money won leaders
1. Dale Jarrett..........$6,649.596
2. Jeff Burton.............5,725,399
3. Jeff Burton ............5,725,399
4. Bobby Labonte ......4,763,615
5. Mark Martin ..........3,509,744
6. Tony Stewart ........3,190,149
7. Dale Earnhardt .....3,149,536
8. Mike Skinner ........2,499,877
9. Terry Labonte .......2,475,365
10. Rusty Wallace........2,454,050

## Pole winners (15)
1. Jeff Gordon ........................7
2. Bobby Labonte ..................5
3. Rusty Wallace ....................4
4. Joe Nemechek ...................3
5. Tony Stewart .....................2
   Mike Skinner .....................2
   Kenny Irwin .......................2
8. Ward Burton ......................1
   Ken Schrader.....................1
   Sterling Marlin ..................1
   Mark Martin.......................1
   John Andretti.....................1
   Kevin Lepage ....................1
   Ricky Rudd .......................1
   David Green.......................1

In 1999, there were 34 NASCAR Winston Cup events

Qualifying was rained out at Fontana, Calif.

# 1998 NASCAR WINSTON CUP SEASON

| Race No. | Location | Date | Winner | Car owner |
|---|---|---|---|---|
| 1. | Daytona Beach, Fla. | Feb. 15 | Dale Earnhardt | Richard Childress |
| 2. | Rockingham, N.C. | Feb. 22 | Jeff Gordon | Rick Hendrick |
| 3. | Las Vegas | Mar. 1 | Mark Martin | Jack Roush |
| 4. | Hampton, Ga. | Mar. 9 | Bobby Labonte | Joe Gibbs |
| 5. | Darlington, S.C. | Mar. 22 | Dale Jarrett | Robert Yates |
| 6. | Bristol, Tenn. | Mar. 29 | Jeff Gordon | Rick Hendrick |
| 7. | Justin, Texas | April 5 | Mark Martin | Jack Roush |
| 8. | Martinsville, Va. | April 20 | Bobby Hamilton | Morgan-McClure |
| 9. | Talladega, Ala. | April 26 | Bobby Labonte | Joe Gibbs |
| 10. | Fontana, Calif. | May 3 | Mark Martin | Jack Roush |
| 11. | Harrisburg, N.C. | May 24 | Jeff Gordon | Rick Hendrick |
| 12. | Dover, Del. | May 31 | Dale Jarrett | Robert Yates |
| 13. | Richmond, Va. | June 6 | Terry Labonte | Rick Hendrick |
| 14. | Brooklyn, Mich. | June 14 | Mark Martin | Jack Roush |
| 15. | Long Pond, Pa. | June 21 | Jeremy Mayfield | Michael Kranefuss |
| 16. | Sonoma, Calif. | June 28 | Jeff Gordon | Rick Hendrick |
| 17. | Loudon, N.H. | July 12 | Jeff Burton | Jack Roush |
| 18. | Long Pond, Pa. | July 26 | Jeff Gordon | Rick Hendrick |
| 19. | Indianapolis | Aug. 1 | Jeff Gordon | Rick Hendrick |
| 20. | Watkins Glen, N.Y. | Aug. 9 | Jeff Gordon | Rick Hendrick |
| 21. | Brooklyn, Mich. | Aug. 16 | Jeff Gordon | Rick Hendrick |
| 22. | Bristol, Tenn. | Aug. 22 | Mark Martin | Jack Roush |
| 23. | Loudon, N.H. | Aug. 30 | Jeff Gordon | Rick Hendrick |
| 24. | Darlington, S.C. | Sept. 6 | Jeff Gordon | Rick Hendrick |
| 25. | Richmond, Va. | Sept. 12 | Jeff Burton | Jack Roush |
| 26. | Dover, Del. | Sept. 20 | Mark Martin | Jack Roush |
| 27. | Martinsville, Va. | Sept. 27 | Ricky Rudd | Ricky Rudd |
| 28. | Harrisburg, N.C. | Oct. 4 | Mark Martin | Jack Roush |
| 29. | Talladega, Ala. | Oct. 11 | Dale Jarrett | Robert Yates |
| 30. | Daytona Beach, Fla. | Oct. 17 | Jeff Gordon | Rick Hendrick |
| 31. | Phoenix | Oct. 25 | Rusty Wallace | Roger Penske |
| 32. | Rockingham, N.C. | Nov. 1 | Jeff Gordon | Rick Hendrick |
| 33. | Hampton, Ga. | Nov. 8 | Jeff Gordon | Rick Hendrick |

## Points standings
1. Jeff Gordon .................5,328
2. Mark Martin ................4,964
3. Dale Jarrett .................4,619
4. Rusty Wallace .............4,501
5. Jeff Burton ..................4,415
6. Bobby Labonte............3,180
7. Jeremy Mayfield .........3,157
8. Dale Earnhardt ............3,928
9. Terry Labonte ..............3,901
10. Bobby Hamilton .........3,786

## Race winners (11)
1. J. Gordon...........................13
2. M. Martin............................7
3. D. Jarrett ............................3
4. J. Burton ............................2
    B. Labonte .........................2
6. D. Earnhardt ......................1
    B. Hamilton ........................1
    T. Labonte .........................1
    J. Mayfield .........................1
    R. Rudd .............................1
    R. Wallace .........................1

## Money won leaders
1. J. Gordon ............$9,306,584
2. M. Martin ............4,309,006
3. D. Jarrett .............4,019,657
4. D. Earnhardt .......2,990,749
5. B. Labonte ..........2,980,052
6. R. Wallace ..........2,667,889
7. J. Burton .............2,626,987
8. J. Mayfield ..........2,332,034
9. B. Hamilton .........2,089,566
10. T. Labonte ..........2,054,163

## Pole winners (15)
1. J. Gordon ..............................7
2. R. Wallace .............................4
3. E. Irvan ..................................3
    B. Labonte .............................3
    M. Martin.................................3
6. W. Burton ...............................2
    D. Jarrett .................................2
    K. Schrader ............................2
9. J. Andretti ...............................1
    D. Cope ..................................1
    R. Craven ................................1
    B. Hamilton .............................1
    K. Irwin ....................................1
    R. Mast ...................................1
    J. Mayfield...............................1

In 1998, there were 33 NASCAR Winston Cup events

# 1997 NASCAR WINSTON CUP SEASON

| Race No. | Location | Date | Winner | Car owner |
|---|---|---|---|---|
| 1. | Daytona Beach, Fla. | Feb. 16 | Jeff Gordon | Rick Hendrick |
| 2. | Rockingham, N.C. | Feb. 23 | Jeff Gordon | Rick Hendrick |
| 3. | Richmond, Va. | Mar. 2 | Rusty Wallace | Roger Penske |
| 4. | Hampton, Ga. | Mar. 9 | Dale Jarrett | Robert Yates |
| 5. | Darlington, S.C. | Mar. 23 | Dale Jarrett | Robert Yates |
| 6. | Justin, Texas | April 6 | Jeff Burton | Jack Roush |
| 7. | Bristol, Tenn. | April 13 | Jeff Gordon | Rick Hendrick |
| 8. | Martinsville, Va. | Apr. 20 | Jeff Gordon | Rick Hendrick |
| 9. | Sonoma, Calif. | May 5 | Mark Martin | Jack Roush |
| 10. | Talladega, Ala. | May 10 | Mark Martin | Jack Roush |
| 11. | Harrisburg, N.C. | May 25 | Jeff Gordon | Rick Hendrick |
| 12. | Dover, Del. | June 1 | Ricky Rudd | Ricky Rudd |
| 13. | Long Pond, Pa. | June 8 | Jeff Gordon | Rick Hendrick |
| 14. | Brooklyn, Mich. | June 15 | Ernie Irvan | Robert Yates |
| 15. | Fontana, Calif. | June 22 | Jeff Gordon | Rick Hendrick |
| 16. | Daytona Beach, Fla. | July 5 | John Andretti | Cale Yarborough |
| 17. | Loudon, N.H. | July 13 | Jeff Burton | Jack Roush |
| 18. | Long Pond, Pa. | July 20 | Dale Jarrett | Robert Yates |
| 19. | Indianapolis | Aug. 2 | Ricky Rudd | Ricky Rudd |
| 20. | Watkins Glen, N.Y. | Aug. 10 | Jeff Gordon | Rick Hendrick |
| 21. | Brooklyn, Mich. | Aug. 17 | Mark Martin | Jack Roush |
| 22. | Bristol, Tenn. | Aug. 23 | Dale Jarrett | Robert Yates |
| 23. | Darlington, S.C. | Aug. 31 | Jeff Gordon | Rick Hendrick |
| 24. | Richmond, Va. | Sept. 6 | Dale Jarrett | Robert Yates |
| 25. | Loudon, N.H. | Sept. 14 | Jeff Gordon | Rick Hendrick |
| 26. | Dover, Del. | Sept. 21 | Mark Martin | Jack Roush |
| 27. | Martinsville, Va. | Sept. 29 | Jeff Burton | Jack Roush |
| 28. | Harrisburg, N.C. | Oct. 5 | Dale Jarrett | Robert Yates |
| 29. | Talladega, Ala. | Oct. 12 | Terry Labonte | Rick Hendrick |
| 30. | Rockingham, N.C. | Oct. 27 | Bobby Hamilton | Richard Petty |
| 31. | Phoenix | Nov. 2 | Dale Jarrett | Robert Yates |
| 32. | Hampton, Ga. | Nov. 16 | Bobby Labonte | Joe Gibbs |

## Points standings
1. Jeff Gordon .................4,710
2. Dale Jarrett .................4,696
3. Mark Martin .................4,681
4. Jeff Burton ..................4,285
5. Dale Earnhardt ............4,216
6. Terry Labonte...............4,177
7. Bobby Labonte.............4,101
8. Bill Elliott .....................3,836
9. Rusty Wallace .............3,598
10. Ken Schrader .............3,576

## Race winners (11)
1. J. Gordon......................10
2. D. Jarrett .......................7
3. M. Martin .......................4
4. J. Burton .......................3
5. R. Rudd .........................2
6. T. Labonte .....................1
   B. Labonte .....................1
   R. Wallace .....................1
   E. Irvan ..........................1
   B. Hamilton ....................1
   J. Andretti .....................1

## Money won leaders
1. J. Gordon ...........$6,375,658
2. D. Jarrett .............3,240,542
3. M. Martin .............2,532,484
4. J. Burton ..............2,296,614
5. T. Labonte............2,270,144
6. B. Labonte ...........2,217,999
7. D. Earnhardt ........2,151,909
8. R. Rudd ...............1,975,981
9. R. Wallace ...........1,705,625
10. E. Irvan................1,614,281
11. B. Elliott ..............1,607,827
12. B. Hamilton .........1,478,843
13. K. Schrader .........1,355,292
14. S. Marlin..............1,301,370
15. R. Craven ............1,259,550
16. T. Musgrave ........1,256,680
17. J. Benson ............1,256,457
18. J. Andretti............1,143,725
19. M. Waltrip............1,138,599
20. G. Bodine .............1,092,734

## Pole winners (18)
1. M. Martin.......................3
   B. Labonte .....................3
3. M. Skinner.....................2
   D. Jarrett .......................2
   G. Bodine.......................2
   B. Hamilton ....................2
   E. Irvan ..........................2
   J. Nemechek .................2
   K. Schrader ...................2
   K. Wallace .....................2
11. R. Gordon.....................1
    R. Wallace .....................1
    J. Andretti .....................1
    J. Gordon ......................1
    T. Bodine .......................1
    J. Benson ......................1
    B. Elliott ........................1
    W. Burton ......................1

In 1997, there were 32 NASCAR Winston Cup events

Qualifying was rained out at Richmond (1) and Texas

# 1996 NASCAR WINSTON CUP SEASON

| Race No. | Location | Date | Winner | Car owner |
|---|---|---|---|---|
| 1. | Daytona Beach, Fla. | Feb. 18 | Dale Jarrett | Robert Yates |
| 2. | Rockingham, N.C. | Feb. 25 | Dale Earnhardt | Richard Childress |
| 3. | Richmond, Va. | Mar. 3 | Jeff Gordon | Rick Hendrick |
| 4. | Hampton, Ga. | Mar. 10 | Dale Earnhardt | Richard Childress |
| 5. | Darlington, S.C. | Mar. 24 | Jeff Gordon | Rick Hendrick |
| 6. | Bristol, Tenn. | Mar. 31 | Jeff Gordon | Rick Hendrick |
| 7. | N. Wilkesboro, N.C. | Apr. 14 | Terry Labonte | Rick Hendrick |
| 8. | Martinsville, Va. | Apr. 21 | Rusty Wallace | Roger Penske |
| 9. | Talladega, Ala. | Apr. 28 | Sterling Marlin | Morgan-McClure |
| 10. | Sonoma, Calif. | May 5 | Rusty Wallace | Roger Penske |
| 11. | Harrisburg, N.C. | May 26 | Dale Jarrett | Robert Yates |
| 12. | Dover, Del. | June 2 | Jeff Gordon | Rick Hendrick |
| 13. | Long Pond, Pa. | June 16 | Jeff Gordon | Rick Hendrick |
| 14. | Brooklyn, Mich. | June 23 | Rusty Wallace | Roger Penske |
| 15. | Daytona Beach, Fla. | July 6 | Sterling Marlin | Morgan-McClure |
| 16. | Loudon, N.H. | July 14 | Ernie Irvan | Robert Yates |
| 17. | Long Pond, Pa. | July 21 | Rusty Wallace | Roger Penske |
| 18. | Talladega, Ala. | July 28 | Jeff Gordon | Rick Hendrick |
| 19. | Indianapolis | Aug. 3 | Dale Jarrett | Robert Yates |
| 20. | Watkins Glen, N.Y. | Aug. 11 | Geoff Bodine | Geoff Bodine |
| 21. | Brooklyn, Mich. | Aug. 18 | Dale Jarrett | Robert Yates |
| 22. | Bristol, Tenn. | Aug. 24 | Rusty Wallace | Roger Penske |
| 23. | Darlington, S.C. | Sept. 1 | Jeff Gordon | Rick Hendrick |
| 24. | Richmond, Va. | Sept. 7 | Ernie Irvan | Robert Yates |
| 25. | Dover, Del. | Sept. 15 | Jeff Gordon | Rick Hendrick |
| 26. | Martinsville, Va. | Sept. 22 | Jeff Gordon | Rick Hendrick |
| 27. | N. Wilkesboro, N.C. | Sept. 29 | Jeff Gordon | Rick Hendrick |
| 28. | Harrisburg, N.C. | Oct. 6 | Terry Labonte | Rick Hendrick |
| 29. | Rockingham, N.C. | Oct. 20 | Ricky Rudd | Ricky Rudd |
| 30. | Phoenix | Oct. 27 | Bobby Hamilton | Richard Petty |
| 31. | Hampton, Ga. | Nov. 10 | Bobby Labonte | Joe Gibbs |

## Points standings
1. Terry Labonte ............... 4,657
2. Jeff Gordon ................. 4,620
3. Dale Jarrett ................ 4,568
4. Dale Earnhardt .............. 4,327
5. Mark Martin ................. 4,278
6. Ricky Rudd .................. 3,845
7. Rusty Wallace ............... 3,717
8. Sterling Marlin ............. 3,682
9. Bobby Hamilton .............. 3,639
10. Ernie Irvan ................ 3,632

## Race winners (11)
1. J. Gordon ................... 10
2. R. Wallace .................. 5
3. D. Jarrett .................. 4
4. D. Earnhardt ................ 2
   S. Marlin ................... 2
   E. Irvan .................... 2
   T. Labonte .................. 2
8. G. Bodine ................... 1
   R. Rudd ..................... 1
   B. Hamilton ................. 1
   B. Labonte .................. 1

## Money won leaders
1. T. Labonte ........... $4,030,648
2. J. Gordon ............. 3,428,485
3. D. Jarrett ............ 2,985,418
4. D. Earnhardt .......... 2,285,926
5. M. Martin ............. 1,887,396
6. R. Rudd ............... 1,503,025
7. R. Wallace ............ 1,665,315
8. S. Marlin ............. 1,588,425
9. B. Hamilton ........... 1,475,196
10. E. Irvan ............. 1,683,313
11. B. Labonte ........... 1,475,196
12. K. Schrader .......... 1,089,603
13. J. Burton ............... 884,303
14. M. Waltrip ........... 1,182,811
15. J. Spencer ........... 1,090,876
16. T. Musgrave ............. 961,512
17. G. Bodine ............ 1,031,762
18. R. Mast ................. 924,559
19. M. Shepherd ............. 719,059
20. R. Craven ............... 941,959

## Pole winners (14)
1. J. Gordon ................... 5
2. T. Labonte .................. 4
   B. Labonte .................. 4
   M. Martin ................... 4
5. D. Earnhardt ................ 2
   B. Hamilton ................. 2
   D. Jarrett .................. 2
   R. Craven ................... 2
9. J. Benson ................... 1
   J. Mayfield ................. 1
   J. Burton ................... 1
   W. Burton ................... 1
   T. Musgrave ................. 1
   E. Irvan .................... 1

In 1996, there were 31 NASCAR Winston Cup events

# 1995 NASCAR WINSTON CUP SEASON

| Race No. | Location | Date | Winner | Car owner |
|---|---|---|---|---|
| 1. | Daytona Beach, Fla. | Feb. 19 | Sterling Marlin | Morgan-McClure |
| 2. | Rockingham, N.C. | Feb. 26 | Jeff Gordon | Rick Hendrick |
| 3. | Richmond, Va. | Mar. 5 | Terry Labonte | Rick Hendrick |
| 4. | Hampton, Ga. | Mar. 12 | Jeff Gordon | Rick Hendrick |
| 5. | Darlington, S.C. | Mar. 26 | Sterling Marlin | Morgan-McClure |
| 6. | Bristol, Tenn. | Apr. 2 | Jeff Gordon | Rick Hendrick |
| 7. | N. Wilkesboro, N.C. | Apr. 9 | Dale Earnhardt | Richard Childress |
| 8. | Martinsville, Va. | Apr. 23 | Rusty Wallace | Roger Penske |
| 9. | Talladega, Ala. | Apr. 30 | Mark Martin | Jack Roush |
| 10. | Sonoma, Calif. | May 7 | Dale Earnhardt | Richard Childress |
| 11. | Harrisburg, N.C. | May 28 | Bobby Labonte | Joe Gibbs |
| 12. | Dover, Del. | June 4 | Kyle Petty | Felix Sabates |
| 13. | Long Pond, Pa. | June 11 | Terry Labonte | Rick Hendrick |
| 14. | Brooklyn, Mich. | June 18 | Bobby Labonte | Joe Gibbs |
| 15. | Daytona Beach, Fla. | July 1 | Jeff Gordon | Rick Hendrick |
| 16. | Loudon, N.H. | July 9 | Jeff Gordon | Rick Hendrick |
| 17. | Long Pond, Pa. | July 16 | Dale Jarrett | Robert Yates |
| 18. | Talladega, Ala. | July 23 | Sterling Marlin | Morgan-McClure |
| 19. | Indianapolis | Aug. 5 | Dale Earnhardt | Richard Childress |
| 20. | Watkins Glen, N.Y. | Aug. 13 | Mark Martin | Jack Roush |
| 21. | Brooklyn, Mich. | Aug. 20 | Bobby Labonte | Joe Gibbs |
| 22. | Bristol, Tenn. | Aug. 26 | Terry Labonte | Rick Hendrick |
| 23. | Darlington, S.C. | Sept. 3 | Jeff Gordon | Rick Hendrick |
| 24. | Richmond, Va. | Sept. 9 | Rusty Wallace | Roger Penske |
| 25. | Dover, Del. | Sept. 17 | Jeff Gordon | Rick Hendrick |
| 26. | Martinsville, Va. | Sept. 24 | Dale Earnhardt | Richard Childress |
| 27. | N. Wilkesboro, N.C. | Oct. 1 | Mark Martin | Jack Roush |
| 28. | Harrisburg, N.C. | Oct. 8 | Mark Martin | Jack Roush |
| 29. | Rockingham, N.C. | Oct. 22 | Ward Burton | Bill Davis |
| 30. | Phoenix | Oct. 29 | Ricky Rudd | Ricky Rudd |
| 31. | Hampton, Ga. | Nov. 12 | Dale Earnhardt | Richard Childress |

## Points standings
1. Jeff Gordon .................4,614
2. Dale Earnhardt ............4,580
3. Sterling Marlin .............4,361
4. Mark Martin .................4,320
5. Rusty Wallace .............4,240
6. Terry Labonte...............4,146
7. Ted Musgrave .............3,949
8. Bill Elliott .....................3,746
9. Ricky Rudd .................3,734
10. Bobby Labonte...........3,718

## Race winners (11)
1. J. Gordon.........................7
2. D. Earnhardt ....................5
3. M. Martin .........................4
4. S. Marlin ..........................3
   T. Labonte .......................3
   B. Labonte .......................3
7. R. Wallace .......................2
8. R. Rudd ...........................1
   W. Burton .........................1
   K. Petty ............................1
   D. Jarrett ..........................1

## Money won leaders
1. J. Gordon ..........$4,347,343
2. D. Earnhardt .........3,154,241
3. S. Marlin................2,253,502
4. M. Martin ...............1,893,519
5. R. Wallace ............1,642,837
6. T. Labonte.............1,558,659
7. B. Labonte ............1,413,682
8. D. Jarrett ..............1,363,158
9. R. Rudd ................1,337,703
10. T. Musgrave ........1,147,445
11. G. Bodine ............1,011,090
12. B. Elliott...................996,816
13. M. Shepherd ...........966,374
14. M. Waltrip ................898,338
15. B. Bodine .................893,029
16. K. Schrader ..............886,566
17. D. Waltrip .................850,632
18. B. Hamilton ..............804,505
19. R. Mast ....................749,550
20. K. Petty ...................698,875

## Pole winners (15)
1. J. Gordon .........................8
2. M. Martin..........................4
3. D. Earnhardt ....................3
4. B. Elliott...........................2
   R. Rudd ...........................2
   B. Labonte .......................2
7. T. Labonte .......................1
   S. Marlin ..........................1
   T. Musgrave.....................1
   D. Jarrett ..........................1
   K. Schrader ......................1
   J. Andretti ........................1
   D. Waltrip .........................1
   R. Mast .............................1
   H. Stricklin........................1

In 1995, there were 31 NASCAR Winston Cup events

# 1994 NASCAR WINSTON CUP SEASON

| Race No. | Location | Date | Winner | Car owner |
|---|---|---|---|---|
| 1. | Daytona Beach, Fla. | Feb. 20 | Sterling Marlin | Morgan-McClure |
| 2. | Rockingham, N.C. | Feb. 27 | Rusty Wallace | Roger Penske |
| 3. | Richmond, Va. | Mar. 6 | Ernie Irvan | Robert Yates |
| 4. | Hampton, Ga. | Mar. 13 | Ernie Irvan | Robert Yates |
| 5. | Darlington, S.C. | Mar. 27 | Dale Earnhardt | Richard Childress |
| 6. | Bristol, Tenn. | Apr. 10 | Dale Earnhardt | Richard Childress |
| 7. | N. Wilkesboro, N.C. | Apr. 17 | Terry Labonte | Rick Hendrick |
| 8. | Martinsville, Va. | Apr. 24 | Rusty Wallace | Roger Penske |
| 9. | Talladega, Ala. | May 1 | Dale Earnhardt | Richard Childress |
| 10. | Sonoma, Calif. | May 15 | Ernie Irvan | Robert Yates |
| 11. | Harrisburg, N.C. | May 29 | Jeff Gordon | Rick Hendrick |
| 12. | Dover, Del. | June 5 | Rusty Wallace | Roger Penske |
| 13. | Long Pond, Pa. | June 12 | Rusty Wallace | Roger Penske |
| 14. | Brooklyn, Mich. | June 19 | Rusty Wallace | Roger Penske |
| 15. | Daytona Beach, Fla. | July 2 | Jimmy Spencer | Junior Johnson |
| 16. | Loudon, N.H. | July 10 | Ricky Rudd | Ricky Rudd |
| 17. | Long Pond, Pa. | July 17 | Geoff Bodine | Geoff Bodine |
| 18. | Talladega, Ala. | July 24 | Jimmy Spencer | Junior Johnson |
| 19. | Indianapolis | Aug. 6 | Jeff Gordon | Rick Hendrick |
| 20. | Watkins Glen, N.Y. | Aug. 14 | Mark Martin | Jack Roush |
| 21. | Brooklyn, Mich. | Aug. 21 | Geoff Bodine | Geoff Bodine |
| 22. | Bristol, Tenn. | Aug. 27 | Rusty Wallace | Roger Penske |
| 23. | Darlington, S.C. | Sept. 4 | Bill Elliott | Junior Johnson |
| 24. | Richmond, Va. | Sept. 10 | Terry Labonte | Rick Hendrick |
| 25. | Dover, Del. | Sept. 18 | Rusty Wallace | Roger Penske |
| 26. | Martinsville, Va. | Sept. 25 | Rusty Wallace | Roger Penske |
| 27. | N. Wilkesboro, N.C. | Oct. 2 | Geoff Bodine | Geoff Bodine |
| 28. | Harrisburg, N.C. | Oct. 9 | Dale Jarrett | Joe Gibbs |
| 29. | Rockingham, N.C. | Oct. 23 | Dale Earnhardt | Richard Childress |
| 30. | Phoenix | Oct. 30 | Terry Labonte | Rick Hendrick |
| 31. | Hampton, Ga. | Nov. 13 | Mark Martin | Jack Roush |

## Points standings
1. Dale Earnhardt ............4,694
2. Mark Martin .................4,250
3. Rusty Wallace .............4,207
4. Ken Schrader ..............4,060
5. Ricky Rudd .................4,050
6. Morgan Shepherd ........4,029
7. Terry Labonte ..............3,876
8. Jeff Gordon .................3,776
9. Darrell Waltrip .............3,688
10. Bill Elliott ....................3,617

## Race winners (12)
1. Rusty Wallace ..................8
2. Dale Earnhardt ..................4
3. Ernie Irvan .......................3
   Terry Labonte ..................3
   Geoff Bodine ....................3
6. Jeff Gordon ......................2
   Jimmy Spencer ................2
   Mark Martin ......................2
9. Sterling Marlin ..................1
   Ricky Rudd ......................1
   Bill Elliott ........................1
   Dale Jarrett .....................1

## Money won leaders
1. D. Earnhardt ........$3,300,733
2. R. Wallace ...........1,914,072
3. J. Gordon .............1,779,523
4. M. Martin .............1,628,906
5. G. Bodine ............1,276,126
6. K. Schrader ..........1,171,062
7. S. Marlin ..............1,127,683
8. T. Labonte ............1,125,921
9. M. Shepherd.........1,089,038
10. R. Rudd ..............1,044,441
11. B. Elliott ................936,779
12. D. Jarrett ...............881,754
13. D. Waltrip ..............835,680
14. L. Speed ...............832,463
15. K. Petty .................806,332
16. B. Bodine ..............791,444
17. R. Mast .................722,361
18. M. Waltrip .............706,426
19. T. Musgrave ..........656,187
20. T. Bodine ..............494,316

## Pole winners (17)
1. Geoff Bodine .......................5
   Ernie Irvan ...........................5
3. Loy Allen .............................3
   Ted Musgrave ......................3
5. Rusty Wallace .....................2
   Dale Earnhardt ....................2
7. Bill Elliott ............................1
   Chuck Bown ........................1
   Jeff Gordon .........................1
   Rick Mast ............................1
   Mark Martin .........................1
   Harry Gant ..........................1
   Jimmy Spencer ....................1
   Ward Burton ........................1
   Ricky Rudd .........................1
   Sterling Marlin .....................1
   Greg Sacks .........................1

In 1994, there were 31 NASCAR Winston Cup events

# 1993 NASCAR WINSTON CUP SEASON

| Race No. | Location | Date | Winner | Car owner |
|---|---|---|---|---|
| 1. | Daytona Beach, Fla. | Feb. 14 | Dale Jarrett | Joe Gibbs |
| 2. | Rockingham, N.C. | Feb. 28 | Rusty Wallace | Roger Penske |
| 3. | Richmond, Va. | Mar. 7 | Davey Allison | Robert Yates |
| 4. | Hampton, Ga. | Mar. 20 | Morgan Shepherd | Wood Brothers |
| 5. | Darlington, S.C. | Mar. 28 | Dale Earnhardt | Richard Childress |
| 6. | Bristol, Tenn. | Apr. 4 | Rusty Wallace | Roger Penske |
| 7. | N. Wilkesboro, N.C. | Apr. 18 | Rusty Wallace | Roger Penske |
| 8. | Martinsville, Va. | Apr. 25 | Rusty Wallace | Roger Penske |
| 9. | Talladega, Ala. | May 2 | Ernie Irvan | Morgan-McClure |
| 10. | Sonoma, Calif. | May 16 | Geoff Bodine | Bud Moore |
| 11. | Harrisburg, N.C. | May 30 | Dale Earnhardt | Richard Childress |
| 12. | Dover, Del. | June 6 | Dale Earnhardt | Richard Childress |
| 13. | Long Pond, Pa. | June 13 | Kyle Petty | Felix Sabates |
| 14. | Brooklyn, Mich. | June 20 | Ricky Rudd | Rick Hendrick |
| 15. | Daytona Beach, Fla. | July 3 | Dale Earnhardt | Richard Childress |
| 16. | Loudon, N.H. | July 11 | Rusty Wallace | Roger Penske |
| 17. | Long Pond, Pa. | July 18 | Dale Earnhardt | Richard Childress |
| 18. | Talladega, Ala. | July 25 | Dale Earnhardt | Richard Childress |
| 19. | Watkins Glen, N.Y. | Aug. 8 | Mark Martin | Jack Roush |
| 20. | Brooklyn, Mich. | Aug. 15 | Mark Martin | Jack Roush |
| 21. | Bristol, Tenn. | Aug. 28 | Mark Martin | Jack Roush |
| 22. | Darlington, S.C. | Sept. 5 | Mark Martin | Jack Roush |
| 23. | Richmond, Va. | Sept. 11 | Rusty Wallace | Roger Penske |
| 24. | Dover, Del. | Sept. 19 | Rusty Wallace | Roger Penske |
| 25. | Martinsville, Va. | Sept. 26 | Ernie Irvan | Robert Yates |
| 26. | N. Wilkesboro, N.C. | Oct. 3 | Rusty Wallace | Roger Penske |
| 27. | Harrisburg, N.C. | Oct. 10 | Ernie Irvan | Robert Yates |
| 28. | Rockingham, N.C. | Oct. 24 | Rusty Wallace | Roger Penske |
| 29. | Phoenix | Oct. 31 | Mark Martin | Jack Roush |
| 30. | Hampton, Ga. | Nov. 14 | Rusty Wallace | Roger Penske |

## Points standings
1. Dale Earnhardt ............. 4,526
2. Rusty Wallace ............. 4,446
3. Mark Martin ................ 4,150
4. Dale Jarrett ................. 4,000
5. Kyle Petty ..................... 3,860
6. Ernie Irvan .................. 3,834
7. Morgan Shepherd ....... 3,807
8. Bill Elliott ..................... 3,774
9. Ken Schrader .............. 3,715
10. Ricky Rudd ................. 3,644

## Race winners (10)
1. Rusty Wallace ................. 10
2. Dale Earnhardt ................. 6
3. Mark Martin ....................... 5
4. Ernie Irvan ......................... 3
5. Davey Allison .................... 1
   Geoff Bodine ..................... 1
   Dale Jarrett ....................... 1
   Kyle Petty .......................... 1
   Ricky Rudd ........................ 1
   Morgan Shepherd ............. 1

## Money won leaders
1. D. Earnhardt .......... 3,353,789
2. R. Wallace ............. 1,702,154
3. M. Martin ............... 1,657,662
4. E. Irvan .................. 1,400,468
5. D. Jarrett ............... 1,242,394
6. B. Elliott ..................... 955,859
7. K. Schrader ............... 952,748
8. K. Petty ...................... 914,662
9. G. Bodine ................... 783,762
10. M. Shepherd ............ 782,523
11. H. Gant ..................... 772,832
12. J. Gordon .................. 765,168
13. R. Rudd ..................... 752,562
14. D. Waltrip ................. 746,646
15. J. Spencer ................ 686,026
16. S. Marlin ................... 628,835
17. B. Bodine .................. 582,014
18. R. Mast ..................... 568,095
19. T. Labonte ................ 531,717
20. M. Waltrip ................ 529,923

## Pole winners (12)
1. Ken Schrader ..................... 6
2. Mark Martin ....................... 5
3. Ernie Irvan ......................... 4
4. Rusty Wallace .................... 3
5. Brett Bodine ...................... 2
   Dale Earnhardt .................. 2
   Bill Elliott ........................... 2
8. Geoff Bodine ..................... 1
   Jeff Gordon ....................... 1
   Bobby Labonte .................. 1
   Kyle Petty .......................... 1
   Harry Gant......................... 1

In 1993, there were 30 NASCAR Winston Cup events

# 1992 NASCAR WINSTON CUP SEASON

| Race No. | Location | Date | Winner | Car owner |
|---|---|---|---|---|
| 1. | Daytona Beach, Fla. | Feb. 16 | Davey Allison | Robert Yates |
| 2. | Rockingham, N.C. | Mar. 1 | Bill Elliott | Junior Johnson |
| 3. | Richmond, Va. | Mar. 8 | Bill Elliott | Junior Johnson |
| 4. | Hampton, Ga. | Mar. 15 | Bill Elliott | Junior Johnson |
| 5. | Darlington, S.C. | Mar. 29 | Bill Elliott | Junior Johnson |
| 6. | Bristol, Tenn. | Apr. 5 | Alan Kulwicki | Alan Kulwicki |
| 7. | N. Wilkesboro, N.C. | Apr. 12 | Davey Allison | Robert Yates |
| 8. | Martinsville, Va. | Apr. 26 | Mark Martin | Jack Roush |
| 9. | Talladega, Ala. | May 3 | Davey Allison | Robert Yates |
| 10. | Harrisburg, N.C. | May 24 | Dale Earnhardt | Richard Childress |
| 11. | Dover, Del. | May 31 | Harry Gant | Leo Jackson |
| 12. | Sonoma, Calif. | June 7 | Ernie Irvan | Morgan-McClure |
| 13. | Long Pond, Pa. | June 14 | Alan Kulwicki | Alan Kulwicki |
| 14. | Brooklyn, Mich. | June 21 | Davey Allison | Robert Yates |
| 15. | Daytona Beach, Fla. | July 4 | Ernie Irvan | Morgan-McClure |
| 16. | Long Pond, Pa. | July 19 | Darrell Waltrip | Darrell Waltrip |
| 17. | Talladega, Ala. | July 26 | Ernie Irvan | Morgan-McClure |
| 18. | Watkins Glen, N.Y. | Aug. 9 | Kyle Petty | Felix Sabates |
| 19. | Brooklyn, Mich. | Aug. 16 | Harry Gant | Leo Jackson |
| 20. | Bristol, Tenn. | Aug. 29 | Darrell Waltrip | Darrell Waltrip |
| 21. | Darlington, S.C. | Sept. 6 | Darrell Waltrip | Darrell Waltrip |
| 22. | Richmond, Va. | Sept. 12 | Rusty Wallace | Roger Penske |
| 23. | Dover, Del. | Sept. 20 | Ricky Rudd | Rick Hendrick |
| 24. | Martinsville, Va. | Sept. 28 | Geoff Bodine | Bud Moore |
| 25. | N. Wilkesboro, N.C. | Oct. 5 | Geoff Bodine | Bud Moore |
| 26. | Harrisburg, N.C. | Oct. 11 | Mark Martin | Jack Roush |
| 27. | Rockingham, N.C. | Oct. 25 | Kyle Petty | Felix Sabates |
| 28. | Phoenix | Nov. 1 | Davey Allison | Robert Yates |
| 29. | Hampton, Ga. | Nov. 15 | Bill Elliott | Junior Johnson |

## Points standings
1. Alan Kulwicki ................4,078
2. Bill Elliott .......................4,068
3. Davey Allison ................4,015
4. Harry Gant ....................3,955
5. Kyle Petty ......................3,945
6. Mark Martin ..................3,887
7. Ricky Rudd ...................3,735
8. Terry Labonte ................3,674
9. Darrell Waltrip ...............3,659
10. Sterling Marlin ..............3,063

## Race winners (12)
1. Davey Allison ......................5
   Bill Elliott .............................5
3. Ernie Irvan ..........................3
   Darrell Waltrip .....................3
   Geoff Bodine .......................2
6. Harry Gant ..........................2
   Alan Kulwicki ......................2
   Mark Martin ........................2
   Kyle Petty ............................2
10. Dale Earnhardt ...................1
    Ricky Rudd .........................1
    Rusty Wallace ....................1

## Money won leaders
1. Alan Kulwicki ......$2,322,561
2. Davey Allison .........1,955,628
3. Bill Elliott ................1,692,381
4. Harry Gant .............1,122,776
5. Kyle Petty ...............1,107,063
6. Mark Martin ...........1,000,571
7. Ernie Irvan ...............996,885
8. Dale Earnhardt ........915,463
9. Darrell Waltrip .........876,492
10. Ricky Rudd .............793,903
11. Geoff Bodine ...........716,583
12. Rusty Wallace .........657,925
13. Sterling Marlin .........649,048
14. Ken Schrader ...........639,679
15. Morgan Shepherd ....634,222
16. Terry Labonte ..........600,381
17. Brett Bodine ............495,224
18. Ted Musgrave .........449,121
19. Dick Trickle .............429,521
20. Dale Jarrett .............418,648
21. Michael Waltrip ........410,545
22. Bobby Hamilton .......367,065
23. Rick Mast ................350,740
24. Richard Petty ...........348,870
25. Hut Stricklin ............336,965

## Pole winners (14)
1. Alan Kulwicki ........................6
2. Sterling Marlin ......................3
3. Ernie Irvan ............................3
   Kyle Petty .............................3
5. Davey Allison .......................2
   Bill Elliott ..............................2
7. Brett Bodine .........................1
   Dale Earnhardt .....................1
   Mark Martin ..........................1
   Rick Mast .............................1
   Ricky Rudd ...........................1
   Ken Schrader .......................1
   Rusty Wallace ......................1
   Darrell Waltrip ......................1

In 1992, there were 29 NASCAR Winston Cup events

# 1991 NASCAR WINSTON CUP SEASON

| Race No. | Location | Date | Winner | Car owner |
|---|---|---|---|---|
| 1. | Daytona Beach, Fla. | Feb. 17 | Ernie Irvan | Morgan-McClure |
| 2. | Richmond, Va. | Feb. 24 | Dale Earnhardt | Richard Childress |
| 3. | Rockingham, N.C. | Mar. 3 | Kyle Petty | Felix Sabates |
| 4. | Hampton, Ga. | Mar. 17 | Ken Schrader | Rick Hendrick |
| 5. | Darlington, S.C. | Apr. 7 | Ricky Rudd | Rick Hendrick |
| 6. | Bristol, Tenn. | Apr. 14 | Rusty Wallace | Roger Penske |
| 7. | N. Wilkesboro, N.C. | Apr. 21 | Darrell Waltrip | Darrell Waltrip |
| 8. | Martinsville, Va. | Apr. 28 | Dale Earnhardt | Richard Childress |
| 9. | Talladega, Ala. | May 6 | Harry Gant | Leo Jackson |
| 10. | Harrisburg, N.C. | May 26 | Davey Allison | Robert Yates |
| 11. | Dover, Del. | June 2 | Ken Schrader | Rick Hendrick |
| 12. | Sonoma, Calif. | June 9 | Davey Allison | Robert Yates |
| 13. | Long Pond, Pa. | June 16 | Darrell Waltrip | Darrell Waltrip |
| 14. | Brooklyn, Mich. | June 23 | Davey Allison | Robert Yates |
| 15. | Daytona Beach, Fla. | July 6 | Bill Elliott | Harry Melling |
| 16. | Long Pond, Pa. | July 21 | Rusty Wallace | Roger Penske |
| 17. | Talladega, Ala. | July 28 | Dale Earnhardt | Richard Childress |
| 18. | Watkins Glen, N.Y. | Aug. 11 | Ernie Irvan | Morgan-McClure |
| 19. | Brooklyn, Mich. | Aug. 18 | Dale Jarrett | Wood Brothers |
| 20. | Bristol, Tenn. | Aug. 24 | Alan Kulwicki | Alan Kulwicki |
| 21. | Darlington, S.C. | Sept. 1 | Harry Gant | Leo Jackson |
| 22. | Richmond, Va. | Sept. 7 | Harry Gant | Leo Jackson |
| 23. | Dover, Del. | Sept. 15 | Harry Gant | Leo Jackson |
| 24. | Martinsville, Va. | Sept. 22 | Harry Gant | Leo Jackson |
| 25. | N. Wilkesboro, N.C. | Sept. 29 | Dale Earnhardt | Richard Childress |
| 26. | Harrisburg, N.C. | Oct. 6 | Geoff Bodine | Junior Johnson |
| 27. | Rockingham, N.C. | Oct. 20 | Davey Allison | Robert Yates |
| 28. | Phoenix | Nov. 3 | Davey Allison | Robert Yates |
| 29. | Hampton, Ga. | Nov. 17 | Mark Martin | Jack Roush |

## Points standings
1. Dale Earnhardt .............4,287
2. Ricky Rudd .................4,092
3. Davey Allison ...............4,088
4. Harry Gant ..................3,985
5. Ernie Irvan ..................3,925
6. Mark Martin ................3,914
7. Sterling Marlin .............3,839
8. Darrell Waltrip .............3,711
9. Ken Schrader ..............3,690
10. Rusty Wallace ............3,582

## Race winners (14)
1. Davey Allison .....................5
   Harry Gant .........................5
3. Dale Earnhardt ...................4
4. Ernie Irvan .........................2
   Ken Schrader ....................2
   Rusty Wallace ...................2
   Darrell Waltrip ...................2
8. Geoff Bodine .....................1
   Bill Elliott ............................1
   Alan Kulwicki ....................1
   Dale Jarrett .......................1
   Mark Martin .......................1
   Ricky Rudd ........................1
   Kyle Petty ..........................1

## Money won leaders
1. Dale Earnhardt ....$2,396,685
2. Davey Allison ........1,732,924
3. Harry Gant ............1,194,033
4. Ricky Rudd............1,093,765
5. Ernie Irvan .............1,079,017
6. Mark Martin ...........1,039,991
7. Ken Schrader...........722,434
8. Bill Elliott .................705,605
9. Sterling Marlin..........633,690
10. Geoff Bodine ..........625,256
11. Darrell Waltrip ........604,854
12. Alan Kulwicki ..........595,614
13. Morgan Shepherd ...521,147
14. Rusty Wallace ..........502,073
15. Dale Jarrett ..............444,256
16. Michael Waltrip ........440,812
17. Hut Stricklin .............426,524
18. Derrike Cope ...........419,380
19. Kyle Petty ................413,727
20. Brett Bodine ............376,220
21. Joe Ruttman ............361,661
22. Terry Labonte ..........348,898
23. Rick Mast ................344,020
24. Jimmy Spencer ........283,620
25. Richard Petty............268,035

## Pole winners (14)
1. Mark Martin......................5
2. Alan Kulwicki ..................4
3. Davey Allison..................3
4. Geoff Bodine ..................2
   Bill Elliott ..........................2
   Sterling Marlin..................2
   Kyle Petty ........................2
   Rusty Wallace ..................2
   Michael Waltrip ................2
10. Brett Bodine ...................1
    Harry Gant......................1
    Ernie Irvan ......................1
    Terry Labonte .................1
    Ricky Rudd ......................1

In 1991, there were 29 NASCAR Winston Cup events

# 1990 NASCAR WINSTON CUP SEASON

| Race No. | Location | Date | Winner | Car owner |
|---|---|---|---|---|
| 1. | Daytona Beach, Fla. | Feb. 18 | Derrike Cope | Bob Whitcomb |
| 2. | Richmond, Va. | Feb. 25 | Mark Martin | Jack Roush |
| 3. | Rockingham, N.C. | Mar. 4 | Kyle Petty | Felix Sabates |
| 4. | Hampton, Ga. | Mar. 18 | Dale Earnhardt | Richard Childress |
| 5. | Darlington, S.C. | Apr. 1 | Dale Earnhardt | Richard Childress |
| 6. | Bristol, Tenn. | Apr. 8 | Davey Allison | Robert Yates |
| 7. | N. Wilkesboro, N.C. | Apr. 22 | Brett Bodine | Kenny Bernstein |
| 8. | Martinsville, Va. | Apr. 29 | Geoff Bodine | Junior Johnson |
| 9. | Talladega, Ala. | May 6 | Dale Earnhardt | Richard Childress |
| 10. | Harrisburg, N.C. | May 27 | Rusty Wallace | Raymond Beadle |
| 11. | Dover, Del. | June 3 | Derrike Cope | Bob Whitcomb |
| 12. | Sonoma, Calif. | June 10 | Rusty Wallace | Raymond Beadle |
| 13. | Long Pond, Pa. | June 17 | Harry Gant | Leo Jackson |
| 14. | Brooklyn, Mich. | June 24 | Dale Earnhardt | Richard Childress |
| 15. | Daytona Beach, Fla. | July 7 | Dale Earnhardt | Richard Childress |
| 16. | Long Pond, Pa. | July 22 | Geoff Bodine | Junior Johnson |
| 17. | Talladega, Ala. | July 29 | Dale Earnhardt | Richard Childress |
| 18. | Watkins Glen, N.Y. | Aug. 12 | Ricky Rudd | Rick Hendrick |
| 19. | Brooklyn, Mich. | Aug. 19 | Mark Martin | Jack Roush |
| 20. | Bristol, Tenn. | Aug. 25 | Ernie Irvan | Morgan-McClure |
| 21. | Darlington, S.C. | Sept. 2 | Dale Earnhardt | Richard Childress |
| 22. | Richmond, Va. | Sept. 9 | Dale Earnhardt | Richard Childress |
| 23. | Dover, Del. | Sept. 16 | Bill Elliott | Harry Melling |
| 24. | Martinsville, Va. | Sept. 23 | Geoff Bodine | Junior Johnson |
| 25. | N. Wilkesboro, N.C. | Sept. 30 | Mark Martin | Jack Roush |
| 26. | Harrisburg, N.C. | Oct. 7 | Davey Allison | Robert Yates |
| 27. | Rockingham, N.C. | Oct. 21 | Alan Kulwicki | Alan Kulwicki |
| 28. | Phoenix | Nov. 4 | Dale Earnhardt | Richard Childress |
| 29. | Hampton, Ga. | Nov. 18 | Morgan Shepherd | Bud Moore |

## Points standings
1. Dale Earnhardt .............4,430
2. Mark Martin .................4,404
3. Geoff Bodine ................4,017
4. Bill Elliott .....................3,999
5. Morgan Shepherd .......3,689
6. Rusty Wallace .............3,676
7. Ricky Rudd .................3,601
8. Alan Kulwicki ..............3,599
9. Ernie Irvan ..................3,593
10. Ken Schrader .............3,572

## Race winners (14)
1. Dale Earnhardt ...................9
2. Geoff Bodine ......................3
   Mark Martin ........................3
4. Derrike Cope ......................2
   Rusty Wallace .....................2
   Davey Allison ......................2
7. Kyle Petty ...........................1
   Brett Bodine ........................1
   Harry Gant ..........................1
   Ricky Rudd ..........................1
   Ernie Irvan ..........................1
   Bill Elliott ............................1
   Alan Kulwicki ......................1
   Morgan Shepherd ..............1

## Money won leaders
1. Dale Earnhardt ....$3,083,056
2. Mark Martin ..........1,302,958
3. Geoff Bodine .........1,131,222
4. Bill Elliott ..............1,090,730
5. Rusty Wallace ..........954,129
6. Ken Schrader ............769,934
7. Kyle Petty .................746,326
8. Morgan Shepherd ....666,915
9. Davey Allison ............640,684
10. Ricky Rudd ..............573,650
11. Derrike Cope ............569,451
12. Alan Kulwicki ...........550,936
13. Ernie Irvan ............. 535,280
14. Darrell Waltrip ..........530,420
15. Harry Gant ................522,519
16. Terry Labonte ...........450,230
17. Brett Bodine ..............442,681
18. Michael Waltrip .........395,507
19. Sterling Marlin...........369,167
20. Dick Trickle ...............350,990
21. Bobby Hillin ...............339,366
22. Dave Marcis...............242,724
23. Rick Wilson ...............242,067
24. Jimmy Spencer .........219,775
25. Greg Sacks ...............216,148

## Pole winners (13)
1. Dale Earnhardt......................4
2. Ernie Irvan ..........................3
   Mark Martin ........................3
   Ken Schrader ......................3
5. Geoff Bodine ......................2
   Ricky Rudd ..........................2
   Bill Elliott ............................2
   Kyle Petty ...........................2
   Rusty Wallace .....................2
10. Dick Trickle ........................1
    Greg Sacks .........................1
    Alan Kulwicki ......................1
    Brett Bodine .......................1

In 1990, there were 29 NASCAR Winston Cup Events

# 1989 NASCAR WINSTON CUP SEASON

| Race No. | Location | Date | Winner | Car owner |
|---|---|---|---|---|
| 1. | Daytona Beach, Fla. | Feb. 19 | Darrell Waltrip | Rick Hendrick |
| 2. | Rockingham, N.C. | Mar. 5 | Rusty Wallace | Raymond Beadle |
| 3. | Hampton, Ga. | Mar. 19 | Darrell Waltrip | Rick Hendrick |
| 4. | Richmond, Va. | Mar. 26 | Rusty Wallace | Raymond Beadle |
| 5. | Darlington, S.C. | Apr. 2 | Harry Gant | Leo Jackson |
| 6. | Bristol, Tenn. | Apr. 9 | Rusty Wallace | Raymond Beadle |
| 7. | N. Wilkesboro, N.C. | Apr. 16 | Dale Earnhardt | Richard Childress |
| 8. | Martinsville, Va. | Apr. 23 | Darrell Waltrip | Rick Hendrick |
| 9. | Talladega, Ala. | May 7 | Davey Allison | Robert Yates |
| 10. | Harrisburg, N.C. | May 28 | Darrell Waltrip | Rick Hendrick |
| 11. | Dover, Del. | June 4 | Dale Earnhardt | Richard Childress |
| 12. | Sonoma, Calif. | June 11 | Ricky Rudd | Kenny Bernstein |
| 13. | Long Pond, Pa. | June 18 | Terry Labonte | Junior Johnson |
| 14. | Brooklyn, Mich. | June 25 | Bill Elliott | Harry Melling |
| 15. | Daytona Beach, Fla. | July 1 | Davey Allison | Robert Yates |
| 16. | Long Pond, Pa. | July 23 | Bill Elliott | Harry Melling |
| 17. | Talladega, Ala. | July 30 | Terry Labonte | Junior Johnson |
| 18. | Watkins Glen, N.Y. | Aug. 13 | Rusty Wallace | Raymond Beadle |
| 19. | Brooklyn, Mich. | Aug. 20 | Rusty Wallace | Raymond Beadle |
| 20. | Bristol, Tenn. | Aug. 26 | Darrell Waltrip | Rick Hendrick |
| 21. | Darlington, S.C. | Sept. 3 | Dale Earnhardt | Richard Childress |
| 22. | Richmond, Va. | Sept. 10 | Rusty Wallace | Raymond Beadle |
| 23. | Dover, Del. | Sept. 17 | Dale Earnhardt | Richard Childress |
| 24. | Martinsville, Va. | Sept. 24 | Darrell Waltrip | Rick Hendrick |
| 25. | Harrisburg, N.C. | Oct. 8 | Ken Schrader | Rick Hendrick |
| 26. | N. Wilkesboro, N.C. | Oct. 15 | Geoff Bodine | Rick Hendrick |
| 27. | Rockingham, N.C. | Oct. 22 | Mark Martin | Jack Roush |
| 28. | Phoenix | Nov. 5 | Bill Elliott | Harry Melling |
| 29. | Hampton, Ga. | Nov. 19 | Dale Earnhardt | Richard Childress |

## Points standings
1. Rusty Wallace ..............4,176
2. Dale Earnhardt............4,164
3. Mark Martin .................4,053
4. Darrell Waltrip .............3,971
5. Ken Schrader ..............3,786
6. Bill Elliott ......................3,774
7. Harry Gant ...................3,610
8. Ricky Rudd .................3,608
9. Geoff Bodine ...............3,600
10. Terry Labonte.............3,569

## Race winners (11)
1. Rusty Wallace ....................6
   Darrell Waltrip ....................6
3. Dale Earnhardt....................5
4. Bill Elliott ............................3
5. Davey Allison .....................2
   Terry Labonte ....................2
7. Ricky Rudd ........................1
   Harry Gant .........................1
   Ken Schrader .....................1
   Geoff Bodine ......................1
   Mark Martin ........................1

## Money won leaders
1. Rusty Wallace......$2,247,950
2. Dale Earnhardt ......1,435,730
3. Darrell Waltrip .......1,323,079
4. Ken Schrader ........1,039,441
5. Mark Martin ..........1,019,250
6. Bill Elliott ................854,570
7. Terry Labonte ..........704,806
8. Harry Gant...............641,092
9. Davey Allison ..........640,956
10. Geoff Bodine ..........620,594
11. Morgan Shepherd ...544,255
12. Ricky Rudd .............534,824
13. Alan Kulwicki...........501,295
14. Sterling Marlin..........473,267
15. Dick Trickle .............343,728
16. Rick Wilson .............312,402
17. Phil Parsons ............285,012
18. Bobby Hillin .............283,181
19. Brett Bodine ............281,274
20. Neil Bonnett.............271,628
21. Michael Waltrip ........249,233
22. Dale Jarrett .............232,317
23. Lake Speed .............201,227

## Pole winners (9)
1. Mark Martin * .......................6
   Alan Kulwicki........................6
3. Rusty Wallace .....................4
   Ken Schrader.......................4
   Geoff Bodine .......................3
   Bill Elliott ..............................2
   Morgan Shepherd ................1
   Davey Allison.......................1
   Jimmy Hensley ....................1

In 1988, there were 29 NASCAR Winston Cup events.

Time trials for Holly Farms 400 at North Wilkesboro rained out. Starting order determined by car owner points.

# 1988 NASCAR WINSTON CUP SEASON

| Race No. | Location | Date | Winner | Car owner |
|---|---|---|---|---|
| 1. | Daytona Beach, Fla. | Feb. 14 | Bobby Allison | Stavola Brothers |
| 2. | Richmond, Va. | Feb. 21 | Neil Bonnett | Rahilly-Mock |
| 3. | Rockingham, N.C. | Mar. 6 | Neil Bonnett | Rahilly-Mock |
| 4. | Hampton, Ga. | Mar. 20 | Dale Earnhardt | Richard Childress |
| 5. | Darlington, S.C. | Mar. 27 | Lake Speed | Lake Speed |
| 6. | Bristol, Tenn. | Apr. 10 | Bill Elliott | Harry Melling |
| 7. | N. Wilkesboro, N.C. | Apr. 17 | Terry Labonte | Junior Johnson |
| 8. | Martinsville, Va. | Apr. 24 | Dale Earnhardt | Richard Childress |
| 9. | Talladega, Ala. | May 1 | Phil Parsons | Jackson Brothers |
| 10. | Harrisburg, N.C. | May 29 | Darrell Waltrip | Rick Hendrick |
| 11. | Dover, Del. | June 5 | Bill Elliott | Harry Melling |
| 12. | Riverside, Calif. | June 12 | Rusty Wallace | Raymond Beadle |
| 13. | Long Pond, Pa. | June 19 | Geoff Bodine | Rick Hendrick |
| 14. | Brooklyn, Mich. | June 26 | Rusty Wallace | Raymond Beadle |
| 15. | Daytona Beach, Fla. | July 2 | Bill Elliott | Harry Melling |
| 16. | Long Pond, Pa. | July 24 | Bill Elliott | Harry Melling |
| 17. | Talladega, Ala. | July 31 | Ken Schrader | Rick Hendrick |
| 18. | Watkins Glen, N.Y. | Aug. 14 | Ricky Rudd | Kenny Bernstein |
| 19. | Brooklyn, Mich. | Aug. 21 | Davey Allison | Harry Ranier |
| 20. | Bristol, Tenn. | Aug. 27 | Dale Earnhardt | Richard Childress |
| 21. | Darlington, S.C. | Sept. 4 | Bill Elliott | Harry Melling |
| 22. | Richmond, Va. | Sept. 11 | Davey Allison | Harry Ranier |
| 23. | Dover, Del. | Sept. 18 | Bill Elliott | Harry Melling |
| 24. | Martinsville, Va. | Sept. 25 | Darrell Waltrip | Rick Hendrick |
| 25. | Harrisburg, N.C. | Oct. 9 | Rusty Wallace | Raymond Beadle |
| 26. | N. Wilkesboro, N.C. | Oct. 16 | Rusty Wallace | Raymond Beadle |
| 27. | Rockingham, N.C. | Oct. 23 | Rusty Wallace | Raymond Beadle |
| 28. | Phoenix | Nov. 6 | Alan Kulwicki | Alan Kulwicki |
| 29. | Hampton, Ga. | Nov. 20 | Rusty Wallace | Raymond Beadle |

## Points standings
1. Bill Elliott .....................4,488
2. Rusty Wallace ..............4,464
3. Dale Earnhardt............4,256
4. Terry Labonte...............4,007
5. Ken Schrader ...............3,858
6. Geoff Bodine ................3,799
7. Darrell Waltrip .............3,764
8. Davey Allison ...............3,631
9. Phil Parsons ................3,630
10. Sterling Marlin ............3,621

## Race winners (14)
1. Bill Elliott ............................6
   Rusty Wallace ...................6
3. Dale Earnhardt ..................3
4. Neil Bonnett......................2
   Davey Allison ....................2
   Darrell Waltrip ..................2
7. Bobby Allison ....................1
   Terry Labonte ...................1
   Phil Parsons .....................1
   Lake Speed .......................1
   Geoff Bodine ....................1
   Ken Schrader ....................1
   Ricky Rudd ........................1
   Alan Kulwicki ....................1

## Money won leaders
1. Bill Elliott ............$1,574,639
2. Rusty Wallace.......1,411,567
3. Dale Earnhardt .....1,214,089
4. Terry Labonte .........950,781
5. Davey Allison...........844,532
6. Darrell Waltrip .........731,659
7. Ken Schrader............631,544
8. Geoff Bodine ............570,643
9. Phil Parsons ............532,043
10. Sterling Marlin........521,464
11. Alan Kulwicki...........448,547
12. Neil Bonnett.............440,139
13. Brett Bodine ............433,658
14. Ricky Rudd ..............410,954
15. Kyle Petty ................377,092
16. Bobby Hillin, Jr. ........330,217
17. Lake Speed ..............260,500
18. Michael Waltrip ........240,400
19. Mark Martin..............223,630
20. Dave Marcis.............212,485

## Pole winners (12)
1. Bill Elliott ..............................6
2. Alan Kulwicki ........................4
3. Davey Allison........................3
   Geoff Bodine .......................3
5. Ken Schrader ........................2
   Ricky Rudd ...........................2
   Morgan Shepherd ................2
   Darrell Waltrip .....................2
   Rusty Wallace ......................2
10. Rick Wilson ..........................1
    Terry Labonte ......................1
    Mark Martin ........................1

In 1988, there were 29 NASCAR Winston Cup events.

# 1987 NASCAR WINSTON CUP SEASON

| Race No. | Location | Date | Winner | Car owner |
|---|---|---|---|---|
| 1. | Daytona Beach, Fla. | Feb. 15 | Bill Elliott | Harry Melling |
| 2. | Rockingham, N.C. | Mar. 1 | Dale Earnhardt | Richard Childress |
| 3. | Richmond, Va. | Mar. 8 | Dale Earnhardt | Richard Childress |
| 4. | Hampton, Ga. | Mar. 15 | Ricky Rudd | Bud Moore |
| 5. | Darlington, S.C. | Mar. 29 | Dale Earnhardt | Richard Childress |
| 6. | N. Wilkesboro, N.C. | Apr. 5 | Dale Earnhardt | Richard Childress |
| 7. | Bristol, Tenn. | Apr. 12 | Dale Earnhardt | Richard Childress |
| 8. | Martinsville, Va. | Apr. 26 | Dale Earnhardt | Richard Childress |
| 9. | Talladega, Ala. | May 3 | Davey Allison | Harry Ranier |
| 10. | Harrisburg, N.C. | May 24 | Kyle Petty | Wood Brothers |
| 11. | Dover, Del. | May 31 | Davey Allison | Harry Ranier |
| 12. | Long Pond, Pa. | June 14 | Tim Richmond | Rick Hendrick |
| 13. | Riverside, Calif. | June 21 | Tim Richmond | Rick Hendrick |
| 14. | Brooklyn, Mich. | June 28 | Dale Earnhardt | Richard Childress |
| 15. | Daytona Beach, Fla. | July 4 | Bobby Allison | Stavola Brothers |
| 16. | Long Pond, Pa. | July 19 | Dale Earnhardt | Richard Childress |
| 17. | Talladega, Ala. | July 26 | Bill Elliott | Harry Melling |
| 18. | Watkins Glen, N.Y. | Aug. 10 | Rusty Wallace | Raymond Beadle |
| 19. | Brooklyn, Mich. | Aug. 16 | Bill Elliott | Harry Melling |
| 20. | Bristol, Tenn. | Aug. 22 | Dale Earnhardt | Richard Childress |
| 21. | Darlington, S.C. | Sept. 6 | Dale Earnhardt | Richard Childress |
| 22. | Richmond, Va. | Sept. 13 | Dale Earnhardt | Richard Childress |
| 23. | Dover, Del. | Sept. 20 | Ricky Rudd | Bud Moore |
| 24. | Martinsville, Va. | Sept. 27 | Darrell Waltrip | Rick Hendrick |
| 25. | N. Wilkesboro, N.C. | Oct. 4 | Terry Labonte | Junior Johnson |
| 26. | Harrisburg, N.C. | Oct. 11 | Bill Elliott | Harry Melling |
| 27. | Rockingham, N.C. | Oct. 25 | Bill Elliott | Harry Melling |
| 28. | Riverside, Calif. | Nov. 8 | Rusty Wallace | Raymond Beadle |
| 29. | Hampton, Ga. | Nov. 22 | Bill Elliott | Harry Melling |

## Points standings
1. Dale Earnhardt ............4,696
2. Bill Elliott .....................4,207
3. Terry Labonte ..............4,007
4. Darrell Waltrip .............3,911
5. Rusty Wallace ..............3,818
6. Ricky Rudd ..................3,742
7. Kyle Petty ....................3,737
8. Richard Petty ...............3,708
9. Bobby Allison ...............3,530
10. Ken Schrader ..............3,405

## Race winners (10)
1. Dale Earnhardt ..................11
2. Bill Elliott ...........................6
3. Davey Allison .....................2
   Tim Richmond ....................2
   Ricky Rudd .........................2
   Rusty Wallace ....................2
7. Kyle Petty ..........................1
   Bobby Allison .....................1
   Darrell Waltrip ...................1
   Terry Labonte ....................1

## Money won leaders
1. Dale Earnhardt ....$2,099,243
2. Bill Elliott ..............1,619,210
3. Terry Labonte ..........825,369
4. Rusty Wallace ..........690,652
5. Ricky Rudd ...............653,508
6. Benny Parsons .........566,484
7. Kyle Petty ................544,437
8. Bobby Allison ...........515,894
9. Darrell Waltrip ..........511,768
10. Richard Petty...........468,702
11. Geoff Bodine ...........449,816
12. Neil Bonnett.............401,541
13. Ken Schrader............375,918
14. Alan Kulwicki............369,889
15. Davey Allison ...........361,060
16. Bobby Hillin, Jr. ........346,735
17. Morgan Shepherd ....317,034
18. Sterling Marlin..........306,412
19. Dave Marcis .............256,354
20. Buddy Baker .............255,320
21. Michael Waltrip ........205,370
22. Harry Gant................197,645
23. Phil Parsons .............180,261
24. Jimmy Means ...........154,055
25. Tim Richmond..........151,850

## Pole winners (12)
1. Bill Elliott ..............................8
2. Davey Allison......................5
3. Terry Labonte .....................4
4. Alan Kulwicki ......................3
5. Geoff Bodine ......................2
6. Dale Earnhardt....................1
   Ken Schrader......................1
   Harry Gant..........................1
   Morgan Shepherd ...............1
   Rusty Wallace .....................1
   Tim Richmond......................1
   Bobby Allison ......................1

In 1987, there were 29 NASCAR Winston Cup events.

# 1986 NASCAR WINSTON CUP SEASON

| Race No. | Location | Date | Winner | Car owner |
|---|---|---|---|---|
| 1. | Daytona Beach, Fla. | Feb. 16 | Geoff Bodine | Rick Hendrick |
| 2. | Richmond, Va. | Feb. 23 | Kyle Petty | Wood Brothers |
| 3. | Rockingham, N.C. | Mar. 2 | Terry Labonte | Billy Hagan |
| 4. | Hampton, Ga. | Mar. 16 | Morgan Shepherd | Jack Beebe |
| 5. | Bristol, Tenn. | Apr. 6 | Rusty Wallace | Raymond Beadle |
| 6. | Darlington, S.C. | Apr. 13 | Dale Earnhardt | Richard Childress |
| 7. | N. Wilkesboro, N.C. | Apr. 20 | Dale Earnhardt | Richard Childress |
| 8. | Martinsville, Va. | Apr. 27 | Ricky Rudd | Bud Moore |
| 9. | Talladega, Ala. | May 4 | Bobby Allison | Stavola Brothers |
| 10. | Dover, Del. | May 18 | Geoff Bodine | Rick Hendrick |
| 11. | Harrisburg, N.C. | May 25 | Dale Earnhardt | Richard Childress |
| 12. | Riverside, Calif. | June 1 | Darrell Waltrip | Junior Johnson |
| 13. | Long Pond, Pa. | June 8 | Tim Richmond | Rick Hendrick |
| 14. | Brooklyn, Mich. | June 15 | Bill Elliott | Harry Melling |
| 15. | Daytona Beach, Fla. | July 4 | Tim Richmond | Rick Hendrick |
| 16. | Long Pond, Pa. | July 20 | Tim Richmond | Rick Hendrick |
| 17. | Talladega, Ala. | July 27 | Bobby Hillin, Jr. | Stavola Brothers |
| 18. | Watkins Glen, N.Y. | Aug. 10 | Tim Richmond | Rick Hendrick |
| 19. | Brooklyn, Mich. | Aug. 17 | Bill Elliott | Harry Melling |
| 20. | Bristol, Tenn. | Aug. 23 | Darrell Waltrip | Junior Johnson |
| 21. | Darlington, S.C. | Aug. 31 | Tim Richmond | Rick Hendrick |
| 22. | Richmond, Va. | Sept. 7 | Tim Richmond | Rick Hendrick |
| 23. | Dover, Del. | Sept. 14 | Ricky Rudd | Bud Moore |
| 24. | Martinsville, Va. | Sept. 21 | Rusty Wallace | Raymond Beadle |
| 25. | N. Wilkesboro, N.C. | Sept. 28 | Darrell Waltrip | Junior Johnson |
| 26. | Harrisburg, N.C. | Oct. 5 | Dale Earnhardt | Richard Childress |
| 27. | Rockingham, N.C. | Oct. 19 | Neil Bonnett | Junior Johnson |
| 28. | Hampton, Ga. | Nov. 2 | Dale Earnhardt | Richard Childress |
| 29. | Riverside, Calif. | Nov. 16 | Tim Richmond | Rick Hendrick |

## Point standings
1. Dale Earnhardt ............4,468
2. Darrell Waltrip ............4,180
3. Tim Richmond ............4,174
4. Bill Elliott ............3,844
5. Ricky Rudd ............3,823
6. Rusty Wallace ............3,762
7. Bobby Allison ............3,698
8. Geoff Bodine ............3,678
9. Bobby Hillin Jr. ............3,546
10. Kyle Petty ............3,537

## Race winners (13)
1. Tim Richmond ............7
2. Dale Earnhardt ............5
3. Darrell Waltrip ............3
4. Rusty Wallace ............2
   Geoff Bodine ............2
   Bill Elliott ............2
   Ricky Rudd ............2
8. Terry Labonte ............1
   Morgan Shepherd ............1
   Bobby Allison ............1
   Kyle Petty ............1
   Bobby Hillin, Jr. ............1
   Neil Bonnett ............1

## Money won leaders
1. Dale Earnhardt ....$1,768,880
2. Darrell Waltrip ......1,099,735
3. Bill Elliott ............1,049,142
4. Tim Richmond ............973,221
5. Geoff Bodine ............795,111
6. Ricky Rudd ............671,548
7. Harry Gant ............583,024
8. Rusty Wallace ............557,354
9. Terry Labonte ............522,235
10. Bobby Allison ............503,095
11. Neil Bonnett ............485,930
12. Bobby Hillin, Jr. ............448,452
13. Kyle Petty ............403,242
14. Richard Petty ............280,657
15. Joe Ruttman ............259,263
16. Morgan Shepherd ....244,146
17. Kenny Schrader ........235,905
18. Dave Marcis ............220,461
19. Buddy Arrington ......186,588
20. Benny Parsons ........176,985
21. Jimmy Means ............157,940
22. Buddy Baker ............138,600
23. Cale Yarborough ............137,010
24. Sterling Marlin ............113,070
25. Mike Waltrip ............108,767
26. Ron Bouchard ............106,835
27. J.D. McDuffie ............106,115

## Pole winners (10)
1. Tim Richmond* ............8
   Geoff Bodine ............8
3. Bill Elliott ............4
4. Harry Gant ............2
5. Ricky Rudd ............1
   Terry Labonte ............1
   Dale Earnhardt ............1
   Darrell Waltrip ............1
   Cale Yarborough ............1
   Benny Parsons ............1

In 1986, there were 29 NASCAR Winston Cup events.
*Won Busch Pole Award based on tie-breaker rule.
   Time trials for the Miller 400 at Richmond Fairgrounds were rained out. Starting order determined by car owner points.

# 1985 NASCAR WINSTON CUP SEASON

| Race No. | Location | Date | Winner | Car owner |
|---|---|---|---|---|
| 1. | Daytona Beach, Fla. | Feb. 17 | Bill Elliott | Harry Melling |
| 2. | Richmond, Va. | Feb. 24 | Dale Earnhardt | Richard Childress |
| 3. | Rockingham, N.C. | Mar. 3 | Neil Bonnett | Junior Johnson |
| 4. | Hampton, Ga. | Mar. 17 | Bill Elliott | Harry Melling |
| 5. | Bristol, Tenn. | Apr. 6 | Dale Earnhardt | Richard Childress |
| 6. | Darlington, S.C. | Apr. 14 | Bill Elliott | Harry Melling |
| 7. | N. Wilkesboro, N.C. | Apr. 21 | Neil Bonnett | Junior Johnson |
| 8. | Martinsville, Va. | Apr. 28 | Harry Gant | Needham-Reynolds |
| 9. | Talladega, Ala. | May 5 | Bill Elliott | Harry Melling |
| 10. | Dover, Del. | May 19 | Bill Elliott | Harry Melling |
| 11. | Harrisburg, N.C. | May 26 | Darrell Waltrip | Junior Johnson |
| 12. | Riverside, Calif. | June 2 | Terry Labonte | Billy Hagan |
| 13. | Long Pond, Pa. | June 9 | Bill Elliott | Harry Melling |
| 14. | Brooklyn, Mich. | June 16 | Bill Elliott | Harry Melling |
| 15. | Daytona Beach, Fla. | July 4 | Greg Sacks | Bill Gardner |
| 16. | Long Pond, Pa. | July 21 | Bill Elliott | Harry Melling |
| 17. | Talladega, Ala. | July 28 | Cale Yarborough | Harry Ranier |
| 18. | Brooklyn, Mich. | Aug. 11 | Bill Elliott | Harry Melling |
| 19. | Bristol, Tenn. | Aug. 24 | Dale Earnhardt | Richard Childress |
| 20. | Darlington, S.C. | Sept. 1 | Bill Elliott | Harry Melling |
| 21. | Richmond, Va. | Sept. 8 | Darrell Waltrip | Junior Johnson |
| 22. | Dover, Del. | Sept. 15 | Harry Gant | Needham-Reynolds |
| 23. | Martinsville, Va. | Sept. 22 | Dale Earnhardt | Richard Childress |
| 24. | N. Wilkesboro, N.C. | Sept. 29 | Harry Gant | Needham-Reynolds |
| 25. | Harrisburg, N.C. | Oct. 6 | Cale Yarborough | Harry Ranier |
| 26. | Rockingham, N.C. | Oct. 20 | Darrell Waltrip | Junior Johnson |
| 27. | Hampton, Ga. | Nov. 3 | Bill Elliott | Harry Melling |
| 28. | Riverside, Calif. | Nov. 17 | Ricky Rudd | Bud Moore |

## Points standings
1. Darrell Waltrip ..............4,292
2. Bill Elliott ....................4,191
3. Harry Gant ..................4,033
4. Neil Bonnett ................3,902
5. Geoff Bodine ...............3,862
6. Ricky Rudd .................3,857
7. Terry Labonte..............3,683
8. Dale Earnhardt ............3,561
9. Kyle Petty....................3,528
10. Lake Speed ...............3,507

## Race winners (9)
1. Bill Elliott .........................11
2. Dale Earnhardt...................4
3. Harry Gant .......................3
   Darrell Waltrip ..................3
5. Neil Bonnett .....................2
   Cale Yarborough ...............2
7. Terry Labonte ...................1
   Ricky Rudd .......................1
   Greg Sacks .......................1

## Money won leaders
1. Bill Elliott ............$2,383,187
2. Darrell Waltrip ......1,318,735
3. Harry Gant.............804,287
4. Terry Labonte .........694,510
5. Geoff Bodine ..........565,865
6. Dale Earnhardt........546,596
7. Neil Bonnett............530,145
8. Ricky Rudd .............512,441
9. Cale Yarborough .....310,465
10. Richard Petty..........306,142
11. Lake Speed .............300,326
12. Kyle Petty ...............296,367
13. Tim Richmond..........290,284
14. Bobby Allison ..........272,536
15. Ron Bouchard ..........240,304
16. Buddy Baker ...........235,479
17. Greg Sacks ..............234,141
18. Rusty Wallace ..........233,670
19. Ken Schrader...........211,523
20. Dave Marcis.............173,467
21. Buddy Arrington ......153,222
22. Bobby Hillin, Jr..........145,070
23. Jimmy Means ..........132,130
24. Clark Dwyer.............128,710
25. Phil Parsons ............104,840
26. E. Bierschwale..........102,650

## Pole winners (7)
1. Bill Elliott ..........................11
2. Terry Labonte .....................4
   Darrell Waltrip ....................4
4. Geoff Bodine ......................3
   Harry Gant .........................3
6. Neil Bonnett........................1
   Dale Earnhardt....................1

In 1985, there were 28 NASCAR Winston Cup events.

Time trials for the Miller 400 at Michigan International Speedway were rained out and the NASCAR Winston Cup car owners' point standings were used to determine the starting lineup.

# 1984 NASCAR WINSTON CUP SEASON

| Race No. | Location | Date | Winner | Car owner |
|---|---|---|---|---|
| 1. | Daytona Beach, Fla. | Feb. 19 | Cale Yarborough | Harry Ranier |
| 2. | Richmond, Va. | Feb. 26 | Ricky Rudd | Bud Moore |
| 3. | Rockingham, N.C. | Mar. 4 | Bobby Allison | Bill Gardner |
| 4. | Hampton, Ga. | Mar. 18 | Benny Parsons | Johnny Hayes |
| 5. | Bristol, Tenn. | Apr. 1 | Darrell Waltrip | Junior Johnson |
| 6. | N. Wilkesboro, N.C. | Apr. 8 | Tim Richmond | Raymond Beadle |
| 7. | Darlington, S.C. | Apr. 15 | Darrell Waltrip | Junior Johnson |
| 8. | Martinsville, Va. | Apr. 29 | Geoff Bodine | Rick Hendrick |
| 9. | Talladega, Ala. | May 6 | Cale Yarborough | Harry Ranier |
| 10. | Nashville | May 12 | Darrell Waltrip | Junior Johnson |
| 11. | Dover, Del. | May 20 | Richard Petty | Mike Curb |
| 12. | Harrisburg, N.C. | May 27 | Bobby Allison | Bill Gardner |
| 13. | Riverside, Calif. | June 3 | Terry Labonte | Billy Hagan |
| 14. | Long Pond, Pa. | June 10 | Cale Yarborough | Harry Ranier |
| 15. | Brooklyn, Mich. | June 17 | Bill Elliott | Harry Melling |
| 16. | Daytona Beach, Fla. | July 4 | Richard Petty | Mike Curb |
| 17. | Nashville | July 14 | Geoff Bodine | Rick Hendrick |
| 18. | Long Pond, Pa. | July 22 | Harry Gant | Needham-Reynolds |
| 19. | Talladega, Ala. | July 29 | Dale Earnhardt | Richard Childress |
| 20. | Brooklyn, Mich. | Aug. 12 | Darrell Waltrip | Junior Johnson |
| 21. | Bristol, Tenn. | Aug. 25 | Terry Labonte | Billy Hagan |
| 22. | Darlington, S.C. | Sept. 2 | Harry Gant | Needham-Reynolds |
| 23. | Richmond, Va. | Sept. 9 | Darrell Waltrip | Junior Johnson |
| 24. | Dover, Del. | Sept. 16 | Harry Gant | Needham-Reynolds |
| 25. | Martinsville, Va. | Sept. 23 | Darrell Waltrip | Junior Johnson |
| 26. | Harrisburg, N.C. | Oct. 7 | Bill Elliott | Harry Melling |
| 27. | N. Wilkesboro, N.C.. | Oct. 14 | Darrell Waltrip | Junior Johnson |
| 28. | Rockingham, N.C. | Oct. 21 | Bill Elliott | Harry Melling |
| 29. | Hampton, Ga. | Nov. 11 | Dale Earnhardt | Richard Childress |
| 30. | Riverside, Calif. | Nov. 18 | Geoff Bodine | Rick Hendrick |

## Points standings
1. Terry Labonte..............4,508
2. Harry Gant..................4,443
3. Bill Elliott .....................4,377
4. Dale Earnhardt.............4,265
5. Darrell Waltrip .............4,230
6. Bobby Allison...............4,094
7. Ricky Rudd .................3,918
8. Neil Bonnett.................3,802
9. Geoff Bodine ...............3,734
10. Richard Petty .............3,643

## Race winners (12)
1. Darrell Waltrip ....................7
2. Geoff Bodine .....................3
   Bill Elliott ............................3
   Harry Gant .........................3
   Cale Yarborough ................3
6. Bobby Allison .....................2
   Dale Earnhardt...................2
   Terry Labonte ....................2
   Richard Petty .....................2
10. Benny Parsons .................1
    Tim Richmond ...................1
    Ricky Rudd .......................1

## Money won leaders
1. Terry Labonte ........$713,010
2. Darrell Waltrip ..........703,876
3. Bill Elliott .................660,226
4. Harry Gant................650,707
5. Bobby Allison ...........627,637
6. Dale Earnhardt..........616,788
7. Ricky Rudd ..............476,602
8. Geoff Bodine ............393,924
9. Cale Yarborough ......385,853
10. Dave Marcis............330,766
11. Tim Richmond..........329,589
12. Kyle Petty ................324,555
13. Richard Petty............251,226
14. Benny Parsons ........241,665
15. Ron Bouchard ..........229,528
16. Neil Bonnett..............223,592
17. Rusty Wallace ..........195,927
18. Dick Brooks..............186,819
19. Trevor Boys ..............160,235
20. Joe Ruttman ............150,068
21. Buddy Baker ............133,635
22. Buddy Arrington ......128,802
23. Clark Dwyer..............114,335
24. Jimmy Means ..........100,885

## Pole winners (11)
1. Bill Elliott* ..............................4
   Darrell Waltrip .......................4
   Ricky Rudd ...........................4
   Cale Yarborough ...................4
5. Geoff Bodine ........................3
   Harry Gant ............................3
7. Terry Labonte .......................2
   Benny Parsons ....................2
9. Buddy Baker ........................1
   David Pearson ......................1
   Joe Ruttman ........................1

In 1984, there were 30 NASCAR Winston Cup events.

*Elliott won the $25,000 Busch Pole award via the tie breaker — the driver points standings. Time trials were rained out at Dover Downs International Speedway at Dover, Del.

# 1983 NASCAR WINSTON CUP SEASON

| Race No. | Location | Date | Winner | Car owner |
|---|---|---|---|---|
| 1. | Daytona Beach, Fla. | Feb. 20 | Cale Yarborough | Harry Ranier |
| 2. | Richmond, Va. | Feb. 27 | Bobby Allison | Bill Gardner |
| 3. | Rockingham, N.C. | Mar. 13 | Richard Petty | Petty Enterprises |
| 4. | Hampton, Ga. | Mar. 27 | Cale Yarborough | Harry Ranier |
| 5. | Darlington, S.C. | Apr. 10 | Harry Gant | Needham-Reynolds |
| 6. | N. Wilkesboro, N.C. | Apr. 17 | Darrell Waltrip | Junior Johnson |
| 7. | Martinsville, Va. | Apr. 24 | Darrell Waltrip | Junior Johnson |
| 8. | Talladega, Ala. | May 1 | Richard Petty | Petty Enterprises |
| 9. | Nashville | May 7 | Darrell Waltrip | Junior Johnson |
| 10. | Dover, Del. | May 15 | Bobby Allison | Bill Gardner |
| 11. | Bristol, Tenn. | May 21 | Darrell Waltrip | Junior Johnson |
| 12. | Harrisburg, N.C. | May 29 | Neil Bonnett | Rahilly-Mock |
| 13. | Riverside, Calif. | June 5 | Ricky Rudd | Richard Childress |
| 14. | Long Pond, Pa. | June 12 | Bobby Allison | Bill Gardner |
| 15. | Brooklyn, Mich. | June 19 | Cale Yarborough | Harry Ranier |
| 16. | Daytona Beach, Fla. | July 4 | Buddy Baker | Wood Brothers |
| 17. | Nashville | July 16 | Dale Earnhardt | Bud Moore |
| 18. | Long Pond, Pa. | July 24 | Tim Richmond | Raymond Beadle |
| 19. | Talladega, Ala. | July 31 | Dale Earnhardt | Bud Moore |
| 20. | Brooklyn, Mich. | Aug. 21 | Cale Yarborough | Harry Ranier |
| 21. | Bristol, Tenn. | Aug. 27 | Darrell Waltrip | Junior Johnson |
| 22. | Darlington, S.C. | Sept. 5 | Bobby Allison | Bill Gardner |
| 23. | Richmond, Va. | Sept. 11 | Bobby Allison | Bill Gardner |
| 24. | Dover, Del. | Sept. 18 | Bobby Allison | Bill Gardner |
| 25. | Martinsville, Va. | Sept. 25 | Ricky Rudd | Richard Childress |
| 26. | N. Wilkesboro, N.C. | Oct. 2 | Darrell Waltrip | Junior Johnson |
| 27. | Harrisburg, N.C. | Oct. 9 | Richard Petty | Petty Enterprises |
| 28. | Rockingham, N.C. | Oct. 30 | Terry Labonte | Billy Hagan |
| 29. | Hampton, Ga. | Nov. 6 | Neil Bonnett | Rahilly-Mock |
| 30. | Riverside, Calif. | Nov. 20 | Bill Elliott | Harry Melling |

## Points standings
1. Bobby Allison..............4,667
2. Darrell Waltrip ............4,620
3. Bill Elliott .....................4,279
4. Richard Petty ...............4,042
5. Terry Labonte...............4,004
6. Neil Bonnett .................3,842
7. Harry Gant ...................3,790
8. Dale Earnhardt.............3,732
9. Ricky Rudd ..................3,693
10. Tim Richmond ............3,612

## Race winners (12)
1. Bobby Allison ....................6
   Darrell Waltrip ...................6
3. Cale Yarborough ...............4
4. Richard Petty ....................3
5. Neil Bonnett ......................2
   Dale Earnhardt..................2
   Ricky Rudd ........................2
8. Buddy Baker .....................1
   Bill Elliott ...........................1
   Harry Gant ........................1
   Terry Labonte ...................1
   Tim Richmond ...................1

## Money won leaders
1. Bobby Allison .........$828,355
2. Darrell Waltrip ..........824,858
3. Richard Petty............491,022
4. Bill Elliott ..................479,965
5. Neil Bonnett..............455,662
6. Dale Earnhardt.........446,272
7. Harry Gant ................390,189
8. Terry Labonte ...........362,790
9. Dave Marcis..............306,355
10. Morgan Shepherd ....270,851
11. Ricky Rudd ................257,585
12. Cale Yarborough ......245,535
13. Tim Richmond...........245,664
14. Joe Ruttman .............217,557
15. Buddy Baker .............206,355
16. Geoff Bodine .............194,476
17. Dick Brooks ...............176,471
18. Kyle Petty .................157,820
19. Sterling Marlin..........143,564
20. Ron Bouchard ..........142,314
21. Buddy Arrington ......138,429
22. Jimmy Means ...........132,915
23. Benny Parsons ........119,760

## Pole winners (10)
1. Darrell Waltrip .....................7
2. Tim Richmond.....................4
   Ricky Rudd .........................4
   Neil Bonnett.........................4
5. Terry Labonte ....................3
   Cale Yarborough ................3
7. Joe Ruttman ......................2
8. Buddy Baker ......................1
   Geoff Bodine ......................1
   Ron Bouchard ....................1

In 1983, there were 30 NASCAR Winston Cup events.

**HISTORY**

# 1982 NASCAR WINSTON CUP SEASON

| Race No. | Location | Date | Winner | Car owner |
|---|---|---|---|---|
| 1. | Daytona Beach, Fla. | Feb. 14 | Bobby Allison | Bill Gardner |
| 2. | Richmond, Va. | Feb. 21 | Dave Marcis | Dave Marcis |
| 3. | Bristol, Tenn. | Mar. 14 | Darrell Waltrip | Junior Johnson |
| 4. | Hampton, Ga. | Mar. 21 | Darrell Waltrip | Junior Johnson |
| 5. | Rockingham, N.C. | Mar. 28 | Cale Yarborough | M.C. Anderson |
| 6. | Darlington, S.C. | Apr. 4 | Dale Earnhardt | Bud Moore |
| 7. | N. Wilkesboro, N.C. | Apr. 18 | Darrell Waltrip | Junior Johnson |
| 8. | Martinsville, Va. | Apr. 25 | Harry Gant | Needham-Reynolds |
| 9. | Talladega, Ala. | May 2 | Darrell Waltrip | Junior Johnson |
| 10. | Nashville | May 8 | Darrell Waltrip | Junior Johnson |
| 11. | Dover, Del. | May 16 | Bobby Allison | Bill Gardner |
| 12. | Harrisburg, N.C. | May 30 | Neil Bonnett | Wood Brothers |
| 13. | Long Pond, Pa. | June 6 | Bobby Allison | Bill Gardner |
| 14. | Riverside, Calif. | June 13 | Tim Richmond | Jim Stacy |
| 15. | Brooklyn, Mich. | June 20 | Cale Yarborough | M.C. Anderson |
| 16. | Daytona Beach, Fla. | July 4 | Bobby Allison | Bill Gardner |
| 17. | Nashville | July 10 | Darrell Waltrip | Junior Johnson |
| 18. | Long Pond, Pa. | July 25 | Bobby Allison | Bill Gardner |
| 19. | Talladega, Ala. | Aug. 1 | Darrell Waltrip | Junior Johnson |
| 20. | Brooklyn, Mich. | Aug. 22 | Bobby Allison | Bill Gardner |
| 21. | Bristol, Tenn. | Aug. 28 | Darrell Waltrip | Junior Johnson |
| 22. | Darlington, S.C. | Sept. 6 | Cale Yarborough | M.C. Anderson |
| 23. | Richmond, Va. | Sept. 12 | Bobby Allison | Bill Gardner |
| 24. | Dover, Del. | Sept. 19 | Darrell Waltrip | Junior Johnson |
| 25. | N. Wilkesboro, N.C. | Oct. 3 | Darrell Waltrip | Junior Johnson |
| 26. | Harrisburg, N.C. | Oct. 10 | Harry Gant | Needham-Reynolds |
| 27. | Martinsville, Va. | Oct. 17 | Darrell Waltrip | Junior Johnson |
| 28. | Rockingham, N.C. | Oct. 31 | Darrell Waltrip | Junior Johnson |
| 29. | Hampton, Ga. | Nov. 7 | Bobby Allison | Bill Gardner |
| 30. | Riverside, Calif. | Nov. 21 | Tim Richmond | Jim Stacy |

## Points standings
1. Darrell Waltrip ............4,489
2. Bobby Allison ..............4,417
3. Terry Labonte ..............4,211
4. Harry Gant ..................3,877
5. Richard Petty ..............3,817
6. Dave Marcis .................3,666
7. Buddy Arrington ..........3,642
8. Ron Bouchard ..............3,545
9. Ricky Rudd ..................3,537
10. Morgan Shepherd ......3,451

## Race winners (8)
1. Darrell Waltrip ..................12
2. Bobby Allison ......................8
3. Cale Yarborough .................3
4. Harry Gant ...........................2
   Tim Richmond .....................2
6. Dave Marcis .........................1
   Dale Earnhardt ....................1
   Neil Bonnett ........................1

## Money won leaders
1. Darrell Waltrip .......$873,118
2. Bobby Allison .........726,562
3. Richard Petty ..........453,832
4. Dale Earnhardt........375,325
5. Terry Labonte .........363,970
6. Ron Bouchard ........356,582
7. Harry Gant ..............311,769
8. Jody Ridley .............304,960
9. Geoff Bodine ..........258,500
10. Buddy Baker .........253,675
11. Benny Parsons ......248,564
12. Dave Marcis..........239,027
13. Bill Elliott ...............226,780
14. Cale Yarborough ......219,090
15. Ricky Rudd ...........206,130
16. Joe Ruttman .........191,634
17. Buddy Arrington ...178,159
18. Tim Richmond..........176,730
19. Morgan Shepherd ....150,475
20. Jimmy Means .........148,905
21. Neil Bonnett ..........140,494
22. Mark Martin ..........126,655
23. Kyle Petty ..............120,730
24. Lake Speed ............114,754
25. J.D. McDuffie ..........112,744
26. Tommy Gale ..........102,235

## Pole winners (15)
1. Darrell Waltrip .....................7
2. Benny Parsons ......................3
3. Cale Yarborough .................2
   Terry Labonte ......................2
   Ricky Rudd ...........................2
   Geoff Bodine ........................2
   Morgan Shepherd ................2
   David Pearson .....................2
9. Dale Earnhardt....................1
   Buddy Baker ........................1
   Ron Bouchard .....................1
   Bill Elliott .............................1
   Tim Richmond.....................1
   Bobby Allison ......................1
   Harry Gant...........................1

In 1982, there were 30 NASCAR Winston Cup events.

Time trials were rained out at the Van Scoy Diamond Mine 500 at Pocono (Pa.) International Raceway.

# 1981 NASCAR WINSTON CUP SEASON

| Race No. | Location | Date | Winner | Car owner |
|---|---|---|---|---|
| 1. | Riverside, Calif. | Jan. 11 | Bobby Allison | Harry Ranier |
| 2. | Daytona Beach, Fla. | Feb. 15 | Richard Petty | Petty Enterprises |
| 3. | Richmond, Va. | Feb. 22 | Darrell Waltrip | Junior Johnson |
| 4. | Rockingham, N.C. | Mar. 1 | Darrell Waltrip | Junior Johnson |
| 5. | Hampton, Ga. | Mar. 15 | Cale Yarborough | M.C. Anderson |
| 6. | Bristol, Tenn. | Mar. 29 | Darrell Waltrip | Junior Johnson |
| 7. | N. Wilkesboro, N.C. | Apr. 5 | Richard Petty | Petty Enterprises |
| 8. | Darlington, S.C. | Apr. 12 | Darrell Waltrip | Junior Johnson |
| 9. | Martinsville, Va. | Apr. 26 | Morgan Shepherd | Cliff Stewart |
| 10. | Talladega, Ala. | May 3 | Bobby Allison | Harry Ranier |
| 11. | Nashville | May 9 | Benny Parsons | Bud Moore |
| 12. | Dover, Del. | May 17 | Jody Ridley | Junie Donlavey |
| 13. | Harrisburg, N.C. | May 24 | Bobby Allison | Harry Ranier |
| 14. | Bryan, Texas | June 7 | Benny Parsons | Bud Moore |
| 15. | Riverside, Calif. | June 14 | Darrell Waltrip | Junior Johnson |
| 16. | Brooklyn, Mich. | June 21 | Bobby Allison | Harry Ranier |
| 17. | Daytona Beach, Fla. | July 4 | Cale Yarborough | M.C. Anderson |
| 18. | Nashville | July 11 | Darrell Waltrip | Junior Johnson |
| 19. | Long Pond, Pa. | July 26 | Darrell Waltrip | Junior Johnson |
| 20. | Talladega, Ala. | Aug. 2 | Ron Bouchard | Jack Beebe |
| 21. | Brooklyn, Mich. | Aug. 16 | Richard Petty | Petty Enterprises |
| 22. | Bristol, Tenn. | Aug. 22 | Darrell Waltrip | Junior Johnson |
| 23. | Darlington, S.C. | Sept. 7 | Neil Bonnett | Wood Brothers |
| 24. | Richmond, Va. | Sept. 13 | Benny Parsons | Bud Moore |
| 25. | Dover, Del. | Sept. 20 | Neil Bonnett | Wood Brothers |
| 26. | Martinsville, Va. | Sept. 27 | Darrell Waltrip | Junior Johnson |
| 27. | N. Wilkesboro, N.C. | Oct. 4 | Darrell Waltrip | Junior Johnson |
| 28. | Harrisburg, N.C. | Oct. 11 | Darrell Waltrip | Junior Johnson |
| 29. | Rockingham, N.C. | Nov. 1 | Darrell Waltrip | Junior Johnson |
| 30. | Hampton, Ga. | Nov. 8 | Neil Bonnett | Wood Brothers |
| 31. | Riverside, Calif. | Nov. 22 | Bobby Allison | Harry Ranier |

## Points standings
1. Darrell Waltrip ............4,880
2. Bobby Allison...............4,827
3. Harry Gant ..................4,210
4. Terry Labonte...............4,052
5. Jody Ridley ..................4,002
6. Ricky Rudd ..................3,988
7. Dale Earnhardt .............3,975
8. Richard Petty ...............3,880
9. Dave Marcis .................3,507
10. Benny Parsons...........3,449

## Race winners (9)
1. Darrell Waltrip ................12
2. Bobby Allison ...................5
3. Richard Petty ....................3
   Benny Parsons .................3
   Neil Bonnett......................3
6. Cale Yarborough ..............2
7. Jody Ridley .......................1
   Morgan Shepherd ............1
   Ron Bouchard ..................1

## Money won leaders
1. Darrell Waltrip ........$693,352
2. Bobby Allison ..........644,311
3. Richard Petty...........389,214
4. Ricky Rudd .............381,968
5. Dale Earnhardt........347,113
6. Terry Labonte..........334,987
7. Benny Parsons........287,949
8. Harry Gant...............280,047
9. Jody Ridley ..............257,318
10. Neil Bonnett............181,670
11. Morgan Shepherd ....165,329
12. Dave Marcis............162,213
13. Ron Bouchard .........152,855
14. Cale Yarborough ......150,840
15. Joe Millikan .............148,400
16. Joe Ruttman............137,275
17. Buddy Arrington ......133,928
18. Buddy Baker ...........115,095
19. Kyle Petty ................112,289
20. J.D. McDuffie ..........105,499
21. Tommy Gale ...........105,474
22. Jimmy Means ..........100,484

## Pole winners (13)
1. Darrell Waltrip ...............11
2. Ricky Rudd .......................3
   Harry Gant.........................3
4. Bobby Allison ...................2
   Terry Labonte...................2
   Cale Yarborough ..............2
   Mark Martin......................2
8. Morgan Shepherd ............1
   Dave Marcis......................1
   Bill Elliott..........................1
   David Pearson ..................1
   Neil Bonnett .....................1
   Ron Bouchard ...................1

In 1981, there were 31 NASCAR Winston Cup events.

# 1980 NASCAR WINSTON CUP SEASON

| Race No. | Location | Date | Winner | Car owner |
|---|---|---|---|---|
| 1. | Riverside, Calif. | Jan. 19 | Darrell Waltrip | Bill Gardner |
| 2. | Daytona Beach, Fla. | Feb. 17 | Buddy Baker | Harry Ranier |
| 3. | Richmond, Va. | Feb. 24 | Darrell Waltrip | Bill Gardner |
| 4. | Rockingham, N.C. | Mar. 9 | Cale Yarborough | Junior Johnson |
| 5. | Hampton, Ga. | Mar. 16 | Dale Earnhardt | Rod Osterlund |
| 6. | Bristol, Tenn. | Mar. 30 | Dale Earnhardt | Rod Osterlund |
| 7. | Darlington, S.C. | Apr. 13 | David Pearson | Hoss Ellington |
| 8. | N. Wilkesboro, N.C. | Apr. 20 | Richard Petty | Petty Enterprises |
| 9. | Martinsville, Va. | Apr. 27 | Darrell Waltrip | Bill Gardner |
| 10. | Talladega, Ala. | May 4 | Buddy Baker | Harry Ranier |
| 11. | Nashville | May 10 | Richard Petty | Petty Enterprises |
| 12. | Dover, Del. | May 18 | Bobby Allison | Bud Moore |
| 13. | Harrisburg, N.C. | May 25 | Benny Parsons | M.C. Anderson |
| 14. | Bryan, Texas | June 1 | Cale Yarborough | Junior Johnson |
| 15. | Riverside, Calif. | June 8 | Darrell Waltrip | Bill Gardner |
| 16. | Brooklyn, Mich. | June 15 | Benny Parsons | M.C. Anderson |
| 17. | Daytona Beach, Fla. | July 4 | Bobby Allison | Bud Moore |
| 18. | Nashville | July 12 | Dale Earnhardt | Rod Osterlund |
| 19. | Long Pond, Pa. | July 27 | Neil Bonnett | Wood Brothers |
| 20. | Talladega, Ala. | Aug. 3 | Neil Bonnett | Wood Brothers |
| 21. | Brooklyn, Mich. | Aug. 17 | Cale Yarborough | Junior Johnson |
| 22. | Bristol, Tenn. | Aug. 23 | Cale Yarborough | Junior Johnson |
| 23. | Darlington, S.C. | Sept. 1 | Terry Labonte | Billy Hagan |
| 24. | Richmond, Va. | Sept. 7 | Bobby Allison | Bud Moore |
| 25. | Dover, Del. | Sept. 14 | Darrell Waltrip | Bill Gardner |
| 26. | N. Wilkesboro, N.C. | Sept. 21 | Bobby Allison | Bud Moore |
| 27. | Martinsville, Va. | Sept. 28 | Dale Earnhardt | Rod Osterlund |
| 28. | Harrisburg, N.C. | Oct. 5 | Dale Earnhardt | Rod Osterlund |
| 29. | Rockingham, N.C. | Oct. 19 | Cale Yarborough | Junior Johnson |
| 30. | Hampton, Ga. | Nov. 2 | Cale Yarborough | Junior Johnson |
| 31. | Fontana, Calif. | Nov. 15 | Benny Parsons | M.C. Anderson |

## Points standings
1. Dale Earnhardt ............4,661
2. Cale Yarborough ........4,642
3. Benny Parsons............4,278
4. Richard Petty ...............4,255
5. Darrell Waltrip ............4,239
6. Bobby Allison..............4,019
7. Jody Ridley ................3,972
8. Terry Labonte...............3,766
9. Dave Marcis.................3,745
10. Richard Childress ......3,742

## Race winners (10)
1. Cale Yarborough ................6
2. Dale Earnhardt ...................5
   Darrell Waltrip ...................5
4. Bobby Allison ....................4
5. Benny Parsons ...................3
6. Richard Petty.....................2
   Neil Bonnett ......................2
   Buddy Baker .....................2
9. Terry Labonte ...................1
   David Pearson ..................1

## Money won leaders
1. Dale Earnhardt........$588,926
2. Cale Yarborough ......537,358
3. Benny Parsons ........385,140
4. Darrell Waltrip ..........382,138
5. Richard Petty...........374,092
6. Bobby Allison ..........356,050
7. Buddy Baker ...........264,200
8. Terry Labonte .........215,889
9. Neil Bonnett.............210,547
10. Jody Ridley .............196,617
11. Harry Gant..............162,190
12. Richard Childress ....157,420
13. Dave Marcis............150,165
14. Buddy Arrington ......120,355
15. James Hylton ..........109,230

## Pole winners (7)
1. Cale Yarborough ................14
2. Buddy Baker .......................6
3. Darrell Waltrip .....................5
4. Benny Parsons ..................2
   Bobby Allison ....................2
6. David Pearson ...................1
   Donnie Allison ...................1

In 1980, there were 31 NASCAR Winston Cup events

# 1979 NASCAR WINSTON CUP SEASON

| Race No. | Location | Date | Winner | Car owner |
|---|---|---|---|---|
| 1. | Riverside, Calif. | Jan. 14 | Darrell Waltrip | Bill Gardner |
| 2. | Daytona Beach, Fla. | Feb. 18 | Richard Petty | Petty Enterprises |
| 3. | Rockingham, N.C. | Mar. 4 | Bobby Allison | Bud Moore |
| 4. | Richmond, Va. | Mar. 11 | Cale Yarborough | Junior Johnson |
| 5. | Hampton, Ga. | Mar. 18 | Buddy Baker | Harry Ranier |
| 6. | N. Wilkesboro, N.C. | Mar. 25 | Bobby Allison | Bud Moore |
| 7. | Bristol, Tenn. | Apr. 1 | Dale Earnhardt | Rod Osterlund |
| 8. | Darlington, S.C. | Apr. 8 | Darrell Waltrip | Bill Gardner |
| 9. | Martinsville, Va. | Apr. 22 | Richard Petty | Petty Enterprises |
| 10. | Talladega, Ala. | May 6 | Bobby Allison | Bud Moore |
| 11. | Nashville | May 12 | Cale Yarborough | Junior Johnson |
| 12. | Dover, Del. | May 20 | Neil Bonnett | Wood Brothers |
| 13. | Harrisburg, N.C. | May 27 | Darrell Waltrip | Bill Gardner |
| 14. | Bryan, Texas | June 3 | Darrell Waltrip | Bill Gardner |
| 15. | Riverside, Calif. | June 10 | Bobby Allison | Bud Moore |
| 16. | Brooklyn, Mich. | June 17 | Buddy Baker | Harry Ranier |
| 17. | Daytona Beach, Fla. | July 4 | Neil Bonnett | Wood Brothers |
| 18. | Nashville | July 14 | Darrell Waltrip | Bill Gardner |
| 19. | Long Pond, Pa. | July 30 | Cale Yarborough | Junior Johnson |
| 20. | Talladega, Ala. | Aug. 5 | Darrell Waltrip | Bill Gardner |
| 21. | Brooklyn, Mich. | Aug. 19 | Richard Petty | Petty Enterprises |
| 22. | Bristol, Tenn. | Aug. 25 | Darrell Waltrip | Bill Gardner |
| 23. | Darlington, S.C. | Sept. 3 | David Pearson | Rod Osterlund |
| 24. | Richmond, Va. | Sept. 9 | Bobby Allison | Bud Moore |
| 25. | Dover, Del. | Sept. 16 | Richard Petty | Petty Enterprises |
| 26. | Martinsville, Va. | Sept. 23 | Buddy Baker | Harry Ranier |
| 27. | Harrisburg, N.C. | Oct. 7 | Cale Yarborough | Junior Johnson |
| 28. | N. Wilkesboro, N.C. | Oct. 14 | Benny Parsons | M.C. Anderson |
| 29. | Rockingham, N.C. | Oct. 21 | Richard Petty | Petty Enterprises |
| 30. | Hampton, Ga. | Nov. 4 | Neil Bonnett | Wood Brothers |
| 31. | Fontana, Calif. | Nov. 18 | Benny Parsons | M.C. Anderson |

## Points standings
1. Richard Petty ............. 4,830
2. Darrell Waltrip ............ 4,819
3. Bobby Allison .............. 4,633
4. Cale Yarborough .......... 4,604
5. Benny Parsons ............ 4,256
6. Joe Millikan ................ 4,014
7. Dale Earnhardt ............ 3,749
8. Richard Childress ........ 3,735
9. Ricky Rudd ................. 3,642
10. Terry Labonte ............. 3,615

## Race winners (9)
1. Darrell Waltrip ..................... 7
2. Richard Petty ...................... 5
   Bobby Allison ...................... 5
4. Cale Yarborough ................. 4
5. Buddy Baker ....................... 3
   Neil Bonnett ........................ 3
7. Benny Parsons ................... 2
8. Dale Earnhardt .................... 1
   David Pearson .................... 1

## Money won leaders
1. Richard Petty .......... $531,292
2. Darrell Waltrip .......... 523,691
3. Cale Yarborough ...... 413,872
4. Bobby Allison ........... 403,014
5. Buddy Baker ............ 287,552
6. Dale Earnhardt ......... 264,086
7. Benny Parsons ........ 241,205
8. Joe Millikan .............. 222,053
9. Ricky Rudd .............. 146,302
10. Donnie Allison ......... 144,770
11. Neil Bonnett ............. 140,735
12. Richard Childress .... 132,922
13. Buddy Arrington ...... 131,833
14. Terry Labonte .......... 130,057
15. D.K. Ulrich ............... 108,862
16. J.D. McDuffie .......... 103,478

## Pole winners (12)
1. Buddy Baker ....................... 7
2. Darrell Waltrip ..................... 5
3. Neil Bonnett ........................ 4
   Dale Earnhardt .................... 4
5. Bobby Allison ...................... 3
6. David Pearson .................... 2
7. Donnie Allison ..................... 1
   Harry Gant .......................... 1
   Joe Millikan ......................... 1
   Benny Parsons ................... 1
   Richard Petty ...................... 1
   Cale Yarborough ................. 1

In 1979, there were 31 NASCAR Winston Cup events.

# 1978 NASCAR WINSTON CUP SEASON

| Race No. | Location | Date | Winner | Car owner |
|---|---|---|---|---|
| 1. | Riverside, Calif. | Jan. 22 | Cale Yarborough | Junior Johnson |
| 2. | Daytona Beach, Fla. | Feb. 19 | Bobby Allison | Bud Moore |
| 3. | Richmond, Va. | Feb. 26 | Benny Parsons | L.G. DeWitt |
| 4. | Rockingham, N.C. | Mar. 5 | David Pearson | Wood Brothers |
| 5. | Hampton, Ga. | Mar. 19 | Bobby Allison | Bud Moore |
| 6. | Bristol, Tenn. | Apr. 2 | Darrell Waltrip | Bill Gardner |
| 7. | Darlington, S.C. | Apr. 9 | Benny Parsons | L.G. DeWitt |
| 8. | N. Wilkesboro, N.C. | Apr. 16 | Darrell Waltrip | Bill Gardner |
| 9. | Martinsville, Va. | Apr. 23 | Darrell Waltrip | Bill Gardner |
| 10. | Talladega, Ala. | May 14 | Cale Yarborough | Junior Johnson |
| 11. | Dover, Del. | May 21 | David Pearson | Wood Brothers |
| 12. | Harrisburg, N.C. | May 28 | Darrell Waltrip | Bill Gardner |
| 13. | Nashville | June 3 | Cale Yarborough | Junior Johnson |
| 14. | Riverside, Calif. | June 11 | Benny Parsons | L.G. DeWitt |
| 15. | Brooklyn, Mich. | June 18 | Cale Yarborough | Junior Johnson |
| 16. | Daytona Beach, Fla. | July 4 | David Pearson | Wood Brothers |
| 17. | Nashville | July 15 | Cale Yarborough | Junior Johnson |
| 18. | Long Pond, Pa. | July 30 | Darrell Waltrip | Bill Gardner |
| 19. | Talladega, Ala. | Aug. 6 | Lennie Pond | Harry Ranier |
| 20. | Brooklyn, Mich. | Aug. 20 | David Pearson | Wood Brothers |
| 21. | Bristol, Tenn. | Aug. 26 | Cale Yarborough | Junior Johnson |
| 22. | Darlington, S.C. | Sept. 4 | Cale Yarborough | Junior Johnson |
| 23. | Richmond, Va. | Sept. 10 | Darrell Waltrip | Bill Gardner |
| 24. | Dover, Del. | Sept. 17 | Bobby Allison | Bud Moore |
| 25. | Martinsville, Va. | Sept. 24 | Cale Yarborough | Junior Johnson |
| 26. | N. Wilkesboro, N.C. | Oct. 1 | Cale Yarborough | Junior Johnson |
| 27. | Harrisburg, N.C. | Oct. 8 | Bobby Allison | Bud Moore |
| 28. | Rockingham, N.C. | Oct. 22 | Cale Yarborough | Junior Johnson |
| 29. | Hampton, Ga. | Nov. 5 | Donnie Allison | Hoss Ellington |
| 30. | Fontana, Calif. | Nov. 19 | Bobby Allison | Bud Moore |

## Point standings
1. Cale Yarborough ..........4,841
2. Bobby Allison................4,367
3. Darrell Waltrip ..............4,362
4. Benny Parsons.............4,350
5. Dave Marcis .................4,335
6. Richard Petty ................3,949
7. Lennie Pond..................3,794
8. Richard Brooks ............3,769
9. Buddy Arrington ..........3,626
10. Richard Childress ......3,566

## Race winners (7)
1. Cale Yarborough ..............10
2. Darrell Waltrip ....................6
3. Bobby Allison .....................5
4. David Pearson ...................4
5. Benny Parsons ..................3
6. Lennie Pond ......................1
   Donnie Allison ...................1

## Money won leaders
1. Cale Yarborough ....$530,751
2. Darrell Waltrip ..........343,367
3. Bobby Allison ...........335,635
4. Benny Parsons ........288,458
5. Richard Petty............215,491
6. Dave Marcis..............178,725
7. Lennie Pond .............160,627
8. Neil Bonnett..............155,875
9. David Pearson ..........151,837
10. Richard Brooks ........131,474
11. Buddy Arrington ......112,959
12. Richard Childress ...108,106
13. Buddy Baker ............104,265

## Pole winners (9)
1. Cale Yarborough .................8
2. David Pearson .....................7
3. Lennie Pond ........................5
4. Neil Bonnett.........................3
5. Benny Parsons ...................2
   Darrell Waltrip .....................2
7. Bobby Allison ......................1
   Buddy Baker .......................1
   J.D. McDuffie ......................1

In 1978, there were 30 NASCAR Winston Cup events.

# 1977 NASCAR WINSTON CUP SEASON

| Race No. | Location | Date | Winner | Car owner |
|---|---|---|---|---|
| 1. | Riverside, Calif. | Jan. 16 | David Pearson | Wood Brothers |
| 2. | Daytona Beach, Fla. | Feb. 20 | Cale Yarborough | Junior Johnson |
| 3. | Richmond, Va. | Feb. 27 | Cale Yarborough | Junior Johnson |
| 4. | Rockingham, N.C. | Mar. 13 | Richard Petty | Petty Enterprises |
| 5. | Hampton, Ga. | Mar. 20 | Richard Petty | Petty Enterprises |
| 6. | N. Wilkesboro, N.C | Mar. 27 | Cale Yarborough | Junior Johnson |
| 7. | Darlington, S.C. | Apr. 3 | Darrell Waltrip | Bill Gardner |
| 8. | Bristol, Tenn. | Apr. 17 | Cale Yarborough | Junior Johnson |
| 9. | Martinsville, Va. | Apr. 24 | Cale Yarborough | Junior Johnson |
| 10. | Talladega, Ala. | May 1 | Darrell Waltrip | Bill Gardner |
| 11. | Nashville | May 7 | Benny Parsons | L.G. DeWitt |
| 12. | Dover, Del. | May 15 | Cale Yarborough | Junior Johnson |
| 13. | Harrisburg, N.C. | May 29 | Richard Petty | Petty Enterprises |
| 14. | Riverside, Calif. | June 12 | Richard Petty | Petty Enterprises |
| 15. | Brooklyn, Mich. | June 19 | Cale Yarborough | Junior Johnson |
| 16. | Daytona Beach, Fla. | July 4 | Richard Petty | Petty Enterprises |
| 17. | Nashville | July 16 | Darrell Waltrip | Bill Gardner |
| 18. | Long Pond, Pa. | July 31 | Benny Parsons | L.G. DeWitt |
| 19. | Talladega, Ala. | Aug. 7 | Donnie Allison | Hoss Ellington |
| 20. | Brooklyn, Mich. | Aug. 22 | Darrell Waltrip | Bill Gardner |
| 21. | Bristol, Tenn. | Aug. 28 | Cale Yarborough | Junior Johnson |
| 22. | Darlington, S.C. | Sept. 5 | David Pearson | Wood Brothers |
| 23. | Richmond, Va. | Sept. 11 | Neil Bonnett | Jim Stacy |
| 24. | Dover, Del. | Sept. 18 | Benny Parsons | L.G. DeWitt |
| 25. | Martinsville, Va. | Sept. 25 | Cale Yarborough | Junior Johnson |
| 26. | N. Wilkesboro, N.C | Oct. 2 | Darrell Waltrip | Bill Gardner |
| 27. | Harrisburg, N.C. | Oct. 9 | Benny Parsons | L.G. DeWitt |
| 28. | Rockingham, N.C. | Oct. 23 | Donnie Allison | Hoss Ellington |
| 29. | Hampton, Ga. | Nov. 6 | Darrell Waltrip | Bill Gardner |
| 30. | Fontana, Calif. | Nov. 20 | Neil Bonnett | Jim Stacy |

## Points standings
1. Cale Yarborough ..........5,000
2. Richard Petty ...............4,614
3. Benny Parsons.............4,570
4. Darrell Waltrip ..............4,498
5. Buddy Baker ................3,961
6. Richard Brooks ............3,742
7. James Hylton................3,476
8. Bobby Allison................3,467
9. Richard Childress ........3,463
10. Cecil Gordon ..............3,294

## Race winners (7)
1. Cale Yarborough ................9
2. Darrell Waltrip ...................6
3. Richard Petty .....................5
4. Benny Parsons ..................4
5. David Pearson ...................2
   Neil Bonnett .......................2
   Donnie Allison ....................2

## Money won leaders
1. Cale Yarborough ....$477,498
2. Richard Petty...........345,886
3. Benny Parsons .......297,421
4. Darrell Waltrip .........276,312
5. Buddy Baker ...........205,803
6. David Pearson .........180,999
7. Richard Brooks ........141,421
8. Donnie Allison .........124,785
9. Neil Bonnett.............110,672
10. James Hylton ..........108,398

## Pole winners (9)
1. Neil Bonnett......................6
2. Richard Petty....................5
   David Pearson ....................5
4. Cale Yarborough ...............3
   Donnie Allison ....................3
   Benny Parsons ...................3
   Darrell Waltrip ....................3
8. A.J. Foyt ...........................1
   Sam Sommers ...................1

In 1977, there were 30 NASCAR Winston Cup events.

# 1976 NASCAR WINSTON CUP SEASON

| Race No. | Location | Date | Winner | Car owner |
|---|---|---|---|---|
| 1. | Riverside, Calif. | Jan. 18 | David Pearson | Wood Brothers |
| 2. | Daytona Beach, Fla. | Feb. 15 | David Pearson | Wood Brothers |
| 3. | Rockingham, N.C. | Feb. 29 | Richard Petty | Petty Enterprises |
| 4. | Richmond, Va. | Mar. 7 | Dave Marcis | Nord Krauskopf |
| 5. | Bristol, Tenn. | Mar. 14 | Cale Yarborough | Junior Johnson |
| 6. | Hampton, Ga. | Mar. 21 | David Pearson | Wood Brothers |
| 7. | N. Wilkesboro, N.C. | Apr. 4 | Cale Yarborough | Junior Johnson |
| 8. | Darlington, S.C. | Apr. 11 | David Pearson | Wood Brothers |
| 9. | Martinsville, Va. | Apr. 25 | Darrell Waltrip | Bill Gardner |
| 10. | Talladega, Ala. | May 2 | Buddy Baker | Bud Moore |
| 11. | Nashville | May 8 | Cale Yarborough | Junior Johnson |
| 12. | Dover, Del. | May 16 | Benny Parsons | L.G. DeWitt |
| 13. | Harrisburg, N.C. | May 30 | David Pearson | Wood Brothers |
| 14. | Riverside, Calif. | June 13 | David Pearson | Wood Brothers |
| 15. | Brooklyn, Mich. | June 20 | David Pearson | Wood Brothers |
| 16. | Daytona Beach, Fla. | July 4 | Cale Yarborough | Junior Johnson |
| 17. | Nashville | July 17 | Benny Parsons | L.G. DeWitt |
| 18. | Long Pond, Pa. | Aug. 1 | Richard Petty | Petty Enterprises |
| 19. | Talladega, Ala. | Aug. 8 | Dave Marcis | Nord Krauskopf |
| 20. | Brooklyn, Mich. | Aug. 22 | David Pearson | Wood Brothers |
| 21. | Bristol, Tenn. | Aug. 29 | Cale Yarborough | Junior Johnson |
| 22. | Darlington, S.C. | Sept. 6 | David Pearson | Wood Brothers |
| 23. | Richmond, Va. | Sept. 12 | Cale Yarborough | Junior Johnson |
| 24. | Dover, Del. | Sept. 19 | Cale Yarborough | Junior Johnson |
| 25. | Martinsville, Va. | Sept. 26 | Cale Yarborough | Junior Johnson |
| 26. | N. Wilkesboro, N.C. | Oct. 3 | Cale Yarborough | Junior Johnson |
| 27. | Harrisburg, N.C. | Oct. 10 | Donnie Allison | Hoss Ellington |
| 28. | Rockingham, N.C. | Oct. 24 | Richard Petty | Petty Enterprises |
| 29. | Hampton, Ga. | Nov. 7 | Dave Marcis | Nord Krauskopf |
| 30. | Fontana, Calif. | Nov. 21 | David Pearson | Wood Brothers |

## Points standings
1. Cale Yarborough ..........4,644
2. Richard Petty ...............4,449
3. Benny Parsons.............4,304
4. Bobby Allison................4,097
5. Lennie Pond.................3,930
6. Dave Marcis .................3,875
7. Buddy Baker  ...............3,745
8. Darrell Waltrip ..............3,505
9. David Pearson ..............3,483
10. Richard Brooks ..........3,447

## Race winners (8)
1. David Pearson ...................10
2. Cale Yarborough ................9
3. Richard Petty .....................3
    Dave Marcis.......................3
5. Benny Parsons ..................2
6. Buddy Baker ......................1
    Darrell Waltrip ...................1
    Donnie Allison ...................1

## Money won leaders
1. Cale Yarborough ......387,173
2. Richard Petty..........338,265
3. David Pearson ..........283,686
4. Benny Parsons  ........242,970
5. Buddy Baker ............214,439
6. Bobby Allison ...........210,376
7. Dave Marcis..............198,199
8. Darrell Waltrip ..........191,501
9. Richard Brooks ........105,917

## Pole winners (11)
1. David Pearson ......................8
2. Dave Marcis..........................7
3. Darrell Waltrip ......................3
4. Bobby Allison  .....................2
    Buddy Baker  .....................2
    Benny Parsons ...................2
    Cale Yarborough .................2
8. Richard Petty.......................1
    Neil Bonnett.........................1
    A.J. Foyt  .............................1
    Ramo Stott .........................1

In 1976, there were 30 NASCAR Winston Cup events.

# 1975 NASCAR WINSTON CUP SEASON

| Race No. | Location | Date | Winner | Car owner |
|---|---|---|---|---|
| 1. | Riverside, Calif. | Jan. 19 | Bobby Allison | Roger Penske |
| 2. | Daytona Beach, Fla. | Feb. 16 | Benny Parsons | L.G. DeWitt |
| 3. | Richmond, Va. | Feb. 23 | Richard Petty | Petty Enterprises |
| 4. | Rockingham, N.C. | Mar. 2 | Cale Yarborough | Junior Johnson |
| 5. | Bristol, Tenn. | Mar. 16 | Richard Petty | Petty Enterprises |
| 6. | Hampton, Ga. | Mar. 23 | Richard Petty | Petty Enterprises |
| 7. | N. Wilkesboro, N.C. | Apr. 6 | Richard Petty | Petty Enterprises |
| 8. | Darlington, S.C. | Apr. 13 | Bobby Allison | Roger Penske |
| 9. | Martinsville, Va. | Apr. 27 | Richard Petty | Petty Enterprises |
| 10. | Talladega, Ala. | May 4 | Buddy Baker | Bud Moore |
| 11. | Nashville | May 10 | Darrell Waltrip | Darrell Waltrip |
| 12. | Dover, Del. | May 19 | David Pearson | Wood Brothers |
| 13. | Harrisburg, N.C. | May 25 | Richard Petty | Petty Enterprises |
| 14. | Riverside, Calif. | June 8 | Richard Petty | Petty Enterprises |
| 15. | Brooklyn, Mich. | June 15 | David Pearson | Wood Brothers |
| 16. | Daytona Beach, Fla. | July 4 | Richard Petty | Petty Enterprises |
| 17. | Nashville | July 20 | Cale Yarborough | Junior Johnson |
| 18. | Long Pond, Pa. | Aug. 3 | David Pearson | Wood Brothers |
| 19. | Talladega, Ala. | Aug. 17 | Buddy Baker | Bud Moore |
| 20. | Brooklyn, Mich. | Aug. 24 | Richard Petty | Petty Enterprises |
| 21. | Darlington, S.C. | Sept. 1 | Bobby Allison | Roger Penske |
| 22. | Dover, Del. | Sept. 14 | Richard Petty | Petty Enterprises |
| 23. | N. Wilkesboro, N.C. | Sept. 21 | Richard Petty | Petty Enterprises |
| 24. | Martinsville, Va. | Sept. 28 | Dave Marcis | Nord Krauskopf |
| 25. | Harrisburg, N.C. | Oct. 5 | Richard Petty | Petty Enterprises |
| 26. | Richmond, Va. | Oct. 12 | Darrell Waltrip | Bill Gardner |
| 27. | Rockingham, N.C. | Oct. 19 | Cale Yarborough | Junior Johnson |
| 28. | Bristol, Tenn. | Nov. 2 | Richard Petty | Petty Enterprises |
| 29. | Hampton, Ga. | Nov. 9 | Buddy Baker | Bud Moore |
| 30. | Fontana, Calif. | Nov. 23 | Buddy Baker | Bud Moore |

## Points standings
1. Richard Petty ............4,783
2. Dave Marcis ..............4,061
3. James Hylton ............3,914
4. Benny Parsons...........3,820
5. Richard Childress ......3,818
6. Cecil Gordon .............3,702
7. Darrell Waltrip ...........3,462
8. Elmo Langley ............3,399
9. Cale Yarborough .......3,295
10. Richard Brooks ........3,182

## Race winners (8)
1. Richard Petty .................13
2. Buddy Baker .....................4
3. David Pearson ..................3
   Cale Yarborough ...............3
   Bobby Allison ....................3
6. Darrell Waltrip ..................2
7. Benny Parsons .................1
   Dave Marcis ......................1

## Money won leaders
1. Richard Petty..........$378,865
2. David Pearson ..........179,207
3. Buddy Baker ............169,917
4. Dave Marcis..............149,202
5. Benny Parsons .........140,199
6. Cale Yarborough .......139,257
7. Bobby Allison ...........122,435
8. James Hylton ...........101,141
9. Darrell Waltrip ..........100,191

## Pole winners (9)
1. David Pearson ......................7
2. Dave Marcis.........................4
3. Bobby Allison ......................3
   Richard Petty.......................3
   Buddy Baker .......................3
   Benny Parsons ...................3
   Cale Yarborough .................3
8. Donnie Allison .....................2
   Darrell Waltrip ................... 2

In 1975, there were 30 NASCAR Winston Cup events.

# 1974 NASCAR WINSTON CUP SEASON

| Race No. | Location | Date | Winner | Car owner |
|---|---|---|---|---|
| 1. | Riverside, Calif. | Jan. 26 | Cale Yarborough | Junior Johnson |
| 2. | Daytona Beach, Fla. | Feb. 17 | Richard Petty | Petty Enterprises |
| 3. | Richmond, Va. | Feb. 24 | Bobby Allison | Bobby Allison |
| 4. | Rockingham, N.C. | Mar. 3 | Richard Petty | Petty Enterprises |
| 5. | Bristol, Tenn. | Mar. 17 | Cale Yarborough | Junior Johnson |
| 6. | Hampton, Ga. | Mar. 24 | Cale Yarborough | Junior Johnson |
| 7. | Darlington, S.C. | Apr. 7 | David Pearson | Wood Brothers |
| 8. | N. Wilkesboro, N.C. | Apr. 21 | Richard Petty | Petty Enterprises |
| 9. | Martinsville, Va. | Apr. 28 | Cale Yarborough | Junior Johnson |
| 10. | Talladega, Ala. | May 5 | David Pearson | Wood Brothers |
| 11. | Nashville | May 11 | Richard Petty | Petty Enterprises |
| 12. | Dover, Del. | May 19 | Cale Yarborough | Junior Johnson |
| 13. | Harrisburg, N.C. | May 26 | David Pearson | Wood Brothers |
| 14. | Riverside, Calif. | June 9 | Cale Yarborough | Junior Johnson |
| 15. | Brooklyn, Mich. | June 16 | Richard Petty | Petty Enterprises |
| 16. | Daytona Beach, Fla. | July 4 | David Pearson | Wood Brothers |
| 17. | Bristol, Tenn. | July 14 | Cale Yarborough | Junior Johnson |
| 18. | Nashville | July 20 | Cale Yarborough | Junior Johnson |
| 19. | Hampton, Ga. | July 28 | Richard Petty | Petty Enterprises |
| 20. | Long Pond, Pa. | Aug. 4 | Richard Petty | Petty Enterprises |
| 21. | Talladega, Ala. | Aug. 11 | Richard Petty | Petty Enterprises |
| 22. | Brooklyn, Mich. | Aug. 25 | David Pearson | Wood Brothers |
| 23. | Darlington, S.C. | Sept. 2 | Cale Yarborough | Junior Johnson |
| 24. | Richmond, Va. | Sept. 8 | Richard Petty | Petty Enterprises |
| 25. | Dover, Del. | Sept. 15 | Richard Petty | Petty Enterprises |
| 26. | N. Wilkesboro, N.C. | Sept. 22 | Cale Yarborough | Junior Johnson |
| 27. | Martinsville, Va. | Sept. 29 | Earl Ross | Allan Brooke |
| 28. | Harrisburg, N.C. | Oct. 6 | David Pearson | Wood Brothers |
| 29. | Rockingham, N.C. | Oct. 20 | David Pearson | Wood Brothers |
| 30. | Fontana, Calif. | Nov. 24 | Bobby Allison | Roger Penske |

## Points standings
1. Richard Petty ........5,037.750
2. Cale Yarborough ....4,470.300
3. David Pearson........2,389.250
4. Bobby Allison .......2,019.195
5. Benny Parsons ......1,591.500
6. Dave Marcis ..........1,378.200
7. Buddy Baker ..........1,016.880
8. Earl Ross ...............1,009.470
9. Cecil Gordon..........1,000.650
10. David Sisco ............956.200

## Race winners (5)
1. Richard Petty....................10
   Cale Yarborough ..............10
3. David Pearson ....................7
4. Bobby Allison .....................2
5. Earl Ross ............................1

## Money won leaders
1. Richard Petty.........$330,347
2. Cale Yarborough ......272,946
3. David Pearson ..........233,567
4. Bobby Allison ..........129,768

## Pole winners (8)
1. David Pearson ....................11
2. Richard Petty.......................7
3. Bobby Allison ......................3
   Cale Yarborough .................3
5. Donnie Allison ....................2
   Buddy Baker .......................2
7. Darrell Waltrip ....................1
   George Follmer ...................1

In 1974, there were 30 NASCAR Winston Cup events.

# 1973 NASCAR WINSTON CUP SEASON

| Race No. | Location | Date | Winner | Car owner |
|---|---|---|---|---|
| 1. | Riverside, Calif. | Jan. 21 | Mark Donohue | Roger Penske |
| 2. | Daytona Beach, Fla. | Feb. 18 | Richard Petty | Petty Enterprises |
| 3. | Richmond, Va. | Feb. 25 | Richard Petty | Petty Enterprises |
| 4. | Rockingham, N.C. | Mar. 18 | David Pearson | Wood Brothers |
| 5. | Bristol, Tenn. | Mar. 25 | Cale Yarborough | Junior Johnson |
| 6. | Hampton, Ga. | Apr. 1 | David Pearson | Wood Brothers |
| 7. | N. Wilkesboro, N.C. | Apr. 8 | Richard Petty | Petty Enterprises |
| 8. | Darlington, S.C. | Apr. 15 | David Pearson | Wood Brothers |
| 9. | Martinsville, Va. | Apr. 29 | David Pearson | Wood Brothers |
| 10. | Talladega, Ala. | May 6 | David Pearson | Wood Brothers |
| 11. | Nashville | May 12 | Cale Yarborough | Junior Johnson |
| 12. | Harrisburg, N.C. | May 27 | Buddy Baker | Nord Krauskopf |
| 13. | Dover, Del. | June 3 | David Pearson | Wood Brothers |
| 14. | Bryan, Texas | June 10 | Richard Petty | Petty Enterprises |
| 15. | Riverside, Calif. | June 17 | Bobby Allison | Bobby Allison |
| 16. | Brooklyn, Mich. | June 24 | David Pearson | Wood Brothers |
| 17. | Daytona Beach, Fla. | July 4 | David Pearson | Wood Brothers |
| 18. | Bristol, Tenn. | July 8 | Benny Parsons | L.G. DeWitt |
| 19. | Hampton, Ga. | July 22 | David Pearson | Wood Brothers |
| 20. | Talladega, Ala. | Aug. 12 | Dick Brooks | Crawford Brothers |
| 21. | Nashville | Aug. 25 | Buddy Baker | Nord Krauskopf |
| 22. | Darlington, S.C. | Sept. 3 | Cale Yarborough | Junior Johnson |
| 23. | Richmond, Va. | Sept. 9 | Richard Petty | Petty Enterprises |
| 24. | Dover, Del. | Sept. 16 | David Pearson | Wood Brothers |
| 25. | N. Wilkesboro, N.C. | Sept. 23 | Bobby Allison | Bobby Allison |
| 26. | Martinsville, Va. | Sept. 30 | Richard Petty | Petty Enterprises |
| 27. | Harrisburg, N.C. | Oct. 7 | Cale Yarborough | Junior Johnson |
| 28. | Rockingham, N.C. | Oct. 21 | David Pearson | Wood Brothers |

## Points standings
1. Benny Parsons ........7,173.80
2. Cale Yarborough ......7,106.65
3. Cecil Gordon ............7,046.80
4. James Hylton ..........6,972.75
5. Richard Petty ........6,877.955
6. Buddy Baker ............6,327.60
7. Bobby Allison ..........6,272.30
8. Walter Ballard ..........5,955.70
9. Elmo Langley ..........5,826.85
10. J.D. McDuffie ........5,743.90

## Race winners (8)
1. David Pearson .................11
2. Richard Petty .....................6
3. Cale Yarborough ................4
4. Buddy Baker ......................2
   Bobby Allison ......................2
6. Benny Parsons ..................1
   Richard Brooks ..................1
   Mark Donohue....................1

## Money won leaders
1. David Pearson ........$216,737
2. Cale Yarborough ......181,574
3. Richard Petty............171,122
4. Benny Parsons ........114,345
5. Buddy Baker ............132,988
6. Bobby Allison ..........107,299

## Pole winners (5)
1. David Pearson ......................8
2. Bobby Allison ......................6
3. Buddy Baker ........................5
   Cale Yarborough ..................5
5. Richard Petty .................... 3

In 1973, there were 28 NASCAR Winston Cup events.

# 1972 NASCAR WINSTON CUP SEASON

| Race No. | Location | Date | Winner | Car owner |
|---|---|---|---|---|
| 1. | Riverside, Calif. | Jan. 23 | Richard Petty | Petty Enterprises |
| 2. | Daytona Beach, Fla. | Feb. 20 | A.J. Foyt | Wood Brothers |
| 3. | Richmond, Va. | Feb. 27 | Richard Petty | Petty Enterprises |
| 4. | Fontana, Calif. | Mar. 5 | A.J. Foyt | Wood Brothers |
| 5. | Rockingham, N.C. | Mar. 12 | Bobby Isaac | Nord Krauskopf |
| 6. | Hampton, Ga. | Mar. 26 | Bobby Allison | Junior Johnson |
| 7. | Bristol, Tenn. | Apr. 9 | Bobby Allison | Junior Johnson |
| 8. | Darlington, S.C. | Apr. 16 | David Pearson | Wood Brothers |
| 9. | N. Wilkesboro, N.C. | Apr. 23 | Richard Petty | Petty Enterprises |
| 10. | Martinsville, Va. | Apr. 30 | Richard Petty | Petty Enterprises |
| 11. | Talladega, Ala. | May 7 | David Pearson | Wood Brothers |
| 12. | Harrisburg, N.C. | May 28 | Buddy Baker | Petty Enterprises |
| 13. | Dover, Del. | June 4 | Bobby Allison | Junior Johnson |
| 14. | Brooklyn, Mich. | June 11 | David Pearson | Wood Brothers |
| 15. | Riverside, Calif. | June 18 | Ray Elder | Fred Elder |
| 16. | Bryan, Texas | June 25 | Richard Petty | Petty Enterprises |
| 17. | Daytona Beach, Fla. | July 4 | David Pearson | Wood Brothers |
| 18. | Bristol, Tenn. | July 9 | Bobby Allison | Junior Johnson |
| 19. | Trenton, N.J. | July 16 | Bobby Allison | Junior Johnson |
| 20. | Hampton, Ga. | July 23 | Bobby Allison | Junior Johnson |
| 21. | Talladega, Ala. | Aug. 6 | James Hylton | James Hylton |
| 22. | Brooklyn, Mich. | Aug. 20 | David Pearson | Wood Brothers |
| 23. | Nashville | Aug. 26 | Bobby Allison | Junior Johnson |
| 24. | Darlington, S.C. | Sept. 4 | Bobby Allison | Junior Johnson |
| 25. | Richmond, Va. | Sept. 10 | Richard Petty | Petty Enterprises |
| 26. | Dover, Del. | Sept. 17 | David Pearson | Wood Brothers |
| 27. | Martinsville, Va. | Sept. 24 | Richard Petty | Petty Enterprises |
| 28. | N. Wilkesboro, N.C. | Oct. 1 | Richard Petty | Petty Enterprises |
| 29. | Harrisburg, N.C. | Oct. 8 | Bobby Allison | Junior Johnson |
| 30. | Rockingham, N.C. | Oct. 22 | Bobby Allison | Junior Johnson |
| 31. | Bryan, Texas | Nov. 12 | Buddy Baker | Nord Krauskopf |

## Points standings
1. Richard Petty ..........8,701.40
2. Bobby Allison ..........8,573.50
3. James Hylton ..........8,158.70
4. Cecil Gordon ............7,326.05
5. Benny Parsons ........6,844.15
6. Walter Ballard ..........6,781.45
7. Elmo Langley ..........6,656.25
8. John Sears ..............6,298.50
9. Dean Dalton ............6,295.05
10. Ben Arnold ............6,179.00

## Race winners (8)
1. Bobby Allison ..................10
2. Richard Petty ....................8
3. David Pearson ...................6
4. Buddy Baker ......................2
    A.J. Foyt ............................2
6. James Hylton ....................1
    Bobby Isaac......................1
    Ray Elder ..........................1

## Money won leaders
1. Bobby Allison ........$284,467
2. Richard Petty..........265,460
3. David Pearson ..........139,599
4. James Hylton ..........113,705

## Pole winners (6)
1. Bobby Allison ..................11
2. Bobby Isaac........................9
3. David Pearson .....................4
4. Richard Petty......................3
    A.J. Foyt ............................3
6. Buddy Baker ......................1

In 1972, there were 31 NASCAR Winston Cup events.

# 1971 NASCAR WINSTON CUP SEASON

| Race No. | Location | Date | Winner | Car owner |
|---|---|---|---|---|
| 1. | Riverside, Calif. | Jan. 10 | Ray Elder | Fred Elder |
| 2. | Daytona Beach, Fla. | Feb. 11 | Pete Hamilton | Cotton Owens |
| 3. | Daytona Beach, Fla. | Feb. 11 | David Pearson | Holman-Moody |
| 4. | Daytona Beach, Fla. | Feb. 14 | Richard Petty | Petty Enterprises |
| 5. | Ontario, Calif. | Feb. 28 | A.J. Foyt | Wood Brothers |
| 6. | Richmond, Va. | Mar. 7 | Richard Petty | Petty Enterprises |
| 7. | Rockingham, N.C. | Mar. 14 | Richard Petty | Petty Enterprises |
| 8. | Hickory, N.C. | Mar. 21 | Richard Petty | Petty Enterprises |
| 9. | Bristol, Tenn. | Mar. 28 | David Pearson | Holman-Moody |
| 10. | Hampton, Ga. | Apr. 4 | A.J. Foyt | Wood Brothers |
| 11. | Columbia, S.C. | Apr. 8 | Richard Petty | Petty Enterprises |
| 12. | Greenville, S.C. | Apr. 10 | Bobby Isaac | Nord Krauskopf |
| 13. | Maryville, Tenn. | Apr. 15 | Richard Petty | Petty Enterprises |
| 14. | North Wilkesboro, N.C. | Apr. 18 | Richard Petty | Petty Enterprises |
| 15. | Martinsville, Va. | Apr. 25 | Richard Petty | Petty Enterprises |
| 16. | Darlington, S.C. | May 2 | Buddy Baker | Petty Enterprises |
| 17. | South Boston, Va. | May 9 | Benny Parsons | L.G. DeWitt |
| 18. | Talladega, Ala. | May 16 | Donnie Allison | Wood Brothers |
| 19. | Asheville, N.C. | May 21 | Richard Petty | Petty Enterprises |
| 20. | Kingsport, Tenn. | May 23 | Bobby Isaac | Nord Krauskopf |
| 21. | Concord, N.C. | May 30 | Bobby Allison | Holman-Moody |
| 22. | Dover, Del. | Jun. 6 | Bobby Allison | Holman-Moody |
| 23. | Brooklyn, Mich. | Jun. 13 | Bobby Allison | Holman-Moody |
| 24. | Riverside, Calif. | Jun. 20 | Bobby Allison | Bobby Allison |
| 25. | Houston, Texas | Jun. 23 | Bobby Allison | Bobby Allison |
| 26. | Greenville, S.C. | Jun. 26 | Richard Petty | Petty Enterprises |
| 27. | Daytona Beach, Fla. | Jul. 4 | Bobby Isaac | Nord Krauskopf |
| 28. | Bristol, Tenn. | Jul. 11 | Charlie Glotzbach | Jr. Johnson/R. Howard |
| 29. | Malta, N.Y. | Jul. 14 | Richard Petty | Petty Enterprises |
| 30. | Islip, N.Y. | Jul. 15 | Richard Petty | Petty Enterprises |
| 31. | Trenton, N.J. | Jul. 18 | Richard Petty | Petty Enterprises |
| 32. | Nashville, Tenn. | Jul. 24 | Richard Petty | Petty Enterprises |
| 33. | Hampton, Ga. | Aug. 1 | Richard Petty | Petty Enterprises |
| 34. | Winston-Salem, N.C. | Aug. 6 | Bobby Allison | Melvin Joseph |
| 35. | Ona, W.Va. | Aug. 8 | Richard Petty | Petty Enterprises |
| 36. | Brooklyn, Mich. | Aug. 15 | Bobby Allison | Holman-Moody |
| 37. | Talladega, Ala. | Aug. 22 | Bobby Allison | Holman-Moody |
| 38. | Columbia, S.C. | Aug. 27 | Richard Petty | Petty Enterprises |
| 39. | Hickory, N.C. | Aug. 28 | Tiny Lund | Ronnie Hopkins |
| 40. | Darlington, S.C. | Sep. 6 | Bobby Allison | Holman-Moody |
| 41. | Martinsville, Va. | Sep. 26 | Bobby Isaac | Nord Krauskopf |
| 42. | Concord, N.C. | Oct. 10 | Bobby Allison | Holman-Moody |
| 43. | Dover, Del. | Oct. 17 | Richard Petty | Petty Enterprises |
| 44. | Rockingham, N.C. | Oct. 24 | Richard Petty | Petty Enterprises |
| 45. | Macon, Ga. | Nov. 7 | Bobby Allison | Holman-Moody |
| 46. | Richmond, Va. | Nov. 14 | Richard Petty | Petty Enterprises |
| 47. | North Wilkesboro, N.C. | Nov. 22 | Tiny Lund | Ronnie Hopkins |
| 48. | College Station, Texas | Dec. 12 | Richard Petty | Petty Enterprises |

## Points standings
1. Richard Petty ........4,435.00
2. James Hylton ........4,071.00
3. Cecil Gordon .........3,677.00
4. Bobby Allison ........3,636.00
5. Elmo Langley ........3,356.00
6. Jabe Thomas ........3,200.00
7. Bill Champion ........3,058.00
8. Frank Warren ........2,886.00
9. J.D. McDuffie ........2,862.00
10. Walter Ballard ........2,633.00

## Race winners (12)
1. Richard Petty ..................21
2. Bobby Allison .................11
3. Bobby Isaac ....................4
4. Tiny Lund............................2
   A.J. Foyt ............................2
   David Pearson ..................2
7. Benny Parsons ..................1
   Buddy Baker ......................1
   Donnie Allison ....................1
   Ray Elder ...........................1
   Pete Hamilton ....................1
   Charlie Glotzbach...............1

## Money won leaders
1. Richard Petty.........$269,225
2. Bobby Allison ..........235,795
3. Buddy Baker ...........115,150
4. Bobby Isaac............106,426
5. Donnie Allison..........69,995
6. Pete Hamilton ..........60,440
7. James Hylton ...........55,860
8. Benny Parsons .........48,517
9. Fred Lorenzen ..........45,100
10. Cecil Gordon ...........42,949

## Pole winners (14)
1. Richard Petty.....................9
   Bobby Allison .....................9
3. Bobby Isaac.......................5
   Donnie Allison ....................5
5. Charlie Glotzbach .............4
   A.J. Foyt ............................4
7. Dave Marcis.......................2
   David Pearson ...................2
   Pete Hamilton ....................2
   Friday Hassler ...................2
   Buddy Baker ......................1
   Bill Dennis ..........................1
   James Hylton .....................1
   Fred Lorenzen ...................1

# 1970 NASCAR WINSTON CUP SEASON

| Race No. | Location | Date | Winner | Car owner |
|---|---|---|---|---|
| 1. | Riverside, Calif. | Jan. 18 | A.J. Foyt | Jack Bowsher |
| 2. | Daytona Beach, Fla. | Feb. 19 | Cale Yarborough | Wood Brothers |
| 3. | Daytona Beach, Fla. | Feb. 19 | Charlie Glotzbach | Ray Nichels |
| 4. | Daytona Beach, Fla. | Feb. 22 | Pete Hamilton | Petty Enterprises |
| 5. | Richmond, Va. | Mar. 1 | James Hylton | James Hylton |
| 6. | Rockingham, N.C. | Mar. 8 | Richard Petty | Petty Enterprises |
| 7. | Savannah, Ga. | Mar. 15 | Richard Petty | Petty Enterprises |
| 8. | Hampton, Ga. | Mar. 29 | Bobby Allison | Mario Rossi |
| 9. | Bristol, Tenn. | Apr. 5 | Donnie Allison | Banjo Matthews |
| 10. | Talladega, Ala. | Apr. 12 | Pete Hamilton | Petty Enterprises |
| 11. | North Wilkesboro, N.C. | Apr. 18 | Richard Petty | Petty Enterprises |
| 12. | Columbia, S.C. | Apr. 30 | Richard Petty | Donald Robertson |
| 13. | Darlington, S.C. | May. 9 | David Pearson | Holman-Moody |
| 14. | Beltsville, Md. | May. 15 | Bobby Isaac | Nord Krauskopf |
| 15. | Hampton, Va. | May. 18 | Bobby Isaac | Nord Krauskopf |
| 16. | Concord, N.C. | May. 24 | Donnie Allison | Banjo Matthews |
| 17. | Maryville, Tenn. | May. 28 | Bobby Isaac | Nord Krauskopf |
| 18. | Martinsville, Va. | May. 31 | Bobby Isaac | Nord Krauskopf |
| 19. | Brooklyn, Mich. | Jun. 7 | Cale Yarborough | Wood Brothers |
| 20. | Riverside, Calif. | Jun. 14 | Richard Petty | Petty Enterprises |
| 21. | Hickory, N.C. | Jun. 20 | Bobby Isaac | Nord Krauskopf |
| 22. | Kingsport, Tenn. | Jun. 26 | Richard Petty | Petty Enterprises |
| 23. | Greenville, S.C. | Jun. 27 | Bobby Isaac | Nord Krauskopf |
| 24. | Daytona Beach, Fla. | Jul. 4 | Donnie Allison | Banjo Matthews |
| 25. | Malta, N.Y. | Jul. 7 | Richard Petty | Petty Enterprises |
| 26. | Thompson, Conn. | Jul. 9 | Bobby Isaac | Nord Krauskopf |
| 27. | Trenton, N.J. | Jul. 12 | Richard Petty | Petty Enterprises |
| 28. | Bristol, Tenn. | Jul. 19 | Bobby Allison | Bobby Allison |
| 29. | Maryville, Tenn. | Jul. 24 | Richard Petty | Petty Enterprises |
| 30. | Nashville, Tenn. | Jul. 25 | Bobby Isaac | Nord Krauskopf |
| 31. | Hampton, Ga. | Aug. 2 | Richard Petty | Petty Enterprises |
| 32. | Columbia, S.C. | Aug. 6 | Bobby Isaac | Nord Krauskopf |
| 33. | Ona, W.Va. | Aug. 11 | Richard Petty | Petty Enterprises |
| 34. | Brooklyn, Mich. | Aug. 16 | Charlie Glotzbach | Ray Nichels |
| 35. | Talladega, Ala. | Aug. 23 | Pete Hamilton | Petty Enterprises |
| 36. | Winston-Salem, N.C. | Aug. 28 | Richard Petty | Petty Enterprises |
| 37. | South Boston, Va. | Aug. 29 | Richard Petty | Petty Enterprises |
| 38. | Darlington, S.C. | Sep. 7 | Buddy Baker | Cotton Owens |
| 39. | Hickory, N.C. | Sep. 11 | Bobby Isaac | Nord Krauskopf |
| 40. | Richmond, Va. | Sep. 13 | Richard Petty | Petty Enterprises |
| 41. | Dover, Del. | Sep. 20 | Richard Petty | Petty Enterprises |
| 42. | Raleigh, N.C. | Sep. 30 | Richard Petty | Donald Robertson |
| 43. | North Wilkesboro, N.C. | Oct. 4 | Bobby Isaac | Nord Krauskopf |
| 44. | Concord, N.C. | Oct. 11 | LeeRoy Yarbrough | Junior Johnson |
| 45. | Martinsville, Va. | Oct. 18 | Richard Petty | Petty Enterprises |
| 46. | Macon, Ga. | Nov. 8 | Richard Petty | Petty Enterprises |
| 47. | Rockingham, N.C. | Nov. 15 | Cale Yarborough | Wood Brothers |
| 48. | Hampton, Va. | Nov. 22 | Bobby Allison | Bobby Allison |

## Points standings
1. Bobby Isaac ..........3,911.00
2. Bobby Allison ........3,860.00
3. James Hylton ........3,788.00
4. Richard Petty ........3,447.00
5. Neil Castles ...........3,158.00
6. Elmo Langley .......3,154.00
7. Jabe Thomas ........3,120.00
8. Benny Parsons ......2,993.00
9. Dave Marcis .........2,820.00
10. Frank Warren ......2,697.00

## Race winners (12)
1. Richard Petty ................18
2. Bobby Isaac ...................11
3. Pete Hamilton .................3
   Cale Yarborough ..............3
   Bobby Allison ...................3
   Donnie Allison ..................3
7. Charlie Glotzbach ............2
8. LeeRoy Yarbrough ............1
   David Pearson ...................1
   A.J. Foyt ............................1
   James Hylton.....................1
   Buddy Baker .....................1

## Money won leaders
1. Richard Petty..........$138,969
2. Bobby Allison ..........131,965
3. Pete Hamilton ..........131,406
4. Bobby Isaac..............121,470
5. Cale Yarborough .......115,875
6. Donnie Allison ...........92,606
7. David Pearson ............87,118
8. Buddy Baker ..............62,928
9. LeeRoy Yarbrough......61,930
10. James Hylton ............59,705

## Pole winners (16)
1. Bobby Isaac................13
2. Richard Petty................9
3. Cale Yarborough ..........5
   Bobby Allison ...............5
5. Charlie Glotzbach .........4
6. David Pearson ..............2
7. LeeRoy Yarbrough.......1
   Benny Parsons .............1
   John Sears ....................1
   Fred Lorenzen ..............1
   Larry Baumel................1
   Buddy Baker ................1
   Donnie Allison .............1
   James Hylton ...............1
   Pete Hamilton ..............1
   Dan Gurney ..................1

# 1969 NASCAR WINSTON CUP SEASON

| Race No. | Location | Date | Winner | Car owner |
|---|---|---|---|---|
| 1. | Macon, Ga. | Nov. 17 | Richard Petty | Petty Enterprises |
| 2. | Montgomery, Ala. | Dec. 8 | Bobby Allison | Mario Rossi |
| 3. | Riverside, Calif. | Feb. 1 | Richard Petty | Petty Enterprises |
| 4. | Daytona Beach, Fla. | Feb. 20 | David Pearson | Holman-Moody |
| 5. | Daytona Beach, Fla. | Feb. 20 | Bobby Isaac | Nord Krauskopf |
| 6. | Daytona Beach, Fla. | Feb. 23 | LeeRoy Yarbrough | Junior Johnson |
| 7. | Rockingham, N.C. | Mar. 9 | David Pearson | Holman-Moody |
| 8. | Augusta, Ga. | Mar. 16 | David Pearson | Holman-Moody |
| 9. | Bristol, Tenn. | Mar. 23 | Bobby Allison | Mario Rossi |
| 10. | Hampton, Ga. | Mar. 30 | Cale Yarborough | Wood Brothers |
| 11. | Columbia, S.C. | Apr. 3 | Bobby Isaac | Nord Krauskopf |
| 12. | Hickory, N.C. | Apr. 6 | Bobby Isaac | Nord Krauskopf |
| 13. | Greenville, S.C. | Apr. 8 | Bobby Isaac | Nord Krauskopf |
| 14. | Richmond, Va. | Apr. 13 | David Pearson | Holman-Moody |
| 15. | North Wilkesboro, N.C. | Apr. 20 | Bobby Allison | Mario Rossi |
| 16. | Martinsville, Va. | Apr. 27 | Richard Petty | Petty Enterprises |
| 17. | Weaverville, N.C. | May. 4 | Bobby Isaac | Nord Krauskopf |
| 18. | Darlington, S.C. | May. 10 | LeeRoy Yarbrough | Junior Johnson |
| 19. | Beltsville, Md. | May. 16 | Bobby Isaac | Nord Krauskopf |
| 20. | Hampton, Va. | May. 17 | David Pearson | Holman-Moody |
| 21. | Concord, N.C. | May. 25 | LeeRoy Yarbrough | Junior Johnson |
| 22. | Macon, Ga. | Jun. 1 | Bobby Isaac | Nord Krauskopf |
| 23. | Maryville, Tenn. | Jun. 5 | Bobby Isaac | Nord Krauskopf |
| 24. | Brooklyn, Mich. | Jun. 15 | Cale Yarborough | Wood Brothers |
| 25. | Kingsport, Tenn. | Jun. 19 | Richard Petty | Petty Enterprises |
| 26. | Greenville, S.C. | Jun. 21 | Bobby Isaac | Nord Krauskopf |
| 27. | Raleigh, N.C. | Jun. 26 | David Pearson | Holman-Moody |
| 28. | Daytona Beach, Fla. | Jul. 4 | LeeRoy Yarbrough | Junior Johnson |
| 29. | Dover, Del. | Jul. 6 | Richard Petty | Petty Enterprises |
| 30. | Thompson, Conn. | Jul. 10 | David Pearson | Holman-Moody |
| 31. | Trenton, N.J. | Jul. 13 | David Pearson | Holman-Moody |
| 32. | Beltsville, Md. | Jul. 15 | Richard Petty | Petty Enterprises |
| 33. | Bristol, Tenn. | Jul. 20 | David Pearson | Holman-Moody |
| 34. | Nashville, Tenn. | Jul. 26 | Richard Petty | Petty Enterprises |
| 35. | Maryville, Tenn. | Jul. 27 | Richard Petty | Petty Enterprises |
| 36. | Hampton, Ga. | Aug. 10 | LeeRoy Yarbrough | Junior Johnson |
| 37. | Brooklyn, Mich. | Aug. 17 | David Pearson | Holman-Moody |
| 38. | South Boston, Va. | Aug. 21 | Bobby Isaac | Nord Krauskopf |
| 39. | Winston-Salem, N.C. | Aug. 22 | Richard Petty | Petty Enterprises |
| 40. | Weaverville, N.C. | Aug. 24 | Bobby Isaac | Nord Krauskopf |
| 41. | Darlington, S.C. | Sep. 1 | LeeRoy Yarbrough | Junior Johnson |
| 42. | Hickory, N.C. | Sep. 5 | Bobby Isaac | Nord Krauskopf |
| 43. | Richmond, Va. | Sep. 7 | Bobby Allison | Mario Rossi |
| 44. | Talladega, Ala. | Sep. 14 | Richard Brickhouse | Ray Nichels |
| 45. | Columbia, S.C. | Sep. 18 | Bobby Isaac | Nord Krauskopf |
| 46. | Martinsville, Va. | Sep. 28 | Richard Petty | Petty Enterprises |
| 47. | North Wilkesboro, N.C. | Oct. 5 | David Pearson | Holman-Moody |
| 48. | Concord, N.C. | Oct. 12 | Donnie Allison | Banjo Matthews |
| 49. | Savannah, Ga. | Oct. 17 | Bobby Isaac | Nord Krauskopf |
| 50. | Augusta, Ga. | Oct. 19 | Bobby Isaac | Nord Krauskopf |
| 51. | Rockingham, N.C. | Oct. 26 | LeeRoy Yarbrough | Junior Johnson |
| 52. | Jefferson, Ga. | Nov. 2 | Bobby Isaac | Nord Krauskopf |
| 53. | Macon, Ga. | Nov. 9 | Bobby Allison | Mario Rossi |
| 54. | College Station, Texas | Dec. 7 | Bobby Isaac | Nord Krauskopf |

## Points standings
1. David Pearson........4,170.00
2. Richard Petty ........3,813.00
3. James Hylton ........3,750.00
4. Neil Castles ...........3,530.00
5. Elmo Langley .......3,383.00
6. Bobby Isaac ..........3,301.00
7. John Sears ............3,166.00
8. Jabe Thomas ........3,103.00
9. Wendell Scott .......3,015.00
10. Cecil Gordon ..........3,002.00

## Race winners (8)
1. Bobby Isaac ................17
2. David Pearson ................11
3. Richard Petty ................10
4. LeeRoy Yarbrough ................7
5. Bobby Allison ................5
6. Cale Yarborough ................2
7. Richard Brickhouse ................1
   Donnie Allison ................1

## Money won leaders
1. LeeRoy Yarbrough..$188,105
2. David Pearson ..........183,700
3. Richard Petty...........109,180
4. Bobby Isaac...............80,560
5. Donnie Allison ...........74,255
6. Cale Yarborough ........73,540
7. Bobby Allison ............66,775
8. Buddy Baker ..............57,910
9. James Hylton ............55,992
10. Richard Brickhouse ....45,312

## Pole winners (9)
1. Bobby Isaac.......................20
2. David Pearson ..................13
3. Cale Yarborough .................6
   Richard Petty.....................6
5. Buddy Baker ......................3
6. Donnie Allison ...................2
   Charlie Glotzbach .............2
8. Bobby Allison .....................1
   A.J. Foyt .............................1

# 1968 NASCAR WINSTON CUP SEASON

| Race No. | Location | Date | Winner | Car owner |
|---|---|---|---|---|
| 1. | Macon, Ga. | Nov. 12 | Bobby Allison | Holman-Moody |
| 2. | Montgomery, Ala. | Nov. 26 | Richard Petty | Petty Enterprises |
| 3. | Riverside, Calif. | Jan. 21 | Dan Gurney | Wood Brothers |
| 4. | Daytona Beach, Fla. | Feb. 25 | Cale Yarborough | Wood Brothers |
| 5. | Bristol, Tenn. | Mar. 17 | David Pearson | Holman-Moody |
| 6. | Richmond, Va. | Mar. 24 | David Pearson | Holman-Moody |
| 7. | Hampton, Ga. | Mar. 31 | Cale Yarborough | Wood Brothers |
| 8. | Hickory, N.C. | Apr. 7 | Richard Petty | Petty Enterprises |
| 9. | Greenville, S.C. | Apr. 13 | Richard Petty | Petty Enterprises |
| 10. | Columbia, S.C. | Apr. 18 | Bobby Isaac | Nord Krauskopf |
| 11. | North Wilkesboro, N.C. | Apr. 21 | David Pearson | Holman-Moody |
| 12. | Martinsville, Va. | Apr. 28 | Cale Yarborough | Wood Brothers |
| 13. | Augusta, Ga. | May. 3 | Bobby Isaac | Nord Krauskopf |
| 14. | Weaverville, N.C. | May. 5 | David Pearson | Holman-Moody |
| 15. | Darlington, S.C. | May. 11 | David Pearson | Holman-Moody |
| 16. | Beltsville, Md. | May. 17 | David Pearson | Holman-Moody |
| 17. | Hampton, Va. | May. 18 | David Pearson | Holman-Moody |
| 18. | Concord, N.C. | May. 26 | Buddy Baker | Raymond Fox |
| 19. | Asheville, N.C. | May. 31 | Richard Petty | Petty Enterprises |
| 20. | Macon, Ga. | Jun. 2 | David Pearson | Holman-Moody |
| 21. | Maryville, Tenn. | Jun. 6 | Richard Petty | Petty Enterprises |
| 22. | Birmingham, Ala. | Jun. 8 | Richard Petty | Petty Enterprises |
| 23. | Rockingham, N.C. | Jun. 16 | Donnie Allison | Banjo Matthews |
| 24. | Greenville, S.C. | Jun. 22 | Richard Petty | Petty Enterprises |
| 25. | Daytona Beach, Fla. | Jul. 4 | Cale Yarborough | Wood Brothers |
| 26. | Islip, N.Y. | Jul. 7 | Bobby Allison | Bobby Allison |
| 27. | Oxford, Maine | Jul. 9 | Richard Petty | Petty Enterprises |
| 28. | Fonda, N.Y. | Jul. 11 | Richard Petty | Petty Enterprises |
| 29. | Trenton, N.J. | Jul. 14 | LeeRoy Yarbrough | Junior Johnson |
| 30. | Bristol, Tenn. | Jul. 21 | David Pearson | Holman-Moody |
| 31. | Maryville, Tenn. | Jul. 25 | Richard Petty | Petty Enterprises |
| 32. | Nashville, Tenn. | Jul. 27 | David Pearson | Holman-Moody |
| 33. | Hampton, Ga. | Aug. 4 | LeeRoy Yarbrough | Junior Johnson |
| 34. | Columbia, S.C. | Aug. 8 | David Pearson | Holman-Moody |
| 35. | Winston-Salem, N.C. | Aug. 10 | David Pearson | Holman-Moody |
| 36. | Weaverville, N.C. | Aug. 18 | David Pearson | Holman-Moody |
| 37. | South Boston, Va. | Aug. 23 | Richard Petty | Petty Enterprises |
| 38. | Hampton, Va. | Aug. 24 | David Pearson | Holman-Moody |
| 39. | Darlington, S.C. | Sep. 2 | Cale Yarborough | Wood Brothers |
| 40. | Hickory, N.C. | Sep. 6 | David Pearson | Holman-Moody |
| 41. | Richmond, Va. | Sep. 8 | Richard Petty | Petty Enterprises |
| 42. | Beltsville, Md. | Sep. 13 | Bobby Isaac | Nord Krauskopf |
| 43. | Hillsboro, N.C. | Sep. 15 | Richard Petty | Petty Enterprises |
| 44. | Martinsville, Va. | Sep. 22 | Richard Petty | Petty Enterprises |
| 45. | North Wilkesboro, N.C. | Sep. 29 | Richard Petty | Petty Enterprises |
| 46. | Augusta, Ga. | Oct. 5 | David Pearson | Holman-Moody |
| 47. | Concord, N.C. | Oct. 20 | Charlie Glotzbach | Cotton Owens |
| 48. | Rockingham, N.C. | Oct. 27 | Richard Petty | Petty Enterprises |
| 49. | Jefferson, Ga. | Nov. 3 | Cale Yarborough | Wood Brothers |

## Points standings
1. David Pearson........3,499.00
2. Bobby Isaac ..........3,373.00
3. Richard Petty ........3,123.00
4. Clyde Lynn ...........3,041.00
5. John Sears ............3,017.00
6. Elmo Langley ........2,823.00
7. James Hylton ........2,719.00
8. Jabe Thomas ........2,687.00
9. Wendell Scott ........2,685.00
10. Roy Tyner .............2,504.00

## Race winners (10)
1. Richard Petty ....................16
   David Pearson ..................16
3. Cale Yarborough ................6
4. Bobby Isaac ........................3
5. Bobby Allison .....................2
   LeeRoy Yarbrough .............2
7. Buddy Baker ......................1
   Donnie Allison ....................1
   Dan Gurney .........................1
   Charlie Glotzbach................1

## Money won leaders
1. Cale Yarborough ....$134,136
2. David Pearson ..........118,487
3. Richard Petty ............89,103
4. LeeRoy Yarbrough......86,604
5. Buddy Baker .............54,125
6. Donnie Allison ...........50,815
7. Bobby Allison ...........50,391
8. Bobby Isaac ...............44,530
9. Charlie Glotzbach ......41,835
10. James Hylton ...........27,865

## Pole winners (11)
1. Richard Petty .....................12
   David Pearson ..................12
3. LeeRoy Yarbrough...............6
4. Cale Yarborough ..................4
   Buddy Baker .......................4
6. Bobby Isaac.........................3
   Charlie Glotzbach ..............3
8. Bobby Allison .....................2
9. Donnie Allison ....................1
   Darel Dieringer ....................1
   Dan Gurney .........................1

# 1967 NASCAR WINSTON CUP SEASON

| Race No. | Location | Date | Winner | Car owner |
|---|---|---|---|---|
| 1. | Augusta, Ga. | Nov. 13 | Richard Petty | Petty Enterprises |
| 2. | Riverside, Calif. | Jan. 29 | Parnelli Jones | William Stroppe |
| 3. | Daytona Beach, Fla. | Feb. 24 | LeeRoy Yarbrough | Jon Thorne |
| 4. | Daytona Beach, Fla. | Feb. 24 | Fred Lorenzen | Holman-Moody |
| 5. | Daytona Beach, Fla. | Feb. 26 | Mario Andretti | Holman-Moody |
| 6. | Weaverville, N.C. | Mar. 5 | Richard Petty | Petty Enterprises |
| 7. | Bristol, Tenn. | Mar. 19 | David Pearson | Cotton Owens |
| 8. | Greenville, S.C. | Mar. 25 | David Pearson | Cotton Owens |
| 9. | Winston-Salem, N.C. | Mar. 27 | Bobby Allison | Bobby Allison |
| 10. | Hampton, Ga. | Apr. 2 | Cale Yarborough | Wood Brothers |
| 11. | Columbia, S.C. | Apr. 6 | Richard Petty | Petty Enterprises |
| 12. | Hickory, N.C. | Apr. 9 | Richard Petty | Petty Enterprises |
| 13. | North Wilkesboro, N.C. | Apr. 16 | Darel Dieringer | Junior Johnson |
| 14. | Martinsville, Va. | Apr. 23 | Richard Petty | Petty Enterprises |
| 15. | Savannah, Ga. | Apr. 28 | Bobby Allison | Bobby Allison |
| 16. | Richmond, Va. | Apr. 30 | Richard Petty | Petty Enterprises |
| 17. | Darlington, S.C. | May 13 | Richard Petty | Petty Enterprises |
| 18. | Beltsville, Md. | May 19 | Jim Paschal | Thomas Friedkin |
| 19. | Hampton, Va. | May 20 | Richard Petty | Petty Enterprises |
| 20. | Concord, N.C. | May 28 | Jim Paschal | Thomas Friedkin |
| 21. | Asheville, N.C. | Jun. 2 | Jim Paschal | Thomas Friedkin |
| 22. | Macon, Ga. | Jun. 6 | Richard Petty | Petty Enterprises |
| 23. | Maryville, Tenn. | Jun. 8 | Richard Petty | Petty Enterprises |
| 24. | Birmingham, Ala. | Jun. 10 | Bobby Allison | Cotton Owens |
| 25. | Rockingham, N.C. | Jun. 18 | Richard Petty | Petty Enterprises |
| 26. | Greenville, S.C. | Jun. 24 | Richard Petty | Petty Enterprises |
| 27. | Montgomery, Ala. | Jun. 27 | Jim Paschal | Thomas Friedkin |
| 28. | Daytona Beach, Fla. | Jul. 4 | Cale Yarborough | Wood Brothers |
| 29. | Trenton, N.J. | Jul. 9 | Richard Petty | Petty Enterprises |
| 30. | Oxford, Maine | Jul. 11 | Bobby Allison | Bobby Allison |
| 31. | Fonda, N.Y. | Jul. 13 | Richard Petty | Petty Enterprises |
| 32. | Islip, N.Y. | Jul. 15 | Richard Petty | Petty Enterprises |
| 33. | Bristol, Tenn. | Jul. 23 | Richard Petty | Petty Enterprises |
| 34. | Maryville, Tenn. | Jul. 27 | Dick Hutcherson | Bondy Long |
| 35. | Nashville, Tenn. | Jul. 29 | Richard Petty | Petty Enterprises |
| 36. | Hampton, Ga. | Aug. 6 | Dick Hutcherson | Bondy Long |
| 37. | Winston-Salem, N.C. | Aug. 12 | Richard Petty | Petty Enterprises |
| 38. | Columbia, S.C. | Aug. 17 | Richard Petty | Petty Enterprises |
| 39. | Savannah, Ga. | Aug. 25 | Richard Petty | Petty Enterprises |
| 40. | Darlington, S.C. | Sep. 4 | Richard Petty | Petty Enterprises |
| 41. | Hickory, N.C. | Sep. 8 | Richard Petty | Petty Enterprises |
| 42. | Richmond, Va. | Sep. 10 | Richard Petty | Petty Enterprises |
| 43. | Beltsville, Md. | Sep. 15 | Richard Petty | Petty Enterprises |
| 44. | Hillsboro, N.C. | Sep. 17 | Richard Petty | Petty Enterprises |
| 45. | Martinsville, Va. | Sep. 24 | Richard Petty | Petty Enterprises |
| 46. | North Wilkesboro, N.C. | Oct. 1 | Richard Petty | Petty Enterprises |
| 47. | Concord, N.C. | Oct. 15 | Buddy Baker | Raymond Fox |
| 48. | Rockingham, N.C. | Oct. 29 | Bobby Allison | Holman-Moody |
| 49. | Weaverville, N.C. | Nov. 5 | Bobby Allison | Holman-Moody |

## Points standings
1. Richard Petty ......42,472.00
2. James Hylton ......36,444.00
3. Dick Hutcherson ..33,658.00
4. Bobby Allison ......30,812.00
5. John Sears ..........29,078.00
6. Jim Paschal ........27,624.00
7. David Pearson......26,302.00
8. Neil Castles ........23,218.00
9. Elmo Langley ......22,286.00
10. Wendell Scott ......20,700.00

## Race winners (12)
1. Richard Petty....................27
2. Bobby Allison ...................6
3. Jim Paschal .......................4
4. David Pearson ...................2
   Dick Hutcherson ................2
   Cale Yarborough ................2
7. LeeRoy Yarbrough..............1
   Buddy Baker .....................1
   Mario Andretti ...................1
   Darel Dieringer...................1
   Fred Lorenzen ...................1
   Parnelli Jones ....................1

## Money won leaders
1. Richard Petty.........$130,275
2. Dick Hutcherson ........75,965
3. David Pearson ...........69,585
4. Cale Yarborough ........56,685
5. Bobby Allison ............53,415
6. Jim Paschal................53,380
7. Buddy Baker .............45,110
8. James Hylton ............39,005
9. Paul Goldsmith ..........35,360
10. Darel Dieringer ..........32,870

## Pole winners (11)
1. Richard Petty.....................19
2. Dick Hutcherson .................9
3. Darel Dieringer ...................6
4. Cale Yarborough .................4
5. David Pearson .....................2
   Bobby Allison ......................2
   Curtis Turner ......................2
8. John Sears ........................1
   James Hunter ....................1
   James Hylton ....................1
   Jim Paschal.......................1

# 1966 NASCAR WINSTON CUP SEASON

| Race No. | Location | Date | Winner | Car owner |
|---|---|---|---|---|
| 1. | Augusta, Ga. | Nov. 14 | Richard Petty | Petty Enterprises |
| 2. | Riverside, Calif. | Jan. 23 | Dan Gurney | Wood Brothers |
| 3. | Daytona Beach, Fla. | Feb. 25 | Paul Goldsmith | Ray Nichels |
| 4. | Daytona Beach, Fla. | Feb. 25 | Earl Balmer | Raymond Fox |
| 5. | Daytona Beach, Fla. | Feb. 27 | Richard Petty | Petty Enterprises |
| 6. | Rockingham, N.C. | Mar. 13 | Paul Goldsmith | Ray Nichels |
| 7. | Bristol, Tenn. | Mar. 20 | Dick Hutcherson | Holman-Moody |
| 8. | Hampton, Ga. | Mar. 27 | Jim Hurtubise | Norm Nelson |
| 9. | Hickory, N.C. | Apr. 3 | David Pearson | Cotton Owens |
| 10. | Columbia, S.C. | Apr. 7 | David Pearson | Cotton Owens |
| 11. | Greenville, S.C. | Apr. 9 | David Pearson | Cotton Owens |
| 12. | Winston-Salem, N.C. | Apr. 11 | David Pearson | Cotton Owens |
| 13. | North Wilkesboro, N.C. | Apr. 17 | Jim Paschal | Thomas Friedkin |
| 14. | Martinsville, Va. | Apr. 24 | Jim Paschal | Thomas Friedkin |
| 15. | Darlington, S.C. | Apr. 30 | Richard Petty | Petty Enterprises |
| 16. | Hampton, Va. | May. 7 | Richard Petty | Petty Enterprises |
| 17. | Macon, Ga. | May. 10 | Richard Petty | Petty Enterprises |
| 18. | Monroe, N.C. | May. 13 | Darel Dieringer | Reid Shaw |
| 19. | Richmond, Va. | May. 15 | David Pearson | Cotton Owens |
| 20. | Concord, N.C. | May. 22 | Marvin Panch | Petty Enterprises |
| 21. | Moyock, N.C. | May. 29 | David Pearson | Cotton Owens |
| 22. | Asheville, N.C. | Jun. 3 | David Pearson | Cotton Owens |
| 23. | Spartanburg, S.C. | Jun. 4 | Elmo Langley | E. Langley/H. Woodfield |
| 24. | Maryville, Tenn. | Jun. 9 | David Pearson | Cotton Owens |
| 25. | Weaverville, N.C. | Jun. 12 | Richard Petty | Petty Enterprises |
| 26. | Beltsville, Md. | Jun. 15 | Tiny Lund | Lyle Stelter |
| 27. | Greenville, S.C. | Jun. 25 | David Pearson | Cotton Owens |
| 28. | Daytona Beach, Fla. | Jul. 4 | Sam McQuagg | Ray Nichels |
| 29. | Manassas, Va. | Jul. 7 | Elmo Langley | E. Langley/H. Woodfield |
| 30. | Bridgehampton, N.Y. | Jul. 10 | David Pearson | Cotton Owens |
| 31. | Oxford, Maine | Jul. 12 | Bobby Allison | Bobby Allison |
| 32. | Fonda, N.Y. | Jul. 14 | David Pearson | Cotton Owens |
| 33. | Islip, N.Y. | Jul. 16 | Bobby Allison | Bobby Allison |
| 34. | Bristol, Tenn. | Jul. 24 | Paul Goldsmith | Ray Nichels |
| 35. | Maryville, Tenn. | Jul. 28 | Paul Lewis | Paul Lewis |
| 36. | Nashville, Tenn. | Jul. 30 | Richard Petty | Petty Enterprises |
| 37. | Hampton, Ga. | Aug. 7 | Richard Petty | Petty Enterprises |
| 38. | Columbia, S.C. | Aug. 18 | David Pearson | Cotton Owens |
| 39. | Weaverville, N.C. | Aug. 21 | Darel Dieringer | Walter "Bud" Moore |
| 40. | Beltsville, Md. | Aug. 24 | Bobby Allison | Bobby Allison |
| 41. | Winston-Salem, N.C. | Aug. 27 | David Pearson | Cotton Owens |
| 42. | Darlington, S.C. | Sep. 5 | Darel Dieringer | Walter "Bud" Moore |
| 43. | Hickory, N.C. | Sep. 9 | David Pearson | Cotton Owens |
| 44. | Richmond, Va. | Sep. 11 | David Pearson | Cotton Owens |
| 45. | Hillsboro, N.C. | Sep. 18 | Dick Hutcherson | Bondy Long |
| 46. | Martinsville, Va. | Sep. 25 | Fred Lorenzen | Holman-Moody |
| 47. | North Wilkesboro, N.C. | Oct. 2 | Dick Hutcherson | Bondy Long |
| 48. | Concord, N.C. | Oct. 16 | LeeRoy Yarbrough | Jon Thorne |
| 49. | Rockingham, N.C. | Oct. 30 | Fred Lorenzen | Holman-Moody |

## Points standings
1. David Pearson......35,638.00
2. James Hylton ......33,688.00
3. Richard Petty .....22,952.00
4. Henley Gray .......22,468.00
5. Paul Goldsmith ...22,078.00
6. Wendell Scott .....21,702.00
7. John Sears ........21,432.00
8. J.T. Putney .......21,208.00
9. Neil Castles ......20,446.00
10. Bobby Allison ....19,910.00

## Race winners (17)
1. David Pearson ..................15
2. Richard Petty ....................8
3. Bobby Allison ...................3
   Dick Hutcherson ................3
   Darel Dieringer .................3
   Paul Goldsmith ..................3
7. Jim Paschal .......................2
   Fred Lorenzen ...................2
   Elmo Langley ....................2
10. Marvin Panch ...................1
    LeeRoy Yarbrough .............1
    Sam McQuagg ...................1
    Dan Gurney ......................1
    Earl Balmer ......................1
    Jim Hurtubise ...................1
    Tiny Lund..........................1
    Paul Lewis ........................1

## Money won leaders
1. Richard Petty...........$78,840
2. David Pearson ..........59,205
3. Darel Dieringer .........50,960
4. Paul Goldsmith .........48,075
5. Marvin Panch ...........37,385
6. Fred Lorenzen ..........36,310
7. James Hylton ...........29,575
8. Jim Paschal ..............29,415
9. Sam McQuagg ..........27,960
10. G.C. Spencer ...........25,675

## Pole winners (15)
1. Richard Petty......................16
2. David Pearson .....................7
3. Tom Pistone ........................4
   Bobby Allison ......................4
5. Junior Johnson ....................3
6. Jim Paschal..........................2
   Curtis Turner .......................2
   LeeRoy Yarbrough..............2
   Dick Hutcherson .................2
   Fred Lorenzen .....................2
11. Buddy Baker .......................1
    Paul Goldsmith ...................1
    Tiny Lund.............................1
    Elmo Langley......................1
    James Hylton .....................1

# 1965 NASCAR WINSTON CUP SEASON

| Race No. | Location | Date | Winner | Car owner |
|---|---|---|---|---|
| 1. | Riverside, Calif. | Jan. 17 | Dan Gurney | Wood Brothers |
| 2. | Daytona Beach, Fla. | Feb. 12 | Darel Dieringer | Walter "Bud" Moore |
| 3. | Daytona Beach, Fla. | Feb. 12 | Junior Johnson | Rex Lovette |
| 4. | Daytona Beach, Fla. | Feb. 14 | Fred Lorenzen | Holman-Moody |
| 5. | Spartanburg, S.C. | Feb. 27 | Ned Jarrett | Bondy Long |
| 6. | Weaverville, N.C. | Feb. 28 | Ned Jarrett | Bondy Long |
| 7. | Richmond, Va. | Mar. 7 | Junior Johnson | Rex Lovette |
| 8. | Hillsboro, N.C. | Mar. 14 | Ned Jarrett | Bondy Long |
| 9. | Hampton, Ga. | Apr. 11 | Marvin Panch | Wood Brothers |
| 10. | Greenville, S.C. | Apr. 17 | Dick Hutcherson | Holman-Moody |
| 11. | North Wilkesboro, N.C. | Apr. 18 | Junior Johnson | Rex Lovette |
| 12. | Martinsville, Va. | Apr. 25 | Fred Lorenzen | Holman-Moody |
| 13. | Columbia, S.C. | Apr. 28 | Tiny Lund | Lyle Stelter |
| 14. | Bristol, Tenn. | May. 2 | Junior Johnson | Rex Lovette |
| 15. | Darlington, S.C. | May. 8 | Junior Johnson | Rex Lovette |
| 16. | Hampton, Va. | May. 14 | Ned Jarrett | Bondy Long |
| 17. | Winston-Salem, N.C. | May. 15 | Junior Johnson | Rex Lovette |
| 18. | Hickory, N.C. | May. 16 | Junior Johnson | Rex Lovette |
| 19. | Concord, N.C. | May. 23 | Fred Lorenzen | Holman-Moody |
| 20. | Shelby, N.C. | May. 27 | Ned Jarrett | Bondy Long |
| 21. | Asheville, N.C. | May. 29 | Junior Johnson | Rex Lovette |
| 22. | Harris, N.C. | May. 30 | Ned Jarrett | Bondy Long |
| 23. | Nashville, Tenn. | Jun. 3 | Dick Hutcherson | Holman-Moody |
| 24. | Birmingham, Ala. | Jun. 6 | Ned Jarrett | Bondy Long |
| 25. | Hampton, Ga. | Jun. 13 | Marvin Panch | Wood Brothers |
| 26. | Greenville, S.C. | Jun. 19 | Dick Hutcherson | Holman-Moody |
| 27. | Myrtle Beach, S.C. | Jun. 24 | Dick Hutcherson | Holman-Moody |
| 28. | Valdosta, Ga. | Jun. 27 | Cale Yarborough | Kenny Myler |
| 29. | Daytona Beach, Fla. | Jul. 4 | A.J. Foyt | Wood Brothers |
| 30. | Manassas, Va. | Jul. 8 | Junior Johnson | Rex Lovette |
| 31. | Old Bridge, N.J. | Jul. 9 | Junior Johnson | Rex Lovette |
| 32. | Islip, N.Y. | Jul. 14 | Marvin Panch | Wood Brothers |
| 33. | Watkins Glen, N.Y. | Jul. 18 | Marvin Panch | Wood Brothers |
| 34. | Bristol, Tenn. | Jul. 25 | Ned Jarrett | Bondy Long |
| 35. | Nashville, Tenn. | Jul. 31 | Richard Petty | Petty Enterprises |
| 36. | Shelby, N.C. | Aug. 5 | Ned Jarrett | Bondy Long |
| 37. | Weaverville, N.C. | Aug. 8 | Richard Petty | Petty Enterprises |
| 38. | Maryville, Tenn. | Aug. 13 | Dick Hutcherson | Holman-Moody |
| 39. | Spartanburg, S.C. | Aug. 14 | Ned Jarrett | Bondy Long |
| 40. | Augusta, Ga. | Aug. 15 | Dick Hutcherson | Holman-Moody |
| 41. | Columbus, Ga. | Aug. 19 | David Pearson | Cotton Owens |
| 42. | Moyock, N.C. | Aug. 24 | Dick Hutcherson | Holman-Moody |
| 43. | Beltsville, Md. | Aug. 25 | Ned Jarrett | Bondy Long |
| 44. | Winston-Salem, N.C. | Aug. 28 | Junior Johnson | Rex Lovette |
| 45. | Darlington, S.C. | Sep. 6 | Ned Jarrett | Bondy Long |
| 46. | Hickory, N.C. | Sep. 10 | Richard Petty | Petty Enterprises |
| 47. | New Oxford, Pa. | Sep. 14 | Dick Hutcherson | Holman-Moody |
| 48. | Manassas, Va. | Sep. 17 | Richard Petty | Petty Enterprises |
| 49. | Richmond, Va. | Sep. 18 | David Pearson | Cotton Owens |
| 50. | Martinsville, Va. | Sep. 26 | Junior Johnson | Rex Lovette |
| 51. | North Wilkesboro, N.C. | Oct. 3 | Junior Johnson | Rex Lovette |
| 52. | Concord, N.C. | Oct. 17 | Fred Lorenzen | Holman-Moody |
| 53. | Hillsboro, N.C. | Oct. 24 | Dick Hutcherson | Holman-Moody |
| 54. | Rockingham, N.C. | Oct. 31 | Curtis Turner | Wood Brothers |
| 55. | Moyock, N.C. | Nov. 7 | Ned Jarrett | Bondy Long |

## Points standings
1. Ned Jarrett.............38,824.00
2. Dick Hutcherson ....35,790.00
3. Darel Dieringer.......24,696.00
4. G.C. Spencer .........24,314.00
5. Marvin Panch..........22,798.00
6. Bob Derrington ......21,394.00
7. J.T. Putney.............20,928.00
8. Neil Castles ...........20,848.00
9. Buddy Baker...........20,672.00
10. Cale Yarborough ....20,192.00

## Race winners (13)
1. Ned Jarrett ........................13
   Junior Johnson...................13
3. Dick Hutcherson ..................9
4. Richard Petty ......................4
   Marvin Panch ......................4
   Fred Lorenzen .....................4
7. David Pearson .....................2
8. Darel Dieringer ....................1
   Curtis Turner .......................1
   Cale Yarborough ..................1
   Tiny Lund .............................1
   A.J. Foyt ..............................1
   Dan Gurney..........................1

## Money won leaders
1. Ned Jarrett ................$77,966
2. Fred Lorenzen............77,115
3. Junior Johnson ...........57,925
4. Marvin Panch .............54,045
5. Dick Hutcherson .........49,420
6. Darel Dieringer ...........47,775
7. Buddy Baker ...............25,390
8. Cale Yarborough .........24,040
9. Bobby Johns ...............23,695
10. G.C. Spencer ............23,030

## Pole winners (13)
1. Junior Johnson.....................10
2. Ned Jarrett ...........................9
   Dick Hutcherson ...................9
4. Richard Petty .......................7
5. Fred Lorenzen......................6
6. Marvin Panch .......................5
7. Darel Dieringer ....................2
8. Tom Pistone ........................1
   G.C. Spencer .......................1
   David Pearson .....................1
   Bobby Isaac ........................1
   Bud Moore ..........................1
   Paul Lewis ..........................1

# 1964 NASCAR WINSTON CUP SEASON

| Race No. | Location | Date | Winner | Car owner |
|---|---|---|---|---|
| 1. | Concord, N.C. | Nov. 10 | Ned Jarrett | Charles Robinson |
| 2. | Augusta, Ga. | Nov. 17 | Fireball Roberts | Holman-Moody |
| 3. | Jacksonville, Fla. | Dec. 1 | Wendell Scott | Wendell Scott |
| 4. | Savannah, Ga. | Dec. 29 | Richard Petty | Petty Enterprises |
| 5. | Riverside, Calif. | Jan. 19 | Dan Gurney | Wood Brothers |
| 6. | Daytona Beach, Fla. | Feb. 21 | Junior Johnson | Raymond Fox |
| 7. | Daytona Beach, Fla. | Feb. 21 | Bobby Isaac | Ray Nichels |
| 8. | Daytona Beach, Fla. | Feb. 23 | Richard Petty | Petty Enterprises |
| 9. | Richmond, Va. | Mar. 10 | David Pearson | Cotton Owens |
| 10. | Bristol, Tenn. | Mar. 22 | Fred Lorenzen | Holman-Moody |
| 11. | Greenville, S.C. | Mar. 28 | David Pearson | Cotton Owens |
| 12. | Winston-Salem, N.C. | Mar. 30 | Marvin Panch | Wood Brothers |
| 13. | Hampton, Ga. | Apr. 5 | Fred Lorenzen | Holman-Moody |
| 14. | Weaverville, N.C. | Apr. 11 | Marvin Panch | Wood Brothers |
| 15. | Hillsboro, N.C. | Apr. 12 | David Pearson | Cotton Owens |
| 16. | Spartanburg, S.C. | Apr. 14 | Ned Jarrett | Bondy Long |
| 17. | Columbia, S.C. | Apr. 16 | Ned Jarrett | Bondy Long |
| 18. | North Wilkesboro, N.C. | Apr. 19 | Fred Lorenzen | Holman-Moody |
| 19. | Martinsville, Va. | Apr. 26 | Fred Lorenzen | Holman-Moody |
| 20. | Savannah, Ga. | May 1 | LeeRoy Yarbrough | Louie Weathersby |
| 21. | Darlington, S.C. | May 9 | Fred Lorenzen | Holman-Moody |
| 22. | Hampton, Va. | May 15 | Ned Jarrett | Bondy Long |
| 23. | Hickory, N.C. | May 16 | Ned Jarrett | Bondy Long |
| 24. | South Boston, Va. | May 17 | Richard Petty | Petty Enterprises |
| 25. | Concord, N.C. | May 24 | Jim Paschal | Petty Enterprises |
| 26. | Greenville, S.C. | May 30 | LeeRoy Yarbrough | Louie Weathersby |
| 27. | Asheville, N.C. | May 31 | Ned Jarrett | Bondy Long |
| 28. | Hampton, Ga. | Jun. 7 | Ned Jarrett | Bondy Long |
| 29. | Concord, N.C. | Jun. 11 | Richard Petty | Petty Enterprises |
| 30. | Nashville, Tenn. | Jun. 14 | Richard Petty | Petty Enterprises |
| 31. | Chattanooga, Tenn. | Jun. 19 | David Pearson | Cotton Owens |
| 32. | Birmingham, Ala. | Jun. 21 | Ned Jarrett | Bondy Long |
| 33. | Valdosta, Ga. | Jun. 23 | Buck Baker | Raymond Fox |
| 34. | Spartanburg, S.C. | Jun. 26 | Richard Petty | Petty Enterprises |
| 35. | Daytona Beach, Fla. | Jul. 4 | A.J. Foyt | Ray Nichels |
| 36. | Manassas, Va. | Jul. 8 | Ned Jarrett | Bondy Long |
| 37. | Old Bridge, N.J. | Jul. 10 | Billy Wade | Walter "Bud" Moore |
| 38. | Bridgehampton, N.Y. | Jul. 12 | Billy Wade | Walter "Bud" Moore |
| 39. | Islip, N.Y. | Jul. 15 | Billy Wade | Walter "Bud" Moore |
| 40. | Watkins Glen, N.Y. | Jul. 19 | Billy Wade | Walter "Bud" Moore |
| 41. | New Oxford, Pa. | Jul. 21 | David Pearson | Cotton Owens |
| 42. | Bristol, Tenn. | Jul. 26 | Fred Lorenzen | Holman-Moody |
| 43. | Nashville, Tenn. | Aug. 2 | Richard Petty | Petty Enterprises |
| 44. | Myrtle Beach, S.C. | Aug. 7 | David Pearson | Cotton Owens |
| 45. | Weaverville, N.C. | Aug. 9 | Ned Jarrett | Bondy Long |
| 46. | Moyock, N.C. | Aug. 13 | Ned Jarrett | Bondy Long |
| 47. | Huntington, W.Va. | Aug. 16 | Richard Petty | Petty Enterprises |
| 48. | Columbia, S.C. | Aug. 21 | David Pearson | Cotton Owens |
| 49. | Winston-Salem, N.C. | Aug. 22 | Junior Johnson | Banjo Matthews |
| 50. | Roanoke, Va. | Aug. 23 | Junior Johnson | Banjo Matthews |
| 51. | Darlington, S.C. | Sep. 7 | Buck Baker | Raymond Fox |
| 52. | Hickory, N.C. | Sep. 11 | David Pearson | Cotton Owens |
| 53. | Richmond, Va. | Sep. 14 | Cotton Owens | Cotton Owens |
| 54. | Manassas, Va. | Sep. 18 | Ned Jarrett | Bondy Long |
| 55. | Hillsboro, N.C. | Sep. 20 | Ned Jarrett | Bondy Long |
| 56. | Martinsville, Va. | Sep. 27 | Fred Lorenzen | Holman-Moody |
| 57. | Savannah, Ga. | Oct. 9 | Ned Jarrett | Bondy Long |
| 58. | North Wilkesboro, N.C. | Oct. 11 | Marvin Panch | Wood Brothers |
| 59. | Concord, N.C. | Oct. 18 | Fred Lorenzen | Holman-Moody |
| 60. | Harris, N.C. | Oct. 25 | Richard Petty | Petty Enterprises |
| 61. | Augusta, Ga. | Nov. 1 | Darel Dieringer | Walter "Bud" Moore |
| 62. | Jacksonville, N.C. | Nov. 8 | Ned Jarrett | Bondy Long |

## Points standings
1. Richard Petty............40,252.00
2. Ned Jarrett ..............34,950.00
3. David Pearson ........32,146.00
4. Billy Wade ...............28,474.00
5. Jimmy Pardue .........26,570.00
6. Curtis Crider ............25,606.00
7. Jim Paschal.............25,450.00
8. Larry Thomas ..........22,950.00
9. Buck Baker ..............22,366.00
10. Marvin Panch .........21,480.00

## Race winners (17)
1. Ned Jarrett .................15
2. Richard Petty ...............9
3. Fred Lorenzen ..............8
   David Pearson ..............8
5. Billy Wade .....................4
6. Junior Johnson .............3
   Marvin Panch ................3
8. LeeRoy Yarbrough ........2
   Buck Baker ....................2
10. Wendell Scott ...............1
    Fireball Roberts .............1
    Dan Gurney ...................1
    A.J. Foyt .........................1
    Darel Dieringer ..............1
    Jim Paschal....................1
    Cotton Owens ................1
    Bobby Isaac ...................1

## Money won leaders
1. Richard Petty ..............$98,810
2. Fred Lorenzen ..............72,385
3. Ned Jarrett ......................63,330
4. Jim Paschal ....................54,960
5. Buck Baker ......................41,080
6. David Pearson ...............38,175
7. Jimmy Pardue ................36,440
8. Marvin Panch ..................32,135
9. Billy Wade ........................29,710
10. Fireball Roberts .............28,345

## Pole winners (14)
1. David Pearson ................12
2. Ned Jarrett ........................9
   Richard Petty ....................9
4. Fred Lorenzen ..................7
5. Marvin Panch ....................5
   Billy Wade ..........................5
   Junior Johnson .................5
8. Paul Goldsmith ................2
   Dick Hutcherson ..............2
   Jimmy Pardue ..................2
11. Glen Wood .......................1
    Doug Yates ......................1
    Jack Smith .......................1
    Darel Dieringer ................1

# 1963 NASCAR WINSTON CUP SEASON

| Race No. | Location | Date | Winner | Car owner |
|---|---|---|---|---|
| 1. | Birmingham, Ala. | Nov. 4 | Jim Paschal | Petty Enterprises |
| 2. | Tampa, Fla. | Nov. 11 | Richard Petty | Petty Enterprises |
| 3. | Randleman, N.C. | Nov. 22 | Jim Paschal | Petty Enterprises |
| 4. | Riverside, Calif. | Jan. 20 | Dan Gurney | Holman-Moody |
| 5. | Daytona Beach, Fla. | Feb. 22 | Junior Johnson | Raymond Fox |
| 6. | Daytona Beach, Fla. | Feb. 22 | Johnny Rutherford | Smokey Yunick |
| 7. | Daytona Beach, Fla. | Feb. 24 | Tiny Lund | Wood Brothers |
| 8. | Spartanburg, S.C. | Mar. 2 | Richard Petty | Petty Enterprises |
| 9. | Weaverville, N.C. | Mar. 3 | Richard Petty | Petty Enterprises |
| 10. | Hillsboro, N.C. | Mar. 10 | Junior Johnson | Raymond Fox |
| 11. | Hampton, Ga. | Mar. 17 | Fred Lorenzen | Holman-Moody |
| 12. | Hickory, N.C. | Mar. 24 | Junior Johnson | Raymond Fox |
| 13. | Bristol, Tenn. | Mar. 31 | Fireball Roberts | Holman-Moody |
| 14. | Augusta, Ga. | Apr. 4 | Ned Jarrett | Charles Robinson |
| 15. | Richmond, Va. | Apr. 7 | Joe Weatherly | Walter "Bud" Moore |
| 16. | Greenville, S.C. | Apr. 13 | Buck Baker | Buck Baker |
| 17. | South Boston, Va. | Apr. 14 | Richard Petty | Petty Enterprises |
| 18. | Winston-Salem, N.C. | Apr. 15 | Jim Paschal | Petty Enterprises |
| 19. | Martinsville, Va. | Apr. 21 | Richard Petty | Petty Enterprises |
| 20. | North Wilkesboro, N.C. | Apr. 28 | Richard Petty | Petty Enterprises |
| 21. | Columbia, S.C. | May. 2 | Richard Petty | Petty Enterprises |
| 22. | Randleman, N.C. | May. 5 | Jim Paschal | Petty Enterprises |
| 23. | Darlington, S.C. | May. 11 | Joe Weatherly | Walter "Bud" Moore |
| 24. | Manassas, Va. | May. 18 | Richard Petty | Petty Enterprises |
| 25. | Richmond, Va. | May. 19 | Ned Jarrett | Charles Robinson |
| 26. | Concord, N.C. | Jun. 2 | Fred Lorenzen | Holman-Moody |
| 27. | Birmingham, Ala. | Jun. 9 | Richard Petty | Petty Enterprises |
| 28. | Hampton, Ga. | Jun. 30 | Junior Johnson | Raymond Fox |
| 29. | Daytona Beach, Fla. | Jul. 4 | Fireball Roberts | Holman-Moody |
| 30. | Myrtle Beach, S.C. | Jul. 7 | Ned Jarrett | Charles Robinson |
| 31. | Savannah, Ga. | Jul. 10 | Ned Jarrett | Charles Robinson |
| 32. | Moyock, N.C. | Jul. 11 | Jimmy Pardue | Peter Stewart |
| 33. | Winston-Salem, N.C. | Jul. 13 | Glen Wood | Wood Brothers |
| 34. | Asheville, N.C. | Jul. 14 | Ned Jarrett | Charles Robinson |
| 35. | Old Bridge, N.J. | Jul. 19 | Fireball Roberts | Holman-Moody |
| 36. | Bridgehampton, N.Y. | Jul. 21 | Richard Petty | Petty Enterprises |
| 37. | Bristol, Tenn. | Jul. 28 | Fred Lorenzen | Holman-Moody |
| 38. | Greenville, S.C. | Jul. 30 | Richard Petty | Petty Enterprises |
| 39. | Nashville, Tenn. | Aug. 4 | Jim Paschal | Petty Enterprises |
| 40. | Columbia, S.C. | Aug. 8 | Richard Petty | Petty Enterprises |
| 41. | Weaverville, N.C. | Aug. 11 | Fred Lorenzen | Holman-Moody |
| 42. | Spartanburg, S.C. | Aug. 14 | Ned Jarrett | Charles Robinson |
| 43. | Winston-Salem, N.C. | Aug. 16 | Junior Johnson | Raymond Fox |
| 44. | Huntington, W.Va. | Aug. 18 | Fred Lorenzen | Holman-Moody |
| 45. | Darlington, S.C. | Sep. 2 | Fireball Roberts | Holman-Moody |
| 46. | Hickory, N.C. | Sep. 6 | Junior Johnson | Raymond Fox |
| 47. | Richmond, Va. | Sep. 8 | Ned Jarrett | Charles Robinson |
| 48. | Martinsville, Va. | Sep. 22 | Fred Lorenzen | Holman-Moody |
| 49. | Moyock, N.C. | Sep. 24 | Ned Jarrett | Charles Robinson |
| 50. | North Wilkesboro, N.C. | Sep. 29 | Marvin Panch | Wood Brothers |
| 51. | Randleman, N.C. | Oct. 5 | Richard Petty | Petty Enterprises |
| 52. | Concord, N.C. | Oct. 13 | Junior Johnson | Raymond Fox |
| 53. | South Boston, Va. | Oct. 20 | Richard Petty | Petty Enterprises |
| 54. | Hillsboro, N.C. | Oct. 27 | Joe Weatherly | Walter "Bud" Moore |
| 55. | Riverside, Calif. | Nov. 3 | Darel Dieringer | William Stroppe |

## Points standings
1. Joe Weatherly .............33,398.00
2. Richard Petty.............31,170.00
3. Fred Lorenzen ...........29,684.00
4. Ned Jarrett ................27,214.00
5. Fireball Roberts .........22,642.00
6. Jimmy Pardue ...........22,228.00
7. Darel Dieringer .........21,418.00
8. David Pearson ...........21,156.00
9. Rex White .................20,976.00
10. Tiny Lund ..................19,624.00

## Race winners (15)
1. Richard Petty .........................14
2. Ned Jarrett ..............................8
3. Junior Johnson .......................7
4. Fred Lorenzen .........................6
5. Jim Paschal ..............................5
6. Fireball Roberts ......................4
7. Joe Weatherly ..........................3
8. Glen Wood ...............................1
Johnny Rutherford ......................1
Dan Gurney .................................1
Darel Dieringer ............................1
Buck Baker ..................................1
Jimmy Pardue .............................1
Marvin Panch ..............................1
Tiny Lund .....................................1

## Money won leaders
1. Fred Lorenzen ............$113,570
2. Fireball Roberts ..............67,320
3. Junior Johnson ...............65,710
4. Joe Weatherly .................57,710
5. Richard Petty ..................47,765
6. Tiny Lund .........................40,930
7. Ned Jarrett .......................38,740
8. Marvin Panch ..................37,461
9. Darel Dieringer ................25,575
10. Rex White .......................24,235

## Pole winners (15)
1. Junior Johnson ........................9
2. Fred Lorenzen .........................9
3. Richard Petty ............................8
4. Joe Weatherly ..........................6
5. Ned Jarrett ................................4
6. Rex White .................................3
Marvin Panch ..............................3
8. Glen Wood ...............................2
Jack Smith ...................................2
Fireball Roberts ..........................2
David Pearson ............................2
12. Paul Goldsmith.......................1
LeeRoy Yarbrough .....................1
Jim Paschal .................................1
Jimmy Pardue .............................1

# 1962 NASCAR WINSTON CUP SEASON

| Race No. | Location | Date | Winner | Car owner |
|---|---|---|---|---|
| 1. | Concord, N.C. | Nov. 5 | Jack Smith | Jack Smith |
| 2. | Weaverville, N.C. | Nov. 12 | Rex White | Rex White |
| 3. | Daytona Beach, Fla. | Feb. 16 | Fireball Roberts | Jim Stephens |
| 4. | Daytona Beach, Fla. | Feb. 16 | Joe Weatherly | Walter "Bud" Moore |
| 5. | Daytona Beach, Fla. | Feb. 18 | Fireball Roberts | Jim Stephens |
| 6. | Concord, N.C. | Feb. 25 | Joe Weatherly | Walter "Bud" Moore |
| 7. | Weaverville, N.C. | Mar. 4 | Joe Weatherly | Walter "Bud" Moore |
| 8. | Savannah, Ga. | Mar. 17 | Jack Smith | Jack Smith |
| 9. | Hillsboro, N.C. | Mar. 18 | Rex White | Rex White |
| 10. | Richmond, Va. | Apr. 1 | Rex White | Rex White |
| 11. | Columbia, S.C. | Apr. 13 | Ned Jarrett | Bee Gee Holloway |
| 12. | North Wilkesboro, N.C. | Apr. 15 | Richard Petty | Petty Enterprises |
| 13. | Greenville, S.C. | Apr. 19 | Ned Jarrett | Bee Gee Holloway |
| 14. | Myrtle Beach, S.C. | Apr. 21 | Jack Smith | Jack Smith |
| 15. | Martinsville, Va. | Apr. 22 | Richard Petty | Petty Enterprises |
| 16. | Winston-Salem, N.C. | Apr. 23 | Rex White | Rex White |
| 17. | Bristol, Tenn. | Apr. 29 | Bobby Johns | Shorty Johns |
| 18. | Richmond, Va. | May 4 | Jimmy Pardue | Jimmy Pardue |
| 19. | Hickory, N.C. | May 5 | Jack Smith | Jack Smith |
| 20. | Concord, N.C. | May 6 | Joe Weatherly | Walter "Bud" Moore |
| 21. | Darlington, S.C. | May 12 | Nelson Stacy | Holman-Moody |
| 22. | Spartanburg, S.C. | May 19 | Ned Jarrett | Bee Gee Holloway |
| 23. | Concord, N.C. | May 27 | Nelson Stacy | Holman-Moody |
| 24. | Hampton, Ga. | Jun. 10 | Fred Lorenzen | Holman-Moody |
| 25. | Winston-Salem, N.C. | Jun. 16 | Johnny Allen | Fred Lovette |
| 26. | Augusta, Ga. | Jun. 19 | Joe Weatherly | Walter "Bud" Moore |
| 27. | Richmond, Va. | Jun. 22 | Jim Paschal | Cliff Stewart |
| 28. | South Boston, Va. | Jun. 23 | Rex White | Rex White |
| 29. | Daytona Beach, Fla. | Jul. 4 | Fireball Roberts | Banjo Matthews |
| 30. | Columbia, S.C. | Jul. 7 | Rex White | Rex White |
| 31. | Asheville, N.C. | Jul. 13 | Jack Smith | Jack Smith |
| 32. | Greenville, S.C. | Jul. 14 | Richard Petty | Petty Enterprises |
| 33. | Augusta, Ga. | Jul. 17 | Joe Weatherly | Walter "Bud" Moore |
| 34. | Savannah, Ga. | Jul. 20 | Joe Weatherly | Walter "Bud" Moore |
| 35. | Myrtle Beach, S.C. | Jul. 21 | Ned Jarrett | Bee Gee Holloway |
| 36. | Bristol, Tenn. | Jul. 29 | Jim Paschal | Petty Enterprises |
| 37. | Chattanooga, Tenn. | Aug. 3 | Joe Weatherly | Walter "Bud" Moore |
| 38. | Nashville, Tenn. | Aug. 5 | Jim Paschal | Petty Enterprises |
| 39. | Huntsville, Ala. | Aug. 8 | Richard Petty | Petty Enterprises |
| 40. | Weaverville, N.C. | Aug. 12 | Jim Paschal | Petty Enterprises |
| 41. | Roanoke, Va. | Aug. 15 | Richard Petty | Petty Enterprises |
| 42. | Winston-Salem, N.C. | Aug. 18 | Richard Petty | Petty Enterprises |
| 43. | Spartanburg, S.C. | Aug. 21 | Richard Petty | Petty Enterprises |
| 44. | Valdosta, Ga. | Aug. 25 | Ned Jarrett | Bee Gee Holloway |
| 45. | Darlington, S.C. | Sep. 3 | Larry Frank | Ratus Walters |
| 46. | Hickory, N.C. | Sep. 7 | Rex White | Rex White |
| 47. | Richmond, Va. | Sep. 9 | Joe Weatherly | Walter "Bud" Moore |
| 48. | Moyock, N.C. | Sep. 11 | Ned Jarrett | Bee Gee Holloway |
| 49. | Augusta, Ga. | Sep. 13 | Fred Lorenzen | Mamie Reynolds |
| 50. | Martinsville, Va. | Sep. 23 | Nelson Stacy | Holman-Moody |
| 51. | North Wilkesboro, N.C. | Sep. 30 | Richard Petty | Petty Enterprises |
| 52. | Concord, N.C. | Oct. 14 | Junior Johnson | Raymond Fox |
| 53. | Hampton, Ga. | Oct. 28 | Rex White | Rex White |

## Points standings
1. Joe Weatherly ............30,836.00
2. Richard Petty............28,440.00
3. Ned Jarrett ................25,336.00
4. Jack Smith ................22,870.00
5. Rex White ..................19,424.00
6. Jim Paschal ..............18,128.00
7. Fred Lorenzen ..........17,554.00
8. Fireball Roberts ........16,380.00
9. Marvin Panch ...........15,138.00
10. David Pearson ..........14,404.00

## Race winners (14)
1. Joe Weatherly .........................9
2. Richard Petty ..........................8
   Rex White ................................8
4. Ned Jarrett ..............................6
5. Jack Smith ...............................5
6. Jim Paschal ..............................4
7. Nelson Stacy ...........................3
   Fireball Roberts .......................3
9. Fred Lorenzen ........................2
10. Larry Frank ..............................1
    Johnny Allen ............................1
    Bobby Johns ............................1
    Jimmy Pardue ..........................1
    Junior Johnson ........................1

## Money won leaders
1. Joe Weatherly ................$55,055
2. Richard Petty ..................52,885
3. Fireball Roberts ...............51,970
4. Fred Lorenzen .................42,948
5. Nelson Stacy ...................42,515
6. Ned Jarrett .......................35,320
7. Junior Johnson ................33,940
8. Larry Frank......................31,410
9. Rex White ........................30,643
10. Jack Smith .......................28,485

## Pole winners (13)
1. Fireball Roberts .........................9
   Rex White ................................9
3. Jack Smith ................................7
   Joe Weatherly ...........................7
5. Richard Petty ............................4
   Ned Jarrett ................................4
7. Fred Lorenzen ..........................3
8. Junior Johnson .........................2
   Banjo Matthews ........................2
10. Wendell Scott ............................1
    Johnny Allen .............................1
    Darel Dieringer .........................1
    Cotton Owens ...........................1

# 1961 NASCAR WINSTON CUP SEASON

| Race No. | Location | Date | Winner | Car owner |
|---|---|---|---|---|
| 1. | Charlotte, N.C. | Nov. 6 | Joe Weatherly | Dr. Bradford White |
| 2. | Jacksonville, Fla. | Nov. 20 | Lee Petty | Petty Enterprises |
| 3. | Daytona Beach, Fla. | Feb. 24 | Fireball Roberts | Jim Stephens |
| 4. | Daytona Beach, Fla. | Feb. 24 | Joe Weatherly | Walter "Bud" Moore |
| 5. | Daytona Beach, Fla. | Feb. 26 | Marvin Panch | Smokey Yunick |
| 6. | Spartanburg, S.C. | Mar. 4 | Cotton Owens | Cotton Owens |
| 7. | Weaverville, N.C. | Mar. 5 | Rex White | Rex White |
| 8. | Hanford, Calif. | Mar. 12 | Fireball Roberts | J.D. Braswell |
| 9. | Hampton, Ga. | Mar. 26 | Bob Burdick | Roy Burdick |
| 10. | Greenville, S.C. | Apr. 1 | Emanuel Zervakis | Monroe Shook |
| 11. | Hillsboro, N.C. | Apr. 2 | Cotton Owens | Cotton Owens |
| 12. | Winston-Salem, N.C. | Apr. 3 | Rex White | Rex White |
| 13. | Martinsville, Va. | Apr. 9 | Fred Lorenzen | Holman-Moody |
| 14. | North Wilkesboro, N.C. | Apr. 16 | Rex White | Rex White |
| 15. | Columbia, S.C. | Apr. 20 | Cotton Owens | Cotton Owens |
| 16. | Hickory, N.C. | Apr. 22 | Junior Johnson | Rex Lovette |
| 17. | Richmond, Va. | Apr. 23 | Richard Petty | Petty Enterprises |
| 18. | Martinsville, Va. | Apr. 30 | Junior Johnson | Rex Lovette |
| 19. | Darlington, S.C. | May. 6 | Fred Lorenzen | Holman-Moody |
| 20. | Concord, N.C. | May. 21 | Richard Petty | Petty Enterprises |
| 21. | Concord, N.C. | May. 21 | Joe Weatherly | Walter "Bud" Moore |
| 22. | Riverside, Calif. | May. 21 | Lloyd Dane | Lloyd Dane |
| 23. | Los Angles, Calif. | May. 27 | Eddie Gray | Eddie Gray |
| 24. | Concord, N.C. | May. 28 | David Pearson | John Masoni |
| 25. | Spartanburg, S.C. | Jun. 2 | Jim Paschal | J.H. Petty |
| 26. | Birmingham, Ala. | Jun. 4 | Ned Jarrett | Bee Gee Holloway |
| 27. | Greenville, S.C. | Jun. 8 | Jack Smith | Jack Smith |
| 28. | Winston-Salem, N.C. | Jun. 10 | Rex White | Rex White |
| 29. | Norwood, Mass. | Jun. 17 | Emanuel Zervakis | Monroe Shook |
| 30. | Hartsville, S.C. | Jun. 23 | Buck Baker | Buck Baker |
| 31. | Roanoke, Va. | Jun. 24 | Junior Johnson | Rex Lovette |
| 32. | Daytona Beach, Fla. | Jul. 4 | David Pearson | John Masoni |
| 33. | Hampton, Ga. | Jul. 9 | Fred Lorenzen | Holman-Moody |
| 34. | Columbia, S.C. | Jul. 20 | Cotton Owens | Cotton Owens |
| 35. | Myrtle Beach, S.C. | Jul. 22 | Joe Weatherly | Walter "Bud" Moore |
| 36. | Bristol, Tenn. | Jul. 30 | Jack Smith | Jack Smith |
| 37. | Nashville, Tenn. | Aug. 6 | Jim Paschal | J.H. Petty |
| 38. | Winston-Salem, N.C. | Aug. 9 | Rex White | Rex White |
| 39. | Weaverville, N.C. | Aug. 13 | Junior Johnson | Rex Lovette |
| 40. | Richmond, Va. | Aug. 18 | Junior Johnson | Rex Lovette |
| 41. | South Boston, Va. | Aug. 27 | Junior Johnson | Rex Lovette |
| 42. | Darlington, S.C. | Sep. 4 | Nelson Stacy | Dudley Farrell |
| 43. | Hickory, N.C. | Sep. 8 | Rex White | Rex White |
| 44. | Richmond, Va. | Sep. 10 | Joe Weatherly | Walter "Bud" Moore |
| 45. | Sacramento, Calif. | Sep. 10 | Eddie Gray | Eddie Gray |
| 46. | Hampton, Ga. | Sep. 17 | David Pearson | John Masoni |
| 47. | Martinsville, Va. | Sep. 24 | Joe Weatherly | Walter "Bud" Moore |
| 48. | North Wilkesboro, N.C. | Oct. 1 | Rex White | Rex White |
| 49. | Concord, N.C. | Oct. 15 | Joe Weatherly | Walter "Bud" Moore |
| 50. | Bristol, Tenn. | Oct. 22 | Joe Weatherly | Walter "Bud" Moore |
| 51. | Greenville, S.C. | Oct. 28 | Junior Johnson | Rex Lovette |
| 52. | Hillsboro, N.C. | Oct. 29 | Joe Weatherly | Walter "Bud" Moore |

## Points standings
1. Ned Jarrett ..............27,272.00
2. Rex White ................26,442.00
3. Emanuel Zervakis ....22,312.00
4. Joe Weatherly ..........17,894.00
5. Fireball Roberts ........17,600.00
6. Junior Johnson ........17,178.00
7. Jack Smith ................15,186.00
8. Richard Petty.............14,984.00
9. Jim Paschal...............13,922.00
10. Buck Baker ...............13,746.00

## Race winners (19)
1. Joe Weatherly .........................9
2. Junior Johnson .......................7
   Rex White.................................7
4. Cotton Owens...........................4
5. David Pearson .........................3
   Fred Lorenzen ..........................3
7. Richard Petty ...........................2
   Emanuel Zervakis ....................2
   Jack Smith ................................2
   Fireball Roberts .......................2
   Eddie Gray ................................2
   Jim Paschal ..............................2
13. Lloyd Dane...............................1
    Bob Burdick ..............................1
    Buck Baker ...............................1
    Nelson Stacy ............................1
    Marvin Panch ...........................1
    Ned Jarrett ................................1
    Lee Petty ...................................1

## Money won leaders
1. David Pearson ..............$49,580
2. Rex White .......................48,830
3. Joe Weatherly ................39,965
4. Fireball Roberts .............38,300
5. Fred Lorenzen ................29,655
6. Marvin Panch .................28,865
7. Ned Jarrett ......................27,235
8. Nelson Stacy ..................26,760
9. Junior Johnson ...............25,310
10. Richard Petty .................22,671

## Pole winners (21)
1. Junior Johnson .......................10
2. Rex White...................................7
3. Fireball Roberts .......................6
4. Joe Weatherly ..........................4
   Fred Lorenzen ..........................4
   Ned Jarrett ................................4
7. Cotton Owens...........................2
   Richard Petty ...........................2
9. Emanuel Zervakis ...................1
   Danny Weinberg .......................1
   Glen Wood .................................1
   Bob Ross ...................................1
   Lee Petty ...................................1
   Buck Baker ...............................1
   Eddie Gray ................................1
   Johnny Allen .............................1
   Bill Amick ..................................1
   Jim Paschal ..............................1
   David Pearson ..........................1
   Bobby Johns .............................1
   Marvin Panch ...........................1

# 1960 NASCAR WINSTON CUP SEASON

| Race No. | Location | Date | Winner | Car owner |
|---|---|---|---|---|
| 1. | Charlotte, N.C. | Nov. 8 | Jack Smith | Jack Smith |
| 2. | Columbia, S.C. | Nov. 26 | Ned Jarrett | Ned Jarrett |
| 3. | Daytona Beach, Fla. | Feb. 12 | Fireball Roberts | John Hines |
| 4. | Daytona Beach, Fla. | Feb. 12 | Jack Smith | Jack Smith |
| 5. | Daytona Beach, Fla. | Feb. 14 | Junior Johnson | John Masoni |
| 6. | Charlotte, N.C. | Feb. 28 | Richard Petty | Petty Enterprises |
| 7. | North Wilkesboro, N.C. | Mar. 27 | Lee Petty | Petty Enterprises |
| 8. | Phoenix, Ariz. | Apr. 3 | John Rostek | John Rostek |
| 9. | Columbia, S.C. | Apr. 5 | Rex White | Rex White |
| 10. | Martinsville, Va. | Apr. 10 | Richard Petty | Petty Enterprises |
| 11. | Hickory, N.C. | Apr. 16 | Joe Weatherly | Holman-Moody |
| 12. | Wilson, N.C. | Apr. 17 | Joe Weatherly | Holman-Moody |
| 13. | Winston-Salem, N.C. | Apr. 18 | Glen Wood | Wood Brothers |
| 14. | Greenville, S.C. | Apr. 23 | Ned Jarrett | Ned Jarrett |
| 15. | Weaverville, N.C. | Apr. 24 | Lee Petty | Petty Enterprises |
| 16. | Darlington, S.C. | May. 14 | Joe Weatherly | Holman-Moody |
| 17. | Spartanburg, S.C. | May. 28 | Ned Jarrett | Ned Jarrett |
| 18. | Hillsboro, N.C. | May. 29 | Lee Petty | Petty Enterprises |
| 19. | Richmond, Va. | Jun. 5 | Lee Petty | Petty Enterprises |
| 20. | Hanford, Calif. | Jun. 12 | Marvin Porter | Vel Miletich |
| 21. | Concord, N.C. | Jun. 19 | Joe Lee Johnson | Paul McDuffie |
| 22. | Winston-Salem, N.C. | Jun. 26 | Glen Wood | Wood Brothers |
| 23. | Daytona Beach, Fla. | Jul. 4 | Jack Smith | Jack Smith |
| 24. | Heidelburg, Pa. | Jul. 10 | Lee Petty | Petty Enterprises |
| 25. | Montgomery, N.Y. | Jul. 17 | Rex White | Rex White |
| 26. | Myrtle Beach, S.C. | Jul. 23 | Buck Baker | Buck Baker |
| 27. | Hampton, Ga. | Jul. 31 | Fireball Roberts | John Hines |
| 28. | Birmingham, Ala. | Aug. 3 | Ned Jarrett | Ned Jarrett |
| 29. | Nashville, Tenn. | Aug. 7 | Johnny Beauchamp | Dale Swanson |
| 30. | Weaverville, N.C. | Aug. 14 | Rex White | Rex White |
| 31. | Spartanburg, S.C. | Aug. 16 | Cotton Owens | Cotton Owens |
| 32. | Columbia, S.C. | Aug. 18 | Rex White | Rex White |
| 33. | South Boston, Va. | Aug. 20 | Junior Johnson | John Masoni |
| 34. | Winston-Salem, N.C. | Aug. 23 | Glen Wood | Wood Brothers |
| 35. | Darlington, S.C. | Sep. 5 | Buck Baker | Jack Smith |
| 36. | Hickory, N.C. | Sep. 9 | Junior Johnson | John Masoni |
| 37. | Sacramento, Calif. | Sep. 11 | Jim Cook | Floyd Johnson |
| 38. | Sumter, S.C. | Sep. 15 | Ned Jarrett | Ned Jarrett |
| 39. | Hillsboro, N.C. | Sep. 18 | Richard Petty | Petty Enterprises |
| 40. | Martinsville, Va. | Sep. 25 | Rex White | Rex White |
| 41. | North Wilkesboro, N.C. | Oct. 2 | Rex White | Rex White |
| 42. | Concord, N.C. | Oct. 16 | Speedy Thompson | Wood Brothers |
| 43. | Richmond, Va. | Oct. 23 | Speedy Thompson | Wood Brothers |
| 44. | Hampton, Ga. | Oct. 30 | Bobby Johns | Cotton Owens |

## Points standings
1. Rex White ............21,164.00
2. Richard Petty ....17,228.00
3. Bobby Johns ........14,964.00
4. Buck Baker ..........14,674.00
5. Ned Jarrett ..........14,660.00
6. Lee Petty .............14,510.00
7. Junior Johnson ......9,932.00
8. Emanuel Zervakis ..9,720.00
9. Jim Paschal ..........8,968.00
10. Banjo Matthews ....8,458.00

## Race winners (18)
1. Rex White .....................6
2. Ned Jarrett....................5
    Lee Petty .......................5
4. Junior Johnson ............3
    Richard Petty ................3
    Jack Smith .....................3
    Glen Wood ....................3
    Joe Weatherly ...............3
9. Fireball Roberts ............2
    Buck Baker ....................2
    Speedy Thompson........2
12. John Rostek ..................1
     Bobby Johns ..................1
     Joe Lee Johnson ...........1
     Jim Cook ........................1
     Marvin Porter ................1
     Johnny Beauchamp .......1
     Cotton Owens ...............1

## Money won leaders
1. Rex White .........$45,280
2. Bobby Johns .........40,840
3. Richard Petty........35,180
4. Buck Baker ...........33,915
5. Joe Lee Johnson ..33,388
6. Junior Johnson .....30,775
7. Lee Petty ...............26,650
8. Jack Smith .............23,590
9. Ned Jarrett ............20,540
10. Fireball Roberts ....19,895

## Pole winners (19)
1. Fireball Roberts ..............6
2. Ned Jarrett .......................5
3. Jack Smith .......................4
    Glen Wood .......................4
5. Cotton Owens ..................3
    Lee Petty ...........................3
    Rex White .........................3
    Junior Johnson ................3
9. Richard Petty ...................2
    Buck Baker ........................2
11. Jim Cook ..........................1
     Curtis Turner ....................1
     Doug Yates .......................1
     Emanuel Zervakis ............1
     Mel Larson .......................1
     David Pearson .................1
     John Rostek .....................1
     Tommy Irwin ....................1
     Frank Secrist ....................1

# 1959 NASCAR WINSTON CUP SEASON

| Race No. | Location | Date | Winner | Car owner |
|---|---|---|---|---|
| 1. | Fayetteville, N.C. | Nov. 9 | Bob Welborn | J.H. Petty |
| 2. | Daytona Beach, Fla. | Feb. 20 | Bob Welborn | W.J. Ridgeway |
| 3. | Daytona Beach, Fla. | Feb. 22 | Lee Petty | Petty Enterprises |
| 4. | Hillsboro, N.C. | Mar. 1 | Curtis Turner | Dr. Bradford White |
| 5. | Concord, N.C. | Mar. 8 | Curtis Turner | Dr. Bradford White |
| 6. | Atlanta, Ga. | Mar. 22 | Johnny Beauchamp | Roy Burdick |
| 7. | Wilson, N.C. | Mar. 29 | Junior Johnson | Paul Spaulding |
| 8. | Winston-Salem, N.C. | Mar. 30 | Jim Reed | Jim Reed |
| 9. | Columbia, S.C. | Apr. 4 | Jack Smith | Jack Smith |
| 10. | North Wilkesboro, N.C. | Apr. 5 | Lee Petty | Petty Enterprises |
| 11. | Reading, Pa. | Apr. 26 | Junior Johnson | Paul Spaulding |
| 12. | Hickory, N.C. | May. 2 | Junior Johnson | Paul Spaulding |
| 13. | Martinsville, Va. | May. 3 | Lee Petty | Petty Enterprises |
| 14. | Trenton, N.J. | May. 17 | Tom Pistone | Carl Rupert |
| 15. | Charlotte, N.C. | May. 22 | Lee Petty | Petty Enterprises |
| 16. | Nashville, Tenn. | May. 24 | Rex White | Rex White |
| 17. | Los Angles, Calif. | May. 30 | Parnelli Jones | Vel Miletich |
| 18. | Spartenburg, S.C. | Jun. 5 | Jack Smith | Jack Smith |
| 19. | Greenville, S.C. | Jun. 13 | Junior Johnson | Paul Spaulding |
| 20. | Atlanta, Ga. | Jun. 14 | Lee Petty | Petty Enterprises |
| 21. | Columbia, S.C. | Jun. 18 | Lee Petty | Petty Enterprises |
| 22. | Wilson, N.C. | Jun. 20 | Junior Johnson | Paul Spaulding |
| 23. | Richmond, Va. | Jun. 21 | Tom Pistone | Carl Rupert |
| 24. | Winston-Salem, N.C. | Jun. 27 | Rex White | Rex White |
| 25. | Weaverville, N.C. | Jun. 28 | Rex White | Rex White |
| 26. | Daytona Beach, Fla. | Jul. 4 | Fireball Roberts | Jim Stephens |
| 27. | Pittsburgh, Pa. | Jul. 21 | Jim Reed | Jim Reed |
| 28. | Charlotte, N.C. | Jul. 26 | Jack Smith | Jack Smith |
| 29. | Myrtle Beach, S.C. | Aug. 1 | Ned Jarrett | Ned Jarrett |
| 30. | Charlotte, N.C. | Aug. 2 | Ned Jarrett | Ned Jarrett |
| 31. | Nashville, Tenn. | Aug. 9 | Joe Lee Johnson | Joe Lee Johnson |
| 32. | Weaverville, N.C. | Aug. 16 | Bob Welborn | Bob Welborn |
| 33. | Winston-Salem, N.C. | Aug. 21 | Rex White | Rex White |
| 34. | Greenville, S.C. | Aug. 22 | Buck Baker | Lynton Tyson |
| 35. | Columbia, S.C. | Aug. 29 | Lee Petty | Petty Enterprises |
| 36. | Darlington, S.C. | Sep. 7 | Jim Reed | Jim Reed |
| 37. | Hickory, N.C. | Sep. 11 | Lee Petty | Petty Enterprises |
| 38. | Richmond, Va. | Sep. 13 | Cotton Owens | Cotton Owens |
| 39. | Sacramento, Calif. | Sep. 13 | Eddie Gray | Vel Miletich |
| 40. | Hillsboro, N.C. | Sep. 20 | Lee Petty | Petty Enterprises |
| 41. | Martinsville, Va. | Sep. 27 | Rex White | White-Clements |
| 42. | Weaverville, N.C. | Oct. 11 | Lee Petty | Petty Enterprises |
| 43. | North Wilkesboro, N.C. | Oct. 18 | Lee Petty | Petty Enterprises |
| 44. | Concord, N.C. | Oct. 25 | Jack Smith | Jack Smith |

## Points standings
1. Lee Petty..............11,792.00
2. Cotton Owens.........9,962.00
3. Speedy Thompson 7,684.00
4. Herman Beam.........7,396.00
5. Buck Baker ............7,170.00
6. Tom Pistone ..........7,050.00
7. L.D. Austin .............6,519.00
8. Jack Smith .............6,150.00
9. Jim Reed................5,744.00
10. Rex White ............5,526.00

## Race winners (16)
1. Lee Petty ..........................11
2. Junior Johnson ..................5
   Rex White .........................5
4. Jack Smith .........................4
5. Jim Reed ............................3
   Bob Welborn ......................3
7. Tom Pistone.......................2
   Ned Jarrett.........................2
   Curtis Turner .....................2
10. Fireball Roberts ................1
    Eddie Gray ........................1
    Johnny Beauchamp ............1
    Buck Baker ........................1
    Cotton Owens ....................1
    Parnelli Jones ....................1
    Joe Lee Johnson ................1

## Money won leaders
1. Lee Petty ..................$43,590
2. Jim Reed .....................22,784
3. Cotton Owens .............11,925
4. Jack Smith ..................11,850
5. Rex White ...................11,560
6. Tom Pistone ................10,885
7. Fireball Roberts ..........10,865
8. Bob Burdick................10,050
9. Buck Baker ..................9,540
10. Joe Weatherly ............9,495

## Pole winners (16)
1. Rex White ..........................5
   Bob Welborn ......................5
3. Buck Baker ........................4
4. Fireball Roberts .................3
   Jack Smith .........................3
   Glen Wood .........................3
7. Lee Petty ...........................2
   Bob Burdick........................2
   Cotton Owens ....................2
10. Curtis Turner ....................1
    Tommy Irwin .....................1
    Dick Bailey........................1
    Junior Johnson ..................1
    Jim Reed ...........................1
    Speedy Thompson .............1
    Bobby Johns .....................1

# 1958 NASCAR WINSTON CUP SEASON

| Race No. | Location | Date | Winner | Car owner |
|---|---|---|---|---|
| 1. | Fayetteville, N.C. | Nov. 3 | Rex White | J.H. Petty |
| 2. | Daytona Beach, Fla. | Feb. 23 | Paul Goldsmith | Smokey Yunick |
| 3. | Concord, N.C. | Mar. 2 | Lee Petty | Petty Enterprises |
| 4. | Fayetteville, N.C. | Mar. 15 | Curtis Turner | Holman-Moody |
| 5. | Wilson, N.C. | Mar. 16 | Lee Petty | Petty Enterprises |
| 6. | Hillsboro, N.C. | Mar. 23 | Buck Baker | Buck Baker |
| 7. | Fayetteville, N.C. | Apr. 5 | Bob Welborn | J.H. Petty |
| 8. | Columbia, S.C. | Apr. 10 | Speedy Thompson | Alfred "Speedy" Thompson |
| 9. | Spartenburg, S.C. | Apr. 12 | Speedy Thompson | Alfred "Speedy" Thompson |
| 10. | Atlanta, Ga. | Apr. 13 | Curtis Turner | Holman-Moody |
| 11. | Charlotte, N.C. | Apr. 18 | Curtis Turner | Holman-Moody |
| 12. | Martinsville, Va. | Apr. 20 | Bob Welborn | J.H. Petty |
| 13. | Manassas, Va. | Apr. 25 | Frankie Schneider | Frankie Schneider |
| 14. | Old Bridge, N.J. | Apr. 27 | Jim Reed | Jim Reed |
| 15. | Greenville, S.C. | May. 3 | Jack Smith | Jack Smith |
| 16. | Greensboro, N.C. | May. 11 | Bob Welborn | J.H. Petty |
| 17. | Roanoke, Va. | May. 15 | Jim Reed | Jim Reed |
| 18. | North Wilkesboro, N.C. | May. 18 | Junior Johnson | Paul Spaulding |
| 19. | Winston-Salem, N.C. | May. 24 | Bob Welborn | J.H. Petty |
| 20. | Trenton, N.J. | May. 30 | Fireball Roberts | Frank Strickland |
| 21. | Riverside, Calif. | Jun. 1 | Eddie Gray | Eddie Gray |
| 22. | Columbia, S.C. | Jun. 5 | Junior Johnson | Paul Spaulding |
| 23. | Bradford, Pa. | Jun. 12 | Junior Johnson | Paul Spaulding |
| 24. | Reading, Pa. | Jun. 15 | Junior Johnson | Paul Spaulding |
| 25. | New Oxford, Pa. | Jun. 25 | Lee Petty | Petty Enterprises |
| 26. | Hickory, N.C. | Jun. 28 | Lee Petty | Petty Enterprises |
| 27. | Weaverville, N.C. | Jun. 29 | Rex White | J.H. Petty |
| 28. | Raleigh, N.C. | Jul. 4 | Fireball Roberts | Frank Strickland |
| 29. | Asheville, N.C. | Jul. 12 | Jim Paschal | J.H. Petty |
| 30. | Busti, N.Y. | Jul. 16 | Shorty Rollins | Shorty Rollins |
| 31. | Toronto, Ontario, Canada | Jul. 18 | Lee Petty | Petty Enterprises |
| 32. | Buffalo, N.Y. | Jul. 19 | Jim Reed | Jim Reed |
| 33. | Rochester, N.Y. | Jul. 25 | Cotton Owens | Jim Stephens |
| 34. | Belmar, N.J. | Jul. 26 | Jim Reed | Jim Reed |
| 35. | Bridgehampton, N.Y. | Aug. 2 | Jack Smith | Jack Smith |
| 36. | Columbia, S.C. | Aug. 7 | Speedy Thompson | Alfred "Speedy" Thompson |
| 37. | Nashville, Tenn. | Aug. 10 | Joe Weatherly | Holman-Moody |
| 38. | Weaverville, N.C. | Aug. 17 | Fireball Roberts | Frank Strickland |
| 39. | Winston-Salem, N.C. | Aug. 22 | Lee Petty | Petty Enterprises |
| 40. | Myrtle Beach, S.C. | Aug. 23 | Bob Welborn | J.H. Petty |
| 41. | Darlington, S.C. | Sep. 1 | Fireball Roberts | Frank Strickland |
| 42. | Charlotte, N.C. | Sep. 5 | Buck Baker | Buck Baker |
| 43. | Birmingham, Ala. | Sep. 7 | Fireball Roberts | Frank Strickland |
| 44. | Sacramento, Calif. | Sep. 7 | Parnelli Jones | Vel Miletich |
| 45. | Gastonia, N.C. | Sep. 12 | Buck Baker | Buck Baker |
| 46. | Richmond, Va. | Sep. 14 | Speedy Thompson | Alfred "Speedy" Thompson |
| 47. | Hillsboro, N.C. | Sep. 28 | Joe Eubanks | Jim Stephens |
| 48. | Salisbury, N.C. | Oct. 5 | Lee Petty | Petty Enterprises |
| 49. | Martinsville, Va. | Oct. 12 | Fireball Roberts | Frank Strickland |
| 50. | North Wilkesboro, N.C. | Oct. 19 | Junior Johnson | Paul Spaulding |
| 51. | Atlanta, Ga. | Oct. 26 | Junior Johnson | Paul Spaulding |

## Points standings
1. Lee Petty .................12,232.00
2. Buck Baker ..............11,588.00
3. Speedy Thompson ......8,792.00
4. Shorty Rollins .............8,124.00
5. Jack Smith .................7,666.00
6. L.D. Austin .................6,972.00
7. Rex White ...................6,552.00
8. Junior Johnson ...........6,380.00
9. Eddie Pagan ...............4,910.00
10. Jim Reed ...................4,762.00

## Race winners (19)
1. Lee Petty ............................7
2. Junior Johnson ...................6
   Fireball Roberts ..................6
4. Bob Welborn .......................5
5. Speedy Thompson ..............4
   Jim Reed .............................4
7. Curtis Turner ......................3
   Buck Baker ..........................3
9. Rex White ............................2
   Jack Smith ...........................2
11. Joe Eubanks .......................1
    Joe Weatherly .....................1
    Frankie Schneider ...............1
    Parnelli Jones .....................1
    Jim Paschal ........................1
    Cotton Owens .....................1
    Shorty Rollins ......................1
    Paul Goldsmith....................1
    Eddie Gray ..........................1

## Money won leaders
1. Fireball Roberts ..........$31,755
2. Buck Baker ....................22,740
3. Lee Petty ........................21,550
4. Speedy Thompson .......12,985
5. Junior Johnson .............12,420
6. Shorty Rollins ................11,315
7. Jack Smith .....................11,090
8. Rex White ......................11,075
9. Curtis Turner ...................9,720
10. Jim Reed ........................8,795

## Pole winners (23)
1. Rex White................................7
   Speedy Thompson .................7
3. Lee Petty ...............................4
   Jack Smith .............................4
5. Buck Baker ............................3
   Glen Wood ..............................3
7. Eddie Pagan ..........................2
   Marvin Panch .........................2
   Cotton Owens ........................2
   Parnelli Jones ........................2
   Tiny Lund ...............................2
   Jim Reed .................................2
13. Gober Sosebee .....................1
    Bob Welborn .........................1
    Joe Weatherly .......................1
    Curtis Turner .........................1
    Paul Goldsmith......................1
    George Dunn ........................1
    Bob Duell ...............................1
    Possum Jones ......................1
    Ken Rush ...............................1
    Jim Paschal ..........................1
    Jimmy Massey ......................1

# 1957 NASCAR WINSTON CUP SEASON

| Race No. | Location | Date | Winner | Car owner |
|---|---|---|---|---|
| 1. | Lancaster, Calif. | Nov. 11 | Marvin Panch | Pete DePaolo |
| 2. | Concord, N.C. | Dec. 2 | Marvin Panch | Pete DePaolo |
| 3. | Titusville, Fla. | Dec. 30 | Fireball Roberts | Pete DePaolo |
| 4. | Daytona Beach, Fla. | Feb. 17 | Cotton Owens | Ray Nichels |
| 5. | Concord, N.C. | Mar. 3 | Jack Smith | Hugh Babb |
| 6. | Wilson, N.C. | Mar. 17 | Ralph Moody | Pete DePaolo |
| 7. | Hillsboro, N.C. | Mar. 24 | Buck Baker | Hugh Babb |
| 8. | Weaverville, N.C. | Mar. 31 | Buck Baker | Hugh Babb |
| 9. | North Wilkesboro, N.C. | Apr. 7 | Fireball Roberts | Pete DePaolo |
| 10. | Langhorne, Pa. | Apr. 14 | Fireball Roberts | Pete DePaolo |
| 11. | Charlotte, N.C. | Apr. 19 | Fireball Roberts | Pete DePaolo |
| 12. | Spartenburg, S.C. | Apr. 27 | Marvin Panch | Pete DePaolo |
| 13. | Greensboro, N.C. | Apr. 28 | Paul Goldsmith | Smokey Yunick |
| 14. | Portland, Ore. | Apr. 28 | Art Watts | Al Schmidhamer |
| 15. | Shelby, N.C. | May 4 | Fireball Roberts | Pete DePaolo |
| 16. | Richmond, Va. | May 5 | Paul Goldsmith | Pete DePaolo |
| 17. | Martinsville, Va. | May 19 | Buck Baker | Hugh Babb |
| 18. | Portland, Ore. | May 26 | Eddie Pagan | Eddie Pagan |
| 19. | Eureka, Calif. | May 30 | Lloyd Dane | Lloyd Dane |
| 20. | New Oxford, Pa. | May 30 | Buck Baker | Hugh Babb |
| 21. | Lancaster, S.C. | Jun. 1 | Paul Goldsmith | Smokey Yunick |
| 22. | Los Angeles, Calif. | Jun. 8 | Eddie Pagan | Eddie Pagan |
| 23. | Newport, Tenn. | Jun. 15 | Fireball Roberts | Edward "Fireball" Robert |
| 24. | Columbia, S.C. | Jun. 20 | Jack Smith | Jack Smith |
| 25. | Sacramento, Calif. | Jun. 22 | Bill Amick | William Amick |
| 26. | Spartenburg, S.C. | Jun. 29 | Lee Petty | Petty Enterprises |
| 27. | Jacksonville, N.C. | Jun. 30 | Buck Baker | Buck Baker |
| 28. | Raleigh, N.C. | Jul. 4 | Paul Goldsmith | Smokey Yunick |
| 29. | Charlotte, N.C. | Jul. 12 | Marvin Panch | Marvin Panch |
| 30. | LeHi, Ark. | Jul. 14 | Marvin Panch | Herb Thomas |
| 31. | Portland, Ore. | Jul. 14 | Eddie Pagan | Eddie Pagan |
| 32. | Hickory, N.C. | Jul. 20 | Jack Smith | Jack Smith |
| 33. | Norfolk, Va. | Jul. 24 | Buck Baker | Buck Baker |
| 34. | Lancaster, S.C. | Jul. 30 | Speedy Thompson | Alfred "Speedy" Thompson |
| 35. | Watkins Glen, N.Y. | Aug. 4 | Buck Baker | Buck Baker |
| 36. | Bremerton, Wash. | Aug. 4 | Parnelli Jones | Oscar Maples |
| 37. | New Oxford, Pa. | Aug. 10 | Marvin Panch | Marvin Panch |
| 38. | Old Bridge, N.J. | Aug. 16 | Lee Petty | Petty Enterprises |
| 39. | Myrtle Beach, S.C. | Aug. 26 | Gwyn Staley | J.H. Petty |
| 40. | Darlington, S.C. | Sep. 2 | Speedy Thompson | Alfred "Speedy" Thompson |
| 41. | Syracuse, N.Y. | Sep. 5 | Gwyn Staley | J.H. Petty |
| 42. | Weaverville, N.C. | Sep. 8 | Lee Petty | Petty Enterprises |
| 43. | Sacramento, Calif. | Sep. 8 | Danny Graves | Danny Graves |
| 44. | San Jose, Calif. | Sep. 15 | Marvin Porter | Marvin Porter |
| 45. | Langhorne, Pa. | Sep. 15 | Gwyn Staley | J.H. Petty |
| 46. | Columbia, S.C. | Sep. 19 | Buck Baker | Buck Baker |
| 47. | Shelby, N.C. | Sep. 21 | Buck Baker | Buck Baker |
| 48. | Charlotte, N.C. | Oct. 5 | Lee Petty | Petty Enterprises |
| 49. | Martinsville, Va. | Oct. 6 | Bob Welborn | Bob Welborn |
| 50. | Newberry, S.C. | Oct. 12 | Fireball Roberts | Edward "Fireball" Robert |
| 51. | Concord, N.C. | Oct. 13 | Fireball Roberts | Edward "Fireball" Robert |
| 52. | North Wilkesboro, N.C. | Oct. 20 | Jack Smith | Jack Smith |
| 53. | Greensboro, N.C. | Oct. 27 | Buck Baker | Buck Baker |

## Points standings
1. Buck Baker .............. 10,716.00
2. Marvin Panch ............ 9,956.00
3. Speedy Thompson ...... 8,580.00
4. Lee Petty ................. 8,528.00
5. Jack Smith ............... 8,464.00
6. Fireball Roberts ......... 8,268.00
7. Johnny Allen ............. 7,068.00
8. L.D. Austin ............... 6,532.00
9. Brownie King ............ 5,740.00
10. Jim Paschal ............. 5,136.00

## Race winners (18)
1. Buck Baker .......................... 10
2. Fireball Roberts .................... 8
3. Marvin Panch ....................... 6
4. Lee Petty ............................. 4
   Jack Smith ........................... 4
   Paul Goldsmith ..................... 4
7. Eddie Pagan ........................ 3
   Gwyn Staley ........................ 3
9. Speedy Thompson ................ 2
10. Bill Amick ........................... 1
    Lloyd Dane ......................... 1
    Art Watts ........................... 1
    Bob Welborn ....................... 1
    Ralph Moody ....................... 1
    Cotton Owens ...................... 1
    Parnelli Jones ...................... 1
    Danny Graves ...................... 1
    Marvin Porter ...................... 1

## Money won leaders
1. Buck Baker ................ $25,665
2. Speedy Thompson ......... 24,710
3. Marvin Panch ............... 19,980
4. Fireball Roberts ............ 17,425
5. Lee Petty .................... 15,945
6. Cotton Owens .............. 12,325
7. Paul Goldsmith ............. 11,950
8. Jack Smith ................... 11,335
9. Johnny Allen .................. 8,075
10. Bill Amick .................... 8,030

## Pole winners (24)
1. Buck Baker .......................... 6
2. Art Watts ............................ 5
3. Speedy Thompson ................ 4
   Marvin Panch ....................... 4
   Paul Goldsmith ..................... 4
   Fireball Roberts .................... 4
7. Tiny Lund ............................ 3
   Lee Petty ............................ 3
9. Eddie Pagan ........................ 2
   Gwyn Staley ........................ 2
   Bill Amick ............................ 2
   Jack Smith .......................... 2
13. Rex White ........................... 1
    Curtis Turner ....................... 1
    Ken Rush ............................ 1
    Frankie Schneider ................. 1
    Danny Graves ...................... 1
    Russ Hepler ........................ 1
    Johnny Allen ....................... 1
    Lloyd Dane ......................... 1
    Banjo Matthews ................... 1
    Cotton Owens ...................... 1
    Parnelli Jones ...................... 1
    Mel Larson .......................... 1

# 1956 NASCAR WINSTON CUP SEASON

| Race No. | Location | Date | Winner | Car owner |
|---|---|---|---|---|
| 1. | Hickory, N.C. | Nov. 13 | Tim Flock | Carl Kiekhafer |
| 2. | Charlotte, N.C. | Nov. 20 | Fonty Flock | Carl Kiekhafer |
| 3. | Lancaster, Calif. | Nov. 20 | Chuck Stevenson | Carl Dane |
| 4. | West Palm Beach, Fla. | Dec. 11 | Herb Thomas | Herb Thomas |
| 5. | Phoenix, Ariz. | Jan. 22 | Buck Baker | Carl Kiekhafer |
| 6. | Daytona Beach, Fla. | Feb. 26 | Tim Flock | Carl Kiekhafer |
| 7. | West Palm Beach, Fla. | Mar. 4 | Billy Myers | William Stroppe |
| 8. | Wilson, N.C. | Mar. 18 | Herb Thomas | Smokey Yunick |
| 9. | Atlanta, Ga. | Mar. 25 | Buck Baker | Carl Kiekhafer |
| 10. | North Wilkesboro, N.C. | Apr. 8 | Tim Flock | Carl Kiekhafer |
| 11. | Langhorne, Pa. | Apr. 22 | Buck Baker | Carl Kiekhafer |
| 12. | Richmond, Va. | Apr. 29 | Buck Baker | Carl Kiekhafer |
| 13. | Columbia, S.C. | May. 5 | Speedy Thompson | Carl Kiekhafer |
| 14. | Concord, N.C. | May. 6 | Speedy Thompson | Carl Kiekhafer |
| 15. | Greenville, S.C. | May. 10 | Buck Baker | Carl Kiekhafer |
| 16. | Hickory, N.C. | May. 12 | Speedy Thompson | Carl Kiekhafer |
| 17. | Hillsboro, N.C. | May. 13 | Buck Baker | Carl Kiekhafer |
| 18. | Martinsville, Va. | May. 20 | Buck Baker | Carl Kiekhafer |
| 19. | New Oxford, Pa. | May. 25 | Buck Baker | Carl Kiekhafer |
| 20. | Charlotte, N.C. | May. 27 | Speedy Thompson | Carl Kiekhafer |
| 21. | Portland, Ore. | May. 27 | Herb Thomas | Carl Kiekhafer |
| 22. | Eureka, Calif. | May. 30 | Herb Thomas | Carl Kiekhafer |
| 23. | Syracuse, N.Y. | May. 30 | Buck Baker | Carl Kiekhafer |
| 24. | Merced, Calif. | Jun. 3 | Herb Thomas | Carl Kiekhafer |
| 25. | LeHi, Ark. | Jun. 10 | Ralph Moody | Pete DePaolo |
| 26. | Charlotte, N.C. | Jun. 15 | Speedy Thompson | Carl Kiekhafer |
| 27. | Rochester, N.Y. | Jun. 22 | Speedy Thompson | Carl Kiekhafer |
| 28. | Portland, Ore. | Jun. 24 | John Kieper | John Kieper |
| 29. | Weaverville, N.C. | Jul. 1 | Lee Petty | Petty Enterprises |
| 30. | Raleigh, N.C. | Jul. 4 | Fireball Roberts | Pete DePaolo |
| 31. | Spartanburg, S.C. | Jul. 7 | Lee Petty | Petty Enterprises |
| 32. | Sacramento, Calif. | Jul. 8 | Lloyd Dane | Lloyd Dane |
| 33. | Chicago, Ill. | Jul. 21 | Fireball Roberts | Pete DePaolo |
| 34. | Shelby, N.C. | Jul. 27 | Speedy Thompson | Carl Kiekhafer |
| 35. | Montgomery, Ala. | Jul. 29 | Marvin Panch | Tom Harbison |
| 36. | Oklahoma City, Okla. | Aug. 3 | Jim Paschal | Frank Hayworth |
| 37. | Elkhart Lakes, Wis. | Aug. 12 | Tim Flock | William Stroppe |
| 38. | Old Bridge, N.J. | Aug. 17 | Ralph Moody | Pete DePaolo |
| 39. | San Mateo, Calif. | Aug. 19 | Eddie Pagan | Eddie Pagan |
| 40. | Norfolk, Va. | Aug. 22 | Billy Myers | William Stroppe |
| 41. | Spartanburg, S.C. | Aug. 23 | Ralph Moody | Pete DePaolo |
| 42. | Myrtle Beach, S.C. | Aug. 25 | Fireball Roberts | Pete DePaolo |
| 43. | Portland, Ore. | Aug. 26 | Royce Haggerty | Curly Weida |
| 44. | Darlington, S.C. | Sep. 3 | Curtis Turner | Charles Schwam |
| 45. | Montgomery, Ala. | Sep. 9 | Buck Baker | Carl Kiekhafer |
| 46. | Charlotte, N.C. | Sep. 12 | Ralph Moody | Pete DePaolo |
| 47. | Langhorne, Pa. | Sep. 23 | Paul Goldsmith | Smokey Yunick |
| 48. | Portland, Ore. | Sep. 23 | Lloyd Dane | Lloyd Dane |
| 49. | Columbia, S.C. | Sep. 29 | Buck Baker | Carl Kiekhafer |
| 50. | Hillsboro, N.C. | Sep. 30 | Fireball Roberts | Pete DePaolo |
| 51. | Newport, Tenn. | Oct. 7 | Fireball Roberts | Pete DePaolo |
| 52. | Charlotte, N.C. | Oct. 17 | Buck Baker | Carl Kiekhafer |
| 53. | Shelby, N.C. | Oct. 23 | Buck Baker | Carl Kiekhafer |
| 54. | Martinsville, Va. | Oct. 28 | Jack Smith | Carl Kiekhafer |
| 55. | Hickory, N.C. | Nov. 11 | Speedy Thompson | Carl Kiekhafer |
| 56. | Wilson, N.C. | Nov. 18 | Buck Baker | Carl Kiekhafer |

## Points standings
1. Buck Baker .................9,272.00
2. Herb Thomas..............8,568.00
3. Speedy Thompson .....8,328.00
4. Lee Petty ....................8,324.00
5. Jim Paschal ................7,878.00
6. Billy Myers ..................6,920.00
7. Fireball Roberts ..........5,794.00
8. Ralph Moody ..............5,548.00
9. Tim Flock ....................5,062.00
10. Marvin Panch ............4,680.00

## Race winners (19)
1. Buck Baker ........................14
2. Speedy Thompson ..............8
3. Herb Thomas ......................5
   Fireball Roberts ..................5
5. Tim Flock ............................4
   Ralph Moody ......................4
7. Billy Myers ..........................2
   Lee Petty ............................2
   Lloyd Dane .........................2
10. Jack Smith .........................1
    Curtis Turner .....................1
    Chuck Stevenson ..............1
    Royce Haggerty ................1
    Paul Goldsmith..................1
    Fonty Flock .......................1
    John Kieper ......................1
    Jim Paschal ......................1
    Marvin Panch ...................1
    Eddie Pagan .....................1

## Money won leaders
1. Buck Baker....................$29,140
2. Speedy Thompson ..........24,670
3. Herb Thomas ...................17,695
4. Jim Paschal .....................16,540
5. Tim Flock .........................15,409
6. Billy Myers .......................15,320
7. Ralph Moody ...................14,545
8. Fireball Roberts ...............14,395
9. Curtis Turner ...................14,295
10. Lee Petty .......................13,455

## Pole winners (22)
1. Buck Baker ...............................11
2. Speedy Thompson .....................7
3. Tim Flock ....................................5
   Ralph Moody ..............................5
5. Fireball Roberts .........................3
   John Kieper ................................3
   Herb Thomas .............................3
8. Jim Reed ....................................2
   Eddie Pagan ..............................2
   Fonty Flock ................................2
   Joe Eubanks..............................2
12. Lee Petty ..................................1
    Joe Weatherly ...........................1
    Rex White..................................1
    Jim Paschal ..............................1
    Royce Haggerty ........................1
    Ralph Earnhardt ........................1
    Doug Cox ..................................1
    Junior Johnson .........................1
    Marvin Panch ............................1
    Billy Myers ................................1
    Frank Mundy ............................1

# 1955 NASCAR WINSTON CUP SEASON

| Race No. | Location | Date | Winner | Car owner |
|---|---|---|---|---|
| 1. | High Point, N.C. | Nov. 7 | Lee Petty | Petty Enterprises |
| 2. | West Palm Beach, Fla. | Feb. 6 | Herb Thomas | Herb Thomas |
| 3. | Jacksonville, Fla. | Feb. 13 | Lee Petty | Petty Enterprises |
| 4. | Daytona Beach, Fla. | Feb. 27 | Tim Flock | Carl Kiekhafer |
| 5. | Savannah, Ga. | Mar. 6 | Lee Petty | Petty Enterprises |
| 6. | Columbia, S.C. | Mar. 26 | Fonty Flock | Frank Christian |
| 7. | Hillsboro, N.C. | Mar. 27 | Jim Paschal | Ernest Woods |
| 8. | North Wilkesboro, N.C. | Apr. 3 | Buck Baker | Bobby Griffin |
| 9. | Montgomery, Ala. | Apr. 17 | Tim Flock | Carl Kiekhafer |
| 10. | Langhorne, Pa. | Apr. 24 | Tim Flock | Carl Kiekhafer |
| 11. | Charlotte, N.C. | May. 1 | Buck Baker | Buck Baker |
| 12. | Hickory, N.C. | May. 7 | Junior Johnson | Carl Beckham/Jim Lowe |
| 13. | Phoenix, Ariz. | May. 8 | Tim Flock | Carl Kiekhafer |
| 14. | Tucson, Ariz. | May. 15 | Danny Letner | Cos Concilla |
| 15. | Martinsville, Va. | May. 15 | Tim Flock | Carl Kiekhafer |
| 16. | Richmond, Va. | May. 22 | Tim Flock | Carl Kiekhafer |
| 17. | Raleigh, N.C. | May. 28 | Junior Johnson | Carl Beckham/Jim Lowe |
| 18. | Winston-Salem, N.C. | May. 29 | Lee Petty | Petty Enterprises |
| 19. | New Oxford, Pa. | Jun. 10 | Junior Johnson | Carl Beckham/Jim Lowe |
| 20. | Rochester, N.Y. | Jun. 17 | Tim Flock | Carl Kiekhafer |
| 21. | Fonda, N.Y. | Jun. 18 | Junior Johnson | Carl Beckham/Jim Lowe |
| 22. | Plattsburg, N.Y. | Jun. 19 | Lee Petty | Petty Enterprises |
| 23. | Charlotte, N.C. | Jun. 24 | Tim Flock | Carl Kiekhafer |
| 24. | Spartanburg, S.C. | Jul. 6 | Tim Flock | Carl Kiekhafer |
| 25. | Columbia, S.C. | Jul. 9 | Jim Paschal | Ernest Woods |
| 26. | Weaverville, N.C. | Jul. 10 | Tim Flock | Carl Kiekhafer |
| 27. | Morristown, N.J. | Jul. 15 | Tim Flock | Carl Kiekhafer |
| 28. | Altamont, N.Y. | Jul. 29 | Junior Johnson | Carl Beckham/Jim Lowe |
| 29. | Syracuse, N.Y. | Jul. 30 | Tim Flock | Carl Kiekhafer |
| 30. | San Mateo, Calif. | Jul. 31 | Tim Flock | Carl Kiekhafer |
| 31. | Charlotte, N.C. | Aug. 5 | Jim Paschal | Ernest Woods |
| 32. | Winston-Salem, N.C. | Aug. 7 | Lee Petty | Petty Enterprises |
| 33. | LeHi, Ark. | Aug. 14 | Fonty Flock | Carl Kiekhafer |
| 34. | Raleigh, N.C. | Aug. 20 | Herb Thomas | Herb Thomas |
| 35. | Darlington, S.C. | Sep. 5 | Herb Thomas | Herb Thomas |
| 36. | Montgomery, Ala. | Sep. 11 | Tim Flock | Carl Kiekhafer |
| 37. | Langhorne, Pa. | Sep. 18 | Tim Flock | Carl Kiekhafer |
| 38. | Raleigh, N.C. | Sep. 30 | Fonty Flock | Carl Kiekhafer |
| 39. | Greenville, S.C. | Oct. 6 | Tim Flock | Carl Kiekhafer |
| 40. | LeHi, Ark. | Oct. 9 | Speedy Thompson | Pete DePaolo |
| 41. | Columbia, S.C. | Oct. 15 | Tim Flock | Carl Kiekhafer |
| 42. | Martinsville, Va. | Oct. 16 | Speedy Thompson | Carl Kiekhafer |
| 43. | Las Vegas, Nev. | Oct. 16 | Norm Nelson | Carl Kiekhafer |
| 44. | North Wilkesboro, N.C. | Oct. 23 | Buck Baker | Pete DePaolo |
| 45. | Hillsboro, N.C. | Oct. 30 | Tim Flock | Carl Kiekhafer |

## Points standings
1. Tim Flock ............9,596.00
2. Buck Baker ...........8,088.00
3. Lee Petty.............7,194.00
4. Bob Welborn..........5,460.00
5. Herb Thomas ........5,186.00
6. Junior Johnson ......4,810.00
7. Eddie Skinner ........4,652.00
8. Jim Paschal ..........4,572.00
9. Jimmy Lewallen ....4,526.00
10. Gwyn Staley .........4,360.00

## Race winners (10)
1. Tim Flock.........................18
2. Lee Petty..........................6
3. Junior Johnson .................5
4. Buck Baker .......................3
   Jim Paschal .......................3
   Fonty Flock .......................3
   Herb Thomas ....................3
8. Speedy Thompson.............2
9. Danny Letner ....................1
   Norm Nelson .....................1

## Money won leaders
1. Tim Flock...............$33,275
2. Buck Baker ..............17,590
3. Lee Petty ..................16,775
4. Herb Thomas............16,320
5. Fonty Flock ..............12,690
6. Junior Johnson ..........10,055
7. Jim Paschal................9,700
8. Bob Welborn ..............8,275
9. Speedy Thompson ......6,680
10. Gwyn Staley ...............5,815

## Pole winners (14)
1. Tim Flock...........................17
2. Fonty Flock .........................6
3. Dick Rathmann ....................3
4. Jim Paschal..........................2
   Herb Thomas.......................2
   Buck Baker ..........................2
   Bill Amick ............................2
   Junior Johnson ....................2
9. Dink Widenhouse .................1
   Bob Welborn .......................1
   Fireball Roberts ...................1
   Jimmy Lewallen ...................1
   Norm Nelson .......................1
   Lee Petty .............................1

# 1954 NASCAR WINSTON CUP SEASON

| Race No. | Location | Date | Winner | Car owner |
|---|---|---|---|---|
| 1. | West Palm Beach, Fla. | Feb. 7 | Herb Thomas | Herb Thomas |
| 2. | Daytona Beach, Fla. | Feb. 21 | Lee Petty | Petty Enterprises |
| 3. | Jacksonville, Fla. | Mar. 7 | Herb Thomas | Herb Thomas |
| 4. | Atlanta, Ga. | Mar. 21 | Herb Thomas | Herb Thomas |
| 5. | Savannah, Ga. | Mar. 28 | Al Keller | George Miller |
| 6. | Oakland, Calif. | Mar. 28 | Dick Rathmann | Ray Erickson |
| 7. | North Wilkesboro, N.C. | Apr. 4 | Dick Rathmann | John Ditz |
| 8. | Hillsboro, N.C. | Apr. 18 | Herb Thomas | Herb Thomas |
| 9. | Macon, Ga. | Apr. 25 | Gober Sosebee | Gober Sosebee |
| 10. | Langhorne, Pa. | May. 2 | Herb Thomas | Herb Thomas |
| 11. | Wilson, N.C. | May. 9 | Buck Baker | Ernest Woods |
| 12. | Martinsville, Va. | May. 16 | Jim Paschal | Bobby Griffin |
| 13. | Sharon, Pa. | May. 23 | Lee Petty | Petty Enterprises |
| 14. | Raleigh, N.C. | May. 29 | Herb Thomas | Herb Thomas |
| 15. | Charlotte, N.C. | May. 30 | Buck Baker | Bobby Griffin |
| 16. | Gardena, Calif. | May. 30 | John Soares | Charles Vance |
| 17. | Columbia, S.C. | Jun. 6 | Curtis Turner | Elmer Brooks |
| 18. | Linden, N.J. | Jun. 13 | Al Keller | Paul Whiteman |
| 19. | Mechanicsburg, Pa. | Jun. 17 | Herb Thomas | Herb Thomas |
| 20. | Hickory, N.C. | Jun. 19 | Herb Thomas | Herb Thomas |
| 21. | Rochester, N.Y. | Jun. 25 | Lee Petty | Petty Enterprises |
| 22. | Spartanburg, S.C. | Jul. 3 | Herb Thomas | Herb Thomas |
| 23. | Weaverville, N.C. | Jul. 4 | Herb Thomas | Herb Thomas |
| 24. | Willow Springs, Ill. | Jul. 10 | Dick Rathmann | John Ditz |
| 25. | Grand Rapids, Mich. | Jul. 11 | Lee Petty | Petty Enterprises |
| 26. | Morristown, N.J. | Jul. 30 | Buck Baker | Ernest Woods |
| 27. | Oakland, Calif. | Aug. 1 | Danny Letner | Joseph Bearscheck |
| 28. | Charlotte, N.C. | Aug. 13 | Lee Petty | Petty Enterprises |
| 29. | San Mateo, Calif. | Aug. 22 | Hershel McGriff | Frank Christian |
| 30. | Corbin, Ky. | Aug. 29 | Lee Petty | Petty Enterprises |
| 31. | Darlington, S.C. | Sep. 6 | Herb Thomas | Herb Thomas |
| 32. | Macon, Ga. | Sep. 12 | Hershel McGriff | Frank Christian |
| 33. | Charlotte, N.C. | Sep. 24 | Hershel McGriff | Frank Christian |
| 34. | Langhorne, Pa. | Sep. 26 | Herb Thomas | Herb Thomas |
| 35. | LeHi, Ark. | Oct. 10 | Buck Baker | Bobby Griffin |
| 36. | Martinsville, Va. | Oct. 17 | Lee Petty | Petty Enterprises |
| 37. | North Wilkesboro, N.C. | Oct. 24 | Hershel McGriff | Frank Christian |

### Points standings
1. Lee Petty ................8,649.00
2. Herb Thomas ..........8,366.00
3. Buck Baker .............6,893.00
4. Dick Rathmann ......6,760.00
5. Joe Eubanks ...........5,467.00
6. Hershel McGriff......5,137.00
7. Jim Paschal ............3,903.00
8. Jimmy Lewallen ....3,233.00
9. Curtis Turner .........2,994.00
10. Ralph Liguori ........2,905.00

### Race winners (11)
1. Herb Thomas ....................12
2. Lee Petty ............................7
3. Hershel McGriff ..................4
   Buck Baker .........................4
5. Dick Rathmann ..................3
6. Al Keller .............................2
7. Danny Letner .....................1
   Curtis Turner ......................1
   Gober Sosebee ...................1
   Jim Paschal ........................1
   John Soares .......................1

### Money won leaders
1. Herb Thomas............$27,540
2. Lee Petty ...................19,125
3. Buck Baker ................18,015
4. Dick Rathmann .........14,910
5. Hershel McGriff .........11,625
6. Curtis Turner ...............9,820
7. Joe Eubanks ................7,160
8. Jim Paschal .................4,585
9. Marvin Panch ..............4,530
10. Jimmy Lewallen ..........3,965

### Pole winners (13)
1. Herb Thomas ........................8
2. Buck Baker ...........................7
3. Hershel McGriff ....................5
4. Dick Rathmann .....................4
5. Lee Petty ...............................3
6. Jim Paschal ...........................2
7. Curtis Turner ........................1
   Gober Sosebee ......................1
   Junior Johnson .....................1
   Tim Flock...............................1
   Al Keller.................................1
   Marvin Panch ........................1
   Danny Letner.........................1

# 1953 NASCAR WINSTON CUP SEASON

| Race No. | Location | Date | Winner | Car owner |
|---|---|---|---|---|
| 1. | West Palm Beach, Fla. | Feb. 1 | Lee Petty | Petty Enterprises |
| 2. | Daytona Beach, Fla. | Feb. 15 | Bill Blair | Bill Blair |
| 3. | Spring Lake, N.C. | Mar. 8 | Herb Thomas | Herb Thomas |
| 4. | North Wilkesboro, N.C. | Mar. 29 | Herb Thomas | Herb Thomas |
| 5. | Charlotte, N.C. | Apr. 5 | Dick Passwater | Frank Arford |
| 6. | Richmond, Va. | Apr. 19 | Lee Petty | Petty Enterprises |
| 7. | Macon, Ga. | Apr. 26 | Dick Rathmann | Walt Chapman |
| 8. | Langhorne, Pa. | May. 3 | Buck Baker | Bobby Griffin |
| 9. | Columbia, S.C. | May. 9 | Buck Baker | Bobby Griffin |
| 10. | Hickory, N.C. | May. 16 | Tim Flock | Ted Chester |
| 11. | Martinsville, Va. | May. 17 | Lee Petty | Petty Enterprises |
| 12. | Columbus, Ohio | May. 24 | Herb Thomas | Herb Thomas |
| 13. | Raleigh, N.C. | May. 30 | Fonty Flock | Frank Christian |
| 14. | Shreveport, La. | Jun. 7 | Lee Petty | Petty Enterprises |
| 15. | Pensacola, Fla. | Jun. 14 | Herb Thomas | Herb Thomas |
| 16. | Langhorne, Pa. | Jun. 21 | Dick Rathmann | Walt Chapman |
| 17. | High Point, N.C. | Jun. 26 | Herb Thomas | Herb Thomas |
| 18. | Wilson, N.C. | Jun. 28 | Fonty Flock | Frank Christian |
| 19. | Rochester, N.Y. | Jul. 3 | Herb Thomas | Herb Thomas |
| 20. | Spartanburg, S.C. | Jul. 4 | Lee Petty | Petty Enterprises |
| 21. | Morristown, N.J. | Jul. 10 | Dick Rathmann | Walt Chapman |
| 22. | Atlanta, Ga. | Jul. 12 | Herb Thomas | Herb Thomas |
| 23. | Rapid City, S.D. | Jul. 22 | Herb Thomas | Herb Thomas |
| 24. | North Platte, Neb. | Jul. 26 | Dick Rathmann | Walt Chapman |
| 25. | Davenport, Iowa | Aug. 2 | Herb Thomas | Herb Thomas |
| 26. | Hillsboro, N.C. | Aug. 9 | Curtis Turner | Frank Christian |
| 27. | Weaverville, N.C. | Aug. 16 | Fonty Flock | Frank Christian |
| 28. | Norfolk, Va. | Aug. 23 | Herb Thomas | Herb Thomas |
| 29. | Hickory, N.C. | Aug. 29 | Fonty Flock | Frank Christian |
| 30. | Darlington, S.C. | Sep. 7 | Buck Baker | Bobby Griffin |
| 31. | Macon, Ga. | Sep. 13 | Speedy Thompson | Buckshot Morris |
| 32. | Langhorne, Pa. | Sep. 20 | Dick Rathmann | Walt Chapman |
| 33. | Bloomsburg, Pa. | Oct. 3 | Herb Thomas | Herb Thomas |
| 34. | Wilson, N.C. | Oct. 4 | Herb Thomas | Herb Thomas |
| 35. | North Wilkesboro, N.C. | Oct. 11 | Speedy Thompson | Buckshot Morris |
| 36. | Martinsville, Va. | Oct. 13 | Jim Paschal | George Hutchens |
| 37. | Atlanta, Ga. | Nov. 1 | Buck Baker | Bobby Griffin |

## Points standings
1. Herb Thomas ........8,460.00
2. Lee Petty .............7,814.00
3. Dick Rathmann ......7,362.00
4. Buck Baker ...........6,713.00
5. Fonty Flock ...........6,174.00
6. Tim Flock .............5,011.00
7. Jim Paschal .........4,211.00
8. Joe Eubanks .........3,603.00
9. Jimmy Lewallen ....3,508.00
10. Curtis Turner .........3,373.00

## Race winners (11)
1. Herb Thomas ...................12
2. Dick Rathmann ................5
   Lee Petty .........................5
4. Fonty Flock .....................4
   Buck Baker ......................4
6. Speedy Thompson.............2
7. Curtis Turner ...................1
   Tim Flock .........................1
   Bill Blair ...........................1
   Dick Passwater .................1
   Jim Paschal .......................1

## Money won leaders
1. Herb Thomas............$24,300
2. Dick Rathmann .........19,205
3. Lee Petty ..................17,225
4. Fonty Flock ..............16,440
5. Buck Baker ..............16,220
6. Tim Flock...................7,365
7. Speedy Thompson ......6,150
8. Jim Paschal.................4,935
9. Joe Eubanks ...............4,725
10. Bill Blair......................3,970

## Pole winners (11)
1. Herb Thomas.....................11
2. Buck Baker ........................4
3. Fonty Flock ........................3
   Curtis Turner .......................3
   Tim Flock.............................3
6. Dick Rathmann ...................2
7. Slick Smith ........................1
   Lloyd Shaw ........................1
   Joe Eubanks ......................1
   Jim Paschal........................1
   Bob Pronger .......................1

# 1952 NASCAR WINSTON CUP SEASON

| Race No. | Location | Date | Winner | Car owner |
|---|---|---|---|---|
| 1. | West Palm Beach, Fla. | Jan. 20 | Tim Flock | Ted Chester |
| 2. | Daytona Beach, Fla. | Feb. 10 | Marshall Teague | Marshall Teague |
| 3. | Jacksonville, Fla. | Mar. 6 | Marshall Teague | Marshall Teague |
| 4. | North Wilkesboro, N.C. | Mar. 30 | Herb Thomas | Herb Thomas |
| 5. | Martinsville, Va. | Apr. 6 | Dick Rathmann | Walt Chapman |
| 6. | Columbia, S.C. | Apr. 12 | Buck Baker | B.A. Pless |
| 7. | Atlanta, Ga. | Apr. 20 | Bill Blair | George Hutchens |
| 8. | Macon, Ga. | Apr. 27 | Herb Thomas | Herb Thomas |
| 9. | Langhorne, Pa. | May. 4 | Dick Rathmann | Walt Chapman |
| 10. | Darlington, S.C. | May. 10 | Dick Rathmann | Walt Chapman |
| 11. | Dayton, Ohio | May. 18 | Dick Rathmann | Walt Chapman |
| 12. | Canfield, Ohio | May. 30 | Herb Thomas | Herb Thomas |
| 13. | Augusta, Ga. | Jun. 1 | Gober Sosebee | Sam Knox |
| 14. | Toledo, Ohio | Jun. 1 | Tim Flock | Ted Chester |
| 15. | Hillsboro, N.C. | Jun. 8 | Tim Flock | Ted Chester |
| 16. | Charlotte, N.C. | Jun. 15 | Herb Thomas | Herb Thomas |
| 17. | Detroit, Mich. | Jun. 29 | Tim Flock | Ted Chester |
| 18. | Niagara Falls, Ontario, Canada | Jul. 1 | Buddy Shuman | B.A. Pless |
| 19. | Oswego, N.Y. | Jul. 4 | Tim Flock | Ted Chester |
| 20. | Monroe, Mich. | Jul. 6 | Tim Flock | Ted Chester |
| 21. | Morristown, N.J. | Jul. 11 | Lee Petty | Petty Enterprises |
| 22. | South Bend, Ind. | Jul. 20 | Tim Flock | Ted Chester |
| 23. | Rochester, N.Y. | Aug. 15 | Tim Flock | Ted Chester |
| 24. | Weaverville, N.C. | Aug. 17 | Bob Flock | Ted Chester |
| 25. | Darlington, S.C. | Sep. 1 | Fonty Flock | Frank Christian |
| 26. | Macon, Ga. | Sep. 7 | Lee Petty | Petty Enterprises |
| 27. | Langhorne, Pa. | Sep. 14 | Lee Petty | Petty Enterprises |
| 28. | Dayton, Ohio | Sep. 21 | Dick Rathmann | Walt Chapman |
| 29. | Wilson, N.C. | Sep. 28 | Herb Thomas | Herb Thomas |
| 30. | Hillsboro, N.C. | Oct. 12 | Fonty Flock | Frank Christian |
| 31. | Martinsville, Va. | Oct. 19 | Herb Thomas | Herb Thomas |
| 32. | North Wilkesboro, N.C. | Oct. 26 | Herb Thomas | Herb Thomas |
| 33. | Atlanta, Ga. | Nov. 16 | Donald Thomas | Herb Thomas |
| 34. | West Palm Beach, Fla. | Nov. 30 | Herb Thomas | Herb Thomas |

## Points standings
1. Tim Flock .............. 6,858.50
2. Herb Thomas ........ 6,752.50
3. Lee Petty ............... 6,498.50
4. Fonty Flock ........... 5,183.50
5. Dick Rathmann ..... 3,952.50
6. Bill Blair ................. 3,499.00
7. Joe Eubanks ......... 3,090.50
8. Ray Duhigg ........... 2,986.50
9. Donald Thomas .... 2,574.00
10. Buddy Shuman .... 2,483.50

## Race winners (12)
1. Tim Flock ........................ 8
   Herb Thomas .................. 8
3. Dick Rathmann ............... 5
4. Lee Petty ........................ 3
5. Marshall Teague ............. 2
   Fonty Flock ..................... 2
7. Donald Thomas ............... 1
   Buck Baker ..................... 1
   Gober Sosebee ............... 1
   Bob Flock ........................ 1
   Bill Blair .......................... 1
   Buddy Shuman ............... 1

## Money won leaders
1. Tim Flock ............... $20,210
2. Fonty Flock ............. 18,040
3. Herb Thomas .......... 17,625
4. Lee Petty ................ 15,670
5. Dick Rathmann ...... 10,309
6. Bill Blair ................... 7,095
7. Buddy Shuman ........ 4,210
8. Donald Thomas ....... 4,075
9. Johnny Patterson .... 3,350
10. Ray Duhigg ............ 3,275

## Pole winners (12)
1. Herb Thomas ................ 10
2. Fonty Flock .................... 7
3. Tim Flock ....................... 4
4. Buck Baker .................... 2
   Dick Rathmann .............. 2
6. Jack Smith ..................... 1
   Donald Thomas .............. 1
   Marshall Teague ............. 1
   Perk Brown .................... 1
   Bill Blair .......................... 1
   Tommy Moon .................. 1
   Pat Kirkwood .................. 1

# 1951 NASCAR WINSTON CUP SEASON

| Race No. | Location | Date | Winner | Car owner |
|---|---|---|---|---|
| 1. | Daytona Beach, Fla. | Feb. 11 | Marshall Teague | Marshall Teague |
| 2. | Charlotte, N.C. | Apr. 1 | Curtis Turner | Nash Motor Company |
| 3. | Mobile, Ala. | Apr. 8 | Tim Flock | Ted Chester |
| 4. | Gardena, Calif. | Apr. 8 | Marshall Teague | Marshall Teague |
| 5. | Hillsboro, N.C. | Apr. 15 | Fonty Flock | Frank Christian |
| 6. | Phoenix, Ariz. | Apr. 22 | Marshall Teague | Marshall Teague |
| 7. | North Wilkesboro, N.C. | Apr. 29 | Fonty Flock | Frank Christian |
| 8. | Martinsville, Va. | May 6 | Curtis Turner | John Eanes |
| 9. | Canfield, Ohio | May 30 | Marshall Teague | Marshall Teague |
| 10. | Columbus, Ga. | Jun. 10 | Tim Flock | Ted Chester |
| 11. | Columbia, S.C. | Jun. 16 | Frank Mundy | Perry Smith |
| 12. | Dayton, Ohio | Jun. 24 | Curtis Turner | John Eanes |
| 13. | Gardena, Calif. | Jun. 30 | Lou Figaro | Jack Gaynor |
| 14. | Grand Rapids, Mich. | Jul. 1 | Marshall Teague | Marshall Teague |
| 15. | Bainbridge, Ohio | Jul. 8 | Fonty Flock | Frank Christian |
| 16. | Carnegie, Pa. | Jul. 15 | Herb Thomas | Hubert Westmoreland |
| 17. | Weaverville, N.C. | Jul. 29 | Fonty Flock | Frank Christian |
| 18. | Rochester, N.Y. | Jul. 31 | Lee Petty | Petty Enterprises |
| 19. | Altamont, N.Y. | Aug. 1 | Fonty Flock | Frank Christian |
| 20. | Detroit, Mich. | Aug. 12 | Tommy Thompson | Tommy Thompson |
| 21. | Toledo, Ohio | Aug. 19 | Tim Flock | Ted Chester |
| 22. | Morristown, N.J. | Aug. 24 | Tim Flock | Ted Chester |
| 23. | Greenville, S.C. | Aug. 25 | Bob Flock | Ted Chester |
| 24. | Darlington, S.C. | Sep. 3 | Herb Thomas | Herb Thomas |
| 25. | Columbia, S.C. | Sep. 7 | Tim Flock | Ted Chester |
| 26. | Macon, Ga. | Sep. 8 | Herb Thomas | Herb Thomas |
| 27. | Langhorne, Pa. | Sep. 15 | Herb Thomas | Herb Thomas |
| 28. | Charlotte, N.C. | Sep. 23 | Herb Thomas | Herb Thomas |
| 29. | Dayton, Ohio | Sep. 23 | Fonty Flock | Frank Christian |
| 30. | Wilson, N.C. | Sep. 30 | Fonty Flock | Frank Christian |
| 31. | Hillsboro, N.C. | Oct. 7 | Herb Thomas | Herb Thomas |
| 32. | Thompson, Conn. | Oct. 12 | Neil Cole | John Golabek |
| 33. | Shippenville, Pa. | Oct. 14 | Tim Flock | Ted Chester |
| 34. | Martinsville, Va. | Oct. 14 | Frank Mundy | Ted Chester |
| 35. | Oakland, Calif. | Oct. 14 | Marvin Burke | Bob Phillippi |
| 36. | North Wilkesboro, N.C. | Oct. 21 | Fonty Flock | Ted Chester |
| 37. | Hanford, Calif. | Oct. 28 | Danny Weinberg | Tony Sampo |
| 38. | Jacksonville, Fla. | Nov. 4 | Herb Thomas | Marshall Teague |
| 39. | Atlanta, Ga. | Nov. 11 | Tim Flock | Ted Chester |
| 40. | Gardena, Calif. | Nov. 11 | Bill Norton | Larry Bettinger |
| 41. | Mobile, Ala. | Nov. 25 | Frank Mundy | Perry Smith |

## Points standings
1. Herb Thomas ........4,208.45
2. Fonty Flock ...........4,062.25
3. Tim Flock .............3,722.50
4. Lee Petty...............2,392.25
5. Frank Mundy..........1,963.50
6. Buddy Shuman ......1,368.75
7. Jesse James Taylor 1,214.00
8. Dick Rathmann ......1,040.00
9. Bill Snowden..........1,009.25
10. Joe Eubanks .........1,005.50

## Race winners (14)
1. Fonty Flock .......................8
2. Tim Flock ..........................7
   Herb Thomas ....................7
4. Marshall Teague................5
5. Curtis Turner ....................3
   Frank Mundy ....................3
7. Tommy Thompson............1
   Neil Cole ...........................1
   Danny Weinberg ...............1
   Marvin Burke .....................1
   Bill Norton .........................1
   Bob Flock..........................1
   Lou Figaro .........................1
   Lee Petty ...........................1

## Money won leaders
1. Herb Thomas...........$19,425
2. Fonty Flock ...............14,770
3. Tim Flock..................14,670
4. Lee Petty ....................7,250
5. Frank Mundy ..............6,470
6. Tommy Thompson .....5,225
7. Bob Flock ...................3,375
8. Jesse James Taylor ......3,175
9. Dick Rathmann ...........3,105
10. Joe Eubanks ..............3,085

## Pole winners (12)
1. Fonty Flock ......................12
2. Tim Flock ..........................6
3. Frank Mundy .....................4
   Herb Thomas......................4
5. Billy Carden .......................2
6. Gober Sosebee .................1
   Marshall Teague ................1
   Neil Cole ............................1
   Bill Rexford ........................1
   Bob Flock ..........................1
   Lou Figaro ..........................1
   Andy Pierce .......................1

## 1950 NASCAR WINSTON CUP SEASON

| Race No. | Location | Date | Winner | Car owner |
|---|---|---|---|---|
| 1. | Daytona Beach, Fla. | Feb. 5 | Harold Kite | Harold Kite |
| 2. | Charlotte, N.C. | Apr. 2 | Tim Flock | Harold Kite |
| 3. | Langhorne, Pa. | Apr. 16 | Curtis Turner | John Eanes |
| 4. | Martinsville, Va. | May. 21 | Curtis Turner | John Eanes |
| 5. | Canfield, Ohio | May. 30 | Bill Rexford | Julian Buesink |
| 6. | Vernon, N.Y. | Jun. 18 | Bill Blair | Sam Rice |
| 7. | Dayton, Ohio | Jun. 25 | Jimmy Florian | Jimmy Florian |
| 8. | Rochester, N.Y. | Jul. 2 | Curtis Turner | John Eanes |
| 9. | Charlotte, N.C. | Jul. 23 | Curtis Turner | John Eanes |
| 10. | Hillsboro, N.C. | Aug. 13 | Fireball Roberts | Sam Rice |
| 11. | Dayton, Ohio | Aug. 20 | Dick Linder | Don Rogalla |
| 12. | Hamburg, N.Y. | Aug. 27 | Dick Linder | Don Rogalla |
| 13. | Darlington, S.C. | Sep. 4 | Johnny Mantz | Westmoreland/France Sr. |
| 14. | Langhorne, Pa. | Sep. 17 | Fonty Flock | Frank Christian |
| 15. | North Wilkesboro, N.C. | Sep. 24 | Leon Sales | Hubert Westmoreland |
| 16. | Vernon, N.Y. | Oct. 1 | Dick Linder | Don Rogalla |
| 17. | Martinsville, Va. | Oct. 15 | Herb Thomas | Herb Thomas |
| 18. | Winchester, Ind. | Oct. 15 | Lloyd Moore | Julian Buesink |
| 19. | Hillsboro, N.C. | Oct. 29 | Lee Petty | Petty Enterprises |

**Points standings**
1. Bill Rexford ............ 1,959.00
2. Fireball Roberts ...... 1,848.50
3. Lee Petty ............... 1,590.00
4. Lloyd Moore ........... 1,398.00
5. Curtis Turner ......... 1,375.50
6. Johnny Mantz ........ 1,282.00
7. Chuck Mahoney ..... 1,217.50
8. Dick Linder ............ 1,121.00
9. Jimmy Florian ........... 801.00
10. Bill Blair ................... 766.00

**Race winners (14)**
1. Curtis Turner ................. 4
2. Dick Linder .................... 3
3. Bill Rexford .................... 1
   Lee Petty ........................ 1
   Herb Thomas ................. 1
   Leon Sales ..................... 1
   Fireball Roberts ............. 1
   Lloyd Moore ................... 1
   Fonty Flock .................... 1
   Tim Flock ....................... 1
   Bill Blair ......................... 1
   Johnny Mantz ................ 1
   Harold Kite .................... 1
   Jimmy Florian ................ 1

**Money won leaders**
1. Johnny Mantz ........ $10,560
2. Curtis Turner ............ 7,195
3. Fireball Roberts ......... 6,475
4. Lee Petty .................. 6,375
5. Dick Linder ............... 5,450
6. Lloyd Moore .............. 5,300
7. Bill Rexford ............... 5,175
8. Bill Blair .................... 4,200
9. Tim Flock .................. 3,975
10. Herb Thomas ........... 2,825

**Pole winners (11)**
1. Dick Linder .................... 5
2. Curtis Turner ................. 4
3. Fonty Flock .................... 2
4. Joe Littlejohn ................. 1
   Fireball Roberts ............. 1
   Chuck Mahoney ............. 1
   Red Byron ...................... 1
   Buck Baker ..................... 1
   Wally Campbell .............. 1
   Jimmy Florian ................ 1
   Tim Flock ....................... 1

## 1949 NASCAR WINSTON CUP SEASON

| Race No. | Location | Date | Winner | Car owner |
|---|---|---|---|---|
| 1. | Charlotte, N.C. | Jun. 19 | Jim Roper | R.B. McIntosh |
| 2. | Daytona Beach, Fla. | Jul. 10 | Red Byron | Raymond Parks |
| 3. | Hillsboro, N.C. | Aug. 7 | Bob Flock | Frank Christian |
| 4. | Langhorne, Pa. | Sep. 11 | Curtis Turner | Hubert Westmoreland |
| 5. | Hamburg, N.Y. | Sep. 18 | Jack White | Dailey Moyer |
| 6. | Martinsville, Va. | Sep. 25 | Red Byron | Raymond Parks |
| 7. | Carnegie, Pa. | Oct. 2 | Lee Petty | Petty Enterprises |
| 8. | North Wilkesboro, N.C. | Oct. 16 | Bob Flock | Frank Christian |

**Points standings**
1. Red Byron ................ 842.50
2. Lee Petty .................. 725.00
3. Bob Flock ................. 704.00
4. Bill Blair ................... 567.50
5. Fonty Flock .............. 554.50
6. Curtis Turner ........... 430.00
7. Ray Erickson ............ 422.00
8. Tim Flock ................. 421.00
9. Glenn Dunnaway ..... 384.00
10. Frank Mundy ........... 370.00

**Race winners (6)**
1. Bob Flock ........................ 2
   Red Byron ....................... 2
3. Curtis Turner ................. 1
   Jack White ..................... 1
   Lee Petty ........................ 1
   Jim Roper ....................... 1

**Money won leaders**
1. Red Byron ............... $4,800
2. Bob Flock ................... 4,550
3. Lee Petty ................... 3,375
4. Curtis Turner ............. 2,475
5. Jim Roper .................. 2,050
6. Fonty Flock ................ 1,775
7. Jack White ................. 1,500
8. Tim Flock ................... 1,350
9. Gober Sosebee .......... 1,225
10. Frank Mundy ............ 1,000

**Pole winners (6)**
1. Red Byron ....................... 2
2. Curtis Turner ................. 1
   Ken Wagner .................... 1
   Gober Sosebee .............. 1
   Al Bonnell ....................... 1
   Bob Flock ........................ 1

HISTORY

# 1948 NASCAR WINSTON CUP SEASON

| Location | Date | Winner | Car owner |
|---|---|---|---|
| Daytona Beach, Fl. | Feb. 15 | Red Byron | Raymond Parks |
| Jacksonville, Fl. | Feb. 24 | Fonty Flock | H.B. Babb & Elmer Fields |
| Atlanta, Ga. | Mar. 27 | Fonty Flock | H.B. Babb & Elmer Fields |
| Macon, Ga. | Apr. 4 | Fonty Flock | H.B. Babb & Elmer Fields |
| Augusta, Ga. | Apr. 11 | Bob Flock | Raymond Parks |
| Jacksonville, Fl. | Apr. 18 | Skimp Hersey | Mac Richardson |
| Greensboro, N.C. | Apr. 18 | Fonty Flock | H.B. Babb & Elmer Fields |
| N. Wilkesboro, N.C. | Apr. 25 | Red Byron | Raymond Parks |
| Lexington, N.C. | May 2 | Red Byron | Raymond Parks |
| Wadesboro, N.C. | May 9 | Red Byron | Raymond Parks |
| Richmond, Va. | May 16 | Red Byron | Raymond Parks |
| Macon, Ga. | May 23 | Gober Sosebee | Gober Sosebee |
| Danville, Va. | May 23 | Bill Blair | Bill Blair |
| Dover, N.J. | May 23 | Johnny Rogers | N/A |
| Greensboro, N.C. | May 29 | Bob Flock | Raymond Parks |
| N. Wilkesboro, N.C. | May 30 | Marshall Teague | Marshall Teague |
| Jacksonville, Fl. | May 30 | Paul Pappy | N/A |
| Danville, Va. | June 4 | Bob Flock | Raymond Parks |
| Greensboro, N.C. | June 5 | Red Byron | Raymond Parks |
| Lexington, N.C. | June 6 | Bob Flock | Raymond Parks |
| Wadesboro, N.C. | June 13 | Fonty Flock | H.B. Babb & Elmer Fields |
| Birmingham, Al. | June 20 | Fonty Flock | H.B. Babb & Elmer Fields |
| Columbus, Ga. | June 20 | Bob Flock | Raymond Parks |
| Greensboro, N.C. | June 20 | Tim Flock | Charlie Mobley |
| Occoneechee, N.C. | June 27 | Fonty Flock | H. B. Babb & Elmer Fields |
| Martinsville, Va. | July 4 | Fonty Flock | H B. Babb & Elmer Fields |
| Charlotte, N.C. | July 11 | Red Byron | Raymond Parks |
| N. Wilkesboro, N.C. | July 18 | Curtis Turner | Bob Smith |
| Greensboro, N.C. | July 25 | Curtis Turner | Bob Smith |
| Columbus, Ga. | July 25 | Billy Carden | N/A |
| Lexington, N.C. | Aug. 1 | Curtis Turner | Bob Smith |
| Daytona Beach, Fl. | Aug. 8 | Fonty Flock | H.B. Babb & Elmer Fields |
| Langhorne, Pa. | Aug. 15 | Al Keller | N/A |
| Columbus, Ga. | Sept. 5 | Gober Sosebee | Gober Sosebee |
| N. Wilkesboro, N.C. (1) | Sept. 5 | Curtis Turner | Bob Smith |
| N. Wilkesboro, N.C. (2) | Sept. 5 | Curtis Turner | Bob Smith |
| Charlotte, N.C. (1) | Sept. 12 | Curtis Turner | Bob Smith |
| Charlotte, N.C. (2) | Sept. 12 | Buddy Shuman | Shuman-Thompson |
| Occoneechee, N.C. (1) | Sept. 19 | Fonty Flock | H.B. Babb & Elmer Fields |
| Occoneechee, N.C. (2) | Sept. 19 | Fonty Flock | H.B. Babb & Elmer Fields |
| Lexington, N.C. (1) | Sept. 26 | Fonty Flock | H.B. Babb & Elmer Fields |
| Lexington, N.C. (2) | Sept. 26 | Gober Sosebee | Gober Sosebee |
| Elkin, N.C. (1) | Oct. 3 | Buddy Shuman | Shuman-Thompson |
| Elkin, N.C. (2) | Oct. 3 | Curtis Turner | Bob Smith |
| Macon, Ga. (1) | Oct. 3 | Billy Carden | N/A |
| Macon, Ga. (2) | Oct. 3 | Red Byron | Raymond Parks |
| Greensboro, N.C. | Oct. 10 | Fonty Flock | Joe Wolf |
| Greensboro, N.C. | Oct. 16 | Fonty Flock | Joe Wolf |
| N. Wilkesboro, N.C. | Oct. 17 | Red Byron | Raymond Parks |
| Charlotte, N.C. | Oct. 24 | Red Byron | Raymond Parks |
| Winston-Salem, N.C. | Oct. 31 | Fonty Flock | Joe Wolf |
| Columbus, Ga. | Nov. 14 | Red Byron | Raymond Parks |

## Race winners (14)

1. Fonty Flock .......................... 15
2. Red Byron .......................... 11
3. Curtis Turner ....................... 7
4. Bob Flock ........................... 5
5. Gober Sosebee ..................... 3
6. Billy Carden ........................ 2
   Buddy Shuman ..................... 2
8. Bill Blair ............................ 1
   Tim Flock ........................... 1
   Skimp Hersey ...................... 1
   Al Keller ............................. 1
   Paul Pappy ......................... 1
   Johnny Rogers ..................... 1
   Marshall Teague ................... 1

## Points standings

1. Red Byron ........................... 2996.5
2. Fonty Flock ........................ 2963.75
3. Tim Flock ........................... 1759.5
4. Curtis Turner ...................... 1540.5
5. Buddy Shuman .................... 1350
6. Bill Blair ............................ 1188.5
7. Bob Flock ........................... 1181.5
8. Marshall Teague .................. 1134.25
9. Bill Snowden ....................... 1092.5
10. Buck Baker ........................ 952.5
11. Billy Carden ....................... 866.5
12. Johnny Grubb ..................... 733
13. Speedy Thompson ................ 623
14. Roscoe Thompson ................ 471
15. Jimmy Lewallen .................. 437
16. Al Keller ........................... 415
17. Jimmy Thompson ................. 386
18. Jack Smith ........................ 384.75
19. Pee Wee Martin .................. 354
20. Fred Mahon ....................... 353

## Money won

$1,250.00
$600.00
$400.00
$350.00
$300.00
$250.00
$200.00
$150.00
$150.00
$150.00
$150.00
$150.00
$150.00
$150.00
$100.00
$100.00
$100.00
$100.00
$100.00
$100.00

# All-time race winners

| # | | Driver | Wins | # | | Driver | Wins | # | | Driver | Wins | # | | Driver | Wins |
|---|---|---|---|---|---|---|---|---|---|---|---|---|---|---|---|
| 1. | * | Richard Petty | 200 | 43. | # | Dick Rathmann | 13 | | # | Dick Linder | 3 | | * | Lloyd Moore | 1 |
| 2. | * | David Pearson | 105 | | # | Tim Richmond | 13 | | # | Tiny Lund | 3 | | * | Norm Nelson | 1 |
| 3. | * | Bobby Allison | 84 | 45. | | Sterling Marlin | 10 | | # | Bill Blair | 3 | | * | Bill Norton | 1 |
| | * | Darrell Waltrip | 84 | | * | Donnie Allison | 10 | 88. | | Jimmy Spencer | 2 | | * | Dick Passwater | 1 |
| 5. | * | Cale Yarborough | 83 | 47. | | Dale Earnhardt Jr. | 9 | | | Steve Park | 2 | | * | Lennie Pond | 1 |
| 6. | # | Dale Earnhardt | 76 | | | Ryan Newman | 9 | | | John Andretti | 2 | | * | Jody Ridley | 1 |
| 7. | | Jeff Gordon | 64 | | * | Paul Goldsmith | 9 | | | Derrike Cope | 2 | | * | Earl Ross | 1 |
| 8. | # | Lee Petty | 55 | | * | Cotton Owens | 9 | | | Ricky Craven | 2 | | * | John Rostek | 1 |
| 9. | | Rusty Wallace | 54 | 51. | | Kyle Petty | 8 | | * | Tom Pistone | 2 | | * | Johnny Rutherford | 1 |
| 10. | * | Ned Jarrett | 50 | | | Kurt Busch | 8 | | * | Danny Letner | 2 | | * | Leon Sales | 1 |
| | * | Junior Johnson | 50 | 53. | | Matt Kenseth | 7 | | * | Emanuel Zervakis | 2 | | * | Frankie Schneider | 1 |
| 12. | # | Herb Thomas | 48 | | * | A.J. Foyt | 7 | | * | Ray Elder | 2 | | * | John Soares Jr. | 1 |
| 13. | # | Buck Baker | 46 | | * | Jim Reed | 7 | | * | James Hylton | 2 | | * | Chuck Stevenson | 1 |
| 14. | | Bill Elliott | 44 | | # | Marshall Teague | 7 | | * | Bobby Johns | 2 | | * | Tommy Thompson | 1 |
| 15. | # | Tim Flock | 40 | | # | Bob Welborn | 7 | | # | Marvin Porter | 2 | | * | Art Watts | 1 |
| 16. | * | Bobby Isaac | 37 | | # | Darel Dieringer | 7 | | * | Jimmy Pardue | 2 | | * | Danny Weinberg | 1 |
| 17. | | Mark Martin | 33 | 59. | # | Jimmie Johnson | 6 | | | Gober Sosebee | 2 | | * | Jack White | 1 |
| 18. | #† | Fireball Roberts | 32 | 60. | | Ward Burton | 5 | | # | Gwyn Staley | 2 | | * | Mario Andretti | 1 |
| 19. | | Dale Jarrett | 31 | | * | Dave Marcis | 5 | | # | Red Byron | 2 | | * | Earl Balmer | 1 |
| 20. | *† | Rex White | 26 | | * | Ralph Moody | 5 | | # | Johnny Beauchamp | 2 | | * | Ron Bouchard | 1 |
| | * | Fred Lorenzen | 26 | | * | Dan Gurney | 5 | | * | Al Keller | 2 | | * | Johnny Allen | 1 |
| 22. | * | Jim Paschal | 25 | | # | Alan Kulwicki | 5 | | * | Billy Myers | 2 | | * | Neil Cole | 1 |
| 23. | # | Joe Weatherly | 24 | 65. | | Ken Schrader | 4 | | # | Elmo Langley | 2 | | * | Bob Burdick | 1 |
| 24. | | Ricky Rudd | 23 | | | Bobby Hamilton | 4 | 108. | | Greg Sacks | 1 | | * | Richard Brickhouse | 1 |
| 25. | | Terry Labonte | 22 | | | Morgan Shepherd | 4 | | | Brett Bodine | 1 | | * | Marvin Burke | 1 |
| 26. | | Bobby Labonte | 21 | | | Kevin Harvick | 4 | | | Jerry Nadeau | 1 | | * | June Cleveland | 1 |
| | * | Benny Parsons | 21 | | | Michael Waltrip | 4 | | | Johnny Benson | 1 | | # | Bobby Courtwright | 1 |
| | # | Jack Smith | 21 | | * | Parnelli Jones | 4 | | | Jamie McMurray | 1 | | # | Mark Donohue | 1 |
| 29. | # | Speedy Thompson | 20 | | * | Glen Wood | 4 | | | Elliott Sadler | 1 | | # | Joe Eubanks | 1 |
| 30. | * | Buddy Baker | 19 | | * | Lloyd Dane | 4 | | | Greg Biffle | 1 | | # | Lou Figaro | 1 |
| | # | Fonty Flock | 19 | | * | Charlie Glotzbach | 4 | | * | Phil Parsons | 1 | | # | Jimmy Florian | 1 |
| | # | Davey Allison | 19 | | * | Pete Hamilton | 4 | | * | Bobby Hillin Jr. | 1 | | # | Jim Hurtubise | 1 |
| 33. | | Geoffrey Bodine | 18 | | * | Hershel McGriff | 4 | | | Lake Speed | 1 | | * | Harold Kite | 1 |
| | * | Harry Gant | 18 | | # | Bob Flock | 4 | | | Dick Brooks | 1 | | * | Johnny Mantz | 1 |
| | # | Neil Bonnett | 18 | | # | Eddie Gray | 4 | | | Jim Cook | 1 | | # | Bill Rexford | 1 |
| 36. | | Jeff Burton | 17 | | # | Billy Wade | 4 | | | Larry Frank | 1 | | # | Shorty Rollins | 1 |
| | | Tony Stewart | 17 | | # | Eddie Pagan | 4 | | | Danny Graves | 1 | | # | Jim Roper | 1 |
| | * | Marvin Panch | 17 | | | Nelson Stacy | 4 | | | Royce Hagerty | 1 | | # | Wendell Scott | 1 |
| | # | Curtis Turner | 17 | 81. | | Jeremy Mayfield | 3 | | * | Joe Lee Johnson | 1 | | # | Buddy Shuman | 1 |
| 40. | * | Ernie Irvan | 15 | | | Joe Nemechek III | 3 | | * | John Kieper | 1 | | # | Donald Thomas | 1 |
| 41. | * | Dick Hutcherson | 14 | | | Robby Gordon | 3 | | * | Paul Lewis | 1 | | # | Bill Amick | 1 |
| | # | Lee Roy Yarbrough | 14 | | * | Frank Mundy | 3 | | | Sam McQuagg | 1 | | | | |

**167 DRIVERS**     **2,022**

* Retired
# Deceased
** 1,998 races; 6 wins by Convertible Division, 3 by Grand American Division, 3 by Short Track Division in combined races
† Rex White & Fireball Roberts had two convertible wins not included in total above..

# NMPA Driver of the Year

| Year | Drivers | Year | Drivers | Year | Drivers | Year | Drivers |
|---|---|---|---|---|---|---|---|
| 1969 | Lee Roy Yarbrouch | 1978 | Cale Yarborough | 1987 | Dale Earnhardt | 1996 | Terry Labonte |
| 1970 | Bobby Isaac | 1979 | Richard Petty | 1988 | Rusty Wallace | 1997 | Dale Jarrett |
| 1971 | Bobby Allison | 1980 | Dale Earnhardt | 1989 | Mark Martin | 1998 | Jeff Gordon |
| 1972 | Bobby Allison | 1981 | Darrell Waltrip | 1990 | Dale Earnhardt | 1999 | Dale Jarrett |
| 1973 | David Pearson | 1982 | Darrell Waltrip | 1991 | Harry Gant | 2000 | Bobby Labonte |
| 1974 | Richard Petty | 1983 | Bobby Allison | 1992 | Davey Allison | 2001 | Kevin Harvick |
| 1975 | Richard Petty | 1984 | Terry Labonte | 1993 | Rusty Wallace | 2002 | Tony Stewart |
| 1976 | Cale Yarborough | 1985 | Bill Elliott | 1994 | Dale Earnhardt | 2003 | To be announced |
| 1977 | Darrell Waltrip | 1986 | Dale Earnhardt & Tim Richmond | 1995 | Jeff Gordon | | |

# Superspeedway race winners

## (1950–2003)

| Driver | Wins | Driver | Wins | Driver | Wins | Driver | Wins | Driver | Wins | Driver | Wins |
|---|---|---|---|---|---|---|---|---|---|---|---|
| 1. Richard Petty | 55 | Fred Lorenzen | 12 | Ward Burton | 5 | Morgan Shepherd | 3 | Darel Dieringer | 1 | Jack Smith | 1 |
| 2. David Pearson | 49 | Benny Parsons | 12 | Matt Kenseth | 6 | Bobby Isaac | 3 | Larry Frank | 1 | Mario Andretti | 1 |
| 3. Dale Earnhardt | 48 | 21. L. Yarbrough | 11 | 39. Ken Schrader | 4 | 57. Derrike Cope | 2 | Jim Hurtubise | 1 | T. Thompson | 1 |
| 4. C. Yarborough | 47 | Fireball Roberts | 11 | Buck Baker | 4 | Jimmy Spencer | 2 | Dick Hutcherson | 1 | Rex White | 1 |
| Bobby Allison | 47 | 23. Terry Labonte | 11 | Marvin Panch | 4 | Dave Marcis | 2 | James Hylton | 1 | Bob Burdick | 1 |
| 6. Jeff Gordon | 44 | Sterling Marlin | 10 | Michael Waltrip | 4 | Charlie Glotzbach | 2 | Bobby Johns | 1 | R. Brickhouse | 1 |
| 7. Bill Elliott | 40 | Tony Stewart | 10 | Kurt Busch | 4 | Ned Jarrett | 2 | Joe Lee Johnson | 1 | Lake Speed | 1 |
| 8. Darrell Waltrip | 32 | 25. Donnie Allison | 9 | Kevin Harvick | 4 | Jim Paschal | 2 | Tiny Lund | 1 | Ron Bouchard | 1 |
| 9. Dale Jarrett | 27 | 26. Ernie Irvan | 8 | 45. Bobby Hamilton | 3 | Lee Petty | 2 | Johnny Mantz | 1 | Greg Sacks | 1 |
| 10. Rusty Wallace | 24 | D. Earnhardt Jr. | 8 | Jeremy Mayfield | 3 | Curtis Turner | 2 | Hershel McGriff | 1 | Johnny Benson | 1 |
| 11. Mark Martin | 22 | Ryan Newman | 8 | Alan Kulwicki | 3 | Joe Nemechek III | 2 | Sam McQuagg | 1 | Jamie McMurray | 1 |
| 12. Bobby Labonte | 20 | 30. Geoff Bodine | 7 | Nelson Stacy | 3 | 66. John Andretti | 1 | Ralph Moody | 1 | Ricky Craven | 1 |
| 13. Buddy Baker | 17 | 31. Kyle Petty | 6 | S. Thompson | 3 | Phil Parsons | 1 | Eddie Pagan | 1 | Greg Biffle | 1 |
| 14. Jeff Burton | 15 | Tim Richmond | 6 | Joe Weatherly | 3 | Steve Park | 1 | Lennie Pond | 1 | | |
| Neil Bonnett | 15 | A.J. Foyt | 6 | Paul Goldsmith | 3 | Jerry Nadeau | 1 | Marvin Porter | 1 | **103 DRIVERS** | **\*\*819** |
| 16. Davey Allison | 14 | Jimmie Johnson | 6 | Fonty Flock | 3 | Robby Gordon | 1 | Dick Rathmann | 1 | \*\*1 win by Convertible | |
| 17. Harry Gant | 13 | 35. Junior Johnson | 5 | Tim Flock | 3 | Dick Brooks | 1 | Jim Reed | 1 | Division in a combined | |
| 18. Ricky Rudd | 12 | Herb Thomas | 5 | Pete Hamilton | 3 | Bobby Hillin Jr. | 1 | Jody Ridley | 1 | race. Total Races: 820 | |

# Short track winners

## (Through 2003)

| Driver | Wins | Driver | Wins | Driver | Wins | Driver | Wins | Driver | Wins | Driver | Wins |
|---|---|---|---|---|---|---|---|---|---|---|---|
| 1. Richard Petty | 139 | 23. Fred Lorenzen | 14 | Ernie Irvan | 4 | Jimmy Pardue | 2 | Jimmy Florian | 1 | Frankie Schneider | 1 |
| 2. David Pearson | 52 | 24. Dick Hutcherson | 13 | Ralph Moody | 4 | Tim Richmond | 2 | Danny Graves | 1 | Wendell Scott | 1 |
| Lee Petty | 52 | Jeff Gordon | 13 | Kurt Busch | 4 | Gober Sosebee | 2 | Royce Hagerty | 1 | Buddy Shuman | 1 |
| 4. Ned Jarrett | 48 | 26. Dick Rathmann | 12 | 48. Lloyd Dane | 3 | Gwyn Staley | 2 | Pete Hamilton | 1 | John Soares Jr. | 1 |
| 5. Darrell Waltrip | 47 | 27. Marvin Panch | 11 | Neil Bonnett | 3 | Billy Wade | 2 | James Hylton | 1 | Nelson Stacy | 1 |
| 6. Junior Johnson | 45 | 28. Terry Labonte | 9 | Eddie Gray | 3 | Emanuel Zervakis | 2 | Bobby Johns | 1 | Donald Thomas | 1 |
| 7. Herb Thomas | 43 | 29. Geoff Bodine | 8 | Dick Linder | 3 | Buddy Baker | 2 | Parnelli Jones | 1 | Art Watts | 1 |
| 8. Buck Baker | 41 | Cotton Owens | 8 | Hershel McGriff | 3 | J. Beauchamp | 2 | Al Keller | 1 | Danny Weinberg | 1 |
| 9. Bobby Isaac | 34 | Benny Parsons | 8 | Eddie Pagan | 3 | 75. Brett Bodine | 1 | John Kieper | 1 | Jack White | 1 |
| Tim Flock | 34 | 32. Mark Martin | 7 | L. Yarbrough | 3 | Bobby Hamilton | 1 | Paul Lewis | 1 | Bill Amick | 1 |
| 11. C. Yarborough | 33 | Bob Welborn | 7 | Dave Marcis | 3 | Kyle Petty | 1 | Lloyd Moore | 1 | John Rostek | 1 |
| 12. Bobby Allison | 31 | 34. Jim Reed | 6 | Frank Mundy | 3 | Dale Earnhardt Jr. | 1 | Norm Nelson | 1 | Leon Sales | 1 |
| 13. Dale Earnhardt | 27 | 35. Ricky Rudd | 5 | 57. Jeff Burton | 2 | Donnie Allison | 1 | Bill Norton | 1 | Marvin Burke | 1 |
| 14. Rex White | 25 | Darel Dieringer | 5 | Bill Elliott | 2 | Morgan Shepherd | 1 | Dick Passwater | 1 | Earl Balmer | 1 |
| 15. Rusty Wallace | 24 | Paul Goldsmith | 5 | Bill Blair | 2 | Johnny Allen | 1 | Marvin Porter | 1 | J. Rutherford | 1 |
| 16. Jim Paschal | 23 | Marshall Teague | 5 | Charlie Glotzbach | 2 | Red Byron | 1 | Bill Rexford | 1 | Matt Kenseth | 1 |
| 17. Joe Weatherly | 21 | Harry Gant | 5 | Tom Pistone | 2 | June Cleveland | 1 | Shorty Rollins | 1 | Bobby Labonte | 1 |
| 18. Jack Smith | 19 | Tony Stewart | 5 | Alan Kulwicki | 2 | Neil Cole | 1 | Jim Roper | 1 | Joe Nemechek | 1 |
| Fireball Roberts | 19 | 41. Dale Jarrett | 4 | Elmo Langley | 2 | Jim Cook | 1 | Earl Ross | 1 | Ryan Newman | 1 |
| 20. S. Thompson | 17 | Davey Allison | 4 | Danny Letner | 2 | B. Courtwright | 1 | Elliot Sadler | 1 | **129 DRIVERS** | **1,097** |
| 21. Fonty Flock | 16 | Bob Flock | 4 | Tiny Lund | 2 | Joe Eubanks | 1 | John Andretti | 1 | **TOTAL RACES** | **2,008** |
| 22. Curtis Turner | 15 | Glen Wood | 4 | Billy Myers | 2 | Lou Figaro | 1 | Ricky Craven | 1 | | |

# Road race winners

## (Through 2003)

| Driver | Wins | Driver | Wins | Driver | Wins | Driver | Wins | Driver | Wins | Driver | Wins |
|---|---|---|---|---|---|---|---|---|---|---|---|
| 1. Jeff Gordon | 7 | 9. Mark Martin | 4 | Fireball Roberts | 2 | Buck Baker | 1 | A.J. Foyt | 1 | Kyle Petty | 1 |
| 2. Rusty Wallace | 6 | David Pearson | 4 | Marshall Teague | 2 | Dale Earnhardt | 1 | Paul Goldsmith | 1 | Jack Smith | 1 |
| Richard Petty | 6 | 11. Geoff Bodine | 3 | Billy Wade | 2 | Davey Allison | 1 | Eddie Gray | 1 | Chuck Stevenson | 1 |
| Bobby Allison | 6 | Ernie Irvan | 3 | Ray Elder | 2 | Red Byron | 1 | Al Keller | 1 | Bill Blair | 1 |
| Ricky Rudd | 6 | Cale Yarborough | 3 | Parnelli Jones | 2 | Lloyd Dane | 1 | Harold Kite | 1 | | |
| 6. Darrell Waltrip | 5 | Tim Flock | 3 | Tony Stewart | 2 | Darel Dieringer | 1 | Cotton Owens | 1 | **44 DRIVERS** | **105** |
| Dan Gurney | 5 | 15. Terry Labonte | 2 | Robby Gordon | 2 | Mark Donohue | 1 | Benny Parsons | 1 | | |
| Tim Richmond | 5 | Marvin Panch | 2 | 24. Steve Park | 1 | Bill Elliott | 1 | Lee Petty | 1 | | |

# All-time pole winners

| # | Driver | Poles |
|---|---|---|
| 1. | Richard Petty | 126 |
| 2. | David Pearson | 113 |
| 3. | Cale Yarborough | 70 |
| 4. | Darrell Waltrip | 59 |
| 5. | Bobby Allison | 57 |
| 6. | Bill Elliott | 55 |
| 7. | Bobby Isaac | 51 |
| 8. | Junior Johnson | 47 |
| 9. | Jeff Gordon | 46 |
| 10. | Buck Baker | 44 |
| 11. | Mark Martin | 41 |
| 12. | Buddy Baker | 40 |
| 13. | Tim Flock | 39 |
|  | Herb Thomas | 39 |
| 15. | Geoff Bodine | 37 |
| 16. | Rusty Wallace | 36 |
| 17. | Fireball Roberts | 35 |
|  | Ned Jarrett | 35 |
|  | Rex White | 35 |
| 20. | Fonty Flock | 34 |
| 21. | Fred Lorenzen | 33 |
| 22. | Ricky Rudd | 28 |
| 23. | Terry Labonte | 27 |
| 24. | Bobby Labonte | 25 |
| 25. | Jack Smith | 24 |
|  | Alan Kulwicki | 24 |
| 27. | Ken Schrader | 23 |
| 28. | Dale Earnhardt | 22 |
|  | Ernie Irvan | 22 |
|  | Dick Hutcherson | 22 |
| 31. | Marvin Panch | 21 |
| 32. | Neil Bonnett | 20 |
|  | Benny Parsons | 20 |
| 34. | Joe Weatherly | 19 |
|  | Speedy Thompson | 19 |
| 36. | Lee Petty | 18 |
|  | Ryan Newman | 18 |
| 38. | Harry Gant | 17 |
|  | Curtis Turner | 17 |
|  | Donnie Allison | 17 |
| 41. | Dale Jarrett | 15 |
| 42. | Tim Richmond | 14 |
|  | Davey Allison | 14 |
|  | Dave Marcis | 14 |
| 45. | Dick Rathmann | 13 |
| 46. | Charlie Glotzbach | 12 |
|  | Jim Paschal | 12 |
| 48. | Sterling Marlin | 11 |
|  | Darel Dieringer | 11 |
|  | Lee Roy Yarbrough | 11 |
|  | Cotton Owens | 11 |
|  | Glen Wood | 11 |
| 53. | A.J. Foyt | 10 |
| 54. | Kyle Petty | 8 |
|  | Paul Goldsmith | 8 |
| 56. | Morgan Shepherd | 7 |
|  | Bob Welborn | 7 |
|  | Ward Burton | 7 |
|  | Tony Stewart | 7 |
|  | Jeremy Mayfield | 7 |
| 61. | Joe Nemechek III | 6 |
|  | Tiny Lund | 6 |
|  | Eddie Pagan | 6 |
|  | Dale Earnhardt Jr. | 6 |
|  | Ricky Craven | 6 |
|  | Bobby Hamilton | 6 |
|  | Jimmie Johnson | 6 |
| 68. | Ted Musgrave | 5 |
|  | Mike Skinner | 5 |
|  | Brett Bodine | 5 |
|  | Dick Linder | 5 |
|  | Hershel McGriff | 5 |
|  | Ralph Moody | 5 |
|  | Tom Pistone | 5 |
|  | Lennie Pond | 5 |
|  | Billy Wade | 5 |
|  | Art Watts | 5 |
|  | Bill Amick | 5 |
|  | Joe Eubanks | 5 |
|  | Todd Bodine | 5 |
| 81. | John Andretti | 4 |
|  | Rick Mast | 4 |
|  | James Hylton | 4 |
|  | Gober Sosebee | 4 |
|  | Jim Reed | 4 |
|  | Steve Park | 4 |
| 87. | Loy Allen Jr | 3 |
|  | Joe Ruttman | 3 |
|  | Ron Bouchard | 3 |
|  | Frank Mundy | 3 |
|  | Jimmy Pardue | 3 |
|  | Marshall Teague | 3 |
|  | Bob Flock | 3 |
|  | Johnny Allen | 3 |
|  | Pete Hamilton | 3 |
|  | Parnelli Jones | 3 |
|  | Banjo Matthews | 3 |
|  | Kenny Irwin Jr | 3 |
|  | Kenny Wallace | 3 |
|  | Matt Kenseth | 3 |
| 101. | Johnny Benson Jr | 2 |
|  | Michael Waltrip | 2 |
|  | Jeff Burton | 2 |
|  | Dan Gurney | 2 |
|  | Friday Hassler | 2 |
|  | Tommy Irwin | 2 |
|  | Bobby Johns | 2 |
|  | John Kieper | 2 |
|  | Mel Larson | 2 |
|  | Ken Rush | 2 |
|  | John Sears | 2 |
|  | Billy Carden | 2 |
|  | Stacy Compton | 2 |
|  | Greg Sacks | 2 |
|  | Danny Graves | 2 |
|  | Doug Yates | 2 |
|  | Emanuel Zervakis | 2 |
|  | Gwyn Staley | 2 |
|  | Bob Burdick | 2 |
|  | Red Byron | 2 |
|  | Kurt Busch | 2 |
|  | Jeff Green | 2 |
|  | Kevin Harvick | 2 |
|  | Elliott Sadler | 2 |
| 125. | Jimmy Spencer | 1 |
|  | Robby Gordon | 1 |
|  | Jimmy Hensley | 1 |
|  | Hut Stricklin | 1 |
|  | Dick Trickle | 1 |
|  | Derrike Cope | 1 |
|  | Rick Wilson | 1 |
|  | David Green | 1 |
|  | Kevin Lepage | 1 |
|  | Wally Campbell | 1 |
|  | Neil Cole | 1 |
|  | Jim Cook | 1 |
|  | Bobby Courtwright | 1 |
|  | Doug Cox | 1 |
|  | Bill Dennis | 1 |
|  | Bob Duell | 1 |
|  | Glenn Dunaway | 1 |
|  | Ralph Earnhardt | 1 |
|  | Lou Figaro | 1 |
|  | Jimmy Florian | 1 |
|  | George Follmer | 1 |
|  | Eddie Gray | 1 |
|  | Royce Hagerty | 1 |
|  | Russ Hepler | 1 |
|  | Jim Hunter | 1 |
|  | Possum Jones | 1 |
|  | Al Keller | 1 |
|  | Pat Kirkwood | 1 |
|  | Elmo Langley | 1 |
|  | Danny Letner | 1 |
|  | Jimmie Lewallen | 1 |
|  | Paul Lewis | 1 |
|  | Joe Littlejohn | 1 |
|  | Chuck Mahoney | 1 |
|  | Jim Massey | 1 |
|  | J.D McDuffie | 1 |
|  | Joe Millikan | 1 |
|  | Tommy Moon | 1 |
|  | Paul "Bud" Moore | 1 |
|  | Billy Myers | 1 |
|  | Norm Nelson | 1 |
|  | Andy Pierce | 1 |
|  | Don Porter | 1 |
|  | Bob Pronger | 1 |
|  | Chuck Bown | 1 |
|  | Jason Leffler | 1 |
|  | Al Bonnell | 1 |
|  | Bob Ross | 1 |
|  | Slick Smith | 1 |
|  | Donald Thomas | 1 |
|  | John Rostek | 1 |
|  | Sam Sommers | 1 |
|  | Larry Baumel | 1 |
|  | Frankie Schneider | 1 |
|  | G.C. Spencer | 1 |
|  | Ken Wagner | 1 |
|  | Wendell Scott | 1 |
|  | Ramo Stott | 1 |
|  | Danny Weinberg | 1 |
|  | Frank Secrist | 1 |
|  | Dick Bailey | 1 |
|  | Bill Rexford | 1 |
|  | Lloyd Shaw | 1 |
|  | Lyle Tadlock | 1 |
|  | Perk Brown | 1 |
|  | Bill Benson | 1 |
|  | Dink Widenhouse | 1 |
|  | Bill Blair | 1 |
|  | Dave Blaney | 1 |
|  | Boris Said | 1 |
|  | Jamie McMurray | 1 |
|  | **195 DRIVERS** | ***1,980** |

*1,998 races; no time trials for 46 races; 5 poles by Convertible Division, 1 by Grand American Division, 2 by Short Track Division in combined races.

**HISTORY**

# Superspeedway pole winners

## (1950–2003)

| # | Driver | Wins |
|---|---|---|
| 1. | David Pearson | 58 |
| 2. | Bill Elliott | 48 |
| 3. | C. Yarborough | 46 |
| 4. | Buddy Baker | 29 |
|  | Jeff Gordon | 29 |
| 6. | Richard Petty | 23 |
|  | Bobby Labonte | 23 |
| 8. | Mark Martin | 22 |
|  | Ken Schrader | 22 |
| 10. | Geoff Bodine | 21 |
| 11. | Fireball Roberts | 20 |
| 12. | Rusty Wallace | 19 |
| 13. | Bobby Allison | 18 |
| 14. | Alan Kulwicki | 17 |
| 15. | Ryan Newman | 16 |
| 16. | Donnie Allison | 15 |
|  | Darrell Waltrip | 15 |
|  | Bobby Isaac | 15 |
| 19. | Fred Lorenzen | 14 |
|  | Dale Jarrett | 14 |
| 21. | Terry Labonte | 13 |
|  | Ernie Irvan | 13 |
| 23. | Ricky Rudd | 12 |
|  | Dale Earnhardt | 12 |
|  | Harry Gant | 12 |
|  | Davey Allison | 12 |
| 27. | Sterling Marlin | 11 |
|  | C. Glotzbach | 11 |
|  | Neil Bonnett | 11 |
| 30. | Benny Parsons | 10 |
| 31. | Dave Marcis | 9 |
|  | Tim Richmond | 9 |
| 33. | A.J. Foyt | 7 |
|  | Jeremy Mayfield | 7 |
| 35. | Kyle Petty | 6 |
|  | Marvin Panch | 6 |
|  | Junior Johnson | 6 |
|  | L. Yarborough | 6 |
|  | Dale Earnhardt Jr. | 6 |
| 40. | Ward Burton | 5 |
|  | Joe Nemechek | 5 |
|  | Fonty Flock | 5 |
|  | Rick Craven | 5 |
|  | Jimmie Johnson | 5 |
| 45. | John Andretti | 4 |
|  | Mike Skinner | 4 |
|  | Rick Mast | 4 |
|  | Darel Dieringer | 4 |
|  | Herb Thomas | 4 |
| 50. | Bobby Hamilton | 3 |
|  | John Andretti | 3 |
|  | Cotton Owens | 3 |
|  | Curtis Turner | 3 |
|  | Buck Baker | 3 |
|  | Loy Allen Jr. | 3 |
|  | Kenny Irwin Jr. | 3 |
|  | Pete Hamilton | 3 |
|  | Todd Bodine | 3 |
|  | Tony Stewart | 3 |
|  | Steve Park | 3 |
| 61. | J. Benson Jr. | 2 |
|  | Morgan Shepherd | 2 |
|  | Michael Waltrip | 2 |
|  | Greg Sacks | 2 |
|  | Ron Bouchard | 2 |
|  | Paul Goldsmith | 2 |
|  | Eddie Pagan | 2 |
|  | Banjo Matthews | 2 |
|  | Jimmy Spencer | 2 |
|  | Stacy Compton | 2 |
|  | Kurt Busch | 2 |
|  | Kevin Harvick | 2 |
|  | Elliott Sadler | 2 |
| 74. | Jeff Burton | 1 |
|  | Hut Stricklin | 1 |
|  | Dick Trickle | 1 |
|  | Joe Ruttman | 1 |
|  | Robby Gordon | 1 |
|  | Derrike Cope | 1 |
|  | Dick Hutcherson | 1 |
|  | Hershel McGriff | 1 |
|  | Frank Mundy | 1 |
|  | Jimmy Pardue | 1 |
|  | Lee Petty | 1 |
|  | Dick Rathmann | 1 |
|  | Bob Ross | 1 |
|  | Tim Flock | 1 |
|  | Frank Secrist | 1 |
|  | Jack Smith | 1 |
|  | Slick Smith | 1 |
|  | Sam Sommers | 1 |
|  | Ramo Stott | 1 |
|  | Marshall Teague | 1 |
|  | S. Thompson | 1 |
|  | Bob Welborn | 1 |
|  | Frankie Schneider | 1 |
|  | Friday Hassler | 1 |
|  | J.D. McDuffie | 1 |
|  | Kevin Lepage | 1 |
|  | David Green | 1 |
|  | Kenny Wallace | 1 |
|  | Jason Leffler | 1 |
|  | Casey Atwood | 1 |
|  | Matt Kenseth | 1 |
|  | Jamie McMurray | 1 |
|  | Jeff Green | 1 |
|  | Dave Blaney | 1 |

**107 DRIVERS   **801**

# Short track pole winners

## (Through 2003)

| # | Driver | Wins |
|---|---|---|
| 1. | Richard Petty | 97 |
| 2. | David Pearson | 47 |
| 3. | Junior Johnson | 40 |
| 4. | Buck Baker | 38 |
| 5. | Bobby Isaac | 36 |
| 6. | Darrell Waltrip | 35 |
|  | Ned Jarrett | 35 |
|  | Herb Thomas | 35 |
|  | Rex White | 35 |
|  | Tim Flock | 35 |
| 11. | Bobby Allison | 34 |
| 12. | Fonty Flock | 29 |
| 13. | C. Yarborough | 22 |
|  | Jack Smith | 22 |
| 15. | D. Hutcherson | 20 |
| 16. | Joe Weatherly | 19 |
| 17. | S. Thompson | 18 |
| 18. | Fred Lorenzen | 17 |
| 19. | Lee Petty | 16 |
| 20. | Mark Martin | 15 |
|  | Fireball Roberts | 15 |
| 22. | Rusty Wallace | 14 |
|  | Marvin Panch | 14 |
|  | Curtis Turner | 14 |
|  | Geoff Bodine | 14 |
| 26. | Jim Paschal | 12 |
|  | Dick Rathmann | 12 |
|  | Jeff Gordon | 12 |
| 29. | Buddy Baker | 11 |
|  | Glenn Wood | 11 |
| 31. | Ricky Rudd | 10 |
|  | Benny Parsons | 10 |
| 33. | Neil Bonnett | 9 |
| 34. | Ernie Irvan | 8 |
|  | Cotton Owens | 8 |
| 36. | Bill Elliott | 7 |
|  | Darrell Dieringer | 7 |
|  | Alan Kulwicki | 7 |
|  | Bob Welborn | 6 |
|  | Tiny Lund | 6 |
|  | Terry Labonte | 6 |
| 42. | Ted Musgrave | 5 |
|  | Dave Marcis | 5 |
|  | Harry Gant | 5 |
|  | Ralph Moody | 5 |
|  | Tom Pistone | 5 |
|  | Lennie Pond | 5 |
|  | Bill Amick | 5 |
|  | Joe Eubanks | 5 |
|  | Dick Linder | 5 |
|  | L. Yarborough | 5 |
|  | Dale Earnhardt | 5 |
| 53. | James Hylton | 4 |
|  | Hershel McGriff | 4 |
|  | Eddie Pagan | 4 |
|  | Billy Wade | 4 |
|  | Art Watts | 4 |
|  | M. Shepherd | 4 |
| 59. | Tony Stewart | 3 |
|  | Jim Reed | 3 |
|  | Tim Richmond | 3 |
|  | Bob Flock | 3 |
|  | Gober Sosebee | 3 |
|  | Paul Goldsmith | 3 |
|  | Johnny Allen | 3 |
| 66. | Bobby Labonte | 2 |
|  | Kyle Petty | 2 |
|  | Kenny Wallace | 2 |
|  | Bobby Hamilton | 2 |
|  | Joe Ruttman | 2 |
|  | Brett Bodine | 2 |
|  | Davey Allison | 2 |
|  | Donnie Allison | 2 |
|  | Tommy Irwin | 2 |
|  | Bobby Johns | 2 |
|  | John Sears | 2 |
|  | Frank Mundy | 2 |
|  | Bob Burdick | 2 |
|  | Mel Larson | 2 |
|  | Red Byron | 2 |
|  | Gwyn Staley | 2 |
|  | Marshall Teague | 2 |
|  | John Kieper | 2 |
|  | Jimmy Pardue | 2 |
|  | Billy Carden | 2 |
|  | Doug Yates | 2 |
|  | E. Zervakis | 2 |
|  | Ken Rush | 2 |
|  | Parnelli Jones | 2 |
|  | Ward Burton | 2 |
|  | Mike Skinner | 2 |
|  | Ryan Newman | 2 |
| 93. | Ricky Craven | 1 |
|  | Ken Schrader | 1 |
|  | Jimmy Spencer | 1 |
|  | Rick Wilson | 1 |
|  | Chuck Bown | 1 |
|  | Jimmy Hensley | 1 |
|  | Ron Bouchard | 1 |
|  | Jeff Burton | 1 |
|  | Steve Park | 1 |
|  | Bill Benson | 1 |
|  | Bill Blair | 1 |
|  | Al Bonnell | 1 |
|  | Perk Brown | 1 |
|  | Wally Campbell | 1 |
|  | Neil Cole | 1 |
|  | Jim Cook | 1 |
|  | B. Courtwright | 1 |
|  | Doug Cox | 1 |
|  | Bill Dennis | 1 |
|  | Bob Duell | 1 |
|  | Joe Nemechek | 1 |
|  | Jeff Green | 1 |
|  | Todd Bodine | 1 |
|  | A.J. Foyt | 1 |
|  | Charlie Glotzbach | 1 |
|  | Danny Graves | 1 |
|  | Royce Hagerty | 1 |
|  | Friday Hassler | 1 |
|  | Russ Hepler | 1 |
|  | Jim Hunter | 1 |
|  | Possum Jones | 1 |
|  | Al Keller | 1 |
|  | Elmo Langley | 1 |
|  | Danny Letner | 1 |
|  | Jimmie Lewallen | 1 |
|  | Paul Lewis | 1 |
|  | Chuck Mahoney | 1 |
|  | Jim Massey | 1 |
|  | Tommy Moon | 1 |
|  | Paul "Bud" Moore | 1 |
|  | Billy Myers | 1 |
|  | Norm Nelson | 1 |
|  | Andy Pierce | 1 |
|  | Don Porter | 1 |
|  | Bill Rexford | 1 |
|  | John Rostek | 1 |
|  | Wendell Scott | 1 |
|  | Lloyd Shaw | 1 |
|  | G.C. Spencer | 1 |
|  | Lyle Tadlock | 1 |
|  | Donald Thomas | 1 |
|  | Ken Wagner | 1 |
|  | Danny Weinberg | 1 |
|  | Dink Widenhouse | 1 |
|  | Glenn Dunaway | 1 |
|  | Ralph Earnhardt | 1 |
|  | Joe Millikan | 1 |
|  | Dick Bailey | 1 |
|  | Larry Baumel | 1 |
|  | Lou Figaro | 1 |
|  | Jimmy Florian | 1 |
|  | Jimmy Johnson | 1 |

**154 DRIVERS   1,080**
**TOTAL RACES   2,008**

# Road race pole winners

## (Through 2003)

| # | Driver | Wins |
|---|---|---|
| 1. | Darrell Waltrip | 9 |
| 2. | Terry Labonte | 8 |
|  | David Pearson | 8 |
| 4. | Richard Petty | 6 |
|  | Ricky Rudd | 6 |
| 6. | Dale Earnhardt | 5 |
|  | Bobby Allison | 5 |
|  | Jeff Gordon | 5 |
| 9. | Mark Martin | 4 |
| 10. | Rusty Wallace | 3 |
|  | Tim Flock | 3 |
|  | Paul Goldsmith | 3 |
|  | Buck Baker | 3 |
| 14. | Geoff Bodine | 2 |
|  | Fred Lorenzen | 2 |
|  | Tim Richmond | 2 |
|  | Cale Yarborough | 2 |
|  | Dan Gurney | 2 |
|  | A.J. Foyt | 2 |
| 20. | Todd Bodine | 1 |
|  | Dale Jarrett | 1 |
|  | Eddie Gray | 1 |
|  | Dick Hutcherson | 1 |
|  | Ernie Irvan | 1 |
|  | Junior Johnson | 1 |
|  | Parnelli Jones | 1 |
|  | Pat Kirkwood | 1 |
|  | Tony Stewart | 1 |
|  | Joe Littlejohn | 1 |
|  | Banjo Matthews | 1 |
|  | Marvin Panch | 1 |
|  | Lee Petty | 1 |
|  | Bob Pronger | 1 |
|  | Jim Reed | 1 |
|  | Morgan Shepherd | 1 |
|  | Jack Smith | 1 |
|  | Gober Sosebee | 1 |
|  | Billy Wade | 1 |
|  | Art Watts | 1 |
|  | George Follmer | 1 |
|  | Danny Graves | 1 |
|  | Boris Said | 1 |

**No time trials in 17 races; 1 pole by Convertible Division in a combined race. Total races: 819.

## Races won from the pole (1949-2003)

| | Driver | Wins | | Driver | Wins | | Driver | Wins | | Driver | Wins |
|---|---|---|---|---|---|---|---|---|---|---|---|
| 1. | Richard Petty | 61 | | Speedy Thompson | 7 | | Cotton Owens | 3 | | Art Watts | 1 |
| 2. | David Pearson | 37 | 21. | Jack Smith | 6 | | Ryan Newman | 3 | | Ralph Moody | 1 |
| 3. | Darrell Waltrip | 24 | | Marvin Panch | 6 | 41. | Dale Jarrett | 2 | | Norm Nelson | 1 |
| 4. | Bobby Isaac | 21 | | Joe Weatherly | 6 | | Harry Gant | 2 | | Danny Graves | 1 |
| 5. | Bobby Allison | 20 | | Fireball Roberts | 6 | | Jim Reed | 2 | | Parnelli Jones | 1 |
| 6. | Herb Thomas | 19 | 25. | Terry Labonte | 4 | | Paul Goldsmith | 2 | | Jim Cook | 1 |
| 7. | Cale Yarborough | 16 | | Bobby Labonte | 4 | | Eddie Pagan | 2 | | Lee Roy Yarbrough | 1 |
| | Tim Flock | 16 | | Tim Richmond | 4 | | Dick Linder | 2 | | Dan Gurney | 1 |
| 9. | Bill Elliott | 15 | | Curtis Turner | 4 | | Donnie Allison | 2 | | Dave Marcis | 1 |
| | Jeff Gordon | 15 | | Buddy Baker | 4 | | Charlie Glotzbach | 2 | | Neil Cole | 1 |
| 11. | Buck Baker | 12 | | Dick Hutcherson | 4 | | Bob Welborn | 2 | | Alan Kulwicki | 1 |
| | Junior Johnson | 12 | | Jim Paschal | 4 | | Davey Allison | 2 | | Lou Figaro | 1 |
| 13. | Ned Jarrett | 11 | 32. | Dale Earnhardt | 3 | | Darel Dieringer | 2 | | Marshall Teague | 1 |
| | Fred Lorenzen | 11 | | Kyle Petty | 3 | | Ernie Irvan | 2 | | Gwyn Staley | 1 |
| 15. | Rusty Wallace | 9 | | Glen Wood | 3 | 53. | Bobby Hamilton | 1 | | Donald Thomas | 1 |
| | Fonty Flock | 9 | | Billy Wade | 3 | | Tony Stewart | 1 | | Frank Mundy | 1 |
| 17. | Mark Martin | 7 | | Hershel McGriff | 3 | | Sterling Marlin | 1 | | Kurt Busch | 1 |
| | Rex White | 7 | | Geoff Bodine | 3 | | Ricky Rudd | 1 | | Kevin Harvick | 1 |
| | Lee Petty | 7 | | A.J. Foyt | 3 | | Benny Parsons | 1 | | **75 DRIVERS** | **460** |

## All-time money leaders (through 2003)

| Rank | | Driver | Career Starts | Career Winnings | Average Per Start |
|---|---|---|---|---|---|
| 1 | | Jeff Gordon | 365 | $58,525,057 | $160,342 |
| 2 | | Dale Jarrett | 531 | 41,818,270 | 78,753 |
| 3 | # | Dale Earnhardt | 676 | 41,742,384 | 61,749 |
| 4 | | Mark Martin | 566 | 40,656,775 | 71,831 |
| 5 | | Rusty Wallace | 634 | 38,689,400 | 61,024 |
| 6 | | Bill Elliott | 731 | 36,427,403 | 49,832 |
| 7 | | Bobby Labonte | 366 | 35,641,757 | 97,381 |
| 8 | | Terry Labonte | 781 | 34,064,557 | 43,616 |
| 9 | | Ricky Rudd | 803 | 32,215,451 | 40,118 |
| 10 | | Jeff Burton | 331 | 31,588,107 | 95,432 |
| 11 | | Sterling Marlin | 604 | 28,512,919 | 47,206 |
| 12 | | Tony Stewart | 176 | 27,069,354 | 153,803 |
| 13 | | Michael Waltrip | 570 | 22,945,465 | 40,255 |
| 14 | | Ken Schrader | 596 | 22,571,841 | 37,872 |
| 15 | | Ward Burton | 322 | 21,551,794 | 66,931 |
| 16 | | Dale Earnhardt Jr. | 147 | 20,742,359 | 141,104 |
| 17 | * | Darrell Waltrip | 809 | 19,416,618 | 24,000 |
| 18 | | Matt Kenseth | 148 | 19,096,585 | 129,030 |
| 19 | | Kyle Petty | 678 | 17,822,861 | 26,287 |
| 20 | | Jeremy Mayfield | 309 | 17,595,675 | 56,943 |
| 21 | | Jimmy Spencer | 439 | 17,449,974 | 39,479 |
| 22 | | John Andretti | 327 | 17,123,759 | 52,366 |
| 23 | | Johnny Benson | 264 | 16,204,439 | 61,380 |
| 24 | | Geoffrey Bodine | 565 | 16,131,920 | 28,552 |
| 25 | | Bobby Hamilton | 368 | 15,187,015 | 41,269 |
| 26 | | Joe Nemechek | 322 | 14,982,115 | 46,528 |
| 27 | | Kevin Harvick | 106 | 14,388,537 | 135,740 |
| 28 | | Brett Bodine | 480 | 13,575,991 | 28,283 |
| 29 | | Elliott Sadler | 177 | 13,184,295 | 74,487 |
| 30 | | Kurt Busch | 114 | 13,183,351 | 115,643 |
| 31 | | Mike Skinner | 229 | 13,032,500 | 56,910 |
| 32 | | Ricky Craven | 252 | 12,871,864 | 51,078 |
| 33 | | Steve Park | 181 | 12,477,058 | 68,934 |
| 34 | | Ryan Newman | 80 | 11,950,629 | 149,382 |
| 35 | | Kenny Wallace | 300 | 11,763,969 | 39,213 |
| 36 | | Jimmie Johnson | 75 | 11,656,118 | 155,414 |
| 37 | * | Ernie Irvan | 313 | 11,625,817 | 37,143 |
| 38 | | Robby Gordon | 134 | 10,226,462 | 76,316 |
| 39 | | Rick Mast | 364 | 9,229,910 | 25,356 |
| 40 | | Jerry Nadeau | 177 | 9,634,007 | 54,429 |

Note: Career winnings include race winnings, postseason awards, non-points race winnings and special bonuses.
*Retired.
#Deceased.

# Driver records (1949-2003)

### ALL RACES

Most wins, career – 200, Richard Petty (1958-92).
Most wins, season – 27, Richard Petty (1967).
Most consecutive wins – 10, Richard Petty (1967).
Most wins from pole, career – 61, Richard Petty (1958-92).
Most wins from pole, season – 15, Richard Petty (1967).
Oldest driver to win a race – Harry Gant, 52 years, 219 days (Aug. 16, 1992).
Youngest driver to win a race – Donald Thomas, 20 years, 129 days (Nov. 16, 1952).
Most consecutive races won from pole, Individual – 4, Richard Petty (1967) and Darrell Waltrip (1981).
Most years won at least one race from pole – 16, Richard Petty (1958-92).
Most consecutive wins at one track – 7, Richard Petty, Richmond Fairgrounds Raceway (1970-73) and Darrell Waltrip, Bristol International Raceway (1981-84).

### MODERN RECORDS (1972-2003) ALL RACES

Most wins – 84, Darrell Waltrip (1972-00).
Most wins, season – 13, Richard Petty (1975) and Jeff Gordon (1998).
Most consecutive wins – 4, Cale Yarborough (1976); Darrell Waltrip (1981); Dale Earnhardt (1987); Harry Gant (1991); Bill Elliott (1992); Mark Martin (1993); Jeff Gordon (1998).
Most wins from pole, career – 24, Darrell Waltrip (1972-00).
Most wins from pole, season – 8, Darrell Waltrip (1981).
Most consecutive races won from pole – 4, Darrell Waltrip (1981).
Most years won at least one race from pole – 9, Darrell Waltrip (1972-00).
Most consecutive years won at least one race from pole – 7, Darrell Waltrip (1978-84).
Most consecutive wins at one track – 7, Darrell Waltrip, Bristol Raceway (1981-84).
Most races, career – 1,177, Richard Petty, 1958-92.
Most years leading circuit in wins – 7, Richard Petty, 1958-92.
Most consecutive years leading circuit in wins – 5, Jeff Gordon, 1995-99
Best winning percentage, career – 21.2, Tim Flock (40 wins, 189 starts), 1949-1961.
Best winning percentage, season – 61.1, David Pearson (11 wins, 18 starts), 1973.
Most races started without a win – 653, J.D. McDuffie, 1963-91.

# All-time driver records—qualifying

### ALL RACES

Most poles, career – 126, Richard Petty (1958-92).
Most poles, season – 20, Bobby Isaac (1969).
Most consecutive poles – 5, Bobby Allison (1972); Cale Yarborough (1980); Bill Elliott (1985).
Most years won at least 1 pole – 23, David Pearson (1960-86).
Most consecutive years won at least 1 pole – 20, David Pearson (1963-82).
Most consecutive poles won at one track – 11, David Pearson (1973-78), Charlotte Motor Speedway.
Most poles at one track – 14, David Pearson, Charlotte Motor Speedway.

### MODERN QUALIFYING RECORDS (1972-2003) ALL RACES

Most poles, career – 59, Darrell Waltrip (1972-00).
Most poles, season – 14, Cale Yarborough (1980).
Most consecutive poles – 5, Bobby Allison (1972); Cale Yarborough (1980); Bill Elliott (1985).
Most years won at least one pole – 16, Darrell Waltrip (1972-00).
Most consecutive years won at least one pole – 13, Darrell Waltrip (1974-86).
Most consecutive poles won at one track – 11, David Pearson

# First-time wins on the Cup circuit

| Year | Drivers |
|---|---|
| 1972 | None |
| 1973 | Dick Brooks, Mark Donohue |
| 1974 | Earl Ross |
| 1975 | Dave Marcis, Darrell Waltrip |
| 1976 | None |
| 1977 | Neil Bonnett |
| 1978 | Lennie Pond |
| 1979 | Dale Earnhardt |
| 1980 | Terry Labonte |
| 1981 | Morgan Shepherd, Jody Ridley, Ron Bouchard |
| 1982 | Harry Gant, Tim Richmond |
| 1983 | Ricky Rudd, Bill Elliott |
| 1984 | Geoff Bodine |
| 1985 | Greg Sacks |
| 1986 | Kyle Petty, Rusty Wallace, Bobby Hillin, Jr. |
| 1987 | Davey Allison |
| 1988 | Lake Speed, Phil Parsons, Ken Schrader, Alan Kulwicki |
| 1989 | Mark Martin |
| 1990 | Derrike Cope, Brett Bodine, Ernie Irvan |
| 1991 | Dale Jarrett |
| 1992 | None |
| 1993 | None |
| 1994 | Sterling Marlin, Jeff Gordon, Jimmy Spencer |
| 1995 | Bobby Labonte, Ward Burton |
| 1996 | Bobby Hamilton |
| 1997 | Jeff Burton, John Andretti |
| 1998 | Jeremy Mayfield |
| 1999 | Tony Stewart, Joe Nemechek |
| 2000 | Dale Earnhardt, Jr.; Matt Kenseth; Steve Park; Jerry Nadeau |
| 2001 | Michael Waltrip, Kevin Harvick, Elliott Sadler, Ricky Craven, Robby Gordon |
| 2002 | Kurt Busch, Jimmie Johnson, Ryan Newman, Jamie McMurray, Johnny Benson |
| 2003 | Greg Biffle |

# Drivers with 500 starts (1949-2003)

| | Driver | 500th Start | Total Starts | | Driver | 500th Start | Total Starts |
|---|---|---|---|---|---|---|---|
| 1. | * Richard Petty | †1970 | 1,177 | 17. | * David Pearson | 1978 | 574 |
| 2. | * Dave Marcis | 1985 | 882 | 18. | Michael Waltrip | 2002 | 570 |
| 3. | * Darrell Waltrip | 1990 | 809 | 19. | Mark Martin | 2002 | 566 |
| 4. | Ricky Rudd | 1994 | 803 | 20. | Geoff Bodine | 1998 | 565 |
| 5. | Terry Labonte | 1995 | 781 | 21. | * Buddy Arrington | 1985 | 560 |
| 6. | Bill Elliott | 1997 | 731 | 22. | * Cale Yarborough | 1984 | 559 |
| 7. | * Bobby Allison | 1981 | 717 | 23. | # Elmo Langley | 1975 | 533 |
| 8. | * Buddy Baker | 1980 | 698 | 24. | Dale Jarrett | 2003 | 531 |
| 9. | Kyle Petty | 1997 | 678 | 25. | * Benny Parsons | 1988 | 526 |
| 10. | # Dale Earnhardt | 1995 | 676 | | | | |
| 11. | # J.D. McDuffie | 1981 | 653 | | | | |
| 12. | Rusty Wallace | 2000 | 634 | | | | |
| 13. | # Buck Baker | 1964 | 631 | | | | |
| 14. | Sterling Marlin | 2000 | 604 | | | | |
| 15. | * James Hylton | 1979 | 602 | | | | |
| 16. | Ken Schrader | 2001 | 596 | | | | |

* Retired.
† Entered 1,000th race in 1986.
# Deceased.

**Drivers closing in**

| | |
|---|---|
| Morgan Shepherd | 488 |
| Brett Bodine | 480 |
| Jimmy Spencer | 439 |

# Drivers with at least 300 consecutive starts
## (Through 2003)

| Rank | Driver | Start | End | Races |
|---|---|---|---|---|
| 1. | Ricky Rudd | Jan. 11, 1981 | — | 716 |
| 2. | Terry Labonte | Jan. 14, 1979 | Aug. 5, 2000 | 655 |
| 3. | # Dale Earnhardt | Sept. 9, 1979 | Feb. 25, 2001 | 648 |
| 4. | Rusty Wallace | Feb. 19, 1984 | — | 625 |
| 5. | Ken Schrader | Feb. 17, 1985 | August 3, 2003 | 579 |
| 6. | * Richard Petty | Nov. 14, 1971 | March 19, 1989 | 513 |
| 7. | Mark Martin | Feb. 14, 1988 | — | 509 |
| 8. | * Darrell Waltrip | Jan. 18, 1976 | June 24, 1990 | 431 |
| 9. | Michael Waltrip | Feb. 23, 1986 | Oct. 17, 1998 | 421 |
| 10. | Bill Elliott | Oct. 31, 1982 | April 28, 1996 | 395 |
| 11. | * Bobby Allison | Nov. 9, 1975 | June 19, 1988 | 374 |
| 12. | Jeff Gordon | Nov. 12, 1992 | — | 365 |
| 13. | Sterling Marlin | Feb. 15, 1987 | March 1, 1998 | 332 |
| 14. | * Benny Parsons | Nov. 14, 1971 | July 4, 1982 | 321 |

* Retired.
# Deceased.

# NMPA Most Popular Drivers (1953-2003)

| Year | Driver | Year | Driver | Year | Driver | Year | Driver |
|---|---|---|---|---|---|---|---|
| 1953 | Lee Petty | 1966 | Darel Dieringer | 1980 | David Pearson | 1993 | Bill Elliott |
| 1954 | Lee Petty | 1967 | Cale Yarborough | 1981 | Bobby Allison | 1994 | Bill Elliott |
| 1955 | Tim Flock | 1969 | Bobby Isaac | 1982 | Bobby Allison | 1995 | Bill Elliott |
| 1956 | Curtis Turner | 1970 | Richard Petty | 1983 | Bobby Allison | 1996 | Bill Elliott |
| 1957 | Fireball Roberts | 1971 | Bobby Allison | 1984 | Bill Elliott | 1997 | Bill Elliott |
| 1958 | Glen Wood | 1972 | Bobby Allison | 1985 | Bill Elliott | 1998 | Bill Elliott |
| 1959 | Jack Smith | 1973 | Bobby Allison | 1986 | Bill Elliott | 1999 | Bill Elliott |
| 1960 | Rex White | 1974 | Richard Petty | 1987 | Bill Elliott | 2000 | Bill Elliott |
| 1961 | Joe Weatherly | 1975 | Richard Petty | 1988 | Bill Elliott | 2001 | Dale Earnhardt |
| 1962 | Richard Petty | 1976 | Richard Petty | 1989 | Darrell Waltrip | 2002 | Bill Elliott |
| 1963 | Fred Lorenzen | 1977 | Richard Petty | 1990 | Darrell Waltrip | 2003 | Dale Earnhardt Jr. |
| 1964 | Richard Petty | 1978 | Richard Petty | 1991 | Bill Elliott | | |
| 1965 | Fred Lorenzen | 1979 | David Pearson | 1992 | Bill Elliott | | |

# Winning streaks

## MOST CONSECUTIVE WINS (1972–2003): Four

| Year | Driver | Sites |
|---|---|---|
| 1976 | Cale Yarborough | Richmond, Va. – Dover, Del. – Martinsville, Va. – N. Wilkesboro, N.C. in fall |
| 1981 | Darrell Waltrip | Martinsville, Va. – N. Wilkesboro, N.C. – Charlotte, N.C. – Rockingham, N.C. in fall |
| 1987 | Dale Earnhardt | Darlington, S.C. – N.Wilkesboro, N.C. – Bristol, Tenn. – Martinsville, Va. in spring |
| 1991 | Harry Gant | Darlington, S.C. – Richmond, Va. – Dover, Del. – Martinsville, Va, in summer/fall |
| 1992 | Bill Elliott | Rockingham, N.C. – Richmond, Va. – Atlanta – Darlington, S.C. in spring |
| 1993 | Mark Martin | Watkins Glen, N.Y. – Michigan – Bristol, Tenn. – Darlington, S.C. |
| 1998 | Jeff Gordon | Pocono, Pa. – Indianapolis – Watkins Glen, N.Y. – Michigan |

Note: In 1971, both Bobby Allison and Richard Petty won five straight races in 48-race season.

## WINNING STREAKS (1972–2002)

| Year | Drivers |
|---|---|
| 1972 | Bobby Allison - 3; Bobby Allison - 2 (three times); Richard Petty - 2 (twice). |
| 1973 | David Pearson - 3; David Pearson - 2; Richard Petty - 2. |
| 1974 | Richard Petty - 3; Richard Petty - 2; David Pearson - 2; Cale Yarborough - 2 (twice). |
| 1975 | Richard Petty - 3; Richard Petty - 2 (twice); Buddy Baker - 2. |
| 1976 | Cale Yarborough - 4; David Pearson - 3. |
| 1977 | Cale Yarborough - 2 (twice); Richard Petty - 2 (twice). |
| 1978 | Cale Yarborough - 2 (twice); Darrell Waltrip - 2. |
| 1979 | Darrell Waltrip - 2. |
| 1980 | Dale Earnhardt - 2 (twice); Cale Yarborough - 2 (twice); Neil Bonnett - 2. |
| 1981 | Darrell Waltrip - 4; Darrell Waltrip - 2 (twice). |
| 1982 | Darrell Waltrip - 2 (four times). |
| 1983 | Bobby Allison - 3; Darrell Waltrip - 2. |
| 1984 | No one won two races in a row. |
| 1985 | Bill Elliott - 2 (twice). |
| 1986 | Tim Richmond - 2 (twice); Dale Earnhardt - 2. |
| 1987 | Dale Earnhardt - 4, Dale Earnhardt - 3, Dale Earnhardt - 2; Tim Richmond - 2; Bill Elliott - 2. |
| 1988 | Neil Bonnett - 2; Bill Elliott - 2. |
| 1989 | Rusty Wallace - 2. |
| 1990 | Dale Earnhardt - 2 (three times). |
| 1991 | Harry Gant - 4; Davey Allison - 2. |
| 1992 | Bill Elliott - 4; Darrell Waltrip - 2; Geoff Bodine - 2. |
| 1993 | Mark Martin - 4; Rusty Wallace - 3; Dale Earnhardt - 2 (twice). |
| 1994 | Rusty Wallace - 3; Wallace - 2; Ernie Irvan - 2; Dale Earnhardt - 2. |
| 1995 | Jeff Gordon - 2; Mark Martin - 2. |
| 1996 | Jeff Gordon - 3; Jeff Gordon - 2 (twice). |
| 1997 | Jeff Gordon - 2 (twice); Dale Jarrett - 2; Mark Martin - 2. |
| 1998 | Jeff Gordon - 4; Jeff Gordon - 2; Jeff Gordon - 2. |
| 1999 | Jeff Gordon - 2; Tony Stewart - 2. |
| 2000 | Tony Stewart - 2 (twice); Rusty Wallace - 2. |
| 2001 | Jeff Gordon - 2 (twice); Dale Jarrett - 2. |
| 2002 | Bill Elliott - 2; Kurt Busch - 2. |
| 2003 | Jeff Gordon - 2. |

## LONGEST STREAKS OF DIFFERENT RACE WINNERS IN WINSTON CUP HISTORY (Before 1972)

| Races | First Race in Streak | Last Race in Streak |
|---|---|---|
| 13 | April 30, 1961 — Martinsville, Va. | June 23, 1961 — Hartsville, S.C. |
| 13 | May 6, 1961 — Darlington, S.C. | June 24, 1961 — Roanoke, Va. |
| 11 | June 2, 1961 — Spartanburg, S.C. | July 22, 1961 — Myrtle Beach, S.C. |
| 10 | July 7, 1956 — Spartanburg, S.C. | Aug. 22, 1956 — Norfolk, Va. |
| 10 | June 11, 1960 — Hanford, Calif. | Aug. 7, 1960 — Nashville |
| 10 | June 17, 1960 — Norwood, Mass. | Aug. 9, 1961 — Winston – Salem, N.C. |
| 9 | Oct. 27, 1963 — Hillsboro, N.C. | Feb. 21, 1964 — Daytona Beach, Fla. |
| 9 | Oct. 3, 1965 — N. Wilkesboro, N.C. | Feb. 25, 1966 — Daytona Beach, Fla. |

## LONGEST STREAKS OF DIFFERENT RACE WINNERS IN WINSTON CUP HISTORY (1972–2003)

| Races | First Race in Streak | Last Race in Streak |
|---|---|---|
| 11 | Sept. 22, 1985 — Martinsville, Va. | April 13, 1986 — Darlington, S.C. |
| 11 | Sept. 29, 1985 — N. Wilkesboro, N.C. | April 20, 1986 — N. Wilkesboro, N.C. |
| 10 | May 5, 2002 — Richmond, Va. | July 28, 2002 — Long Pond, Pa. |
| 10 | Feb. 20, 2000 — Daytona Beach, Fla. | April 30, 2000 — Los Angeles, Calif. |
| 10 | Oct. 2, 1983 — N. Wilkesboro, N.C. | April 8, 1984 — N. Wilkesboro, N.C. |
| 9 | June 16, 1981 — Pocono, Pa. | Sept. 1, 1991 — Darlington, S.C. |
| 9 | May 27, 1984 — Charlotte, N.C. | Aug. 12, 1984 — Brooklyn, Mich. |
| 9 | February 6, 2003 — Daytona Beach, Fla. | April 13, 2003 — Martinsville, Va. |

HISTORY

# Inactive drivers with 50-plus victories

## Bobby Allison

**(1961 through 1988)**
**ALL WINSTON CUP RACES**

| Year | Car Owner | Races | Won | 2nd | 3rd | 4th | 5th | 6-10th | 11-31st | DNF | Poles | Outside Poles | Money Won |
|---|---|---|---|---|---|---|---|---|---|---|---|---|---|
| 1961 | Bobby Allison | 4 | 0 | 0 | 0 | 0 | 0 | 0 | 2 | 2 | 0 | 0 | $ 650 |
| 1965 | Bobby Allison | 8 | 0 | 0 | 0 | 0 | 0 | 3 | 1 | 4 | 0 | 0 | 4,780 |
| 1966 | Bobby Allison | 34 | 3 | 0 | 3 | 1 | 2 | 5 | 3 | 17 | 4 | 1 | 21,850 |
| 1967 | Bobby Allison | 28 | 3 | 2 | 2 | 3 | 2 | 4 | 1 | 11 | 1 | 2 | 12,840 |
|  | Cotton Owens | 9 | 1 | 2 | 3 | 1 | 0 | 1 | 0 | 1 | 0 | 2 | 16,130 |
|  | Bud Moore | 4 | 0 | 0 | 0 | 0 | 0 | 1 | 1 | 2 | 0 | 0 | 2,520 |
|  | Nord Krauskopf | 2 | 0 | 0 | 0 | 0 | 0 | 0 | 0 | 2 | 0 | 0 | 2,375 |
|  | Holman-Moody | 2 | 2 | 0 | 0 | 0 | 0 | 0 | 0 | 0 | 1 | 0 | 19,550 |
| 1968 | Bobby Allison | 22 | 1 | 2 | 3 | 3 | 1 | 2 | 0 | 10 | 0 | 1 | 21,263 |
|  | Bondy Long | 8 | 0 | 0 | 1 | 1 | 0 | 0 | 0 | 6 | 0 | 0 | 17,433 |
|  | Bill Ellis | 5 | 0 | 1 | 0 | 2 | 1 | 0 | 0 | 1 | 2 | 0 | 7,795 |
|  | Holman-Moody | 2 | 1 | 1 | 0 | 0 | 0 | 0 | 0 | 0 | 0 | 2 | 3,900 |
| 1969 | Mario Rossi | 23 | 4 | 3 | 1 | 1 | 2 | 1 | 0 | 11 | 1 | 2 | 64,710 |
|  | Bill Ellis | 2 | 1 | 0 | 0 | 0 | 0 | 0 | 0 | 1 | 0 | 0 | 1,275 |
|  | Bobby Allison | 2 | 0 | 0 | 0 | 0 | 0 | 1 | 0 | 1 | 0 | 0 | 790 |
| 1970 | Mario Rossi | 20 | 1 | 6 | 4 | 1 | 0 | 2 | 2 | 4 | 2 | 3 | 95,495 |
|  | Bobby Allison | 26 | 2 | 9 | 4 | 3 | 0 | 3 | 2 | 3 | 3 | 2 | 36,470 |
| 1971 | Holman-Moody | 22 | 8 | 5 | 3 | 2 | 0 | 1 | 0 | 3 | 5 | 5 | 194,665 |
|  | Bobby Allison | 18 | 2 | 1 | 0 | 3 | 1 | 3 | 2 | 6 | 3 | 2 | 44,630 |
| 1972 | Junior Johnson | 31 | 10 | 12 | 2 | 1 | 0 | 2 | 1 | 3 | 11 | 8 | 271,395 |
| 1973 | Bobby Allison | 27 | 2 | 2 | 6 | 4 | 1 | 1 | 1 | 10 | 6 | 6 | 101,380 |
| 1974 | Bobby Allison | 17 | 1 | 3 | 4 | 1 | 2 | 0 | 0 | 6 | 3 | 2 | 74,915 |
|  | Roger Penske | 10 | 1 | 0 | 1 | 1 | 3 | 0 | 0 | 4 | 0 | 3 | 42,485 |
| 1975 | Roger Penske | 19 | 3 | 3 | 1 | 2 | 1 | 0 | 0 | 9 | 3 | 2 | 122,435 |
| 1976 | Roger Penske | 30 | 0 | 2 | 6 | 5 | 2 | 4 | 2 | 9 | 2 | 4 | 210,377 |
| 1977 | Bobby Allison | 30 | 0 | 1 | 0 | 2 | 2 | 10 | 3 | 12 | 0 | 2 | 87,740 |
| 1978 | Bud Moore | 30 | 5 | 3 | 4 | 0 | 2 | 8 | 1 | 7 | 1 | 5 | 335,636 |
| 1979 | Bud Moore | 31 | 5 | 7 | 2 | 3 | 0 | 4 | 3 | 7 | 3 | 6 | 403,014 |
| 1980 | Bud Moore | 31 | 4 | 2 | 4 | 1 | 1 | 6 | 0 | 13 | 2 | 2 | 356,050 |
| 1981 | Ranier Racing | 31 | 5 | 7 | 4 | 3 | 2 | 5 | 2 | 3 | 2 | 5 | 644,311 |
| 1982 | DiGard Racing | 30 | 8 | 2 | 1 | 2 | 1 | 5 | 3 | 8 | 1 | 3 | 726,562 |
| 1983 | DiGard Racing | 30 | 6 | 5 | 6 | 1 | 0 | 7 | 3 | 2 | 0 | 0 | 828,355 |
| 1984 | DiGard Racing | 30 | 2 | 1 | 2 | 4 | 4 | 6 | 7 | 4 | 0 | 0 | 627,637 |
| 1985 | DiGard Racing | 15 | 0 | 0 | 3 | 2 | 1 | 3 | 4 | 2 | 0 | 1 | 217,690 |
|  | Bobby Allison | 13 | 0 | 0 | 0 | 1 | 0 | 1 | 5 | 6 | 0 | 0 | 54,846 |
| 1986 | Stavola Bros. | 29 | 1 | 2 | 1 | 1 | 1 | 8 | 9 | 6 | 0 | 1 | 503,095 |
| 1987 | Stavola Bros. | 29 | 1 | 1 | 0 | 1 | 1 | 9 | 7 | 9 | 1 | 2 | 515,894 |
| 1988 | Stavola Bros. | 13 | 1 | 1 | 0 | 0 | 1 | 3 | 6 | 1 | 0 | 0 | 409,295 |
| **TOTAL** |  | 717 | 84 | 86 | 71 | 56 | 34 | 109 | 71 | 206 | 57 | 74 | $7,102,233 |

## Dale Earnhardt

**(1975 through 2001)**
**ALL WINSTON CUP RACES**

| Year | Car Owner | Races | Won | 2nd | 3rd | 4th | 5th | 6-10th | 11-31st | DNF | Poles | Outside Poles | Money Won |
|---|---|---|---|---|---|---|---|---|---|---|---|---|---|
| 1975 | Ed Negre | 1 | 0 | 0 | 0 | 0 | 0 | 0 | 1 | 0 | 0 | 0 | 1,925 |
| 1976 | W. Ballard | 1 | 0 | 0 | 0 | 0 | 0 | 0 | 0 | 1 | 0 | 0 | 1,725 |
|  | Johnny Ray | 1 | 0 | 0 | 0 | 0 | 0 | 0 | 0 | 1 | 0 | 0 | 1,360 |
| 1977 | Henley Gray | 1 | 0 | 0 | 0 | 0 | 0 | 0 | 0 | 1 | 0 | 0 | 1,375 |
| 1978 | W. Cronkrite | 4 | 0 | 0 | 0 | 0 | 0 | 1 | 3 | 0 | 0 | 0 | 13,245 |
|  | R. Osterlund | 1 | 0 | 0 | 0 | 0 | 1 | 0 | 0 | 0 | 0 | 0 | 6,900 |
| 1979 | R. Osterlund | 27 | 1 | 1 | 3 | 4 | 2 | 6 | 6 | 4 | 4 | 0 | 264,086 |
| 1980 | R. Osterlund | 31 | 5 | 3 | 4 | 3 | 4 | 4 | 4 | 4 | 0 | 1 | 588,926 |

| Year | Car Owner | Races | Won | 2nd | 3rd | 4th | 5th | 6-10th | 11-31st | DNF | Poles | Outside Poles | Money Won |
|---|---|---|---|---|---|---|---|---|---|---|---|---|---|
| 1981 | R. Osterlund | 16 | 0 | 2 | 3 | 0 | 2 | 3 | 2 | 4 | 0 | 1 | 220,085 |
|  | Jim Stacy | 4 | 0 | 0 | 0 | 0 | 0 | 1 | 1 | 2 | 0 | 0 | 34,300 |
|  | R. Childress | 11 | 0 | 0 | 0 | 2 | 0 | 4 | 1 | 4 | 0 | 2 | 92,728 |
| 1982 | Bud Moore | 30 | 1 | 1 | 3 | 2 | 0 | 5 | 0 | 18 | 1 | 0 | 375,325 |
| 1983 | Bud Moore | 30 | 2 | 3 | 0 | 3 | 1 | 5 | 3 | 13 | 0 | 1 | 446,272 |
| 1984 | R. Childress | 30 | 2 | 4 | 2 | 0 | 4 | 10 | 6 | 2 | 0 | 1 | 616,788 |
| 1985 | R. Childress | 28 | 4 | 0 | 0 | 4 | 2 | 6 | 3 | 9 | 1 | 0 | 546,596 |
| 1986 | R. Childress | 29 | 5 | 5 | 3 | 1 | 2 | 7 | 2 | 4 | 1 | 3 | 1,783,880 |
| 1987 | R. Childress | 29 | 11 | 5 | 1 | 2 | 2 | 3 | 3 | 2 | 1 | 4 | 2,099,243 |
| 1988 | R. Childress | 29 | 3 | 2 | 3 | 3 | 2 | 6 | 9 | 1 | 0 | 5 | 1,214,089 |
| 1989 | R. Childress | 29 | 5 | 3 | 5 | 1 | 0 | 5 | 8 | 2 | 0 | 1 | 1,435,730 |
| 1990 | R. Childress | 29 | 9 | 3 | 3 | 1 | 2 | 5 | 5 | 1 | 4 | 2 | 3,083,056 |
| 1991 | R. Childress | 29 | 4 | 3 | 4 | 1 | 2 | 7 | 6 | 2 | 0 | 1 | 2,396,685 |
| 1992 | R. Childress | 29 | 1 | 2 | 2 | 1 | 0 | 9 | 10 | 4 | 1 | 1 | 915,463 |
| 1993 | R. Childress | 30 | 6 | 5 | 3 | 3 | 0 | 4 | 7 | 2 | 2 | 1 | 3,353,789 |
| 1994 | R. Childress | 31 | 4 | 7 | 6 | 1 | 2 | 5 | 3 | 3 | 2 | 2 | 3,300,733 |
| 1995 | R. Childress | 31 | 5 | 6 | 5 | 1 | 2 | 4 | 6 | 2 | 3 | 2 | 3,154,241 |
| 1996 | R. Childress | 31 | 2 | 3 | 3 | 4 | 0 | 4 | 12 | 2 | 2 | 0 | 2,285,926 |
| 1997 | R. Childress | 32 | 0 | 4 | 1 | 1 | 1 | 9 | 16 | 0 | 0 | 1 | 2,151,909 |
| 1998 | R. Childress | 33 | 1 | 0 | 1 | 2 | 1 | 8 | 17 | 3 | 0 | 1 | 2,990,749 |
| 1999 | R. Childress | 34 | 3 | 3 | 0 | 0 | 1 | 14 | 10 | 3 | 0 | 0 | 3,149,536 |
| 2000 | R. Childress | 34 | 2 | 5 | 4 | 2 | 0 | 11 | 10 | 0 | 0 | 0 | 4,918,886 |
| 2001 | R. Childress | 1 | 0 | 0 | 0 | 0 | 0 | 0 | 0 | 1 | 0 | 0 | $ 296,833 |
| TOTAL |  | 676 | 76 | 70 | 59 | 43 | 33 | 146 | 154 | 95 | 22 | 30 | $41,708,384 |

## Ned Jarrett

(1953 through 1966)
ALL WINSTON CUP RACES

| Year | Car Owner | Races | Won | 2nd | 3rd | 4th | 5th | 6-10th | 11-31st | DNF | Poles | Outside Poles | Money Won |
|---|---|---|---|---|---|---|---|---|---|---|---|---|---|
| 1953 | Ned Jarrett | 2 | 0 | 0 | 0 | 0 | 0 | 0 | 0 | 2 | 0 | 0 | $ 125 |
| 1954 | Ned Jarrett | 2 | 0 | 0 | 0 | 0 | 0 | 0 | 1 | 1 | 0 | 0 | 25 |
| 1955 | Mellie Bernard | 3 | 0 | 0 | 0 | 0 | 0 | 0 | 1 | 2 | 0 | 0 | 260 |
| 1956 | Ned Jarrett | 2 | 0 | 0 | 0 | 0 | 0 | 0 | 1 | 1 | 0 | 0 | 60 |
| 1957 | Ned Jarrett | 1 | 0 | 0 | 0 | 0 | 0 | 0 | 0 | 1 | 0 | 0 | 50 |
| 1959 | Paul Spaulding | 1 | 0 | 1 | 0 | 0 | 0 | 0 | 0 | 0 | 0 | 0 | 525 |
|  | Ned Jarrett | 15 | 2 | 0 | 1 | 0 | 0 | 2 | 3 | 7 | 0 | 0 | 3,285 |
| 1960 | Ned Jarrett | 40 | 5 | 3 | 4 | 4 | 4 | 6 | 2 | 12 | 5 | 2 | 20,540 |
| 1961 | Ned Jarrett | 2 | 0 | 0 | 0 | 0 | 0 | 0 | 0 | 2 | 0 | 0 | 110 |
|  | W.G. Holloway | 44 | 1 | 4 | 8 | 4 | 6 | 10 | 2 | 9 | 4 | 3 | 27,125 |
| 1962 | W.G. Holloway | 51 | 6 | 2 | 3 | 3 | 5 | 13 | 5 | 14 | 4 | 4 | $ 34,890 |
|  | J.C. Parker | 1 | 0 | 0 | 0 | 0 | 0 | 1 | 0 | 0 | 0 | 0 | 430 |
| 1963 | W.G. Holloway | 2 | 0 | 0 | 0 | 0 | 0 | 0 | 0 | 2 | 0 | 0 | 200 |
|  | Burton-Robinson | 50 | 8 | 7 | 5 | 7 | 4 | 7 | 3 | 9 | 4 | 6 | 38,265 |
|  | Herman Beam | 1 | 0 | 0 | 0 | 0 | 1 | 0 | 0 | 0 | 0 | 0 | 275 |
| 1964 | Burton-Robinson | 4 | 1 | 0 | 0 | 0 | 1 | 0 | 0 | 2 | 1 | 0 | 3,275 |
|  | Bondy Long | 55 | 14 | 7 | 4 | 5 | 3 | 2 | 0 | 20 | 8 | 9 | 60,055 |
| 1965 | Bondy Long | 54 | 13 | 13 | 10 | 4 | 2 | 2 | 1 | 9 | 9 | 6 | 77,966 |
| 1966 | Bondy Long | 8 | 0 | 0 | 1 | 1 | 1 | 2 | 0 | 3 | 0 | 0 | 8,685 |
|  | Henley Gray | 2 | 0 | 0 | 0 | 0 | 0 | 0 | 0 | 2 | 0 | 0 | 2,375 |
|  | Larry Hess | 10 | 0 | 0 | 2 | 0 | 0 | 0 | 1 | 7 | 0 | 0 | 9,720 |
|  | Bernard Alvarez | 1 | 0 | 0 | 0 | 0 | 0 | 0 | 0 | 1 | 0 | 0 | 905 |
| TOTAL |  | 351 | 50 | 37 | 38 | 28 | 27 | 45 | 20 | 106 | 35 | 30 | $289,146 |

## Junior Johnson

(1953 through 1966)
ALL WINSTON CUP RACES

| Year | Car Owner | Races | Won | 2nd | 3rd | 4th | 5th | 6-10th | 11-31st | DNF | Poles | Outside Poles | Money Won |
|---|---|---|---|---|---|---|---|---|---|---|---|---|---|
| 1953 | Gwyn Staley | 1 | 0 | 0 | 0 | 0 | 0 | 0 | 0 | 1 | 0 | 0 | $ 110 |
| 1954 | George Miller | 1 | 0 | 0 | 0 | 0 | 1 | 0 | 0 | 0 | 0 | 0 | 300 |
|  | Paul Whiteman | 3 | 0 | 0 | 0 | 0 | 0 | 0 | 1 | 2 | 1 | 0 | 250 |
| 1955 | Junior Johnson | 1 | 0 | 0 | 0 | 0 | 0 | 0 | 0 | 1 | 0 | 0 | 25 |
|  | Buchan-Lowe | 33 | 5 | 0 | 2 | 1 | 3 | 5 | 1 | 16 | 2 | 3 | 9,280 |

| Year | Car Owner | Races | Won | 2nd | 3rd | 4th | 5th | 6-10th | 11-31st | DNF | Poles | Outside Poles | Money Won |
|---|---|---|---|---|---|---|---|---|---|---|---|---|---|
| | Henry Ford | 1 | 0 | 0 | 0 | 0 | 0 | 0 | 0 | 1 | 0 | 0 | 50 |
| | Bob Welborn | 1 | 0 | 1 | 0 | 0 | 0 | 0 | 0 | 0 | 0 | 0 | 700 |
| 1956 | A.L. Bumgarner | 8 | 0 | 0 | 0 | 0 | 0 | 0 | 0 | 8 | 1 | 0 | 200 |
| | Jim Stephens | 1 | 0 | 0 | 0 | 0 | 0 | 0 | 0 | 1 | 0 | 0 | 50 |
| | Carl Kiekhaefer | 1 | 0 | 1 | 0 | 0 | 0 | 0 | 0 | 0 | 0 | 1 | 700 |
| | Pete DePaolo | 2 | 0 | 0 | 0 | 0 | 0 | 0 | 0 | 2 | 0 | 0 | 200 |
| | Smokey Yunick | 1 | 0 | 0 | 0 | 0 | 0 | 0 | 1 | 0 | 0 | 0 | 200 |
| 1957 | A.L. Bumgarner | 1 | 0 | 0 | 0 | 0 | 0 | 0 | 0 | 1 | 0 | 0 | 50 |
| 1958 | Paul Spaulding | 26 | 6 | 2 | 3 | 1 | 0 | 3 | 1 | 10 | 0 | 2 | 12,205 |
| | Dick Beaty | 1 | 0 | 0 | 0 | 0 | 0 | 1 | 0 | 0 | 0 | 0 | 215 |
| 1959 | Paul Spaulding | 26 | 5 | 1 | 3 | 2 | 2 | 1 | 3 | 9 | 1 | 0 | 8,330 |
| | Wood Brothers | 2 | 0 | 0 | 0 | 1 | 0 | 0 | 0 | 1 | 0 | 0 | 275 |
| 1960 | Paul Spaulding | 2 | 0 | 0 | 0 | 0 | 0 | 0 | 0 | 2 | 1 | 0 | 50 |
| | John Masoni | 2 | 1 | 0 | 0 | 0 | 1 | 0 | 0 | 0 | 0 | 0 | 19,875 |
| | Wood Brothers | 2 | 0 | 0 | 0 | 1 | 0 | 0 | 0 | 1 | 1 | 0 | 345 |
| | Rex Lovette | 26 | 2 | 2 | 4 | 1 | 2 | 4 | 1 | 10 | 1 | 4 | 10,320 |
| | Bob Welborn | 1 | 0 | 0 | 0 | 0 | 0 | 0 | 0 | 1 | 0 | 0 | 75 |
| | Tom Pistone | 1 | 0 | 0 | 0 | 0 | 0 | 0 | 0 | 1 | 0 | 0 | 110 |
| 1961 | Rex Lovette | 40 | 7 | 2 | 2 | 3 | 1 | 3 | 2 | 20 | 9 | 9 | 24,785 |
| | John Masoni | 1 | 0 | 1 | 0 | 0 | 0 | 0 | 0 | 0 | 1 | 0 | 525 |
| 1962 | Rex Lovette | 11 | 0 | 0 | 2 | 1 | 1 | 0 | 0 | 7 | 1 | 3 | 3,960 |
| | Buck Baker | 1 | 0 | 0 | 0 | 0 | 0 | 0 | 0 | 1 | 0 | 0 | 50 |
| | Ray Nichels | 1 | 0 | 0 | 0 | 0 | 0 | 0 | 0 | 1 | 0 | 0 | 200 |
| | Cotton Owens | 4 | 0 | 1 | 0 | 0 | 0 | 1 | 0 | 2 | 0 | 1 | 7,345 |
| | Ray Fox | 6 | 1 | 1 | 0 | 0 | 0 | 0 | 0 | 4 | 1 | 1 | 22,385 |
| 1963 | Ray Fox | 2 | 1 | 0 | 0 | 0 | 0 | 0 | 0 | 1 | 0 | 1 | 3,200 |
| | Rex Lovette | 30 | 6 | 2 | 2 | 0 | 0 | 0 | 0 | 20 | 9 | 6 | 61,210 |
| | Bill Stroppe | 1 | 0 | 0 | 0 | 0 | 1 | 0 | 0 | 0 | 0 | 0 | 1,300 |
| 1964 | Rex Lovette | 2 | 0 | 0 | 0 | 0 | 0 | 0 | 0 | 2 | 0 | 1 | 675 |
| | Ray Fox | 9 | 1 | 1 | 0 | 3 | 0 | 1 | 0 | 3 | 0 | 1 | 8,265 |
| | Banjo Matthews | 17 | 2 | 1 | 4 | 0 | 0 | 0 | 0 | 10 | 4 | 1 | 16,460 |
| | Holman-Moody | 1 | 0 | 0 | 0 | 0 | 0 | 0 | 0 | 1 | 1 | 0 | 100 |
| 1965 | Rex Lovette | 36 | 13 | 2 | 1 | 1 | 0 | 1 | 0 | 19 | 10 | 9 | 57,925 |
| 1966 | Junior Johnson | 7 | 0 | 0 | 0 | 0 | 1 | 0 | 0 | 6 | 3 | 2 | 3,610 |
| **TOTAL** | | 313 | 50 | 18 | 23 | 15 | 13 | 19 | 10 | 165 | 47 | 45 | $ 275,910 |

## David Pearson

**(1960 through 1986)**
**ALL WINSTON CUP RACES**

| Year | Car Owner | Races | Won | 2nd | 3rd | 4th | 5th | 6-10th | 11-31st | DNF | Poles | Outside Poles | Money Won |
|---|---|---|---|---|---|---|---|---|---|---|---|---|---|
| 1960 | David Pearson | 22 | 0 | 1 | 0 | 1 | 1 | 2 | 6 | 11 | 1 | 0 | $ 5,030 |
| 1961 | Ray Fox Sr. | 7 | 3 | 0 | 1 | 0 | 0 | 0 | 0 | 3 | 1 | 2 | 47,790 |
| | David Pearson | 12 | 0 | 0 | 1 | 1 | 1 | 0 | 3 | 6 | 0 | 0 | 1,790 |
| 1962 | Ray Fox Sr. | 6 | 0 | 0 | 0 | 0 | 0 | 3 | 0 | 3 | 0 | 1 | 8,315 |
| | Cotton Owens | 4 | 0 | 0 | 0 | 1 | 0 | 0 | 1 | 2 | 0 | 1 | 5,185 |
| | David Pearson | 2 | 0 | 0 | 0 | 0 | 0 | 1 | 0 | 1 | 0 | 1 | 2,075 |
| 1963 | Cotton Owens | 41 | 0 | 3 | 2 | 5 | 3 | 6 | 6 | 16 | 2 | 1 | 21,160 |
| 1964 | Cotton Owens | 61 | 9 | 8 | 3 | 7 | 2 | 9 | 1 | 22 | 12 | 10 | 38,175 |
| 1965 | Cotton Owens | 14 | 2 | 2 | 1 | 1 | 0 | 1 | 0 | 7 | 1 | 2 | 8,925 |
| 1966 | Cotton Owens | 42 | 14 | 5 | 4 | 1 | 0 | 8 | 2 | 8 | 7 | 10 | 59,205 |
| 1967 | Holman-Moody | 12 | 0 | 5 | 1 | 1 | 0 | 0 | 0 | 5 | 2 | 0 | 53,650 |
| | Cotton Owens | 10 | 2 | 0 | 1 | 1 | 0 | 2 | 0 | 4 | 0 | 4 | 16,260 |
| 1968 | Holman-Moody | 48 | 16 | 12 | 4 | 2 | 2 | 2 | 1 | 9 | 12 | 17 | 118,842 |
| 1969 | Holman-Moody | 51 | 11 | 18 | 7 | 2 | 2 | 2 | 0 | 9 | 14 | 11 | 183,700 |
| 1970 | Holman-Moody | 19 | 1 | 2 | 2 | 3 | 1 | 1 | 0 | 9 | 2 | 4 | 87,118 |
| 1971 | Holman-Moody | 10 | 2 | 3 | 1 | 2 | 0 | 0 | 0 | 2 | 2 | 2 | 25,950 |
| | Chris Vallo | 7 | 0 | 0 | 0 | 0 | 0 | 1 | 0 | 6 | 0 | 0 | 6,085 |
| 1972 | Wood Brothers | 14 | 6 | 1 | 3 | 1 | 0 | 0 | 0 | 3 | 4 | 6 | 131,415 |
| | Bud Moore | 2 | 0 | 0 | 0 | 1 | 0 | 0 | 0 | 1 | 0 | 0 | 5,860 |
| | Junie Donlavey | 1 | 0 | 0 | 0 | 0 | 0 | 0 | 0 | 1 | 0 | 0 | 430 |
| 1973 | Wood Brothers | 18 | 11 | 2 | 1 | 0 | 0 | 0 | 0 | 4 | 8 | 5 | 213,966 |
| 1974 | Wood Brothers | 19 | 7 | 5 | 2 | 1 | 0 | 0 | 0 | 4 | 11 | 1 | 221,615 |
| 1975 | Wood Brothers | 21 | 3 | 6 | 2 | 2 | 0 | 0 | 0 | 8 | 7 | 5 | 179,208 |

| Year | Car Owner | Races | Won | 2nd | 3rd | 4th | 5th | 6-10th | 11-31st | DNF | Poles | Outside Poles | Money Won |
|---|---|---|---|---|---|---|---|---|---|---|---|---|---|
| 1976 | Wood Brothers | 22 | 10 | 3 | 2 | 1 | 0 | 2 | 0 | 4 | 8 | 5 | 283,686 |
| 1977 | Wood Brothers | 22 | 2 | 7 | 2 | 2 | 3 | 0 | 0 | 6 | 5 | 1 | 180,999 |
| 1978 | Wood Brothers | 22 | 4 | 2 | 1 | 1 | 3 | 0 | 0 | 11 | 7 | 1 | 151,837 |
| 1979 | Wood Brothers | 5 | 0 | 1 | 0 | 0 | 0 | 0 | 0 | 4 | 1 | 0 | 22,815 |
| | Rod Osterlund | 4 | 1 | 1 | 0 | 1 | 0 | 1 | 0 | 0 | 1 | 1 | 64,865 |
| 1980 | Hoss Ellington | 9 | 1 | 2 | 1 | 0 | 0 | 1 | 0 | 4 | 1 | 3 | 94,330 |
| 1981 | Joel Halpern | 4 | 0 | 0 | 0 | 0 | 0 | 1 | 0 | 3 | 0 | 0 | 9,625 |
| | Kennie Childers | 1 | 0 | 0 | 0 | 0 | 0 | 0 | 0 | 1 | 1 | 0 | 2,675 |
| | Hoss Ellington | 1 | 0 | 0 | 0 | 0 | 0 | 1 | 0 | 0 | 0 | 0 | 4,850 |
| 1982 | Bobby Hawkins | 6 | 0 | 0 | 1 | 0 | 1 | 0 | 0 | 4 | 2 | 0 | 47,945 |
| 1983 | Bobby Hawkins | 10 | 0 | 0 | 1 | 0 | 0 | 3 | 0 | 6 | 0 | 0 | 59,720 |
| 1984 | Bobby Hawkins | 11 | 0 | 0 | 0 | 0 | 0 | 3 | 1 | 7 | 1 | 0 | 54,125 |
| 1985 | Hoss Ellington | 8 | 0 | 0 | 0 | 0 | 0 | 1 | 1 | 6 | 0 | 1 | 48,090 |
| | David Pearson | 4 | 0 | 0 | 0 | 0 | 0 | 0 | 0 | 4 | 0 | 1 | 7,535 |
| 1986 | David Pearson | 2 | 0 | 0 | 0 | 0 | 0 | 1 | 0 | 1 | 0 | 0 | 8,405 |
| **TOTAL** | | **574** | **105** | **89** | **44** | **38** | **19** | **52** | **22** | **205** | **113** | **96** | **$2,482,596** |

## Lee Petty

(1949 through 1964)
ALL WINSTON CUP RACES

| Year | Car Owner | Races | Won | 2nd | 3rd | 4th | 5th | 6-10th | 11-31st | DNF | Poles | Outside Poles | Money Won |
|---|---|---|---|---|---|---|---|---|---|---|---|---|---|
| 1949 | Petty Enter. | 8 | 1 | 2 | 0 | 0 | 0 | 4 | 0 | 1 | 0 | 0 | $ 3,475 |
| 1950 | Petty Enter. | 18 | 2 | 1 | 2 | 3 | 1 | 4 | 1 | 4 | 0 | 1 | 7,375 |
| 1951 | Petty Enter. | 32 | 1 | 4 | 2 | 1 | 3 | 8 | 7 | 6 | 0 | 0 | 7,225 |
| 1952 | Petty Enter. | 32 | 3 | 6 | 5 | 5 | 2 | 5 | 0 | 6 | 0 | 0 | 15,620 |
| 1953 | Petty Enter. | 36 | 5 | 4 | 10 | 4 | 3 | 5 | 2 | 3 | 0 | 2 | 17,225 |
| 1954 | Petty Enter. | 33 | 7 | 5 | 4 | 3 | 3 | 8 | 0 | 3 | 3 | 3 | 18,775 |
| | Gary Drake | 1 | 0 | 0 | 0 | 1 | 0 | 0 | 0 | 0 | 0 | 0 | 350 |
| 1955 | Petty Enter. | 41 | 6 | 4 | 5 | 4 | 1 | 9 | 3 | 9 | 1 | 4 | 16,760 |
| | Henry Ford | 1 | 0 | 0 | 0 | 0 | 0 | 0 | 0 | 1 | 0 | 0 | 50 |
| 1956 | Petty Enter. | 46 | 2 | 1 | 6 | 2 | 5 | 10 | 5 | 15 | 1 | 3 | 13,380 |
| | Fred Frazier | 1 | 0 | 0 | 0 | 0 | 0 | 0 | 1 | 0 | 0 | 0 | 175 |
| 1957 | Petty Enter. | 41 | 4 | 4 | 3 | 3 | 6 | 12 | 3 | 6 | 3 | 3 | 15,670 |
| 1958 | Petty Enter. | 49 | 7 | 5 | 3 | 9 | 3 | 13 | 4 | 5 | 4 | 6 | 20,600 |
| 1959 | Petty Enter. | 42 | 11 | 5 | 7 | 4 | 0 | 6 | 1 | 8 | 2 | 5 | 43,590 |
| 1960 | Petty Enter. | 39 | 5 | 7 | 2 | 6 | 1 | 8 | 1 | 9 | 3 | 3 | 26,650 |
| 1961 | Petty Enter. | 3 | 1 | 0 | 1 | 0 | 0 | 0 | 0 | 1 | 1 | 0 | 1,260 |
| 1962 | Petty Enter. | 1 | 0 | 0 | 0 | 0 | 1 | 0 | 0 | 0 | 0 | 0 | 750 |
| 1963 | Petty Enter. | 3 | 0 | 0 | 0 | 1 | 0 | 1 | 0 | 1 | 0 | 0 | 600 |
| 1964 | Petty Enter. | 2 | 0 | 0 | 0 | 0 | 0 | 0 | 0 | 2 | 0 | 0 | 250 |
| **TOTAL** | | **429** | **55** | **48** | **50** | **46** | **29** | **93** | **28** | **80** | **18** | **30** | **$209,780** |

## Richard Petty

(1958 through 1992)
ALL WINSTON CUP RACES

| Year | Car Owner | Races | Won | 2nd | 3rd | 4th | 5th | 6-10th | 11-31st | DNF | Poles | Outside Poles | Money Won |
|---|---|---|---|---|---|---|---|---|---|---|---|---|---|
| 1958 | Petty Enter. | 8 | 0 | 0 | 0 | 0 | 0 | 1 | 2 | 5 | 0 | 0 | $ 645 |
| 1959 | Petty Enter. | 16 | 0 | 0 | 2 | 1 | 1 | 3 | 1 | 8 | 0 | 1 | 5,605 |
| 1960 | Petty Enter. | 40 | 3 | 7 | 3 | 3 | 1 | 13 | 2 | 8 | 2 | 3 | 35,180 |
| 1961 | Petty Enter. | 42 | 2 | 4 | 4 | 5 | 3 | 4 | 2 | 18 | 2 | 2 | 22,671 |
| 1962 | Petty Enter. | 52 | 8 | 9 | 8 | 5 | 2 | 6 | 3 | 11 | 5 | 7 | 52,885 |
| 1963 | Petty Enter. | 54 | 14 | 10 | 2 | 4 | 1 | 8 | 4 | 12 | 8 | 7 | 47,765 |
| 1964 | Petty Enter. | 61 | 9 | 14 | 11 | 0 | 2 | 5 | 1 | 19 | 9 | 17 | 98,810 |
| 1965 | Petty Enter. | 14 | 4 | 4 | 2 | 0 | 0 | 0 | 0 | 4 | 7 | 4 | 16,450 |
| 1966 | Petty Enter. | 39 | 8 | 9 | 3 | 0 | 0 | 1 | 1 | 17 | 16 | 6 | 78,840 |
| 1967 | Petty Enter. | 48 | 27 | 7 | 2 | 1 | 1 | 1 | 1 | 8 | 19 | 15 | 130,275 |
| 1968 | Petty Enter. | 49 | 16 | 6 | 5 | 2 | 2 | 2 | 0 | 16 | 12 | 12 | 89,003 |
| 1969 | Petty Enter. | 50 | 10 | 9 | 9 | 0 | 3 | 4 | 0 | 15 | 6 | 10 | 109,180 |
| 1970 | Petty Enter. | 40 | 18 | 5 | 0 | 0 | 2 | 4 | 1 | 10 | 9 | 8 | 138,969 |
| 1971 | Petty Enter. | 46 | 21 | 8 | 7 | 2 | 0 | 3 | 0 | 5 | 9 | 11 | 309,225 |
| 1972 | Petty Enter. | 31 | 8 | 9 | 5 | 2 | 1 | 2 | 0 | 4 | 3 | 6 | 227,015 |

| Year | Car Owner | Races | Won | 2nd | 3rd | 4th | 5th | 6-10th | 11-31st | DNF | Poles | Outside Poles | Money Won |
|---|---|---|---|---|---|---|---|---|---|---|---|---|---|
| 1973 | Petty Enter. | 28 | 6 | 6 | 1 | 2 | 0 | 1 | 2 | 10 | 3 | 3 | 159,655 |
| 1974 | Petty Enter. | 30 | 10 | 8 | 4 | 0 | 0 | 1 | 0 | 7 | 7 | 8 | 299,175 |
| 1975 | Petty Enter. | 30 | 13 | 5 | 3 | 0 | 0 | 3 | 0 | 6 | 3 | 5 | 378,865 |
| 1976 | Petty Enter. | 30 | 3 | 9 | 3 | 4 | 0 | 3 | 0 | 8 | 1 | 5 | 338,265 |
| 1977 | Petty Enter. | 30 | 5 | 6 | 6 | 2 | 1 | 3 | 1 | 6 | 5 | 5 | 345,886 |
| 1978 | Petty Enter. | 30 | 0 | 3 | 3 | 3 | 2 | 6 | 1 | 12 | 0 | 1 | 215,491 |
| 1979 | Petty Enter. | 31 | 5 | 7 | 2 | 4 | 5 | 4 | 1 | 3 | 1 | 2 | 531,292 |
| 1980 | Petty Enter. | 31 | 2 | 4 | 3 | 2 | 4 | 3 | 3 | 10 | 0 | 0 | 374,092 |
| 1981 | Petty Enter. | 31 | 3 | 1 | 4 | 3 | 1 | 4 | 0 | 14 | 0 | 0 | 389,214 |
| 1982 | Petty Enter. | 30 | 0 | 5 | 2 | 1 | 1 | 7 | 1 | 13 | 0 | 0 | 453,832 |
| 1983 | Petty Enter. | 30 | 3 | 1 | 1 | 1 | 3 | 12 | 4 | 5 | 0 | 0 | 491,022 |
| 1984 | Mike Curb | 30 | 2 | 0 | 0 | 2 | 1 | 8 | 10 | 7 | 0 | 0 | 251,226 |
| 1985 | Mike Curb | 28 | 0 | 0 | 1 | 0 | 0 | 12 | 3 | 12 | 0 | 0 | 306,142 |
| 1986 | Petty Enter. | 29 | 0 | 1 | 2 | 1 | 0 | 7 | 8 | 10 | 0 | 1 | 280,657 |
| 1987 | Petty Enter. | 28 | 0 | 1 | 3 | 2 | 3 | 5 | 10 | 5 | 0 | 0 | 468,602 |
| 1988 | Petty Enter. | 29 | 0 | 0 | 1 | 0 | 0 | 4 | 9 | 15 | 0 | 0 | 190,155 |
| 1989 | Petty Enter. | 25 | 0 | 0 | 0 | 0 | 0 | 0 | 13 | 12 | 0 | 0 | 133,050 |
| 1990 | Petty Enter. | 29 | 0 | 0 | 0 | 0 | 0 | 1 | 16 | 12 | 0 | 0 | 169,465 |
| 1991 | Petty Enter. | 29 | 0 | 0 | 0 | 0 | 0 | 1 | 18 | 10 | 0 | 0 | 268,035 |
| 1992 | Petty Enter. | 29 | 0 | 0 | 0 | 0 | 0 | 0 | 24 | 5 | 0 | 1 | 348,870 |
| TOTAL | | 1,177 | 200 | 155 | 102 | 52 | 40 | 144 | 141 | 343 | 127 | 140 | $7,755,409 |

# Darrell Waltrip

(1972 through 1999)
ALL WINSTON CUP RACES

| Year | Car Owner | Races | Won | 2nd | 3rd | 4th | 5th | 6-10th | 11-31st | DNF | Poles | Outside Poles | Money Won |
|---|---|---|---|---|---|---|---|---|---|---|---|---|---|
| 1972 | D. Waltrip | 5 | 0 | 0 | 1 | 0 | 0 | 2 | 0 | 2 | 0 | 0 | $ 8,615 |
| 1973 | D. Waltrip | 14 | 0 | 1 | 0 | 0 | 0 | 3 | 3 | 7 | 0 | 0 | 27,775 |
|  | Bud Moore | 5 | 0 | 0 | 0 | 0 | 0 | 1 | 0 | 4 | 0 | 1 | 5,691 |
| 1974 | D. Waltrip | 16 | 0 | 1 | 3 | 2 | 1 | 4 | 0 | 5 | 1 | 0 | 57,690 |
| 1975 | D. Waltrip | 17 | 1 | 2 | 0 | 3 | 2 | 2 | 0 | 7 | 2 | 1 | 79,762 |
|  | Bill Gardner | 11 | 1 | 0 | 2 | 0 | 0 | 1 | 0 | 7 | 0 | 3 | 20,430 |
| 1976 | Bill Gardner | 30 | 1 | 3 | 4 | 1 | 1 | 2 | 2 | 16 | 3 | 1 | 191,501 |
| 1977 | Bill Gardner | 30 | 6 | 4 | 3 | 1 | 2 | 6 | 1 | 7 | 3 | 3 | 276,312 |
| 1978 | Bill Gardner | 30 | 6 | 6 | 4 | 1 | 1 | 1 | 2 | 9 | 2 | 7 | 343,367 |
| 1979 | Bill Gardner | 31 | 7 | 4 | 6 | 2 | 1 | 3 | 7 | 1 | 5 | 3 | 523,691 |
| 1980 | Bill Gardner | 31 | 5 | 3 | 2 | 6 | 0 | 1 | 2 | 12 | 5 | 5 | 382,138 |
| 1981 | Junior Johnson | 31 | 12 | 6 | 3 | 0 | 0 | 4 | 2 | 4 | 11 | 4 | 693,342 |
| 1982 | Junior Johnson | 30 | 12 | 1 | 3 | 0 | 1 | 2 | 3 | 8 | 7 | 6 | 873,118 |
| 1983 | Junior Johnson | 30 | 6 | 8 | 4 | 2 | 2 | 3 | 1 | 4 | 7 | 3 | 824,858 |
| 1984 | Junior Johnson | 30 | 7 | 2 | 3 | 1 | 0 | 7 | 7 | 3 | 4 | 2 | 703,876 |
| 1985 | Junior Johnson | 28 | 3 | 6 | 6 | 2 | 1 | 3 | 2 | 5 | 4 | 1 | 1,318,735 |
| 1986 | Junior Johnson | 29 | 3 | 2 | 4 | 6 | 6 | 1 | 1 | 6 | 1 | 4 | 1,099,735 |
| 1987 | Rick Hendrick | 29 | 1 | 1 | 1 | 2 | 1 | 10 | 11 | 2 | 0 | 2 | 511,768 |
| 1988 | Rick Hendrick | 29 | 2 | 1 | 1 | 2 | 4 | 4 | 11 | 4 | 2 | 1 | 731,659 |
| 1989 | Rick Hendrick | 29 | 6 | 2 | 2 | 2 | 2 | 4 | 8 | 3 | 0 | 6 | 1,323,079 |
| 1990 | Rick Hendrick | 23 | 0 | 1 | 1 | 2 | 1 | 7 | 11 | 0 | 0 | 0 | 530,420 |
| 1991 | D. Waltrip | 29 | 2 | 2 | 1 | 0 | 0 | 12 | 6 | 6 | 0 | 0 | 604,854 |
| 1992 | D. Waltrip | 29 | 3 | 2 | 3 | 0 | 2 | 3 | 12 | 4 | 1 | 0 | 876,492 |
| 1993 | D. Waltrip | 30 | 0 | 0 | 2 | 1 | 1 | 6 | 15 | 5 | 0 | 0 | 746,646 |
| 1994 | D. Waltrip | 31 | 0 | 0 | 2 | 2 | 0 | 9 | 17 | 1 | 0 | 0 | 835,680 |
| 1995 | D. Waltrip | 31 | 0 | 0 | 1 | 3 | 0 | 4 | 12 | 11 | 1 | 0 | 850,632 |
| 1996 | D. Waltrip | 31 | 0 | 0 | 0 | 0 | 0 | 2 | 18 | 11 | 0 | 0 | 740,745 |
| 1997 | D. Waltrip | 31 | 0 | 0 | 0 | 0 | 1 | 3 | 22 | 5 | 0 | 0 | 958,679 |
| 1998 | D. Waltrip | 5 | 0 | 0 | 0 | 0 | 0 | 0 | 3 | 2 | 0 | 0 | 222,865 |
|  | D. Earnhardt | 13 | 0 | 0 | 0 | 0 | 1 | 1 | 9 | 2 | 0 | 0 | 398,615 |
|  | T. Beverly | 15 | 0 | 0 | 0 | 0 | 0 | 0 | 14 | 1 | 0 | 0 | 434,995 |
| 1999 | T. Carter | 27 | 0 | 0 | 0 | 0 | 0 | 0 | 23 | 4 | 0 | 0 | 973,133 |
| 2000 | T. Carter | 29 | 0 | 0 | 0 | 0 | 0 | 0 | 11 | 7 | 0 | 1 | 1,246,280 |
| TOTAL | | 809 | 84 | 58 | 62 | 41 | 31 | 111 | 236 | 177 | 59 | 54 | $ 19,416,618 |

# Cale Yarborough

(1957 through 1988)
ALL WINSTON CUP RACES

| Year | Car Owner | Races | Won | 2nd | 3rd | 4th | 5th | 6-10th | 11-31st | DNF | Poles | Outside Poles | Money Won |
|---|---|---|---|---|---|---|---|---|---|---|---|---|---|
| 1957 | B. Weatherly | 1 | 0 | 0 | 0 | 0 | 0 | 0 | 0 | 1 | 0 | 0 | $ 100 |
| 1959 | C. Yarborough | 1 | 0 | 0 | 0 | 0 | 0 | 0 | 0 | 1 | 0 | 0 | 150 |
| 1960 | C. Yarborough | 1 | 0 | 0 | 0 | 0 | 0 | 0 | 0 | 1 | 0 | 0 | 85 |
| 1961 | C. Yarborough | 1 | 0 | 0 | 0 | 0 | 0 | 0 | 0 | 1 | 0 | 0 | 200 |
| 1962 | C. Yarborough | 8 | 0 | 0 | 0 | 0 | 0 | 1 | 1 | 6 | 0 | 0 | 2,725 |
| 1963 | Herman Beam | 14 | 0 | 0 | 0 | 0 | 3 | 4 | 7 | 0 | 0 | 0 | 4,100 |
|  | C. Yarborough | 4 | 0 | 0 | 0 | 0 | 0 | 0 | 2 | 2 | 0 | 0 | 1,450 |
| 1964 | Herman Beam | 20 | 0 | 0 | 0 | 0 | 1 | 4 | 5 | 10 | 0 | 0 | 7,680 |
|  | C. Yarborough | 4 | 0 | 0 | 0 | 0 | 0 | 2 | 0 | 2 | 0 | 0 | 1,615 |
| 1965 | C. Yarborough | 21 | 0 | 0 | 1 | 0 | 0 | 5 | 1 | 14 | 0 | 0 | 6,540 |
|  | Ken Myler | 18 | 1 | 1 | 0 | 5 | 3 | 2 | 2 | 4 | 0 | 0 | 6,305 |
|  | B. Matthews | 7 | 0 | 2 | 0 | 0 | 0 | 0 | 0 | 5 | 0 | 1 | 12,295 |
| 1966 | B. Matthews | 8 | 0 | 2 | 0 | 0 | 0 | 3 | 0 | 3 | 0 | 0 | 18,290 |
|  | Ken Myler | 1 | 0 | 0 | 0 | 0 | 0 | 1 | 0 | 0 | 0 | 0 | 390 |
|  | Wood Brothers | 5 | 0 | 0 | 0 | 1 | 0 | 0 | 1 | 3 | 0 | 0 | 4,350 |
| 1967 | Wood Brothers | 16 | 2 | 3 | 1 | 1 | 0 | 0 | 0 | 9 | 4 | 2 | 56,685 |
| 1968 | Wood Brothers | 21 | 6 | 2 | 1 | 0 | 3 | 0 | 0 | 9 | 4 | 2 | 136,786 |
| 1969 | Wood Brothers | 19 | 2 | 2 | 1 | 2 | 0 | 1 | 0 | 11 | 6 | 2 | 74,240 |
| 1970 | Wood Brothers | 18 | 3 | 4 | 2 | 0 | 1 | 1 | 0 | 7 | 5 | 1 | 114,675 |
|  | Banjo Matthews | 1 | 0 | 0 | 0 | 0 | 0 | 0 | 0 | 1 | 0 | 0 | 1,200 |
| 1971 | C. Yarborough | 4 | 0 | 0 | 0 | 0 | 0 | 1 | 0 | 3 | 0 | 0 | 3,869 |
| 1972 | C. Yarborough | 5 | 0 | 0 | 0 | 0 | 1 | 3 | 0 | 1 | 0 | 0 | 11,332 |
| 1973 | Junior Johnson | 28 | 4 | 6 | 4 | 1 | 1 | 3 | 1 | 8 | 5 | 4 | 162,235 |
| 1974 | Junior Johnson | 30 | 10 | 4 | 5 | 1 | 1 | 1 | 1 | 7 | 3 | 6 | 255,525 |
| 1975 | Junior Johnson | 27 | 3 | 3 | 3 | 3 | 1 | 0 | 0 | 14 | 3 | 0 | 139,258 |
| 1976 | Junior Johnson | 30 | 9 | 6 | 3 | 1 | 2 | 1 | 3 | 5 | 2 | 3 | 387,173 |
| 1977 | Junior Johnson | 30 | 9 | 6 | 4 | 3 | 3 | 2 | 3 | 0 | 3 | 7 | 477,499 |
| 1978 | Junior Johnson | 30 | 10 | 6 | 1 | 5 | 1 | 1 | 4 | 2 | 8 | 7 | 530,751 |
| 1979 | Junior Johnson | 31 | 4 | 2 | 6 | 4 | 2 | 3 | 4 | 6 | 1 | 4 | 413,872 |
| 1980 | Junior Johnson | 31 | 6 | 4 | 4 | 4 | 1 | 3 | 4 | 5 | 14 | 6 | 537,358 |
| 1981 | M.C. Anderson | 18 | 2 | 1 | 2 | 0 | 1 | 3 | 2 | 7 | 2 | 3 | 150,840 |
| 1982 | M.C. Anderson | 16 | 3 | 2 | 1 | 2 | 0 | 0 | 0 | 8 | 2 | 0 | 219,090 |
| 1983 | Harry Ranier | 16 | 4 | 0 | 0 | 0 | 0 | 4 | 0 | 8 | 3 | 1 | 254,535 |
| 1984 | Harry Ranier | 16 | 3 | 1 | 3 | 1 | 2 | 0 | 4 | 2 | 4 | 0 | 385,853 |
| 1985 | Harry Ranier | 16 | 2 | 2 | 2 | 0 | 0 | 1 | 0 | 9 | 0 | 4 | 310,465 |
| 1986 | Harry Ranier | 16 | 0 | 0 | 2 | 0 | 0 | 3 | 1 | 10 | 1 | 0 | 137,010 |
| 1987 | C. Yarborough | 16 | 0 | 0 | 0 | 1 | 1 | 2 | 3 | 9 | 0 | 0 | 111,025 |
| 1988 | C. Yarborough | 10 | 0 | 0 | 0 | 0 | 0 | 3 | 3 | 4 | 0 | 0 | 66,065 |
| TOTAL |  | 559 | 83 | 59 | 46 | 35 | 28 | 58 | 52 | 198 | 70 | 53 | $5,003,616 |

HISTORY

# Owner wins (1949-2003)

| | | | | | | | | | |
|---|---|---|---|---|---|---|---|---|---|
| 1. | Petty Enterprises | 271 | | # Banjo Matthews | 9 | * Kenny Bernstein | 3 | Joe Hendrick | 1 | * Mamie Reynolds | 1 |
| 2. | * Junior Johnson | 139 | 42. | * John Eanes | 8 | # Jim Stephens | 3 | * Junie Donlavey | 1 | * John Rostek | 1 |
| 3. | Rick Hendrick | 113 | | * Ray Fox | 8 | # Bradford White | 3 | * Pete Stewart | 1 | * Tony Sampo | 1 |
| 4. | Wood Brothers | 97 | | * Johnny Griffin | 8 | * Vel Miletich | 3 | * Tommy Thompson | 1 | * Al Schmidhamer | 1 |
| 5. | * Holman-#Moody | 92 | 45. | Felix Sabates | 7 | # Fireball Roberts | 3 | * Charles Vance | 1 | * Joe Bearscheck | 1 |
| 6. | Richard Childress | 76 | | * Ned Jarrett | 7 | 85. Andy Petree | 2 | * David Vaughn | 1 | * W.H. Watson | 1 |
| 7. | * Bud Moore | 63 | | * Rod Osterlund | 7 | * Roy Burdick | 2 | * Ratus Walters | 1 | * Reid Shaw | 1 |
| 8. | Jack Roush | 61 | | * Jim Reed | 7 | * Jack Beebe | 2 | * Cale Yarborough | 1 | # Westmoreland | |
| 9. | # Carl Kiekhaefer | 54 | | * Bobby Allison | 7 | * Mike Curb | 2 | * Lake Speed | 1 | France | 1 |
| | Robert Yates | 54 | | * J.D. Bracken | 7 | * John Hines | 2 | * Richard Jackson | 1 | # Gober Sosebee | 1 |
| 11. | Roger Penske | 50 | | # W.G. Holloway Jr. | 7 | * George Hutchens | 2 | * Max Welborn | 1 | # Nelson Stacy | 1 |
| 12. | * Bill Gardner | 43 | 52. | * Darrell Waltrip | 6 | * Marvin Panch | 2 | * Larry Bettinger | 1 | # Dale Swanson | 1 |
| | # Nord Krauskopf | 43 | | * Billy Hagan | 6 | * Raymond Parks | 2 | * Jack Bowsher | 1 | * Bill Blair | 1 |
| 14. | * Cotton Owens | 40 | | * Ricky Rudd | 6 | * B.A. Pless | 2 | * J.D. Braswell | 1 | # Millard Clothier | 1 |
| 15. | # Herb Thomas | 39 | | * Tom Friedkin | 6 | * Marvin Porter | 2 | * Allan Brooke | 1 | # Bobby Courtwright | 1 |
| 16. | Joe Gibbs | 36 | | # Speedy Thompson | 6 | * Monroe Shook | 2 | * Elmer Brooks | 1 | # Carl Dane | 1 |
| 17. | # Harry Melling | 34 | | # Frank Strickland | 6 | * Lyle Stelter | 2 | * Marvin Burke | 1 | # Shorty Johns | 1 |
| 18. | * Bondy Long | 31 | 58. | Bill Davis | 5 | * Cliff Stewart | 2 | * Cos Cancilla | 1 | * Harold Kite | 1 |
| 19. | * Rex Lovette | 29 | | Chip Ganassi | 5 | * Louie Weathersby | 2 | * June Cleveland | 1 | # James Mulgrew | 1 |
| 20. | * White-Clements | #24 | | * Hoss Ellington | 5 | * Bob Whitcomb | 2 | * Crawford Brothers | 1 | * Ken Myler | 1 |
| | * Harry Ranier | 24 | | * Hugh Babb | 5 | * Rex White | 2 | * John Edmunds | 1 | # Jimmy Pardue | 1 |
| 22. | * Raymond Beadle | 20 | | * Buchan-Lowe | 5 | * Guy Wilson | 2 | * Buddy Elliott | 1 | # Shorty Rollins | 1 |
| | * Jack Smith | 20 | | # Mario Rossi | 5 | * James Hylton | 2 | * Bill Ellis | 1 | # Charlie Schwam | 1 |
| 24. | # Frank Christian | 19 | | # Ernest Woods | 5 | # Fred Elder | 2 | * Ray Erickson | 1 | # Frank Arford | 1 |
| 25. | # Pete DePaolo | 18 | | # Alan Kulwicki | 5 | # Eddie Gray | 2 | * Jack Gaynor | 1 | # Wendell Scott | 1 |
| 26. | # Ted Chester | 17 | | # Bob Flock | 5 | # Elmo Langley | 2 | * John Golabek | 1 | * Bill Amick | 1 |
| 27. | D. Earnhardt, Inc. | 15 | 67. | Geoff Bodine | 4 | # Buckshot Morris | 2 | * Danny Graves | 1 | # Paul Whiteman | 1 |
| 28. | Morgan-McClure | 14 | | Georgetta Roush | 4 | # Sam Rice | 2 | * Tom Harbison | 1 | | |
| | # Buck Baker | 14 | | * Lloyd Dane | 4 | # Carl Rupert | 2 | * Johnny Hayes | 1 | **183 OWNERS** | **2,022** |
| 30. | * Marshall Teague | 12 | | * Stavola Brothers | 4 | * Perry Smith | 2 | * Frank Hayworth | 1 | | |
| | * L.G. DeWitt | 12 | | * Rahilly-Mock | 4 | * Bill Stroppe | 2 | * Floyd Johnson | 1 | * Team/owner(s) quit or | |
| 32. | * Paul Spaulding | 11 | | * Jim Stacy | 4 | * Jon Thorne | 2 | * John Kieper | 1 | retired | |
| 33. | * Ray Nichels | 10 | | # Eddie Pagan | 4 | * Bob Welborn | 2 | * Sam Knox | 1 | # Deceased | |
| | # M.C. Anderson | 10 | | # John Masoni | 4 | # John Dietz | 2 | * Paul Lewis | 1 | a 1,998 races from 1949- | |
| | # T.W. Chapman | 10 | 75. | Jeff Gordon | 5 | # Julian Buesink | 2 | * Oscar Maples | 1 | 2002. | |
| | # Smokey Yunick | 10 | | Ray Evernham | 4 | 115. Nelson Bowers | 1 | * George Miller | 1 | b 6 wins by Convertible | |
| 37. | * Needham-Reynolds | 9 | | * Penske-Kranefuss | 3 | Cal Wells, III | 2 | * Lee Moyer | 1 | Division, 3 by Grand | |
| | * J.H. Petty | 9 | | * Don Rogala | 3 | Dave Marcis | 1 | * Norm Nelson | 1 | American Division, 3 by | |
| | * Leo Jackson | 9 | | * Hubert | | Mark Martin | 1 | * W.M. Packer | 1 | Short Track Division in | |
| | # Burton-Robinson | 9 | | Westmoreland | 3 | Geoff Smith | 1 | * Jim Paschal | 1 | combined races. | |

# NASCAR Busch Series

# Milestones

The NASCAR Busch Series, Grand National Division, which enters its 22nd season in 2003, has established itself as the No. 2 motorsports series in the United States, second only to the NASCAR Winston Cup Series.

The NASCAR Busch Series represents the middle rung in NASCAR's national series, situated between the top NASCAR Winston Cup Series and NASCAR Craftsman Truck Series. The NASCAR Busch Series has proven to be an outstanding series for competitors who aspire to become NASCAR Winston Cup Series drivers, with many of today's premier drivers having competed in the series over the years. However, many drivers also have chosen to spend their entire careers in this division due to the competitive nature and popularity of the series.

The series was formed in 1982 when NASCAR consolidated the old Late Model Sportsman division into a touring series of nearly 30 races per year. The series, however, has roots dating back more than five decades ago. The series debuted in 1950 as the NASCAR Sportsman Division and remained as so until 1968 before being renamed the NASCAR Late Model Sportsman Division. In 1982, Anheuser-Busch, Inc. joined with NASCAR to create the evolving touring circuit now commonly known as the NASCAR Busch Series, Grand National Division.

Below are some of the milestones in the history of the series:

**1950** The origin of the NASCAR Busch Series, Grand National Division traces back to this year when the series was known as the NASCAR Sportsman Division. Drivers would frequently compete in three to four races per week approximately 60 races per year throughout the East Coast region of the United States. Some of the notable names that claimed championships in this division during these early years were: Ralph Earnhardt (1956) and Ned Jarrett (1957-58), fathers of future NASCAR Winston Cup champions Dale Earnhardt and Dale Jarrett.

**1968** The NASCAR Sportsman Division undergoes its first name change, now known as the NASCAR Late Model Sportsman Division.

**1982** NASCAR Late Model Sportsman Division is consolidated into a national touring series. The inaugural season consisted of 29 races in the first season and was renamed the NASCAR Budweiser Late Model Sportsman Series.

**February 13, 1982** First race of the new touring series was held at Daytona International Speedway the Goody's 300. Mike Porter took the pole position and Dale Earnhardt won the inaugural race in a Pontiac. This race also marked the first superspeedway event in the history of the series.

**February 20, 1982** Series has its first short track race, the Eastern 150 at Richmond (Va.) International Raceway. Tommy Houston won the event.

**March 28, 1982** Diane Teel becomes the first female driver to start a NASCAR Busch Series race, competing at Martinsville (Va.) Speedway and finishing 26th.

**October 31, 1982** The series championship comes down to the final race of the season at Martinsville Speedway between Jack Ingram and Sam Ard. Ingram, despite a 26th-place finish, holds off Ard, who finished sixth, to claim the first series title by 49 points.

**October 8, 1983** Sam Ard establishes a series record with four consecutive wins during the season. Ard won at South Boston (Va.) Speedway (9/17); Martinsville Speedway (9/24); Orange County (N.C.) Speedway (10/1); and Charlotte Motor Speedway (10/8). The series record still stands.

**1984** One of the most important milestones in series history as Anheuser-Busch switches its series sponsorship from its Budweiser brand to Busch. The NASCAR Budweiser Late Model Sportsman Series is renamed the NASCAR Busch Grand National Series.

**May 26-27, 1984** Bobby Allison becomes the first driver to sweep a race weekend, winning the NASCAR Busch Series and NASCAR Winston Cup Series races at Charlotte Motor Speedway. He won the NASCAR Busch race the Mello Yello 300 on Saturday and came back the next day to win the NASCAR Winston Cup event, the World 600.

**October 20, 1984** Sam Ard clinches his second consecutive NASCAR Busch Series title, becoming the first driver in history to win back-to-back championships. He also becomes the first multiple champion in the series.

**1985** Jack Ingram captures his second NASCAR Busch Series Grand National title, joining two-time champ Ard as the only champions in the four-year-old series.

**July 6, 1986** The series' first road course race is held at Road Atlanta in Braselton, Ga. The race was won by Darrell Waltrip.

**1987** Larry Pearson, son of the legendary David Pearson, wins his second consecutive series championship, joining Sam Ard (1983-84) as the only drivers at this stage to win back-to-back titles.

**1989** The Raybestos Rookie of the Year award is established, with Kenny Wallace claiming the inaugural honor. Wallace edged Bobby Hamilton for the award, posting 16 top-10 finishes in 29 starts en route to a sixth-place finish in the championship. ... Jack Ingram earns the achievement of first driver in the NASCAR Busch Series to earn $1 million in his career.

**1992** Joe Nemechek earns the NASCAR Busch Series championship in the closest battle in series history. Nemechek defeated runner-up Bobby Labonte by just three points for the crown. The margin remains the closest in series history. ... Jeff Gordon becomes the first driver to win $100,000 in a NASCAR Busch Series race at Charlotte Motor Speedway.

**1995** The series name is altered slightly, changing to the present NASCAR Busch Series, Grand National Division.

**Oct. 19, 1996** Tommy Houston, a 15-year series veteran, makes his final NASCAR Busch Series start at the season finale at North Carolina Speedway in Rockingham, N.C. Houston, who finished 39th that day, concludes his career with a series-record 417 starts.

**1997** Randy LaJoie becomes the third driver in history to win back-to-back NASCAR Busch Series championships, joining Sam Ard (1983-84) and Larry Pearson (1986-87). LaJoie also enjoyed another piece of history, becoming the first driver to earn $1 million in a single season.

**March 15, 1997** The NASCAR Busch Series travels to the West Coast for the Las Vegas 300 at Las Vegas Motor Speedway, marking the first race west of the Mississippi River in history. California Speedway, Texas Motor Speedway and Gateway International Raceway near St. Louis also were added to the series schedule that season.

**September 5, 1998** Dick Trickle, at 56 years, 11 months, becomes the oldest driver to win a NASCAR Busch Series race, at Darlington (S.C.) Raceway.

**October 17, 1998** The Petty racing legacy is extended to a fourth generation as Adam Petty, son of Kyle, makes his NASCAR Busch Series debut at Gateway International Raceway in Madison, Ill. Petty finished 27th.

**November 13, 1998** NASCAR and Anheuser-Busch announce a multi-year renewal of the Busch beer title sponsorship. With this announcement came an increase in the series' point fund ($650,000 to $1.5 million); a Busch beer marketing campaign and an integrated, media-driven marketing plan which includes: new series logo; aggressive national and market-specific public relations efforts; comprehensive coverage on NASCAR Online; and additional inclusion on licensed TV, radio and print media.

**January 1999** Final attendance figures are announced for the 1998 season and the numbers reveal that more than 2 million attended races that year.

**June 27, 1999** At Watkins Glen (N.Y.) International, Bill Lester makes history as the first African-American driver to start a NASCAR Busch Series race. Lester finished 21st after starting 24th.

**July 4, 1999** Casey Atwood, at 18 years, 11 months, wins at The Milwaukee (Wis.) Mile, becoming the youngest winner of a NASCAR Busch Series race in history. Atwood easily eclipses the mark set by Rob Moroso, who was 19 years, nine months old when he won previously at Myrtle Beach (S.C.) Speedway on July 2, 1988.

**November 11, 1999** NASCAR announces a six-year television contract with NBC Sports and Turner Sports (a joint venture) and an eight-year agreement with FOX and its FX cable network, beginning with the 2001 NASCAR Winston Cup Series and NASCAR Busch Series seasons.

**November 13, 1999** Dale Earnhardt Jr. is crowned the 1999 series champion, becoming the fourth driver to win consecutive titles and second in a row. Earnhardt Jr. joins Sam Ard (1983-84), Larry Pearson (1986-87) and Randy LaJoie (1996-97).

**November 2000** Jeff Green earns his first NASCAR Busch Series championship and enhances the family racing legacy. Coupled with his brother David's series title in 1994, the Greens become the first brothers to win NASCAR Busch Series titles. ... For the first time in NASCAR Busch Series history, three rookies (Kevin Harvick, Ron Hornaday and Jimmie Johnson) finish in the top 10 in the final driver point standings.

**2001** As a result of increased broadcast and cable coverage on NBC/TNT and FOX/FX, the NASCAR Busch Series enjoys tremendous increases in television ratings and viewership. The number of households tuning in to watch NASCAR Busch Series races increases 33 percent compared to the previous year. The NASCAR Busch Series is establishing itself as the No. 2 motorsports series in the United States.

**November 3, 2001** Kevin Harvick becomes the 15th different NASCAR Busch Series champion since 1982 in what becomes an incredible season. While chasing the title, team owner Richard Childress asks Harvick to take over the team's NASCAR Winston Cup ride of Dale Earnhardt, who was involved in a fatal accident in the season opener. Harvick responded by finishing ninth in the NASCAR Winston Cup championship and capturing the NASCAR Winston Cup Raybestos Rookie-of-the-Year award. ... Childress becomes the only car owner ever to win championships in all three of NASCAR's national series: NASCAR Winston Cup (1986-87, '90-91, '93-94 with Dale Earnhardt); NASCAR Craftsman Truck Series (1995 with Mike Skinner); and NASCAR Busch Series with Harvick.

**2002** Greg Biffle of Roush Racing captures the NASCAR Busch Series crown, becoming the first driver in history to win titles in the NASCAR Craftsman Series and this series. Biffle becomes the first driver in NASCAR Busch Series history to top $2 million in single-season earnings.

**2002** Brian Vickers is NASCAR's youngest champion ever at 20 years old. He edges runnerup David Green by 14 points. The No. 5 Chevrolet that Vickers drives is fielded by Hendrick Motorsports, which joins Roush Racing and Richard Childress Racing as the only teams to have won championships in each of NASCAR's top three series— Craftsman Trucks, Busch and what becomes NEXTEL Cup.

# NASCAR Busch Series drivers

## Casey Atwood
**Birthdate:** 8/25/80 **Birth place:** Antioch, Tenn.
**Car:** Chevrolet **Car owner:** Fitz/Bradshaw

### CAREER STATISTICS

| Year | Rank | Starts | Wins | Poles | Top 5 | Top 10 | Races Led | Laps Led |
|---|---|---|---|---|---|---|---|---|
| 1998 | 38 | 13 | 0 | 2 | 1 | 1 | 2 | 129 |
| 1999 | 13 | 31 | 2 | 2 | 5 | 9 | 5 | 244 |
| 2000 | 8 | 32 | 0 | 2 | 0 | 8 | 3 | 108 |
| 2003 | 37 | 14 | 0 | 0 | 0 | 4 | 0 | 0 |
| Totals | | 90 | 2 | 6 | 6 | 22 | 10 | 481 |

## Stanton Barrett
**Birthdate:** 12/01/72 **Birth place:** Bishop, Calif.
**Car:** Ford **Car owner:** Stanton Barrett

### CAREER STATISTICS

| Year | Rank | Starts | Wins | Poles | Top 5 | Top 10 | Races Led | Laps Led |
|---|---|---|---|---|---|---|---|---|
| 1992 | 99 | 1 | 0 | 0 | 0 | 0 | 0 | 0 |
| 1993 | 121 | 1 | 0 | 0 | 0 | 0 | 0 | 0 |
| 1994 | 77 | 3 | 0 | 0 | 0 | 0 | 0 | 0 |
| 1995 | 119 | 1 | 0 | 0 | 0 | 0 | 0 | 0 |
| 1996 | 64 | 2 | 0 | 0 | 1 | 1 | 0 | 0 |
| 1997 | 60 | 6 | 0 | 0 | 0 | 0 | 0 | 0 |
| 1998 | 49 | 10 | 0 | 0 | 0 | 1 | 0 | 0 |
| 1999 | 48 | 12 | 0 | 0 | 0 | 0 | 0 | 0 |
| 2001 | 74 | 6 | 0 | 0 | 0 | 0 | 0 | 0 |
| 2002 | 46 | 12 | 0 | 0 | 0 | 0 | 0 | 0 |
| 2003 | 25 | 22 | 0 | 0 | 0 | 4 | 1 | 15 |
| Totals | | 76 | 0 | 0 | 1 | 6 | 1 | 15 |

## Mike Bliss
**Birthdate:** 4/5/65 **Birth place:** Milwaukie, Ore.
**Car:** Chevrolet **Car owner:** Joe Gibbs

### CAREER STATISTICS

| Year | Rank | Starts | Wins | Poles | Top 5 | Top 10 | Races Led | Laps Led |
|---|---|---|---|---|---|---|---|---|
| 1998 | 71 | 2 | 0 | 0 | 0 | 1 | 0 | 0 |
| 1999 | 84 | 3 | 0 | 0 | 0 | 0 | 0 | 0 |
| 2000 | 100 | 1 | 0 | 0 | 0 | 0 | 0 | 0 |
| 2001 | 143 | 1 | 0 | 0 | 0 | 0 | 0 | 0 |
| 2003 | 10 | 34 | 0 | 0 | 8 | 14 | 3 | 136 |
| Totals | | 41 | 0 | 0 | 8 | 15 | 3 | 136 |

## Chad Blount
**Birthdate:** 9/4/79 **Birth place:** Walkerton, Ind.
**Car:** Dodge **Car owner:** Jessel Motorsports

### CAREER STATISTICS

| Year | Rank | Starts | Wins | Poles | Top 5 | Top 10 | Races Led | Laps Led |
|---|---|---|---|---|---|---|---|---|
| 2003 | 33 | 19 | 0 | 0 | 1 | 2 | 1 | 28 |
| Totals | | 19 | 0 | 0 | 1 | 2 | 1 | 28 |

## Clint Bowyer
**Birth place:** Emporia, Kan. **Car:** Chevrolet **Car owner:** Richard Childress

Midwestern short track ace is 24 years old.

## Conrad Burr
**Birthdate:** 11/23/68. **Birth place:** Concord, N.C.
**Car:** Chevrolet **Car owner:** Black Cat Racing

Ran 4 Craftsman Truck Series races in 2003.

## Kyle Busch
**Birthdate:** 5/2/85 **Birth place:** Las Vegas **Car:** No. 5 Chevrolet **Car owner:** Ricky Hendrick

### CAREER STATISTICS

| Year | Rank | Starts | Wins | Poles | Top 5 | Top 10 | Races Led | Laps Led |
|---|---|---|---|---|---|---|---|---|
| 2003 | 48 | 7 | 0 | 0 | 2 | 3 | 2 | 39 |
| Totals | | 7 | 0 | 0 | 2 | 3 | 2 | 39 |

## Stacy Compton
**Birthdate:** 5/26/67 **Birth place:** Grit, Va. **Car:** Ford **Car owner:** Tad Geschickter

### CAREER STATISTICS

| Year | Rank | Starts | Wins | Poles | Top 5 | Top 10 | Races Led | Laps Led |
|---|---|---|---|---|---|---|---|---|
| 2001 | 96 | 1 | 0 | 0 | 0 | 1 | 0 | 0 |
| 2002 | 9 | 34 | 0 | 0 | 5 | 11 | 6 | 82 |
| 2003 | 11 | 34 | 0 | 1 | 3 | 11 | 6 | 49 |
| Totals | | 69 | 0 | 1 | 8 | 23 | 12 | 131 |

## Kerry Earnhardt

**Birthdate:** 12/8/69 **Birth place:** Kannapolis, N.C. **Car:** Chevrolet

### CAREER STATISTICS

| Year | Rank | Starts | Wins | Poles | Top 5 | Top 10 | Races Led | Laps Led |
|---|---|---|---|---|---|---|---|---|
| 1998 | 73 | 3 | 0 | 0 | 0 | 0 | 0 | 0 |
| 1999 | 81 | 4 | 0 | 0 | 0 | 0 | 0 | 0 |
| 2001 | 73 | 3 | 0 | 0 | 0 | 0 | 0 | 0 |
| 2002 | 22 | 34 | 0 | 0 | 2 | 5 | 1 | 9 |
| 2003 | 27 | 21 | 0 | 0 | 0 | 0 | 2 | 4 |
| Totals | | 65 | 0 | 0 | 2 | 5 | 3 | 13 |

## Tim Fedewa

**Birthdate:** 5/9/67 **Birth place:** Holt, Mich. **Car:** Chevrolet **Car owner:** FitzBradshaw Racing

### CAREER STATISTICS

| Year | Rank | Starts | Wins | Poles | Top 5 | Top 10 | Races Led | Laps Led |
|---|---|---|---|---|---|---|---|---|
| 1992 | 60 | 4 | 0 | 0 | 0 | 0 | 1 | 5 |
| 1993 | 18 | 25 | 0 | 0 | 1 | 4 | 1 | 8 |
| 1994 | 10 | 28 | 0 | 0 | 1 | 8 | 3 | 13 |
| 1995 | 7 | 26 | 1 | 1 | 4 | 4 | 6 | 145 |
| 1996 | 20 | 25 | 0 | 0 | 1 | 2 | 1 | 14 |
| 1997 | 9 | 30 | 0 | 1 | 4 | 11 | 4 | 88 |
| 1998 | 7 | 31 | 2 | 1 | 4 | 10 | 4 | 231 |
| 1999 | 14 | 30 | 0 | 0 | 3 | 9 | 5 | 73 |
| 2000 | 18 | 30 | 1 | 1 | 3 | 6 | 1 | 118 |
| 2001 | 25 | 25 | 0 | 0 | 2 | 6 | 1 | 1 |
| 2002 | 51 | 9 | 0 | 0 | 1 | 1 | 1 | 2 |
| 2003 | 36 | 15 | 0 | 0 | 0 | 0 | 0 | 0 |
| Totals | | 278 | 4 | 4 | 24 | 61 | 28 | 698 |

## David Green

**Birthdate:** 1/28/58 **Birth place:** Owensboro, Ky. **Car:** Chevrolet **Car owner:** Clarence Brewer

### CAREER STATISTICS

| Year | Rank | Starts | Wins | Poles | Top 5 | Top 10 | Races Led | Laps Led |
|---|---|---|---|---|---|---|---|---|
| 1989 | 96 | 1 | 0 | 0 | 0 | 0 | 0 | 0 |
| 1990 | 85 | 2 | 0 | 0 | 0 | 0 | 0 | 0 |
| 1991 | 13 | 29 | 1 | 1 | 6 | 9 | 5 | 210 |
| 1993 | 3 | 28 | 0 | 0 | 6 | 16 | 5 | 94 |
| 1994 | 1 | 28 | 1 | 9 | 10 | 14 | 11 | 380 |
| 1995 | 12 | 26 | 1 | 4 | 4 | 6 | 7 | 271 |
| 1996 | 2 | 26 | 2 | 4 | 13 | 18 | 10 | 501 |
| 1998 | 26 | 19 | 0 | 0 | 7 | 8 | 1 | 32 |

| Year | Rank | Starts | Wins | Poles | Top 5 | Top 10 | Races Led | Laps Led |
|---|---|---|---|---|---|---|---|---|
| 1999 | 27 | 17 | 0 | 1 | 1 | 7 | 0 | 0 |
| 2000 | 9 | 32 | 0 | 0 | 2 | 11 | 6 | 88 |
| 2001 | 13 | 33 | 0 | 0 | 0 | 6 | 1 | 1 |
| 2002 | 40 | 12 | 0 | 0 | 3 | 4 | 1 | 9 |
| 2003 | 2 | 34 | 3 | 2 | 11 | 21 | 10 | 122 |
| Totals | | 287 | 8 | 21 | 63 | 120 | 57 | 1708 |

## Mark Green

**Birthdate:** 4/8/59 **Birth place:** Owensboro, Ky. **Car:** Dodge **Car owner:** Akins Motorsports

### CAREER STATISTICS

| Year | Rank | Starts | Wins | Poles | Top 5 | Top 10 | Races Led | Laps Led |
|---|---|---|---|---|---|---|---|---|
| 1995 | 78 | 2 | 0 | 0 | 0 | 0 | 0 | 0 |
| 1996 | 46 | 10 | 0 | 0 | 0 | 1 | 0 | 0 |
| 1997 | 11 | 30 | 0 | 0 | 1 | 5 | 1 | 6 |
| 1998 | 13 | 31 | 0 | 0 | 0 | 4 | 1 | 66 |
| 1999 | 21 | 30 | 0 | 0 | 0 | 1 | 0 | 0 |
| 2000 | 26 | 30 | 0 | 0 | 0 | 1 | 0 | 0 |
| 2001 | 40 | 14 | 0 | 0 | 0 | 1 | 0 | 0 |
| 2002 | 32 | 21 | 0 | 0 | 0 | 0 | 0 | 0 |
| 2003 | 70 | 5 | 0 | 0 | 0 | 0 | 0 | 0 |
| Totals | | 173 | 0 | 0 | 1 | 13 | 2 | 72 |

## Larry Gunselman

**Birthdate:** 12/1/64 **Birth place:** Sierra Village, Calif. **Car:** Chevrolet **Car owner:** Wayne Day

### CAREER STATISTICS

| Year | Rank | Starts | Wins | Poles | Top 5 | Top 10 | Races Led | Laps Led |
|---|---|---|---|---|---|---|---|---|
| 2002 | 41 | 17 | 0 | 0 | 0 | 0 | 2 | 2 |
| 2003 | 21 | 34 | 0 | 0 | 0 | 0 | 0 | 0 |
| Totals | | 51 | 0 | 0 | 0 | 0 | 2 | 2 |

## Bobby Hamilton Jr.

**Birthdate:** 1/8/78 **Birth place:** Nashville **Car:** Ford **Car owner:** Ed Rensi

### CAREER STATISTICS

| Year | Rank | Starts | Wins | Poles | Top 5 | Top 10 | Races Led | Laps Led |
|---|---|---|---|---|---|---|---|---|
| 1998 | 87 | 2 | 0 | 0 | 0 | 0 | 1 | 4 |
| 1999 | 39 | 18 | 0 | 0 | 0 | 1 | 1 | 1 |
| 2000 | 19 | 32 | 0 | 1 | 1 | 3 | 0 | 0 |
| 2001 | 17 | 33 | 0 | 1 | 2 | 5 | 3 | 40 |
| 2002 | 8 | 34 | 1 | 0 | 6 | 15 | 11 | 357 |
| 2003 | 4 | 34 | 4 | 1 | 13 | 22 | 13 | 643 |
| Totals | | 153 | 5 | 3 | 22 | 46 | 29 | 1045 |

## Mike Harmon

**Birthdate:** 1/24/58 **Birth place:** Birmingport, Ala. **Car:** Chevrolet **Car owner:** Greg Mixon

### CAREER STATISTICS

| Year | Rank | Starts | Wins | Poles | Top 5 | Top 10 | Races Led | Laps Led |
|---|---|---|---|---|---|---|---|---|
| 1996 | 56 | 7 | 0 | 0 | 0 | 0 | 0 | 0 |
| 2001 | 51 | 15 | 0 | 0 | 0 | 0 | 1 | 1 |
| 2002 | 38 | 25 | 0 | 0 | 0 | 0 | 0 | 0 |
| 2003 | 23 | 32 | 0 | 0 | 0 | 0 | 0 | 0 |
| Totals | | 79 | 0 | 0 | 0 | 0 | 1 | 1 |

## Ron Hornaday Jr.

**Birthdate:** 6/20/58 **Birth place:** Palmdale, Calif. **Car:** Chevrolet **Car owner:** Richard Childress

### CAREER STATISTICS

| Year | Rank | Starts | Wins | Poles | Top 5 | Top 10 | Races Led | Laps Led |
|---|---|---|---|---|---|---|---|---|
| 1998 | 61 | 4 | 0 | 0 | 0 | 1 | 0 | 0 |
| 1999 | 68 | 4 | 0 | 0 | 0 | 1 | 1 | 98 |
| 2000 | 5 | 32 | 2 | 0 | 6 | 13 | 8 | 246 |
| 2001 | 36 | 12 | 0 | 0 | 1 | 3 | 2 | 26 |
| 2002 | 18 | 30 | 0 | 1 | 5 | 8 | 6 | 231 |
| 2003 | 3 | 34 | 1 | 0 | 8 | 17 | 12 | 403 |
| Totals | | 116 | 3 | 1 | 20 | 43 | 29 | 1004 |

## Kasey Kahne

**Birthdate:** 4/10/80 **Birth place:** Enumclaw, Wash. **Car:** Dodge **Car owner:** Akins Motorsports.

### CAREER STATISTICS

| Year | Rank | Starts | Wins | Poles | Top 5 | Top 10 | Races Led | Laps Led |
|---|---|---|---|---|---|---|---|---|
| 2002 | 33 | 20 | 0 | 0 | 0 | 1 | 0 | 0 |
| 2003 | 7 | 34 | 1 | 1 | 4 | 14 | 6 | 47 |
| Totals | | 54 | 1 | 1 | 4 | 15 | 6 | 47 |

## Jason Keller

**Birthdate:** 4/23/70 **Birth place:** Greenville, S.C. **Car:** FORD **Car owner:** Keith Barnwell

### CAREER STATISTICS

| Year | Rank | Starts | Wins | Poles | Top 5 | Top 10 | Races Led | Laps Led |
|---|---|---|---|---|---|---|---|---|
| 1991 | 105 | 1 | 0 | 0 | 0 | 0 | 0 | 0 |
| 1992 | 53 | 5 | 0 | 0 | 0 | 0 | 0 | 0 |
| 1993 | 33 | 12 | 0 | 0 | 0 | 1 | 0 | 0 |
| 1994 | 17 | 27 | 0 | 3 | 1 | 7 | 3 | 99 |
| 1995 | 4 | 26 | 1 | 1 | 6 | 12 | 4 | 176 |
| 1996 | 6 | 26 | 0 | 0 | 3 | 10 | 1 | 1 |
| 1997 | 13 | 29 | 0 | 0 | 2 | 9 | 1 | 26 |
| 1998 | 16 | 31 | 0 | 0 | 2 | 8 | 1 | 1 |
| 1999 | 8 | 32 | 2 | 3 | 5 | 12 | 8 | 503 |
| 2000 | 2 | 32 | 1 | 0 | 13 | 19 | 6 | 104 |
| 2001 | 3 | 33 | 1 | 0 | 14 | 22 | 6 | 106 |
| 2002 | 2 | 34 | 4 | 2 | 17 | 22 | 15 | 785 |
| 2003 | 5 | 34 | 1 | 2 | 10 | 17 | 8 | 145 |
| Totals | | 322 | 10 | 11 | 73 | 139 | 53 | 1946 |

## Tammy Jo Kirk

**Birthdate:** 5/6/62 **Birth place:** Dalton, Ga. **Car:** Ford **Car owner:** Jay Robinson

### CAREER STATISTICS

| Year | Rank | Starts | Wins | Poles | Top 5 | Top 10 | Races Led | Laps Led |
|---|---|---|---|---|---|---|---|---|
| 2003 | 45 | 15 | 0 | 0 | 0 | 0 | 0 | 0 |
| Totals | | 15 | 0 | 0 | 0 | 0 | 0 | 0 |

## Jason Leffler

**Birthdate:** 9/16/75 **Birth place:** Long Beach, Calif. **Car:** Chevrolet **Car owner:** Gene Haas

### CAREER STATISTICS

| Year | Rank | Starts | Wins | Poles | Top 5 | Top 10 | Races Led | Laps Led |
|---|---|---|---|---|---|---|---|---|
| 1999 | 74 | 4 | 0 | 0 | 0 | 0 | 0 | 0 |
| 2000 | 20 | 31 | 0 | 3 | 2 | 4 | 3 | 47 |
| 2003 | 52 | 6 | 0 | 0 | 1 | 1 | 2 | 6 |
| Totals | | 41 | 0 | 3 | 3 | 5 | 5 | 53 |

## Ashton Lewis

**Birthdate:** 1/22/72 **Birth place:** Chesapeake, Va. **Car:** Chevrolet **Car owner:** Lewis Motorsports.

## Damon Lusk

**Birthdate:** 9/18/77 **Birth place:** Kennewick, Wash. **Car:** Chevrolet **Car owner:** Bill Baumgardner

### CAREER STATISTICS

| Year | Rank | Starts | Wins | Poles | Top 5 | Top 10 | Races Led | Laps Led |
|---|---|---|---|---|---|---|---|---|
| 1993 | 107 | 1 | 0 | 0 | 0 | 0 | 0 | 0 |
| 1994 | 93 | 1 | 0 | 0 | 0 | 0 | 0 | 0 |
| 1995 | 92 | 1 | 0 | 0 | 0 | 0 | 0 | 0 |
| 1998 | 53 | 8 | 0 | 0 | 1 | 1 | 1 | 3 |
| 2000 | 51 | 11 | 0 | 0 | 0 | 0 | 0 | 0 |
| 2001 | 20 | 32 | 0 | 0 | 2 | 3 | 0 | 0 |
| 2002 | 17 | 34 | 0 | 0 | 1 | 7 | 2 | 12 |
| 2003 | 12 | 34 | 0 | 1 | 2 | 10 | 2 | 45 |
| Totals | | 122 | 0 | 1 | 6 | 21 | 5 | 60 |

## Paul Menard

**Birthdate:** 8/21/80 **Birth place:** EauClaire, Wis. **Car:** Chevrolet **Car owner:** Andy Petree

### CAREER STATISTICS

| Year | Rank | Starts | Wins | Poles | Top 5 | Top 10 | Races Led | Laps Led |
|---|---|---|---|---|---|---|---|---|
| 1999 | 127 | 1 | 0 | 0 | 0 | 0 | 0 | 0 |
| 2002 | 92 | 2 | 0 | 0 | 0 | 0 | 0 | 0 |
| 2003 | 47 | 11 | 0 | 0 | 0 | 0 | 0 | 0 |
| Totals | | 14 | 0 | 0 | 0 | 0 | 0 | 0 |

## Billy Parker

**Car:** Dodge **Car owner:** Rusty Wallace

Short track star will run for rookie title with new team.

## Robert Pressley

**Birthdate:** 4/8/59 **Birth place:** Asheville, N.C. **Car:** Ford **Car owner:** Tad Geschickter

### CAREER STATISTICS

| Year | Rank | Starts | Wins | Poles | Top 5 | Top 10 | Races Led | Laps Led |
|---|---|---|---|---|---|---|---|---|
| 2003 | 60 | 6 | 0 | 0 | 0 | 1 | 0 | 0 |
| Totals | | 6 | 0 | 0 | 0 | 1 | 0 | 0 |

## Johnny Sauter

### CAREER STATISTICS

| Year | Rank | Starts | Wins | Poles | Top 5 | Top 10 | Races Led | Laps Led |
|---|---|---|---|---|---|---|---|---|
| 1984 | 109 | 1 | 0 | 0 | 0 | 0 | 0 | 0 |
| 1989 | 18 | 19 | 1 | 0 | 1 | 3 | 1 | 108 |
| 1990 | 12 | 31 | 0 | 0 | 5 | 9 | 4 | 183 |
| 1991 | 3 | 31 | 1 | 1 | 8 | 15 | 7 | 441 |
| 1992 | 5 | 31 | 5 | 2 | 11 | 16 | 10 | 736 |
| 1993 | 8 | 28 | 3 | 0 | 8 | 13 | 9 | 382 |
| 1994 | 12 | 28 | 0 | 1 | 2 | 9 | 3 | 74 |
| 1997 | 33 | 15 | 0 | 0 | 2 | 3 | 2 | 39 |
| 1998 | 31 | 18 | 0 | 2 | 0 | 6 | 3 | 169 |
| 1999 | 77 | 3 | 0 | 0 | 0 | 0 | 0 | 0 |
| Totals | | 205 | 10 | 6 | 37 | 74 | 39 | 2132 |

**Birthdate:** 5/1/78 **Birth place:** Necedah, Wis. **Car:** Chevrolet **Car owner:** Brewco Motorsports

### CAREER STATISTICS

| Year | Rank | Starts | Wins | Poles | Top 5 | Top 10 | Races Led | Laps Led |
|---|---|---|---|---|---|---|---|---|
| 2001 | 55 | 5 | 0 | 0 | 1 | 1 | 1 | 13 |
| 2002 | 15 | 33 | 1 | 1 | 3 | 6 | 5 | 86 |
| 2003 | 8 | 34 | 1 | 0 | 6 | 14 | 10 | 231 |
| Totals | | 72 | 2 | 1 | 10 | 21 | 16 | 330 |

## David Stremme

**Birthdate:** 6/19/77 **Birth place:** South Bend, Ind. **Car:** Dodge **Car owner:** James Finch

### CAREER STATISTICS

| Year | Rank | Starts | Wins | Poles | Top 5 | Top 10 | Races Led | Laps Led |
|---|---|---|---|---|---|---|---|---|
| 2003 | 22 | 18 | 0 | 0 | 3 | 7 | 6 | 86 |
| Totals | | 18 | 0 | 0 | 3 | 7 | 6 | 86 |

## Martin Truex Jr.

**Birthdate:** 6/29/80 **Birth place:** Mayetta, N.J. **Car:** Chevrolet **Car owner:** Chance 2 Motorsports

### CAREER STATISTICS

| Year | Rank | Starts | Wins | Poles | Top 5 | Top 10 | Races Led | Laps Led |
|---|---|---|---|---|---|---|---|---|
| 2001 | 133 | 1 | 0 | 0 | 0 | 0 | 0 | 0 |
| 2002 | 65 | 4 | 0 | 0 | 0 | 0 | 0 | 0 |
| 2003 | 40 | 10 | 0 | 0 | 2 | 3 | 1 | 11 |
| Totals | | 15 | 0 | 0 | 2 | 3 | 1 | 11 |

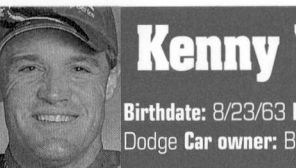

## Kenny Wallace

**Birthdate:** 8/23/63 **Birth place:** St. Louis, **Car:** Dodge **Car owner:** Bill Davis

### CAREER STATISTICS

| Year | Rank | Starts | Wins | Poles | Top 5 | Top 10 | Races Led | Laps Led |
|---|---|---|---|---|---|---|---|---|
| 1988 | 81 | 1 | 0 | 0 | 0 | 0 | 0 | 0 |
| 1989 | 6 | 29 | 0 | 3 | 4 | 16 | 4 | 259 |
| 1990 | 7 | 31 | 0 | 1 | 4 | 14 | 4 | 131 |
| 1991 | 2 | 31 | 2 | 1 | 11 | 17 | 10 | 745 |
| 1992 | 6 | 31 | 1 | 2 | 7 | 15 | 7 | 238 |
| 1994 | 4 | 28 | 3 | 1 | 11 | 15 | 12 | 865 |
| 1995 | 27 | 15 | 1 | 0 | 5 | 7 | 3 | 205 |
| 1996 | 41 | 10 | 1 | 0 | 3 | 4 | 2 | 380 |
| 1997 | 101 | 1 | 0 | 0 | 0 | 0 | 0 | 0 |
| 1999 | 23 | 18 | 0 | 0 | 2 | 8 | 1 | 4 |
| 2000 | 30 | 15 | 0 | 0 | 2 | 8 | 1 | 3 |
| 2001 | 10 | 33 | 1 | 2 | 7 | 13 | 4 | 20 |
| 2002 | 7 | 34 | 0 | 0 | 2 | 13 | 1 | 8 |
| 2003 | 155 | 1 | 0 | 0 | 0 | 1 | 0 | 0 |
| Totals | | 278 | 9 | 10 | 58 | 131 | 49 | 2858 |

## Mike Wallace

**Birthdate:** 3/10/59 **Birth place:** St. Louis **Car:** No. 4 Chevrolet **Car owner:** Fred Biagi

### CAREER STATISTICS

| Year | Rank | Starts | Wins | Poles | Top 5 | Top 10 | Races Led | Laps Led |
|---|---|---|---|---|---|---|---|---|
| 1990 | 82 | 1 | 0 | 0 | 0 | 1 | 0 | 0 |
| 1991 | 39 | 9 | 0 | 0 | 1 | 2 | 1 | 4 |

| Year | Rank | Starts | Wins | Poles | Top 5 | Top 10 | Races Led | Laps Led |
|---|---|---|---|---|---|---|---|---|
| 1992 | 22 | 17 | 0 | 0 | 1 | 3 | 1 | 110 |
| 1993 | 12 | 28 | 0 | 0 | 1 | 9 | 1 | 4 |
| 1994 | 19 | 22 | 3 | 0 | 6 | 9 | 7 | 338 |
| 1995 | 20 | 19 | 0 | 0 | 4 | 9 | 8 | 148 |
| 1996 | 26 | 17 | 0 | 0 | 2 | 5 | 0 | 0 |
| 1997 | 59 | 6 | 0 | 0 | 0 | 0 | 0 | 0 |
| 1998 | 57 | 6 | 0 | 0 | 0 | 1 | 0 | 0 |
| 1999 | 136 | 1 | 0 | 0 | 0 | 0 | 0 | 0 |
| 2000 | 59 | 8 | 0 | 0 | 0 | 0 | 0 | 0 |
| 2001 | 50 | 8 | 0 | 0 | 0 | 1 | 0 | 0 |
| 2002 | 37 | 17 | 0 | 0 | 0 | 0 | 2 | 10 |
| 2003 | 13 | 32 | 0 | 0 | 1 | 3 | 0 | 0 |
| Totals | | 191 | 3 | 0 | 16 | 43 | 20 | 614 |

## Brian Weber

**Birthdate:** 11/12/66 **Birth place:** Mooresville, N.C. **Car:** Chevrolet **Car owner:** Brian Weber

### CAREER STATISTICS

| Year | Rank | Starts | Wins | Poles | Top 5 | Top 10 | Races Led | Laps Led |
|---|---|---|---|---|---|---|---|---|
| 1988 | 105 | 1 | 0 | 0 | 0 | 0 | 0 | 0 |
| 2001 | 141 | 1 | 0 | 0 | 0 | 0 | 0 | 0 |
| 2002 | 50 | 13 | 0 | 0 | 0 | 0 | 0 | 0 |
| 2003 | 116 | 5 | 0 | 0 | 0 | 0 | 0 | 0 |
| Totals | | 20 | 0 | 0 | 0 | 0 | 0 | 0 |

## J.J. Yeley

**Birthdate:** 10/5/76 **Birth place:** Phoenix **Car:** Chevrolet **Car owner:** Joe Gibbs

USAC triple crown winner is a big talent.

# NASCAR NEXTEL Cup/Busch Series drivers

## Greg Biffle

**Birthdate:** 12/23/69 **Birth place:** Vancouver, Wash. **Car:** Chevrolet **Car owner:** Ed Evans

### CAREER STATISTICS

| Year | Rank | Starts | Wins | Poles | Top 5 | Top 10 | Races Led | Laps Led |
|---|---|---|---|---|---|---|---|---|
| 1996 | 77 | 2 | 0 | 0 | 0 | 0 | 0 | 0 |
| 2001 | 4 | 33 | 5 | 2 | 16 | 21 | 19 | 948 |
| 2002 | 1 | 34 | 4 | 5 | 20 | 25 | 22 | 1061 |
| 2003 | 35 | 14 | 2 | 2 | 3 | 4 | 4 | 222 |
| Totals | | 83 | 11 | 9 | 39 | 50 | 45 | 2231 |

## Dave Blaney

**Birthdate:** 10/24/62 **Birth place:** Hartford, Ohio

### CAREER STATISTICS

| Year | Rank | Starts | Wins | Poles | Top 5 | Top 10 | Races Led | Laps Led |
|---|---|---|---|---|---|---|---|---|
| 1998 | 29 | 20 | 0 | 1 | 0 | 3 | 1 | 5 |
| 1999 | 7 | 31 | 0 | 4 | 5 | 12 | 6 | 139 |
| 2000 | 46 | 8 | 0 | 1 | 2 | 4 | 1 | 24 |
| 2001 | 155 | 1 | 0 | 0 | 0 | 0 | 0 | 0 |
| 2002 | 114 | 1 | 0 | 0 | 0 | 0 | 1 | 3 |
| 2003 | 43 | 10 | 0 | 0 | 0 | 3 | 0 | 0 |
| Totals | | 71 | 0 | 6 | 7 | 22 | 9 | 171 |

## Todd Bodine

**Birthdate:** 2/27/64 **Birth place:** Chemung, N.Y.

### CAREER STATISTICS

| Year | Rank | Starts | Wins | Poles | Top 5 | Top 10 | Races Led | Laps Led |
|---|---|---|---|---|---|---|---|---|
| 1986 | 114 | 1 | 0 | 0 | 0 | 0 | 0 | 0 |
| 1990 | 40 | 8 | 0 | 0 | 1 | 3 | 1 | 3 |
| 1991 | 7 | 31 | 1 | 2 | 7 | 15 | 7 | 214 |
| 1992 | 3 | 31 | 3 | 2 | 11 | 19 | 9 | 277 |
| 1993 | 9 | 28 | 3 | 1 | 9 | 13 | 12 | 502 |
| 1994 | 118 | 1 | 0 | 0 | 0 | 0 | 0 | 0 |
| 1995 | 59 | 3 | 1 | 0 | 1 | 1 | 1 | 1 |
| 1996 | 3 | 26 | 1 | 0 | 3 | 9 | 7 | 290 |
| 1997 | 2 | 30 | 1 | 0 | 9 | 22 | 10 | 186 |
| 1998 | 33 | 13 | 0 | 0 | 5 | 7 | 1 | 2 |
| 1999 | 4 | 32 | 0 | 0 | 10 | 21 | 7 | 178 |
| 2000 | 4 | 32 | 1 | 1 | 14 | 19 | 7 | 185 |
| 2001 | 29 | 16 | 2 | 0 | 6 | 7 | 5 | 283 |
| 2002 | 23 | 28 | 1 | 1 | 6 | 8 | 5 | 98 |
| 2003 | 17 | 22 | 1 | 0 | 6 | 11 | 6 | 102 |
| Totals | | 302 | 15 | 7 | 88 | 155 | 78 | 2321 |

## Jeff Burton

**Birthdate:** 6/29/67 **Birth place:** South Boston, Va. **Car:** Ford
**Car owner:** Jack Roush

### CAREER STATISTICS

| Year | Rank | Starts | Wins | Poles | Top 5 | Top 10 | Races Led | Laps Led |
|---|---|---|---|---|---|---|---|---|
| 1988 | 44 | 5 | 0 | 0 | 0 | 0 | 0 | 0 |
| 1989 | 13 | 27 | 0 | 0 | 2 | 6 | 1 | 14 |
| 1990 | 15 | 31 | 1 | 1 | 3 | 5 | 4 | 154 |
| 1991 | 12 | 31 | 1 | 2 | 3 | 10 | 4 | 210 |
| 1992 | 9 | 31 | 1 | 0 | 4 | 10 | 7 | 101 |
| 1993 | 14 | 28 | 1 | 0 | 3 | 10 | 6 | 330 |
| 1996 | 113 | 1 | 0 | 0 | 0 | 0 | 0 | 0 |
| 1997 | 26 | 13 | 2 | 1 | 9 | 10 | 9 | 714 |
| 1998 | 30 | 13 | 3 | 2 | 7 | 9 | 7 | 441 |
| 1999 | 25 | 14 | 1 | 1 | 7 | 12 | 4 | 116 |
| 2000 | 29 | 14 | 4 | 0 | 11 | 13 | 6 | 833 |
| 2001 | 33 | 11 | 1 | 1 | 4 | 9 | 4 | 163 |
| 2002 | 31 | 13 | 5 | 2 | 8 | 9 | 7 | 586 |
| 2003 | 76 | 4 | 0 | 0 | 0 | 0 | 1 | 24 |
| Totals | | 236 | 20 | 10 | 61 | 103 | 63 | 3686 |

## Derrike Cope

**Birthdate:** 11/03/58 **Birth place:** Spanaway, Wash.

### CAREER STATISTICS

| Year | Rank | Starts | Wins | Poles | Top 5 | Top 10 | Races Led | Laps Led |
|---|---|---|---|---|---|---|---|---|
| 1990 | 109 | 1 | 0 | 0 | 0 | 0 | 0 | 0 |
| 1994 | 32 | 11 | 1 | 1 | 2 | 3 | 3 | 56 |
| 1995 | 52 | 5 | 0 | 0 | 0 | 2 | 0 | 0 |
| 1996 | 40 | 12 | 0 | 0 | 0 | 3 | 1 | 9 |

| Year | Rank | Starts | Wins | Poles | Top 5 | Top 10 | Races Led | Laps Led |
|---|---|---|---|---|---|---|---|---|
| 1998 | 91 | 2 | 0 | 0 | 0 | 0 | 0 | 0 |
| 1999 | 70 | 5 | 0 | 0 | 0 | 0 | 0 | 0 |
| 2001 | 71 | 4 | 0 | 0 | 0 | 0 | 0 | 0 |
| 2002 | 54 | 8 | 0 | 0 | 0 | 0 | 0 | 0 |
| 2003 | 62 | 7 | 0 | 0 | 0 | 0 | 0 | 0 |
| Totals | | 55 | 1 | 1 | 2 | 8 | 4 | 65 |

## Dale Earnhardt Jr.

**Birthdate:** 10/10/74 **Birth place:** Kannapolis, N.C. **Car:** Chevrolet **Car owner:** Chance 2 Motorsports

### CAREER STATISTICS

| Year | Rank | Starts | Wins | Poles | Top 5 | Top 10 | Races Led | Laps Led |
|---|---|---|---|---|---|---|---|---|
| 1996 | 79 | 1 | 0 | 0 | 0 | 0 | 0 | 0 |
| 1997 | 47 | 8 | 0 | 0 | 0 | 1 | 1 | 22 |
| 1998 | 1 | 31 | 7 | 3 | 16 | 22 | 19 | 1615 |
| 1999 | 1 | 32 | 6 | 3 | 18 | 22 | 23 | 725 |
| 2001 | 118 | 1 | 0 | 0 | 0 | 0 | 0 | 0 |
| 2002 | 60 | 3 | 2 | 1 | 2 | 2 | 2 | 249 |
| 2003 | 66 | 3 | 3 | 1 | 3 | 3 | 3 | 227 |
| Totals | | 79 | 18 | 8 | 39 | 50 | 48 | 2838 |

## Robby Gordon

**Birthdate:** 1/2/69 **Birth place:** Cerritos, Calif. **Car:** Chevrolet
**Car owner:** Robby Gordon

### CAREER STATISTICS

| Year | Rank | Starts | Wins | Poles | Top 5 | Top 10 | Races Led | Laps Led |
|---|---|---|---|---|---|---|---|---|
| 2001 | 60 | 3 | 0 | 0 | 1 | 1 | 2 | 31 |
| Totals | | 3 | 0 | 0 | 1 | 1 | 2 | 31 |

## Jeff Green

**Birthdate:** 9/6/62 **Birth place:** Owensboro, Ky.

### CAREER STATISTICS

| Year | Rank | Starts | Wins | Poles | Top 5 | Top 10 | Races Led | Laps Led |
|---|---|---|---|---|---|---|---|---|
| 1990 | 84 | 2 | 0 | 0 | 0 | 0 | 0 | 0 |
| 1991 | 29 | 14 | 0 | 0 | 0 | 1 | 0 | 0 |
| 1992 | 30 | 13 | 0 | 0 | 0 | 1 | 0 | 0 |
| 1993 | 40 | 11 | 0 | 1 | 1 | 1 | 0 | 0 |
| 1994 | 62 | 3 | 0 | 0 | 1 | 2 | 0 | 0 |
| 1995 | 5 | 26 | 0 | 1 | 6 | 12 | 6 | 345 |
| 1996 | 4 | 26 | 0 | 1 | 5 | 13 | 5 | 112 |
| 1997 | 28 | 14 | 1 | 2 | 6 | 7 | 8 | 272 |
| 1998 | 52 | 7 | 0 | 0 | 1 | 1 | 0 | 0 |
| 1999 | 2 | 31 | 3 | 4 | 15 | 19 | 16 | 975 |
| 2000 | 1 | 32 | 6 | 7 | 25 | 27 | 19 | 1480 |
| 2001 | 2 | 33 | 4 | 2 | 16 | 26 | 22 | 726 |
| 2002 | 19 | 22 | 2 | 5 | 12 | 16 | 14 | 696 |
| 2003 | 72 | 6 | 0 | 0 | 0 | 0 | 0 | 0 |
| Totals | | 240 | 16 | 23 | 87 | 126 | 90 | 4606 |

## Kevin Harvick

**Birthdate:** 12/8/75 **Birth place:** Bakersfield, Calif. **Car:** Chevrolet **Car owner:** Richard Childress

### CAREER STATISTICS

| Year | Rank | Starts | Wins | Poles | Top 5 | Top 10 | Races Led | Laps Led |
|---|---|---|---|---|---|---|---|---|
| 1999 | 138 | 1 | 0 | 0 | 0 | 0 | 0 | 0 |
| 2000 | 3 | 31 | 3 | 2 | 8 | 16 | 11 | 665 |
| 2001 | 1 | 33 | 5 | 4 | 20 | 24 | 18 | 1265 |
| 2002 | 64 | 4 | 0 | 0 | 0 | 1 | 2 | 54 |
| 2003 | 16 | 19 | 3 | 5 | 12 | 18 | 15 | 971 |
| Totals | | 88 | 11 | 11 | 40 | 59 | 46 | 2955 |

## Matt Kenseth

**Birthdate:** 3/10/72 **Birth place:** Cambridge, Wis. **Car:** Ford **Car owners:** Jack Roush, Robbie Reiser

### CAREER STATISTICS

| Year | Rank | Starts | Wins | Poles | Top 5 | Top 10 | Races Led | Laps Led |
|---|---|---|---|---|---|---|---|---|
| 1996 | 101 | 1 | 0 | 0 | 0 | 0 | 0 | 0 |
| 1997 | 22 | 21 | 0 | 0 | 2 | 7 | 2 | 29 |
| 1998 | 2 | 31 | 3 | 1 | 17 | 23 | 10 | 437 |
| 1999 | 3 | 32 | 4 | 2 | 14 | 20 | 15 | 874 |
| 2000 | 17 | 20 | 4 | 2 | 10 | 17 | 12 | 331 |
| 2001 | 18 | 23 | 1 | 3 | 12 | 14 | 13 | 413 |
| 2002 | 77 | 4 | 0 | 0 | 1 | 2 | 0 | 0 |
| 2003 | 24 | 14 | 2 | 0 | 7 | 9 | 8 | 515 |
| Totals | | 146 | 14 | 8 | 63 | 92 | 60 | 2599 |

## Mark Martin

**Birthdate:** 1/9/59 **Birth place:** Batesville, Ark. **Car:** Ford **Car owner:** Jack Roush

### CAREER STATISTICS

| Year | Rank | Starts | Wins | Poles | Top 5 | Top 10 | Races Led | Laps Led |
|---|---|---|---|---|---|---|---|---|
| 1982 | 162 | 1 | 0 | 0 | 0 | 0 | 0 | 0 |
| 1987 | 8 | 27 | 3 | 6 | 5 | 13 | 8 | 257 |
| 1988 | 29 | 13 | 1 | 0 | 2 | 6 | 1 | 5 |
| 1989 | 20 | 17 | 1 | 1 | 6 | 8 | 8 | 353 |
| 1990 | 32 | 12 | 1 | 0 | 3 | 5 | 3 | 216 |
| 1991 | 102 | 1 | 0 | 0 | 0 | 0 | 0 | 0 |
| 1992 | 21 | 14 | 1 | 2 | 5 | 9 | 9 | 429 |
| 1993 | 24 | 14 | 7 | 1 | 7 | 7 | 11 | 990 |
| 1994 | 20 | 15 | 3 | 3 | 8 | 11 | 14 | 1120 |
| 1995 | 22 | 15 | 3 | 1 | 9 | 11 | 11 | 851 |
| 1996 | 21 | 14 | 6 | 2 | 11 | 12 | 14 | 991 |
| 1997 | 24 | 15 | 6 | 3 | 10 | 12 | 11 | 598 |
| 1998 | 27 | 15 | 2 | 1 | 6 | 9 | 8 | 211 |
| 1999 | 26 | 14 | 6 | 3 | 9 | 10 | 12 | 746 |
| 2000 | 27 | 13 | 5 | 4 | 12 | 13 | 12 | 969 |
| Totals | | 200 | 45 | 27 | 93 | 126 | 122 | 7736 |

## Jeremy Mayfield

**Birthdate:** 5/27/69 **Birth place:** Owensboro, Ky.

### CAREER STATISTICS

| Year | Rank | Starts | Wins | Poles | Top 5 | Top 10 | Races Led | Laps Led |
|---|---|---|---|---|---|---|---|---|
| 1995 | 50 | 7 | 0 | 0 | 0 | 0 | 1 | 10 |
| 1996 | 43 | 13 | 0 | 0 | 0 | 2 | 1 | 2 |
| 2003 | 99 | 1 | 0 | 0 | 1 | 1 | 1 | 14 |
| Totals | | 21 | 0 | 0 | 1 | 3 | 3 | 26 |

## Jamie McMurray

**Birthdate:** 6/3/76 **Birth place:** Joplin, Mo. **Car:** Dodge **Car owner:** James Finch

### CAREER STATISTICS

| Year | Rank | Starts | Wins | Poles | Top 5 | Top 10 | Races Led | Laps Led |
|---|---|---|---|---|---|---|---|---|
| 2000 | 93 | 2 | 0 | 0 | 0 | 0 | 0 | 0 |
| 2001 | 16 | 33 | 0 | 0 | 0 | 3 | 1 | 1 |
| 2002 | 6 | 34 | 2 | 0 | 6 | 14 | 9 | 87 |
| 2003 | 20 | 19 | 2 | 0 | 6 | 10 | 4 | 400 |
| Totals | | 88 | 4 | 0 | 12 | 27 | 14 | 488 |

## Casey Mears

**Birthdate:** 3/12/78 **Birth place:** Bakersfield, Calif. **Car:** Dodge **Car owner:** Todd Braun

### CAREER STATISTICS

| Year | Rank | Starts | Wins | Poles | Top 5 | Top 10 | Races Led | Laps Led |
|---|---|---|---|---|---|---|---|---|
| 2001 | 114 | 1 | 0 | 0 | 0 | 0 | 0 | 0 |
| 2002 | 21 | 34 | 0 | 0 | 1 | 2 | 2 | 5 |
| 2003 | 34 | 14 | 0 | 1 | 1 | 4 | 1 | 2 |
| Totals | | 49 | 0 | 1 | 2 | 6 | 3 | 7 |

## Joe Nemechek

**Birthdate:** 9/26/63 **Birth place:** Lakeland, Fla. **Car:** Chevrolet **Car owner:** Joe Nemechek

### CAREER STATISTICS

| Year | Rank | Starts | Wins | Poles | Top 5 | Top 10 | Races Led | Laps Led |
|---|---|---|---|---|---|---|---|---|
| 1989 | 98 | 1 | 0 | 0 | 0 | 0 | 0 | 0 |
| 1990 | 17 | 28 | 0 | 0 | 2 | 5 | 1 | 20 |
| 1991 | 6 | 31 | 0 | 0 | 5 | 16 | 4 | 34 |
| 1992 | 1 | 31 | 2 | 1 | 13 | 18 | 8 | 241 |
| 1993 | 5 | 28 | 0 | 3 | 8 | 11 | 14 | 627 |
| 1994 | 38 | 12 | 1 | 0 | 1 | 2 | 4 | 190 |
| 1995 | 43 | 6 | 0 | 1 | 2 | 4 | 2 | 71 |
| 1996 | 38 | 11 | 0 | 1 | 3 | 6 | 5 | 115 |
| 1997 | 40 | 9 | 2 | 3 | 5 | 6 | 6 | 430 |
| 1998 | 39 | 9 | 2 | 1 | 5 | 7 | 4 | 308 |

| Year | Rank | Starts | Wins | Poles | Top 5 | Top 10 | Races Led | Laps Led |
|---|---|---|---|---|---|---|---|---|
| 1999 | 33 | 12 | 1 | 0 | 6 | 7 | 5 | 82 |
| 2000 | 32 | 14 | 1 | 0 | 6 | 8 | 4 | 215 |
| 2001 | 35 | 13 | 2 | 2 | 4 | 6 | 7 | 181 |
| 2002 | 34 | 14 | 1 | 2 | 6 | 7 | 5 | 122 |
| 2003 | 31 | 16 | 3 | 2 | 5 | 6 | 4 | 133 |
| Totals | | 235 | 15 | 16 | 71 | 109 | 73 | 2769 |

# Tony Raines

**Birthdate:** 4/14/64 **Birth place:** LaPorte, Ind.

## CAREER STATISTICS

| Year | Rank | Starts | Wins | Poles | Top 5 | Top 10 | Races Led | Laps Led |
|---|---|---|---|---|---|---|---|---|
| 1999 | 12 | 31 | 0 | 0 | 1 | 3 | 0 | 0 |
| 2000 | 15 | 32 | 0 | 0 | 1 | 1 | 5 | 154 |
| 2001 | 6 | 33 | 0 | 1 | 4 | 13 | 4 | 26 |
| 2002 | 12 | 34 | 0 | 0 | 5 | 11 | 5 | 28 |
| 2003 | 39 | 12 | 0 | 0 | 2 | 5 | 0 | 0 |
| Totals | | 142 | 0 | 1 | 13 | 33 | 14 | 208 |

# Elliott Sadler

**Birthdate:** 4/30/75 **Birth place:** Emporia, Va.

## CAREER STATISTICS

| Year | Rank | Starts | Wins | Poles | Top 5 | Top 10 | Races Led | Laps Led |
|---|---|---|---|---|---|---|---|---|
| 1995 | 70 | 2 | 0 | 0 | 0 | 1 | 0 | 0 |
| 1996 | 35 | 13 | 0 | 0 | 1 | 3 | 1 | 2 |
| 1997 | 5 | 30 | 3 | 4 | 6 | 10 | 9 | 317 |
| 1998 | 8 | 31 | 2 | 1 | 5 | 10 | 7 | 256 |
| 1999 | 36 | 15 | 0 | 0 | 1 | 3 | 2 | 34 |
| 2000 | 80 | 3 | 0 | 0 | 0 | 0 | 0 | 0 |
| 2003 | 144 | 1 | 0 | 0 | 0 | 0 | 0 | 0 |
| Totals | | 95 | 5 | 5 | 13 | 27 | 19 | 609 |

# Jimmy Spencer

**Birthdate:** 2/15/57 **Birth place:** Berwick, Pa.

## CAREER STATISTICS

| Year | Rank | Starts | Wins | Poles | Top 5 | Top 10 | Races Led | Laps Led |
|---|---|---|---|---|---|---|---|---|
| 1985 | 84 | 1 | 0 | 0 | 0 | 0 | 0 | 0 |
| 1987 | 75 | 2 | 0 | 0 | 0 | 0 | 0 | 0 |
| 1988 | 7 | 30 | 0 | 0 | 5 | 13 | 5 | 102 |
| 1989 | 15 | 22 | 3 | 1 | 4 | 11 | 3 | 377 |
| 1990 | 44 | 6 | 0 | 0 | 1 | 2 | 2 | 9 |
| 1991 | 43 | 6 | 0 | 0 | 1 | 2 | 0 | 0 |
| 1992 | 17 | 25 | 2 | 0 | 6 | 10 | 9 | 456 |
| 1993 | 42 | 9 | 0 | 0 | 0 | 2 | 0 | 0 |
| 1994 | 64 | 3 | 0 | 0 | 1 | 1 | 1 | 20 |
| 1995 | 34 | 12 | 0 | 0 | 1 | 5 | 2 | 30 |
| 1996 | 32 | 13 | 0 | 0 | 1 | 6 | 4 | 118 |
| 1997 | 30 | 12 | 2 | 0 | 7 | 7 | 5 | 327 |
| 1998 | 43 | 8 | 1 | 0 | 5 | 6 | 5 | 195 |
| 1999 | 43 | 9 | 0 | 0 | 5 | 6 | 4 | 131 |
| 2000 | 65 | 6 | 0 | 0 | 0 | 1 | 1 | 19 |
| 2001 | 26 | 18 | 3 | 2 | 5 | 10 | 9 | 493 |
| 2002 | 26 | 23 | 1 | 0 | 2 | 10 | 6 | 181 |
| 2003 | 86 | 2 | 0 | 0 | 0 | 1 | 0 | 0 |
| Totals | | 207 | 12 | 3 | 44 | 93 | 56 | 2458 |

# Tony Stewart

**Birthdate:** 5/20/71 **Birth place:** Rushville, Ind.

## CAREER STATISTICS

| Year | Rank | Starts | Wins | Poles | Top 5 | Top 10 | Races Led | Laps Led |
|---|---|---|---|---|---|---|---|---|
| 1996 | 49 | 9 | 0 | 0 | 0 | 0 | 0 | 0 |
| 1997 | 58 | 5 | 0 | 0 | 1 | 2 | 0 | 0 |
| 1998 | 21 | 22 | 0 | 2 | 5 | 5 | 6 | 157 |
| 2003 | 109 | 1 | 0 | 0 | 0 | 0 | 1 | 86 |
| Totals | | 37 | 0 | 2 | 6 | 7 | 7 | 243 |

# Michael Waltrip

**Birthdate:** 4/30/63 **Birth place:** Owensboro, Ky. **Car:** Chevrolet
**Car owner:** Michael Waltrip

## CAREER STATISTICS

| Year | Rank | Starts | Wins | Poles | Top 5 | Top 10 | Races Led | Laps Led |
|---|---|---|---|---|---|---|---|---|
| 1988 | 41 | 5 | 1 | 0 | 2 | 2 | 2 | 8 |
| 1989 | 22 | 14 | 1 | 4 | 5 | 8 | 6 | 201 |
| 1990 | 30 | 13 | 2 | 2 | 4 | 4 | 5 | 306 |
| 1991 | 34 | 10 | 0 | 0 | 5 | 5 | 5 | 75 |
| 1992 | 26 | 11 | 1 | 1 | 3 | 6 | 4 | 83 |
| 1993 | 30 | 10 | 2 | 0 | 4 | 5 | 8 | 194 |
| 1994 | 41 | 9 | 0 | 1 | 2 | 4 | 5 | 47 |
| 1995 | 48 | 6 | 0 | 1 | 2 | 2 | 3 | 56 |
| 1996 | 34 | 13 | 0 | 1 | 3 | 3 | 5 | 66 |
| 1997 | 29 | 16 | 0 | 1 | 4 | 5 | 5 | 36 |
| 1998 | 34 | 15 | 0 | 0 | 1 | 6 | 2 | 29 |
| 1999 | 29 | 15 | 1 | 0 | 3 | 7 | 2 | 27 |
| 2000 | 37 | 12 | 0 | 0 | 2 | 4 | 2 | 19 |
| 2001 | 41 | 12 | 0 | 0 | 1 | 3 | 1 | 55 |
| 2002 | 27 | 19 | 1 | 2 | 6 | 11 | 9 | 389 |
| 2003 | 18 | 20 | 1 | 2 | 8 | 13 | 9 | 419 |
| Totals | | 200 | 10 | 15 | 55 | 88 | 73 | 2010 |

# Selected drivers who competed in 2003

## A.J. Alsup

**Birthdate:** 1/16/76

### CAREER STATISTICS

| Year | Rank | Starts | Wins | Poles | Top 5 | Top 10 | Races Led | Laps Led |
|---|---|---|---|---|---|---|---|---|
| 2001 | 76 | 4 | 0 | 0 | 0 | 0 | 0 | 0 |
| 2003 | 151 | 1 | 0 | 0 | 0 | 0 | 0 | 0 |
| Totals | | 5 | 0 | 0 | 0 | 0 | 0 | 0 |

## Joe Aramendia

**Birthdate:** 4/23/63 **Birth place:** SanAntonio

### CAREER STATISTICS

| Year | Rank | Starts | Wins | Poles | Top 5 | Top 10 | Races Led | Laps Led |
|---|---|---|---|---|---|---|---|---|
| 2003 | 82 | 3 | 0 | 0 | 0 | 0 | 0 | 0 |
| Totals | | 3 | 0 | 0 | 0 | 0 | 0 | 0 |

## Justin Ashburn

**Birthdate:** 12/23/81 **Birth place:** Joelton, Tenn.

### CAREER STATISTICS

| Year | Rank | Starts | Wins | Poles | Top 5 | Top 10 | Races Led | Laps Led |
|---|---|---|---|---|---|---|---|---|
| 2003 | 58 | 14 | 0 | 0 | 0 | 0 | 0 | 0 |
| Totals | | 14 | 0 | 0 | 0 | 0 | 0 | 0 |

## Brad Baker

**Birthdate:** 8/3/74 **Birth place:** Bristol, Tenn.

### CAREER STATISTICS

| Year | Rank | Starts | Wins | Poles | Top 5 | Top 10 | Races Led | Laps Led |
|---|---|---|---|---|---|---|---|---|
| 1999 | 129 | 1 | 0 | 0 | 0 | 0 | 0 | 0 |
| 2000 | 95 | 2 | 0 | 0 | 0 | 0 | 0 | 0 |
| 2001 | 38 | 16 | 0 | 0 | 0 | 0 | 0 | 0 |
| 2002 | 59 | 5 | 0 | 0 | 0 | 0 | 0 | 0 |
| 2003 | 59 | 9 | 0 | 0 | 0 | 0 | 0 | 0 |
| Totals | | 33 | 0 | 0 | 0 | 0 | 0 | 0 |

## Bruce Bechtel

**Birthdate:** 2/13/55 **Birth place:** Corona, Calif.

### CAREER STATISTICS

| Year | Rank | Starts | Wins | Poles | Top 5 | Top 10 | Races Led | Laps Led |
|---|---|---|---|---|---|---|---|---|
| 2002 | 76 | 4 | 0 | 0 | 0 | 0 | 0 | 0 |
| 2003 | 84 | 4 | 0 | 0 | 0 | 0 | 0 | 0 |
| Totals | | 8 | 0 | 0 | 0 | 0 | 0 | 0 |

## Robby Benton

**Birthdate:** 6/28/79 **Birth place:** Charlotte, N.C.

### CAREER STATISTICS

| Year | Rank | Starts | Wins | Poles | Top 5 | Top 10 | Races Led | Laps Led |
|---|---|---|---|---|---|---|---|---|
| 2003 | 93 | 3 | 0 | 0 | 0 | 0 | 0 | 0 |
| Totals | | 3 | 0 | 0 | 0 | 0 | 0 | 0 |

## Chris Bingham

**Birthdate:** 12/15/71 **Birth place:** Bellvue, Wash.

### CAREER STATISTICS

| Year | Rank | Starts | Wins | Poles | Top 5 | Top 10 | Races Led | Laps Led |
|---|---|---|---|---|---|---|---|---|
| 2003 | 55 | 11 | 0 | 0 | 0 | 0 | 0 | 0 |
| Totals | | 11 | 0 | 0 | 0 | 0 | 0 | 0 |

## Joe Buford

**Birthdate:** 6/19/67 **Birth place:** Antioch, Tenn.

### CAREER STATISTICS

| Year | Rank | Starts | Wins | Poles | Top 5 | Top 10 | Races Led | Laps Led |
|---|---|---|---|---|---|---|---|---|
| 1998 | 126 | 1 | 0 | 0 | 0 | 0 | 0 | 0 |
| 1999 | 82 | 3 | 0 | 0 | 0 | 0 | 0 | 0 |
| 2002 | 52 | 11 | 0 | 0 | 0 | 0 | 1 | 1 |
| 2003 | 104 | 3 | 0 | 0 | 0 | 0 | 0 | 0 |
| Totals | | 18 | 0 | 0 | 0 | 0 | 1 | 1 |

## Rick Carelli

**Birthdate:** 11/9/55 **Birth place:** Denver

### CAREER STATISTICS

| Year | Rank | Starts | Wins | Poles | Top 5 | Top 10 | Races Led | Laps Led |
|---|---|---|---|---|---|---|---|---|
| 1998 | 134 | 1 | 0 | 0 | 0 | 0 | 0 | 0 |
| 2003 | 119 | 1 | 0 | 0 | 0 | 0 | 0 | 0 |
| Totals | | 2 | 0 | 0 | 0 | 0 | 0 | 0 |

## Dion Ciccarelli
**Birthdate:** 9/13/67 **Birth place:** Severn, Md.

### CAREER STATISTICS

| Year | Rank | Starts | Wins | Poles | Top 5 | Top 10 | Races Led | Laps Led |
|---|---|---|---|---|---|---|---|---|
| 2001 | 124 | 1 | 0 | 0 | 0 | 0 | 0 | 0 |
| 2002 | 82 | 4 | 0 | 0 | 0 | 0 | 0 | 0 |
| 2003 | 80 | 4 | 0 | 0 | 0 | 0 | 0 | 0 |
| Totals | | 9 | 0 | 0 | 0 | 0 | 0 | 0 |

## Joey Clanton
**Birthdate:** 11/1/72 **Birth place:** Stockbridge, Ga.

### CAREER STATISTICS

| Year | Rank | Starts | Wins | Poles | Top 5 | Top 10 | Races Led | Laps Led |
|---|---|---|---|---|---|---|---|---|
| 2003 | 30 | 18 | 0 | 0 | 1 | 1 | 1 | 2 |
| Totals | | 18 | 0 | 0 | 1 | 1 | 1 | 2 |

## Carlos Contreras
**Birthdate:** 6/8/70 **Birth place:** Mexico City, Mexico

### CAREER STATISTICS

| Year | Rank | Starts | Wins | Poles | Top 5 | Top 10 | Races Led | Laps Led |
|---|---|---|---|---|---|---|---|---|
| 2003 | 138 | 1 | 0 | 0 | 0 | 0 | 0 | 0 |
| Totals | | 1 | 0 | 0 | 0 | 0 | 0 | 0 |

## Wally Dallenbach Jr.
**Birthdate:** 5/23/63 **Birth place:** Basalt, Colo.

### CAREER STATISTICS

| Year | Rank | Starts | Wins | Poles | Top 5 | Top 10 | Races Led | Laps Led |
|---|---|---|---|---|---|---|---|---|
| 2002 | 62 | 3 | 0 | 0 | 0 | 2 | 0 | 0 |
| 2003 | 73 | 5 | 0 | 0 | 0 | 0 | 0 | 0 |
| Totals | | 8 | 0 | 0 | 0 | 2 | 0 | 0 |

## Tim Edwards
**Birthdate:** 4/4/66 **Birth place:** Mill Springs, S.C.

### CAREER STATISTICS

| Year | Rank | Starts | Wins | Poles | Top 5 | Top 10 | Races Led | Laps Led |
|---|---|---|---|---|---|---|---|---|
| 2003 | 149 | 1 | 0 | 0 | 0 | 0 | 0 | 0 |
| Totals | | 1 | 0 | 0 | 0 | 0 | 0 | 0 |

## Jeff Fuller
**Birthdate:** 3/27/57 **Birth place:** Auburn, Mass.

### CAREER STATISTICS

| Year | Rank | Starts | Wins | Poles | Top 5 | Top 10 | Races Led | Laps Led |
|---|---|---|---|---|---|---|---|---|
| 1992 | 96 | 1 | 0 | 0 | 0 | 0 | 0 | 0 |
| 1995 | 10 | 26 | 0 | 0 | 1 | 6 | 1 | 6 |
| 1996 | 17 | 24 | 1 | 1 | 1 | 4 | 1 | 145 |
| 1997 | 21 | 28 | 0 | 0 | 1 | 4 | 1 | 66 |
| 1998 | 48 | 11 | 0 | 0 | 0 | 0 | 0 | 0 |
| 1999 | 22 | 27 | 0 | 0 | 0 | 0 | 0 | 0 |
| 2000 | 98 | 1 | 0 | 0 | 0 | 0 | 0 | 0 |
| 2001 | 147 | 1 | 0 | 0 | 0 | 0 | 0 | 0 |
| 2002 | 105 | 2 | 0 | 0 | 0 | 0 | 0 | 0 |
| 2003 | 54 | 13 | 0 | 0 | 0 | 0 | 0 | 0 |
| Totals | | 134 | 1 | 1 | 3 | 14 | 3 | 217 |

## Jeff Fultz
**Birthdate:** 12/14/68 **Birth place:** Blue Ash, Ohio

### CAREER STATISTICS

| Year | Rank | Starts | Wins | Poles | Top 5 | Top 10 | Races Led | Laps Led |
|---|---|---|---|---|---|---|---|---|
| 2001 | 137 | 1 | 0 | 0 | 0 | 0 | 0 | 0 |
| 2002 | 83 | 3 | 0 | 0 | 0 | 0 | 0 | 0 |
| 2003 | 77 | 3 | 0 | 0 | 0 | 0 | 0 | 0 |
| Totals | | 7 | 0 | 0 | 0 | 0 | 0 | 0 |

## Coy Gibbs
**Birthdate:** 12/9/72 **Birth place:** Mooresville, N.C.

### CAREER STATISTICS

| Year | Rank | Starts | Wins | Poles | Top 5 | Top 10 | Races Led | Laps Led |
|---|---|---|---|---|---|---|---|---|
| 2002 | 61 | 5 | 0 | 0 | 0 | 0 | 0 | 0 |
| 2003 | 14 | 34 | 0 | 0 | 0 | 2 | 1 | 1 |
| Totals | | 39 | 0 | 0 | 0 | 2 | 1 | 1 |

## Tina Gordon
**Birthdate:** 3/14/69 **Birth place:** Cedar Bluff, Ala.

### CAREER STATISTICS

| Year | Rank | Starts | Wins | Poles | Top 5 | Top 10 | Races Led | Laps Led |
|---|---|---|---|---|---|---|---|---|
| 2001 | 154 | 1 | 0 | 0 | 0 | 0 | 0 | 0 |
| 2003 | 110 | 1 | 0 | 0 | 0 | 1 | 0 | 0 |
| Totals | | 2 | 0 | 0 | 0 | 1 | 0 | 0 |

## Steve Grissom

**Birthdate:** 6/26/63  **Birth place:** Gadsden, Ala.

### CAREER STATISTICS

| Year | Rank | Starts | Wins | Poles | Top 5 | Top 10 | Races Led | Laps Led |
|------|------|--------|------|-------|-------|--------|-----------|----------|
| 1986 | 78 | 2 | 0 | 0 | 0 | 0 | 0 | 0 |
| 1987 | 51 | 2 | 0 | 0 | 0 | 0 | 0 | 0 |
| 1988 | 13 | 29 | 0 | 0 | 1 | 4 | 0 | 0 |
| 1989 | 12 | 29 | 0 | 0 | 2 | 5 | 1 | 1 |
| 1990 | 3 | 31 | 4 | 1 | 11 | 15 | 9 | 486 |
| 1991 | 10 | 31 | 1 | 1 | 7 | 13 | 3 | 147 |
| 1992 | 12 | 31 | 1 | 1 | 2 | 7 | 5 | 199 |
| 1993 | 1 | 28 | 2 | 0 | 11 | 18 | 7 | 120 |
| 1994 | 43 | 11 | 0 | 0 | 1 | 1 | 0 | 0 |
| 1995 | 26 | 15 | 2 | 0 | 4 | 7 | 4 | 105 |
| 1996 | 45 | 8 | 1 | 0 | 3 | 4 | 2 | 57 |
| 1997 | 116 | 1 | 0 | 0 | 0 | 0 | 0 | 0 |
| 1998 | 78 | 2 | 0 | 1 | 0 | 0 | 1 | 88 |
| 1999 | 52 | 12 | 0 | 0 | 0 | 0 | 0 | 0 |
| 2000 | 113 | 1 | 0 | 0 | 0 | 0 | 0 | 0 |
| 2001 | 151 | 1 | 0 | 0 | 0 | 0 | 0 | 0 |
| 2002 | 56 | 7 | 0 | 0 | 0 | 0 | 0 | 0 |
| 2003 | 67 | 6 | 0 | 0 | 0 | 0 | 1 | 1 |
| Totals | | 247 | 11 | 4 | 42 | 74 | 33 | 1204 |

## Kevin Grubb

**Birthdate:** 4/19/78  **Birth place:** Mechanicsville, Va.

### CAREER STATISTICS

| Year | Rank | Starts | Wins | Poles | Top 5 | Top 10 | Races Led | Laps Led |
|------|------|--------|------|-------|-------|--------|-----------|----------|
| 1997 | 80 | 4 | 0 | 0 | 0 | 0 | 0 | 0 |
| 1998 | 35 | 18 | 0 | 1 | 2 | 5 | 2 | 26 |
| 1999 | 17 | 28 | 0 | 0 | 1 | 5 | 2 | 21 |
| 2000 | 13 | 31 | 0 | 0 | 2 | 6 | 3 | 31 |
| 2001 | 14 | 33 | 0 | 0 | 3 | 7 | 6 | 22 |
| 2002 | 24 | 30 | 0 | 0 | 2 | 6 | 2 | 19 |
| 2003 | 19 | 25 | 0 | 0 | 0 | 2 | 0 | 0 |
| Totals | | 169 | 0 | 1 | 10 | 31 | 15 | 119 |

## Shane Hall

**Birthdate:** 8/25/69  **Birth place:** Greenville, S.C.

### CAREER STATISTICS

| Year | Rank | Starts | Wins | Poles | Top 5 | Top 10 | Races Led | Laps Led |
|------|------|--------|------|-------|-------|--------|-----------|----------|
| 1995 | 80 | 2 | 0 | 0 | 0 | 0 | 0 | 0 |
| 1996 | 42 | 14 | 0 | 0 | 0 | 0 | 0 | 0 |
| 1997 | 23 | 28 | 0 | 1 | 0 | 1 | 1 | 12 |
| 1998 | 19 | 31 | 0 | 1 | 0 | 3 | 3 | 31 |
| 1999 | 24 | 25 | 0 | 0 | 1 | 1 | 1 | 1 |
| 2000 | 92 | 2 | 0 | 0 | 0 | 0 | 0 | 0 |
| 2001 | 23 | 33 | 0 | 0 | 0 | 0 | 1 | 4 |
| 2002 | 29 | 24 | 0 | 0 | 0 | 1 | 1 | 1 |
| 2003 | 85 | 5 | 0 | 0 | 0 | 0 | 2 | 4 |
| Totals | | 164 | 0 | 2 | 1 | 6 | 9 | 53 |

## John Hayden

**Birthdate:** 12/2/68  **Birth place:** Owensboro, Ky.

### CAREER STATISTICS

| Year | Rank | Starts | Wins | Poles | Top 5 | Top 10 | Races Led | Laps Led |
|------|------|--------|------|-------|-------|--------|-----------|----------|
| 2002 | 113 | 1 | 0 | 0 | 0 | 0 | 0 | 0 |
| 2003 | 57 | 10 | 0 | 0 | 0 | 0 | 0 | 0 |
| Totals | | 11 | 0 | 0 | 0 | 0 | 0 | 0 |

## Derek Hayes

**Birthdate:** 12/8/77  **Birth place:** Dungannon, Ireland

### CAREER STATISTICS

| Year | Rank | Starts | Wins | Poles | Top 5 | Top 10 | Races Led | Laps Led |
|------|------|--------|------|-------|-------|--------|-----------|----------|
| 2003 | 90 | 3 | 0 | 0 | 0 | 0 | 0 | 0 |
| Totals | | 3 | 0 | 0 | 0 | 0 | 0 | 0 |

## Jimmy Henderson

**Birthdate:** 2/24/83  **Birth place:** Conyers, Ga.

### CAREER STATISTICS

| Year | Rank | Starts | Wins | Poles | Top 5 | Top 10 | Races Led | Laps Led |
|------|------|--------|------|-------|-------|--------|-----------|----------|
| 2003 | 139 | 1 | 0 | 0 | 0 | 0 | 0 | 0 |
| Totals | | 1 | 0 | 0 | 0 | 0 | 0 | 0 |

## Bill Hoff

**Birthdate:** 8/2/60  **Birth place:** Ivyland, Pa.

### CAREER STATISTICS

| Year | Rank | Starts | Wins | Poles | Top 5 | Top 10 | Races Led | Laps Led |
|------|------|--------|------|-------|-------|--------|-----------|----------|
| 1996 | 93 | 2 | 0 | 0 | 0 | 0 | 0 | 0 |
| 1997 | 111 | 1 | 0 | 0 | 0 | 0 | 0 | 0 |
| 2001 | 62 | 9 | 0 | 0 | 0 | 0 | 0 | 0 |
| 2002 | 81 | 5 | 0 | 0 | 0 | 0 | 0 | 0 |
| 2003 | 91 | 3 | 0 | 0 | 0 | 0 | 0 | 0 |
| Totals | | 20 | 0 | 0 | 0 | 0 | 0 | 0 |

## David Keith

### CAREER STATISTICS

| Year | Rank | Starts | Wins | Poles | Top 5 | Top 10 | Races Led | Laps Led |
|------|------|--------|------|-------|-------|--------|-----------|----------|
| 2003 | 118 | 2 | 0 | 0 | 0 | 0 | 0 | 0 |
| Totals | | 2 | 0 | 0 | 0 | 0 | 0 | 0 |

## Jimmy Kitchens

**Birthdate:** 4/26/62 **Birth place:** Hueytown, Ala.

### CAREER STATISTICS

| Year | Rank | Starts | Wins | Poles | Top 5 | Top 10 | Races Led | Laps Led |
|---|---|---|---|---|---|---|---|---|
| 1994 | 101 | 1 | 0 | 0 | 0 | 0 | 0 | 0 |
| 1996 | 112 | 1 | 0 | 0 | 0 | 0 | 0 | 0 |
| 1998 | 116 | 1 | 0 | 0 | 0 | 0 | 0 | 0 |
| 1999 | 72 | 6 | 0 | 0 | 0 | 0 | 0 | 0 |
| 2002 | 43 | 14 | 0 | 0 | 0 | 1 | 0 | 0 |
| 2003 | 78 | 7 | 0 | 0 | 0 | 0 | 0 | 0 |
| Totals | | 30 | 0 | 0 | 0 | 1 | 0 | 0 |

## Justin Labonte

**Birthdate:** 2/5/81 **Birth place:** Thomasville, N.C.

### CAREER STATISTICS

| Year | Rank | Starts | Wins | Poles | Top 5 | Top 10 | Races Led | Laps Led |
|---|---|---|---|---|---|---|---|---|
| 1999 | 58 | 9 | 0 | 0 | 0 | 0 | 0 | 0 |
| 2000 | 48 | 13 | 0 | 0 | 0 | 0 | 0 | 0 |
| 2003 | 135 | 1 | 0 | 0 | 0 | 0 | 0 | 0 |
| Totals | | 23 | 0 | 0 | 0 | 0 | 0 | 0 |

## Randy LaJoie

**Birthdate:** 8/28/61 **Birth place:** Norwalk, Conn.

### CAREER STATISTICS

| Year | Rank | Starts | Wins | Poles | Top 5 | Top 10 | Races Led | Laps Led |
|---|---|---|---|---|---|---|---|---|
| 1986 | 49 | 4 | 0 | 0 | 0 | 1 | 0 | 0 |
| 1987 | 86 | 1 | 0 | 0 | 0 | 1 | 0 | 0 |
| 1988 | 72 | 2 | 0 | 0 | 1 | 1 | 1 | 1 |
| 1989 | 25 | 15 | 0 | 0 | 1 | 3 | 0 | 0 |
| 1990 | 57 | 6 | 0 | 0 | 0 | 0 | 0 | 0 |
| 1993 | 36 | 8 | 0 | 0 | 3 | 4 | 1 | 8 |
| 1994 | 16 | 27 | 0 | 1 | 4 | 7 | 8 | 156 |
| 1995 | 37 | 9 | 0 | 1 | 1 | 3 | 1 | 20 |
| 1996 | 1 | 26 | 5 | 2 | 11 | 20 | 12 | 784 |
| 1997 | 1 | 30 | 5 | 2 | 15 | 21 | 13 | 1037 |
| 1998 | 4 | 31 | 1 | 0 | 7 | 12 | 3 | 153 |
| 1999 | 10 | 32 | 1 | 0 | 6 | 7 | 6 | 313 |
| 2000 | 7 | 32 | 1 | 0 | 4 | 9 | 6 | 140 |
| 2001 | 12 | 33 | 2 | 0 | 4 | 8 | 5 | 93 |
| 2002 | 11 | 34 | 0 | 1 | 3 | 14 | 3 | 43 |
| 2003 | 26 | 19 | 0 | 2 | 2 | 4 | 2 | 63 |
| Totals | | 309 | 15 | 9 | 62 | 115 | 61 | 2811 |

## Jody Lavender

**Birthdate:** 12/29/79 **Birth place:** Hartsville, S.C.

### CAREER STATISTICS

| Year | Rank | Starts | Wins | Poles | Top 5 | Top 10 | Races Led | Laps Led |
|---|---|---|---|---|---|---|---|---|
| 2003 | 125 | 1 | 0 | 0 | 0 | 0 | 0 | 0 |
| Totals | | 1 | 0 | 0 | 0 | 0 | 0 | 0 |

## Anthony Lazzaro

**Birthdate:** 8/26/66 **Birth place:** Acworth, Ga.

### CAREER STATISTICS

| Year | Rank | Starts | Wins | Poles | Top 5 | Top 10 | Races Led | Laps Led |
|---|---|---|---|---|---|---|---|---|
| 2000 | 55 | 10 | 0 | 0 | 0 | 0 | 0 | 0 |
| 2003 | 127 | 1 | 0 | 0 | 0 | 0 | 0 | 0 |
| Totals | | 11 | 0 | 0 | 0 | 0 | 0 | 0 |

## Dwayne Leik

**Birthdate:** 2/9/67 **Birth place:** Skyland, N.C.

### CAREER STATISTICS

| Year | Rank | Starts | Wins | Poles | Top 5 | Top 10 | Races Led | Laps Led |
|---|---|---|---|---|---|---|---|---|
| 2001 | 125 | 1 | 0 | 0 | 0 | 0 | 0 | 0 |
| 2002 | 79 | 4 | 0 | 0 | 0 | 0 | 0 | 0 |
| 2003 | 88 | 3 | 0 | 0 | 0 | 0 | 0 | 0 |
| Totals | | 8 | 0 | 0 | 0 | 0 | 0 | 0 |

## Mardy Lindley

**Birthdate:** 7/10/72 **Birth place:** Taylors, S.C.

### CAREER STATISTICS

| Year | Rank | Starts | Wins | Poles | Top 5 | Top 10 | Races Led | Laps Led |
|---|---|---|---|---|---|---|---|---|
| 2003 | 117 | 1 | 0 | 0 | 0 | 0 | 0 | 0 |
| Totals | | 1 | 0 | 0 | 0 | 0 | 0 | 0 |

## Brad Loney

**Birthdate:** 1/21/68 **Birth place:** Cedar Rapids, Iowa

### CAREER STATISTICS

| Year | Rank | Starts | Wins | Poles | Top 5 | Top 10 | Races Led | Laps Led |
|---|---|---|---|---|---|---|---|---|
| 1997 | 77 | 3 | 0 | 0 | 0 | 0 | 0 | 0 |
| 1998 | 60 | 6 | 0 | 0 | 0 | 0 | 0 | 0 |
| 1999 | 40 | 17 | 0 | 0 | 1 | 2 | 0 | 0 |
| 2003 | 103 | 2 | 0 | 0 | 0 | 0 | 0 | 0 |
| Totals | | 28 | 0 | 0 | 1 | 2 | 0 | 0 |

## Carl Long

**Birthdate:** 9/20/67  **Birth place:** Roxboro, N.C.

### CAREER STATISTICS

| Year | Rank | Starts | Wins | Poles | Top 5 | Top 10 | Races Led | Laps Led |
|------|------|--------|------|-------|-------|--------|-----------|----------|
| 2001 | 146  | 1      | 0    | 0     | 0     | 0      | 0         | 0        |
| 2003 | 114  | 2      | 0    | 0     | 0     | 0      | 0         | 0        |
| Totals |    | 3      | 0    | 0     | 0     | 0      | 0         | 0        |

## Randy MacDonald

**Birthdate:** 7/26/62  **Birth place:** Oshawa, Ontario

### CAREER STATISTICS

| Year | Rank | Starts | Wins | Poles | Top 5 | Top 10 | Races Led | Laps Led |
|------|------|--------|------|-------|-------|--------|-----------|----------|
| 1986 | 112  | 1      | 0    | 0     | 0     | 0      | 0         | 0        |
| 1987 | 91   | 1      | 0    | 0     | 0     | 0      | 0         | 0        |
| 1990 | 105  | 1      | 0    | 0     | 0     | 0      | 0         | 0        |
| 1991 | 84   | 1      | 0    | 0     | 0     | 1      | 0         | 0        |
| 1992 | 77   | 2      | 0    | 0     | 0     | 0      | 0         | 0        |
| 1993 | 69   | 2      | 0    | 0     | 0     | 0      | 0         | 0        |
| 1994 | 61   | 4      | 0    | 0     | 0     | 0      | 0         | 0        |
| 1995 | 102  | 1      | 0    | 0     | 0     | 0      | 0         | 0        |
| 2003 | 81   | 5      | 0    | 0     | 0     | 0      | 0         | 0        |
| Totals |    | 18     | 0    | 0     | 0     | 1      | 0         | 0        |

## Blake Mallory

**Birthdate:** 3/2/80  **Birth place:** Joshua, Texas

### CAREER STATISTICS

| Year | Rank | Starts | Wins | Poles | Top 5 | Top 10 | Races Led | Laps Led |
|------|------|--------|------|-------|-------|--------|-----------|----------|
| 2003 | 100  | 3      | 0    | 0     | 0     | 0      | 0         | 0        |
| Totals |    | 3      | 0    | 0     | 0     | 0      | 0         | 0        |

## Rick Markle

**Birthdate:** 2/3/72  **Birth place:** Fowlerville, Mich.

### CAREER STATISTICS

| Year | Rank | Starts | Wins | Poles | Top 5 | Top 10 | Races Led | Laps Led |
|------|------|--------|------|-------|-------|--------|-----------|----------|
| 2001 | 110  | 2      | 0    | 0     | 0     | 0      | 0         | 0        |
| 2002 | 99   | 3      | 0    | 0     | 0     | 0      | 0         | 0        |
| 2003 | 75   | 5      | 0    | 0     | 0     | 0      | 0         | 0        |
| Totals |    | 10     | 0    | 0     | 0     | 0      | 0         | 0        |

## Steadman Marlin

**Birthdate:** 10/29/80  **Birth place:** Columbia, Tenn.

### CAREER STATISTICS

| Year | Rank | Starts | Wins | Poles | Top 5 | Top 10 | Races Led | Laps Led |
|------|------|--------|------|-------|-------|--------|-----------|----------|
| 2000 | 104  | 1      | 0    | 0     | 0     | 0      | 0         | 0        |
| 2001 | 53   | 8      | 0    | 0     | 0     | 0      | 0         | 0        |
| 2002 | 55   | 6      | 0    | 0     | 0     | 0      | 1         | 7        |
| 2003 | 63   | 7      | 0    | 0     | 0     | 0      | 0         | 0        |
| Totals |    | 22     | 0    | 0     | 0     | 0      | 1         | 7        |

## Eric McClure

### CAREER STATISTICS

| Year | Rank | Starts | Wins | Poles | Top 5 | Top 10 | Races Led | Laps Led |
|------|------|--------|------|-------|-------|--------|-----------|----------|
| 2003 | 130  | 1      | 0    | 0     | 0     | 0      | 0         | 0        |
| Totals |    | 1      | 0    | 0     | 0     | 0      | 0         | 0        |

## Mike McLaughlin

**Birthdate:** 10/6/56  **Birth place:** Waterloo, N.Y.

### CAREER STATISTICS

| Year | Rank | Starts | Wins | Poles | Top 5 | Top 10 | Races Led | Laps Led |
|------|------|--------|------|-------|-------|--------|-----------|----------|
| 1984 | 72   | 2      | 0    | 0     | 0     | 0      | 0         | 0        |
| 1985 | 66   | 2      | 0    | 0     | 0     | 0      | 1         | 1        |
| 1990 | 45   | 6      | 0    | 0     | 2     | 3      | 1         | 18       |
| 1991 | 45   | 8      | 0    | 0     | 0     | 0      | 0         | 0        |
| 1992 | 49   | 5      | 0    | 0     | 0     | 0      | 0         | 0        |
| 1993 | 58   | 3      | 0    | 0     | 0     | 1      | 0         | 0        |
| 1994 | 13   | 26     | 0    | 0     | 3     | 8      | 3         | 9        |
| 1995 | 3    | 26     | 1    | 1     | 9     | 14     | 5         | 82       |
| 1996 | 10   | 26     | 0    | 0     | 7     | 10     | 6         | 99       |
| 1997 | 4    | 30     | 2    | 2     | 7     | 14     | 8         | 206      |
| 1998 | 3    | 31     | 2    | 2     | 11    | 16     | 9         | 165      |
| 1999 | 9    | 32     | 0    | 0     | 3     | 8      | 4         | 53       |
| 2000 | 24   | 31     | 0    | 0     | 3     | 5      | 0         | 0        |
| 2001 | 7    | 33     | 1    | 0     | 5     | 12     | 5         | 38       |
| 2002 | 4    | 34     | 0    | 0     | 7     | 17     | 5         | 128      |
| 2003 | 61   | 7      | 0    | 0     | 0     | 1      | 0         | 0        |
| Totals |    | 302    | 6    | 5     | 57    | 109    | 47        | 799      |

## Chase Montgomery

**Birthdate:** 9/29/83  **Birth place:** Lebanon, Tenn.

### CAREER STATISTICS

| Year | Rank | Starts | Wins | Poles | Top 5 | Top 10 | Races Led | Laps Led |
|------|------|--------|------|-------|-------|--------|-----------|----------|
| 2003 | 41   | 15     | 0    | 0     | 0     | 1      | 0         | 0        |
| Totals |    | 15     | 0    | 0     | 0     | 1      | 0         | 0        |

## Brent Moore

**Birthdate:** 2/8/78 **Birth place:** Pickens, S.C.

### CAREER STATISTICS

| Year | Rank | Starts | Wins | Poles | Top 5 | Top 10 | Races Led | Laps Led |
|---|---|---|---|---|---|---|---|---|
| 2002 | 125 | 1 | 0 | 0 | 0 | 0 | 0 | 0 |
| 2003 | 132 | 1 | 0 | 0 | 0 | 0 | 0 | 0 |
| Totals | | 2 | 0 | 0 | 0 | 0 | 0 | 0 |

## Jamie Mosley

**Birthdate:** 12/9/69 **Birth place:** London, Ky.

### CAREER STATISTICS

| Year | Rank | Starts | Wins | Poles | Top 5 | Top 10 | Races Led | Laps Led |
|---|---|---|---|---|---|---|---|---|
| 2003 | 65 | 8 | 0 | 0 | 0 | 0 | 0 | 0 |
| Totals | | 8 | 0 | 0 | 0 | 0 | 0 | 0 |

## Ted Musgrave

**Birthdate:** 12/18/55 **Birth place:** Franklin, Wis.

### CAREER STATISTICS

| Year | Rank | Starts | Wins | Poles | Top 5 | Top 10 | Races Led | Laps Led |
|---|---|---|---|---|---|---|---|---|
| 1989 | 70 | 2 | 0 | 0 | 0 | 0 | 0 | 0 |
| 1995 | 93 | 1 | 0 | 0 | 0 | 0 | 0 | 0 |
| 1997 | 79 | 2 | 0 | 0 | 0 | 0 | 0 | 0 |
| 1999 | 105 | 1 | 0 | 0 | 0 | 0 | 0 | 0 |
| 2000 | 53 | 9 | 0 | 0 | 0 | 1 | 0 | 0 |
| 2003 | 98 | 1 | 0 | 0 | 1 | 1 | 0 | 0 |
| Totals | | 16 | 0 | 0 | 1 | 2 | 0 | 0 |

## Donnie Neuenberger

**Birthdate:** 8/10/62 **Birth place:** Brandywine, Md.

### CAREER STATISTICS

| Year | Rank | Starts | Wins | Poles | Top 5 | Top 10 | Races Led | Laps Led |
|---|---|---|---|---|---|---|---|---|
| 2002 | 103 | 1 | 0 | 0 | 0 | 0 | 0 | 0 |
| 2003 | 74 | 6 | 0 | 0 | 0 | 0 | 0 | 0 |
| Totals | | 7 | 0 | 0 | 0 | 0 | 0 | 0 |

## Lance Norick

**Birthdate:** 9/20/68 **Birth place:** Oklahoma City, Okla.

### CAREER STATISTICS

| Year | Rank | Starts | Wins | Poles | Top 5 | Top 10 | Races Led | Laps Led |
|---|---|---|---|---|---|---|---|---|
| 2003 | 64 | 7 | 0 | 0 | 0 | 0 | 0 | 0 |
| Totals | | 7 | 0 | 0 | 0 | 0 | 0 | 0 |

## Steve Park

**Birthdate:** 8/23/67 **Birth place:** East Northport, N.Y.

### CAREER STATISTICS

| Year | Rank | Starts | Wins | Poles | Top 5 | Top 10 | Races Led | Laps Led |
|---|---|---|---|---|---|---|---|---|
| 1990 | 101 | 1 | 0 | 0 | 0 | 0 | 0 | 0 |
| 1995 | 109 | 1 | 0 | 0 | 0 | 0 | 0 | 0 |
| 1996 | 98 | 1 | 0 | 0 | 0 | 0 | 0 | 0 |
| 1997 | 3 | 30 | 3 | 1 | 12 | 20 | 14 | 477 |
| 2000 | 43 | 9 | 0 | 0 | 0 | 3 | 2 | 25 |
| 2001 | 46 | 7 | 0 | 0 | 2 | 5 | 1 | 40 |
| 2003 | 102 | 1 | 0 | 0 | 1 | 1 | 0 | 0 |
| Totals | | 50 | 3 | 1 | 15 | 29 | 17 | 542 |

## Hank Parker Jr.

**Birthdate:** 10/7/74 **Birth place:** Denver, N.C.

### CAREER STATISTICS

| Year | Rank | Starts | Wins | Poles | Top 5 | Top 10 | Races Led | Laps Led |
|---|---|---|---|---|---|---|---|---|
| 1997 | 94 | 1 | 0 | 0 | 0 | 0 | 0 | 0 |
| 1998 | 67 | 3 | 0 | 0 | 0 | 1 | 1 | 4 |
| 1999 | 18 | 27 | 0 | 0 | 2 | 4 | 1 | 32 |
| 2000 | 14 | 32 | 0 | 1 | 2 | 8 | 1 | 4 |
| 2001 | 15 | 33 | 1 | 0 | 2 | 6 | 6 | 38 |
| 2002 | 14 | 34 | 1 | 0 | 3 | 8 | 3 | 42 |
| 2003 | 51 | 6 | 0 | 0 | 2 | 4 | 2 | 7 |
| Totals | | 136 | 2 | 1 | 11 | 31 | 14 | 127 |

## Toby Porter

**Birthdate:** 11/22/74 **Birth place:** Greenville, S.C.

### CAREER STATISTICS

| Year | Rank | Starts | Wins | Poles | Top 5 | Top 10 | Races Led | Laps Led |
|---|---|---|---|---|---|---|---|---|
| 2003 | 128 | 1 | 0 | 0 | 0 | 0 | 0 | 0 |
| Totals | | 1 | 0 | 0 | 0 | 0 | 0 | 0 |

## Mike Potter

**Birthdate:** 7/4/49 **Birth place:** Johnson City, Tenn.

### CAREER STATISTICS

| Year | Rank | Starts | Wins | Poles | Top 5 | Top 10 | Races Led | Laps Led |
|---|---|---|---|---|---|---|---|---|
| 1982 | 173 | 1 | 0 | 0 | 0 | 0 | 0 | 0 |
| 1985 | 106 | 1 | 0 | 0 | 0 | 0 | 0 | 0 |
| 2001 | 144 | 1 | 0 | 0 | 0 | 0 | 0 | 0 |
| 2003 | 68 | 11 | 0 | 0 | 0 | 0 | 0 | 0 |
| Totals | | 14 | 0 | 0 | 0 | 0 | 0 | 0 |

## Jerry Reary

**Birthdate:** 12/4/61 **Birth place:** Matthews, N.C.

### CAREER STATISTICS

| Year | Rank | Starts | Wins | Poles | Top 5 | Top 10 | Races Led | Laps Led |
|---|---|---|---|---|---|---|---|---|
| 2003 | 95 | 3 | 0 | 0 | 0 | 0 | 0 | 0 |
| Totals | | 3 | 0 | 0 | 0 | 0 | 0 | 0 |

## David Reutimann

**Birthdate:** 3/2/70 **Birth place:** Zephyr Hills, Fla.

### CAREER STATISTICS

| Year | Rank | Starts | Wins | Poles | Top 5 | Top 10 | Races Led | Laps Led |
|---|---|---|---|---|---|---|---|---|
| 2002 | 63 | 4 | 0 | 0 | 0 | 0 | 1 | 12 |
| 2003 | 50 | 7 | 0 | 0 | 2 | 3 | 1 | 22 |
| Totals | | 11 | 0 | 0 | 2 | 3 | 2 | 34 |

## Josh Richeson

**Birthdate:** 9/4/81 **Birth place:** Davidson, N.C.

### CAREER STATISTICS

| Year | Rank | Starts | Wins | Poles | Top 5 | Top 10 | Races Led | Laps Led |
|---|---|---|---|---|---|---|---|---|
| 2001 | 105 | 2 | 0 | 0 | 0 | 0 | 0 | 0 |
| 2002 | 57 | 9 | 0 | 0 | 0 | 0 | 0 | 0 |
| 2003 | 79 | 8 | 0 | 0 | 0 | 0 | 0 | 0 |
| Totals | | 19 | 0 | 0 | 0 | 0 | 0 | 0 |

## Scott Riggs

**Birthdate:** 1/1/71 **Birth place:** Bahama, N.C.

### CAREER STATISTICS

| Year | Rank | Starts | Wins | Poles | Top 5 | Top 10 | Races Led | Laps Led |
|---|---|---|---|---|---|---|---|---|
| 2002 | 10 | 34 | 2 | 2 | 8 | 13 | 12 | 415 |
| 2003 | 6 | 34 | 2 | 0 | 11 | 17 | 14 | 505 |
| Totals | | 68 | 4 | 2 | 19 | 30 | 26 | 920 |

## Jason Rudd

**Birthdate:** 4/15/79 **Birth place:** Norfolk, Va.

### CAREER STATISTICS

| Year | Rank | Starts | Wins | Poles | Top 5 | Top 10 | Races Led | Laps Led |
|---|---|---|---|---|---|---|---|---|
| 2001 | 64 | 6 | 0 | 0 | 0 | 0 | 0 | 0 |
| 2003 | 107 | 2 | 0 | 0 | 0 | 0 | 0 | 0 |
| Totals | | 8 | 0 | 0 | 0 | 0 | 0 | 0 |

## Hermie Sadler

**Birthdate:** 4/24/69 **Birth place:** Emporia, Va.

### CAREER STATISTICS

| Year | Rank | Starts | Wins | Poles | Top 5 | Top 10 | Races Led | Laps Led |
|---|---|---|---|---|---|---|---|---|
| 1992 | 51 | 5 | 0 | 0 | 0 | 0 | 0 | 0 |
| 1993 | 10 | 28 | 1 | 0 | 4 | 8 | 1 | 8 |
| 1994 | 5 | 28 | 1 | 0 | 6 | 11 | 7 | 291 |
| 1995 | 13 | 26 | 0 | 0 | 3 | 6 | 2 | 114 |
| 1996 | 15 | 26 | 0 | 1 | 1 | 5 | 4 | 184 |
| 1997 | 10 | 30 | 0 | 2 | 2 | 7 | 5 | 54 |
| 1998 | 10 | 31 | 0 | 0 | 2 | 5 | 3 | 18 |
| 1999 | 37 | 17 | 0 | 0 | 0 | 1 | 0 | 0 |
| 2000 | 35 | 16 | 0 | 0 | 0 | 1 | 2 | 4 |
| 2002 | 66 | 6 | 0 | 0 | 0 | 0 | 0 | 0 |
| 2003 | 44 | 13 | 0 | 0 | 0 | 0 | 0 | 0 |
| Totals | | 226 | 2 | 3 | 18 | 44 | 24 | 673 |

## Jay Sauter

**Birthdate:** 6/22/62 **Birth place:** West Salem, Wis.

### CAREER STATISTICS

| Year | Rank | Starts | Wins | Poles | Top 5 | Top 10 | Races Led | Laps Led |
|---|---|---|---|---|---|---|---|---|
| 1997 | 86 | 1 | 0 | 0 | 0 | 0 | 0 | 0 |
| 2000 | 16 | 31 | 0 | 0 | 1 | 8 | 3 | 25 |
| 2001 | 19 | 31 | 0 | 1 | 2 | 7 | 2 | 13 |
| 2002 | 36 | 14 | 0 | 0 | 1 | 4 | 4 | 47 |
| 2003 | 49 | 10 | 0 | 0 | 0 | 1 | 1 | 2 |
| Totals | | 87 | 0 | 1 | 4 | 20 | 10 | 87 |

## Tim Sauter

**Birthdate:** 10/13/64 **Birth place:** Necedah, Wis.

### CAREER STATISTICS

| Year | Rank | Starts | Wins | Poles | Top 5 | Top 10 | Races Led | Laps Led |
|---|---|---|---|---|---|---|---|---|
| 2000 | 73 | 3 | 0 | 0 | 0 | 0 | 0 | 0 |
| 2001 | 32 | 18 | 0 | 0 | 0 | 2 | 0 | 0 |
| 2002 | 13 | 34 | 0 | 0 | 0 | 7 | 4 | 12 |
| 2003 | 46 | 12 | 0 | 0 | 0 | 0 | 1 | 4 |
| Totals | | 67 | 0 | 0 | 0 | 9 | 5 | 16 |

## Jason Schuler

**Birthdate:** 2/24/72 **Birth place:** Cambridge, Wis.

### CAREER STATISTICS

| Year | Rank | Starts | Wins | Poles | Top 5 | Top 10 | Races Led | Laps Led |
|---|---|---|---|---|---|---|---|---|
| 2000 | 44 | 11 | 0 | 0 | 0 | 0 | 1 | 2 |
| 2001 | 104 | 2 | 0 | 0 | 0 | 0 | 0 | 0 |
| 2002 | 78 | 5 | 0 | 0 | 0 | 0 | 0 | 0 |
| 2003 | 28 | 27 | 0 | 0 | 0 | 0 | 2 | 12 |
| Totals | | 45 | 0 | 0 | 0 | 0 | 3 | 14 |

## Morgan Shepherd

**Birthdate:** 10/21/41 **Birth place:** Conover, N.C.

### CAREER STATISTICS

| Year | Rank | Starts | Wins | Poles | Top 5 | Top 10 | Races Led | Laps Led |
|---|---|---|---|---|---|---|---|---|
| 1982 | 11 | 12 | 2 | 2 | 8 | 8 | 0 | 0 |
| 1983 | 18 | 18 | 2 | 1 | 9 | 13 | 2 | 145 |
| 1984 | 22 | 15 | 3 | 1 | 4 | 6 | 7 | 379 |
| 1985 | 28 | 11 | 0 | 0 | 2 | 3 | 3 | 13 |
| 1986 | 25 | 14 | 4 | 1 | 5 | 6 | 6 | 431 |
| 1987 | 24 | 14 | 3 | 0 | 6 | 8 | 6 | 245 |
| 1988 | 24 | 17 | 1 | 0 | 3 | 6 | 8 | 149 |
| 1989 | 47 | 7 | 0 | 1 | 0 | 2 | 1 | 54 |
| 1990 | 34 | 12 | 0 | 0 | 3 | 4 | 1 | 22 |
| 1991 | 32 | 16 | 0 | 0 | 1 | 3 | 2 | 9 |
| 1992 | 37 | 11 | 0 | 0 | 2 | 4 | 2 | 38 |
| 1993 | 106 | 1 | 0 | 0 | 0 | 0 | 1 | 3 |
| 1994 | 45 | 8 | 0 | 0 | 0 | 1 | 1 | 5 |
| 1995 | 45 | 7 | 0 | 0 | 1 | 2 | 2 | 23 |
| 1996 | 90 | 2 | 0 | 0 | 0 | 0 | 0 | 0 |
| 1997 | 87 | 3 | 0 | 0 | 0 | 0 | 0 | 0 |
| 1998 | 118 | 1 | 0 | 0 | 0 | 0 | 0 | 0 |
| 1999 | 96 | 1 | 0 | 0 | 0 | 1 | 0 | 0 |
| 2003 | 53 | 14 | 0 | 0 | 0 | 0 | 0 | 0 |
| Totals | | 184 | 15 | 6 | 44 | 67 | 42 | 1516 |

## Regan Smith

**Birthdate:** 9/23/83 **Birth place:** Cato, N.Y.

### CAREER STATISTICS

| Year | Rank | Starts | Wins | Poles | Top 5 | Top 10 | Races Led | Laps Led |
|---|---|---|---|---|---|---|---|---|
| 2002 | 118 | 1 | 0 | 0 | 0 | 0 | 0 | 0 |
| 2003 | 38 | 18 | 0 | 0 | 0 | 0 | 0 | 0 |
| Totals | | 19 | 0 | 0 | 0 | 0 | 0 | 0 |

## Jeff Streeter

**Birthdate:** 11/25/79 **Birth place:** Vinton, Iowa

### CAREER STATISTICS

| Year | Rank | Starts | Wins | Poles | Top 5 | Top 10 | Races Led | Laps Led |
|---|---|---|---|---|---|---|---|---|
| 2001 | 88 | 4 | 0 | 0 | 0 | 0 | 0 | 0 |
| 2003 | 87 | 5 | 0 | 0 | 0 | 0 | 0 | 0 |
| Totals | | 9 | 0 | 0 | 0 | 0 | 0 | 0 |

## Brad Teague

**Birthdate:** 12/9/47 **Birth place:** Johnson City, Tenn.

### CAREER STATISTICS

| Year | Rank | Starts | Wins | Poles | Top 5 | Top 10 | Races Led | Laps Led |
|---|---|---|---|---|---|---|---|---|
| 1982 | 107 | 1 | 0 | 0 | 1 | 1 | 0 | 0 |
| 1983 | 136 | 1 | 0 | 0 | 0 | 0 | 0 | 0 |
| 1984 | 27 | 10 | 0 | 0 | 4 | 8 | 1 | 34 |
| 1985 | 13 | 24 | 0 | 2 | 2 | 7 | 8 | 129 |
| 1986 | 19 | 20 | 0 | 0 | 1 | 10 | 3 | 52 |
| 1987 | 7 | 27 | 1 | 0 | 1 | 10 | 2 | 97 |
| 1988 | 23 | 17 | 0 | 0 | 1 | 5 | 4 | 101 |
| 1989 | 52 | 6 | 0 | 0 | 1 | 1 | 0 | 0 |
| 1990 | 49 | 6 | 0 | 0 | 0 | 0 | 1 | 4 |
| 1991 | 98 | 1 | 0 | 0 | 0 | 0 | 0 | 0 |
| 1995 | 66 | 2 | 0 | 0 | 0 | 1 | 0 | 0 |
| 1996 | 62 | 3 | 0 | 0 | 0 | 0 | 0 | 0 |
| 1997 | 56 | 5 | 0 | 0 | 0 | 0 | 0 | 0 |
| 1999 | 110 | 1 | 0 | 0 | 0 | 0 | 0 | 0 |
| 2001 | 47 | 16 | 0 | 0 | 0 | 0 | 0 | 0 |
| 2002 | 42 | 19 | 0 | 0 | 0 | 0 | 0 | 0 |
| 2003 | 32 | 26 | 0 | 0 | 0 | 0 | 1 | 1 |
| Totals | | 185 | 1 | 2 | 11 | 43 | 20 | 418 |

## Brian Vickers

**Birthdate:** 10/24/83 **Birth place:** Thomasville, N.C.

### CAREER STATISTICS

| Year | Rank | Starts | Wins | Poles | Top 5 | Top 10 | Races Led | Laps Led |
|---|---|---|---|---|---|---|---|---|
| 2001 | 72 | 4 | 0 | 0 | 0 | 0 | 0 | 0 |
| 2002 | 30 | 21 | 0 | 0 | 0 | 1 | 1 | 12 |
| 2003 | 1 | 34 | 3 | 1 | 13 | 21 | 14 | 623 |
| Totals | | 59 | 3 | 1 | 13 | 22 | 15 | 635 |

## Shane Wallace

**Birthdate:** 1/11/84 **Birth place:** Utica, N.Y.

### CAREER STATISTICS

| Year | Rank | Starts | Wins | Poles | Top 5 | Top 10 | Races Led | Laps Led |
|---|---|---|---|---|---|---|---|---|
| 2003 | 142 | 1 | 0 | 0 | 0 | 0 | 0 | 0 |
| Totals | | 1 | 0 | 0 | 0 | 0 | 0 | 0 |

## Gus Wasson

**Birthdate:** 3/20/74 **Birth place:** Lincoln, N.C.

### CAREER STATISTICS

| Year | Rank | Starts | Wins | Poles | Top 5 | Top 10 | Races Led | Laps Led |
|---|---|---|---|---|---|---|---|---|
| 1998 | 102 | 1 | 0 | 0 | 0 | 0 | 0 | 0 |
| 1999 | 73 | 5 | 0 | 0 | 0 | 0 | 1 | 7 |
| 2000 | 84 | 3 | 0 | 0 | 0 | 0 | 0 | 0 |
| 2001 | 123 | 1 | 0 | 0 | 0 | 0 | 0 | 0 |
| 2002 | 127 | 1 | 0 | 0 | 0 | 0 | 0 | 0 |
| 2003 | 56 | 9 | 0 | 0 | 0 | 0 | 0 | 0 |
| Totals | | 20 | 0 | 0 | 0 | 0 | 1 | 7 |

## Dana White

**Birthdate:** 3/31/58 **Birth place:** Wake Forest, N.C.

### CAREER STATISTICS

| Year | Rank | Starts | Wins | Poles | Top 5 | Top 10 | Races Led | Laps Led |
|---|---|---|---|---|---|---|---|---|
| 2002 | 87 | 3 | 0 | 0 | 0 | 0 | 0 | 0 |
| 2003 | 71 | 7 | 0 | 0 | 0 | 0 | 0 | 0 |
| Totals | | 10 | 0 | 0 | 0 | 0 | 0 | 0 |

## Jason White

**Birthdate:** 6/5/79 **Birth place:** Powhatan, Va.

### CAREER STATISTICS

| Year | Rank | Starts | Wins | Poles | Top 5 | Top 10 | Races Led | Laps Led |
|---|---|---|---|---|---|---|---|---|
| 1999 | 102 | 2 | 0 | 0 | 0 | 0 | 0 | 0 |
| 2000 | 86 | 2 | 0 | 0 | 0 | 0 | 0 | 0 |
| 2002 | 75 | 4 | 0 | 0 | 0 | 0 | 0 | 0 |
| 2003 | 29 | 23 | 0 | 0 | 0 | 0 | 0 | 0 |
| Totals | | 31 | 0 | 0 | 0 | 0 | 0 | 0 |

## Scott Wimmer

**Birthdate:** 1/26/76 **Birth place:** Wausau, Wis.

### CAREER STATISTICS

| Year | Rank | Starts | Wins | Poles | Top 5 | Top 10 | Races Led | Laps Led |
|---|---|---|---|---|---|---|---|---|
| 2000 | 78 | 3 | 0 | 0 | 0 | 0 | 1 | 2 |
| 2001 | 11 | 33 | 0 | 0 | 2 | 8 | 6 | 53 |
| 2002 | 3 | 34 | 4 | 0 | 11 | 17 | 7 | 191 |
| 2003 | 9 | 34 | 1 | 0 | 4 | 12 | 6 | 133 |
| Totals | | 104 | 5 | 0 | 17 | 37 | 20 | 379 |

## Paul Wolfe

### CAREER STATISTICS

| Year | Rank | Starts | Wins | Poles | Top 5 | Top 10 | Races Led | Laps Led |
|---|---|---|---|---|---|---|---|---|
| 2003 | 89 | 2 | 0 | 0 | 0 | 0 | 0 | 0 |
| Totals | | 2 | 0 | 0 | 0 | 0 | 0 | 0 |

## Jon Wood

**Birthdate:** 10/25/81 **Birth place:** Stuart, Va.

### CAREER STATISTICS

| Year | Rank | Starts | Wins | Poles | Top 5 | Top 10 | Races Led | Laps Led |
|---|---|---|---|---|---|---|---|---|
| 2002 | 88 | 1 | 0 | 0 | 0 | 1 | 0 | 0 |
| 2003 | 122 | 1 | 0 | 0 | 0 | 0 | 0 | 0 |
| Totals | | 2 | 0 | 0 | 0 | 1 | 0 | 0 |

## Ron Young

**Birthdate:** 7/22/70 **Birth place:** Conyers, Ga.

### CAREER STATISTICS

| Year | Rank | Starts | Wins | Poles | Top 5 | Top 10 | Races Led | Laps Led |
|---|---|---|---|---|---|---|---|---|
| 2000 | 106 | 1 | 0 | 0 | 0 | 0 | 0 | 0 |
| 2001 | 86 | 3 | 0 | 0 | 0 | 0 | 0 | 0 |
| 2002 | 45 | 12 | 0 | 0 | 0 | 0 | 0 | 0 |
| 2003 | 42 | 13 | 0 | 0 | 0 | 0 | 0 | 0 |
| Totals | | 29 | 0 | 0 | 0 | 0 | 0 | 0 |

# 2003 race results

| No. | Date | Race | Track | Pole winner | Race winner |
|---|---|---|---|---|---|
| 1 | February 15 | Koolerz 300 | Daytona International Speedway | Joe Nemechek | Dale Earnhardt Jr. |
| 2 | February 24 | Rockingham 200 | North Carolina Speedway | David Green | Jamie McMurray |
| 3 | March 1 | Sam's Town 300 | Las Vegas Motor Speedway | Stanton Barrett (rain) | Joe Nemechek |
| 4 | March 17 | Darlingtonraceway.com 200 | Darlington Raceway | Stanton Barrett (rain) | Todd Bodine |
| 5 | March 22 | Channellock 250 | Bristol Motor Speedway | David Green | Kevin Harvick |
| 6 | March 29 | O'Reilly 300 | Texas Motor Speedway | Jason Keller | Joe Nemechek |
| 7 | April 5 | Aaron's 312 | Talladega Superspeedway | Joe Nemechek | Dale Earnhardt Jr. |
| 8 | April 12 | Pepsi 300 | Nashville Superspeedway | Randy LaJoie | David Green |
| 9 | April 26 | 1-800-PIT-SHOP.COM 300 | California Speedway | Kevin Harvick | Matt Kenseth |
| 10 | May 2 | Hardee's 250 | Richmond International Raceway | Michael Waltrip | Kevin Harvick |
| 11 | May 10 | Charter Pipeline 250 | Gateway International Raceway | Ashton Lewis Jr. | Scott Riggs |
| 12 | May 18 | Goulds Pumps ITT Industries 200 | Nazareth Speedway | Randy LaJoie | Ron Hornaday |
| 13 | May 24 | CARQUEST Auto Parts 300 | Lowe's Motor Speedway | Kevin Harvick | Matt Kenseth |
| 14 | May 31 | MBNA Armed Forces Family 200 | Dover International Speedway | Joe Nemechek | Joe Nemechek |
| 15 | June 7 | Trace Adkins Chrome 300 | Nashville Superspeedway | Johnny Sauter (rain) | Scott Riggs |
| 16 | June 14 | Meijer 300 | Kentucky Speedway | Stacy Compton | Bobby Hamilton Jr. |
| 17 | June 29 | GNC Live Well 250 | The Milwaukee Mile | Johnny Sauter (rain) | Jason Keller |
| 18 | July 4 | Winn-Dixie 250 | Daytona International Speedway | Dale Earnhardt Jr. | Dale Earnhardt Jr. |
| 19 | July 12 | Tropicana Twister 300 | Chicagoland Speedway | Casey Mears | Bobby Hamilton Jr. |
| 20 | July 19 | New England 200 | New Hampshire Int'l Speedway | Kevin Harvick (rain) | David Green |
| 21 | July 26 | TrimSpa Dream Body 250 | Pikes Peak International Raceway | Bobby Hamilton Jr. | Scott Wimmer |
| 22 | August 2 | Kroger 200 | Indianapolis Raceway Park | Shane Hmiel | Brian Vickers |
| 23 | August 16 | Cabela's 250 | Michigan International Speedway | Kasey Kahne | Kevin Harvick |
| 24 | August 22 | Food City 250 | Bristol Motor Speedway | Jason Keller | Michael Waltrip |
| 25 | August 30 | Winn-Dixie 200 | Darlington Raceway | Kevin Harvick | Brian Vickers |
| 26 | September 5 | Funai 250 | Richmond International Raceway | Kevin Harvick (rain) | Johnny Sauter |
| 27 | September 20 | Dover 200 | Dover International Speedway | Kevin Harvick (rain) | Brian Vickers |
| 28 | October 4 | Mr. Goodcents 300 | Kansas Speedway | Michael Waltrip | David Green |
| 29 | October 11 | Little Trees 300 | Lowe's Motor Speedway | Kevin Harvick | Greg Biffle |
| 30 | October 18 | Sam's Town 250 | Memphis Motorsports Park | David Reutimann | Bobby Hamilton Jr. |
| 31 | October 25 | Aaron's 312 | Atlanta Motor Speedway | Greg Biffle | Greg Biffle |
| 32 | November 1 | Bashas' Supermarkets 200 | Phoenix International Raceway | Kevin Harvick | Bobby Hamilton Jr. |
| 33 | November 8 | Target House 200 | North Carolina Speedway | Brian Vickers | Jamie McMurray |
| 34 | November 15 | Ford 300 | Homestead-Miami Speedway | Greg Biffle | Kasey Kahne |

# 2003 points standings

| Pos. | Driver | Points | Behind | Starts | Wins | Top 5 | Top 10 | Money won |
|---|---|---|---|---|---|---|---|---|
| 1 | Brian Vickers | 4,637 | — | 34 | 3 | 13 | 21 | $1,112,250 |
| 2 | David Green | 4,623 | -14 | 34 | 3 | 11 | 21 | $1,135,360 |
| 3 | Ron Hornaday | 4,591 | -46 | 34 | 1 | 8 | 17 | $957,270 |
| 4 | Bobby Hamilton Jr. | 4,588 | -49 | 34 | 4 | 13 | 22 | $1,167,460 |
| 5 | Jason Keller | 4,528 | -109 | 34 | 1 | 10 | 17 | $1,117,840 |
| 6 | Scott Riggs | 4,462 | -175 | 34 | 2 | 11 | 17 | $1,122,030 |
| 7 | Kasey Kahne | 4,104 | -533 | 34 | 1 | 4 | 14 | $831,415 |
| 8 | Johnny Sauter | 4,098 | -539 | 34 | 1 | 6 | 14 | $756,225 |
| 9 | Scott Wimmer | 4,059 | -578 | 34 | 1 | 4 | 12 | $973,910 |
| 10 | Mike Bliss | 3,932 | -705 | 34 | 0 | 8 | 14 | $766,885 |
| 11 | Stacy Compton | 3,893 | -744 | 34 | 0 | 3 | 11 | $724,040 |
| 12 | Ashton Lewis | 3,801 | -836 | 34 | 0 | 2 | 10 | $730,845 |
| 13 | Mike Wallace | 3,489 | -1,148 | 32 | 0 | 1 | 3 | $643,850 |
| 14 | Coy Gibbs* | 3,213 | -1,424 | 34 | 0 | 0 | 2 | $642,915 |
| 15 | Shane Hmiel | 3,160 | -1,477 | 26 | 0 | 4 | 10 | $591,000 |
| 16 | Kevin Harvick | 3,077 | -1,560 | 19 | 3 | 12 | 18 | $584,170 |
| 17 | Todd Bodine | 2,763 | -1,874 | 22 | 1 | 6 | 11 | $499,072 |
| 18 | Michael Waltrip | 2,637 | -2,000 | 20 | 1 | 8 | 13 | $496,295 |
| 19 | Kevin Grubb | 2,498 | -2,139 | 25 | 0 | 0 | 2 | $482,425 |
| 20 | Jamie McMurray | 2,478 | -2,159 | 19 | 2 | 6 | 10 | $468,940 |
| 21 | Larry Gunselman | 2,371 | -2,266 | 34 | 0 | 0 | 0 | $576,930 |
| 22 | David Stremme* | 2,354 | -2,283 | 18 | 0 | 3 | 7 | $377,890 |
| 23 | Mike Harmon | 2,207 | -2,430 | 32 | 0 | 0 | 0 | $520,176 |
| 24 | Matt Kenseth | 1,925 | -2,712 | 14 | 2 | 7 | 9 | $439,755 |
| 25 | Stanton Barrett | 1,877 | -2,760 | 22 | 0 | 0 | 4 | $484,255 |
| 26 | Randy LaJoie | 1,863 | -2,774 | 19 | 0 | 2 | 4 | $383,400 |
| 27 | Kerry Earnhardt | 1,767 | -2,870 | 21 | 0 | 0 | 0 | $400,905 |
| 28 | Jason Schuler | 1,765 | -2,872 | 27 | 0 | 0 | 0 | $433,158 |
| 29 | Jason White* | 1,754 | -2,883 | 23 | 0 | 0 | 0 | $351,265 |
| 30 | Joey Clanton* | 1,716 | -2,921 | 18 | 0 | 1 | 1 | $343,845 |
| 31 | Joe Nemechek | 1,704 | -2,933 | 16 | 3 | 5 | 6 | $413,984 |
| 32 | Brad Teague | 1,647 | -2,990 | 26 | 0 | 0 | 0 | $392,210 |
| 33 | Chad Blount* | 1,581 | -3,056 | 19 | 0 | 1 | 2 | $353,520 |
| 34 | Casey Mears | 1,525 | -3,112 | 14 | 0 | 1 | 4 | $230,490 |
| 35 | Greg Biffle | 1,502 | -3,135 | 14 | 2 | 3 | 4 | $334,715 |
| 36 | Tim Fedewa | 1,491 | -3,146 | 15 | 0 | 0 | 0 | $245,825 |
| 37 | Casey Atwood | 1,422 | -3,215 | 14 | 0 | 0 | 4 | $214,886 |
| 38 | Regan Smith* | 1,313 | -3,324 | 18 | 0 | 0 | 0 | $298,980 |
| 39 | Tony Raines | 1,230 | -3,407 | 12 | 0 | 2 | 5 | $218,005 |
| 40 | Martin Truex, Jr | 1,228 | -3,409 | 10 | 0 | 2 | 3 | $186,500 |
| 41 | Chase Montgomery* | 1,219 | -3,418 | 15 | 0 | 0 | 1 | $315,620 |
| 42 | Ron Young | 1,201 | -3,436 | 13 | 0 | 0 | 0 | $188,520 |
| 43 | Dave Blaney | 1,133 | -3,504 | 10 | 0 | 0 | 3 | $146,660 |
| 44 | Hermie Sadler | 1,066 | -3,571 | 13 | 0 | 0 | 0 | $232,830 |
| 45 | Tammy Jo Kirk | 1,062 | -3,575 | 15 | 0 | 0 | 0 | $227,485 |
| 46 | Tim Sauter | 1,028 | -3,609 | 12 | 0 | 0 | 0 | $154,945 |
| 47 | Damon Lusk* | 950 | -3,687 | 11 | 0 | 0 | 0 | $193,572 |
| 48 | Kyle Busch | 827 | -3,810 | 7 | 0 | 2 | 3 | $136,330 |
| 49 | Jay Sauter | 818 | -3,819 | 10 | 0 | 0 | 1 | $132,360 |
| 50 | David Reutimann | 805 | -3,832 | 7 | 0 | 2 | 3 | $129,050 |
| 51 | Hank Parker, Jr | 783 | -3,854 | 6 | 0 | 2 | 4 | $127,410 |
| 52 | Jason Leffler | 739 | -3,898 | 6 | 0 | 1 | 1 | $113,345 |
| 53 | Morgan Shepherd | 727 | -3,910 | 14 | 0 | 0 | 0 | $182,970 |
| 54 | Jeff Fuller | 688 | -3,949 | 13 | 0 | 0 | 0 | $200,322 |
| 55 | Chris Bingham* | 680 | -3,957 | 11 | 0 | 0 | 0 | $166,610 |
| 56 | Gus Wasson | 672 | -3,965 | 9 | 0 | 0 | 0 | $130,440 |
| 57 | John Hayden | 663 | -3,974 | 10 | 0 | 0 | 0 | $131,739 |
| 58 | Justin Ashburn | 646 | -3,991 | 14 | 0 | 0 | 0 | $176,579 |
| 59 | Brad Baker | 639 | -3,998 | 9 | 0 | 0 | 0 | $139,325 |
| 60 | Paul Menard | 629 | -4,008 | 6 | 0 | 0 | 1 | $92,710 |
| 61 | Mike McLaughlin | 615 | -4,022 | 7 | 0 | 0 | 1 | $126,050 |
| 62 | Derrike Cope | 601 | -4,036 | 7 | 0 | 0 | 0 | $135,655 |
| 63 | Steadman Marlin | 580 | -4,057 | 7 | 0 | 0 | 0 | $106,975 |
| 64 | Lance Norick | 577 | -4,060 | 7 | 0 | 0 | 0 | $118,990 |
| 65 | Jamie Mosley | 563 | -4,074 | 8 | 0 | 0 | 0 | $111,650 |
| 66 | Dale Earnhardt Jr. | 555 | -4,082 | 3 | 3 | 3 | 3 | $201,625 |
| 67 | Steve Grissom | 482 | -4,155 | 6 | 0 | 0 | 0 | $83,825 |
| 68 | Mike Potter | 473 | -4,164 | 11 | 0 | 0 | 0 | $139,330 |
| 69 | Ron Barfield | 472 | -4,165 | 7 | 0 | 0 | 0 | $82,360 |
| 70 | Mark Green | 467 | -4,170 | 5 | 0 | 0 | 0 | $66,975 |
| 71 | Dana White | 466 | -4,171 | 7 | 0 | 0 | 0 | $101,095 |
| 72 | Jeff Green | 447 | -4,190 | 6 | 0 | 0 | 0 | $105,195 |
| 73 | Wally Dallenbach | 434 | -4,203 | 5 | 0 | 0 | 0 | $78,790 |
| 74 | Donnie Neuenberger | 408 | -4,229 | 6 | 0 | 0 | 0 | $116,330 |
| 75 | Rick Markle | 362 | -4,275 | 5 | 0 | 0 | 0 | $65,565 |
| 76 | Jeff Burton | 330 | -4,307 | 4 | 0 | 0 | 0 | $56,085 |

| Pos. | Driver | Points | Behind | Starts | Wins | Top 5 | Top 10 | Money won |
|---|---|---|---|---|---|---|---|---|
| 77 | Jeff Fultz | 318 | -4,319 | 3 | 0 | 0 | 0 | $59,565 |
| 78 | Jimmy Kitchens | 318 | -4,319 | 7 | 0 | 0 | 0 | $102,668 |
| 79 | Josh Richeson | 316 | -4,321 | 8 | 0 | 0 | 0 | $107,345 |
| 80 | Dion Ciccarelli | 304 | -4,333 | 4 | 0 | 0 | 0 | $45,735 |
| 81 | Randy MacDonald | 287 | -4,350 | 5 | 0 | 0 | 0 | $80,230 |
| 82 | Joe Aramendia | 285 | -4,352 | 3 | 0 | 0 | 0 | $49,005 |
| 83 | Kenny Hendrick | 280 | -4,357 | 5 | 0 | 0 | 0 | $70,450 |
| 84 | Bruce Bechtel | 274 | -4,363 | 4 | 0 | 0 | 0 | $76,740 |
| 85 | Shane Hall | 254 | -4,383 | 5 | 0 | 0 | 0 | $68,360 |
| 86 | Jimmy Spencer | 241 | -4,396 | 2 | 0 | 0 | 1 | $39,190 |
| 87 | Jeff Streeter | 241 | -4,396 | 5 | 0 | 0 | 0 | $76,255 |
| 88 | Dwayne Leik | 231 | -4,406 | 3 | 0 | 0 | 0 | $46,555 |
| 89 | Paul Wolfe | 221 | -4,416 | 2 | 0 | 0 | 0 | $23,170 |
| 90 | Derek Hayes | 204 | -4,433 | 3 | 0 | 0 | 0 | $47,315 |
| 91 | Bill Hoff | 201 | -4,436 | 3 | 0 | 0 | 0 | $35,690 |
| 92 | Carlos Contreras | 197 | -4,440 | 2 | 0 | 0 | 0 | $38,395 |
| 93 | Robby Benton | 189 | -4,448 | 3 | 0 | 0 | 0 | $60,870 |
| 94 | J.R. Robbs | 189 | -4,448 | 3 | 0 | 0 | 0 | $40,985 |
| 95 | Jerry Reary | 174 | -4,463 | 3 | 0 | 0 | 0 | $42,580 |
| 96 | Lowell Bennett | 170 | -4,467 | 2 | 0 | 0 | 0 | $22,375 |
| 97 | Jimmy Vasser | 167 | -4,470 | 2 | 0 | 0 | 0 | $45,175 |
| 98 | Ted Musgrave | 165 | -4,472 | 1 | 0 | 1 | 1 | $26,900 |
| 99 | Jeremy Mayfield | 165 | -4,472 | 1 | 0 | 1 | 1 | $16,500 |
| 100 | Blake Mallory | 162 | -4,475 | 3 | 0 | 0 | 0 | $38,140 |
| 101 | Larry Hollenbeck | 161 | -4,476 | 2 | 0 | 0 | 0 | $33,620 |
| 102 | Steve Park | 160 | -4,477 | 1 | 0 | 1 | 1 | $31,650 |
| 103 | Brad Loney | 155 | -4,482 | 2 | 0 | 0 | 0 | $22,290 |
| 104 | Joe Buford | 153 | -4,484 | 3 | 0 | 0 | 0 | $36,215 |
| 105 | Clint Vahsholtz | 152 | -4,485 | 2 | 0 | 0 | 0 | $34,840 |
| 106 | Mike Skinner | 146 | -4,491 | 1 | 0 | 0 | 1 | $13,880 |
| 107 | Jason Rudd | 143 | -4,494 | 2 | 0 | 0 | 0 | $27,950 |
| 108 | Caleb Holman | 143 | -4,494 | 2 | 0 | 0 | 0 | $23,140 |
| 109 | Tony Stewart | 140 | -4,497 | 1 | 0 | 0 | 0 | $15,575 |
| 110 | Tina Gordon | 134 | -4,503 | 1 | 0 | 0 | 1 | $20,925 |
| 111 | Ryck Sanders | 131 | -4,506 | 2 | 0 | 0 | 0 | $33,845 |
| 112 | Troy Cline | 131 | -4,506 | 2 | 0 | 0 | 0 | $29,870 |
| 113 | Brian Tyler | 128 | -4,509 | 2 | 0 | 0 | 0 | $26,839 |
| 114 | Carl Long | 125 | -4,512 | 2 | 0 | 0 | 0 | $21,985 |
| 115 | Jeff Spraker | 119 | -4,518 | 2 | 0 | 0 | 0 | $28,535 |
| 116 | Brian Weber | 117 | -4,520 | 5 | 0 | 0 | 0 | $63,229 |
| 117 | Mardy Lindley | 115 | -4,522 | 1 | 0 | 0 | 0 | $10,655 |
| 118 | David Keith | 107 | -4,530 | 2 | 0 | 0 | 0 | $31,120 |
| 119 | Rick Carelli | 106 | -4,531 | 1 | 0 | 0 | 0 | $19,335 |
| 120 | Shelby Howard | 103 | -4,534 | 1 | 0 | 0 | 0 | $20,275 |
| 121 | Norm Benning | 98 | -4,539 | 2 | 0 | 0 | 0 | $21,180 |
| 122 | Dude Teate | 97 | -4,540 | 1 | 0 | 0 | 0 | $10,620 |
| 123 | Jon Wood | 97 | -4,540 | 1 | 0 | 0 | 0 | $16,670 |
| 124 | Jody Lavender | 94 | -4,543 | 1 | 0 | 0 | 0 | $11,780 |
| 125 | Stan Boyd | 94 | -4,543 | 1 | 0 | 0 | 0 | $12,895 |
| 126 | Bobby Gerhart | 91 | -4,546 | 1 | 0 | 0 | 0 | $18,005 |
| 127 | Anthony Lazzaro | 88 | -4,549 | 1 | 0 | 0 | 0 | $16,950 |
| 128 | Toby Porter | 85 | -4,552 | 1 | 0 | 0 | 0 | $32,500 |
| 129 | Mike Garvey | 85 | -4,552 | 1 | 0 | 0 | 0 | $16,550 |
| 130 | Eric McClure | 85 | -4,552 | 1 | 0 | 0 | 0 | $11,300 |
| 131 | Brent Moore | 82 | -4,555 | 1 | 0 | 0 | 0 | $10,170 |
| 132 | Justin Hobgood | 82 | -4,555 | 1 | 0 | 0 | 0 | $18,880 |
| 133 | Jay Sommers | 79 | -4,558 | 1 | 0 | 0 | 0 | $17,115 |
| 134 | Justin Labonte | 76 | -4,561 | 1 | 0 | 0 | 0 | $13,775 |
| 135 | Billy Boat | 76 | -4,561 | 1 | 0 | 0 | 0 | $16,400 |
| 136 | Vern Slagh | 73 | -4,564 | 1 | 0 | 0 | 0 | $13,825 |
| 137 | Jeremy Clements | 70 | -4,567 | 1 | 0 | 0 | 0 | $15,785 |
| 138 | Jimmy Henderson | 64 | -4,573 | 1 | 0 | 0 | 0 | $14,920 |
| 139 | Kevin Conway | 64 | -4,573 | 1 | 0 | 0 | 0 | $11,745 |
| 140 | Michael Lewis | 61 | -4,576 | 1 | 0 | 0 | 0 | $14,550 |
| 141 | Lyndon Amick | 55 | -4,582 | 1 | 0 | 0 | 0 | $14,775 |
| 142 | Gene Albert | 55 | -4,582 | 1 | 0 | 0 | 0 | $9,980 |
| 143 | Shane Wallace | 55 | -4,582 | 1 | 0 | 0 | 0 | $11,190 |
| 144 | Elliott Sadler | 55 | -4,582 | 1 | 0 | 0 | 0 | $15,355 |
| 145 | Brett Oakley | 49 | -4,588 | 1 | 0 | 0 | 0 | $11,035 |
| 146 | Jamie Aube | 49 | -4,588 | 1 | 0 | 0 | 0 | $9,940 |
| 147 | Rich Bickle | 49 | -4,588 | 1 | 0 | 0 | 0 | $16,010 |
| 148 | Eddy McKean | 46 | -4,591 | 1 | 0 | 0 | 0 | $17,420 |
| 149 | Timothy Edwards | 46 | -4,591 | 1 | 0 | 0 | 0 | $10,980 |
| 150 | Phil Bonifield | 43 | -4,594 | 1 | 0 | 0 | 0 | $12,630 |
| 151 | Andy Belmont | 37 | -4,600 | 1 | 0 | 0 | 0 | $16,460 |
| 152 | Don Satterfield | 37 | -4,600 | 1 | 0 | 0 | 0 | $12,755 |
| 153 | A J Alsup | 37 | -4,600 | 1 | 0 | 0 | 0 | $11,000 |
| 154 | Wayne Edwards | 34 | -4,603 | 1 | 0 | 0 | 0 | $16,981 |
| 155 | Kenny Wallace | 0 | -4,637 | 1 | 0 | 0 | 1 | $22,425 |
| 156 | Jerry Robertson | 0 | -4,637 | 1 | 0 | 0 | 0 | $15,050 |

*Rookie

## 2003 miles leaders

| Rank | Driver | Miles Led | Times Led | Races Led | Miles Run | Possible Miles | Unfinished Miles | Laps Led | Wins | Starts |
|---|---|---|---|---|---|---|---|---|---|---|
| 1 | Kevin Harvick | 1037.82 | 24 | 14 | 4703.85 | 4706.35 | 2.50 | 953 | 3 | 20 |
| 2 | Bobby Hamilton Jr. | 965.63 | 23 | 14 | 7602.74 | 8347.84 | 745.09 | 646 | 4 | 34 |
| 3 | Brian Vickers | 626.79 | 27 | 14 | 7756.92 | 8347.84 | 290.92 | 561 | 3 | 34 |
| 4 | Michael Waltrip | 625.18 | 32 | 10 | 4629.50 | 5091.53 | 462.04 | 490 | 1 | 21 |
| 5 | Matt Kenseth | 587.65 | 21 | 8 | 3135.36 | 3487.45 | 352.09 | 494 | 2 | 14 |
| 6 | Scott Riggs | 560.15 | 23 | 14 | 7921.88 | 8347.84 | 425.96 | 502 | 2 | 34 |
| 7 | Dale Earnhardt Jr. | 497.48 | 3 | 3 | 705.96 | 705.96 | 0.00 | 227 | 3 | 3 |
| 8 | Jamie McMurray | 436.76 | 7 | 3 | 4549.99 | 4841.41 | 291.43 | 395 | 2 | 20 |
| 9 | Greg Biffle | 333.86 | 9 | 4 | 3083.34 | 3472.75 | 389.41 | 221 | 2 | 15 |
| 10 | Johnny Sauter | 245.66 | 14 | 10 | 7607.26 | 8160.34 | 553.07 | 231 | 1 | 33 |
| 11 | Ron Hornaday | 241.59 | 17 | 10 | 8153.02 | 8191.88 | 38.85 | 250 | 1 | 33 |
| 12 | Joe Nemechek | 176.32 | 9 | 4 | 2706.31 | 3948.34 | 1242.03 | 133 | 3 | 16 |
| 13 | Mike Bliss | 152.75 | 4 | 3 | 7599.51 | 8347.84 | 748.33 | 136 | 0 | 34 |
| 14 | David Green | 146.40 | 15 | 10 | 7887.56 | 8347.84 | 460.28 | 122 | 3 | 34 |
| 15 | Todd Bodine | 141.99 | 13 | 6 | 5504.75 | 5797.51 | 292.76 | 102 | 1 | 22 |
| 16 | Jason Keller | 138.12 | 9 | 8 | 7882.82 | 8347.84 | 165.02 | 145 | 1 | 34 |
| 17 | Randy LaJoie | 130.34 | 3 | 1 | 3900.72 | 4809.46 | 908.75 | 49 | 0 | 19 |
| 18 | Shane Hmiel | 125.07 | 5 | 3 | 5819.35 | 6366.64 | 547.29 | 164 | 0 | 26 |
| 19 | Mike McLaughlin | 118.00 | 3 | 1 | 1671.16 | 1943.46 | 272.30 | 59 | 0 | 8 |
| 20 | Scott Wimmer | 112.40 | 8 | 6 | 7564.04 | 8347.84 | 483.79 | 133 | 1 | 34 |
| 21 | Kenny Hendrick | 103.82 | 2 | 1 | 583.57 | 711.53 | 127.95 | 76 | 0 | 4 |
| 22 | Kyle Busch | 90.70 | 5 | 3 | 1372.82 | 1735.12 | 362.30 | 72 | 0 | 8 |
| 23 | David Stremme | 86.60 | 7 | 6 | 4441.18 | 4503.42 | 62.24 | 85 | 0 | 18 |
| 24 | Chad Blount | 74.48 | 1 | 1 | 4096.17 | 4945.58 | 849.41 | 28 | 0 | 19 |
| 25 | Kasey Kahne | 64.22 | 5 | 5 | 7566.31 | 8147.03 | 580.72 | 41 | 1 | 33 |
| 26 | Stacy Compton | 55.09 | 0 | 0 | 7709.15 | 8347.84 | 638.69 | 49 | 0 | 34 |
| 27 | Jon Wood | 49.50 | 1 | 1 | 298.50 | 300.00 | 1.50 | 66 | 0 | 1 |
| 28 | Ashton Lewis | 47.55 | 2 | 2 | 7864.38 | 8347.84 | 483.46 | 45 | 0 | 34 |
| 29 | Jeff Burton | 36.00 | 1 | 1 | 775.75 | 1070.00 | 294.25 | 24 | 0 | 4 |
| 30 | Stanton Barrett | 20.49 | 1 | 1 | 3775.33 | 5493.96 | 1468.63 | 15 | 0 | 29 |
| 31 | Jermey Mayfield | 14.00 | 1 | 1 | 197.00 | 197.00 | 0.00 | 14 | 0 | 1 |
| 32 | Jason Schuler | 12.33 | 2 | 2 | 3307.71 | 5930.76 | 2623.05 | 12 | 0 | 27 |
| 33 | Jason Leffler | 9.04 | 2 | 2 | 1587.12 | 1593.70 | 6.58 | 6 | 0 | 6 |
| 34 | Hank Parker Jr. | 9.00 | 2 | 2 | 1618.36 | 1763.77 | 145.41 | 7 | 0 | 7 |
| 35 | Shane Hall | 8.73 | 2 | 2 | 504.22 | 1385.93 | 881.71 | 4 | 0 | 4 |
| 36 | Martin Truex | 8.25 | 1 | 1 | 2502.23 | 2553.45 | 51.22 | 11 | 0 | 10 |
| 37 | Ronnie Hornaday | 6.67 | 1 | 1 | 155.96 | 155.96 | 0.00 | 5 | 0 | 1 |
| 38 | Kerry Earnhardt | 4.38 | 2 | 2 | 4170.61 | 5068.96 | 898.36 | 4 | 0 | 21 |
| 39 | Tim Sauter | 4.00 | 1 | 1 | 2456.53 | 2906.52 | 449.99 | 4 | 0 | 13 |
| 40 | Casey Mears | 3.00 | 1 | 1 | 3291.49 | 3535.25 | 243.76 | 2 | 0 | 15 |
| 41 | Jay Sauter | 2.67 | 1 | 1 | 1861.11 | 2474.43 | 613.32 | 2 | 0 | 10 |
| 42 | Joey Clanton | 2.00 | 1 | 1 | 3577.05 | 4077.78 | 500.73 | 2 | 0 | 18 |
| 43 | Coy Gibbs | 1.50 | 1 | 1 | 7612.68 | 8347.84 | 735.15 | 1 | 0 | 34 |
| 43 | Steve Grissom | 1.50 | 1 | 1 | 1185.97 | 1769.25 | 583.28 | 1 | 0 | 6 |
| 45 | Brad Teague | 1.33 | 1 | 1 | 3212.54 | 6100.84 | 2888.30 | 1 | 0 | 26 |

# 2003 champion

## Brian Vickers

**Car:** No. 5 Chevrolet. **Team Owner:** Ricky Hendrick. **Birthdate:** Oct. 24, 1983. **Hometown:** Thomasville, N.C.

### NASCAR BUSCH SERIES STATISTICS

**Seasons Competed:** 2001-2003
**Career Starts:** 59  **Career Wins:** 3  **Career Poles:** 1
**Championship Season Recap:** Vickers became the youngest winner ever of a NASCAR series title, capturing the NASCAR Busch Series crown at 20 years old. In a close battle for the points championship, Vickers finished 11th in the last race of the season at Homestead-Miami Speedway after gaining back a lost lap. That kept Vickers just 14 points ahead of 1995 series champion David Green, who finished ninth at Homestead. It was the second-closest title race in series history.

### CHAMPIONSHIP LINESCORE

| Starts | Wins | Poles | Top 5 | Top 10 | Races Led | Laps Led |
|---|---|---|---|---|---|---|
| 34 | 4 | 5 | 20 | 25 | 22 | 1061 |

## Brian Vickers 2003 race by race

| Race No. | Race | Start | Finish | Points | Total points | Pos. | Laps/Completed | Money won | Status |
|---|---|---|---|---|---|---|---|---|---|
| 1 | Koolerz 300 | 21 | 42 | 37 | 37 | 42 | 30/120 | $40,825 | Accident |
| 2 | Rockingham 200 | 15 | 8 | 142 | 179 | 20 | 197/197 | $23,400 | Running |
| 3 | Sam's Town 300 | 6 | 13 | 124 | 303 | 17 | 200/200 | $31,705 | Running |
| 4 | darlingtonraceway.com 200 | 6 | 7 | 151 | 454 | 14 | 147/147 | $22,800 | Running |
| 5 | Channellock 250 | 10 | 14 | 121 | 575 | 12 | 249/250 | $23,905 | Running |
| 6 | O'Reilly 300 | 5 | 25 | 98 | 673 | 12 | 190/200 | $27,600 | Accident |
| 7 | Aaron's 312 | 13 | 23 | 94 | 767 | 12 | 100/117 | $25,875 | Running |
| 8 | Pepsi 300 | 19 | 9 | 143 | 910 | 10 | 225/225 | $23,280 | Running |
| 9 | 1-800-PIT-SHOP.COM 300 | 6 | 19 | 106 | 1,016 | 11 | 149/150 | $29,795 | Running |
| 10 | Hardee's 250 | 21 | 16 | 115 | 1,131 | 10 | 250/250 | $21,580 | Running |
| 11 | Charter Pipeline 250 | 21 | 4 | 165 | 1,296 | 9 | 200/200 | $38,550 | Running |
| 12 | Goulds Pumps ITT Industries 200 | 15 | 2 | 170 | 1,466 | 9 | 200/200 | $38,400 | Running |
| 13 | CARQUEST Auto Parts 300 | 18 | 14 | 121 | 1,587 | 8 | 199/200 | $24,800 | Running |
| 14 | MBNA Armed Forces Family 200 | 13 | 5 | 160 | 1,747 | 7 | 200/200 | $27,990 | Running |
| 15 | Trace Adkins Chrome 300 | 9 | 10 | 134 | 1,881 | 5 | 223/225 | $26,130 | Running |
| 16 | Meijer 300 presented by Oreo | 19 | 6 | 150 | 2,031 | 6 | 200/200 | $34,875 | Running |
| 17 | GNC 250 | 8 | 2 | 175 | 2,206 | 6 | 250/250 | $42,500 | Running |
| 18 | Winn-Dixie 250 presented by PepsiCo | 9 | 7 | 146 | 2,352 | 6 | 100/100 | $35,700 | Running |
| 19 | Tropicana Twister 300 | 8 | 3 | 170 | 2,522 | 4 | 200/200 | $58,385 | Running |
| 20 | New England 200 | 6 | 4 | 160 | 2,682 | 3 | 200/200 | $30,960 | Running |
| 21 | TrimSpa Dream Body 250 presented by Dodge | 4 | 29 | 76 | 2,758 | 5 | 29/250 | $25,555 | Accident |
| 22 | Kroger 200 presented by Tom Raper RVs | 3 | 1 | 180 | 2,938 | 5 | 200/200 | $52,120 | Running |
| 23 | Cabela's 250 | 9 | 19 | 106 | 3,044 | 5 | 110/110 | $25,025 | Running |
| 24 | Food City 250 | 3 | 7 | 151 | 3,195 | 5 | 250/250 | $29,215 | Running |
| 25 | Winn-Dixie 200 presented by PepsiCo | 4 | 1 | 180 | 3,375 | 3 | 147/147 | $49,470 | Running |
| 26 | Funai 250 | 4 | 4 | 160 | 3,535 | 2 | 250/250 | $27,770 | Running |
| 27 | Stacker 200 presented by YJ Stinger | 3 | 1 | 185 | 3,720 | 1 | 200/200 | $50,295 | Running |
| 28 | Mr. Goodcents 300 | 17 | 32 | 67 | 3,787 | 3 | 148/200 | $25,490 | Running |
| 29 | Little Trees 300 | 2 | 4 | 165 | 3,952 | 2 | 200/200 | $42,850 | Running |
| 30 | Sam's Town 250 benefiting St. Jude | 3 | 5 | 165 | 4,117 | 1 | 250/250 | $33,645 | Running |
| 31 | Aaron's 312 | 5 | 31 | 70 | 4,187 | 5 | 189/203 | $19,230 | Running |
| 32 | Bashas' Supermarkets 200 | 6 | 3 | 165 | 4,352 | 3 | 181/181 | $44,035 | Running |
| 33 | Target House 200 | 1 | 6 | 155 | 4,507 | 1 | 197/197 | $28,300 | Running |
| 34 | Ford 300 | 6 | 11 | 130 | 4,637 | 1 | 200/200 | $30,100 | Running |

# Series champions (1950-2003)

The NASCAR Busch Series, Grand National Division started in 1982, but the circuit's roots date back more than five decades. Originally formed as the NASCAR Sportsman Division in 1950, the series competed until 1968 under that name before becoming the NASCAR Late Model Sportsman Division. Fourteen years later, Anheuser-Busch, Inc. joined with NASCAR to create the NASCAR Busch Series.

## ALL-TIME CHAMPIONS

| | | | | |
|---|---|---|---|---|
| 1950: Mike Klapak * | 1961: Dick Nephew | 1972: Jack Ingram | 1983: Sam Ard | 1994: David Green |
| 1951: Mike Klapak | 1962: Rene Charland | 1973: Jack Ingram | 1984: Sam Ard ∞ | 1995: Johnny Benson § |
| 1952: Mike Klapak | 1963: Rene Charland | 1974: Jack Ingram | 1985: Jack Ingram | 1996: Randy LaJoie |
| 1953: Johnny Roberts | 1964: Rene Charland | 1975: L.D. Ottinger | 1986: Larry Pearson | 1997: Randy LaJoie |
| 1954: Danny Graves | 1965: Rene Charland | 1976: L.D. Ottinger | 1987: Larry Pearson | 1998: Dale Earnhardt Jr. |
| 1955: Billy Myers | 1966: Don MacTavish | 1977: Butch Lindley | 1988: Tommy Ellis | 1999: Dale Earnhardt Jr. |
| 1956: Ralph Earnhardt | 1967: Pete Hamilton | 1978: Butch Lindley | 1989: Rob Moroso | 2000: Jeff Green |
| 1957: Ned Jarrett | 1968: Joe Thurman † | 1979: Gene Glover | 1990: Chuck Bown | 2001: Kevin Harvick |
| 1958: Ned Jarrett | 1969: Red Farmer | 1980: Morgan Shepherd | 1991: Bobby Labonte | 2002: Greg Biffle |
| 1959: Rick Henderson | 1970: Red Farmer | 1981: Tommy Ellis | 1992: Joe Nemechek | |
| 1960: Bill Wimble | 1971: Red Farmer | 1982: Jack Ingram ‡ | 1993: Steve Grissom | |

*NASCAR Sportsman Division was formed in 1950
†Series changed name to NASCAR Late Model Sportsman Division in 1968
‡Series changed name to NASCAR Budweiser Late Model Sportsman Series in 1982
∞Series changed name to NASCAR Busch Grand National Series in 1984
§Series changed name to NASCAR Busch Series, Grand National Division in 1995

## Season by season champions (1982-2003)

| Year | Car No. | Driver | Car Owner | Car Make | Wins | Poles | Winnings | Runner-Up | Margin of Victory |
|---|---|---|---|---|---|---|---|---|---|
| 1982 | 11 | Jack Ingram | Aline Ingram | Olds/Pont. | 7 | 1 | $122,100 | Sam Ard | 49 |
| 1983 | 00 | Sam Ard | Howard Thomas | Oldsmobile | 10 | 10 | 192,362 | Jack Ingram | 87 |
| 1984 | 00 | Sam Ard | Howard Thomas | Oldsmobile | 8 | 7 | 217,531 | Jack Ingram | 426 |
| 1985 | 11 | Jack Ingram | Aline Ingram | Pontiac | 5 | 2 | 164,710 | Jimmy Hensley | 29 |
| 1986 | 21 | Larry Pearson | David Pearson | Pontiac | 1 | 1 | 184,344 | Brett Bodine | 20 |
| 1987 | 21 | Larry Pearson | David Pearson | Chevrolet | 6 | 3 | 256,372 | Jimmy Hensley | 382 |
| 1988 | 99 | Tommy Ellis | John Jackson | Buick | 3 | 5 | 200,003 | Rob Moroso | 239 |
| 1989 | 25 | Rob Moroso | Dick Moroso | Oldsmobile | 4 | 6 | 346,739 | Tommy Houston | 55 |
| 1990 | 63 | Chuck Bown | Hubert Hensley | Pontiac | 6 | 4 | 323,399 | Jimmy Hensley | 200 |
| 1991 | 44 | Bobby Labonte | Bobby Labonte | Oldsmobile | 2 | 2 | 246,368 | Kenny Wallace | 74 |
| 1992 | 87 | Joe Nemechek | Joe Nemechek | Chevrolet | 2 | 1 | 285,008 | Bobby Labonte | 3 |
| 1993 | 31 | Steve Grissom | Wayne Grissom | Chevrolet | 2 | 0 | 336,432 | Ricky Craven | 253 |
| 1994 | 44 | David Green | Bobby Labonte | Chevrolet | 1 | 9 | 391,670 | Ricky Craven | 46 |
| 1995 | 74 | Johnny Benson | William Baumgardner | Chevrolet | 2 | 0 | 469,129 | Chad Little | 404 |
| 1996 | 74 | Randy LaJoie | William Baumgardner | Chevrolet | 5 | 2 | 532,823 | David Green | 29 |
| 1997 | 74 | Randy LaJoie | William Baumgardner | Chevrolet | 5 | 2 | 1,105,201 | Todd Bodine | 266 |
| 1998 | 3 | Dale Earnhardt Jr. | Dale Earnhardt | Chevrolet | 5 | 3 | 1,332,701 | Matt Kenseth | 48 |
| 1999 | 3 | Dale Earnhardt Jr. | Dale Earnhardt | Chevrolet | 6 | 3 | 1,680,549 | Jeff Green | 280 |
| 2000 | 10 | Jeff Green | Greg Pollex | Chevrolet | 6 | 7 | 1,929,937 | Jason Keller | 616 |
| 2001 | 2 | Kevin Harvick | Richard Childress | Chevrolet | 5 | 5 | 1,833,570 | Jeff Green | 124 |
| 2002 | 60 | Greg Biffle | Jack Roush | Ford | 4 | 5 | 2,337,255 | Jason Keller | 264 |
| 2003 | 5 | Brian Vickers | Rick Hendrick | Chevrolet | 3 | 1 | 1,112,250 | David Green | 14 |

# 2002 champion

## Greg Biffle

**Car:** No. 60 Ford. **Team Owner:** Jack Roush. **Birthdate:** Dec. 23, 1969. **Hometown:** Vancouver, Wash.

### NASCAR BUSCH SERIES STATISTICS

**Seasons Competed:** 4 (1996, 2001-2003)
**Career Starts:** 83
**Career Wins:** 11
**Career Poles:** 8
**Championship Season Recap:** Biffle became the first driver in history to win the crown in the NASCAR Busch Series and the NASCAR Craftsman Truck Series (2000), both coming with Roush Racing. He was a model of consistency en route to the title, posting a series-leading 25 top-10 finishes in 34 starts, including four wins. He also led the series in top five efforts (20) and laps led (1,058) and co-shared the series lead for poles (5). He was among the top eight in the championship for all but one race during the 34-race season—the season opener at Daytona—and took the lead for good following a runnerup finish at the July event at Daytona. He held the top spot for the remaining 16 races of the season en route to a 264-point advantage over runnerup Jason Keller.

### CHAMPIONSHIP LINESCORE

| Starts | Wins | Poles | Top 5 | Top 10 | Races Led | Laps Led |
|---|---|---|---|---|---|---|
| 34 | 4 | 5 | 20 | 25 | 22 | 1061 |

# 2001 champion

## Kevin Harvick

**Car:** No. 2 Chevrolet. **Team Owner:** Richard Childress. **Birthdate:** Dec. 8, 1975. **Hometown:** Bakersfield, Calif.

### NASCAR BUSCH SERIES STATISTICS

**Seasons Competed:** 5 (1999-2003)
**Career Starts:** 88
**Career Wins:** 11
**Career Poles:** 11
**Championship Season Recap:** Harvick followed up his rookie-of-the-year campaign with a championship. He was powered by a co-series-leading five wins, four poles, a series-leading 20 top five finishes and a series-leading 1,265 laps led in 33 starts for a 124-point margin over runnerup and defending series champion Jeff Green. Harvick was extremely consistent throughout as he never fell outside the top three in the championship race during the entire season. He regained the championship lead after the 15th race following a third-place finish at Dover and did not relinquish it the remainder of the season. His performance was even more impressive considering that team owner Richard Childress called upon him to replace the late Dale Earnhardt in the NASCAR Winston Cup Series and responded with an incredible performance. He earned NASCAR Winston Cup Raybestos Rookie-of-the-Year honors and finished ninth in the NASCAR Winston Cup championship while chasing the NASCAR Busch Series crown.

### CHAMPIONSHIP LINESCORE

| Starts | Wins | Poles | Top 5 | Top 10 | Races Led | Laps Led |
|---|---|---|---|---|---|---|
| 33 | 5 | 4 | 20 | 24 | 18 | 1 |

## 2000 champion

### Jeff Green

**Car:** No. 10 Chevrolet. **Team Owner:** Greg Pollex. **Birthdate:** Sept. 6, 1962. **Hometown:** Owensboro, Ky.

#### NASCAR BUSCH SERIES STATISTICS

**Seasons Competed:** 14 (1990-2003)
**Career Starts:** 240  **Career Wins:** 16  **Career Poles:** 23

Championship Season Recap: Green, who finished runner-up in the championship the previous year, would not be denied this season as he constructed the most dominant performance in NASCAR Busch Series history. He led the series in wins (6), poles (7), top 5s (25) and top 10s (27) en route to the largest points differential in history, 616 over runner-up Jason Keller. Matt Kenseth led the championship for the first seven races and then Todd Bodine took over after the eighth, with Green situated in third. Green finished fifth in the following race at Talladega to claim the championship lead and he held the top spot for the final 23 races.

#### CHAMPIONSHIP LINESCORE

| Starts | Wins | Poles | Top 5 | Top 10 | Races Led | Laps Led |
|---|---|---|---|---|---|---|
| 32 | 6 | 7 | 25 | 27 | 19 | 2 |

## 1999 and 1998 champion

### Dale Earnhardt Jr.

**Car:** No. 3 Chevrolet. **Team Owner:** Dale Earnhardt. **Birthdate:** Oct. 10, 1974. **Hometown:** Kannapolis, N.C.

#### NASCAR BUSCH SERIES STATISTICS

**Seasons Competed:** 7 (1996-99, 2001-2003)
**Career Starts:** 79  **Career Wins:** 18  **Career Poles:** 8

**1999 Championship season recap:** Earnhardt Jr. became the fourth driver—and second in a row—in NASCAR Busch Series history to win consecutive championships. He followed up Randy LaJoie's feat in 1996-97 and joined the company of Sam Ard (1982-83) and Larry Pearson (1986-87) as a two-time champion. Earnhardt Jr. enjoyed a strong campaign as he led the series in wins (6), top 5s (18) and top 10s (22) and rolled to a 280-point advantage over runner-up Jeff Green. Earnhardt Jr.'s fourth win of the season – Gateway – allowed him to overtake Matt Kenseth for the championship lead, one he would not surrender.

#### 1999 CHAMPIONSHIP LINESCORE

| Starts | Wins | Poles | Top 5 | Top 10 | Races Led | Laps Led |
|---|---|---|---|---|---|---|
| 32 | 6 | 3 | 18 | 22 | 23 | 4 |

**1998 Championship season recap:** Earnhardt Jr., after just nine career starts in the previous two seasons, stormed into title contention. Earnhardt Jr. led the series in wins (7) and poles (3), and ranked second in top-five (16) and top-10 (22) finishes. Earnhardt's win at California Speedway handed him the championship lead and kept Matt Kenseth at bay the rest of the way. His second-place finish at Atlanta gave him a 166-point lead heading into the season finale, and he needed it. He finished 42nd because of an engine failure while Kenseth finished fourth, but Earnhardt Jr. had enough cushion to secure the title.

#### 1998 CHAMPIONSHIP LINESCORE

| Starts | Wins | Poles | Top 5 | Top 10 | Races Led | Laps Led |
|---|---|---|---|---|---|---|
| 31 | 7 | 3 | 16 | 22 | 19 | 3 |

# 1997 and 1996 champion

## Randy LaJoie

**Car:** No. 74 Chevrolet. **Team Owner:** William Baumgardner. **Birthdate:** Aug. 28, 1961. **Hometown:** South Norwalk, Conn.

### NASCAR BUSCH SERIES STATISTICS

**Seasons Competed:** 16 (1986-90, '93-2003)
**Career Starts:** 309   **Career Wins:** 15   **Career Poles:** 9

**1997 Championship Season Recap:** LaJoie made history, becoming the third driver to win consecutive NASCAR Busch Series titles and fourth multiple champion. He joined Sam Ard (1983-84) and Larry Pearson (1986-87) as back-to-back series titliests. LaJoie led the series with 15 top five finishes and was second in wins (5) and top 10 efforts (21), coasting by runnerup Todd Bodine by 266 points. LaJoie's win at Milwaukee in the 18th race gave him the championship lead, which he held the rest of the season. He earned $1,105,201, becoming the first NASCAR Busch Series champion to top the $1 million mark in single-season earnings. Owner William Baumgardner also made history as the only owner to win three consecutive NASCAR Busch series crowns.

### 1997 CHAMPIONSHIP LINESCORE

| Starts | Wins | Poles | Top 5 | Top 10 | Races Led | Laps Led |
|---|---|---|---|---|---|---|
| 30 | 5 | 2 | 15 | 21 | 13 | 1 |

**1996 Championship Season Recap:** In the third-closest championship race in history, LaJoie nipped 1994 NASCAR Busch Series champion David Green by 29 points. LaJoie was paced by five wins, which ranked second in the series, and a series-leading 20 top 10 efforts. LaJoie overtook Green for the points lead by virtue of a sixth-place finish at Charlotte with two races left. LaJoie held a 33-point lead going into the season-ending race at Miami, and used a 10th-place finish to offset a ninth-place performance by Green to secure the title.

### 1996 CHAMPIONSHIP LINESCORE

| Starts | Wins | Poles | Top 5 | Top 10 | Races Led | Laps Led |
|---|---|---|---|---|---|---|
| 26 | 5 | 2 | 11 | 20 | 12 | 4 |

# 1995 champion

## Johnny Benson

**Car:** No. 74 Chevrolet. **Team Owner:** William Baumgardner. **Birthdate:** June 27, 1963. **Hometown:** Grand Rapids, Mich.

### NASCAR BUSCH SERIES STATISTICS

**Seasons Competed:** 7 (1993-96, '98-99, '02)
**Career Starts:** 75   **Career Wins:** 3   **Career Poles:** 0

**Championship Season Recap:** Benson posted just a pair of wins, but his consistency in placing among the top 10 let him roll to his first NASCAR Busch Series crown. He recorded 19 top 10 finishes—12 among the top five—to outdistance runnerup Chad Little by 404 points, the third-largest margin in series history. Benson won the fourth race of the season, Atlanta, to grab the points lead from Terry Labonte and relinquished the top spot just once the rest of the season.

### CHAMPIONSHIP LINESCORE

| Starts | Wins | Poles | Top 5 | Top 10 | Races Led | Laps Led |
|---|---|---|---|---|---|---|
| 26 | 2 | 0 | 12 | 19 | 13 | 1 |

# 1994 champion

## David Green

**Car:** No. 44 Chevrolet. **Team Owner:** Bobby Labonte. **Birthdate:** Jan. 28, 1958. **Hometown:** Owensboro, Ky.

### NASCAR BUSCH SERIES STATISTICS

**Seasons Competed:** 13 (1989-91, '93-96, '98-2003)
**Career Starts:** 287   **Career Wins:** 8   **Career Poles:** 21
**Championship Season Recap:** Green became only the second driver to register one victory yet win the title. Green edged Ricky Craven by 46 points. Green's fourth-place finish at South Boston in the 17th race pushed him past Craven as the leader, and he maintained the lead. Green was boosted by 10 top five finishes and just one DNF. He had a series-leading nine poles.

### CHAMPIONSHIP LINESCORE

| Starts | Wins | Poles | Top 5 | Top 10 | Races Led | Laps Led |
|---|---|---|---|---|---|---|
| 28 | 1 | 9 | 10 | 14 | 11 | 1 |

# 1993 champion

## Steve Grissom

**Car:** No. 31 Chevrolet. **Team Owner:** Wayne Grissom. **Birthdate:** June 26, 1963. **Hometown:** Gadsden, Ala.

### NASCAR BUSCH SERIES STATISTICS

**Seasons Competed:** 17 (1986-2003)
**Career Starts:** 247   **Career Wins:** 11   **Career Poles:** 4
**Championship Season Recap:** Grissom's consistency among the top five paved the way to his first championship. His series-leading 11 top five finishes boosted him to a 253-point spread over runnerup Ricky Craven. Grissom took the lead from David Green with a fourth-place finish at Michigan, the 18th race of the season, and held the top spot for the rest of the year.

### CHAMPIONSHIP LINESCORE

| Starts | Wins | Poles | Top 5 | Top 10 | Races Led | Laps Led |
|---|---|---|---|---|---|---|
| 28 | 2 | 0 | 11 | 18 | 7 | 4 |

# 1992 champion

## Joe Nemecheck

**Car:** No. 87 Chevrolet. **Team Owner:** Joe Nemechek. **Birthdate:** Sept. 26, 1963. **Hometown:** Lakeland, Fla.

### NASCAR BUSCH SERIES STATISTICS

**Seasons Competed:** 15 (1989-2003)
**Career Starts:** 235   **Career Wins:** 15   **Career Poles:** 17
**Championship Season Recap:** Nemechek took on defending series champion, Bobby Labonte, and outlasted him in the closest championship battle in NASCAR Busch Series history. Nemechek wrestled the lead from Todd Bodine with three races remaining. Labonte won two of the final three races, including the season finale at Hickory, but Nemechek finished sixth at Hickory to edge him by three points.

### CHAMPIONSHIP LINESCORE

| Starts | Wins | Poles | Top 5 | Top 10 | Races Led | Laps Led |
|---|---|---|---|---|---|---|
| 31 | 2 | 1 | 13 | 18 | 8 | 2 |

# 1991 champion

## Bobby Labonte

**Car:** No. 44 Oldsmobile. **Team Owner:** Bobby Labonte. **Birthdate:** May 8, 1964. **Hometown:** Corpus Christi, Texas

### NASCAR BUSCH SERIES STATISTICS

**Seasons Competed:** 13 (1982, '85, '88-94, '96-99)
**Career Starts:** 161   **Career Wins:** 9   **Career Poles:** 10
**Championship Season Recap:** Kenny Wallace took the lead from Labonte with three races to go, but Labonte overcame the 33-point deficit. Labonte had a pair of top five finishes coupled with an eighth-place effort while Wallace cracked the top 20 just once in that span. With two to go, Labonte held a 42-point lead and clinched finishing fifth in the finale at Martinsville.

### CHAMPIONSHIP LINESCORE

| Starts | Wins | Poles | Top 5 | Top 10 | Races Led | Laps Led |
|---|---|---|---|---|---|---|
| 31 | 2 | 2 | 10 | 21 | 10 | 3 |

# 1990 champion

## Chuck Bown

**Car:** No. 63 Pontiac. **Team Owner:** Hubert Hensley. **Birthdate:** Feb. 22, 1954. **Hometown:** Portland, Ore.

### NASCAR BUSCH SERIES STATISTICS

**Seasons Competed:** 11 (1986-93, '95-96, '99)
**Career Starts:** 187   **Career Wins:** 11   **Career Poles:** 13
**Championship Season Recap:** Bown, buoyed by a series-high six wins, earned his first NASCAR Busch Series title by a 200-point margin over Jimmy Hensley. Bown took the lead after a win at Hickory in the 11th race of the season and never relinquished the top spot.

### CHAMPIONSHIP LINESCORE

| Starts | Wins | Poles | Top 5 | Top 10 | Races Led | Laps Led |
|---|---|---|---|---|---|---|
| 31 | 6 | 4 | 13 | 18 | 14 | 2 |

# 1989 champion

## Rob Moroso

**Car:** No. 25 Oldsmobile. **Team Owner:** Dick Moroso. **Birthdate:** Sept. 28, 1968. **Hometown:** Madison, Conn.

### NASCAR BUSCH SERIES STATISTICS

**Seasons Competed:** 4 (1986-89)
**Career Starts:** 86   **Career Wins:** 6   **Career Poles:** 8
**Championship Season Recap:** Moroso overcame Tommy Houston to capture his first NASCAR Busch Series crown. Moroso topped Houston by 55 points, but was trailing him down the stretch.

Moroso grabbed the lead from Houston with a win at Charlotte, but lost it the following race at Rockingham after finishing 12th. Houston came into the season finale at Martinsville with a 19-point lead, but lost the title when he finished 24th due to engine failure as Moroso finished third. Moroso had a series-leading four wins and series-high six poles.

### CHAMPIONSHIP LINESCORE

| Starts | Wins | Poles | Top 5 | Top 10 | Races Led | Laps Led |
|---|---|---|---|---|---|---|
| 29 | 4 | 6 | 12 | 16 | 11 | 3 |

## 1988 champion

### Tommy Ellis

**Car:** No. 99 Buick. **Team Owner:** John Jackson. **Birthdate:** Aug. 8, 1947. **Hometown:** Richmond, Va.

#### NASCAR BUSCH SERIES STATISTICS

**Seasons Competed:** 14 (1982-1995)
**Career Starts:** 235  **Career Wins:** 22  **Career Poles:** 28
**Championship Season Recap:** Ellis, after a stint in the NASCAR Winston Cup Series, returned to the NASCAR Busch Series and promptly captured his first championship. He posted a 239-point spread over runnerup Rob Moroso. Ellis was tied for second in the series in wins with three – trailing only Harry Gant (5) – and notched 20 top 10 finishes in 30 starts. He also had a series-leading five poles.

### CHAMPIONSHIP LINESCORE

| Starts | Wins | Poles | Top 5 | Top 10 | Races Led | Laps Led |
|---|---|---|---|---|---|---|
| 30 | 3 | 5 | 12 | 20 | 13 | 4 |

## 1987 and 1986 champion

### Larry Pearson

**Car:** No. 21 Chevrolet. **Team Owner:** David Pearson. **Birthdate:** Nov. 2, 1953. **Hometown:** Spartanburg, S.C.

#### NASCAR BUSCH SERIES STATISTICS

**Seasons Competed:** 16 (1982-90, '93-99)
**Career Starts:** 259  **Career Wins:** 15  **Career Poles:** 11
**1987 Championship Season Recap:** Pearson became the second driver to win consecutive NASCAR Busch Series crowns and the third multiple champion in the series. While his first title run was one of the closest in history, he rolled to his second as he outdistanced runnerup Jimmy Hensley by 382 points. Pearson led the series with six wins and registered 20 top 10 finishes. He joined Sam Ard as the only back-to-back champions.

### 1987 CHAMPIONSHIP LINESCORE

| Starts | Wins | Poles | Top 5 | Top 10 | Races Led | Laps Led |
|---|---|---|---|---|---|---|
| 27 | 6 | 3 | 16 | 20 | 13 | 3 |

**1986 Championship Season Recap:** Pearson rallied late to claim his first NASCAR Busch Series title, edging Brett Bodine by 20 points. The points battle would be the second closest in series history. Bodine led Pearson by 19 points with five races to go, but two races later Pearson grabbed the lead by six points. Pearson extended the lead to 30 heading into the season finale at Martinsville and clinched with a runnerup showing while Bodine made a final gasp with a victory.

### 1986 CHAMPIONSHIP LINESCORE

| Starts | Wins | Poles | Top 5 | Top 10 | Races Led | Laps Led |
|---|---|---|---|---|---|---|
| 31 | 1 | 1 | 17 | 24 | 7 | 2 |

# 1985 and 1982 champion

## Jack Ingram

**Car:** No. 11 Pontiac. **Team Owner:** Aline Ingram. **Birthdate:** Dec. 28, 1936. **Hometown:** Asheville, N.C.

### NASCAR BUSCH SERIES STATISTICS

**Seasons Competed:** 10 (1982-91)
**Career Starts:** 274  **Career Wins:** 31  **Career Poles:** 5

**Championship Season Recap:** Ingram joined Sam Ard as a multiple champion in the NASCAR Busch Series, adding this crown to the one he captured in the inaugural 1982 season. Ingram had another tough battle en route to this title as well, edging Jimmy Hensley by 29 points. Ard owned a 39-point lead with one to go, and iced it with a fifth-place finish in the season finale at Martinsville. The points margin is tied for the third-closest in NASCAR Busch Series history. Ingram was boosted by five wins – which tied for the series lead with Tommy Ellis – and 22 top-10 finishes in 27 starts.

#### 1985 CHAMPIONSHIP LINESCORE

| Starts | Wins | Poles | Top 5 | Top 10 | Races Led | Laps Led |
|---|---|---|---|---|---|---|
| 27 | 5 | 2 | 17 | 22 | 15 | 4 |

**Championship Season Recap:** Ingram became the inaugural NASCAR Busch Series, Grand National Division champion, edging Sam Ard by 49 points. Ingram had an incredible run of consistency as he posted 23 top five finishes, including a series leading seven victories. Ard, with four wins, was trailing by 58 points with three races remaining, but never was able to get closer to Ingram than 43 points over that span.

#### 1982 CHAMPIONSHIP LINESCORE

| Starts | Wins | Poles | Top 5 | Top 10 | Races Led | Laps Led |
|---|---|---|---|---|---|---|
| 29 | 7 | 1 | 23 | 24 | NA | 4 |

# 1984 and 1983 champion

## Sam Ard

**Car:** No. 00 Oldsmobile. **Team Owner:** Howard Thomas. **Birthdate:** Feb. 14, 1939. **Hometown:** Asheboro, N.C.

### NASCAR BUSCH SERIES STATISTICS

**Seasons Competed:** 3 (1982-84)
**Career Starts:** 92  **Career Wins:** 22  **Career Poles:** 25

**1984 Championship Season Recap:** Ard and Jack Ingram had squared off for the championship the first two seasons, with each earning a title, but the third battle between the two was no contest. Ard became the series' first multiple and back-to-back champion by rolling to a 426-point spread over Ingram, the second-largest points difference in history. Ard and Ingram tied for the series lead in wins with eight each, but it was Ard's consistency that allowed him to coast to the crown. He recorded 24 top-five finishes in 28 starts and finished outside the top 10 just twice.

#### 1984 CHAMPIONSHIP LINESCORE

| Starts | Wins | Poles | Top 5 | Top 10 | Races Led | Laps Led |
|---|---|---|---|---|---|---|
| 28 | 8 | 7 | 24 | 26 | 26 | 1 |

**1983 Championship Season Recap:** It was a battle between the top two contenders – Ard and defending champion Jack Ingram – from the inaugural 1982 season, but this time Ard prevailed. He needed a NASCAR Busch Series history record 10 victories to fend off Ingram and claim the title by 87 points. He also led the series with 10 poles. Ingram stayed in the hunt though behind five wins and 29 top-10 efforts, but could not run down the dominating Ard in the end.

#### 1983 CHAMPIONSHIP LINESCORE

| Starts | Wins | Poles | Top 5 | Top 10 | Races Led | Laps Led |
|---|---|---|---|---|---|---|
| 35 | 10 | 10 | 23 | 30 | NA | 3 |

# 2003 Raybestos Rookie of the Year

## David Stremme

**Truck:** No. 30 Dodge. **Team Owner:** James Finch. **Birthdate:** June 19, 1977. **Hometown:** South Bend, Ind.

### NASCAR BUSCH SERIES STATISTICS

**Seasons Competed:** 1 (2003)
**Career Starts:** 18
**Career Wins:** 0
**Career Poles:** 0
**Rookie Season Recap:** Stremme didn't even start in 16 of the NASCAR Busch Series races in 2003 but still pulled out a solid freshman season. He put himself in position to finish strong each week by starting in the 12th position, on average. And he managed to capitalize on those strong qualifying efforts by conserving his equipment (he suffered only one DNF) and winding up with three top five finishes. He led all rookies in top 10 finishes. The Raybestos Rookie of the Year title in NASCAR Busch Series racing is Stremme's fourth rookie title: He also was a quick performer in the Street Stock and Late Model divisions at South Bend Speedway and won the 2002 ASA rookie title.

## Rookie of the Year winners

| Year | Driver | Points | Finish | Races | Poles | Wins | Top 5 | Top 10 | Winnings | Hometown |
|------|--------|--------|--------|-------|-------|------|-------|--------|----------|----------|
| 2003 | David Stremme | 2,354 | 22 | 18 | 0 | 0 | 3 | 7 | $377,890 | South Bend, Ind. |
| 2002 | Scott Riggs | 4,023 | 10 | 34 | 2 | 2 | 8 | 13 | $1,170,846 | Bahama, N.C. |
| 2001 | Greg Biffle | 4,509 | 4 | 33 | 2 | 5 | 16 | 21 | 1,623,546 | Vancouver, Wash. |
| 2000 | Kevin Harvick | 4,113 | 3 | 31 | 2 | 3 | 8 | 16 | 995,274 | Bakersfield, Calif. |
| 1999 | Tony Raines | 3,142 | 12 | 31 | 0 | 0 | 1 | 3 | 657,220 | LaPorte, Ind. |
| 1998 | Andy Santerre | 2,598 | 20 | 29 | 1 | 0 | 1 | 2 | 307,835 | Cherryfield, Maine |
| 1997 | Steve Park | 4,080 | 3 | 30 | 1 | 3 | 12 | 20 | 677,921 | East Northport, N.Y. |
| 1996 | Glenn Allen | 2,593 | 14 | 26 | 0 | 0 | 0 | 2 | 176,372 | Cincinnati, Ohio |
| 1995 | Jeff Fuller | 2,845 | 10 | 26 | 1 | 0 | 1 | 6 | 174,950 | Auburn, Mass. |
| 1994 | Johnny Benson | 3,303 | 6 | 28 | 0 | 1 | 6 | 9 | 190,011 | Grand Rapids, Mich. |
| 1993 | Hermie Sadler | 3,362 | 10 | 28 | 0 | 1 | 4 | 8 | 149,596 | Emporia, Va. |
| 1992 | Ricky Craven | 3,456 | 14 | 31 | 1 | 0 | 0 | 5 | 167,618 | Newburgh, Maine |
| 1991 | Jeff Gordon | 3,582 | 11 | 30 | 1 | 0 | 5 | 10 | 111,608 | Pittsboro, Ind. |
| 1990 | Joe Nemechek | 3,022 | 17 | 28 | 0 | 0 | 2 | 5 | 70,279 | Lakeland, Fla. |
| 1989 | Kenny Wallace | 3,750 | 6 | 29 | 3 | 0 | 4 | 16 | 88,423 | St. Louis, Mo. |

# Miscellaneous records

Most Races Started: 417, Tommy Houston (1982-1996)
Most Wins, Season: 10, Sam Ard (1983)
Most Wins, Career: 45, Mark Martin (1982-2000)
Most Superspeedway Wins, Season: 5, Dale Earnhardt Jr. (1998)
  Mark Martin (1993, '96, '97, '00)
  Chad Little (1995)
  Greg Biffle (2001)
Most Superspeedway Wins, Career: 36, Mark Martin (1982-2000)
Most Short Track Wins, Season: 9, Sam Ard (1983)
Most Short Track Wins, Career: 29, Jack Ingram (1982-1991)
Most Years Winning At Least One Race: 13, Dale Earnhardt, Mark Martin
Most Different Race Winners, Season: 18 (1988, 89)
Most Wins At One Track: 11, Mark Martin, Rockingham
Most Races Won From Pole, Career: 9, Sam Ard (1982-84),
  Mark Martin (1987-2000)
Most Races Won From Pole, Season: 4, Sam Ard (1983)
Oldest Driver To Win: Dick Trickle (56 years, 11 months) Darlington, Sept. 5, 1998
Youngest Driver To Win: Casey Atwood (18 years, 10 months), Milwaukee, July 4, 1999

Most Races Started Without Winning: Ed Berrier, 208 (1984-1997)
Most Top-Five Finishes, Season: 25, Jeff Green (2000)
Most Top-Five Finishes, Career: 123, Tommy Houston (1982-1996)
Most Top-10 Finishes, Season: 30, Sam Ard (1983)
Most Top-10 Finishes, Career: 198, Tommy Houston (1982-1996)
Most Pole Awards, Season: 11, Jeff Gordon (1992)
Most Pole Awards, Career: 28, Tommy Ellis (1982-1995)
Most Years Winning At Least One Pole: 11, Mark Martin
Most Different Pole Winners, Season: 24 (1998)
Most Poles At One Track: 7, Tommy Ellis, Hickory
  Mark Martin, Darlington
Most Money Won, Season: $2,337,254, Greg Biffle (2002)
Most Money Won, Career: $7,680,119, Jason Keller (1991-current)
Most Money Won, Race: $113,844, Jeff Gordon, Charlotte, May 23, 1982
Largest Purse, Superspeedway: $1,789,282, Daytona (2002)
Largest Purse, Short Track: $1,054,532, Memphis (2002)
Largest Margin of Victory by Series Champion: 616 points, Jeff Green over Jason Keller (2000)
Smallest Margin of Victory by Series Champion: 3 points, Joe Nemechek over Bobby Labonte (1992)

## Series Race Records

Longest Race, Distance: 400 miles, Charlotte, Oct. 5, 1985
Longest Race, Time: 3 hrs., 41 min., 58 sec., New Hampshire, July 15, 1990
Shortest Race, Distance: 56.25 miles, Orange County, 1985-1988
Shortest Race, Time: 38 min., 4 sec., Orange County, June 14, 1986
Fastest Average Speed: 169.571 mph, Michigan, Aug. 19, 1995
Slowest Average Speed: 48.842 mph, Orange County, Aug. 13, 1982
Most Caution Flags, Race: 26, Hickory, April 18, 1992
Most Caution Laps, Race: 132, Hickory, April 18, 1992
Fewest Caution Flags, Race: 0, Five times – most recent, Michigan, Aug. 15, 1998
Fewest Caution Laps, Race: 0, Five times – most-recent, Michigan, Aug. 15, 1998

Most Lead Changes, Race: 35, Three times – most recent, Rockingham, Feb. 22, 1997
Most Cars Finishing On Lead Lap, Race: 28, Watkins Glen, 1998; Daytona, 2001
Fewest Cars Finishing On Lead Lap: 1, 12 times – most recent, Orange County, Aug. 10, 1991
Largest Starting Field: 47, Oxford, Maine, July 10, 1988
Smallest Starting Field: 17, Hampton, Va., May 8, 1982
Most Cars Running At Finish: 43, Michigan, Aug. 15, 1998
Fewest DNF's, Race: 0, Michigan, Aug. 15, 1998
Fewest Cars Running At Finish: 10, North Wilkesboro, April 8, 1983
Most DNF's, Race: 26, Charlotte, Nov., 10, 1987

## Records Set In Consecutive Years

Most Consecutive Starts: 360, Tommy Houston (Feb. 13, 1982 - Feb. 26, 1994)
Most Consecutive Races Won: 4, Sam Ard (1983)
Most Consecutive Years Winning at Least One Race: 10, Dale Earnhardt (1985-1994)
Most Consecutive Different Race Winners, Season: 13 (1988)
Most Consecutive Wins at One Track: 5, Dale Earnhardt, Daytona (1990-94); Jack Ingram, South Boston (1986)
Most Consecutive Wins by a Car Manufacturer: 11, Chevrolet (2000)

Most Consecutive Races Running at Finish: 60, Kevin Harvick (Mar. 18, 2000 - Nov. 3, 2001)
Most Consecutive Poles: 3, Four drivers (most recent, Jeff Gordon, 1992)
Most Consecutive Different Pole Winners, Season: 15 (1995)
Most Consecutive Poles at One Track: 4, David Green, Hickory (1994-1996)
Most Consecutive Years Winning at Least One Pole: 9, Mark Martin (1992-2000)

First Race: Daytona International Speedway; Feb. 13, 1982
First Winner: Dale Earnhardt
First Pole Winner: Mike Porter; Daytona, Feb. 9, 1982
First Superspeedway Race: Daytona; Feb. 13, 1982
First Superspeedway Winner: Dale Earnhardt Daytona; Feb. 13, 1982
First Short Track Race: Richmond; Feb. 20, 1982
First Short Track Winner: Tommy Houston; Richmond, Feb. 20, 1982
First Road Course Race: Road Atlanta, July 6, 1986
First Road Course Winner: Darrell Waltrip, Road Atlanta, July 6, 1986
First Chevrolet Win: Tommy Houston, Hickory, Aug. 1, 1982

## Series Firsts

First Dodge Win: Hank Parker Jr., Pikes Peak, July 27, 2002
First Ford Win: Mark Martin, Dover, May 30, 1987
First Champion: Jack Ingram, 1982
First Rookie of the Year: Kenny Wallace, 1989
First Driver to Win $1 Million in Career: Jack Ingram 1989
First Driver to Win $1 Million in a Season: Randy LaJoie 1997
First Driver to Win $100,000 in a Race: Jeff Gordon 1992
First Race West of Mississippi River: Las Vegas 300, March 15, 1997
First Brothers to Win Championships: David Green (1994), Jeff Green (2000)

## Race winners

### 1982 - 2003 (664 Races)

| DRIVER | Tot. | DRIVER | Tot. | DRIVER | Tot. | DRIVER | Tot. | DRIVER | Tot. |
|---|---|---|---|---|---|---|---|---|---|
| Mark Martin | 45 | Terry Labonte | 11 | Ward Burton | 4 | Sterling Marlin | 2 | Bill Elliott | 1 |
| Jack Ingram | 31 | Greg Biffle | 11 | Ricky Craven | 4 | Butch Miller | 2 | Jeff Fuller | 1 |
| Tommy Houston | 24 | Kevin Harvick | 11 | Tim Fedewa | 4 | Hank Parker Jr. | 2 | Bobby Hamilton | 1 |
| Sam Ard | 22 | Robert Pressley | 10 | Jeff Purvis | 4 | Phil Parsons | 2 | Tracy Leslie | 1 |
| Tommy Ellis | 22 | Jason Keller | 10 | Jamie McMurray | 4 | Tim Richmond | 2 | Dick McCabe | 1* |
| Dale Earnhardt | 21 | Michael Waltrip | 10 | Scott Riggs | 4 | Johnny Rumley | 2 | David Pearson | 1 |
| Harry Gant | 21 | Jimmy Hensley | 9 | Johnny Benson | 3 | Hermie Sadler | 2 | Larry Pollard | 1 |
| Jeff Burton | 20 | Bobby Labonte | 9 | Ron Fellows | 3 | Elton Sawyer | 2 | Ricky Rudd | 1 |
| Dale Earnhardt Jr. | 18 | Rick Mast | 9 | Ernie Irvan | 3 | Ken Schrader | 2 | Joe Ruttman | 1 |
| Jeff Green | 16 | Kenny Wallace | 9 | L.D. Ottinger | 3 | Dennis Setzer | 2 | Greg Sacks | 1 |
| Larry Pearson | 15 | David Green | 8 | Steve Park | 3 | Ronnie Silver | 2 | Andy Santerre | 1 |
| Morgan Shepherd | 15 | Geoffrey Bodine | 6 | Mike Wallace | 3 | Dick Trickle | 2 | John Settlemyre | 1 |
| Randy LaJoie | 15 | Butch Lindley | 6 | Ron Hornaday | 3 | Rick Wilson | 2 | Mike Skinner | 1 |
| Todd Bodine | 15 | Chad Little | 6 | Brian Vickers | 3 | Johnny Sauter | 2 | Jack Sprague | 1 |
| Joe Nemechek | 15 | Mike McLaughlin | 6 | Mike Alexander | 2 | Jamie Aube | 1* | Brad Teague | 1 |
| Matt Kenseth | 14 | Rob Moroso | 6 | Bobby Allison | 2 | Ed Berrier | 1 | Ryan Newman | 1 |
| Darrell Waltrip | 13 | Brett Bodine | 5 | Casey Atwood | 2 | Joe Bessey | 1 | Jimmy Johnson | 1 |
| Jimmy Spencer | 12 | Jeff Gordon | 5 | Ron Bouchard | 2 | Neil Bonnett | 1 | Kasey Kahne | 1 |
| Chuck Bown | 11 | Elliott Sadler | 5 | Bobby Hillin | 2 | Ronald Cooper | 1 | | |
| Steve Grissom | 11 | Scott Wimmer | 5 | Buckshot Jones | 2 | Derrike Cope | 1 | | |
| Dale Jarrett | 11 | Bobby Hamilton Jr. | 5 | Kevin Lepage | 2 | Bobby Dotter | 1 | | |

* Busch North Series, NASCAR Touring wins in "combination" races

## Pole winners

### 1982 - 2003 (663 races*^)

| DRIVER | Totals | DRIVER | Totals | DRIVER | Totals | DRIVER | Totals | DRIVER | Totals |
|---|---|---|---|---|---|---|---|---|---|
| Tommy Ellis | 28 | Rob Moroso | 8 | Bobby Hamilton Jr. | 3 | Elton Sawyer | 2 | Sterling Marlin | 1 |
| Mark Martin | 27 | Todd Bodine | 7 | Shane Hmiel | 3 | Tony Stewart | 2 | Casey Mears | 1 |
| Sam Ard | 24 | Ward Burton | 7 | Terry Labonte | 4 | Hut Stricklin | 2 | Gary Niece | 1 |
| Jeff Green | 23 | Dale Earnhardt | 7 | Kevin Lepage | 4 | Brad Teague | 2 | Steve Park | 1 |
| David Green | 21 | Dale Earnhardt Jr | 7 | Butch Miller | 4 | Rusty Wallace | 2 | Hank Parker Jr. | 1 |
| Tommy Houston | 18 | Dick Trickle | 7 | L.D. Ottinger | 4 | Stanton Barrett | 2 | Randy Porter | 1 |
| Joe Nemechek | 17 | Casey Atwood | 6 | Darrell Waltrip | 4 | Johnny Sauter | 2 | Scott Pruett | 1 |
| Brett Bodine | 16 | Dave Blaney | 6 | Mike Alexander | 3 | Tim Bender | 1 | Tony Raines | 1 |
| Jimmy Hensley | 15 | Ryan Newman | 6 | Buckshot Jones | 3 | Ed Berrier | 1 | Stevie Reeves | 1 |
| Michael Waltrip | 15 | Phil Parsons | 6 | Jason Leffler | 3 | Rich Bickle | 1 | David Reutimann | 1 |
| Harry Gant | 14 | Robert Pressley | 6 | David Pearson | 3 | Jim Bown | 1 | Shawna Robinson | 1 |
| Dale Jarrett | 14 | Jeff Purvis | 6 | Hermie Sadler | 3 | Stacy Compton | 1 | Johnny Rumley | 1 |
| Geoffrey Bodine | 13 | Tim Richmond | 6 | Mike Skinner | 3 | Derrike Cope | 1 | Boris Said | 1 |
| Chuck Bown | 12 | Morgan Shepherd | 6 | Jimmy Spencer | 3 | Dave Dion | 1 | Andy Santerre | 1 |
| Jeff Gordon | 12 | Jack Ingram | 5 | Davey Allison | 2 | Eddie Falk | 1^ | Jay Sauter | 1 |
| Kevin Harvick | 11 | Ernie Irvan | 5 | Joe Bessey | 2 | Jeff Fuller | 1 | Dennis Setzer | 1 |
| Jason Keller | 11 | Butch Lindley | 5 | Bill Elliott | 2 | Wayne Grubb | 1 | Bob Shreeves | 1 |
| Larry Pearson | 11 | Rick Mast | 5 | Ron Fellows | 2 | Kevin Grubb | 1 | Jack Sprague | 1 |
| Jeff Burton | 10 | Mike McLaughlin | 5 | Shane Hall | 2 | Ron Hornaday | 1 | Mike Swaim | 1 |
| Bobby Labonte | 10 | Elliott Sadler | 5 | Tracy Leslie | 2 | Robert Ingram | 1 | Brian Vickers | 1 |
| Kenny Wallace | 10 | Ken Schrader | 5 | Dave Mader III | 2 | Kasey Kahne | 1 | Rick Wilson | 1 |
| Greg Biffle | 9 | Ron Bouchard | 4 | Kelly Moore | 2^ | Alan Kulwicki | 1 | | |
| Randy LaJoie | 9 | Bobby Dotter | 4 | Mike Porter | 2 | Ashton Lewis | 1 | | |
| Ricky Craven | 8 | Tim Fedewa | 4 | Scott Riggs | 2 | Chad Little | 1 | | |
| Matt Kenseth | 8 | Steve Grissom | 4 | Greg Sacks | 2 | Curtis Markham | 1 | | |

* Includes races where qualifying rained out; 25 races started by points.
^ Busch North Series, NASCAR Touring Poles in "combination" races.

## 200 or more career starts

### 1982 - 2003

| DRIVER | STARTS | DATE | 200th START AT |
|---|---|---|---|
| Tommy Houston | 417 | 8/18/88 | Rougemont |
| Elton Sawyer | 392 | 3/19/95 | Nashville |
| Dale Jarrett | 324 | 10/07/89 | Charlotte |
| Jason Keller | 322 | 5/5/00 | Richmond |
| Randy LaJoie | 309 | 4/15/00 | Talladega |
| Todd Bodine | 302 | 9/25/99 | Dover |
| Mike McLaughlin | 302 | 3/11/00 | Atlanta |
| David Green | 287 | 8/25/00 | Bristol |
| Phil Parsons | 285 | 5/09/98 | New Hampshire |
| Tim Fedewa | 278 | 2/19/00 | Daytona Beach |
| Kenny Wallace | 277 | 3/25/00 | Bristol |
| Jack Ingram | 274 | 9/03/88 | Darlington |
| Larry Pearson | 259 | 6/10/95 | Myrtle Beach |
| Jimmy Hensley | 255 | 8/11/90 | Rougemont |
| Ed Berrier | 250 | 10/25/97 | Rockingham |
| Steve Grissom | 247 | 7/22/95 | Talladega |
| Rick Mast | 243 | 3/25/90 | Hickory |
| Jeff Green | 240 | 7/28/01 | Pikes Peak |
| Jeff Burton | 236 | 4/29/00 | California |
| Tommy Ellis | 235 | 2/17/91 | Daytona Beach |
| Joe Nemechek | 235 | 9/07/01 | Richmond |
| Hermie Sadler | 226 | 8/19/00 | Michigan |
| Bobby Dotter | 208 | 8/02/96 | Indianapolis |
| Jimmy Spencer | 207 | 9/21/02 | Dover |
| Tracy Leslie | 206 | 8/21/98 | Bristol |
| L.D. Ottinger | 206 | 9/15/90 | Dover |
| Robert Pressley | 205 | 10/31/98 | Rockingham |
| Mark Martin | 200 | 11/11/00 | Homestead |
| Michael Waltrip | 200 | 11/15/03 | Homestead |

Notes: Houston's 300th start was 2/15/92 at Daytona Beach
Sawyer's 300th start was 4/10/99 at Bristol
Bodine's 300th start was 10/4/03 at Kansas
Houston's 400th start was 3/9/96 at Atlanta
Jarrett's 300th start was 2/22/97 at Rockingham
LaJoie's 300th start was 5/2/03 at Richmond
McLaughlin's 300th start was 07/19/03

## Career money leaders

### 1982 - 2003

| RK | DRIVER | STARTS | POLES | WINS | TOP 5 | TOP 10 | MONEY |
|---|---|---|---|---|---|---|---|
| 1 | Jason Keller | 322 | 11 | 10 | 73 | 139 | $7,680,115 |
| 2 | Randy LaJoie | 290 | 9 | 15 | 62 | 115 | $6,715,577 |
| 3 | Jeff Green | 240 | 23 | 16 | 87 | 126 | $6,656,649 |
| 4 | Mike McLaughlin | 302 | 5 | 6 | 57 | 109 | $5,941,791 |
| 5 | Todd Bodine | 302 | 7 | 15 | 88 | 155 | $5,273,249 |
| 6 | David Green | 287 | 21 | 8 | 63 | 120 | $4,829,492 |
| 7 | Elton Sawyer | 392 | 2 | 2 | 51 | 131 | $4,704,263 |
| 8 | Greg Biffle | 83 | 9 | 11 | 39 | 50 | $4,307,861 |
| 9 | Matt Kenseth | 146 | 8 | 14 | 63 | 92 | $4,403,417 |
| 10 | Tim Fedewa | 278 | 4 | 4 | 24 | 61 | $3,565,921 |
| 11 | Bobby Hamilton Jr | 153 | 3 | 5 | 22 | 46 | $3,538,785 |
| 12 | Kevin Harvick | 88 | 11 | 11 | 40 | 59 | $3,486,644 |
| 13 | Dale Earnhardt Jr | 79 | 8 | 18 | 39 | 50 | $3,388,179 |
| 14 | Kenny Wallace | 277 | 10 | 9 | 58 | 130 | $3,330,126 |
| 15 | Jeff Purvis | 186 | 6 | 4 | 25 | 57 | $3,307,732 |
| 16 | Tony Raines | 142 | 1 | 0 | 13 | 33 | $3,164,502 |
| 17 | Joe Nemechek | 235 | 16 | 15 | 71 | 109 | $3,145,805 |
| 18 | Scott Wimmer | 104 | 4 | 1 | 17 | 37 | $3,043,533 |
| 19 | Mark Martin | 200 | 27 | 45 | 93 | 126 | $2,882,780 |
| 20 | Kevin Grubb | 169 | 1 | 0 | 10 | 31 | $2,832,962 |
| 21 | Jeff Burton | 236 | 10 | 20 | 61 | 103 | $2,832,919 |
| 22 | Phil Parsons | 285 | 6 | 2 | 38 | 96 | $2,765,979 |
| 23 | Hank Parker Jr | 136 | 1 | 2 | 11 | 31 | $2,886,383 |
| 24 | Ron Hornaday | 116 | 1 | 3 | 20 | 43 | $2,879,681 |
| 25 | Kevin Lepage | 188 | 4 | 2 | 19 | 50 | $2,461,313 |

# 2003 performance chart

| Pos. | Driver | Points | Starts | Poles | Wins | Top 5 | Top 10 | Winnings |
|---|---|---|---|---|---|---|---|---|
| 1. | Brian Vickers | 4637 | 34 | 1 | 3 | 13 | 21 | $1,112,250 |
| 2. | David Green | 4623 | 34 | 2 | 3 | 11 | 21 | $1,135,360 |
| 3. | Ron Hornaday | 4591 | 34 | 0 | 1 | 8 | 17 | $957,270 |
| 4. | Bobby Hamilton Jr. | 4588 | 34 | 1 | 4 | 13 | 22 | $1,167,460 |
| 5. | Jason Keller | 4528 | 34 | 1 | 1 | 10 | 17 | $1,117,840 |
| 6. | Scott Riggs | 4462 | 34 | 0 | 2 | 11 | 17 | $1,122,030 |
| 7. | Kasey Kahne | 4104 | 34 | 1 | 1 | 4 | 14 | $831,415 |
| 8. | Johnny Sauter | 4098 | 34 | 0 | 1 | 6 | 14 | $756,225 |
| 9. | Scott Wimmer | 4059 | 34 | 0 | 1 | 4 | 12 | $973,910 |
| 10. | Mike Bliss | 3932 | 34 | 0 | 0 | 8 | 14 | $766,885 |
| 11. | Stacy Compton | 3893 | 34 | 1 | 0 | 3 | 11 | $724,040 |
| 12. | Ashton Lewis | 3801 | 34 | 1 | 0 | 2 | 10 | $730,845 |
| 13. | Mike Wallace | 3489 | 32 | 0 | 0 | 1 | 3 | $643,850 |
| 14. | Coy Gibbs* | 3213 | 34 | 0 | 0 | 0 | 2 | $642,915 |
| 15. | Shane Hmiel | 3160 | 26 | 1 | 0 | 4 | 10 | $591,000 |
| 16. | Kevin Harvick | 3077 | 19 | 5 | 3 | 12 | 18 | $584,170 |
| 17. | Todd Bodine | 2763 | 22 | 0 | 1 | 6 | 11 | $499,072 |
| 18. | Michael Waltrip | 2637 | 20 | 2 | 1 | 8 | 13 | $496,295 |
| 19. | Kevin Grubb | 2498 | 25 | 0 | 0 | 0 | 2 | $482,425 |
| 20. | Jamie McMurray | 2478 | 19 | 0 | 2 | 6 | 10 | $468,940 |
| 21. | Larry Gunselman | 2371 | 34 | 0 | 0 | 0 | 0 | $576,930 |
| 22. | David Stremme* | 2354 | 18 | 0 | 0 | 3 | 7 | $377,890 |
| 23. | Mike Harmon | 2207 | 32 | 0 | 0 | 0 | 0 | $520,176 |
| 24. | Matt Kenseth | 1925 | 14 | 0 | 2 | 7 | 9 | $439,755 |
| 25. | Stanton Barrett | 1877 | 22 | 0 | 0 | 0 | 4 | $484,255 |

*Raybestos Rookie of the Year candidate

### Race winners (17)
Bobby Hamilton Jr. .....................4
Brian Vickers ...............................3
David Green ................................3
Kevin Harvick ..............................3
Dale Earnhardt Jr. .......................3
Joe Nemechek ............................3
Scott Riggs ..................................2
Jamie Mc Murray ........................2
Matt Kenseth ..............................2
Greg Biffle ...................................2
Ron Hornaday ............................1
Jason Keller ................................1
Kasey Kahne ...............................1
Johnny Sauter ............................1
Scott Wimmer ............................1
Todd Bodine ...............................1
Michael Waltrip ..........................1

### Season winnings
Bobby Hamilton Jr. ........$1,167,460
David Green ....................1,135,260
Scott Riggs ......................1,122,030
Jason Keller ....................1,117,840
Brian Vickers ...................1,112,250
Scott Wimmer ....................973,910
Ron Hornaday ...................957,270
Kasey Kahne ......................831,415
Mike Bliss ..........................766,885
Johnny Sauter ...................756,225

### Pole winners (16)
Kevin Harvick.................................5
Joe Nemechek...............................3
David Green..................................2
Randy LaJoie.................................2
Michael Waltrip ............................2
Greg Biffle .....................................2
Stacy Compton .............................1
Dale Earnhardt Jr. ........................1
Bobby Hamilton Jr. ......................1
Shane Hmiel .................................1
Kasey Kahne .................................1
Jason Keller...................................1
Ashton Lewis Jr. ...........................1
Casey Mears .................................1
David Reutimann .........................1
Brian Vickers ................................1

# 2002 performance chart

| Pos. | Driver | Points | Starts | Poles | Wins | Top 5 | Top 10 | Winnings |
|---|---|---|---|---|---|---|---|---|
| 1. | Greg Biffle | 4919 | 34 | 5 | 4 | 20 | 25 | $2,337,254 |
| 2. | Jason Keller | 4655 | 34 | 2 | 4 | 17 | 22 | 1,669,642 |
| 3. | Scott Wimmer | 4488 | 34 | 0 | 4 | 11 | 17 | 1,332,409 |
| 4. | Mike McLaughlin | 4253 | 34 | 0 | 0 | 7 | 17 | 1,281,356 |
| 5. | Jack Sprague | 4206 | 34 | 0 | 1 | 9 | 15 | 1,103,989 |
| 6. | Jamie McMurray | 4147 | 34 | 0 | 2 | 6 | 14 | 1,044,282 |
| 7. | Kenny Wallace | 4078 | 34 | 0 | 0 | 2 | 13 | 882,800 |
| 8. | Bobby Hamilton Jr. | 4058 | 34 | 0 | 1 | 6 | 15 | 1,072,280 |
| 9. | Stacy Compton | 4042 | 34 | 0 | 0 | 5 | 11 | 861,924 |
| 10. # | Scott Riggs | 4023 | 34 | 2 | 2 | 8 | 13 | 1,170,846 |

# Raybestos Rookie of the Year candidate

### Race winners (17)
Jeff Burton .................................5
Scott Wimmer ..........................4
Greg Biffle ................................4
Jason Keller .............................4
Dale Earnhardt Jr. ...................2
Jeff Green ................................2
Jamie McMurray ......................2
Scott Riggs ..............................2
Bobby Hamilton Jr. ..................1
Joe Nemechek .........................1
Todd Bodine ............................1
Hank Parker Jr. .......................1
Jeff Purvis ...............................1
Johnny Sauter .........................1
Jimmy Spencer ........................1
Jack Sprague ...........................1
Michael Waltrip .......................1

### Season winnings
Greg Biffle ...................$2,337,254
Jason Keller ..................1,669,642
Scott Wimmer ...............1,332,409
Mike McLaughlin ...........1,281,356
Scott Riggs ..................1,170,846
Bobby Hamilton Jr. .......1,072,280
Jamie McMurray ...........1,044,282
Randy LaJoie ................1,018,629
Johnny Sauter..................991,534
Kenny Wallace ................882,800

Note:
No qualifying was held at California, Richmond (May), Nazareth, Darlington (Aug. 31), and Atlanta due to rain.

### Pole winners (14)
Greg Biffle ................................5
Jeff Green ................................5
Jeff Burton ...............................2
Shane Hmiel .............................2
Jason Keller .............................2
Kevin Lepage ...........................2
Joe Nemechek .........................2
Scott Riggs ..............................2
Michael Waltrip .......................2
Dale Earnhardt Jr. ...................1
Todd Bodine ............................1
Ron Hornaday ..........................1
Randy LaJoie ...........................1
Johnny Sauter .........................1

## 2001 performance chart

| Pos. | Driver | Points | Starts | Poles | Wins | Top 5 | Top 10 | Winnings |
|---|---|---|---|---|---|---|---|---|
| 1. | Kevin Harvick | 4813 | 33 | 5 | 5 | 20 | 24 | $1,833,570 |
| 2. | Jeff Green | 4689 | 33 | 2 | 4 | 16 | 26 | 1,797,836 |
| 3. | Jason Keller | 4637 | 33 | 0 | 1 | 14 | 22 | 1,519,811 |
| 4. # | Greg Biffle | 4509 | 33 | 2 | 5 | 16 | 21 | 1,623,546 |
| 5. | Elton Sawyer | 4100 | 33 | 0 | 0 | 6 | 19 | 1,079,093 |
| 6. | Tony Raines | 3975 | 33 | 1 | 0 | 4 | 13 | 921,777 |
| 7. | Mike McLaughlin | 3962 | 33 | 0 | 1 | 5 | 12 | 951,682 |
| 8. | Jimmie Johnson | 3871 | 33 | 0 | 1 | 4 | 9 | 920,192 |
| 9. | Chad Little | 3846 | 33 | 0 | 0 | 2 | 6 | 690,321 |
| 10. | Kenny Wallace | 3799 | 33 | 2 | 1 | 7 | 13 | 821,665 |

# Raybestos Rookie of the Year candidate

### Race winners (17)
Greg Biffle ................................5
Kevin Harvick ..........................5
Jeff Green ................................4
Jimmy Spencer ........................3
Todd Bodine ............................2
Randy LaJoie ...........................2
Joe Nemechek .........................2
Jeff Burton ...............................1
Ron Fellows .............................1
Jimmie Johnson .......................1
Jason Keller .............................1
Matt Kenseth ...........................1
Mike McLaughlin .....................1
Rayn Newman .........................1
Hank Parker Jr. .......................1
Jeff Purvis ...............................1
Kenny Wallace .........................1

### Season winnings
Kevin Harvick ...............$1,833,570
Jeff Green ....................1,797,836
Greg Biffle ....................1,623,546
Jason Keller ..................1,519,811
Elton Sawyer ................1,079,093
Mike McLaughlin ..............951,682
Hank Parker Jr. ...............936,819
Tony Raines ....................921,777
Jimmie Johnson ...............920,192
Randy LaJoie ...................917,791

### Pole winners (15)
Ryan Newman ..........................6
Kevin Harvick ..........................5
Matt Kenseth ...........................3
Greg Biffle ................................2
Jeff Green ................................2
Joe Nemechek .........................2
Kenny Wallace .........................2
Jeff Burton ...............................1
Bobby Hamilton Jr. ..................1
Kevin Lepage ...........................1
Scott Pruett ............................1
Tony Raines .............................1
Jay Sauter ...............................1
Mike Skinner ............................1
Jimmy Spencer ........................1

## 2000 performance chart

| Pos. | Driver | Points | Starts | Poles | Wins | Top 5 | Top 10 | Winnings |
|---|---|---|---|---|---|---|---|---|
| 1. | Jeff Green | 5005 | 32 | 7 | 6 | 25 | 27 | $1,929,937 |
| 2. | Jason Keller | 4389 | 32 | 0 | 1 | 13 | 19 | 1,174,448 |
| 3. # | Kevin Harvick | 4113 | 31 | 2 | 3 | 8 | 16 | 995,274 |
| 4. | Todd Bodine | 4075 | 32 | 1 | 1 | 14 | 19 | 935,269 |
| 5. # | Ron Hornaday | 3870 | 32 | 0 | 2 | 6 | 13 | 958,836 |
| 6. | Elton Sawyer | 3776 | 32 | 0 | 0 | 5 | 14 | 925,919 |
| 7. | Randy LaJoie | 3670 | 32 | 0 | 1 | 4 | 9 | 873,179 |
| 8. | Casey Atwood | 3404 | 32 | 2 | 0 | 0 | 8 | 775,615 |
| 9. | David A Green | 3316 | 32 | 0 | 0 | 2 | 11 | 759,269 |
| 10. # | Jimmie Johnson | 3264 | 31 | 0 | 0 | 0 | 6 | 549,271 |

# Raybestos Rookie of the Year candidate

### Race winners (14)
Jeff Green ..................................6
Mark Martin ...............................5
Jeff Burton .................................4
Matt Kenseth .............................4
Kevin Harvick .............................3
Ron Hornaday ............................2
Todd Bodine ...............................1
Tim Fedewa ................................1
Ron Fellows ................................1
Jeff Gordon .................................1
Jason Keller ................................1
Randy LaJoie ..............................1
Sterling Marlin ............................1
Joe Nemechek ...........................1

### Season winnings
Jeff Green .....................$1,929,937
Jason Keller ..................1,174,448
Kevin Harvick ...................995,274
Ron Hornaday ..................958,836
Todd Bodine .....................935,269
Elton Sawyer ....................925,919
Randy LaJoie ...................873,179
Matt Kenseth ...................839,305
Casey Atwood .................775,615
David Green ....................759,269

### Pole winners (16)
Jeff Green ..................................7
Mark Martin ...............................4
Jason Leffler ...............................3
Casey Atwood ............................2
Kevin Harvick .............................2
Matt Kenseth .............................2
Dave Blaney ...............................1
Todd Bodine ...............................1
Tim Fedewa ................................1
Ron Fellows ................................1
Bobby Hamilton Jr. ...................1
Buckshot Jones ..........................1
Hank Parker Jr. ..........................1
Jeff Purvis ..................................1
Hut Stricklin ...............................1
Mike Skinner ..............................1

## 1999 performance chart

| Pos. | Driver | Points | Starts | Poles | Wins | Top 5 | Top 10 | Winnings |
|---|---|---|---|---|---|---|---|---|
| 1. | Dale Earnhardt Jr. | 4647 | 32 | 3 | 6 | 18 | 22 | $985,195 |
| 2. | Jeff Green | 4367 | 31 | 3 | 3 | 15 | 19 | 735,040 |
| 3. | Matt Kenseth | 4327 | 32 | 2 | 4 | 14 | 20 | 859,660 |
| 4. | Todd Bodine | 4029 | 32 | 0 | 0 | 10 | 21 | 541,860 |
| 5. | Elton Sawyer | 3891 | 32 | 0 | 1 | 4 | 14 | 599,105 |
| 6. | Jeff Purvis | 3658 | 32 | 0 | 0 | 4 | 12 | 631,416 |
| 7. | Dave Blaney | 3582 | 31 | 4 | 0 | 5 | 12 | 499,660 |
| 8. | Jason Keller | 3537 | 32 | 3 | 2 | 5 | 12 | 631,850 |
| 9. | Mike McLaughlin | 3478 | 32 | 0 | 0 | 3 | 8 | 631,950 |
| 10. | Randy LaJoie | 3379 | 32 | 0 | 1 | 6 | 7 | 695,210 |

### Race winners (15)
Dale Earnhardt Jr. ....................6
Mark Martin ...............................6
Matt Kenseth .............................4
Jeff Green ..................................3
Casey Atwood ...........................2
Jason Keller ...............................2
Jeff Burton .................................1
Jeff Gordon .................................1
Terry Labonte .............................1
Randy LaJoie ..............................1
Joe Nemechek ...........................1
Andy Santerre ............................1
Elton Sawyer ..............................1
Mike Skinner ..............................1
Michael Waltrip .........................1

### Season winnings
Dale Earnhardt Jr. ...........$985,195
Matt Kenseth ...................859,660
Jeff Green .........................735,040
Randy LaJoie ...................695,210
Mike McLaughlin ............631,950
Jason Keller ....................631,850
Jeff Purvis .......................631,416
Elton Sawyer ...................599,105
Tony Raines .....................555,820
Todd Bodine ....................541,860

### Pole winners (14)
Dave Blaney ...............................4
Dale Earnhardt Jr. ....................3
Jeff Green ..................................3
Jason Keller ...............................3
Mark Martin ...............................3
Ken Schrader .............................3
Casey Atwood ............................2
David Green ...............................2
Matt Kenseth .............................2
Jeff Burton .................................1
Ward Burton ..............................1
Ron Fellows ................................1
Hut Stricklin ...............................1
Dick Trickle ................................1

## 1998 performance chart

| Pos. | Driver | Points | Starts | Poles | Wins | Top 5 | Top 10 | Winnings |
|---|---|---|---|---|---|---|---|---|
| 1. | Dale Earnhardt Jr. | 4469 | 31 | 3 | 7 | 16 | 22 | $1,332,701 |
| 2. | Matt Kenseth | 4421 | 31 | 1 | 3 | 17 | 23 | 991,965 |
| 3. | Mike McLaughlin | 4045 | 31 | 1 | 2 | 11 | 16 | 828,313 |
| 4. | Randy LaJoie | 3543 | 31 | 0 | 1 | 7 | 12 | 783,703 |
| 5. | Elton Sawyer | 3533 | 31 | 0 | 0 | 4 | 10 | 576,089 |
| 6. | Phil Parsons | 3525 | 31 | 0 | 0 | 5 | 9 | 550,352 |
| 7. | Tim Fedewa | 3515 | 31 | 1 | 2 | 4 | 10 | 526,520 |
| 8. | Elliott Sadler | 3470 | 31 | 1 | 2 | 5 | 10 | 635,058 |
| 9. | Buckshot Jones | 3453 | 31 | 0 | 1 | 6 | 9 | 484,932 |
| 10. | Hermie Sadler | 3340 | 31 | 0 | 0 | 2 | 5 | 405,691 |

### Race Winners (16)
D. Earnhardt Jr. ...... 7
J. Burton ............. 3
M. Kenseth ........... 3
T. Fedewa ............ 2
M. Martin ............. 2
M. McLaughlin ....... 2
J. Nemechek ......... 2
E. Sadler ............. 2
E. Berrier ............. 1
R. Fellows ............ 1
B. Jones .............. 1
B. Labonte ........... 1
R. LaJoie ............. 1
K. Lepage ............ 1
J. Spencer ........... 1
D. Trickle ............ 1

### Season Winnings
D. Earnhardt Jr. ...... $1,332,701
M. Kenseth ........... 991,965
M. McLaughlin ....... 828,313
R. LaJoie ............. 783,703
E. Sadler ............. 635,058
E. Sawyer ............ 576,089
P. Parsons ............ 550,352
J. Purvis .............. 536,415
T. Fedewa ............ 526,520
B. Jones .............. 484,932

### Busch Pole Winners (24)
D. Earnhardt Jr. ...... 3
C. Atwood ............ 2
J. Burton ............. 2
R. Pressley ........... 2
J. Nemechek ......... 2
T. Stewart ............ 2
J. Bessey ............. 1
D. Blaney ............. 1
T. Fedewa ............ 1
S. Grissom ........... 1
K. Grubb .............. 1
W. Grubb ............. 1
S. Hall ................ 1
B. Jones .............. 1
M. Kenseth ........... 1
B. Labonte ........... 1
K. Lepage ............ 1
M. Martin ............. 1
M. McLaughlin ....... 1
J. Purvis .............. 1
E. Sadler ............. 1
B. Said ................ 1
A. Santerre .......... 1
D. Trickle ............ 1

# 1997 performance chart

| Pos. | Driver | Points | Starts | Poles | Wins | Top 5 | Top 10 | Winnings |
|---|---|---|---|---|---|---|---|---|
| 1. | Randy LaJoie | 4,381 | 30 | 2 | 5 | 15 | 21 | $1,105,201 |
| 2. | Todd Bodine | 4,115 | 30 | 0 | 1 | 9 | 22 | 658,295 |
| 3. # | Steve Park | 4,080 | 30 | 1 | 3 | 12 | 20 | 677,921 |
| 4. | Mike McLaughlin | 3,614 | 30 | 2 | 2 | 7 | 14 | 585,173 |
| 5. | Elliott Sadler | 3,534 | 30 | 4 | 3 | 6 | 10 | 556,372 |
| 6. | Phil Parsons | 3,523 | 30 | 0 | 0 | 5 | 12 | 411,026 |
| 7. | Buckshot Jones | 3,437 | 30 | 0 | 0 | 5 | 14 | 446,637 |
| 8. | Elton Sawyer | 3,419 | 30 | 0 | 0 | 6 | 9 | 349,229 |
| 9. | Tim Fedewa | 3,398 | 30 | 1 | 0 | 4 | 11 | 346,424 |
| 10. | Hermie Sadler | 3,340 | 30 | 2 | 0 | 2 | 7 | 328,154 |

# Raybestos Rookie of the Year candidate

### Race winners (13)
M. Martin ............. 6
R. LaJoie ............. 5
S. Park ............... 3
E. Sadler ............. 3
J. Burton ............. 2
M. McLaughlin ....... 2
J. Nemechek ......... 2
J. Spencer ........... 2
J. Bessey ............. 1
T. Bodine ............. 1
J. Green .............. 1
B. Labonte ........... 1
D. Trickle ............ 1

### Season winnings
R. LaJoie ............. $1,105,201
S. Park ............... 677,921
T. Bodine ............. 658,295
M. McLaughlin ....... 585,173
E. Sadler ............. 556,372
B. Jones .............. 446,637
P. Parsons ............ 411,026
K. Lepage ............ 396,937
M. Martin ............. 373,469
J. Keller .............. 372,681

### Pole winners (15)
E. Sadler ............. 4
M. Martin ............. 3
J. Nemechek ......... 3
J. Green .............. 2
R. LaJoie ............. 2
M. McLaughlin ....... 2
H. Sadler ............. 2
D. Trickle ............ 2
T. Bender ............. 1
J. Bessey ............. 1
J. Burton ............. 1
T. Fedewa ............ 1
S. Hall ................ 1
S. Park ............... 1
M. Waltrip ........... 1

# 1996 performance chart

| Pos. | Driver | Points | Starts | Poles | Wins | Top 5 | Top 10 | Winnings |
|---|---|---|---|---|---|---|---|---|
| 1. | Randy LaJoie | 3,714 | 26 | 2 | 5 | 11 | 20 | $532,823 |
| 2. | David Green | 3,685 | 26 | 4 | 2 | 13 | 18 | 469,118 |
| 3. | Todd Bodine | 3,064 | 26 | 0 | 1 | 3 | 9 | 281,616 |
| 4. | Jeff Green | 3,059 | 26 | 1 | 0 | 5 | 13 | 369,285 |
| 5. | Chad Little | 2,984 | 26 | 1 | 0 | 2 | 7 | 317,394 |
| 6. | Jason Keller | 2,900 | 26 | 0 | 0 | 3 | 10 | 281,902 |
| 7. | Jeff Purvis | 2,894 | 26 | 2 | 2 | 4 | 7 | 266,026 |
| 8. | Kevin Lepage | 2,870 | 26 | 0 | 1 | 3 | 10 | 254,925 |
| 9. | Phil Parsons | 2,854 | 26 | 0 | 0 | 5 | 6 | 215,023 |
| 10. | Mike McLaughlin | 2,853 | 26 | 0 | 0 | 7 | 10 | 290,701 |

### Race winners (13)
M. Martin .................................. 6
R. LaJoie .................................. 5
T. Labonte ................................ 3
D. Green .................................. 2
J. Purvis .................................. 2
T. Bodine ................................. 1
J. Fuller .................................... 1
S. Grissom ............................... 1
B. Jones .................................. 1
B. Labonte ............................... 1
K. Lepage ................................ 1
G. Sacks ................................. 1
K. Wallace ............................... 1

### Season winnings
R. Lajoie .................... $532,823
D. Green ...................... 469,118
C. Little ....................... 317,394
M. McLaughlin ............ 290,701
J. Keller ...................... 281,902
T. Bodine ................... 281,616
J. Green ..................... 269,285
J. Purvis .................... 266,026
K. Lepage .................. 254,925
H. Sadler ................... 238,511

### Pole winners (16)
D. Green .................................. 4
B. Labonte ............................... 3
R. Craven ................................ 2
R. LaJoie ................................. 2
M. Martin ................................. 2
J. Purvis .................................. 2
J. Fuller ................................... 1
J. Green .................................. 1
D. Jarrett ................................. 1
B. Jones .................................. 1
C. Little ................................... 1
S. Marlin .................................. 1
J. Nemechek ........................... 1
H. Sadler ................................. 1
D. Trickle ................................. 1
M. Waltrip ................................ 1

## 1995 performance chart

| Pos. | Driver | Points | Starts | Poles | Wins | Top 5 | Top 10 | Winnings |
|---|---|---|---|---|---|---|---|---|
| 1. | Johnny Benson | 3,688 | 26 | 0 | 2 | 12 | 19 | $469,129 |
| 2. | Chad Little | 3,284 | 26 | 0 | 6 | 11 | 13 | 529,056 |
| 3. | Mike McLaughlin | 3,273 | 26 | 1 | 1 | 9 | 14 | 317,075 |
| 4. | Jason Keller | 3,211 | 26 | 1 | 1 | 6 | 12 | 257,880 |
| 5. | Jeff Green | 3,182 | 26 | 1 | 0 | 6 | 12 | 241,187 |
| 6. | Larry Pearson | 3,029 | 26 | 1 | 2 | 5 | 8 | 276,057 |
| 7. | Tim Fedewa | 3,022 | 26 | 1 | 1 | 4 | 4 | 253,907 |
| 8. | Phil Parsons | 2,985 | 26 | 0 | 0 | 3 | 9 | 177,358 |
| 9. | Elton Sawyer | 2,952 | 26 | 1 | 0 | 2 | 9 | 250,833 |
| 10. | # Jeff Fuller | 2,845 | 26 | 0 | 0 | 1 | 6 | 174,950 |

# Raybestos Rookie of the Year candidate

### Race winners (14)
C. Little ................................... 6
D. Jarrett ................................ 3
M. Martin ................................ 3
J. Benson ............................... 2
S. Grissom ............................. 2
L. Pearson .............................. 2
T. Bodine ................................ 1
T. Fedewa .............................. 1
D. Green ................................. 1
J. Keller .................................. 1
T. Labonte .............................. 1
M. McLaughlin ........................ 1
J. Rumley ............................... 1
K. Wallace .............................. 1

### Season winnings
C. Little ..................... $529,056
J. Benson .................... 469,129
M. McLaughlin ............ 317,075
L. Pearson ................. 276,057
D. Green .................... 274,628
J. Keller ..................... 257,880
T. Fedewa ................. 253,907
E. Sawyer .................. 250,833
J. Green .................... 241,187
M. Martin ................... 210,475

### Pole winners (21)
D. Green .................................. 4
R. Bickle ................................. 1
B. Dotter ................................. 1
T. Fedewa ............................... 1
J. Green .................................. 1
D. Jarrett ................................ 1
J. Keller .................................. 1
T. Labonte .............................. 1
R. LaJoie ................................. 1
T. Leslie ................................. 1
C. Markham ............................ 1
M. Martin ................................ 1
M. McLaughlin ........................ 1
J. Nemechek ........................... 1
L. Pearson .............................. 1
J. Purvis ................................. 1
S. Reeves ............................... 1
E. Sawyer ............................... 1
D. Setzer ................................. 1
D. Waltrip ................................ 1
M. Waltrip ............................... 1

## 1994 performance chart

| Pos. | Driver | Points | Starts | Poles | Wins | Top 5 | Top 10 | Winnings |
|---|---|---|---|---|---|---|---|---|
| 1. | David Green | 3,725 | 28 | 9 | 1 | 10 | 14 | $391,670 |
| 2. | Ricky Craven | 3,679 | 28 | 1 | 2 | 8 | 16 | 273,000 |
| 3. | Chad Little | 3,662 | 28 | 0 | 0 | 10 | 14 | 234,022 |
| 4. | Kenny Wallace | 3,554 | 28 | 1 | 3 | 11 | 15 | 307,017 |
| 5. | Hermie Sadler | 3,466 | 28 | 0 | 1 | 6 | 11 | 238,204 |
| 6. | # Johnny Benson | 3,303 | 28 | 0 | 1 | 6 | 9 | 190,011 |
| 7. | Bobby Dotter | 3,299 | 28 | 0 | 0 | 2 | 8 | 176,093 |
| 8. | Larry Pearson | 3,277 | 27 | 0 | 0 | 3 | 12 | 161,859 |
| 9. | # Dennis Setzer | 3,273 | 28 | 0 | 2 | 4 | 11 | 214,246 |
| 10. | Tim Fedewa | 3,125 | 28 | 0 | 0 | 1 | 8 | 142,034 |

# Raybestos Rookie of the Year candidate

### Race Winners (17)
- T. Labonte .......... 4
- M. Martin .......... 3
- K. Wallace .......... 3
- M. Wallace .......... 3
- R. Craven .......... 2
- D. Setzer .......... 2
- J. Benson .......... 1
- D. Cope .......... 1
- D. Earnhardt .......... 1
- H. Gant .......... 1
- D. Green .......... 1
- B. Labonte .......... 1
- J. Nemechek .......... 1
- P. Parsons .......... 1
- H. Sadler .......... 1
- E. Sawyer .......... 1
- K. Schrader .......... 1

### Season Winnings
- D. Green .......... $391,670
- K. Wallace .......... 307,017
- R. Craven .......... 273,000
- H. Sadler .......... 238,204
- C. Little .......... 234,022
- T. Labonte .......... 215,438
- D. Setzer .......... 214,246
- M. Martin .......... 200,608
- J. Benson .......... 190,011
- T. Leslie .......... 188,567

### Busch Pole Winners (14)
- D. Green .......... 9
- J. Keller .......... 3
- M. Martin .......... 3
- H. Gant .......... 2
- D. Cope .......... 1
- R. Craven .......... 1
- B. Labonte .......... 1
- R. LaJoie .......... 1
- R. Pressley .......... 1
- J. Purvis .......... 1
- S. Robinson .......... 1
- M. Skinner .......... 1
- K. Wallace .......... 1
- M. Waltrip .......... 1

## 1993 performance chart

| Pos. | Driver | Points | Starts | Poles | Wins | Top 5 | Top 10 | Winnings |
|---|---|---|---|---|---|---|---|---|
| 1. | Steve Grissom | 3,846 | 28 | 0 | 2 | 11 | 18 | $336,432 |
| 2. | Ricky Craven | 3,593 | 28 | 1 | 0 | 6 | 17 | 197,829 |
| 3. | David Green | 3,584 | 28 | 0 | 0 | 6 | 16 | 225,747 |
| 4. | Chuck Bown | 3,532 | 28 | 1 | 1 | 5 | 13 | 195,961 |
| 5. | Joe Nemechek | 3,443 | 28 | 3 | 0 | 8 | 11 | 254,346 |
| 6. | Ward Burton | 3,413 | 28 | 4 | 3 | 9 | 10 | 293,622 |
| 7. | Bobby Dotter | 3,406 | 28 | 2 | 0 | 3 | 8 | 160,003 |
| 8. | Robert Pressley | 3,389 | 28 | 0 | 3 | 8 | 13 | 254,723 |
| 9. | Todd Bodine | 3,387 | 28 | 1 | 3 | 9 | 13 | 240,899 |
| 10. # | Hermie Sadler | 3,362 | 28 | 0 | 1 | 4 | 8 | 149,596 |

# Raybestos Rookie of the Year candidate

### Race winners (13)
- M. Martin .......... 7
- T. Bodine .......... 3
- W. Burton .......... 3
- R. Pressley .......... 3
- D. Earnhardt .......... 2
- S. Grissom .......... 2
- M. Waltrip .......... 2
- C. Bown .......... 1
- J. Burton .......... 1
- B. Elliott .......... 1
- T. Leslie .......... 1
- J. Rumley .......... 1
- H. Sadler .......... 1

### Season winnings
- S. Grissom .......... $336,432
- W. Burton .......... 293,622
- R. Pressley .......... 254,723
- J. Nemechek .......... 254,346
- T. Bodine .......... 240,899
- M. Martin .......... 230,703
- D. Green .......... 225,747
- J. Burton .......... 212,843
- R. Craven .......... 197,829
- C. Bown .......... 195,961

### Pole winners (16)
- W. Burton .......... 4
- E. Irvan .......... 3
- J. Nemechek .......... 3
- B. Dotter .......... 2
- B. Elliott .......... 2
- T. Bodine .......... 1
- C. Bown .......... 1
- R. Craven .......... 1
- J. Green .......... 1
- B. Labonte .......... 1
- T. Labonte .......... 1
- T. Leslie .......... 1
- M. Martin .......... 1
- R. Mast .......... 1
- B. Miller .......... 1
- K. Schrader .......... 1

## 1992 performance chart

| Pos. | Driver | Points | Starts | Poles | Wins | Top 5 | Top 10 | Winnings |
|---|---|---|---|---|---|---|---|---|
| 1. | Joe Nemechek | 4,275 | 31 | 1 | 2 | 13 | 18 | $285,008 |
| 2. | Bobby Labonte | 4,272 | 31 | 0 | 3 | 13 | 19 | 329,985 |
| 3. | Todd Bodine | 4,212 | 31 | 2 | 3 | 11 | 19 | 284,284 |
| 4. | Jeff Gordon | 4,053 | 31 | 11 | 3 | 10 | 15 | 412,293 |
| 5. | Robert Pressley | 3,988 | 31 | 2 | 5 | 11 | 16 | 299,303 |
| 6. | Kenny Wallace | 3,966 | 31 | 2 | 1 | 7 | 15 | 166,167 |
| 7. | Butch Miller | 3,725 | 31 | 2 | 0 | 4 | 10 | 131,991 |
| 8. | Ward Burton | 3,648 | 31 | 0 | 1 | 3 | 10 | 203,116 |
| 9. | Jeff Burton | 3,609 | 31 | 0 | 1 | 4 | 10 | 202,775 |
| 10. | Tommy Houston | 3,599 | 31 | 0 | 1 | 2 | 10 | 133,065 |

HISTORY

### Race winners (17)
R. Pressley .................................... 5
T. Bodine ...................................... 3
J. Gordon ...................................... 3
B. Labonte .................................... 3
H. Gant ........................................ 2
E. Irvan ........................................ 2
J. Nemechek ................................. 2
J. Spencer .................................... 2
J. Burton ...................................... 1
W. Burton .................................... 1
B. Dotter ...................................... 1
D. Earnhardt ................................. 1
S. Grissom ................................... 1
T. Houston ................................... 1
M. Martin ..................................... 1
K. Wallace .................................... 1
M. Waltrip .................................... 1

### Season winnings
J. Gordon ........................ $412,293
B. Labonte ........................ 329,985
R. Pressley ....................... 299,303
J. Nemechek .................... 285,008
T. Bodine ......................... 284,284
W. Burton ........................ 203,116
J. Burton ......................... 202,775
S. Grissom ....................... 170,716
C. Bown ........................... 169,513
K. Wallace ....................... 166,167

### Pole winners (14)
J. Gordon .................................... 11
T. Bodine ...................................... 2
M. Martin ..................................... 2
B. Miller ....................................... 2
R. Pressley ................................... 2
K. Wallace .................................... 2
J. Bown ........................................ 1
R. Craven ..................................... 1
D. Earnhardt ................................. 1
S. Grissom ................................... 1
E. Irvan ........................................ 1
J. Nemechek ................................. 1
J. Rumley ..................................... 1
M. Waltrip .................................... 1

## 1991 performance chart

| Pos. | Driver | Points | Starts | Poles | Wins | Top 5 | Top 10 | Winnings |
|---|---|---|---|---|---|---|---|---|
| 1. | Bobby Labonte | 4,264 | 31 | 2 | 2 | 10 | 21 | $246,368 |
| 2. | Kenny Wallace | 4,190 | 31 | 1 | 2 | 11 | 17 | 274,506 |
| 3. | Robert Pressley | 3,929 | 31 | 1 | 1 | 8 | 15 | 171,256 |
| 4. | Chuck Bown | 3,922 | 31 | 5 | 3 | 9 | 14 | 244,739 |
| 5. | Jimmy Hensley | 3,916 | 31 | 4 | 3 | 9 | 17 | 227,739 |
| 6. | Joe Nemechek | 3,902 | 31 | 0 | 0 | 5 | 16 | 124,255 |
| 7. | Todd Bodine | 3,825 | 31 | 2 | 1 | 7 | 15 | 136,273 |
| 8. | Tommy Houston | 3,777 | 31 | 0 | 0 | 5 | 11 | 163,827 |
| 9. | Tom Peck | 3,746 | 31 | 0 | 0 | 2 | 13 | 163,189 |
| 10. | Steve Grissom | 3,689 | 31 | 1 | 1 | 7 | 13 | 152,206 |

### Race winners (16)
H. Gant ........................................ 5
C. Bown ....................................... 3
D. Earnhardt ................................. 3
J. Hensley .................................... 3
D. Jarrett ..................................... 3
R. Craven ..................................... 2
B. Labonte .................................... 2
K. Wallace .................................... 2
T. Bodine ...................................... 1
J. Burton ...................................... 1
D. Green ...................................... 1
S. Grissom ................................... 1
E. Irvan ........................................ 1
T. Labonte .................................... 1
B. Miller ....................................... 1
R. Pressley ................................... 1

### Season winnings
K. Wallace ....................... $274,506
B. Labonte ....................... 246,368
C. Bown ........................... 244,739
J. Hensley ....................... 227,969
R. Pressley ....................... 171,256
T. Houston ....................... 163,827
T. Peck ............................ 163,189
S. Grissom ....................... 152,206
J. Burton ......................... 144,798
T. Bodine ......................... 136,273

### Pole winners (20)
C. Bown ........................................ 5
J. Hensley .................................... 4
T. Bodine ...................................... 2
J. Burton ...................................... 2
B. Labonte .................................... 2
W. Burton .................................... 1
R. Craven ..................................... 1
D. Earnhardt ................................. 1
H. Gant ........................................ 1
J. Gordon ..................................... 1
D. Green ...................................... 1
S. Grissom ................................... 1
E. Irvan ........................................ 1
T. Labonte .................................... 1
D. Mader ...................................... 1
B. Miller ....................................... 1
R. Pressley ................................... 1
E. Sawyer ..................................... 1
J. Sprague .................................... 1
K. Wallace .................................... 1

## 1990 performance chart

| Pos. | Driver | Points | Starts | Poles | Wins | Top 5 | Top 10 | Winnings |
|---|---|---|---|---|---|---|---|---|
| 1. | Chuck Bown | 4,372 | 31 | 4 | 6 | 13 | 18 | $323,399 |
| 2. | Jimmy Hensley | 4,172 | 31 | 4 | 1 | 9 | 17 | 201,877 |
| 3. | Steve Grissom | 3,982 | 31 | 1 | 4 | 11 | 15 | 166,842 |
| 4. | Bobby Labonte | 3,977 | 31 | 2 | 0 | 6 | 17 | 136,936 |
| 5. | Tom Peck | 3,868 | 31 | 0 | 0 | 2 | 12 | 109,821 |
| 6. | Tommy Ellis | 3,829 | 31 | 3 | 1 | 5 | 13 | 205,863 |
| 7. | Kenny Wallace | 3,829 | 31 | 1 | 0 | 4 | 14 | 112,781 |
| 8. | L.D. Ottinger | 3,693 | 31 | 0 | 1 | 5 | 7 | 156,674 |
| 9. | Tommy Houston | 3,667 | 31 | 0 | 4 | 9 | 14 | 200,350 |
| 10. | Rick Mast | 3,617 | 31 | 1 | 3 | 8 | 10 | 127,965 |

**Race winners (13)**
- C. Bown ............ 6
- S. Grissom ........ 4
- T. Houston ........ 4
- R. Mast ............ 3
- H. Gant ............ 2
- D. Jarrett ......... 2
- M. Waltrip ........ 2
- J. Burton .......... 1
- T. Ellis ............. 1
- J. Hensley ......... 1
- S. Marlin .......... 1
- M. Martin .......... 1
- L. Ottinger ........ 1

**Season winnings**
- C. Bown ............ $323,399
- T. Ellis ............. 205,863
- J. Hensley ......... 201,877
- T. Houston ........ 200,350
- S. Grissom ........ 166,842
- L. Ottinger ........ 156,674
- B. Hamilton ....... 156,281
- E. Sawyer .......... 144,699
- B. Labonte ........ 136,936
- R. Mast ............ 127,965

**Pole winners (17)**
- C. Bown ............ 4
- J. Hensley ......... 4
- T. Ellis ............. 3
- R. Craven .......... 2
- B. Labonte ........ 2
- M. Waltrip ........ 2
- D. Allison ......... 1
- E. Berrier ......... 1
- J. Burton .......... 1
- H. Gant ............ 1
- S. Grissom ........ 1
- D. Mader .......... 1
- R. Mast ............ 1
- G. Sacks ........... 1
- D. Trickle ......... 1
- K. Wallace ......... 1
- D. Waltrip ......... 1

# 1989 performance chart

| Pos. | Driver | Points | Starts | Poles | Wins | Top 5 | Top 10 | Winnings |
|---|---|---|---|---|---|---|---|---|
| 1. | Rob Moroso | 4,001 | 29 | 6 | 4 | 12 | 16 | $346,849 |
| 2. | Tommy Houston | 3,946 | 29 | 1 | 3 | 12 | 17 | 184,734 |
| 3. | Tommy Ellis | 3,945 | 29 | 1 | 3 | 11 | 19 | 202,141 |
| 4. | L.D. Ottinger | 3,916 | 29 | 0 | 1 | 7 | 16 | 109,821 |
| 5. | Jack Ingram | 3,802 | 29 | 0 | 0 | 7 | 14 | 144,436 |
| 6. # | Kenny Wallace | 3,750 | 29 | 3 | 0 | 4 | 16 | 88,423 |
| 7. | Rick Mast | 3,558 | 29 | 2 | 2 | 9 | 13 | 127,028 |
| 8. | Ronald Cooper | 3,557 | 29 | 0 | 1 | 4 | 10 | 106,068 |
| 9. | Chuck Bown | 3,349 | 29 | 2 | 0 | 5 | 12 | 103,294 |
| 10. | Tom Peck | 3,171 | 28 | 0 | 0 | 2 | 7 | 58,441 |

# Raybestos Rookie of the Year candidate

**Race winners (18)**
- R. Moroso .......... 4
- T. Ellis ............. 3
- T. Houston ........ 3
- J. Spencer ......... 3
- D. Earnhardt ...... 2
- H. Gant ............ 2
- R. Mast ............ 2
- R. Wilson .......... 2
- G. Bodine .......... 1
- R. Cooper .......... 1
- B. Hamilton ....... 1
- B. Hillin ........... 1
- M. Martin .......... 1
- L. Ottinger ........ 1
- R. Pressley ........ 1
- K. Schrader ....... 1
- D. Waltrip ......... 1
- M. Waltrip ........ 1

**Season winnings**
- R. Moroso .......... $346,849
- T. Ellis ............. 202,141
- T. Houston ........ 184,735
- J. Ingram .......... 144,436
- R. Mast ............ 127,028
- L. Ottinger ........ 109,821
- R. Cooper .......... 106,068
- J. Spencer ......... 103,726
- C. Bown ............ 103,294
- M. Waltrip ........ 90,487

**Pole winners (17)**
- R. Moroso .......... 6
- M. Waltrip ........ 4
- K. Wallace ......... 3
- C. Bown ............ 2
- R. Mast ............ 2
- G. Bodine .......... 1
- T. Ellis ............. 1
- H. Gant ............ 1
- J. Hensley ......... 1
- T. Houston ........ 1
- D. Jarrett ......... 1
- M. Martin .......... 1
- G. Sacks ........... 1
- K. Schrader ....... 1
- J. Spencer ......... 1
- M. Shepherd ...... 1
- R. Wilson .......... 1

# 1988 performance chart

| Pos. | Driver | Points | Starts | Poles | Wins | Top 5 | Top 10 | Winnings |
|---|---|---|---|---|---|---|---|---|
| 1. | Tommy Ellis | 4,310 | 30 | 5 | 3 | 12 | 20 | $200,003 |
| 2. | Rob Moroso | 4,071 | 30 | 2 | 2 | 10 | 19 | 181,618 |
| 3. | Mike Alexander | 4,053 | 30 | 1 | 1 | 10 | 17 | 151,303 |
| 4. | Larry Pearson | 4,050 | 30 | 5 | 3 | 13 | 16 | 164,593 |
| 5. | Tommy Houston | 4,042 | 30 | 2 | 3 | 11 | 17 | 123,385 |
| 6. | Jimmy Hensley | 3,904 | 30 | 0 | 1 | 7 | 13 | 125,615 |
| 7. | Jimmy Spencer | 3,839 | 30 | 0 | 0 | 5 | 13 | 64,112 |
| 8. | Rick Mast | 3,809 | 30 | 0 | 2 | 5 | 13 | 116,557 |
| 9. | L.D. Ottinger | 3,732 | 30 | 1 | 0 | 5 | 11 | 66,640 |
| 10. | Jack Ingram | 3,610 | 30 | 0 | 0 | 10 | 12 | 100,497 |

### Race winners (18)
H. Gant ............................5
T. Ellis .............................3
T. Houston ......................3
L. Pearson ......................3
R. Mast ...........................2
R. Moroso .......................2
M. Alexander ..................1
B. Allison ........................1
G. Bodine ........................1
D. Earnhardt ...................1
J. Hensley ......................1
B. Hillin ...........................1
D. Jarrett ........................1
M. Martin ........................1
D. McCabe ......................1
M. Shepherd ...................1
D. Waltrip .......................1
M. Waltrip .......................1

### Season winnings
T. Ellis ....................$200,003
R. Moroso ................. 181,618
L. Pearson ................ 164,593
M. Alexander ............. 151,303
J. Hensley ................. 125,615
T. Houston ................ 123,385
R. Mast ..................... 116,557
J. Ingram .................. 100,497
H. Gant ...................... 88,847
L. Ottinger ................. 66,640

### Pole winners (12)
T. Ellis .............................5
L. Pearson ......................5
H. Gant ...........................4
G. Bodine ........................3
T. Houston ......................2
R. Moroso .......................2
M. Alexander ..................1
B. Dotter ........................1
D. Earnhardt ...................1
D. Jarrett ........................1
L. Ottinger ......................1
M. Swaim ........................1

## 1987 performance chart

| Pos. | Driver | Points | Starts | Poles | Wins | Top 5 | Top 10 | Winnings |
|---|---|---|---|---|---|---|---|---|
| 1. | Larry Pearson | 3,999 | 27 | 3 | 6 | 16 | 20 | $185,124 |
| 2. | Jimmy Hensley | 3,617 | 27 | 2 | 1 | 8 | 14 | 66,505 |
| 3. | Brett Bodine | 3,611 | 27 | 5 | 0 | 8 | 17 | 115,889 |
| 4. | Jack Ingram | 3,598 | 27 | 0 | 1 | 6 | 14 | 105,530 |
| 5. | Mike Alexander | 3,497 | 27 | 1 | 1 | 8 | 13 | 51,598 |
| 6. | Dale Jarrett | 3,444 | 27 | 0 | 1 | 5 | 11 | 84,025 |
| 7. | Brad Teague | 3,391 | 27 | 0 | 1 | 1 | 9 | 94,960 |
| 8. | Mark Martin | 3,349 | 27 | 6 | 3 | 5 | 13 | 65,208 |
| 9. | Rick Mast | 3,319 | 27 | 1 | 2 | 4 | 9 | 69,704 |
| 10. | L.D. Ottinger | 3,318 | 27 | 0 | 0 | 6 | 10 | 95,440 |

### Race winners (15)
L. Pearson ......................6
H. Gant ...........................3
M. Martin ........................3
M. Shepherd ...................3
R. Mast ...........................2
M. Alexander ..................1
J. Aube ...........................1
G. Bodine ........................1
D. Earnhardt ...................1
T. Ellis .............................1
J. Hensley ......................1
J. Ingram ........................1
D. Jarrett ........................1
L. Pollard ........................1
B. Teague .......................1

### Season winnings
L. Pearson ...............$256,372
B. Bodine .................. 138,551
J. Ingram .................. 124,929
B. Teague ................. 106,172
L. Ottinger ................ 102,702
D. Jarrett ................... 97,499
J. Hensley .................. 94,504
T. Houston ................. 90,340
H. Gant ...................... 85,722
D. Waltrip .................. 77,684

### Pole winners (13)
M. Martin .........................6
B. Bodine ........................5
L. Pearson ......................3
H. Gant ...........................2
J. Hensley ......................2
T. Houston ......................2
M. Alexander ..................1
G. Bodine ........................1
D. Dion ............................1
D. Earnhardt ...................1
R. Ingram ........................1
R. Mast ...........................1
R. Wallace ......................1

## 1986 performance chart

| Pos. | Driver | Points | Starts | Poles | Wins | Top 5 | Top 10 | Winnings |
|---|---|---|---|---|---|---|---|---|
| 1. | Larry Pearson | 4,551 | 31 | 1 | 1 | 17 | 24 | $127,488 |
| 2. | Brett Bodine | 4,531 | 31 | 8 | 2 | 16 | 24 | 146,233 |
| 3. | Jack Ingram | 4,301 | 29 | 1 | 5 | 16 | 22 | 152,229 |
| 4. | Dale Jarrett | 4,261 | 31 | 5 | 1 | 14 | 19 | 71,463 |
| 5. | L.D. Ottinger | 4,153 | 31 | 0 | 1 | 12 | 20 | 79,363 |
| 6. | Tommy Houston | 4,121 | 31 | 4 | 4 | 12 | 18 | 108,038 |
| 7. | Ronnie Silver | 3,967 | 31 | 0 | 1 | 9 | 12 | 85,584 |
| 8. | Jimmy Hensley | 3,950 | 31 | 0 | 0 | 3 | 9 | 86,019 |
| 9. | Charlie Luck | 3,847 | 31 | 0 | 0 | 1 | 14 | 51,518 |
| 10. | Larry Pollard | 3,726 | 30 | 0 | 0 | 1 | 11 | 45,029 |

### Race winners (13)
D. Earnhardt .................... 5
J. Ingram ........................ 5
T. Houston ...................... 4
M. Shepherd .................... 4
D. Waltrip ....................... 4
B. Bodine ........................ 2
C. Bown .......................... 1
D. Jarrett ........................ 1
B. Miller ......................... 1
L. Ottinger ...................... 1
L. Pearson ...................... 1
T. Richmond .................... 1
R. Silver ......................... 1

### Season winnings
L. Pearson ............... $184,344
J. Ingram ................. 174,482
B. Bodine ................. 173,181
D. Earnhardt ............. 150,558
T. Houston ............... 121,706
L. Ottinger ............... 96,476
R. Silver .................. 96,262
J. Hensley ................ 95,148
D. Jarrett ................. 90,701
D. Waltrip ................ 87,873

### Pole winners (14)
B. Bodine ........................ 8
D. Jarrett ........................ 5
T. Houston ...................... 4
T. Richmond .................... 3
D. Waltrip ....................... 2
M. Alexander ................... 1
D. Allison ....................... 1
G. Bodine ....................... 1
D. Earnhardt .................... 1
J. Ingram ........................ 1
T. Labonte ...................... 1
L. Pearson ...................... 1
R. Porter ........................ 1
M. Shepherd .................... 1

# 1985 performance chart

| Pos. | Driver | Points | Starts | Poles | Wins | Top 5 | Top 10 | Winnings |
|---|---|---|---|---|---|---|---|---|
| 1. | Jack Ingram | 4,106 | 27 | 2 | 5 | 17 | 22 | $115,798 |
| 2. | Jimmy Hensley | 4,077 | 27 | 4 | 3 | 15 | 23 | 92,808 |
| 3. | Larry Pearson | 3,951 | 27 | 0 | 2 | 15 | 19 | 101,438 |
| 4. | Tommy Houston | 3,936 | 27 | 4 | 1 | 17 | 21 | 81,258 |
| 5. | Dale Jarrett | 3,774 | 27 | 0 | 0 | 9 | 17 | 51,323 |
| 6. | L.D. Ottinger | 3,732 | 27 | 0 | 0 | 6 | 19 | 65,748 |
| 7. | Rick Mast | 3,589 | 27 | 0 | 0 | 5 | 15 | 52,380 |
| 8. | Ronnie Silver | 3,425 | 27 | 0 | 1 | 3 | 13 | 49,758 |
| 9. | Larry Pollard | 3,197 | 24 | 0 | 0 | 2 | 12 | 30,235 |
| 10. | Eddie Falk | 3,044 | 27 | 0 | 0 | 0 | 4 | 30,145 |

### Race winners (12)
T. Ellis ........................... 5
J. Ingram ........................ 5
B. Bodine ........................ 3
J. Hensley ....................... 3
D. Waltrip ....................... 3
L. Pearson ...................... 2
G. Bodine ....................... 1
D. Earnhardt .................... 1
T. Houston ...................... 1
T. Labonte ...................... 1
T. Richmond .................... 1
R. Silver ......................... 1

### Season winnings
J. Ingram ............... $164,709
L. Pearson ............... 120,453
J. Hensley ............... 115,963
T. Houston ............... 97,932
L. Ottinger ............... 77,291
T. Ellis .................... 73,936
G. Bodine ................ 71,433
D. Jarrett ................. 65,566
R. Mast ................... 61,977
R. Silver .................. 57,470

### Pole winners (13)
J. Hensley ....................... 4
T. Houston ...................... 4
B. Bodine ........................ 3
T. Ellis ........................... 3
G. Bodine ....................... 2
J. Ingram ........................ 2
T. Richmond .................... 2
B. Teague ....................... 2
R. Bouchard .................... 1
D. Earnhardt .................... 1
A. Kulwicki ..................... 1
M. Porter ........................ 1
R. Wallace ...................... 1

# 1984 performance chart

| Pos. | Driver | Points | Starts | Poles | Wins | Top 5 | Top 10 | Winnings |
|---|---|---|---|---|---|---|---|---|
| 1. | Sam Ard | 4,552 | 28 | 7 | 8 | 24 | 26 | $217,531 |
| 2. | Jack Ingram | 4,126 | 29 | 0 | 8 | 17 | 19 | 122,953 |
| 3. | Tommy Houston | 4,070 | 29 | 4 | 2 | 15 | 22 | 104,778 |
| 4. | Dale Jarrett | 4,014 | 29 | 1 | 0 | 9 | 19 | 72,503 |
| 5. | Ronnie Silver | 3,398 | 26 | 0 | 0 | 8 | 14 | 52,133 |
| 6. | Joe Thurman | 3,221 | 27 | 0 | 0 | 2 | 8 | 51,383 |
| 7. | Charlie Luck | 3,172 | 26 | 0 | 0 | 1 | 9 | 40,279 |
| 8. | L.D. Ottinger | 3,069 | 26 | 3 | 0 | 3 | 10 | 43,264 |
| 9. | Jeff Hensley | 3,032 | 26 | 0 | 0 | 1 | 7 | 29,629 |
| 10. | Bob Shreeves | 2,869 | 25 | 0 | 0 | 0 | 7 | 33,739 |

HISTORY

| Race winners (10) | Season winnings | Pole winners (11) |
|---|---|---|
| S. Ard .................... 8 | S. Ard .................. $217,531 | S. Ard .................... 7 |
| J. Ingram ................ 8 | J. Ingram ............... 122,953 | T. Ellis .................. 4 |
| M. Shepherd ........... 3 | T. Houston ............. 104,778 | T. Houston ............. 4 |
| R. Bouchard ........... 2 | D. Jarrett ............... 72,503 | G. Bodine .............. 3 |
| T. Houston ............. 2 | R. Silver ................ 52,133 | R. Bouchard .......... 3 |
| D. Waltrip .............. 2 | J. Thurman ............ 51,383 | L. Ottinger ............ 3 |
| B. Allison ............... 1 | D. Waltrip .............. 50,280 | E. Falk .................. 1 |
| G. Bodine .............. 1 | L. Ottinger ............ 43,264 | D. Jarrett ............... 1 |
| T. Ellis .................. 1 | G. Bodine .............. 42,950 | T. Richmond .......... 1 |
| L. Pearson ............. 1 | C. Luck ................. 40,279 | M. Shepherd .......... 1 |
| | | D. Trickle .............. 1 |

## 1983 performance chart

| Pos. | Driver | Points | Starts | Poles | Wins | Top 5 | Top 10 | Winnings |
|---|---|---|---|---|---|---|---|---|
| 1. | Sam Ard | 5,454 | 35 | 10 | 10 | 23 | 30 | $192,362 |
| 2. | Jack Ingram | 5,367 | 35 | 1 | 5 | 23 | 29 | 126,956 |
| 3. | Tommy Houston | 4,933 | 35 | 1 | 4 | 14 | 22 | 104,561 |
| 4. | Tommy Ellis | 4,929 | 35 | 7 | 7 | 16 | 21 | 97,251 |
| 5. | Dale Jarrett | 4,837 | 35 | 4 | 0 | 17 | 21 | 55,360 |
| 6. | Ronnie Silver | 4,058 | 32 | 0 | 0 | 6 | 16 | 35,705 |
| 7. | Pete Silva | 3,945 | 31 | 0 | 0 | 6 | 13 | 42,900 |
| 8. | Jimmy Hensley | 3,716 | 29 | 0 | 0 | 5 | 16 | 26,305 |
| 9. | Eddie Falk | 3,617 | 30 | 0 | 0 | 1 | 13 | 21,162 |
| 10. | Jeff Hensley | 3,444 | 28 | 0 | 0 | 1 | 9 | 18,875 |

| Race winners (10) | Season winnings | Pole winners (11) |
|---|---|---|
| S. Ard .................. 10 | S. Ard .................. $192,362 | S. Ard .................. 10 |
| T. Ellis .................. 7 | J. Ingram ............... 126,956 | T. Ellis .................. 7 |
| J. Ingram ............... 5 | T. Houston ............. 104,561 | D. Jarrett ............... 4 |
| T. Houston ............. 4 | T. Ellis .................. 97,251 | P. Parsons ............. 4 |
| D. Earnhardt .......... 2 | D. Jarrett ............... 55,360 | B. Lindley .............. 3 |
| B. Lindley .............. 2 | B. Lindley .............. 44,488 | D. Earnhardt .......... 1 |
| M. Shepherd ......... 2 | P. Silva .................. 42,900 | T. Houston ............. 1 |
| N. Bonnett ............. 1 | P. Parsons ............. 40,976 | J. Ingram ............... 1 |
| R. Rudd ................. 1 | M. Shepherd ......... 36,570 | D. Pearson ............ 1 |
| D. Waltrip .............. 1 | R. Silver ................ 35,705 | L. Pearson ............. 1 |
| | | M. Shepherd ......... 1 |

## 1982 performance chart

| Pos. | Driver | Points | Starts | Poles | Wins | Top 5 | Top 10 | Winnings |
|---|---|---|---|---|---|---|---|---|
| 1. | Jack Ingram | 4,495 | 29 | 1 | 7 | 23 | 24 | $122,100 |
| 2. | Sam Ard | 4,446 | 29 | 7 | 4 | 20 | 23 | 122,099 |
| 3. | Tommy Ellis | 3,873 | 29 | 5 | 1 | 13 | 16 | 78,782 |
| 4. | Tommy Houston | 3,827 | 29 | 0 | 2 | 11 | 18 | 67,792 |
| 5. | Phil Parsons | 3,783 | 29 | 2 | 1 | 5 | 18 | 62,839 |
| 6. | Dale Jarrett | 3,332 | 29 | 0 | 0 | 1 | 15 | 27,260 |
| 7. | Pete Silva | 2,349 | 18 | 0 | 0 | 5 | 8 | 18,127 |
| 8. | Jimmy Lawson | 2,106 | 18 | 0 | 0 | 0 | 5 | 12,458 |
| 9. | Bob Shreeves | 1,928 | 15 | 1 | 0 | 5 | 8 | 13,785 |
| 10. | Butch Lindley | 1,581 | 14 | 2 | 4 | 9 | 10 | 38,170 |

| Race winners (14) | Season winnings | Pole winners (12) |
|---|---|---|
| J. Ingram ............... 7 | J. Ingram ............... $122,100 | S. Ard .................... 7 |
| S. Ard .................... 4 | S. Ard .................. 122,099 | T. Ellis .................. 5 |
| B. Lindley .............. 4 | T. Ellis .................. 78,782 | H. Gant ................. 3 |
| D. Earnhardt .......... 2 | T. Houston ............. 67,792 | G. Bodine .............. 2 |
| T. Houston ............. 2 | P. Parsons ............. 62,839 | B. Lindley .............. 2 |
| M. Shepherd ......... 2 | B. Lindley .............. 38,170 | P. Parsons ............. 2 |
| G. Bodine .............. 1 | D. Earnhardt .......... 29,980 | D. Pearson ............ 2 |
| T. Ellis .................. 1 | G. Bodine .............. 29,005 | M. Shepherd ......... 2 |
| H. Gant ................. 1 | D. Jarrett ............... 27,260 | J. Ingram ............... 1 |
| P. Parsons ............. 1 | M. Shepherd ......... 23,955 | G. Neice ............... 1 |
| D. Pearsons .......... 1 | | M. Porter .............. 1 |
| J. Ruttman ............ 1 | | B. Shreeves .......... 1 |
| J. Settlemyre ......... 1 | | |
| D. Waltrip .............. 1 | | |

NASCAR Craftsman Truck Series

# Milestones

**1993** Four off-road racing enthusiasts — Dick Landfield, Jimmy Smith, Jim Venable and Frank "Scoop" Vessels — build prototype racing pickup truck

**February 1994** Group seeks NASCAR sanction for truck racing

**May 14, 1994** NASCAR President Bill France announces creation of NASCAR Craftsman Truck Series, then titled NASCAR SuperTruck Series, during news conference at Sears Point Raceway in Sonoma, Calif.

**July 30, 1994** First of four demonstration races is held at Mesa Marin Raceway in Bakersfield, Calif. P.J. Jones is first NASCAR Craftsman Truck Series winner in a Ford owned by Vessels

**Late 1994** Craftsman agrees to present series. A 20-race schedule is released. Total posted awards of $1.6 million are announced, along with complete national television package

**Nov. 20, 1994** Rick Carelli wins first of three preview races held at Tucson Raceway Park. Each is broadcast live by TNN as part of its Winter Heat package

**Feb. 5, 1995** NASCAR Craftsman Truck Series begins at Phoenix International Raceway. Mike Skinner, driving the GM Goodwrench Service Chevrolet is the first winner of a championship race, beating former NASCAR Winston Cup Series champion Terry Labonte by just 0.09-second

**June 3, 1995** Skinner's Ford Credit 200 victory at the Louisville Motor Speedway makes him first in the series to win two consecutive races

**June 23, 1995** Joe Ruttman and Irvan-Simo Racing give Ford its first series win, in the Pizza Plus 150 at the Bristol Motor Speedway

**July 15, 1995** Butch Miller, Raybestos Ford, edges Skinner in closest finish to date — 0.0001-second — at Colorado National Speedway

**July 29, 1995** Ron Hornaday Jr. drives Teresa Earnhardt's Papa John's Pizza Chevrolet to victory in series' first road race, at Heartland Park Topeka

**Aug. 17, 1995** Hornaday's win at Flemington Speedway clinches first series manufacturer championship for Chevrolet

**Oct. 27, 1995** Skinner wins first NASCAR Craftsman Truck Series championship at Phoenix, by 126 points over Ruttman. Championship is worth $428,096

**Nov. 18, 1995** Second season of 24 races announced during awards banquet at Fairmont Hotel in San Francisco. Total posted awards increase to $4 million

**February 1996** Sears Craftsman agrees to become title sponsor of NASCAR Craftsman Truck Series under new, three-year agreement

**March 17, 1996** Dave Rezendes wins then-record $44,550 with victory in Florida Dodge Dealers 400 at Homestead-Miami Speedway

**May 3, 1996** Rich Bickle, qualifying for the Craftsman 200 at Portland Speedway, drives Richard Petty-owned Cummins Engine Company Dodge to company's first fast qualifying time since the late 1970s in a major NASCAR series

**June 9, 1996** Skinner's road racing victory, at Heartland Park Topeka, completes first three-wins-in-a-row streak in series history

**July 6, 1996** 17 lead changes in Sears Auto Center 200 at The Milwaukee Mile sets series record

**Sept. 8, 1996** Hornaday's New Hampshire International Speedway victory makes him first in series to win on short track, road course and superspeedway in single season

**Oct. 26, 1996** Crowd of 58,000 for GM Goodwrench/Delco Battery 300 at Phoenix International Raceway sets series attendance record

**Nov. 1, 1996** Bryan Reffner becomes fastest driver in series history, winning the Busch Pole at the Las Vegas Motor Speedway with a lap of 157.909 mph in the 1-800-COLLECT Ford. Sixty-one teams which attempt to qualify for the Carquest Auto Parts 420K is a series record

**Nov. 3, 1996** Jack Sprague, driving the Quaker State Chevrolet, wins fastest race in series history at 120.782 mph. His $79,825 sets a single-race money won mark. Reffner becomes first Rookie of the Year

**Nov. 16, 1996** Hornaday, celebrating 1996 NASCAR Craftsman Truck Series championship at Fairmont Hotel, sets season winnings mark of $625,634. Skinner's third-place awards make him first series millionaire. A $6 million, 26-race schedule is announced for the 1997 season, including events at Walt Disney World Speedway, the California Speedway and Texas Motor Speedway

**Jan. 19, 1997** Walt Disney World Speedway near Orlando, Fla. hosts opening race of third season

**March 1, 1997** Hornaday's win at Tucson Raceway Park makes him first competitor to win in all three seasons of the NASCAR Craftsman Truck Series

**March 16, 1997** Kenny Irwin becomes first Rookie-of-the-Year candidate to win a race, capturing the Florida Dodge Dealers 400 at Homestead-Miami Speedway

**May 24, 1997** Dodge gets its first victory in the NASCAR Craftsman Truck Series as Tony Raines wins Western Auto/Parts America 200 at I-70 Speedway in Kansas City, Mo.

**June 6, 1997** Mike Bliss, who laps Texas Motor Speedway at 175.667 mph, heads fastest field in series history. Starting field for the Pronto Auto Parts 400 averages 171.209. Hornaday, despite failing to finish, becomes NASCAR Craftsman Truck Series leading money winner at $1,051,221

**Aug. 9, 1997** Hornaday's fifth consecutive short track victory, at Flemington Speedway, gives the Palmdale, Calif. driver the all time series win record at 17

**Oct. 18, 1997** Bliss wins fastest race in series history, averaging 137.195 mph in The No Fear Challenge at the California Speedway

**Nov. 9, 1997** Sprague becomes third different NASCAR Craftsman Truck Series champion by a record, 232 points over Bickle. Ruttman's victory in the Carquest Auto Parts 420K is worth a record $83,000

**Dec. 13, 1997** Sprague boosts the single-season, money-won record to $880,835. He also becomes the tour's all-time leading money winner. Five different drivers – Sprague, Hornaday, Ruttman, Skinner and Bliss – now have won more than $1 million during their NCTS careers

**Jan. 18, 1998** Hornaday becomes the first driver to win a race in all four years of the NASCAR Craftsman Truck Series

**June 20, 1998** Sprague records 21st consecutive top-10 finish at Bristol Motor Speedway. The mark eventually reaches 23. Hornaday's victory is his 13th on a short track, most in series history

**July 18, 1998** Sprague wins the fastest race in series history, capturing The No Fear Challenge at California Speedway with an average speed of 141.844 mph

**July 25, 1998** Series adopts "live" pit stop format for most venues

**Sept. 19, 1998** Sprague finishes fourth at Gateway International Raceway to become the tour's first $2 million career winner

**Oct. 10, 1998** Tom Hubert wins Bud Pole for Kragen/Exide 151 at Sears Point Raceway. He's record 15th different driver to record a fast time

**Oct. 18, 1998** Dennis Setzer's victory at Mesa Marin Raceway establishes a single-season record for series winners – 14

**Oct. 24, 1998** Bliss wins GM Goodwrench Service Plus/AC Delco 300 at Phoenix International Raceway to become the series' 12th consecutive different winner

**Nov. 8, 1998** Hornaday becomes first two-time NASCAR Craftsman Truck Series champion, beating Sprague by three points. The pair finishes one-two in the season-ending Sam's Town 250 at Las Vegas Motor Speedway, with Sprague winning a race record $84,725

**Dec. 11, 1998** Hornaday collects nearly $400,000 in post-season awards to set career and single season money won records of $2,442,586 and $915,407, respectively

**March 20, 1999** The CART FedEx Championship Series and NASCAR Craftsman Truck Series share a weekend for the first time

**March 27, 1999** Hornaday becomes first driver to win in all five seasons of the series when he captures Chevy Trucks NASCAR 150 at Phoenix International Raceway

**April 3, 1999** Hornaday wins the series' 100th race, at Evergreen Speedway near Seattle, and $100,000 Craftsman bonus award

**June 11, 1999** Dodge scores first NASCAR Craftsman Truck Series superspeedway victory when Dennis Setzer captures Pronto Auto Parts 400 at Texas Motor Speedway

**July 24, 1999** The NASCAR Craftsman Truck Series visits Michigan Speedway for the first time. Greg Biffle wins the goracing.com 200

**Sept. 13, 1999** Chevrolet, Dodge and Ford drivers participate in NASCAR test at Daytona International Speedway to lay the groundwork for a Speedweeks visit to the historic venue in 2000

**Sept. 24, 1999** Biffle's victory in The Orleans 250 at Las Vegas Motor Speedway hands Ford its first series manufacturer championship. Biffle's ninth win of the year sets a single-season record

**Oct. 15, 1999** The fastest field in NASCAR Craftsman Truck Series history, qualifying at an average speed of 175.373 mph, takes the green flag at Texas Motor Speedway

**Oct. 30, 1999** Three drivers – Biffle, Sprague and Setzer – enter the season finale just 25 points apart in the series' closest three-way showdown. Sprague wins NAPA Auto Parts 200 to clinch his second NCTS title and post his 100th lead lap finish. His eight-point cushion, over Biffle, was the tour's second tightest

**Dec. 10, 1999** Postseason awards distributed at the fifth Annual Champion's Banquet make Sprague and Hornaday the first drivers to win $3 million in the NASCAR Craftsman Truck Series.

**Feb. 18, 2000** The World Center of Racing, Daytona International Speedway, hosts its first NASCAR Craftsman Truck Series event. The lead changes a record, 31 times before Mike Wallace drafts past Andy Houston entering the final set of turns of the 100th and final lap.

**June 17, 2000** The NASCAR Craftsman Truck Series opens Kentucky Speedway to the delight of a sell-out crowd.

**July 8, 2000** Kurt Busch becomes the first rookie to win back-to-back races on the series.

**Oct. 13, 2000** Greg Biffle closes out the championship race for the first time prior to the final race of the season. He is the first champion to drive a Ford to the title. It is the first NASCAR championship for team owner Jack Roush.

**Nov. 2, 2000** Greg Biffle is the first one-season millionaire, winning $1,002,510. He is the youngest champion at 30 years nine months 22 days and the first who didn't compete on the tour in 1995.

**April 4, 2001** Series celebrates 150th race at Martinsville Speedway in Virginia. Scott Riggs scores first NCTS victory for Jim Smith, an owner who has fielded at least one entry in every event.

**June 2, 2001** Dodge's eighth consecutive victory, at Dover Downs International Speedway, matches series record set in 1995 by Chevrolet.

**June 8, 2001** In winning for the first time at Texas Motor Speedway, Jack Sprague becomes the only competitor to win in six consecutive seasons on the NASCAR Craftsman Truck Series.

**June 29, 2001** Jack Sprague records 16th career Bud Pole at The Milwaukee Mile to become the series' all-time qualifying leader. He extends the mark to 20 by season's end.

**July 7, 2001** Ricky Hendrick becomes youngest winner In NCTS history (21 years three months five days) with his victory at Kansas Speedway.

**July 14, 2001** Jack Sprague finishes third at Kentucky Speedway and becomes the first $4 million winner in NCTS history.

**Sept. 28, 2001** Ted Musgrave's victory at South Boston Speedway gives Dodge its first NCTS manufacturer title.

**Oct. 14, 2001** Ted Musgrave's sixth win of 2001 gives Ultra Motorsports 11 victories on the season, breaking Roush Racing's record set in 1999.

**Nov. 3, 2001** By starting the final race of the season at California Speedway, Jack Sprague wraps up an unprecedented third NASCAR Craftsman Truck Series championship.

**2002** The NASCAR Craftsman Truck Series, the NASCAR Winston Cup Series and NASCAR Busch Series, Grand National Division, will begin and end the season on the same weekend at the same tracks – Daytona International Speedway and Homestead-Miami Speedway, respectively.

**Feb. 15, 2002** Robert Pressley becomes second competitor (and first since the series' inaugural race) to win in his first NASCAR Craftsman Truck Series appearance. Pressley wins the Florida Dodge Dealers 250 at Daytona International Speedway.

**April 15, 2002** Winning from the 33rd starting position at Martinsville Speedway, Dennis Setzer races to victory from deepest in the field for a series race. Setzer is only the second provisional starter to win on the series.

**Sept. 13, 2002** Brendan Gaughan, the Raybestos Rookie-of-the-Year, completes sweep of two series races held at Texas Motor Speedway. Gaughan is the first repeat winner of any NASCAR race at the 1.5-mile superspeedway.

**Oct. 13, 2002** David Starr's victory at Las Vegas Motor Speedway gives owner Wayne Spears first win in team's 187th series appearance. That's the longest any owner has waited for win No. 1.

**Nov. 15, 2002** Mike Bliss becomes fifth NASCAR Craftsman Truck Series champion with fifth-place finish at Homestead-Miami Speedway. Finish is closest among top-three in series history – 51 points. Xpress Motorsports is first championship team without NASCAR Winston Cup Series owner or driver affiliation.

**Feb. 12, 2003** NASCAR announces that Toyota will join the Craftsman Truck Series in 2004, marking the first time a NASCAR series will include a foreign automaker.

**March 25, 2003** Dennis Setzer won the Lucas Oil 250 at Mesa Marin Raceway to match the NASCAR Craftsman Truck Series record for victories in consecutive seasons. Setzer won for the sixth straight season, matching the mark set by Jack Sprague in 2001.

**Oct. 10, 2003** Brendan Gaughan made NASCAR Craftsman Truck Series history, winning his fourth consecutive race at Texas Motor Speedway. It completed his second straight season sweep at the track.

**Nov. 14, 2003** Travis Kvapil, 27 and a native of Janesville, Wis., is the youngest driver to win the NASCAR Craftsman Truck Series championship. His nine-point margin of victory is the closest in NASCAR Craftsman Truck Series history. Kvapil set another NASCAR Craftsman Truck Series record by completing all but a single lap in 2003 – and that on the half-mile Mesa Marin Raceway. Xpress Motorsports' Steve Coulter becomes the first owner to win consecutive championships in the NASCAR Craftsman Truck Series.

# NASCAR Craftsman Truck Series drivers

## Jamie Aube

**Birthdate:** 8/4/53 **Birth place:** North Ferrisburg, Vt. **Truck:** No team assigned

### CAREER STATISTICS

| Year | Rank | Starts | Wins | Poles | Top 5 | Top 10 | Races Led | Laps Led |
|---|---|---|---|---|---|---|---|---|
| 2003 | 31 | 11 | 0 | 0 | 0 | 0 | 0 | 0 |
| Totals | | 11 | 0 | 0 | 0 | 0 | 0 | 0 |

## Randy Briggs

**Birthdate:** 3/10/65 **Birth place:** Kansas City, Mo. **Truck:** No. 53 Ford **Truck owner:** Mary Ward

### CAREER STATISTICS

| Year | Rank | Starts | Wins | Poles | Top 5 | Top 10 | Races Led | Laps Led |
|---|---|---|---|---|---|---|---|---|
| 1999 | 69 | 1 | 0 | 0 | 0 | 0 | 0 | 0 |
| 2001 | 73 | 2 | 0 | 0 | 0 | 0 | 0 | 0 |
| 2002 | 45 | 5 | 0 | 0 | 0 | 0 | 0 | 0 |
| 2003 | 19 | 17 | 0 | 0 | 0 | 0 | 0 | 0 |
| Totals | | 25 | 0 | 0 | 0 | 0 | 0 | 0 |

## Chad Chaffin

**Birthdate:** 7/20/68 **Birth place:** Nashville **Truck:** No. 18 Dodge **Truck owner:** Bobby Hamilton

### CAREER STATISTICS

| Year | Rank | Starts | Wins | Poles | Top 5 | Top 10 | Races Led | Laps Led |
|---|---|---|---|---|---|---|---|---|
| 2000 | 55 | 3 | 0 | 0 | 1 | 1 | 0 | 0 |
| 2001 | 60 | 2 | 0 | 0 | 1 | 1 | 0 | 0 |
| 2002 | 77 | 2 | 0 | 0 | 0 | 0 | 0 | 0 |
| 2003 | 10 | 25 | 0 | 2 | 2 | 9 | 5 | 115 |
| Totals | | 32 | 0 | 2 | 4 | 11 | 5 | 115 |

## Terry Cook

**Birthdate:** 2/26/68 **Birth place:** Sylvania, Ohio **Truck:** Ford **Truck owner:** Jack Roush

### CAREER STATISTICS

| Year | Rank | Starts | Wins | Poles | Top 5 | Top 10 | Races Led | Laps Led |
|---|---|---|---|---|---|---|---|---|
| 1996 | 60 | 3 | 0 | 0 | 0 | 0 | 0 | 0 |
| 1997 | 24 | 15 | 0 | 1 | 0 | 0 | 0 | 0 |
| 1998 | 20 | 27 | 1 | 1 | 3 | 6 | 2 | 42 |
| 1999 | 15 | 25 | 0 | 0 | 1 | 3 | 1 | 15 |
| 2000 | 14 | 24 | 0 | 0 | 1 | 8 | 5 | 25 |
| 2001 | 7 | 24 | 0 | 1 | 5 | 16 | 5 | 67 |
| 2002 | 8 | 22 | 4 | 2 | 9 | 17 | 9 | 490 |
| 2003 | 9 | 25 | 0 | 2 | 0 | 13 | 4 | 84 |
| Totals | | 165 | 5 | 7 | 19 | 63 | 26 | 723 |

## Matt Crafton

**Birthdate:** 6/11/76 **Birth place:** Tulare, Calif. **Truck:** No. 6 Chevrolet **Truck owner:** Kevin Harvick

### CAREER STATISTICS

| Year | Rank | Starts | Wins | Poles | Top 5 | Top 10 | Races Led | Laps Led |
|---|---|---|---|---|---|---|---|---|
| 2000 | 83 | 1 | 0 | 0 | 0 | 1 | 0 | 0 |
| 2001 | 12 | 24 | 0 | 0 | 0 | 11 | 3 | 29 |
| 2002 | 15 | 22 | 0 | 0 | 0 | 6 | 0 | 0 |
| 2003 | 11 | 25 | 0 | 0 | 0 | 11 | 2 | 11 |
| Totals | | 72 | 0 | 0 | 0 | 29 | 5 | 40 |

## Rick Crawford

**Birthdate:** 7/26/58 **Birth place:** Mobile, Ala. **Truck:** No. 14 Ford **Truck owner:** Tom Mitchell

### CAREER STATISTICS

| Year | Rank | Starts | Wins | Poles | Top 5 | Top 10 | Races Led | Laps Led |
|---|---|---|---|---|---|---|---|---|
| 1997 | 12 | 26 | 0 | 0 | 1 | 10 | 2 | 24 |
| 1998 | 18 | 27 | 1 | 0 | 4 | 5 | 1 | 31 |
| 1999 | 14 | 25 | 0 | 0 | 3 | 10 | 4 | 46 |
| 2000 | 11 | 24 | 0 | 0 | 2 | 12 | 2 | 20 |
| 2001 | 8 | 24 | 0 | 0 | 10 | 16 | 10 | 201 |
| 2002 | 2 | 22 | 0 | 2 | 12 | 17 | 12 | 476 |
| 2003 | 7 | 25 | 1 | 0 | 10 | 16 | 8 | 256 |
| Totals | | 173 | 2 | 2 | 42 | 86 | 39 | 1054 |

DRIVERS

## Bobby Dotter

**Birthdate:** 7/11/60 **Birth place:** Chicago
**Truck:** No. 07 Chevrolet **Truck owners:** Gene Christensen, Bobby Dotter

### CAREER STATISTICS

| Year | Rank | Starts | Wins | Poles | Top 5 | Top 10 | Races Led | Laps Led |
|---|---|---|---|---|---|---|---|---|
| 1996 | 96 | 1 | 0 | 0 | 0 | 0 | 0 | 0 |
| 1997 | 36 | 7 | 0 | 0 | 0 | 0 | 0 | 0 |
| 1998 | 81 | 1 | 0 | 0 | 0 | 0 | 0 | 0 |
| 2000 | 72 | 2 | 0 | 0 | 0 | 0 | 0 | 0 |
| 2001 | 15 | 24 | 0 | 0 | 0 | 1 | 2 | 2 |
| 2002 | 14 | 22 | 0 | 0 | 1 | 4 | 0 | 0 |
| 2003 | 29 | 10 | 0 | 0 | 0 | 0 | 1 | 1 |
| Totals | | 67 | 0 | 0 | 1 | 5 | 3 | 3 |

## Carl Edwards

**Birthdate:** 8/15/79 **Birth place:** Columbia, Mo.
**Truck:** No. 99 Ford **Truck owner:** Jack Roush

### CAREER STATISTICS

| Year | Rank | Starts | Wins | Poles | Top 5 | Top 10 | Races Led | Laps Led |
|---|---|---|---|---|---|---|---|---|
| 2002 | 33 | 7 | 0 | 0 | 0 | 1 | 0 | 0 |
| 2003 | 8 | 25 | 3 | 1 | 13 | 15 | 13 | 363 |
| Totals | | 32 | 3 | 1 | 13 | 16 | 13 | 363 |

## Brendan Gaughan

**Birthdate:** 7/10/75 **Birth place:** Los Angeles
**Truck:** No. 62 Dodge **Truck owner:** Michael Gaughan

### CAREER STATISTICS

| Year | Rank | Starts | Wins | Poles | Top 5 | Top 10 | Races Led | Laps Led |
|---|---|---|---|---|---|---|---|---|
| 1997 | 99 | 1 | 0 | 0 | 0 | 0 | 0 | 0 |
| 1998 | 75 | 2 | 0 | 0 | 0 | 0 | 0 | 0 |
| 1999 | 75 | 2 | 0 | 0 | 0 | 0 | 0 | 0 |
| 2000 | 40 | 5 | 0 | 0 | 0 | 0 | 0 | 0 |
| 2001 | 31 | 7 | 0 | 0 | 2 | 3 | 4 | 56 |
| 2002 | 11 | 22 | 2 | 0 | 5 | 9 | 4 | 87 |
| 2003 | 4 | 25 | 6 | 3 | 14 | 18 | 16 | 652 |
| Totals | | 64 | 8 | 3 | 21 | 30 | 24 | 795 |

## Tina Gordon

**Birthdate:** 3/14/69 **Birth place:** Cedar Bluff, Ala. **Truck:** No team assigned

### CAREER STATISTICS

| Year | Rank | Starts | Wins | Poles | Top 5 | Top 10 | Races Led | Laps Led |
|---|---|---|---|---|---|---|---|---|
| 2003 | 25 | 11 | 0 | 0 | 0 | 0 | 0 | 0 |
| Totals | | 11 | 0 | 0 | 0 | 0 | 0 | 0 |

## Bobby Hamilton

**Birthdate:** 5/29/57 **Birth place:** Nashville
**Truck:** No. 4 Dodge **Truck owner:** Bobby Hamilton

### CAREER STATISTICS

| Year | Rank | Starts | Wins | Poles | Top 5 | Top 10 | Races Led | Laps Led |
|---|---|---|---|---|---|---|---|---|
| 1996 | 82 | 2 | 0 | 1 | 0 | 0 | 1 | 116 |
| 1997 | 56 | 2 | 0 | 0 | 1 | 2 | 0 | 0 |
| 1998 | 59 | 3 | 0 | 0 | 0 | 0 | 0 | 0 |
| 1999 | 36 | 5 | 0 | 1 | 1 | 1 | 2 | 89 |
| 2000 | 42 | 5 | 1 | 1 | 1 | 2 | 4 | 278 |
| 2001 | 38 | 5 | 1 | 0 | 2 | 3 | 2 | 258 |
| 2002 | 66 | 2 | 0 | 0 | 0 | 0 | 0 | 0 |
| 2003 | 6 | 25 | 2 | 1 | 10 | 18 | 13 | 394 |
| Totals | | 49 | 4 | 4 | 15 | 26 | 22 | 1135 |

## Tracy Hines

**Birthdate:** 5/1/72 **Birth place:** New Castle, Ind. **Truck:** No team assigned

### CAREER STATISTICS

| Year | Rank | Starts | Wins | Poles | Top 5 | Top 10 | Races Led | Laps Led |
|---|---|---|---|---|---|---|---|---|
| 2003 | 54 | 4 | 0 | 0 | 0 | 0 | 0 | 0 |
| Totals | | 4 | 0 | 0 | 0 | 0 | 0 | 0 |

## Andy Houston

**Birthdate:** 11/7/70 **Birth place:** Hickory, N.C.
**Truck:** No. 2 Dodge **Truck owner:** Marlene Smith

### Career Statistics

| Year | Rank | Starts | Wins | Poles | Top 5 | Top 10 | Races Led | Laps Led |
|---|---|---|---|---|---|---|---|---|
| 1997 | 48 | 4 | 0 | 0 | 0 | 0 | 0 | 0 |
| 1998 | 12 | 27 | 1 | 1 | 6 | 9 | 6 | 103 |
| 1999 | 8 | 25 | 0 | 1 | 5 | 14 | 3 | 17 |
| 2000 | 3 | 24 | 2 | 1 | 13 | 18 | 14 | 222 |
| 2002 | 38 | 5 | 0 | 0 | 0 | 0 | 0 | 0 |
| 2003 | 21 | 11 | 0 | 1 | 3 | 7 | 3 | 75 |
| Totals | | 96 | 3 | 4 | 27 | 48 | 26 | 417 |

## Marty Houston

**Birthdate:** 1/07/68 **Birth place:** Hickory, N.C. **Truck:** Dodge **Truck owner:** Ultra Motorsports

### Career Statistics

| Year | Rank | Starts | Wins | Poles | Top 5 | Top 10 | Races Led | Laps Led |
|---|---|---|---|---|---|---|---|---|
| 1999 | 23 | 19 | 0 | 0 | 0 | 1 | 1 | 4 |
| 2000 | 12 | 24 | 0 | 0 | 1 | 10 | 7 | 27 |
| 2003 | 120 | 1 | 0 | 0 | 0 | 0 | 0 | 0 |
| Totals | | 44 | 0 | 0 | 1 | 11 | 8 | 31 |

## Doug Keller

**Birthdate:** 12/4/72 **Birth place:** St. Joseph, Mo. **Truck:** No. 27 Chevrolet **Truck owner:** Doug Keller

### Career Statistics

| Year | Rank | Starts | Wins | Poles | Top 5 | Top 10 | Races Led | Laps Led |
|---|---|---|---|---|---|---|---|---|
| 2001 | 55 | 4 | 0 | 0 | 0 | 0 | 0 | 0 |
| 2002 | 41 | 5 | 0 | 0 | 0 | 0 | 0 | 0 |
| 2003 | 34 | 8 | 0 | 0 | 0 | 0 | 0 | 0 |
| Totals | | 17 | 0 | 0 | 0 | 0 | 0 | 0 |

## Travis Kvapil

**Birthdate:** 3/1/76 **Birth place:** Janesville, Wis. **Truck:** No. 24 Toyota **Truck owner:** Bang Racing

### Career Statistics

| Year | Rank | Starts | Wins | Poles | Top 5 | Top 10 | Races Led | Laps Led |
|---|---|---|---|---|---|---|---|---|
| 2001 | 4 | 24 | 1 | 0 | 11 | 18 | 9 | 55 |
| 2002 | 9 | 22 | 1 | 0 | 10 | 14 | 7 | 170 |
| 2003 | 1 | 25 | 1 | 0 | 13 | 22 | 11 | 49 |
| Totals | | 71 | 3 | 0 | 34 | 54 | 27 | 274 |

## Jody Lavender

**Birthdate:** 12/29/79 **Birth place:** Hartsville, S.C. **Truck:** No. 08 Chevrolet **Truck owners:** Gene Christensen, Bobby Dotter

### Career Statistics

| Year | Rank | Starts | Wins | Poles | Top 5 | Top 10 | Races Led | Laps Led |
|---|---|---|---|---|---|---|---|---|
| 2002 | 99 | 1 | 0 | 0 | 0 | 0 | 0 | 0 |
| 2003 | 17 | 21 | 0 | 0 | 0 | 0 | 1 | 1 |
| Totals | | 22 | 0 | 0 | 0 | 0 | 1 | 1 |

## Bill Lester

**Birthdate:** 2/6/61 **Birth place:** Oakland **Truck:** Toyota **Truck owner:** Bill Davis

### Career Statistics

| Year | Rank | Starts | Wins | Poles | Top 5 | Top 10 | Races Led | Laps Led |
|---|---|---|---|---|---|---|---|---|
| 2000 | 86 | 1 | 0 | 0 | 0 | 0 | 0 | 0 |
| 2001 | 59 | 5 | 0 | 0 | 0 | 0 | 0 | 0 |
| 2002 | 17 | 22 | 0 | 0 | 0 | 0 | 0 | 0 |
| 2003 | 14 | 25 | 0 | 1 | 0 | 1 | 2 | 17 |
| Totals | | 53 | 0 | 1 | 0 | 1 | 2 | 17 |

## Ted Musgrave

**Birthdate:** 12/18/55 **Birth place:** Franklin, Wis. **Truck:** No. 1 Dodge **Truck owner:** Jim Smith

### Career Statistics

| Year | Rank | Starts | Wins | Poles | Top 5 | Top 10 | Races Led | Laps Led |
|---|---|---|---|---|---|---|---|---|
| 1995 | 66 | 1 | 0 | 0 | 1 | 1 | 0 | 0 |
| 1996 | 69 | 2 | 0 | 0 | 1 | 1 | 0 | 0 |
| 2001 | 2 | 24 | 7 | 2 | 13 | 18 | 15 | 810 |
| 2002 | 3 | 22 | 3 | 3 | 12 | 16 | 15 | 757 |
| 2003 | 3 | 25 | 3 | 4 | 14 | 18 | 18 | 796 |
| Totals | | 74 | 13 | 9 | 41 | 54 | 48 | 2363 |

## Hank Parker Jr.

**Birthdate:** 10/7/74 **Birth place:** Denver, N.C. **Truck:** No. 21 Toyota **Truck owner:** George deBidart

## Buddy Rice

**Birthdate:** 1/31/76 **Birth place:** Phoenix **Truck:** Chevrolet **Truck owner:** Duke Thorson

### CAREER STATISTICS

| Year | Rank | Starts | Wins | Poles | Top 5 | Top 10 | Races Led | Laps Led |
|---|---|---|---|---|---|---|---|---|
| 2003 | 44 | 4 | 0 | 0 | 0 | 2 | 0 | 0 |
| Totals | | 4 | 0 | 0 | 0 | 2 | 0 | 0 |

## Buddy Rice

**Birthdate:** 1/31/76 **Birth place:** Phoenix **Truck:** Chevrolet **Truck owner:** Duke Thorson

### CAREER STATISTICS

| Year | Rank | Starts | Wins | Poles | Top 5 | Top 10 | Races Led | Laps Led |
|---|---|---|---|---|---|---|---|---|
| 2003 | 102 | 1 | 0 | 0 | 0 | 0 | 0 | 0 |
| Totals | | 1 | 0 | 0 | 0 | 0 | 0 | 0 |

## Ken Schrader

**Birthdate:** 5/29/55 **Birth place:** Fenton, Mo. **Truck:** No. 52 Chevrolet **Truck owner:** Ken Schrader

### CAREER STATISTICS

| Year | Rank | Starts | Wins | Poles | Top 5 | Top 10 | Races Led | Laps Led |
|---|---|---|---|---|---|---|---|---|
| 1995 | 29 | 7 | 1 | 0 | 3 | 3 | 1 | 54 |
| 1996 | 44 | 4 | 0 | 0 | 0 | 2 | 0 | 0 |
| 1997 | 61 | 2 | 0 | 0 | 0 | 1 | 1 | 48 |
| 1999 | 118 | 1 | 0 | 0 | 0 | 0 | 0 | 0 |
| 2000 | 35 | 5 | 0 | 0 | 1 | 3 | 1 | 59 |
| 2001 | 28 | 8 | 0 | 0 | 1 | 5 | 0 | 0 |
| 2002 | 27 | 8 | 0 | 0 | 0 | 3 | 0 | 0 |
| 2003 | 23 | 11 | 0 | 0 | 0 | 3 | 0 | 0 |
| Totals | | 46 | 1 | 0 | 5 | 20 | 3 | 161 |

## Dennis Setzer

**Birthdate:** 2/27/60 **Birth place:** Newton, N.C. **Truck:** No. 46 Chevrolet **Truck owners:** RobMorgan, David Dollar

### CAREER STATISTICS

| Year | Rank | Starts | Wins | Poles | Top 5 | Top 10 | Races Led | Laps Led |
|---|---|---|---|---|---|---|---|---|
| 1995 | 28 | 8 | 0 | 0 | 1 | 2 | 1 | 27 |
| 1997 | 124 | 1 | 0 | 0 | 0 | 0 | 0 | 0 |
| 1998 | 28 | 13 | 1 | 0 | 1 | 5 | 2 | 31 |
| 1999 | 3 | 25 | 3 | 1 | 11 | 19 | 12 | 427 |
| 2000 | 7 | 24 | 1 | 0 | 8 | 16 | 4 | 73 |
| 2001 | 9 | 24 | 1 | 2 | 8 | 15 | 7 | 99 |
| 2002 | 6 | 22 | 1 | 0 | 8 | 14 | 6 | 142 |
| 2003 | 2 | 25 | 3 | 0 | 15 | 23 | 8 | 437 |
| Totals | | 142 | 10 | 3 | 52 | 94 | 40 | 1236 |

## Mike Skinner

**Birthdate:** 6/28/57 **Birth place:** Susanville, Calif. **Truck:** No. 42 Toyota **Truck owner:** Bang Racing

### CAREER STATISTICS

| Year | Rank | Starts | Wins | Poles | Top 5 | Top 10 | Races Led | Laps Led |
|---|---|---|---|---|---|---|---|---|
| 1995 | 1 | 20 | 8 | 10 | 17 | 18 | 13 | 1053 |
| 1996 | 3 | 24 | 8 | 5 | 17 | 20 | 18 | 1533 |
| 1997 | 44 | 4 | 0 | 0 | 2 | 2 | 2 | 40 |
| 1998 | 49 | 2 | 0 | 0 | 1 | 1 | 1 | 4 |
| 2003 | 48 | 4 | 0 | 0 | 0 | 0 | 1 | 3 |
| Totals | | 54 | 16 | 15 | 37 | 41 | 35 | 2633 |

## Jack Sprague

**Birthdate:** 8/8/64 **Birth place:** Spring Lake, Mich. **Truck:** No. 16 Chevrolet **Truck owner:** Steve Coulter

### CAREER STATISTICS

| Year | Rank | Starts | Wins | Poles | Top 5 | Top 10 | Races Led | Laps Led |
|---|---|---|---|---|---|---|---|---|
| 1995 | 5 | 20 | 0 | 1 | 4 | 15 | 3 | 55 |
| 1996 | 2 | 24 | 5 | 2 | 18 | 21 | 10 | 733 |
| 1997 | 1 | 26 | 3 | 5 | 16 | 23 | 13 | 1004 |
| 1998 | 2 | 27 | 5 | 4 | 16 | 23 | 13 | 837 |
| 1999 | 1 | 25 | 3 | 1 | 16 | 19 | 15 | 581 |
| 2000 | 5 | 24 | 3 | 0 | 13 | 15 | 10 | 492 |
| 2001 | 1 | 24 | 4 | 7 | 15 | 17 | 19 | 1386 |
| 2003 | 66 | 2 | 0 | 0 | 2 | 2 | 0 | 0 |
| Totals | | 172 | 23 | 20 | 100 | 135 | 83 | 5088 |

## Darrell Waltrip

**Birthdate:** 2/5/47 **Birth place:** Owensboro, Ky. **Truck:** No. 17 Toyota **Truck owner:** Darrell Waltrip

### CAREER STATISTICS

| Year | Rank | Starts | Wins | Poles | Top 5 | Top 10 | Races Led | Laps Led |
|---|---|---|---|---|---|---|---|---|
| 1995 | 41 | 4 | 0 | 0 | 0 | 2 | 0 | 0 |
| 1996 | 34 | 5 | 0 | 0 | 1 | 3 | 0 | 0 |
| 2002 | 62 | 2 | 0 | 0 | 0 | 1 | 0 | 0 |
| 2003 | 59 | 3 | 0 | 0 | 0 | 2 | 0 | 0 |
| Totals | | 14 | 0 | 0 | 1 | 8 | 0 | 0 |

## Brandon Whitt

**Birthdate:** 10/15/82 **Birth place:** El Cajon, Calif. **Truck:** No. 38 Chevrolet **Truck owner:** Dan Whitt

### CAREER STATISTICS

| Year | Rank | Starts | Wins | Poles | Top 5 | Top 10 | Races Led | Laps Led |
|---|---|---|---|---|---|---|---|---|
| 2003 | 40 | 7 | 0 | 0 | 0 | 0 | 0 | 0 |
| Totals | | 7 | 0 | 0 | 0 | 0 | 0 | 0 |

## Jon Wood

**Birthdate:** 10/25/81 **Birth place:** Stuart, Va. **Truck:** Ford **Truck owner:** Jack Roush

### CAREER STATISTICS

| Year | Rank | Starts | Wins | Poles | Top 5 | Top 10 | Races Led | Laps Led |
|---|---|---|---|---|---|---|---|---|
| 2001 | 17 | 16 | 0 | 0 | 2 | 4 | 3 | 31 |
| 2002 | 12 | 22 | 0 | 0 | 0 | 10 | 1 | 13 |
| 2003 | 5 | 25 | 2 | 2 | 10 | 20 | 10 | 349 |
| Totals | | 63 | 2 | 2 | 12 | 34 | 14 | 393 |

# Selected drivers who competed in 2003

## T.J. Bell

**Birthdate:** 8/25/81 **Birth place:** Reno, Nev.

### CAREER STATISTICS

| Year | Rank | Starts | Wins | Poles | Top 5 | Top 10 | Races Led | Laps Led |
|---|---|---|---|---|---|---|---|---|
| 2003 | 26 | 12 | 0 | 0 | 0 | 0 | 0 | 0 |
| Totals | | 12 | 0 | 0 | 0 | 0 | 0 | 0 |

## Rick Bogart

**Birthdate:** 12/27/74 **Birth place:** El Cajon, Calif.

### CAREER STATISTICS

| Year | Rank | Starts | Wins | Poles | Top 5 | Top 10 | Races Led | Laps Led |
|---|---|---|---|---|---|---|---|---|
| 2002 | 109 | 1 | 0 | 0 | 0 | 0 | 0 | 0 |
| 2003 | 93 | 2 | 0 | 0 | 0 | 0 | 0 | 0 |
| Totals | | 3 | 0 | 0 | 0 | 0 | 0 | 0 |

## Robby Benton

**Birthdate:** 6/28/79 **Birth place:** Charlotte

### CAREER STATISTICS

| Year | Rank | Starts | Wins | Poles | Top 5 | Top 10 | Races Led | Laps Led |
|---|---|---|---|---|---|---|---|---|
| 2003 | 84 | 3 | 0 | 0 | 0 | 0 | 0 | 0 |
| Totals | | 3 | 0 | 0 | 0 | 0 | 0 | 0 |

## Phil Bonifield

**Birthdate:** 6/23/63 **Birth place:** Napa, Calif.

### CAREER STATISTICS

| Year | Rank | Starts | Wins | Poles | Top 5 | Top 10 | Races Led | Laps Led |
|---|---|---|---|---|---|---|---|---|
| 1999 | 31 | 14 | 0 | 0 | 0 | 0 | 0 | 0 |
| 2000 | 39 | 8 | 0 | 0 | 0 | 0 | 0 | 0 |
| 2001 | 33 | 12 | 0 | 0 | 0 | 0 | 0 | 0 |
| 2002 | 31 | 11 | 0 | 0 | 0 | 0 | 0 | 0 |
| 2003 | 20 | 21 | 0 | 0 | 0 | 0 | 0 | 0 |
| Totals | | 66 | 0 | 0 | 0 | 0 | 0 | 0 |

## Rich Bickle

**Birthdate:** 5/13/61 **Birth place:** Edgerton, Wis.

### CAREER STATISTICS

| Year | Rank | Starts | Wins | Poles | Top 5 | Top 10 | Races Led | Laps Led |
|---|---|---|---|---|---|---|---|---|
| 1996 | 11 | 24 | 0 | 2 | 5 | 9 | 3 | 180 |
| 1997 | 2 | 26 | 3 | 4 | 15 | 17 | 7 | 630 |
| 1998 | 40 | 4 | 0 | 0 | 1 | 3 | 0 | 0 |
| 1999 | 66 | 2 | 0 | 0 | 0 | 1 | 0 | 0 |
| 2002 | 28 | 6 | 0 | 0 | 0 | 1 | 0 | 0 |
| 2003 | 22 | 12 | 0 | 0 | 0 | 2 | 0 | 0 |
| Totals | | 74 | 3 | 6 | 21 | 33 | 10 | 810 |

## Stan Boyd

**Birthdate:** 9/16/70 **Birth place:** Holly, Mich.

### CAREER STATISTICS

| Year | Rank | Starts | Wins | Poles | Top 5 | Top 10 | Races Led | Laps Led |
|---|---|---|---|---|---|---|---|---|
| 1998 | 73 | 2 | 0 | 0 | 0 | 0 | 0 | 0 |
| 1999 | 43 | 5 | 0 | 0 | 0 | 0 | 0 | 0 |

| Year | Rank | Starts | Wins | Poles | Top 5 | Top 10 | Races Led | Laps Led |
|---|---|---|---|---|---|---|---|---|
| 2000 | 51 | 5 | 0 | 0 | 0 | 0 | 0 | 0 |
| 2001 | 35 | 10 | 0 | 0 | 0 | 0 | 0 | 0 |
| 2002 | 25 | 13 | 0 | 0 | 0 | 0 | 1 | 4 |
| 2003 | 32 | 12 | 0 | 0 | 0 | 0 | 0 | 0 |
| Totals | | 47 | 0 | 0 | 0 | 0 | 1 | 4 |

## Trevor Boys

**Birthdate:** 11/3/57 **Birth place:** Calgary Alberta, Canada

### CAREER STATISTICS

| Year | Rank | Starts | Wins | Poles | Top 5 | Top 10 | Races Led | Laps Led |
|---|---|---|---|---|---|---|---|---|
| 2003 | 49 | 6 | 0 | 0 | 0 | 0 | 0 | 0 |
| Totals | | 6 | 0 | 0 | 0 | 0 | 0 | 0 |

## Charlie Bradberry

**Birthdate:** 6/28/82 **Birth place:** Chelsea, Ala.

### CAREER STATISTICS

| Year | Rank | Starts | Wins | Poles | Top 5 | Top 10 | Races Led | Laps Led |
|---|---|---|---|---|---|---|---|---|
| 2003 | 53 | 5 | 0 | 0 | 0 | 0 | 0 | 0 |
| Totals | | 5 | 0 | 0 | 0 | 0 | 0 | 0 |

## Conrad Burr

**Birthdate:** 11/23/68 **Birth place:** Concord, N.C.

### CAREER STATISTICS

| Year | Rank | Starts | Wins | Poles | Top 5 | Top 10 | Races Led | Laps Led |
|---|---|---|---|---|---|---|---|---|
| 2000 | 84 | 1 | 0 | 0 | 0 | 0 | 0 | 0 |
| 2001 | 101 | 1 | 0 | 0 | 0 | 0 | 0 | 0 |
| 2002 | 46 | 5 | 0 | 0 | 0 | 0 | 0 | 0 |
| 2003 | 58 | 4 | 0 | 0 | 0 | 0 | 0 | 0 |
| Totals | | 11 | 0 | 0 | 0 | 0 | 0 | 0 |

## Johnny Chapman

**Birthdate:** 12/14/67 **Birth place:** Stony Point, N.C.

### CAREER STATISTICS

| Year | Rank | Starts | Wins | Poles | Top 5 | Top 10 | Races Led | Laps Led |
|---|---|---|---|---|---|---|---|---|
| 1996 | 57 | 4 | 0 | 0 | 0 | 0 | 0 | 0 |
| 1998 | 62 | 2 | 0 | 0 | 0 | 0 | 0 | 0 |
| 2003 | 45 | 6 | 0 | 0 | 0 | 0 | 0 | 0 |
| Totals | | 12 | 0 | 0 | 0 | 0 | 0 | 0 |

## Aaron Daniel

**Birthdate:** 2/24/67 **Birth place:** Kansas City, Mo.

### CAREER STATISTICS

| Year | Rank | Starts | Wins | Poles | Top 5 | Top 10 | Races Led | Laps Led |
|---|---|---|---|---|---|---|---|---|
| 2001 | 94 | 1 | 0 | 0 | 0 | 0 | 0 | 0 |
| 2002 | 43 | 6 | 0 | 0 | 0 | 0 | 0 | 0 |
| 2003 | 57 | 4 | 0 | 0 | 0 | 0 | 0 | 0 |
| Totals | | 11 | 0 | 0 | 0 | 0 | 0 | 0 |

## Michael Dokken

**Birthdate:** 6/4/71 **Birth place:** Clearwater, Fla.

### CAREER STATISTICS

| Year | Rank | Starts | Wins | Poles | Top 5 | Top 10 | Races Led | Laps Led |
|---|---|---|---|---|---|---|---|---|
| 1995 | 32 | 7 | 0 | 0 | 0 | 0 | 0 | 0 |
| 1996 | 19 | 20 | 0 | 0 | 0 | 3 | 0 | 0 |
| 1997 | 26 | 14 | 0 | 1 | 2 | 2 | 1 | 95 |
| 1999 | 44 | 5 | 0 | 0 | 0 | 0 | 0 | 0 |
| 2000 | 43 | 4 | 0 | 0 | 0 | 1 | 1 | 5 |
| 2001 | 34 | 10 | 0 | 0 | 0 | 0 | 0 | 0 |
| 2002 | 36 | 8 | 0 | 0 | 0 | 0 | 0 | 0 |
| 2003 | 56 | 6 | 0 | 0 | 0 | 0 | 0 | 0 |
| Totals | | 74 | 0 | 1 | 2 | 6 | 2 | 100 |

## Wayne Edwards

**Birthdate:** 6/23/67 **Birth place:** Shepherdsville, Ky.

### CAREER STATISTICS

| Year | Rank | Starts | Wins | Poles | Top 5 | Top 10 | Races Led | Laps Led |
|---|---|---|---|---|---|---|---|---|
| 2000 | 26 | 13 | 0 | 0 | 0 | 0 | 0 | 0 |
| 2001 | 91 | 2 | 0 | 0 | 0 | 0 | 0 | 0 |
| 2002 | 57 | 4 | 0 | 0 | 0 | 0 | 0 | 0 |
| 2003 | 39 | 8 | 0 | 0 | 0 | 0 | 0 | 0 |
| Totals | | 27 | 0 | 0 | 0 | 0 | 0 | 0 |

## Jay Godley

**Birthdate:** 5/21/81 **Birth place:** Concord, N.C.

### CAREER STATISTICS

| Year | Rank | Starts | Wins | Poles | Top 5 | Top 10 | Races Led | Laps Led |
|---|---|---|---|---|---|---|---|---|
| 2003 | 80 | 2 | 0 | 0 | 0 | 0 | 0 | 0 |
| Totals | | 2 | 0 | 0 | 0 | 0 | 0 | 0 |

## Kevin Harvick

**Birthdate:** 12/8/75 **Birth place:** Bakersfield, Calif.

### CAREER STATISTICS

| Year | Rank | Starts | Wins | Poles | Top 5 | Top 10 | Races Led | Laps Led |
|---|---|---|---|---|---|---|---|---|
| 1995 | 89 | 1 | 0 | 0 | 0 | 0 | 0 | 0 |
| 1996 | 55 | 4 | 0 | 0 | 0 | 0 | 0 | 0 |
| 1997 | 27 | 13 | 0 | 0 | 0 | 2 | 0 | 0 |
| 1998 | 17 | 26 | 0 | 0 | 3 | 5 | 5 | 19 |
| 1999 | 12 | 25 | 0 | 0 | 6 | 11 | 6 | 214 |
| 2001 | 122 | 1 | 0 | 0 | 1 | 1 | 1 | 1 |
| 2002 | 30 | 5 | 1 | 0 | 3 | 4 | 3 | 189 |
| 2003 | 30 | 6 | 1 | 0 | 3 | 4 | 4 | 300 |
| Totals | | 81 | 2 | 0 | 16 | 27 | 19 | 723 |

## Ryan Hemphill

**Birthdate:** 12/30/81 **Birth place:** Apollo, Pa.

### CAREER STATISTICS

| Year | Rank | Starts | Wins | Poles | Top 5 | Top 10 | Races Led | Laps Led |
|---|---|---|---|---|---|---|---|---|
| 2002 | 35 | 6 | 0 | 0 | 0 | 1 | 1 | 5 |
| 2003 | 68 | 3 | 0 | 0 | 0 | 0 | 0 | 0 |
| Totals | | 9 | 0 | 0 | 0 | 1 | 1 | 5 |

## Kenny Hendrick

**Birthdate:** 9/10/69 **Birth place:** Chino, Calif.

### CAREER STATISTICS

| Year | Rank | Starts | Wins | Poles | Top 5 | Top 10 | Races Led | Laps Led |
|---|---|---|---|---|---|---|---|---|
| 1996 | 59 | 4 | 0 | 0 | 0 | 0 | 0 | 0 |
| 1997 | 51 | 4 | 0 | 0 | 0 | 0 | 0 | 0 |
| 2003 | 35 | 12 | 0 | 0 | 0 | 0 | 0 | 0 |
| Totals | | 20 | 0 | 0 | 0 | 0 | 0 | 0 |

## Gary Higgs

**Birthdate:** 6/29/62 **Birth place:** Lakewood, Colo.

### CAREER STATISTICS

| Year | Rank | Starts | Wins | Poles | Top 5 | Top 10 | Races Led | Laps Led |
|---|---|---|---|---|---|---|---|---|
| 1997 | 108 | 1 | 0 | 0 | 0 | 0 | 0 | 0 |
| 2003 | 122 | 1 | 0 | 0 | 0 | 0 | 0 | 0 |
| Totals | | 2 | 0 | 0 | 0 | 0 | 0 | 0 |

## Jerry Hill

**Birthdate:** 7/25/61 **Birth place:** Port Tobacco, Md.

### CAREER STATISTICS

| Year | Rank | Starts | Wins | Poles | Top 5 | Top 10 | Races Led | Laps Led |
|---|---|---|---|---|---|---|---|---|
| 2001 | 25 | 13 | 0 | 0 | 0 | 0 | 0 | 0 |
| 2002 | 23 | 21 | 0 | 0 | 0 | 0 | 0 | 0 |
| 2003 | 18 | 22 | 0 | 0 | 0 | 0 | 0 | 0 |
| Totals | | 56 | 0 | 0 | 0 | 0 | 0 | 0 |

## Andy Hillenburg

**Birthdate:** 4/30/63 **Birth place:** Indianapolis

### CAREER STATISTICS

| Year | Rank | Starts | Wins | Poles | Top 5 | Top 10 | Races Led | Laps Led |
|---|---|---|---|---|---|---|---|---|
| 1995 | 98 | 1 | 0 | 0 | 0 | 0 | 0 | 0 |
| 1996 | 74 | 2 | 0 | 0 | 0 | 0 | 0 | 0 |
| 2003 | 97 | 1 | 0 | 0 | 0 | 0 | 0 | 0 |
| Totals | | 4 | 0 | 0 | 0 | 0 | 0 | 0 |

## Lance Hooper

**Birthdate:** 6/1/67 **Birth place:** Palmdale, Calif.

### CAREER STATISTICS

| Year | Rank | Starts | Wins | Poles | Top 5 | Top 10 | Races Led | Laps Led |
|---|---|---|---|---|---|---|---|---|
| 2000 | 28 | 13 | 0 | 0 | 0 | 0 | 0 | 0 |
| 2001 | 19 | 18 | 0 | 0 | 0 | 1 | 0 | 0 |
| 2002 | 20 | 22 | 0 | 0 | 0 | 0 | 1 | 1 |
| 2003 | 24 | 17 | 0 | 0 | 0 | 0 | 1 | 4 |
| Totals | | 70 | 0 | 0 | 0 | 1 | 2 | 5 |

## Chris Horn

**Birthdate:** 11/2/73 **Birth place:** Cedar Rapids, Iowa

### CAREER STATISTICS

| Year | Rank | Starts | Wins | Poles | Top 5 | Top 10 | Races Led | Laps Led |
|---|---|---|---|---|---|---|---|---|
| 1998 | 48 | 3 | 0 | 0 | 0 | 0 | 0 | 0 |
| 1999 | 51 | 4 | 0 | 0 | 0 | 0 | 0 | 0 |
| 2000 | 52 | 4 | 0 | 0 | 0 | 0 | 0 | 0 |
| 2001 | 52 | 5 | 0 | 0 | 0 | 0 | 1 | 3 |
| 2002 | 39 | 6 | 0 | 0 | 0 | 0 | 0 | 0 |
| 2003 | 36 | 7 | 0 | 0 | 0 | 0 | 0 | 0 |
| Totals | | 29 | 0 | 0 | 0 | 0 | 1 | 3 |

## Ronnie Hornaday

**Birthdate:** 8/1/79 **Birth place:** Palmdale, Calif.

### Career Statistics

| Year | Rank | Starts | Wins | Poles | Top 5 | Top 10 | Races Led | Laps Led |
|------|------|--------|------|-------|-------|--------|-----------|----------|
| 1999 | 37   | 5      | 0    | 0     | 0     | 0      | 0         | 0        |
| 2000 | 93   | 1      | 0    | 0     | 0     | 0      | 0         | 0        |
| 2001 | 45   | 5      | 0    | 0     | 0     | 0      | 0         | 0        |
| 2002 | 90   | 1      | 0    | 0     | 0     | 0      | 0         | 0        |
| 2003 | 91   | 2      | 0    | 0     | 0     | 0      | 0         | 0        |
| Totals | | 14 | 0 | 0 | 0 | 0 | 0 | 0 |

## Roland Isaacs

**Birthdate:** 6/10/57 **Birth place:** La Grange, Ky.

### Career Statistics

| Year | Rank | Starts | Wins | Poles | Top 5 | Top 10 | Races Led | Laps Led |
|------|------|--------|------|-------|-------|--------|-----------|----------|
| 2001 | 112  | 1      | 0    | 0     | 0     | 0      | 0         | 0        |
| 2003 | 38   | 9      | 0    | 0     | 0     | 0      | 0         | 0        |
| Totals | | 10 | 0 | 0 | 0 | 0 | 0 | 0 |

## Eric Jones

**Birthdate:** 7/12/77 **Birth place:** Granger, Iowa

### Career Statistics

| Year | Rank | Starts | Wins | Poles | Top 5 | Top 10 | Races Led | Laps Led |
|------|------|--------|------|-------|-------|--------|-----------|----------|
| 2001 | 54   | 4      | 0    | 0     | 0     | 0      | 0         | 0        |
| 2002 | 29   | 9      | 0    | 0     | 0     | 0      | 0         | 0        |
| 2003 | 27   | 9      | 0    | 0     | 0     | 1      | 0         | 0        |
| Totals | | 22 | 0 | 0 | 0 | 1 | 0 | 0 |

## P.J. Jones

**Birthdate:** 4/23/69 **Birth place:** Torrance, Calif.

### Career Statistics

| Year | Rank | Starts | Wins | Poles | Top 5 | Top 10 | Races Led | Laps Led |
|------|------|--------|------|-------|-------|--------|-----------|----------|
| 1995 | 17   | 13     | 0    | 0     | 1     | 2      | 2         | 10       |
| 2003 | 92   | 1      | 0    | 0     | 0     | 1      | 0         | 0        |
| Totals | | 14 | 0 | 0 | 1 | 3 | 2 | 10 |

## Frank Kimmel

**Birthdate:** 4/30/62 **Birth place:** Clarksville, Ind.

### Career Statistics

| Year | Rank | Starts | Wins | Poles | Top 5 | Top 10 | Races Led | Laps Led |
|------|------|--------|------|-------|-------|--------|-----------|----------|
| 1995 | 80   | 1      | 0    | 0     | 0     | 0      | 0         | 0        |
| 1996 | 45   | 4      | 0    | 0     | 0     | 1      | 0         | 0        |
| 1997 | 119  | 1      | 0    | 0     | 0     | 0      | 0         | 0        |
| 1998 | 79   | 1      | 0    | 0     | 0     | 0      | 0         | 0        |
| 2001 | 97   | 1      | 0    | 0     | 0     | 0      | 0         | 0        |
| 2003 | 117  | 1      | 0    | 0     | 0     | 0      | 0         | 0        |
| Totals | | 9 | 0 | 0 | 0 | 1 | 0 | 0 |

## Gilbert King

**Birthdate:** 2/24/65 **Birth place:** Chesterfield, S.C.

### Career Statistics

| Year | Rank | Starts | Wins | Poles | Top 5 | Top 10 | Races Led | Laps Led |
|------|------|--------|------|-------|-------|--------|-----------|----------|
| 2003 | 118  | 1      | 0    | 0     | 0     | 0      | 0         | 0        |
| Totals | | 1 | 0 | 0 | 0 | 0 | 0 | 0 |

## Stuart Kirby

**Birthdate:** 5/9/81 **Birth place:** Bowling Green, Ky.

### Career Statistics

| Year | Rank | Starts | Wins | Poles | Top 5 | Top 10 | Races Led | Laps Led |
|------|------|--------|------|-------|-------|--------|-----------|----------|
| 2003 | 82   | 2      | 0    | 0     | 0     | 0      | 0         | 0        |
| Totals | | 2 | 0 | 0 | 0 | 0 | 0 | 0 |

## Patrick Lawler

**Birthdate:** 10/24/63 **Birth place:** Colleyville, Texas

### Career Statistics

| Year | Rank | Starts | Wins | Poles | Top 5 | Top 10 | Races Led | Laps Led |
|------|------|--------|------|-------|-------|--------|-----------|----------|
| 2000 | 59   | 3      | 0    | 0     | 0     | 0      | 0         | 0        |
| 2001 | 105  | 1      | 0    | 0     | 0     | 0      | 0         | 0        |
| 2002 | 106  | 1      | 0    | 0     | 0     | 0      | 0         | 0        |
| 2003 | 101  | 2      | 0    | 0     | 0     | 0      | 0         | 0        |
| Totals | | 7 | 0 | 0 | 0 | 0 | 0 | 0 |

## Jason Leffler

**Birthdate:** 9/16/75 **Birth place:** Long Beach, Calif.

### Career Statistics

| Year | Rank | Starts | Wins | Poles | Top 5 | Top 10 | Races Led | Laps Led |
|------|------|--------|------|-------|-------|--------|-----------|----------|
| 2000 | 103  | 1      | 0    | 0     | 0     | 0      | 0         | 0        |
| 2002 | 4    | 22     | 0    | 8     | 11    | 15     | 15        | 494      |
| 2003 | 16   | 16     | 1    | 2     | 5     | 10     | 11        | 214      |
| Totals | | 39 | 1 | 10 | 16 | 25 | 26 | 708 |

## Jon Lemke

**Birthdate:** 6/25/68 **Birth place:** Greenfield, Minn.

### CAREER STATISTICS

| Year | Rank | Starts | Wins | Poles | Top 5 | Top 10 | Races Led | Laps Led |
|------|------|--------|------|-------|-------|--------|-----------|----------|
| 2003 | 123  | 1      | 0    | 0     | 0     | 0      | 0         | 0        |
| Totals |    | 1      | 0    | 0     | 0     | 0      | 0         | 0        |

## Carl Long

**Birthdate:** 9/20/67 **Birth place:** Roxboro, N.C.

### CAREER STATISTICS

| Year | Rank | Starts | Wins | Poles | Top 5 | Top 10 | Races Led | Laps Led |
|------|------|--------|------|-------|-------|--------|-----------|----------|
| 1998 | 101  | 1      | 0    | 0     | 0     | 0      | 0         | 0        |
| 1999 | 61   | 2      | 0    | 0     | 0     | 0      | 0         | 0        |
| 2000 | 70   | 1      | 0    | 0     | 0     | 0      | 0         | 0        |
| 2002 | 91   | 2      | 0    | 0     | 0     | 0      | 0         | 0        |
| 2003 | 130  | 1      | 0    | 0     | 0     | 0      | 0         | 0        |
| Totals |    | 7      | 0    | 0     | 0     | 0      | 0         | 0        |

## Scott Lynch

**Birthdate:** 5/14/80 **Birth place:** Burley, Idaho

### CAREER STATISTICS

| Year | Rank | Starts | Wins | Poles | Top 5 | Top 10 | Races Led | Laps Led |
|------|------|--------|------|-------|-------|--------|-----------|----------|
| 2003 | 74   | 2      | 0    | 0     | 0     | 0      | 0         | 0        |
| Totals |    | 2      | 0    | 0     | 0     | 0      | 0         | 0        |

## Randy MacDonald

**Birthdate:** 7/26/62 **Birth place:** Oshawa, Ontario

### CAREER STATISTICS

| Year | Rank | Starts | Wins | Poles | Top 5 | Top 10 | Races Led | Laps Led |
|------|------|--------|------|-------|-------|--------|-----------|----------|
| 1996 | 112  | 1      | 0    | 0     | 0     | 0      | 0         | 0        |
| 1997 | 52   | 4      | 0    | 0     | 0     | 0      | 0         | 0        |
| 1998 | 32   | 10     | 0    | 0     | 0     | 1      | 0         | 0        |
| 1999 | 40   | 5      | 0    | 0     | 0     | 0      | 0         | 0        |
| 2000 | 19   | 24     | 0    | 0     | 0     | 1      | 0         | 0        |
| 2001 | 107  | 1      | 0    | 0     | 0     | 0      | 0         | 0        |
| 2002 | 19   | 22     | 0    | 0     | 0     | 0      | 0         | 0        |
| 2003 | 15   | 25     | 0    | 0     | 0     | 0      | 0         | 0        |
| Totals |    | 92     | 0    | 0     | 0     | 2      | 0         | 0        |

## Teri MacDonald

**Birthdate:** 11/8/63 **Birth place:** Whitby, Ontario

## CAREER STATISTICS

| Year | Rank | Starts | Wins | Poles | Top 5 | Top 10 | Races Led | Laps Led |
|------|------|--------|------|-------|-------|--------|-----------|----------|
| 2002 | 55   | 4      | 0    | 0     | 0     | 0      | 0         | 0        |
| 2003 | 119  | 1      | 0    | 0     | 0     | 0      | 0         | 0        |
| Totals |    | 5      | 0    | 0     | 0     | 0      | 0         | 0        |

## Doug Mahlik

**Birthdate:** 5/20/68 **Birth place:** Green Bay

### CAREER STATISTICS

| Year | Rank | Starts | Wins | Poles | Top 5 | Top 10 | Races Led | Laps Led |
|------|------|--------|------|-------|-------|--------|-----------|----------|
| 2003 | 103  | 1      | 0    | 0     | 0     | 0      | 0         | 0        |
| Totals |    | 1      | 0    | 0     | 0     | 0      | 0         | 0        |

## Blake Mallory

**Birthdate:** 3/2/80 **Birth place:** Joshua, Texas

### CAREER STATISTICS

| Year | Rank | Starts | Wins | Poles | Top 5 | Top 10 | Races Led | Laps Led |
|------|------|--------|------|-------|-------|--------|-----------|----------|
| 2002 | 67   | 2      | 0    | 0     | 0     | 0      | 0         | 0        |
| 2003 | 62   | 4      | 0    | 0     | 0     | 0      | 0         | 0        |
| Totals |    | 6      | 0    | 0     | 0     | 0      | 0         | 0        |

## Steadman Marlin

**Birthdate:** 10/29/80 **Birth place:** Columbia, Tenn.

### CAREER STATISTICS

| Year | Rank | Starts | Wins | Poles | Top 5 | Top 10 | Races Led | Laps Led |
|------|------|--------|------|-------|-------|--------|-----------|----------|
| 2003 | 133  | 1      | 0    | 0     | 0     | 0      | 0         | 0        |
| Totals |    | 1      | 0    | 0     | 0     | 0      | 0         | 0        |

## Matt McCall

**Birthdate:** 7/3/81 **Birth place:** Denver, N.C.

### CAREER STATISTICS

| Year | Rank | Starts | Wins | Poles | Top 5 | Top 10 | Races Led | Laps Led |
|------|------|--------|------|-------|-------|--------|-----------|----------|
| 2003 | 105  | 1      | 0    | 0     | 0     | 0      | 0         | 0        |
| Totals |    | 1      | 0    | 0     | 0     | 0      | 0         | 0        |

## Mark McFarland

**Birthdate:** 2/1/78

### CAREER STATISTICS

| Year | Rank | Starts | Wins | Poles | Top 5 | Top 10 | Races Led | Laps Led |
|---|---|---|---|---|---|---|---|---|
| 2003 | 67 | 3 | 0 | 0 | 0 | 0 | 0 | 0 |
| Totals | | 3 | 0 | 0 | 0 | 0 | 0 | 0 |

## Ryan McGlynn
**Birthdate:** 11/22/74 **Birth place:** Shickshinny, Pa.

### CAREER STATISTICS

| Year | Rank | Starts | Wins | Poles | Top 5 | Top 10 | Races Led | Laps Led |
|---|---|---|---|---|---|---|---|---|
| 1998 | 67 | 2 | 0 | 0 | 0 | 0 | 0 | 0 |
| 1999 | 29 | 13 | 0 | 0 | 0 | 0 | 0 | 0 |
| 2000 | 25 | 18 | 0 | 0 | 0 | 0 | 0 | 0 |
| 2001 | 58 | 3 | 0 | 0 | 0 | 0 | 0 | 0 |
| 2002 | 60 | 3 | 0 | 0 | 0 | 0 | 0 | 0 |
| 2003 | 60 | 5 | 0 | 0 | 0 | 0 | 0 | 0 |
| Totals | | 44 | 0 | 0 | 0 | 0 | 0 | 0 |

## Paul Menard
**Birthdate:** 8/21/80 **Birth place:** EauClaire, Wis.

### CAREER STATISTICS

| Year | Rank | Starts | Wins | Poles | Top 5 | Top 10 | Races Led | Laps Led |
|---|---|---|---|---|---|---|---|---|
| 2003 | 42 | 5 | 0 | 0 | 0 | 1 | 0 | 0 |
| Totals | | 5 | 0 | 0 | 0 | 1 | 0 | 0 |

## G.J. Mennen
**Birthdate:** 5/13/72 **Birth place:** Austin, Texas

### CAREER STATISTICS

| Year | Rank | Starts | Wins | Poles | Top 5 | Top 10 | Races Led | Laps Led |
|---|---|---|---|---|---|---|---|---|
| 2001 | 70 | 1 | 0 | 0 | 0 | 0 | 0 | 0 |
| 2003 | 89 | 2 | 0 | 0 | 0 | 0 | 0 | 0 |
| Totals | | 3 | 0 | 0 | 0 | 0 | 0 | 0 |

## Brandon Miller
**Birthdate:** 8/28/81 **Birth place:** Bakersfield, Calif.

### CAREER STATISTICS

| Year | Rank | Starts | Wins | Poles | Top 5 | Top 10 | Races Led | Laps Led |
|---|---|---|---|---|---|---|---|---|
| 2003 | 51 | 4 | 0 | 0 | 0 | 1 | 0 | 0 |
| Totals | | 4 | 0 | 0 | 0 | 1 | 0 | 0 |

## Jerry Miller
**Birthdate:** 2/16/58 **Birth place:** Allentown, Pa.

### CAREER STATISTICS

| Year | Rank | Starts | Wins | Poles | Top 5 | Top 10 | Races Led | Laps Led |
|---|---|---|---|---|---|---|---|---|
| 1999 | 105 | 1 | 0 | 0 | 0 | 0 | 0 | 0 |
| 2000 | 87 | 1 | 0 | 0 | 0 | 0 | 0 | 0 |
| 2001 | 96 | 2 | 0 | 0 | 0 | 0 | 0 | 0 |
| 2002 | 103 | 1 | 0 | 0 | 0 | 0 | 0 | 0 |
| 2003 | 109 | 1 | 0 | 0 | 0 | 0 | 0 | 0 |
| Totals | | 6 | 0 | 0 | 0 | 0 | 0 | 0 |

## L.W. Miller
**Birthdate:** 7/20/73 **Birth place:** Dushore, Pa.

### CAREER STATISTICS

| Year | Rank | Starts | Wins | Poles | Top 5 | Top 10 | Races Led | Laps Led |
|---|---|---|---|---|---|---|---|---|
| 2003 | 43 | 6 | 0 | 0 | 0 | 0 | 0 | 0 |
| Totals | | 6 | 0 | 0 | 0 | 0 | 0 | 0 |

## Chase Montgomery
**Birthdate:** 9/29/83 **Birth place:** Lebanon, Tenn.

### CAREER STATISTICS

| Year | Rank | Starts | Wins | Poles | Top 5 | Top 10 | Races Led | Laps Led |
|---|---|---|---|---|---|---|---|---|
| 2003 | 106 | 1 | 0 | 0 | 0 | 0 | 0 | 0 |
| Totals | | 1 | 0 | 0 | 0 | 0 | 0 | 0 |

## Alex Mueller
**Birthdate:** 1/20/79 **Birth place:** Rees, Germany

### CAREER STATISTICS

| Year | Rank | Starts | Wins | Poles | Top 5 | Top 10 | Races Led | Laps Led |
|---|---|---|---|---|---|---|---|---|
| 2003 | 88 | 2 | 0 | 0 | 0 | 0 | 0 | 0 |
| Totals | | 2 | 0 | 0 | 0 | 0 | 0 | 0 |

## Donnie Neuenberger
**Birthdate:** 8/10/62 **Birth place:** Brandywine, Md.

### CAREER STATISTICS

| Year | Rank | Starts | Wins | Poles | Top 5 | Top 10 | Races Led | Laps Led |
|---|---|---|---|---|---|---|---|---|
| 2000 | 60 | 2 | 0 | 0 | 0 | 1 | 0 | 0 |
| 2001 | 50 | 6 | 0 | 0 | 0 | 0 | 0 | 0 |
| 2002 | 71 | 2 | 0 | 0 | 0 | 0 | 0 | 0 |
| 2003 | 86 | 2 | 0 | 0 | 0 | 0 | 0 | 0 |
| Totals | | 12 | 0 | 0 | 0 | 1 | 0 | 0 |

## Andy Petree

**Birthdate:** 8/15/58 **Birth place:** Newton, N.C.

### CAREER STATISTICS

| Year | Rank | Starts | Wins | Poles | Top 5 | Top 10 | Races Led | Laps Led |
|---|---|---|---|---|---|---|---|---|
| 2002 | 64 | 2 | 0 | 0 | 0 | 0 | 1 | 13 |
| 2003 | 50 | 4 | 0 | 0 | 0 | 1 | 0 | 0 |
| Totals | | 6 | 0 | 0 | 0 | 1 | 1 | 13 |

## Tom Pistone III

**Birthdate:** 7/9/74 **Birth place:** Charlotte

### CAREER STATISTICS

| Year | Rank | Starts | Wins | Poles | Top 5 | Top 10 | Races Led | Laps Led |
|---|---|---|---|---|---|---|---|---|
| 2002 | 85 | 1 | 0 | 0 | 0 | 0 | 0 | 0 |
| 2003 | 112 | 1 | 0 | 0 | 0 | 0 | 0 | 0 |
| Totals | | 2 | 0 | 0 | 0 | 0 | 0 | 0 |

## Ron Polodna

### CAREER STATISTICS

| Year | Rank | Starts | Wins | Poles | Top 5 | Top 10 | Races Led | Laps Led |
|---|---|---|---|---|---|---|---|---|
| 2003 | 114 | 1 | 0 | 0 | 0 | 0 | 0 | 0 |
| Totals | | 1 | 0 | 0 | 0 | 0 | 0 | 0 |

## Andy Ponstein

**Birthdate:** 5/22/76 **Birth place:** Hudsonville, Mich.

### CAREER STATISTICS

| Year | Rank | Starts | Wins | Poles | Top 5 | Top 10 | Races Led | Laps Led |
|---|---|---|---|---|---|---|---|---|
| 2003 | 83 | 2 | 0 | 0 | 0 | 0 | 0 | 0 |
| Totals | | 2 | 0 | 0 | 0 | 0 | 0 | 0 |

## Robert Pressley

**Birthdate:** 4/8/59 **Birth place:** Asheville, N.C.

### CAREER STATISTICS

| Year | Rank | Starts | Wins | Poles | Top 5 | Top 10 | Races Led | Laps Led |
|---|---|---|---|---|---|---|---|---|
| 2002 | 7 | 22 | 2 | 0 | 7 | 15 | 8 | 185 |
| 2003 | 12 | 22 | 0 | 0 | 4 | 9 | 2 | 10 |
| Totals | | 44 | 2 | 0 | 11 | 24 | 10 | 195 |

## Jonathon Price

**Birthdate:** 12/3/73 **Birth place:** Buffalo

### CAREER STATISTICS

| Year | Rank | Starts | Wins | Poles | Top 5 | Top 10 | Races Led | Laps Led |
|---|---|---|---|---|---|---|---|---|
| 2001 | 46 | 8 | 0 | 0 | 0 | 0 | 0 | 0 |
| 2002 | 74 | 2 | 0 | 0 | 0 | 0 | 0 | 0 |
| 2003 | 70 | 4 | 0 | 0 | 0 | 0 | 0 | 0 |
| Totals | | 14 | 0 | 0 | 0 | 0 | 0 | 0 |

## Bryan Reffner

**Birthdate:** 11/6/63 **Birth place:** Wisconsin Rapids, Wis.

### CAREER STATISTICS

| Year | Rank | Starts | Wins | Poles | Top 5 | Top 10 | Races Led | Laps Led |
|---|---|---|---|---|---|---|---|---|
| 1996 | 9 | 24 | 0 | 3 | 3 | 9 | 1 | 3 |
| 1997 | 19 | 26 | 0 | 0 | 0 | 2 | 1 | 1 |
| 1998 | 22 | 26 | 0 | 0 | 2 | 8 | 1 | 2 |
| 1999 | 26 | 13 | 0 | 0 | 0 | 0 | 2 | 6 |
| 2000 | 9 | 24 | 1 | 2 | 3 | 16 | 6 | 148 |
| 2001 | 30 | 8 | 0 | 0 | 1 | 3 | 2 | 2 |
| 2002 | 63 | 3 | 0 | 0 | 0 | 0 | 0 | 0 |
| 2003 | 81 | 2 | 0 | 0 | 0 | 0 | 0 | 0 |
| Totals | | 126 | 1 | 5 | 9 | 38 | 13 | 162 |

## Randy Renfrow

**Birthdate:** 1/28/58 **Birth place:** Wilson, N.C.

### CAREER STATISTICS

| Year | Rank | Starts | Wins | Poles | Top 5 | Top 10 | Races Led | Laps Led |
|---|---|---|---|---|---|---|---|---|
| 1996 | 36 | 7 | 0 | 0 | 0 | 0 | 0 | 0 |
| 1997 | 78 | 2 | 0 | 0 | 0 | 0 | 0 | 0 |
| 1998 | 30 | 12 | 0 | 0 | 0 | 1 | 3 | 64 |
| 1999 | 30 | 9 | 0 | 0 | 0 | 1 | 4 | 61 |
| 2000 | 23 | 15 | 0 | 0 | 1 | 4 | 1 | 8 |
| 2003 | 76 | 3 | 0 | 0 | 0 | 0 | 0 | 0 |
| Totals | | 48 | 0 | 0 | 1 | 6 | 8 | 133 |

## Stephen Rhodes

**Birthdate:** 3/27/84 **Birth place:** Goldsboro, N.C.

### CAREER STATISTICS

| Year | Rank | Starts | Wins | Poles | Top 5 | Top 10 | Races Led | Laps Led |
|---|---|---|---|---|---|---|---|---|
| 2003 | 87 | 2 | 0 | 0 | 0 | 0 | 0 | 0 |
| Totals | | 2 | 0 | 0 | 0 | 0 | 0 | 0 |

## Loni Richardson

**Birthdate:** 11/11/70 **Birth place:** Paris, Texas

### CAREER STATISTICS

| Year | Rank | Starts | Wins | Poles | Top 5 | Top 10 | Races Led | Laps Led |
|---|---|---|---|---|---|---|---|---|
| 2001 | 57 | 4 | 0 | 0 | 0 | 0 | 0 | 0 |
| 2002 | 42 | 7 | 0 | 0 | 0 | 0 | 0 | 0 |
| 2003 | 73 | 3 | 0 | 0 | 0 | 0 | 0 | 0 |
| Totals | | 14 | 0 | 0 | 0 | 0 | 0 | 0 |

## Jarod Robie

**Birthdate:** 12/11/79 **Birth place:** Candia, N.H.

### CAREER STATISTICS

| Year | Rank | Starts | Wins | Poles | Top 5 | Top 10 | Races Led | Laps Led |
|---|---|---|---|---|---|---|---|---|
| 2003 | 113 | 1 | 0 | 0 | 0 | 0 | 0 | 0 |
| Totals | | 1 | 0 | 0 | 0 | 0 | 0 | 0 |

## Shawna Robinson

**Birthdate:** 11/30/64 **Birth place:** Des Moines, Iowa

### CAREER STATISTICS

| Year | Rank | Starts | Wins | Poles | Top 5 | Top 10 | Races Led | Laps Led |
|---|---|---|---|---|---|---|---|---|
| 2003 | 72 | 3 | 0 | 0 | 0 | 0 | 0 | 0 |
| Totals | | 3 | 0 | 0 | 0 | 0 | 0 | 0 |

## Brian Rose

**Birthdate:** 10/19/79 **Birth place:** Bowling Green, Ky.

### CAREER STATISTICS

| Year | Rank | Starts | Wins | Poles | Top 5 | Top 10 | Races Led | Laps Led |
|---|---|---|---|---|---|---|---|---|
| 2001 | 22 | 15 | 0 | 0 | 0 | 0 | 1 | 7 |
| 2002 | 22 | 21 | 0 | 0 | 1 | 5 | 3 | 28 |
| 2003 | 78 | 2 | 0 | 0 | 0 | 0 | 0 | 0 |
| Totals | | 38 | 0 | 0 | 1 | 5 | 4 | 35 |

## Ricky Sanders

**Birthdate:** 7/30/66 **Birth place:** Stockbridge, Ga.

### CAREER STATISTICS

| Year | Rank | Starts | Wins | Poles | Top 5 | Top 10 | Races Led | Laps Led |
|---|---|---|---|---|---|---|---|---|
| 2000 | 36 | 5 | 0 | 0 | 0 | 0 | 0 | 0 |
| 2001 | 27 | 13 | 0 | 0 | 0 | 0 | 0 | 0 |
| 2002 | 58 | 3 | 0 | 0 | 0 | 0 | 0 | 0 |
| 2003 | 41 | 6 | 0 | 0 | 0 | 0 | 0 | 0 |
| Totals | | 27 | 0 | 0 | 0 | 0 | 0 | 0 |

## Scotty Sands

**Birthdate:** 11/17/71 **Birth place:** Henryville, Ind.

### CAREER STATISTICS

| Year | Rank | Starts | Wins | Poles | Top 5 | Top 10 | Races Led | Laps Led |
|---|---|---|---|---|---|---|---|---|
| 1999 | 70 | 1 | 0 | 0 | 0 | 0 | 0 | 0 |
| 2003 | 129 | 1 | 0 | 0 | 0 | 0 | 0 | 0 |
| Totals | | 2 | 0 | 0 | 0 | 0 | 0 | 0 |

## Tim Sauter

**Birthdate:** 10/13/64 **Birth place:** Necedah, Wis.

### CAREER STATISTICS

| Year | Rank | Starts | Wins | Poles | Top 5 | Top 10 | Races Led | Laps Led |
|---|---|---|---|---|---|---|---|---|
| 2003 | 77 | 3 | 0 | 0 | 0 | 0 | 0 | 0 |
| Totals | | 3 | 0 | 0 | 0 | 0 | 0 | 0 |

## Morgan Shepherd

**Birthdate:** 10/21/41 **Birth place:** Conover, N.C.

### CAREER STATISTICS

| Year | Rank | Starts | Wins | Poles | Top 5 | Top 10 | Races Led | Laps Led |
|---|---|---|---|---|---|---|---|---|
| 1997 | 110 | 1 | 0 | 0 | 0 | 0 | 0 | 0 |
| 2000 | 47 | 3 | 0 | 0 | 0 | 0 | 1 | 1 |
| 2001 | 26 | 16 | 0 | 0 | 0 | 0 | 2 | 17 |
| 2002 | 24 | 15 | 0 | 0 | 0 | 0 | 0 | 0 |
| 2003 | 28 | 16 | 0 | 0 | 0 | 0 | 1 | 7 |
| Totals | | 51 | 0 | 0 | 0 | 0 | 4 | 25 |

## Jay Sherston

**Birthdate:** 4/25/61 **Birth place:** Howell, Mich.

### CAREER STATISTICS

| Year | Rank | Starts | Wins | Poles | Top 5 | Top 10 | Races Led | Laps Led |
|---|---|---|---|---|---|---|---|---|
| 2003 | 110 | 1 | 0 | 0 | 0 | 0 | 0 | 0 |
| Totals | | 1 | 0 | 0 | 0 | 0 | 0 | 0 |

## Shane Sieg
**Birthdate:** 8/23/82 **Birth place:** Tucker, Ga.

### CAREER STATISTICS

| Year | Rank | Starts | Wins | Poles | Top 5 | Top 10 | Races Led | Laps Led |
|---|---|---|---|---|---|---|---|---|
| 2003 | 52 | 4 | 0 | 0 | 0 | 0 | 0 | 0 |
| Totals | | 4 | 0 | 0 | 0 | 0 | 0 | 0 |

## Jason Small
**Birthdate:** 6/7/79 **Birth place:** Bakersfield, Calif.

### CAREER STATISTICS

| Year | Rank | Starts | Wins | Poles | Top 5 | Top 10 | Races Led | Laps Led |
|---|---|---|---|---|---|---|---|---|
| 2000 | 102 | 2 | 0 | 0 | 0 | 0 | 0 | 0 |
| 2001 | 53 | 5 | 0 | 0 | 0 | 0 | 0 | 0 |
| 2002 | 21 | 22 | 0 | 0 | 0 | 2 | 0 | 0 |
| 2003 | 64 | 3 | 0 | 0 | 0 | 1 | 0 | 0 |
| Totals | | 32 | 0 | 0 | 0 | 3 | 0 | 0 |

## Brian Sockwell
**Birthdate:** 6/7/68 **Birth place:** Brown Summit, N.C.

### CAREER STATISTICS

| Year | Rank | Starts | Wins | Poles | Top 5 | Top 10 | Races Led | Laps Led |
|---|---|---|---|---|---|---|---|---|
| 1999 | 45 | 3 | 0 | 0 | 0 | 0 | 0 | 0 |
| 2000 | 50 | 4 | 0 | 0 | 0 | 0 | 0 | 0 |
| 2001 | 51 | 5 | 0 | 0 | 0 | 0 | 0 | 0 |
| 2002 | 47 | 5 | 0 | 0 | 0 | 0 | 0 | 0 |
| 2003 | 61 | 4 | 0 | 0 | 0 | 0 | 0 | 0 |
| Totals | | 21 | 0 | 0 | 0 | 0 | 0 | 0 |

## Jimmy Spencer
**Birthdate:** 2/15/57 **Birth place:** Berwick, Pa.

### CAREER STATISTICS

| Year | Rank | Starts | Wins | Poles | Top 5 | Top 10 | Races Led | Laps Led |
|---|---|---|---|---|---|---|---|---|
| 2003 | 55 | 3 | 1 | 1 | 1 | 2 | 2 | 125 |
| Totals | | 3 | 1 | 1 | 1 | 2 | 2 | 125 |

## David Starr
**Birthdate:** 10/11/67 **Birth place:** Houston

### CAREER STATISTICS

| Year | Rank | Starts | Wins | Poles | Top 5 | Top 10 | Races Led | Laps Led |
|---|---|---|---|---|---|---|---|---|
| 1998 | 43 | 5 | 0 | 0 | 0 | 0 | 1 | 1 |
| 1999 | 22 | 24 | 0 | 0 | 0 | 0 | 1 | 8 |
| 2000 | 29 | 13 | 0 | 0 | 0 | 0 | 1 | 6 |
| 2001 | 47 | 5 | 0 | 0 | 3 | 4 | 0 | 0 |
| 2002 | 5 | 22 | 1 | 2 | 8 | 16 | 8 | 111 |
| 2003 | 13 | 21 | 0 | 0 | 5 | 13 | 3 | 16 |
| Totals | | 90 | 1 | 2 | 16 | 33 | 14 | 142 |

## Tony Stewart
**Birthdate:** 5/20/71 **Birth place:** Rushville, Ind.

### CAREER STATISTICS

| Year | Rank | Starts | Wins | Poles | Top 5 | Top 10 | Races Led | Laps Led |
|---|---|---|---|---|---|---|---|---|
| 1996 | 87 | 1 | 0 | 0 | 0 | 1 | 0 | 0 |
| 2002 | 69 | 1 | 1 | 0 | 1 | 1 | 1 | 34 |
| 2003 | 85 | 1 | 1 | 0 | 1 | 1 | 1 | 32 |
| Totals | | 3 | 2 | 0 | 2 | 3 | 2 | 66 |

## John Stout
**Birthdate:** 9/15/83 **Birth place:** Castile, N.Y.

### CAREER STATISTICS

| Year | Rank | Starts | Wins | Poles | Top 5 | Top 10 | Races Led | Laps Led |
|---|---|---|---|---|---|---|---|---|
| 2003 | 75 | 3 | 0 | 0 | 0 | 0 | 0 | 0 |
| Totals | | 3 | 0 | 0 | 0 | 0 | 0 | 0 |

## David Stover
**Birthdate:** 12/13/79 **Birth place:** Tulsa, Okla.

### CAREER STATISTICS

| Year | Rank | Starts | Wins | Poles | Top 5 | Top 10 | Races Led | Laps Led |
|---|---|---|---|---|---|---|---|---|
| 2003 | 37 | 7 | 0 | 0 | 0 | 0 | 0 | 0 |
| Totals | | 7 | 0 | 0 | 0 | 0 | 0 | 0 |

## Kelly Sutton
**Birthdate:** 9/24/71 **Birth place:** Crownsville, Md.

## Brad Teague

**Birthdate:** 12/9/47 **Birth place:** Johnson City, Tenn.

### CAREER STATISTICS

| Year | Rank | Starts | Wins | Poles | Top 5 | Top 10 | Races Led | Laps Led |
|------|------|--------|------|-------|-------|--------|-----------|----------|
| 2003 | 63 | 4 | 0 | 0 | 0 | 0 | 0 | 0 |
| Totals | | 4 | 0 | 0 | 0 | 0 | 0 | 0 |

## Jeremy Thompson

**Birthdate:** 8/19/74 **Birth place:** Kilgore, Texas

### CAREER STATISTICS

| Year | Rank | Starts | Wins | Poles | Top 5 | Top 10 | Races Led | Laps Led |
|------|------|--------|------|-------|-------|--------|-----------|----------|
| 1997 | 47 | 4 | 0 | 0 | 0 | 0 | 0 | 0 |
| 1998 | 52 | 2 | 0 | 0 | 0 | 0 | 0 | 0 |
| 2003 | 98 | 1 | 0 | 0 | 0 | 0 | 0 | 0 |
| Totals | | 7 | 0 | 0 | 0 | 0 | 0 | 0 |

## Joe Varde

**Birthdate:** 4/3/50 **Birth place:** Tampa

### CAREER STATISTICS

| Year | Rank | Starts | Wins | Poles | Top 5 | Top 10 | Races Led | Laps Led |
|------|------|--------|------|-------|-------|--------|-----------|----------|
| 2003 | 104 | 1 | 0 | 0 | 0 | 0 | 0 | 0 |
| Totals | | 1 | 0 | 0 | 0 | 0 | 0 | 0 |

## Tyler Walker

**Birthdate:** 7/16/79 **Birth place:** North Hills, Calif.

### CAREER STATISTICS

| Year | Rank | Starts | Wins | Poles | Top 5 | Top 10 | Races Led | Laps Led |
|------|------|--------|------|-------|-------|--------|-----------|----------|
| 2003 | 135 | 1 | 0 | 0 | 0 | 0 | 0 | 0 |
| Totals | | 1 | 0 | 0 | 0 | 0 | 0 | 0 |

## Mike Wallace

**Birthdate:** 3/10/59 **Birth place:** St. Louis

### CAREER STATISTICS

| Year | Rank | Starts | Wins | Poles | Top 5 | Top 10 | Races Led | Laps Led |
|------|------|--------|------|-------|-------|--------|-----------|----------|
| 2003 | 71 | 3 | 0 | 0 | 0 | 0 | 0 | 0 |
| Totals | | 3 | 0 | 0 | 0 | 0 | 0 | 0 |

### CAREER STATISTICS

| Year | Rank | Starts | Wins | Poles | Top 5 | Top 10 | Races Led | Laps Led |
|------|------|--------|------|-------|-------|--------|-----------|----------|
| 1995 | 92 | 1 | 0 | 0 | 0 | 0 | 0 | 0 |
| 1997 | 22 | 15 | 0 | 0 | 1 | 7 | 2 | 95 |
| 1998 | 13 | 27 | 0 | 1 | 3 | 11 | 5 | 64 |
| 1999 | 6 | 25 | 2 | 0 | 12 | 14 | 10 | 261 |
| 2000 | 4 | 24 | 2 | 2 | 13 | 16 | 9 | 416 |
| 2002 | 44 | 4 | 0 | 0 | 1 | 2 | 1 | 3 |
| 2003 | 46 | 4 | 0 | 0 | 0 | 1 | 1 | 2 |
| Totals | | 100 | 4 | 3 | 30 | 51 | 28 | 841 |

## Shane Wallace

**Birthdate:** 1/11/84 **Birth place:** Utica, N.Y.

### CAREER STATISTICS

| Year | Rank | Starts | Wins | Poles | Top 5 | Top 10 | Races Led | Laps Led |
|------|------|--------|------|-------|-------|--------|-----------|----------|
| 2003 | 33 | 7 | 0 | 0 | 0 | 0 | 0 | 0 |
| Totals | | 7 | 0 | 0 | 0 | 0 | 0 | 0 |

## Rick Ware

**Birthdate:** 8/6/63 **Birth place:** Los Angeles

### CAREER STATISTICS

| Year | Rank | Starts | Wins | Poles | Top 5 | Top 10 | Races Led | Laps Led |
|------|------|--------|------|-------|-------|--------|-----------|----------|
| 1999 | 71 | 1 | 0 | 0 | 0 | 0 | 0 | 0 |
| 2000 | 24 | 14 | 0 | 0 | 0 | 0 | 0 | 0 |
| 2003 | 131 | 1 | 0 | 0 | 0 | 0 | 0 | 0 |
| Totals | | 16 | 0 | 0 | 0 | 0 | 0 | 0 |

## Ken Weaver

**Birthdate:** 2/10/56 **Birth place:** Dallas

### CAREER STATISTICS

| Year | Rank | Starts | Wins | Poles | Top 5 | Top 10 | Races Led | Laps Led |
|------|------|--------|------|-------|-------|--------|-----------|----------|
| 2003 | 47 | 5 | 0 | 0 | 0 | 0 | 0 | 0 |
| Totals | | 5 | 0 | 0 | 0 | 0 | 0 | 0 |

## Dana White

**Birthdate:** 3/31/58 **Birth place:** Wake Forest, N.C.

### CAREER STATISTICS

| Year | Rank | Starts | Wins | Poles | Top 5 | Top 10 | Races Led | Laps Led |
|------|------|--------|------|-------|-------|--------|-----------|----------|
| 2001 | 48 | 6 | 0 | 0 | 0 | 0 | 0 | 0 |
| 2002 | 32 | 9 | 0 | 0 | 0 | 0 | 0 | 0 |
| 2003 | 65 | 6 | 0 | 0 | 0 | 0 | 0 | 0 |
| Totals | | 21 | 0 | 0 | 0 | 0 | 0 | 0 |

## Jason White

**Birthdate:** 6/5/79 **Birth place:** Powhatan, Va.

### CAREER STATISTICS

| Year | Rank | Starts | Wins | Poles | Top 5 | Top 10 | Races Led | Laps Led |
|---|---|---|---|---|---|---|---|---|
| 2001 | 43 | 7 | 0 | 0 | 0 | 0 | 0 | 0 |
| 2002 | 73 | 2 | 0 | 0 | 0 | 0 | 0 | 0 |
| 2003 | 134 | 1 | 0 | 0 | 0 | 0 | 0 | 0 |
| Totals | | 10 | 0 | 0 | 0 | 0 | 0 | 0 |

## Craig Wood

### CAREER STATISTICS

| Year | Rank | Starts | Wins | Poles | Top 5 | Top 10 | Races Led | Laps Led |
|---|---|---|---|---|---|---|---|---|
| 2003 | 124 | 1 | 0 | 0 | 0 | 0 | 0 | 0 |
| Totals | | 1 | 0 | 0 | 0 | 0 | 0 | 0 |

## Tim Woods III

**Birthdate:** 10/11/74 **Birth place:** Chino Hills, Calif.

### CAREER STATISTICS

| Year | Rank | Starts | Wins | Poles | Top 5 | Top 10 | Races Led | Laps Led |
|---|---|---|---|---|---|---|---|---|
| 2001 | 77 | 2 | 0 | 0 | 0 | 0 | 0 | 0 |
| 2003 | 111 | 2 | 0 | 0 | 0 | 0 | 0 | 0 |
| Totals | | 4 | 0 | 0 | 0 | 0 | 0 | 0 |

## Nick Woodward

**Birthdate:** 11/29/79 **Birth place:** High Point, N.C.

### CAREER STATISTICS

| Year | Rank | Starts | Wins | Poles | Top 5 | Top 10 | Races Led | Laps Led |
|---|---|---|---|---|---|---|---|---|
| 2001 | 69 | 2 | 0 | 0 | 0 | 0 | 0 | 0 |
| 2003 | 96 | 1 | 0 | 0 | 0 | 0 | 0 | 0 |
| Totals | | 3 | 0 | 0 | 0 | 0 | 0 | 0 |

## Nathan Wulff

**Birthdate:** 12/2/76 **Birth place:** Escondido, Calif.

### CAREER STATISTICS

| Year | Rank | Starts | Wins | Poles | Top 5 | Top 10 | Races Led | Laps Led |
|---|---|---|---|---|---|---|---|---|
| 2003 | 79 | 2 | 0 | 0 | 0 | 0 | 0 | 0 |
| Totals | | 2 | 0 | 0 | 0 | 0 | 0 | 0 |

## Jason York

**Birthdate:** 6/12/75 **Birth place:** Reidsville, N.C.

### CAREER STATISTICS

| Year | Rank | Starts | Wins | Poles | Top 5 | Top 10 | Races Led | Laps Led |
|---|---|---|---|---|---|---|---|---|
| 2003 | 132 | 2 | 0 | 0 | 0 | 0 | 1 | 1 |
| Totals | | 2 | 0 | 0 | 0 | 0 | 1 | 1 |

## 2003 race by race

| No. | Date | Race | Track | Pole winner | Race winner |
|---|---|---|---|---|---|
| 1 | February 14 | Florida Dodge Dealers 250 | Daytona International Speedway | Jason Leffler | Rick Crawford |
| 2 | March 14 | Craftsman 200 | Darlington Raceway | Travis Kvapil (rain) | Bobby Hamilton |
| 3 | March 23 | Lucas Oil 250 | Mesa Marin Raceway | Ted Musgrave | Dennis Setzer |
| 4 | April 12 | Advance Auto Parts 250 | Martinsville Speedway | Ted Musgrave | Dennis Setzer |
| 5 | May 16 | Hardee's 200 | Lowe's Motor Speedway | Bill Lester | Ted Musgrave |
| 6 | May 30 | MBNA Armed Forces Family 200 | Dover International Speedway | Bobby Hamilton (rain) | Jason Leffler |
| 7 | June 6 | O'Reilly 400K | Texas Motor Speedway | Bobby Hamilton (rain) | Brendan Gaughan |
| 8 | June 21 | O'Reilly 200 | Memphis Motorsports Park | Jon Wood | Ted Musgrave |
| 9 | June 28 | GNC Live Well 200 | The Milwaukee Mile | Terry Cook | Brendan Gaughan |
| 10 | July 5 | O'Reilly Auto Parts 250 | Kansas Speedway | Chad Chaffin | Jon Wood |
| 11 | July 12 | Built Ford Tough 225 | Kentucky Speedway | Jon Wood | Carl Edwards |
| 12 | July 19 | Dodge Ram Tough 200 | Gateway International Raceway | Travis Kvapil (rain) | Brendan Gaughan |
| 13 | July 26 | Sears 200 | Michigan International Speedway | Jason Leffler | Brendan Gaughan |
| 14 | August 1 | Power Stroke Diesel 200 | Indianapolis Raceway Park | Terry Cook | Carl Edwards |
| 15 | August 8 | Federated Auto Parts 200 | Nashville Superspeedway | Chad Chaffin | Carl Edwards |
| 16 | August 20 | O'Reilly 200 | Bristol Motor Speedway | Ted Musgrave | Travis Kvapil |
| 17 | September 4 | Virginia Is For Lovers 200 | Richmond International Raceway | Travis Kvapil (rain) | Tony Stewart |
| 18 | September 13 | New Hampshire 200 | New Hampshire Int'l Speedway | Jimmy Spencer | Jimmy Spencer |
| 19 | September 20 | American Racing Wheels 200 | California Speedway | Brendan Gaughan | Ted Musgrave |
| 20 | September 27 | Las Vegas 350 | Las Vegas Motor Speedway | Brendan Gaughan | Brendan Gaughan |
| 21 | October 4 | John Boy & Billy 250 | Big Daddy's S. Boston Speedway | Brendan Gaughan | Dennis Setzer |
| 22 | October 11 | Silverado 350 | Texas Motor Speedway | Andy Houston | Brendan Gaughan |
| 23 | October 18 | Advance Auto Parts 200 | Martinsville Speedway | Carl Edwards | Jon Wood |
| 24 | October 31 | Chevy Silverado 150 | Phoenix International Raceway | Ted Musgrave | Kevin Harvick |
| 25 | November 14 | Ford 200 | Homestead-Miami Speedway | Bobby Hamilton | Bobby Hamilton |

## 2003 miles leaders

| Rank | Driver | Miles Led | Times Led | Races Led | Miles Run | Possible Miles | Unfinished Miles | Laps Led | Wins | Starts |
|---|---|---|---|---|---|---|---|---|---|---|
| 1 | Brendan Gaughan | 898.29 | 31 | 16 | 4452.65 | 4605.55 | 152.90 | 652 | 6 | 25 |
| 2 | Ted Musgrave | 829.95 | 38 | 18 | 4383.95 | 4605.55 | 221.60 | 796 | 3 | 25 |
| 3 | Bobby Hamilton | 470.58 | 23 | 13 | 4514.77 | 4605.55 | 90.78 | 394 | 2 | 25 |
| 4 | Carl Edwards | 420.52 | 21 | 13 | 4168.49 | 4605.55 | 437.07 | 363 | 3 | 25 |
| 5 | Rick Crawford | 386.50 | 18 | 8 | 4291.19 | 4605.55 | 314.36 | 256 | 1 | 25 |
| 6 | Jon Wood | 309.61 | 18 | 10 | 4578.72 | 4605.55 | 26.84 | 349 | 2 | 25 |
| 7 | Kevin Harvick | 286.61 | 10 | 4 | 704.48 | 992.90 | 288.42 | 300 | 1 | 6 |
| 8 | Dennis Setzer | 236.72 | 12 | 8 | 4428.94 | 4605.55 | 176.62 | 437 | 3 | 25 |
| 9 | Jason Leffler | 229.64 | 13 | 11 | 2680.86 | 3048.55 | 367.70 | 214 | 1 | 16 |
| 10 | Jimmy Spencer | 131.94 | 4 | 2 | 432.30 | 466.80 | 34.50 | 125 | 1 | 3 |
| 11 | Chad Chaffin | 87.94 | 8 | 5 | 4333.84 | 4605.55 | 271.72 | 115 | 0 | 25 |
| 12 | Terry Cook | 73.13 | 5 | 4 | 4471.59 | 4605.55 | 133.96 | 84 | 0 | 25 |
| 13 | Andy Houston | 64.20 | 5 | 3 | 1839.49 | 2019.00 | 179.52 | 75 | 0 | 11 |
| 14 | Travis Kvapil | 54.12 | 12 | 11 | 4605.05 | 4605.55 | 0.50 | 49 | 1 | 25 |
| 15 | David Starr | 25.00 | 4 | 3 | 3116.27 | 3580.05 | 463.78 | 16 | 0 | 20 |
| 16 | Tony Stewart | 24.00 | 3 | 1 | 150.00 | 150.00 | 0.00 | 32 | 1 | 1 |
| 17 | Bill Lester | 24.00 | 2 | 2 | 4348.90 | 4605.55 | 256.66 | 17 | 0 | 25 |
| 18 | Morgan Shepherd | 10.50 | 1 | 1 | 708.29 | 2938.35 | 2230.06 | 7 | 0 | 16 |
| 19 | Robert Pressley | 9.00 | 3 | 2 | 3728.48 | 4055.55 | 327.07 | 10 | 0 | 22 |
| 20 | Lance Hooper | 8.00 | 1 | 1 | 1029.65 | 3007.60 | 1977.96 | 4 | 0 | 16 |
| 21 | Matt Crafton | 7.25 | 2 | 2 | 4395.07 | 4605.55 | 210.48 | 11 | 0 | 25 |
| 22 | Mike Wallace | 5.00 | 1 | 1 | 807.12 | 815.95 | 8.83 | 2 | 0 | 4 |
| 23 | Jeremy Mayfield | 4.50 | 1 | 1 | 204.00 | 204.00 | 0.00 | 3 | 0 | 1 |
| 23 | Mike Skinner | 4.50 | 1 | 1 | 755.96 | 762.20 | 6.24 | 3 | 0 | 4 |
| 24 | Bobby Dotter | 1.50 | 1 | 1 | 1250.84 | 1806.60 | 555.76 | 1 | 0 | 10 |
| 25 | Jody Lavender | 1.50 | 1 | 1 | 3426.36 | 3709.95 | 283.59 | 1 | 0 | 21 |
| 27 | Jason York | 1.06 | 1 | 1 | 355.12 | 361.60 | 6.48 | 1 | 0 | 2 |

# 2003 points standings

| Rk. | Driver | Points | Behind | Starts | Wins | Top5 | Top10 | Winnings |
|---|---|---|---|---|---|---|---|---|
| 1 | Travis Kvapil | 3,837 | Leader | 25 | 1 | 13 | 22 | $872,395 |
| 2 | Dennis Setzer | 3,828 | -9 | 25 | 3 | 15 | 23 | $654,455 |
| 3 | Ted Musgrave | 3,819 | -18 | 25 | 3 | 14 | 18 | $764,195 |
| 4 | Brendan Gaughan | 3,797 | -40 | 25 | 6 | 14 | 18 | $771,290 |
| 5 | Jon Wood | 3,659 | -178 | 25 | 2 | 10 | 20 | $545,965 |
| 6 | Bobby Hamilton | 3,627 | -210 | 25 | 2 | 10 | 18 | $521,915 |
| 7 | Rick Crawford | 3,578 | -259 | 25 | 1 | 10 | 16 | $505,240 |
| 8 | Carl Edwards* | 3,416 | -421 | 25 | 3 | 13 | 15 | $608,080 |
| 9 | Terry Cook | 3,212 | -625 | 25 | 0 | 0 | 13 | $337,160 |
| 10 | Chad Chaffin | 3,143 | -694 | 25 | 0 | 2 | 9 | $333,770 |
| 11 | Matt Crafton | 3,074 | -763 | 25 | 0 | 0 | 11 | $322,891 |
| 12 | Robert Pressley | 2,773 | -1,064 | 22 | 0 | 4 | 9 | $337,085 |
| 13 | David Starr | 2,768 | -1,069 | 21 | 0 | 5 | 13 | $305,225 |
| 14 | Bill Lester | 2,712 | -1,125 | 25 | 0 | 0 | 1 | $298,800 |
| 15 | Randy MacDonald | 2,458 | -1,379 | 25 | 0 | 0 | 0 | $296,895 |
| 16 | Jason Leffler | 2,209 | -1,628 | 16 | 1 | 5 | 10 | $309,890 |
| 17 | Jody Lavender* | 2,168 | -1,669 | 21 | 0 | 0 | 0 | $243,693 |
| 18 | Jerry Hill | 1,882 | -1,955 | 22 | 0 | 0 | 0 | $212,125 |
| 19 | Randy Briggs* | 1,618 | -2,219 | 17 | 0 | 0 | 0 | $190,485 |
| 20 | Phil Bonifield | 1,524 | -2,313 | 21 | 0 | 0 | 0 | $187,345 |
| 21 | Andy Houston | 1,487 | -2,350 | 11 | 0 | 3 | 7 | $150,079 |
| 22 | Rich Bickle | 1,288 | -2,549 | 12 | 0 | 0 | 2 | $131,957 |
| 23 | Ken Schrader | 1,286 | -2,551 | 11 | 0 | 0 | 3 | $99,665 |
| 24 | Lance Hooper | 1,191 | -2,646 | 17 | 0 | 0 | 0 | $136,545 |
| 25 | Tina Gordon* | 1,112 | -2,725 | 11 | 0 | 0 | 0 | $108,465 |
| 26 | T.J. Bell* | 1,059 | -2,778 | 12 | 0 | 0 | 0 | $114,940 |
| 27 | Eric Jones | 1,058 | -2,779 | 9 | 0 | 0 | 1 | $89,050 |
| 28 | Morgan Shepherd | 991 | -2,846 | 16 | 0 | 0 | 0 | $125,855 |
| 29 | Bobby Dotter | 939 | -2,898 | 10 | 0 | 0 | 0 | $100,904 |
| 30 | Kevin Harvick | 807 | -3,030 | 6 | 1 | 3 | 4 | $89,760 |
| 31 | Jamie Aube | 800 | -3,037 | 11 | 0 | 0 | 0 | $85,477 |
| 32 | Stan Boyd | 799 | -3,038 | 12 | 0 | 0 | 0 | $113,474 |
| 33 | Shane Wallace | 685 | -3,152 | 7 | 0 | 0 | 0 | $59,565 |
| 34 | Doug Keller* | 674 | -3,163 | 8 | 0 | 0 | 0 | $62,015 |
| 35 | Kenny Hendrick | 656 | -3,181 | 12 | 0 | 0 | 0 | $91,293 |
| 36 | Chris Horn | 625 | -3,212 | 7 | 0 | 0 | 0 | $64,170 |
| 37 | David Stover | 607 | -3,230 | 7 | 0 | 0 | 0 | $57,505 |
| 38 | Roland Isaacs | 600 | -3,237 | 9 | 0 | 0 | 0 | $55,410 |
| 39 | Wayne Edwards | 595 | -3,242 | 8 | 0 | 0 | 0 | $57,195 |
| 40 | Brandon Whitt | 592 | -3,245 | 7 | 0 | 0 | 0 | $58,830 |
| 41 | Ricky Sanders | 573 | -3,264 | 6 | 0 | 0 | 0 | $56,190 |
| 42 | Paul Menard | 572 | -3,265 | 5 | 0 | 0 | 1 | $47,295 |
| 43 | L W Miller | 558 | -3,279 | 6 | 0 | 0 | 0 | $56,090 |
| 44 | Hank Parker, Jr | 524 | -3,313 | 4 | 0 | 0 | 2 | $54,855 |
| 45 | Johnny Chapman | 513 | -3,324 | 6 | 0 | 0 | 0 | $56,976 |
| 46 | Mike Wallace | 500 | -3,337 | 4 | 0 | 0 | 1 | $47,895 |
| 47 | Ken Weaver | 482 | -3,355 | 5 | 0 | 0 | 0 | $41,950 |
| 48 | Mike Skinner | 471 | -3,366 | 4 | 0 | 0 | 0 | $46,860 |
| 49 | Trevor Boys | 471 | -3,366 | 6 | 0 | 0 | 0 | $50,794 |
| 50 | Andy Petree | 467 | -3,370 | 4 | 0 | 0 | 1 | $32,770 |
| 51 | Brandon Miller | 454 | -3,383 | 4 | 0 | 0 | 1 | $32,945 |
| 52 | Shane Sieg | 451 | -3,386 | 4 | 0 | 0 | 0 | $48,485 |
| 53 | Charlie Bradberry | 446 | -3,391 | 5 | 0 | 0 | 0 | $33,600 |
| 54 | Tracy Hines | 445 | -3,392 | 4 | 0 | 0 | 0 | $30,925 |
| 55 | Jimmy Spencer | 416 | -3,421 | 3 | 1 | 1 | 2 | $77,530 |
| 56 | Michael Dokken | 410 | -3,427 | 6 | 0 | 0 | 0 | $59,135 |

# 2003 champion

## Travis Kvapil

**Truck:** No. 16 Chevrolet. **Team Owner:** Steve Coulter. **Birthdate:** March 1, 1976. **Hometown:** Janesville, Wis.

### NASCAR CRAFTSMAN TRUCK SERIES STATISTICS

**Seasons Competed:** 3 (2001, 2002, 2003)
**Career Starts:** 71
**Career Wins:** 3
**Career Poles:** 0

**Championship Season Recap:** Kvapil spun on the opening lap of the final race of the season at Homestead-Miami Speedway but recovered to secure the title with a sixth-place finish. He began the race third in points. Brendan Gaughan entered the race as the points leader but lost his chance because of a late-race accident. Kvapil beat out Dennis Setzer, who finished seventh in the race, by nine points for the title, the closest battle in NASCAR Craftsman Truck Series history. Kvapil's season included one victory, at Bristol in August, and 22 top 10s. He led in 11 races for 49 laps and set a NASCAR Craftsman Truck Series record by finishing every lap of the season except one—that at the half-mile Mesa Marin Raceway.

## Travis Kvapil 2003 race by race

| Race No. | Race | Start | Finish | Points | Total points | Pos. | Laps/ Completed | Money won | Status |
|---|---|---|---|---|---|---|---|---|---|
| 1 | Florida Dodge Dealers 250 | 7 | 2 | 175 | 175 | 2 | 106/106 | $53,725 | Running |
| 2 | Craftsman 200 | 1 | 4 | 165 | 340 | 2 | 147/147 | $12,525 | Running |
| 3 | Lucas Oil 250 presented by Glidden | 11 | 16 | 115 | 455 | 4 | 254/255 | $8,290 | Running |
| 4 | Advance Auto Parts 250 | 3 | 18 | 114 | 569 | 6 | 250/250 | $9,365 | Running |
| 5 | Hardee's 200 | 16 | 4 | 160 | 729 | 5 | 136/136 | $14,800 | Running |
| 6 | MBNA Armed Forces Family 200 | 5 | 5 | 155 | 884 | 3 | 200/200 | $17,000 | Running |
| 7 | O'Reilly 400K | 3 | 4 | 160 | 1,044 | 4 | 167/167 | $20,850 | Running |
| 8 | O'Reilly 200 | 4 | 2 | 175 | 1,219 | 2 | 200/200 | $31,250 | Running |
| 9 | GNC 200 | 12 | 6 | 150 | 1,369 | 4 | 200/200 | $11,675 | Running |
| 10 | O'Reilly Auto Parts 250 | 9 | 4 | 160 | 1,529 | 1 | 167/167 | $15,550 | Running |
| 11 | Built Ford Tough 225 presented by the Greater Cin. Ford Dealers | 14 | 6 | 155 | 1,684 | 1 | 150/150 | $18,825 | Running |
| 12 | Ram Tough 200 | 1 | 3 | 165 | 1,849 | 1 | 160/160 | $28,790 | Running |
| 13 | Sears 200 | 18 | 7 | 151 | 2,000 | 2 | 100/100 | $12,475 | Running |
| 14 | Power Stroke Diesel 200 | 9 | 2 | 170 | 2,170 | 1 | 200/200 | $28,325 | Running |
| 15 | Federated Auto Parts 200 | 10 | 9 | 138 | 2,308 | 2 | 150/150 | $9,100 | Running |
| 16 | O'Reilly 200 presented by Valvoline Maxlife | 12 | 1 | 180 | 2,488 | 1 | 200/200 | $42,310 | Running |
| 17 | Virginia is for Lovers 200 | 1 | 9 | 138 | 2,626 | 2 | 200/200 | $8,900 | Running |
| 18 | New Hampshire 200 | 11 | 7 | 151 | 2,777 | 2 | 200/200 | $11,675 | Running |
| 19 | American Racing Wheels 200 | 12 | 8 | 147 | 2,924 | 2 | 100/100 | $14,000 | Running |
| 20 | Las Vegas 350 | 6 | 4 | 160 | 3,084 | 2 | 146/146 | $14,750 | Running |
| 21 | John Boy and Billy 250 | 4 | 2 | 170 | 3,254 | 2 | 253/253 | $25,550 | Running |
| 22 | Silverado 350 | 11 | 2 | 175 | 3,429 | 2 | 146/146 | $41,600 | Running |
| 23 | Advance Auto Parts 200 | 11 | 16 | 115 | 3,544 | 2 | 200/200 | $8,265 | Running |
| 24 | Chevy Silverado 150 | 8 | 9 | 143 | 3,687 | 3 | 150/150 | $10,425 | Running |
| 25 | Ford 200 | 4 | 6 | 150 | 3,837 | 1 | 134/134 | $15,125 | Running |

# 2002 champion

## Mike Bliss

**Birthdate:** April 5, 1965  **Hometown:** Milwaukie, Ore.

### NASCAR CRAFTSMAN TRUCK SERIES STATISTICS

**Years of competition:** 1995-1999, 2001-2002.
**Titles:** 1. **Year:** 2002.
**Victories:** 12. **Bud poles:** 18
**Career winnings:** $2,679,872
**Career highlights:** Fourth series champion to have competed in first NASCAR Craftsman Truck Series event … Ranks second all-time in Bud Poles with 18 … One of three series competitors with at least one victory in six different seasons.

# 2001, 1999 and 1997 champion

## Jack Sprague

**Birthdate:** August 8, 1964  **Hometown:** Spring Lake, Mich.

### NASCAR CRAFTSMAN TRUCK SERIES STATISTICS

**Years of competition:** 1995-2001, 2003
**Titles:** 3. **Years:** 1997, 1999, 2001.
**Victories:** 23. **Bud poles:** 20
**Career winnings:** $4,717,914
**Career highlights:** First three time NASCAR Craftsman Truck Series champion … Most Bud Poles (23) in series history … One of three competitors to win a race in six different seasons … Leading money winner in NASCAR Craftsman Truck Series competition ($4,691,664).

# 2000 champion

## Greg Biffle

**Birthdate:** December 23, 1969  **Hometown:** Vancouver, Wash.

### NASCAR CRAFTSMAN TRUCK SERIES STATISTICS

**Years of competition:** 1998-2001.
**Titles:** 1. **Year:** 2000.
**Victories:** 16. **Bud poles:** 12.
**Career winnings:** $2,242,844
**Career highlights:** 1998 Raybestos Rookie of the Year … Set season record for most victories – nine – in 1999 … First series competitor to win $1 million in season (2000) … 2001 NASCAR Busch Series Raybestos Rookie of the Year and 2002 NASCAR Busch Series champion.

# 1998 and 1996 champion

## Ron Hornaday Jr.

**Birthdate:** June 20, 1958  **Hometown:** Palmdale, Calif.

### NASCAR CRAFTSMAN TRUCK SERIES STATISTICS

**Years of competition:** 1995-1999, 2002
**Titles:** 2. **Years:** 1996, 1998
**Victories:** 26. **Bud Poles:** 11
**Career winnings:** $3,079,853
**Career highlights:** Sat on Bud Pole for first NASCAR Craftsman Truck Series race at Phoenix International Raceway … First two time series champion … Most victories in NASCAR Craftsman Truck Series history.

# 1995 champion

## Mike Skinner

**Birthdate:** June 28, 1957  **Hometown:** Susanville, Calif.

### NASCAR CRAFTSMAN TRUCK SERIES STATISTICS

**Years of competition:** 1995-1998, 2003
**Titles:** 1. **Year:** 1995
**Victories:** 16. **Bud poles:** 15
**Career winnings:** $1,129,640
**Career highlights:** Won first NASCAR Craftsman Truck Series race held on Feb. 5, 1995 at Phoenix International Raceway … Holds record for most Bud Poles in season, 10 in 1995 … First NASCAR Craftsman Truck Series champion (1995) … Daytona 500 Bud Pole winner (1997).

## Series champions

### (1995–2003)

| Year | Truck No. | Driver | Owner | Truck | Wins | Poles | Winnings |
|---|---|---|---|---|---|---|---|
| 1995 | 3 | Mike Skinner | Richard Childress | Chevrolet | 8 | 10 | $428,096 |
| 1996 | 16 | Ron Hornaday Jr. | Teresa Earnhardt | Chevrolet | 4 | 2 | $625,634 |
| 1997 | 24 | Jack Sprague | Rick Hendrick | Chevrolet | 3 | 5 | $880,835 |
| 1998 | 16 | Ron Hornaday Jr. | Teresa Earnhardt | Chevrolet | 6 | 2 | $915,407 |
| 1999 | 24 | Jack Sprague | Rick Hendrick | Chevrolet | 3 | 1 | $834,016 |
| 2000 | 50 | Greg Biffle | Jack Roush | Ford | 5 | 4 | $1,002,510 |
| 2001 | 24 | Jack Sprague | Rick Hendrick | Chevrolet | 4 | 7 | $967,493 |
| 2002 | 16 | Mike Bliss | Steve Coulter | Chevrolet | 5 | 4 | $894,388 |
| 2003 | 16 | Travis Kvapil | Steve Coulter | Chevrolet | 1 | 0 | $872,395 |

# 2003 Raybestos Rookie of the Year

## Carl Edwards

**Truck:** No. 63 Ford. **Team Owner:** Jack Roush. **Birthdate:** August 15, 1979. **Hometown:** Columbia, Mo.

### NASCAR CRAFTSMAN TRUCK SERIES STATISTICS

**Seasons competed:** 2 (2002, 2003)
**Career starts:** 32
**Career wins:** 3
**Career poles:** 1
**Championship season recap:** A hot July and August — with six consecutive top five finishes, including three victories — pushed Edwards to the front of the 2003 rookie class. In his first year driving for Roush Racing, Edwards' particularly strong superspeedway program led to consistently strong performances at the larger tracks. He also finished the season strong, with six top 10 finishes in the final eight races of the season. Edwards won his first career Bud Pole position in the 23rd race of the season at Martinsville, becoming the first rookie to win a pole in the NASCAR Craftsman Truck Series since Kurt Busch (October 2000 at California Speedway). The third Roush driver to win a NASCAR Craftsman Truck Series rookie title (joining Busch and Greg Biffle), Edwards ended the Raybestos Rookie of the Year contest with a commanding 147-point advantage over Jody Lavender.

## Rookie of the Year winners

| Year | Driver | Points | Rank | Races | Poles | Wins | Top 5 | Top 10 | Winnings | Hometown |
|---|---|---|---|---|---|---|---|---|---|---|
| 1996 | Bryan Reffner | 2,961 | 9th | 24 | 2 | 0 | 3 | 9 | $200,898 | Wisconsin Rapids, Wis. |
| 1997 | Kenny Irwin | 3,220 | 10th | 26 | 0 | 2 | 7 | 10 | $349,645 | Indianapolis, Ind. |
| 1998 | Greg Biffle | 3,276 | 8th | 27 | 4 | 0 | 8 | 12 | $459,782 | Vancouver, Wash. |
| 1999 | Mike Stefanik | 3,074 | 13th | 25 | 0 | 0 | 1 | 9 | $287,981 | Coventry, R.I. |
| 2000 | Kurt Busch | 3,596 | 2nd | 24 | 4 | 4 | 13 | 16 | $745,632 | Las Vegas, Nev. |
| 2001 | Travis Kvapil | 3,547 | 4th | 24 | 0 | 1 | 11 | 19 | $560,661 | Janesville, Wis. |
| 2002 | Brendan Gaughan | 2,893 | 11th | 22 | 0 | 2 | 5 | 9 | $422,647 | Las Vegas, Nev. |
| 2003 | Carl Edwards | 3,416 | 8th | 25 | 1 | 3 | 13 | 15 | $608,080 | Columbia, Mo. |

## Rookie records

Most Rookies (Race) - 14 - multiple times, most recent, Loudon, N.H., May 31, 1997
Fewest Rookies (Race) - 2 - multiple times, most recent, Homestead, Nov. 13, 2003
Best Finish, Rookie - 1st - Kenny Irwin (2 times, 1997); Tony Raines (1997); Randy Tolsma (1997); Andy Houston (1998); Kurt Busch (4 times, 2000); Ricky Hendrick (2001); Travis Kvapil (2001); Brendan Gaughan (2 times, 2002); Carl Edwards (3 times, 2003)
Most Wins by Rookie – 4 – Kurt Busch, 2000
Most Rookie Winners (season) – 3 – 1997
Quickest Win by Rookie – 5th Start — Tony Raines, 1997
Most Top-5 Finishes by Rookie – 13 – Carl Edwards, 2003; Kurt Busch, 2000
Most Top-10 Finishes by Rookie – 19 – Ricky Hendrick, 2001
Most Bud Poles by Rookie – 4 – Greg Biffle, 1998; Kurt Busch, 2000
Most Consecutive Bud Poles by Rookie – 3 –Greg Biffle, 1998
Most Starts – 27 – Greg Biffle, Andy Houston, Scot Walters, 1998
Most Money Won – $745,632 – Kurt Busch, 2000
Best Championship Finish – 2nd – Kurt Busch, 2000

# Miscellaneous records

## Series Records, Season—Drivers

Most Wins - 9 – Greg Biffle - 1999
Most Wins on Short Track - 7 - Mike Skinner - 1996; Ron Hornaday Jr. - 1997
Most Wins on Road Course - 2 - Ron Hornaday Jr. - 1995, Joe Ruttman - 1997
Most Wins on Superspeedway - 6 - Brendan Gaughan - 2003
Most Consecutive Wins - 3 - Mike Skinner - 1996 (Tucson, Colorado, Topeka,); Ron Hornaday Jr. - 1997 (Milwaukee, Louisville, Colorado); Greg Biffle – 2000 (Texas, Kentucky, Watkins Glen)
Most Consecutive Wins on Short Track - 5 - Ron Hornaday Jr. - 1997 (Bristol, Louisville, Colorado, Indianapolis, Flemington)
Most Wins Leading All Laps - 2 - Mike Skinner - 1995; Ron Hornaday Jr. - 1997
Most Bud Poles - 10 - Mike Skinner - 1995
Most Consecutive Bud Poles - 10 - Mike Skinner - 1995
Most Bud Poles, Rookie - 4 - Greg Biffle – 1998; Kurt Busch – 2000
Most Wins from Bud Pole - 4 - Mike Skinner - 1995 and 1996
Most Top 5 Finishes – 18 – Ron Hornaday Jr., Jack Sprague – 1996;
Most Laps Completed - 4,939 - Jay Sauter - 1998
Most Miles Completed - 4,520.33 - Joe Ruttman - 2001
Best Miles Completed Percentage - 99.9676% - Ron Hornaday Jr. - 1996

Fewest Uncompleted Laps - 2 - Joe Ruttman - 1995, Ron Hornaday Jr. - 1996
Fewest Uncompleted Miles - 0.666-mile - Joe Ruttman - 1995
Best Laps Completed Percentage - 99.9995% - Ron Hornaday Jr. - 1996
Most Laps Led - 1,533 - Mike Skinner - 1996
Most Miles Led - 1,443.02 – Jack Sprague – 2001
Most Times Led - 52 – Jack Sprague – 2001
Most Races Led - 19 – Greg Biffle – 2000, Jack Sprague – 2001
Consecutive Races Led - 11 - Jack Sprague – 2001 (May 6, 2001 - Aug. 3, 2001)
Most Races Completed - 27 - Joe Ruttman, Jay Sauter - 1998
Best Races Completed Percentage - 100% - Joe Ruttman - 1995; Ron Hornaday Jr.- 1996; Mike Bliss - 1997; Jay Sauter, Joe Ruttman - 1998
Most Races Completed/Lead Lap - 24 - Jack Sprague - 1997
Most Money Won (Race) - $84,475 - Jack Sprague, Las Vegas, Nev., Nov. 8, 1998
Most Money Won (Season) - $1,002,510 – Greg Biffle – 2000
Most Money Won (Season, Race Winnings Only) - $634,235 – Greg Biffle – 2000

## Series Racing Records—Wins

Most Wins - 26 - Ron Hornaday Jr.
Most Short Track Wins - 15 - Ron Hornaday Jr.
Most Road Course Wins - 3 - Ron Hornaday Jr., Joe Ruttman
Most Superspeedway Wins - 13 - Jack Sprague
Most Wins (Track) - 3 - Jack Sprague - Phoenix, Ariz. – Ron Hornaday Jr. – Phoenix Ariz.
Most Consecutive Short Track Wins - 5 - Ron Hornaday Jr. - Bristol, Louisville, Denver, Indianapolis, Flemington 1997
Most Consecutive Road Course Wins - 2 - Ron Hornaday Jr. - Topeka, Sonoma 1995
Most Consecutive Superspeedway Wins - 3 - Mike Skinner - Phoenix, Milwaukee, Phoenix 1995
Most Consecutive Wins (Track) - 4 - Brendan Gaughan - Texas. - 2002-2003
Win From Furthest Back - 33rd - Dennis Setzer - Martinsville, Va. - April 13, 2002

Most Wins From Bud Pole - 8 - Mike Skinner
Most Wins Leading All Laps - 3 - Mike Skinner (Most recent, Ron Hornaday Jr., Louisville, July 12, 1997)
Consecutive Wins From Bud Pole - 2 - Rich Bickle - Portland, Ore. May 3, 1997 and Evergreen, Wash. May 10, 1997
Most Winners (Season) - 14 - 1998
Most Consecutive Different Winners (Same Season) - 12 - 1998 (Aug. 1, New Hampshire, through Oct. 24, Phoenix)
Most Races Before First Win – 120 – Rick Crawford (Win came at Daytona, February 14, 2003
Most Races Between Wins – 73 – Randy Tolsma – Win #1 Bakersfield, Calif. Oct. 12, 1997; Win #2 Nashville, Tenn. Aug. 12, 2000)
Most Races Without Win (Since Most Recent Win) – 120 - Rick Crawford (Last Win, Miami, Fla. - April 4, 1998)
Most Races Without Win – 154 – Lance Norick

## Bud Poles/Speeds

Most Bud Poles - 20 - Jack Sprague
Most Bud Poles (Superspeedway) - 17 - Jack Sprague
Most Bud Poles (Road Course) - 4 - Ron Fellows
Most Bud Poles (Short Track) - 11 - Mike Skinner
Most Bud Poles (Track) – 3 - Jack Sprague - Phoenix, Ariz.; Ron Fellows – Watkins Glen, N.Y.
Most Fast Qualifiers/Bud Pole Winners - 15 - 1998
Most Consecutive Different Bud Pole Winners (same season) - 8 - 1997, 1998
Most Consecutive Different Bud Pole Winners (continuing) - 9 - 1995-96

Consecutive Bud Poles (Superspeedway) - 3 - Jack Sprague, Jason Leffler
Most Wins (Season) by Bud Pole Winner – 10 – 2000
Fastest Official Lap – 187.563 mph – Joe Ruttman – Daytona Beach, Fla. – Feb. 16, 2000
Fastest Official Lap (Superspeedway) – 187.563 mph – Joe Ruttman – Daytona Beach, Fla. – Feb. 16, 2000
Fastest Official Lap (Road Course) - 117.366 mph - Ron Fellows - Watkins Glen, N.Y. - Aug. 24, 1997
Fastest Official Lap (Short Track) - 123.378 mph - Jason Leffler - Richmond, Va. - Sept. 5, 2002

## Race winners (1995-2003)

### (217 Races)

| Driver | Total | Driver | Total | Driver | Total |
|---|---|---|---|---|---|
| Ron Hornaday Jr. | 26 | Jay Sauter | 4 | Tony Stewart | 2 |
| Jack Sprague | 23 | Mike Wallace | 4 | Jon Wood | 2 |
| Mike Skinner | 16 | Rich Bickle | 3 | Ricky Hendrick | 1 |
| Greg Biffle | 16 | Carl Edwards | 3 | Bob Keselowski | 1 |
| Ted Musgrave | 13 | Andy Houston | 3 | Terry Labonte | 1 |
| Joe Ruttman | 13 | Travis Kvapil | 3 | Jason Leffler | 1 |
| Mike Bliss | 12 | Dave Rezendes | 3 | Mark Martin | 1 |
| Dennis Setzer | 10 | Stacy Compton | 2 | Butch Miller | 1 |
| Brendan Gaughan | 8 | Ron Fellows | 2 | Bryan Reffner | 1 |
| Terry Cook | 5 | Jimmy Hensley | 2 | Boris Said | 1 |
| Scott Riggs | 5 | Kenny Irwin | 2 | Ken Schrader | 1 |
| Kurt Busch | 4 | Robert Pressley | 2 | Jimmy Spencer | 1 |
| Rick Carelli | 4 | Randy Tolsma | 2 | David Starr | 1 |
| Bobby Hamilton | 4 | Rick Crawford | 2 | **Different Winners** | **43** |
| Tony Raines | 4 | Kevin Harvick | 2 | **# of Races** | **217** |

## Pole winners (1995-2003)

### (217 Races)

| Driver | Total | Driver | Total | Driver | Total |
|---|---|---|---|---|---|
| Jack Sprague | 20 | Andy Houston | 4 | Tobey Butler | 1 |
| Mike Bliss | 18 | Ron Fellows | 3 | Michael Dokken | 1 |
| Joe Ruttman | 17 | Brendan Gaughan | 3 | Carl Edwards | 1 |
| Mike Skinner | 15 | Dennis Setzer | 3 | Tom Hubert | 1 |
| Greg Biffle | 12 | Mike Wallace | 3 | Kenny Irwin | 1 |
| Ron Hornaday Jr. | 11 | Chad Chaffin | 2 | Terry Labonte | 1 |
| Jason Leffler | 10 | Rick Crawford | 2 | Bill Lester | 1 |
| Stacy Compton | 9 | Jamie McMurray | 2 | Butch Miller | 1 |
| Ted Musgrave | 9 | Boris Said | 2 | Steve Park | 1 |
| Terry Cook | 7 | Jay Sauter | 2 | Tony Raines | 1 |
| Rich Bickle | 6 | David Starr | 2 | Dave Rezendes | 1 |
| Bryan Reffner | 5 | Randy Tolsma | 2 | Bill Sedgwick | 1 |
| Scott Riggs | 5 | Jon Wood | 2 | Jimmy Spencer | 1 |
| Kurt Busch | 4 | Johnny Benson | 1 | Tim Steele | 1 |
| Bobby Hamilton | 4 | Geoffrey Bodine | 1 | **Different Winners** | **46** |
| Jimmy Hensley | 4 | Chuck Bown | 1 | * Time trials held in 206 events | |

**Ron Hornaday Jr.**

**Jack Sprague**

## Most starts (1995-2003)

1. Rick Crawford — 173
2. Jack Sprague — 172
3. Joe Ruttman* — 168
4. Terry Cook — 165
5. Lance Norick* — 153
6. Jimmy Hensley* — 146
7. Mike Bliss* — 144
8. Dennis Setzer — 142
9. Rick Carelli* — 134
10. Ron Hornaday Jr.* — 12

*Did not participate in 2003

## Total miles run (1995-2003)

| | Driver | 1995 | 1996 | 1997 | 1998 | 1999 | 2000 | 2001 | 2002 | 2003 | Total |
|---|---|---|---|---|---|---|---|---|---|---|---|
| 1 | Jack Sprague | 1817.826 | 3172.849 | 4017.740 | 4411.746 | 4034.482 | 3725.810 | 4333.360 | | 420.000 | 25933.813 |
| 2 | Rick Crawford | | | 3796.652 | 4033.439 | 3743.686 | 4116.694 | 4349.490 | 4237.617 | 4291.192 | 28563.769 |
| 3 | Terry Cook | | 450.732 | 1808.834 | 3855.616 | 3950.447 | 4010.012 | 4399.080 | 4103.980 | 4468.591 | 27047.291 |
| 4 | Joe Ruttman | 1863.545 | 3051.353 | 4026.776 | 4484.463 | 2842.610 | 4147.254 | 4520.330 | 679.810 | | 25616.140 |
| 5 | Dennis Setzer | 643.500 | | 34.900 | 2296.320 | 3952.648 | 3788.55 | 4429.860 | 3088.841 | 4428.250 | 23662.871 |
| 6 | Lance Norick | | 2076.895 | 2101.401 | 3797.464 | 3317.930 | 3574.964 | 4383.540 | 3994.019 | | 23246.209 |
| 7 | Jimmy Hensley | 230.643 | 2824.390 | 3992.190 | 4188.661 | 3908.386 | 3867.782 | 2593.470 | | | 21605.520 |
| 8 | Mike Bliss | 1738.198 | 3035.088 | 3976.747 | 4062.962 | 3828.641 | | 100.000 | 4095.091 | | 20836.731 |
| 9 | Ron Hornaday Jr. | 1852.752 | 3176.021 | 3807.734 | 4449.090 | 4105.842 | | | 448.500 | | 17839.940 |
| 10 | Rick Carelli | 1796.587 | 2949.781 | 3474.154 | 4024.580 | 785.450 | 3674.206 | 848.672 | 250.000 | | 17803.432 |

## Total miles led (1995-2003)

| | Driver | 1995 | 1996 | 1997 | 1998 | 1999 | 2000 | 2001 | 2002 | 2003 | Total |
|---|---|---|---|---|---|---|---|---|---|---|---|
| 1 | Jack Sprague | 37.563 | 765.127 | 1074.627 | 845.959 | 524.045 | 496.690 | 1443.02 | | | 5187.031 |
| 2 | Ron Hornaday Jr. | 628.328 | 582.284 | 713.283 | 848.915 | 1000.214 | | | 31.500 | | 3804.524 |
| 3 | Ted Musgrave | | | | | | | 827.22 | 886.310 | 829.950 | 2545.480 |
| 4 | Greg Biffle | | | | 345.776 | 556.572 | 1128.422 | 290.17 | | | 2320.940 |
| 5 | Mike Bliss | 13.125 | 196.119 | 770.158 | 666.246 | 126.663 | | | 442.780 | | 2215.091 |
| 6 | Mike Skinner | 635.054 | 1136.902 | 64.768 | 8 | | | | | 4.50 | 1849.224 |
| 7 | Rick Crawford | | | 38.325 | 46.5 | 46.5 | 200 | 244.83 | 587.840 | 386.50 | 1550.495 |
| 8 | Kevin Harvick | | | | 21 | 161.632 | | .75 | 188.410 | 286.61 | 1235.307 |
| 9 | Joe Ruttman | 71.376 | 103.931 | 171.734 | 78.872 | 3.372 | 440.72 | 216.73 | 2.500 | | 1089.238 |
| 10 | Brendan Gaughan | | | | | | | 59.00 | 131.00 | 898.29 | 1088.290 |

# 1995 season top 10

| Pos. | Driver | Points | Starts | Poles | Wins | Top 5 | Top 10 | Winnings |
|---|---|---|---|---|---|---|---|---|
| 1 | Mike Skinner | 3,224 | 20 | 10 | 8 | 17 | 18 | $428,096 |
| 2 | Joe Ruttman | 3,098 | 20 | 1 | 2 | 9 | 18 | 264,798 |
| 3 | Ron Hornaday Jr. | 2,986 | 20 | 4 | 6 | 10 | 14 | 296,715 |
| 4 | Butch Miller | 2,812 | 20 | | 1 | 9 | 14 | 182,633 |
| 5 | Jack Sprague | 2,740 | 20 | 1 | 0 | 4 | 15 | 116,501 |
| 6 | Rick Carelli | 2,683 | 20 | | 0 | 5 | 10 | 132,013 |
| 7 | Bill Sedgwick | 2,681 | 20 | 1 | 0 | 6 | 13 | 119,918 |
| 8 | Mike Bliss | 2,626 | 19 | | 1 | 5 | 12 | 144,354 |
| 9 | Scott Lagasse | 2,470 | 20 | | 0 | 2 | 7 | 88,100 |
| 10 | Tobey Butler | 2,358 | 20 | | 0 | 3 | 5 | 86,146 |

### Race winners
| | |
|---|---|
| Mike Skinner | 8 |
| Ron Hornaday Jr. | 6 |
| Joe Ruttman | 2 |
| Mike Bliss | 1 |
| Terry Labonte | 1 |
| Butch Miller | 1 |
| Ken Schrader | 1 |

### Race winnings
| | |
|---|---|
| Mike Skinner | $428,096 |
| Ron Hornaday Jr. | 296,715 |
| Joe Ruttman | 264,798 |
| Butch Miller | 182,633 |
| Mike Bliss | 144,354 |
| Rick Carelli | 132,013 |
| Bill Sedgwick | 119,918 |
| Jack Sprague | 116,501 |
| Dave Rezendes | 90,814 |
| Scott Lagasse | 88,100 |

### Pole winners
| | |
|---|---|
| Mike Skinner | 10 |
| Ron Hornaday Jr. | 4 |
| Terry Labonte | 1 |
| Joe Ruttman | 1 |
| Bill Sedgwick | 1 |
| Jack Sprague | 1 |

# 1996 season top 10

| Pos. | Driver | Points | Starts | Poles | Wins | Top 5 | Top 10 | Winnings |
|---|---|---|---|---|---|---|---|---|
| 1 | Ron Hornaday Jr. | 3,831 | 24 | 2 | 4 | 18 | 23 | $625,634 |
| 2 | Jack Sprague | 3,778 | 24 | 2 | 5 | 18 | 21 | 580,112 |
| 3 | Mike Skinner | 3,771 | 24 | 4 | 8 | 17 | 20 | 602,495 |
| 4 | Joe Ruttman | 3,275 | 24 | 0 | 0 | 7 | 16 | 276,013 |
| 5 | Mike Bliss | 3,190 | 24 | 2 | 2 | 9 | 11 | 345,322 |
| 6 | Dave Rezendes | 3,179 | 24 | 0 | 3 | 9 | 13 | 335,840 |
| 7 | Butch Miller | 3,126 | 24 | 1 | 0 | 7 | 11 | 258,333 |
| 8 | Jimmy Hensley | 3,029 | 24 | 1 | 0 | 5 | 14 | 228,936 |
| 9 | #Bryan Reffner | 2,961 | 24 | 3 | 0 | 3 | 9 | 200,898 |
| 10 | Rick Carelli | 2,953 | 24 | 0 | 1 | 2 | 9 | 227,575 |

# Rookie of the Year contenders

### Race winners
| | |
|---|---|
| Mike Skinner | 8 |
| Jack Sprague | 5 |
| Ron Hornaday Jr. | 4 |
| Dave Rezendes | 3 |
| Mike Bliss | 2 |
| Rick Carelli | 1 |
| Mark Martin | 1 |

### Race winnings
| | |
|---|---|
| Ron Hornaday Jr. | $625,634 |
| Mike Skinner | 602,495 |
| Jack Sprague | 580,112 |
| Mike Bliss | 345,322 |
| Dave Rezendes | 335,840 |
| Joe Ruttman | 276,013 |
| Butch Miller | 258,333 |
| Jimmy Hensley | 228,936 |
| Rick Carelli | 227,575 |
| Rich Bickle | 204,169 |

### Pole winners
| | |
|---|---|
| Mike Skinner | 5 |
| Bryan Reffner | 3 |
| Rich Bickle | 2 |
| Mike Bliss | 2 |
| Ron Hornaday Jr. | 2 |
| Jack Sprague | 2 |
| Johnny Benson | 1 |
| Geoffrey Bodine | 1 |
| Tobey Butler | 1 |
| Bobby Hamilton | 1 |
| Jimmy Hensley | 1 |
| Kenny Irwin | 1 |
| Butch Miller | 1 |
| Steve Park | 1 |

## 1997 season top 10

| Pos. | Driver | Points | Starts | Poles | Wins | Top 5 | Top 10 | Winnings |
|---|---|---|---|---|---|---|---|---|
| 1 | Jack Sprague | 3,969 | 26 | 5 | 3 | 16 | 23 | $880,835 |
| 2 | Rich Bickle | 3,737 | 26 | 4 | 3 | 15 | 17 | 485,180 |
| 3 | Joe Ruttman | 3,736 | 26 | 2 | 5 | 13 | 17 | 641,444 |
| 4 | Mike Bliss | 3,611 | 26 | 6 | 1 | 11 | 18 | 541,555 |
| 5 | Ron Hornaday Jr. | 3,574 | 26 | 3 | 7 | 13 | 17 | 604,830 |
| 6 | Jay Sauter | 3,467 | 26 | 0 | 1 | 10 | 15 | 412,264 |
| 7 | Rick Carelli | 3,461 | 26 | 0 | 0 | 6 | 17 | 331,325 |
| 8 | Jimmy Hensley | 3,385 | 26 | 2 | 0 | 4 | 13 | 312,820 |
| 9 | Chuck Bown | 3,320 | 26 | 0 | 0 | 4 | 13 | 290,921 |
| 10 | #Kenny Irwin | 3,220 | 26 | 0 | 2 | 7 | 10 | 349,645 |

# Rookie of the Year contenders

### Race winners
| | |
|---|---|
| Ron Hornaday Jr. | 7 |
| Joe Ruttman | 5 |
| Rich Bickle | 3 |
| Jack Sprague | 3 |
| Kenny Irwin | 2 |
| Mike Bliss | 1 |
| Ron Fellows | 1 |
| Bob Keselowski | 1 |
| Tony Raines | 1 |
| Jay Sauter | 1 |
| Tandy Tolsma | 1 |

### Race winnings
| | |
|---|---|
| Jack Sprague | $880,835 |
| Joe Ruttman | 641,444 |
| Ron Hornaday Jr. | 604,830 |
| Mike Bliss | 541,555 |
| Rich Bickle | 485,180 |
| Jay Sauter | 412,264 |
| Kenny Irwin | 349,645 |
| Rick Carelli | 331,325 |
| Jimmy Hensley | 312,820 |
| Butch Miller | 298,225 |

### Pole winners
| | |
|---|---|
| Mike Bliss | 6 |
| Jack Sprague | 5 |
| Rich Bickle | 4 |
| Ron Hornaday Jr. | 3 |
| Jimmy Hensley | 2 |
| Joe Ruttman | 2 |
| Terry Cook | 1 |
| Michael Dokken | 1 |
| Ron Fellows | 1 |
| Dave Rezendes | 1 |

## 1998 season top 10

| Pos. | Driver | Points | Starts | Poles | Wins | Top 5 | Top 10 | Winnings |
|---|---|---|---|---|---|---|---|---|
| 1 | Ron Hornaday Jr. | 4,072 | 27 | 2 | 6 | 16 | 22 | $915,407 |
| 2 | Jack Sprague | 4,069 | 27 | 4 | 5 | 16 | 23 | 745,171 |
| 3 | Joe Ruttman | 3,874 | 27 | 2 | 1 | 14 | 19 | 547,933 |
| 4 | Jay Sauter | 3,672 | 27 | 0 | 1 | 7 | 14 | 457,765 |
| 5 | Tony Raines | 3,596 | 27 | 1 | 3 | 9 | 15 | 453,846 |
| 6 | Jimmy Hensley | 3,570 | 27 | 0 | 1 | 9 | 15 | 430,328 |
| 7 | Stacy Compton | 3,542 | 27 | 2 | 2 | 9 | 14 | 433,855 |
| 8 | #Greg Biffle | 3,276 | 27 | 4 | 0 | 8 | 12 | 459,782 |
| 9 | Ron Barfield | 3,227 | 27 | 0 | 0 | 2 | 10 | 268,910 |
| 10 | Mike Bliss | 3,216 | 27 | 4 | 2 | 5 | 9 | 395,844 |

# Rookie of the Year contenders

### Race winners
| | |
|---|---|
| Ron Hornaday Jr. | 6 |
| Jack Sprague | 5 |
| Tony Raines | 3 |
| Mike Bliss | 2 |
| Stacy Compton | 2 |
| Rick Carelli | 1 |
| Terry Cook | 1 |
| Rick Crawford | 1 |
| Jimmy Hensley | 1 |
| Andy Houston | 1 |
| Joe Ruttman | 1 |
| Boris Said | 1 |
| Jay Sauter | 1 |
| Dennis Setzer | 1 |

### Race winnings
| | |
|---|---|
| Ron Hornaday Jr. | $915,407 |
| Jack Sprague | 745,171 |
| Joe Ruttman | 547,933 |
| Greg Biffle | 459,782 |
| Jay Sauter | 457,765 |
| Tony Raines | 453,846 |
| Stacy Compton | 433,855 |
| Jimmy Hensley | 430,328 |
| Mike Bliss | 395,844 |
| Andy Houston | 350,487 |

### Pole winners
| | |
|---|---|
| Greg Biffle | 4 |
| Mike Bliss | 4 |
| Jack Sprague | 4 |
| Stacy Compton | 2 |
| Ron Hornaday Jr. | 2 |
| Joe Ruttman | 2 |
| Chuck Bown | 1 |
| Terry Cook | 1 |
| Ron Fellows | 1 |
| Andy Houston | 1 |
| Tom Hubert | 1 |
| Tony Raines | 1 |
| Boris Said | 1 |
| Randy Tolsma | 1 |
| Mike Wallace | 1 |

## 1999 season top 10

| Pos. | Driver | Points | Starts | Poles | Wins | Top 5 | Top 10 | Winnings |
|---|---|---|---|---|---|---|---|---|
| 1 | Jack Sprague | 3,747 | 25 | 1 | 3 | 16 | 19 | $834,016 |
| 2 | Greg Biffle | 3,739 | 25 | 4 | 9 | 14 | 19 | 763,238 |
| 3 | Dennis Setzer | 3,639 | 25 | 1 | 3 | 11 | 19 | 628,835 |
| 4 | Stacy Compton | 3,623 | 25 | 6 | 0 | 12 | 17 | 481,922 |
| 5 | Jay Sauter | 3,543 | 25 | 2 | 2 | 8 | 16 | 482,118 |
| 6 | Mike Wallace | 3,494 | 25 | 0 | 2 | 12 | 14 | 478,900 |
| 7 | Ron Hornaday Jr. | 3,488 | 25 | 0 | 2 | 7 | 16 | 576,152 |
| 8 | Andy Houston | 3,359 | 25 | 1 | 0 | 5 | 14 | 312,323 |
| 9 | Mike Bliss | 3,294 | 25 | 3 | 1 | 6 | 13 | 349,284 |
| 10 | Jimmy Hensley | 3,280 | 25 | 0 | 1 | 7 | 14 | 332,170 |

# Rookie of the Year contenders

### Race winners
| | |
|---|---|
| Greg Biffle | 9 |
| Sennis Setzer | 3 |
| Jack Sprague | 3 |
| Ron Hornaday Jr. | 2 |
| Jay Sauter | 2 |
| Mike Wallace | 2 |
| Mike Bliss | 1 |
| Rick Carelli | 1 |
| Ron Fellows | 1 |
| Jimmy Hensley | 1 |

### Race winnings
| | |
|---|---|
| Jack Sprague | $834,016 |
| Greg Biffle | 763,238 |
| Dennis Setzer | 628,835 |
| Ron Hornaday Jr. | 576,152 |
| Jay Sauter | 482,118 |
| Stacy Compton | 481,922 |
| Mike Wallace | 478,900 |
| Terry Cook | 438,676 |
| Mike Bliss | 349,284 |
| Jimmy Hensley | 332,170 |

### Pole winners
| | |
|---|---|
| Stacy Compton | 6 |
| Greg Biffle | 4 |
| Mike Bliss | 3 |
| Boris Said | 2 |
| Jay Sauter | 2 |
| Ron Fellows | 1 |
| Bobby Hamilton | 1 |
| Andy Houston | 1 |
| Dennis Setzer | 1 |
| Jack Sprague | 1 |
| Tim Steele | 1 |
| Randy Tolsma | 1 |

## 2000 season top 10

| Pos. | Driver | Points | Starts | Poles | Wins | Top 5 | Top 10 | Winnings |
|---|---|---|---|---|---|---|---|---|
| 1 | Greg Biffle | 3,826 | 24 | 4 | 5 | 18 | 18 | $1,002,510 |
| 2 | #Kurt Busch | 3,596 | 24 | 4 | 4 | 13 | 16 | 745,632 |
| 3 | Andy Houston | 3,566 | 24 | 1 | 2 | 13 | 18 | 614,539 |
| 4 | Mike Wallace | 3,450 | 24 | 2 | 2 | 13 | 16 | 624,505 |
| 5 | Jack Sprague | 3,316 | 24 | 0 | 3 | 13 | 15 | 567,536 |
| 6 | Joe Ruttman | 3,278 | 24 | 8 | 3 | 10 | 11 | 578,086 |
| 7 | Dennis Setzer | 3,214 | 24 | 0 | 1 | 8 | 16 | 431,711 |
| 8 | Randy Tolsma | 3,157 | 24 | 0 | 1 | 6 | 15 | 447,892 |
| 9 | Bryan Reffner | 3,153 | 24 | 2 | 1 | 3 | 16 | 375,542 |
| 10 | Steve Grissom | 3,113 | 24 | 0 | 0 | 6 | 11 | 310,529 |

# Rookie of the Year contenders

### Race winners
| | |
|---|---|
| Greg Biffle | 5 |
| Kurt Busch | 4 |
| Joe Ruttman | 3 |
| Jack Sprague | 3 |
| Andy Houston | 2 |
| Mike Wallace | 2 |
| Rick Carelli | 1 |
| Bobby Hamilton | 1 |
| Bryan Reffner | 1 |
| Dennis Setzer | 1 |
| Randy Tolsma | 1 |

### Race winnings
| | |
|---|---|
| Greg Biffle | $1,002,510 |
| Kurt Busch | 745,632 |
| Mike Wallace | 624,505 |
| Andy Houston | 614,539 |
| Joe Ruttman | 578,086 |
| Jack Sprague | 567,536 |
| Randy Tolsma | 447,892 |
| Dennis Setzer | 431,711 |
| Bryan Reffner | 375,542 |
| Jimmy Hensley | 317,936 |

### Pole winners
| | |
|---|---|
| Joe Ruttman | 8 |
| Greg Biffle | 4 |
| Kurt Busch | 4 |
| Mike Wallace | 2 |
| Jamie McMurray | 2 |
| Bryan Reffner | 2 |
| Bobby Hamilton | 1 |
| Andy Houston | 1 |

## 2001 season top 10

| Pos. | Driver | Points | Starts | Poles | Wins | Top 5 | Top 10 | Winnings |
|---|---|---|---|---|---|---|---|---|
| 1 | Jack Sprague | 3,670 | 24 | 7 | 4 | 15 | 17 | $967,493 |
| 2 | Ted Musgrave | 3,597 | 24 | 2 | 7 | 13 | 18 | 726,406 |
| 3 | Joe Ruttman | 3,570 | 24 | 4 | 2 | 10 | 20 | 597,129 |
| 4 | Travis Kvapil # | 3,547 | 24 | 0 | 1 | 11 | 18 | 560,661 |
| 5 | Scott Riggs | 3,526 | 24 | 4 | 5 | 14 | 16 | 677,888 |
| 6 | Ricky Hendrick # | 3,412 | 24 | 0 | 1 | 8 | 19 | 442,031 |
| 7 | Terry Cook | 3,327 | 24 | 1 | 0 | 5 | 16 | 427,773 |
| 8 | Rick Crawford | 3,320 | 24 | 0 | 0 | 10 | 16 | 423,761 |
| 9 | Dennis Setzer | 3,306 | 24 | 2 | 1 | 8 | 15 | 416,492 |
| 10 | Coy Gibbs | 2,875 | 24 | 0 | 0 | 2 | 7 | 290,922 |

# Raybestos Rookie of the Year contenders

### Race winners

| | |
|---|---|
| Ted Musgrave | 7 |
| Scott Riggs | 5 |
| Jack Sprague | 4 |
| Greg Biffle | 2 |
| Joe Ruttman | 2 |
| Bobby Hamilton | 1 |
| Travis Kvapil | 1 |
| Ricky Hendrick | 1 |
| Dennis Setzer | 1 |

### Race winnings

| | |
|---|---|
| Jack Sprague | $967,493 |
| Ted Musgrave | 726,406 |
| Scott Riggs | 677,888 |
| Joe Ruttman | 597,129 |
| Travis Kvapil | 560,661 |
| Ricky Hendrick | 442,031 |
| Terry Cook | 427,773 |
| Rick Crawford | 423,761 |
| Dennis Setzer | 416,492 |
| Lance Norick | 303,697 |

### Pole winners

| | |
|---|---|
| Jack Sprague | 7 |
| Scott Riggs | 4 |
| Joe Ruttman | 4 |
| Ted Musgrave | 2 |
| Dennis Setzer | 2 |
| Stacy Compton | 1 |
| Terry Cook | 1 |

## 2002 season top 10

| Pos. | Driver | Points | Starts | Poles | Wins | Top 5 | Top 10 | Winnings |
|---|---|---|---|---|---|---|---|---|
| 1 | Mike Bliss | 3,259 | 22 | 4 | 5 | 13 | 18 | $894,388 |
| 2 | Rick Crawford | 3,313 | 22 | 2 | 0 | 12 | 17 | 544,359 |
| 3 | Ted Musgrave | 3,308 | 22 | 3 | 3 | 12 | 16 | 651,797 |
| 4 | Jason Leffler | 3,156 | 22 | 8 | 0 | 11 | 15 | 525,619 |
| 5 | David Starr | 3,144 | 22 | 2 | 1 | 8 | 16 | 473,712 |
| 6 | Dennis Setzer | 3,132 | 22 | 0 | 1 | 8 | 14 | 502,040 |
| 7 | Robert Pressley | 3,097 | 22 | 0 | 2 | 7 | 15 | 495,817 |
| 8 | Terry Cook | 3,070 | 22 | 2 | 4 | 9 | 17 | 521,465 |
| 9 | Travis Kvapil | 3,039 | 22 | 0 | 1 | 10 | 14 | 414,326 |
| 10 | Coy Gibbs | 3,010 | 22 | 0 | 0 | 4 | 14 | 364,907 |

# Raybestos Rookie of the Year contenders

### Race winners

| | |
|---|---|
| Mike Bliss | 5 |
| Terry Cook | 4 |
| Ted Musgrave | 3 |
| Brendan Gaughan | 2 |
| Robert Pressley | 2 |
| Kevin Harvick | 1 |
| Ron Hornaday Jr. | 1 |
| Travis Kvapil | 1 |
| Dennis Setzer | 1 |
| David Starr | 1 |
| Tony Stewart | 1 |

### Race winnings

| | |
|---|---|
| Mike Bliss | $894,388 |
| Ted Musgrave | 651,797 |
| Rick Crawford | 544,359 |
| Jason Leffler | 525,619 |
| Terry Cook | 521,465 |
| Dennis Setzer | 502,040 |
| Robert Pressley | 495,817 |
| Brendan Gaughan | 414,326 |
| Travis Kvapil | 414,326 |

### Pole winners

| | |
|---|---|
| Jason Leffler | 8 |
| Mike Bliss | 4 |
| Ted Musgrave | 3 |
| Terry Cook | 2 |
| Rick Crawford | 2 |
| David Starr | 2 |

# NASCAR tracks

# Atlanta Motor Speedway

## TRACK FACTS
**Date Opened:** 1960
**Owner:** Speedway Motorsports, Inc.
**President/GM:** Ed Clark
**Distance:** 1.54 milesl
**Banking in Turns:** 24 degrees
**Banking in Straights:** 5 degrees
**Length of Frontstretch:** 2,332 feet
**Length of Backstretch:** 1,800 feet
**Grandstand Seating:** 124,000
**Tickets:** (770) 946-4211
www.gospeedway.com

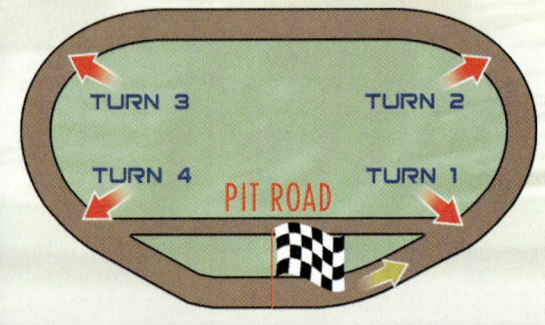

## NEXTEL CUP

### TRACK RECORDS
**Most Wins:** 8—Dale Earnhardt
**Oldest Winner:** Morgan Shepherd, 51 years, 4 months, 27 days, 03/20/1993
**Youngest Winner:** Jeff Gordon, 23 years, 7 months, 8 days, 03/12/1995
**Most Lead Changes:** 45—11/7/82
**Fewest Lead Changes:** 6—3 times, most recently, 6/30/63
**Most Leaders:** 17—3/12/00
**Fewest Leaders:** 3—6/30/63
**Most Laps Led in a 400 Miles race:** 167, Banjo Matthews, 09/17/1961
**Most Laps Led in a 500 Miles race:** 308, Cale Yarborough, 03/30/1969
**Most Cautions:** 11—3 times, most recently, 11/14/93
**Fewest Cautions:** 1—7/9/61
**Most Caution Laps:** 99—11/6/77
**Fewest Caution Laps:** 7—11/2/86
**Most on the Lead Lap:** 32—11/8/98
**Fewest on the Lead Lap:** 1—11 times, most recently, 11/2/86
**Most Running at the Finish:** 39—10/27/02
**Fewest Running at the Finish:** 10—4/5/64
**Most Laps Led by a Race Winner:** 308—Cale Yarborough, 3/30/69
**Fewest Laps Led by a Race Winner:** 1—David Pearson, 9/17/61
**Closest Margin of Victory:** 0.006 seconds, Kevin Harvick defeated Jeff Gordon 03/11/01
**Greatest Margin of Victory:** 1 Lap, 3 seconds, Dale Earnhardt defeated Richard Petty 11/02/86

### QUALIFYING AND RACE RECORDS
**QUALIFYING**
**Track:** Geoffrey Bodine, Ford, 197.478 mph, 28.074 seconds, Nov. 15, 1997 (NAPA 500).
**Spring Race (Golden Corral 500):** Bobby Labonte, Pontiac, 194.957 mph, 28.437 seconds, March 12, 1999.
**FALL RACE (Bass Pro Shops MBNA 500):** Geoffrey Bodine, Ford, 197.478 mph, 28.074 seconds, Nov. 15, 1997.

**RACE**
**Track:** Dale Earnhardt, Chevrolet, 163.633 mph, Nov. 12, 1995 (NAPA 500).
**Spring Race (Golden Corral 500):** Dale Earnhardt, Chevrolet, 161.298 mph, March 10, 1996.
**Fall Race (Bass Pro Shops MBNA 500):** Dale Earnhardt, Chevrolet, 163.633 mph, Nov. 12, 1995.
**Dixie 400:** Richard Petty, Plymouth, 130.244 mph, Aug. 7, 1966.
**Dixie 300:** Glenn "Fireball" Roberts, Pontiac, 112.653 mph, July 31, 1960.
**Festival 250:** Fred Lorenzen, Ford, 118.098 mph, July 9, 1961.

## 2004 SCHEDULE

### NEXTEL Cup
**Golden Corral 500**
**Race:** No. 4 of 36
**Date:** March 14
**TV:** FOX. **Radio:** PRN
**Bass Pro Shops MBNA 500**
**Race:** No. 33 of 36
**Date:** October 31
**TV:** NBC. **Radio:** PRN

### Busch Series
**Aaron's 312**
Race No. 31 of 34
Date: October 30
TV: TNT. Radio: PRN

### Craftsman Truck Series
**Atlanta 200***
**Race:** No. 2 of 25
**Date:** March 13
**TV:** Speed. **Radio:** PRN

*Inaugural event

## YEAR BY YEAR WINNERS

| Year | Event | Race Winner | Car Make | Avg. Speed | Start Pos. | Winning Car Owner | Pole Winner |
|---|---|---|---|---|---|---|---|
| 2003 | Bass/MBNA 500 | J. Gordon | Chevrolet | 127.769 | 19 | Rick Hendrick | R. Newman |
|  | Bass/MBNA 500 | B. Labonte | Chevrolet | 146.037 | 4 | Joe Gibbs | R. Newman |
| 2002 | NAPA 500 | K. Busch | Ford | 127.519 | 8 | Jack Roush | Trials Rained Out |
|  | MBNA America 500 | T. Stewart | Pontiac | 148..443 | 9 | Joe Gibbs | B. Elliott |
| 2001 | NAPA 500 | B. Labonte | Pontiac | 151.756 | 39 | Joe Gibbs | D. Earnhardt Jr. |
|  | Cracker Barrel 500 | K. Harvick | Chevrolet | 143.273 | 5 | Richard Childress | D. Jarrett |
| 2000 | NAPA 500 | J. Nadeau | Chevrolet | 141.296 | 2 | Joe Hendrick | J. Gordon |
|  | Cracker Barrel 500 | D. Earnhardt | Chevrolet | 131.759 | 35 | Richard Childress | D. Jarrett |
| 1999 | NAPA 500 | B. Labonte | Pontiac | 137.932 | 37 | Joe Gibbs | K. Lepage |
|  | Cracker Barrel 500 | J. Gordon | Chevrolet | 143.296 | 8 | Rick Hendrick | B. Labonte |
| 1998 | NAPA 500 | J. Gordon | Chevrolet | 114.915 | 21 | Rick Hendrick | K. Irwin |
|  | Primestar 500 | B. Labonte | Pontiac | 139.501 | 14 | Joe Gibbs | J. Andretti |
| 1997 | NAPA 500 | B. Labonte | Pontiac | 159.904 | 21 | Joe Gibbs | G. Bodine |
|  | Primestar 500 | D. Jarrett | Ford | 132.731 | 9 | Robert Yates | R. Gordon |
| 1996 | NAPA 500 | B. Labonte | Chevrolet | 134.661 | 1 | Joe Gibbs | B. Labonte |
|  | Purolator 500 | D. Earnhardt | Chevrolet | 161.298 | 18 | Richard Childress | J. Benson |
| 1995 | NAPA 500 | D. Earnhardt | Chevrolet | 163.633 | 11 | Richard Childress | D. Waltrip |
|  | Purolator 500 | J. Gordon | Chevrolet | 150.115 | 3 | Rick Hendrick | D. Earnhardt |
| 1994 | Hooters 500 | M. Martin | Ford | 148.982 | 5 | Jack Roush | G. Sacks |
|  | Purolator 500 | E. Irvan | Ford | 146.136 | 7 | Robert Yates | L. Allen |
| 1993 | Hooters 500 | R. Wallace | Pontiac | 125.221 | 20 | Roger Penske | H. Gant |
|  | Motorcraft 500 | M. Shepherd | Ford | 150.442 | 7 | Wood Brothers | R. Wallace |
| 1992 | Hooters 500 | Elliott | Ford | 133.322 | 11 | Junior Johnson | Mast |
|  | Motorcraft 500 | Elliott | Ford | 147.746 | 4 | Junior Johnson | Martin |

| Year | Event | Race Winner | Car Make | Avg. Speed | Start Pos. | Winning Car Owner | Pole Winner |
|---|---|---|---|---|---|---|---|
| 1991 | Hardee's 500 | Martin | Ford | 137.968 | 4 | Jack Roush | Elliott |
| g | Motorcraft 500 | Schrader | Chevrolet | 140.470 | 5 | Rick Hendrick | Kulwicki |
| 1990 | Atl. Journal 500 | Shepherd | Ford | 140.911 | 20 | Bud Moore | Wallace |
| f | Motorcraft 500 | Earnhardt | Chevrolet | 156.849 | 1 | Richard Childress | Trials Rained Out |
| 1989 | Atl. Journal 500 | Earnhardt | Chevrolet | 140.229 | 3 | Richard Childress | Kulwicki |
|  | Motorcraft 500 | D. Waltrip | Chevrolet | 139.684 | 4 | Rick Hendrick | Kulwicki |
| 1988 | Atl. Journal 500 | Wallace | Pontiac | 129.024 | 1 | Blue Max | Wallace |
|  | Motorcraft 500 | Earnhardt | Chevrolet | 137.588 | 2 | Richard Childress | G. Bodine |
| 1987 | Atl. Journal 500 | Elliott | Ford | 139.047 | 1 | Melling Racing | Elliott |
|  | Motorcraft 500 | Rudd | Ford | 133.689 | 6 | Bud Moore | Earnhardt |
| 1986 | Atl. Journal 500 | Earnhardt | Chevrolet | 152.523 | 4 | Richard Childress | Elliott |
|  | Motorcraft 500 | Shepherd | Buick | 132.126 | 3 | Jack Beebe | Earnhardt |
| 1985 | Atl. Journal 500 | Elliott | Ford | 139.597 | 3 | Harry Melling | Gant |
|  | Coca-Cola 500 | Elliott | Ford | 140.273 | 1 | Harry Melling | Bonnett |
| 1984 | Atl. Journal 500 | Earnhardt | Chevrolet | 134.610 | 10 | Richard Childress | Elliott |
|  | Coca-Cola 500 | Parsons | Chevrolet | 144.945 | 8 | Johnny Hayes | Buddy Baker |
| 1983 | Atl. Journal 500 | Bonnett | Chevrolet | 137.643 | 15 | Hodg./Rahmoc | Richmond |
|  | Coca-Cola 500 | C. Yarborough | Chevrolet | 124.055 | 22 | Ranier Racing | G. Bodine |
| 1982 | Atl. Journal 500 | B. Allison | Buick | 130.884 | 9 | DiGard Rac. Co. | Shepherd |
| e | Coca-Cola 500 | Waltrip | Buick | 124.824 | 14 | Junior Johnson | Earnhardt |
| 1981 | Atl. Journal 500 | Bonnett | Ford | 130.391 | 5 | Wood Brothers | Gant |
|  | Coca-Cola 500 | C. Yarborough | Buick | 133.619 | 17 | M.C. Anderson | Labonte |
| 1980 | Atl. Journal 500 | C. Yarborough | Chevrolet | 131.190 | 12 | Junior Johnson | B. Allison |
|  | Atlanta 500 | Earnhardt | Chevrolet | 134.808 | 31 | Osterlund Rac. | Buddy Baker |
| 1979 | Dixie 500 | Bonnett | Mercury | 140.120 | 4 | Wood Brothers | Buddy Baker |
|  | Atlanta 500 | Buddy Baker | Oldsmobile | 135.136 | 1 | Ranier Racing | Buddy Baker |
| 1978 | Dixie 500 | D. Allison | Chevrolet | 124.312 | 13 | Hoss Ellington | C. Yarborough |
|  | Atlanta 500 | B. Allison | Ford | 142.520 | 4 | Bud Moore | C. Yarborough |
| d 1977 | Dixie 500 | Waltrip | Chevrolet | 110.052 | 8 | DiGard Rac. Co. | Sommers |
|  | Atlanta 500 | R. Petty | Dodge | 144.093 | 1 | Petty Eng. | R. Petty |
| 1976 | Dixie 500 | Marcis | Dodge | 127.396 | 2 | Nord Krauskopf | Buddy Baker |
|  | Atlanta 500 | Pearson | Mercury | 128.904 | 2 | Wood Brothers | Marcis |
| 1975 | Dixie 500 | Buddy Baker | Ford | 130.900 | 3 | Bud Moore | Marcis |
|  | Atlanta 500 | R. Petty | Dodge | 133.496 | 1 | Petty Eng. | R. Petty |
| 1974 | Dixie 500 | R. Petty | Dodge | 131.651 | 2 | Petty Eng. | C. Yarborough |
|  | Atlanta 500 | C. Yarborough | Chevrolet | 136.910 | 9 | Junior Johnson | Pearson |
| 1973 | Dixie 500 | Pearson | Mercury | 130.211 | 5 | Wood Brothers | R. Petty |
| * | Atlanta 500 | Pearson | Mercury | 139.351 | 9 | Wood Brothers | NONE |
| 1972 | Dixie 500 | B. Allison | Chevrolet | 131.295 | 3 | Junior Johnson | Pearson |
|  | Atlanta 500 | B. Allison | Chevrolet | 128.214 | 1 | Junior Johnson | B. Allison |
| 1971 | Dixie 500 | R. Petty | Plymouth | 129.061 | 3 | Petty Eng. | Buddy Baker |
|  | Atlanta 500 | Foyt | Mercury | 131.375 | 1 | Wood Brothers | Foyt |
| 1970 | Dixie 500 | R. Petty | Plymouth | 142.712 | 6 | Petty Eng. | Lorenzen |
| c | Atlanta 500 | B. Allison | Dodge | 139.554 | 9 | Mario Rossi | C. Yarborough |
| 1969 | Dixie 500 | L. Yarbrough | Ford | 133.001 | 2 | Junior Johnson | C. Yarborough |
| † | Atlanta 500 | C. Yarborough | Mercury | 132.191 | 5 | Wood Brothers | Pearson |
| 1968 | Dixie 500 | L. Yarbrough | Mercury | 127.068 | 5 | Junior Johnson | Buddy Baker |
|  | Atlanta 500 | C. Yarborough | Mercury | 125.564 | 4 | Wood Brothers | L. Yarbrough |
| 1967 | Dixie 500 | Hutcherson | Ford | 132.286 | 8 | Bondy Long | Dieringer |
|  | Atlanta 500 | C. Yarborough | Ford | 131.238 | 1 | Wood Brothers | C. Yarborough |
| 1966 | Dixie 400 | R. Petty | Plymouth | 130.244 | 5 | Petty Eng. | Turner |
|  | Atlanta 500 | Hurtubise | Plymouth | 131.266 | 5 | Norm Nelson | R. Petty |
| 1965 | Dixie 400 | Panch | Ford | 110.120 | 2 | Wood Brothers | Lorenzen |
|  | Atlanta 500 | Panch | Ford | 129.410 | 1 | Wood Brothers | Panch |
| 1964 | Dixie 400 | Jarrett | Ford | 112.535 | 17 | Bondy Long | Johnson |
|  | Atlanta 500 | Lorenzen | Ford | 132.959 | 1 | Holman-Moody | Lorenzen |
| 1963 | Dixie 400 | Johnson | Chevrolet | 121.139 | 2 | Ray Fox | Panch |
|  | Atlanta 500 | Lorenzen | Ford | 130.582 | 2 | Holman-Moody | Johnson |
| 1962 | Dixie 400 | White | Chevrolet | 124.896 | 5 | Louis Clements | Roberts |
| b | Atlanta 500 | Lorenzen | Ford | 101.983 | 7 | Holman-Moody | Matthews |
| 1961 | Dixie 400 | Pearson | Pontiac | 125.384 | 5 | Ray Fox | Roberts |
| a | Festival 250 | Lorenzen | Ford | 118.007 | 5 | Holman-Moody | Roberts |
|  | Atlanta 500 | Burdick | Pontiac | 124.172 | 7 | Bob Burdick | Panch |
| 1960 | Atlanta 500 | Johns | Pontiac | 134.596 | 5 | Cotton Owens | Roberts |
|  | Dixie 300 | Roberts | Pontiac | 112.653 | 1 | Smokey Yunick | Roberts |

* Qualifying rained out; drivers drew for starting positions; Gordon Johncock started on pole.
† Pearson won pole but elected to start 40th; Glotzbach started on pole.
a Special, one-shot race.
b Race cut to 328.5 miles by rain.
c Track remeasured, changed from 1.5-mile to 1.522-mile circuit.
d Race cut to 407.89 miles by rain and darkness.
e Race cut to 436.814 miles by rain.
f Name changed to Atlanta Motor Speedway.
g First 47 laps run on Sunday, March 17; final 281 on March 18.
h First race on redesigned 1.54-mile track with backstretch now the start-finish line.
i Race cut short to 340.34 miles by rain.
j Race was red-flagged after the second caution and completed on October 27.

## ALL ATLANTA RACES

### POLE WINNERS

| | | | |
|---|---|---|---|
| Buddy Baker | 7 | Yarbrough | 1 |
| Yarborough | 6 | Turner | 1 |
| Roberts | 5 | Diering | 1 |
| Elliott | 5 | Matthews | 1 |
| R. Petty | 4 | T. Labonte | 1 |
| Earnhardt | 4 | Shepherd | 1 |
| R. Wallace | 3 | Richmond | 1 |
| G. Bodine | 3 | Martin | 1 |
| Pearson | 3 | Bonnett | 1 |
| Gant | 3 | Mast | 1 |
| Lorenzen | 3 | Allen | 1 |
| Panch | 3 | Sacks | 1 |
| Kulwicki | 3 | D. Waltrip | 1 |
| B. Labonte | 2 | Benson | 1 |
| D. Jarrett | 2 | J. Gordon | 1 |
| Jr. Johnson | 2 | R. Gordon | 1 |
| B. Allison | 2 | J. Andretti | 1 |
| Marcis | 2 | K. Irwin | 1 |
| Newman | 2 | Lepage | 1 |
| Foyt | 1 | Earnhardt Jr. | 1 |
| Sommers | 1 | Earnhardt | 9 |

### RACE WINNERS

| | | | |
|---|---|---|---|
| C. Yarborough | 7 | Roberts | 1 |
| R. Petty | 6 | N. Jarrett | 1 |
| B. Labonte | 6 | Hutcherson | 1 |
| B. Allison | 5 | Johns | 1 |
| Elliott | 5 | Burdick | 1 |
| Lorenzen | 4 | D. Allison | 1 |
| Pearson | 4 | Parsons | 1 |
| J. Gordon | 4 | Rudd | 1 |
| D. Waltrip | 3 | Schrader | 1 |
| Bonnett | 3 | E. Irvan | 1 |
| Shepherd | 3 | D. Jarrett | 1 |
| R. Wallace | 3 | J. Nadeau | 1 |
| M. Martin | 2 | K. Harvick | 1 |
| L. Yarbrough | 2 | T. Stewart | 1 |
| Panch | 2 | K. Busch | 1 |
| Buddy Baker | 2 | | |
| Marcis | 1 | | |
| Foyt | 1 | | |
| Jr. Johnson | 1 | | |
| White | 1 | | |
| Hurtubise | 1 | | |

## SPRING: Golden Corral 500

### POLE WINNERS

| | | | |
|---|---|---|---|
| Earnhardt | 4 | Jr. Johnson | 1 |
| Buddy Baker | 3 | Matthews | 1 |
| R. Petty | 3 | T. Labonte | 1 |
| Yarborough | 3 | Bonnett | 1 |
| D. Jarrett | 2 | B. Allison | 1 |
| G. Bodine | 2 | Martin | 1 |
| Pearson | 2 | R. Wallace | 1 |
| Panch | 2 | Allen | 1 |
| Kulwicki | 2 | Benson | 1 |
| Foyt | 1 | R. Gordon | 1 |
| Yarbrough | 1 | J. Andretti | 1 |
| Lorenzen | 1 | B. Labonte | 1 |
| Marcis | 1 | Elliott | 1 |
| Roberts | 1 | R. Newman | 1 |

### RACE WINNERS

| | | | |
|---|---|---|---|
| Yarborough | 6 | Johns | 1 |
| Earnhardt | 5 | Burdick | 1 |
| Lorenzen | 3 | Buddy Baker | 1 |
| B. Allison | 3 | Parsons | 1 |
| J. Gordon | 2 | Rudd | 1 |
| Pearson | 2 | Schrader | 1 |
| R. Petty | 2 | Irvan | 1 |
| D. Waltrip | 2 | D. Jarrett | 1 |
| Elliott | 2 | Harvick | 1 |
| Shepherd | 2 | Stewart | 1 |
| B. Labonte | 2 | | |
| Foyt | 1 | | |
| Panch | 1 | | |
| Hurtubise | 1 | | |

## FALL: Bass Pro Shops MBNA 500

### POLE WINNERS

| | | | |
|---|---|---|---|
| Buddy Baker | 4 | B. Allison | 1 |
| Elliott | 4 | Shepherd | 1 |
| Gant | 3 | Richmond | 1 |
| Yarborough | 3 | Kulwicki | 1 |
| Roberts | 3 | Mast | 1 |
| R. Wallace | 2 | Sacks | 1 |
| Lorenzen | 2 | D. Waltrip | 1 |
| Pearson | 1 | B. Labonte | 1 |
| R. Petty | 1 | G. Bodine | 1 |
| Marcis | 1 | K. Irwin | 1 |
| Panch | 1 | Lepage | 1 |
| Sommers | 1 | J. Gordon | 1 |
| Turner | 1 | Earnhardt Jr. | 1 |
| Jr. Johnson | 1 | Newman | 1 |
| Dieringer | 1 | | |

### RACE WINNERS

| | | | |
|---|---|---|---|
| B. Labonte | 4 | Roberts | 1 |
| R. Petty | 4 | Hutcherson | 1 |
| Earnhardt | 4 | Jr. Johnson | 1 |
| Bonnett | 3 | White | 1 |
| Elliott | 3 | Jarrett | 1 |
| R. Wallace | 2 | D. Allison | 1 |
| Martin | 2 | Yarborough | 1 |
| Pearson | 2 | Shepherd | 1 |
| B. Allison | 2 | Nadeau | 1 |
| Yarborough | 2 | Busch | 1 |
| J. Gordon | 2 | | |
| Buddy Baker | 1 | | |
| D. Waltrip | 1 | | |
| Marcis | 1 | | |
| Panch | 1 | | |

## Festival 250

### POLE WINNERS

| | |
|---|---|
| Roberts | 1 |

### RACE WINNERS

| | |
|---|---|
| Lorenzen | 1 |

## BUSCH SERIES

### YEAR BY YEAR WINNERS

| Year | Event | Pole Winner | Speed | Race Winner | Started | Year | Event | Pole Winner | Speed | Race Winner | Started |
|------|-------|-------------|-------|-------------|---------|------|-------|-------------|-------|-------------|---------|
| 1992 | Atlanta 300 | J. Gordon | 173.821 | J. Gordon | 1 | 1998 | Stihl 300 | D. Trickle | 186.673 | M. Martin | 10 |
| 1993 | Slick 50 300 | M. Martin | 174.286 | W. Burton | 5 | 1999 | Yellow Freight 300 | D. Blaney | 186.775 | M. Skinner | 17 |
| 1994 | Busch Light 300 | S. Robinson | 174.330 | H. Gant | 23 | 2000* | Aaron's 312 | M. Kenseth | 185.704 | M. Martin | 4 |
| 1995 | Busch Light 300 | M. Martin | 176.623 | J. Benson | 10 | 2001 | Aaron's 312 | R. Newman | 191.661 | J. Nemechek | 3 |
| 1996 | Busch Light 300 | D. Trickle | 177.544 | T. Labonte | 11 | 2002 | Aaron's 312 | Qualifying Rained Out | — | J. McMurray | 8 |
| 1997 | Stihl 300 | T. Bender | 179.835 | M. Martin | 13 | 2003 | Aaron's 312 | G. Biffle | 193.300 | G. Biffle | 1 |

*race changed to 203 laps

### POLE WINNERS
| | | | | |
|---|---|---|---|---|
| Mark Martin 2 | Dave Blaney 1 | Ryan Newman 1 | Greg Biffle 1 | |
| Dick Trickle 2 | Jeff Gordon 1 | Shawna Robinson 1 | | |
| Tim Bender 1 | Matt Kenseth 1 | | | |

### RACE WINNERS
| | | | |
|---|---|---|---|
| Mark Martin 3 | Harry Gant 1 | Jamie McMurray 1 | Mike Skinner 1 |
| Johnny Benson 1 | Jeff Gordon 1 | | Greg Biffle 1 |
| Ward Burton 1 | Terry Labonte 1 | Joe Nemechek 1 | |

### QUALIFYING RECORD
Greg Biffle, Chevrolet; 192.300 mph; October 24, 2003

### RACE RECORD
Mark Martin, Ford; 151.751 mph (1 hr., 58 min., 55 sec.); March 8, 1997

# Bristol Motor Speedway

## TRACK FACTS
**Date Opened:** 1961
**Owner:** Speedway Motorsports, Inc.
**President/GM:** Jeff Byrd
**Distance:** .533 miles
**Banking in Turns:** 36 degrees
**Banking on Straights:** 16 degrees
**Length of Frontstretch:** 650 feet
**Length of Backstretch:** 650 feet
**Grandstand Seating:** 160,000
**Tickets:** (423) 764-1161
**Website:** www.bristolmotorspeedway.com

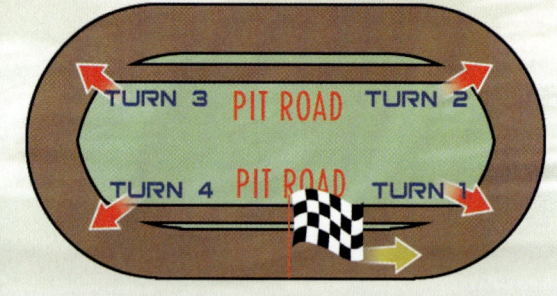

## 2004 SCHEDULE

### NEXTEL Cup
**Food City 500**
Race: No. 6 of 36
Date: March 28
TV: FOX. Radio: PRN

**Sharpie 500**
Race: No. 24 of 36
Date: August 28
TV: TNT. Radio: PRN

### Busch Series
**Channellock 250**
Race: No. 5 of 34
Date: March 27
TV: FX. Radio: PRN

**Food City 250**
Race: No. 24 of 34
Date: August 27
TV: TNT. Radio: PRN

### Craftsman Truck Series
**O'Reilly 200 by Valvoline**
Race: No. 16 of 25
Date: August 25
TV: Speed. Radio: MRN

## NEXTEL CUP

### TRACK RECORDS
**Most Wins:** 12—Darrell Waltrip
**Oldest Winner:** Dale Earnhardt, 48 years, 3 months, 30 days, 8/28/1999
**Youngest Winner:** Kurt Busch, 23 years, 7 months, 20 days, 3/24/2002
**Most Lead Changes:** 40—4/14/91
**Fewest Lead Changes:** 0—3/25/73
**Most Leaders:** 20—Twice, most recently, 8/26/95
**Fewest Leaders:** 1—3/25/73
**Most Cautions:** 20—Three times, most recently, 8/23/03
**Fewest Cautions:** 0—Twice, most recently, 4/2/95
**Most Caution Laps:** 167—7/25/65
**Fewest Caution Laps:** 0—Twice, most recently, 4/2/95
**Most on the Lead Lap:** 25—3/25/01
**Fewest on the Lead Lap:** 1—22 times, most recently, 8/22/81
**Most Running at the Finish:** 40—4/11/99
**Fewest Running at the Finish:** 7—3/20/66
**Most Laps Led by a Race Winner:** 500—Cale Yarborough, 3/25/73
**Fewest Laps Led by a Race Winner:** 1—Fred Lorenzen, 7/26/64
**Closest Margin of Victory:** 0.100 seconds, Terry Labonte defeated Dale Earnhardt 08/26/95
**Greatest Margin of Victory:** 7 laps, Cale Yarborough defeated Dick Brooks 04/17/77

### QUALIFYING AND RACE RECORDS
**QUALIFYING**
Track: Ryan Newman, Dodge, 128.709 mph, March 21, 2003.
Spring Race (Food City 500): Ryan Newman, Dodge, 128.709 mph, March 21, 2003.
Fall Race (Sharpie 500): Jeff Gordon, Chevrolet, 127.597 mph, August 21, 2003.

**RACE**
Track: Charlie Glotzbach, Chevrolet, 101.074 mph, 2 hours, 38 minutes, 12 seconds, July 11, 1971 (Volunteer 500).
Spring Race (Food City 500): Cale Yarborough, Chevrolet, 100.989 mph, 2 hours, 38 minutes, 20 seconds, April 17, 1977.
Fall Race (Sharpie 500): Charlie Glotzbach, Chevrolet, 101.074 mph, 2 hours, 38 minutes, 12 seconds, July 11, 1971.

## YEAR BY YEAR WINNERS

| Year | Event | Race Winner | Car Make | Avg. Speed | Start Pos. | Winning Car Owner | Pole Winner |
|---|---|---|---|---|---|---|---|
| * 2003 | Sharpie 500 | K. Busch | Ford | 77.421 | 5 | Jack Roush | J. Gordon |
| | Food City 500 | K. Busch | Ford | 76.185 | 9 | Jack Roush | R. Newman |
| * 2002 | Sharpie 500 | J. Gordon | Chevrolet | 77.097 | 1 | Rick Hendrick | J. Gordon |
| | Food City 500 | K. Busch | Ford | 82.281 | 27 | Jack Roush | J. Gordon |
| * 2001 | Sharpie 500 | T. Stewart | Pontiac | 85.106 | 18 | Joe Gibbs | J. Green |
| | Food City 500 | E. Sadler | Ford | 86.949 | 38 | Wood Brothers | M. Martin |
| * 2000 | GoRacing.com 500 | R. Wallace | Ford | 85.394 | 1 | Roger Penske | R. Wallace |
| | Food City 500 | R. Wallace | Ford | 88.018 | 6 | Roger Penske | S. Park |
| * 1999 | Goody's 500 | D. Earnhardt | Chevrolet | 91.276 | 26 | Richard Childress | T. Stewart |
| | Food City 500 | R. Wallace | Ford | 93.363 | 1 | Roger Penske | R. Wallace |
| * 1998 | Goody's 500 | M. Martin | Ford | 86.918 | 4 | Jack Roush | R. Wallace |
| | Food City 500 | J. Gordon | Chevrolet | 82.850 | 2 | Rick Hendrick | R. Wallace |
| * 1997 | Goody's 500 | D. Jarrett | Ford | 80.013 | 3 | Robert Yates | K. Wallace |
| | Food City 500 | J. Gordon | Chevrolet | 75.035 | 5 | Rick Hendrick | R. Wallace |
| *h 1996 | Goody's 500 | R. Wallace | Ford | 91.267 | 5 | Roger Penske | M. Martin |
| g | Food City 500 | J. Gordon | Chevrolet | 91.308 | 8 | Rick Hendrick | M. Martin |
| * 1995 | Goody's 500 | T. Labonte | Chevrolet | 81.979 | 2 | Rick Hendrick | M. Martin |
| | Food City 500 | J. Gordon | Chevrolet | 92.011 | 2 | Rick Hendrick | M. Martin |
| * 1994 | Goody's 500 | R. Wallace | Ford | 91.363 | 4 | Roger Penske | H. Gant |
| | Food City 500 | D. Earnhardt | Chevrolet | 89.647 | 24 | Richard Childress | C. Brown |
| * 1993 | Bud 500 | Martin | Ford | 88.172 | 1 | Jack Roush | Martin |
| | Food City 500 | R. Wallace | Pontiac | 84.730 | 1 | Roger Penske | R. Wallace |
| *f 1992 | Bud 500 | D. Waltrip | Chevrolet | 91.198 | 9 | Darrell Waltrip | Irvan |
| | Food City 500 | Kulwicki | Ford | 86.316 | 1 | Alan Kulwicki | Kulwicki |
| * 1991 | Bud 500 | Kulwicki | Ford | 82.028 | 5 | Alan Kulwicki | Elliott |
| | Valleydale 500 | R. Wallace | Pontiac | 72.809 | 1 | Roger Penske | R. Wallace |
| * 1990 | Busch 500 | Irvan | Chevrolet | 91.782 | 6 | Morgan-McClure | Earnhardt |
| | Valleydale 500 | Da. Allison | Ford | 87.258 | 19 | Robert Yates | Irvan |
| * 1989 | Busch 500 | D. Waltrip | Chevrolet | 78.775 | 9 | Rick Hendrick | Kulwicki |
| | Valleydale 500 | Wallace | Pontiac | 76.034 | 8 | Blue Max | Martin |
| * 1988 | Busch 500 | Earnhardt | Chevrolet | 78.775 | 5 | Richard Childress | Kulwicki |
| | Valleydale 500 | Elliott | Ford | 83.115 | 13 | Melling Racing | R. Wilson |
| * 1987 | Busch 500 | Earnhardt | Chevrolet | 90.373 | 6 | Richard Childress | Labonte |
| | Valleydale 500 | Earnhardt | Chevrolet | 75.621 | 3 | Richard Childress | Gant |
| * 1986 | Busch 500 | Waltrip | Chevrolet | 86.934 | 10 | Junior Johnson | Bodine |
| | Valleydale 500 | Wallace | Pontiac | 89.747 | 14 | Blue Max | Bodine |
| * 1985 | Busch 500 | Earnhardt | Chevrolet | 81.388 | 1 | Richard Childress | Earnhardt |
| | Valleydale 500 | Earnhardt | Chevrolet | 81.790 | 12 | Richard Childress | Gant |
| * 1984 | Busch 500 | Labonte | Chevrolet | 85.365 | 6 | Billy Hagan | Bodine |
| | Valleydale 500 | Waltrip | Chevrolet | 93.967 | 3 | Junior Johnson | Rudd |
| * 1983 | Busch 500 | Waltrip | Chevrolet | 89.430 | 2 | Junior Johnson | Rutman |
| | Valleydale 500 | Waltrip | Chevrolet | 93.445 | 13 | Junior Johnson | Bonnett |
| * 1982 | Busch 500 | Waltrip | Buick | 94.318 | 8 | Junior Johnson | Richmond |
| | Valleydale 500 | Waltrip | Buick | 94.025 | 1 | Junior Johnson | Waltrip |
| * 1981 | Busch 500 | Waltrip | Buick | 84.723 | 1 | Junior Johnson | Waltrip |
| | Valleydale 500 | Waltrip | Buick | 89.530 | 1 | Junior Johnson | Waltrip |
| * 1980 | Busch Vol. 500 | C. Yarborough | Chevrolet | 86.973 | 1 | Junior Johnson | C. Yarborough |
| e | Valleydale SE 500 | Earnhardt | Chevrolet | 96.977 | 4 | Osterlund Rac. | C. Yarborough |
| * 1979 | Volunteer 500 | Waltrip | Chevrolet | 91.493 | 5 | DiGard Rac. Co. | R. Petty |
| | Southeastern 500 | Earnhardt | Chevrolet | 91.033 | 9 | Osterlund Rac. | Buddy Baker |
| * 1978 | Volunteer 500 | C. Yarborough | Oldsmobile | 88.628 | 4 | Junior Johnson | Pond |
| d | Southeastern 500 | Waltrip | Chevrolet | 92.401 | 7 | DiGard Rac. Co. | Bonnett |
| 1977 | Volunteer 400 | C. Yarborough | Chevrolet | 79.726 | 1 | Junior Johnson | C. Yarborough |
| | Southeastern 500 | C. Yarborough | Chevrolet | 100.989 | 1 | Junior Johnson | C. Yarborough |
| 1976 | Volunteer 400 | C. Yarborough | Chevrolet | 99.175 | 2 | Junior Johnson | Waltrip |
| | Southeastern 400 | C. Yarborough | Chevrolet | 87.377 | 3 | Junior Johnson | Buddy Baker |
| 1975 | Volunteer 500 | R. Petty | Dodge | 97.016 | 4 | Petty Eng. | C. Yarborough |
| | Southeastern 500 | R. Petty | Dodge | 97.053 | 2 | Petty Eng. | Buddy Baker |
| 1974 | Volunteer 500 | C. Yarborough | Chevrolet | 75.430 | 3 | Junior Johnson | R. Petty |
| | Southeastern 500 | C. Yarborough | Chevrolet | 64.533 | 3 | Junior Johnson | D. Allison |
| 1973 | Volunteer 500 | Parsons | Chevrolet | 91.342 | 2 | L.G. DeWitt | C. Yarborough |
| c | Southeastern 500 | C. Yarborough | Chevrolet | 88.952 | 1 | Junior Johnson | C. Yarborough |
| 1972 | Volunteer 500 | B. Allison | Chevrolet | 92.735 | 1 | Junior Johnson | B. Allison |
| | Southeastern 500 | B. Allison | Chevrolet | 92.826 | 1 | Junior Johnson | B. Allison |
| b 1971 | Volunteer 500 | Glotzbach | Chevrolet | 101.074 | 2 | Junior Johnson | R. Petty |
| | Southeastern 500 | Pearson | Ford | 91.704 | 1 | Holman-Moody | Pearson |
| 1970 | Volunteer 500 | B. Allison | Dodge | 84.880 | 10 | Bobby Allison | C. Yarborough |
| | Southeastern 500 | Do. Allison | Ford | 87.543 | 2 | Banjo Matthews | Pearson |
| a 1969 | Volunteer 500 | Pearson | Ford | 79.737 | 3 | Holman-Moody | C. Yarborough |
| | Southeastern 500 | B. Allison | Dodge | 81.455 | 4 | Mario Rossi | Isaac |
| 1968 | Volunteer 500 | Pearson | Ford | 76.310 | 6 | Holman-Moody | L. Yarbrough |
| | Southeastern 500 | Pearson | Ford | 77.247 | 2 | Holman-Moody | R. Petty |
| 1967 | Volunteer 500 | R. Petty | Plymouth | 78.705 | 1 | Petty Eng. | R. Petty |
| | Southeastern 500 | Pearson | Dodge | 75.930 | 14 | Cotton Owens | Dieringer |
| 1966 | Volunteer 500 | Goldsmith | Plymouth | 77.963 | 4 | Ray Nichels | Turner |
| | Southeastern 500 | Hutcherson | Ford | 69.952 | 6 | Bondy Long | Pearson |

## ALL BRISTOL RACES

### POLE WINNERS

| | | | |
|---|---|---|---|
| Yarborough | 9 | Isaac | 1 |
| R. Wallace | 7 | Dieringer | 1 |
| Martin | 7 | Yarbrough | 1 |
| R. Petty | 6 | Turner | 1 |
| Lorenzen | 4 | Johns | 1 |
| D. Waltrip | 4 | Richmond | 1 |
| G. Bodine | 3 | Ruttman | 1 |
| Kulwicki | 3 | Rudd | 1 |
| Buddy Baker | 3 | T. Labonte | 1 |
| J. Gordon | 3 | Wilson | 1 |
| Pearson | 2 | Elliott | 1 |
| B. Allison | 2 | Gant | 1 |
| Bonnett | 2 | Bown | 1 |
| Earnhardt | 2 | K. Wallace | 1 |
| Irvan | 2 | Stewart | 1 |
| Roberts | 2 | Park | 1 |
| Panch | 2 | Green | 1 |
| Pond | 1 | Newman | 1 |
| D. Allison | 1 | | |

### RACE WINNERS

| | | | |
|---|---|---|---|
| D. Waltrip | 12 | Roberts | 1 |
| Yarborough | 9 | Johns | 1 |
| Earnhardt | 9 | Paschal | 1 |
| R. Wallace | 9 | Smith | 1 |
| Pearson | 5 | Weatherly | 1 |
| J. Gordon | 5 | Elliott | 1 |
| B. Allison | 4 | Da. Allison | 1 |
| R. Petty | 3 | Irvan | 1 |
| Lorenzen | 3 | Parsons | 1 |
| K. Busch | 3 | D. Jarrett | 1 |
| T. Labonte | 2 | E. Sadler | 1 |
| Martin | 2 | T. Stewart | 1 |
| Kulwicki | 2 | | |
| D. Allison | 1 | | |
| Glotzbach | 1 | | |
| Hutcherson | 1 | | |
| Goldsmith | 1 | | |
| Jr. Johnson | 1 | | |
| Jarrett | 1 | | |

## SPRING: Food City 500

### POLE WINNERS

| | | | |
|---|---|---|---|
| R. Wallace | 5 | B. Allison | 1 |
| M. Martin | 4 | Isaac | 1 |
| Buddy Baker | 3 | Dieringer | 1 |
| Pearson | 3 | Roberts | 1 |
| Yarborough | 3 | Rudd | 1 |
| Waltrip | 2 | R. Wilson | 1 |
| Bonnett | 2 | Irvan | 1 |
| Gant | 2 | Kulwicki | 1 |
| G. Bodine | 2 | C. Brown | 1 |
| Lorenzen | 2 | S. Park | 1 |
| Panch | 2 | J. Gordon | 1 |
| D. Allison | 1 | Newman | 1 |

### RACE WINNERS

| | | | |
|---|---|---|---|
| R. Wallace | 6 | Lorenzen | 1 |
| D. Waltrip | 5 | Roberts | 1 |
| Earnhardt | 5 | Johns | 1 |
| Yarborough | 4 | Smith | 1 |
| J. Gordon | 4 | Elliott | 1 |
| Pearson | 3 | Da. Allison | 1 |
| B. Allison | 2 | Kulwicki | 1 |
| K. Busch | 2 | E. Sadler | 1 |
| R. Petty | 1 | | |
| D. Allison | 1 | | |
| Hutcherson | 1 | | |
| Jr. Johnson | 1 | | |

## FALL: Sharpie 500

### POLE WINNERS

| | | | |
|---|---|---|---|
| Yarborough | 6 | Turner | 1 |
| R. Petty | 5 | Johns | 1 |
| Martin | 3 | Pond | 1 |
| Waltrip | 2 | Richmond | 1 |
| Bodine | 2 | Ruttman | 1 |
| Kulwicki | 2 | Labonte | 1 |
| Earnhardt | 2 | Elliott | 1 |
| Lorenzen | 2 | Irvan | 1 |
| R. Wallace | 2 | Gant | 1 |
| J. Gordon | 2 | K. Wallace | 1 |
| B. Allison | 1 | Stewart | 1 |
| Yarbrough | 1 | Green | 1 |
| Roberts | 1 | | |

### RACE WINNERS

| | | | |
|---|---|---|---|
| D. Waltrip | 7 | Pascal | 1 |
| Yarborough | 5 | Weatherly | 1 |
| Earnhardt | 4 | Irvan | 1 |
| R. Wallace | 3 | Kulwicki | 1 |
| R. Petty | 2 | Parsons | 1 |
| B. Allison | 2 | D. Jarrett | 1 |
| Pearson | 2 | Stewart | 1 |
| Lorenzen | 2 | J. Gordon | 1 |
| T. Labonte | 2 | Busch | 1 |
| Martin | 2 | | |
| Glotzbach | 1 | | |
| Goldsmith | 1 | | |
| Jarrett | 1 | | |

| Year | Event | Race Winner | Car Make | Avg. Speed | Start Pos. | Winning Car Owner | Pole Winner |
|---|---|---|---|---|---|---|---|
| 1965 | Volunteer 500 | Jarrett | Ford | 61.826 | 6 | Bondy Long | Lorenzen |
| | Southeastern 500 | Johnson | Ford | 74.938 | 3 | Junior Johnson | Panch |
| 1964 | Volunteer 500 | Lorenzen | Ford | 78.044 | 8 | Holman-Moody | R. Petty |
| | Southeastern 500 | Lorenzen | Ford | 72.196 | 2 | Holman-Moody | Panch |
| 1963 | Volunteer 500 | Lorenzen | Ford | 74.844 | 1 | Holman-Moody | Lorenzen |
| | Southeastern 500 | Roberts | Ford | 76.910 | 3 | Holman-Moody | Lorenzen |
| 1962 | Southeastern 500 | Paschal | Plymouth | 75.280 | 12 | Petty Eng. | Roberts |
| | Volunteer 500 | Johns | Pontiac | 73.320 | 6 | Shorty Johns | Roberts |
| 1961 | Southeastern 500 | Weatherly | Pontiac | 72.450 | 2 | Bud Moore | Johns |
| | Volunteer 500 | Smith | Pontiac | 68.370 | 12 | Jack Smith | Lorenzen |

*Night races. a Track reshaped and remeasured; turns banked from 22 to 36 degrees and track measured at .533 of a mile; 500 laps now cover 266.5 miles; prior to the change it was a .5-mile track and the distance was 500 laps, 250 miles. b Race run without a caution. c Yarborough led all 500 laps, 266.5 miles (March 25, 1973). d Name changed from Bristol International Speedway to Bristol International Raceway. e Called after 419 laps, rain. f Track surface is concrete. g Called after 342 laps, rain. h Name of track changed from Bristol International Raceway to Bristol Motor Speedway.

# BUSCH SERIES

## YEAR BY YEAR WINNERS

| Year | Event | Pole Winner | Speed | Race Winner | Started | Year | Event | Pole Winner | Speed | Race Winner | Started |
|---|---|---|---|---|---|---|---|---|---|---|---|
| 1982 | Southeastern 150 | D. Pearson | 114.816 | P. Parsons | 7 | 1993 | Budweiser 250 | W. Burton | 122.945 | M. Waltrip | 9 |
| | Pet Dairy 150 | M. Shepherd | 115.132 | J. Ingram | 6 | | Food City 250 | None - weather | | T. Bodine | 12 |
| 1983 | Southeastern 150 | None - weather | | M. Shepherd | 7 | 1994 | Goody's 250 | M. Martin | 123.746 | D. Green | 3 |
| | Free Service 150 | P. Parsons | 115.231 | S. Ard | 2 | | Food City 250 | H. Gant | 123.364 | K. Wallace | 7 |
| 1984* | No Spring race held | | | | | 1995 | Goody's 250 | D. Green | 122.474 | S. Grissom | 18 |
| | Free Service 200 | M. Shepherd | 116.045 | M. Shepherd | 1 | | Food City 250 | S. Reeves | 122.560 | S. Grissom | 28 |
| 1985 | Budweiser 200 | T. Ellis | 116.829 | D. Waltrip | 16 | 1996 | Goody's 250 | C. Little | 121.198 | M. Martin | 10 |
| | Tri-City Pont. 200 | R. Bouchard | 116.964 | B. Bodine | 4 | | Food City 250 | J. Fuller | 121.029 | J. Fuller | 1 |
| 1986 | Budweiser 200 | G. Bodine | 117.293 | M. Shepherd | 2 | 1997 | Moore's Snacks 250 | H. Sadler | 120.938 | J. Burton | 3 |
| | Tri-City Pont. 200 | B. Bodine | 116.171 | B. Bodine | 1 | | Food City 250 | R. LaJoie | 121.267 | J. Spencer | 16 |
| 1987 | Budweiser 200 | D. Earnhardt | 117.653 | M. Shepherd | 11 | 1998 | Moore's Snacks 250 | D. Earnhardt, Jr. | 122.217 | E. Sadler | 3 |
| | Tri-City Pont. 200 | M. Martin | 117.754 | L. Pearson | 4 | | Ford City 250 | S. Grissom | 121.512 | K. Lepage | 5 |
| 1988 | Budweiser 200 | L. Pearson | 117.057 | D. Earnhardt | 4 | 1999 | Moore's Snacks 250 | J. Keller | 123.024 | J. Keller | 1 |
| | Tri-City Pont. 200 | T. Ellis | 113.761 | L. Pearson | 7 | | Food City 250 | J. Green | 122.537 | M. Kenseth | 3 |
| 1989 | Budweiser 200 | R. Wilson | 119.299 | R. Wilson | 1 | 2000 | Cheez-It 250 | J. Green | 124.428 | S. Marlin | 16 |
| | Jay Johnson 200 | M. Shepherd | 116.368 | M. Martin | 8 | | Food City 250 | K. Harvick | 123.356 | K. Harvick | 1 |
| 1990# | Budweiser 250 | None - weather | | L. Ottinger | 13 | 2001 | Cheez-It 250 | K. Harvick | 125.264 | M. Kenseth | 2 |
| | Jay Johnson 250 | B. Labonte | 114.850 | R. Mast | 12 | | Food City 250 | M. Skinner | 124.460 | K. Harvick | 2 |
| 1991 | Budweiser 250 | J. Burton | 117.286 | B. Labonte | 21 | 2002 | Channellock 250 | S. Riggs | 126.270 | J. Green | 2 |
| | Jay Johnson 250 | C. Bown | 116.737 | D. Jarrett | 11 | | Food City 250 | J. Keller | 124.428 | J. Spencer | 10 |
| 1992 | Budweiser 250 | B. Miller | 121.267 | H. Gant | 18 | 2003 | Channellock 250 | D. Green | 126.495 | K. Harvick | 11 |
| | Food City 250 | K. Wallace | 118.189 | T. Bodine | 11 | | Food City 250 | J. Keller | 126.021 | M. Waltrip | 4 |

* Race length changed to 200 laps

### POLE WINNERS

| | | | | | | | | | |
|---|---|---|---|---|---|---|---|---|---|
| Shepherd | 3 | G. Bodine | 1 | Gant | 1 | L. Pearson | 1 | Ottinger | 1 |
| Ellis | 2 | Bouchard | 1 | Grissom | 1 | Reeves | 1 | P. Parsons | 1 |
| J. Green | 2 | J. Burton | 1 | B. Labonte | 1 | Riggs | 1 | E. Sadler | 1 |
| Harvick | 2 | W. Burton | 1 | LaJoie | 1 | H. Sadler | 1 | K. Wallace | 1 |
| Keller | 3 | Bown | 1 | Little | 1 | Skinner | 1 | D. Waltrip | 1 |
| Martin | 2 | Earnhardt | 1 | Miller | 1 | K. Wallace | 1 | Wilson | 1 |
| D. Green | 2 | Earnhardt Jr. | 1 | P. Parsons | 1 | Wilson | 1 | | |
| B. Bodine | 1 | Fuller | 1 | D. Pearson | 1 | | | | |

### RACE WINNERS

| | | | | | | | | | |
|---|---|---|---|---|---|---|---|---|---|
| Shepherd | 4 | Spencer | 2 | J. Green | 1 | | | | | | |
| Harvick | 3 | M. Waltrip | 2 | Ingram | 1 | | | | | | |
| B. Bodine | 2 | Ard | 1 | D. Jarrett | 1 | | | | | | |
| T. Bodine | 2 | J. Burton | 1 | Keller | 1 | | | | | | |
| Grissom | 2 | Earnhardt | 1 | Lepage | 1 | | | | | | |
| Kenseth | 2 | Fuller | 1 | B. Labonte | 1 | | | | | | |
| Martin | 2 | Gant | 1 | Str. Marlin | 1 | | | | | | |
| L. Pearson | 2 | D. Green | 1 | Mast | 1 | | | | | | |

**QUALIFYING RECORD**
David Green, Pontiac, 126.495 mph, March 21, 2003

**RACE RECORD**
Harry Gant, Buick; 92.929 mph (1 hr., 26 min., 02 sec.); April 4, 1992

# CRAFTSMAN TRUCK SERIES

## YEAR BY YEAR WINNERS

| Year | Event | Pole Winner | Speed | Race Winner | Started |
|---|---|---|---|---|---|
| 1995 | Pizza Plus 15 | Mike Skinner | 118,738 | Joe Ruttman | 3 |
| 1996 | Coca-Cola 200 | Mike Skinner | 117,805 | Rick Carelli | 2 |
| 1997 | Loadhandler 200 | Ron Hornaday Jr. | 121.213 | Ron Hornaday Jr. | 1 |
| 1998 | Loadhandler 200 | Ron Hornaday Jr. | 119.910 | Ron Hornaday Jr. | 1 |
| 1999 | Coca-Cola 200 | Greg Biffle | 120.831 | Jack Sprague | 3 |
| 2003 | O'Reilly 200 | Ted Musgrave | 123.562 | Travis Kvapil | 12 |

**QUALIFYING RECORD**
Ted Musgrave, Dodge, 123.562 mph, August 20, 2003.

**RACE RECORD**
Travis Kvapil, Chevrolet, 88.813 mph (1 hr., 12 min., 1 sec.), August 20, 2003.

### POLE WINNERS

| | | | | | |
|---|---|---|---|---|---|
| Hornaday | 2 | Sprague | 1 | | |
| Skinner | 2 | Musgrave | 1 | | |
| Biffle | 1 | | | | |

### RACE WINNERS

| | | | |
|---|---|---|---|
| Honraday | 2 | Kvapil | 1 |
| Carelli | 1 | | |
| Ruttman | 1 | | |

# California Speedway

## TRACK FACTS
**Date Opened:** June 20, 1997
**Owner:** ISC
**President:** Bill Miller
**Distance:** 2.0 miles
**Banking in Turns 1-4:** 14 degrees
**Banking in Trioval:** 11 degrees
**Banking on Backstretch:** 3 degrees
**Length of Frontstretch:** 3,100 feet
**Length of Backstretch:** 2,500 feet
**Grandstand Seating:** 92,000
**Tickets:** (800) 944-7223
**Website:** www.californiaspeedway.com

## NEXTEL CUP

### TRACK RECORDS
**Most Wins:** 2—Jeff Gordon
**Oldest Winner:** Rusty Wallace, 44 years, 8 months, 15 days, 04/29/2001
**Youngest Winner:** Kurt Busch, 24 years, 8 months, 23 days, 4/27/03
**Most Lead Changes:** 27—5/2/99
**Fewest Lead Changes:** 18—5/3/98
**Most Leaders:** 15—4/30/00
**Fewest Leaders:** 8—Twice, most recently, 4/28/02
**Most Cautions:** 8—4/27/03
**Fewest Cautions:** 4—6/22/97
**Most Caution Laps:** 35—5/3/98
**Fewest Caution Laps:** 22—Twice, most recently, 4/30/00
**Most on the Lead Lap:** 26—4/29/01
**Fewest on the Lead Lap:** 9—Twice, most recently, 5/2/99
**Most Running at the Finish:** 40—4/29/01
**Fewest Running at the Finish:** 32—6/22/97
**Most Laps Led by a Race Winner:** 165—Mark Martin, 5/3/98
**Fewest Laps Led by a Race Winner:** 26—Jeremy Mayfield, 4/30/00
**Closest Margin of Victory:** 0.270 seconds, Rusty Wallace defeated Jeff Gordon 04/29/01
**Greatest Margin of Victory:** 4.492 seconds, Jeff Gordon defeated Jeff Burton 05/02/99

### QUALIFYING AND RACE RECORDS
**QUALIFYING**
**Track:** Ryan Newman, Chevrolet, 187.432 mph, 38.414 seconds, April 26, 2002.
**RACE**
**Track:** Jeff Gordon, Chevrolet, 155.012 mph, 3 hours, 13 minutes, 32 seconds, June 22, 1997.

### ALL CALIFORNIA RACES

| POLE WINNERS | | RACE WINNERS | |
|---|---|---|---|
| J. Nemechek | 1 | B. Labonte | 1 | J. Gordon | 2 | R. Wallace | 1 |
| J. Gordon | 1 | R. Newman | 1 | M. Martin | 1 | J. Johnson | 1 |
| M. Skinner | 1 | | | J. Mayfield | 1 | | |

### 2004 SCHEDULE

**NEXTEL Cup**
Auto Club 500
**Race:** No. 10 of 36
**Date:** May 2
**TV:** FOX.
**Radio:** PRN

Pop Secret 500*
**Race:** No. 25 of 36
**Date:** September 5
**TV:** TNT.
**Radio:** PRN

**Busch Series**
1-800-PIT-SHOP.com 300
**Race:** No. 9 of 34
**Date:** May 1
**TV:** FOX. Radio: MRN

CaliforniaSpeedway.com 300
**Race:** No. 25 of 34
**Date:** September 4
**Radio:** MRN

**Craftsman Truck Series**
American Racing Wheels 200
**Race:** No. 20 of 25
**Date:** October 2
**TV:** Speed.
**Radio:** MRN

*Inaugural event

### YEAR BY YEAR WINNERS

| Year | Event | Race Winner | Car Make | Avg. Speed | Start Pos. | Winning Car Owner | Pole Winner |
|---|---|---|---|---|---|---|---|
| 2003 | Auto Club 500 | K. Busch | Ford | 140.111 | 16 | Jack Roush | S. Park |
| 2002 | NAPA Auto Parts 500 | J. Johnson | Chevrolet | 150.088 | 4 | Rick Hendrick | R. Newman |
| 2002 | NAPA Auto Parts 500 | J. Johnson | Chevrolet | 150.088 | 4 | Rick Hendrick | R. Newman |
| 2001 | NAPA Auto Parts 500 | R. Wallace | Ford | 143.118 | 19 | Roger Penske | B. Labonte |
| 2000 | NAPA Auto Parts 500 | J. Mayfield | Ford | 149.378 | 24 | Roger Penske | M. Skinner |
| 1999 | California 500 | J. Gordon | Chevrolet | 150.276 | 5 | Rick Hendrick | Trials Rained Out |
| 1998 | California 500 | M. Martin | Ford | 140.220 | 3 | Jack Roush | J. Gordon |
| 1997 | California 500 | J. Gordon | Chevrolet | 155.012 | 3 | Rick Hendrick | J. Nemechek |

## BUSCH SERIES

### YEAR BY YEAR WINNERS

| Year | Event | Pole Winner | Speed | Race Winner | Started |
|---|---|---|---|---|---|
| 1997 | Kenwood 300 | S. Park | 175.157 | T. Bodine | 28 |
| 1998 | Kenwood 300 | R. Pressley | 174.073 | D. Earnhardt Jr. | 2 |
| 1999 | Auto Club 300 | None - weather | — | M. Kenseth | 2 |
| 2000 | Auto Club 300 | J. Green | 178.258 | M. Kenseth | 8 |
| 2001 | Auto Club 300 | B. Hamilton Jr. | 179.198 | H. Parker Jr. | 26 |
| 2002 | Auto Club 300 | None - weather | — | S. Riggs | 6 |
| 2003 | 1-800-PIT-SHOP.COM 300 | Kevin Harvick | 183.941 | Matt Kenseth | 19 |

| POLE WINNERS | | RACE WINNERS | | | | | |
|---|---|---|---|---|---|---|---|
| Jeff Green | 1 | Robert Pressley | 1 | Matt Kenseth | 3 | Hank Parker Jr. | 1 |
| Bobby Hamilton, Jr. | 1 | Kevin Harvick | 1 | Todd Bodine | 1 | Scott Riggs | 1 |
| Steve Park | 1 | | | Dale Earnhardt Jr. | 1 | | |

**BUSCH SERIES QUALIFYING RECORD**
Kevin Harvick, Chevrolet; 183.941 mph; April 25, 2003

**BUSCH SERIES RACE RECORD**
Hank Parker, Jr., Chevrolet; 155.957 mph (1 hr., 55 min., 25 sec.); April 28, 2001

## CRAFTSMAN TRUCK SERIES

### YEAR BY YEAR WINNERS

| Year | Event | Pole Winner | Speed | Race Winner | Started |
|---|---|---|---|---|---|
| 1997 | The No Fear Challenge | Mike Bliss | 173.198 | Mike Bliss | 1 |
| 1998 | The No Fear Challenge | Andy Houston | 172.022 | Jack Sprague | 10 |
| 1999 | NAPA Auto Parts 200 | Andy Houston | 173.561 | Jack Sprague | 3 |
| 2000 | Motorola 200 | Kurt Busch | 177.388 | Kurt Busch | 1 |
| 2001 | Auto Club 200 | Scott Riggs | 173.678 | Ted Musgrave | 12 |
| 2002 | Am. Racing Wheels 200 | David Starr | 175.850 | Ted Musgrave | 11 |
| 2003 | Am. Racing Wheels 200 | Brendan Gaughan | 173.716 | Ted Musgrave | 10 |

**QUALIFYING RECORD**
Kurt Busch, Ford; 177.388 mph (40.589 sec.); October 27, 2000.

**RACE RECORD**
Ted Musgrave, Dodge; 145.926 mph (1 hr., 22 min., 14 sec.); September 20, 2003.

### POLE WINNERS

| | |
|---|---|
| Andy Houston | 2 |
| David Starr | 2 |
| Mike Bliss | 1 |
| Kurt Busch | 1 |
| Scott Riggs | 1 |

### RACE WINNERS

| | |
|---|---|
| Ted Musgrave | 3 |
| Jack Sprague | 2 |
| Mike Bliss | 1 |
| Kurt Busch | 1 |

# Chicagoland Speedway

### TRACK FACTS
**Date Opened:** 2001
**Owner:** Raceway Associates, LLC
**VP/GM:** Matthew T. Alexander
**Distance:** 1.5 miles
**Banking in Turns:** 18 degrees
**Banking on Trioval:** 11 degrees
**Banking on Backstretch:** 5 degrees
**Length of Frontstretch:** 2,400 feet
**Length of Backstretch:** 1,700 feet
**Grandstand Seating:** 75,000
**Tickets:** (815) 727-7223
**Website:** www.chicagolandspeedway.com

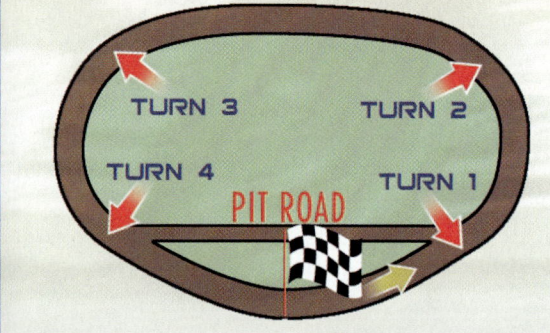

### 2004 SCHEDULE

#### NEXTEL Cup
**Tropicana 400**
**Race:** No. 18 of 36
**Date:** Juy 11
**TV:** NBC. **Radio:** MRN

#### Busch Series
**Twister 300**
**Race:** No. 19 of 34
**Date:** July 10
**TV:** NBC. **Radio:** MRN

## NEXTEL CUP

### TRACK RECORDS
**Most Wins:** 2—Kevin Harvick
**Oldest Winner:** Kevin Harvick, 26 years, 7 months, 6 days, 07/14/2002
**Youngest Winner:** Ryan Newman, 25 years, 7 months, 5 days, 7/13/03
**Most Lead Changes:** 19—7/14/02
**Fewest Lead Changes:** 13—7/13/03
**Most Leaders:** 11—7/14/02
**Fewest Leaders:** 7—7/13/03
**Most Cautions:** 10—7/15/01
**Fewest Cautions:** 7—Twice, most recently 7/13/03
**Most Caution Laps:** 56—7/15/01
**Fewest Caution Laps:** 35—7/14/02
**Most on the Lead Lap:** 17—7/15/01
**Fewest on the Lead Lap:** 11—7/13/03
**Most Running at the Finish:** 34—7/15/01
**Fewest Running at the Finish:** 33—7/14/02
**Most Laps Led by a Race Winner:** 113—Kevin Harvick 7/15/01
**Fewest Laps Led by a Race Winner:** 29—Kevin Harvick 7/14/02
**Closest Margin of Victory:**—0.649 second, Kevin Harvick defeated Robert Pressley 07/15/01
**Greatest Margin of Victory:**—2.633 seconds, Ryan Newman defeated Tony Stewart, 7/13/03

### QUALIFYING AND RACE RECORDS
**QUALIFYING**
**Track:** Tony Stewart, Chevrolet, 184.786 mph, July 11, 2003.
**RACE**
**Track:** Kevin Harvick, Chevrolet, 136.832 mph, 2:55:37, July 14, 2002.

### YEAR BY YEAR WINNERS

| Year | Event | Race Winner | Car Make | Avg. Speed | Start Pos. | Winning Car Owner | Pole Winner |
|---|---|---|---|---|---|---|---|
| 2003 | Tropicana 400 | R. Newman | Dodge | 134.059 | 14 | Roger Penske | T. Stewart |
| 2002 | Tropicana 400 | K. Harvick | Chevrolet | 136.832 | 32 | Richard Childress | R. Newman |
| 2001 | Tropicana 400 | K. Harvick | Chevrolet | 131.759 | 6 | Richard Childress | T. Bodine |

### ALL CHICAGOLAND RACES

| POLE WINNERS | | | RACE WINNERS | |
|---|---|---|---|---|
| T. Bodine | 1 | Stewart | 1 | K. Harvick | 2 |
| Newman | 1 | | | Newman | 1 |

## BUSCH SERIES

### YEAR BY YEAR WINNERS

| Year | Event | Pole Winner | Speed | Race Winner | START Pos |
|------|-------|-------------|-------|-------------|-----------|
| 2001 | Sam's Club 300 | R. Newman | 181.886 | J. Johnson | 6 |
| 2002 | Tropicana 300 | T. Bodine | 178.772 | Jo. Sauter | 20 |
| 2003 | Tropicana Twister 300 | Casey Mears | 181.757 | Bobby Hamilton Jr. | 3 |

**POLE WINNERS**
Ryan Newman 1
Todd Bodine 1
Mears 1

**RACE WINNERS**
Jimmie Johnson 1
Johnny Sauter 1
Hamilton Jr. 1

**QUALIFYING RECORD**
Ryan Newman, Ford; 181.886 mph (29.689 sec.); July 13, 2001

**RACE RECORD**
Bobby Hamilton Jr., Ford; 129.73 mph; July 12, 2003

# Darlington Raceway

## TRACK FACTS
**Date Opened:** 1950
**Owner:** ISC
**President/GM:** Andrew Gurtis
**Distance:** 1.366 miles
**Banking in Turns 1-2:** 25 degrees
**Banking in Turns 3-4:** 23 degrees
**Banking in Straights:** 2 degrees
**Length of Frontstretch:** 1,229 feet
**Length of Backstretch:** 1,229 feet
**Grandstand Seating:** 60,000
**Tickets:** (843) 395-8499
**Website:** www.darlingtonraceway.com

## 2004 SCHEDULE

### NEXTEL Cup
**Carolina Dodge Dealers 400**
**Race:** No. 5 of 36
**Date:** March 21
**TV:** FOX. **Radio:** MRN
**Southern 500**
**Race:** No. 35 of 36
**Date:** November 14
**TV:** NBC. **Radio:** MRN

### Busch Series
**Diamond Hill Plywood 200**
**Race:** No. 4 of 34
**Date:** March 20
**TV:** FX. **Radio:** MRN
**South Carolina 200**
**Race:** No. 33 of 34
**Date:** November 13
**TV:** TNT. **Radio:** MRN

### Craftsman Truck Series
**Darlington 200**
**Race:** No. 24 of 25
**Date:** November 12
**TV:** Speed. **Radio:** MRN

## NEXTEL CUP

### TRACK RECORDS
**Most Wins:** 9—David Pearson and Dale Earnhardt
**Oldest Winner:** Harry Gant, 51 years, 7 months, 22 days, 09/01/91
**Youngest Winner:** Terry Labonte, 23 years, 9 months, 16 days, 09/01/80
**Most Lead Changes:** 41—9/6/82
**Fewest Lead Changes:** 4—9/4/50
**Most Leaders:** 20—9/4/94
**Fewest Leaders:** 2—5/9/64
**Most Laps Led in a 300 Miles Race:** 197, Once, Junior Johnson, 05/08/1965
**Most Laps Led in a 400 Miles race:** 281, Once, Richard Petty, 04/30/1966
**Most Laps Led in a 500 Miles race:** 351, Once, Johnny Mantz, 09/04/1950
**Most Cautions:** 15—3/26/95
**Fewest Cautions:** 0—9/2/63
**Most Caution Laps:** 101—9/2/74
**Fewest Caution Laps:** 0—9/2/63
**Most on the Lead Lap:** 23—9/1/02
**Fewest on the Lead Lap:** 1—24 times, most recently, 9/3/79
**Most Running at the Finish:** 41—3/21/99
**Fewest Running at the Finish:** 12—9/2/74
**Most Laps Led by a Race Winner:** 351—Johnny Mantz, 9/4/50
**Fewest Laps Led by a Race Winner:** 1—Ricky Craven, 3/16/03
**Closest Margin of Victory:**—0.002 second, Ricky Craven defeated Kurt Busch 03/16/03
**Greatest Margin of Victory:**—2 Laps, 4 seconds, David Pearson defeated Bill Elliott 09/03/79

### QUALIFYING AND RACE RECORDS
**QUALIFYING**
**Track:** Ward Burton, Pontiac, 173.797 mph, 28.295 seconds, March 22, 1996 (TranSouth 400).
**Spring Race (Carolina Dodge Dealers 400):** Ward Burton, Pontiac, 173.797 mph, 28.295 seconds, March 22, 1996.
**Fall Race (Southern 500):** Kenny Irwin, Ford, 170.970 mph, 28.763 seconds, Sept. 3, 1999.

**RACE**
**Track:** Dale Earnhardt, Chevrolet, 139.958 mph, 3 hours, 33 minutes, 29 seconds, March 28, 1993 (TranSouth 500).
**Spring Race (Carolina Dodge Dealers 400):** Dale Earnhardt, Chevrolet, 139.958 mph, 3 hours, 33 minutes, 29 seconds, March 28, 1993.
**Fall Race (Southern 500):** Jeff Gordon, Chevrolet, 139.031 mph, 3 hours, 36 minutes, 21 seconds, Sept. 6, 1998.
**400 Miles:** David Pearson, Ford, 132.699 mph, 3 hours, 0 minutes, 54 seconds, May 11, 1968 (Rebel 400).
**300 Miles:** Fred Lorenzen, Ford, 130.013 mph, 2 hours, 18 minutes, 51 seconds, May 9, 1964 (Rebel 300).
**100 Miles:** Dick Rathmann, Hudson, 83.818 mph, 1 hour, 11 minutes, 35 seconds, May 10, 1952 (Grand National 100).

## YEAR BY YEAR WINNERS

| Year | Event | Race Winner | Car Make | Avg. Speed | Start Pos. | Winning Car Owner | Pole Winner |
|---|---|---|---|---|---|---|---|
| 2003 | Mtn Dew Southern 500 | T. Labonte | Chevrolet | 120.744 | 3 | Rick Hendrick | R. Newman |
|  | Carolina Dodge Dealers | R. Craven | Pontiac | 126.214 | 31 | Cal Wells | E. Sadler |
| 2002 | Mtn Dew Southern 500 | J. Gordon | Chevrolet | 118.617 | 3 | Rick Hendrick | Trials Rained Out |
|  | Caro. Dodge Dlrs 400 | S. Marlin | Dodge | 126.070 | 11 | Chip Ganassi | R. Craven |
| 2001 | Mtn Dew Southern 500 | W. Burton | Dodge | 122.773 | 37 | Bill Davis | K. Busch |
|  | Caro. Dodge Dlrs 400 | D. Jarrett | Ford | 126.588 | 2 | Robert Yates | Trials Rained Out |
| 2000 | Pepsi Southern 500 | B. Labonte | Pontiac | 108.273 | 37 | Joe Gibbs | J. Mayfield |
|  | Mall.com 400 | W. Burton | Pontiac | 128.076 | 3 | Bill Davis | J. Gordon |
| 1999 | Pepsi Southern 500 | J. Burton | Ford | 107.816 | 15 | Jack Roush | K. Irwin |
|  | TranSouth 400 | J. Burton | Ford | 121.294 | 9 | Jack Roush | J. Gordon |
| 1998 | Pepsi 500 | J. Gordon | Chevrolet | 139.031 | 5 | Rick Hendrick | D. Jarrett |
|  | TranSouth 400 | D. Jarrett | Ford | 127.962 | 3 | Robert Yates | M. Martin |
| 1997 | Mt. Dew 500 | J. Gordon | Chevrolet | 121.149 | 7 | Rick Hendrick | B. Labonte |
|  | TranSouth 400 | D. Jarrett | Ford | 121.162 | 1 | Robert Yates | D. Jarrett |
| 1996 | Mt. Dew 500 | J. Gordon | Chevrolet | 135.757 | 2 | Rick Hendrick | D. Jarrett |
|  | TranSouth 400 | J. Gordon | Chevrolet | 124.792 | 2 | Rick Hendrick | W. Burton |
| 1995 | Mt. Dew 500 | J. Gordon | Chevrolet | 121.231 | 5 | Rick Hendrick | J. Andretti |
|  | TranSouth 400 | S. Marlin | Chevrolet | 111.392 | 5 | Morgan McClure | J. Gordon |
| 1994 | Mt. Dew 500 | B. Elliott | Ford | 127.952 | 9 | Junior Johnson | G. Bodine |
|  | TranSouth 400 | D. Earnhardt | Chevrolet | 132.432 | 9 | Richard Childress | B. Elliott |
| 1993 | Mt. Dew 500 | Martin | Ford | 137.932 | 4 | Jack Roush | Schrader |
|  | TranSouth 500 | Earnhardt | Chevrolet | 139.958 | 1 | Richard Childress | Trials Rained Out |
| 1992 | Mt. Dew 500 | D. Waltrip | Chevrolet | 129.114 | 5 | Darrell Waltrip | S. Marlin |
|  | TranSouth 500 | Elliott | Ford | 139.364 | 2 | Junior Johnson | S. Marlin |
| 1991 | Heinz 500 | Gant | Oldsmobile | 133.508 | 5 | Leo Jackson | Da. Allison |
|  | TranSouth 500 | Rudd | Chevrolet | 135.594 | 13 | Rick Hendrick | G. Bodine |
| 1990 | Heinz 500 | Earnhardt | Chevrolet | 123.141 | 1 | Richard Childress | Earnhardt |
|  | TranSouth 500 | Earnhardt | Chevrolet | 124.073 | 15 | Richard Childress | G. Bodine |
| 1989 | Heinz 500 | Earnhardt | Chevrolet | 135.462 | 10 | Richard Childress | Kulwicki |
|  | TranSouth 500 | Gant | Oldsmobile | 115.475 | 10 | Jackson Bros. | Martin |
| 1988 | Southern 500 | Elliott | Ford | 128.297 | 1 | Melling Racing | Elliott |
|  | TranSouth 500 | Speed | Oldsmobile | 131.284 | 8 | Lake Speed | Schrader |
| 1987 | Southern 500 | Earnhardt | Chevrolet | 115.520 | 5 | Richard Childress | Da. Allison |
|  | TranSouth 500 | Earnhardt | Chevrolet | 122.540 | 2 | Richard Childress | Schrader |
| 1986 | Southern 500 | Richmond | Chevrolet | 121.068 | 1 | Rick Hendrick | Richmond |
|  | TranSouth 500 | Earnhardt | Chevrolet | 128.994 | 4 | Richard Childress | Bodine |
| 1985 | Southern 500 | Elliott | Ford | 121.254 | 1 | Melling Racing | Elliott |
|  | TranSouth 500 | Elliott | Ford | 126.295 | 1 | Melling Racing | Elliott |
| 1984 | Southern 500 | Gant | Chevrolet | 128.270 | 1 | Mach 1 | Gant |
|  | TranSouth 500 | Waltrip | Chevrolet | 119.925 | 9 | Junior Johnson | B. Parsons |
| 1983 | Southern 500 | B. Allison | Buick | 123.343 | 14 | DiGard Rac. Co. | Bonnett |
|  | TranSouth 500 | Gant | Buick | 130.406 | 5 | Mach 1 | Richmond |
| 1982 | Southern 500 | C. Yarborough | Buick | 115.224 | 9 | M. C. Anderson | Pearson |
|  | CRC Rebel 500 | Earnhardt | Ford | 123.554 | 5 | Bud Moore | Buddy Baker |
| 1981 | Southern 500 | Bonnett | Ford | 126.410 | 3 | Wood Brothers | Gant |
|  | CRC Rebel 500 | Waltrip | Buick | 126.703 | 3 | Bill Gardner | Elliott |
| 1980 | Southern 500 | Labonte | Chevrolet | 115.210 | 10 | Stratagraph Rac. | Waltrip |
|  | CRC Rebel 500 | Pearson | Chevrolet | 112.397 | 2 | Hoss Ellington | Parsons |
| 1979 | Southern 500 | Pearson | Chevrolet | 126.259 | 5 | Osterlund Rac. | B. Allison |
|  | CRC Rebel 500 | Waltrip | Chevrolet | 121.721 | 5 | DiGard Rac. Co. | D. Allison |
| 1978 | Southern 500 | C. Yarborough | Oldsmobile | 116.828 | 6 | Junior Johnson | Pearson |
|  | Rebel 500 | Parsons | Chevrolet | 127.544 | 8 | L. G. DeWitt | B. Allison |
| 1977 | Southern 500 | Pearson | Mercury | 106.797 | 5 | Wood Brothers | Waltrip |
|  | Rebel 500 | Waltrip | Chevrolet | 128.817 | 4 | DiGard Rac. Co. | Pearson |
| 1976 | Southern 500 | Pearson | Mercury | 120.534 | 1 | Wood Brothers | Pearson |
|  | Rebel 500 | Pearson | Mercury | 122.973 | 1 | Wood Brothers | Pearson |
| 1975 | Southern 500 | B. Allison | Matador | 116.825 | 3 | Roger Penske | Pearson |
|  | Rebel 500 | B. Allison | Matador | 117.597 | 5 | Roger Penske | Pearson |
| 1974 | Southern 500 | C. Yarborough | Chevrolet | 111.075 | 4 | Junior Johnson | R. Petty |
|  | Rebel 500 | Pearson | Mercury | 117.543 | 2 | Wood Brothers | D. Allison |
| 1973 | Southern 500 | C. Yarborough | Chevrolet | 134.033 | 8 | Junior Johnson | Pearson |
|  | Rebel 500 | Pearson | Mercury | 122.655 | 1 | Wood Brothers | Pearson |
| 1972 | Southern 500 | B. Allison | Chevrolet | 128.124 | 1 | Junior Johnson | B. Allison |
|  | Rebel 400 | Pearson | Mercury | 124.406 | 1 | Wood Brothers | Pearson |
| 1971 | Southern 500 | B. Allison | Mercury | 131.398 | 1 | Holman-Moody | B. Allison |
|  | Rebel 400 | Buddy Baker | Dodge | 130.678 | 5 | Petty Eng. | D. Allison |
| 1970 | Southern 500 | Buddy Baker | Dodge | 128.817 | 2 | Cotton Owens | Pearson |
|  | Rebel 400 | Pearson | Ford | 129.668 | 3 | Holman-Moody | Glotzbach |
| 1969 | Southern 500 | L. Yarbrough | Ford | 105.612 | 4 | Junior Johnson | C. Yarborough |
|  | Rebel 400 | L. Yarbrough | Mercury | 131.572 | 4 | Junior Johnson | C. Yarborough |
| 1968 | Southern 500 | C. Yarborough | Mercury | 126.132 | 2 | Wood Brothers | Glotzbach |
|  | Rebel 400 | Pearson | Ford | 132.699 | 2 | Holman-Moody | L. Yarbrough |
| 1967 | Southern 500 | R. Petty | Plymouth | 130.423 | 1 | Petty Eng. | R. Petty |
|  | Rebel 400 | R. Petty | Plymouth | 125.738 | 2 | Petty Eng. | Pearson |
| 1966 | Southern 500 | Dieringer | Mercury | 114.830 | 3 | Bud Moore | L. Yarbrough |
|  | Rebel 400 | R. Petty | Plymouth | 131.993 | 1 | Petty Eng. | R. Petty |
| 1965 | Southern 500 | N. Jarrett | Ford | 115.924 | 10 | Bondy Long | Johnson |
|  | Rebel 300 | Johnson | Ford | 111.849 | 3 | Holly Farms | Lorenzen |
| 1964 | Southern 500 | Buck Baker | Dodge | 117.757 | 6 | Ray Fox | R. Petty |
|  | Rebel 300 | Lorenzen | Ford | 130.013 | 1 | Holman-Moody | Lorenzen |

## ALL DARLINGTON RACES

| POLE WINNERS | | RACE WINNERS | |
|---|---|---|---|
| Pearson | 12 | Martin | 2 | Pearson | 10 | T. Labonte | 2 |
| Roberts | 7 | B. Labonte | 1 | Earnhardt | 9 | Dieringer | 1 |
| Lorenzen | 6 | Goldsmith | 1 | J. Gordon | 6 | Frank | 1 |
| Elliott | 5 | Jr. Johnson | 1 | Yarborough | 5 | N. Jarrett | 1 |
| R. Petty | 4 | Mundy | 1 | B. Allison | 5 | Mantz | 1 |
| B. Allison | 4 | Owens | 1 | D. Waltrip | 5 | Reed | 1 |
| G. Bodine | 4 | Pagan | 1 | Elliott | 5 | Thompson | 1 |
| Schrader | 3 | Thompson | 1 | Roberts | 4 | F. Flock | 1 |
| D. Jarrett | 3 | Buddy Baker | 1 | Gant | 4 | Parsons | 1 |
| D. Allison | 3 | Bonnett | 1 | R. Petty | 3 | Bonnett | 1 |
| J. Gordon | 3 | Buck Baker | 1 | Thomas | 3 | Richmond | 1 |
| F. Flock | 2 | Kulwicki | 1 | Buck Baker | 3 | Speed | 1 |
| Glotzbach | 2 | Earnhardt | 1 | D. Jarrett | 3 | Rudd | 1 |
| Turner | 2 | J. Andretti | 1 | J. Burton | 2 | Martin | 1 |
| Yarborough | 2 | W. Burton | 1 | W. Burton | 2 | Jr. Johnson | 1 |
| D. Waltrip | 2 | K. Irwin | 1 | Lorenzen | 2 | B. Labonte | 1 |
| Parsons | 2 | Mayfield | 1 | Weatherly | 2 | Craven | 1 |
| Gant | 2 | Busch | 1 | Stacy | 2 | | |
| Richmond | 2 | Craven | 1 | Yarbrough | 2 | | |
| Yarbrough | 2 | Newman | 1 | Turner | 2 | | |
| Da. Allison | 2 | Sadler | 1 | Buddy Baker | 2 | | |
| Marlin | 2 | | | Marlin | 2 | | |

## SPRING: Carolina Dodge Dealers 400

| POLE WINNERS | | RACE WINNERS | |
|---|---|---|---|
| Pearson | 6 | R. Petty | 1 | Pearson | 7 | Jr. Johnson | 1 |
| Lorenzen | 5 | Turner | 1 | Earnhardt | 6 | Stacy | 1 |
| Elliott | 3 | Yarborough | 1 | Waltrip | 4 | Turner | 1 |
| D. Allison | 3 | B. Allison | 1 | D. Jarrett | 3 | Yarbrough | 1 |
| G. Bodine | 3 | Yarbrough | 1 | Lorenzen | 2 | Parsons | 1 |
| J. Gordon | 3 | Buddy Baker | 1 | Roberts | 2 | B. Allison | 1 |
| Schrader | 2 | Richmond | 1 | R. Petty | 2 | Speed | 1 |
| Martin | 2 | Marlin | 1 | Gant | 2 | Rudd | 1 |
| Parsons | 2 | W. Burton | 1 | Elliott | 2 | J. Gordon | 1 |
| Roberts | 2 | D. Jarrett | 1 | Weatherly | 2 | J. Burton | 1 |
| Glotzbach | 1 | Craven | 1 | Marlin | 2 | W. Burton | 1 |
| Goldsmith | 1 | Sadler | 1 | Buddy Baker | 1 | Craven | 1 |

## FALL: Southern 500

| POLE WINNERS | | RACE WINNERS | |
|---|---|---|---|
| Pearson | 6 | Turner | 1 | Yarborough | 5 | Thompson | 1 |
| Roberts | 5 | Yarborough | 1 | J. Gordon | 5 | Turner | 1 |
| R. Petty | 3 | Yarbrough | 1 | B. Allison | 4 | Yarbrough | 1 |
| B. Allison | 3 | Bonnett | 1 | Earnhardt | 3 | T. Labonte | 1 |
| Elliott | 2 | Richmond | 1 | Buck Baker | 3 | Bonnett | 1 |
| D. Jarrett | 2 | Buck Baker | 1 | Thomas | 3 | Buddy Baker | 1 |
| Waltrip | 2 | Kulwicki | 1 | Pearson | 3 | Richmond | 1 |
| Gant | 2 | Earnhardt | 1 | Elliott | 3 | D. Waltrip | 1 |
| F. Flock | 2 | Marlin | 1 | Roberts | 2 | Martin | 1 |
| Da. Allison | 2 | Schrader | 1 | Gant | 2 | F. Flock | 1 |
| Glotzbach | 1 | G. Bodine | 1 | Dieringer | 1 | J. Burton | 1 |
| Jr. Johnson | 1 | J. Andretti | 1 | Frank | 1 | B. Labonte | 1 |
| Lorenzen | 1 | B. Labonte | 1 | N. Jarrett | 1 | W. Burton | 1 |
| Mundy | 1 | K. Irwin | 1 | R. Petty | 1 | Newman | 1 |
| Owens | 1 | Mayfield | 1 | Mantz | 1 | | |
| Pagan | 1 | Busch | 1 | Reed | 1 | | |
| Thompson | 1 | T. Labonte | 1 | Stacy | 1 | | |

| Year | Event | Race Winner | Car Make | Avg. Speed | Start Pos. | Winning Car Owner | Pole Winner |
|---|---|---|---|---|---|---|---|
| 1963 | Southern 500 | Roberts | Ford | 129.784 | 9 | Holman-Moody | Lorenzen |
| e | Rebel 300 | Weatherly | Pontiac | 122.745 | 6 | Bud Moore | Lorenzen |
| 1962 | Southern 500 | Frank | Ford | 117.965 | 10 | Ratus Walters | Roberts |
| d | Rebel 300 | Stacy | Ford | 117.864 | 3 | Holman-Moody | Lorenzen |
| 1961 | Southern 500 | Stacy | Ford | 117.880 | 3 | Nelson Stacy | Roberts |
| | Rebel 300 | Lorenzen | Ford | 119.529 | 1 | Holman-Moody | Lorenzen |
| 1960 | Southern 500 | Buck Baker | Pontiac | 105.901 | 2 | Jack Smith | Roberts |
| c | Rebel 300 | Weatherly | Ford | 102.646 | 2 | Holman-Moody | Roberts |
| 1959 | Southern 500 | Reed | Chevrolet | 111.836 | 14 | Jim Reed | Roberts |
| | Rebel 300 | Roberts | Chevrolet | 115.380 | 10 | Ogden-Ridgeway | Turner |
| 1958 | Southern 500 | Roberts | Chevrolet | 102.590 | 2 | Frank Strickland | Pagan |
| | Rebel 300 | Turner | Ford | 109.624 | 12 | Holman-Moody | Roberts |
| 1957 | Southern 500 | S. Thompson | Chevrolet | 100.100 | 7 | S. Thompson | Owens |
| | Rebel 300 | Roberts | Ford | 107.540 | 4 | Holman-Moody | Goldsmith |
| 1956 | Southern 500 | Turner | Ford | 95.067 | 11 | Holman-Moody | S. Thompson |
| 1955 | Southern 500 | Thomas | Chevrolet | 92.281 | 8 | Smokey Yunick | Roberts |
| 1954 | Southern 500 | Thomas | Hudson | 94.930 | 23 | Herb Thomas | Buck Baker |
| b 1953 | Southern 500 | Buck Baker | Oldsmobile | 92.780 | 7 | Johnny Griffin | F. Flock |
| 1952 | Grand National 100 | D. Rathmann | Hudson | | 4 | | F. Roberts |
| | Southern 500 | F. Flock | Oldsmobile | 74.510 | 1 | Frank Christian | F. Flock |
| 1951 | Southern 500 | Thomas | Hudson | 76.900 | 2 | Marshall-Teague | Mundy |
| a 1950 | Southern 500 | Mantz | Plymouth | 76.260 | 43 | Bill France, Sr. – Turner, etc. | Turner |

\* Qualifying speeds of Charlie Glotzbach and Cale Yarborough were identical, Glotzbach won the pole because he qualified ahead of Yarborough, but each was credited as being the fastest qualifier.
† Cut by 50 miles due to energy shortage.
a Bill France, Sr.; Hubert Westmoreland; Curtis Turner and Alvin Hawkins were co-owners of the car.
b Changed from 1.25-mile to 1.375-mile track.
c Race halted after 57 laps; completed following Saturday.
d Last convertible race.
e 300-mile race divided into two 150-milers.
f Cut to 316.25 miles, rain and darkness.
g Track remeasured at 1.386 miles (367 laps for 500-mile race).
h Cut to 258.17 miles, rain and darkness.
i Cut to 275.932 miles, rain.
j Cut to 407.068 miles, rain.
k Cut to 479.466 miles, rain and darkness.
l Track changed. Front and back straightaway flip-flopped.
m Cut to 224.024 miles, rain.
n Cut to 368.82 miles, rain and darkness.
o Cut to 448.048 miles, rain.

# BUSCH SERIES
## YEAR BY YEAR WINNERS

| Year | Event | Pole Winner | Speed | Race Winner | Started | Year | Event | Pole Winner | Speed | Race Winner | Started |
|---|---|---|---|---|---|---|---|---|---|---|---|
| 1982 | TranSouth 200 | H. Gant | 154.259 | G. Bodine | 3 | 1993 | Mark III Vans 200 | None - weather | | R. Pressley | 7 |
| | No Fall race held | | | | | | Gatorade 200 | R. Craven | 157.909 | M. Martin | 3 |
| 1983 | No Spring race held | | | | | 1994 | Mark III Vans 200 | M. Martin | 161.011 | M. Martin | 1 |
| | Darlington 250 | J. Ingram | 152.630 | N. Bonnett | 2 | | Gatorade 200 | R. LaJoie | 161.022 | M. Martin | 2 |
| 1984 | Dixie Cup 200 | R. Bouchard | 151.815 | R. Bouchard | 1 | 1995 | Mark III Vans 200 | T. Fedewa | 162.905 | L. Pearson | 36 |
| | Darlington 200 | R. Bouchard | 153.392 | R. Bouchard | 1 | | Gatorade 200 | L. Pearson | 161.429 | M. Martin | 5 |
| 1985 | Dixie Cup 200 | D. Earnhardt | 154.341 | J. Ingram | 11 | 1996 | Dura Lube 200 | J. Green | 166.337 | M. Martin | 2 |
| | Pontiac 200 | T. Richmond | 155.704 | D. Waltrip | 6 | | Dura Lube 200 | M. Martin | 165.799 | T. Labonte | 2 |
| 1986 | Dixie Cup 200 | T. Richmond | 157.298 | D. Waltrip | 5 | 1997 | Diamond Hill 200 | E. Sadler | 166.051 | R. LaJoie | 11 |
| | Gatorade 200 | T. Richmond | 154.749 | D. Earnhardt | 2 | | Dura Lube 200 | M. Martin | 163.745 | J. Burton | 10 |
| 1987 | Country Squire 200 | G. Bodine | 157.646 | D. Earnhardt | 2 | 1998 | Diamond Hill 300 | J. Burton | 162.577 | B. Labonte | 9 |
| | Gatorade 200 | L. Pearson | 154.978 | H. Gant | 20 | | DuraLube 200 | M. McLaughlin | 164.661 | D. Trickle | 4 |
| 1988 | Country Squire 200 | G. Bodine | 156.826 | G. Bodine | 1 | 1999 | Diamond Hill 300 | M. Martin | 166.568 | M. Kenseth | 9 |
| | Gatorade 200 | G. Bodine | 156.422 | H. Gant | 2 | | DuraLube 200 | W. Burton | 167.676 | M. Martin | 2 |
| 1989 | Country Squire 200 | G. Bodine | 156.631 | G. Bodine | 1 | 2000 | SunCom 200 | M. Martin | 167.038 | M. Martin | 1 |
| | Gatorade 200 | K. Schrader | 156.597 | H. Gant | 3 | | Bumper to Bumper 200 | M. Martin | 164.965 | M. Martin | 1 |
| 1990 | Pontiac 200 | K. Wallace | 156.821 | H. Gant | 3 | 2001 | SunCom 200 | R. Newman | 170.301 | J. Green | 13 |
| | Gatorade 200 | G. Sacks | 155.056 | D. Jarrett | 28 | | South Carolina 200 | R. Newman | 169.246 | J. Burton | 24 |
| 1991 | Pontiac 200 | J. Hensley | 158.894 | D. Jarrett | 6 | 2002 | Darlington.com 200 | J. Burton | 168.250 | J. Burton | 1 |
| | Gatorade 200 | H. Gant | 158.899 | D. Earnhardt | 16 | | Gatorade 200 | None - weather | — | J. Burton | 33 |
| 1992 | Mark III Vans 200 | M. Martin | 159.068 | R. Pressley | 2 | 2003 | Darlingtonraceway.com 200 | Stanton Barrett | — | T. Bodine | 13 |
| | Gatorade 200 | M. Martin | 159.652 | M. Waltrip | 15 | | Winn-Dixie 200 | K. Harvick | 167.516 | B. Vickers | 4 |

**QUALIFYING RECORD**
Ryan Newman, Ford; 170.301 mph (28.876 sec.); March 16, 2001

**RACE RECORD**
Michael Waltrip, Pontiac; 138.140 mph (1 hr., 27 min., 13 sec.); Sept. 5, 1992.

## BUSCH SERIES POLE WINNERS

| | | | | | | | |
|---|---|---|---|---|---|---|---|
| Mark Martin | 8 | Ward Burton | 1 | Mike McLaughlin | 1 | | |
| Geoffrey Bodine | 4 | Ricky Craven | 1 | Greg Sacks | 1 | | |
| Tim Richmond | 3 | Dale Earnhardt | 1 | Elliott Sadler | 1 | | |
| Ron Bouchard | 2 | Tim Fedewa | 1 | Ken Schrader | 1 | | |
| Jeff Burton | 2 | Jeff Green | 1 | Kenny Wallace | 1 | | |
| Harry Gant | 2 | Jimmy Hensley | 1 | Stanton Barrett | 1 | | |
| Ryan Newman | 2 | Jack Ingram | 1 | Kevin Harvick | 1 | | |
| Larry Pearson | 2 | Randy LaJoie | 1 | | | | |

## BUSCH SERIES RACE WINNERS

| | | | | | |
|---|---|---|---|---|---|
| Mark Martin | 8 | Darrell Waltrip | 2 | Larry Pearson | 1 |
| Jeff Burton | 4 | Neil Bonnett | 1 | Dick Trickle | 1 |
| Harry Gant | 4 | Jeff Green | 1 | Michael Waltrip | 1 |
| Geoffrey Bodine | 3 | Jack Ingram | 1 | Brian Vickers | 1 |
| Dale Earnhardt | 3 | Matt Kenseth | 1 | T. Bodine | 1 |
| Ron Bouchard | 2 | Bobby Labonte | 1 | | |
| Dale Jarrett | 2 | Terry Labonte | 1 | | |
| Robert Pressley | 2 | Randy LaJoie | 1 | | |

# CRAFTSMAN TRUCK SERIES

## YEAR BY YEAR WINNERS

| Year | Event | Pole Winner | Speed | Race Winner | START Pos |
|---|---|---|---|---|---|
| 2001 | Darlington 200 | Jack Sprague | 162.878 mph | Bobby Hamilton | 3 |
| 2002 | Craftsman 200 | Jason Leffler | 163.702 mph | Ted Musgrave | 2 |
| 2003 | Craftsman 200 | Travis Kvapil | — | Bobby Hamilton | 14 |

**QUALIFYING RECORD**
Jason Leffler, Dodge; 163.703 mph (30.040 sec.); March 14, 2002

**RACE RECORD**
Bobby Hamilton, Dodge, 133.645 mph, (1 hour, 30 min., 9 sec.); March 14, 2003

### POLE WINNERS
Jason Leffler 1
Jack Sprague 1
Travis Kvapil 1

### RACE WINNERS
Bobby Hamilton 2
Ted Musgrave 1

# Daytona International Speedway

## TRACK FACTS
**Date Opened:** 1959
**Owner:** ISC
**President/GM:** Robin Braig
**Distance:** 2.5 miles
**Banking in Turns:** 31 degrees
**Banking in Trioval:** 18 degrees
**Banking on Backstretch:** 3 degrees
**Length of Frontstretch:** 3,800 feet
**Length of Backstretch:** 3,400 feet
**Grandstand Seating:** 168,000
**Tickets:** (386) 253-7223
**Website:** www.daytonausa.com

## 2004 SCHEDULE

### NEXTEL Cup
**Daytona 500**
Race: No. 1 of 36
Date: February 15
TV: NBC. Radio: MRN
**Pepsi 400**
Race: No. 17 of 36
Date: July 3
TV: FOX. Radio: MRN

### Busch Series
**Hershey's Kisses 300**
Race: No. 1 of 34
Date: February 14
TV: NBC. Radio: MRN
**Winn-Dixie 250**
Race: No. 18 of 34
Date: July 2
TV: FX. Radio: MRN

### Craftsman Truck Series
**Florida Dodge Dealers 250**
Race: No. 1 of 25
Date: February 13
TV: Speed. Radio: MRN

## NEXTEL CUP

### TRACK RECORDS
**Most Wins:** 10—Richard Petty
**Most Top 5s:** 28—Richard Petty
**Most Top 10s:** 37—Richard Petty
**Oldest Winner:** Bobby Allison, 50 years, 2 months, 11 days, 02/14/1988
**Youngest Winner:** Jeff Gordon, 23 years, 10 months, 27 days, 07/01/1995
**Most Lead Changes:** 59—Once, 2/17/74
**Fewest Lead Changes:** 1—Twice, most recently, 2/22/63
**Most Leaders:** 15—3 times, most recently, 2/18/96
**Fewest Leaders:** 1—Twice, most recently, 2/22/63
**Most Laps Led in a 400 Miles Race:** 142, Once, Cale Yarborough, 07/04/1968
**Most Laps Led in a 500 Miles Race:** 184, Once, Richard Petty, 02/23/1964
**Most Cautions:** 12—7/1/89
**Fewest Cautions:** 0—12 times, most recently, 2/11/71
**Most Caution Laps:** 60—2/25/68
**Fewest Caution Laps:** 0—12 times, most recently, 2/11/71
**Most on the Lead Lap:** 33—2/16/03*
**Fewest on the Lead Lap:** 1—8 times, most recently, 2/15/76
**Most Running at the Finish:** 40—7/5/03*
**Fewest Running at the Finish:** 7—2/12/65
**Most Laps Led by a Race Winner:** 184—Richard Petty, 2/23/64
**Fewest Laps Led by a Race Winner:** 1—Jimmy Spencer, 7/2/94
**Closest Margin of Victory:** 0.029 Second, John Andretti defeated Terry Labonte 07/05/97
**Greatest Margin of Victory:** 33.2 Seconds, Bobby Allison defeated Cale Yarborough 02/19/78

*rain-shortened, 109-lap, 272.5-mile race

### QUALIFYING AND RACE RECORDS
**QUALIFYING**
**Track:** Bill Elliott, Ford, 210.364 mph, 42.783 seconds, Feb. 9, 1987 (Daytona 500).
**Spring Race (Daytona 500):** Bill Elliott, Ford, 210.364 mph, 42.783 seconds, Feb. 9, 1987.
**Fall Race (Pepsi 400):** Sterling Marlin, Chevrolet,

# NEXTEL CUP

203.666 mph, 44.198 seconds, July 3, 1986.
**Firecracker 250:** Edwin "Banjo" Matthews, Pontiac, 160.490 mph, July 1, 1962.

## RACE

**Spring Race (Daytona 500):** Buddy Baker, Oldsmobile, 177.602 mph, 2:48:55, (5 cautions for 15 laps), Feb. 17, 1980.
**Fall Race (Pepsi 400):** Bobby Allison, Mercury, 173.473 mph, 2:18:21, (3 cautions for 11 laps), July 4, 1980.
**Firecracker 250:** David Pearson, Pontiac, 154.194 mph, July 4, 1961.
**Qualifying Race, 125 miles:** Terry Labonte, Ford, 189.554 mph, Feb. 16, 1989.
**Qualifying Race, 100 miles:** Fred Lorenzen, Ford, 174.583 mph, Feb. 24, 1967.

*World closed course auto race record.

## ALL DAYTONA RACES

### POLE WINNERS

| Driver | Wins | Driver | Wins |
|---|---|---|---|
| Yarborough | 12 | R. Petty | 1 |
| Buddy Baker | 5 | Smith | 1 |
| Roberts | 5 | Turner | 1 |
| Elliott | 5 | Yarbrough | 1 |
| D. Allison | 4 | Wellborn | 1 |
| Marlin | 4 | Stott | 1 |
| Schrader | 4 | Bonnett | 1 |
| Dieringer | 3 | Parsons | 1 |
| Earnhardt | 3 | Bodine | 1 |
| D. Jarrett | 3 | Rudd | 1 |
| Skinner | 2 | Martin | 1 |
| B. Labonte | 2 | Sacks | 1 |
| J. Gordon | 2 | K. Petty | 1 |
| Foyt | 2 | D. Waltrip | 1 |
| B. Allison | 2 | Irvan | 1 |
| Da. Allison | 2 | Allen | 1 |
| Pearson | 2 | Glotzbach | 1 |
| Goldsmith | 1 | Nemechek | 1 |
| Jr. Johnson | 1 | Ji. Johnson | 1 |
| Matthews | 1 | K. Harvick | 1 |
| Owens | 1 | J. Green | 1 |
| Panch | 1 | Park | 1 |

### RACE WINNERS

| Driver | Wins | Driver | Wins |
|---|---|---|---|
| R. Petty | 10 | Panch | 1 |
| Yarborough | 8 | McQuagg | 1 |
| Pearson | 6 | Smith | 1 |
| B. Allison | 6 | Bonnett | 1 |
| J. Gordon | 4 | L. Petty | 1 |
| Roberts | 4 | Sacks | 1 |
| Elliott | 4 | Bodine | 1 |
| D. Jarrett | 4 | Richmond | 1 |
| D. Earnhardt | 3 | D. Waltrip | 1 |
| Foyt | 3 | Cope | 1 |
| Marlin | 3 | Andretti | 1 |
| Irvan | 2 | D. Allison | 1 |
| Buddy Baker | 2 | J. Andretti | 1 |
| Yarbrough | 2 | Spencer | 1 |
| Da. Allison | 2 | J. Burton | 1 |
| M. Waltrip | 2 | Earnhardt Jr. | 1 |
| Parsons | 1 | W. Burton | 1 |
| Hamilton | 1 | Biffle | 1 |
| Jr. Johnson | 1 | | |
| Lorenzen | 1 | | |
| Lund | 1 | | |

## SPRING: Daytona 500

### POLE WINNERS

| Driver | Wins | Driver | Wins |
|---|---|---|---|
| Buddy Baker | 4 | Stott | 1 |
| Yarborough | 4 | B. Allison | 1 |
| Elliott | 4 | Parsons | 1 |
| Roberts | 3 | Rudd | 1 |
| Schrader | 3 | Da. Allison | 1 |
| D. Allison | 2 | Marlin | 1 |
| D. Jarrett | 2 | K. Petty | 1 |
| Foyt | 2 | Allen | 1 |
| Pearson | 1 | Earnhardt | 1 |
| Dieringer | 1 | M. Skinner | 1 |
| Goldsmith | 1 | B. Labonte | 1 |
| Isaac | 1 | J. Gordon | 1 |
| Owens | 1 | Ji. Johnson | 1 |
| R. Petty | 1 | Green | 1 |
| Turner | 1 | | |
| Welborn | 1 | | |

### RACE WINNERS

| Driver | Wins | Driver | Wins |
|---|---|---|---|
| R. Petty | 7 | L. Yarbrough | 1 |
| C. Yarborough | 4 | Buddy Baker | 1 |
| B. Allison | 3 | Andretti | 1 |
| D. Jarrett | 3 | Bodine | 1 |
| Elliott | 2 | D. Waltrip | 1 |
| S. Marlin | 2 | Cope | 1 |
| J. Gordon | 2 | Irvan | 1 |
| M. Waltrip | 2 | Da. Allison | 1 |
| Foyt | 1 | Parsons | 1 |
| Lund | 1 | Pearson | 1 |
| Hamilton | 1 | D. Earnhardt | 1 |
| Jr. Johnson | 1 | W. Burton | 1 |
| Lorenzen | 1 | | |
| Panch | 1 | | |
| L. Petty | 1 | | |
| Roberts | 1 | | |

## YEAR BY YEAR WINNERS

| | Year | Event | Race Winner | Car Make | Avg. Speed | Start Pos. | Winning Car Owner | Pole Winner |
|---|---|---|---|---|---|---|---|---|
| | 2003 | Pepsi 400 | G. Biffle | Ford | 166.109 | 30 | Jack Roush | S. Park |
| f | | Daytona 500 | M. Waltrip | Chevrolet | 133.870 | 4 | Dale Earnhardt, Inc. | J. Green |
| | 2002 | Pepsi 400 | M. Waltrip | Chevrolet | 135.952 | 7 | Dale Earnhardt, Inc. | K. Harvick |
| | | Daytona 500 | W. Burton | Dodge | 142.971 | 19 | Bill Davis | J. Johnson |
| # | 2001 | Pepsi 400 | D. Earnhardt Jr. | Chevrolet | 157.601 | 13 | Dale Earnhardt, Inc. | S. Marlin |
| | | Daytona 500 | M. Waltrip | Chevrolet | 161.783 | 19 | Dale Earnhardt, Inc. | B. Elliott |
| | 2000 | Pepsi 400 | J. Burton | Ford | 148.576 | 9 | Jack Roush | D. Jarrett |
| | | Daytona 500 | D. Jarrett | Ford | 155.669 | 1 | Robert Yates | D. Jarrett |
| # | 1999 | Pepsi 400 | D. Jarrett | Ford | 169.213 | 12 | Robert Yates | J. Nemechek |
| | | Daytona 500 | J. Gordon | Chevrolet | 161.551 | 1 | Rick Hendrick | J. Gordon |
| e | 1998 | Pepsi 400 | J. Gordon | Chevrolet | 144.549 | 8 | Rick Hendrick | B. Labonte |
| | | Daytona 500 | D. Earnhardt | Chevrolet | 172.712 | 4 | Richard Childress | B. Labonte |
| | 1997 | Pepsi 400 | J. Andretti | Ford | 167.791 | 3 | Cale Yarborough | M. Skinner |
| | | Daytona 500 | J. Gordon | Chevrolet | 148.295 | 6 | Rick Hendrick | M. Skinner |
| d | 1996 | Pepsi 400 | S. Marlin | Chevrolet | 161.602 | 2 | Morgan-McClure | J. Gordon |
| | | Daytona 500 | D. Jarrett | Ford | 154.308 | 7 | Robert Yates | D. Earnhardt |
| | 1995 | Pepsi 400 | J. Gordon | Chevrolet | 166.976 | 3 | Rick Hendrick | D. Earnhardt |
| | | Daytona 500 | S. Marlin | Chevrolet | 141.710 | 3 | Morgan-McClure | D. Jarrett |
| | 1994 | Pepsi 400 | J. Spencer | Ford | 155.558 | 3 | Junior Johnson | D. Earnhardt |
| | | Daytona 500 | S. Marlin | Chevrolet | 156.931 | 4 | Morgan-McClure | L. Allen |
| | 1993 | Pepsi 400 | D. Earnhardt | Chevrolet | 151.755 | 5 | Richard Childress | E. Irvan |
| | | Daytona 500 | D. Jarrett | Chevrolet | 154.972 | 2 | Joe Gibbs | K. Petty |
| | 1992 | Pepsi 400 | Irvan | Chevrolet | 170.457 | 6 | Morgan-McClure | S. Marlin |
| | | Daytona 500 | Da. Allison | Ford | 160.256 | 6 | Robert Yates | S. Marlin |
| | 1991 | Pepsi 400 | Elliott | Ford | 159.116 | 10 | Melling Racing | S. Marlin |
| | | Daytona 500 | Irvan | Chevrolet | 148.148 | 2 | Morgan-McClure | Da. Allison |
| | 1990 | Pepsi 400 | Earnhardt | Chevrolet | 160.894 | 3 | Richard Childress | Sacks |
| | | Daytona 500 | Cope | Chevrolet | 165.761 | 12 | Bob Whitcomb | Schrader |
| | 1989 | Pepsi 400 | Da. Allison | Ford | 132.207 | 8 | Robert Yates | Martin |
| | | Daytona 500 | D. Waltrip | Chevrolet | 148.466 | 2 | Rick Hendrick | Schrader |
| | 1988 | Pepsi Firecracker 400 | Elliott | Ford | 163.302 | 38 | Melling Racing | D. Waltrip |
| | | Daytona 500 | B. Allison | Buick | 137.531 | 3 | Stavola Brothers | Schrader |
| | 1987 | Pepsi Firecracker 400 | B. Allison | Buick | 161.074 | 11 | Stavola Brothers | Da. Allison |
| | | Daytona 500 | Elliott | Ford | 176.263 | 1 | Melling Racing | Elliott |
| | 1986 | Pepsi Firecracker 400 | Richmond | Chevrolet | 131.916 | 9 | Rick Hendrick | C. Yarborough |
| | | Daytona 500 | Bodine | Chevrolet | 148.124 | 2 | Rick Hendrick | Elliott |
| | 1985 | Pepsi Firecracker 400 | Sacks | Chevrolet | 158.730 | 9 | Bill Gardner | Elliott |
| | | Daytona 500 | Elliott | Ford | 172.265 | 1 | Melling Racing | Elliott |
| | 1984 | Pepsi Firecracker 400 | R. Petty | Pontiac | 171.204 | 6 | Curb Racing | C. Yarborough |
| | | Daytona 500 | C. Yarborough | Chevrolet | 150.994 | 1 | Ranier Racing | C. Yarborough |
| | 1983 | Firecracker 400 | Buddy Baker | Ford | 167.442 | 8 | Wood Brothers | C. Yarborough |
| | | Daytona 500 | C. Yarborough | Pontiac | 155.979 | 8 | Ranier Racing | Rudd |
| | 1982 | Firecracker 400 | B. Allison | Buick | 163.099 | 9 | DiGard Rac. Co. | Bodine |
| | | Daytona 500 | B. Allison | Buick | 153.991 | 7 | DiGard Rac. Co. | Parsons |
| | 1981 | Firecracker 400 | C. Yarborough | Buick | 142.588 | 1 | M.C. Anderson | C. Yarborough |
| | | Daytona 500 | R. Petty | Buick | 169.651 | 8 | Petty Eng. | B. Allison |
| | 1980 | Firecracker 400 | B. Allison | Mercury | 173.473 | 14 | Bud Moore | C. Yarborough |
| | | Daytona 500 | Buddy Baker | Oldsmobile | 177.602 | 1 | Ranier Racing | Buddy Baker |
| | 1979 | Firecracker 400 | Bonnett | Mercury | 172.890 | 2 | Wood Brothers | Buddy Baker |
| | | Daytona 500 | R. Petty | Oldsmobile | 143.977 | 13 | Petty Eng. | Buddy Baker |
| | 1978 | Firecracker 400 | Pearson | Mercury | 154.340 | 3 | Wood Brothers | C. Yarborough |
| | | Daytona 500 | B. Allison | Ford | 159.730 | 33 | Bud Moore | C. Yarborough |
| | 1977 | Firecracker 400 | R. Petty | Dodge | 142.716 | 5 | Petty Eng. | Bonnett |
| | | Daytona 500 | C. Yarborough | Chevrolet | 153.218 | 4 | Junior Johnson | D. Allison |
| | 1976 | Firecracker 400 | C. Yarborough | Chevrolet | 160.966 | 2 | Junior Johnson | Foyt |
| | | Daytona 500 | Pearson | Mercury | 152.181 | 7 | Wood Brothers | Stott |
| | 1975 | Firecracker 400 | R. Petty | Dodge | 158.381 | 13 | Petty Eng. | D. Allison |
| | | Daytona 500 | Parsons | Chevrolet | 153.649 | 32 | L.G. DeWitt | D. Allison |
| | 1974 | Firecracker 400 | Pearson | Mercury | 138.301 | 1 | Wood Brothers | Pearson |
| c | | Daytona 500 | R. Petty | Dodge | 140.894 | 2 | Petty Eng. | Pearson |
| | 1973 | Firecracker 400 | Pearson | Mercury | 158.468 | 6 | Wood Brothers | B. Allison |
| | | Daytona 500 | R. Petty | Dodge | 157.205 | 7 | Petty Eng. | Buddy Baker |
| | 1972 | Firecracker 400 | Pearson | Mercury | 160.821 | 2 | Wood Brothers | Isaac |
| | | Daytona 500 | Foyt | Mercury | 161.550 | 2 | Wood Brothers | Isaac |
| | 1971 | Firecracker 400 | Isaac | Dodge | 161.947 | 21 | Nord Krauskopf | D. Allison |
| | | Daytona 500 | R. Petty | Plymouth | 144.462 | 5 | Petty Eng. | Foyt |
| | 1970 | Firecracker 400 | D. Allison | Ford | 162.235 | 15 | Banjo Matthews | C. Yarborough |
| | | Daytona 500 | Hamilton | Plymouth | 149.601 | 9 | Petty Eng. | C. Yarborough |
| | 1969 | Firecracker 400 | L. Yarbrough | Ford | 160.875 | 2 | Junior Johnson | C. Yarborough |
| | | Daytona 500 | L. Yarbrough | Ford | 157.950 | 19 | Junior Johnson | Buddy Baker |
| | 1968 | Firecracker 400 | C. Yarborough | Mercury | 167.247 | 4 | Wood Brothers | Glotzbach |
| | | Daytona 500 | C. Yarborough | Mercury | 143.251 | 1 | Wood Brothers | C. Yarborough |
| | 1967 | Firecracker 400 | C. Yarborough | Ford | 143.583 | 2 | Wood Brothers | Dieringer |
| | | Daytona 500 | Andretti | Ford | 146.926 | 12 | Holman-Moody | Turner |
| | 1966 | Firecracker 400 | McQuagg | Dodge | 153.813 | 4 | Ray Nichels | L. Yarbrough |
| b | | Daytona 500 | R. Petty | Plymouth | 160.627 | 1 | Petty Eng. | R. Petty |

365

## FALL: Pepsi 400/250 races

### POLE WINNERS
| | | | | | |
|---|---|---|---|---|---|
| Yarborough | 8 | Bodine | 1 | | |
| Marlin | 3 | Elliott | 1 | | |
| D. Allison | 2 | Da. Allison | 1 | | |
| Roberts | 2 | D. Waltrip | 1 | | |
| Dieringer | 2 | Martin | 1 | | |
| Earnhardt | 2 | Sacks | 1 | | |
| Yarbrough | 1 | Irvan | 1 | | |
| B. Allison | 1 | Pearson | 1 | | |
| Isaac | 1 | J. Gordon | 1 | | |
| Foyt | 1 | Skinner | 1 | | |
| Smith | 1 | B. Labonte | 1 | | |
| Jr. Johnson | 1 | Nemechek | 1 | | |
| Panch | 1 | D. Jarrett | 1 | | |
| Matthews | 1 | Harvick | 1 | | |
| Glotzbach | 1 | Park | 1 | | |
| Bonnett | 1 | | | | |
| Buddy Baker | 1 | | | | |

### RACE WINNERS
| | | | |
|---|---|---|---|
| Pearson | 5 | L. Yarborough | 1 |
| C. Yarborough | 4 | Da. Allison | 1 |
| R. Petty | 3 | Irvan | 1 |
| B. Allison | 3 | J. Spencer | 1 |
| Roberts | 3 | S. Marlin | 1 |
| Foyt | 2 | J. Andretti | 1 |
| Elliott | 2 | D. Jarrett | 1 |
| Earnhardt | 2 | J. Burton | 1 |
| J. Gordon | 2 | Earnhardt Jr. | 1 |
| D. Allison | 1 | M. Waltrip | 1 |
| Isaac | 1 | Biffle | 1 |
| McQuagg | 1 | | |
| Smith | 1 | | |
| Bonnett | 1 | | |
| Buddy Baker | 1 | | |
| Sacks | 1 | | |
| Richmond | 1 | | |

| Year | Event | Race Winner | Car Make | Avg. Speed | Start Pos. | Winning Car Owner | Pole Winner |
|---|---|---|---|---|---|---|---|
| 1965 | Firecracker 400 | Foyt | Ford | 150.046 | 11 | Banjo Matthews | Panch |
| a | Daytona 500 | Lorenzen | Ford | 141.539 | 4 | Holman-Moody | Dieringer |
| 1964 | Firecracker 400 | Foyt | Dodge | 151.451 | 19 | Ray Nichels | Dieringer |
| | Daytona 500 | R. Petty | Plymouth | 154.334 | 2 | Petty Eng. | Goldsmith |
| 1963 | Firecracker 400 | Roberts | Ford | 150.927 | 3 | Holman-Moody | Jr. Johnson |
| | Daytona 500 | Lund | Ford | 151.566 | 12 | Wood Brothers | Roberts |
| 1962 | Firecracker 250 | Roberts | Pontiac | 153.688 | 4 | Smokey Yunick | Matthews |
| * | Daytona 500 | Roberts | Pontiac | 152.529 | 1 | Smokey Yunick | Roberts |
| * 1961 | Firecracker 250 | Pearson | Pontiac | 154.294 | 2 | Ray Fox | Roberts |
| * | Daytona 500 | Panch | Pontiac | 149.601 | 4 | Smokey Yunick | Roberts |
| * 1960 | Firecracker 250 | Smith | Pontiac | 146.842 | 1 | Jack Smith | Smith |
| | Daytona 500 | Jr. Johnson | Chevrolet | 124.740 | 9 | John Masoni | Owens |
| * 1959 | Firecracker 250 | Roberts | Pontiac | 140.581 | 1 | Smokey Yunick | Roberts |
| | Daytona 500 | L. Petty | Oldsmobile | 135.521 | 15 | Petty Eng. | Welborn |

\* Caution-free race.
\# Night race.
a Reduced to 332.5 miles, rain.
b Reduced to 495 miles, rain.
c Reduced to 450 miles, energy shortage.
d Reduced to 293 miles, rain.
e Took place in October, rather than July.
f Reduced to 272.500 miles, rain.

## BUSCH SERIES

### YEAR BY YEAR WINNERS

| Year | Event | Pole Winner | Speed | Race Winner | Started | Year | Event | Pole Winner | Speed | Race Winner | Started |
|---|---|---|---|---|---|---|---|---|---|---|---|
| 1982 | Goody's 300 | M. Porter | 184.569 | D. Earnhardt | 5 | 1994 | Goody's 300 | M. Waltrip | 184.555 | D. Earnhardt | 7 |
| 1983 | Goody's 300 | S. Ard | 185.774 | D. Waltrip | 5 | 1995 | Goody's 300 | M. Waltrip | 185.326 | C. Little | 42 |
| 1984 | Goody's 300 | L. Ottinger | 187.682 | D. Waltrip | 12 | 1996 | Goody's 300 | J. Purvis | 189.733 | S. Grissom | 4 |
| 1985 | Goody's 300 | R. Wallace | 187.438 | G. Bodine | 2 | 1997 | Gargoyles 300 | E. Sadler | 190.508 | R. LaJoie | 14 |
| 1986 | Goody's 300 | L. Pearson | 191.310 | D. Earnhardt | 9 | 1998 | Napa Auto Parts 300 | M. McLaughlin | 190.134 | J. Nemechek | 1 |
| 1987 | Goody's 300 | T. Houston | 194.389 | G. Bodine | 5 | 1999 | Napa Auto Parts 300 | K. Schrader | 189.865 | R. LaJoie | 2 |
| 1988 | Goody's 300 | M. Swaim | 189.825 | B. Allison | 9 | 2000 | Napa Auto Parts 300 | H. Stricklin | 187.336 | M. Kenseth | 8 |
| 1989 | Goody's 300 | K. Wallace | 192.271 | D. Waltrip | 9 | 2001 | NAPA Auto Parts 300 | J. Nemechek | 186.966 | R. LaJoie | 2 |
| 1990 | Goody's 300 | D. Waltrip | 188.945 | D. Earnhardt | 2 | 2002 | EAS/GNC 300 | J. Nemechek | 186.254 | D. Earnhardt Jr. | 4 |
| 1991 | Goody's 300 | D. Green | 188.675 | D. Earnhardt | 3 | | Stacker/GNC 250 | J. Nemechek | 185.793 | J. Nemechek | 1 |
| 1992 | Goody's 300 | M. Waltrip | 186.556 | D. Earnhardt | 4 | 2003 | Daytona 250 | D. Earnhardt Jr. | 186.308 | D. Earnhardt Jr. | 1 |
| 1993 | Goody's 300 | K. Schrader | 186.513 | D. Earnhardt | 5 | | Koolerz 300 | J. Nemechek | 186.050 | D. Earnhardt Jr. | 2 |

### QUALIFYING RECORD
Tommy Houston, Buick; 194.389 mph (46.298 sec.); February 10, 1987.

### RACE RECORD
Geoffrey Bodine, Pontiac; 157.137 mph (1 hr., 54 min., 33 sec.); February 16, 1985.

### POLE WINNERS
| | | | | | | | |
|---|---|---|---|---|---|---|---|
| Joe Nemechek | 5 | L.D. Ottinger | 1 | Mike Swaim | 1 | | |
| Michael Waltrip | 3 | Larry Pearson | 1 | Kenny Wallace | 1 | | |
| Ken Schrader | 2 | Mike Porter | 1 | Rusty Wallace | 1 | | |
| Sam Ard | 1 | Jeff Purvis | 1 | Darrell Waltrip | 1 | | |
| David Green | 1 | Elliott Sadler | 1 | Dale Earnhardt Jr. | 1 | | |
| Tommy Houston | 1 | Hut Stricklin | 1 | | | | |

### RACE WINNERS
| | | | |
|---|---|---|---|
| Dale Earnhardt | 7 | Dale Earnhardt Jr. | 3 |
| Randy LaJoie | 3 | Steve Grissom | 1 |
| Darrell Waltrip | 3 | M. Kenseth | 1 |
| Geoffrey Bodine | 2 | Chad Little | 1 |
| Joe Nemechek | 2 | | |
| Bobby Allison | 1 | | |

## CRAFTSMAN TRUCK SERIES

### YEAR BY YEAR WINNERS

| Year | Event | Pole Winner | Speed | Race Winner | Started |
|---|---|---|---|---|---|
| 2000 | Daytona 250 | Joe Ruttman | 187.563 | Mike Wallace | 2 |
| 2001 | Fla Dodge Dealers 250 | Joe Ruttman | 186.123 | Joe Ruttman | 1 |
| 2002 | Fla Dodge Dealers 250 | Ted Musgrave | 187.215 | Robert Pressley | 2 |
| 2003 | Fla. Dodge Dealers 250 | Jason Leffler | 182.994 | Rick Crawford | 19 |

### QUALIFYING RECORD
Joe Ruttman, Dodge; 187.563 mph (47.984 sec.); February 16, 2000

### RACE RECORD
Robert Pressley, Dodge; 140.121 mph (1 hr., 47 min., 3 sec.); February 15, 2002

### POLE WINNERS
| | | | |
|---|---|---|---|
| Joe Ruttman | 2 | Jason Leffler | 1 |
| Ted Musgrave | 1 | | |

### RACE WINNERS
| | | | |
|---|---|---|---|
| Robert Pressley | 1 | Rick Crawford | 1 |
| Joe Ruttman | 1 | | |

# Dover International Speedway

## TRACK FACTS
**Date Opened:** 1969
**Owner:** Dover Downs Ent., Inc.
**President & CEO:** Denis McGlynn
**Distance:** 1 mile
**Banking in Turns:** 24 degrees
**Banking in Straights:** 9 degrees
**Length of Frontstretch:** 1,076 feet
**Length of Backstretch:** 1,076 feet
**Grandstand Seating:** 140,000
**Tickets:** (800) 441-7223
**Website:** www.doverspeedway.com

## 2004 SCHEDULE

### NEXTEL Cup
**MBNA America 400**
**Race:** No. 13 of 36
**Date:** June 6
**TV:** FX. **Radio:** MRN

**MBNA America 400**
**Race:** No. 28 of 36
**Date:** September 26
**TV:** TNT. **Radio:** MRN

### Busch Series
**MBNA America 200**
**Race:** No. 14 of 34
**Date:** June 5
**TV:** FX. **Radio:** MRN

**Stacker 200 by YJ Stinger**
**Race:** No. 27 of 34
**Date:** September 25
**TV:** TNT. **Radio:** MRN

### Craftsman Truck Series
**MBNA America 200**
**Race:** No. 6 of 25
**Date:** June 4
**TV:** Speed. *Radio:* MRN

## NEXTEL CUP

### TRACK RECORDS
**Most Wins:** 7—Richard Petty and Bobby Allison
**Oldest Winner:** Harry Gant, 52 years, 4 months, 21 days, 05/31/1992
**Youngest Winner:** Jeff Gordon, 24 years, 1 month, 13 days, 09/17/1995
**Most Lead Changes:** 29—Twice, most recently, 5/18/86
**Fewest Lead Changes:** 3—10/17/71
**Most Leaders:** 13—Twice, most recently, 9/24/00
**Fewest Leaders:** 3—5 times, most recently, 5/16/82
**Most Laps Led in a 300 Miles Race:** 186, Richard Petty, 09/20/1970
**Most Laps Led in a 400 Miles Race:** 381, Jeff Gordon, 06/03/2001
**Most Laps Led in a 500 Miles Race:** 491, Richard Petty, 09/15/1974
**Most Cautions:** 16—9/19/93
**Fewest Cautions:** 0—6/6/71
**Most Caution Laps:** 103—9/19/93
**Fewest Caution Laps:** 0—6/6/71
**Most on the Lead Lap:** 17—6/2/02
**Fewest on the Lead Lap:** 1—11 times, most recently, 9/15/91
**Most Running at the Finish:** 39—6/2/02
**Fewest Running at the Finish:** 13—5/17/81
**Most Laps Led by a Race Winner:** 491—Richard Petty, 9/15/74
**Fewest Laps Led by a Race Winner:** 8—Dale Jarrett, 5/31/98
**Closest Margin of Victory:**—0.091 second, Ricky Rudd defeated Mark Martin 06/01/97
**Greatest Margin of Victory:**—3 Laps, 6 seconds, Bobby Allison defeated Dave Marcis 05/16/82

### QUALIFYING AND RACE RECORDS
**QUALIFYING**
**Track:** Rusty Wallace, Ford, 159.964 mph, 22.505 seconds, Sept. 24, 1999 (MBNA Gold 400).
**Spring Race (MBNA America 400):** Bobby Labonte, Pontiac, 159.320 mph, 22.596 seconds, June 4, 1999.
**Fall Race (MBNA America 400):** Rusty Wallace, Ford, 159.964 mph, 22.505 seconds, Sept. 25, 1999.

**RACE**
**Track:** (400 miles): Mark Martin, Ford, 132.719 mph, 3 hours, 0 minutes, 50 seconds, Sept. 21, 1997 (MBNA 400).
**Spring Race (MBNA America 400):** Mark Martin, Ford, 132.719 mph, 3 hours, 0 minutes, 50 seconds, Sept. 21, 1997.
**Fall Race (MBNA America 400):** Bobby Labonte, Pontiac, 120.603 mph, 3 hours, 19 minutes, 0 seconds, June 6, 1999.
**Track Record (500 miles):** Bill Elliott, Ford, 125.945 mph, 3 hours, 58 minutes, 0 seconds, Sept. 16, 1990 (MBNA 500).
**Miller 500:** Derrike Cope, Chevrolet, 123.960 mph, 4 hours, 2 minutes, 1 second, June 3, 1990.

## ALL DOVER RACES

### POLE WINNERS

| Driver | Wins | Driver | Wins | Driver | Wins |
|---|---|---|---|---|---|
| Pearson | 6 | D. Waltrip | 2 | Trickle | 1 |
| R. Wallace | 5 | T. Labonte | 2 | M. Waltrip | 1 |
| Rudd | 4 | R. Petty | 2 | B. Bodine | 1 |
| Kulwicki | 4 | G. Bodine | 2 | McDuffie | 1 |
| M. Martin | 4 | Irvan | 2 | R. Mast | 1 |
| C. Yarborough | 3 | Isaac | 2 | J. Mayfield | 1 |
| Elliott | 3 | J. Gordon | 2 | D. Jarrett | 1 |
| B. Labonte | 3 | Bonnett | 1 | M. Kenseth | 1 |
| B. Allison | 2 | Earnhardt | 1 | Newman | 1 |
| Buddy Baker | 2 | Ruttman | 1 | | |
| Marcis | 2 | Da. Allison | 1 | | |

### RACE WINNERS

| Driver | Wins | Driver | Wins | Driver | Wins |
|---|---|---|---|---|---|
| B. Allison | 7 | Waltrip | 2 | B. Labonte | 1 |
| R. Petty | 7 | Parsons | 2 | D. Earnhardt Jr. | 1 |
| Pearson | 5 | Bonnett | 2 | D. Jarrett | 1 |
| J. Gordon | 4 | T. Stewart | 2 | Newman | 2 |
| Elliott | 4 | J. Johnson | 2 | | |
| R. Rudd | 4 | Bodine | 1 | | |
| Gant | 4 | Cope | 1 | | |
| Earnhardt | 3 | Schrader | 1 | | |
| R. Wallace | 3 | D. Allison | 1 | | |
| C. Yarborough | 3 | K. Petty | 1 | | |
| M. Martin | 3 | Ridley | 1 | | |

## YEAR BY YEAR WINNERS

| Year | Event | Race Winner | Car Make | Avg. Speed | Start Pos. | Winning Car Owner | Pole Winner |
|---|---|---|---|---|---|---|---|
| 2003 | MBNA America 400 | R. Newman | Dodge | 108.82 | 5 | Roger Penske | Trials Rained Out |
|  | MBNA Armed Forces 400 | R. Newman | Dodge | 106.896 | 1 | Roger Penske | R. Newman |
| 2002 | MBNA Am. Heroes 400 | J. Johnson | Chevrolet | 120.805 | 19 | Rick Hendrick | R. Wallace |
|  | MBNA Platinum 400 | J. Johnson | Chevrolet | 117.551 | 10 | Rick Hendrick | M. Kenseth |
| 2001 | MBNA Cal Ripken 400 | D. Earnhardt Jr. | Chevrolet | 101.559 | 27 | Dale Earnhardt | D. Jarrett |
|  | MBNA Platinum 400 | J. Gordon | Chevrolet | 120.361 | 2 | Rick Hendrick | Trials Rained Out |
| 2000 | MBNA.com 400 | T. Stewart | Pontiac | 115.191 | 27 | Joe Gibbs | J. Mayfield |
|  | MBNA Platinum 400 | T. Stewart | Pontiac | 109.514 | 16 | Joe Gibbs | R. Wallace |
| 1999 | MBNA Gold 400 | M. Martin | Ford | 127.434 | 8 | Jack Roush | R. Wallace |
|  | MBNA Platinum 400 | B. Labonte | Pontiac | 120.603 | 1 | Joe Gibbs | B. Labonte |
| 1998 | MBNA Gold 400 | M. Martin | Ford | 113.834 | 1 | Jack Roush | M. Martin |
|  | MBNA Platinum 400 | D. Jarrett | Ford | 119.522 | 4 | Robert Yates | R. Wallace |
| 1997 | MBNA 400 | M. Martin | Ford | 132.719 | 1 | Jack Roush | M. Martin |
|  | Miller 500 | R. Rudd | Ford | 114.635 | 13 | Ricky Rudd | B. Labonte |
| 1996 | MBNA 500 | J. Gordon | Chevrolet | 105.646 | 3 | Rick Hendrick | B. Labonte |
|  | Miller 500 | J. Gordon | Chevrolet | 122.741 | 1 | Rick Hendrick | J. Gordon |
| 1995 | MBNA 500 | J. Gordon | Chevrolet | 124.740 | 2 | Rick Hendrick | R. Mast |
|  | Miller 500 | K. Petty | Pontiac | 119.880 | 37 | Felix Sabates | J. Gordon |
| 1994 | SpitFire 500 | R. Wallace | Ford | 112.556 | 10 | Roger Penske | G. Bodine |
|  | Budweiser 500 | R. Wallace | Ford | 102.529 | 6 | Roger Penske | E. Irvan |
| 1993 | SpitFire 500 | R. Wallace | Pontiac | 100.334 | 1 | Roger Penske | R. Wallace |
|  | Budweiser 500 | Earnhardt | Chevrolet | 105.600 | 8 | Richard Childress | Irvan |
| 1992 | Peak 500 | Rudd | Chevrolet | 115.289 | 6 | Rick Hendrick | Kulwicki |
|  | Budweiser 500 | Gant | Oldsmobile | 109.456 | 15 | Leo Jackson | B. Bodine |
| 1991 | Peak 500 | Gant | Oldsmobile | 110.179 | 10 | Leo Jackson | Kulwicki |
|  | Budweiser 500 | Schrader | Chevrolet | 120.152 | 19 | Rick Hendrick | M. Waltrip |
| 1990 | Peak 500 | Elliot | Ford | 125.945 | 1 | Melling Racing | Elliott |
|  | Budweiser 500 | Cope | Chevrolet | 123.960 | 15 | Bob Whitcomb | Trickle |
| 1989 | Peak 500 | Earnhardt | Chevrolet | 122.909 | 15 | Richard Childress | Da. Allison |
|  | Budweiser 500 | Earnhardt | Chevrolet | 121.670 | 2 | Richard Childress | Martin |
| 1988 | Delaware 500 | Elliott | Ford | 109.349 | 3 | Melling Racing | Martin |
|  | Budweiser 500 | Elliott | Ford | 118.726 | 17 | Melling Racing | Kulwicki |
| 1987 | Delaware 500 | Rudd | Ford | 124.706 | 13 | Bud Moore | Kulwicki |
|  | Budweiser 500 | Da. Allison | Ford | 112.958 | 2 | Ranier Racing | Elliott |
| 1986 | Delaware 500 | Rudd | Ford | 114.329 | 11 | Bud Moore | Bodine |
|  | Budweiser 500 | Bodine | Chevrolet | 115.009 | 3 | Rick Hendrick | Rudd |
| 1985 | Delaware 500 | Gant | Chevrolet | 120.538 | 4 | Mach 1 | Elliott |
|  | Budweiser 500 | Elliott | Ford | 123.094 | 4 | Melling Racing | Labonte |
| 1984 d | Delaware 500 | Gant | Chevrolet | 111.856 | 4 | Mach 1 | Trials Rained Out |
|  | Budweiser 500 | R. Petty | Pontiac | 118.717 | 5 | Curb Racing | Rudd |
| 1983 | Budweiser 500 | B. Allison | Buick | 116.077 | 7 | DiGard Rac. Co. | Labonte |
|  | Mason-Dixon 500 | B. Allison | Buick | 114.847 | 10 | DiGard Rac. Co. | Ruttman |
| 1982 | CRC Chemicals 500 | Waltrip | Buick | 107.642 | 3 | Junior Johnson | Rudd |
|  | Mason-Dixon 500 | B. Allison | Chevrolet | 120.136 | 3 | DiGard Rac. Co. | Waltrip |
| 1981 | CRC Chemicals 500 | Bonnett | Ford | 119.561 | 3 | Wood Brothers | Rudd |
|  | Mason-Dixon 500 | Ridley | Ford | 116.595 | 11 | Junie Donlavey | Pearson |
| 1980 | CRC Chemicals 500 | Waltrip | Chevrolet | 116.024 | 2 | DiGard Rac. Co. | C. Yarborough |
|  | Mason-Dixon 500 | B. Allison | Ford | 113.866 | 8 | Bud Moore | C. Yarborough |
| 1979 | CRC Chemicals 500 | R. Petty | Chevrolet | 114.366 | 4 | Petty Eng. | Earnhardt |
|  | Mason-Dixon 500 | Bonnett | Mercury | 111.269 | 5 | Wood Brothers | Waltrip |
| 1978 | Delaware 500 | B. Allison | Ford | 119.323 | 2 | Bud Moore | McDuffie |
|  | Mason-Dixon 500 | Pearson | Mercury | 114.664 | 5 | Wood Brothers | Buddy Baker |
| 1977 | Delaware 500 | Parsons | Chevrolet | 114.708 | 7 | L. G. DeWitt | Bonnett |
|  | Mason-Dixon 500 | C. Yarborough | Chevrolet | 123.327 | 6 | Junior Johnson | R. Petty |
| 1976 | Delaware 500 | C. Yarborough | Chevrolet | 115.740 | 1 | Junior Johnson | C. Yarborough |
|  | Mason-Dixon 500 | Parsons | Chevrolet | 115.436 | 7 | L. G. DeWitt | Marcis |
| 1975 | Delaware 500 | R. Petty | Dodge | 111.372 | 3 | Petty Eng. | Marcis |
| c | Mason-Dixon 500 | Pearson | Mercury | 100.820 | 1 | Wood Brothers | Pearson |
| 1974 | Delaware 500 | R. Petty | Dodge | 113.640 | 2 | Petty Eng. | Buddy Baker |
| b | Mason-Dixon 500 | C. Yarborough | Chevrolet | 119.990 | 3 | Junior Johnson | Pearson |
| 1973 | Delaware 500 | Pearson | Mercury | 112.852 | 1 | Wood Brothers | Pearson |
|  | Mason-Dixon 500 | Pearson | Mercury | 119.745 | 1 | Wood Brothers | Pearson |
| 1972 | Delaware 500 | Pearson | Mercury | 120.506 | 2 | Wood Brothers | B. Allison |
|  | Mason-Dixon 500 | B. Allison | Chevrolet | 118.019 | 2 | Junior Johnson | Isaac |
| 1971 | Delaware 500 | R. Petty | Plymouth | 123.254 | 4 | Petty Eng. | B. Allison |
| a | Mason-Dixon 500 | B. Allison | Ford | 123.119 | 2 | Holman-Moody | R. Petty |
| 1970 | Mason-Dixon 300 | R. Petty | Plymouth | 112.103 | 2 | Petty Eng. | Isaac |
| 1969 | Mason-Dixon 300 | R. Petty | Ford | 115.772 | 3 | Petty Eng. | Pearson |

a Caution-free race.
b Reduced to 450 miles, energy shortage.
c First 140 miles run on Sunday, May 18; final 360 miles run on Monday, May 19.
d Starting lineup determined by Winston Cup car owner point standings.

## SPRING: MBNA AMERICA 400

### POLE WINNERS

| | | | |
|---|---|---|---|
| Pearson | 5 | T. Labonte | 1 |
| R. Petty | 2 | Elliott | 1 |
| D. Waltrip | 2 | Kulwicki | 1 |
| Rudd | 2 | Martin | 1 |
| Irvan | 2 | Trickle | 1 |
| Isaac | 2 | M. Waltrip | 1 |
| J. Gordon | 2 | B. Bodine | 1 |
| B. Labonte | 2 | Marcis | 1 |
| R. Wallace | 2 | Kenseth | 1 |
| Buddy Baker | 1 | Newman | 1 |
| Yarborough | 1 | | |
| Ruttman | 1 | | |

### RACE WINNERS

| | | | |
|---|---|---|---|
| B. Allison | 5 | Cope | 1 |
| R. Petty | 3 | Schrader | 1 |
| Pearson | 3 | Gant | 1 |
| J. Gordon | 2 | R. Wallace | 1 |
| Elliott | 2 | K. Petty | 1 |
| Earnhardt | 2 | Rudd | 1 |
| Yarborough | 2 | D. Jarrett | 1 |
| Parsons | 1 | B. Labonte | 1 |
| Bonnett | 1 | Stewart | 1 |
| Ridley | 1 | Ji. Johnson | 1 |
| G. Bodine | 1 | Newman | 1 |
| Da. Allison | 1 | | |

## FALL: DOVER 400

### POLE WINNERS

| | | | |
|---|---|---|---|
| M. Martin | 3 | Marcis | 1 |
| Kulwicki | 3 | McDuffie | 1 |
| R. Wallace | 3 | Earnhardt | 1 |
| B. Allison | 2 | T. Labonte | 1 |
| Yarborough | 2 | Pearson | 1 |
| Rudd | 2 | Da. Allison | 1 |
| Elliott | 2 | Mast | 1 |
| G. Bodine | 2 | B. Labonte | 1 |
| Buddy Baker | 1 | Mayfield | 1 |
| Bonnett | 1 | D. Jarrett | 1 |

### RACE WINNERS

| | | | |
|---|---|---|---|
| R. Petty | 4 | Parsons | 1 |
| Gant | 3 | Bonnett | 1 |
| Rudd | 3 | Earnhardt | 1 |
| Martin | 3 | Yarborough | 1 |
| B. Allison | 2 | Stewart | 1 |
| Pearson | 2 | Earnhardt Jr. | 1 |
| Waltrip | 2 | Ji. Johnson | 1 |
| Elliott | 2 | Newman | 1 |
| R. Wallace | 2 | | |
| J. Gordon | 2 | | |

# BUSCH SERIES

## YEAR BY YEAR WINNERS

| Year | Event | Pole Winner | Speed | Race Winner | Started |
|---|---|---|---|---|---|
| 1982 | Sportsman 200 | H. Gant | 138.021 | J. Ruttman | 9 |
| | No Fall race held | | | | |
| 1983 | Sportsman 200 | D. Pearson | 137.504 | R. Rudd | 12 |
| | No Fall race held | | | | |
| 1984 | Budweiser 200 | R. Bouchard | 139.184 | S. Ard | 2 |
| | No Fall race held | | | | |
| 1985 | Budweiser 200 | J. Ingram | 135.941 | D. Waltrip | 8 |
| | No Fall race held | | | | |
| 1986 | Budweiser 200 | B. Bodine | 137.546 | D. Waltrip | 2 |
| | Grand National 200 | M. Shepherd | 141.093 | M. Shepherd | 1 |
| 1987 | Budweiser 200 | R. Mast | 141.995 | M. Martin | 5 |
| | Grand National 200 | H. Gant | 140.685 | R. Mast | 3 |
| 1988 | Budweiser 200 | M. Alexander | 143.192 | B. Hillin | 15 |
| | Grand National 200 | H. Gant | 143.896 | M. Waltrip | 5 |
| 1989 | Budweiser 200 | H. Gant | 142.006 | R. Wilson | 8 |
| | Ames/Peak 200 | M. Waltrip | 143.209 | K. Schrader | 14 |
| 1990 | Budweiser 200 | B. Labonte | 143.885 | M. Waltrip | 4 |
| | Ames/Splitfire 200 | T. Ellis | 144.289 | H. Gant | 3 |
| 1991 | Budweiser 200 | D. Mader | 142.510 | T. Bodine | 9 |
| | Splitfire 200 | B. Miller | 145.396 | H. Gant | 16 |
| 1992 | Goodwrench 200 | T. Bodine | 143.604 | R. Pressley | 4 |
| | Splitfire 200 | J. Gordon | 143.079 | R. Pressley | 4 |
| 1993 | Goodw./Delco 200 | W. Burton | 145.926 | T. Bodine | 5 |
| | Splitfire 200 | T. Labonte | 147.366 | T. Bodine | 22 |
| 1994 | Goodw./Delco 200 | R. Craven | 146.425 | M. Wallace | 19 |
| | Splitfire 200 | H. Gant | 149.638 | J. Benson | 20 |
| 1995 | Goodw./Delco 200 | T. Leslie | 147.832 | M. McLaughlin | 5 |
| | MBNA 200 | J. Keller | 149.409 | J. Rumley | 24 |
| 1996 | Goodw./Delco 200 | B. Labonte | 149.963 | R. LaJoie | 16 |
| | MBNA 200 | R. Craven | 150.069 | R. LaJoie | 24 |
| 1997 | Goodw./Delco 200 | D. Trickle | 148.926 | B. Labonte | 2 |
| | MBNA 200 | D. Trickle | 147.656 | J. Bessey | 6 |
| 1998 | MBNA Platinum 200 | K. Lepage | 151.688 | D. Earnhardt Jr. | 16 |
| | MBNA Gold 200 | K. Grubb | 153.498 | M. Kenseth | 4 |
| 1999 | MBNA Platinum 200 | D. Trickle | 155.213 | D. Earnhardt Jr. | 15 |
| | MBNA Gold 200 | M. Kenseth | 155.293 | C. Atwood | 5 |
| 2000 | MBNA Platinum 200 | K. Harvick | 154.912 | J. Keller | 22 |
| | MBNA.com 200 | M. Skinner | 155.932 | M. Kenseth | 14 |
| 2001 | MBNA Platinum 200 | None - weather | | J. Spencer | 21 |
| | MBNA.COM 200 | R. Newman | 155.635 | J. Green | 2 |
| 2002 | MBNA Platinum 200 | J. Green | 155.347 | G. Biffle | 3 |
| | MBNA All-American 200 | K. Lepage | 155.757 | S. Wimmer | 26 |
| 2003 | MBNA Armed Forces 200 | Joe Nemechek | 156.747 | Joe Nemechek | 1 |
| | Stacker 200 by YJ Stinger | None - weather | | B. Vickers | 3 |

**QUALIFYING RECORD**
Mike Skinner, Chevrolet; 155.932 mph (23.087 sec.); September 22, 2000.

**RACE RECORD**
Dale Earnhardt Jr., Chevrolet; 130.152 mph (1 hr., 32 min., 12 sec.); May 30, 1998.

### POLE WINNERS

| | | | | | | | |
|---|---|---|---|---|---|---|---|
| Harry Gant | 5 | Jeff Gordon | 1 | Butch Miller | 1 | | |
| Dick Trickle | 3 | Jeff Green | 1 | Ryan Newman | 1 | | |
| Ricky Craven | 2 | Kevin Grubb | 1 | David Pearson | 1 | | |
| Bobby Labonte | 2 | Kevin Harvick | 1 | Morgan Shepherd | 1 | | |
| Kevin LePage | 2 | Jack Ingram | 1 | Mike Skinner | 1 | | |
| Mike Alexander | 1 | Jason Keller | 1 | Michael Waltrip | 1 | | |
| Brett Bodine | 1 | Matt Kenseth | 1 | Joe Nemechek | 1 | | |
| Todd Bodine | 1 | Terry Labonte | 1 | | | | |
| Ron Bouchard | 1 | Tracy Leslie | 1 | | | | |
| Ward Burton | 1 | Dave Mader III | 1 | | | | |
| Tommy Ellis | 1 | Rick Mast | 1 | | | | |

### RACE WINNERS

| | | | | | | |
|---|---|---|---|---|---|---|
| Todd Bodine | 3 | Joe Bessey | 1 | Joe Ruttman | 1 |
| Dale Earnhardt Jr. | 2 | Greg Biffle | 1 | Ken Schrader | 1 |
| Harry Gant | 2 | Jeff Green | 1 | Morgan Shepherd | 1 |
| Matt Kenseth | 2 | Bobby Hillin | 1 | Jimmy Spencer | 1 |
| Randy LaJoie | 2 | Jason Keller | 1 | Mike Wallace | 1 |
| Robert Pressley | 2 | Bobby Labonte | 1 | Rick Wilson | 1 |
| Darrell Waltrip | 2 | Mark Martin | 1 | Scott Wimmer | 1 |
| Michael Waltrip | 1 | Rick Mast | 1 | Joe Nemechek | 1 |
| Sam Ard | 1 | Mike McLaughlin | 1 | Brian Vickers | 1 |
| Casey Atwood | 1 | Ricky Rudd | 1 | | |
| Johnny Benson | 1 | Johnny Rumley | 1 | | |

# CRAFTSMAN TRUCK SERIES

## YEAR BY YEAR WINNERS

| Year | Event | Pole Winner | Speed | Race Winner | Started |
|---|---|---|---|---|---|
| 2000 | MBNA E-Commerce.com 200 | Kurt Busch | 151.764 | Kurt Busch | 1 |
| 2001 | MBNA E-Commerce 200 | Scott Riggs | 150.288 | Scott Riggs | 1 |
| 2002 | MBNA America 200 | Rick Crawford | 150.414 | Ted Musgrave | 2 |
| 2003 | MBNA Armed Forces 200 | Bobby Hamilton | — | Jason Leffler | 26 |

**QUALIFYING RECORD**
Kurt Busch, Ford; 151.764 mph (23.721 sec.); September 21, 2000

**RACE RECORD**
Ted Musgrave, Dodge; 104.545 mph (1 hr., 54 min., 47 sec.); May 31, 2002

### POLE WINNERS

| | | | |
|---|---|---|---|
| Kurt Busch | 1 | Scott Riggs | 1 |
| Rick Crawford | 1 | | |

### RACE WINNERS

| | | | |
|---|---|---|---|
| Ted Musgrave | 1 | Scott Riggs | 1 |
| Kurt Busch | 1 | Jason Leffler | 1 |

TRACKS

# Homestead-Miami Speedway

## TRACK FACTS
**Date Opened:** Fall 1995
**Owner:** ISC
**President:** Curtis Gray
**Distance:** 1.5 miles
**Banking in Turns:** Variable, 18 to 20 degrees
**Banking in Straights:** 3 degrees
**Length of Frontstretch:** 1,760 feet
**Length of Backstretch:** 1,760 feet
**Grandstand Seating:** 73,000
**Tickets:** (305) 230-7223
**Website:** www.homesteadmiamispeedway.com

## 2004 SCHEDULE

### NEXTEL Cup
**Ford 400**
**Race:** No. 36 of 36
**Date:** November 21
**TV:** NBC. **Radio:** MRN

### Busch Series
**Ford 300**
**Race:** No. 34 of 34
**Date:** November 20
**TV:** NBC. **Radio:** MRN

### Craftsman Truck Series
**Ford 200**
**Race:** No. 25 of 25
**Date:** November 19
**TV:** Speed. **Radio:** MRN

## NEXTEL CUP

### TRACK RECORDS
**Most Wins:** 2—Tony Stewart
**Oldest Winner:** Bill Elliott, 46 years, 1 month, 3 days, 11/11/2001
**Youngest Winner:** Kurt Busch, 24 years, 3 months, 13 days, 11/17/2002
**Most Lead Changes:** 21—11/16/03
**Fewest Lead Changes:** 12—11/17/02
**Most Leaders:** 12—11/14/03
**Fewest Leaders:** 6—11/17/02
**Most Cautions:** 10—11/16/03
**Fewest Cautions:** 1—11/14/99
**Most Caution Laps:** 60—11/16/03
**Fewest Caution Laps:** 5—11/14/99
**Most on the Lead Lap:** 25—11/11/01
**Fewest on the Lead Lap:** 6—11/12/00
**Most Running at the Finish:** 42—11/11/01
**Fewest Running at the Finish:** 35—11/12/00
**Most Laps Led by a Race Winner:** 1—Bobby Labonte, 11/16/03
**Fewest Laps Led by a Race Winner:** 28—Kurt Busch, 11/17/02
**Closest Margin of Victory:** 1.420 second, Bill Elliott defeated Michael Waltrip 11/11/01
**Greatest Margin of Victory:** 5.289 seconds, Tony Stewart defeated Bobby Labonte 11/14/99

### QUALIFYING AND RACE RECORDS
**QUALIFYING**
**Track:** Jamie McMurray, Dodge, 181.111 mph, Nov. 14, 2003.
**RACE**
**Track:** Tony Stewart, Pontiac, 140.335 mph, 2 hours, 51 minutes, 14 seconds, Nov. 14, 1999.

### YEAR BY YEAR WINNERS

| Year | Event | Race Winner | Car Make | Avg. Speed | Start Pos. | Winning Car Owner | Pole Winner |
|---|---|---|---|---|---|---|---|
| 2003 | Ford 400 | B. Labonte | Chevrolet | 116.868 | 2 | Joe Gibbs | J. McMurray |
| 2002 | Ford 400 | K. Busch | Ford | 116.462 | 1 | Jack Roush | K. Busch |
| 2001 | Pennzoil Freedom 400 | B. Elliott | Dodge | 117.449 | 1 | Ray Evernham | B. Elliott |
| 2000 | Pennzoil 400 | T. Stewart | Pontiac | 127.480 | 13 | Joe Gibbs | S. Park |
| 1999 | Pennzoil 400 | T. Stewart | Pontiac | 140.335 | 7 | Joe Gibbs | D. Green |

### ALL HOMESTEAD RACES

| POLE WINNERS | | RACE WINNERS | |
|---|---|---|---|
| D. Green | 1 | Stewart | 2 |
| Park | 1 | B. Elliott | 1 |
| B. Elliott | 1 | K. Busch | 1 |
| Busch | 1 | B. Labonte | 1 |
| McMurray | | | |

## BUSCH SERIES

### YEAR BY YEAR WINNERS

| Year | Event | Pole Winner | Speed | Race Winner | Started |
|---|---|---|---|---|---|
| 1995 | Jiffy Lube 300 | J. Nemechek | 134.628 | D. Jarrett | 26 |
| 1996 | Jiffy Lube 300 | B. Labonte | 139.074 | K. Lepage | 10 |
| 1997 | Jiffy Lube 300 | M. McLaughlin | 147.771 | J. Nemechek | 3 |
| 1998 | Jiffy Lube 300 | C. Atwood | 148.262 | J. Bruton | 23 |
| 1999 | Hotwheels.com 300 | H. Stricklin | 149.456 | J. Nemechek | 12 |
| 2000 | Miami 300 | B. Hamilton Jr. | 151.490 | J. Gordon | 6 |
| 2001 | GNC Live Well 300 | J. Green | 150.939 | J. Nemechek | 20 |
| 2002 | Ford 300 | J. Green | 152.031 | S. Wimmer | 26 |
| 2003 | Ford 300 | G. Biffle | 177.416 | K. Kahne | 3 |

**QUALIFYING RECORD**
Kevin Lepage, Chev.; 185.644 mph (38.784 sec.); Aug. 16, 2002

**RACE RECORD**
Joe Nemechek, Chev.; 132.191 mph (2 hrs. 16 min. 10 sec.); Nov. 11, 2001

### POLE WINNERS

| | | | | | |
|---|---|---|---|---|---|
| Jeff Green | 2 | Bobby Labonte | 1 | Hut Stricklin | 1 |
| Casey Atwood | 1 | Mike McLaughlin | 1 | Greg Biffle | 1 |
| Bobby Hamilton Jr. | 1 | Joe Nemechek | 1 | | |

### RACE WINNERS

| | | | | | |
|---|---|---|---|---|---|
| Joe Nemechek | 3 | Dale Jarrett | 1 | Kasey Kahne | 1 |
| Jeff Burton | 1 | Kevin Lepage | 1 | | |
| Jeff Gordon | 1 | Scott Wimmer | 1 | | |

# CRAFTSMAN TRUCK SERIES

## YEAR BY YEAR WINNERS

| Year | Event | Pole Winner | Speed | Race Winner | Started |
|---|---|---|---|---|---|
| 1996 | Florida Dodge Dealers 400 | Geoff Bodine | 135.598 | Dave Rezendes | 10 |
| 1997 | Florida Dodge Dealers 400 | Joe Ruttman | 140.221 | Kenny Irwin | 5 |
| 1998 | Florida Dodge Dealers 400 | Jack Sprague | 149.283 | Rick Crawford | 12 |
| 1999 | Florida Dodge Dealers 400 | Randy Tolsma | 149.813 | Mike Wallace | 10 |
| 2000 | Florida Dodge Dealers 400 | Joe Ruttman | 146.727 | Andy Houston | 3 |
| 2001 | Florida Dodge Dealers 400 | Scott Riggs | 146.017 | Ted Musgrave | 3 |
| 2002 | Ford 200 | Mike Bliss | 147.111 | Ron Hornaday Jr. | 5 |
| 2003 | Ford 200 | Bobby Hamilton | 169.252 | Bobby Hamilton | 1 |

**QUALIFYING RECORD**
Bobby Hamilton, Dodge; 169.252 mph; November 13, 2003

**RACE RECORD**
Ron Hornaday Jr., Chevrolet; 133.260 mph (1 hr., 30 min., 30 sec.); November 15, 2002

### POLE WINNERS
| | | | | | |
|---|---|---|---|---|---|
| Joe Ruttman | 2 | Jack Sprague | 1 | | |
| Mike Bliss | 1 | Randy Tolsma | 1 | | |
| Geoffrey Bodine | 1 | Rick Crawford | 1 | | |
| Scott Riggs | 1 | Hamilton | 1 | | |

### RACE WINNERS
| | | | |
|---|---|---|---|
| Ron Hornaday Jr. | 1 | Dave Rezendes | 1 |
| Andy Houston | 1 | Hamilton | 1 |
| Kenny Irwin | 1 | | |
| Ted Musgrave | 1 | | |

# Indianapolis Motor Speedway

## TRACK FACTS
**Date Opened:** 1909
**Owner:** Hulman-George Family, Hulman & Co., Terre Haute
**President/CEO:** Anton H. George
**Distance:** 2.5 miles
**Banking in Turns:** 9 degrees
**Banking on Straights:** 0 degrees
**Length of Frontstretch:** 3,300 feet
**Length of Backstretch:** 3,300 feet
**Length of Short Straightaways:** 660 feet
**Grandstand Seating:** 250,000
**Tickets:** (317) 481-6700
**Website:** www.brickyard400.com

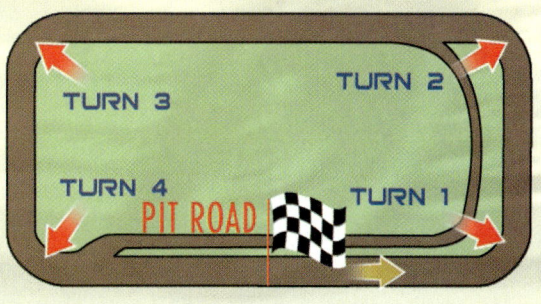

## NEXTEL CUP

### TRACK RECORDS
**Most Wins:** 3—Jeff Gordon
**Oldest Winner:** Bill Elliott, 46 years, 9 months, 27 days, 08/04/2002
**Youngest Winner:** Jeff Gordon, 23 years, 2 days, 08/06/1994
**Most Lead Changes:** 21—8/6/94
**Fewest Lead Changes:** 9—8/5/00
**Most Leaders:** 13—Twice, most recently, 8/3/96
**Fewest Leaders:** 5—8/5/00
**Most Cautions:** 9—8/1/98
**Fewest Cautions:** 1—8/5/95
**Most Caution Laps:** 36—8/4/02
**Fewest Caution Laps:** 4—8/5/95
**Most on the Lead Lap:** 30—8/4/02
**Fewest on the Lead Lap:** 14—8/5/00
**Most Running at the Finish:** 39—Twice, most recently, 8/5/00
**Fewest Running at the Finish:** 31—8/1/98
**Most Laps Led by a Race Winner:** 117—Dale Jarrett, 8/7/99
**Fewest Laps Led by a Race Winner:** 11—Dale Jarrett, 8/3/96
**Closest Margin of Victory:** 0.183 second, Ricky Rudd defeated Bobby Labonte 08/02/97
**Greatest Margin of Victory:** 4.229 seconds, Bobby Labonte defeated Rusty Wallace 08/05/00

### QUALIFYING AND RACE RECORDS
**QUALIFYING**
Kevin Harvick, Chevrolet, 184.343 mph, August 1, 2003.
**RACE**
Bobby Labonte, Pontiac, 155.912 mph, 2 hours, 33 minutes, 56 seconds, August 5, 2000.

### 2004 SCHEDULE
**NEXTEL Cup**
**Brickyard 400**
**Race:** No. 21 of 36
**Date:** August 8
**TV:** NBC. **Radio:** IMS

### YEAR BY YEAR WINNERS

| Year | Event | Race Winner | Car Make | Avg. Speed | Start Pos. | Winning Car Owner | Pole Winner |
|---|---|---|---|---|---|---|---|
| 2003 | Brickyard 400 | K. Harvick | Chevrolet | 134.544 | 1 | Richard Childress | K. Harvick |
| 2002 | Brickyard 400 | B. Elliott | Dodge | 125.033 | 2 | Ray Evernham | T. Stewart |
| 2001 | Brickyard 400 | J. Gordon | Chevrolet | 130.790 | 27 | Rick Hendrick | J. Spencer |
| 2000 | Brickyard 400 | B. Labonte | Pontiac | 155.912 | 3 | Joe Gibbs | R. Rudd |
| 1999 | Brickyard 400 | D. Jarrett | Ford | 148.194 | 4 | Robert Yates | J. Gordon |
| 1998 | Brickyard 400 | J. Gordon | Chevrolet | 126.770 | 3 | Rick Hendrick | E Irvan |
| 1997 | Brickyard 400 | R. Rudd | Ford | 130.814 | 7 | Ricky Rudd | E. Irvan |
| 1996 | Brickyard 400 | D. Jarrett | Ford | 139.508 | 24 | Robert Yates | J. Gordon |
| 1995 | Brickyard 400 | D. Earnhardt | Chevrolet | 155.206 | 13 | Richard Childress | J. Gordon |
| 1994 | Brickyard 400 | J. Gordon | Chevrolet | 131.977 | 3 | Rick Hendrick | R. Mast |

### ALL INDIANAPOLIS RACES

| POLE WINNERS | | RACE WINNERS | |
|---|---|---|---|
| J. Gordon | 3 | J. Gordon | 3 |
| Irvan | 2 | D. Jarrett | 2 |
| Mast | 1 | Earnhardt | 1 |
| Rudd | 1 | Rudd | 1 |
| Spencer | 1 | B. Labonte | 1 |
| Stewart | 1 | Elliott | 1 |
| Harvick | 1 | Harvick | 1 |

# Infineon Raceway

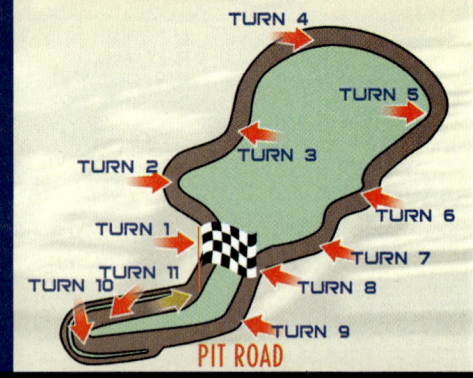

## TRACK FACTS
**Date Opened:** 1968
**Owner:** Speedway Motorsports, Inc.
**President:** Steve Page
**Distance:** 1.99-mile road course
**Turns:** 11, with varying lengths and degrees of banking.
**The chute:** 890 feet, 2.8 degrees banking
**Grandstand Seating:** 30,000
**Tickets:** (800) 870-7223
**Website:** www.infineonraceway.com

## NEXTEL CUP

### TRACK RECORDS
**Most Wins:** 3—Jeff Gordon
**Most Top 5s:** 6—Ricky Rudd
**Most Top 10s:** 7—Dale Earnhardt, Mark Martin and Ricky Rudd
**Oldest Winner:** Ricky Rudd, 45 years, 9 months, 11 days, 06/23/2002
**Youngest Winner:** Jeff Gordon, 26 years, 10 months, 24 days, 06/28/1998
**Most Lead Changes:** 10—4 times, most recently, 6/23/02
**Fewest Lead Changes:** 3—6/11/89
**Most Leaders:** 9—Twice, most recently, 6/23/02
**Fewest Leaders:** 3—6/11/89
**Most Cautions:** 9—6/10/90
**Fewest Cautions:** 3—4 times, most recently, 6/23/02
**Most Caution Laps:** 26—6/27/99
**Fewest Caution Laps:** 7—6/7/92
**Most on the Lead Lap:** 29—4 times, most recently, 6/22/03
**Fewest on the Lead Lap:** 14—Twice, most recently, 5/16/93
**Most Running at the Finish:** 42—5/5/96
**Fewest Running at the Finish:** 32—5/16/93
**Most Laps Led by a Race Winner:** 81—Robby Gordon 6/22/03
**Fewest Laps Led by a Race Winner:** 2—Davey Allison 6/9/91
**Closest Margin of Victory:** 0.05 seconds, Ricky Rudd defeated Rusty Wallace 06/11/89
**Greatest Margin of Victory:** 9.56 seconds, Ernie Irvan defeated Geoffrey Bodine 05/15/94

### QUALIFYING AND RACE RECORDS
**QUALIFYING**
**Track Record (1.99 miles):** Tony Stewart, Pontiac, 93.4/6 mph, 76.640 seconds, June 23, 2002.
**RACE**
**Track Record (1.99 miles):** Ricky Rudd, Ford, 81.007 mph, 2 hours, 42 minutes, 08 seconds, June 23, 2002.

### 2004 SCHEDULE
**NEXTEL Cup**
**Dodge/Save Mart 350**
**Race:** No. 16 of 36
**Date:** June 27
**TV:** FOX. **Radio:** PRN

## YEAR BY YEAR WINNERS

|   | Year | Event | Race Winner | Car Make | Avg. Speed | Start Pos. | Winning Car Owner | Pole Winner |
|---|------|-------|-------------|----------|------------|------------|-------------------|-------------|
|   | 2003 | Dodge/Save Mart 350 | R. Gordon | Chevrolet | 73.821 | 2 | Richard Childress | B. Said |
| c | 2002 | Dodge/Save Mart 350 | R. Rudd | Ford | 81.007 | 7 | Robert Yates | T. Stewart |
| b | 2001 | Dodge/Save Mart 350 | T. Stewart | Pontiac | 75.889 | 3 | Joe Gibbs | J. Gordon |
|   | 2000 | Save Mart/Kragen 350 | J. Gordon | Chevrolet | 78.789 | 5 | Rick Hendrick | R. Wallace |
| a | 1999 | Save Mart 350 | J. Gordon | Chevrolet | 70.378 | 1 | Rick Hendrick | J. Gordon |
|   | 1998 | Save Mart 350 | J. Gordon | Chevrolet | 72.387 | 1 | Rick Hendrick | J. Gordon |
|   | 1997 | Save Mart 300 | M. Martin | Ford | 75.788 | 1 | Jack Roush | M. Martin |
|   | 1996 | Save Mart 300 | R. Wallace | Ford | 77.673 | 7 | Roger Penske | T. Labonte |
|   | 1995 | Save Mart 300 | Earnhardt | Chevrolet | 70.681 | 4 | Richard Childress | R. Rudd |
|   | 1994 | Save Mart 300 | E. Irvan | Ford | 77.458 | 1 | Robert Yates | E. Irvan |
|   | 1993 | Save Mart 300 | G. Bodine | Ford | 77.013 | 3 | Bud Moore | Earnhardt |
|   | 1992 | Save Mart 300 | Irvan | Chevrolet | 81.413 | 2 | Morgan-McClure | Rudd |
|   | 1991 | Banquet 300 | Da. Allison | Ford | 72.970 | 13 | Robert Yates | Rudd |
|   | 1990 | Banquet 300 | Wallace | Pontiac | 69.245 | 11 | Blue Max | Rudd |
|   | 1989 | Banquet 300 | Rudd | Buick | 76.088 | 4 | King Racing | Wallace |

a Track reconfigured from 2.52 miles to 1.949 miles.
b Track reconfigured from 1.949 miles to 2 miles.
c Track reconfigured from 2 miles to 1.99 miles.

## ALL SONOMA RACES

| POLE WINNERS | | RACE WINNERS | |
|---|---|---|---|
| Rudd | 4 | T. Labonte | 1 | J. Gordon | 3 | G. Bodine | 1 |
| J. Gordon | 3 | Martin | 1 | Irvan | 2 | Earnhardt | 1 |
| R. Wallace | 2 | Stewarat | 1 | R. Wallace | 2 | Martin | 1 |
| Earnhardt | 1 | Said | 1 | Rudd | 2 | Stewart | 1 |
| Irvan | 1 | | | Da. Allison | 1 | R. Gordon | 1 |

# Kansas Speedway

## TRACK FACTS

**Date Opened:** July 6, 2001
**Owner:** ISC
**President:** W. Grant Lynch, Jr.
**Distance:** 1.5 miles
**Banking in Turns:** 15 degrees
**Banking on Frontstretch:** 10.4 degrees
**Banking on Backstretch:** 5 degrees
**Length of Frontstretch:** 2,685 feet
**Length of Backstretch:** 2,207 feet
**Grandstand Seating:** 80,187
**Tickets:** (913) 328-7223
**Website:** www.kansasspeedway.com

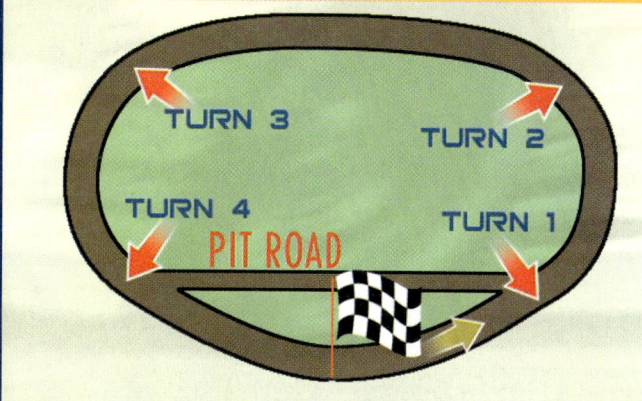

## 2004 SCHEDULE

### NEXTEL Cup
**Banquet 400**
**Race:** No. 30 of 36
**Date:** October 10
**TV:** NBC. **Radio:** MRN

### Busch Series
**Mr. Goodcents 300**
**Race:** No. 28 of 34
**Date:** October 9
**TV:** TNT. **Radio:** MRN

### Craftsman Truck Series
**O'Reilly Auto Parts 250**
**Race:** No. 10 of 25
**Date:** July 3
**TV:** Speed. **Radio:** MRN

# NEXTEL CUP

## TRACK RECORDS

**Most Wins:** 2—Jeff Gordon
**Oldest Winner:** Jeff Gordon, 31 years, 1 month, 25 days, 09/29/2002
**Youngest Winner:** Ryan Newman, 26 years, 9 months, 27 days, 10/5/03
**Most Lead Changes:** 23—10/5/03
**Fewest Lead Changes:** 13—9/29/02
**Most Leaders:** 12—9/30/01
**Fewest Leaders:** 10—9/29/02
**Most Cautions:** 13—9/30/01
**Fewest Cautions:** 9—10/5/03
**Most Caution Laps:** 70—9/30/01
**Fewest Caution Laps:** 47—10/5/03
**Most on the Lead Lap:** 24—10/5/03
**Fewest on the Lead Lap:** 9—9/29/02
**Most Running at the Finish:** 34—10/5/03
**Fewest Running at the Finish:** 27—9/29/02
**Most Laps Led by a Race Winner:** 116—Jeff Gordon, 9/29/02
**Fewest Laps Led by a Race Winner:** 28—Ryan Newman, 10/5/03
**Closest Margin of Victory:** 0.413 second, Jeff Gordon defeated Ryan Newman 09/30/01
**Greatest Margin of Victory:** 0.863 second, Ryan Newman defeated Bill Elliott 10/5/03

## QUALIFYING AND RACE RECORDS

### QUALIFYING
**Track:** Jimmy Johnson, Chevrolet, 180.373 mph, October 3, 2003

### RACE
**Track:** Ryan Newman, Dodge, 121.630 mph (3 hours, 17 min., 34 sec.); October 5, 2003

## YEAR BY YEAR WINNERS

| Year | Event | Race Winner | Car Make | Avg. Speed | Start Pos. | Winning Car Owner | Pole Winner |
|---|---|---|---|---|---|---|---|
| 2003 | Banquet 400 | R. Newman | Dodge | 121.630 | 11 | Roger Penske | J. Johnson |
| 2002 | Protection One 400 | J. Gordon | Chevrolet | 119.394 | 10 | R. Hendrick | D. Earnhardt Jr. |
| 2001 | Protection One 400 | J. Gordon | Chevrolet | 110.576 | 2 | R. Hendrick | J. Leffler |

## ALL KANSAS RACES

| POLE WINNERS | | RACE WINNERS | |
|---|---|---|---|
| R. Rudd | 4 | J. Gordon | 2 |
| J. Leffler | 1 | Newman | 1 |
| D. Earnhardt Jr. | 1 | | |
| Ji. Johnson | 1 | | |

# BUSCH SERIES

## YEAR BY YEAR WINNERS

| Year | Event | Pole Winner | Speed | Race Winner | Started |
|---|---|---|---|---|---|
| 2001 | Mr. Goodcents 300 | K. Lepage | 174.210 | J. Green | 12 |
| 2002 | Mr. Goodcents 300 | M. Waltrip | 174.831 | J. Burton | 2 |
| 2003 | Mr. Goodcents 300 | M. Waltrip | 178.365 | D. Green | 3 |

### QUALIFYING RECORD
Michael Waltrip, Chevrolet; 178.365 mph; October 3, 2003

### RACE RECORD
Jeff Green, Ford; 129.125 (2 hrs., 19 min., 24 sec.); Sept. 29, 2001

| POLE WINNERS | | RACE WINNERS | | | |
|---|---|---|---|---|---|
| Kevin Lepage | 1 | Jeff Green | 1 | D. Green | 1 |
| Michael Waltrip | 2 | Jeff Burton | 1 | | |

# CRAFTSMAN TRUCK SERIES

## YEAR BY YEAR WINNERS

| Year | Event | Pole Winner | Speed | Race Winner | Started |
|---|---|---|---|---|---|
| 2001 | O'Reilly Auto Parts 250 | Dennis Setzer | 162.411 mph | Ricky Hendrick | 2 |
| 2002 | O'Reilly Auto Parts 250 | Jason Leffler | 165.812 mph | Mike Bliss | 4 |
| 2003 | O'Reilly Auto Parts 250 | Chad Chaffin | 166.323 mph | Jon Wood | 3 |

### QUALIFYING RECORD
Chad Chaffin, Dodge; 166.323 mph; July 4, 2003

### RACE RECORD
Ricky Hendrick, Chevrolet; 125.094 mph (2 hrs., 0 min., 9 sec.); July 7, 2001

### POLE WINNERS
| | | | |
|---|---|---|---|
| Jason Leffler | 1 | Chad Chaffin | 1 |
| Dennis Setzer | 1 | | |

### RACE WINNERS
| | | | |
|---|---|---|---|
| Mike Bliss | 1 | Jon Wood | 1 |
| Ricky Hendrick | 1 | | |

# Las Vegas Motor Speedway

## TRACK FACTS
**Date Opened:** June 25, 1996
**Owner:** Speedway Motorsports, Inc.
**President & GM:** Chris Powell
**Distance:** 1.5 miles
**Banking in Turns:** 12 degrees
**Banking on Frontstretch:** 9 degrees
**Banking on Backstretch:** 3 degrees
**Length of Frontstretch:** 2,275 feet
**Length of Backstretch:** 1,572 feet
**Grandstand Seating:** 137,000
**Tickets:** (702) 644-4444
**Website:** www.lvms.com

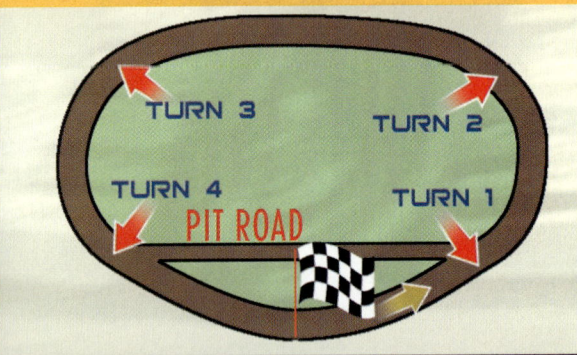

## 2004 SCHEDULE

### NEXTEL Cup
**UAW-DaimlerChrysler 400**
Race: No. 3 of 36
Date: March 7
TV: FOX. Radio: PRN

### Busch Series
**Sam's Town 300**
Race: No. 3 of 34
Date: March 6
TV: FX. Radio: PRN

### Craftsman Truck Series
**O'Reilly Auto Parts 250**
Race: No. 10 of 25
Date: July 3
TV: Speed. Radio: MRN

## NEXTEL CUP

### TRACK RECORDS
**Most Wins:** 2—Jeff Burton
**Oldest Winner:** Sterling Marlin, 44 years, 8 months, 1 days, 03/03/2002
**Youngest Winner:** Jeff Gordon, 29 years, 7 months, 03/04/2001
**Most Lead Changes:** 25—3/7/99
**Fewest Lead Changes:** 13—3/5/00
**Most Leaders:** 13—Twice, most recently, 3/3/02
**Fewest Leaders:** 7—3/5/00
**Most Cautions:** 6—Twice, most recently, 3/3/02
**Fewest Cautions:** 2—Twice, most recently, 3/5/00
**Most Caution Laps:** 28—3/5/00
**Fewest Caution Laps:** 9—3/1/98
**Most on the Lead Lap:** 20—3/3/02
**Fewest on the Lead Lap:** 10—Twice, most recently, 3/7/99
**Most Running at the Finish:** 42—3/5/00
**Fewest Running at the Finish:** 35—3/7/99
**Most Laps Led by a Race Winner:** 111—Jeff Burton, 3/7/99
**Fewest Laps Led by a Race Winner:** 33—Jeff Gordon, 3/4/01
**Closest Margin of Victory:** 1.065 seconds, Mark Martin defeated Jeff Burton 03/01/98
**Greatest Margin of Victory:** 9.104 seconds, Matt Kenseth defeated Dale Earnhardt Jr. 3/2/03

### QUALIFYING AND RACE RECORDS
**QUALIFYING**
Track: Bobby Labonte, Chevrolet; 173.016 mph; February 28, 2003
**RACE**
Track: Mark Martin, Ford, 146.554 mph, 2 hours, 43 minutes, 58 seconds, March 1, 1998.

## YEAR BY YEAR WINNERS

| Year | Event | Race Winner | Car Make | Avg. Speed | Start Pos. | Winning Car Owner | Pole Winner |
|---|---|---|---|---|---|---|---|
| 2003 | UAW-DaimlerChrysler 400 | M. Kenseth | Ford | 132.934 | 17 | Jack Roush | B. Labonte |
| 2002 | UAW-DaimlerChrysler 400 | S. Maratin | Dodge | 136.754 | 24 | Chip Ganassi | T. Bodine |
| 2001 | UAW-DaimlerChrysler 400 | J. Gordon | Chevrolet | 135.546 | 24 | Rick Hendrick | D. Jarrett |
| a 2000 | CarsDirect.com 400 | J. Burton | Ford | 119.982 | 11 | Jack Roush | R. Rudd |
| 1999 | Las Vegas 400 | J. Burton | Ford | 137.537 | 19 | Jack Roush | B. Labonte |
| 1998 | Las Vegas 400 | M. Martin | Ford | 146.554 | 7 | Jack Roush | D. Jarrett |

a Reduced to 222.0 miles, rain

## ALL LAS VEGAS RACES

### POLE WINNERS
| | |
|---|---|
| D. Jarrett | 2 |
| B. Labonte | 2 |
| Rudd | 1 |
| T. Bodine | 1 |

### RACE WINNERS
| | |
|---|---|
| J. Burton | 2 |
| Martin | 1 |
| J. Gordon | 1 |
| Marlin | 1 |
| Kenseth | 1 |

## BUSCH SERIES

### YEAR BY YEAR WINNERS

| Year | Event | Pole Winner | Speed | Race Winner | Started |
|------|-------|-------------|-------|-------------|---------|
| 1997 | Las Vegas 300 | J. Green | 159.311 | J. Green | 1 |
| 1998 | Sam's Town 300 | M. Martin | 162.577 | J. Spencer | 7 |
| 1999 | Sam's Town 300 | M. Martin | 165.715 | M. Martin | 1 |
| 2000 | Sam's Town 300 | H. Parker Jr. | 166.328 | J. Burton | 7 |
| 2001 | Sam's Town 300 | M. Kenseth | 169.385 | T. Bodine | 2 |
| 2002 | Sam's Town 300 | J. Burton | 169.168 | J. Burton | 1 |
| 2003 | Sam's Town 300 | S. Barrett | — | J. Nemechek | 29 |

**QUALIFYING RECORD**
Matt Kenseth, Chevrolet; 169.385 (31.880 sec.); March 2, 2001

**RACE RECORD**
Jeff Burton, Ford; 135.118 mph (2 hrs., 13 min., 13 sec.); March 4, 2000.

### POLE WINNERS

| | | | | | |
|---|---|---|---|---|---|
| Mark Martin | 2 | Matt Kenseth | 1 | | |
| Jeff Burton | 1 | Hank Parker Jr. | 1 | | |
| Jeff Green | 1 | | | | |

### RACE WINNERS

| | | | | |
|---|---|---|---|---|
| Jeff Burton | 2 | Mark Martin | 1 | |
| Todd Bodine | 1 | Jimmy Spencer | 1 | |
| Jeff Green | 1 | Joe Nemechek | 1 | |

## CRAFTSMAN TRUCK SERIES

### YEAR BY YEAR WINNERS

| Year | Event | Pole Winner | Speed | Race Winner | Started |
|------|-------|-------------|-------|-------------|---------|
| 1996 | Carquest Auto Parts 420K | Bryan Reffner | 157.909 mph | Jack Sprague | 3 |
| 1997 | Carquest Auto Parts 420K | Jack Sprague | 161.310 mph | Joe Ruttman | 8 |
| 1998 | Sam's Town 250 | Jack Sprague | 161.749 mph | Jack Sprague | 1 |
| 1999 | The Orleans 250 | Stacy Compton | 161.796 mph | Greg Biffle | 5 |
| 2001 | The Orleans 350 | Jack Sprague | 161.803 mph | Ted Musgrave | 10 |
| 2002 | Las Vegas 350 | David Starr | 163.112 mph | David Starr | 1 |
| 2003 | Las Vegas 350 | Brendan Gaughan | 162.152 mph | Brendan Gaughan | 1 |

**QUALIFYING RECORD**
David Starr, Chevrolet; 163.112 mph (33.106 sec.); October 12, 2002

**RACE RECORD**
David Starr, Chevrolet; 135.394 mph (1 hr., 37 min., 3 sec.); October 13, 2002

### POLE WINNERS

| | | | | | |
|---|---|---|---|---|---|
| Jack Sprague | 3 | David Starr | 1 | | |
| Stacy Compton | 1 | Brendan Gaughan | 1 | | |
| Bryan Reffner | 1 | | | | |

### RACE WINNERS

| | | | | |
|---|---|---|---|---|
| Jack Sprague | 2 | Joe Ruttman | 1 | |
| Greg Biffle | 1 | Brendan Gaughan | 1 | |
| Ted Musgrave | 1 | | | |

# Lowe's Motor Speedway

## TRACK FACTS

**Date Opened:** June 1960
**Owner:** Speedway Motorsports, Inc.
**President:** H.A. "Humpy" Wheeler
**Distance:** 1.5 Mile Oval
**Banking in Turns:** 24 degrees
**Banking in Straights:** 5 degrees
**Length of Frontstretch:** 1,952 feet
**Length of Backstretch:** 1,360 feet
**Grandstand Seating:** 171,000
**Tickets:** (704) 455-3267
**Website:** www.lowesmotorspeedway.com

## 2004 SCHEDULE

### NEXTEL Cup
**NASCAR NEXTEL All-Star Challenge***
**Date:** May 22
**TV:** FX. **Radio:** MRN
**Coca-Cola 600**
**Race:** No. 12 of 36
**Date:** May 30
**TV:** FOX. **Radio:** PRN
**UAW-GM Quality 500**
**Race:** No. 31 of 36
**Date:** October 16
**TV:** NBC. **Radio:** PRN

### Busch Series
**Carquest Auto Parts 300**
**Race:** No. 13 of 34
**Date:** May 29
**TV:** FX. **Radio:** PRN
**"Little Trees" 300**
**Race:** No. 29 of 34
**Date:** October 15
**TV:** TNT. **Radio:** PRN

### Craftsman Truck Series
**Hardee's 200**
**Race:** No. 5 of 25
**Date:** May 21
**TV:** Speed. **Radio:** MRN
*Non-points event

## NEXTEL CUP

### TRACK RECORDS
**Most Wins:** 6 - Darrell Waltrip and Bobby Allison
**Oldest Winner:** Cale Yarborough, 46 years, 6 months, 9 days, 10/06/1985
**Youngest Winner:** Jeff Gordon, 22 years, 9 months, 25 days, 05/29/1994
**Most Lead Changes:** 59—5/27/79
**Fewest Lead Changes:** 2—5/21/61
**Most Leaders:** 18—5/29/88
**Fewest Leaders:** 3—5/21/61

**Most Laps Led in a 400 Miles race:** 209, Once, Junior Jonson, 10/13/1963
**Most Laps Led in a 500 Miles race:** 328, Once, Ernie Irvan, 10/10/1993
**Most Laps Led in a 600 Miles race:** 335, Once, Jim Paschal, 5/28/1967
**Most Cautions:** 14—5/25/80
**Fewest Cautions:** 0—5/21/61
**Most Caution Laps:** 113—5/25/80
**Fewest Caution Laps:** 0—5/21/61
**Most on the Lead Lap:** 19—10/8/00

## YEAR BY YEAR WINNERS

| Year | Event | Race Winner | Car Make | Avg. Speed | Start Pos. | Winning Car Owner | Pole Winner |
|---|---|---|---|---|---|---|---|
| 2003 | UAW-GM Quality 500 | T. Stewart | Chevrolet | 142.871 | 6 | Joe Gibbs | R. Newman |
| d | Coca-Cola 600 | J. Johnson | Chevrolet | 126.198 | 37 | Rick Hendrick | R. Newman |
| 2002 | UAW-GM Quality 500 | J. McMurray | Dodge | 141.481 | 5 | Chip Ganassi | Trials Rained Out |
|  | Coca-Cola 600 | M. Martin | Ford | 137.729 | 25 | Jack Roush | J. Johnson |
| 2001 | UAW-GM Quality 500 | S. Marlin | Dodge | 139.006 | 13 | Chip Ganassi | J. Spencer |
| * | Coca-Cola 600 | J. Burton | Ford | 138.107 | 18 | Jack Roush | R. Newman |
| 2000 | UAW-GM Quality 500 | B. Labonte | Pontiac | 133.630 | 2 | Joe Gibbs | J. Gordon |
|  | Coca-Cola 600 | M. Kenseth | Ford | 142.640 | 21 | Jack Roush | D. Earnhardt Jr. |
| 1999 | UAW-GM Quality 500 | J. Gordon | Chevrolet | 160.306 | 22 | Rick Hendrick | B. Labonte |
| * | Coca-Cola 600 | J. Burton | Ford | 151.367 | 2 | Jack Roush | B. Labonte |
| 1998 | UAW-GM Quality 500 | M. Martin | Ford | 123.188 | 2 | Jack Roush | D. Cope |
| * | Coca-Cola 600 | J. Gordon | Chevrolet | 136.424 | 1 | Rick Hendrick | J. Gordon |
| 1997 | UAW-GM Quality 500 | D. Jarrett | Ford | 144.323 | 5 | Robert Yates | G. Bodine |
| *c | Coca-Cola 600 | J. Gordon | Chevrolet | 136.745 | 1 | Rick Hendrick | J. Gordon |
| 1996 | UAW-GM Quality 500 | T. Labonte | Chevrolet | 143.143 | 16 | Rick Hendrick | B. Labonte |
| * | Coca-Cola 600 | D. Jarrett | Ford | 147.581 | 15 | Robert Yates | J. Gordon |
| 1995 | UAW-GM Quality 500 | M. Martin | Ford | 145.358 | 5 | Jack Roush | R. Rudd |
| * | Coca-Cola 600 | B. Labonte | Chevrolet | 151.952 | 2 | Joe Gibbs | J. Gordon |
| 1994 | Mello Yello 500 | D. Jarrett | Chevrolet | 145.920 | 22 | Joe Gibbs | W. Burton |
|  | Coca-Cola 600 | J. Gordon | Chevrolet | 139.445 | 1 | Rick Hendrick | J. Gordon |
| 1993 | Mello Yello 500 | Irvan | Ford | 154.537 | 2 | Robert Yates | J. Gordon |
| * | Coca-Cola 600 | Earnhardt | Chevrolet | 145.504 | 14 | Richard Childress | Schrader |
| 1992 | Mello Yello 500 | Martin | Ford | 153.537 | 4 | Jack Roush | Kulwicki |
|  | Coca-Cola 600 | Earnhardt | Chevrolet | 132.980 | 13 | Richard Childress | Elliott |
| 1991 | Mello Yello 500 | G. Bodine | Ford | 138.984 | 6 | Junior Johnson | Martin |
|  | Coca-Cola 600 | Da. Allison | Ford | 138.951 | 10 | Robert Yates | Martin |
| 1990 | Mello Yello 500 | Da. Allison | Ford | 137.428 | 5 | Robert Yates | B. Bodine |
|  | Coca-Cola 600 | Wallace | Pontiac | 137.650 | 9 | Raymond Beadle | Schrader |
| 1989 | All Pro 500 | Schrader | Chevrolet | 149.863 | 2 | Rick Hendrick | Elliott |
|  | Coca-Cola 600 | D. Waltrip | Chevrolet | 144.077 | 4 | Rick Hendrick | Kulwicki |
| 1988 | Oakwood 500 | Wallace | Pontiac | 130.677 | 3 | Raymond Beadle | Kulwicki |
|  | Coca-Cola 600 | D. Waltrip | Chevrolet | 124.460 | 5 | Rick Hendrick | Da. Allison |
| 1987 | Oakwood 500 | Elliott | Ford | 128.443 | 7 | Melling Racing | B. Allison |
|  | Coca-Cola 600 | K. Petty | Ford | 131.483 | 7 | Wood Brothers | Elliott |
| 1986 | Oakwood 500 | Earnhardt | Chevrolet | 132.403 | 3 | Richard Childress | Richmond |
|  | Coca-Cola 600 | Earnhardt | Chevrolet | 140.406 | 3 | Richard Childress | Bodine |
| 1985 | Miller 500 | C. Yarborough | Ford | 136.761 | 7 | Ranier Racing | Gant |
|  | World 600 | Waltrip | Chevrolet | 141.807 | 5 | Junior Johnson | Elliott |
| 1984 | Miller 500 | Elliott | Ford | 146.861 | 2 | Melling Racing | Parsons |
|  | World 600 | B. Allison | Buick | 129.233 | 16 | DiGard Rac. Co. | Gant |
| 1983 | Miller 500 | R. Petty | Pontiac | 139.998 | 20 | Petty Eng. | Richmond |
|  | World 600 | Bonnett | Chevrolet | 140.707 | 5 | Rahmoc | Buddy Baker |
| 1982 | National 500 | Gant | Buick | 137.208 | 1 | Mach 1 | Gant |
|  | World 600 | Bonnett | Ford | 130.058 | 13 | Wood Brothers | Pearson |
| 1981 | National 500 | Waltrip | Buick | 117.483 | 1 | Junior Johnson | Waltrip |
|  | World 600 | B. Allison | Buick | 129.326 | 7 | Ranier Racing | Bonnett |
| 1980 | National 500 | Earnhardt | Chevrolet | 135.243 | 0 | Osterlund Rac. | Buddy Baker |
|  | World 600 | Parsons | Chevrolet | 119.265 | 6 | M.C. Anderson | C. Yarborough |
| 1979 | NAPA 500 | C. Yarborough | Chevrolet | 134.266 | 4 | Junior Johnson | Bonnett |
|  | World 600 | Waltrip | Chevrolet | 136.674 | 5 | DiGard Rac. Co. | Bonnett |
| 1978 | NAPA 500 | B. Allison | Ford | 141.826 | 8 | Bud Moore | Pearson |
|  | World 600 | Waltrip | Chevrolet | 138.355 | 17 | DiGard Rac. Co. | Pearson |
| 1977 | NAPA 500 | Parsons | Chevrolet | 142.780 | 8 | L.G. DeWitt | Pearson |
|  | World 600 | R. Petty | Dodge | 137.676 | 2 | Petty Eng. | Pearson |
| 1976 | National 500 | D. Allison | Chevrolet | 141.226 | 15 | Hoss Ellington | Pearson |
|  | World 600 | Pearson | Mercury | 137.352 | 1 | Wood Brothers | Pearson |
| 1975 | National 500 | R. Petty | Dodge | 132.209 | 9 | Petty Eng. | Pearson |
|  | World 600 | R. Petty | Dodge | 145.327 | 3 | Petty Eng. | Pearson |
| 1974 | National 500 | Pearson | Mercury | 119.912 | 1 | Wood Brothers | Pearson |
|  | World 600 | Pearson | Mercury | 135.720 | 1 | Wood Brothers | Pearson |
| 1973 | National 500 | C. Yarborough | Chevrolet | 145.240 | 2 | Junior Johnson | Pearson |
|  | World 600 | Buddy Baker | Dodge | 134.890 | 1 | Nord Krauskopf | Buddy Baker |
| 1972 | National 500 | B. Allison | Chevrolet | 133.234 | 4 | Junior Johnson | Pearson |
|  | World 600 | Buddy Baker | Dodge | 142.255 | 6 | Petty Eng. | B. Allison |
| b 1971 | National 500 | B. Allison | Mercury | 126.140 | 3 | Holman-Moody | Glotzbach |
|  | World 600 | B. Allison | Mercury | 140.442 | 3 | Holman-Moody | Glotzbach |
| 1970 | National 500 | L. Yarbrough | Mercury | 123.246 | 5 | Junior Johnson | Glotzbach |
|  | World 600 | D. Allison | Ford | 129.680 | 9 | Banjo Matthews | Isaac |
| 1969 | National 500 | D. Allison | Ford | 131.271 | 1 | Banjo Matthews | C. Yarborough |
|  | World 600 | L. Yarbrough | Mercury | 134.361 | 2 | Junior Johnson | D. Allison |
| 1968 | National 500 | Glotzbach | Dodge | 135.324 | 1 | Cotton Owens | Glotzbach |
| a | World 600 | Buddy Baker | Dodge | 104.207 | 12 | Ray Fox | D. Allison |
| 1967 | National 500 | Buddy Baker | Dodge | 130.317 | 1 | Ray Fox | C. Yarborough |
|  | World 600 | Paschal | Plymouth | 135.832 | 10 | Tom Friedkin | C. Yarborough |
| 1966 | National 400 | L. Yarbrough | Dodge | 130.743 | 1 | Jon Thorne | Lorenzen |
|  | World 600 | Panch | Plymouth | 135.042 | 0 | Petty Eng. | R. Petty |
| 1965 | National 400 | Lorenzen | Ford | 119.118 | 1 | Holman-Moody | Lorenzen |
|  | | Lorenzen | Ford | 121.772 | 1 | Holman-Moody | Lorenzen |
| 1964 | National 400 | Lorenzen | Ford | 134.559 | 3 | Holman-Moody | R. Petty |
|  | World 600 | Paschal | Plymouth | 125.772 | 12 | Petty Eng. | Pardue |

## NEXTEL CUP

**Fewest on the Lead Lap:** 1—14 times, most recently, 5/24/87
**Most Running at the Finish:** 39—10/11/03
**Fewest Running at the Finish:** 10—5/21/61
**Most Laps Led by a Race Winner:** 335—Jim Paschal, 5/28/67
**Fewest Laps Led by a Race Winner:** 3—Joe Weatherly, 5/21/61
**Closest Margin of Victory:** 0.24 second, Darrell Waltrip defeated Rusty Wallace 05/29/88
**Greatest Margin of Victory:** 1 lap, 5 seconds, Cale Yarborough defeated Bobby Allison 10/07/79

### QUALIFYING AND RACE RECORDS

**QUALIFYING**
**Track:** Ryan Newman, Dodge, 186.657 mph, October 9, 2003.
**Spring Race (Coca-Cola 600):** Jimmie Johnson, Chevrolet, 186.464 mph, 28.960 seconds, May 24, 2000.
**Fall Race (UAW-GM Quality 500):** Ryan Newman, Dodge, 186.657 mph, October 9, 2003.

**RACE**
**Track:** Jeff Gordon, Chevrolet, 160.306 mph, 3 hours, 7 minutes, 31 seconds, Oct. 11, 1999. (UAW-GM Quality 500).
**Spring Race (Coca-Cola 600):** Bobby Labonte, Chevrolet, 151.952 mph, 3 hours, 56 minutes, 55 seconds, May 28, 1995.
**Fall Race (UAW-GM Quality 500):** Jeff Gordon, Chevrolet, 160.306 mph, 3 hours, 7 minutes, 31 seconds, Oct. 11, 1999.
**National 400:** Fred Lorenzen, Ford, 134.559 mph, Oct. 18, 1964.
**100-Mile Qualifying Race:** Richard Petty, Plymouth, 132.86 mph, May 21, 1961.

## ALL CHARLOTTE RACES

### POLE WINNERS

| | | | |
|---|---|---|---|
| Pearson | 14 | Panch | 1 |
| J. Gordon | 7 | Isaac | 1 |
| Elliott | 4 | Pardue | 1 |
| Yarborough | 4 | Parsons | 1 |
| Glotzbach | 4 | Waltrip | 1 |
| B. Labonte | 3 | Da. Allison | 1 |
| R. Petty | 3 | B. Bodine | 1 |
| Lorenzen | 3 | Jr. Johnson | 1 |
| Bonnett | 3 | W. Burton | 1 |
| Buddy Baker | 3 | Rudd | 1 |
| Gant | 3 | Cope | 1 |
| Kulwicki | 3 | Earnhardt Jr. | 1 |
| Roberts | 3 | Newman | 1 |
| D. Allison | 2 | Spencer | 1 |
| B. Allison | 2 | Ji. Johnson | 1 |
| Martin | 2 | | |
| Schrader | 2 | | |
| Richmond | 2 | | |
| G. Bodine | 2 | | |
| Newman | 2 | | |

### RACE WINNERS

| | | | |
|---|---|---|---|
| B. Allison | 6 | B. Labonte | 2 |
| Waltrip | 6 | J. Burton | 2 |
| Earnhardt | 5 | J. L. Johnson | 1 |
| J. Gordon | 4 | Weatherly | 1 |
| Pearson | 4 | Thompson | 1 |
| Buddy Baker | 4 | Gant | 1 |
| Lorenzen | 4 | K. Petty | 1 |
| R. Petty | 4 | Schrader | 1 |
| M. Martin | 4 | Glotzbach | 1 |
| D. Jarrett | 3 | G. Bodine | 1 |
| D. Allison | 3 | Panch | 1 |
| Yarbrough | 3 | Irvan | 1 |
| Yarborough | 3 | Stacy | 1 |
| Bonnett | 2 | T. Labonte | 1 |
| Parsons | 2 | Kenseth | 1 |
| Wallace | 2 | Marlin | 1 |
| Elliott | 2 | McMurray | 1 |
| Jr. Johnson | 1 | Stewart | 1 |
| Paschal | 2 | Ji. Johnson | 1 |
| Da. Allison | 2 | | |

| Year | Event | Race Winner | Car Make | Avg. Speed | Start Pos. | Winning Car Owner | Pole Winner |
|---|---|---|---|---|---|---|---|
| 1963 | National 400 | Johnson | Chevrolet | 132.105 | 2 | Ray Fox | Panch |
|  | World 600 | Lorenzen | Ford | 132.418 | 2 | Holman-Moody | Jr. Johnson |
| 1962 | National 400 | Johnson | Pontiac | 132.085 | 3 | Ray Fox | Roberts |
|  | World 600 | Stacy | Ford | 125.552 | 18 | Holman-Moody | Roberts |
| 1961 | National 400 | Weatherly | Pontiac | 119.800 | 6 | Bud Moore | Pearson |
|  | World 600 | Pearson | Pontiac | 111.634 | 3 | Ray Fox | R. Petty |
| 1960 | National 400 | S. Thompson | Ford | 112.760 | 4 | Wood Brothers | Roberts |
|  | World 600 | J.L. Johnson | Chevrolet | 107.752 | 20 | Frank Strickland | Roberts |

\* Twilight.
a Race shortened to 382.5 miles, rain.
b Race shortened to 357 miles, rain.
c Race shortened to 499.5 miles, rain.
d Race shortened to 414.0 miles, rain.

## SPRING: Coca-Cola 600

| POLE WINNERS | | | | RACE WINNERS | | | |
|---|---|---|---|---|---|---|---|
| Pearson | 6 | Isaac | 1 | Waltrip | 5 | Stacy | 1 |
| J. Gordon | 5 | Pardue | 1 | Pearson | 3 | J. L. Johnson | 1 |
| Elliott | 3 | Gant | 1 | Buddy Baker | 3 | Parsons | 1 |
| D. Allison | 2 | G. Bodine | 1 | B. Allison | 3 | K. Petty | 1 |
| R. Petty | 2 | Da. Allison | 1 | Earnhardt | 3 | Wallace | 1 |
| C. Yarborough | 2 | Kulwicki | 1 | J. Gordon | 3 | Da. Allison | 1 |
| Bonnett | 2 | Martin | 1 | J. Burton | 2 | B. Labonte | 1 |
| Buddy Baker | 2 | Roberts | 1 | R. Petty | 2 | D. Jarrett | 1 |
| Schrader | 2 | B. Labonte | 1 | Lorenzen | 2 | M. Kenseth | 1 |
| R. Newman | 2 | Earnhardt Jr. | 1 | Paschal | 2 | M. Martin | 1 |
| B. Allison | 2 | Ji. Johnson | 1 | Bonnett | 2 | Ji. Johnson | 1 |
| Glotzbach | 1 | | | D. Allison | 1 | | |
| Lorenzen | 1 | | | L. Yarborough | 1 | | |
| Jr. Johnson | 1 | | | Panch | 1 | | |

# BUSCH SERIES
## YEAR BY YEAR WINNERS

| Year | Event | Pole Winner | Speed | Race Winner | Started |
|---|---|---|---|---|---|
| 1982 | Mello Yello 300 | H. Gant | 162.847 | H. Gant | 1 |
|  | Miller 300 | P. Parsons | 162.191 | D. Waltrip | 3 |
| 1983 | Mello Yello 300 | M. Shepherd | 161.565 | D. Earnhardt | 3 |
|  | Miller Time 300 | L. Pearson | 162.235 | S. Ard | 10 |
| 1984 | Mello Yello 300 | L. Ottinger | 162.421 | B. Allison | 8 |
|  | Miller Time 300 | T. Richmond | 163.676 | D. Waltrip | 6 |
| 1985 | Winn-Dixie 300 | T. Richmond | 160.633 | T. Richmond | 1 |
|  | Miller 400* | G. Bodine | 162.656 | T. Labonte | 14 |
| 1986 | Winn-Dixie 300 | T. Richmond | 163.711 | T. Richmond | 1 |
|  | All Pro 300 | D. Earnhardt | 161.599 | D. Earnhardt | 1 |
| 1987 | Winn-Dixie 300 | B. Bodine | 167.328 | H. Gant | 16 |
|  | All Pro 300 | H. Gant | 168.940 | H. Gant | 1 |
| 1988 | Winn-Dixie 300 | G. Bodine | 168.099 | D. Jarrett | 6 |
|  | All Pro 300 | H. Gant | 169.710 | R. Moroso | 13 |
| 1989 | Champion 300 | G. Sacks | 167.214 | R. Moroso | 4 |
|  | All Pro 300 | M. Waltrip | 168.993 | R. Moroso | 4 |
| 1990 | Champion 300 | D. Trickle | 168.219 | D. Jarrett | 3 |
|  | All Pro 300 | None - weather | | S. Marlin | 32 |
| 1991 | Champion 300 | J. Sprague | 167.167 | D. Earnhardt | 19 |
|  | All Pro 300 | W. Burton | 172.574 | H. Gant | 33 |
| 1992 | Champion 300 | J. Gordon | 170.638 | J. Gordon | 1 |
|  | All Pro 300 | J. Gordon | 173.566 | J. Gordon | 1 |
| 1993 | Champion 300 | T. Leslie | 172.574 | M. Waltrip | 12 |
|  | All Pro 300 | B. Dotter | 174.390 | M. Martin | 5 |
| 1994 | Champion 300 | M. Skinner | 172.480 | P. Parsons | 12 |
|  | All Pro 300 | M. Martin | 176.696 | T. Labonte | 16 |
| 1995 | Red Dog 300 | R. Bickle | 173.193 | C. Little | 7 |
|  | All Pro 300 | B. Dotter | 172.051 | M. Martin | 3 |
| 1996 | Red Dog 300 | D. Jarrett | 171.996 | M. Martin | 17 |
|  | All Pro 300 | B. Labonte | 174.272 | M. Martin | 2 |
| 1997 | Carquest Auto. Parts 300 | M. Martin | 175.012 | J. Nemechek | 2 |
|  | All Pro 300 | J. Nemechek | 176.378 | J. Spencer | 4 |
| 1998 | Carquest A.uto 300 | B. Labonte | 172.822 | M. Martin | 6 |
|  | All Pro 300 | D. Blaney | 177.247 | M. McLaughlin | 3 |
| 1999 | Carquest Auto Parts 300 | D. Green | 176.569 | M. Martin | 2 |
|  | All Pro 300 | M. Kenseth | 177.328 | M. Waltrip | 31 |
| 2000 | Carquest Auto Parts 300 | D. Blaney | 177.608 | J. Burton | 4 |
|  | All Pro 300 | M. Kenseth | 178.956 | M. Kenseth | 1 |
| 2001 | Carquest Auto Parts 300 | None - weather | | J. Green | 2 |
|  | Little Trees 300 | J. Burton | 179.485 | G. Biffle | 3 |
| 2002 | Carquest Auto. Parts 300 | R. Hornaday | 182.094 | J. Green | 4 |
|  | Little Trees 300 | M. Waltrip | 180.343 | J. Burton | 2 |
| 2003 | Carquest Auto Parts 300 | K. Harvick | 184.445 | M. Kenseth | 9 |
|  | Little Trees 300 | K. Harvick | 184.313 | G. Biffle | 4 |

\* 400-mile race

## FALL: UAW-GM Quality 500

| POLE WINNERS | | | | RACE WINNERS | | | |
|---|---|---|---|---|---|---|---|
| Pearson | 8 | Waltrip | 1 | M. Martin | 3 | Thompson | 1 |
| Glotzbach | 3 | Parsons | 1 | B. Allison | 3 | Gant | 1 |
| B. Labonte | 2 | B. Allison | 1 | Yarborough | 3 | Wallace | 1 |
| C. Yarborough | 2 | Elliott | 1 | R. Petty | 2 | Schrader | 1 |
| Gant | 2 | B. Bodine | 1 | Earnhardt | 2 | Waltrip | 1 |
| Kulwicki | 2 | Martin | 1 | Elliott | 2 | G. Bodine | 1 |
| Richmond | 2 | W. Burton | 1 | D. Allison | 2 | Da. Allison | 1 |
| Lorenzen | 2 | R. Rudd | 1 | Yarborough | 2 | Irvan | 1 |
| Roberts | 2 | G. Bodine | 1 | Jr. Johnson | 2 | T. Labonte | 1 |
| J. Gordon | 2 | Cope | 1 | D. Jarrett | 2 | J. Gordon | 1 |
| R. Petty | 1 | Spencer | 1 | Pearson | 1 | B. Labonte | 1 |
| Panch | 1 | Newman | 1 | Buddy Baker | 1 | Marlin | 1 |
| Bonnett | 1 | | | Parsons | 1 | McMurray | 1 |
| Buddy Baker | 1 | | | Glotzbach | 1 | Stewart | 1 |
| | | | | Weatherly | 1 | | |

### QUALIFYING RECORD
Kevin Harvick, Chevrolet, 184.445 mph, May 23, 2003.

### RACE RECORD
Mark Martin, Ford; 155.996 mph (1 hr., 55 min., 32 sec.), May 25, 1996.

| POLE WINNERS | | | | RACE WINNERS | | | |
|---|---|---|---|---|---|---|---|
| Gant | 3 | Green | 1 | Martin | 6 | Ard | 1 |
| Richmond | 3 | Hornaday | 1 | Gant | 4 | Little | 1 |
| Blaney | 2 | Jarrett | 1 | Earnhardt | 3 | Marlin | 1 |
| Bodine | 2 | Leslie | 1 | Moroso | 3 | McLaughlin | 1 |
| Dotter | 2 | Nemechek | 1 | J. Burton | 2 | Nemechek | 1 |
| Gordon | 2 | Ottinger | 1 | J. Gordon | 2 | Parsons | 1 |
| Kenseth | 2 | Parsons | 1 | J. Green | 2 | Spencer | 1 |
| Martin | 2 | Pearson | 1 | Jarrett | 2 | | |
| B. Labonte | 2 | Sacks | 1 | T. Labonte | 2 | | |
| Waltrip | 2 | Shepherd | 1 | Richmond | 2 | | |
| Bickle | 1 | Skinner | 1 | D. Waltrip | 2 | | |
| Bodine | 1 | Sprague | 1 | M. Waltrip | 2 | | |
| J. Burton | 1 | Trickle | 1 | Biffle | 2 | | |
| W. Burton | 1 | Harvick | 2 | Kenseth | 2 | | |
| Earnhardt | 1 | | | B. Allison | 1 | | |

# CRAFTSMAN TRUCK SERIES
## YEAR BY YEAR WINNERS

| Year | Event | Pole Winner | Speed | Race Winner | Started |
|---|---|---|---|---|---|
| 2003 | Hardee's 200 | Ted Musgrave | 91.297 | Dennis Setzer | 5 |

### QUALIFYING RECORD
Ted Musgrave, Dodge, 91.297 mph, May 15, 2003.

### RACE RECORD
Dennis Setzer, Chevrolet, 66.921 mph, 1 hour, 57 min., 54 sec., May 16, 2003

| POLE WINNERS | | RACE WINNERS | |
|---|---|---|---|
| Musgrave | 1 | Setzer | 1 |

# Martinsville Speedway

## TRACK FACTS
**Date Opened:** 1947
**Owner:** W. Clay Campbell
**President:** W. Clay Campbell
**Distance:** .526 miles
**Banking in Turns:** 12 degrees
**Banking on Straights:** None
**Length of Frontstretch:** 800 feet
**Length of Backstretch:** 800 feet
**Grandstand Seating:** 91,000
**Tickets:** (276) 956-3151 or (877) 722-3849
**Website:** www.martinsvillespeedway.com

## NEXTEL CUP

### TRACK RECORDS
**Most Wins:** 11—Darrell Waltrip
**Oldest Winner:** Harry Gant, 51 years, 8 months, 12 days, 9/22/1991
**Youngest Winner:** Richard Petty, 22 years, 9 months, 8 days, 4/10/1960
**Most Lead Changes:** 25—9/28/80
**Fewest Lead Changes:** 1—3 times, most recently, 4/9/61
**Most Leaders:** 14—10/15/01
**Fewest Leaders:** 2—11 times, most recently, 9/26/76
**Most Laps Led in a 200 Laps race:** 193, Jim Paschal, 05/16/1954
**Most Laps Led in a 500 Laps race:** 493, Fred Lorenzen, 09/27/1964
**Most Cautions:** 18—10/1/00
**Fewest Cautions:** 1—3 times, most recently, 4/25/71
**Most Caution Laps:** 119—10/19/03
**Fewest Caution Laps:** 3—4/25/71

**Most on the Lead Lap:** 20—4/14/02
**Fewest on the Lead Lap:** 1—27 times, most recently, 4/27/86
**Most Running at the Finish:** 42—4/18/99
**Fewest Running at the Finish:** 4—5/6/51
**Most Laps Led by a Race Winner:** 493—Fred Lorenzen, 9/27/64
**Fewest Laps Led by a Race Winner:** 4—Richard Petty, 4/25/71
**Closest Margin of Victory:** 0.19 second, Geoffrey Bodine defeated Rusty Wallace 09/28/92
**Greatest Margin of Victory:** 1 Lap, 1 second, Harry Gant defeated Butch Lindley 04/25/82

### QUALIFYING AND RACE RECORDS
**QUALIFYING**
**Track:** Tony Stewart, Pontiac, 95.371 mph, 19.855 seconds, September 29, 2000 (NAPA 500).
**Spring Race (Advance Auto Parts 500):** Tony Stewart, Pontiac, 95.275 mph, 19.875 seconds, April 16, 1999.
**Fall Race (Subway 500):** Tony Stewart, Pontiac, 95.371 mph, 19.855 seconds, Sept. 29, 2000.

**RACE**
**Track:** Jeff Gordon, Chevrolet, 82.223 mph, 3 hours, 11 minutes, 54 seconds, Sept. 22, 1996 (Hanes 500).
**Spring Race (Advance Auto Parts 500):** Rusty Wallace, Ford, 81.410 mph, 3 hours, 13 minutes, 50 seconds, April 21, 1996.
**Fall Race (Subway 500):** Jeff Gordon, Chevrolet, 82.223 mph, 3 hours, 11 minutes, 54 seconds, Sept. 22, 1996.

## 2004 SCHEDULE

### NEXTEL Cup
**Advance Auto Parts 500**
**Race:** No. 8 of 36
**Date:** April 18
**TV:** FOX. **Radio:** MRN
**Subway 500**
**Race:** No. 32 of 36
**Date:** October 24
**TV:** NBC. **Radio:** MRN

### Craftsman Truck Series
**Martinsville 250**
**Race:** No. 3 of 25
**Date:** March 27
**TV:** Speed. **Radio:** MRN
**Martinsville 200**
**Race:** No. 22 of 25
**Date:** October 23
**TV:** Speed. **Radio:** MRN

## YEAR BY YEAR WINNERS

| Year | Event | Race Winner | Car Make | Avg. Speed | Start Pos. | Winning Car Owner | Pole Winner |
|---|---|---|---|---|---|---|---|
| 2003 | Subway 500 | J. Gordon | Chevrolet | 67.658 | 1 | Rick Hendrick | J. Gordon |
|  | Virginia 500 | J. Gordon | Chevrolet | 75.557 | 1 | Rick Hendrick | J. Gordon |
| 2002 | Old Dominion 500 | K. Busch | Ford | 74.651 | 36 | Jack Roush | R. Newman |
|  | Virginia 500 | B. Labonte | Pontiac | 73.951 | 15 | J. Gibbs | J. Gordon |
| 2001 | Old Dominion 500 | R. Craven | Ford | 75.750 | 6 | Cal Wells III | T. Bodine |
|  | Virginia 500 | D. Jarrett | Ford | 70.799 | 13 | Robert Yates | J. Gordon |
| 2000 | NAPA 500 | T. Stewart | Pontiac | 73.859 | 1 | Joe Gibbs | T. Stewart |
|  | Goody's 500 | M. Martin | Ford | 71.161 | 21 | Jack Roush | R. Wallace |
| 1999 | NAPA 500 | J. Gordon | Chevrolet | 72.347 | 5 | Rick Hendrick | J. Nemechek |
|  | Goody's 500 | J. Andretti | Pontiac | 75.653 | 21 | Petty Eng. | T. Stewart |
| 1998 | NAPA 500 | R. Rudd | Ford | 73.350 | 2 | Ricky Rudd | E. Irvan |
|  | Goody's 500 | B. Hamilton | Chevrolet | 70.709 | 1 | Morgan-McClure | B. Hamilton |
| 1997 | Hanes 500 | J. Burton | Ford | 73.078 | 10 | Jack Roush | W. Burton |
|  | Goody's 500 | J. Gordon | Chevrolet | 70.347 | 4 | Rick Hendrick | K. Wallace |
| 1996 | Hanes 500 | J. Gordon | Chevrolet | 82.223 | 10 | Rick Hendrick | B. Hamilton |
|  | Goody's 500 | R. Wallace | Ford | 81.410 | 5 | Roger Penske | R. Craven |
| 1995 | Goody's 500 | Earnhardt | Chevrolet | 73.946 | 2 | Richard Childress | Trials Rained Out |
|  | Hanes 500 | R. Wallace | Ford | 72.145 | 15 | Roger Penske | B. Labonte |
| 1994 | Goody's 500 | R. Wallace | Ford | 77.139 | 7 | Roger Penske | T. Musgrave |
|  | Hanes 500 | R. Wallace | Ford | 76.700 | 1 | Roger Penske | R. Wallace |
| 1993 | Goody's 500 | E. Irvan | Ford | 74.101 | 1 | Robert Yates | E. Irvan |
|  | Hanes 500 | R. Wallace | Pontiac | 79.078 | 5 | Roger Penske | G. Bodine |

| Year | Event | Race Winner | Car Make | Avg. Speed | Start Pos. | Winning Car Owner | Pole Winner |
|---|---|---|---|---|---|---|---|
| k 1992 | Goody's 500 | G. Bodine | Ford | 75.424 | 7 | Bud Moore | K. Petty |
|  | Hanes 500 | Martin | Ford | 78.086 | 12 | Jack Roush | D. Waltrip |
| 1991 | Goody's 500 | Gant | Oldsmobile | 74.535 | 12 | Leo Jackson | Martin |
|  | Hanes 500 | Earnhardt | Chevrolet | 75.139 | 10 | Richard Childress | Martin |
| 1990 | Goody's 500 | G. Bodine | Ford | 76.386 | 14 | Junior Johnson | Martin |
|  | Hanes 500 | G. Bodine | Ford | 77.423 | 1 | Junior Johnson | G. Bodine |
| 1989 | Goody's 500 | D. Waltrip | Chevrolet | 76.571 | 2 | Rick Hendrick | Hensley |
|  | Pannill 500 | D. Waltrip | Chevrolet | 79.025 | 10 | Rick Hendrick | G. Bodine |
| 1988 | Goody's 500 | Waltrip | Chevrolet | 74.988 | 20 | Rick Hendrick | Wallace |
|  | Pannill 500 | Earnhardt | Chevrolet | 74.740 | 14 | Richard Childress | Rudd |
| 1987 | Goody's 500 | Waltrip | Chevrolet | 76.410 | 14 | Rick Hendrick | G. Bodine |
|  | Sovran Bank 500 | Earnhardt | Chevrolet | 72.808 | 4 | Richard Childress | Shepherd |
| 1986 | Goody's 500 | Wallace | Pontiac | 73.191 | 8 | Blue Max | G. Bodine |
|  | Sovran Bank 500 | Rudd | Ford | 76.882 | 4 | Bud Moore | Richmond |
| 1985 | Goody's 500 | Earnhardt | Chevrolet | 70.694 | 11 | Richard Childress | G. Bodine |
|  | Sovran Bank 500 | Gant | Chevrolet | 73.072 | 13 | Mach I | Waltrip |
| 1984 | Goody's 500 | Waltrip | Chevrolet | 75.532 | 3 | Junior Johnson | G. Bodine |
|  | Sovran Bank 500 | G. Bodine | Chevrolet | 73.264 | 6 | Rick Hendrick | Ruttman |
| 1983 | Goody's 500 | Rudd | Chevrolet | 76.134 | 2 | Richard Childress | Waltrip |
|  | Va. Nat'l Bank 500 | Waltrip | Chevrolet | 66.460 | 3 | Junior Johnson | Rudd |
| 1982 | Old Dominion 500 | Waltrip | Buick | 71.315 | 3 | Junior Johnson | Rudd |
|  | Va. Nat'l Bank 500 | Gant | Buick | 75.073 | 2 | Mach I | Labonte |
| 1981 | Old Dominion 500 | Waltrip | Buick | 70.089 | 1 | Junior Johnson | Waltrip |
|  | Virginia 500 | Shepherd | Pontiac | 75.019 | 12 | Cliff Stewart | Rudd |
| 1980 | Old Dominion 500 | Earnhardt | Chevrolet | 69.654 | 7 | Osterlund Racing | Buddy Baker |
|  | Virginia 500 | Waltrip | Chevrolet | 69.049 | 1 | DiGard Rac. Co. | Waltrip |
| 1979 | Old Dominion 500 | Buddy Baker | Chevrolet | 75.119 | 5 | Ranier Racing | Waltrip |
|  | Virginia 500 | R. Petty | Chevrolet | 76.562 | 2 | Petty Eng. | Waltrip |
| 1978 | Old Dominion 500 | C. Yarborough | Oldsmobile | 79.185 | 6 | Junior Johnson | Pond |
|  | Virginia 500 | Waltrip | Chevrolet | 78.025 | 3 | DiGard Rac. Co. | Pond |
| 1977 | Old Dominion 500 | C. Yarborough | Chevrolet | 73.447 | 3 | Junior Johnson | Bonnett |
|  | Virginia 500 | C. Yarborough | Chevrolet | 77.405 | 5 | Junior Johnson | Bonnett |
| i 1976 | Old Dominion 500 | C. Yarborough | Chevrolet | 75.370 | 4 | Junior Johnson | Waltrip |
|  | Virginia 500 | Waltrip | Chevrolet | 71.759 | 4 | DiGard Rac. Co. | Marcis |
| 1975 | Old Dominion 500 | Marcis | Dodge | 75.800 | 7 | Nord Krauskopf | C. Yarborough |
|  | Virginia 500 | R. Petty | Dodge | 69.282 | 6 | Petty Eng. | Parsons |
| h 1974 | Old Dominion 500 | Ross | Chevrolet | 66.232 | 11 | Allan Brooke | R. Petty |
|  | Virginia 500 | C. Yarborough | Chevrolet | 69.936 | 1 | Junior Johnson | C. Yarborough |
| g 1973 | Old Dominion 500 | R. Petty | Dodge | 68.831 | 6 | Petty Eng. | C. Yarborough |
|  | Virginia 500 | Pearson | Mercury | 70.251 | 1 | Wood Brothers | Pearson |
| 1972 | Old Dominion 500 | R. Petty | Plymouth | 69.989 | 4 | Petty Eng. | B. Allison |
|  | Virginia 500 | R. Petty | Plymouth | 72.657 | 3 | Petty Eng. | B. Allison |
| 1971 | Old Dominion 500 | Isaac | Dodge | 73.681 | 1 | Nord Krauskopf | Isaac |
|  | Virginia 500 | R. Petty | Plymouth | 77.077 | 3 | Petty Eng. | D. Allison |
| 1970 | Old Dominion 500 | R. Petty | Plymouth | 72.159 | 4 | Petty Eng. | B. Allison |
| f | Virginia 500 | Isaac | Dodge | 68.512 | 2 | Nord Krauskopf | L. Yarborough |
| e 1969 | Old Dominion 500 | R. Petty | Ford | 63.127 | 6 | Petty Eng. | Pearson |
|  | Virginia 500 | R. Petty | Ford | 64.405 | 6 | Petty Eng. | B. Allison |
| 1968 | Old Dominion 500 | R. Petty | Plymouth | 72.159 | 6 | Petty Eng. | C. Yarborough |
|  | Virginia 500 | C. Yarborough | Mercury | 66.686 | 3 | Wood Brothers | Pearson |
| 1967 | Old Dominion 500 | R. Petty | Plymouth | 69.606 | 5 | Petty Eng. | C. Yarborough |
|  | Virginia 500 | R. Petty | Plymouth | 67.446 | 2 | Petty Eng. | Dieringer |
| 1966 | Old Dominion 500 | Lorenzen | Ford | 69.177 | 2 | Holman-Moody | Jr. Johnson |
|  | Virginia 500 | Paschal | Plymouth | 69.156 | 1 | Tom Friedkin | Paschal |
| 1965 | Old Dominion 500 | Johnson | Ford | 67.056 | 3 | Junior Johnson | R. Petty |
|  | Virginia 500 | Lorenzen | Ford | 66.765 | 2 | Holman-Moody | Jr. Johnson |
| 1964 | Old Dominion 500 | Lorenzen | Ford | 67.320 | 1 | Holman-Moody | Lorenzen |
|  | Virginia 500 | Lorenzen | Ford | 70.098 | 1 | Holman-Moody | Lorenzen |
| 1963 | Old Dominion 500 | Lorenzen | Ford | 67.486 | 2 | Holman-Moody | Johnson |
|  | Virginia 500 | R. Petty | Plymouth | 64.823 | 8 | Petty Eng. | White |
| 1962 | Old Dominion 500 | Stacy | Ford | 66.870 | 3 | Holman-Moody | Roberts |
|  | Virginia 500 | R. Petty | Plymouth | 66.430 | 7 | Petty Eng. | Lorenzen |
| 1961 | Old Dominion 500 | Weatherly | Pontiac | 62.590 | 4 | Bud Moore | Lorenzen |
|  | Virginia 500 | Johnson | Pontiac | 66.280 | 17 | Rex Lovette | White |
| cd | Grand Nat'l. 200 | Lorenzen | Ford | 68.370 | 2 | Holman-Moody | White |
| 1960 | Old Dominion 500 | White | Chevrolet | 60.440 | 1 | Louis Clements | Wood |
| * 1959 | Old Dominion 500 | R. Petty | Plymouth | 63.940 | 4 | Petty Eng. | Wood |
|  | Virginia 500 | White | Chevrolet | 60.500 | 14 | Louis Clements | Wood |
| *b 1958 | Old Dominion 500 | L. Petty | Oldsmobile | 59.440 | 24 | Petty Eng. | Johns |
|  | Virginia 500 | Roberts | Chevrolet | 64.340 | 4 | Frank Strickland | Wood(C) |
| * 1957 | Old Dominion 500 | Welborn(C) | Chevrolet(C) | 61.160 | 20 | Bob Welborn | Buck Baker |
| a | Virginia 500 | Buck Baker | Chevrolet | 63.030 | 2 | Hugh Babb | Pagan |
| 1956 | Old Dominion 400 | J. Smith | Dodge | NO TIME | 6 | Buck Baker | Goldsmith |
|  | Virginia 500 | Buck Baker | Dodge | 61.140 | 23 | Carl Kiekhaefer | Buck Baker |
|  |  |  |  | 60.950 | 1 |  |  |

(C) Convertible
* Sweepstakes race, included Grand Nationals and Convertibles (with regular points).
a 220.5 miles (441 laps), rain.
b 175 miles (350 laps), rain.
c 74.5 miles (149 laps), rain; scheduled for 100 miles.
d Special 100-mile point race.
e Last year of 500-lap, 250-miles races; track remeasured at .525 of a mile and distance increased to 262.5 miles (500 laps) beginning with '69 OD 500.
f 197.925 miles (377 laps), rain.
g 252 miles (480 laps), rain.
h Race cut by 26.25 miles, energy shortage.
i 178.5 miles (340 laps), rain.
j 201.6 miles (384 laps), rain.
k Postponed 9-27 – 9-28 due to rain.
m All pit stalls now located on front straightaway.
n Single Pit Road; Garages added.

## ALL MARTINSVILLE RACES

### POLE WINNERS
| | | | |
|---|---|---|---|
| D. Waltrip | 8 | Isaac | 1 |
| G. Bodine | 7 | Dieringer | 1 |
| Yarborough | 5 | Paschal | 1 |
| Wood | 5 | Roberts | 1 |
| B. Allison | 4 | Johns | 1 |
| Lorenzen | 4 | Welborn | 1 |
| Rudd | 4 | Goldsmith | 1 |
| J. Gordon | 4 | Amick | 1 |
| Pearson | 3 | Pagan | 1 |
| Jr. Johnson | 3 | Nemechek | 1 |
| Buck Baker | 3 | Turner | 1 |
| Martin | 3 | Ruttman | 1 |
| R. Wallace | 3 | Richmond | 1 |
| R. Petty | 2 | Shepherd | 1 |
| B. Hamilton | 2 | Hensley | 1 |
| Irvan | 2 | T. Labonte | 1 |
| Pond | 2 | K. Petty | 1 |
| White | 2 | Musgrave | 1 |
| Bonnett | 2 | B. Labonte | 1 |
| Stewart | 2 | Craven | 1 |
| Buddy Baker | 1 | K. Wallace | 1 |
| Marcis | 1 | W. Burton | 1 |
| Parsons | 1 | T. Bodine | 1 |
| D. Allison | 1 | Newman | 1 |
| Yarborough | 1 | | |

### RACE WINNERS
| | | | |
|---|---|---|---|
| R. Petty | 15 | L. Petty | 1 |
| Waltrip | 11 | Ross | 1 |
| Yarborough | 6 | Smith | 1 |
| Earnhardt | 6 | Irvan | 1 |
| R. Wallace | 2 | J. Burton | 1 |
| J. Gordon | 5 | B. Hamilton | 1 |
| Lorenzen | 5 | J. Andretti | 1 |
| G. Bodine | 4 | D. Jarrett | 1 |
| Rudd | 3 | Stewart | 1 |
| Gant | 2 | Craven | 1 |
| Jr. Johnson | 2 | Busch | 1 |
| White | 2 | B. Labonte | 1 |
| Buck Baker | 2 | | |
| Welborn | 2 | | |
| Isaac | 2 | | |
| Martin | 2 | | |
| Roberts | 1 | | |
| Shepherd | 1 | | |
| Buddy Baker | 1 | | |
| Marcis | 1 | | |
| Pearson | 1 | | |
| Paschal | 1 | | |
| Stacy | 1 | | |
| Weatherly | 1 | | |

## SPRING: Advance Auto Parts 500

### POLE WINNERS
| | | | |
|---|---|---|---|
| Waltrip | 4 | L. Yarborough | 1 |
| Rudd | 3 | Dieringer | 1 |
| G. Bodine | 3 | Paschal | 1 |
| J. Gordon | 3 | Jr. Johnson | 1 |
| B. Allison | 2 | Wood | 1 |
| Pearson | 2 | Johns | 1 |
| Lorenzen | 2 | Goldsmith | 1 |
| White | 2 | Ruttman | 1 |
| Buck Baker | 2 | Richmond | 1 |
| R. Wallace | 2 | Shepherd | 1 |
| Labonte | 2 | Martin | 1 |
| Pond | 1 | B. Labonte | 1 |
| Bonnett | 1 | R. Craven | 1 |
| Marcis | 1 | K. Wallace | 1 |
| Parsons | 1 | | |
| C. Yarborough | 1 | B. Hamilton | 1 |
| D. Allison | 1 | T. Stewart | 1 |

### RACE WINNERS
| | | | |
|---|---|---|---|
| R. Petty | 9 | Welborn | 1 |
| Waltrip | 5 | Rudd | 1 |
| R. Wallace | 4 | B. Hamilton | 1 |
| Earnhardt | 3 | J. Andretti | 1 |
| C. Yarborough | 3 | D. Jarrett | 1 |
| G. Bodine | 2 | B. Labonte | 1 |
| Lorenzen | 2 | | |
| Buck Baker | 2 | | |
| Gant | 1 | | |
| Martin | 1 | | |
| J. Gordon | 2 | | |
| Shepherd | 1 | | |
| Pearson | 1 | | |
| Isaac | 1 | | |
| Paschal | 1 | | |
| Jr. Johnson | 1 | | |
| L. Petty | 1 | | |

## FALL: Subway 500

### POLE WINNERS
| | | | |
|---|---|---|---|
| Waltrip | 4 | Amick | 1 |
| Yarborough | 4 | Pagan | 1 |
| Wood | 4 | Turner | 1 |
| Bodine | 4 | Buck Baker | 1 |
| R. Petty | 2 | Wallace | 1 |
| B. Allison | 2 | Hensley | 1 |
| Jr. Johnson | 2 | Rudd | 1 |
| Lorenzen | 2 | K. Petty | 1 |
| Martin | 2 | Musgrave | 1 |
| Irvan | 2 | B. Hamilton | 1 |
| Buddy Baker | 1 | W. Burton | 1 |
| Pond | 1 | Nemechek | 1 |
| Bonnett | 1 | Stewart | 1 |
| Pearson | 1 | T. Bodine | 1 |
| Isaac | 1 | | |
| Roberts | 1 | Newman | 1 |
| Welborn | 1 | J. Gordon | 1 |

### RACE WINNERS
| | | | |
|---|---|---|---|
| R. Petty | 6 | Weatherly | 1 |
| Waltrip | 6 | Pistone | 1 |
| Earnhardt | 4 | Amick | 1 |
| Lorenzen | 3 | Welborn | 1 |
| Yarborough | 3 | Massey | 1 |
| J. Gordon | 3 | Smith | 1 |
| G. Bodine | 2 | Gant | 1 |
| R. Wallace | 2 | Irvan | 1 |
| White | 2 | J. Burton | 1 |
| Roberts | 1 | Stewart | 1 |
| Rudd | 2 | Craven | 1 |
| Buddy Baker | 1 | Busch | 1 |
| Marcis | 1 | | |
| Ross | 1 | | |
| Isaac | 1 | | |
| Jr. Johnson | 1 | | |
| Stacy | 1 | | |

## CRAFTSMAN TRUCK SERIES
### YEAR BY YEAR WINNERS

| Year | Event | Pole Winner | Speed | Race Winner | Started |
|---|---|---|---|---|---|
| 1995 | Goody's 150 | Not held | Not held | Joe Ruttman | 2 |
| 1996 | Hanes 250 | Bobby Hamilton | 92.101 | Mike Skinner | 16 |
| 1997 | Hanes 250 | Rich Bickle | 92.796 | Rich Bickle | 1 |
| 1998 | NAPA 250 | Greg Biffle | 91.891 | Jay Sauter | 10 |
| 1999 | NAPA 250 | Mike Bliss | 94.275 | Jimmy Hensley | 9 |
| 2000 | NAPA 250 | Mike Wallace | 93.070 | Bobby Hamilton | 2 |
| 2001 | Advance Auto Parts 250 | Joe Ruttman | 92.411 | Scott Riggs | 2 |
| 2002 | Advance Auto Parts 250 | Ted Musgrave | 92.864 | Dennis Setzer | 33 |
| 2003 | Advance Auto Parts 250 | Ted Musgrave | 91.297 | Dennis Setzer | 5 |

**QUALIFYING RECORD**
Mike Bliss, Ford; 94.275 mph (20.086 sec.); April 16, 1999

**RACE RECORD**
Jimmy Hensley, Dodge; 74.294 (1 hr., 46 min., 12 sec.); April 17, 1999

### POLE WINNERS

| | | | | | |
|---|---|---|---|---|---|
| Ted Musgrave | 2 | Bobby Hamilton | 1 | | |
| Rich Bickle | 1 | Joe Ruttman | 1 | | |
| Greg Biffle | 1 | Mike Wallace | 1 | | |
| Mike Bliss | 1 | | | | |

### RACE WINNERS

| | | | | | |
|---|---|---|---|---|---|
| Dennis Setzer | 2 | Scott Riggs | 1 |
| Rich Bickle | 1 | Joe Ruttman | 1 |
| Bobby Hamilton | 1 | Jay Sauter | 1 |
| Jimmy Hensley | 1 | Mike Skinner | 1 |

# Michigan International Speedway

## TRACK FACTS
**Date Opened:** 1968
**Owner:** ISC
**President:** Brett Shelton
**Distance:** 2 miles
**Banking in Turns:** 18 degrees
**Banking on Frontstretch:** 12 degrees
**Banking on Backstretch:** 5 degrees
**Length of Frontstretch:** 3,600 feet
**Length of Backstretch:** 2,242 feet
**Grandstand Seating:** 136,373
**Tickets:** (800) 354-1010
**Website:** www.mispeedway.com

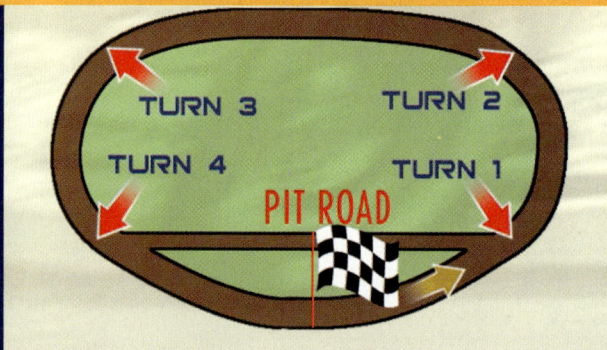

## 2004 SCHEDULE

### NEXTEL Cup
**Michigan 400**
Race: No. 16 of 36
Date: June 20
TV: FOX. Radio: MRN

**Michigan 400**
Race: No. 24 of 36
Date: August 22
TV: TNT. Radio: MRN

### Busch Series
**Cabela's 250**
Race: No. 22 of 34
Date: August 21
TV: FOX. Radio: MRN

### Craftsman Truck Series
**Michigan 200**
Race: No. 12 of 25
Date: July 31
TV: SPEED. Radio: MRN

## NEXTEL CUP
### TRACK RECORDS
**Most Wins:** 9—David Pearson
**Oldest Winner:** Harry Gant, 52 years, 7 months, 6 days, 8/16/1992
**Youngest Winner:** Kurt Busch, 24 years, 10 months, 11 days, 6/15/03
**Most Lead Changes:** 65—8/16/81
**Fewest Lead Changes:** 7—8/12/84
**Most Leaders:** 16—8/20/95
**Fewest Leaders:** 5—six times, most recently, 8/12/84
**Most Laps Led in a 400 Miles race:** 162, Once, Rusty Wallace, 08/20/1989
**Most Laps Led in a 500 Miles race:** 136, Once, LeeRoy Yarbrough, 06/15/1969
**Most Cautions:** 9—Twice, most recently 6/15/03
**Fewest Cautions:** 0—4 times, most recently, 6/11/00
**Most Caution Laps:** 63—8/24/75
**Fewest Caution Laps:** 0—4 times, most recently, 6/11/00
**Most on the Lead Lap:** 32—8/18/02
**Fewest on the Lead Lap:** 2—5 times, most recently, 6/15/75
**Most Running at the Finish:** 41—3 times, most recently, 6/13/99
**Fewest Running at the Finish:** 14—6/16/74
**Most Laps Led by a Race Winner:** 162—Rusty Wallace, 8/20/89
**Fewest Laps Led by a Race Winner:** 7—Dale Jarrett, 8/18/02
**Closest Margin of Victory:** 0.085 second, Jeff Gordon defeated Ricky Rudd 06/10/01
**Greatest Margin of Victory:** 15.71 seconds, Rusty Wallace defeated Morgan Shepherd 08/20/89

### QUALIFYING AND RACE RECORDS
**QUALIFYING**
**Track:** Dale Earnhardt Jr., Chevrolet, 191.149 mph, 37.667 seconds, Aug. 18, 2000 (Pepsi 400)
**Spring Race (Michigan 400):** Bobby Labonte, Chevrolet, 190.365 mph; June 13, 2003.
**Fall Race (Michigan 400):** Dale Earnhardt Jr., Chevrolet, 191.149 mph, 37.667 seconds, Aug. 18, 2000.
**RACE**
**Track:** Dale Jarrett, Ford, 173.997 mph, 2 hours, 17 minutes, 56 seconds, June 13, 1999 (Kmart 400)
**Spring Race (Michigan 400):** Dale Jarrett, Ford, 173.997 mph, 2 hours, 17 minutes, 56 seconds, June 13, 1999.

## YEAR BY YEAR WINNERS

| Year | Event | Race Winner | Car Make | Avg. Speed | Start Pos. | Winning Car Owner | Pole Winner |
|---|---|---|---|---|---|---|---|
| 2003 | GFS Marketplace 400 | R. Newman | Dodge | 127.310 | 8 | Roger Penske | B. Labonte |
| | Sirius 400 | K. Busch | Ford | 131.219 | 4 | Jack Roush | B. Labonte |
| 2002 | Pepsi 400 | D. Jarrett | Ford | 140.566 | 8 | Robert Yates | D. Earnhardt Jr. |
| | Sirius 400 | M. Kenseth | Ford | 154.822 | 20 | Jack Roush | D. Jarrett |
| g 2001 | Pepsi 400 | S. Marlin | Dodge | 140.513 | 15 | Chip Ganassi | R. Craven |
| | Kmart 400 | J. Gordon | Chevrolet | 134.203 | 1 | Rick Hendrick | J. Gordon |
| 2000 | Pepsi 400 | R. Wallace | Ford | 132.597 | 10 | Roger Penske | D. Earnhardt Jr. |
| f | Kmart 400 | T. Stewart | Pontiac | 143.926 | 28 | Joe Gibbs | B. Labonte |
| 1999 | Pepsi 400 | B. Labonte | Pontiac | 144.332 | 19 | Joe Gibbs | W. Burton |
| b | Kmart 400 | D. Jarrett | Ford | 173.997 | 6 | Robert Yates | J. Gordon |
| 1998 | Pepsi 400 | J. Gordon | Chevrolet | 151.995 | 3 | Rick Hendrick | E. Irvan |
| | Miller 400 | M. Martin | Ford | 158.695 | 7 | Jack Roush | W. Burton |
| 1997 | DeVilbiss 400 | M. Martin | Ford | 126.880 | 2 | Jack Roush | J. Benson, Jr. |
| | Miller 400 | E. Irvan | Ford | 153.338 | 20 | Robert Yates | D. Jarrett |
| 1996 | Goodwrench 400 | D. Jarrett | Ford | 139.792 | 11 | Robert Yates | J. Burton |
| | Miller 400 | R. Wallace | Ford | 166.033 | 18 | Roger Penske | B. Hamilton |
| 1995 | Goodwrench 400 | B. Labonte | Chevrolet | 157.739 | 1 | Joe Gibbs | B. Labonte |
| | Miller 400 | B. Labonte | Chevrolet | 134.141 | 19 | Joe Gibbs | J. Gordon |
| 1994 | Goodwrench 400 | G. Bodine | Ford | 139.914 | 1 | Geoff Bodine | G. Bodine |
| | Miller 400 | R. Wallace | Ford | 125.022 | 5 | Roger Penske | L. Allen |
| 1993 | Champion 400 | Martin | Ford | 144.564 | 12 | Jack Roush | Schrader |
| | Miller 400 | Rudd | Chevrolet | 148.484 | 2 | Rick Hendrick | B. Bodine |
| 1992 | Champion 400 | Gant | Oldsmobile | 146.056 | 24 | Leo Jackson | Kulwicki |
| | Miller 400 | Da. Allison | Ford | 152.672 | 1 | Robert Yates | Da. Allison |
| 1991 | Champion 400 | D. Jarrett | Ford | 142.972 | 11 | Wood Brothers | Kulwicki |
| | Miller 400 | Da. Allison | Ford | 160.912 | 4 | Robert Yates | M. Waltrip |
| 1990 | Champion 400 | Martin | Ford | 138.822 | 5 | Jack Roush | Kulwicki |
| | Miller 400 | Earnhardt | Chevrolet | 150.219 | 5 | Richard Childress | Trials Rained Out |
| 1989 | Champion 400 | Wallace | Pontiac | 157.704 | 2 | Blue Max | G. Bodine |
| | Miller 400 | Elliott | Ford | 139.023 | 2 | Melling Racing | Schrader |
| 1988 | Champion 400 | Da. Allison | Ford | 156.863 | 4 | Ranier Racing | Elliott |
| | Miller 400 | Wallace | Pontiac | 153.551 | 5 | Blue Max | Elliott |
| 1987 | Champion 400 | Elliott | Ford | 138.648 | 3 | Melling Racing | Da. Allison |
| | Miller Am. 400 | Earnhardt | Chevrolet | 148.454 | 5 | Richard Childress | Wallace |
| 1986 | Champion 400 | Elliott | Ford | 135.376 | 3 | Melling Racing | B. Parsons |
| | Miller Am. 400 | Elliott | Ford | 138.851 | 8 | Melling Racing | Richmond |
| 1985 | Champion 400 | Elliott | Ford | 137.430 | 1 | Melling Racing | Elliott |
| e | Miller 400 | Elliott | Ford | 144.724 | 1 | Melling Racing | Trials Rained Out |
| d 1984 | Champion 400 | Waltrip | Chevrolet | 153.863 | 7 | Junior Johnson | Elliott |
| | Miller 400 | Elliott | Ford | 134.705 | 1 | Melling Racing | Elliott |
| 1983 | Champion 400 | C. Yarborough | Chevrolet | 147.511 | 7 | Ranier Racing | Labonte |
| | Gabriel 400 | C. Yarborough | Chevrolet | 138.728 | 9 | Ranier Racing | Labonte |
| 1982 | Champion 400 | B. Allison | Buick | 136.454 | 10 | DiGard Rac. Co. | Elliott |
| | Gabriel 400 | C. Yarborough | Buick | 118.101 | 4 | M.C. Anderson | Bouchard |
| 1981 | Champion 400 | R. Petty | Buick | 123.457 | 7 | Petty Eng. | Bouchard |
| | Gabriel 400 | B. Allison | Buick | 130.589 | 4 | Ranier Racing | Waltrip |
| 1980 | Champion 400 | C. Yarborough | Chevrolet | 145.352 | 2 | Junior Johnson | Buddy Baker |
| | Gabriel 400 | Parsons | Chevrolet | 131.808 | 1 | M.C. Anderson | Parsons |
| 1979 | Champion 400 | R. Petty | Chevrolet | 130.376 | 5 | Petty Eng. | Pearson |
| | Gabriel 400 | Buddy Baker | Chevrolet | 135.798 | 3 | Ranier Racing | Bonnett |
| 1978 | Champion 400 | Pearson | Mercury | 129.566 | 1 | Wood Brothers | Pearson |
| | Gabriel 400 | C. Yarborough | Oldsmobile | 149.563 | 3 | Junior Johnson | Pearson |
| 1977 | Champion 400 | Waltrip | Chevrolet | 137.944 | 3 | DiGard Rac. Co. | Pearson |
| | CAM2 400 | C. Yarborough | Chevrolet | 135.033 | 4 | Junior Johnson | Pearson |
| 1976 | Champion 400 | Pearson | Mercury | 140.078 | 1 | Wood Brothers | Pearson |
| | CAM2 400 | Pearson | Mercury | 141.148 | 8 | Wood Brothers | R. Petty |
| 1975 | Champion 400 | R. Petty | Dodge | 107.583 | 4 | Petty Eng. | Pearson |
| | Motor State 400 | Pearson | Mercury | 131.398 | 3 | Wood Brothers | C. Yarborough |
| 1974 | Yankee 400 | Pearson | Mercury | 133.045 | 1 | Wood Brothers | Pearson |
| c | Motor State 400 | R. Petty | Dodge | 127.987 | 4 | Petty Eng. | Pearson |
| b 1973 | Motor State 400 | Pearson | Mercury | 153.485 | 2 | Wood Brothers | Buddy Baker |
| 1972 | Yankee 400 | Pearson | Mercury | 134.416 | 4 | Wood Brothers | R. Petty |
| | Motor State 400 | Pearson | Mercury | 146.639 | 3 | Wood Brothers | Isaac |
| 1971 | Yankee 400* | B. Allison | Mercury | 149.862 | 2 | Holman-Moody | Hamilton |
| | Motor State 400* | B. Allison | Mercury | 149.567 | 1 | Holman-Moody | B. Allison |
| 1970 | Yankee 400* | Glotzbach | Dodge | 147.571 | 2 | Ray Nichels | Glotzbach |
| | Motor State 400 | C. Yarborough | Mercury | 138.302 | 5 | Wood Brothers | Hamilton |
| a 1969 | Yankee 600 | Pearson | Ford | 115.508 | 1 | Holman-Moody | Pearson |
| | Motor State 500 | C. Yarborough | Mercury | 139.254 | 4 | Wood Brothers | D. Allison |

*3 races were 197 laps instead of 200; track measured at 2.04 miles. **a** Race shortened to 330 miles, rain and darkness. **b** Race run without a caution. **c** Race reduced to 360 miles, energy shortage. **d** Race run without a caution. **e** Starting lineup determined by Winston Cup car owner standings. **f** Race shortened to 388 miles, rain. **g** Race shortened to 324 miles, rain.

## NEXTEL CUP

**Fall Race (Michigan 400):** Bobby Labonte, Chevrolet, 157.739 mph, 2 hours, 32 minutes, 9 seconds, Aug. 20, 1995.

**500 miles:** Cale Yarborough, Mercury, 139.254 mph, 3 hours, 35 minutes, 26 seconds, June 15, 1969 (Motor State 500).

***600 miles:** David Pearson, Ford, 115.508 mph, 2 hours, 51 minutes, 25 seconds, Aug. 17, 1969 (Yankee 600).
*Race cut to 330 miles, rain and darkness.

## ALL MICHIGAN RACES

### POLE WINNERS / RACE WINNERS

| Pole Winner | | Pole Winner | | Race Winner | | Race Winner | |
|---|---|---|---|---|---|---|---|
| Pearson | 10 | Yarborough | 1 | Pearson | 9 | Parsons | 1 |
| Elliott | 6 | Glotzbach | 1 | Yarborough | 8 | Irvan | 1 |
| Kulwicki | 3 | D. Allison | 1 | Elliott | 7 | Stewart | 1 |
| J. Gordon | 3 | Isaac | 1 | R. Wallace | 5 | Marlin | 1 |
| R. Petty | 2 | Bonnett | 1 | R. Petty | 4 | Kenseth | 1 |
| Buddy Baker | 2 | D. Waltrip | 1 | B. Allison | 4 | Busch | 1 |
| Bouchard | 2 | Richmond | 1 | Martin | 4 | Newman | 1 |
| T. Labonte | 2 | Wallace | 1 | D. Jarrett | 4 | | |
| Schrader | 2 | B. Allison | 1 | B. Labonte | 3 | | |
| G. Bodine | 2 | M. Waltrip | 1 | Da. Allison | 3 | | |
| Da. Allison | 2 | B. Bodine | 1 | J. Gordon | 2 | | |
| Parsons | 2 | L. Allen | 1 | D. Waltrip | 2 | | |
| P. Hamilton | 2 | B. Hamilton | 1 | Earnhardt | 2 | | |
| W. Burton | 2 | J. Burton | 1 | Glotzbach | 1 | | |
| B. Labonte | 2 | J. Benson Jr. | 1 | Baker | 1 | | |
| D. Jarrett | 2 | Irvan | 1 | Gant | 1 | | |
| Earnhardt Jr. | 2 | Craven | 1 | Rudd | 1 | | |
| B. Labonte | 2 | | | G. Bodine | 1 | | |

## SPRING: Sirius 400

### POLE WINNERS / RACE WINNERS

| Pole Winner | | Pole Winner | | Race Winner | | Race Winner | |
|---|---|---|---|---|---|---|---|
| Pearson | 3 | Parsons | 1 | Yarborough | 6 | Martin | 1 |
| J. Gordon | 3 | D. Waltrip | 1 | Pearson | 4 | D. Jarrett | 1 |
| Elliott | 2 | Bouchard | 1 | Elliott | 4 | Stewart | 1 |
| D. Jarrett | 2 | T. Labonte | 1 | R. Wallace | 2 | J. Gordon | 1 |
| B. Labonte | 2 | Richmond | 1 | Earnhardt | 2 | Kenseth | 1 |
| Yarborough | 1 | Wallace | 1 | Da. Allison | 2 | Newman | 1 |
| R. Petty | 1 | Schrader | 1 | B. Allison | 2 | | |
| B. Allison | 1 | M. Waltrip | 1 | R. Petty | 1 | | |
| D. Allison | 1 | Da. Allison | 1 | Buddy Baker | 1 | | |
| Buddy Baker | 1 | B. Bodine | 1 | Parsons | 1 | | |
| Hamilton | 1 | Allen | 1 | Rudd | 1 | | |
| Isaac | 1 | B. Hamilton | 1 | B. Labonte | 1 | | |
| Bonnett | 1 | W. Burton | 1 | Irvan | 1 | | |

## FALL: Pepsi 400

### POLE WINNERS / RACE WINNERS

| Pole Winner | | Pole Winner | | Race Winner | | Race Winner | |
|---|---|---|---|---|---|---|---|
| Pearson | 7 | Da. Allison | 1 | Pearson | 5 | Gant | 1 |
| Elliott | 4 | R. Petty | 1 | Martin | 3 | G. Bodine | 1 |
| Kulwicki | 3 | Schrader | 1 | R. Petty | 3 | J. Gordon | 1 |
| G. Bodine | 2 | J. Burton | 1 | Elliott | 3 | Marlin | 1 |
| Earnhardt Jr. | 2 | J. Benson Jr. | 1 | D. Jarrett | 3 | Busch | 1 |
| B. Labonte | 2 | Irvan | 1 | B. Allison | 2 | | |
| Hamilton | 1 | W. Burton | 1 | Yarborough | 2 | | |
| Glotzbach | 1 | Craven | 1 | D. Waltrip | 2 | | |
| Buddy Baker | 1 | | | B. Labonte | 2 | | |
| Bouchard | 1 | | | R. Wallace | 2 | | |
| T. Labonte | 1 | | | Da. Allison | 1 | | |
| Parsons | 1 | | | Glotzbach | 1 | | |

## BUSCH SERIES

### YEAR BY YEAR WINNERS

| Year | Event | Pole Winner | Speed | Race Winner | Started | Year | Event | Pole Winner | Speed | Race Winner | Started |
|---|---|---|---|---|---|---|---|---|---|---|---|
| 1992 | Detroit Gasket 200 | J. Gordon | 173.135 | T. Bodine | 12 | 1999 | NAPA 200 | D. Blaney | 180.054 | D. Earnhardt Jr. | 3 |
| 1993 | Detroit Gasket 200 | B. Elliott | 175.447 | M. Martin | 2 | 2000 | NAPAonline.com 250 | B. Jones | 184.786 | T. Bodine. | 16 |
| 1994 | Detroit Gasket 200 | D. Cope | 175.426 | B. Labonte | 7 | 2001 | NAPAonline.com 250 | J. Spencer | 184.824 | R. Newman | 2 |
| 1995 | Detroit Gasket 200 | D. Jarrett | 174.199 | M. Martin | 2 | 2002 | Cabela's 250 | K. Lepage | 185.644 | M. Waltrip | 2 |
| 1996 | Detroit Gasket 200 | R. Craven | 174.965 | J. Purvis | 27 | 2003 | Cabela's 250 | K. Kahne | 186.490 | K. Harvick | 5 |
| 1997 | Detroit Gasket 200 | H. Sadler | 175.511 | S. Park | 4 | | | | | | |
| 1998 | Pepsi 200 | J. Burton | 177.052 | J. Burton | 1 | | | | | | |

*race length changed to 125 laps

### POLE WINNERS

| Blaney | 1 | Craven | 1 | D. Jarrett | 1 | Sadler | 1 |
| J. Burton | 1 | Elliott | 1 | Jones | 1 | Spencer | 1 |
| Cope | 1 | J. Gordon | 1 | Lepage | 1 | Kahne | 1 |

### RACE WINNERS

| Bodine | 2 | Earnhardt Jr. | 1 | Purvis | 1 | Harvick | 1 |
| Martin | 2 | B. Labonte | 1 | Park | 1 | | |
| J. Burton | 1 | Newman | 1 | Waltrip | 1 | | |

### QUALIFYING RECORD
Kasey Kahne, Ford, 186.490; August 15, 2003

### RACE RECORD
Mark Martin, Ford; 169.571 mph (1 hr, 10 min, 46 sec.); August 19, 1995.

## CRAFTSMAN TRUCK SERIES

### YEAR BY YEAR WINNERS

| Year | Event | Pole Winner | Speed | Race Winner | Started |
|---|---|---|---|---|---|
| 1999 | goracing.com200 | Stacy Compton | 175.717 | Greg Biffle | 11 |
| 2000 | Michigan 200 | Jamie McMurray | 177.144 | Greg Biffle | 2 |
| 2002 | Michigan 200 | | Not held | Robert Pressley | 8 |
| 2003 | Sears 200 | Jason Leffler | 178.037 | Brendan Gaughan | 6 |

### QUALIFYING RECORD
Jason Leffler, Dodge; 178.037 mph, July 25, 2003

### RACE RECORD
Brendan Gaughan, Dodge; 154.044 mph (1 hour, 17 min., 54 sec.), July 26, 2003

### POLE WINNERS

| Stacy Comptom | 1 | Jason Leffler | 1 |
| Jamie McMurray | 1 | | |

### RACE WINNERS

| Greg Biffle | 2 | Brendan Gaughan | 1 |
| Robert Pressley | 1 | | |

# New Hampshire International Speedway

## TRACK FACTS
**Date Opened:** June 5, 1990
**Owner/Chairman:** Bob Bahre
**Owner/President:** Gary G. Bahre
**Distance:** 1.058 miles
**Banking in Turns:** 12 degrees
**Banking on Straights:** 2 degrees
**Length of Frontstretch:** 1,500 feet
**Length of Backstretch:** 1,500 feet
**Grandstand Seating:** 91,000
**Tickets:** (603) 783-4931
**Website:** www.nhis.com

## 2004 SCHEDULE

### NEXTEL Cup
**New England 300**
**Race:** No. 19 of 36
**Date:** July 25
**TV:** TNT. **Radio:** MRN

**Sylvania 300**
**Race:** No. 27 of 36
**Date:** September 19
**TV:** TNT. **Radio:** MRN

### Busch Series
**New England 200**
**Race:** No. 20 of 34
**Date:** July 24
**TV:** TNT. **Radio:** MRN

### Craftsman Truck Series
**New Hampshire 200**
**Race:** No. 18 of 25
**Date:** September 18
**TV:** Speed. **Radio:** MRN

## NEXTEL CUP

### TRACK RECORDS
**Most Wins:** 4—Jeff Burton
**Oldest Winner:** Dale Jarrett, 44 years, 7 months, 26 days, 7/22/2001
**Youngest Winner:** Jeff Gordon, 23 years, 11 months, 5 days, 7/09/1995
**Most Lead Changes:** 23—7/14/96
**Fewest Lead Changes:** 1—9/17/00
**Most Leaders:** 15—7/14/96
**Fewest Leaders:** 1—9/17/00
**Most Cautions:** 17—7/10/94
**Fewest Cautions:** 2—7/13/97
**Most Caution Laps:** 78—7/10/94
**Fewest Caution Laps:** 10—7/13/97
**Most on the Lead Lap:** 30—7/21/02
**Fewest on the Lead Lap:** 7—7/11/93
**Most Running at the Finish:** 39—

# NEXTEL CUP

Three times, most recently 7/20/03
**Fewest Running at the Finish:** 30—Twice, most recently, 9/17/00
**Most Laps Led by a Race Winner:** 300—Jeff Burton, 9/17/00
**Fewest Laps Led by a Race Winner:** 2—Jeff Burton, 7/11/99
**Closest Margin of Victory:**—0.664 second, Jeff Gordon defeated Mark Martin 08/20/98
**Greatest Margin of Victory:**—6.240 seconds, Jimmie Johnson defeated Ricky Rudd 09/14/03

## QUALIFYING AND RACE RECORDS
### QUALIFYING
**Track:** Ryan Newman, Ford, 133.357 mph, September 12, 2003.
**Summer Race (New England 300):** Ryan Newman, Ford, 132.241 mph, 28.802 seconds, Sept. 13, 2002.
**Fall Race (Sylvania 300):** Ryan Newman, Ford, 133.357 mph, September 12, 2003.

### RACE
**Track:** Jeff Burton, Ford, 117.134 mph, 2 hours, 42 minutes, 35 seconds, July 13, 1997 (Jiffy Lube 300).
**Summer Race (New England 300):** Jeff Burton, Ford, 117.134 mph, 2 hours, 42 minutes, 35 seconds, July 13, 1997.
**Fall Race (Sylvania 300):** Jeff Gordon, Chevrolet, 112.078 mph, 2 hours, 45 minutes, 55 seconds, Aug. 28, 1998.

## YEAR BY YEAR WINNERS

| Year | Event | Race Winner | Car Make | Avg. Speed | Start Pos. | Winning Car Owner | Pole Winner |
|---|---|---|---|---|---|---|---|
| 2003 | Sylvania 500 | J. Johnson | Chevrolet | 106.580 | 8 | Rick Hendrick | R. Newman |
| | New England 300 | J. Johnson | Chevrolet | 96.924 | 6 | Rick Hendrick | Trials raned out |
| 2002 | New Hampshire 300 | R. Newman | Ford | 105.081 | 1 | Roger Penske | R. Newman |
| | New England 300 | W. Burton | Dodge | 92.342 | 31 | Bill Davis | B. Elliott |
| b 2001 | New Hampshire 300 | R. Gordon | Chevrolet | 103.594 | 31 | Richard Childress | Trials Canceled |
| | New England 300 | D. Jarrett | Ford | 102.131 | 9 | Robert Yates | J. Gordon |
| 2000 | Dura-Lube/Kmart 300 | J. Burton | Ford | 102.003 | 2 | Jack Roush | B. Labonte |
| a | thatlook.com 300 | T. Stewart | Pontiac | 103.145 | 6 | Joe Gibbs | R. Wallace |
| 1999 | Dura-Lube/Kmart 300 | J. Nemechek | Chevrolet | 100.673 | 11 | Felix Sebates | R. Wallace |
| | Jiffy Lube 300 | J. Burton | Ford | 101.876 | 38 | Jack Roush | J. Gordon |
| 1998 | CMT 300 | J. Gordon | Chevrolet | 112.078 | 1 | Rick Hendrick | J. Gordon |
| | Jiffy Lube 300 | J. Burton | Ford | 102.996 | 5 | Jack Roush | R. Craven |
| 1997 | CMT 300 | J. Gordon | Chevrolet | 100.364 | 13 | Rick Hendrick | K. Schrader |
| | Jiffy Lube 300 | J. Burton | Ford | 117.194 | 15 | Jack Roush | K. Schrader |
| 1996 | Jiffy Lube 300 | E. Irvan | Ford | 98.930 | 6 | Robert Yates | R. Craven |
| 1995 | Slick 50 300 | J. Gordon | Chevrolet | 107.029 | 21 | Rick Hendrick | M. Martin |
| 1994 | Slick 50 300 | R. Rudd | Ford | 87.599 | 3 | Ricky Rudd | E. Irvan |
| 1993 | Slick 50 300 | R. Wallace | Pontiac | 105.947 | 33 | Roger Penske | M. Martin |

a Race cut to 273 laps, rain.
b Time trails had been called off after the terrorist attacks, then the race was rescheduled for November 23, 2001.

## ALL NEW HAMPSHIRE RACES

| POLE WINNERS | | | | RACE WINNERS | | | |
|---|---|---|---|---|---|---|---|
| J. Gordon | 3 | B. Labonte | 1 | J. Burton | 4 | R. Rudd | 1 |
| M. Martin | 2 | E. Irvan | 1 | J. Gordon | 3 | D. Jarrett | 1 |
| K. Schrader | 2 | B. Elliott | 1 | R. Wallace | 1 | R. Gordon | 1 |
| R. Craven | 2 | | | E. Irvan | 1 | W. Burton | 1 |
| R. Wallace | 2 | | | J. Nemechek | 1 | R. Newman | 1 |
| R. Newman | 2 | | | T. Stewart | 1 | Ji. Johnson | 2 |

## SUMMER: New England 300

| POLE WINNERS | | | | RACE WINNERS | | | |
|---|---|---|---|---|---|---|---|
| M. Martin | 2 | K. Schrader | 1 | J. Burton | 3 | T. Stewart | 1 |
| R. Craven | 2 | R. Wallace | 1 | R. Wallace | 1 | D. Jarrett | 1 |
| J. Gordon | 2 | B. Elliott | 1 | R. Rudd | 1 | W. Burton | 1 |
| E. Irvan | 1 | | | J. Gordon | 1 | Ji. Johnson | 1 |
| | | | | E. Irvan | 1 | | |

## FALL: New Hampshire 300

| POLE WINNERS | | | | RACE WINNERS | | | |
|---|---|---|---|---|---|---|---|
| R. Newman | 2 | R. Wallace | 1 | J. Gordon | 2 | R. Gordon | 1 |
| K. Schrader | 1 | B. Labonte | 1 | J. Nemechek | 1 | R. Newman | 1 |
| J. Gordon | 1 | | | J. Burton | 1 | Ji. Johnson | 1 |

# BUSCH SERIES

## YEAR BY YEAR WINNERS

| Year | Event | Pole Winner | Speed | Race Winner | Started |
|---|---|---|---|---|---|
| 1990 | Budweiser 300 | J. Hensley | 123.410 | T. Ellis | 4 |
| | NE Chevy 250 | R. Craven | 122.085 | R. Mast | 18 |
| 1991 | Budweiser 300 | J. Hensley | 128.470 | K. Wallace | 3 |
| | NE Chevy 250 | R. Craven | 121.800 | R. Craven | 1 |
| 1992 | Budweiser 300 | K. Wallace | 122.532 | J. Burton | 23 |
| | NE Chevy 250 | E. Irvan | 122.422 | J. Nemechek | 10 |
| 1993 | NE Chevy 250 | J. Nemechek | 124.875 | R. Pressley | 3 |
| 1994 | NE Chevy 250 | B. Labonte | 124.871 | D. Cope | 14 |
| 1995 | NE Chevy 250 | M. McLaughlin | 124.903 | C. Little | 9 |

| Year | Event | Pole Winner | Speed | Race Winner | Started |
|---|---|---|---|---|---|
| 1996* | Stanley 200 | None - weather | | R. LaJoie | 2 |
| 1997 | U.S. Cellular 200 | None - weather | | M. McLaughlin | 12 |
| 1998 | Gumout 200 | J. Bessey | 127.701 | B. Jones | 26 |
| 1999 | NASCAR Busch Series 200 | J. Green | 128.637 | E. Sawyer | 2 |
| 2000 | Busch 200 | T. Fedewa | 130.247 | T. Fedewa | 1 |
| 2001 | CVS Pharmacy 200 | K. Harvick | 130.716 | J. Keller | 4 |
| 2002 | Busch 200 | S. Hmiel | 129.406 | B. Hamilton Jr. | 2 |
| 2003 | 200 | None-weather | | D. Green | 37 |

* race shortened to 200 laps

## POLE WINNERS

| | | | | | |
|---|---|---|---|---|---|
| Ricky Craven | 2 | Kevin Harvick | 1 | Joe Nemechek | 1 |
| Jimmy Hensley | 2 | Shane Hmiel | 1 | Kenny Wallace | 1 |
| Joe Bessey | 1 | Ernie Irvan | 1 | | |
| Tim Fedewa | 1 | Bobby Labonte | 1 | | |
| Jeff Green | 1 | M. McLaughlin | 1 | | |

## RACE WINNERS

| | | | | | |
|---|---|---|---|---|---|
| Jeff Burton | 1 | B. Hamilton Jr. | 1 | Rick Mast | 1 | Kenny Wallace | 1 |
| Derrike Cope | 1 | Buckshot Jones | 1 | M. McLaughlin | 1 | David Green | 1 |
| Ricky Craven | 1 | Jason Keller | 1 | Joe Nemechek | 1 | | |
| Tommy Ellis | 1 | Randy LaJoie | 1 | Robert Pressley | 1 | | |
| Tim Fedewa | 1 | Chad Little | 1 | Elton Sawyer | 1 | | |

### QUALIFYING RECORD
Kevin Harvick, Chevrolet; 130.716 mph (29.138 sec.); May 11, 2001

### RACE RECORD
Bobby Hamilton Jr., Ford; 110.368 mph (1 hr., 55 min., 2 sec.); May 11, 2002

## CRAFTSMAN TRUCK SERIES

### YEAR BY YEAR WINNERS

| Year | Event | Pole Winner | Speed | Race Winner | Starter |
|---|---|---|---|---|---|
| 1996 | Pennzoil Tripleheader | Mike Skinner | 124.891 | Ron Hornaday Jr. | 8 |
| 1997 | Pennzoil Tripleheader | Jack Sprague | 126.985 | Jay Sauter | 26 |
| 1998 | Pennzoil Tripleheader | Mike Wallace | 126.994 | Andy Houston | 7 |
| 1999 | Pennzoil Tripleheader | Stacy Compton | 126.745 | Dennis Setzer | 10 |
| 2000 | thatlook.com 200 | Joe Ruttman | 127.885 | Kurt Busch | 5 |
| 2001 | New England 200 | Jack Sprague | 128.091 | Jack Sprague | 1 |
| 2002 | New England 200 | Jason Leffler | 128.424 | Terry Cook | 2 |
| 2003 | New Hampshire 200 | Jimmy Spencer | 127.346 | Jimmy Spencer | 1 |

**QUALIFYING RECORD**
Jack Sprague, Chevrolet; 128.091 mph (29.735 sec.); July 20, 2001

**RACE RECORD**
Jack Sprague, Chevrolet; 109.244 mph (1 hr, 56 min., 13 sec.); July 21, 2001

### POLE WINNERS

| | | | | |
|---|---|---|---|---|
| Jack Sprague | 2 | Mike Skinner | 1 | |
| Stacy Compton | 1 | Mike Wallace | 1 | |
| Jason Leffler | 1 | Jimmy Spencer | 1 | |
| Joe Ruttman | 1 | | | |

### RACE WINNERS

| | | | |
|---|---|---|---|
| Kurt Busch | 1 | Jay Sauter | 1 |
| Terry Cook | 1 | Dennis Setzer | 1 |
| Ron Hornaday Jr. | 1 | Jack Sprague | 1 |
| Andy Houston | 1 | Jimmy Spencer | 1 |

# North Carolina Speedway

### TRACK FACTS
**Date Opened:** 1965
**Owner:** ISC
**Executive VP & GM:** Chris Browning
**Distance:** 1.017 miles
**Banking in Turns 1-2:** 22 degrees
**Banking in Turns 3-4:** 25 degrees
**Banking on Straights:** 8 degrees
**Length of Frontstretch:** 1,300 feet
**Length of Backstretch:** 1,367 feet
**Grandstand Seating:** 60,113
**Tickets:** (910) 582-2861
**Website:** www.northcarolinaspeedway.com

### 2004 SCHEDULE

**NEXTEL Cup**
**Subway 400**
**Race:** No. 2 of 36
**Date:** February 22
**TV:** FOX. **Radio:** MRN

**Busch Series**
**Rockingham 200**
**Race:** No. 2 of 34
**Date:** March 21
**TV:** FX. **Radio:** MRN

## NEXTEL CUP

### TRACK RECORDS
**Most Wins:** 9—Richard Petty
**Oldest Winner:** Bill Elliott, 48 years, 1 month, 1 day, 11/9/2003
**Youngest Winner:** Jeff Gordon, 23 years, 6 months, 22 days, 02/26/1995
**Most Lead Changes:** 36—Twice, most recently, 10/30/83
**Fewest Lead Changes:** 2—3/18/73
**Most Leaders:** 13—10/22/78
**Fewest Leaders:** 2—Twice, most recently, 3/18/73
**Most Laps Led in a 400 Miles race:** 323, Once, Dale Jarrett, 02/23/1997
**Most Laps Led in a 500 Miles race:** 491, Once, David Pearson, 03/18/1973
**Most Cautions:** 14—Twice, most recently, 10/22/89
**Fewest Cautions:** 2—3 times, most recently, 11/4/01
**Most Caution Laps:** 118—3/13/77
**Fewest Caution Laps:** 12—10/25/92
**Most on the Lead Lap:** 19—Twice, most recently, 2/24/02
**Fewest on the Lead Lap:** 1—15 times, most recently, 3/28/82
**Most Running at the Finish:** 42—2/27/00
**Fewest Running at the Finish:** 13—Twice, most recently, 10/29/67
**Most Laps Led by a Race Winner:** 491—David Pearson 3/18/73
**Fewest Laps Led by a Race Winner:** 13—Darrell Waltrip 3/1/81
**Closest Margin of Victory:** 0.06 second, Dale Earnhardt defeated Rick Mast 10/23/94
**Greatest Margin of Victory:** 2 Laps, Richard Petty defeated Darrell Waltrip 02/29/76

### QUALIFYING AND RACE RECORDS
#### QUALIFYING
**Track:** Rusty Wallace, Ford, 158.035 mph, 23.167 seconds, Feb. 25, 2000 (Dura-Lube/Kmart 400).
**Subway 400:** Rusty Wallace, Ford, 158.035 mph, 23.167 seconds, Feb. 25, 2000.
**Pop Secret 400:** Mark Martin, Ford, 157.383 mph, 23.263 seconds, Oct. 22, 1999.
#### RACE
**Track Record (400 miles):** Jeff Burton, Ford, 131.103 mph, 3 hours, 2 minutes, 55 seconds, Oct. 24, 1999 (Pop Secret 400).

# NEXTEL CUP

**Subway 400:** Bobby Labonte, Pontiac, 127.875 mph, 3 hours, 7 minutes, 32 seconds, Feb. 27, 2000.
**Pop Secret 400:** Jeff Burton, Ford, 131.103 mph, 3 hours, 2 minutes, 55 seconds, Oct. 24, 1999.

## ALL NORTH CAROLINA RACES

### POLE WINNERS
| | | | |
|---|---|---|---|
| M. Martin | 5 | J. Gordon | 2 |
| K. Petty | 5 | R. Newman | 2 |
| Pearson | 5 | Hutcherson | 1 |
| C. Yarborough | 5 | Goldsmith | 1 |
| T. Labonte | 4 | Isaac | 1 |
| R. Rudd | 3 | Parsons | 1 |
| R. Petty | 3 | Gant | 1 |
| Glotzbach | 3 | Richmond | 1 |
| D. Allison | 3 | Kulwicki | 1 |
| Marcis | 2 | L. Yarborough | 1 |
| Lorenzen | 2 | Schrader | 1 |
| Buddy Baker | 2 | H. Stricklin | 1 |
| Waltrip | 2 | D. Jarrett | 1 |
| Bonnett | 2 | B. Labonte | 1 |
| Da. Allison | 2 | R. Mast | 1 |
| Elliott | 2 | J. Mayfield | 1 |
| G. Bodine | 2 | K. Wallace | 1 |
| B. Allison | 2 | R. Craven | 1 |
| R. Wallace | 2 | Blaney | 1 |

### RACE WINNERS
| | | | |
|---|---|---|---|
| R. Petty | 11 | L. Yarborough | 1 |
| C. Yarborough | 7 | Kulwicki | 1 |
| R. Wallace | 5 | Da. Allison | 1 |
| Pearson | 5 | W. Burton | 1 |
| J. Gordon | 4 | R. Rudd | 1 |
| B. Allison | 4 | B. Hamilton | 1 |
| Waltrip | 4 | J. Burton | 1 |
| B. Elliott | 4 | B. Labonte | 1 |
| K. Petty | 3 | S. Park | 1 |
| Bonnett | 3 | J. Nemechek | 1 |
| D. Earnhardt | 3 | M. Kenseth | 1 |
| T. Labonte | 2 | J. Benson | 1 |
| M. Martin | 2 | | |
| D. Allison | 2 | | |
| D. Jarrett | 2 | | |
| Goldsmith | 1 | | |
| Lorenzen | 1 | | |
| Isaac | 1 | | |
| Turner | 1 | | |

## Subway 400

### POLE WINNERS
| | | | |
|---|---|---|---|
| K. Petty | 3 | L. Yarborough | 1 |
| T. Labonte | 3 | Bonnett | 1 |
| M. Martin | 2 | D. Waltrip | 1 |
| R. Rudd | 2 | Isaac | 1 |
| Pearson | 2 | Parsons | 1 |
| C. Yarborough | 2 | Gant | 1 |
| B. Allison | 2 | Da. Allison | 1 |
| R. Wallace | 2 | Elliott | 1 |
| J. Gordon | 1 | D. Allison | 1 |
| Buddy Baker | 1 | G. Bodine | 1 |
| Marcis | 1 | R. Mast | 1 |
| Goldsmith | 1 | R. Craven | 1 |
| Hutcherson | 1 | Blaney | 1 |
| Lorenzen | 1 | | |

### RACE WINNERS
| | | | |
|---|---|---|---|
| R. Petty | 7 | Elliott | 1 |
| R. Wallace | 3 | M. Martin | 1 |
| J. Gordon | 3 | B. Labonte | 1 |
| C. Yarborough | 3 | S. Park | 1 |
| B. Allison | 3 | M. Kenseth | 1 |
| Bonnett | 2 | D. Jarrett | 1 |
| K. Petty | 2 | | |
| Earnhardt | 2 | | |
| Goldsmith | 1 | | |
| Isaac | 1 | | |
| T. Labonte | 1 | | |
| D. Allison | 1 | | |
| D. Waltrip | 1 | | |

## Pop Secret 400

### POLE WINNERS
| | | | |
|---|---|---|---|
| M. Martin | 3 | Bodine | 1 |
| Pearson | 3 | Labonte | 1 |
| R. Petty | 3 | Richmond | 1 |
| Glotzbach | 3 | Da. Allison | 1 |
| C. Yarborough | 3 | Elliott | 1 |
| K. Petty | 2 | Kulwicki | 1 |
| D. Allison | 2 | Schrader | 1 |
| R. Newman | 2 | R. Rudd | 1 |
| Marcis | 1 | H. Stricklin | 1 |
| Lorenzen | 1 | D. Jarrett | 1 |
| Buddy Baker | 1 | B. Labonte | 1 |
| D. Waltrip | 1 | J. Mayfield | 1 |
| Bonnett | 1 | K. Wallace | 1 |

### RACE WINNERS
| | | | |
|---|---|---|---|
| R. Petty | 4 | Martin | 1 |
| C. Yarborough | 4 | Kulwicki | 1 |
| D. Waltrip | 3 | Da. Allison | 1 |
| Elliott | 3 | K. Petty | 1 |
| B. Allison | 2 | D. Earnhardt | 1 |
| Pearson | 2 | W. Burton | 1 |
| R. Wallace | 2 | R. Rudd | 1 |
| D. Allison | 1 | B. Hamilton | 1 |
| Turner | 1 | J. Gordon | 1 |
| Lorenzen | 1 | J. Burton | 1 |
| L. Yarborough | 1 | D. Jarrett | 1 |
| T. Labonte | 1 | J. Nemechek | 1 |
| Bonnett | 1 | J. Benson | 1 |

## YEAR BY YEAR WINNERS

| | Year | Event | Race Winner | Car Make | Avg. Speed | Start Pos. | Winning Car Owner | Pole Winner |
|---|---|---|---|---|---|---|---|---|
| | 2003 | Pop Secret 400 | B. Elliott | Dodge | 111.677 | 32 | Ray Evernham | R. Newman |
| | | Subway 400 | D. Jarrett | Ford | 117.852 | 9 | Robert Yates | D. Blaney |
| | 2002 | Pop Secret 400 | J. Benson | Pontiac | 128.526 | 26 | Nelson Bowers | R. Newman |
| | | Subway 400 | M. Kenseth | Ford | 115.478 | 25 | Jack Roush | R. Craven |
| | 2001 | Pop Secret 400 | J. Nemechek | Chevrolet | 128.941 | 13 | Andy Petree | K. Wallace |
| | | Dura-Lube 400 | S. Park | Chevrolet | 111.877 | 2 | Dale Earnhardt | J. Gordon |
| | 2000 | Pop Secret 400 | D. Jarrett | Ford | 110.418 | 21 | Robert Yates | J. Mayfield |
| | | Dura-Lube/Kmart 400 | B. Labonte | Pontiac | 127.875 | 3 | Joe Gibbs | R. Wallace |
| d | 1999 | Pop Secret 400 | J. Burton | Ford | 131.103 | 6 | Jack Roush | M. Martin |
| | | Dura-Lube 400 | M. Martin | Ford | 120.750 | 5 | Jack Roush | R. Rudd |
| | 1998 | AC Delco 400 | J. Gordon | Chevrolet | 128.423 | 9 | Rick Hendrick | M. Martin |
| | | Goodwrench 400 | J. Gordon | Chevrolet | 117.065 | 1 | Rick Hendrick | R. Mast |
| | 1997 | AC Delco 400 | B. Hamilton | Pontiac | 121.730 | 28 | Petty Eng. | B. Labonte |
| | | Goodwrench 400 | J. Gordon | Chevrolet | 125.927 | 4 | Rick Hendrick | M. Martin |
| | 1996 | AC Delco 400 | R. Rudd | Ford | 122.320 | 2 | Ricky Rudd | D. Jarrett |
| | | Goodwrench 400 | D. Earnhardt | Chevrolet | 113.959 | 18 | R. Childress | T. Labonte |
| | 1995 | AC Delco 400 | W. Burton | Pontiac | 114.778 | 3 | Bill Davis | H. Stricklin |
| | | Goodwrench 500 | J. Gordon | Chevrolet | 125.305 | 1 | Rick Hendrick | J. Gordon |
| | 1994 | AC Delco 500 | D. Earnhardt | Chevrolet | 126.408 | 20 | R. Childress | R. Rudd |
| | | Goodwrench 500 | R. Wallace | Ford | 125.239 | 15 | Roger Penske | G. Bodine |
| | 1993 | AC Delco 500 | R. Wallace | Pontiac | 114.036 | 18 | Roger Penske | M. Martin |
| | | Goodwrench 500 | R. Wallace | Pontiac | 124.486 | 10 | Roger Penske | M. Martin |
| | 1992 | AC Delco 500 | K. Petty | Pontiac | 130.748 | 1 | Felix Sabates | K. Petty |
| | | Goodwrench 500 | Elliott | Ford | 126.125 | 2 | Junior Johnson | K. Petty |
| | 1991 | AC Delco 500 | Da. Allison | Ford | 127.292 | 10 | Robert Yates | K. Petty |
| | | Goodwrench 500 | K. Petty | Pontiac | 124.083 | 1 | Felix Sabates | K. Petty |
| | 1990 | AC Delco 500 | Kulwicki | Ford | 126.452 | 3 | Alan Kulwicki | Schrader |
| | | Goodwrench 500 | K. Petty | Pontiac | 122.864 | 1 | Felix Sabates | K. Petty |
| | 1989 | AC Delco 500 | Martin | Ford | 114.079 | 7 | Jack Roush | Kulwicki |
| | | Goodwrench 500 | Wallace | Pontiac | 115.122 | 1 | Blue Max | Wallace |
| | 1988 | AC Delco 500 | Wallace | Pontiac | 111.557 | 3 | Blue Max | Elliott |
| | | Goodwrench 500 | Bonnett | Pontiac | 120.159 | 30 | Rahmoc | Elliott |
| | 1987 | AC Delco 500 | Elliott | Ford | 118.258 | 3 | Melling Racing | Da. Allison |
| | | Goodwrench 500 | Earnhardt | Chevrolet | 117.556 | 14 | R. Childress | Da. Allison |
| | 1986 | Nationwise 500 | Bonnett | Chevrolet | 120.381 | 6 | Junior Johnson | Richmond |
| | | Goodwrench 500 | T. Labonte | Oldsmobile | 120.488 | 1 | Billy Hagan | Labonte |
| | 1985 | Nationwise 500 | Waltrip | Chevrolet | 118.344 | 20 | Junior Johnson | Labonte |
| | | Carolina 500 | Bonnett | Chevrolet | 114.953 | 4 | Junior Johnson | Labonte |
| | 1984 | Hodg. Amer. 500 | Elliott | Ford | 112.617 | 2 | Melling Racing | Bodine |
| | | Hodg. Car. 500 | B. Allison | Buick | 122.931 | 15 | DiGard Rac. Co. | Gant |
| | 1983 | Hodg. Amer. 500 | T. Labonte | Chevrolet | 119.324 | 3 | Billy Hagan | Bonnett |
| c | | Hodg. Car. 500 | R. Petty | Pontiac | 113.055 | 12 | Petty Eng. | Rudd |
| | 1982 | Hodg. Amer. 500 | Waltrip | Buick | 115.122 | 4 | Junior Johnson | C. Yarborough |
| | | Hodg. Car. 500 | C. Yarborough | Buick | 108.992 | 11 | M.C. Anderson | Parsons |
| | 1981 | American 500 | Waltrip | Buick | 107.399 | 1 | Junior Johnson | Waltrip |
| | | Carolina 500 | Waltrip | Buick | 114.594 | 4 | Junior Johnson | C. Yarborough |
| | 1980 | American 500 | C. Yarborough | Chevrolet | 114.155 | 2 | Junior Johnson | D. Allison |
| | | Carolina 500 | C. Yarborough | Oldsmobile | 108.735 | 21 | Junior Johnson | Waltrip |
| | 1979 | American 500 | R. Petty | Chevrolet | 108.356 | 7 | Petty Eng. | Buddy Baker |
| | | Carolina 500 | B. Allison | Ford | 121.727 | 1 | Bud Moore | B. Allison |
| | 1978 | American 500 | C. Yarborough | Oldsmobile | 117.288 | 1 | Junior Johnson | C. Yarborough |
| | | Carolina 500 | Pearson | Mercury | 116.681 | 9 | Wood Brothers | Bonnett |
| | 1977 | American 500 | D. Allison | Chevrolet | 113.584 | 1 | Hoss Ellington | D. Allison |
| | | Carolina 500 | R. Petty | Dodge | 97.860 | 2 | Petty Eng. | D. Allison |
| | 1976 | American 500 | R. Petty | Dodge | 117.718 | 4 | Petty Eng. | Pearson |
| | | Carolina 500 | R. Petty | Dodge | 113.665 | 3 | Petty Eng. | Marcis |
| | 1975 | American 500 | C. Yarborough | Chevrolet | 120.129 | 4 | Junior Johnson | Marcis |
| | | Carolina 500 | C. Yarborough | Chevrolet | 117.588 | 7 | Junior Johnson | Buddy Baker |
| | 1974 | American 500 | Pearson | Mercury | 118.493 | 3 | Wood Brothers | R. Petty |
| b | | Carolina 500 | R. Petty | Dodge | 121.622 | 2 | Petty Eng. | C. Yarborough |
| | 1973 | American 500 | Pearson | Mercury | 117.749 | 2 | Wood Brothers | R. Petty |
| | | Carolina 500 | Pearson | Mercury | 118.649 | 1 | Wood Brothers | Pearson |
| | 1972 | American 500 | B. Allison | Chevrolet | 118.275 | 5 | Wood Brothers | R. Petty |
| | | Carolina 500 | Isaac | Dodge | 113.895 | 1 | Nord Krauskopf | Isaac |
| | 1971 | American 500 | R. Petty | Plymouth | 113.405 | 5 | Petty Eng. | Glotzbach |
| | | Carolina 500 | R. Petty | Plymouth | 118.696 | 2 | Petty Eng. | Lorenzen |
| | 1970 | American 500 | C. Yarborough | Mercury | 119.811 | 2 | Wood Brothers | Glotzbach |
| | | Carolina 500 | R. Petty | Plymouth | 116.117 | 8 | Petty Eng. | B. Allison |
| a | 1969 | American 500 | L. Yarborough | Ford | 111.938 | 9 | Junior Johnson | Glotzbach |
| | | Carolina 500 | Pearson | Ford | 102.569 | 1 | Holman-Moody | Pearson |
| | 1968 | American 500 | R. Petty | Plymouth | 105.060 | 4 | Petty Eng. | C. Yarborough |
| | | Carolina 500 | D. Allison | Ford | 99.318 | 7 | Banjo Matthews | L. Yarborough |
| | 1967 | American 500 | B. Allison | Ford | 98.420 | 3 | Holman-Moody | Pearson |
| | | Carolina 500 | R. Petty | Plymouth | 104.682 | 2 | Petty Eng. | Hutcherson |
| | 1966 | American 500 | Lorenzen | Ford | 104.348 | 1 | Holman-Moody | Lorenzen |
| | | Pch. Bism. 500 | Goldsmith | Plymouth | 100.072 | 1 | Ray Nichels | Goldsmith |
| | 1965 | American 500 | Turner | Ford | 101.943 | 4 | Wood Brothers | R. Petty |

a  Track reshaped and remeasured at 1.017 miles instead of an even mile; laps reduced from 500 to 492 to keep distance at 500 miles.
b  Reduced to 450 miles, energy shortage
c  First 143 laps run on Sunday, March 6; final 349 laps on March 13.
d  All pit stalls now located on front straightaway.

## BUSCH SERIES

### YEAR BY YEAR WINNERS

| Year | Event | Pole Winner | Speed | Race Winner | Started |
|---|---|---|---|---|---|
| 1982 | Coca-Cola 200 | D. Pearson | 141.054 | D. Pearson | 1 |
| | No Fall race held | — | — | — | |
| 1983 | Coca Cola 200 | D. Earnhardt | 141.027 | D. Earnhardt | 1 |
| | No Fall race held | — | — | — | |
| 1984 | Komfort Koach 200 | S. Ard | 142.726 | S. Ard | 1 |
| | Komfort Koach 200 | G. Bodine | 143.111 | G. Bodine | 1 |
| 1985 | Komfort Koach 200 | G. Bodine | 143.864 | D. Earnhardt | 2 |
| | Sandhills 200 | B. Bodine | 141.011 | B. Bodine | 1 |
| 1986 | Protecta-Liner 200 | B. Bodine | 142.028 | D. Earnhardt | 7 |
| | Sandhills 200 | Da. Allison | 141.638 | M. Shepherd | 10 |
| 1987 | No Spring race (snow) | — | — | — | |
| | AC-Delco 200 | J. Hensley | 144.895 | M. Shepherd | 19 |
| 1988 | Goodwrench 200 | D. Earnhardt | 142.282 | M. Martin | 6 |
| | AC-Delco 200 | H. Gant | 145.534 | H. Gant | 1 |
| 1989 | Goodwrench 200 | R. Moroso | 144.918 | R. Moroso | 1 |
| | AC-Delco 200 | M. Martin | 144.187 | H. Gant | 4 |
| 1990 | Goodwrench 200 | H. Gant | 145.361 | D. Earnhardt | 11 |
| | AC-Delco 200 | D. Mader | 143.915 | S. Grissom | 32 |
| 1991 | Goodwrench 200 | D. Earnhardt | 145.598 | D. Jarrett | 9 |
| | AC-Delco 200 | E. Irvan | 145.627 | E. Irvan | 1 |
| 1992 | Goodwrench 200 | J. Gordon | 145.505 | W. Burton | 10 |
| | AC-Delco 200 | J. Gordon | 147.587 | M. Martin | 4 |
| 1993 | Goodwrench 200 | None - weather | — | M. Martin | 17 |
| | AC-Delco 200 | W. Burton | 147.999 | M. Martin | 2 |
| 1994 | Goodwrench 200 | R. Pressley | 148.257 | T. Labonte | 8 |
| | AC-Delco 200 | D. Green | 153.419 | M. Martin | 4 |
| 1995 | Goodwrench 200 | D. Green | 150.642 | C. Little | 2 |
| | AC-Delco 200 | None - weather | — | T. Bodine | 14 |
| 1996 | Goodwrench 200 | M. Martin | 150.952 | M. Martin | 1 |
| | AC-Delco 200 | B. Jones | 150.425 | M. Martin | 5 |
| 1997 | Goodwrench 200 | M. Martin | 151.264 | M. Martin | 1 |
| | AC-Delco 200 | J. Burton | 151.734 | M. Martin | 6 |
| 1998 | Goodwrench 200 | T. Stewart | 152.119 | M. Kenseth | 27 |
| | AC-Delco 200 | T. Stewart | 152.544 | E. Sadler | 19 |
| 1999 | ALLtel 200 | None - weather | — | J. Burton | 30 |
| | Kmart 200 | M. Martin | 152.486 | M. Martin | 1 |
| 2000 | ALLtel 200 | M. Martin | 154.383 | M. Martin | 1 |
| | Sam's Club 200 | M. Martin | 154.162 | Jeff Green | 4 |
| 2001 | ALLTEL 200 | G. Biffle | 156.368 | T. Bodine | 3 |
| | Sam's Club 200 | R. Newman | 154.007 | K. Wallace | 2 |
| 2002 | 1-866RBCTerm 200 | J. Green | 153.587 | J. Keller | 10 |
| | Sam's Club 200 | J. Green | 153.355 | J. McMurray | 3 |
| 2003 | Rockingham 200 | D. Green | 154.429 | J. McMurray | 2 |
| | Target House 200 | B. Vickers | 155.037 | J. McMurray | 8 |

### POLE WINNERS

| | | | | |
|---|---|---|---|---|
| Mark Martin 6 | Jeff Green 2 | Jeff Burton 1 | Dave Mader III 1 | |
| Dale Earnhardt 3 | Tony Stewart 2 | Ward Burton 1 | Rob Moroso 1 | |
| David Green 3 | Davey Allison 1 | D. Earnhardt Jr. 1 | Ryan Newman 1 | |
| Geoffrey Bodine 2 | Sam Ard 1 | Jimmy Hensley 1 | David Pearson 1 | |
| Harry Gant 2 | Greg Biffle 1 | Ernie Irvan 1 | Robert Pressley 1 | |
| Jeff Gordon 2 | Brett Bodine 1 | Buckshot Jones 1 | Brian Vickers 1 | |

### RACE WINNERS

| | | | |
|---|---|---|---|
| Mark Martin 11 | Sam Ard 1 | Steve Grissom 1 | Chad Little 1 |
| Dale Earnhardt 4 | Brett Bodine 1 | Ernie Irvan 1 | Rob Moroso 1 |
| J. McMurray 3 | Geoffrey Bodine 1 | Dale Jarrett 1 | David Pearson 1 |
| Todd Bodine 2 | Jeff Burton 1 | Jason Keller 1 | Elliott Sadler 1 |
| Harry Gant 2 | Ward Burton 1 | Matt Kenseth 1 | Kenny Wallace 1 |
| M. Shepherd 2 | Jeff Green 1 | Terry Labonte 1 | |

**QUALIFYING RECORD**
Greg Biffle, Ford; 156.368 (23.414 sec.); February 23, 2001.

**RACE RECORD**
Mark Martin, Ford; 124.397 mph (1 hr., 36 min., 38 sec.); October 19, 1996.

# Phoenix International Speedway

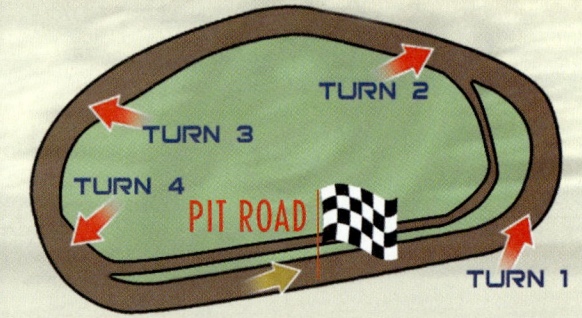

### TRACK FACTS
**Date Opened:** 1964
**Owner:** ISC
**President:** Bryan Sperber
**Distance:** 1 mile
**Banking in Turns 1-2:** 11 degrees
**Banking in Turns 3-4:** 9 degrees
**Banking in Straights:** None
**Length of Frontstretch:** 1,179 feet
**Length of Backstretch:** 1,551 feet
**Grandstand Seating:** 76,812
**Tickets:** (602) 252-2227
**Website:** www.phoenixintlraceway.com

### 2004 SCHEDULE

**NEXTEL Cup**
Checker Auto Parts 500
Race: No. 34 of 36
Date: November 7
TV: NBC. Radio: MRN

Race No. 32 of 34
Date: November 6
TV: FOX. Radio: MRN

**Craftsman Truck Series**
Chevy Silverado 150
Race: No. 23 of 25
Date: November 5
TV: Speed. Radio: MRN

**Busch Series**
Bashas' Supermarkets 200

### NEXTEL CUP
### TRACK RECORDS
**Most Wins:** 2—Jeff Burton and Davey Allison
**Oldest Winner:** Rusty Wallace, 42 years, 2 months, 11 days, 10/25/1998
**Youngest Winner:** Tony Stewart, 28 years, 5 months, 18 days, 11/7/1999
**Most Lead Changes:** 23—11/5/00
**Fewest Lead Changes:** 1—11/4/90
**Most Leaders:** 16—10/29/95
**Fewest Leaders:** 2—11/4/90
**Most Cautions:** 10—Twice, most recently 11/2/03
**Fewest Cautions:** 2—11/7/99
**Most Caution Laps:** 66—11/2/03
**Fewest Caution Laps:** 10—11/7/99

# NEXTEL CUP

**Most on the Lead Lap:** 29—11/2/03
**Fewest on the Lead Lap:** 3—10/30/94
**Most Running at the Finish:** 41—Twice, most recently, 11/7/99
**Fewest Running at the Finish:** 27—11/5/89
**Most Laps Led by a Race Winner:** 262—Dale Earnhardt 11/4/90
**Fewest Laps Led by a Race Winner:** 30—Davey Allison 11/1/92
**Closest Margin of Victory:** 0.17 Seconds, Mark Martin defeated Ernie Irvan 10/31/93
**Greatest Margin of Victory:** 11.44 seconds, Davey Allison defeated Darrell Waltrip 11/03/91

## QUALIFYING AND RACE RECORDS

### QUALIFYING
**Track:** Rusty Wallace, Ford, 134.178 mph, 26.830 seconds, Nov. 3, 2000.

### RACE
**Track Record (312 miles):** Tony Stewart, Pontiac, 118.132 mph, 2 hours, 38 minutes, 28 seconds, Nov. 7, 1999.

## YEAR BY YEAR WINNERS

| Year | Event | Race Winner | Car Make | Avg. Speed | Start Pos. | Winning Car Owner | Pole Winner |
|---|---|---|---|---|---|---|---|
| 2003 | Checker Auto Parts 500 | D. Earnhardt Jr. | Chevrolet | 93.984 | 11 | Dale Earnhardt, Inc. | R. Newman |
| 2002 | Checker Auto Parts 500 | M. Kenseth | Ford | 113.857 | 28 | Jack Roush | R. Newman |
| 2001 | Checker Auto Parts 500 | J. Burton | Ford | 102.613 | 3 | Jack Roush | C. Atwood |
| 2000 | Checker/Dura-Lube 500 | J. Burton | Ford | 105.041 | 2 | Jack Roush | R. Wallace |
| 1999 | Dura-Lube 500 | T. Stewart | Pontiac | 118.132 | 11 | Joe Gibbs | J. Andretti |
| 1998 | Dura-Lube 500 | R. Wallace | Ford | 108.211 | 6 | Roger Penske | K. Schrader |
| 1997 | Dura-Lube 500 | D. Jarrett | Ford | 110.824 | 9 | Robert Yates | B. Hamilton |
| 1996 | Dura-Lube 500 | B. Hamilton | Pontiac | 109.709 | 17 | Petty Enterprises | B. Labonte |
| 1995 | Dura-Lube 500 | R. Rudd | Ford | 100.300 | 29 | Ricky Rudd | B. Elliott |
| 1994 | Slick 50 500 | T. Labonte | Chevrolet | 107.463 | 19 | Rick Hendrick | S. Marlin |
| 1993 | Slick 50 500 | M. Martin | Ford | 100.375 | 3 | Jack Roush | B. Elliott |
| 1992 | Pyroil 500 | Da. Allison | Ford | 103.885 | 12 | Robert Yates | R. Wallace |
| 1991 | Pyroil 500 | Da. Allison | Ford | 95.746 | 13 | Robert Yates | G. Bodine |
| 1990 | | Earnhardt | Chevrolet | 96.786 | 3 | Richard Childress | R. Wallace |
| 1989 | Autoworks 500 | Elliott | | 105.683 | 13 | Melling Racing | Schrader |
| 1988 | Checker 500 | Kulwicki | Ford | 90.457 | 21 | Alan Kulwicki | G. Bodine |

a Race shortened to 257 miles, rain.

## ALL PHOENIX RACES

### POLE WINNERS
| | |
|---|---|
| R. Wallace | 3 |
| G. Bodine | 2 |
| B. Elliott | 2 |
| Schrader | 2 |
| R. Newman | 2 |
| S. Marlin | 1 |
| B. Labonte | 1 |
| B. Hamilton | 1 |
| J. Andretti | 1 |
| C. Atwood | 1 |

### RACE WINNERS
| | |
|---|---|
| J. Burton | 2 |
| Da. Allison | 2 |
| Kulwicki | 1 |
| Elliott | 1 |
| Earnhardt | 1 |
| M. Martin | 1 |
| T. Labonte | 1 |
| B. Hamilton | 1 |
| R. Rudd | 1 |
| D. Jarrett | 1 |
| R. Wallace | 1 |
| T. Stewart | 1 |
| M. Kenseth | 1 |
| Earnhardt Jr. | 1 |

### QUALIFYING RECORD
Kevin Harvick, Chevrolet; 132.930 mph; October 31, 2003

### RACE RECORD
Jeff Burton, Pontiac; 115.145 mph (1 hr., 44 min., 13 sec.); November 4, 2000.

# BUSCH SERIES

## YEAR BY YEAR WINNERS

| Year | Event | Pole Winner | Speed | Race Winner | Started |
|---|---|---|---|---|---|
| 1999 | Outback Steakhouse 200 | K. Schrader | 129.580 | J. Gordon | 3 |
| 2000 | Outback Steakhouse 200 | J. Leffler | 130.957 | J. Burton | 3 |
| 2001 | Outback Steakhouse 200 | J. Spencer | 131.339 | G. Biffle | 4 |
| 2002 | Bashas' Supermarkets 200 | G. Biffle | 132.193 | S. Wimmer | 18 |
| 2003 | Bashas' Supermarkets 200 | K. Harvick | 132.930 | B. Hamilton Jr. | 4 |

### POLE WINNERS
| | | | |
|---|---|---|---|
| Gant | 3 | Ken Schrader | 1 |
| Greg Biffle | 1 | Jimmy Spencer | 1 |
| Jason Leffler | 1 | Kevin Harvick | 1 |

### RACE WINNERS
| | | | |
|---|---|---|---|
| Greg Biffle | 1 | Scott Wimmer | 1 |
| Jeff Burton | 1 | Bobby Hamilton Jr. | 1 |
| Jeff Gordon | 1 | | |

# CRAFTSMAN TRUCK SERIES

## YEAR BY YEAR WINNERS

| Year | Event | Pole Winner | Speed | Race Winner | Started |
|---|---|---|---|---|---|
| 1995 | Skoal Copper World | Ron Hornaday Jr. | 123.665 | Mike Skinner | 16 |
| 1995 | GM Goodwrench 200 | Jack Sprague | 124.378 | Mike Skinner | 3 |
| 1996 | Chevrolet Desert Star Classic | Mike Skinner | 125.257 | Jack Sprague | 2 |
| 1996 | GM Goodwrench 300 | Jack Sprague | 126.957 | Jack Sprague | 1 |
| 1997 | Chevy Trucks Desert Star | Jack Sprague | 121.236 | Jack Sprague | 1 |
| 1997 | GM Goodwrench 300 | Mike Bliss | 127.741 | Joe Ruttman | 7 |
| 1998 | Chevy Trucks Desert Star | Stacy Compton | 127.596 | Ron Hornaday Jr. | 4 |
| 1998 | GM Goodwrench 300 | Mike Bliss | 127.155 | Mike Bliss | 1 |
| 1999 | Chevy Trucks NASCAR 150 | Jack Sprague | 128.402 | Ron Hornaday Jr. | 5 |
| 2000 | Chevy Trucks NASCAR 150 | Joe Ruttman | 129.204 | Joe Ruttman | 1 |
| 2001 | Chevy Silverado 150 | Stacy Compton | 127.700 | Greg Biffle | 11 |
| 2002 | Chevy Silverado 150 | Rick Crawford | 128.329 | Kevin Harvick | 3 |
| 2003 | Chevy Silverado 150 | Ted Musgrave | 129.427 | Kevin Harvick | 2 |

### QUALIFYING RECORD
Ted Musgrave, Dodge; 129.427 mph, October 29, 2003

### RACE RECORD
Kevin Harvick, Chevrolet; 108.014 mph (1 hr., 24 min., 26 sec.); Nov. 8, 2002

### POLE WINNERS
| | |
|---|---|
| Mike Bliss | 2 |
| Stacy Compton | 2 |
| Rick Crawford | 1 |
| Ron Hornaday Jr. | 1 |
| Joe Ruttman | 1 |
| Mike Skinner | 1 |
| Ted Musgrave | 1 |

### RACE WINNERS
| | |
|---|---|
| Jack Sprague | 3 |
| Ron Hornaday Jr. | 2 |
| Joe Ruttman | 2 |
| Mike Skinner | 2 |
| Kevin Harvick | 2 |
| Greg Biffle | 1 |
| Mike Bliss | 1 |

# Pocono Raceway

## TRACK FACTS
**Date Opened:** October 20, 1968
**Owner:** Pocono Raceway, Inc.
**CEO:** Dr. Joseph Mattioli
**Distance:** 2.5 miles
**Banking in Turn 1:** 14 degrees
**Banking in Turn 2:** 8 degrees
**Banking in Turn 3:** 6 degrees
**Length of Frontstretch:** 3,740 feet
**Length of Shortstretch:** 1,780 feet
**Length of Backstretch:** 3,055 feet
**Grandstand Seating:** 70,000
**Tickets:** (800) 722-3939
**Website:** www.poconoraceway.com

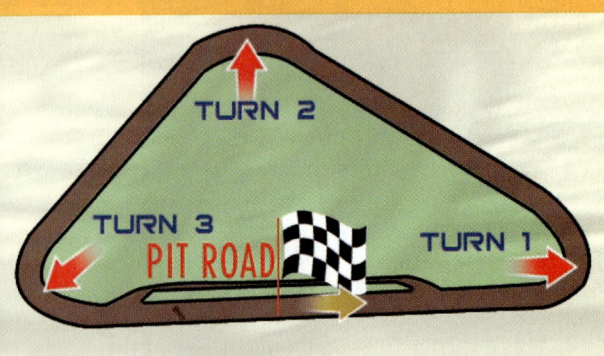

### 2004 SCHEDULE
**NEXTEL Cup**
**Pocono 500**
Race: No. 14 of 36
Date: June 13
TV: FOX. Radio: MRN
**Pennsylvania 500**
Race: No. 20 of 36
Date: August 1
TV: TNT. Radio: MRN

## NEXTEL CUP

### TRACK RECORDS
**Most Wins:** 5—Bill Elliott
**Oldest Winner:** Harry Gant, 50 years, 5 months, 7 days, 6/17/1990
**Youngest Winner:** Jeff Gordon, 24 years, 10 months, 12 days, 6/16/1996
**Most Lead Changes:** 56—7/30/79
**Fewest Lead Changes:** 9—7/26/98
**Most Leaders:** 16—Twice, most recently 6/8/03
**Fewest Leaders:** 4—Twice, most recently, 6/9/85
**Most Cautions:** 13—6/17/90
**Fewest Cautions:** 1—7/30/78
**Most Caution Laps:** 53—6/8/86
**Fewest Caution Laps:** 3—7/30/78
**Most on the Lead Lap:** 26—7/28/02
**Fewest on the Lead Lap:** 2—Twice, most recently, 6/6/82
**Most Running at the Finish:** 39—7/29/01
**Fewest Running at the Finish:** 18—7/25/82
**Most Laps Led by a Race Winner:** 164—Jeff Gordon, 7/26/98
**Fewest Laps Led by a Race Winner:** 4—Bobby Labonte, 7/29/01
**Closest Margin of Victory:** 0.02 Second, Bill Elliott defeated Harry Gant 06/09/85
**Greatest Margin of Victory:** 24 Seconds, Richard Petty defeated Buddy Baker 08/01/76

### QUALIFYING AND RACE RECORDS
**QUALIFYING**
**Track:** Tony Stewart, Pontiac, 172.391 mph, 52.207 seconds, July 21, 2000 (Pennsylvania 500).
**Spring Race (Pocono 500):** Rusty Wallace, Ford, 171.625 mph, 52.440 seconds, June 17, 2000.
**Fall Race (Pennsylvania 500):** Tony Stewart, Pontiac, 172.391 mph, 52.207 seconds, July 21, 2000.

**RACE**
**Track:** Rusty Wallace, Ford, 144.892 mph, 3 hours, 27 minutes, 03 seconds, July 21, 1996 (Miller Genuine Draft 500).
**Spring Race (Pocono 500):** Alan Kulwicki, Ford, 144.023 mph, 3 hours, 28 minutes, 18 seconds, June 14, 1992.
**Fall Race (Pennsylvania 500):** Rusty Wallace, Ford, 144.892 mph, 3 hours, 27 minutes, 3 seconds, July 21, 1996.

## YEAR BY YEAR WINNERS

| Year | Event | Race Winner | Car Make | Avg. Speed | Start Pos. | Winning Car Owner | Pole Winner |
|---|---|---|---|---|---|---|---|
| 2003 | Pennsylvania 500 | R. Newman | Dodge | 127.705 | 1 | Roger Penske | R. Newman |
|  | Pocono 500 | T. Stewart | Chevrolet | 134.892 | 4 | Joe Gibbs | J. Johnson |
| 2002 | Pennsylvania 500 | B. Elliott | Dodge | 125.809 | 1 | Ray Evernham | B. Elliott |
|  | Pocono 500 | D. Jarrett | Ford | 143.426 | 13 | Robert Yates | TrialsRainedOut |
| 2001 | Pennsylvania 500 | B. Labonte | Pontiac | 134.590 | 11 | Joe Gibbs | T. Bodine |
|  | Pocono 500 | R. Rudd | Ford | 134.389 | 1 | Robert Yates | R. Rudd |
| 2000 | Pennsylvania 500 | R. Wallace | Ford | 130.662 | 2 | Roger Penske | T. Stewart |
|  | Pocono 500 | J. Mayfield | Ford | 139.741 | 22 | Penske-Kranefuss | R. Wallace |
| 1999 | Pennsylvania 500 | B. Labonte | Pontiac | 116.982 | 4 | Joe Gibbs | M. Skinner |
|  | Pocono 500 | B. Labonte | Pontiac | 118.898 | 3 | Joe Gibbs | S. Marlin |
| 1998 | Pennsylvania 500 | J. Gordon | Chevrolet | 134.660 | 2 | Rick Hendrick | W. Burton |
|  | Pocono 500 | J. Mayfield | Ford | 117.801 | 3 | Penske-Kranefuss | J. Gordon |
| 1997 | Pennsylvania 500 | D. Jarrett | Ford | 142.068 | 4 | Robert Yates | J. Nemechek |
|  | Pocono 500 | J. Gordon | Chevrolet | 139.828 | 11 | Rick Hendrick | B. Hamilton |
| 1996 | Miller 500 | R. Wallace | Ford | 144.892 | 13 | Roger Penske | M. Martin |
|  | Teamwork 500 | J. Gordon | Chevrolet | 139.104 | 1 | Rick Hendrick | J. Gordon |
| 1995 | Miller 500 | D. Jarrett | Ford | 134.038 | 15 | Robert Yates | B. Elliott |
|  | Teamwork 500 | T. Labonte | Chevrolet | 137.720 | 27 | Rick Hendrick | K. Schrader |
| 1994 | Miller 500 | G. Bodine | Ford | 136.075 | 1 | Geoff Bodine | G. Bodine |
|  | Teamwork 500 | R. Wallace | Ford | 128.801 | 1 | Roger Penske | R. Wallace |

## ALL POCONO RACES

| POLE WINNERS | | | | RACE WINNERS | | | |
|---|---|---|---|---|---|---|---|
| Schrader | 5 | Irvan | 1 | Elliott | 5 | Bonnett | 1 |
| Elliott | 5 | Buddy Baker | 1 | D. Waltrip | 4 | Pearson | 1 |
| D. Waltrip | 3 | Da. Allison | 1 | Richmond | 4 | Kulwicki | 1 |
| Yarborough | 3 | B. Hamilton | 1 | R. Wallace | 4 | K. Petty | 1 |
| M. Martin | 3 | Nemechek | 1 | G. Bodine | 3 | Rudd | 1 |
| R. Wallace | 3 | W. Burton | 1 | J. Gordon | 3 | Newman | 1 |
| Gant | 2 | Marlin | 1 | B. Labonte | 3 | Stewart | 1 |
| Richmond | 2 | M. Skinner | 1 | B. Allison | 3 | | |
| Kulwicki | 2 | Stewart | 1 | D. Jarrett | 3 | | |
| G. Bodine | 2 | Rudd | 1 | Gant | 2 | | |
| J. Gordon | 2 | T. Bodine | 1 | Earnhardt | 2 | | |
| Parsons | 1 | Newman | 1 | R. Petty | 2 | | |
| Pearson | 1 | Ji. Johnson | 1 | Yarborough | 2 | | |
| T. Labonte | 1 | | | T. Labonte | 2 | | |
| Shepherd | 1 | | | Mayfield | 2 | | |
| B. Allison | 1 | | | Parsons | 1 | | |

## YEAR BY YEAR WINNERS

| Year | Event | Race Winner | Car Make | Avg. Speed | Start Pos. | Winning Car Owner | Pole Winner |
|---|---|---|---|---|---|---|---|
| 1993 | Miller 500 | Earnhardt | Chevrolet | 133.343 | 11 | Richard Childress | Schrader |
| | Champion SP 500 | K. Petty | Pontiac | 138.005 | 8 | Felix Sabates | Schrader |
| 1992 | Miller 500 | D. Waltrip | Chevrolet | 134.058 | 8 | D. Waltrip | Da. Allison |
| | Champion SP 500 | Kulwicki | Ford | 144.023 | 6 | Alan Kulwicki | Schrader |
| f 1991 | Miller 500 | R. Wallace | Pontiac | 115.459 | 10 | Roger Penske | Kulwicki |
| | Champion SP 500 | D. Waltrip | Chevrolet | 122.666 | 13 | D. Waltrip | Martin |
| 1990 | AC S. Plug 500 | G. Bodine | Ford | 124.070 | 4 | Junior Johnson | Martin |
| | Miller Draft 500 | Gant | Oldsmobile | 120.600 | 16 | Jackson Bros. | Irvan |
| 1989 | AC S. Plug 500 | Elliott | Ford | 117.847 | 14 | Melling Racing | Schrader |
| | Miller HL 500 | Labonte | Ford | 131.320 | 23 | Junior Johnson | Wallace |
| 1988 | AC S. Plug 500 | Elliott | Ford | 122.866 | 2 | Melling Racing | Shepherd |
| | Miller HL 500 | G. Bodine | Chevrolet | 126.147 | 3 | Rick Hendrick | Kulwicki |
| 1987 | Summer 500 | Earnhardt | Chevrolet | 121.745 | 16 | Richard Childress | Richmond |
| | Miller HL 500 | Richmond | Chevrolet | 122.166 | 3 | Rick Hendrick | Labonte |
| e 1986 | Summer 500 | Richmond | Chevrolet | 124.218 | 5 | Rick Hendrick | Gant |
| | Miller HL 500 | Richmond | Chevrolet | 113.166 | 3 | Rick Hendrick | Bodine |
| d 1985 | Summer 500 | Elliott | Ford | 134.008 | 2 | Melling Racing | Elliott |
| | Van Scoy 500 | Elliott | Ford | 138.974 | 1 | Melling Racing | Elliott |
| 1984 | Like Cola 500 | Gant | Chevrolet | 121.351 | 3 | Mach 1 | Elliott |
| c | Van Scoy 500 | C. Yarborough | Chevrolet | 138.164 | 12 | Ranier Racing | Pearson |
| 1983 | Like Cola 500 | Richmond | Pontiac | 114.818 | 1 | Blue Max | Richmond |
| | Van Scoy 500 | B. Allison | Buick | 128.636 | 7 | DiGard Rac. Co. | Waltrip |
| 1982 | Mt. Dew 500 | B. Allison | Buick | 115.496 | 4 | DiGard Rac. Co. | C. Yarborough |
| b | Van Scoy 500 | B. Allison | Buick | 113.579 | 3 | DiGard Rac. Co. | Rained Out |
| 1981 | Mt. Dew 500 | Waltrip | Buick | 119.111 | 1 | Junior Johnson | Waltrip |
| 1980 | Coca-Cola 500 | Bonnett | Mercury | 124.395 | 2 | Wood Brothers | C. Yarborough |
| * 1979 | Coca-Cola 500 | C. Yarborough | Chevrolet | 115.207 | 2 | Junior Johnson | Gant |
| 1978 | Coca-Cola 500 | Waltrip | Chevrolet | 142.540 | 4 | DiGard Rac. Co. | Parsons |
| 1977 | Coca-Cola 500 | Parsons | Chevrolet | 128.379 | 4 | L.G. DeWitt | Waltrip |
| 1976 | Purolator 500 | R. Petty | Dodge | 115.875 | 5 | Petty Eng. | C. Yarborough |
| 1975 | Purolator 500 | Pearson | Mercury | 111.179 | 2 | Wood Brothers | B. Allison |
| a 1974 | Purolator 500 | R. Petty | Dodge | 115.593 | 3 | Petty Eng. | Buddy Baker |

* Rain delayed event until Monday.
a Race shortened to 480 miles, rain.
b Starting lineup determined by NASCAR Winston Cup car owner point standings.
c Pearson qualified Neil Bonnett's car.
d Elliott awarded pole 2 1/2 weeks after race when test showed pole winner used illegal fuel.
e Race shortened to 375 miles, rain.
f Race shortened to 447.5 miles, rain.
g Race shortened to 437.5 miles, rain.

## SPRING: Pocono 500

### POLE WINNERS
| | | | |
|---|---|---|---|
| Schrader | 3 | Pearson | 1 |
| R. Wallace | 3 | Kulwicki | 1 |
| J. Gordon | 2 | B. Hamilton | 1 |
| Martin | 1 | Marlin | 1 |
| Irvan | 1 | Rudd | 1 |
| T. Labonte | 1 | Ji. Johnson | 1 |
| G. Bodine | 1 | | |
| Elliott | 1 | | |
| D. Waltrip | 1 | | |

### RACE WINNERS
| | | | |
|---|---|---|---|
| J. Gordon | 2 | Yarborough | 1 |
| B. Allison | 2 | Kulwicki | 1 |
| Richmond | 2 | R. Wallace | 1 |
| T. Labonte | 2 | B. Labonte | 1 |
| Mayfield | 2 | K. Petty | 1 |
| Gant | 1 | Rudd | 1 |
| D. Waltrip | 1 | D. Jarrett | 1 |
| G. Bodine | 1 | Stewart | 1 |
| Elliott | 1 | | |

## FALL: Pennsylvania 500

### POLE WINNERS
| | | | |
|---|---|---|---|
| Elliott | 4 | Buddy Baker | 1 |
| Yarborough | 3 | Kulwicki | 1 |
| D. Waltrip | 2 | Da. Allison | 1 |
| Schrader | 2 | G. Bodine | 1 |
| Gant | 2 | W. Burton | 1 |
| Richmond | 2 | Skinner | 1 |
| Martin | 2 | Stewart | 1 |
| Shepherd | 1 | Nemechek | 1 |
| B. Parsons | 1 | T. Bodine | 1 |
| B. Allison | 1 | Newman | 1 |

### RACE WINNERS
| | | | |
|---|---|---|---|
| Elliott | 4 | B. Parsons | 1 |
| D. Waltrip | 3 | Pearson | 1 |
| R. Wallace | 3 | Yarborough | 1 |
| B. Labonte | 2 | Bonnett | 1 |
| Earnhardt | 2 | B. Allison | 1 |
| G. Bodine | 2 | J. Gordon | 1 |
| R. Petty | 2 | Newman | 1 |
| Richmond | 2 | | |
| D. Jarrett | 2 | | |
| Gant | 1 | | |

# Richmond International Raceway

## TRACK FACTS
**Date Opened:** October 12, 1946
**Owner:** ISC
**President:** Douglas S. Fritz
**Distance:** .750 miles
**Banking in Turns:** 14 degrees
**Banking on Frontstretch:** 8 degrees
**Banking on Backstretch:** 2 degrees
**Length of Frontstretch:** 1,290 feet
**Length of Backstretch:** 860 feet
**Grandstand Seating:** 105,000
**Tickets:** (804) 345-7223
**Website:** www.rir.com

## 2004 SCHEDULE

### NEXTEL Cup
**Richmond 400**
Race: No. 11 of 36
Date: May 15
TV: FX. Radio: MRN

**Chevy Monte Carlo 400**
Race: No. 26 of 36
Date: September 11
TV: TNT. Radio: MRN

### Busch Series
**TBD**
Race: No. 11 of 34
Date: May 14
TV: FX. Radio: MRN

**Funai 250**
Race: No. 26 of 34
Date: September 10
TV: TNT. Radio: MRN

### Craftsman Truck Series
**NASCAR Craftsman Truck Series 200**
Race: No. 17 of 25
Date: September 9
TV: SPEED. Radio: MRN

## NEXTEL CUP
### TRACK RECORDS
**Most Wins:** 9—Richard Petty
**Oldest Winner:** Harry Gant, 51 Years, 7 months, 28 days, 9/7/1991
**Youngest Winner:** Richard Petty, 23 years, 9 months, 21 days, 4/23/1961
**Most Lead Changes:** 25—Twice, most recently, 3/3/96
**Fewest Lead Changes:** 2—7 times, most recently, 2/23/75

## YEAR BY YEAR WINNERS

| Year | Event | Race Winner | Car Make | Avg. Speed | Start Pos. | Winning Car Owner | Pole Winner |
|------|-------|-------------|----------|------------|------------|-------------------|-------------|
| 2003 | Chevy Rock & Roll 400 | R. Newman | Dodge | 94.945 | 11 | Roger Penske | M. Skinner |
|      | Pontiac Excitement 400 | J. Nemechek | Chevrolet | 126.511 | 2 | Joe Hendrick | T. Labonte |
| 2002 | Chevrolet 400 | M. Kenseth | Ford | 94.787 | 25 | Jack Roush | J. Johnson |
|      | Pontiac 400 | T. Stewart | Pontiac | 86.824 | 3 | Joe Gibbs | W. Burton |
| 2001 | Chevrolet 400 | R. Rudd | Ford | 95.146 | 9 | Robert Yates | J. Gordon |
|      | Pontiac 400 | T. Stewart | Pontiac | 95.872 | 7 | Joe Gibbs | M. Martin |
| 2000 | Chevrolet 400 | J. Gordon | Chevrolet | 99.871 | 13 | Rick Hendrick | J. Burton |
|      | Pontiac 400 | D. Earnhardt Jr. | Chevrolet | 99.374 | 5 | Dale Earnhardt | R. Wallace |
| 1999 | Exide Batteries 400 | T. Stewart | Pontiac | 104.006 | 2 | Joe Gibbs | M. Skinner |
|      | Pontiac 400 | D. Jarrett | Ford | 100.102 | 21 | Robert Yates | J. Gordon |
| 1998 | Exide Batteries 400 | J. Burton | Ford | 91.985 | 3 | Jack Roush | R. Wallace |
|      | Pontiac 400 | T. Labonte | Chevrolet | 97.044 | 16 | Rick Hendrick | J. Gordon |
| 1997 | Exide Batteries 400 | D. Jarrett | Ford | 108.707 | 23 | Robert Yates | B. Elliott |
|      | Pontiac 400 | R. Wallace | Ford | 108.499 | 3 | Roger Penske | Start Via Points |
| 1996 | Miller 400 | E. Irvan | Ford | 105.469 | 16 | Robert Yates | M. Martin |
|      | Pontiac 400 | J. Gordon | Chevrolet | 102.750 | 2 | Rick Hendrick | T. Labonte |
| 1995 | Miller 400 | R. Wallace | Ford | 104.459 | 7 | Roger Penske | D. Earnhardt |
|      | Pontiac 400 | T. Labonte | Chevrolet | 106.425 | 24 | Rick Hendrick | J. Gordon |
| 1994 | Miller 400 | T. Labonte | Chevrolet | 104.156 | 3 | Rick Hendrick | T. Musgrave |
|      | Pontiac 400 | E. Irvan | Ford | 98.334 | 7 | Robert Yates | T. Musgrave |
| 1993 | Miller 400 | R. Wallace | Pontiac | 99.917 | 3 | Roger Penske | B. Labonte |
|      | Da. Allison | | Ford | 107.709 | 14 | Robert Yates | Schrader |
| 1992 | Miller 400 | R. Wallace | Pontiac | 104.661 | 3 | Roger Penske | Irvan |
|      | Pontiac 400 | Elliott | Ford | 104.378 | 1 | Junior Johnson | Elliott |
| 1991 | Miller 400 | Gant | Oldsmobile | 101.361 | 13 | Leo Jackson | R. Wallace |
|      | Pontiac 400 | Earnhardt | Chevrolet | 105.397 | 19 | Richard Childress | Da. Allison |
| 1990 | Miller High Life 400 | Earnhardt | Chevrolet | 95.567 | 6 | Richard Childress | Irvan |
|      | Pontiac 400 | Martin | Ford | 92.158 | 6 | Jack Roush | Rudd |
| 1989 | Miller High Life 400 | R. Wallace | Pontiac | 88.380 | 6 | Blue Max | Elliott |
|      | Pontiac 400 | R. Wallace | Pontiac | 89.619 | 2 | Blue Max | G. Bodine |
| 1988 | Miller High Life 400 | Da. Allison | Ford | 95.770 | 1 | Ranier Racing | Da. Allison |
|      | Pontiac 400 | Bonnett | Pontiac | 66.401 | 3 | Rahmoc | Shepherd |
| 1987 | Wrangler Indigo 400 | Earnhardt | Chevrolet | 67.074 | 8 | Richard Childress | Kulwicki |
|      | Miller High Life 400 | Earnhardt | Chevrolet | 81.520 | 3 | Richard Childress | Kulwicki |
| 1986 | Wrangler Indigo 400 | Richmond | Chevrolet | 70.161 | 4 | Rick Hendrick | Gant |
|      | Miller High Life 400 | K. Petty | Ford | 71.078 | 12 | Wood Brothers | Start Via Points |
| 1985 | Wrangler SanforSet 400 | Waltrip | Chevrolet | 72.508 | 22 | Junior Johnson | Bodine |
|      | Miller High Life 400 | Earnhardt | Chevrolet | 67.945 | 4 | Richard Childress | Waltrip |
| 1984 | Wrangler SanforSet 400 | Waltrip | Chevrolet | 74.780 | 1 | Junior Johnson | Waltrip |
|      | Miller High Life 400 | Rudd | Ford | 76.736 | 4 | Bud Moore | Waltrip |
| 1983 | Wrangler SanforSet 400 | B. Allison | Buick | 79.381 | 6 | DiGard Rac. Co. | Waltrip |
|      | Richmond 400 | B. Allison | Chevrolet | 79.584 | 6 | DiGard Rac. Co. | Rudd |
| 1982 | Wrangler SanforSet 400 | B. Allison | Chevrolet | 82.800 | 1 | DiGard Rac. Co. | B. Allison |
|      | Richmond 400 | Marcis | Chevrolet | 72.914 | 6 | Dave Marcis | Waltrip |
| 1981 | Wrangler SanforSet 400 | Parsons | Ford | 69.998 | 4 | Bud Moore | Martin |
|      | Richmond 400 | Waltrip | Buick | 76.570 | 7 | Junior Johnson | Shepherd |
| 1980 | Capital City 400 | B. Allison | Ford | 79.722 | 2 | Bud Moore | C. Yarborough |
|      | Richmond 400 | Waltrip | Chevrolet | 67.703 | 5 | DiGard Rac. Co. | Waltrip |
| 1979 | Capital City 400 | B. Allison | Ford | 80.604 | 2 | Bud Moore | Earnhardt |
|      | Richmond 400 | C. Yarborough | Oldsmobile | 83.608 | 9 | Junior Johnson | B. Allison |
| 1978 | Capital City 400 | Waltrip | Chevrolet | 79.568 | 2 | DiGard Rac. Co. | Waltrip |
|      | Richmond 400 | Parsons | Chevrolet | 80.304 | 3 | L.G. DeWitt | Bonnett |
| 1977 | Capital City 400 | Bonnett | Dodge | 80.644 | 2 | Jim Stacy | Parsons |
|      | Richmond 400 | C. Yarborough | Chevrolet | 73.084 | 7 | Junior Johnson | Bonnett |
| 1976 | Capital City 400 | C. Yarborough | Chevrolet | 77.993 | 6 | Junior Johnson | Parsons |
|      | Richmond 400 | Marcis | Dodge | 72.792 | 2 | Nord Krauskopf | B. Allison |
| 1975 | Capital City 500 | Waltrip | Chevrolet | 81.886 | 5 | DiGard Rac. Co. | Parsons |
|      | Richmond 500 | R. Petty | Dodge | 74.913 | 1 | Petty Eng. | R. Petty |
| 1974 | Capital City 500 | R. Petty | Dodge | 64.430 | 1 | Petty Eng. | R. Petty |
|      | Richmond 500 | B. Allison | Chevrolet | 80.095 | 1 | Bobby Allison | B. Allison |
| 1973 | Capital City 500 | R. Petty | Dodge | 63.215 | 5 | Petty Eng. | B. Allison |
|      | Richmond 500 | R. Petty | Dodge | 74.764 | 8 | Petty Eng. | B. Allison |
| 1972 | Capital City 500 | R. Petty | Plymouth | 75.899 | 3 | Petty Eng. | B. Allison |
|      | Richmond 500 | R. Petty | Plymouth | 76.258 | 3 | Petty Eng. | B. Allison |
| 1971 | Capital City 500 | R. Petty | Plymouth | 80.025 | 11 | Petty Eng. | B. Allison |
|      | Richmond 500 | R. Petty | Plymouth | 79.836 | 28 | Petty Eng. | Marcis |
| 1970 | Capital City 500 | R. Petty | Plymouth | 81.476 | 1 | Petty Eng. | R. Petty |
|      | Richmond 500 | Hylton | Ford | 82.044 | 3 | Hylton Eng. | R. Petty |
| 1969 | Capital City 500 | B. Allison | Dodge | 76.388 | 26 | Mario Rossi | R. Petty |
|      | Richmond 250 | Pearson | Ford | 73.752 | 1 | Holman-Moody | Pearson |
| 1968 | Capital City 300 | R. Petty | Plymouth | 85.659 | 1 | Petty Eng. | R. Petty |
|      | Richmond 250 | Pearson | Ford | 65.217 | 16 | Holman-Moody | Isaac |
| 1967 | Capital City 300 | R. Petty | Plymouth | 57.631 | 2 | Petty Eng. | Draw Position |
|      | Richmond 250 | R. Petty | Plymouth | 65.982 | 1 | Petty Eng. | R. Petty |
| 1966 | Capital City 300 | Pearson | Dodge | 62.886 | 1 | Cotton Owens | Pearson |
|      | Richmond 250 | Pearson | Dodge | 66.539 | 4 | Cotton Owens | Pistone |
| 1965 | Capital City 300 | Pearson | Dodge | 60.983 | 2 | Cotton Owens | Hutcherson |
|      | Richmond 250 | Johnson | Ford | 61.416 | 1 | Junior Johnson | Johnson |
| 1964 | Capital City 300 | Owens | Dodge | 61.955 | 3 | Cotton Owens | Jarrett |
|      | Richmond 250 | Pearson | Dodge | 58.660 | 10 | Cotton Owens | Jarrett |
| 1963 | Capital City 300 | Jarrett | Ford | 66.339 | 7 | Bob Robinson | Weatherly |
|      | Richmond 250 | Weatherly | Pontiac | 58.624 | 3 | Bud Moore | White |

## NEXTEL CUP

**Most Leaders:** 16—9/10/94
**Fewest Leaders:** 2—8 times, most recently, 3/11/79
**Most Laps Led in a 400 Laps race:** 369, Bobby Allison, 09/09/1979
**Most Cautions:** 15—5/3/03
**Fewest Cautions:** 0—3/7/76
**Most Caution Laps:** 123—Twice, most recently, 9/8/74
**Fewest Caution Laps:** 0—3/7/76
**Most on the Lead Lap:** 22—5/6/00
**Fewest on the Lead Lap:** 1—22 times, most recently, 10/12/75
**Most Running at the Finish:** 39—3 times, most recently, 9/11/99
**Fewest Running at the Finish:** 1—4/19/53
**Most Laps Led by a Race Winner:** 488—David Pearson 9/13/70
**Fewest Laps Led by a Race Winner:** 4—Kyle Petty 2/23/86
**Closest Margin of Victory:** 0.051 second, Jeff Burton defeated Jeff Gordon 09/12/98
**Greatest Margin of Victory:** 6 Laps plus, Richard Petty defeated Lennie Pond 02/23/75

## QUALIFYING AND RACE RECORDS

### QUALIFYING
**Track:** Ward Burton, Dodge, 127.389 mph, 21.195 seconds, May 4, 2002 (Pontiac Excitement 400).
**Spring Race (Pontiac Excitement 400):** Ward Burton, Dodge, 127.389 mph, 21.195 seconds, May 4, 2002.
**Fall Race (Chevy Rock & Roll 400):** Jimmie Johnson, Chevrolet, 126.145 mph, 21.404 seconds, Sept. 6, 2002.
**Dirt:** Tom Pistone, Ford, 70.978 mph, 25.360 seconds, May 15, 1966, .5-mile track (Richmond 250).

### RACE
**Track Record (300 miles):** Dale Jarrett, Ford, 109.047 mph, 2 hours, 45 minutes, 04 seconds, Sept. 6, 1997 (Exide Batteries 400).
**Spring Race (Pontiac Excitement 400):** Rusty Wallace, Ford, 108.499 mph, 2 hours, 45 minutes, 54 seconds, March 2, 1997.
**Fall Race (Chevy Rock & Roll 400):** Dale Jarrett, Ford, 109.047 mph, 2 hours, 45 minutes, 04 seconds, Sept. 6, 1997.
**271 Miles:** James Hylton, Ford, 82.044 mph, March 1, 1970, .542-mile track (Richmond 500).
**250 Miles:** Bobby Allison, Dodge, 76.388 mph, Sept. 7, 1969, .5625-mile track (Capital City 250).
**216.8 Miles:** Cale Yarborough, Oldsmobile, 83.608 mph, March 11, 1979, .542-mile track (Richmond 400).
**187.5 Miles:** Richard Petty, Plymouth, 85.659 mph, Sept. 8, 1968, .625-mile track (Capital City 300).
**150 Miles:** Ned Jarrett, Ford, 66.339 mph, Sept. 8, 1963, .5-mile dirt track (Capital City 300).
**125 Miles:** David Pearson, Dodge 66.539 mph, May 15, 1966, .5-mile dirt track (Richmond 250).

# YEAR BY YEAR WINNERS

| Year | Event | Race Winner | Car Make | Avg. Speed | Start Pos. | Winning Car Owner | Pole Winner |
|---|---|---|---|---|---|---|---|
| | 1962 | Capital City 300 | Weatherly | Pontiac | 64.980 | 2 | Bud Moore | White |
| b | | Richmond 250 | White | Chevrolet | 51.360 | 20 | Louis Clements | Draw Position |
| | 1961 | Capital City 250 | Weatherly | Pontiac | 61.680 | 7 | Bud Moore | Johnson |
| a | | Richmond 200 | R. Petty | Plymouth | 62.460 | 1 | Petty Eng. | R. Petty |
| | 1960 | Capital City 200 | S. Thompson | | | 3 | | N. Jarrett |
| | | Richmond 300 | Lee Petty | | | 10 | Petty Eng. | N. Jarrett |
| | 1959 | Capital City 200 | C. Owens | | | 1 | | C. Owens |
| | | Richmond 200 | T. Pistone | | | 12 | | Buck Baker |
| | 1958 | Capital City 200 | S. Thompson | | | 1 | | S. Thompson |
| | 1957 | Richmond 200 | P. Goldsmith | | | 7 | | Hepler |
| | 1956 | Richmond 200 | Buck Baker | | | 1 | | Buck Baker |
| | 1955 | Richmond 200 | Tim Flock | | | 22 | | No Time Trials |
| | 1953 | Richmond 200 | Lee Petty | | | | Petty Eng. | Buck Baker |

\* Night race.
a Last 100-mile, 200-lap race.
b Time trials called off, too wet; race called after 90 miles, 180 laps, darkness.
c Time trials called off; too wet.
d Last race on .5-mile dirt track; distance was 125 miles, 250 laps.
e Track asphalted and remeasured at .625-mile; Distance changed to 187.5 miles, 300 laps.
f Track remeasured at .5625-mile; distance was 250 miles, 462 laps.
g Track remeasured at .5-mile; distance was 250 miles, 500 laps.
h Track remeasured at .542-mile, 500 laps, 271 miles.
i Distance changed from 500 laps, 271 miles, to 400 laps, 216.8 miles.
j Race called after 132.79 miles, 245 laps; rain.
k Race called after 135.5 miles, 250 laps; rain.
l Time trials rained out.
m Track rebuilt to .75 miles.
n Postponed 2-26 – 3-26 due to snow.
o Time trials rained out.
p Race called after 294.75 miles, 393 laps, rain.

# BUSCH SERIES
## YEAR BY YEAR WINNERS

| Year | Event | Pole Winner | Speed | Race Winner | Started |
|---|---|---|---|---|---|
| 1982 | Eastern 150 | G. Bodine | 96.207 | T. Houston | 15 |
| * | Spring 220 | S. Ard | 96.671 | B. Lindley | 3 |
| | Harvest 150 | T. Ellis | 97.046 | B. Lindley | 7 |
| 1983 | Eastern 150 | S. Ard | 96.800 | S. Ard | 1 |
| | Miller Time 150 | T. Ellis | 96.204 | M. Shepherd | 3 |
| 1984 | Wrangler 150 | T. Ellis | 97.814 | S. Ard | 3 |
| | Miller Time 150 | T. Ellis | 97.702 | T. Ellis | 1 |
| 1985 | No Spring race | — | — | — | — |
| | 7-Eleven 150 | J. Hensley | 97.638 | T. Ellis | 3 |
| 1986 | No Spring race | — | — | — | — |
| ** | Freedlander 200 | B. Bodine | 98.218 | D. Earnhardt | 4 |
| 1987 | No Spring race | — | — | — | — |
| | Freedlander 200 | L. Pearson | 98.312 | M. Martin | 16 |
| 1988 | No Spring race | — | — | — | — |
| *** | Commonwealth 200 | H. Gant | 121.218 | H. Gant | 1 |
| 1989 | No Spring race held (snow) | — | — | — | — |
| | Commonwealth 200 | T. Ellis | 118.953 | B. Hamilton | 29 |
| 1990 | Pontiac 200 | M. Waltrip | 118.561 | M. Waltrip | 1 |
| | Autolite 200 | M. Waltrip | 118.974 | R. Mast | 22 |
| 1991 | Pontiac 200 | J. Burton | 118.848 | H. Gant | 11 |
| | Autolite 200 | B. Labonte | 119.617 | H. Gant | 29 |
| 1992 | Hardee's 200 | J. Gordon | 120.466 | H. Gant | 28 |
| | Autolite 200 | T. Bodine | 118.561 | R. Pressley | 14 |
| 1993 | Hardee's 200 | R. Mast | 120.876 | M. Martin | 2 |
| **** | Autolite 250 | C. Bown | 120.903 | M. Martin | 4 |
| 1994 | Hardee's 250 | D. Green | 121.841 | J. Nemechek | 3 |
| | Autolite 250 | J. Keller | 121.968 | K. Wallace | 6 |
| 1995 | Hardee's 250 | None - weather | — | K. Wallace | 21 |
| | Autolite 250 | R. LaJoie | 119.846 | D. Jarrett | 6 |
| 1996 | Hardee's 250 | J. Purvis | 121.114 | J. Purvis | 1 |
| | Autolite 250 | M. Waltrip | 120.444 | K. Wallace | 3 |
| 1997 | Hardee's 250 | None - weather | — | M. Martin | 18 |
| | Autolite 250 | M. Waltrip | 122.227 | S. Park | 2 |
| 1998 | Hardee's 250 | W. Grubb | 123.212 | J. Burton | 8 |
| | Autolite 250 | A. Santerre | 123.604 | D. Earnhardt Jr. | 2 |
| 1999 | Hardee's 250 | J. Keller | 124.907 | M. Martin | 2 |
| | Autolite 250 | J. Burton | 121.984 | D. Earnhardt Jr. | 20 |
| 2000 | Hardee's 250 | D. Green | 123.085 | J. Green | 1 |
| | Autolite/Fram 250 | T. Bodine | 123.768 | J. Burton | 2 |
| 2001 | Hardee's 250 | M. Kenseth | 125.780 | J. Spencer | 3 |
| | Autolite/Fram 250 | J. Green | 125.122 | J. Spencer | 3 |
| 2002 | Hardee's 250 | None - weather | — | J. Keller | |
| | Funai 250 | D. Earnhardt Jr. | 126.868 | D. Earnhardt Jr. | 1 |
| 2003 | Hardee's 250 | M. Waltrip | 125.523 | K. Harvick | 15 |
| | Funai 250 | None-weather | — | Johnny Sauter | 30 |

\* special, one-time race
\*\* race length increased to 200 laps
\*\*\* track enlarged to .750 mile
\*\*\*\* race length increased to 250 laps

# ALL RICHMOND RACES

## POLE WINNERS

| | | | | | |
|---|---|---|---|---|---|
| *B. Allison | 8 | Irvan | 2 | R. Petty | 13 |
| R. Petty | 8 | Musgrave | 2 | B. Allison | 7 |
| Waltrip | 7 | Earnhardt | 2 | R. Wallace | 6 |
| Elliott | 3 | M. Skinner | 2 | Pearson | 6 |
| J. Gordon | 3 | T. Labonte | 2 | Waltrip | 6 |
| Parsons | 3 | Weatherly | 1 | Earnhardt | 5 |
| R. Wallace | 3 | Hutcherson | 1 | T. Labonte | 3 |
| Martin | 3 | Isaac | 1 | Yarborough | 3 |
| Pearson | 2 | *Dennis | 1 | Weatherly | 3 |
| Bonnett | 2 | Yarborough | 1 | Stewart | 3 |
| Kulwicki | 2 | Pistone | 1 | D. Jarrett | 2 |
| Shepherd | 2 | Gant | 1 | Rudd | 2 |
| G. Bodine | 2 | Marcis | 1 | Parsons | 2 |
| Rudd | 2 | Schrader | 1 | Marcis | 2 |
| N. Jarrett | 2 | B. Labonte | 1 | Da. Allison | 2 |
| Johnson | 2 | J. Burton | 1 | Bonnett | 2 |
| White | 2 | W. Burton | 1 | Irvan | 2 |
| Da. Allison | 2 | | | J. Gordon | 2 |

## RACE WINNERS

| | | | |
|---|---|---|---|
| L. Petty | 2 | | |
| Owens | 1 | | |
| Jarrett | 1 | | |
| White | 1 | | |
| K. Petty | 1 | | |
| Richmond | 1 | | |
| Martin | 1 | | |
| Gant | 1 | | |
| Elliott | 1 | | |
| Johnson | 1 | | |
| Hylton | 1 | | |
| J. Burton | 1 | | |
| Earnhardt Jr. | 1 | | |
| Nemechek | 1 | | |
| Newman | 1 | | |

\* The Pole Winner was the Fastest Qualifier in every race except the 1971 Capital City 500. Bill Dennis won the pole, but Bobby Allison was the fastest qualifier.

# SPRING: Richmond 400

## POLE WINNERS

| | | | |
|---|---|---|---|
| B. Allison | 5 | Jarrett | 1 |
| R. Petty | 4 | White | 1 |
| Waltrip | 4 | Kulwicki | 1 |
| J. Gordon | 3 | G. Bodine | 1 |
| Shepherd | 2 | Da. Allison | 1 |
| Rudd | 2 | Elliott | 1 |
| Bonnett | 2 | Schrader | 1 |
| T. Labonte | 2 | Musgrave | 1 |
| Jr. Johnson | 1 | R. Wallace | 1 |
| Marcis | 1 | Martin | 1 |
| Pearson | 1 | W. Burton | 1 |
| Isaac | 1 | | |
| Pistone | 1 | | |

## RACE WINNERS

| | | | |
|---|---|---|---|
| R. Petty | 6 | Jr. Johnson | 1 |
| Pearson | 4 | White | 1 |
| Earnhardt | 3 | Rudd | 1 |
| R. Wallace | 2 | K. Petty | 1 |
| T. Labonte | 2 | Bonnett | 1 |
| Waltrip | 2 | Martin | 1 |
| Yarborough | 2 | Elliott | 1 |
| Marcis | 2 | Da. Allison | 1 |
| B. Allison | 2 | E. Irvan | 1 |
| Stewart | 2 | D. Jarrett | 1 |
| Weatherly | 1 | Earnhardt Jr. | 1 |
| Parsons | 1 | Nemecheck | 1 |
| Hylton | 1 | | |

# FALL: Chevrolet 400

## POLE WINNERS

| | | | |
|---|---|---|---|
| R. Petty | 4 | Jr. Johnson | 1 |
| *B. Allison | 4 | C. Yarborough | 1 |
| Parsons | 3 | Pearson | 1 |
| Waltrip | 3 | Bodine | 1 |
| Irvan | 2 | Gant | 1 |
| Earnhardt | 2 | Kulwicki | 1 |
| Martin | 2 | Da. Allison | 1 |
| B. Elliott | 2 | B. Labonte | 1 |
| R. Wallace | 2 | T. Musgrave | 1 |
| *Dennis | 1 | M. Skinner | 2 |
| Hutcherson | 1 | J. Burton | 1 |
| Jarrett | 1 | J. Gordon | 1 |
| White | 1 | J. Johnson | 1 |
| Weatherly | 1 | | |

## RACE WINNERS

| | | | |
|---|---|---|---|
| R. Petty | 7 | Gant | 1 |
| B. Allison | 5 | T. Labonte | 1 |
| Waltrip | 4 | E. Irvan | 1 |
| R. Wallace | 4 | D. Jarrett | 1 |
| Earnhardt | 2 | J. Burton | 1 |
| Pearson | 2 | T. Stewart | 1 |
| Weatherly | 2 | J. Gordon | 1 |
| C. Yarborough | 1 | R. Rudd | 1 |
| Bonnett | 1 | M. Kenseth | 1 |
| Owens | 1 | Newman | 1 |
| Jarrett | 1 | | |
| Parsons | 1 | | |
| Richmond | 1 | | |
| Da. Allison | 1 | | |

\* The Pole Winner was the Fastest Qualifier in every race.

**BUSCH QUALIFYING RECORD**
Dale Earnhardt Jr., Chevrolet; 126.868 mph (21.282 sec.); September 6, 2002

**BUSCH RACE RECORD**
Dale Jarrett, Ford; 104.928 mph (1 hr., 47 min., 13 sec.); September 8, 1995.

| POLE WINNERS | | | | | RACE WINNERS | | | | | |
|---|---|---|---|---|---|---|---|---|---|---|
| Tommy Ellis | 5 | Chuck Bown | 1 | Randy LaJoie | 1 | Mark Martin | 5 | Dale Earnhardt | 1 | Robert Pressley | 1 |
| Michael Waltrip | 5 | Dale Earnhardt Jr. | 1 | Rick Mast | 1 | Harry Gant | 4 | Jeff Green | 1 | Jeff Purvis | 1 |
| Sam Ard | 2 | Harry Gant | 1 | Larry Pearson | 1 | Kenny Wallace | 3 | Bobby Hamilton | 1 | Morgan Shepherd | 1 |
| Todd Bodine | 2 | Jeff Gordon | 1 | Jeff Purvis | 1 | Sam Ard | 2 | Tommy Houston | 1 | Kenny Wallace | 1 |
| Jeff Burton | 2 | David Green | 1 | Andy Santerre | 1 | Jeff Burton | 2 | Dale Jarrett | 1 | Michael Waltrip | 1 |
| Jeff Green | 2 | Wayne Grubb | 1 | | | Dale Earnhardt Jr. | 2 | Jason Keller | 1 | Kevin Harvick | 1 |
| Jason Keller | 2 | Jimmy Hensley | 1 | | | Tommy Ellis | 2 | Rick Mast | 1 | Johnny Sauter | 1 |
| Brett Bodine | 1 | Matt Kenseth | 1 | | | Butch Lindley | 2 | Joe Nemechek | 1 | | |
| Geoffrey Bodine | 1 | Bobby Labonte | 1 | | | Jimmy Spencer | 2 | Steve Park | 1 | | |

## CRAFTSMAN TRUCK SERIES

### YEAR BY YEAR WINNERS

| Year | Event | Pole Winner | Speed | Race Winner | START Pos |
|---|---|---|---|---|---|
| 1995 | Fas Mart Shootout | Terry Labonte | 116.797 mph | Terry Labonte | 1 |
| 1996 | Fas Mart Shootout | Kenny Irwin | 119.888 mph | Mike Skinner | 2 |
| 1997 | Virginia is for Lovers 200 | Ron Hornaday Jr. | 121.726 mph | Bob Keselowski | 10 |
| 1998 | Virginia is for Lovers 200 | Joe Ruttman | 121.633 mph | Jack Sprague | 2 |
| 1999 | Virginia is for Lovers 200 | Bobby Hamilton | 121.408 mph | Greg Biffle | 4 |
| 2000 | Kroger 200 | Kurt Busch | 121.457 mph | Rick Carelli | 10 |
| 2001 | Kroger 200 | Dennis Setzer | 121.359 mph | Jack Sprague | 2 |
| 2002 | Virginia is for Lovers 200 | Jason Leffler | 123.378 mph | Tony Stewart | 25 |
| 2003 | Virginia is for Lovers 200 | None - weather | | Tony Stewart | 27 |

**QUALIFYING RECORD**
Jason Leffler, Dodge; 123.378 mph (21.884 sec.); September 5, 2002

**RACE RECORD**
Bob Keselowski, Dodge; 104.167 mph (1 hr., 26 min., 24 sec.); September 4, 1997

| POLE WINNERS | | RACE WINNERS | |
|---|---|---|---|
| Kurt Busch | 1 | Jack Sprague | 2 |
| Bobby Hamilton | 1 | Tony Stewart | 2 |
| Ron Hornaday Jr. | 1 | Greg Biffle | 1 |
| Kenny Irwin | 1 | Rick Carelli | 1 |
| Terry Labonte | 1 | Bob Keselowski | 1 |
| Jason Leffler | 1 | Terry Labonte | 1 |
| Joe Ruttman | 1 | Jack Sprague | 1 |
| Dennis Setzer | 1 | | |

# Talladega Superspeedway

## TRACK FACTS
**Date Opened:** September, 1969
**Owner:** ISC
**President:** Grant Lynch
**Distance:** 2.66 miles
**Banking in Turns:** 33 degrees
**Banking on Trioval:** 18 degrees
**Banking on Backstretch:** 2 degrees
**Length of Frontstretch:** 4,300 feet
**Length of Backstretch:** 4,000 feet
**Grandstand Seating:** 143,000
**Tickets:** (256) 362-7223
**Website:** www.talladegasuperspeedway.com

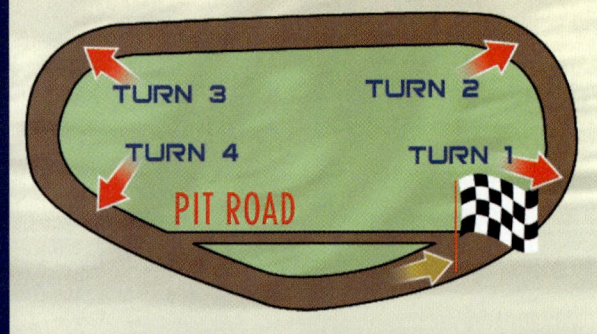

## 2004 SCHEDULE

### NEXTEL Cup
**Aaron's 499**
**Race:** No. 9 of 36
**Date:** April 25
**TV:** FOX. **Radio:** MRN

**EA Sports 500**
**Race:** No. 29 of 36
**Date:** October 3
**TV:** NBC. **Radio:** MRN

### Busch Series
**Aaron's 312**
**Race:** No. 8 of 34
**Date:** April 24
**TV:** FOX. **Radio:** MRN

## NEXTEL CUP

### TRACK RECORDS
**Most Wins:** 10—Dale Earnhardt
**Oldest Winner:** Harry Gant, 51 years, 3 months, 26 days, 05/06/1991
**Youngest Winner:** Bobby Hillin Jr, 22 years, 1 month, 22 days, 07/27/1986
**Most Lead Changes:** 75—5/6/84
**Fewest Lead Changes:** 13—5/6/73
**Most Leaders:** 26—Twice, most recently, 4/22/01
**Fewest Leaders:** 4—5/16/71
**Most Cautions:** 40—8/23/70
**Fewest Cautions:** 0—3 times, most recently, 10/6/02
**Most Caution Laps:** 62—5/7/72
**Fewest Caution Laps:** 0—3 times, most recently, 10/6/02
**Most on the Lead Lap:** 29—4/22/01
**Fewest on the Lead Lap:** 1—Twice, most recently, 5/6/79
**Most Running at the Finish:** 40—4/22/01
**Fewest Running at the Finish:** 14—7/27/86
**Most Laps Led by a Race Winner:** 153—Pete Hamilton 8/23/70
**Fewest Laps Led by a Race Winner:** 3—Twice, most recently, Bobby Hamilton, 4/22/01
**Closest Margin of Victory:** 0.005 second, Dale Earnhardt defeated Ernie Irvan 07/25/93
**Greatest Margin of Victory:** 1 Lap, 50 seconds, Bobby Allison defeated Darrell Waltrip 05/06/79

# NEXTEL CUP
## QUALIFYING AND RACE RECORDS

**QUALIFYING**
**Track:** Bill Elliott, Ford, 212.809 mph, 44.998 seconds, April 30, 1987 (Winston 500).
**Winston 500:** Bill Elliott, Ford, 212.809 mph, 44.998 seconds, April 30, 1987.
**Diehard 500:** Bill Elliott, Ford, 209.005 mph, 45.817 seconds, July 24, 1986.

**RACE**
**Track:** Mark Martin, Ford, 188.354 mph, 2 hours, 39 minutes, 18 seconds, May 10, 1997 (Winston 500).
**Winston 500:** Mark Martin, Ford, 188.354 mph, 2 hours, 39 minutes, 18 seconds, May 10, 1997.
**EA Sports 500:** Dale Earnhardt Jr., Chevrolet, 183.665 mph, 2 hours, 43 minutes, 22 seconds, Oct. 6 2002.

## ALL TALLADEGA RACES

### POLE WINNERS
| | | | | | |
|---|---|---|---|---|---|
| Elliott | 8 | Compton | 2 | Earnhardt | 10 |
| Yarborough | 6 | Foyt | 1 | D. Waltrip | 4 |
| Isaac | 5 | Bonnett | 1 | Buddy Baker | 4 |
| Irvan | 5 | Gant | 1 | B. Allison | 4 |
| Earnhardt | 3 | Bodine | 1 | Earnhardt Jr. | 4 |
| Marlin | 3 | Da. Allison | 1 | Da. Allison | 3 |
| Marcis | 3 | T. Labonte | 1 | Pearson | 3 |
| Pearson | 3 | J. Andretti | 1 | Yarborough | 3 |
| Buddy Baker | 3 | B. Labonte | 1 | D. Allison | 2 |
| Mayfield | 3 | Ji. Johnson | 1 | Hamilton | 2 |
| Martin | 2 | Sadler | 1 | R. Petty | 2 |
| Schrader | 2 | | | Elliott | 2 |
| D. Waltrip | 2 | | | Irvan | 2 |
| D. Allison | 2 | | | Marlin | 2 |
| B. Allison | 2 | | | T. Labonte | 2 |
| Parsons | 2 | | | Martin | 2 |
| Nemechek | 2 | | | J. Gordon | 2 |

### RACE WINNERS (continued)
| | |
|---|---|
| Brooks | 1 |
| Hylton | 1 |
| Brickhouse | 1 |
| Pond | 1 |
| Bonnett | 1 |
| Bouchard | 1 |
| Hillin | 1 |
| P. Parsons | 1 |
| Schrader | 1 |
| Gant | 1 |
| J. Spencer | 1 |
| Marcis | 1 |
| B. Labonte | 1 |
| D. Jarrett | 1 |
| B. Hamilton | 1 |
| M. Waltrip | 1 |

## SPRING: Aaron's 499

### POLE WINNERS
| | | | |
|---|---|---|---|
| Elliott | 4 | Buddy Baker | 1 |
| C. Yarborough | 3 | Gant | 1 |
| Isaac | 3 | Bodine | 1 |
| S. Marlin | 3 | D. Waltrip | 1 |
| J. Mayfield | 3 | Martin | 1 |
| Earnhardt | 2 | E. Irvan | 1 |
| K. Schrader | 2 | S. Compton | 1 |
| Marcis | 2 | J. Johnson | 1 |
| B. Allison | 1 | | |
| D. Allison | 1 | | |
| Pearson | 1 | | |
| Parsons | 1 | | |
| Bonnett | 1 | | |

### RACE WINNERS
| | | | |
|---|---|---|---|
| Earnhardt | 6 | Brickhouse | 1 |
| T. Labonte | 2 | Pond | 1 |
| Waltrip | 2 | Bonnett | 1 |
| J. Gordon | 2 | Bouchard | 1 |
| Earnhardt Jr. | 2 | C. Yarborough | 1 |
| R. Petty | 1 | Hillin | 1 |
| Marcis | 1 | Elliott | 1 |
| B. Allison | 1 | Schrader | 1 |
| D. Allison | 1 | Irvan | 1 |
| Buddy Baker | 1 | J. Spencer | 1 |
| Brooks | 1 | S. Marlin | 1 |
| Hylton | 1 | B. Labonte | 1 |
| Hamilton | 1 | B. Hamilton | 1 |

## FALL: EA Sports 500

### POLE WINNERS
| | | | |
|---|---|---|---|
| Elliott | 4 | B. Allison | 1 |
| Irvan | 4 | Parsons | 1 |
| Yarborough | 3 | Da. Allison | 1 |
| Buddy Baker | 2 | Martin | 1 |
| Pearson | 2 | Earnhardt | 1 |
| Nemechek | 2 | T. Labonte | 1 |
| Isaac | 2 | J. Andretti | 1 |
| D. Allison | 1 | B. Labonte | 1 |
| Marcis | 1 | Compton | 1 |
| Foyt | 1 | Sadler | 1 |
| D. Waltrip | 1 | | |

### RACE WINNERS
| | | | |
|---|---|---|---|
| Earnhardt | 4 | R. Petty | 1 |
| Da. Allison | 3 | Elliott | 1 |
| Pearson | 3 | Parsons | 1 |
| Buddy Baker | 3 | Gant | 1 |
| B. Allison | 3 | Irvan | 1 |
| Martin | 2 | Marlin | 1 |
| Yarborough | 2 | D. Jarrett | 1 |
| D. Waltrip | 2 | M. Waltrip | 1 |
| Earnhardt Jr. | 2 | | |
| D. Allison | 1 | | |
| Hamilton | 1 | | |

## YEAR BY YEAR WINNERS

| Year | Event | Race Winner | Car Make | Avg. Speed | Start Pos. | Winning Car Owner | Pole Winner |
|---|---|---|---|---|---|---|---|
| 2003 | EA Sports 500 | M. Waltrip | Chevrolet | 156.045 | 18 | Dale Earnhardt Inc. | E. Sadler |
| | Aaron's 499 | D. Earnhardt Jr. | Chevrolet | 144.625 | 2 | Dale Earnhardt Inc. | J. Mayfield |
| c 2002 | EA Sports 500 | D. Earnhardt Jr. | Chevrolet | 183.665 | 13 | Dale Earnhardt | Trials Rained Out |
| | Aaron's 499 | D. Earnhardt Jr. | Chevrolet | 159.022 | 4 | Dale Earnhardt | J. Johnson |
| 2001 | EA Sports 500 | D. Earnhardt Jr. | Chevrolet | 164.185 | 6 | Dale Earnhardt | S. Compton |
| c | Talladega 500 | B. Hamilton | Chevrolet | 184.003 | 14 | Andy Petree | S. Compton |
| 2000 | Winston 500 | D. Earnhardt | Chevrolet | 165.681 | 20 | Richard Childress | J. Nemechek |
| | DieHard 500 | J. Gordon | Chevrolet | 161.157 | 36 | Rick Hendrick | J. Mayfield |
| 1999 | Winston 500 | D. Earnhardt | Chevrolet | 166.632 | 27 | Richard Childress | J. Nemechek |
| | DieHard 500 | D. Earnhardt | Chevrolet | 163.395 | 17 | Richard Childress | K. Schrader |
| 1998 | Winston 500 | D. Jarrett | Ford | 159.317 | 3 | Robert Yates | K. Schrader |
| | DieHard 500 | B. Labonte | Pontiac | 163.439 | 1 | Joe Gibbs | B. Labonte |
| 1997 | DieHard 500 | T. Labonte | Chevrolet | 156.601 | 6 | Rick Hendrick | E. Irvan |
| c | Winston 500 | M. Martin | Ford | 188.354 | 18 | Jack Roush | J. Andretti |
| b 1996 | DieHard 500 | J. Gordon | Chevrolet | 133.387 | 2 | Rick Hendrick | J. Mayfield |
| | Winston Select 500 | S. Marlin | Chevrolet | 149.999 | 4 | Morgan-McClure | E. Irvan |
| 1995 | DieHard 500 | S. Marlin | Chevrolet | 173.188 | 1 | Morgan-McClure | S. Marlin |
| | Winston Select 500 | M. Martin | Ford | 178.902 | 3 | Jack Roush | T. Labonte |
| 1994 | DieHard 500 | J. Spencer | Ford | 163.217 | 2 | Junior Johnson | D. Earnhardt |
| | Winston Select 500 | D. Earnhardt | Chevrolet | 157.478 | 4 | Richard Childress | E. Irvan |
| 1993 | DieHard 500 | Earnhardt | Chevrolet | 153.858 | 11 | Richard Childress | B. Elliott |
| | Winston 500 | Irvan | Chevrolet | 155.412 | 16 | Morgan-McClure | Earnhardt |
| 1992 | DieHard 500 | Irvan | Chevrolet | 176.309 | 7 | Morgan-McClure | S. Marlin |
| | Winston 500 | Da. Allison | Ford | 167.609 | 2 | Robert Yates | Irvan |
| 1991 | DieHard 500 | Earnhardt | Chevrolet | 147.383 | 4 | Richard Childress | S. Marlin |
| | Winston 500 | Gant | Oldsmobile | 165.620 | 2 | Leo Jackson | Irvan |
| 1990 | DieHard 500 | Earnhardt | Chevrolet | 174.430 | 1 | Richard Childress | Earnhardt |
| | Winston 500 | Earnhardt | Chevrolet | 159.571 | 5 | Richard Childress | Elliott |
| 1989 | DieHard 500 | Labonte | Ford | 157.354 | 5 | Junior Johnson | Martin |
| | Winston 500 | Da. Allison | Ford | 155.869 | 2 | Robert Yates | Martin |
| 1988 | Talladega DieHard 500 | Schrader | Chevrolet | 154.505 | 7 | Rick Hendrick | D. Waltrip |
| | Winston 500 | P. Parsons | Oldsmobile | 156.547 | 3 | Jackson Bros. | Da. Allison |
| 1987 | Talladega 500 | Elliott | Ford | 171.293 | 1 | Melling Racing | Elliott |
| a | Winston 500 | Da. Allison | Ford | 154.228 | 3 | Ranier Racing | Elliott |
| 1986 | Talladega 500 | Hillin | Buick | 151.552 | 13 | Stavola Bros. | Elliott |
| | Winston 500 | B. Allison | Buick | 157.698 | 2 | Stavola Bros. | Elliott |
| 1985 | Talladega 500 | C. Yarborough | Ford | 148.772 | 2 | Ranier Racing | Elliott |
| | Winston 500 | Elliott | Ford | 186.288 | 1 | Melling Racing | Elliott |
| 1984 | Talladega 500 | Earnhardt | Chevrolet | 155.485 | 3 | Richard Childress | C. Yarborough |
| | Winston 500 | C. Yarborough | Chevrolet | 172.988 | 1 | Ranier Racing | C. Yarborough |
| 1983 | Talladega 500 | Earnhardt | Ford | 170.611 | 4 | Bud Moore | C. Yarborough |
| | Winston 500 | R. Petty | Pontiac | 153.936 | 15 | Petty Eng. | C. Yarborough |
| 1982 | Talladega 500 | Waltrip | Buick | 168.157 | 2 | Junior Johnson | Bodine |
| | Winston 500 | Waltrip | Buick | 156.697 | 2 | Junior Johnson | Parsons |
| 1981 | Talladega 500 | Bouchard | Buick | 156.737 | 10 | Race Hill Farm | Gant |
| | Winston 500 | B. Allison | Buick | 149.376 | 1 | Ranier Racing | B. Allison |
| 1980 | Talladega 500 | Bonnett | Mercury | 166.894 | 2 | Wood Brothers | Buddy Baker |
| | Winston 500 | Buddy Baker | Oldsmobile | 170.481 | 2 | Ranier Racing | Pearson |
| 1979 | Talladega 500 | Waltrip | Oldsmobile | 161.229 | 8 | DiGard Rac. Co. | Bonnett |
| | Winston 500 | B. Allison | Ford | 154.770 | 12 | Bud Moore | D. Waltrip |
| 1978 | Talladega 500 | Pond | Oldsmobile | 174.700 | 5 | Ranier Racing | C. Yarborough |
| | Winston 500 | C. Yarborough | Oldsmobile | 159.669 | 1 | Junior Johnson | C. Yarborough |
| 1977 | Talladega 500 | D. Allison | Chevrolet | 162.524 | 7 | Hoss Ellington | Parsons |
| | Winston 500 | Waltrip | Chevrolet | 164.877 | 11 | DiGard Rac. Co. | Foyt |
| 1976 | Talladega 500 | Marcis | Dodge | 157.547 | 1 | Nord Krauskopf | Marcis |
| | Winston 500 | Buddy Baker | Ford | 169.887 | 12 | Bud Moore | Marcis |
| 1975 | Talladega 500 | Buddy Baker | Ford | 130.892 | 2 | Bud Moore | Marcis |
| | Winston 500 | Buddy Baker | Ford | 144.948 | 1 | Bud Moore | Buddy Baker |
| 1974 | Talladega 500 | R. Petty | Dodge | 148.637 | 3 | Petty Eng. | Pearson |
| | Winston 500 | Pearson | Mercury | 130.220 | 1 | Wood Brothers | Pearson |
| 1973 | Talladega 500 | Brooks | Plymouth | 145.454 | 24 | Crawford Bros. | B. Allison |
| | Winston 500 | Pearson | Mercury | 131.956 | 2 | Wood Brothers | Buddy Baker |
| 1972 | Talladega 500 | Hylton | Mercury | 148.728 | 22 | James Hylton | Isaac |
| | Winston 500 | Pearson | Mercury | 134.400 | 2 | Wood Brothers | Isaac |
| 1971 | Talladega 500 | B. Allison | Mercury | 145.945 | 2 | Holman-Moody | D. Allison |
| | Winston 500 | D. Allison | Mercury | 147.419 | 1 | Wood Brothers | D. Allison |
| 1970 | Talladega 500 | Hamilton | Plymouth | 158.517 | 4 | Petty Eng. | Isaac |
| | Alabama 500 | Hamilton | Plymouth | 152.321 | 6 | Petty Eng. | Isaac |
| 1969 | Talladega 500 | Brickhouse | Dodge | 153.778 | 9 | Ray Nichels | Isaac |

a 473.48 miles (178 laps), darkness.
b 343.14 miles (129 laps), darkness.
c Rescheduled to 5-10, due to rain. Caution-free race.

## BUSCH SERIES

### YEAR BY YEAR WINNERS

| Year | Event | Pole Winner | Speed | Race Winner | START Pos |
|---|---|---|---|---|---|
| 1992 | Fram Filter 500K | D. Earnhardt | 184.733 | E. Irvan | 2 |
| 1993 | Fram Filter 500K | B. Elliott | 188.404 | D. Earnhardt | 22 |
| 1994 | Fram Filter 500K | J. Purvis | 186.703 | K. Schrader | 17 |
| 1995 | Humminbird 500K | J. Purvis | 189.921 | C. Little | 7 |
| 1996 | Humminbird 500K | J. Nemechek | 192.878 | G. Sacks | 7 |
| 1997 | Easy Care 500K | J. Nemechek | 193.517 | M. Martin | 23 |
| 1998* | Touchstone Energy 300 | J. Nemechek | 189.628 | J. Nemechek | 1 |
| 1999 | Touchstone Energy 300 | K. Schrader | 192.455 | T. Labonte | 16 |
| 2000 | Touchstone Energy 300 | None - weather | — | J. Nemechek | 35 |
| 2001 | Subway 300 | J. Nemechek | 189.729 | M. McLaughlin | 14 |
| 2002 | Aaron's 312 | Jo. Sauter | 188.764 | J. Keller | 12 |
| 2003 | Aaron's 312 | J. Nemechek | 188.649 | D. Earnhardt Jr. | 3 |

*changed to 300 miles

**QUALIFYING RECORD**
Joe Nemechek, Chevrolet; 193.517 mph; April 24, 1997.

**RACE RECORD**
Mark Martin, Ford; 168.937 mph (1 hr,. 50 min., 32 sec.); April 26, 1997.

**POLE WINNERS**
- Joe Nemechek 5
- Jeff Purvis 2
- Dale Earnhardt 1
- Bill Elliott 1
- Johnny Sauter 1
- Ken Schrader 1

**RACE WINNERS**
- Joe Nemechek 2
- Dale Earnhardt 1
- Ernie Irvan 1
- Jason Keller 1
- Terry Labonte 1
- Chad Little 1
- Mark Martin 1
- Mike McLaughlin 1
- Greg Sacks 1
- Ken Schrader 1
- Earnhardt Jr. 1

# Texas Motor Speedway

### TRACK FACTS
**Date Opened:** February 5, 1996
**Owner:** Speedway Motorsports, Inc.
**President:** Eddie Gossage
**Distance:** 1.5 miles
**Banking in Turns:** 24 degrees
**Banking in Straightaways:** 5 degrees
**Length of Frontstretch:** 2,250 feet
**Length of Backstretch:** 1,330 feet
**Grandstand Seating:** 154,861
**Tickets:** (817) 215-8500
**Website:** www.texasmotorspeedway.com

### 2004 SCHEDULE

**NEXTEL Cup**
Samsung/RadioShack 500
Race: No. 7 of 36
Date: April 4
TV: FOX. Radio: PRN

**Busch Series**
O'Reilly 300
Race: No. 6 of 34
Date: April 3
TV: FOX. Radio: MRN

**Craftsman Truck Series**
O'Reilly 400K
Race: No. 7 of 25
Date: June 11
TV: Speed. Radio: PRN

Silverado 350K
Race: No. 21 of 25
Date: October 16
TV: Speed. Radio: PRN

## NEXTEL CUP

### TRACK RECORDS
**Most Wins:** 1—Jeff Burton, Dale Earnhardt Jr, Dale Jarrett, Matt Kenseth, Terry Labonte and Mark Martin, Ryan Newman
**Oldest Winner:** Dale Jarrett, 44 years, 4 months, 6 days, 4/1/2001
**Youngest Winner:** Ryan Newman, 25 years, 3 months, 22 days, 3/30/2003
**Most Lead Changes:** 29—4/2/00
**Fewest Lead Changes:** 18—4/1/01
**Most Leaders:** 17—4/2/00
**Fewest Leaders:** 7—4/1/01
**Most Cautions:** 12—4/2/00
**Fewest Cautions:** 7—Twice, most recently, 4/8/02
**Most Caution Laps:** 73—4/6/97
**Fewest Caution Laps:** 39—3/28/99
**Most on the Lead Lap:** 14—4/2/00
**Fewest on the Lead Lap:** 8—4/6/97
**Most Running at the Finish:** 38—4/8/02
**Fewest Running at the Finish:** 29—Twice, most recently, 4/5/98
**Most Laps Led by a Race Winner:** 124—Terry Labonte 3/28/99
**Fewest Laps Led by a Race Winner:** 37—Mark Martin 4/5/98
**Closest Margin of Victory:** 0.573 second, Mark Martin defeated Chad Little 04/05/98
**Greatest Margin of Victory:** 5.920 seconds, Dale Earnhardt Jr defeated Jeff Burton 04/02/00

### QUALIFYING AND RACE RECORDS
**QUALIFYING**
Track: Bill Elliott, Dodge, 194.224 mph, 27.803 seconds, April 8, 2002.

**RACE**
Track: Terry Labonte, Chevrolet, 144.276 mph, 3 hours, 28 minutes, 21 seconds, March 28, 1999.

### YEAR BY YEAR WINNERS

| Year | Event | Race Winner | Car Make | Avg. Speed | Start Pos. | Winning Car Owner | Pole Winner |
|---|---|---|---|---|---|---|---|
| 2003 | Samsung/RadioShack 500 | R. Newman | Dodge | 134.517 | 3 | Roger Penske | B. Labonte |
| 2002 | Samsung/RadioShack 500 | M. Kenseth | Ford | 142.453 | 31 | Jack Roush | B. Elliott |
| 2001 | Harrah's 500 | D. Jarrett | Ford | 141.804 | 3 | Robert Yates | D. EarnhardtJr. |
| 2000 | DirecTV 500 | D. Earnhardt Jr. | Chevrolet | 131.152 | 4 | Dale Earnhardt | T. Labonte |
| 1999 | Primestar 500 | T. Labonte | Chevrolet | 144.276 | 4 | Rick Hendrick | K. Irwin |
| 1998 | Texas 500 | M. Martin | Ford | 136.771 | 7 | Jack Roush | J. Mayfield |
| 1997 | Interstate Batteries 500 | J. Burton | Ford | 125.111 | 5 | Jack Roush | Trials Rained Out |

## ALL TEXAS RACES

### POLE WINNERS
| | | | |
|---|---|---|---|
| J. Mayfield | 1 | D. Earnhardt Jr. | 1 |
| K. Irwin | 1 | B. Elliott | 1 |
| T. Labonte | 1 | B. Labonte | 1 |

### RACE WINNERS
| | | | | | |
|---|---|---|---|---|---|
| J. Burton | 1 | D. Earnhardt Jr. | 1 | R. Newman | 1 |
| M. Martin | 1 | D. Jarrett | 1 | | |
| T. Labonte | 1 | M. Kenseth | 1 | | |

# BUSCH SERIES

## YEAR BY YEAR WINNERS

| Year | Event | Pole Winner | Speed | Race Winner | Started |
|---|---|---|---|---|---|
| 1997 | Coca-Cola 300 | J. Green | 180.054 | M. Martin | 20 |
| 1998 | Coca-Cola 300 | E. Sadler | 179.229 | D. Earnhardt Jr. | 16 |
| 1999 | Coca-Cola 300 | D. Blaney | 183.082 | M. Martin | 2 |
| 2000 | Albertson's 300 | J. Leffler | 184.451 | M. Martin | 2 |
| 2001 | Jani-King 300 | M. Kenseth | 189.880 | K. Harvick | 7 |
| 2002 | O'Reilly 300 | J. Green | 193.483 | J. Purvis | 13 |
| 2003 | O'Reilly 300 | J. Keller | 187.474 | J. Nemechek | 7 |

### POLE WINNERS
| | | | |
|---|---|---|---|
| Jeff Green | 2 | Elliott Sadler | 1 |
| Dave Blaney | 1 | Jason Keller | 1 |
| Matt Kenseth | 1 | | |
| Jason Leffler | 1 | | |

### RACE WINNERS
| | | | |
|---|---|---|---|
| Mark Martin | 3 | Joe Nemechek | 1 |
| Dale Earnhardt Jr. | 1 | | |
| Kevin Harvick | 1 | | |
| Jeff Purvis | 1 | | |

**QUALIFYING RECORD**
Jeff Green, Chevrolet; 193.483 mph (27.908 sec.); April 5, 2002

**RACE RECORD**
Mark Martin, Ford; 127.417 mph (1 hr., 55 min., 08 sec.); March 27, 1999.

# CRAFTSMAN TRUCK SERIES

## YEAR BY YEAR WINNERS

| Year | Event | Pole Winner | Speed | Race Winner | Started |
|---|---|---|---|---|---|
| 1997 | Pronto Auto Parts 400 | Mike Bliss | 175.667 | Kenny Irwin | 5 |
| 1998 | Pronto Auto Parts 400 | Jack Sprague | 178.642 | Tony Raines | 12 |
| 1999 | Pronto Auto Parts 400 | Jay Sauter | 179.718 | Dennis Setzer | 3 |
| 1999 | O'Reilly 400 | Jay Sauter | 179.152 | Jay Sauter | 1 |
| 2000 | Pronto Auto Parts 400 | Greg Biffle | 178.130 | Greg Biffle | 1 |
| 2000 | O'Reilly 400 | Bryan Reffner | 180.373 | Bryan Reffner | 1 |
| 2001 | O'Reilly 400K | Scott Riggs | Not held | Jack Sprague | 3 |
| 2001 | Silverado 350 | Scott Riggs | 181.953 | Travis Kvapil | 7 |
| 2002 | O'Reilly 400K | Jason Leffler | 180.355 | Brendan Gaughan | 10 |
| 2002 | Silverado 350 | Mike Bliss | 179.695 | Brendan Gaughan | 5 |
| 2003 | O'Reilly 400K | None - weather | — | Brendan Gaughan | 5 |
| | Silverado 350 | Andy Houston | 181.531 | Brendan Gaughan | 7 |

### POLE WINNERS
| | |
|---|---|
| Jay Sauter | 2 |
| Mike Bliss | 2 |
| Greg Biffle | 1 |
| Jason Leffler | 1 |
| Bryan Reffner | 1 |
| Scott Riggs | 1 |
| Jack Sprague | 1 |
| Andy Houston | 1 |

### RACE WINNERS
| | |
|---|---|
| Brendan Gaughan | 4 |
| Greg Biffle | 1 |
| Kenny Irwin | 1 |
| Travis Kvapil | 1 |
| Tony Raines | 1 |
| Bryan Reffner | 1 |
| Jay Sauter | 1 |
| Dennis Setzer | 1 |
| Jack Sprague | 1 |

**QUALIFYING RECORD**
Scott Riggs, Dodge; 181.953 mph (29.678 sec.), October 4, 2001

**RACE RECORD**
Brendan Gaughan, Dodge; 140.621 mph (1 hr., 46 min., 53 sec.), June 6, 2003

# Watkins Glen International

## TRACK FACTS
**Date Opened:** September 15, 1956
**Owner:** ISC
**President:** Craig E. Rust
**Distance:** 2.45-mile road course
**Turns:** 11
**Banking:** Ranging from 6 to 10 degrees
**Pit Road Stretch:** 2,141 feet
**Length of Backstretch:** 1,839 feet
**Tickets:** (607) 535-2481
**Website:** www.theglen.com

### 2004 SCHEDULE
**NEXTEL Cup**
Sirius at the Glen
**Race:** No. 22 of 36
**Date:** August 15
**TV:** TNT. **Radio:** MRN

## NEXTEL CUP
### TRACK RECORDS
**Most Wins:** 4—Jeff Gordon
**Oldest Winner:** Geoffrey Bodine, 47 years, 3 months, 24 days, 8/11/1996
**Youngest Winner:** Jeff Gordon, 26 years, 6 days, 8/10/1997
**Most Lead Changes:** 14—8/11/91
**Fewest Lead Changes:** 3—7/18/65

# NEXTEL CUP

Most Leaders: 12—8/13/95
Fewest Leaders: 1—8/4/57
Most Cautions: 8—8/14/88
Fewest Cautions: 0—7/18/65
Most Caution Laps: 36—8/14/88
Fewest Caution Laps: 0—7/18/65
Most on the Lead Lap: 33—8/13/00
Fewest on the Lead Lap: 2—Twice, most recently, 7/18/65
Most Running at the Finish: 39—Three times, most recently 8/10/03
Fewest Running at the Finish: 11—7/18/65
Most Laps Led by a Race Winner: 75—Mark Martin 8/14/94
Fewest Laps Led by a Race Winner: 4—Ricky Rudd 8/14/88
Closest Margin of Victory:—0.172 second, Jeff Gordon defeated Jeff Burton 08/12/01
Greatest Margin of Victory:—12 seconds, Rusty Wallace defeated Terry Labonte 08/10/87

## QUALIFYING AND RACE RECORDS

### QUALIFYING
**Track Record (2.45 mile course):** Jeff Gordon, Chevrolet, 124.580 mph, August 8, 2003
**Track Record (2.428 mile course):** Terry Labonte, Oldsmobile, 121.652 mph, 1 minute, 11.851 seconds, Aug. 9, 1991.
**Track Record (2.3 mile course):** Billy Wade, Mercury, 102.222 mph, 1 minute, 21.000 seconds, July 18, 1964.

### RACE
**Track Record (220.5 miles):** Mark Martin, Ford, 100.303 mph, 2 hours, 11 minutes, 54 seconds, Aug. 13, 1995.
**Track Record (218.52 miles):** Ernie Irvan, Chevrolet, 98.77 mph, Aug. 11, 1991.
**Track Record (151.8 miles):** Marvin Panch, Ford, 98.182 mph, July 18. 1965.
**Track Record (101.2 miles):** Buck Baker, Chevrolet, 82.08 mph, Aug. 4, 1957.

## YEAR BY YEAR WINNERS

| | Year | Event | Race Winner | Car Make | Avg. Speed | Start Pos. | Winning Car Owner | Pole Winner |
|---|---|---|---|---|---|---|---|---|
| | 2003 | Sirius at the Glen | R. Gordon | Chevrolet | 90.441 | 14 | Richard Childress | J. Gordon |
| | 2002 | Sirius at The Glen | T. Stewart | Pontiac | 82.208 | 3 | Joe Gibbs | R. Rudd |
| | 2001 | G. Crossing at The Glen | J. Gordon | Chevrolet | 89.081 | 13 | Rick Henrick | D. Jarrett |
| d | 2000 | G. Crossing at The Glen | S. Park | Chevrolet | 91.336 | 18 | Dale Earnhardt | Trials Rained Out |
| | 1999 | Frontier at The Glen | J. Gordon | Chevrolet | 87.722 | 3 | Rick Hendrick | R. Wallace |
| | 1998 | Bud at Glen | J. Gordon | Chevrolet | 94.466 | 1 | Rick Hendrick | J. Gordon |
| | 1997 | Bud at Glen | J. Gordon | Chevrolet | 91.294 | 11 | Rick Hendrick | T. Bodine |
| | 1996 | Bud at Glen | G. Bodine | Ford | 92.334 | 13 | Geoff Bodine | D. Earnhardt |
| | 1995 | Bud at Glen | M. Martin | Ford | 103.030 | 1 | Jack Roush | M. Martin |
| | 1994 | Bud at Glen | M. Martin | Ford | 93.752 | 1 | Jack Roush | M. Martin |
| | 1993 | Bud at Glen | Martin | Ford | 84.771 | 1 | Jack Roush | M. Martin |
| c | 1992 | Bud at Glen | K. Petty | Pontiac | 85.827 | 2 | Felix Sabates | Earnhardt |
| b | 1991 | Bud at Glen | E. Irvan | Chevrolet | 98.977 | 3 | Morgan-McClure | T. Labonte |
| | 1990 | Bud at Glen | Rudd | Chevrolet | 92.452 | 12 | Rick Hendrick | Earnhardt |
| | 1989 | Bud at Glen | Wallace | Pontiac | 87.242 | 13 | Blue Max | Shepherd |
| | 1988 | Bud at Glen | Rudd | Buick | 74.096 | 6 | King Racing | G. Bodine |
| | 1987 | Bud at Glen | Wallace | Pontiac | 90.682 | 2 | Blue Max | Labonte |
| | 1986 | Bud at Glen | Richmond | Chevrolet | 90.463 | 1 | Rick Hendrick | Richmond |
| *a | 1965 | The Glen 151.8 | Panch | Ford | 98.182 | 3 | Wood Brothers | Trials Rained Out |
| * | 1964 | The Glen 151.8 | Wade | Mercury | 97.988 | 1 | Bud Moore | Wade |
| * | 1957 | The Glen 101.2 | Buck Baker | Chevrolet | 82.08 | 1 | Buck Baker | Buck Baker |

* Miles of event. a Time trials rained out; drew for starting positions. b Last race on 2.428-mile course; it was restructured and is now 2.45 miles. c Race cut to 124.95 miles by rain. d Drivers started via car owner points.

## ALL WATKINS GLEN RACES

| POLE WINNERS | | RACE WINNERS | | | |
|---|---|---|---|---|---|
| Martin | 3 | G. Bodine | 1 | J. Gordon | 4 | Panch | 1 |
| Earnhardt | 3 | Shepherd | 1 | Martin | 3 | Irvan | 1 |
| T. Labonte | 2 | T. Bodine | 1 | Wallace | 2 | K. Petty | 1 |
| J. Gordon | 2 | R. Wallace | 1 | Rudd | 2 | G. Bodine | 1 |
| Richmond | 1 | D. Jarrett | 1 | Richmond | 1 | Park | 1 |
| Buck Baker | 1 | Rudd | 1 | Buck Baker | 1 | Stewart | 1 |
| Wade | 1 | | | Wade | 1 | R. Gordon | 1 |

# Inactive NEXTEL Cup tracks

## Nashville International Raceway

### QUALIFYING AND RACE RECORDS

**QUALIFYING**
**Track Record (35-degree banking):** Bobby Allison, Chevrolet, 116.932 mph, 18.349 seconds, Aug. 26, 1972 (Nashville 420).
**Track Record (18-degree banks):** Cale Yarborough, Chevrolet, 106.581 mph, 20.131 seconds, May 9, 1980 (Music City 420).
**Music City 420 (18 degrees):** Cale Yarborough, Chevrolet, 106.581 mph, 20.131 seconds, May 9, 1980.
**Busch Nashville 420 (18 degrees):** Darrell Waltrip, Chevrolet, 105.430 mph, 20.351 seconds, July 13, 1979.

**RACE**
**Track Record (250 miles):** Cale Yarborough, Chevrolet, 93.419 mph, May 12, 1973 (Melling Tool 420).
**Music City 420:** Cale Yarborough, Chevrolet, 98.419 mph, May 12, 1973.
**Busch Nashville 420:** Dale Earnhardt, Chevrolet, 93.821 mph, July 12, 1980.
**200-Mile Race:** Richard Petty, Ford, 78.740 mph, July 26, 1969.
**100-Mile Race:** Richard Petty, Ford, Plymouth, 76.50 mph, June 14, 1964.

### YEAR BY YEAR WINNERS

| Year | Event | Fastest Qualifier | Race Winner | Start Pos. | | Year | Event | Fastest Qualifier | Race Winner | Start Pos. |
|---|---|---|---|---|---|---|---|---|---|---|
| 1984 | Pepsi 420 | Rudd | Bodine | 5 | | 1973 | Nashville 420 | C. Yarborough | Buddy Baker | 7 |
| | Coors 420 | Waltrip | Waltrip | 1 | g | | Music City 420 | C. Yarborough | C. Yarborough | 1 |
| 1983 | Busch Nashville 420 | Bouchard | Earnhardt | 3 | | 1972 | Nashville 420 | B. Allison | B. Allison | 1 |
| | Marty Robbins 420 | Waltrip | Waltrip | 1 | | 1971 | Nashville 420 | R. Petty | R. Petty | 1 |
| 1982 | Busch Nashville 420 | Shepherd | Waltrip | 3 | f | 1970 | Nashville 420 | L. Yarbrough | Isaac | 2 |
| | Cracker Barrel 420 | Waltrip | Waltrip | 1 | e | 1969 | Nashville 400 | R. Petty | R. Petty | 1 |
| 1981 | Busch Nashville 420 | Marlin | Waltrip | 4 | d | 1968 | Nashville 400 | R. Petty | Pearson | 3 |
| | Melling Tool 420 | Rudd | Parsons | 3 | | 1967 | Nashville 400 | Hutcherson | R. Petty | 2 |
| 1980 | Busch Nashville 420 | C. Yarborough | Earnhardt | 7 | | 1966 | Nashville 400 | R. Petty | R. Petty | 1 |
| | Music City 420 | C. Yarborough | R. Petty | 6 | | 1965 | Nashville 400 | R. Petty | R. Petty | 1 |
| 1979 | Busch Nashville 420 | Waltrip | Waltrip | 1 | | | Music City 200 | Pistone | Hutcherson | 2 |
| | Music City 420 | Milliken | C. Yarborough | 4 | | 1964 | Nashville 400 | R. Petty | R. Petty | 1 |
| 1978 | Nashville 420 | Pond | C. Yarborough | 2 | | | Music City 200 | Pearson | R. Petty | 2 |
| i | Music City 420 | Pond | C. Yarborough | 2 | c | 1963 | Nashville 400 | R. Petty | Paschal | 3 |
| 1977 | Nashville 420 | Parsons | Waltrip | 6 | | 1962 | Nashville 500 | Allen | Paschal | 3 |
| | Music City 420 | Waltrip | Parsons | 2 | b | 1961 | Nashville 500 | White | Paschal | 10 |
| * 1976 | Nashville 420 | Bonnett | Parsons | 6 | a | 1960 | Nashville 500 | White | Beauchamp | 2 |
| | Music City 420 | Parsons | C. Yarborough | 2 | † | 1959 | Nashville 300 | White | J.L. Johnson | 2 |
| 1975 | Nashville 420 | Parsons | C. Yarborough | 3 | | | Music City 200 | White | White | 1 |
| | Music City 420 | Waltrip | Waltrip | 1 | † | 1958 | Nashville 200 | White | Weatherly | 8 |
| 1974 | Nashville 420 | Waltrip | C. Yarborough | 2 | | | | | | |
| h | Music City 420 | B. Allison | R. Petty | 2 | | | | | | |

† Sweepstakes races, combined Grand Nationals and Convertibles; both winners were driving convertibles.
* Neil Bonnett won the pole in Bobby Allison's car, but Allison started the race.
a Race shortened to 333 laps, 166.5 miles; rain.
b Race shortened to 403 laps, 201.5 miles; rain.
c Race shortened to 350 laps, 175 miles; darkness.
d Race shortened to 301 laps, 150.5 miles; rain.
e Last race on a half-mile track.
f Bankings increased to 35 degrees; track remeasured at .596 of a mile.
g Bankings reduced to 18 degrees; track remained at .596 of a mile.
h Race cut by 25 miles, energy shortage.
i Yarborough led all 420 laps, 250 miles (June 3, 1978).

### ALL NASHVILLE RACES

**POLE WINNERS***

| | | | | | | | |
|---|---|---|---|---|---|---|---|
| R. Petty | 7 | B. Allison | 2 | Hutcherson | 1 | Martin | 1 |
| Waltrip | 7 | Rudd | 2 | Pistone | 1 | Shepherd | 1 |
| White | 5 | Pond | 2 | Allen | 1 | Bouchard | 1 |
| Yarborough | 4 | Pearson | 1 | Bonnett | 1 | | |
| Parsons | 3 | L. Yarbrough | 1 | Milikan | 1 | | |

**RACE WINNERS**

| | | | | | | | |
|---|---|---|---|---|---|---|---|
| R. Petty | 9 | Earnhardt | 2 | Buddy Baker | 1 | Bodine | 1 |
| Waltrip | 8 | B. Allison | 1 | J.L. Johnson | 1 | | |
| Yarborough | 7 | Pearson | 1 | White | 1 | | |
| Paschal | 3 | Isaac | 1 | Beauchamp | 1 | | |
| Parsons | 3 | Hutcherson | 1 | Weatherly | 1 | | |

*The pole winner was the fastest qualifier in every race.

# North Wilkesboro Speedway

## QUALIFYING AND RACE RECORDS

### QUALIFYING
**Track:** Ernie Irvan, Ford, 119.016 mph, 18.905 seconds, April 15, 1994 (First Union 400).
**First Union 400:** Ernie Irvan, Ford, 119.016 mph, 18.905 seconds, April 15, 1994.
**Tyson Holly Farms 400:** Jimmy Spencer, Ford, 118.558 mph, 18.978 seconds, Sept. 30, 1994.

### RACE
**Track:** Geoff Bodine, Ford, 107.360 mph, 2 hours, 19 minutes, 43 seconds, Oct. 5, 1992 (Tyson Holly Farms 400).
**First Union 400:** Dale Earnhardt, Chevrolet, 102.424 mph, 2 hours, 26 minutes, 27 seconds, April 9, 1995.
**Tyson Holly Farms 400:** Geoff Bodine, Ford, 107.360 mph, 2 hours, 19 minutes, 43 seconds, Oct. 5, 1992.

## YEAR BY YEAR WINNERS

| Year | Event | Fastest Qualifier | Pole Winner | Race Winner | Start Pos. | Year | Event | Fastest Qualifier | Pole Winner | Race Winner | Start Pos. |
|---|---|---|---|---|---|---|---|---|---|---|---|
| 1996 | Holly Farms 400 | T. Musgrave | T. Musgrave | J. Gordon | 2 | 1978 | Wilkes 400 | D. Waltrip | D. Waltrip | C. Yarborough | 3 |
|  | First Union 400 | T. Labonte | T. Labonte | T. Labonte | 1 |  | Gwyn Staley 400 | B. Parsons | B. Parsons | D. Waltrip | 2 |
| 1995 | Holly Farms 400 | T. Musgrave | T. Musgrave | M. Martin | 2 | 1977 | Wilkes 400 | R. Petty | R. Petty | D. Waltrip | 3 |
|  | First Union 400 | J. Gordon | J. Gordon | D. Earnhardt | 5 |  | Gwyn Staley 400 | N. Bonnett | N. Bonnett | C. Yarborough | 2 |
| 1994 | Holly Farms 400 | J. Spencer | J. Spencer | G. Bodine | 18 | 1976 | Wilkes 400 | D. Waltrip | D. Waltrip | C. Yarborough | 4 |
|  | First Union 400 | E. Irvan | E. Irvan | T. Labonte | 10 |  | Gwyn Staley 400 | D. Marcis | D. Marcis | C. Yarborough | 5 |
| 1993 | Holly Farms 400 | E. Irvan | E. Irvan | R. Wallace | 11 | 1975 | Wilkes 400 | R. Petty | R. Petty | R. Petty | 1 |
|  | First Union 400 | D. Earnhardt | B. Bodine | R. Wallace | 9 |  | Gwyn Staley 400 | D. Waltrip | D. Waltrip | R. Petty | 2 |
| f 1992 | Holly Farms 400 | Kulwicki | Kulwicki | G. Bodine | 3 | 1974 | Wilkes 400 | R. Petty | R. Petty | C. Yarborough | 2 |
|  | First Union 400 | Kulwicki | Kulwicki | Da. Allison | 7 | e | Gwyn Staley 400 | B. Allison | B. Allison | R. Petty | 4 |
| 1991 | Holly Farms 400 | Gant | Gant | D. Earnhardt | 16 | 1973 | Wilkes 400 | B. Allison | B. Allison | B. Allison | 1 |
|  | First Union 400 | B. Bodine | B. Bodine | D. Waltrip | 13 |  | Gwyn Staley 400 | B. Allison | B. Allison | R. Petty | 2 |
| 1990 | Holly Farms 400 | K. Petty | K. Petty | M. Martin | 2 | 1972 | Wilkes 400 | Buddy Baker | Buddy Baker | R. Petty | 3 |
|  | First Union 400 | M. Martin | M. Martin | B. Bodine | 20 |  | Gwyn Staley 400 | B. Isaac | B. Isaac | R. Petty | 3 |
| e 1989 | Holly Farms 400 | Time Trials Rained Out |  | G. Bodine | 11 | d 1971 | Wilkes 400 | C. Glotzbach | C. Glotzbach | T. Lund | 6 |
|  | First Union 400 | R. Wallace | R. Wallace | D. Earnhardt | 3 | c | Gwyn Staley 400 | B. Isaac | B. Isaac | R. Petty | 3 |
| 1988 | Holly Farms 400 | B. Elliott | B. Elliott | R. Wallace | 12 | 1970 | Wilkes 400 | B. Isaac | B. Isaac | B. Isaac | 1 |
|  | First Union 400 | T. Labonte | T. Labonte | T. Labonte | 1 |  | Gwyn Staley 400 | B. Isaac | B. Isaac | R. Petty | 16 |
| 1987 | Holly Farms 400 | B. Elliott | B. Elliott | T. Labonte | 4 | 1969 | Wilkes 400 | B. Allison | B. Allison | D. Pearson | 2 |
|  | First Union 400 | B. Elliott | B. Elliott | D. Earnhardt | 3 |  | Gwyn Staley 400 | B. Isaac | B. Isaac | B. Allison | 11 |
| 1986 | Holly Farms 400 | T. Richmond | T. Richmond | D. Waltrip | 4 | 1968 | Wilkes 400 | B. Allison | B. Allison | R. Petty | 3 |
|  | First Union 400 | G. Bodine | G. Bodine | D. Earnhardt | 5 |  | Gwyn Staley 400 | D. Pearson | D. Pearson | D. Pearson | 1 |
| 1985 | Holly Farms 400 | G. Bodine | G. Bodine | Gant | 11 | 1967 | Wilkes 400 | D. Hutcherson | D. Hutcherson | R. Petty | 5 |
|  | NW Bank 400 | D. Waltrip | D. Waltrip | N. Bonnett | 5 | b | Gwyn Staley 400 | D. Dieringer | D. Dieringer | D. Dieringer | 1 |
| 1984 | Holly Farms 400 | D. Waltrip | D. Waltrip | D. Waltrip | 1 | 1966 | Wilkes 400 | J. Johnson | J. Johnson | D. Hutcherson | 4 |
|  | NW Bank 400 | R. Rudd | R. Rudd | T. Richmond | 17 |  | Gwyn Staley 400 | J. Paschal | J. Paschal | J. Paschal | 1 |
| 1983 | Holly Farms 400 | D. Waltrip | D. Waltrip | D. Waltrip | 1 | 1965 | Wilkes 400 | F. Lorenzen | F. Lorenzen | J. Johnson | 5 |
|  | NW Bank 400 | N. Bonnett | N. Bonnett | D. Waltrip | 10 |  | Gwyn Staley 400 | J. Johnson | J. Johnson | J. Johnson | 1 |
| 1982 | Holly Farms 400 | D. Waltrip | D. Waltrip | D. Waltrip | 1 | 1964 | Wilkes 400 | J. Johnson | J. Johnson | M. Panch | 5 |
|  | NW Bank 400 | D. Waltrip | D. Waltrip | D. Waltrip | 1 |  | Gwyn Staley 400 | F. Lorenzen | F. Lorenzen | F. Lorenzen | 1 |
| 1981 | Holly Farms 400 | D. Waltrip | D. Waltrip | D. Waltrip | 1 | 1963 | Wilkes 400 | F. Lorenzen | F. Lorenzen | M. Panch | 3 |
|  | NW Bank 400 | D. Marcis | D. Marcis | R. Petty | 13 | a | Gwyn Staley 400 | F. Lorenzen | F. Lorenzen | R. Petty | 7 |
| 1980 | Holly Farms 400 | C. Yarborough | C. Yarborough | B. Allison | 2 | * 1962 | Wilkes 320 | F. Lorenzen | F. Lorenzen | R. Petty | 5 |
|  | NW Bank 400 | B. Allison | B. Allison | R. Petty | 7 |  | Gwyn Staley 400 | J. Johnson | J. Johnson | R. Petty | 15 |
| 1979 | Holly Farms 400 | D. Earnhardt | D. Earnhardt | B. Parsons | 5 | 1961 | Wilkes 320* | J. Johnson | J. Johnson | R. White | 3 |
|  | NW Bank 400 | B. Parsons | B. Parsons | B. Allison | 3 |  | Gwyn Staley 400 | J. Johnson | J. Johnson | R. White | 2 |

* 200-mile, 320-lap races.
a 160.625 miles (257 laps), rain.
b Dieringer led all 400 laps, 250 miles (April 16, 1967).
c Combined Grand National-Grand American race; Lund won in '70 Camaro (GA).
d Race run without a caution.
e Race cut by 25 miles, energy shortage.
f Race run without caution.

## ALL MAJOR NORTH WILKSBORO RACES

### POLE WINNERS

| | | | | | |
|---|---|---|---|---|---|
| D. Waltrip | 9 | D. Marcis | 2 | Buddy Baker | 1 |
| J. Johnson | 6 | B. Parsons | 2 | C. Glotzbach | 1 |
| B. Isaac | 6 | A. Kulwicki | 2 | J. Paschal | 1 |
| F. Lorenzen | 5 | T. Labonte | 2 | D. Huterson | 1 |
| B. Allison | 5 | T. Musgrave | 2 | C. Yarborough | 1 |
| B. Elliott | 3 | D. Earnhardt | 1 | D. Dieringer | 1 |
| R. Petty | 3 | R. Wallace | 1 | T. Richmond | 1 |
| G. Bodine | 2 | H. Gant | 1 | J. Spencer | 1 |
| B. Bodine | 2 | K. Petty | 1 | J. Gordon | 1 |
| E. Irvan | 2 | M. Martin | 2 | R. Rudd | 1 |
| N. Bonnett | 2 | D. Pearson | 1 | | |

### RACE WINNERS

| | | | | | |
|---|---|---|---|---|---|
| R. Petty | 15 | M. Panch | 2 | D. Dieringer | 1 |
| D. Waltrip | 10 | M. Martin | 2 | T. Richmond | 1 |
| C. Yarborough | 5 | B. Bodine | 1 | Da. Allison | 1 |
| D. Earnhardt | 5 | H. Gant | 1 | Gordon | 1 |
| B. Allison | 4 | N. Bonnett | 1 | | |
| T. Labonte | 4 | F. Lorenzen | 1 | | |
| R. Wallace | 3 | J. Paschal | 1 | | |
| G. Bodine | 3 | D. Hutcherson | 1 | | |
| D. Pearson | 2 | B. Parsons | 1 | | |
| J. Johnson | 2 | B. Isaac | 1 | | |
| R. White | 2 | T. Lund | 1 | | |

# Ontario Motor Speedway

## QUALIFYING AND RACE RECORDS

**QUALIFYING**
**Track:** Cale Yarborough, Oldsmobile, 156.190 mph, 57.622 seconds, Nov. 17, 1978.

**RACE**
**Track:** Buddy Baker, Ford, 140.712 mph, Nov. 23, 1975.

### YEAR BY YEAR WINNERS

| Year | Event | Fastest Qualifier | Pole Winner | Race Winner | Start Pos. |
|---|---|---|---|---|---|
| 1980 | L.A. Times 500 | C. Yarborough | C. Yarborough | Parsons | 4 |
| 1979 | L.A. Times 500 | C. Yarborough | C. Yarborough | Parsons | 2 |
| 1978 | L.A. Times 500 | C. Yarborough | C. Yarborough | B. Allison | 2 |
| 1977 | L.A. Times 500 | R. Petty | R. Petty | Bonnett | 2 |
| 1976 | L.A. Times 500 | Pearson | Pearson | Pearson | 1 |
| 1975 | L.A. Times 500 | Pearson | Pearson | Buddy Baker | 2 |
| 1974 | L.A. Times 500 | R. Petty | R. Petty | B. Allison | 4 |
| * 1972 | Miller 500 | Foyt | Foyt | Foyt | 1 |
| * 1971 | Miller 500 | Foyt | Foyt | Foyt | 1 |

* Started 51 cars, 17 rows of 3 drivers abreast.

### All Ontario races

| POLE WINNERS | | RACE WINNERS | |
|---|---|---|---|
| R. Petty | 7 | Foyt | 2 |
| C. Yarborough | 3 | B. Allison | 2 |
| Foyt | 2 | Parsons | 2 |
| Pearson | 2 | Pearson | 1 |
| R. Petty | 2 | Buddy Baker | 1 |
| | | Bonnett | 1 |

# Riverside International Raceway

## QUALIFYING AND RACE RECORDS

**QUALIFYING**
**Track:** Ricky Rudd, Buick, 118.484 mph, 1:19.606 seconds, June 10, 1988 (Budweiser 400).
**Budweiser 400:** Ricky Rudd, Buick, 118.484 mph, 1:19.606 seconds, June 10, 1988 (Budweiser 400).
**Winston Western 500:** Tim Richmond, Chevrolet, 118.247 mph, 1:19.765 seconds, Nov. 14, 1986.

**RACE**
**Track:** Darrell Waltrip, Chevrolet, 107.820 mph, Jan. 14, 1979, (500 kilometers).

**500-Mile Record:** Richard Petty, Ford, 105.518 mph, Feb. 1, 1969 (Motor Trend 500).
**500-Kilometer Record (311.78 miles):** Darrell Waltrip, Chevrolet, 107.820 mph, Jan. 14, 1979.
**400-Kilometer Record (248.9 miles):** David Pearson, Mercury, 108.279 mph, June 13, 1976 (Riverside 400).
**400-Mile Record:** Richard Petty, Plymouth, 101.120 mph, June 14, 1970, (Falstaff 400). Cale Yarborough averaged 102.489 mph in winning the Tuborg 400 on June 9, 1974, but the race was reduced to 361.56 miles because of the energy shortage.

### YEAR BY YEAR WINNERS

| Year | Event | Fastest Qualifier | Pole Winner | Race Winner | Start Pos. | | Year | Event | Fastest Qualifier | Pole Winner | Race Winner | Start Pos. |
|---|---|---|---|---|---|---|---|---|---|---|---|---|
| 1988 | Budweiser 400 | Rudd | Rudd | Wallace | 2 | f | 1976 | Riverside 400 | Pearson | Pearson | Pearson | 1 |
| 1987 | Winston West. 500 | G. Bodine | G. Bodine | Wallace | 3 | | | Winston West. 500 | B. Allison | B. Allison | Pearson | 2 |
| | Budweiser 400 | T. Labonte | T. Labonte | Richmond | 5 | | 1975 | Tuborg 400 | B. Allison | B. Allison | R. Petty | 2 |
| 1986 | Winston West. 500 | Richmond | Richmond | Richmond | 1 | | | Winston West. 500 | B. Allison | B. Allison | B. Allison | 1 |
| | Budweiser 400 | Waltrip | Waltrip | Waltrip | 1 | e | 1974 | Tuborg 400 | Follmer | Follmer | C. Yarborough | 3 |
| 1985 | Winston West. 500 | T. Labonte | T. Labonte | Rudd | 4 | d | | Winston West. 500 | Pearson | Pearson | C. Yarborough | 2 |
| | Budweiser 400 | Waltrip | Waltrip | T. Labonte | 2 | | 1973 | Tuborg 400 | R. Petty | R. Petty | B. Allison | 2 |
| 1984 | Winston West. 500 | T. Labonte | T. Labonte | Bodine | 12 | | | Winston West. 500 | Pearson | Pearson | Donohue | 4 |
| | Budweiser 400 | T. Labonte | T. Labonte | T. Labonte | 1 | | 1972 | Golden State 400 | R. Petty | R. Petty | Elder | 7 |
| 1983 | Winston West. 500 | Waltrip | Waltrip | Elliott | 10 | c | | Western 500 | B. Allison | Foyt | R. Petty | 2 |
| | Budweiser 400 | Waltrip | Waltrip | Rudd | 4 | | 1971 | Winston Gold. St. 400 | B. Allison | B. Allison | B. Allison | 1 |
| 1982 | Winston West. 500 | Waltrip | Waltrip | Richmond | 4 | | | Motor Trend 500 | Pearson | R. Petty | Elder | 3 |
| | Budweiser 400 | T. Labonte | T. Labonte | Richmond | 4 | * | 1970 | Falstaff 400 | B. Allison | B. Allison | R. Petty | 2 |
| 1981 | Winston West. 500 | Waltrip | Waltrip | B. Allison | 5 | b | | Motor Trend 500 | Jones | Jones | Foyt | 3 |
| | Hodgdon 400 | Waltrip | Waltrip | Waltrip | 1 | | 1969 | Motor Trend 500x | Foyt | Foyt | R. Petty | 4 |
| | Winston West. 500 | Waltrip | Waltrip | B. Allison | 2 | | 1968 | Motor Trend 500 | Gurney | Gurney | Gurney | 1 |
| 1980 | Hodgdon 500 | C. Yarborough | C. Yarborough | Waltrip | 2 | | 1967 | Motor Trend 500 | Hutcherson | Hutcherson | Jones | 6 |
| h | Winston West. 500 | Waltrip | Waltrip | Waltrip | 1 | | 1966 | Motor Trend 500 | Pearson | Pearson | Gurney | 2 |
| 1979 | NAPA 400 | Earnhardt | Earnhardt | B. Allison | 4 | | 1965 | Motor Trend 500 | Gurney | Jr. Johnson | Gurney | 2 |
| | Winston West. 500 | Pearson | Pearson | Waltrip | 4 | | 1964 | Motor Trend 500 | Lorenzen | Lorenzen | Gurney | 4 |
| 1978 | NAPA 400 | Pearson | Pearson | Parsons | 4 | | 1963 | Golden State 400 | Goldsmith | Panch | Dieringer | 3 |
| | Winston West. 500 | Pearson | Pearson | C. Yarborough | 4 | | | Motor Trend 500 | Gurney | Goldsmith | Gurney | 11 |
| 1977 | NAPA 400 | R. Petty | R. Petty | R. Petty | 1 | | 1961 | Riverside 100 | Gray | Gray | Dane | 2 |
| g | Winston West. 500x | C. Yarborough | C. Yarborough | Pearson | 2 | a | 1958 | Crown America 500 | Jones | Graves | Gray | 6 |

* Won Pole but started 35th.
a Course was 2.631 miles.
b Changed from 2.7-mile to 2.62-mile road course.
c Ended at 390 miles; rain, fog & darkness.
d Red flagged after lap 63, Jan. 20, completed Jan. 26 (Saturday).
e Race reduced to 361.56 miles, energy shortage.
f 400-mile race reduced to 400 kilometers (248.9 miles).
g 500-mile race reduced to 500 kilometers (311.78 miles).
h Red flagged after lap 24, Jan. 13, completed Jan. 19 (Saturday).
x Caution-free races.

## ALL RIVERSIDE RACES

### POLE WINNERS

| | | | | | |
|---|---|---|---|---|---|
| Waltrip | 9 | Foyt | 1 | Lorenzen | 1 |
| Pearson | 7 | Jones | 1 | Panch | 1 |
| T. Labonte | 5 | Follmer | 1 | Graves | 1 |
| B. Allison | 5 | Goldsmith | 1 | Earnhardt | 1 |
| R. Petty | 4 | Gurney | 1 | Rudd | 1 |
| C. Yarborough | 2 | Hutcherson | 1 | | |
| Richmond | 2 | Jr. Johnson | 1 | | |

### RACE WINNERS

| | | | | | |
|---|---|---|---|---|---|
| B. Allison | 6 | Rudd | 2 | Jones | 1 |
| R. Petty | 5 | Labonte | 2 | Donohue | 1 |
| Gurney | 5 | Wallace | 2 | Gray | 1 |
| Waltrip | 5 | Elder | 2 | Elliott | 1 |
| Richmond | 4 | Parsons | 1 | Bodine | 1 |
| Pearson | 3 | Foyt | 1 | | |
| C. Yarborough | 3 | Dieringer | 1 | | |

# Texas World Speedway

## QUALIFYING AND RACE RECORDS

**QUALIFYING**
**Track:** Buddy Baker, Dodge, 176.284 mph, 40.843 seconds, Dec. 4, 1969.

**RACE**
**Track:** Cale Yarborough, Chevrolet, 159.046 mph, June 1, 1980 (NASCAR 400).

### YEAR BY YEAR WINNERS

| Year | Event | Fastest Qualifier | Pole Winner | Race Winner | Start Pos. |
|---|---|---|---|---|---|
| 1981 | Budweiser 400 | T. Labonte | T. Labonte | Parsons | 4 |
| a 1980 | NASCAR 400 | C. Yarborough | C. Yarborough | C. Yarborough | 1 |
| 1979 | Texas 400 | Buddy Baker | Buddy Baker | Waltrip | 4 |
| 1973 | Alamo 500 | Buddy Baker | Buddy Baker | R. Petty | 2 |
| 1972 | Texas 500 | Foyt | Foyt | Buddy Baker | 2 |
| | Lone Star 500 | R. Petty | R. Petty | R. Petty | 1 |
| 1971 | Texas 500 | Hamilton | Hamilton | R. Petty | 3 |
| 1969 | Texas 500 | Buddy Baker | Buddy Baker | Isaac | 7 |

a Caution-free race.

### ALL TEXAS RACES

**POLE WINNERS**

| | | | |
|---|---|---|---|
| Buddy Baker | 3 | C. Yarborough | 1 |
| R. Petty | 1 | T. Labonte | 1 |
| Foyt | 1 | | |
| Hamilton | 1 | | |

**RACE WINNERS**

| | | | |
|---|---|---|---|
| R. Petty | 3 | C. Yarborough | 1 |
| Buddy Baker | 1 | Parsons | 1 |
| Isaac | 1 | | |
| Waltrip | 1 | | |

# Tracks with no NEXTEL Cup race

# Gateway International Raceway

## TRACK FACTS
**Location:** Madison, Ill.
**Length:** 1.25 miles
**Banking in Corners:** 11 degrees—Turn 1 & 2; 9 degrees—Turn 3 & 4
**Length of Frontstretch:** 1,922 feet
**Length of Backstretch:** 1,976 feet
**Website:** www.gatewayraceway.com

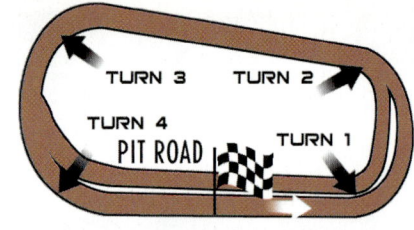

### 2004 SCHEDULE

**Busch Series**
TBD
**Race:** No. 10 of 34
**Date:** May 8
**TV:** FX. **Radio:** MRN

**Craftsman Truck Series**
Missouri/Illinois Dodge Dealers Ram Tough 200
**Race:** No. 12 of 25
**Date:** July 17
**TV:** Speed. **Radio:** MRN

### ALL GATEWAY BUSCH SERIES RACES

**POLE WINNERS**

| | | | |
|---|---|---|---|
| Casey Atwood | 1 | Shane Hall | 1 |
| Joe Bessey | 1 | Randy LaJoie | 1 |
| Greg Biffle | 1 | Ashton Lewis | 1 |

**RACE WINNERS**

| | | | |
|---|---|---|---|
| D. Earnhardt Jr. | 2 | Elliott Sadler | 1 |
| Kevin Harvick | 2 | Scott Riggs | 1 |
| Greg Biffle | 1 | | |

## QUALIFYING AND RACE RECORDS

**QUALIFYING**
**Track:** Casey Atwood, Chevrolet; 132.423 mph (33.982 sec.); July 30, 1999.

**RACE**
**Track:** Kevin Harvick, Chevrolet; 116.595 mph (2 hr., 8 min., 39 sec.); July 29, 2000.

## BUSCH SERIES YEAR BY YEAR WINNERS

| Year | Event | Pole Winner | Speed | Race Winner | Start Pos. |
|---|---|---|---|---|---|
| 1997 | Gateway 300 | J. Bessey | 130.993 | E. Sadler | 12 |
| 1998 | Carquest Auto Parts 250 | S. Hall | 132.361 | D. Earnhardt Jr. | 13 |
| 1999 | Carquest Auto Parts 250 | C. Atwood | 132.423 | D. Earnhardt Jr. | 18 |
| 2000 | Carquest Auto Parts 250 | None - weather | — | K. Harvick | 4 |
| 2001 | Carquest Auto Parts 250 | G. Biffle | 132.357 | K. Harvick | 2 |
| 2002 | Charter Pipeline 250 | R. LaJoie | 131.911 | G. Biffle | 7 |
| 2003 | Charter Pipeline 250 | A. Lewis | 131.903 | S. Riggs | 8 |

## TRUCK SERIES YEAR BY YEAR WINNERS

| Year | Event | Pole Winner | Speed | Race Winner | Start Pos. |
|---|---|---|---|---|---|
| 1998 | Ram Tough 200 | Greg Biffle | 131.218 mph | Rick Carelli | 4 |
| 1999 | Ram Tough 200 | Stacy Compton | 133.093 mph | Greg Biffle | 5 |
| 2000 | Ram Tough 200 | Greg Biffle | 132.279 mph | Jack Sprague | 2 |
| 2001 | Ram Tough 200 | Ted Musgrave | 129.971 mph | Ted Musgrave | 1 |
| 2002 | Ram Tough 200 | Mike Bliss | 129.549 mph | Terry Cook | 8 |
| 2003 | Ram Tough 200 | None - weather | — | Brendan Gaughan | 4 |

## ALL GATEWAY TRUCK SERIES RACES

**POLE WINNERS**
- Casey Atwood 1
- Greg Biffle 2
- Mike Bliss 1
- Stacy Compton 1
- Ted Musgrave 1

**RACE WINNERS**
- Greg Biffle 1
- Rick Carelli 1
- Terry Cook 1
- Ted Musgrave 1
- Jack Sprague 1
- B. Gaughan 1

## QUALIFYING AND RACE RECORDS

**QUALIFYING**
**Track:** Stacy Compton, Dodge; 133.093 mph (33.811 sec.); August 19, 1999.

**RACE**
**Track:** Jack Sprague, Chevrolet; 113.726 mph (1 hr., 35 min., 31 sec.); May 7, 2000.

# Indianapolis Raceway Park

## TRACK FACTS
**Location:** Clermont, Ind.
**Track Length:** .686 miles
**Banking in Corners:** 7.5 degrees
**Banking on Straights:** 2 degrees
**Length of Frontstretch:** 699 feet
**Length of Backstretch:** 699 feet
**Website:** www.irponline.com

## 2004 SCHEDULE

**Busch Series**
Kroger 200
**Race:** No. 22 of 34
**Date:** August 7
**TV:** TNT. **Radio:** MRN

**Craftsman Truck Series**
Power Stroke Diesel 200
**Race:** No. 14 of 25
**Date:** August 6
**TV:** Speed. **Radio:** MRN

## BUSCH SERIES YEAR BY YEAR WINNERS

| Year | Event | Pole Winner | Speed | Race Winner | Start Pos. |
|---|---|---|---|---|---|
| 1982 | Kroger 200 | S. Ard | 104.436 | M. Shepherd | 5 |
| 1983 | Kroger 200 | P. Parsons | 105.201 | T. Houston | 7 |
| 1984 | Kroger 200 | L. Ottinger | 104.246 | M. Shepherd | 3 |
| 1985 | Kroger 200 | B. Bodine | 105.121 | J. Hensley | 2 |
| 1986 | Kroger 200 | D. Waltrip | 104.910 | B. Miller | 18 |
| 1987 | Kroger 200 | M. Alexander | 104.387 | L. Pearson | 11 |
| 1988 | Kroger 200 | K. Moore | 105.895 | M. Shepherd | 2 |
| 1989 | Kroger 200 | M. Waltrip | 108.807 | M. Waltrip | 1 |
| 1990 | Kroger 200 | J. Hensley | 110.260 | S. Grissom | 17 |
| 1991 | Kroger 200 | W. Burton | 110.516 | B. Labonte | 3 |
| 1992 | Kroger 200 | R. Pressley | 109.265 | J. Nemechek | 3 |
| 1993 | Kroger 200 | E. Irvan | 109.828 | T. Leslie | 10 |
| 1994 | Kroger 200 | D. Green | 113.461 | M. Wallace | 5 |
| 1995 | Kroger 200 | E. Sawyer | 109.570 | J. Keller | 3 |
| 1996 | Kroger 200 | R. LaJoie | 109.270 | R. LaJoie | 1 |
| 1997 | Kroger 200 | R. LaJoie | 111.193 | R. LaJoie | 1 |
| 1998 | Kroger 200 | B. Jones | 111.409 | D. Earnhardt Jr. | 16 |
| 1999 | Kroger 200 | J. Keller | 112.352 | J. Keller | 1 |
| 2000 | Kroger 200 | J. Leffler | 112.597 | R. Hornaday | 16 |
| 2001 | Kroger 200 | K. Wallace | 110.635 | K. Harvick | 12 |
| 2002 | Kroger 200 | G. Biffle | 109.521 | G. Biffle | 1 |
| 2003 | Kroger 200 | S. Hmiel | 110.690 | B. Vickers | 3 |

## ALL IRP BUSCH SERIES RACES

**POLE WINNERS**
- Randy LaJoie 2
- Mike Alexander 1
- Sam Ard 1
- Greg Biffle 1
- Brett Bodine 1
- Ward Burton 1
- David Green 1
- Jimmy Hensley 1
- Ernie Irvan 1
- Buckshot Jones 1
- Jason Keller 1
- Jason Leffler 1
- Kelly Moore 1
- L.D. Ottinger 1
- Phil Parsons 1
- Robert Pressley 1
- Elton Sawyer 1
- Kenny Wallace 1
- Darrell Waltrip 1
- Michael Waltrip 1
- Shane Hmiel 1

**RACE WINNERS**
- M. Shepherd 3
- Jason Keller 1
- Randy LaJoie 2
- Greg Biffle 1
- D. Earnhardt Jr. 1
- Steve Grissom 1
- Kevin Harvick 1
- Jimmy Hensley 1
- Ron Hornaday 1
- T. Houston 1
- Bobby Labonte 1
- Tracy Leslie 1
- Butch Miller 1
- Joe Nemechek 1
- Larry Pearson 1
- Mike Wallace 1
- Michael Waltrip 1
- Brian Vickers 1

## QUALIFYING AND RACE RECORDS

**QUALIFYING**
**Track:** David Green, Chevrolet; 113.461 mph (21.766 sec.); August 4, 1994.

**RACE**
**Track:** Jimmy Hensley, Oldsmobile; 96.923 mph (1 hr., 24 min., 56 sec.); June 22, 1985.

### TRUCK SERIES YEAR BY YEAR WINNERS

| Year | Event | Pole Winner | Speed | Race Winner | Start Pos. |
|---|---|---|---|---|---|
| 1995 | Action Packed 150 | Mike Skinner | 108.387 mph | Mike Skinner | 1 |
| 1996 | Cummins 200 | Mike Skinner | 108.855 mph | Mike Skinner | 1 |
| 1997 | Cummins 200 | Jimmy Hensley | 109.750 mph | Ron Hornaday Jr. | 2 |
| 1998 | Cummins 200 | Randy Tolsma | 110.829 mph | Jack Sprague | 3 |
| 1999 | Power Stroke 200 | Dennis Setzer | 111.133 mph | Greg Biffle | 3 |
| 2000 | Power Stroke 200 | Joe Ruttman | 111.843 mph | Joe Ruttman | 1 |
| 2001 | Power Stroke 200 | Joe Ruttman | 109.043 mph | Jack Sprague | 2 |
| 2002 | Power Stroke 200 | Terry Cook | 108.549 mph | Terry Cook | 1 |
| 2003 | Power Stroke 200 | Terry Cook | 107.777 mph | Carl Edwards | 5 |

### ALL IRP TRUCK SERIES RACES

**POLE WINNERS**

| | | | | | |
|---|---|---|---|---|---|
| Joe Ruttman | 2 | Dennis Setzer | 1 | | |
| Mike Skinner | 2 | Randy Tolsma | 1 | | |
| Terry Cook | 2 | | | | |
| Jimmy Hensley | 1 | | | | |

**RACE WINNERS**

| | | | |
|---|---|---|---|
| Mike Skinner | 2 | R. Hornaday Jr. | 1 |
| Jack Sprague | 2 | Joe Ruttman | 1 |
| Greg Biffle | 1 | Carl Edwards | 1 |
| Terry Cook | 1 | | |

## QUALIFYING AND RACE RECORDS

**QUALIFYING**
Track: Joe Ruttman, Dodge; 111.843 mph (222.081 sec.); August 2, 2000.

**RACE**
Track: Greg Biffle, Ford; 88.704 mph (1 hr., 33 min., 16 sec.); August 5, 1999.

# Kentucky Speedway

### TRACK FACTS
**Location:** Sparta, Ky.
**Length:** 1.5 Miles
**Banking in Corners:** 14 degrees
**Banking on Straights:** 8 degrees
**Length of Backstretch:** 1,600 feet
**Website:** www.kentuckyspeedway.com

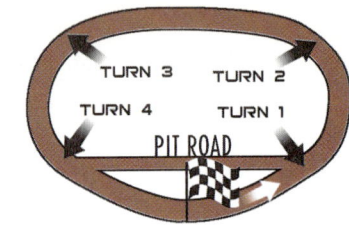

### 2004 SCHEDULE

**Busch Series**
Meijer 300
**Race:** No. 16 of 34
**Date:** June 19
**TV:** FX. **Radio:** MRN

**Craftsman Truck Series**
Built Ford Tough 225
**Race:** No. 11 of 25
**Date:** July 10
**TV:** Speed. **Radio:** MRN

### BUSCH SERIES YEAR BY YEAR WINNERS

| Year | Event | Pole Winner | Speed | Race Winner | Start Pos. |
|---|---|---|---|---|---|
| 2001 | Outback Steakhouse 300 | Ja. Sauter | 171.860 | K. Harvick | 11 |
| 2002 | Kroger 300 | S. Riggs | 174.831 | T. Bodine | 6 |
| 2003 | Meijer 300 | S. Compton | 176.384 | B. Hamilton Jr. | 2 |

### ALL KENTUCKY BUSCH SERIES RACES

**POLE WINNERS**

| | | | |
|---|---|---|---|
| Ja. Sauter | 1 | S. Compton | 1 |
| S. Riggs | 1 | | |

**RACE WINNERS**

| | | | |
|---|---|---|---|
| K. Harvick | 1 | B. Hamilton Jr. | 1 |
| T. Bodine | 1 | | |

## QUALIFYING AND RACE RECORDS

**QUALIFYING**
Track: Stacy Compton, Chevrolet, 176.384 mph; June 13, 2003.

**RACE**
Track: Bobby Hamilton Jr., Ford; 136.123 mph (2 hr., 12 min., 14 sec.); June 14, 2003

### TRUCK SERIES YEAR BY YEAR WINNERS

| Year | Event | Pole Winner | Speed | Race Winner | Start Pos. |
|---|---|---|---|---|---|
| 2000 | Kroger 225 | B. Reffner | 168.460 | G. Biffle | 2 |
| 2001 | Kroger 225 | J. Sprague | 167.115 | S. Riggs | 3 |
| 2002 | Kroger 225 | J. Leffler | 168.303 | M. Bliss | 2 |
| 2003 | Built Ford Tough 225 | J. Wood | 169.641 | C. Edwards | 5 |

### ALL KENTUCKY TRUCK SERIES RACES

**POLE WINNERS**

| | | | |
|---|---|---|---|
| B. Reffner | 1 | J. Leffler | 1 |
| J. Sprague | 1 | J. Wood | 1 |

**RACE WINNERS**

| | | | |
|---|---|---|---|
| G. Biffle | 1 | M. Bliss | 1 |
| S. Riggs | 1 | C. Edwards | 1 |

## QUALIFYING AND RACE RECORDS

**QUALIFYING**
Track: Jon Wood, Ford; 169.641 mph, July 11, 2003.

**RACE**
Track: Carl Edwards, Ford; 122.393 mph (1 hr., 50 min., 18 sec.); July 12, 2003.

# Memphis Motorsports Park

## TRACK FACTS
**Location:** Millington, Tenn.
**Length:** .75 miles
**Banking in Corners:** 11 degrees
**Banking on Straights:** 4 degrees
**Length of Frontstretch:** 1,100 feet
**Length of Backstretch:** 1,100 feet
**Website:** www.memphismotorsportspark.com

### BUSCH SERIES YEAR BY YEAR WINNERS

| Year | Event | Pole Winner | Speed | Race Winner | Start Pos. |
|---|---|---|---|---|---|
| 1999 | Sam's Town 250 | J. Green | 119.311 | J. Green | 1 |
| 2000 | Sam's Town 250 | J. Green | 120.267 | K. Harvick | 2 |
| 2001 | Sam's Town 250 | None - weather | | R. LaJoie | 16 |
| 2002 | Sam's Town 250 | G. Biffle | 116.817 | S. Wimmer | 6 |
| 2003 | Sam's Town 250 | D. Reutimann | 119.766 | B. Hamilton Jr. | 4 |

### 2004 SCHEDULE

**Busch Series**
Sam's Town 250
Race: No. 30 of 34
Date: October 23
TV: TNT. Radio: MRN

**Craftsman Truck Series**
O'Reilly 200
Race: No. 8 of 25
Date: June 19
TV: Speed. Radio: MRN

### BUSCH QUALIFYING AND RACE RECORDS

**QUALIFYING**
Track: Jeff Green, Chevrolet; 120.267 mph (22.450 sec.); October 28, 2000.

**RACE**
Track: Kevin Harvick, Chevrolet; 92.352 mph (2 hrs., 1 min., 49 sec.).

### ALL MEMPHIS BUSCH SERIES RACES

| POLE WINNERS | | RACE WINNERS | |
|---|---|---|---|
| Jeff Green | 2 | Jeff Green | 1 |
| Greg Biffle | 1 | Kevin Harvick | 1 |
| D. Reutimann | 1 | Randy LaJoie | 1 |
| | | Scott Wimmer | 1 |
| | | B. Hamilton Jr. | 1 |

### TRUCK SERIES YEAR BY YEAR WINNERS

| Year | Event | Pole Winner | Speed | Race Winner | Start Pos. |
|---|---|---|---|---|---|
| 1998 | Memphis 200 | Greg Biffle | 118.901 mph | Ron Hornaday Jr. | 3 |
| 1999 | Memphis 200 | Greg Biffle | 120.139 mph | Greg Biffle | 1 |
| 2000 | Quaker State 200 | Bobby Hamilton | 118.043 mph | Jack Sprague | 5 |
| 2001 | Memphis 200 | Jack Sprague | 116.863 mph | Dennis Setzer | 4 |
| 2002 | Memphis 200 | Jason Leffler | 117.971 mph | Travis Kvapil | 3 |
| 2003 | O'Reilly 200 | Jon Wood | 117.407 mph | Ted Musgrave | 3 |

### ALL MEMPHIS TRUCK SERIES RACES

| POLE WINNERS | | | | RACE WINNERS | | | |
|---|---|---|---|---|---|---|---|
| Greg Biffle | 2 | Jack Sprague | 1 | Greg Biffle | 1 | Dennis Setzer | 1 |
| Bobby Hamilton | 1 | Jon Wood | 1 | Ron Hornaday Jr. | 1 | Jack Sprague | 1 |
| Jason Leffler | 1 | | | Travis Kvapil | 1 | Ted Musgrave | 1 |

### QUALIFYING AND RACE RECORDS

**QUALIFYING**
Track: Greg Biffle, Ford; 120.139 mph (22.484 sec.); May 7, 1999.

**RACE**
Track: Travis Kvapil, Chevrolet; 89.065 mph (1 hr., 41 min., 3 sec.); June 22, 2002.

# The Milwaukee Mile

## TRACK FACTS
**Location:** West Allis, Wis.
**Length:** 1 mile
**Banking in Corners:** 9.25 degrees
**Banking on Straights:** 2.5 degrees
**Length of Frontstretch:** 1,265 feet
**Length of Backstretch:** 1,265 feet
**Website:** www.milwaukeemile.com

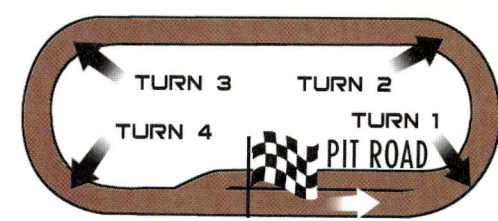

### 2004 SCHEDULE

**Busch Series**
TBD
Race No. 17 of 34
Date: June 26
TV: FX. Radio: MRN

**Craftsman Truck Series**
GNC 200
Race No. 9 of 25
Date: June 26
TV: Speed. Radio: MRN

## BUSCH SERIES YEAR BY YEAR WINNERS

| Year | Event | Pole Winner | Speed | Race Winner | Start Pos. |
|---|---|---|---|---|---|
| 1984 | Red Carpet 200 | D. Trickle | 112.984 | S. Ard | 3 |
| 1985 | Mil. Sentinel 200 | A. Kulwicki | 112.711 | J. Ingram | 8 |
| 1993* | Havoline 250 | B. Dotter | 113.845 | S. Grissom | 14 |
| 1994 | Havoilne 250 | D. Green | 115.407 | M. Wallace | 25 |
| 1995 | Sears Auto Center 250 | D. Setzer | 114.650 | D. Jarrett | 12 |
| 1996 | Sears Auto Center 250 | H. Sadler | 118.320 | B. Jones | 32 |
| 1997 | Sears Auto Center 250 | T. Fedewa | 118.468 | R. LaJoie | 10 |
| 1998 | Diehard 250 | J. Purvis | 119.904 | D. Earnhardt Jr. | 2 |
| 1999 | Diehard 250 | C. Atwood | 121.421 | C. Atwood | 1 |
| 2000 | Sears Diehard 250 | J. Green | 121.572 | J. Green | 1 |
| 2001 | GNC Live Well 250 | K. Harvick | 122.474 | G. Biffle | 2 |
| 2002 | GNC Live Well 250 | G. Biffle | 121.770 | G. Biffle | 1 |
| 2003 | GNC 250 | None - weather | — | J. Keller | 7 |

*race distance increased to 250 miles

## ALL MILWAUKEE BUSCH SERIES RACES

### POLE WINNERS

| | | | | | |
|---|---|---|---|---|---|
| G. Biffle | 2 | T. Fedewa | 1 | | |
| D. Trickle | 1 | J. Purvis | 1 | | |
| A. Kulwicki | 1 | C. Atwood | 1 | | |
| B. Dotter | 1 | J. Green | 1 | | |
| D. Green | 1 | K. Harvick | 1 | | |
| D. Setzer | 1 | | | | |
| H. Sadler | 1 | | | | |

### RACE WINNERS

| | | | | | |
|---|---|---|---|---|---|
| G. Biffle | 2 | R. LaJoie | 1 | | |
| S. Ard | 1 | Earnhardt Jr. | 1 | | |
| J. Ingram | 1 | C. Atwood | 1 | | |
| S. Grissom | 1 | J. Green | 1 | | |
| M. Wallace | 1 | J. Keller | 1 | | |
| D. Jarrett | 1 | | | | |
| B. Jones | 1 | | | | |

## QUALIFYING AND RACE RECORDS

**QUALIFYING**
**Track:** Kevin Harvick, Chevrolet; 122.474 mph (29.394 sec.); June 29, 2001.

**RACE**
**Track:** Jason Keller, Ford; 103.093 mph (2 hrs., 25 min, 30 sec.); June 29, 2003.

## TRUCK SERIES YEAR BY YEAR WINNERS

| Year | Event | Pole Winner | Speed | Race Winner | Start Pos. |
|---|---|---|---|---|---|
| 1995 | Sears Auto 125 | Mike Skinner | 112.535 | Mike Skinner | 1 |
| 1996 | Sears Auto 200 | Mike Bills | 118.265 | Jack Sprague | 8 |
| 1997 | DieHard 200 | Jack Sprague | 119.178 | Ron Hornaday Jr. | 5 |
| 1998 | DieHard 200 | Jack Sprague | 120.530 | Mike Bliss | 2 |
| 1999 | DieHard 200 | Greg Biffle | 121.102 | Greg Biffle | 1 |
| 2000 | DieHard 200 | Kurt Busch | 120.518 | Kurt Busch | 1 |
| 2001 | GNC Live Well 200 | Jack Sprague | 120.692 | Ted Musgrave | 3 |
| 2002 | GNC Live Well 200 | Terry Cook | 119.784 | Terry Cook | 1 |
| 2003 | GNC 200 | Terry Cook | 119.996 | Brendan Gaughan | 2 |

## ALL MILWAUKEE TRUCK SERIES RACES

### POLE WINNERS

| | | | |
|---|---|---|---|
| Jack Sprague | 3 | Greg Biffle | 1 |
| Terry Cook | 2 | Kurt Busch | 1 |
| Mike Sinner | 1 | | |
| Mike Bliss | 1 | | |

### RACE WINNERS

| | | | |
|---|---|---|---|
| Mike Skinner | 1 | Greg Biffle | 1 |
| Jack Sprague | 1 | Kurt Busch | 1 |
| Ron Hornaday Jr. | 1 | Ted Musgrave | 1 |
| Mike Bliss | 1 | Terry Cook | 1 |

## QUALIFYING AND RACE RECORDS

**QUALIFYING**
**Track:** Greg Biffle, Ford; 121.102 mph (29.727 sec.); July 2, 1999.

**RACE**
**Track:** Brendan Gaughan, Dodge; 109.689 mph (1 hr., 49 min., 24 sec.); June 28, 2003.

# Nashville Superspeedway

## TRACK FACTS

**Location:** Nashville
**Length:** 1.333 miles
**Banking in Corners:** 14 degrees
**Banking on Straights:** Front - 9 degrees; Back - 6 degrees
**Length of Frontstretch:** 2,494 feet
**Length of Backstretch:** 2,203 feet
**Website:** www.nashvillesuperspeedway.com

## BUSCH SERIES YEAR BY YEAR WINNERS

| Year | Event | Pole Winner | Speed | Race Winner | Start Pos. |
|---|---|---|---|---|---|
| 2001 | Pepsi 300 | K. Harvick | 159.678 | G. Biffle | 4 |
| 2002 | Pepsi 300 | S. Hmiel | 161.440 | S. Riggs | 3 |
| | Inside Traxx 300 | G. Biffle | 161.288 | J. Sprague | 5 |
| 2003 | Pepsi 300 | R. LaJoie | 163.424 | D. Green | 7 |
| | Trace Adkins Chr. 300 | none - weather | | Scott Riggs | 3 |

## ALL NASHVILLE BUSCH SERIES RACES

### POLE WINNERS

| | | | |
|---|---|---|---|
| Greg Biffle | 1 | Shane Hmiel | 1 |
| K. Harvick | 1 | Randy LaJoie | 1 |

### RACE WINNERS

| | | | |
|---|---|---|---|
| Scott Riggs | 2 | Jack Sprague | 1 |
| Greg Biffle | 1 | David Green | 1 |

## 2004 SCHEDULE

### Busch Series
**Pepsi 300 by Mapco**
**Race:** No. 7 of 34
**Date:** April 10
**TV:** FX. **Radio:** MRN

**Federated Auto Parts 300**
**Race:** No. 15 of 34
**Date:** June 12
**TV:** FX. **Radio:** MRN

### Craftsman Truck Series
**Toyota Tundra 200**
**Race:** No. 15 of 24
**Date:** August 14
**TV:** Speed. **Radio:** MRN

## QUALIFYING AND RACE RECORDS

**QUALIFYING**
Track: Randy LaJoie, Chevrolet; 163.324 mph; April 11, 2003.

**RACE**
Track: David Green, Pontiac; 122.724 mph (2 hrs., 26 min., 38 sec.); April 12, 2003.

### TRUCK SERIES YEAR BY YEAR WINNERS

| Year | Event | Pole Winner | Speed | Race Winner | Start Pos. |
|---|---|---|---|---|---|
| 2001 | Federated Auto 200 | Scott Riggs | 155.477 mph | Scott Riggs | 1 |
| 2002 | Federated Auto 200 | Mike Bliss | 157.322 mph | Mike Bliss | 1 |
| 2003 | Federated Auto 200 | Chad Chaffin | 156.844 | Carl Edwards | 6 |

### ALL NASHVILLE TRUCK SERIES RACES

| POLE WINNERS | | | | RACE WINNERS | | | |
|---|---|---|---|---|---|---|---|
| Mike Bliss | 1 | Chad Chaffin | 1 | Mike Bliss | 1 | Carl Edwards | 1 |
| Scott Riggs | 1 | | | Scott Riggs | 1 | | |

## QUALIFYING AND RACE RECORDS

**QUALIFYING**
Track: Mike Bliss, Chevrolet; 157.322 mph (30.503 sec.); August 9, 2002.

**RACE**
Track: Scott Riggs, Dodge; 132.466 mph (1 hr., 30 min., 34 sec.); August 10, 2001.

# Nazareth Speedway

## TRACK FACTS
**Location:** Nazareth, Pa.
**Length:** 1 mile
**Banking in Corners:** Turn 1 - 3 degrees; Turn 2 - 4 degrees; Turns 3 and 4 - 6 degrees
**Banking on Straights:** Back stretch - 2.7 degrees; Front stretch - 3 degrees
**Length of Frontstretch:** 800 feet
**Length of Backstretch:** 1,200 feet
**Website:** www.nazarethspeedway.com

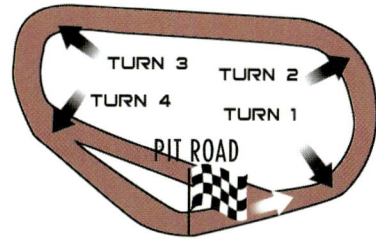

### 2004 SCHEDULE
**Busch Series**
TBD
**Race:** No. 12 of 34
**Date:** May 23
**TV:** FX. **Radio:** MRN

### BUSCH SERIES YEAR BY YEAR WINNERS

| Year | Event | Pole Winner | Speed | Race Winner | Start Pos. |
|---|---|---|---|---|---|
| 1988 | Pennsylvania 300 | None - weather | — | R. Mast | 12 |
| 1989 | GM Parts 300 | T. Houston | 124.031 | B. Hillin | 2 |
| 1990 | Pontiac 300 | Da. Allison | 124.146 | J. Hensley | 2 |
| 1991* | Pontiac 200 | J. Hensley | 126.205 | C. Bown | 2 |
| 1992 | Pontiac 200 | None - weather | — | T. Bodine | 19 |
| 1993 | Laneco 200 | T. Bodine | 126.311 | R. Pressley | 11 |
| 1994 | Meridian Adv. 200 | K. Wallace | 128.834 | R. Craven | 9 |
| 1995 | Meridian Adv. 200 | D. Green | 128.265 | T. Fedewa | 2 |
| 1996 | Meridian Adv. 200 | D. Green | 129.231 | R. LaJoie | 3 |
| 1997 | Core States Adv. 200 | E. Sadler | 129.674 | E. Sadler | 1 |
| 1998 | First Union 200 | D. Earnhardt Jr. | 128.558 | T. Fedewa | 2 |
| 1999** | First Union 200 | J. Green | 130.866 | M. Kenseth | 7 |
| 2000 | EconoLodge 200 | J. Green | 132.402 | R. Hornaday | 4 |
| 2001 | Nazareth 200 | T. Raines | 131.334 | G. Biffle | 7 |
| 2002 | Stacker 2 200 | None - weather | — | J. Keller | 2 |
| 2003 | Goulds Pumps ITT 200 | Randy LaJoie | 133.215 | R. Hornaday | 3 |

\* race length changed to 200 miles.
\*\* race length shortened due to darkness

### ALL NAZARETH BUSCH SERIES RACES

| POLE WINNERS | | | | RACE WINNERS | | | |
|---|---|---|---|---|---|---|---|
| David Green | 2 | Tony Raines | 1 | Tim Fedewa | 2 | Bobby Hillin | 1 |
| Jeff Green | 2 | Elliott Sadler | 1 | Ron Hornaday | 2 | Jason Keller | 1 |
| Davey Allison | 1 | Kenny Wallace | 1 | Gerg Biffle | 1 | Matt Kenseth | 1 |
| Todd Bodine | 1 | Randy LaJoie | 1 | Todd Bodine | 1 | Randy LaJoie | 1 |
| D. Earnhardt Jr. | 1 | | | Chuck Bown | 1 | Rick Mast | 1 |
| Jimmy Hensley | 1 | | | Ricky Craven | 1 | Robert Pressley | 1 |
| T. Houston | 1 | | | Jimmy Hensley | 1 | Elliott Sadler | 1 |

## QUALIFYING AND RACE RECORDS

**QUALIFYING**
Track: Randy LaJoie, Chevrolet; 133.215 mph, May 17, 2003.

**RACE**
Track: (200 miles) Chuck Bown, Pontiac; 104.772 mph (1 hr., 54 min., 32 sec.); May 11, 1991.

# Pikes Peak International Raceway

## TRACK FACTS
**Location:** Fountain, Colo.
**Length:** 1 mile
**Banking in Corners:** 10 degrees
**Banking on Straights:** Front - 7 degrees; Back - 3 degrees
**Length of Frontstretch:** 1,510 feet
**Length of Backstretch:** 1,350 feet
**Website:** www.ppir.com

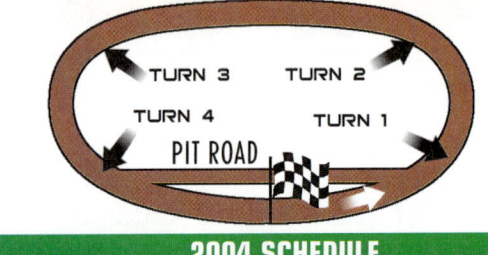

### BUSCH SERIES YEAR BY YEAR WINNERS

| Year | Event | Pole Winner | Speed | Race Winner | Start Pos. |
|---|---|---|---|---|---|
| 1998 | Lycos.com 250 | M. Kenseth | 134.193 | M. Kenseth | 1 |
| 1999 | NAPA Autocare 250 | D. Blaney | 135.318 | A. Santerre | 20 |
| 2000 | NAPA Autocare 250 | J. Purvis | 135.629 | J. Green | 2 |
| 2001 | NAPA Autocare 250 | K. Wallace | 131.062 | J. Purvis | 7 |
| 2002 | Net Zero 250 | J. Keller | 131.801 | H. Parker Jr. | 23 |
| 2003 | TrimSpa 250 | B. Hamilton Jr. | 133.318 | S. Wimmer | 16 |

### 2004 SCHEDULE
**Busch Series**
TBD
**Race:** No. 21 of 34
**Date:** July 31
**TV:** TNT  **Radio:** MRN

### QUALIFYING AND RACE RECORDS
**QUALIFYING**
**Track:** Jeff Purvis, Pontiac; 135.629 mph (26.543 sec.); July 21, 2000.
**RACE**
**Track:** Jeff Purvis, Chevrolet; 120.160 mph (2 hrs., 4 min., 50 sec.); July 28, 2001.

### ALL PIKES PEAK BUSCH SERIES RACES

| POLE WINNERS | | RACE WINNERS | | | |
|---|---|---|---|---|---|
| Dave Blaney | 1 | Jeff Purvis | 1 | Jeff Green | 1 | Jeff Purvis | 1 |
| Jason Keller | 1 | Kenny Wallace | 1 | Matt Kenseth | 1 | Andy Santerre | 1 |
| Matt Kenseth | 1 | B. Hamilton Jr. | 1 | Hank Parker Jr. | 1 | S. Wimmer | 1 |

# Mansfield Motorsports Speedway

## TRACK FACTS
**Location:** Mansfield, Ohio
**Length:** .44 miles
**Banking in Corners:** 12 degrees, 14 degrees and 16 degrees
**Banking on Straights:** 6 degrees
**Length of Straights:** 545 feet
**Website:** www.mansfield-speedway.com

### 2004 SCHEDULE
**Craftsman Truck Series**
Ohio 250
**Race:** No. 4 of 25
**Date:** May 16
**TV:** Speed.  **Radio:** MRN

# NASCAR on television

Ever since the breakthrough of 2001, NASCAR and its broadcast partners have worked hard toward maintaining the position as the No. 2 regular season sport on television and continuing to expand the audience of NASCAR's top series.

After the success of the inaugural season, many observers expected something less in 2002. But NASCAR's broadcast partners delivered outstanding production, innovative technology and unprecedented cross-promotion of the sport. NBC began the 2002 season broadcasting what turned out to be the highest-rated Daytona 500 in history. Drawing a 10.9 rating, it was NBC's first broadcast of the event under the network's six-year deal and was the most watched Daytona 500 since 1979, when CBS aired the event live for the first time on network television.

FOX Sports and cable partner FX carried that momentum into the first half of the 2002 season, picking up the coverage in Rockingham, N.C.: The average per-race audience for NASCAR on FOX "regular season" NASCAR Cup races increased by 70,000 viewers, to 9.334 million. Considering the sport's surge of interest in 2001 surrounding the tragic events at the Daytona 500 and the rainout at Texas Motor Speedway in 2002, FOX's ability to keep the ratings steady in 2002 was quite an accomplishment.

"2002 was a great season and there is no doubt to us that television is a powerful engine that helps drive the sport," said Paul Brooks, vice president of broadcasting for NASCAR. "Our network partners continued to promote and present our sport like never before—attracting new fans, serving our core constituency, and building exposure for all of our drivers, teams, tracks and corporate marketing partners."

NASCAR on FOX has also enjoyed the acclaims of the sports television industry: At its annual awards presentation in 2002, the National Academy of Television Arts and Sciences recognized FOX Sports' inaugural season covering NASCAR. The NASCAR on FOX coverage received three Emmys, more than any single sports series. Despite having never broadcast a single race before 2001, FOX's NASCAR coverage won awards for outstanding live sports series, technical team remote and graphic design.

When NBC returned in July at Chicagoland Speedway, it began a 20-week consecutive sprint for the 2002 NASCAR Winston Cup Series championship.

A highlight was NBC's coverage of the NAPA 500 at the Atlanta Motor Speedway on October 27, 2002, which generated a 5.1 national rating, the highest ever to that point against professional football, according to Nielsen Media Research.

The results were equally impressive on cable television. The Virginia 500, televised from Martinsville on April 14, 2002, attracted 5.3 million viewers, the biggest audience for any program in the history of the FX network. FX and TNT also achieved great results from a business perspective in their second year televising NASCAR. FX increased its overall viewership by 21 million homes since the spring of 2001, whereas TNT brought in 40 new sponsors since it began airing NASCAR races.

Additionally, SPEED Channel's growth continues to lead the sports cable charts, with the network adding more than 10 million homes since the change of ownership and the creation of NASCAR TV, according to Nielsen Media Research. SPEED Channel is now in 59 million homes in the United States and Canada and was rated as the fastest-growing sports cable network in the United States and the ninth-fastest-growing cable network overall by Nielsen.

In 2003, FOX and its family of networks began their third season of NASCAR coverage with comprehensive programming from SpeedWeeks, leading up to live coverage of the 45th annual Daytona 500. The unprecedented coverage, shared by FOX, FX, FOX Sports Net and SPEED Channel, featured nearly 50 hours of on-track coverage and another 20-plus hours of studio programming, marking a dramatic increase in programming hours from 2001, when FOX offered 43 hours during its network premiere from Daytona.

In addition to complete coverage of the Daytona 500, programming was highlighted by live coverage of the 70-lap Budweiser Shootout, presented for the first time in prime time, and the debut of the NASCAR Craftsman Truck Series on SPEED Channel.

For 2004, NBC will kick off its coverage with the first NEXTEL Cup Series race, providing complete coverage of the Daytona 500. TNT will televise SpeedWeeks action, specifically the Budweiser Shootout and both Gatorade 125 races. SPEED Channel also will have a heavy programming presence.

After Daytona, NBC and TNT will next combine efforts to televise the races of the second half of the season, beginning with the Tropicana 400 at Chicagoland Speedway. NBC

and TNT will then follow the NASCAR NEXTEL Cup championship race through the season finale Ford 400 on November 21 at Homestead-Miami Speedway.

In total, NBC Sports will televise 12 NASCAR NEXTEL Cup Series events in 2004, including the prime-time broadcast of the UAW-GM Quality 500 on October 16 at the Lowe's Motor Speedway. TNT Sports returns with a package of eight points races that includes one of the most exciting events in NASCAR: the Sharpie 500 night race at Bristol Motor Speedway.

Allen Bestwick again will call the action and will be joined in the booth by 1973 NASCAR Winston Cup Series champion Benny Parsons and veteran NASCAR competitor Wally Dallenbach.

Bill Weber returns as host of the critically acclaimed NASCAR on NBC/TNT prerace show from pit road that takes viewers to the middle of the action. Weber will also serve as lead pit reporter.

FOX is broadcasting 14 NASCAR NEXTEL Cup Series events, beginning with the Subway 400 at North Carolina Speedway. NASCAR racing legend Darrell Waltrip and former crew chief Larry McReynolds return to provide race analysis, and Mike Joy returns as race announcer. Prerace coverage is hosted by Chris Myers and analyst Jeff Hammond. FOX's extensive coverage will conclude with the Pepsi 400 at Daytona International Speedway.

In addition to being the primary carrier of NASCAR Busch Series races, with 14 events, FX will air three NASCAR NEXTEL Cup events. The FX schedule also includes the NEXTEL All-Star Challenge race live from Lowe's Motor Speedway in Charlotte.

FOX Sports Net, now available in 59 million North American households, returns with its NASCAR programming. *Totally NASCAR* begins its fourth season as the weeknight source for the latest breaking news of NASCAR. John Roberts and the Sunday morning crew at *NASCAR This Morning* return to their posts as well. FOX Sports Net also will cover five rounds of NASCAR NEXTEL Cup qualifying.

NASCAR TV is found exclusively on SPEED Channel and continues to grow in its third season. Live coverage of the NASCAR Craftsman Truck Series anchors the NASCAR TV block, continuing the strategy that created the network's rapid growth—more NASCAR and more live racing. The lineup: *Inside the NASCAR Busch Series*, *Totally NASCAR*, *NASCAR Performance*, *Trackside*, *Men Behind the Wrenches*, *Past Champions*, *NASCAR Victory Lane*, *Legends of Motorsport*, *Stock Car Legends* and *Inside NEXTEL Cup*.

NASCAR TV features complete behind-the-scenes access to NASCAR, enhanced race replays and highlights, and qualifying for NASCAR NEXTEL Cup and NASCAR Busch Series events. Also included in the exclusive block are classic races, season previews and reviews, special event coverage and Racing Across America, which will cover 23 of NASCAR's recently redeveloped NASCAR Grand National Division Series.

## NASCAR offers enhanced viewing options

NASCAR's partnership with iNDEMAND to provide NASCAR IN CAR on iNDEMAND, a multichannel, season-long package, returns to offer fans flag-to-flag in-car camera coverage for NASCAR NEXTEL Cup events. NASCAR IN CAR on iNDEMAND was developed in conjunction with NASCAR's broadcast partners to complement NASCAR's live event coverage on FOX, FX, NBC and TNT, which are free on network and cable television. The package offers an enhanced viewing experience, featuring in-car cameras with live team-audio communications and real-time in-car performance data.

Launched in June 2002 at Michigan International Speedway, NASCAR IN CAR on iNDEMAND begins its second full season offering all 36 NASCAR NEXTEL Cup points races in 2004. The package includes enhancements such as a specially designed NASCAR IN CAR remote control for easier navigation between the in-car camera channels and the network race coverage. Additionally, viewers may participate in an online poll and select the starting lineup of drivers featured on NASCAR IN CAR on iNDEMAND.

## NASCAR continues to grow in global TV distribution

In 2002, NASCAR Broadcasting set a high goal of broadcasting in more than 100 countries to expand NASCAR's growth in international markets.

And it delivered.

Collectively, the NASCAR NEXTEL Cup Series, NASCAR Busch Series and NASCAR Craftsman Truck Series events will continue to be distributed to more than 100 countries around the world.

In addition, in September 2002, NASCAR and Bell Express Vu partnered to launch NASCAR IN CAR on Vu!, which offers Canadian fans who subscribe to Bell ExpressVu flag-to-flag in-camera coverage for NASCAR NEXTEL Cup Series events.